Contemporary Authors®

NEW REVISION SERIES

ISSN 0275-7176

Contemporary
Authors®

**A Bio-Bibliographical Guide to
Current Writers in Fiction, General Nonfiction,
Poetry, Journalism, Drama, Motion Pictures,
Television, and Other Fields**

NEW REVISION SERIES
volume 130

THOMSON
GALE

Detroit • New York • San Francisco • San Diego • New Haven, Conn. • Waterville, Maine • London • Munich

Contemporary Authors, New Revision Series, Vol. 130

Project Editor
Tracey Watson

Editorial
Katy Balcer, Sara Constantakis, Natalie Fulkerson, Michelle Kazensky, Julie Keppen, Joshua Kondek, Lisa Kumar, Mary Ruby, Lemma Shomali, Susan Strickland, Maikue Vang

Permissions
Shalice Shah-Caldwell, Emma Hull, Jacqueline Key

Imaging and Multimedia
Leslie Light, Michael Logusz

Composition and Electronic Capture
Carolyn Roney

Manufacturing
Lori Kessler

LIBRARY OF CONGRESS CATALOG CARD NUMBER 81-640179

ISBN 0-7876-6722-6
ISSN 0275-7176

Printed in the United States of America
10 9 8 7 6 5 4 3 2 1

Contents

> **Indexing note:** All *Contemporary Authors* entries are indexed in the *Contemporary Authors* cumulative index, which is published separately and distributed twice a year.
>
> **As always, the most recent Contemporary Authors cumulative index continues to be the user's guide to the location of an individual author's listing.**

Preface

Contemporary Authors (*CA*) provides information on approximately 115,000 writers in a wide range of media, including:

- Current writers of fiction, nonfiction, poetry, and drama whose works have been issued by commercial publishers, risk publishers, or university presses (authors whose books have been published only by known vanity or author-subsidized firms are ordinarily not included)

- Prominent print and broadcast journalists, editors, photojournalists, syndicated cartoonists, graphic novelists, screenwriters, television scriptwriters, and other media people

- Notable international authors

- Literary greats of the early twentieth century whose works are popular in today's high school and college curriculums and continue to elicit critical attention

A *CA* listing entails no charge or obligation. Authors are included on the basis of the above criteria and their interest to *CA* users. Sources of potential listees include trade periodicals, publishers' catalogs, librarians, and other users.

How to Get the Most out of *CA*: Use the Index

The key to locating an author's most recent entry is the *CA* cumulative index, which is published separately and distributed twice a year. It provides access to *all* entries in *CA* and *Contemporary Authors New Revision Series* (*CANR*). Always consult the latest index to find an author's most recent entry.

For the convenience of users, the *CA* cumulative index also includes references to all entries in these Thomson Gale literary series: *Authors and Artists for Young Adults, Authors in the News, Bestsellers, Black Literature Criticism, Black Literature Criticism Supplement, Black Writers, Children's Literature Review, Concise Dictionary of American Literary Biography, Concise Dictionary of British Literary Biography, Contemporary Authors Autobiography Series, Contemporary Authors Bibliographical Series, Contemporary Dramatists, Contemporary Literary Criticism, Contemporary Novelists, Contemporary Poets, Contemporary Popular Writers, Contemporary Southern Writers, Contemporary Women Poets, Dictionary of Literary Biography, Dictionary of Literary Biography Documentary Series, Dictionary of Literary Biography Yearbook, DISCovering Authors, DISCovering Authors: British, DISCovering Authors: Canadian, DISCovering Authors: Modules* (including modules for Dramatists, Most-Studied Authors, Multicultural Authors, Novelists, Poets, and Popular/Genre Authors), *DISCovering Authors 3.0, Drama Criticism, Drama for Students, Feminist Writers, Hispanic Literature Criticism, Hispanic Writers, Junior DISCovering Authors, Major Authors and Illustrators for Children and Young Adults, Major 20th-Century Writers, Native North American Literature, Novels for Students, Poetry Criticism, Poetry for Students, Short Stories for Students, Short Story Criticism, Something about the Author, Something about the Author Autobiography Series, St. James Guide to Children's Writers, St. James Guide to Crime & Mystery Writers, St. James Guide to Fantasy Writers, St. James Guide to Horror, Ghost & Gothic Writers, St. James Guide to Science Fiction Writers, St. James Guide to Young Adult Writers, Twentieth-Century Literary Criticism, 20th Century Romance and Historical Writers, World Literature Criticism,* and *Yesterday's Authors of Books for Children.*

A Sample Index Entry:

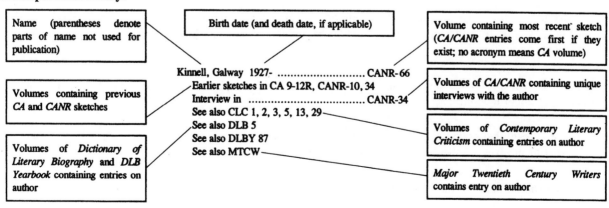

How Are Entries Compiled?

The editors make every effort to secure new information directly from the authors; listees' responses to our questionnaires and query letters provide most of the information featured in *CA*. For deceased writers, or those who fail to reply to requests for data, we consult other reliable biographical sources, such as those indexed in Thomson Gale's *Biography and Genealogy Master Index,* and bibliographical sources, including *National Union Catalog, LC MARC,* and *British National Bibliography.* Further details come from published interviews, feature stories, and book reviews, as well as information supplied by the authors' publishers and agents.

An asterisk (*) at the end of a sketch indicates that the listing has been compiled from secondary sources believed to be reliable but has not been personally verified for this edition by the author sketched.

What Kinds of Information Does An Entry Provide?

Sketches in *CA* contain the following biographical and bibliographical information:

- **Entry heading:** the most complete form of author's name, plus any pseudonyms or name variations used for writing

- **Personal information:** author's date and place of birth, family data, ethnicity, educational background, political and religious affiliations, and hobbies and leisure interests

- **Addresses:** author's home, office, or agent's addresses, plus e-mail and fax numbers, as available

- **Career summary:** name of employer, position, and dates held for each career post; resume of other vocational achievements; military service

- **Membership information:** professional, civic, and other association memberships and any official posts held

- **Awards and honors:** military and civic citations, major prizes and nominations, fellowships, grants, and honorary degrees

- **Writings:** a comprehensive, chronological list of titles, publishers, dates of original publication and revised editions, and production information for plays, television scripts, and screenplays

- **Adaptations:** a list of films, plays, and other media which have been adapted from the author's work

- **Work in progress:** current or planned projects, with dates of completion and/or publication, and expected publisher, when known

- **Sidelights:** a biographical portrait of the author's development; information about the critical reception of the author's works; revealing comments, often by the author, on personal interests, aspirations, motivations, and thoughts on writing

- **Interview:** a one-on-one discussion with authors conducted especially for *CA*, offering insight into authors' thoughts about their craft

- **Autobiographical essay:** an original essay written by noted authors for *CA*, a forum in which writers may present themselves, on their own terms, to their audience

- **Photographs:** portraits and personal photographs of notable authors

- **Biographical and critical sources:** a list of books and periodicals in which additional information on an author's life and/or writings appears

- **Obituary Notices** in *CA* provide date and place of birth as well as death information about authors whose full-length sketches appeared in the series before their deaths. The entries also summarize the authors' careers and writings and list other sources of biographical and death information.

Related Titles in the *CA* Series

Contemporary Authors Autobiography Series complements *CA* original and revised volumes with specially commissioned autobiographical essays by important current authors, illustrated with personal photographs they provide. Common topics include their motivations for writing, the people and experiences that shaped their careers, the rewards they derive from their work, and their impressions of the current literary scene.

Contemporary Authors Bibliographical Series surveys writings by and about important American authors since World War II. Each volume concentrates on a specific genre and features approximately ten writers; entries list works written by and about the author and contain a bibliographical essay discussing the merits and deficiencies of major critical and scholarly studies in detail.

Available in Electronic Formats

GaleNet. *CA* is available on a subscription basis through GaleNet, an online information resource that features an easy-to-use end-user interface, powerful search capabilities, and ease of access through the World-Wide Web. For more information, call 1-800-877-GALE.

Licensing. *CA* is available for licensing. The complete database is provided in a fielded format and is deliverable on such media as disk, CD-ROM, or tape. For more information, contact Thomson Gale's Business Development Group at 1-800-877-GALE, or visit us on our website at www.galegroup.com/bizdev.

Suggestions Are Welcome

The editors welcome comments and suggestions from users on any aspect of the *CA* series. If readers would like to recommend authors for inclusion in future volumes of the series, they are cordially invited to write the Editors at *Contemporary Authors*, Thomson Gale, 27500 Drake Rd., Farmington Hills, MI 48331-3535; or call at 1-248-699-4253; or fax at 1-248-699-8054.

Contemporary Authors Product Advisory Board

The editors of *Contemporary Authors* are dedicated to maintaining a high standard of excellence by publishing comprehensive, accurate, and highly readable entries on a wide array of writers. In addition to the quality of the content, the editors take pride in the graphic design of the series, which is intended to be orderly yet inviting, allowing readers to utilize the pages of *CA* easily and with efficiency. Despite the longevity of the *CA* print series, and the success of its format, we are mindful that the vitality of a literary reference product is dependent on its ability to serve its users over time. As literature, and attitudes about literature, constantly evolve, so do the reference needs of students, teachers, scholars, journalists, researchers, and book club members. To be certain that we continue to keep pace with the expectations of our customers, the editors of *CA* listen carefully to their comments regarding the value, utility, and quality of the series. Librarians, who have firsthand knowledge of the needs of library users, are a valuable resource for us. The *Contemporary Authors* Product Advisory Board, made up of school, public, and academic librarians, is a forum to promote focused feedback about *CA* on a regular basis. The seven-member advisory board includes the following individuals, whom the editors wish to thank for sharing their expertise:

- **Anne M. Christensen,** Librarian II, Phoenix Public Library, Phoenix, Arizona.

- **Barbara C. Chumard,** Reference/Adult Services Librarian, Middletown Thrall Library, Middletown, New York.

- **Eva M. Davis,** Youth Department Manager, Ann Arbor District Library, Ann Arbor, Michigan.

- **Adam Janowski, Jr.,** Library Media Specialist, Naples High School Library Media Center, Naples, Florida.

- **Robert Reginald,** Head of Technical Services and Collection Development, California State University, San Bernadino, California.

- **Stephen Weiner,** Director, Maynard Public Library, Maynard, Massachusetts.

International Advisory Board

Well-represented among the 115,000 author entries published in *Contemporary Authors* are sketches on notable writers from many non-English-speaking countries. The primary criteria for inclusion of such authors has traditionally been the publication of at least one title in English, either as an original work or as a translation. However, the editors of *Contemporary Authors* came to observe that many important international writers were being overlooked due to a strict adherence to our inclusion criteria. In addition, writers who were publishing in languages other than English were not being covered in the traditional sources we used for identifying new listees. Intent on increasing our coverage of international authors, including those who write only in their native language and have not been translated into English, the editors enlisted the aid of a board of advisors, each of whom is an expert on the literature of a particular country or region. Among the countries we focused attention on are Mexico, Puerto Rico, Spain, Italy, France, Germany, Luxembourg, Belgium, the Netherlands, Norway, Sweden, Denmark, Finland, Taiwan, Singapore, Malaysia, Thailand, South Africa, Israel, and Japan, as well as England, Scotland, Wales, Ireland, Australia, and New Zealand. The sixteen-member advisory board includes the following individuals, whom the editors wish to thank for sharing their expertise:

- **Lowell A. Bangerter,** Professor of German, University of Wyoming, Laramie, Wyoming.

- **Nancy E. Berg,** Associate Professor of Hebrew and Comparative Literature, Washington University, St. Louis, Missouri.

- **Frances Devlin-Glass,** Associate Professor, School of Literary and Communication Studies, Deakin University, Burwood, Victoria, Australia.

- **David William Foster,** Regent's Professor of Spanish, Interdisciplinary Humanities, and Women's Studies, Arizona State University, Tempe, Arizona.

- **Hosea Hirata,** Director of the Japanese Program, Associate Professor of Japanese, Tufts University, Medford, Massachusetts.

- **Jack Kolbert,** Professor Emeritus of French Literature, Susquehanna University, Selinsgrove, Pennsylvania.

- **Mark Libin,** Professor, University of Manitoba, Winnipeg, Manitoba, Canada.

- **C. S. Lim,** Professor, University of Malaya, Kuala Lumpur, Malaysia.

- **Eloy E. Merino,** Assistant Professor of Spanish, Northern Illinois University, DeKalb, Illinois.

- **Linda M. Rodríguez Guglielmoni,** Associate Professor, University of Puerto Rico—Mayagüez, Puerto Rico.

- **Sven Hakon Rossel,** Professor and Chair of Scandinavian Studies, University of Vienna, Vienna, Austria.

- **Steven R. Serafin,** Director, Writing Center, Hunter College of the City University of New York, New York City.

- **David Smyth,** Lecturer in Thai, School of Oriental and African Studies, University of London, England.

- **Ismail S. Talib,** Senior Lecturer, Department of English Language and Literature, National University of Singapore, Singapore.

- **Dionisio Viscarri,** Assistant Professor, Ohio State University, Columbus, Ohio.

- **Mark Williams,** Associate Professor, English Department, University of Canterbury, Christchurch, New Zealand.

CA Numbering System and Volume Update Chart

Occasionally questions arise about the *CA* numbering system and which volumes, if any, can be discarded. Despite numbers like "29-32R," "97-100" and "222," the entire *CA* print series consists of only 280 physical volumes with the publication of *CA* Volume 223. The following charts note changes in the numbering system and cover design, and indicate which volumes are essential for the most complete, up-to-date coverage.

***CA* First Revision**	• 1-4R through 41-44R (11 books) *Cover:* Brown with black and gold trim. There will be no further First Revision volumes because revised entries are now being handled exclusively through the more efficient *New Revision Series* mentioned below.
***CA* Original Volumes**	• 45-48 through 97-100 (14 books) *Cover:* Brown with black and gold trim. 101 through 223 (123 books) *Cover:* Blue and black with orange bands. The same as previous *CA* original volumes but with a new, simplified numbering system and new cover design.
***CA* Permanent Series**	• *CAP*-1 and *CAP*-2 (2 books) *Cover:* Brown with red and gold trim. There will be no further Permanent Series volumes because revised entries are now being handled exclusively through the more efficient *New Revision Series* mentioned below.
***CA* New Revision Series**	• CANR-1 through CANR-130 (130 books) *Cover:* Blue and black with green bands. Includes only sketches requiring significant changes; **sketches are taken from any previously published CA, CAP, or CANR volume.**

If You Have:	You May Discard:
CA First Revision Volumes 1-4R through 41-44R and *CA Permanent Series* Volumes 1 and 2	*CA* Original Volumes 1, 2, 3, 4 and Volumes 5-6 through 41-44
CA Original Volumes 45-48 through 97-100 and 101 through 223	**NONE:** These volumes will not be superseded by corresponding revised volumes. Individual entries from these and all other volumes appearing in the left column of this chart may be revised and included in the various volumes of the *New Revision Series*.
CA New Revision Series Volumes *CANR*-1 through *CANR*-130	**NONE:** The *New Revision Series* does not replace any single volume of *CA*. Instead, volumes of *CANR* include entries from many previous *CA* series volumes. All *New Revision Series* volumes must be retained for full coverage.

A Sampling of Authors and Media People
Featured in This Volume

Louis Auchincloss

Auchincloss, a former Wall Street lawyer, is the prolific author of distinguished fiction and nonfiction. Chronicling the business and social life of New York's elite class in novels like *The House of Five Talents* and *The Rector of Justin,* Auchincloss writes in the tradition of the nineteenth-century novel of manners, with elegant and restrained prose but a modern understanding of the complexities of the business world. Among his most recents works are the short stories *Manhattan Monologues,* 2002, and the novel *The Scarlet Letters,* 2003.

Anita Brookner

Brookner is a British author, internationally acclaimed as both an art historian and a novelist and the two-time winner of the prestigious Booker prize for *Hotel du Lac,* in 1984, and for *The Next Big Thing,* in 2002 (published in the U.S. as *Making Things Better*). Critics hail Brookner as a beautiful stylist whose intelligence, wit, and insight transform the mundane into the memorable in her stories. *The Rules of Engagement,* published in 2003, is her most recent novel.

Arthur C. Clarke

Clarke, highly regarded for his scientific writing, is best known for his science fiction. A Grand Master of the Science Fiction Writers of America, Clarke collaborated with director Stanley Kubrick to write the movie classic *2001: A Space Odyssey.* Clarke's forte, according to critics, is his ability to describe the wonders of the universe in a way that is lyrical yet scientifically accurate. In 2000, Clarke published the novel *The Light of Other Days,* in collaboration with Stephen Baxter. *The Collected Stories of Arthur C. Clarke,* was published in 2001.

Nikki Giovanni

Giovanni is a poet and political activist who first came to prominence during the black power movement in the 1960s with works like *Black Feeling, Black Talk.* Over the years her poetry has reflected not only her racial pride but an evolving awareness of a wide range of social issues, especially the importance of the family as the basis of a strong community. Giovanni's recent works include *Prosaic Soul of Nikki Giovanni* and *The Collected Poetry of Nikki Giovanni: 1968-1998,* both published in 2003.

Thomas Keneally

Keneally, a grandson of Irish immigrants, is one of Australia's most distinguished writers. He may be best known for his award-winning novel *Schindler's List,* and the acclaimed motion picture that it became in 1993. In fiction and nonfiction, Keneally's work is characterized by its sensitivity to style and its objectivity as he explores themes as diverse as the American Civil War and the plight of war-torn Ethiopia. In 2003 he published the novel *Office of Innocence* and the biography *Abraham Lincoln.*

Norman Mailer

Mailer burst onto the literary scene with his World War II best-seller *The Naked and the Dead* in 1948 and has remained at the center of attention and controversy ever since. A winner of two Pulitzer Prizes, for *Armies of the Night* and *The Executioner's Song,* Mailer has also been cast as an aging *enfant terrible,* intoxicated with grandiose ideas and preoccupied with sex and violence. Now in the role of literary elder statesman, he reveals a combination of charm and straight talk in *The Spooky Art: Some Thoughts on Writing,* published in 2003.

Mary Stewart

Stewart, one of the most widely read authors of our time, is the author of contemporary romantic suspense novels like the award-winning *My Brother Michael* and *This Rough Magic,* as well as the historical novels *The Crystal Cave, The Hollow Hills,* and *The Last Enchantment* that make up her "Merlin Trilogy." Critics liken the appeal of her suspense novels to that of *Jane Eyre* or *Rebecca,* while praising her extraordinary descriptive prose for its sensuous detail of locale and character. Stewart's most recent novel is 1997's *Rose Cottage.*

Derek Walcott

Walcott, winner of the Nobel Prize for Literature in 1992, is a West Indian poet and playwright. Born of mixed racial and ethnic heritage, Walcott was educated as a British subject. In works like the *The Castaway* and *Dream on Monkey Mountain,* Walcott explores his major theme—the dichotomy between black and white, subject and ruler, and the elements of both Caribbean and Western civilization present in his culture and ancestry. His most recent work includes the poetry collection *Tiepolo's Hound,* published in 2000 and the play *The Haitian Trilogy,* published in 2002.

Acknowledgments

Grateful acknowledgment is made to those publishers, photographers, and artists whose work appear with these authors' essays. Following is a list of the copyright holders who have granted us permission to reproduce material in this volume of *CA*. Every effort has been made to trace copyright, but if omissions have been made, please let us know.

Photographs/Art

Paula Gunn Allen: Allen, photograph. © Jerry Bauer. Reproduced by permission.

Cherie Bennett: Bennett, photograph by Nancy Andrews. Reproduced by permission of Cherie Bennett.

Chris Bohjalian: Bohjalian, photograph by Victoria Blewer. Reproduced by permission.

Arthur C. Clarke: Clarke, photograph. AP/Wide World Photos. Reproduced by permission.

Joe Bob Briggs: Briggs, portrait. The Kobal Collection. Reproduced by permission.

Anita Brookner: Brookner, photograph. © Jerry Bauer. Reproduced by permission.

Brian Castro: Castro, photograph. Reproduced by permission.

Douglas Coupland: Coupland, New York City, 1995, photograph. AP/Wide World Photos. Reproduced by permission.

Thomas Anthony de Paola: de Paola, photograph. © Jon Gilbert Fox. Reproduced by permission.

Christopher Durang: Durang, photograph © Jerry Bauer. Reproduced by permission.

Walker Evans: Evans, photograph. UPI/Corbis-Bettmann. Reproduced by permission.

Mary Lou Fuller: Fuller, photograph by Windswept Acres Studio, Lebanon, ME. Reproduced by permission of Mary Lou Fuller.

Cristina Garcia: Garcia, photograph. © Jerry Bauer. Reproduced by permission.

Laverne M. Gill: Gill, photograph by Photo Generations. Reproduced by permission.

Nikki Giovanni: Giovanni, photograph. AP/Wide World Photos. Reproduced by permission.

Mary Elizabeth Gore: Gore, photograph by Mark Humphery. AP/Wide World Photos. Reproduced by permission.

Catherine Hakim: Hakim, photograph. Reproduced by permission.

Joe Haldeman: Haldeman, photograph by Gay Haldeman. Reproduced by permission.

Steven Harvey: Harvey, photograph. Reproduced by permission.

Chukwuemeka Ike: Ike, photograph. Reproduced by permission.

A

AAKER, David A(llen) 1938-

PERSONAL: Born February 11, 1938, in Fargo, ND; married; children: two. *Education:* Massachusetts Institute of Technology, B.S., 1960; Stanford University, M.S., 1967, Ph.D., 1969.

ADDRESSES: Office—Haas School of Business, University of California, Berkeley, CA 94720; Prophet Brand Strategy, 625 Third St., San Francisco, CA 94107. *E-mail*—aaker@haas.berkeley.edu.

CAREER: Texas Instruments, Inc., Houston, TX, cost engineer, 1960-61, sales engineer, 1961-63, product sales manager, 1963-65; Stanford University, Stanford, CA, instructor in statistics, 1967; University of California, Berkeley, acting assistant professor, 1968-69, assistant professor, 1969-72, associate professor, 1972-76, professor of marketing statistics, 1976-81, J. Gary Shansby Professor of Marketing Strategy, 1981-94, E. T. Grether Professor of Marketing, 1994—, professor emeritus, 2000—; Prophet Brand Strategy, San Francisco, CA, vice chairman, 1999—; Brand Leadership Co., New York, NY, partner.

MEMBER: American Marketing Association, American Statistical Association, Institute of Management Sciences, Tau Beta Pi.

AWARDS, HONORS: Special merit award, Thompson Gold Medal Competition, 1972; *Journal of Marketing* award, 1985.

WRITINGS:

(Editor and contributor) *Multivariate Analysis in Marketing: Theory and Application,* Wadsworth (Belmont, CA), 1971, 2nd edition, 1979.

(Editor, with George S. Day) *Consumerism: Search for the Consumer Interest,* Free Press (New York, NY), 1971, 4th edition, 1982.

(With John G. Meyers) *Advertising Management: An Analytical Approach,* Prentice-Hall (Englewood Cliffs, NJ), 1975, 5th edition, 1996.

(With George S. Day) *Marketing Research: Private and Public Sector Decisions,* Wiley (New York, NY), 1980, 8th edition, with V. Kumar, 2003.

Developing Business Strategies, J. Wiley (New York, NY), 1984, 6th edition, 2001.

Strategic Market Management, J. Wiley (New York, NY), 1984, 6th edition, 2001.

(With Kevin Lane Keller) *Consumer Evaluations of Brand Extensions,* Marketing Science Institute (Cambridge, MA), 1990.

Managing Brand Equity: Capitalizing on the Value of a Brand Name, Maxwell Macmillan International (New York, NY), 1991.

(With Rajeev Batra and John G. Myers) *Advertising Management,* Prentice Hall (Englewood Cliffs, NJ), 1992.

Building Strong Brands, Free Press (New York, NY), 1996.

(With V. Kumar and George S. Day) *Essentials of Marketing Research,* J. Wiley (New York, NY), 1999, 2nd edition, 2002.

(With Erich Joachimsthaler) *Brand Leadership,* Free Press (New York, NY), 2000.

Brand Portfolio Strategy: Creating Relevance, Differentiation, Energy, Leverage, and Clarity, Free Press (New York, NY), 2004.

Contributor of articles and reviews to business journals, including *Planning Review, Management Science, Harvard Business Review, Journal of Advertising Research, Journal of Marketing Research,* and *Journal of Marketing.* Member of editorial board of *Journal of Marketing Research,* 1969—, and *Journal of Business Research,* 1973—; associate editor of *Management Science,* 1971—.

SIDELIGHTS: David A. Aaker "has established a sound reputation for his many contributions to the important topic of marketing strategy," as Peter M. Chisnall noted in the *Journal of the Market Research Society.* Aacker is also "one of the most familiar names in brand strategy in large part thanks to the success of his best-selling *Managing Brand Equity* (1991) and *Building Strong Brands* (1996)," according to a writer for *Brandweek.* The 2000 publication of *Brand Leadership,* according to Arthur J. Kover in the *Journal of Advertising Research,* "completes a trilogy by David Aaker. It is the capstone of his by-now-famous work on brands, branding, and brand equity."

Aaker's view of brands recognizes their importance as a strategic corporate asset. But he argues that corporations should consciously manage their brand identities to encompass areas beyond simple product recognition. Just as a brand like the Harley-Davidson motorcycle, for example, has developed an identity as a symbol of freedom and adventure, other brands can likewise develop themselves in ways that go beyond their actual product to suggest lifestyle choices that emotionally appeal to wider audiences. This development of strong brand names can make for continuing long-term growth of a business.

Aaker's *Building Strong Brands* is grounded in real-life experience, presenting case histories of the creation and development of actual brands such as Saturn automobiles, Kodak, and McDonald's. Barbara Jacobs in *Booklist,* for example, found that the book "presents case examples to which anyone can relate." Speaking of the same volume, Daniel P. Chamberlin in the *Journal of Consumer Marketing* noted that "here in classical textbook format the author takes us through the steps of creating a brand identity. . . . And every one

of his steps is beautifully illustrated by one or more brand histories selected for their pertinence to the particular topic Aaker is addressing at the moment." Similarly, Scott Ferris in *Multichannel News* found that "Aaker does a superb job in laying out contextual cases throughout each chapter."

Aaker's *Brand Leadership* contains advice based on his own studies of some 300 organizations. "The book is studded with marketing insights," according to Kover, who also found it to be "a good read and . . . full of ideas to spark the minds of brand managers." Paul Woolf, writing in *Marketing,* found that "it is his broad range of examples . . . coupled with an uncanny ability to make theory tangible, that makes this book an important addition to any serious marketer's arsenal."

BIOGRAPHICAL AND CRITICAL SOURCES:

PERIODICALS

Booklist, November 15, 1995, review of *Building Strong Brands,* p. 522.
Brandweek, October 2, 1995, excerpt from *Building Strong Brands,* p. 28; February 21, 2000, review of *Brand Leadership,* p. 30.
Industry Week, February 19, 1996, Polly LaBarre, review of *Building Strong Brands,* p. 38.
Journal of Advertising Research, July, 2000, Arthur J. Kover, review of *Brand Leadership,* p. 73.
Journal of Consumer Marketing, winter, 1997, Daniel P. Chamberlin, review of *Building Strong Brands,* p. 92.
Journal of the Market Research Society, July, 1996, Peter M. Chisnall, review of *Developing Business Strategies,* p. 285.
Marketing, February 8, 2001, Paul Woolf, review of *Brand Leadership,* p. 68.
Multichannel News, July 21, 1997, Scott Ferris, review of *Building Strong Brands,* p. A46.
Publishers Weekly, October 16, 1995, review of *Building Strong Brands,* p. 50.*

*   *   *

ALLEN, Paula Gunn 1939-

PERSONAL: Born 1939, in Cubero, NM; daughter of E. Lee (a businessman and politician) and Ethel (Francis); married (divorced); children: three. *Education:* University of Oregon, B.A., 1966, M.F.A., 1968; University of New Mexico, Ph.D., 1975.

Paula Gunn Allen

ADDRESSES: Office—c/o Author Mail, Harper San Francisco, 10 East 53rd Street, New York, NY 10022. *E-mail*—shimanna@mcn.org.

CAREER: Fort Lewis College, Durango, CO, lecturer; San Francisco State University, San Francisco, CA, director of Native-American studies program; University of New Mexico, Albuquerque, lecturer; University of California, Berkeley, lecturer, professor of Native American Studies/Ethnic Studies; University of California, Los Angeles, professor of literature, 1990-99.

AWARDS, HONORS: National Endowment for the Arts fellowship, 1978; postdoctoral fellow in American Indian Studies, University of California, Los Angeles, 1981; postdoctoral fellowship grant, Ford Foundation-National Research Council, 1984; American Book Award, Before Columbus Foundation, 1990, for *Spider Woman's Granddaughters: Traditional Tales and Contemporary Writing by Native American Women;* Susan Koppelman Award, Popular and American Culture Associations, and Native American Prize for Literature, both 1990.

WRITINGS:

POETRY

The Blind Lion, Thorp Springs Press (Berkeley, CA), 1974.
Coyote's Daylight Trip, La Confluencia (Albuquerque, NM), 1978.
A Cannon between My Knees, Strawberry Press (New York, NY), 1981.
Star Child: Poems, Blue Cloud Quarterly (Marvin, SD), 1981.
Shadow Country, University of California American Indian Studies Center (Los Angeles, CA), 1982.
Wyrds, Taurean Horn (San Francisco, CA), 1987.
Skins and Bones, West End (Albuquerque, NM), 1988.
Life Is a Fatal Disease: Collected Poems, 1962-1995, West End (Albuquerque, NM), 1997.

EDITOR

From the Center: A Folio of Native American Art and Poetry, Strawberry Press (New York, NY), 1981.
Studies in American Indian Literature: Critical Essays and Course Designs, Modern Language Association of America (New York, NY), 1983.
Spider Woman's Granddaughters: Traditional Tales and Contemporary Writing by Native American Women, Beacon Press (Boston, MA), 1989.
(And author of introduction) *The Voice of the Turtle: American Indian Literature, 1900-1970,* Ballantine (New York, NY), 1994.
Song of the Turtle: American Indian Fiction, 1974-1994, Ballantine (New York, NY, 1995.
(With Carolyn Dunn Anderson) *Hozho: Walking in Beauty: Native American Stories of Inspiration, Humor, and Life,* Contemporary Books (Chicago, IL), 2001.

OTHER

Sipapu: A Cultural Perspective, University of New Mexico Press (Albuquerque, NM), 1975.
The Woman Who Owned the Shadows (novel), Spinsters Ink (San Francisco, CA), 1983.
(Author of foreword) Brian Swann, *Song of the Sky: Versions of Native American Songs and Poems,* Four Zoas Night House (Boston, MA), 1985.

Grandmothers of the Light: A Medicine Woman's Sourcebook, Beacon Press (Boston, MA), 1991.

Indian Perspectives, Southwest Parks and Monuments Association (Tucson, AZ), 1992.

The Sacred Hoop: Recovering the Feminine in American Indian Traditions (essays), Beacon Press (Boston, MA), 1986, reissued with new preface, 1992.

(With Patricia Clark Smith) *As Long As the Rivers Flow: Nine Stories of Native Americans,* Scholastic (New York, NY), 1996.

Off the Reservation: Reflections on Boundary-Busting Border-Crossing Loose Canons, Beacon Press (Boston, MA), 1998.

Pocahontas: Medicine Woman, Spy, Entrepreneur, Diplomat, HarperSanFrancisco (San Francisco, CA), 2003.

Contributor to *I Tell You Now: Autobiographical Essays by Native American Writers,* edited by Brian Swann and Arnold Krupat, University of Nebraska Press (Lincoln, NE), 1987; and *Columbus and Beyond: Views from Native Americans,* edited by Randolph Jorgen, Southwest Parks and Monuments Association (Tucson, AZ), 1992.

SIDELIGHTS: Paula Gunn Allen is a registered member of the Laguna Pueblo tribe, but her heritage has been enriched by many nationalities. Her father, E. Lee Francis, was born of Lebanese parents at Seboyeta, a Spanish/Mexican land grant village north of Laguna Pueblo. He spoke only Arabic and Spanish until he learned English at the age of ten. He owned the Cubero Trading Company and later served as Lieutenant Governor of New Mexico from 1967 through 1970. Allen's mother, Ethel, was of mixed Laguna Pueblo, Sioux, and Scots ancestry.

Allen grew up in Cubero, New Mexico, where she attended Catholic school. According to Kathy J. Whitson in the book *Native American Literatures,* Allen noted: "Sometimes I get in a dialogue between what the Church taught me, what the nuns taught me, what my mother taught me, what my experience growing up where I grew up taught me. Often you can't reconcile them. I can't reconcile them." In contrast, Allen found stability and what Whitson called the "thematic bedrock" in her New Mexican upbringing: "the land, the family, the road."

Allen married while in college and had two children before divorcing. After the divorce, she went back to school and studied writing. Her work as a writer was initially inspired by the success of N. Scott Momaday, a Native American writer whose novel *House Made of Dawn* has been widely recognized and acclaimed in mainstream American culture.

Although Allen has a diverse ethnic heritage, it is her American Indian roots that inform and direct her work. In an interview with Robin Pogrebin of the *New York Times Book Review,* Allen characterized Native Americans as "something other than victims—mostly what we are is unrecognized." To help remedy this situation, Allen compiled *The Sacred Hoop: Recovering the Feminine in American Indian Traditions,* a collection of seventeen essays covering topics that range from the status of lesbians in Native American cultures, to literature's roots in the soil of tradition and ritual. In the *Los Angeles Times Book Review,* Quannah Karvar complimented the volume's "power and insight as a commentary on the perceptions and priorities of contemporary Native American women." Allen has also gained recognition as a poet. Her first published collection of poems, *The Blind Lion,* appeared in 1974, followed by *Skins and Bones* in 1988 and *Life Is a Fatal Disease: Collected Poems, 1962-1995,* published in 1997.

Allen's novel, 1983's *The Woman Who Owned the Shadows,* received a generally favorable review from Alice Hoffman in the *New York Times Book Review.* "In those sections where the author forsakes the artifice of her style," declared the critic, "an absorbing, often fascinating world is created." The novel's heroine, Ephanie, is emotionally wounded as a young girl and struggles to mend her fractured core "guided," according to Hoffman, "by the traditional tales of spirit women." After several unsuccessful attempts to fit into male-dominated white society, Ephanie attempts suicide, only to cut herself down from the rope by which she is hanging. Struck by a sudden appreciation for life, Ephanie begins her journey toward community and self-acceptance by learning what her woman-centered tribal heritage can mean for her. Within this tradition she finds the Spider Woman, known also as Thought Woman, who "enlightens Ephanie and helps her to enter the shadows of her psyche and to own them, to dream her own dreams and to own them," said Marcia G. Fuchs in *Twentieth-Century Western Writers.*

The Woman Who Owned the Shadows uses a variety of narrative elements, including Native American folklore, letters, dreams, and therapy transcripts to tell

Ephanie's story. While some critics, like Hoffman, found this compilation to be forced, others believed it to be effective and enjoyable. "Allen continues her cultural traditional in her novel by using it in the same way in which the traditional arts have always functioned for the Laguna Pueblo. She has extended traditional storytelling into the modern form of the novel by weaving in the tribal history, cultural traditions, and mythology of the Laguna Pueblo to create a form of curing ceremony for her readers," noted Annette Van Dyke in *Lesbian Texts and Contexts: Radical Revisions.*

A few critics have suggested that the novel represents a vision quest, not only for Ephanie but for her readers, who learn that self-acceptance requires a feeling of connection with the past. Allen affirmed the notion that writing the novel was also a kind of vision quest: "That's what I am searching for, to pull the vision out of me, because it is here, I know it is. . . . That's what a vision quest is for, you know. You go out . . . and you find out who you are. Well, a writer goes into the wilderness and finds out who she is," she remarked in a 1987 interview with Annie O. Eysturoy published in *This Is about Vision: Interviews with Southwestern Writers.*

In 1989 Allen edited *Spider Woman's Granddaughters: Traditional Tales and Contemporary Writing by Native American Women,* which Karvar called "a companion in spirit" to the author's book of essays *The Sacred Hoop.* In *Spider Woman's Granddaughters,* Allen gives space not only to contemporary authors such as Vickie L. Sears, but also to legends of old deities such as the Pueblos' mother goddess of corn. She also includes the words of Pretty Shield, a Crow native who told her life story to ethnographer Frank B. Linderman early in the twentieth century. In the *New York Times Book Review,* Ursula K. Le Guin praised the organization of the book, noting that Allen has arranged the pieces "so that they interact to form larger patterns, giving the book an esthetic wholeness rare in anthologies."

With the 1991 publication of *Grandmothers of the Light: A Medicine Woman's Sourcebook,* Allen again focuses attention on the central role of women in many Native American cultures. A collection of twenty-one stories from the oral tradition of a variety of tribes, the book is divided into three sections that provide information for those seeking to possess something of the goddesses' supernatural and creative powers. In the *Voice Literary Supplement,* Suzanne Ruta asserted that "*goddesses* is probably the wrong word for these divinities, who don't dazzle or attack from distant thrones. Like the cultures that nourished them, they're down to earth, egalitarian, democratic, and resourceful, plunging their arms into the clay, the corn dough, the ashes, to come up with what's needed to create or sustain life."

Many of the stories are told in Allen's own voice as she combines them with her own critical insights into their meaning and their relevance to historical events. While some have noted the lack of critical references in Allen's nonfiction writing, reception generally has been positive. The tribes represented in the stories cover a wide geographic area, including the Navajo, the Cherokee, the Lakota, and the Mayan. While Allen admits that these tribes have very different cultures, she asserts that they all share similar worldviews with respect to the need for balance between the "mundane" and spiritual worlds. This notion of balance, she asserts, is the product of woman-centered societies where models of shared obligations replace struggles for power between men and women. Lucy Patrick said in a *Library Journal* review of *Grandmothers of the Light* that the "recovery of respect for complementary polarity and gynecratic tribal values are central to [Allen's] vision of the interrelationship of the human and supernatural worlds." One of Allen's continuing efforts is to counter the popular notion that Native American culture has been lost in today's world.

In *Off the Reservation: Reflections on Boundary-Busting, Border-Crossing Loose Canons,* Allen draws on her own mixed heritage of mixed Laguna and Lebanese origins to examine contemporary American culture. The collection of essays range widely, from political to spiritual to ecological issues, and are often very personal, as when she considers her Lebanese roots, or describes her return to Laguna Pueblo after a long absence. Writing in *Library Journal,* Faye Powell described the collection as "thought-provoking and informative." A *Booklist* reviewer called the essays "intelligent work from a renegade spirit."

In Allen's 2003 publication, *Pocahontas: Medicine Woman, Spy, Entrepreneur, Diplomat,* she examines the legend of the Native American woman and represents her as other than the tragic and forlorn historical figure who fell in love with Captain John Smith. *Li-*

brary Journal's John Burch criticized the book's lack of "authoritative biographical information," stating "it is the native perspective that apparently gives [Allen] license to construct an image of Pocahontas as a 'shaman priestess, sorcerer, adept pf high degree' without any cited evidence." A *Publishers Weekly* reviewer, however, enjoyed Allen's interpretation of history, and pointed out that Allen's Pocahontas "is a real visionary, a prodigiously gifted young woman fervently devoted to the spiritual traditions of her people." This reviewer praised *Pocahontas,* commenting, "When casting Pocahontas as 'the embodiment of . . . dual culture transformation,' her role, and the book, are at their clearest and are made manifest by Allen's often lyrical and powerful writing."

Allen's "powerful writing" has entranced, enriched, and educated, according to many reviewers, while also offering up many aspects of Native American heritage to culturally enrich readers and add valuable morsels to the collective American history. In *Paula Gunn Allen,* Elizabeth I. Hanson asserted that Allen combines the sacredness of the past with the reality of the present as a means of self-renewal. "Like Allen's own vision of self," said Hanson, "contemporary Native Americans exist not in a romantic past but instead in a community which extends throughout the whole of American experience."

BIOGRAPHICAL AND CRITICAL SOURCES:

BOOKS

Bataille, Gretchen M., and Kathleen M. Sands, editors, *American Indian Women: Telling Their Lives,* University of Nebraska Press (Lincoln, NE), 1984.

Bataille, Gretchen M., and Laurie Lisa, editors, *Native American Women: A Biographical Dictionary,* 2nd edition, Routledge (London, England), 2001.

Bruchac, Joseph, *Survival This Way: Interviews with American Indian Poets,* University of Arizona Press (Tucson, AZ), 1987, pp. 1-24.

Coltelli, Laura, editor, *Winged Words: American Indian Writers Speak,* University of Nebraska Press (Lincoln, NE), 1990, pp. 11-39.

Contemporary Literary Criticism, Volume 84, Gale (Detroit, MI), 1995.

Contemporary Women Poets, St. James Press (Detroit, MI), 1998.

Crawford, C. F., John F. William Balassi, and Annie O. Eysturoy, *This Is about Vision: Interviews with Southwestern Writers,* University of New Mexico Press (Albuquerque, NM), 1990, pp. 95-107.

Encyclopedia of World Biography, 2nd edition, Gale (Detroit, MI), 1998.

Green, Carol Hurd, and Mary Grimley Mason, editors, *American Women Writers,* Continuum (New York, NY), 1994.

Hanson, Elizabeth J., *Paula Gunn Allen,* Boise State University (Boise, ID), 1990.

Jay, Karla and Joanne Glasgow, editors, *Lesbian Texts and Contexts: Radical Revisions,* New York University Press (New York, NY), 1990, pp. 339-354.

Keating, Ana Louise, *Women Reading Women Writing: Self-Invention in Paula Gunn Allen, Gloria Anzaldua, and Audre Lorde,* Temple University Press (Philadelphia, PA), 1996.

Lincoln, Kenneth, *Native American Renaissance,* University of California Press (Los Angeles, CA), 1983, pp. 183-221.

Literature Lover's Companion, Prentice Hall Press (New York, NY), 2001.

Milton, John R., *Four Indian Poets,* [South Dakota], 1974.

Moss, Maria, *We've Been Here Before: Women in Creation Myths and Contemporary Literature of the Native American Southwest,* Lit (Münster, Germany), 1993.

Native North American Literature, Gale (Detroit, MI), 1994.

Pollack, Sandra, and Denise Knight, editors, *Contemporary Lesbian Writers of the United States: A Bio-Bibliographical Critical Sourcebook,* Greenwood Press (Westport, CT), 1993.

Riggs, Thomas, editor, *Reference Guide to American Literature,* 4th edition, St. James Press (Detroit, MI), 2000.

Ruoff, A. La Vonne Brown, *American Indian Literatures: An Introduction, Bibliographic Review, and Selected Bibliography,* Modern Language Association (New York, NY), 1990, pp. 92-94.

Scanlon, Jennifer, editor, *Significant Contemporary American Feminists,* Greenwood Press (Westport, CT).

Twentieth-Century Western Writers, 2nd edition, edited by Geoff Sadler, St. James Press (Detroit, MI), 1991.

Van Dyke, Annette, *The Search for a Woman-Centered Spirituality,* New York University Press (New York, NY), 1992.

Whitson, Kathy J., *Native American Literatures: An Encyclopedia of Works, Characters, Authors, and Themes,* American Bibliographic Center-Clio (Santa Barbara, CA).

PERIODICALS

American Book Review, December, 1992-January, 1993, p. 12.

Belles Lettres, summer, 1990, pp. 40, 42.

Booklist, July, 1994, p. 1917; September 15, 1991, pp. 101-102; March 15, 1998, review of *Spider Woman's Granddaughters: Traditional Tales and Contemporary Writing by Native American Women,* p. 1235; October 1, 1998, review of *Off the Reservation: Reflections on Boundary-Busting Border-Crossing Loose Canons,* p. 303.

Choice, November, 1983, p. 427; September, 1986, p. 114.

Journal of American Folklore, April-June, 1990, pp. 245-247.

Kirkus Reviews, August 1, 1991, p. 976.

Kliatt, November, 2001, review of *Hozho: Walking in Beauty: Native American Stories of Inspiration, Humor, and Life,* p. 23.

Library Journal, January, 1986, p. 89; September 15, 1991, p. 84; November 15, 1998, Faye Powell, review of *Off the Reservation,* p. 74; October 1, 2003, John Burch, review of *Pocahontas: Medicine Woman, Spy, Entrepreneur, Diplomat,* p. 88.

Los Angeles Times, October 19, 1990, pp. E1, E7.

Los Angeles Times Book Review, January 25, 1987, p. 11; July 9, 1989, p. 10.

MELUS, summer, 1983, pp. 3-25.

New York Times Book Review, June 3, 1984, p. 18; May 14, 1989, p. 15.

North Dakota Quarterly, spring, 1989, pp. 149-161.

Parabola, November, 1986, pp. 102, 104; November, 1989, pp. 98, 102.

Publishers Weekly, July 5, 1991, p. 51; October 26, 1998, review of *Off the Reservation,* p. 51; September 1, 2003, review of *Pocahontas,* p. 76.

Village Voice, September 19, 1989, p. 57.

Voice Literary Supplement, November, 1991, p. 26.

Women's Review of Books, March, 1984, p. 8; July, 1989, p. 8; September, 1989, pp. 29-31.

World Literature Today, spring, 1990, pp. 344-345; summer, 1997, Robert L. Berner, review of *Life Is a Fatal Disease: Collected Poems, 1962-1995,* p. 631.*

ANDERS, C. J.
See BENNETT, Cherie

*   *   *

ARRLEY, Richmond
See NOONAN, Tom

*   *   *

AUCHINCLOSS, Louis (Stanton) 1917-
(Andrew Lee)

PERSONAL: Surname pronounced Auk-in-klaus; born September 27, 1917, in New York, NY; son of Joseph Howland (a corporate lawyer) and Priscilla (Stanton) Auchincloss; married Adele Lawrence, 1957; children: John Winthrop, Blake Leay, Andrew Sloane. *Education:* Attended Yale University, 1935-39; University of Virginia Law School, LL.B., 1941. *Religion:* Episcopalian.

ADDRESSES: Home—1111 Park Ave., New York, NY 10128; and Claryville, NY.

CAREER: Admitted to the Bar of New York State, 1941; Sullivan & Cromwell (law firm), New York, NY, associate, 1941-51; Hawkins, Delafield & Wood (law firm), New York, associate, 1954-58, partner, 1958-86. President, Museum of the City of New York; trustee, Josiah Macy, Jr., Foundation; former trustee, St. Barnard's School and New York Society Library; life fellow, Pierpont Morgan Library; former member of administrative committee, Dumbarton Oaks Research Library. *Military service:* U.S. Navy, 1941-45; served in Naval Intelligence and as gunnery officer; became lieutenant senior grade.

MEMBER: National Institute of Arts and Letters, Association of the Bar of the City of New York (former member of executive committee), Phi Beta Kappa, Century Association, American Academy of Arts and Letters (president).

AWARDS, HONORS: D.Litt., New York University, 1974, Pace University, 1979, University of the South, 1986, State University of New York at Geneseo, 2002; New York State Governor's Art Award.

WRITINGS:

NOVELS

(Under pseudonym Andrew Lee) *The Indifferent Children,* Prentice-Hall (Englewood Cliffs, NJ), 1947.

Sybil, Houghton Mifflin (Boston, MA), 1952.

A Law for the Lion, Houghton Mifflin (Boston, MA), 1953.

The Great World and Timothy Colt, Houghton Mifflin (Boston, MA), 1956.

Venus in Sparta, Houghton Mifflin (Boston, MA), 1958.

Pursuit of the Prodigal, Houghton Mifflin (Boston, MA), 1959.

The House of Five Talents, Houghton Mifflin (Boston, MA), 1960.

Portrait in Brownstone, Houghton Mifflin (Boston, MA), 1962.

The Rector of Justin, Houghton Mifflin (Boston, MA), 1964.

The Embezzler, Houghton Mifflin (Boston, MA), 1966.

A World of Profit, Houghton Mifflin (Boston, MA), 1968.

I Come As a Thief, Houghton Mifflin (Boston, MA), 1972.

The Dark Lady, Houghton Mifflin (Boston, MA), 1977.

The Country Cousin, Houghton Mifflin (Boston, MA), 1978.

The House of the Prophet, Houghton Mifflin (Boston, MA), 1980, reprinted, with a new introduction by the author, Transaction Publishers (New Brunswick, NJ), 1991.

The Cat and the King, Houghton Mifflin (Boston, MA), 1981.

Watchfires, Houghton Mifflin (Boston, MA), 1982.

Exit Lady Masham, Houghton Mifflin (Boston, MA), 1983.

The Book Class, Houghton Mifflin (Boston, MA), 1984.

Honourable Men, Houghton Mifflin (Boston, MA), 1986.

Diary of a Yuppie, Houghton Mifflin (Boston, MA), 1987.

The Golden Calves, Houghton Mifflin (Boston, MA), 1988.

Fellow Passengers: A Novel in Portraits, Houghton Mifflin (Boston, MA), 1989.

The Lady of Situations, Houghton Mifflin (Boston, MA), 1990.

Three Lives, Houghton Mifflin (Boston, MA), 1993.

The Education of Oscar Fairfax, Houghton Mifflin (Boston, MA), 1995.

Her Infinite Variety, Houghton Mifflin (Boston, MA), 2000.

The Scarlet Letters, Houghton Mifflin (Boston, MA), 2003.

SHORT STORIES

The Injustice Collectors, Houghton Mifflin (Boston, MA), 1950.

The Romantic Egoists, Houghton Mifflin (Boston, MA), 1954.

Powers of Attorney, Houghton Mifflin (Boston, MA), 1963.

Tales of Manhattan, Houghton Mifflin (Boston, MA), 1967.

Second Chance: Tales of Two Generations, Houghton Mifflin (Boston, MA), 1970.

The Partners, Houghton Mifflin (Boston, MA), 1974.

The Winthrop Covenant, Houghton Mifflin (Boston, MA), 1976.

Narcissa and Other Fables, Houghton Mifflin (Boston, MA), 1982.

Skinny Island: More Tales of Manhattan, Houghton Mifflin (Boston, MA), 1987.

False Gods, Houghton Mifflin (Boston, MA), 1992.

Tales of Yesteryear, Houghton Mifflin (Boston, MA), 1994.

The Collected Stories of Louis Auchincloss, Houghton Mifflin (Boston, MA), 1994.

The Atonement and Other Stories, Houghton Mifflin (Boston, MA), 1997.

The Anniversary and Other Stories, Houghton Mifflin (Boston, MA), 1999.

Manhattan Monologues, Houghton Mifflin (Boston, MA), 2002.

Contributor of stories to the *New Yorker, Harper's, Good Housekeeping, Town and Country,* and *Atlantic.*

NONFICTION

Reflections of a Jacobite (essays), Houghton Mifflin (Boston, MA), 1961.

Edith Wharton, University of Minnesota Press (Minneapolis, MN), 1961.

Ellen Glasgow, University of Minnesota Press (Minneapolis, MN), 1964.

Pioneers and Caretakers: A Study of Nine American Women Novelists, University of Minnesota Press (Minneapolis, MN), 1965.

On Sister Carrie, University of Minnesota Press (Minneapolis, MN), 1968.

Motiveless Malignity (essays), Houghton Mifflin (Boston, MA), 1969.

Henry Adams, University of Minnesota Press (Minneapolis, MN), 1971.

Edith Wharton: A Woman in Her Time (biography), Viking (New York, NY), 1972.

Richelieu (biography), Viking (New York, NY), 1972.

A Writer's Capital (autobiography), University of Minnesota Press (Minneapolis, MN), 1974.

Reading Henry James (essays), University of Minnesota Press (Minneapolis, MN), 1975.

Life, Law, and Letters: Essays and Sketches, Houghton Mifflin (Boston, MA), 1979.

Persons of Consequence: Queen Victoria and Her Circle, Random House (New York, NY), 1979.

Three "Perfect Novels" and What They Have in Common (lecture; first delivered at Pierpont Morgan Library, January, 1981), Bruccoli Clark (Columbia, SC), 1981.

(Editor) Adele Florence Sloane, *Maverick in Mauve: The Diary of a Romantic Age,* Doubleday (New York, NY), 1983.

(Editor) *Quotations from Henry James,* University Press of Virginia (Charlottesville, VA), 1984.

False Dawn: Women in the Age of the Sun King, Anchor Press (New York, NY), 1985.

The Vanderbilt Era: Profiles of a Gilded Age, Scribner (New York, NY), 1989.

(Editor) *Hone & Strong Diaries of Old Manhattan,* Abbeville Press (New York, NY), 1989.

J. P. Morgan: The Financier As Collector, H. N. Abrams (New York, NY), 1990.

Love without Wings: Some Friendships in Literature and Politics, Houghton Mifflin (Boston, MA), 1991.

(Author of text) *Deborah Turbeville's Newport Remembered: A Photographic Portrait of a Gilded Past,* H. N. Abrams (New York, NY), 1994.

The Style's the Man: Reflections on Proust, Fitzgerald, Wharton, Vidal, and Others, Scribner (New York, NY), 1994.

The Man behind the Book: Literary Profiles, Houghton Mifflin (Boston, MA), 1996.

La Gloire: The Roman Empire of Corneille and Racine, University of South Carolina Press (Columbia, SC), 1996.

Woodrow Wilson, Viking (New York, NY), 2000.

Theodore Roosevelt, Times Books (New York, NY), 2001.

Also author of pamphlets *Edith Wharton,* 1961, *Ellen Glasgow,* 1964, and *Henry Adams,* 1971, all published by University of Minnesota Press. Contributor of essays to *Partisan Review* and *Nation.* Member of advisory board, *Dictionary of Literary Biography.*

OTHER

(Editor) Edith Wharton, *An Edith Wharton Reader,* Scribner (New York, NY), 1965.

The Club Bedroom (one-act play; published in *Esquire,* December, 1966), produced on television, 1966, and Off-Off Broadway at The Playwright's Unit, 1967.

(Editor) Anthony Trollope, *The Warden* [and] *Barchester Towers,* Houghton Mifflin (Boston, MA), 1966.

(Editor) *Fables of Wit and Elegance,* Scribner (New York, NY), 1972.

Author of four unproduced full-length plays and several one-act plays.

SIDELIGHTS: Although he also writes short stories and criticism, Louis Auchincloss has established himself as a highly prolific novelist of manners, the chronicler of New York City's old-money elite and those in satellite around such "aristocrats." According to *New York Times* contributor Charlotte Curtis, "Louis Auchincloss . . . is the nearest we have to a Henry James or an Edith Wharton of the East Coast's WASP upper classes. . . . Aside from his books' literary quality, their value has always been the detailed sociological reporting of what life inside these largely invisible families, their networks, their clubs and work places is like." *Christian Science Monitor* correspondent James H. Andrews called Auchincloss "the Anthony Trollope of America's Mayflower set," praising the author for his "urbane, erudite prose . . . and the careful explorations of his characters' intricate psychological landscapes and of the moral quandaries they face."

It is through Henry James, however, that Auchincloss himself claims his genealogy. James Tuttleton, in a *New Criterion* celebration of Auchincloss at 80, reported that "Auchincloss called himself a Jacobite because so much of his youthful reading was 'over the shoulder of Henry James.' To read the fiction of Proust, Trollope, Meredith, Thackeray, George Eliot, and Edith Wharton in the light of the criticism, fiction, and letters of James, Auchincloss observed, is to be exposed to the full range of possibility for the novel of manners, 'to be conducted through the literature of [James's] time, English, American, French and Russian, by a kindly guide of infinitely good manners, who is also infinitely discerning, tasteful and conscientious.' James, for Auchincloss, has been a 'starting point,' a 'common denominator'." Tuttleton went on to observe that "once started, Auchincloss has always gone his own way—often qualifying and contesting, as well as defining and enlarging, the social insights of the nineteenth-century novelist of manners."

While some critics have found fault with Auchincloss for writing almost exclusively about one class of people, others have commended him for, as Tuttleton put it, quoting Anthony Burgess, "the power with which [his] fiction 'presents the real twentieth century world, very sharply, very simply, very elegantly'." Tuttleton continued, "We cannot fully understand the workings of power in the United States—legal, financial, and social—without attending to his fiction, as Gore Vidal has rightly observed." In the *Dictionary of Literary Biography Yearbook: 1980,* Patricia Kane observed how Auchincloss's choice of genre has affected his popularity, noting that his reputation as a writer "has been influenced by factors somewhat external to it. Both the novel of manners and the fictional characters called WASPs are not fashionable." *New York Times Book Review* essayist Webster Schott stated that Auchincloss "is far from the swarming hot center of American literary intellectualism; he's a museum of all that American writing valued before its World War I baptism of despair. . . . Buried in its own riches, his world exists like Shangri-La, lost to inhabitation." But Gore Vidal, writing in the *New York Review of Books,* saw it differently: "The world Auchincloss writes about, the domain of Wall Street bankers and lawyers and stockbrokers, is thought to be irrelevant, a faded and fading genteel-gentile enclave when, in actual fact, this little world comprises the altogether too vigorous and self-renewing ruling class of the United States. . . . Of all our novelists, Auchincloss is the only one who tells us how our rulers behave in their banks and their boardrooms, their law offices and their clubs."

Sandra Salmans reported in the *New York Times* that "some academics and publishers praise him as one of

the few authors who write about the business world with a real understanding of its complexities and conflicts." Michael Upchurch, reviewing Auchincloss's 2002 volume of short stories, *Manhattan Monologues* in the *Seattle Times,* took it a step further, writing, "Still, there's a sense in *Manhattan Monologues*—sharper than in his previous work—that beyond these individual dramas Auchincloss is training his eye on a larger picture: the century-long struggle between totalitarianism, socialism and capitalism that has unfolded in his lifetime. Capitalism clearly is the victor, but he is nothing if not cautionary about where its excesses can lead—which makes Auchincloss, who is sometimes regarded as an old-fashioned writer in his method and content, suddenly feel like a crucial voice of the post-Enron Zeitgeist. Perhaps, decades after his 1960s heyday, his time has come once again."

Auchincloss writes about Manhattan and its wealthy denizens because he himself can lay claim to such a background. The son of a successful attorney, he grew up in a life of privilege, attending the exclusive Groton School and Yale University. Aware that he wanted to be a writer and somewhat uncomfortable among the elite, he nevertheless left Yale after three years and took a law degree at the University of Virginia. After serving in the Navy during World War II he returned to New York City, where he worked as a trust and estate attorney for nearly forty years. A great many of his fifty-plus titles were written while he worked for a Wall Street law firm. According to Morris Dickstein in the *Times Literary Supplement,* Auchincloss's "work on wills and trusts, separation and divorce, gave him access to his characters' business as well as social lives. He got to know Wall Street as [Henry] James wished to but never did, and focused on money as much as on manners, betraying his class simply by writing about it."

The family as a social unit is important to Auchincloss's novels, many of which are multi-generational sagas. *The House of Five Talents,* which *New York Herald Tribune Book Review* critic E. C. Dunn called "the story of human beings, their complexity, their insecurity, [and] their magnificent failure to grasp and hold the full meaning of life," takes an originally middle-class New York family from 1873 to 1948, from a social-climbing grandfather to his heiress granddaughter. In another novel, *Portrait in Brownstone,* the author relates the history of the Denison family from the turn of the century to 1951. Granville Hicks stated in the *Saturday Review* that Auchincloss "tells the story in a neat, dry style that repeatedly gives great pleasure. . . . What distinguishes the novel is its subtlety." And Fanny Butcher wrote in the *Chicago Tribune:* "The warmth of the family ties, the family traditions make the novel a happy reading experience. . . . when *Portrait in Brownstone* is good it is very good. The author has a sensitive eye for human foibles, a sensitive ear for conversation, and a sensitive mind that ferrets out human emotions." Citing an occasionally disjointed plot, however, Butcher added: "If the book were more technically cohesive, it would be a fine novel instead of just a good one."

With *The Rector of Justin,* which critics regard as one of his best works, Auchincloss relates the story of Francis Prescott through the testimony of friends, co-workers, and relations. Hicks explained in another issue of the *Saturday Review* that the subject of *The Rector of Justin* "does not seem to promise excitement—the octogenarian headmaster of a small private school—and yet I was swept along by it, for the revelation of Prescott's character is fascinating. . . . We do come to feel the reality, the complicated reality, of Francis Prescott." On the other hand, Tuttleton noted that "Auchincloss's dramatic technique in this 'conventional novel of character' creates a built-in ambiguity comparable to that of James's *The Awkward Age* or, for that matter, to Faulkner's *Absalom, Absalom!*" *The House of the Prophet* also uses the testimony of other characters to portray Felix Leitner (based, some critics have claimed, on editor and journalist Walter Lippmann), a lawyer, columnist, and public figure, who, in his later years, leaves his wife and betrays his best friend. While admitting that Auchincloss's style and "formal prose [are] so well crafted, so consistent, and so entertaining that you forgive him lapses you wouldn't forgive in a less talented writer," *Christian Science Monitor* reviewer Anne Bernays contended that "the people in this novel . . . don't really breathe; they carry ideas, rather than blood, in their veins." However, *Times Literary Supplement* contributor Charles Wheeler spoke of the novel as "a taut and elegant study of a distinguished American whose closest friends cannot decide whether they like or detest him."

Two of Auchincloss's novels from the 1980s draw on his own background. In *The Book Class,* he exposes the power held by "unliberated" upper-class New York

City wives in the early twentieth century. The story shows the inner workings of a book club's members; the tale is related by the son of the now-deceased founder, through the reminiscences of surviving members. *Washington Post Book World* contributor Jonathan Yardley claimed that while the women "get affectionate and clear-eyed tribute in *The Book Class* . . . Auchincloss never manages to make the reader care about them; they never seem to matter, to be of real consequence, and thus in the end neither does the book. Intelligent and craftsmanlike though it is, *The Book Class* is Auchincloss going through the motions, sticking to his last." With *Honorable Men,* Auchincloss attempted "to come to grips with a long-standing American obsession—how the values, if not the beliefs, of our Puritan forefathers still permeate some of their descendants, and what is won and lost by adhering to them," wrote A. R. Gurney in the *New York Times Book Review.* In a *New York Times Book Review* interview with Herbert Mitgang, Auchincloss explained: "I used to say to my father, 'Everything would be all right if only my class at Yale ran the country.' Well, they did run the country during the Vietnam War and look what happened. . . . [*Honorable Men*] is my ultimate explanation of the Puritan ethic in our time." According to Yardley in the *Washington Post, Honorable Men* is "a novel about politics, but in no way is it a political novel. What concerns Auchincloss is . . . what shaped the men who determined the nature of [America's role in Vietnam] and pressed their cause even against clamorous public opinion. He is considering in fiction, in other words, the same men whom David Halberstam analyzed journalistically in *The Best and the Brightest.*" And while Gurney saw "a tendency toward stuffiness in the writing that can occasionally settle over the book like dust," he added that with *Honorable Men,* "Auchincloss adds a significant work to his long and considerable canon."

Diary of a Yuppie focuses on antihero Robert Service, a man determined to succeed in the world of corporate takeovers and double crosses. Rory Quirk wrote in the *Washington Post Book World:* "Auchincloss unfolds this delightful and disquieting tale with his characteristic deftness, allowing Service to destroy himself in his own words through his damning diary entries. . . . This is contemporary fiction of the absolute first rank. It is fiction, isn't it?" As with some of his other books, *Diary of a Yuppie* has prompted critics to compare Auchincloss to famous predecessors. According to London *Times* contributor Andrew Sinclair: "Not since rereading [Fitzgerald's] *The Great Gatsby* have I felt a whole new class so economically taken apart. . . . [*Diary of a Yuppie* is] the most significant novel Mr. Auchincloss has written in his distinguished career."

Critics also consider the author a skilled short-story writer. *Skinny Island* involves a frequently implemented Auchincloss technique: that of revolving a collection of short stories around a central theme, in this case the "skinny island" of Manhattan. Paul Gray in *Time* suggested another unifying link: "The pieces are not just connected chronologically and geographically but by a common concern as well: the dilemma faced by comfortable people when they must choose between honor and expediency." And *Washington Post Book World* contributor James K. Glassman felt the work "conveys the insular, claustrophobic, dignified and rigid world that obsesses Auchincloss: Old New York." Glassman continued, "The death of society has always been one of Auchincloss's themes, but regular readers will find him here utterly pessimistic, his irony turned to cynicism. This writing on the edge of despair gives *Skinny Island* an urgency and an emotional kick that bring it close to his best books."

A story collection that also stands as a novel, *Fellow Passengers* reveals that the rich "are no different, emotionally or morally, from the rest of us; they just have money left in their checking accounts at the end of the month," according to Edward Hawley in Chicago's *Tribune Books*. *Washington Post* contributor Bruce Bawer called the stories "witty, charming and economical," and stated that "these tales have the pithiness of biblical parables or Aesopian fables," while also delivering a criticism frequently leveled at Auchincloss: "At times the dialogue feels not only formal but unnaturally stilted; and some of the characters' off-the-cuff literary references are hard to buy." Bawer concluded, however: "But no matter. This book—novel, memoir, short-story collection, or what-have-you—is at once a triumph of storytelling and an exemplary meditation upon the standards of conduct by which we live. Auchincloss accomplishes something that's not easy: Even as he delightfully celebrates the voyage of life, he delivers a serious reminder of the responsibilities we all have toward our fellow passenger on the trip." And Hawley advocated: "Readers familiar with Auchincloss's rich body of work will find much pleasure in *Fellow Passengers*, which is full of his characteristic insight and irony. For those who aren't, this is a good place to start."

Auchincloss once told *CA* that his retirement from law in 1986 gave him "lots more time to write . . . perhaps

too much time." He has continued to produce novels, stories, biographies, and criticism, working most often with the publisher Houghton Mifflin. His 1990 novel *The Lady of Situations* was well received by critics, including Linda Gray Sexton, who described the book in the *New York Times Book Review* as "another stinging critique of American society and its poisonous snobbery." Gray Sexton added that the novel "has much in common with other distinguished novels of manners and mores: first impressions cannot be trusted, it tells us, and unexamined impulses can prove treacherous." In the fictitious but loosely autobiographical *The Education of Oscar Fairfax,* published in 1995, a Yale graduate and Wall Street attorney reminisces about the important people and pivotal events in his life. A *Publishers Weekly* reviewer praised the work as "sedate and diverting," concluding that the novel "reliably affirms [Auchincloss's] craft, depicting the maturation of character through time." Auchincloss continues to write, and another novel, *Her Infinite Variety,* was published in 2000, the author's 83rd year. It is the story of what an attractive and determined woman must do to progress in the mid-20th century business world. *Literal Mind* commentator Erin Stringer praised the language of the book but missed a deeper glimpse into the mind and feelings of Clara Hoyt, the protagonist. Carolyn See in the *Washington Post* declared that the heroine "isn't very infinite and doesn't have much variety. In fact, Auchincloss has invented his Clara as a bit of a self-absorbed fiend. Is he being ironic, wicked or simply accurate? At some level, as America's most refined storyteller and most delicate dinosaur, the author remains remarkably opaque in his intentions." The *New York Times*' Megan Harlan saw too much of the soap opera in the fast-paced novel and concluded that "Clara seem[s] like merely the shiniest cog in this glittering yet mechanical tale of money, power and changing mores." Carey Seale, however, in the *Yale Review,* noted that "from *A Law for the Lion*, which depicts socialite Eloise Dilworth's divorce from her unfeeling husband and her consequent ostracism, to 2000's *Her Infinite Variety*, which follows Clara Hoyt, daughter of a Yale college master, as she rises from New Haven obscurity through several marriages and her own considerable ingenuity to command a publishing empire, Auchincloss's novels constitute an admiring chronicle of the ways in which the women of prefeminist Old New York were able to achieve some measure of autonomy and, indeed, to take a central place in the city's cultural and artistic life."

In the short-story collection *The Anniversary and Other Stories,* Auchincloss's "mastery is apparent throughout," argued Patrick Sullivan in *Library Journal*. "These nine previously unpublished stories feature the author's usual preoccupations: the WASP aristocracy confronting moral dilemmas in the boardrooms, prep schools and churches of Manhattan, Westchester and Newport from the Gilded Age to the present," commented a *Publishers Weekly* reviewer. Though the *Publishers Weekly* critic found the stories dated, Mary Ellen Quinn in *Booklist* claimed that Auchincloss's themes are universal, and that it is "easy to get lost in the author's elegant and restrained prose."

Auchincloss has also drawn commendations for his ability to portray the feelings and aspirations of women. "It is when he writes from the point of view of women, . . . rather than about their function from the strategic vantage point of men, that Auchincloss is at his best," declared Andrew Delbanco in a *New Republic* review of the author's *Three Lives*. "[Auchincloss] is on key when he follows the slowly dying spirit of rebellion in rich girls growing up in a world that still honors the principle of dowry. From the first kiss, they are handled with an air of possession by men who seek to purchase them as tickets to social position, and later we see them submitting—sometimes bitterly, sometimes with dignity—to the fact that they are thickening and losing their youth before the desire of their man subsides. It is through such Jamesian portraits of women that Auchincloss best conveys the hurt that sooner or later afflicts even his insulated rich—the . . . discovery that the self is worthless when separated from what it owns." Likewise, *Washington Post Book World* correspondent Arthur Krystal noted in his review of *Three Lives* that Auchincloss "is as adept at creating women as men, as capable of revealing callowness as intelligence, passion as bloodlessness." The critic concluded: "But Auchincloss has never been a mere observer; his fiction has always examined what makes life worth living and in so doing has encouraged us to do the same."

In 1994 Auchincloss released a collection of his favorite short stories, written over four decades. Chicago's *Tribune Books* reviewer Judith Wynn noted that *The Collected Stories of Louis Auchincloss* confirms the author's wisdom in writing about a subject matter some have deemed too exclusive and remote from modern concerns. "His bankers and heiresses gleam with drama and wit," the critic wrote. "His boardrooms, salons and business clubs bask in an affectionately ironic glow. Even his snootiest, least likeable characters are granted their distinctive moments of integrity and insight." Wynn continued: "Auchincloss's elegant prose and his clear-eyed moral acuity reveal the convoluted beauty of an intense social world that is sometimes mistakenly regarded as too WASPy, too exclusive, to interest readers of serious contemporary fiction. *The Collected Stories* makes that fading old Ivy League empire sparkle again, and it may well win this remarkable author the wider audience he deserves."

Further short-story collections have followed: *The Atonement and Other Stories* (published on the occasion of Auchincloss's eightieth birthday) of which Tuttleton remarked, "some sense of the volume is suggested by Auchincloss's recurrent themes: advancing age, moral retrospection, the decline of the WASPs, and the desire to atone for past ills and, toward the end, to set things straight"; *Manhattan Monologues* appeared in 2002, and, according to Upchurch, "In its pages, you can trace the changes in American sexual, marital, legal and corporate manners over the course of a century. If you're wondering what sort of people unleashed the hostile-merger craze on Wall Street or casually moved vast numbers of American industrial jobs overseas, Auchincloss can tell you. If you're speculating about the rules of adultery among our nation's elite in, say, 1937, he can tell you that too." As Reg Stout in the *Journal Sentinel* pointed out, "In these ten highly nuanced portraits, all infected with a Jamesian sense of language, Auchincloss turns to a select group of narrators—attorneys, bankers, diplomats, society matrons and sportsmen—engaged in a private monologue with readers as a way of explaining the true nature of their class."

As well as novels and short stories, Auchincloss has written well-received biographies (Edith Wharton, Theodore Roosevelt, Woodrow Wilson, Cardinal Richelieu, Henry Adams, for instance), an autobiography, literary criticism, historical sketches, essays, and he has edited books of other writers' works. Carey Seale perhaps understood the source of Auchincloss's difficulties especially with popular reviewers when she wrote, "As one might surmise from the list of his nonfiction works, which includes books on Richelieu, on women at Versailles, and on Corneille and Racine and a long essay on Saint-Simon, his roots lie instead in the seventeenth and eighteenth centuries, in an age dominated, especially in France, by the neoclassical ideals of order, economy, and lucidity. It is these ideals that give shape to Auchincloss's work, and he is indeed, as Hortense Calisher has observed, a 'classicist' at heart. Perhaps, then, it is his close attachment to his intellectual antecedents that explains his declining popularity: each new book arrives like a time capsule from some forgotten epoch of grace and intelligence, awkwardly out of place in the world of *Survivor* and Wal-Mart, tract mansions and George W. Bush. But one suspects that Auchincloss might after all be happiest joining that class of writers with whom he has always seemed most intensely sympathetic, those whose half-forgotten books stand regally if dustily to one side, waiting to offer their riches to those who will seek them out."

BIOGRAPHICAL AND CRITICAL SOURCES:

BOOKS

Bryer, Jackson R., *Louis Auchincloss and His Critics: A Bibliographical Record*, G. K. Hall (Boston, MA), 1979.
Dictionary of Literary Biography Yearbook: 1980, Gale (Detroit, MI), 1981.
Gelderman, Carol W., *Louis Auchincloss: A Writer's Life*, Crown (New York, NY), 1993.
Tuttleton, James A., *A Fine Silver Thread: Essays on American Writing and Criticism*, Ivan R. Dee (Chicago, IL), 1998.

PERIODICALS

American Bar Association Journal, February, 1972.
American Literature, January, 1972.
American Prospect, February 11, 2002, p. 43.
Barron's, May 16, 1994.
Biography, fall, 2000, p. 831; winter, 2001, p. 361.
Book, July-August, 2002, p. 81.
Booklist, September 1, 1997, p. 56; May 15, 1999, p. 1666; February 15, 2000, p. 1127; April 15, 2000, p. 1518; June 1, 2000, p. 1847; April 15, 2001, p. 1574; November 15, 2001, p. 543; June 1, 2002, p. 1677; August 2003, p. 1928; October 1, 2003, Mary Ellen Quinn, review of *The Scarlet Letters*, p. 298.
Chicago Tribune, July 15, 1962.
Christian Science Monitor, May 7, 1980; March 15, 1994, p. 14; December 30, 1994, p. 14.
Critique, winter, 1964-65; Volume 15, number 2, 1973.

Entertainment Weekly, October 31, 1997, p. 100.
Kenyon Review, autumn, 1965.
Kirkus Reviews, June 15, 1994, p. 814; September 15, 1994, p. 1218; October 15, 2001, p. 1463; May 1, 2002, p. 588; September 15, 2003, review of *The Scarlet Letters*, p. 1137.
Law Journal, November 8, 1957.
Library Journal, February 1, 1997, p. 78; September 15, 1997, p. 104; June 1, 1999, p. 180; February 1, 2000, p. 115; April 15, 2000, p. 99; March 15, 2001, p. 124; November 14, 2001, p. 74; July 2002, p. 124; October 15, 2003, Robin Nesbitt, review of *The Scarlet Letters*, p. 95.
Life, April 15, 1966.
Los Angeles Times, September 3, 1984; December 30, 2001, p. R-7.
Los Angeles Times Book Review, February 2, 1992.
Lynx, spring, 1966.
National Review, May 1, 2000, p. 50.
New Criterion, October, 1997.
New Republic, March 29, 1993, pp. 36-41.
New Yorker, August 13, 1960.
New York Herald Tribune Book Review, September 11, 1960.
New York Review of Books, July 18, 1974; October 5, 2000, p. 19; April 11, 2002, p. 6.
New York Times, October 28, 1985; April 22, 1986; August 20, 2000; October 27, 2002, p. 29.
New York Times Book Review, March 19, 1967; October 13, 1985; May 24, 1987; May 8, 1988; March 26, 1989; May 28, 1989; July 8, 1990, p. 11; February 10, 1991, p. 7; February 27, 1994; September 11, 1994, p. 26; December 4, 1994; August 1, 1999; April 9, 2000, p. 8.
Publishers Weekly, August 21, 1995, p. 44; August 4, 1997, p. 66; May 17, 1999, p. 54; March 27, 2000, p. 61; June 12, 2000, p. 50; November 19, 2001, p. 55; June 24, 2002, p. 37; September 29, 2003, review of *The Scarlet Letters*, p. 40.
Saturday Review, July 14, 1962; July 11, 1964.
Seattle Times, July 28, 2002, p. K10.
South Atlantic Bulletin, May, 1975.
Spectator, March 4, 1960.
Time, May 11, 1987; December 5, 1994, p. 96.
Times (London, England), January 29, 1987.
Times Literary Supplement, May 2, 1980; June 21, 1991, p. 20.
Tribune Books, (Chicago, IL), March 19, 1989; January 1, 1995, p. 1.
Wall Street Journal, July 5, 2002, p. W7.
Washington Post, September 11, 1985; September 28, 1986; March 28, 1989; August 11, 2000, p. C02.

Washington Post Book World, July 22, 1984; September 28, 1986; May 17, 1987; January 10, 1993, pp. 3, 10.

Yale Review of Books, Volume 6, number 2, spring, 2003.

ONLINE

Atlantic Online, http://www.theatlantic.com/ (October 15, 1997), interview with Auchincloss.

Blogcritics, http://blogcritics.org/ (May 26, 2003), review of *Woodrow Wilson.*

Findlaw's Book Reviews, http://writ.news.findlaw.com/ (February 1, 2002), review of *Theodore Roosevelt.*

JS Online, http://www.jsonline.com/ (July 2, 2002), review of *Manhattan Monologues.*

Literal Mind: Raves, Rants, Reviews, http://literalmind. com/ (March 4, 2004), review of *Her Infinite Variety.**

*   *   *

AUSTEN, Carrie
  See BENNETT, Cherie

B

BAKER, Maureen 1948-

PERSONAL: Born March 9, 1948, in Toronto, Ontario, Canada; daughter of Albert T. and Irene May Baker; married John J. J. Archer (divorced, 1975); married David J. Tippin (a sociologist and consultant), July, 1983. *Ethnicity:* "Canadian." *Education:* University of Toronto, B.A., 1970, M.A., 1972; University of Alberta, Ph.D., 1975. *Hobbies and other interests:* Gardening, piano, reading.

ADDRESSES: *Office*—Department of Sociology, University of Auckland, Auckland, New Zealand; fax: 64-9-373-7439. *E-mail*—ma.baker@auckland.ac.nz.

CAREER: Acadia University, Wolfville, Nova Scotia, Canada, assistant professor, 1974-76; University of Toronto, Toronto, Ontario, Canada, assistant professor, 1978-83; Parliament of Canada, Ottawa, Ontario, senior researcher, 1984-90; McGill University, Montreal, Quebec, Canada, professor of social work, 1990-97; University of Auckland, Auckland, New Zealand, holder of chair in sociology, 1998—.

WRITINGS:

Families: Changing Trends in Canada, McGraw-Hill Ryerson (Toronto, Ontario, Canada), 1984, 4th edition, 2001.

What Will Tomorrow Bring? (monograph), Canadian Advisory Council on the Status of Women (Ottawa, Ontario, Canada), 1985.

Aging in Canadian Society, McGraw-Hill Ryerson (Toronto, Ontario, Canada), 1988.

Families in Canadian Society, McGraw-Hill Ryerson (Toronto, Ontario, Canada), 1989, 2nd edition, 1993.

Canada's Changing Families: Challenges to Public Policy, Vanier Institute of the Family (Ottawa, Ontario, Canada), 1994.

Canadian Family Policies: Cross-national Comparisons, University of Toronto Press (Toronto, Ontario, Canada), 1995.

(With David Tippin) *Poverty, Social Assistance, and the Employability of Mothers: Restructuring Welfare States,* University of Toronto Press (Toronto, Ontario, Canada), 1999.

Families, Labour, and Love: Family Diversity in a Changing World, University of British Columbia Press (Vancouver, British Columbia, Canada), 2001.

WORK IN PROGRESS: *Families, Social Policies, and Globalization,* for University of Toronto Press (Toronto, Ontario, Canada); *Families: Changing Trends in Canada,* 5th edition, McGraw-Hill Ryerson (Toronto, Ontario, Canada).

*   *   *

BAYER, William 1939-
(David Hunt; Leonie St. John, a joint pseudonym)

PERSONAL: Surname is pronounced "buy-er"; born February 20, 1939, in Cleveland, OH; son of Lee G. (a lawyer) and Eleanor Perry (a writer; maiden name,

16

Rosenfeld) Bayer; married Paula Wolfert (a food writer), August 10, 1983. *Education:* Harvard University, B.A. (cum laude), 1960. *Hobbies and other interests:* Photography.

ADDRESSES: Home and office—San Francisco, CA. *Agent*—Fred Hill Associates, 1842 Union St., San Francisco, CA 94123.

CAREER: Novelist. United States Information Agency, Washington, DC, foreign service officer/staff filmmaker in Saigon, Vietnam, and New York City, 1963-68; freelance writer and filmmaker, 1968—.

MEMBER: Authors Guild, Writers Guild of America (East), PEN, International Association of Crime Writers, North America (president, 1991—).

AWARDS, HONORS: American Film Institute grants, 1968, 1969; two Cine Golden Eagle awards; Golden Hugo Award, Chicago International Film Festival, 1970, for *Mississippi Summer;* National Endowment for the Arts research grant, 1973; Edgar Allan Poe Award for best novel, Mystery Writers of America, 1982, for *Peregrine;* Prix Calibre (France), 1994, for translation of *Mirror Maze;* Lambda Literary Award for Best Mystery, 1997, for *The Magician's Tale.*

WRITINGS:

(With Nancy Harmon, under joint pseudonym Leonie St. John) *Love with a Harvard Accent,* Ace (New York, NY), 1962.
In Search of a Hero, World Publishing (New York, NY), 1966.
Breaking Through, Selling Out, Dropping Dead: And Other Notes on Filmmaking (nonfiction), Macmillan (New York, NY), 1971, revised and updated edition, Limelight Editions (New York, NY), 1989.
The Great Movies (nonfiction), Grosset (New York, NY), 1973.
Stardust, Dell (New York, NY), 1974.
Visions of Isabelle, Delacorte (New York, NY), 1976.
Tangier, Dutton (New York, NY), 1978.
Punish Me with Kisses, Congdon & Lattes (New York, NY), 1980.
Peregrine, Congdon & Lattes (New York, NY), 1981.

Switch, Linden/Simon & Schuster (New York, NY), 1984.
Pattern Crimes, Villard (New York, NY), 1987.
(And photographer) *Blind Side,* Villard (New York, NY), 1989.
Wallflower, Villard (New York, NY), 1991.
Mirror Maze, Villard (New York, NY), 1994.
Tarot, French translation from the English (unpublished) by Gérard de Chergé, Rivages (Paris, France), 2001.
The Dream of the Broken Horses, Pocket Books (New York, NY), 2002.

Also author of screenplay for film *Mississippi Summer;* author of teleplays or stories for television films, including *Internal Affairs,* 1988; *Murder Times Seven,* 1990; and *A Silent Betrayal,* 1994, all produced by Columbia Broadcasting System, Inc. (CBS-TV).

Bayer's work has been translated into French, German, Italian, Dutch, Danish, Czech, Norwegian, Portuguese, and Japanese.

NOVELS; UNDER PSEUDONYM DAVID HUNT

The Magician's Tale, Putnam (New York, NY), 1997.
Trick of Light, Putnam (New York, NY), 1998.

ADAPTATIONS: Switch was adapted as the CBC television mini-series *Doubletake,* 1985; *Wallflower* was adapted as the CBS television film *Forget-Me-Not Murders,* 1994.

WORK IN PROGRESS: A new crime novel set in Buenos Aires.

SIDELIGHTS: Although he began his career as a foreign service officer and a documentary filmmaker, William Bayer found his niche as a best-selling crime novelist with the publication of *Tangier* in 1978. For Bayer, who also writes under the pseudonym David Hunt, crime fiction is a family tradition. His father, a lawyer, and his mother, a playwright, coauthored a series of mysteries under their joint pseudonym, Oliver Weld Bayer, in the 1940s. In a *Publishers Weekly* interview, Bayer told Mark Harris: "I remember going to a publicity luncheon for something they did called *Cleveland Murders.* . . . On a table in front of my parents were a gun, a skull, a bottle that said POISON, a dagger. It was so corny. But now I'm a second-generation crime writer."

Tangier was followed by *Punish Me with Kisses* and *Peregrine,* which won the prestigious Edgar Allan Poe Award for best novel in 1982. Bayer captured an even wider audience with his next novel, *Switch,* a psychological thriller that sold more than one million copies in paperback. The crime is a bizarre one: a murderer decapitates two women, one a French teacher in a private school and the other a prostitute, and switches the heads of the two victims. Bayer's detective-hero Frank Janek—first introduced in *Peregrine*—is a sensitive and insightful investigator who repairs and plays accordions in his spare time. In a review for the *Washington Post Book World,* Carolyn Banks described Janek as a well-rounded character, and noted, "By the time Bayer is finished with Janek, we feel we'd recognize him on the street. We'd smile fondly at him, too."

Douglas Hill, who reviewed *Switch* for Toronto's *Globe and Mail,* praised Bayer for the good, solid police work in this novel. "As for the psychology of the book," wrote Hill, "it's not memorable, but it's not excessive either. . . . *Switch* is sensational all right, but it manages to be a decently competent thriller in spite of that." Similarly, Banks concluded that *Switch* satisfied her requirements for a psychological thriller: "I believed it while I was reading it, it frightened me a sufficient number of times, and it didn't haunt me after I'd snapped the covers closed. It's a clean, fast read."

Set in Jerusalem, Bayer's next thriller, *Pattern Crimes,* was described by Peter Gorner in the *Chicago Tribune* as "sort of an Israeli *Gorky Park.*" The story takes place in Israel, where serial murders are known as pattern crimes, and tells the tale of a diverse group of people who are murdered and mutilated in exactly the same way. Although *Pattern Crimes* conforms to the rules of the crime/mystery genre, many critics found that Bayer makes the conventions seem fresh because he writes so convincingly. Of David Bar-Lev, the detective who ultimately solves the case, Gorner said, "He is a most likable hero, this Israeli detective; tough, intense, savvy, obsessed and tormented; the most appealing fictional cop to come along in a long time." Marcel Berlins, writing in the London *Times,* praised *Pattern Crimes* for being "exceptionally well plotted" and for its "exciting action and first-class characterization."

For his next thriller, *Blind Side,* Bayer researched the literature on photography and even included eight of his own original photographs in the published novel. *Blind Side* is the story of a wartime photographer, Geoffrey Barnett, who finds himself unable to photograph human faces until he becomes involved with a mysterious and duplicitous model. Harris, who interviewed Bayer for *Publishers Weekly,* explained the presence of the photos this way: "Interspersed throughout the text are eight photographs, taken by the author—not clues or essential plot points, but views of the unfolding drama through Barnett's eye and lens. Flavored with the brutality and cynicism of *film noir,* the novel draws as much of its inspiration from movies as from books."

Detective Janek returns in *Wallflower,* in which he must find a serial killer whose weapon is a kitchen utensil and whose "signature" is done with a caulking gun. When Janek's goddaughter tragically becomes one of the killer's victims, the detective uncovers startling things about the young woman's private life while risking his career and even his life to solve the case—which he does with the help of a beautiful German psychiatrist whom he meets in Venice. In *Mirror Maze* two crimes confront Janek: the murder of a high-tech components thief, for which a tough prostitute is the chief suspect; and an unsolved homicide from years past. The case brings Janek into the seamy side of the New York City art world and features a climax in which the detective becomes lost in a New Jersey amusement park funhouse.

Past and present again mingle in Bayer's 2002 novel, *The Dream of the Broken Horses.* David Weiss, a forensic sketch artist, returns to his Midwestern hometown to cover a celebrity murder trial for network television. At the same time, he becomes obsessed with a homicide that occurred there twenty-five years earlier, when a rich socialite and her much younger lover were shot to death in the sleazy Flamingo Court motel. Searching old archives for clues, David learns that one of the victims, Barbara Fulraine, had been a patient of his psychoanalyst father, who committed suicide shortly after Barbara's demise. Convinced that his father's death was linked to the Flamingo Court murders, David sets out to find the truth. A *Publishers Weekly* reviewer called the book a "sharp and sexy thriller," and Connie Fletcher of *Booklist* deemed it "richly atmospheric." David Lazarus, in a review of *The Dream of the Broken Horses* for the *San Francisco*

Chronicle, particularly admired Bayer's use of original source material to keep the narrative "shifting underfoot," and called the book a "smart and stylish whodunit" featuring an unusually interesting sleuth. In the *Boston Globe,* Robin W. Winks dubbed *The Dream of the Broken Horses* "a fine book, complex [and] disturbing," and enhanced by "meticulous" plotting and intriguing characters.

Beginning in 1997, Bayer added several more books to his growing oeuvre, these penned under the pseudonym David Hunt. In *The Magician's Tale* color-blind photographer Kay Farrow is shocked when her lover, Tim, turns up dead, his body brutally disfigured. As she begins to trace Tim's recent past, Farrow discovers his roots, and the plot thickens as a devilish brand of magic figures in her friends demise. Noting that the novel "traces a sophisticated puzzle studded with memorable jagged figures jockeying for sexual, financial or artistic power," a *Publishers Weekly* reviewer praised the author's "vibrant, melancholy narrative voice and street-true characters." In a *People* review, Pam Lambert also enjoyed the book, noting that "Bayer mesmerizes with his sleight of hand."

Farrow returns in Bayer's second novel written under the Hunt pseudonym. In *Trick of Light* the San Francisco-based photographer—and cop's daughter—attempts to find the truth behind the hit-and-run death of her mentor, Maddy Yamada. Forced to work in the dark due to her extreme sensitivity to daylight, Farrow nonetheless tracks down motive and more as the clues lead to a secret gun club whose members are bound by something far more sinister than a love of firearms. Praising Farrow as a "tough, smart, likable heroine," *Booklist* contributor Emily Melton praised Bayer's novel for its "high-impact action" and "devilishly clever plot."

BIOGRAPHICAL AND CRITICAL SOURCES:

BOOKS

St. James Guide to Crime and Mystery Writers, 4th edition, St. James Press (Detroit, MI), 1996.

PERIODICALS

Booklist, April 1, 1997, Emily Melton, review of *The Magician's Tale,* p. 1268; September 15, 1998, Emily Melton, review of *Trick of Light,* p. 173; January 1, 2002, Connie Fletcher, review of *The Dream of the Broken Horses,* p. 817.

Boston Globe, March 31, 2002, Robin W. Winks, "The Disturbing Practice of Blurbing," p. B3.
Chicago Tribune, July 15, 1987, Peter Gorner, review of *Pattern Crimes.*
Chicago Tribune Book World, August 9, 1981; July 7, 1985.
Globe and Mail (Toronto, Ontario, Canada), August 10, 1985, Douglas Hill, review of *Switch.*
Kirkus Reviews, December 1, 2001, review of *The Dream of the Broken Horses,* p. 1622.
Library Journal, April 1, 1997, John Noel, review of *The Magician's Tale,* p. 126.
Los Angeles Times, October 14, 1980.
Los Angeles Times Book Review, August 23, 1987; June 4, 1989.
New Yorker, October 29, 1971.
New York Times Book Review, August 19, 1984, p. 20; July 20, 1989; August 11, 1991, p. 25; October 25, 1998, Marilyn Stasio, review of *Trick of Light;* February 17, 2002, Marilyn Stasio, review of *The Dream of the Broken Horses,* p. 21.
People, July 21, 1997, Pam Lambert, review of *The Magician's Tale,* p. 34.
Publishers Weekly, June 9, 1989, Mark Harris, interview with Bayer; March 30, 1990; May 17, 1991; May 5, 1997, review of *The Magician's Tale,* p. 195; September 14, 1998, review of *Trick of Light,* p. 47; January 28, 2002, review of *The Dream of the Broken Horses,* p. 271.
San Francisco Chronicle, February 3, 2002, David Lazarus, review of *The Dream of the Broken Horses,* p. 4.
Times (London, England), December 30, 1987, Marcel Berlins, review of *Pattern Crimes.*
Times Literary Supplement, November 20-26, 1987.
Washington Post, July 21, 1989.
Washington Post Book World, October 5, 1980, p. 6; August 31, 1984; May 17, 1987.

ONLINE

William Bayer Web site, http://www.williambayer.com/ (February 14, 2004).*

*　　*　　*

BENNETT, Cherie 1960-
(Zoey Dean, C. J. Anders, joint pseudonyms; Carrie Austen)

PERSONAL: Born October 6, 1960, in Buffalo, NY; daughter of Bennett Berman (a writer) and Roslyn

Cherie Bennett

(Ozur) Cantor (an educator); married Jeff Gottesfeld (a writer and producer), February 4, 1991; children: Gareth. *Education:* University of Michigan, B.A. *Religion:* Jewish.

ADDRESSES: Home and office—P.O. Box 150326, Nashville, TN 37215. *Agent*—Laura Peterson, Curtis Brown Ltd., 10 Astor Place, New York, NY 10003; Bill Craver, Writers and Artists Agency, 19 West 44th St., New York, NY 10036; Ricki Olshan, Don Buchwald & Associates, 10 East 44th St., New York, NY 10017.

CAREER: Author, playwright, and syndicated columnist. Performer in Broadway, Off-Broadway, and regional theater productions, including *Grease* and *When You Comin' Back, Red Ryder.* Theater director at regional and Off-Broadway productions, including *Anne Frank and Me.* Has performed as a vocalist, singing backup for John Cougar Mellencamp, and in her play *Honky Tonk Angels.* Has appeared on television and radio talk shows and as a lecturer in schools.

MEMBER: Writers Guild East, Dramatists Guild, PEN American Center.

AWARDS, HONORS: First Night award for best new play, RCI Festival of Emerging American Theater award, and Wing Walker Award, all 1993, and first place, Jackie White Memorial National Competition, 1995, all for *John Lennon and Me;* Children's Choice designation, Children's Book Council, and American Library Association distinction, both 1994, both for *Did You Hear about Amber?;* Dallas Shortfest! award, 1994, for *Sex and Rage in a Soho Loft;* Sholem Aleichem Commission award, 1994, and Bonderman Biennial award and First Night award, both 1995, all for *Anne Frank and Me;* New Visions/New Voices award, Kennedy Center for the Performing Arts, 1996, for *Cyra and Rocky;* New Visions/New Voices award, Kennedy Center for the Performing Arts, 1998, for *Searching for David's Heart;* first place, Jackie White Memorial Children's Playwriting Competition, 1998, for *Zink: The Myth, the Legend, the Zebra;* Bonderman biennial certificate of award, 1999, for *David's Heart*; Aurand Harris Memorial Children's Playwriting Award, 1999, for *David's Heart*; ALA Best Books for Young Adults citation, 1999, for *Life in the Fat Lane;* YALSA citations for best audio books, 1999, for *Life in the Fat Lane*; Wilde Award for best fantasy novel, 1999, for *Zink*; Righteous Persons Foundation grant, 1999, for *Anne Frank and Me;* New Jersey Garden State Young Adult Book Award, 2001, for *Life in the Fat Lane,* 2001; Iowa Teen Award List, 2001, for *Life in the Fat Lane;* Delaware 2000 Blue Hen Award for top YA book, for *Zink*; American Alliance of Theater and Education Unpublished Play Reading Project award, for *David's Heart.*

WRITINGS:

YOUNG ADULT NOVELS

Good-Bye, Best Friend, HarperCollins (New York, NY), 1993.
Girls in Love, Scholastic (New York, NY), 1996.
Bridesmaids, Scholastic (New York, NY), 1996.
Searching for David's Heart, Scholastic (New York, NY), 1998.
Life in the Fat Lane, Delacorte (New York, NY), 1998.
The Haunted Heart, Econo-Clad (Minneapolis, MN), 1999.
And the Winner Is, Econo-Clad (Minneapolis, MN), 1999.
The Wedding That Almost Wasn't, Econo-Clad (Minneapolis, MN), 1999.

Zink (novelization of her play; also see below), Delacorte (New York, NY), 1999.

Love Him Forever, Flare, 1999.

(With husband, Jeff Gottesfeld) *Anne Frank and Me,* Putnam (New York, NY), 2001.

(With Jeff Gottesfeld) *A Heart Divided,* Delacorte (New York, NY), 2004.

Also author of *With a Face Like Mine,* c. 1980.

YOUNG ADULT NOVELS; "SUNSET ISLAND" SERIES

Sunset Island, Berkley (New York, NY), 1991.
Sunset Kiss, Berkley (New York, NY), 1991.
Sunset Dreams, Berkley (New York, NY), 1991.
Sunset Farewell, Berkley (New York, NY), 1991.
Sunset Reunion, Berkley (New York, NY), 1991.
Sunset Heat, Berkley (New York, NY), 1992.
Sunset Paradise, Berkley (New York, NY), 1992.
Sunset Promises, Berkley (New York, NY), 1992.
Sunset Scandal, Berkley (New York, NY), 1992.
Sunset Secrets, Berkley (New York, NY), 1992.
Sunset Whispers, Berkley (New York, NY), 1992.
Sunset after Dark, Berkley (New York, NY), 1993.
Sunset after Hours, Berkley (New York, NY), 1993.
Sunset after Midnight, Berkley (New York, NY), 1993.
Sunset Deceptions, Berkley (New York, NY), 1993.
Sunset Embrace, Berkley (New York, NY), 1993.
Sunset on the Road, Berkley (New York, NY), 1993.
Sunset Surf, Berkley (New York, NY), 1993.
Sunset Wishes, Berkley (New York, NY), 1993.
Sunset Touch, Berkley (New York, NY), 1993.
Sunset Wedding, Berkley (New York, NY), 1993.
Sunset Fantasy, Berkley (New York, NY), 1994.
Sunset Fire, Berkley (New York, NY), 1994.
Sunset Glitter, Berkley (New York, NY), 1994.
Sunset Heart, Berkley (New York, NY), 1994.
Sunset Illusions, Berkley (New York, NY), 1994.
Sunset Magic, Berkley (New York, NY), 1994.
Sunset Passion, Berkley (New York, NY), 1994.
Sunset Revenge, Berkley (New York, NY), 1994.
Sunset Sensation, Berkley (New York, NY), 1994.
Sunset Stranger, Berkley (New York, NY), 1994.
Sunset Fling, Berkley (New York, NY), 1995.
Sunset Love, Berkley (New York, NY), 1995.
Sunset Spirit, Berkley (New York, NY), 1995.
Sunset Tears, Berkley (New York, NY), 1995.
Sunset Forever, Berkley (New York, NY), 1997.

"Sunset Island" titles have been translated into several languages.

JUVENILE NOVELS; "CLUB SUNSET ISLAND" TRILOGY

Too Many Boys!, Berkley (New York, NY), 1994.
Dixie's First Kiss, Berkley (New York, NY), 1994.
Tori's Crush, Berkley (New York, NY), 1994.

YOUNG ADULT NOVELS; "SURVIVING SIXTEEN" TRILOGY

Did You Hear about Amber?, Puffin (New York, NY), 1993.
The Fall of the Perfect Girl, Puffin (New York, NY), 1993.
Only Love Can Break Your Heart, Puffin (New York, NY), 1994.

YOUNG ADULT NOVELS; "WILD HEARTS" SERIES

Hot Winter Nights, Pocket Books (New York, NY), 1994.
On the Edge, Pocket Books (New York, NY), 1994.
Passionate Kisses, Pocket Books (New York, NY), 1994.
Wild Hearts, Pocket Books (New York, NY), 1994.
Wild Hearts Forever, Pocket Books (New York, NY), 1994.
Wild Hearts on Fire, Pocket Books (New York, NY), 1994.

YOUNG ADULT NOVELS; "TEEN ANGELS" SERIES; WITH JEFF GOTTESFELD

Heaven Can't Wait, Avon (New York, NY), 1996.
Love Never Dies, Avon (New York, NY), 1996.
Angel Kisses, Avon (New York, NY), 1996.
Heaven Help Us!, Avon (New York, NY), 1996.
Nightmare in Heaven, Avon (New York, NY), 1996.
Love without End, Avon (New York, NY), 1996.

YOUNG ADULT NOVELS; "HOPE HOSPITAL" SERIES

Get Well Soon, Little Sister, Troll Communications (Mahwah, NJ), 1996.
The Initiation, Troll Communications (Mahwah, NJ), 1996.
The Accident, Troll Communications (Mahwah, NJ), 1997.

YOUNG ADULT NOVELS; "TRASH" SERIES; WITH JEFF GOTTESFELD

Trash, Berkley (New York, NY), 1997.
Trash: Love, Lies, and Video, Berkley (New York, NY), 1997.
Trash: Good Girls, Bad Boys, Berkley (New York, NY), 1997.
Dirty Big Secrets, Berkley (New York, NY), 1997.
Trash: The Evil Twin, Berkley (New York, NY), 1997.
Trash: Truth or Scare, Berkley (New York, NY), 1998.

YOUNG ADULT NOVELS; "PAGEANT" SERIES

Southern Girls, Econo-Clad (Minneapolis, MN), 1999.
Midwest Girls, Econo-Clad (Minneapolis, MN), 1999.
Northeast Girls, Econo-Clad (Minneapolis, MN), 1999.
West Coast Girls, Econo-Clad (Minneapolis, MN), 1999.
The National Pageant, Berkley (New York, NY), 1998.
Winners on the Road, Econo-Clad (Minneapolis, MN), 1999.

YOUNG ADULT NOVELS; "MIRROR IMAGE" SERIES; WITH JEFF GOTTESFELD

Stranger in the Mirror, Econo-Clad (Minneapolis, MN), 1999.
Rich Girls in the Mirror, Archway (New York, NY), 2000.
Star in the Mirror, Archway (New York, NY), 2000.
Flirt in the Mirror, Archway (New York, NY), 2000.

YOUNG ADULT NOVELS; "UNIVERSITY HOSPITAL" SERIES; WITH JEFF GOTTESFELD

University Hospital, Berkley (New York, NY), 1999.
Condition Critical, Berkley (New York, NY), 1999.
Crisis Point, Berkley (New York, NY), 2000.
Heart Trauma, Berkley (New York, NY), 2000.

WITH JEFF GOTTESFELD; UNDER PSEUDONYM ZOEY DEAN

The A-List, Little, Brown (New York, NY), 2003.

WITH JEFF GOTTESFELD; UNDER PSEUDONYM C. J. ANDERS

Double Exposure, Pocket Books (New York, NY), 1999.
Too Hot to Handle, Pocket Books (New York, NY), 1999.
Trouble in Paradise, Pocket Books (New York, NY), 1999.
Don't Scream, Pocket Pulse (New York, NY), 2000.
A Capeside Christmas, Pocket Pulse (New York, NY), 2000.
Running on Empty, Pocket Pulse (New York, NY), 2000.

PLAYS

Honky Tonk Angels, produced in New York, NY, 1988.
John Lennon and Me (also known as *Candy Store Window;* adapted from her novel *Good-Bye, Best Friend;* produced in Nashville, TN, 1993), Dramatic Publishing (Woodstock, IL), 1996.
Sex and Rage in a Soho Loft, produced in Nashville, 1994.
Anne Frank and Me (produced in Nashville, 1995, produced Off-Broadway, at American Jewish Theater, 1996), Dramatic Publishing (Woodstock, IL), 1997.
Cyra and Rocky (based on *Cyrano de Bergerac* by Edmund Rostand; produced in Washington, DC, at Kennedy Center for the Performing Arts, 1996), Dramatic Publishing (Woodstock, IL), 1997.
Zink the So-Called Zebra (also known as *Zink: The Myth, the Legend, the Zebra;* produced in Milwaukee, WI, 1997), Dramatic Publishing (Woodstock, IL), 1998.
Searching for David's Heart (play; adapted from novel of the same name), produced in Washington, DC, at Kennedy Center for the Performing Arts, 1998.

SCREENPLAYS

Angel from Montgomery, New Line Cinema, 1993.
Wild Hearts, Lantana Publications, 1995.

Also author of *Samantha Tyler's Younger Sister* (in German translation only), Cora-Verlag Press (Germany). Author of nationally syndicated advice column, "Hey Cherie!" Author of novels in series "The

Party Line," under the pseudonym Carrie Austen. Creator and monitor of America Online's first online reader-written young adult novel, *Horror Ink,* 1997. Has written for National Broadcasting Company (NBC) television daytime drama *Another World* and ABC daytime drama *Port Charles,* and for Warner Brothers television program *Smallville,* 2001-02.

Bennett's works have been translated into several languages, including French, German, Spanish, and Swedish.

ADAPTATIONS: Several novels and plays have been optioned for film and television, including *Honky Tonk Angels, John Lennon and Me, Wild Hearts, Teen Angels, Anne Frank and Me, Hope Hospital,* and *Cyra and Rocky.*

SIDELIGHTS: Cherie Bennett is a popular novelist and advice columnist, read by young teens across the United States. When not writing, she spends a great deal of time meeting with teenagers and discussing with them the difficulties involved in growing up. Her books and talks frequently address issues such as fitting in with peers and worrying about one's appearance. "[Teen girls] worry most whether they are cute enough or thin enough," Bennett explained to *React for Teens* contributor Karen Pritzker. "Their lives become smaller. If I can write one book that saves a girl from that, I'm happy."

Bennett was born in 1960 and grew up in Michigan. Her father was a writer for numerous television series, including *Twilight Zone, Route 66,* and Sid Caesar's *Show of Shows.* She explained to *Blast!* contributor Laura Matter that her own writing began at an early age, but the quality was certainly nothing to brag about: "I wrote really, really bad poetry when I was a teenager," Bennett admitted. "This should give hope to kids out there who write poetry and think, 'This isn't any good.' I mean, my poetry stunk."

Bennett published her first novel, *With a Face Like Mine,* while she was a student at the University of Michigan at the beginning of the 1980s. However, it wasn't until she had graduated from college and spent several years in New York City as a singer and dancer that she returned to her writing seriously, first as a playwright. Bennett's play *Honky Tonk Angels* pro-

vided her with an introduction to the city she would one day call home—Nashville. Featuring a group of women with dreams of becoming country music singing sensations, the play was produced in Nashville in 1988 and sold to Tri Star Pictures in 1992.

Bennett's long-running "Sunset Island" series of young adult novels, which she introduced in 1991, features teens Sam, Emma, and Carrie on a summer vacation that never ends. Taking place on an island off the coast of Maine, the novels follow the teens' efforts to find time for fun and friends while working as summer au pairs for vacationing families. In 1994 Bennett published the "Club Sunset Island" companion trilogy for younger readers. Featuring the novels *Too Many Boys, Dixie's First Kiss,* and *Tori's Crush,* the three-novel series features preteen protagonists coping with their first romantic experiences.

Other Bennett-penned series popular with teen readers include "Surviving Sixteen," a trilogy that debuted in 1993, and "Wild Hearts," which began in 1994. In *Wild Hearts,* the opening novel of the latter series, country music provides the backdrop to a New York City teen's growing appreciation for her new hometown of Nashville. Street-smart and cosmopolitan newcomer Jane McVay and her new friends—Savannah, Kimmy, and Sandra—eventually decide to form the band Wild Hearts, which serves as the series' focus. "Nashville provides a distinctive setting," noted a *Publishers Weekly* reviewer, who added that "Jane's wisecracking, first-person narrative . . . sets a rapid tempo." Silvia Makowski, in her review of the series premier in *Voice of Youth Advocates,* commented that "Bennett is in top form with this first installment. . . . Teens will feel sad and bad for [Jane] and identify with her predicament, caught between two exotic city cultures."

Comprising the novels *Did You Hear about Amber?, The Fall of the Perfect Girl,* and *Only Love Can Break Your Heart,* the "Surviving Sixteen" trilogy was praised by reviewers for its humor and lively style. Bennett's first-hand experience with rheumatoid arthritis serves as inspiration for her book *Did You Hear about Amber?* Published in 1993, the novel follows the beautiful but snobbish Amber, who makes up for living on the poor side of town by excelling at dance. Her talent and good looks gain her entry into the in-crowd until a diagnosis of rheumatoid arthritis cuts Amber's dreams of a career as a dancer short at age sixteen.

In *The Fall of the Perfect Girl,* Bennett introduces readers to a teen with a less-than-ideal personality: Suzanne Elizabeth Wentworth Lafayette. As the length of her name might suggest, Bennett's protagonist is wealthy, worldly, and very spoiled. But the sixteen-year-old's perfect life comes crashing down around her after an indiscretion in her politically prominent father's past is publicly revealed. The family is scandalized by the discovery that Suzanne has a half-sister, Patsy, by her father's old girlfriend, and Suzanne's socialite mother indignantly leaves her husband. While noting that most readers will not find much to sympathize with in the novel's haughty heroine, Elaine S. Patterson stated in her *Kliatt* review that "girls should enjoy . . . [watching] Suzanne becoming more thoughtful and mature." Noting that the novel was a "refreshing change of pace," *Voice of Youth Advocates* critic Beth Andersen maintained that *The Fall of the Perfect Girl* "is a good story about decent teens behaving in believable ways that do *not* involve substance abuse or promiscuity."

Bennett's "Teen Angels" novels, created and coauthored by her writer-producer husband, Jeff Gottesfeld, concern three older teens who meet untimely deaths and wind up in Teen Heaven, sent there by the "Big Guy . . . when they still had lessons of life to learn." The series begins with *Heaven Can't Wait,* as Cisco, Melody, and Nicole attempt to earn "Angel Points" by helping self-destructive musician Shayne Stone straighten out his life and end his dependence on drugs and alcohol. Averting a teen pregnancy becomes the focus of *Love Never Dies,* as angel Nicole is sent to "Ground Zero" (Earth) to convince a sixteen-year-old that motherhood should wait, no matter how much she loves her boyfriend. Observing that the series contains nondenominational references to religion despite its subject matter, Holly M. Ward, writing in *Voice of Youth Advocates,* praised the "Teen Angels" books as a "cute idea." Ward summarized the overall works as "light romance with the idea that one can make a positive difference in another's life." Similar in theme are Bennett's "Hope Hospital" books, which feature a trio of thirteen-year-olds who volunteer at a hospital in Hope, Michigan, and discover a great deal about life, death, and, of course, boys.

Bennett would make writing a family affair again with the "Trash" novel series begun in 1997. Working with her producer-husband Jeff Gottesfeld and drawing heavily on her daytime-drama writing experience, Ben-

nett created series protagonist Chelsea Jennings, the teen-age daughter of a convicted mass murderer. Hoping to conceal her past, Chelsea finds herself with a new boyfriend and a fashionable summer job in New York City, working behind the scenes on a scandalous TV talk show. The author "pulls out all the stops to snare female young adults looking for a read that's, well, just a trifle trashy," according to a *Publishers Weekly* critic in a review of the series' first installment, *Trash.*

Published in 1998, *Life in the Fat Lane* features a sixteen-year-old homecoming queen who lives the life many teens dream about: popularity in school, a perfect boyfriend, and excellent school marks. However, Lara Ardeche's ideal world slowly disintegrates as she begins to add pounds to her beauty pageant figure. Frustrated at her inexplicable weight gain, Lara tries fad diets, intense exercise sessions, and even fasting to shed the added pounds but nothing works. Only after coming to terms with her new size, and the incurable metabolic disorder behind it, is she able to regain her self-confidence and appreciate the few true friends that remain with her. While talking about the damaging effects "unrealistic standards of beauty" have on teenagers, a *Kirkus Reviews* critic claimed that Bennett "lays out the issues with unusual clarity, sharp insight, and cutting irony." Calling the novel an "addicting experience," a contributor to *Publishers Weekly* commented that Bennett's story about Lara's experience "is sure to hit a nerve" with readers.

In addition to her popular novel series, Bennett has written a number of stand-alone novels, and she continues to put her knowledge of the theater to good use in plays written for both adult and teen audiences. *John Lennon and Me,* a drama about a girl with cystic fibrosis based on her 1993 novel *Good-Bye, Best Friend,* received several awards after it was produced for the stage in 1992. Her play *Anne Frank and Me,* about modern American teens, denial of the Holocaust, and the Nazi-occupation of Paris, was produced Off-Broadway by the American Jewish Theater in 1996. Later, the author wrote a novelization of the play. In a review for the *New York Times,* Lawrence Van Gelder hailed Bennett's reflection of Anne Frank's story through the eyes of modern—and skeptical—middle-schoolers assigned to perform a play based on Frank's diaries. The critic called the work "an eloquent and poignant play" that "deserves to be seen."

The theme of *Life in the Fat Lane* was turned upside down in Bennett's book *Stranger in the Mirror.* In this story, Callie Bailey is a self-proclaimed "geek" who wishes to be more like her pretty, popular older sister. A strange rock Callie finds in the woods turns out to have magical properties, and her wish is soon granted. Callie becomes her sister's equal in all outward respects, and even usurps her sister's job and boyfriend. In the end, she learns to be confident as herself instead of having to take on the identity of another. *School Library Journal* contributor Ronni Krasnow found Callie to be "a well-developed and likable heroine with a caustic wit." Helen Rosenberg, a writer for *Booklist,* dismissed the plot as "formulaic," but added: "The story delivers some useful lessons about being true to oneself and finding happiness with who you are."

Zink, like *Anne Frank and Me,* was both a play and a novel. It blends fantasy and realism in a story about a child's battle with leukemia. Inspired by the author's real-life contact with a young person struggling with brain cancer, the book sets the patient's fantasies about a band of imaginary zebras and their spotted leader, Zink. Becky Zaslow finds that when she enters the hospital, her zebras come with her, though only she can see them. Traveling to their homeland, she faces danger in the form of lions and raging rivers. The more fanciful parts of the book are sometimes "bizarre," according to a *Publishers Weekly* writer, but that same writer added: "The hospital scenes stand out for their authenticity, and Becky's bravery in facing cancer becomes all the more poignant as a result of Bennett's candor in setting forth the girl's ordeals."

BIOGRAPHICAL AND CRITICAL SOURCES:

BOOKS

Authors and Artists for Young Adults, Volume 29, Gale (Detroit, MI), 1999.

PERIODICALS

Blast! Magazine (Nashville, TN), April, 1993, pp. 18-19.
Booklist, January 1, 1998, Ilene Cooper, review of *Life in the Fat Lane,* p. 794; February 15, 2000, Helen Rosenberg, review of *Stranger in the Mirror,* p. 1102; February 15, 2001, Frances Bradburn, review of *Anne Frank and Me,* p. 1128.

Bulletin of the Center for Children's Books, February, 1998, pp. 194-195.
Horn Book, January-February, 1998, p. 69.
Indianapolis Star, October 17, 2001, Marion Garmel, review of *Anne Frank and Me,* p. E4.
Kirkus Reviews, December 8, 1997, p. 73.
Kliatt, November, 1993, p. 4; May, 1996, p. 12.
Morning Call (Allentown, PA), March 14, 1997, Geoff Gehman, "Growth and Pain Time-Travel Tale Sparks Teen-Age Awareness of Tragic Holocaust," p. D12.
New York Times, December 11, 1996.
Pensacola News Journal, October 3, 2001, Andy Metzger, "Teen Relives History in *Anne Frank and Me,*" p. 1B.
Publishers Weekly, June 14, 1993, p. 73; January 17, 1994, p. 440; January 8, 1996, Paul Nathan, "Youth Will Be Served," p. 20; May 26, 1997, p. 86; December 8, 1997, review of *Life in the Fat Lane;* December 8, 1997, p. 73; December 15, 1997, p. 1832; June 29, 1998, review of *The Wedding That Almost Wasn't,* p. 59; January 18, 1999, Shannon Maughan, "Changing Hats," p. 198; October 25, 1999, review of *Zink,* p. 81, review of *University Hospital,* p. 82; January 3, 2000, review of *Stranger in the Mirror,* p. 76; March 5, 2001, review of *Anne Frank and Me,* p. 80.
React for Teens, January 15-21, 1996, p. 13.
School Library Journal, September, 1997, Jacqueline Rose, review of *Love, Lies and Video,* p. 213; October, 1997, Jana R. Fine, review of *Trash,* p. 128; March, 1998, Dina Sherman, review of *Life in the Fat Lane,* p. 208; February, 2000, Marilyn Ackerman, review of *Zink,* p. 117; March, 2000, Ronni Krasnow, review of *Stranger in the Mirror,* p. 233; March, 2001, Sharon Grover, review of *Anne Frank and Me,* p. 245.
Tampa Tribune, October 4, 1999, "Personalized Advice," p. 3.
Voice of Youth Advocates, December, 1993, pp. 286-287; February, 1994, p. 364; June, 1994, p. 80; April, 1996, p. 21; June, 1996, p. 92.

ONLINE

Cherie Bennett's Home Page, http://www.cherie bennett.com/ (July 4, 2003).
KidsReads, http://www.kidsreads.com/ (July 5, 2003), interview with Cherie Bennett.*

BENOIT, William L. 1953-

PERSONAL: Born March 17, 1953, in New Castle, IN; son of Garvey J. (an office professional) and Berneice Benoit; married May 18, 1974; wife's name Pamela Jean (a professor); children: Jennifer M. *Ethnicity:* "Caucasian." *Education:* Ball State University, B.S., 1975; Central Michigan University, M.A., 1976; Wayne State University, Ph.D., 1979. *Hobbies and other interests:* Astronomy, blues and rock-and-roll music.

ADDRESSES: Home—Columbia, MO. *Office*—Department of Communication, 115 Switzler Hall, University of Missouri—Columbia, Columbia, MO 65211. *E-mail*—benoitw@missouri.edu.

CAREER: Miami University of Ohio, Oxford, visiting assistant professor of communication, 1979-80; Bowling Green State University, Bowling Green, OH, assistant professor, 1980-84; University of Missouri—Columbia, began as assistant professor, became professor of communication, 1984—.

MEMBER: International Communication Association, National Communication Association, Central States Communication Association.

AWARDS, HONORS: Choice Award for outstanding scholarly book; Rohrer Award for research in argument; Phillips Mentoring Award.

WRITINGS:

(Editor) *Readings in Argumentation,* Mouton Publishers (Hawthorne, NY), 1992.
Accounts, Excuses, Apologies, State University of New York Press (Albany, NY), 1995.
Candidates in Conflict, University of Alabama Press (Tuscaloosa, AL), 1996.
Campaign '96, Praeger (New York, NY), 1998.
Seeing Spots: A Functional Analysis of Presidential Television Advertisements, 1952-1996, Praeger (Westport, CN), 1999.
(With Joseph R. Blaney) *The Clinton Scandals and the Politics of Image Restoration,* Praeger (Westport, CT), 2001.

(With P. M. Pier, LeAnn M. Brazeal, John R. McHale, and others) *The Primary Decision: A Functional Analysis of Debates in Presidential Primaries,* Praeger (Westport, CT), 2001.

SIDELIGHTS: William L. Benoit once told *CA:* "I enjoy doing research to understand how and why communication works—or fails to work. I am motivated primarily by curiosity. I find image repair and politics fascinating."

BIOGRAPHICAL AND CRITICAL SOURCES:

PERIODICALS

Choice, December, 2001, T. M. Jackson, review of *The Clinton Scandals and the Politics of Image Restoration,* p. 759; September, 2002, S. E. Schier, review of *The Primary Decision: A Functional Analysis of Debates in Presidential Primaries,* p. 186.
Presidential Studies Quarterly, March, 2000, Glenn W. Richardson, Jr., review of *Seeing Spots: A Functional Analysis of Presidential Television Advertisements,* p. 197; March, 2002, Henry C. Kenski, review of *The Clinton Scandals and the Politics of Image Restoration,* p. 217.

* * *

BOBRICK, Benson 1947-

PERSONAL: Born 1947. *Education:* Columbia University, Ph.D.

ADDRESSES: Agent—c/o Author Mail, Simon & Schuster, 1230 Avenue of the Americas, New York, NY 10020. *E-mail*—Shiloh98@sover.net.

CAREER: Historian and author.

WRITINGS:

Labyrinths of Iron: A History of the World's Subways, Newsweek Books (New York, NY), 1981, published as *Labyrinths of Iron: Subways in History, Myth, Art, Technology, and War,* Quill (New York, NY), 1986.

Parsons Brinckerhoff: The First Hundred Years, Van Nostrand (New York, NY), 1985.

Fearful Majesty: The Life and Reign of Ivan the Terrible, Putnam (New York, NY), 1987.

East of the Sun: The Epic Conquest and Tragic History of Siberia, Poseidon Press (New York, NY), 1992.

Knotted Tongues: Stuttering in History and the Quest for a Cure, Simon & Schuster (New York, NY), 1995.

Angel in the Whirlwind: The Triumph of the American Revolution, Simon & Schuster (New York, NY), 1997.

Wide As the Waters: The Story of the English Bible and the Revolution It Inspired, Simon & Schuster (New York, NY), 2001, published as *The Making of the English Bible,* Weidenfeld & Nicolson (London, England), 2001.

Testament: A Soldier's Story of the Civil War, Simon & Schuster (New York, NY), 2003.

Fight for Freedom: The American Revolutionary War, Atheneum Books for Young Readers (New York, NY), 2004.

SIDELIGHTS: Praised by *New York Times Book Review* contributor Max Byrd as "perhaps the most interesting—and certainly the least predictable—American historian writing today," independent scholar Benson Bobrick specializes in complex historical events and characters. His first book, *Labyrinths of Iron: Subways in History, Myth, Art, Technology, and War,* is a sociological history of the subway systems of London, Paris, New York, Moscow, and other major world cities. Many reviewers were impressed with the book's scope and engaging writing. A *Publishers Weekly* critic, for one, commented that Bobrick "exploits an unexpectedly rich lode of subject matter with care and enthusiasm," and called the author a "gifted writer." Although a writer for *Choice* criticized Bobrick for sacrificing intellectual complexity for readability, pointing out that the author neglects issues relating to engineering and technology, *New York Times Book Review* critic Richard F. Shepard praised the book's explanation of the psychology involved in making tunnels and recommended *Labyrinths of Iron* as good reading.

Fearful Majesty: The Life and Reign of Ivan the Terrible is Bobrick's biography of the murderous Russian leader and, like *Labyrinths of Iron,* it synthesizes research gathered from many sources. Though *New York Times Book Review* contributor Alfred J. Rieber expressed disappointment that Bobrick does not discuss the role played by economic conditions, or Ivan's reforms in the areas of commerce, government, the military, and the Russian church, he praised the book for its portrayal of Ivan's character. Rieber noted that Bobrick avoids "amateur psychologizing" and concentrates mainly on biology and politics. Philip Longworth, writing in the *Times Literary Supplement,* praised the book's popular appeal but questioned its academic rigor. Bobrick "is insufficiently discriminating," according to Longworth, who pointed out that the author repeats common misunderstandings about Ivan and relies too heavily on "hostile witnesses" in forming his opinions.

Researched during Bobrick's travels in Russia during the last year of the Soviet Union, *East of the Sun: The Epic Conquest and Tragic History of Siberia* traces the history of Siberia from 1581, when the territory was first explored by Russians, to 1991 and the fall of the Soviet empire. Like Bobrick's study of Ivan, this book met with generally positive responses, particularly for its scope and its wealth of information. Jane E. Good, writing in the *Washington Post Book World,* found *East of the Sun* engaging and full of "interesting anecdotes and insights," but added that Bobrick presents little recent information. Norman Davies, in his assessment for the *New York Times Book Review,* acknowledged the scope of research and reader interest in the subject, but faulted Bobrick for ignoring "crucial non-Russian perspectives," particularly that of the Chinese. *Booklist* critic Gilbert Taylor commended Bobrick as a "versatile researcher" who "firmly fixes explorers and conquerors . . . to the native tribes and physical landscape they subdued."

Bobrick tackles a more personal project in *Knotted Tongues: Stuttering in History and the Quest for a Cure,* an examination of an affliction from which Bobrick himself suffers. Critics enjoyed the book, which combines both an historical and a physiological view of the condition. A writer for *Kirkus Reviews* called *Knotted Tongues* "a surprisingly entertaining essay." Reviewing the book for the *Nation,* Edward Hoagland—who is also a stutterer—stated that it "delves into these and other matters more comprehensively and with deeper metaphorical resonance than any of its competitors."

With the critically acclaimed *Angel in the Whirlwind: The Triumph of the American Revolution,* Bobrick returns to political history. *New York Times Book Review* critic Frederick Allen praised the book highly, noting that Bobrick "has studied his subject deeply and writes about it with real understanding and verve." Allen appreciated Bobrick's skill in conveying the "texture of life at the time, with all the necessary sense of how people lived and thought," noting also that while Bobrick draws strong characters—George Washington as epic hero, Benedict Arnold as villain—he does not oversimplify the story as a conflict between good and evil. A *Library Journal* contributor deemed *Angel in the Whirlwind* "a glorious retelling of the American Revolution."

A revolution of a very different kind is explored in Bobrick's *Wide As the Waters: The Story of the English Bible and the Revolution It Inspired.* This 2001 book investigates the many social, religious, and political waves that were created in English history after technological advances allowed the Bible to be translated and printed in English and made available to the general public. As Bobrick relates, for centuries, the Latin version of the Bible had been jealously guarded by the Catholic Church and by royalty in Europe and England for fear that extending access to the scriptures to a larger public would result in unorthodoxy and political upheaval. However, intellectuals such as John Wycliffe felt that it was important to make the Bible accessible, and popular pressure to do so eventually prevailed. Part of the result of the Bible's translation and distribution was, as the clergy and royalty had feared, social upheaval. "Once the people were free to interpret the word of God according to the light of their own understanding," Bobrick explained in an interview with Ray Suarez posted on the Public Broadcasting Service Web site, "they began to question the authority of all their inherited institutions, which led to reform within the Church." The book also explains the political implications of the translation, which caused people to doubt the divine right of kings, thus instigating government reform in England.

In *Wide As the Waters* Bobrick maintains that the English Bible did far more than lead to religious reform. "There was such a hunger and thirst for scripture [in England]," he explained, "to be able to read it, that once it was available in English, people learned how to read their own language in order to read it, and children were then brought up, learned their ABCs from biblical texts, and the rise of literacy . . . owes a great deal of its momentum and growth to the transla-

tion of scripture into English." This education helped make the English citizenry some of the best educated in the West; it also led to the standardization of English and to its evolution into its modern form. Finally, as Bobrick asserted in his interview, the effect of the translation of scripture in England was much more wide-ranging than in European countries such as Germany. "The German Bible doesn't represent an evolutionary process that's at all akin to the English Bible," he explained to Suarez, "nor was the translation of the English Bible and the impetus it gave to free speech and free thought, in the way that it was linked with the constitutional development of England."

Reviews of *Wide As the Waters* were very favorable, Simon Winchester describing the book in the *New York Times Book Review* as "ambitious," as well as "fascinating, readable and scholarly." Calling Bobrick "an exceptionally able writer of popular histories," Winchester went on to maintain that the historian "succeeds entirely in the challenge he sets himself" in *Wide As the Waters.* "Bobrick's message throughout is abundantly clear," the critic continued: "The word of the Scriptures was a formidable ally for all those . . . who demanded the rights of the individual and their primacy in matters of governance."

Still, some minor complaints were noted. Mark Goldblatt, writing in *Reason,* faulted Bobrick for citing too many secondary sources, rather than locating the primary sources, and for his "abominable method of citation" in which he often neglected to provide the name of a scholar within the text itself, forcing the reader to refer to the back of the book. Nevertheless, Goldblatt asserted that "these are quibbles. . . . Bobrick has written a fine, readable study on an important subject." *Harper's* reviewer Guy Davenport likewise praised the book for its importance and readability, calling *Wide As the Waters* an "admirably clear and abundantly informative history of the Bible in English."

In *Testament: A Soldier's Story of the Civil War,* Bobrick mines the letters of his great-grandfather, Benjamin "Webb" Baker, and from those letters creates what *Library Journal* reviewer Edward Metz described as a "thoroughly absorbing survey" of the U.S. Civil War's western theatre and "an intimate, firsthand account of a soldier's travels and hardships." Baker, a member of the 25th Illinois Volunteer Infantry, saw action in the battles of Pea Ridge, Stone's River,

Chickamauga, and General Sherman's devastating March to the Sea. Through his ninety letters home to his mother, as well as what *Booklist* contributor Roland Green described as Bobrick's "excellent narrative continuum," readers gain a sense of the war through the eyes of a thoughtful, intelligent American. Praising Baker as "an impressive person. . . . likeable, brave, admirably selfless," and "idealistic," Max Byrd added in the *New York Times Book Review* that *Testament* "is obviously a labor of love, but it is also, in Robert Frost's lovely phrase, the tribute of the current to the source."

BIOGRAPHICAL AND CRITICAL SOURCES:

PERIODICALS

America, September 27, 1997, p. 2.

Atlantic, August, 1997, p. 96.

Booklist, October 15, 1992, pp. 395-396; April 1, 1995, p. 1368; June 1, 1997, p. 1652; March 1, 2001, Steven Schroeder, review of *Wide As the Waters: The Story of the English Bible and the Revolution It Inspired,* p. 1210; September 15, 2003, Roland Green, review of *Testament: A Soldier's Story of the Civil War,* p. 196.

British Heritage, September, 2002, Katherine Bailey, review of *Wide As the Waters,* p. 60.

Catholic Insight, January-February, 2002, David Dooley, review of *Wide As the Waters,* p. 44.

Choice, January, 1982, review of *Labyrinths of Iron: Subways in History, Myth, Art, Technology, and War,* p. 646.

Christian Century, November 7, 2001, Susan M. Felch, review of *Wide As the Waters,* p. 29.

Harper's, May, 2001, Guy Davenport, review of *Wide As the Waters,* p. 66.

Kirkus Reviews, February 1, 1995, p. 116; May 15, 1997, p. 767; September 1, 2003, review of *Testament,* p. 1108.

Library Journal, August, 1987, p. 119; February 15, 1995, p. 175; June 15, 1997, p. 82l; February 15, 2001, Michael W. Ellis, review of *Wide As the Waters,* p. 174; January, 2002, review of *Wide As the Waters,* p. 48; November 15, 2003, Edward Metz, review of *Testament,* p. 79.

Nation, June 30, 1997, Edward Hoagland, review of *Knotted Tongues: Stuttering in History and the Quest for a Cure,* pp. 32-33.

New Republic, June 12, 1995, p. 42.

Newsweek, November 23, 1981, p. 110.

New Yorker, November 23, 1981, p. 226.

New York Times, July 28, 2001, Edward Rothstein, "When a Demystified Bible Became Anathema to Orthodoxy," pp. A17, B11.

New York Times Book Review, September 7, 1986, p. 36; November 8, 1987, p. 60; November 15, 1992, p. 37; May 7, 1995, p. 14; July 6, 1997, Frederick Allen, review of *Angel in the Whirlwind: The Triumph of the American Revolution,* p. 8; April 8, 2001, Simon Winchester, review of *Wide As the Waters,* p. 8; June 3, 2001, review of *Wide As the Waters,* p. 31; February 17, 2002, Scott Veale, review of *Wide As the Waters,* p. 20; November 16, 2003, Max Byrd, review of *Testament,* p. 9.

Observer (London, England), December 19, 1993, p. 21.

Publishers Weekly, July 24, 1981, review of *Labyrinths of Iron,* p. 138; August 7, 1987, pp. 440-441; February 13, 1995, pp. 68-69; October 6, 1997, p. 2; February 19, 2001, review of *Wide As the Waters,* p. 78.

Reason, December, 2001, Mark Goldblatt, "Revolutionary Book: Did the Vernacular Bible Create Individual Liberty?," p. 73.

Times Literary Supplement, October 12, 1990, Philip Longworth, review of *Fearful Majesty: The Life and Reign of Ivan the Terrible,* p. 1090.

Wall Street Journal, April 4, 2001, Marc Arkin, "The Word in New Words," p. A18.

Washington Post Book World, December 20, 1992, Jane E. Good, review of *East of the Sun: The Epic Conquest and Tragic History of Siberia,* pp. 3, 7.

ONLINE

Public Broadcasting Service Web site, http://www.pbs. org/ (April 3, 2002), Ray Suarez, "Author Benson Bobrick Discusses His New Book, *Wide As the Waters: The Story of the English Bible and the Revolution It Inspired.*"*

*   *   *

BOHJALIAN, Chris(topher A.) 1960-

PERSONAL: Born August 12, 1960, in White Plains, NY; son of Aram (an advertising executive) and Annalee (a homemaker; maiden name, Nelson) Bohjalian; married Victoria Blewer (a photographer and artist),

Chris Bohjalian

October 13, 1984. *Education:* Amherst College, B.A. (summa cum laude), 1982. *Politics:* "I imagine I have some. Generally, I vote Democratic." *Religion:* Episcopalian.

ADDRESSES: Home—Lincoln, VT. *Agent*—Ellen Levine Literary Agency, Suite 1801, 15 East Twenty-sixth St., New York, NY 10010-1505.

CAREER: Burlington Free Press, Burlington, VT, book critic and columnist, 1987—; *Vermont Life* magazine, Montpelier, VT, book critic, 1991—; freelance journalist and novelist. New England Young Writers Conference at Bread Loaf, faculty member, 1991-92; novelist.

MEMBER: League of Vermont Writers, Phi Beta Kappa.

AWARDS, HONORS: Grant in literature finalist, Vermont Council on the Arts, 1990-91; New England Book Award for fiction, New England Booksellers As-

sociation, for *Midwives,* 1998; Oprah Winfrey Book Club selection, 1998, for *Midwives*; Anahid Literary Award, 2000; *Sarasota Herald-Tribune* book club selection, 2003, for *The Buffalo Soldier.*

WRITINGS:

A Killing in the Real World, St. Martin's Press (New York, NY), 1988.
Hangman, Carroll & Graf (New York, NY), 1991.
Past the Bleachers, Carroll & Graf (New York, NY), 1992.
Water Witches, University Press of New England (Hanover, NH), 1995.
Midwives: A Novel, Harmony Books (New York, NY), 1997.
The Law of Similars: A Novel, Harmony Books (New York, NY), 1999.
Trans-Sister Radio, Harmony Books (New York, NY), 2000.
The Buffalo Soldier, Crown (New York, NY), 2002.
Idyll Banter: Weekly Excursions to a Very Small Town, Harmony Books (New York, NY), 2003.
Before You Know Kindness: A Novel, Harmony Books/ Shaye Areheart Books (New York, NY), 2004.

Contributor to numerous magazines, including *Reader's Digest, Cosmopolitan,* and *Boston Globe Magazine.*

ADAPTATIONS: Past the Bleachers was adapted for a Hallmark television movie in 1991; *Midwives* adapted for the stage by Dana Yeaton, October, 2000, and by Lifetime cable channel for a TV movie; *The Buffalo Soldier* also adapted by Lifetime, 2002.

SIDELIGHTS: Chris Bohjalian dismisses his first two novels as "apprentice fiction." Regarding *A Killing in the Real World* he states: "What begins as a vacuous coming-of-age story metamorphoses into a truly horrific mystery." *Hangman* he describes as "a perfectly fine New England ghost story," but goes on to add, "Does the world need another New England ghost story?" Only with his third novel, *Past the Bleachers,* does Bohjalian feel that he found his milieu, writing about "everyday people dealing with the complex moral ambiguities that fill the world." *Past the Bleachers,* which deals with a couple grieving for their eight-year-old son who died of leukemia, became a Hallmark television movie in 1991.

A *Publishers Weekly* reviewer characterized *Water Witches,* Bohjalian's fourth book, as "a moving, life-affirming novel suffused with ecological wisdom." The plot centers around a Vermont ski lodge that wants to develop the wilderness that surrounds it. Environmentalists oppose the development, among them local residents who are the "witches" of the title (modern-day dowsers who can find underground water with a forked stick). Bohjalian's protagonist and narrator, Scott Winston, is a transplanted New York lawyer who represents the interests of the developers. Yet as Scott becomes more aware of the situation and is affected by the New England environment, his allegiance begins to shift. "With wit, insight and mordant irony," the *Publishers Weekly* reviewer noted, "Bohjalian charts Scott's metamorphosis from rationalistic materialist and skeptic to one who believes in higher powers and the interconnectedness of all life." Janet St. John of *Booklist* also praised *Water Witches,* observing that "Bohjalian manages . . . to retain a proper distance from his characters so that they become believable, realistic, and human without submitting to the author's political correctness."

Bohjalian's *Midwives: A Novel* was chosen by *Publishers Weekly* as among the best fiction of the year, and subsequently selected by the Oprah Winfrey television show as a book club pick. Critics were nearly unanimous in their praise. Michelle Green of *People* called *Midwives* "a superbly crafted and astonishingly powerful novel." A reviewer for *Publishers Weekly* commented that "readers will find themselves mesmerized by the irresistible momentum of the narrative and by Bohjalian's graceful and lucid, irony-laced prose." Again set in Vermont, the book tells the story of Sibyl Dansforth, an experienced midwife who performs a caesarean section on a woman who has stopped breathing, to save her unborn infant. However, it turns out that the woman may not have been dead at the time and Sibyl must go on trial for involuntary manslaughter. "The description of the nightmarish Caesarean . . . is harrowing; it is also the book's most effective passage," related Suzanne Berne for the *New York Times.* Narrated as a remembrance by Sibyl's grown daughter, an obstetrician, the novel details the course of Sibyl's trial and the inevitable conflicts it raises between midwifery and the mainstream medical community. Reba Leiding of *Library Journal* praised Bohjalian as a "thorough writer," noting that the book is filled "with information about pregnancy and childbirth, and the characters are well developed, especially Sibyl and her trial lawyer."

In an interview with Rebecca Bain for *J-B Online,* Bohjalian commented, "I don't view *Midwives* as an 'issue' novel. I have no agenda for or against home birth, though I do have a massive amount of respect and affection for midwives and nurse-midwives, and the midwifery model for birth." He added, "About six months after my daughter was born, my wife and I were at a dinner party and I realized I was sitting next to a lay (or independent) midwife. . . . That was the first time I'd ever heard the term 'catching a baby,' and I grew interested fast. And as I got to know this talented and charismatic midwife, I learned that she had attended between 650 and 700 births, which meant she had seen between 650 and 700 sobbing men. I began to realize that she was a part of a profession in which everyone saw their work as a calling (not merely a job), and there was a tremendous amount of beauty and drama every single day. . . . I interviewed over sixty-five people while researching *Midwives,* including (of course) a great many midwives, nurse-midwives, and parents who'd had their children at home. That research was instrumental in all the 'birth' stories in the book, and in the development of the characters and their language." The *BookBrowse* interviewer asked Bohjalian if, having written the novel, he and his wife would consider home birth as an option. He replied, "In a heartbeat. My wife and I would be very comfortable having a baby at home, or using one of the terrific nurse-midwives at the hospital. Certainly we'd see an ob-gyn in the beginning as well, to make sure that Victoria (my wife) was a good candidate for a midwife-attended birth. But assuming it was a low-risk pregnancy, we'd be eager to call our neighbor—now friend and neighbor—who happens to be a midwife, and ask her to help us have our baby."

It was after the publication of *Midwives* that Bohjalian—until then a fairly obscure writer—got the call from Oprah Winfrey telling him she'd picked his novel for her book club. "I understood two things right away. All of a sudden I was on the same short list of writers of the caliber of Toni Morrison, Wally Lamb, and Alice Hoffman (all previous Oprah choices). I also understood that *Midwives* was going to sell a lot more copies, and it was the greatest professional blessing I could have," he told *Grand Rapids Press* reporter Chris Schleier.

In *The Law of Similars,* Bohjalian further explores the central theme of *Midwives,* the conflict between traditional and alternative forms of medicine. Homeopathist

Carissa Lake treats Vermont deputy state attorney Leland Fowler for asthma. Leland is not only cured, he is attracted to Carissa, the first woman he has been drawn to since the death of his wife. Yet when one of Carissa's patients dies, and the man's wife accuses Carissa and demands a criminal investigation, Leland must face the ethical conflict of whether or not he can fairly prosecute a woman with whom he is falling in love. *The Law of Similars* drew considerably less enthusiastic response from critics than *Midwives.* According to Pam Lambert of *People:* "Unlike *Midwives* . . . which builds to a wrenching courtroom climax, this book ends with a disappointing whimper." A *Publishers Weekly* reviewer remarked that the immorality of some of Leland's actions undercut his appeal as a protagonist. Liz Rosenberg of the *New York Times* found the characterizations flat compared to those in *Midwives,* but concluded that "despite its flaws, *The Law of Similars* is fast-paced and absorbing."

Chris Bohjalian told *CA:* "I view myself fundamentally as a novelist. Although I am also a weekly newspaper columnist and freelance journalist, it is my novels that matter to me most. I have no particular agenda for my writing—especially my fiction—no particular goal. I write because it gives me enormous pleasure, and I can't imagine I'd be happy doing anything else.

"I began writing as a genre novelist, producing a mystery, *A Killing in the Real World,* and a ghost story, *Hangman.* It was an accident; it was a mistake. I don't particularly enjoy mysteries. Consequently, my third novel, *Past the Bleachers,* is the first book I've produced that can illuminate the kinds of work I hope to complete over the rest of my career: traditional adult fiction inspired by the work of such contemporary novelists as John Irving, Joyce Carol Oates, and Howard Frank Mosher."

In continuing that career, Bohjalian's prediction that he would be able to write "riskier books" because of his selection for the Oprah book club has come true. He has produced two more novels that explore the edges of what is acceptable societally: *Trans-Sister Radio* and *The Buffalo Soldier.* The first, as Erica Jameson in the *Burlington Free Press* described, "introduces school teacher Allison Banks, her teen-age daughter, her ex-husband and the man who loves her while on his way to surgically becoming a woman." Brisbane *Sunday Mail* writer Robyn Garner pointed out that *Trans-Sister Radio* "is unlikely to top Christian

best-seller lists, as the topic is trans-sexuality. That's trans-sexuality, not transvestism; gender reassignment, not gender exploration. There's a big difference between donning the missus' frock and frilly knickers for a bit of a thrill and spending your whole life knowing you've been born into the wrong skin, be you male or female." Garner continued, "There are dramatic changes in store for all—some expected, some coming out of left field—but they are approached with a refreshing level of honesty and integrity. All credit must go to Chris Bohjalian for this sensitively handled, thought-provoking piece of fiction. Fans of his earlier books, including *Midwives* and *Law of Similars,* will not be surprised to hear that there is nothing camp, overplayed or remotely stereotyped in his portrayal of Dana." "All of my books, at least my good ones, are fictional memoirs," Bohjalian told Jameson. "It's an individual chronicling the seminal event in her life." Jameson added, "For every hour he spends writing, he spends another researching everything from school board meetings to state's attorneys. He interviewed at least thirty-five people for *Trans-Sister Radio,* traveled to Colorado to spend time with people going through gender re-assignment surgery and sent the manuscript to [a woman] doctor . . . who specializes in sex changes as well as once having been a man herself."

According to Robin Vidimos in the *Denver Post,* "Readers seem to be reacting to the book as a love story, even if the lovers are a far cry from Ward and June or even Bill and Hillary." The writer continued, "The book brings to life an alternative kind of partnering that, over the last year, has been increasingly in the mainstream. . . . Bohjalian recognizes the trend, saying, 'I think that's a good thing.'" He added, "Traditionally we've viewed it [gender] as [if] there are men on one side, women on the other. There are people in the world who argue quite convincingly and beautifully that [this view] is narrow-minded, and that it's narrow-minded whether you are gay, straight, or transgendered." "The view of gender as a continuum, and also the impossible psychic conflict that arises from being forced into the wrong gender identity box, come through with clear grace in *Trans-Sister Radio,*" wrote Vidimos.

The Buffalo Soldier is a first departure from Bohjalian's fictional memoir format. He writes it in the third person, with different sections in the voices of different characters. The book, again set in a Vermont town, centers on a couple who have lost their twin daughters to a flood. Struggling to work through their grief, Laura and Terry Sheldon decide to become foster parents since Laura is unable to have more children. Into their home and their all-white community comes Alfred Benoit, a ten-year-old African-American child who has been shunted from home to home and is consequently "secretive, shell-shocked, silent," in the words of *Book* reviewer Paul Evans, who added, "What elevates *The Buffalo Soldier* . . . is the presence of young Alfred. As the adults in his newfound home fret, dissemble and nearly disintegrate, the boy becomes stronger and eventually comes into his own."

Alfred's coming into his own is in large part both because of Laura's kindness and because, as Evans put it, "He is helped by a neighbor, an old man [Paul Hebert] who, like Alfred, feels out of place in the community. He gives Alfred a book on the buffalo soldiers of the 1860s, black riders in the U.S. cavalry. For Alfred, those riders become dream heroes, inspirations. An experienced horseman himself, the old mentor even teaches Alfred to ride." In the meantime, the Sheldon family falls apart as Terry buries himself in his work as a state trooper and has a momentary desperate affair with a woman who becomes pregnant. Evans commented, "While Bohjalian isn't the page-turning storyteller that, say, Stephen King and Alice Hoffman are, he may be something rarer yet equally fine, a remarkably empathetic writer who cares sufficiently about his characters to invest them with genuine warmth, an almost tragic dimension that's rare in mainstream, accessible fiction. With this novel, he's again proved himself a valuable resource—an author of concern and attention."

Robin Vidimos in the *Denver Post* commented, "*The Buffalo Soldier* is a story that pulls at the reader's heart, but it would be nice to see Bohjalian stretch a little more. He's very good at getting into his characters' souls, but there is a sense, this time, that he could be telling a lot more about what makes them tick. He uses a combination of conflicts to drive his plot; it is tempting to wonder how the plot might have deepened if one of them, perhaps the extramarital affair, had been cut." Vidimos concluded though, that the reader should find much to like in this latest novel, despite the fact that Bohjalian has decided to abandon quotation marks to denote speech, which Knight Ridder reporter James Ward Lee characterized as "postmodern cuteness [that] makes the typing easier, but the reading harder."

Lynette Ingram in a *Tennessean* book review wrote, "Distributing the narrative among the perspectives of four major characters, Bohjalian weaves shadings of moral complexity into this richly textured novel. Interspersed with journal entries and correspondence from Captain George Rowe of the Buffalo Soldiers and his Comanche wife, the story of one family's problems expands to explore the wider concepts of unconventional alliances and reconfigured community." *Seattle Times* writer Nancy Pearl, however, judged that "Chris Bohjalian stumbles badly in his eighth novel . . . a coincidence-strewn, credulity-straining tale of a family's redemption from a devastating tragedy." Pearl found that "here even the main characters never seem fully realized, so that it is nearly impossible to feel empathy (or sympathy) for what they're going through." Philip Herter of the *Boston Herald* observed that "opting for a prescription of fresh air and wholesome exercise, *The Buffalo Soldier* raises more questions about race in America than it attempts to answer. As the novel ducks the real social issues that give it weight, it seems the author is exploiting a hot-button topic for effect. . . . Ultimately, the novel puts a happy face on race relations in America, suggesting that in some decent little communities, the storms of prejudice are raging well beyond the cozy farmhouse yards. Putting a black protagonist into an all-white town is a potentially powerful idea for a novel, but in *The Buffalo Soldier* it remains little more than a notion."

In a *BookPage* interview, Bohjalian gave a different view on the purpose of the book: "By design, *The Buffalo Soldier* is about multigenerational love," Bohjalian said. "I hope it illuminates the fact that friendship can transcend age." Interviewer Alden Mudge, responded, "Not only does the book do that, but through the sympathetic portrayal of the widely varying perspectives of its ensemble of characters, *The Buffalo Soldier* sheds light on the whole question of what constitutes a family in contemporary America." Bohjalian told Mudge, "I write domestic dramas. Sometimes that term sounds pejorative, but that's not how I mean it. I write about ordinary people in what I hope are extraordinary circumstances."

A collection of Bohjalian's newspaper columns, titled *Idyll Banter: Weekly Excursions to a Very Small Town,* is a diary of the author's life and of small town America. In a Barnes & Noble Web site interview, Bohjalian said, "I have a novel coming out next autumn. It is tentatively titled *Before You Know a Kindness,* a reference to a lovely poem by Naomi Shihab Nye. It begins: Before you know what kindness really is / you must lose things, / feel the future dissolve in a moment / like salt in a weakened broth."

Denise Civelli in the Melbourne *Herald Sun* remarked of Bohjalian's work, "Author Bohjalian gently develops his characters through their own interpretations of circumstances. His narrative ebbs and swells in the exploration of the people in his landscape—his gift is giving credence to what initially appear to be unlikely scenarios." The popularity of his writing continues to grow as he enables readers to empathize with unlikely characters in complex and challenging situations which he does not belittle or simplify.

BIOGRAPHICAL AND CRITICAL SOURCES:

PERIODICALS

Asheville Citizen-Times (Asheville, NC), May 23, 2003, p. E14.

Book, November, 2000, p. 86; March-April, 2002, p. 67.

Booklist, March 1, 1995, p. 1177; February 15, 1997, p. 1001; December 1, 2000, p. 743; March 1, 2002, p. 1089; November 15, 2002, p. 615.

Boston Herald, March 24, 2002, p. 048.

Burlington Free Press (Burlington VT), May 7, 2000, p. D01; October 19, 2000, p. D03; June 30, 2002, p. D01; August 9, 2002, p. C01.

Cincinnati Enquirer (Cincinnati, OH), April 3, 2003, p. E1.

Daily Variety, March 21, 2002, p. 7.

Denver Post (Denver, CO), May 14, 2000, p. I-06; June 18, 2000, p. F-03; April 14, 2002, p. EE-03.

Grand Rapids Press (Grand Rapids MI), April 7, 2002, p. J1.

Herald Sun (Melbourne, Australia), June 22, 2002, p. W26.

Kirkus Reviews, December 15, 2001, p. 1699; October 1, 2003, review of *Idyll Banter: Weekly Excursions to a Very Small Town,* p. 1206.

Kliatt, November, 2002, p. 42; July, 2003, p. 5.

Knight Ridder/Tribune News Service, April 24, 2002, p. K7220; May 1, 2002, p. K1733.

Lambda Book Report, September, 2000, p. 17.

Library Journal, February 1, 1997, p. 104; December, 1998, p. 152; May 1, 2000, p. 151; August, 2001, p. 186; January, 2002, p. 148; October 1, 2002, p. 143; September 1, 2003, p. 236; November 15, 2003, John McCormick, review of *Idyll Banter,* p. 88.

Maclean's, July 17, 2000, p. 46.

Milwaukee Journal Sentinel, May 14, 2000, p. 06; July 2, 2001, p. 01.

New York Times, May 4, 1997; March 14, 1999.

New York Times Book Review, June 4, 2000, p. 35; March 31, 2002, p. 17.

People, August 25, 1997, p. 41.

Publishers Weekly, January 2, 1995, p. 58; January 20, 1997, p. 390; July 7, 1997, p. 24; October 5, 1998, p. 77; November 9, 1998, p. 21; January 4, 1999, Amy Boaz, "Chris Bohjalian: On the Fringes of Modern Life," p. 67; March 8, 1999, p. 47; April 17, 2000, p. 50; May 6, 2002, p. 22; September 29, 2003, review of *Idyll Banter,* p. 50.

St. Louis Post-Dispatch (St. Louis, MO), March 20, 2000, p. E3.

San Francisco Chronicle, May 14, 2000, p. 11.

Sarasota Herald Tribune (Sarasota, FL), March 2, 2003, p. E4.

Seattle Times (Seattle, WA), March 31, 2002, p. K8.

Star-Ledger (Newark, NJ), April 2, 2001, p. 003.

Sunday Mail (Brisbane, Australia), May 14, 2000, p. 024.

Tennessean (Nashville, TN), April 7, 2002, p. D43.

Us Weekly, April 9, 2001, p. 84.

Washington Post, July 30, 2000, p. X05.

Winston-Salem Journal (Winston-Salem, NC), May 30, 1999, p. A18.

ONLINE

Barnes & Noble, http://btob.barnesandnoble.com/ (March 5, 2004), "Good to Know: Interview."

BookBrowse, http://www.bookbrowse.com/ (March 5, 2004), "An interview with Chris Bohjalian, about *Midwives.*"

BookPage, http://www.bookpage.com/ (March 5, 2004), "Exploring the Trials and Triumphs of an All-American Family: Interview by Alden Mudge."

Chris Bohjalian Home Page, http://www.chris bohjalian.com/ (March 5, 2004).

J-B Online, http://www.josephbeth.com/ (March 5, 2004), Rebecca Bain, author interview.*

BOWERS, Terrell L. 1945-
(Terry Bowers)

PERSONAL: Born July 9, 1945, in LaPorte, IN; son of James L. and Lajetta F. (a corporate president and treasurer; maiden name, Smith) Hansen; married Patricia J. Calhoun (a bakery clerk), January 28, 1967; children: Melanie Williams, Nicole. *Ethnicity:* "White." *Education:* Attended Mesa College, 1976-78.

ADDRESSES: Home—P.O. Box 651, West Jordan, UT 84084. *E-mail*—tlbowers@compuserve.com.

CAREER: Writer. City Market Stores, Delta, CO, clerk, 1966-70; Safeway Stores, Inc., Glenwood Springs, CO, department manager, 1970-74; Bold Petroleum, Grand Junction, CO, store and station manager, 1975-81; Desert Gateway, Mack, CO, proprietor, 1981-85; Questar, Salt Lake City, UT, emergency dispatcher, 1985-98. *Military service:* U.S. National Guard, gunnery sergeant.

WRITINGS:

Noose at Big Iron, Bouregy (New York, NY), 1979.

A Man Called Banker, Bouregy (New York, NY), 1980.

Rio Grande Death Ride, Bouregy (New York, NY), 1980.

Crossfire at Twin Forks, Bouregy (New York, NY), 1980.

Gunfire at Flintlock, Bouregy (New York, NY), 1981.

Frozen Trail, Bouregy (New York, NY), 1981.

Last Stand at Rio Blanco, Bouregy (New York, NY), 1981.

Banyon's War, Bouregy (New York, NY), 1982.

Chase into Mexico, Bouregy (New York, NY), 1982.

Avery's Vengeance, Bouregy (New York, NY), 1982.

Maverick Raid, Bouregy (New York, NY), 1982.

The Fighting Peacemaker, Bouregy (New York, NY), 1983.

Death at Devil's Gap, Bouregy (New York, NY), 1983.

The Fighting McBride, Bouregy (New York, NY), 1983.

The Devil's Badge, Bouregy (New York, NY), 1983.

Gold Trail, Bouregy (New York, NY), 1983.

Dakota Bullets, Bouregy (New York, NY), 1984.

Job for a Gunman, Bouregy (New York, NY), 1984.

Sinclair's Double War, Bouregy (New York, NY), 1984.

Culhane's Code, Bouregy (New York, NY), 1984.

Deadly Bounty, Robert Hale (London, England), 1985.

Blood Vengeance, Robert Hale (London, England), 1985.

Banshee Raiders, Robert Hale (London, England), 1985.

The Masked Cowpoke, Bouregy (New York, NY), 1985.

Skull Mountain Bandit, Bouregy (New York, NY), 1985.

Vendetta, Bouregy (New York, NY), 1985.

The Fighting Lucanes, Bouregy (New York, NY), 1986.

Cheyenne Brothers, Bouregy (New York, NY), 1986.

Trail to Justice, Bouregy (New York, NY), 1986.

The Petticoat War, Robert Hale (London, England), 1986.

Armageddon at Gold Butte, Robert Hale (London, England), 1986.

Delryan's Draw, Robert Hale (London, England), 1986.

Destiny's Trail, Bouregy (New York, NY), 1987.

Lassito's Last War, Bouregy (New York, NY), 1987.

The Railroad War, Bouregy (New York, NY), 1988.

Black Cloud over Gunstock, Bouregy (New York, NY), 1988.

Iron Claw's Revenge, Bouregy (New York, NY), 1988.

The Shadow Killer, Bouregy (New York, NY), 1989.

Justice at Blackwater, Bouregy (New York, NY), 1990.

The Doctor Totes a Six-Gun, Bouregy (New York, NY), 1990.

Tanner's Last Chance, Bouregy (New York, NY), 1990.

The Secret of Snake Canyon, Walker (New York, NY), 1993.

Ride against the Wind, Walker (New York, NY), 1996.

Noose at Sundown, Bouregy (New York, NY), 1997.

Fred at Broken Spoke, Bouregy (New York, NY), 1997.

Gun Law at Broken Spoke, Bouregy (New York, NY), 1998.

Crossfire at Broken Spoke, Bouregy (New York, NY), 1998.

Destiny at Broken Spoke, Avalon Books (New York, NY), 1998.

Yancy's Luck, Robert Hale (London, England), 2002.

Battle at Lost Mesa, Robert Hale (London, England), 2002.

Mystery at Gold Vista, Robert Hale (London, England), 2002.

A Man Called Sundown, Robert Hale (London, England), 2003.

Spenser's Law, Robert Hale (London, England), 2003.

The Shadow Killers, Robert Hale (London, England), 2003.

Some writings appear under the name Terry Bowers.

SIDELIGHTS: Terrell L. Bowers once commented: "I began reading westerns while working with my father, who pulled mobile homes for a living. After the first thousand, I felt some of my ideas for characters and stories were equal to or better than those I was reading.

"Raised on mini-farms, I lived and played cowboys, complete with my own horse. With heroes like Johnny MacBrown, Bob Steele, and John Wayne, it was inevitable that I would one day create my own heroes."

*   *   *

BOWERS, Terry
    See BOWERS, Terrell L.

*   *   *

BOYD, Herb 1938-

PERSONAL: Born November 1, 1938, in Birmingham, AL; son of Clinton and Katherine Boyd; married first wife, Melba Joyce (marriage ended); married second wife, Elza (an author); children: (first marriage) John, Maya. *Education:* Wayne State University, Ph.D., 1969, graduate study, 1972-74; University of Iowa, graduate study, 1982-83.

ADDRESSES: Home—17199 San Juan Ave., Detroit, MI 48221.

CAREER: Wayne State University, Detroit, MI, instructor in Afro-American studies and anthropology, 1967-72; Oberlin College, Oberlin, OH, instructor in anthropology and ethnomusicology, 1970-72; Wayne State University, instructor in black studies, 1972-77; Center for Creative Studies, Detroit, instructor in black history and sociology, 1979; U.S. Census Bureau, De-troit, supervisor of office operations, 1980; *Detroit Metro Times,* Detroit, associate editor, 1981; Wayne State University, instructor in history and sociology, 1982; University of Iowa, Iowa City, instructor in Afro-American studies and history, 1983; African-American history teacher at College of New Rochelle, c. 1997. President of Jazz Research Institute, 1979. Conducted field work in Guatemala, Tanzania, Kenya, the West Indies, and the Middle East.

AWARDS, HONORS: Board of governors scholarship, Wayne State University, 1967-69; faculty research grant, Wayne State University, 1975; grants from Detroit Council of the Arts, 1981, Michigan Council for the Arts, 1983; journalism award, with Michael Eric Dyson, 1993, for article in *Emerge* magazine; American Book Award, Before Columbus Foundation, 1995, for *Brotherman: The Odyssey of Black Men in America.*

WRITINGS:

Detroit: A Young Guide to the City, Writers & Readers (New York, NY), 1971.

(Editor) *Roots: Some Student Perspectives; Readings in Black History and Culture,* Wayne State University Press (Detroit, MI), 1977.

(With Barbara Weinberg) *Jazz Space Detroit,* Jazz Research Institute (Detroit, MI), 1980.

The Former Portuguese Colonies in Africa (for children), F. Watts (New York, NY), 1981.

(With Leni Sinclair) *Detroit Jazz Who's Who,* Jazz Research Institute (Detroit, MI), 1983.

African History for Beginners (nonfiction comic book), Writers & Readers (New York, NY), 1991.

(Editor, with Robert L. Allen) *Brotherman: The Odyssey of Black Men in America,* Ballantine (New York, NY), 1995.

Down the Glory Road (history), Avon (New York, NY), 1995.

(Author of introduction) *The Souls of Black Folk,* Modern Library (New York, NY), 1996.

(Author of introduction) *Strong Men Keep Coming: The Book of African American Men,* J. Wiley (New York, NY), 1999.

(Compiler) *Autobiography of a People: Three Centuries of African-American History Told by Those Who Lived It,* Doubleday (New York, NY), 2000.

(Editor) *Race and Resistance: African Americans in the Twenty-first Century,* South End Press (Cambridge, MA), 2002.

(Editor) *The Harlem Reader: A Celebration of New York's Most Famous Neighborhood, from the Renaissance Years to the Twenty-first Century,* foreword by Howard Dodson, Three Rivers Press (New York, NY), 2003.

Contributor to periodicals, including *Black World, Emerge, Essence, Down Beat, First World,* and *Black Scholar.* Former editor of online magazine *Black World Today.*

WORK IN PROGRESS: Soul's Journey, for Doubleday.

SIDELIGHTS: Herb Boyd is an educator and expert on African and African-American history whose continuing concern for the lack of published writings by black authors has led him to edit a number of anthologies by such writers, including the American Book Award-winning *Brotherman: The Odyssey of Black Men in America,* which he edited with Robert L. Allen. Containing a mix of over one hundred essays by both famous (Malcolm X, Ralph Ellison, James Baldwin, Martin Luther King, Jr., etc.) and new and upcoming black writers, the anthology covers subjects ranging from racism and family relationships to music and sports. Positively received by reviewers—a *Publishers Weekly* contributor called *Brotherman* an "outstanding collection" that is "a distinguished addition to black studies"—the book, Boyd felt, helped to encourage the publishing industry to release more writings by African Americans. Yet he noted in an interview with Claire E. White on the *Writers Write* Web site that "racism still permeates the society and so it is understandable that Black men will not be a topic of concern [in publishing]—unless it is yet another attempt to denigrate us—especially when the hundreds of sales divisions at the publishing houses have already decided that Black men don't buy books. *Brotherman* and other books have dispelled this myth."

Boyd followed *Brotherman* with other anthologies, such as *Autobiography of a People: Three Centuries of African-American History Told by Those Who Lived It* and *Race and Resistance: African Americans in the Twenty-first Century.* The former includes essays, slave narratives, and excerpts from memoirs and autobiographies covering three hundred years of American history, while *Race and Resistance* contains essays by African-American scholars and writers such as Angela Davis and Amiri Baraka. Reviewers have praised these

collections, including *Library Journal* contributor Sherri Barnes, who called *Autobiography of a People* "an original and triumphant collection" that is "remarkable in its inclusiveness."

Boyd has also written books on African-American history, including the unique *African History for Beginners,* which uses the comic-book form to make it more accessible to young reluctant readers. An expert on jazz music, Boyd has written several books on this subject, including *Detroit Jazz Who's Who,* written with Leni Sinclair. He also has been a regular contributing writer to *Down Beat* magazine.

In the late 1990s, Boyd became involved in Internet publishing as the editor of the online *Black World Today,* which addressed issues of interest to the African-American community. Although Boyd told White back in 1997 that the online publication was "among the most prominent Black sites on the Internet" at the time, his prediction that the site would go under because of lack of investors unfortunately proved prophetic. Although African Americans have been buying a lot of computers in recent years, according to Boyd, the problem was whether or not they were using them to surf the Internet for sites that would be relevant to them. As Boyd commented, "When they come online are they supporting Black sites? Getting on the Internet is only half the battle. Where to go when you get there is the most important thing."

Despite the lack of support for his online publication, Boyd continues to help black writers get noticed by editing collections of their works, including, most recently, the well-received *The Harlem Reader: A Celebration of New York's Most Famous Neighborhood, from the Renaissance Years to the Twenty-first Century.*

BIOGRAPHICAL AND CRITICAL SOURCES:

PERIODICALS

American Visions, April-May, 1995, T. Andreas Spelman, review of *Brotherman: The Odyssey of Black Men in America,* p. 34.

Booklist, February 15, 1995, Greg Burkman, review of *Brotherman,* p. 1053.

Library Journal, March 15, 1995, Anita L. Cole, review of *Brotherman,* p. 90; November 1, 1999, Emily J. Jones and Ann Burns, review of *Autobiography of a People: Three Centuries of African-American History Told by Those Who Lived It,* p. 106; January, 2000, Sherri Barnes, review of *Autobiography of a People,* p. 130; November 1, 2002, Ann Burns, review of *Race and Resistance: African Americans in the Twenty-first Century,* p. 115.

New York Times, "Off the Train to Harlem, Street Peddling in SoHo," p. 8.

Publishers Weekly, January 23, 1995, review of *Brotherman,* p. 51.

School Library Journal, August, 1981, Kathleen McCallum, review of *The Former Portuguese Colonies in Africa,* p. 62.

ONLINE

Writers Write, http://www.writerswrite.com/ (November, 1997), Claire E. White, "Interview with Herb Boyd."*

*   *   *

BRIGGS, Joe Bob 1959-

PERSONAL: Born John Bloom, January 27, 1959 (some sources site 1953), in Frontage, TX; son of Joseph Asa (a miner) and Thelma (Whisenhunt) Bloom; married Joyce Karnes, September 2, 1978 (divorced, August 7, 1979); married Paula Leigh Bowen, July 3, 1988. *Education:* Attended Tarleton State College, 1977. *Politics:* Independent. *Religion:* Baptist.

ADDRESSES: Office—P.O. Box 2002, Dallas, TX 75221. *Agent*—Jim Stein, William Morris Agency, 1350 Avenue of the Americas, New York, NY 10019.

CAREER: Television and radio personality, comedian, journalist, and author. Auto mechanic in Hooks, TX, 1974-76; singer in Lawton, OK, 1974-77; *Dallas Times Herald,* Dallas, TX, critic, 1976-77, columnist, 1981-85; *Texas Monthly,* Austin, TX, staff writer, 1978-81; syndicated columnist, Creators Syndicate, beginning 1984, then New York Times Syndicate, and currently with United Press International; stand-up comedian

Joe Bob Briggs

performing an act titled "An Evening with Joe Bob Briggs" (later renamed "Joe Bob Dead in Concert") in cities across the United States, 1985-87. Television host of "Joe Bob's Drive-In Theater," The Movie Channel, 1986-96, and *MonsterVision,* TNT, 1996-2000; appeared as a commentator for television series *The Daily Show,* Comedy Central, 1996-98. Syndicated radio show host of *Media America,* 1988—, and *Joe Bob's Drive-In Review,* 1989-91. Actor in movies, including *The Texas Chainsaw Massacre, Part 2,* 1986, *Great Balls of Fire,* 1989, *Back to Hollywood Boulevard,* 1991, *Casino,* 1995, *Face/Off,* 1997, and *The Storytellers;* actor in videos *The Chiller Theatre Expo Video, Vol. 1,* 1992, and *After Sunset: The Life & Times of the Drive-In Theater,* 1995; actor in television miniseries *The Stand,* 1994, and guest appearance in comedy series *Married . . . with Children;* guest on television programs, including *The Tonight Show.*

MEMBER: Free Press Association (national board member).

AWARDS, HONORS: Named Spot News Reporter of the Year, United Press International, 1976; Robert F. Kennedy Award, 1977, for social reporting; Cable ACE

Award nominations, 1989 and 1990; best commentary track award, DVD Central, for commentary added to film *I Spit on Your Grave.*

WRITINGS:

(With Jim Atkinson) *Evidence of Love,* Texas Monthly Press (Austin, TX), 1984.
Joe Bob Goes to the Drive-In, Delacorte (New York, NY), 1987.
A Guide to Western Civilization; or, My Story, Delacorte (New York, NY), 1988.
Joe Bob Goes Back to the Drive-In, Delacorte (New York, NY), 1990.
The Cosmic Wisdom of Joe Bob Briggs, Random House (New York, NY), 1990.
Iron Joe Bob, Atlantic Monthly Press (New York, NY), 1992.
Profoundly Disturbing: The Shocking Movies That Changed History, Universe Publishing (New York, NY), 2003.

Also author of scripts for *Joe Bob's Drive-In Review,* 1989-91, and for programs aired on Showtime and the Fox television network. Author of biweekly newsletter *We Are the Weird,* Briggs Museum of American Culture, 1985. Syndicated columnist of "Joe Bob Goes to the Drive-In," 1984-98, 2000—, "Joe Bob's America," 1988-98, and "The Vegas Guy," 2000—; wrote humorous sex advice column for *Penthouse,* c. 1999. Contributor to periodicals, including *Playboy, Washingtonian, Texas Monthly, Village Voice, Rolling Stone, Interview, Talk, Maximum Golf,* and *Door;* contributor of theater criticism to *National Review.* Contributing editor, *National Lampoon.*

ADAPTATIONS: Evidence of Love was adapted as the television movie *A Killing in a Small Town.*

SIDELIGHTS: Journalist and television/radio personality Joe Bob Briggs is "an acknowledged king of cult movie history," according to a *Publishers Weekly* writer. After working as a car mechanic and a professional singer for a couple of years, he began his career in journalism at the now-defunct *Dallas Times-Herald,* where he was hired by the paper's entertainment editor, Ron Smith, to write film criticism. Always a fan of B movies, Briggs began writing the column "Joe Bob Goes to the Drive-In" in the early 1980s, which

he later turned into a successful radio show, *Joe Bob's Drive-In Review,* a 1987 book, and its follow-up, 1990's *Joe Bob Goes Back to the Drive-In.*

Briggs has long felt that many B movies such as *The Texas Chainsaw Massacre, The Wild Bunch,* and *I Spit on Your Grave* have been underappreciated by critics, who have snubbed them because of excessive violence (he typically talks and writes about exploitation films) and poor production values. While he admits that many of these movies are flawed, he also insists that some have proved to be groundbreaking films that paved the way for other, more critically accepted films. As he told Gary Crowdus in a *Cineaste* interview, "A great many of the original ideas in film come from the B-movie world and then percolate up into the A-movie world. The filmmakers who work at the Roger Corman level tend to be the young people in their early twenties, who are innovators. *The Great Texas Dynamite Chase* is *Thelma & Louise, I Spit on Your Grave* is *The Accused. The Texas Chainsaw Massacre* became many serial-killer movies, most notably *Silence of the Lambs.*"

Many of Briggs's thoughts on the importance and enjoyment of B movies are aired in his 2003 book, *Profoundly Disturbing: The Shocking Movies That Changed History.* Here he argues for the merits of such movies as *The Curse of Frankenstein, The Creature from the Black Lagoon, And God Created Woman,* and *Blood Feast.* For one of the films in the book, the exploitation flick *I Spit on Your Grave,* Briggs would also provide a commentary track. "Joe Bob makes a passionate defense of the film," noted Crowdus, "and contends with the statements of [Gene] Siskel and [Roger] Ebert, as well as some feminist critics, on a virtual scene-by-scene basis. He makes a convincing case for their misreadings of the film and their utterly wrongheaded condemnations of it." The movie, which is about a woman who is repeatedly raped by several men, exacts revenge on them in several gratuitously bloody scenes, and then escapes without being caught by law enforcement, was criticized by many people for encouraging the exploitation of women. Briggs points out, however, that the movie's producer and director, Meir Zarchi, actually intended to make a film against such exploitation, which is why the female character is victorious in the end. The gruesomeness of the film, however, has been blamed for dooming Zarchi's career and the careers of the actors in it.

Reviewers of *Profoundly Disturbing* found much to admire and enjoy about Briggs's insights into why such previously shunned B movies are deserving of another chance. In what the *Publishers Weekly* contributor called "a wryly amusing, informative study" in which the author "writes with insight and affection" about his subject, *Profoundly Disturbing* does not go so far as to assert that these films make great cinema, but the author admonishes film snobs for not accepting them for what they are. Briggs "both subverts and celebrates these films," noted Andrew Stuttaford in *National Review,* "but who cares? It's better to lighten up, grab a beer, and just see Joe Bob as someone who delights in rummaging through cinema's trash heap and telling us what he's found. He does this brilliantly . . . with a touch of *Cahiers du Cinema* that is all his own."

In addition to his books and newspaper columns, Briggs has also hosted radio and television shows about his favorite movies and has acted in some grizzly flicks himself, including *The Texas Chainsaw Massacre, Part 2* and Stephen King's *The Stand.* Always the comic, he has written the satires *A Guide to Western Civilization; or, My Story, The Cosmic Wisdom of Joe Bob Briggs,* and *Iron Joe Bob,* the last of which parodies the men's movement; and he once had his own stand-up comedy act that toured for two years. More recently, after putting his movie columns on a two-year hiatus, he returned to writing his syndicated "Joe Bob Goes to the Drive-In," as well as a new column, "The Vegas Guy," which is about his travels to various casinos. Today, Briggs continues to find small parts in movies and to contribute articles on gambling, humor, and pop culture to newspapers and national magazines.

BIOGRAPHICAL AND CRITICAL SOURCES:

PERIODICALS

Cineaste, summer, 2003, Gary Crowdus, "Cult Films, Commentary Tracks and Censorious Critics: An Interview with John Bloom," p. 32.
National Review, September 1, 2003, Andrew Stuttaford, "Horror Show."
Publishers Weekly, March 3, 2003, review of *Profoundly Disturbing: The Shocking Movies That Changed History,* p. 65.
Reason, April, 2003, Sara Rimensnyder, "Disturbed Minds," p. 17.
U.S. News & World Report, October 1, 1990, Ann E. Andrews, "X and Mom," p. 17.

ONLINE

The Joe Bob Report, http://www.joebobbriggs.com/ (October 3, 2003).*

* * *

BROOKNER, Anita 1928-

PERSONAL: Born July 16, 1928, in London, England; daughter of Newson (a company director) and Maude (a singer; maiden name, Schiska) Brookner. *Education:* King's College, London, B.A., 1949; Courtauld Institute of Art, London, Ph.D., 1953; three-year postgraduate scholarship in Paris.

ADDRESSES: Agent—A. M. Heath, 79 St. Martin's Lane, London WC2, England.

CAREER: Writer. University of Reading, Reading, England, visiting lecturer in the history of art, 1959-64; Courtauld Institute of Art, London, lecturer, 1964-77, reader in the history of art, 1977-87 (retired); Cambridge University, Slade Professor of Art, 1967-68, New Hall fellow.

AWARDS, HONORS: Royal Society of Literature fellow, 1983; Booker McConnell Prize, National Book League, 1984, for *Hotel du Lac;* Commander, Order of the British Empire, 1990; Booker Prize, 2002, for *The Next Big Thing.*

WRITINGS:

NONFICTION; ART HISTORY AND CRITICISM

(Translator) Waldemar George, *Utrillo,* Oldbourne Press (London, England), 1960.
(Translator) Jean-Paul Crespelle, *The Fauves,* Oldbourne Press (London, England), 1962.
(Translator) Maximilien Gauthier, *Gauguin,* Oldbourne Press (London, England), 1963.
J. A. Dominique Ingres, Purnell (London, England), 1965.
Watteau, Hamlyn (London, England), 1968.

Anita Brookner

The Genius of the Future: Studies in French Art Criticism, Phaidon (London, England), 1971, published as *The Genius of the Future: Essays in French Art Criticism,* Cornell University Press (Ithaca, NY), 1988.

Greuze: The Rise and Fall of an Eighteenth-Century Phenomenon, Elek (London, England), 1972, New York Graphic Society (Greenwich, CT), 1974.

Jacques-Louis David: A Personal Interpretation: Lecture on Aspects of Art, Oxford University Press (London, England), 1974, revised edition, Thames & Hudson (New York, NY), 1987.

Jacques-Louis David, Chatto & Windus (London, England), 1980, Harper (New York, NY), 1981, revised edition, Thames & Hudson (New York, NY), 1987.

Soundings: Studies in Art and Literature (essays; art and literature criticism), Harvill Press (London, England), 1997.

Romanticism and Its Discontents, Farrar, Straus & Giroux (New York, NY), 2000.

Also author of *An Iconography of Cecil Rhodes,* 1956. Contributor of essays on Rigaud, Delacroix, Ingres, and Cezanne to a British Broadcasting Corporation (BBC) production on painters, 1980, published as *Great Paintings,* edited by Edwin Mullins, St. Martin's Press, 1981. Contributor to *The Brothers Goncourt and the Nineteenth-Century Novel,* edited by Richard Faber, Boydell (Wolfeboro, NH), 1988. Also contributor to "The Masters" series, Purnell (London, England), 1965-67.

NOVELS

The Debut, Linden Press (New York, NY), 1981, published as *A Start in Life,* J. Cape (London, England), 1981.

Providence, J. Cape (London, England), 1982, Pantheon (New York, NY), 1984.

Look at Me, Pantheon (New York, NY), 1983.

Hotel du Lac, Pantheon (New York, NY), 1984.

Family and Friends, Pantheon (New York, NY), 1985.

A Misalliance, J. Cape (London, England), 1986, published as *The Misalliance,* Pantheon (New York, NY), 1987.

A Friend from England, Pantheon (New York, NY), 1987.

Latecomers, Random House (New York, NY), 1988.

Lewis Percy, J. Cape (London, England), 1989, Pantheon (New York, NY), 1990.

Brief Lives, J. Cape (London, England), 1990, Random House, (New York, NY), 1991.

A Closed Eye, J. Cape (London, England), 1991, Random House (New York, NY), 1992.

Fraud, J. Cape (London, England), 1992, Random House (New York, NY), 1993.

A Family Romance, J. Cape (London, England), 1993, published as *Dolly,* Random House (New York, NY), 1994.

A Private View, J. Cape (London, England), 1994, Random House (New York, NY), 1995.

Incidents in the Rue Laugier, J. Cape (London, England), 1995, Random House (New York, NY), 1996.

Altered States, J. Cape (London, England), 1996, Random House (New York, NY), 1997.

Visitors, J. Cape (London, England), 1997, Random House (New York, NY), 1998.

Falling Slowly, Viking (London, England), 1998, Random House (New York, NY), 1999.

Undue Influence: A Novel, Viking (London, England), 1999, Random House (New York, NY), 2000.

The Bay of Angels, Viking (London, England), 2001, Random House (New York, NY), 2002.

The Next Big Thing, Viking (London, England), 2002, published as *Making Things Better,* Random House (New York, NY), 2003.

The Rules of Engagement, Random House (New York, NY), 2003.

OTHER

(Author of introduction) *The House of Mirth,* Macmillan (New York, NY), 1987.

(Editor and author of introduction) Edith Wharton, *The Stories of Edith Wharton,* Volume 2, Simon & Schuster (New York, NY), 1988.

(Selector and author of introduction) Edith Wharton, *The Collected Stories of Edith Wharton,* Carroll & Graf (New York, NY), 1998.

(Author of introduction) L. P. Hartley, *Eustace and Hilda: A Trilogy,* New York Review Books (New York, NY), 2001.

Also author of introduction to Margaret Kennedy's *Troy Chimneys,* Virago, 1985, Edith Templeton's *The Island of Desire,* 1985, *Summer in the Country,* 1985, and *Living on Yesterday,* 1986. Contributor of book reviews and articles to periodicals, including *Burlington, London Review of Books, London Standard,* London *Sunday Times, Observer, Spectator, Times Literary Supplement,* and *Writer.*

ADAPTATIONS: An adaptation of *Hotel du Lac* was coproduced in 1985 by the BBC and the Arts and Entertainment Network.

SIDELIGHTS: Anita Brookner is internationally acclaimed for her extensive knowledge and incisive explications of eighteenth- and nineteenth-century French artists and their work. She is an accomplished novelist as well, penning more than twenty novels since 1981, including the Booker McConnell prize-winning *Hotel du Lac.* Critical response to her work has included a great deal of praise, but Phillip Lopate dispelled whatever skepticism a first-time reader might have about the caliber or profusion of Brookner's work in the *New York Times Book Review:* "Yes, she is that good, and she keeps producing quality fiction at a calm,

even rate precisely because she knows what she is doing. Each new Brookner novel seems a guarantee of the pleasures of a mature intelligence, felicitous language, quirky humor, intensely believable characters, bittersweet karma and shapely narrative."

Brookner, the first woman to be named Slade Professor of Art at Cambridge University, once referred to herself in a *Saturday Review* interview as a "speculative" art historian rather than a scholar. Her work attempts to position a subject within a larger context. For instance, *The Genius of the Future: Studies in French Art Criticism,* based upon Brookner's Slade lectures during the late 1960s, offers "paradigmatic" presentations of Diderot, Stendhal, Baudelaire, Zola, the Brothers Goncourt, and Huysmans, and identifies each with a principal idea that becomes a "touchstone for her discussion," wrote Robert E. Hosmer, Jr. in the *Dictionary of Literary Biography Yearbook: 1987.* Hosmer considered *The Genius of the Future* "a work of impeccable scholarship, precise, carefully annotated and designed, whose grace and narrative ease enable the discerning reader, whether art historian or layperson, to read it with pleasure and profit." *Greuze: The Rise and Fall of an Eighteenth-Century Phenomenon* grew out of Brookner's doctoral dissertation and sought to restore Jean-Baptiste Greuze to the historical recognition she believes his work warrants, said Hosmer, who called it "intellectually vital and engagingly written." A *New York Times Book Review* contributor similarly remarked that Brookner's "commanding acquaintance with everything and everybody, minor and major, in art, literature, and philosophy . . . is staggering, and the grace with which she organizes the minutiae to give them an air of spontaneity even more so." Brookner's *Jacques-Louis David: A Personal Interpretation,* the published version of her address to the British Academy in 1974, offers a biographical profile of the artist and traces the progress of his work. "Clearly a blueprint" for her lengthy study six years later, commented Hosmer, the work "testifies to Brookner's powers as a critical scholar and her charms as a lecturer: her text displays learning animated by anecdotal wit." In her subsequent major study, *Jacques-Louis David,* Brookner blends biography, history, and criticism to reveal that the artist's shifts in subject matter and style reflect political changes in France from the Revolution to the restoration of the monarchy twenty-five years later. Calling it "a reciprocal reading," Hosmer explained that Brookner demonstrates "how David was both formed by the sociopolitical/cultural context and how he helped to shape the forces creating that context." Praised by Richard Cobb in the *Times Literary Supplement* as "an art historian of great sensitivity and understanding," Brookner "provides a superb show of investigative work, a thorough and intelligent probing of the meaning of a man's art," maintained Celia Betsky in the *New Republic.*

Soundings: Studies in Art and Literature is a collection of essays written over a span of twenty-five years. The collection begins with essays on three nineteenth-century French artists, Gericault, Ingres, and Delacroix, and goes on to discuss the complex history of and tension between French Neoclassicism and Romanticism. Culled from Brookner's contributions to the *Times Literary Supplement* and the *London Review of Books,* the collection was generally well received by critics. "Her style evinces a contagious love of culture," asserted Douglas F. Smith in *Library Journal.* "It's to her credit that many of these reviews, some dating back to 1975, are far less stale than their one-time targets." "Brookner's survey of the last century can't help but provoke a pang of nostalgia for the classical urge manifested by these characters," wrote a *Publishers Weekly* reviewer.

Published in England as *A Start in Life* and in the United States as *The Debut,* Brookner's first novel concerns Ruth Weiss, a literary scholar in her forties who tries to escape a suffocating life of studying literature and coping with the demands of her aging parents. Disillusioned with literary notions that patience and virtue will triumph in the end, Ruth embraces the opportunistic view of the world expressed by Balzac; after the romantic affair she plans misfires, she returns home to care for her dying parents, and resigns herself to a lonely middle age. "As well as the arm's length of wit, there is a great deal of precision and perception" in Brookner's rendering of Ruth's story, commented Anne Duchene in the *Times Literary Supplement.* And although Duchene believed that Brookner goes too far in blaming literature "for the festering resentments of filial dutifulness," this "hardly matters, given the confidence of the telling." Art Seidenbaum remarked in a *Los Angeles Times* review: "The art historian who studied portraiture and landscapes also knows the terrain of the heart. Her heroine is almost historic, tethered to responsibility, but her technique is modern, hard-edged and as uneuphemistic as today."

With her second novel, *Providence,* Brookner "effectively claims her territory as a writer," suggested

Frances Taliaferro in *Harper's.* The story focuses on another academic—Kitty Maule, a reserved, elegantly dressed professor of Romantic literature at a small, well-funded British college. Never having known her British father, Kitty was raised in the French traditions by her maternal grandparents—French and Russian immigrants, and feels like a foreigner in her native England. She falls in love with a handsome and clever colleague, Maurice Bishop, whose unshakable self-assurance and Catholic faith further impede her desire to assimilate into British culture. The *New York Times'* Michiko Kakutani, who praised Brookner's "sharp eye for the telling detail" and "graceful, economical way with words," pronounced Brookner a "master at creating miniaturist portraits of attenuated lives." However, because Brookner narrates the novel almost exclusively in terms of Kitty and through her perspective alone, according to Joyce Kornblatt in the *Washington Post,* the reader does not see her in a larger context— its "very strength—the vivid creation of Kitty Maule— becomes its limitation." Nonetheless, Kornblatt called the novel "perfectly observed and quietly witty," and praised its craft: "Each expertly paced scene is brought to life through a fastidious accretion of detail, a fine ear for speech, a narrative diction that is always intelligent and often arresting."

In *Look at Me,* her third novel, Brookner portrays the life of Frances Hinton, a young librarian at a British medical institute. Her dreary job of cataloging and filing pictures of death and disease is relieved only by observing the other staff members who frequent the institute's archives. Upon returning to her apartment, bequeathed by her deceased mother, she spends solitary evenings writing about the day's observations. Nick Fraser, an attractive young doctor at the institute, with his glamorous wife, Alix, befriends Frances and welcomes her into their intimate circle of friends. They introduce her to Nick's colleague James, with whom Frances shares a chaste romance; but when Frances and James try to secure some privacy in their relationship, they exclude Alix, who then abandons Frances. Angered, Frances finds release in writing the novel that becomes *Look at Me.* In a *Washington Post Book World* review, Julia Epstein deemed the book "a nearly impossible achievement, a novel about emptiness and vacancy." Believing that the protagonist's novel is "not so much self-reflexive as self-digesting, its material imaged and converted into prose even as it unfolds in Frances' life," Epstein concluded that *Look at Me* is "simultaneously a tragedy of solitude and loss, and a triumph of the sharp-tongued controlling self."

Brookner's fourth novel, *Hotel du Lac,* won the 1984 Booker McConnell Prize, Britain's most prestigious literary award. Like her three earlier novels, it is about romance and loneliness in the life of a discreet, educated, literary woman with conventional dreams of love and marriage; unlike her earlier novels, it suggests that rewards accompany boldness rather than goodness. The story centers on a thirty-nine-year-old London romance novelist, Edith Hope, who jilts her fiancée on her wedding day. Exiled to an off-season Swiss hotel by her family and friends, she spends her time observing the other guests, involving herself in their personal lives, writing letters to her married lover, and working on her latest novel. Edith's popular novels promote the romantic equivalent of Aesop's fable of the tortoise and the hare—that slow and steady wins the race; however, while Edith publicly acknowledges the falsity of the myth, she privately clings to romantic ideals of perfect love. The *New York Times'* John Gross, who considered Brookner "one of the finest novelists of her generation," called *Hotel du Lac* "a novel about romance, and reality, and the gap between them and the way the need for romance persists in the full knowledge of that gap." What distinguishes this novel from Brookner's previous novels, remarked Anne Tyler in the *Washington Post Book World,* is that in *Hotel du Lac,* "the heroine is more philosophical from the outset, more self-reliant, more conscious that a solitary life is not, after all, an unmitigated tragedy."

A Misalliance returns to a type of character familiar from Brookner's earlier novels—a repressed, intellectual woman who finds herself defined by the man she loves. Rejected by her husband of more than twenty years for his secretary, Blanche Vernon still yearns for his occasional visits and spends time in museums contemplating the two contrasting archetypes of woman she sees in paintings: pleasure-loving nymphs of ancient mythology and dutiful saints who personify emotional martyrdom. According to Kakutani, the character sees herself as the inevitable loser in a contest between women who are "calm, sincere, doting and honest in their dealing with men," and those who are "sly, petulant, manipulative and demanding." *Washington Post Book World* columnist Jonathan Yardley thought that what distinguishes this protagonist from her predecessors, though, "is that she had her chance at love and, much though she wanted to seize it, failed to do so out of misunderstanding and uncertainty." Critical consensus confirms that the novel solidified Brookner's status as a master of prose. Yardley believed that "in writing about these lonely women,

she has universal business in mind: the peculiarities and uncertainties of love, the relationship between fate and will, the connections—and disconnections—between art and reality." However, in the *New York Times Book Review,* Fernanda Eberstadt lauded what she thought was the novel's "rather salutary and peculiarly welcome message, namely, that keeping up appearances in hard times is a virtue in itself, that kindness, self-restraint, good housekeeping and a certain cheerful worldliness may after all save the day. To this message, delivered with a lucid and refined intelligence and an invigorating asperity of tone, one can respond only with gratitude and pleasure."

A Friend from England presents a female protagonist who has recovered neither from the loss of her parents nor from a disillusioning love affair with a married man. Part owner of a London bookstore, Rachel lives alone in a bleak apartment and becomes increasingly involved in the sumptuous lifestyle of her accountant's family, the Livingstones, who are recent winners of the football pools. Rachel serves as a companion of sorts to their twenty-seven-year-old daughter, Heather. Although not especially fond of her charge, Rachel encourages her into independence; then, fearful of becoming a surrogate daughter to the Livingstones, reverses herself and tries to persuade Heather to return to her family. Describing Rachel as "repellently cold and cerebral," Deborah Singmaster added in the *Times Literary Supplement* that "she becomes increasingly sinister as the book progresses . . . her blundering insensitivity as she thrusts herself into the disintegrating lives of the Livingstones is mesmerizing." Praising Brookner's "unrivalled eye for the details of appearance and behaviour," Heather Neill added in the *Listener:* "Often she writes like someone describing a painting or a photography. . . . She can take her reader into an environment, conjuring the feel of a place, paying particular attention to light and heat, colour and texture." Although he did not find the novel to be one of Brookner's best, Michael Gorra noted in the *Washington Post Book World* that the beginning of the novel "is as classically elegant as anything Anita Brookner has written and shows why, in its concentration on the limitations of gentility, hers is one of the most characteristically English voices to emerge in the last decade."

Latecomers, considered by critics to be among Brookner's most poignant novels, focuses upon two male characters. Orphaned during the Holocaust, Thomas Fibich and Thomas Hartmann escape Nazi Germany to become schoolmates, friends, and then successful business partners in England. Each character attempts to reconcile himself to the past in a different way, but both rely heavily on the strength and constancy of familial relationships to establish their place in the present. Brookner's "rich, utterly convincing portrayals of Fibich and Hartmann are likely to go a long way in dispelling any labeling of her as a 'women's writer' and in bolstering her reputation for drawing characters with the scrupulousness of a master draftsman," wrote Jocelyn McClurg in the *Los Angeles Times*. Yardley called it "a book not about romantic love but about love in the real world: about accepting and loving people for what they are rather than what one might wish them to be, about the slow, secret ways in which people work themselves so deeply into each other's hearts that extrication is unimaginable, about the acceptance and even celebration of human imperfection." Suggesting that "few writers can offer better, more specific insight than Anita Brookner," Bonnie Burnard maintained in the Toronto *Globe and Mail:* "Her conclusions seem valid, not arrogantly wise or uptown smart. . . . She is in control and has at her disposal a vast, accessible vocabulary of both spoken words and private thought. She can bring to life, calmly and sharply, place, gesture, attitude, intonation; she has mastered the master strokes." Finding the novel "written with grace and elegance that border on the astonishing," Yardley concluded, "At her own pace and in her own fashion, Anita Brookner works a spell on the reader; being under it is both an education and a delight."

Lewis Percy traces an inhibited young man's quest for tranquility; or as Carol Shields put it in her Toronto *Globe and Mail* review, it is "a book about finding an appropriate mode of heroism for our times." Lonely following the death of his mother, Lewis marries Tissy, a library coworker, in an attempt to rescue her from a stifling life. When she falsely suspects him of sleeping with Emmy, the wife of a library colleague, "Lewis struggles to act honorably and keep his marriage vows, thereby antagonizing both women," wrote Lopate. The characterization of Lewis recalls that of Ruth in *A Start in Life,* observed Julian Symons in the *Times Literary Supplement:* "Both are immersed in literature, Ruth an authority on Balzac, Lewis working on a thesis about the concept of heroism in the nineteenth-century novel, which in due time becomes a book and brings him a job in the college library. Both find living a trickier business than reading about it." The

novel "bears the clear imprint of a painterly quality of mind," wrote Tyler: "The plot derives less from a chain of events than from a juxtaposition of portraits, each more detailed than the last. People we'd be unlikely to notice on our own . . . take on texture and dimension, gradually rising right off the page." Although Isabel Raphael considered the novel "less brilliant and distilled" than Brookner's other writings, she added in her London *Times* review, "but for me, it glowed with a new serenity and reality which gave great pleasure, along with a sense that I will return more happily in future to this tender and sympathetic author."

Brookner's eleventh novel, *Brief Lives,* concerns Fay Langdon, a successful but aging businesswoman. After the death of her husband, Fay becomes the mistress of his law partner, thus betraying his wife and her longtime friend, Julia. In recalling the events of her life, Fay begins to question what Nicola Murphy described in the London *Times* as "her immature and foolish supposition that living would be a happy business." In the *Times Literary Supplement,* Lindsay Duguid described Fay as "an intelligent narrator, who is sensitive and shrinking but always sure of the superiority of her judgment. . . . We follow Fay's flat, pathetic first-person story with interest, keen to find out if she will find happiness, suspecting that she will not." Praising Brookner's "infallible precision," Murphy judged the novel "a fine, poised and pointed examination of stoicism in a woman too marginal to be missed. *Brief Lives* is beautifully written."

In *A Closed Eye* and *Fraud,* Brookner continues the theme of female loneliness. In *A Closed Eye,* Harriet, at her parents' urging, marries Freddie, a rich but dull man who is nearly twice her age. They have a daughter, Imogen, who is killed in a car accident. Harriet has only one friend, Tessa, who also has a daughter, Lizzie. At the novel's close, with all other family and friends either dead or withdrawn from their lives, Harriet and Lizzie end up together. Gabriele Annan found the novel "bleak," but considered it "elegantly constructed." Brookner, as Annan explained in the *New York Review of Books,* is often compared to Jane Austen, and although this reviewer found significant differences between Austen's women and Brookner's women, Annan admitted that "*A Closed Eye* does have its Jane Austen side." Namely, noted Annan, "Brookner is a witty and ironic observer of a society she peoples with sharply described characters." What is more, "Brookner has a particular knack for dealing with the sphere where society and locality overlap," capturing "the psyche of each individual [London] *quartier* as she walks her characters through it or settles them in some wickedly specific abode." In the end, believed Annan, Brookner "is an art historian specializing in eighteenth- and early nineteenth-century French art, and her writing recalls—deliberately or not—the elegant cruelty of certain French novels of the period."

The novel *Fraud* begins as a mystery with the disappearance of a middle-aged spinster named Anna Durrant. Through flashbacks, the reader learns that Anna has spent much of her life caring for her sickly mother, that her mother's death was followed by a grim winter and late spring, and that Anna had a mild flirtation with her mother's doctor. Through these events, *New York Times Book Review* contributor Ursula Hegi noted, Brookner offers "unsettling insights into what can happen when the boundaries between aging parents and their children dissolve." In *A Family Romance* (published in the United States as *Dolly*) Brookner explores the relationship between the book's narrator, Jane, and Jane's aunt-by-marriage, Dolly. In this novel Brookner examines the characters' differences from several angles—personality, generational, and ethnic. "Brookner's novel tells the story of how this pair . . . finally develop the bonds that make them a family," Carol Kino noted in the *New York Times Book Review.*

In *A Private View,* as with many of her previous novels, Brookner proves that she is both unafraid of and quite adept at exploring the lives of her contemporaries in England, even as they age and retire. "As newly disenfranchised [retired] workers face the prospect of building a life without the familiar routines of a job, profound questions about identity, activity, and purpose arise," commented Marilyn Gardner in the *Christian Science Monitor.* It is this disenfranchisement that Brookner examines in the life of George Bland of *A Private View.* A bachelor by default, Bland has just retired from his only job as a personnel manager in a London manufacturing company. The event was supposed to be celebrated by a trip to Asia with his longtime friend Putnam, another lifelong bachelor, but Putnam has just died of cancer. Now, though comfortable with his own money and that of his departed friend, Bland has nothing to look forward to or to look back on. He attempts to fill the void with Katy Gibb, a flaky young American occupying his neighbor's flat. She lives and breathes the many manifestations of

New Age self-help and sees Bland as a source of financial support for her business aspirations, to spread the New Age gospel.

As with *Look at Me,* Brookner uses a character in *Incidents in the Rue Laugier* to write the story that becomes her novel. In this case, however, the character is peripheral to the story of the novel. *Incidents in the Rue Laugier* is the tale of a love triangle and its aftermath involving the narrator's mother, father, and another man reconstructed from a few entries in the mother's journals. The mother, Maud, a young French woman, visits her aunt in the country. There, she meets two young Englishmen, falls in love with one, David Tyler, and eventually marries the other, Edward Harrison. The couple is condemned to live, in the words of *Library Journal* contributor Wilda Williams, "thwarted, empty lives." Joan Thomas, writing in the Toronto *Globe and Mail,* found the disparity between the opening love triangle and the couple's ultimate resignation problematic. "Brookner's romantic premise is disastrous to the novel," she wrote. "Unable to deal with Maud and Edward's adult lives in an interesting way, Brookner has nothing to write about for the last half of the book." Still, Thomas conceded, "Brookner has been getting away with writing the same plot with variations for more than a decade because she is a beautiful stylist, with an almost nineteenth-century formality and a fine wit." And, because of Brookner's style and wit, "the reader turns pages compulsively for a dazzling read in which every sentence seems clairvoyant," noted a *Publishers Weekly* reviewer.

Brookner's 1996 novel, *Altered States,* examines the romantic career of Alan Sherwood, a thoroughly conventional middle-aged London solicitor. Flashbacks reveal Alan's many quashed hopes and unfulfilled erotic longings. The novel's dark musings struck a chord with many critics. Calling the novel "unnervingly morbid," Donna Seaman of *Booklist* wrote that Alan Sherwood's "altered states are all forms of loss and compromise, intrinsic aspects of life that Brookner analyzes with brilliant intensity and surprising suspense." This feeling of discomfort coupled with admiration for the author's words was echoed by other reviewers. "Though impressive for its craftsmanship," observed Clare McHugh in *People,* "*Altered States* is unremittingly dark." A reviewer for *Publishers Weekly* found the narrative "alive with tension and heartbreak" while lamenting that Brookner's "view of female nature . . . seems essentially uncharitable and extreme."

Brookner's next novel, *Visitors,* covers similar emotional terrain—this time with a female narrator. Dorothea May is an elderly London widow, who, like many Brookner protagonists, sees her settled life disturbed by unforeseen events. This time it is a visit from her cousin's granddaughter and her wedding party, including a dissolute free spirit who prompts Dorothea to re-examine her own life choices. The very typicality of *Visitors* earned praise from many critics. "Brookner remains an exquisitely subtle observer of how manners bear the imprint of psyches," wrote a critic for *Publishers Weekly.* Brigitte Frase of the *San Francisco Chronicle* praised the book for its subdued prose. "Initially seduced by Brookner's urbane and intelligent language, one is coaxed gradually into an ever more disquieting emotional landscape," Frase wrote. Jacqueline Cary of the *New York Times Book Review* summarized *Visitors* as "the book Brookner has spent her life aiming toward."

Falling Slowly is the story of two sisters, Beatrice Sharpe, a pianist, and Miriam Sharpe, a translator, both of whom are experiencing a form of decline—Beatrice, in the form of an illness, and Miriam, in the form of loneliness. Miriam, once married but now divorced, is disillusioned about romantic endeavors; Beatrice, on the other hand, has always expected one day to meet the man of her dreams. "Like George Bland in Brookner's novel *A Private View,* or Dorothea May in *Visitors,* Miriam and Beatrice are ultimately torn between an idealized hankering for connection and, far more powerfully, an almost greedy complacency about their unruffled existence," summarized *New York Times Book Review* critic Claire Messud. "Women whose empty emotional lives are conducted behind a facade of stoic acceptance are Brookner's stock-in-trade," noted a *Publishers Weekly* critic. But here, in her delineation of the Sharpe sisters, Brookner "evokes an almost palpable atmosphere of resigned regret." Critics were largely positive in their assessment of *Falling Slowly.* "Brookner's impeccable craftsmanship and worldly irony make each of her novels memorable, but here her heroines' passivity becomes exasperating," concluded the critic for *Publishers Weekly.* Donna Seaman in *Booklist* called the novel "a richly figured book," referring to Brookner as a "sagacious and elegant novelist." "The ghastly power of Brookner's novels," argued Messud, "arises from their trenchant accuracy, and in this regard *Falling Slowly* is a further testament to its author's gifts."

Undue Influence focuses on a younger woman, Claire Pitt, twenty-nine, highly intelligent and perceptive of the world she sees around her but blind to her own dysfunctions and vulnerability. Cristina Nehring in the *San Francisco Chronicle* described Claire as "the fruit of feminism triumphant: Independent, unsentimental and intellectually confident, she asserts her sexual needs squarely, refuses romantic mystifications, despises her mother's bond to an invalid husband and her friend's loyalty to a married man. 'She deserves better,' she intones." But Claire, we begin to see, is deceiving herself and those around her. In her affair with Martin Gibson (according to Colin Walters of the *Washington Times,* "a discerning, right-on portrait of the masochistic male)," Claire presents herself as invulnerable, distant, and in charge. Nehring continued, "If these assumptions are convenient for the men, they are encouraged by the women. Claire labors to present herself as a hardened vamp with a 'predator's instinct' and a disdain for 'relationships.' It is she, not Martin—she tells us repeatedly—who 'controls' their affair. But it isn't long before we see that if Claire is masterminding anything, she is masterminding her own destruction." Intelligence, added Nehring, is the undoing rather than the saving of many of Brookner's protagonists.

Nehring maintained that Brookner's focus on similar characters and similar problems in her novels ultimately makes her writing "claustrophobic and repetitive." Kasia Boddy, however, in the London *Daily Mail* argued, "Anita Brookner's . . . novels have so much in common that, in some ways, to consider one is to consider them all. This is not to say that she retells the same story. . . . The arbitrary nature of human entanglements is a common thread." and Melinda Bargreen of the *Seattle Times* considered Anita Brookner "at her most sly and witty in this new novel." Bargreen concluded, "As always, Brookner's prose style gives us a felicitous turn of phrase in nearly every paragraph. And at the end, when Claire 'dispatch(es) naivete forever, consigning it to a prelapsarian time before doubt had set in,' you know she's on the road to self-knowledge." Walters commended the book: "Of Miss Brookner's novels that I've read, this one may have given the most pleasure." Interesting is the difference between those who find humor and those who find no humor in Brookner's work. For instance, a *Christian Science Monitor* reviewer described "some of the novel's most darkly comic moments," whereas Robert Allen Papinchak in the *Milwaukee Journal Sentinel* called this a "relentlessly somber . . . novel."

The protagonist of *The Next Big Thing* is a man, Julius Herz, who is about to retire from an unfulfilling job at age seventy-three. The question is whether he will take up the remainder of his life with vigor and an adventurous spirit or whether it is only death that will be "the next big thing." Sara Maitland in the *Spectator* had equivocal feelings about Brookner's focus: "One of the central themes of Brookner's novels has been 'resignation': Is it possible? Is it virtuous? Is it desirable? What are its compensations? What are the rewards and costs of realism and good behaviour? . . . My problem with Brookner's novels has always been that I feel that resignation is a pseudo-virtue, a vile diminishment preached to the already marginalized." Julius, wrote Maitland, "has endured a thin life; thinner, he rightly feels, than he deserved. . . . What should he do now? How should he fill in the years that will intervene between now and his death? Should he accept that this is all he is going to get, should he practise resignation? Or should he make one last effort to make life deliver its fruit?"

Having warned that Brookner is getting emotionally no easier to read, Ron Charles of the *Christian Science Monitor* found, "The reasons to pay attention to Anita Brookner grow no less compelling. First, she's one of the great English stylists, an artist of such extraordinary precision that her novels serve as an antidote to the overwritten tomes from so many contemporary writers. Second, in a literary marketplace excited by the bizarre, she remains committed to the mundane. No, she can't tell us about a hermaphrodite whose grandparents were siblings—for advice in that situation you must go to Jeffrey Eugenides's widely praised *Middlesex*,—but if you're considering the somewhat more common predicament of getting older, Brookner is as wise a guide as you'll find." Brookner presents Julius as a man who has lost himself in serving others, wrote Charles, and the problem considered is whether, now freed from financial worry and from work, he can make something more exciting of his last years. "A chorus of acquaintances offers advice: His cordial ex-wife admonishes him to cheer up, his lawyer suggests travel, his distractingly beautiful neighbor tells him to stop staring. But none of these courses can solve the problem of learning how to live with an abundance of unaccustomed freedom. 'Keeping one's dignity,' he admits, 'is a lonely business. And how one longs to let it go'." As Charles observed, Julius is in danger of already regarding himself as "posthumous," and the reviewer concluded, "This is bitter medicine for sure, but Brookner draws a portrait of despair so perfectly that it might serve a homeopathic purpose for anyone in or slipping toward 'a pale simulacrum of life.' Only

a writer of her astonishing wit and insight could get us to swallow it."

Observer contributor Adam Mars-Jones, however, found the thinness of descriptive prose and action in the novel a problem. "In a more dynamic novel, the absence of observation wouldn't matter, but here, in a narrative virtually denuded of incident (Herz makes modest perambulations and rambling peregrinations, he remembers, he surmises, he envisages), the thinness of texture is damaging." Rather than seeing Julius Herz as a figure of pathos, as Charles did, Mars-Jones observed, "Herz, wanting company without liking people, sees himself as a stoic, when, in fact, he floats in an admittedly dilute solution of self-pity from the first page to the last. The problem with the psychology on offer is not that it's negative, but that it's dull," concluding, "Brookner once remarked, quoting Freud, that art was a way of turning strong feelings into weak ones. Judge her on that basis, and her success is remarkable. Every trace of urgency has been effaced."

Brookner continues with *The Rules of Engagement*, which follows the lives of two women friends, Elizabeth and Betsy, both born in 1948 and who go at life in very different ways. Elizabeth chooses safety, marrying a kind man much older than herself. Betsy falls in love with a Parisian revolutionary and stays in Paris. The crossing of the two friends' lives thereafter throws a light on the possibilities offered by such choices and such views on the world—Elizabeth's pragmatic and Betsy's romantic. The *Spectator*'s Anne Chisholm noted, "It is, perhaps, a measure of Brookner's great gifts as a writer and her achievement in establishing, over twenty-two novels in thirty years, such a powerful message about the plight of women today that occasionally even her admirers want to fight back. . . . All one can say, perhaps, is that some are and that Anita Brookner knows and understands them. . . . There is beauty as well as courage in Brookner's new book."

BIOGRAPHICAL AND CRITICAL SOURCES:

BOOKS

Contemporary Literary Criticism, Gale (Detroit, MI), Volume 32, 1985, Volume 34, 1985, Volume 51, 1989.
Dictionary of Literary Biography Yearbook: 1987, Gale (Detroit, MI), 1988.

Malcolm, Cheryl Alexander, *Understanding Anita Brookner,* University of South Carolina Press (Columbia, SC), 2001.

Skinner, John, *The Fictions of Anita Brookner: Illusions of Romance,* Macmillan (London, England), 1992.

Soule, George, *Four British Women Novelists: Anita Brookner, Margaret Drabble, Iris Murdoch, Barbara Pym: An Annotated and Critical Secondary Bibliography,* Scarecrow Press (Lanham, MD), 1998.

Werlock, Abby H.P., and Regina Barreca, editors, *British Women Writing Fiction,* University of Alabama Press (Tuscaloosa, AL), 2000.

PERIODICALS

Albuquerque Journal, February 13, 2000, p. F8.

Atlanta Journal-Constitution, March 2, 2003, p. E6.

Atlantic Monthly, March, 1985, p. 124.

Austin American-Statesman, January 30, 2000, p. K6.

Birmingham Post (Birmingham, England), August 7, 1999, p. 60; January 27, 2001, p. 52.

Booklist, November 1, 1997, p. 434; November 1, 1998, p. 450; November 1, 2003, Donna Seaman, review of *Rules of Engagement,* p. 458.

Boston Globe, March 18, 1992, p. 58; May 4, 1993, p. 59.

Boston Herald, April 29, 2001, p. 051; January 26, 2003, p. A24.

Chicago Tribune, March 30, 1989; March 8, 1990.

Christian Science Monitor, March 1, 1985, p. B3; June 18, 1987, p. 26; June 8, 1988, p. 20; May 10, 1989, p. 13; April 26, 1990, p. 14; July 10, 1992, p. 11; February 8, 1993, p. 14; February 22, 1994, p. 11; January 26, 1995; February 18, 1998, p. 14; January 7, 1999, p. 20; January 27, 2000, p. 17; p. B3; April 19, 2001, p. 21; January 2, 2003, p. 12.

Cincinnati Post, May 19, 2001, p. 5C.

Commonweal, September 20, 1985, p. 502.

Contemporary Literature, winter, 2001, p. 825.

Courier-Mail (Brisbane, Australia), April 14, 2001, p. M05.

Critique: Studies in Contemporary Fiction, summer, 1998, p. 325.

Daily, June 28, 2003.

Daily Mail (London, England), July 5, 2002, p. 58; July 4, 2003, p. 58.

Daily Telegraph (London, England), January 20, 2001, p. 06; October 20, 2001; June 22, 2002; April 26, 2003; June 28, 2003.

Deep South, Volume 1, number 3, spring, 1995.

Entertainment Weekly, January 23, 1998, p. 58; January 9, 2004, Lisa Swarzbaum, review of *Rules of Engagement,* p. 87.

English Studies: A Journal of Language and Literature, February 2001, p. 44.

English: The Journal of the English Association, summer, 1993, p. 125; spring 2001, p. 47.

Evening Standard (London, England), June 24, 2002, p. 10; June 23, 2003, p. 39.

Express (London, England), June 29, 2002, p. 52.

Financial Times, October 14, 2000, p. 5.

Globe and Mail (Toronto, Ontario, Canada), November 8, 1986; April 7, 1990; January 13, 1996.

Guardian (London, England), July 31, 1999, p. 10; December 23, 2000, p. 10; February 3, 2001, p. 10; October 27, 2002, p. 11; June 22, 2002, p. 28; July 5, 2003, p. 26.

Harper's, April, 1981; July, 1983.

Herald (Glasgow, Scotland), December 16, 2000, p. 16; January 27, 2001, p. 20; July 5, 2003, p. 12.

Hudson Review, autumn, 1993.

Independent (London, England), July 30, 1999, p. 9; September 9, 2000, p. 11; June 29, 2002, p. 18; July 12, 2003, p. 26.

Independent on Sunday (London, England), September 10, 2000, p. 53; January 28, 2001, p. 45; July 6, 2003, p. 17; July 20, 2003, p. 19.

Irish Times (Dublin, Ireland), August 2, 2003, p. 62; August 16, 2003, p. 60.

Journal of Aging Studies, summer, 1989, p. 177.

Journal of Popular Culture, winter, 1994, p. 1.

Kirkus Reviews, November 1, 2003, review of *Rules of Engagement,* p. 1284.

Knight Ridder/Tribune News Service, April 25, 2001, p. K1955; May 16, 2001, p. K2083; January 8, 2003, p. K4392; January 15, 2003, p. K0748.

Library Journal, November 15, 1994, p. 98; April 1, 1997, p. 145; May 1, 1997, p. 145; September 1, 1997, p. 233; November 1, 1997, p. 115; September 1, 1998, p. 236; October 1, 1998, p. 80; December, 1998, p. 152; January, 2004, Barbara Love, review of *Rules of Engagement,* p. 151.

Listener, August 20, 1987, pp. 18-19.

London Review of Books, September 6, 1984, p. 20; September 5, 1985, p. 13; September 4, 1986, p. 20; October 1, 1987, p. 11; September 1, 1988, p. 24; September 14, 1989, p. 19; September 13, 1990, p. 16; August 29, 1991, p. 18; October 8, 1992, p. 12.

Los Angeles Times, March 18, 1981; May 3, 1983; February 8, 1984; December 25, 1989; March 27, 1992, p. E4; January 12, 1993, p. E2; April 15, 2001, p. 11; January 22, 2003, p. E11.

Los Angeles Times Book Review, October 27, 1985, p. 3; March 20, 1988, p. 2; April 30, 1989, p. 3; March 25, 1990, p. 3; July 7, 1991, p. 3; February 13, 1994, p. 10; January 22, 1995, p. 3; February 19, 1995, p. 11; February 9, 1997, p. 4; January 18, 1998.

Mail on Sunday (London, England), February 18, 2001, p. 66.

Milwaukee Journal Sentinel, January 9, 2000, p. 6E; April 15, 2001, p. 06.

Mosaic, spring, 1991, p. 131; June 1995, p. 123.

Ms., June, 1985, p. 62.

Nation, September 9, 1991, p. 274.

New Leader, October 7-21, 1991, p. 20; December 16-30, 1996, p. 28.

New Republic, May 30, 1981; March 25, 1985, p. 37; April 24, 1995, p. 41; February 9, 2004, Deborah Friedell, review of *Rules of Engagement,* p. 32.

News Letter (Belfast, Northern Ireland), July 1, 2002, p. 34.

New Statesman, May 22, 1981; September 7, 1984; September 6, 1985, p. 30; August 22, 1986, p. 26; August 28, 1987, p. 21; August 19, 1988, p. 39; August 25, 1989, p. 26; August 31, 1990, p. 35; August 23, 1991; August 21, 1992, p. 38; July 9, 1993, p. 33; June 24, 1994, p. 40; August 1, 1997, p. 47.

Newsweek, February 25, 1985, p. 87; March 30, 1987, p. 69.

New Yorker, March 23, 1981; April 9, 1984; February 18, 1985, p. 121; March 10, 1986, p. 121; May 18, 1987, p. 115; May 1, 1989, p. 111; August 23, 1990, p. 115; April 27, 1992, p. 106; February 22, 1993, p. 183; April 11, 1994, p. 99; January 30, 1995, p. 89.

New York Review of Books, January 31, 1985, p. 17; June 1, 1989, p. 34; May 14, 1992, p. 25; January 12, 1995, p. 20.

New York Times, July 4, 1983; February 1, 1984; January 22, 1985; October 12, 1985, p. 18; March 25, 1987, p. C23; February 20, 1988; February 24, 1989, p. C31; February 20, 1990, p. C19; April 6, 1990; February 28, 1992, p. C32; February 2, 2003, p. 17 col. 01.

New York Times Book Review, December 3, 1972; March 29, 1981; May 22, 1983; March 18, 1984; February 3, 1985, p. 1; April 28, 1985, p. 38; November 10, 1985, p. 15; March 29, 1987, p. 10;

March 20, 1988, p. 9; April 2, 1989, p. 3; March 11, 1990, p. 10; July 21, 1991, p. 14; April 12, 1992, p. 12; January 10, 1993, p. 7; February 20, 1994, p. 12; January 8, 1995, p. 9; January 14, 1996, p. 13; January 26, 1997; January 18, 1998; January 31, 1999, p. 7; January 3, 2000, p. 34; November 19, 2000, p. 70; June 3, 2001, p. 23; October 28, 2001, p. 32; April 28, 2002, p. 24; February 2, 2003, p. 17.

Observer (London, England), December 2, 1984, p. 19; September 8, 1985, p. 21; August 24, 1986, p. 20; August 23, 1987, p. 24; August 14, 1988, p. 41; August 27, 1989, p. 38; August 26, 1990, p. 55; August 25, 1991, p. 51; July 11, 1993, p. 61; June 19, 1994, p. 22; June 11, 1995, p. 14; June 18, 1995, p. 17; July 11, 1999, p. 5; August 1, 1999, p. 12; October 29, 2000, p. 13; January 18, 2001, p. 17; June 30, 2002, p. 17.

People, February 20, 1995, p. 31; January 13, 1997, p. 27; February 23, 1998, p. 33.

Plain Dealer (Cleveland, OH), May 27, 2001, p. 12I; January 26, 2003, p. J12.

Publishers Weekly, September 6, 1985; November 20, 1995, p. 66; November 11, 1996; November 17, 1997, p. 53; September 28, 1998, p. 84; October 26, 1998, p. 42; December 22, 2003, review of *Rules of Engagement,* p. 38.

Rocky Mountain News (Denver, CO), May 18, 2001, p. 25D.

St. Louis Post-Dispatch, January 30, 2000, p. F10.

San Francisco Chronicle, January 9, 2000, p. 1; January 23, 2000, p. 4.

Saturday Review, March-April, 1985; May-June, 1985.

Scotland on Sunday (Edinburgh, Scotland), January 28, 2001, p. 9; June 16, 2002, p. 6.

Scotsman (Edinburgh, Scotland), September 4, 1999, p. 11; July 29, 2000, p. 14; January 27, 2001, p. 10; June 29, 2002, p. 9.

Seattle Times, February 20, 2000, p. M7; July 1, 2001, p. J11; January 12, 2003, p. L9.

Spectator, September 14, 1985, p. 28; August 23, 1986, p. 22; August 22, 1987, p. 27; August 20, 1988, p. 24; August 26, 1989, p. 21; September 8, 1990, p. 33; August 31, 1991, p. 25; August 22, 1992, p. 20; June 19, 1993, p. 29; June 18, 1994, p. 33; June 17, 1995, p. 43; June 7, 1997, p. 38; June 29, 2002, p. 40; July 5, 2003, p. 36.

Star Ledger (Newark, NJ), March 5, 2000, p. 004; April 29, 2001, p. 004; January 5, 2003, p. 004.

Sunday Herald (Glasgow, Scotland), January 28, 2001, p. 10.

Sunday Mirror (London, England), July 23, 2000, p. 41.

Sunday Telegraph (London, England), January 21, 2001, p. 15; June 30, 2002, p. 15; June 1, 2003; June 22, 2003, p. 16.

Sunday Times (London, England), July 25, 1999, p. 12; August 8, 1999, p. 6; September 3, 2000, p. 35; January 28, 2001, p. 45; June 30, 2002, p. 45; July 6, 2003, p. 47.

Tampa Tribune, February 13, 2000, p. 4.

Time, October 28, 1985, p. 93; March 21, 1988, p. 76; March 19, 1990, p. 83; June 24, 1991, p. 65; February 8, 1993, p. 83; January 30, 1995, p. 83.

Times (London, England), March 21, 1983; March 31, 1983; September 6, 1984; October 20, 1984; August 21, 1986; August 16, 2000, p. 14; September 6, 2000, p. 12; June 26, 2002, p. 21; July 9, 2003, p. 20; August 2, 2003, p. 20.

Times Educational Supplement, August 6, 1993, p. 20.

Times Literary Supplement, November 26, 1971; January 9, 1981; May 29, 1981; May 28, 1982; March 25, 1983; September 14, 1984; April 26, 1985, p. 479; September 6, 1985, p. 973; August 29, 1986, p. 932; August 21, 1987, p. 897; August 12, 1988, p. 891; August 25, 1989, p. 916; August 24-30, 1990, p. 889; August 23, 1991, p. 20; August 21, 1992, p. 17; June 25, 1993, p. 22; June 17, 1994, p. 22; June 2, 1995, p. 21.

Tribune Books (Chicago, IL), March 1, 1987, p. 7; July 14, 1991, p. 6; March 22, 1992, p. 7; February 14, 1993, p. 4; February 13, 1994, p. 6; February 5, 1995, p. 6.

Twentieth Century Literature, spring, 1995, p. 1.

Village Voice, July 5, 1983; June 25, 1991, p. 70.

Vogue, February, 1985.

Voice Literary Supplement, May, 1987, p. 4; April, 1988, p. 11.

Wall Street Journal, March 30, 1992, p. A9; January 20, 1993, p. A10; December 20, 2000, p. A20(E); April 27, 2001, p. W12.

Washington Post, April 28, 1981; March 9, 1984; January 20, 1999, p. A20(E); November 12, 2000, p. X15; June 20, 2001, p. T04.

Washington Post Book World, July 24, 1983; February 10, 1985, p. 1; October 13, 1985, p. 3; March 8, 1987, p. 3; February 28, 1988, p. 5; March 12, 1989, p. 3; February 18, 1990, p. 3; March 22, 1992, p. 6; January 31, 1993, p. 3; January 9, 1994, p. 3; January 15, 1995, p. 8.

Washington Times, February 20, 2000, p. 6; December 10, 2000, p. 6.

Weekend Australian (Sydney, New South Wales, Australia), September 18, 1999, p. R13; April 7, 2001, p. R15; July 27, 2002, p. B08; October 4, 2003, p. B08.

West Virginia University Philological Papers, 2001-2002, p. 92.

Women's Review of Books, July, 1992, p. 30.

World Literature Today, spring, 1993, p. 380; winter, 1995, p. 138; spring, 1998, p. 367.

ONLINE

Contemporarywriters, http://www.contemporary writers.com/ (March 6, 2004), biography of Brookner.

Deep South, http://www.otago.ac.nz/DeepSouth/ (spring, 1995), Giuliana Giobbi, "Blood Ties: A Case of Mother-Daughter Relationships in Anita Brookner, Sara Maitland and Rosetta Roy."

George Soule Home Page, http://www.people.carleton. edu/˜gsoule/ (March 21, 2000), George Soule, reviews of *Visitors, Altered States,* and *Falling Slowly.*

Pittsburgh Post-Gazette, http://www.post-gazette.com/ (February 27, 2000), Betsy Kline, review of *Undue Influence.**

*   *   *

BROWN, Marc (Tolon) 1946-

PERSONAL: Born November 25, 1946, in Erie, PA; son of LeRoy Edward and Renita (Toulon) Brown; married Stephanie Marini (a ballet dancer and college teacher), September 1, 1968 (marriage ended, 1977); married Laurene Krasny (a psychologist and writer), September 11, 1983; children: (first marriage) Tolon Adam, Tucker Eliot; (second marriage) Eliza Morgan. *Education:* Cleveland Institute of Art, B.F.A., 1969. *Religion:* "Protestant Episcopalian Catholic currently practicing Judaism." *Hobbies and other interests:* Collecting early American art and antiques, gardening, small-scale farming (horses and chickens), baking pies.

ADDRESSES: Home and office—Martha's Vineyard, MA. *Agent*—c/o Author Mail, Little, Brown, and Company Children's Books, 1271 Avenue of the Americas, New York, NY 10020.

CAREER: Author and illustrator of children's books. Worked variously as a truck driver, short-order cook, soda jerk, college professor, gentleman farmer, television art director, actor, and costume and set designer, c. 1960s; WICU-TV (NBC affiliate), Erie, PA, television art director, 1968-69; Garland Junior College, Boston, MA, assistant professor, 1969-76; author and illustrator of children's books, 1976—. *Exhibitions:* Work exhibited widely in the United States and abroad, including numerous one-man shows.

MEMBER: Authors Guild, Authors League of America.

AWARDS, HONORS: Children's Books of the Year citations, Child Study Association of America, 1971, for *What Makes the Sun Shine?,* 1976, for *One Two Three: An Animal Counting Book,* and 1986, for *What's So Funny, Ketu?, Hand Rhymes,* and *The Banza: A Haitian Story;* Children's Choice awards, Children's Book Council (CBC)/International Reading Association, 1976, for *Arthur's Nose,* 1980, for *Arthur's Eyes,* 1981, for *Arthur's Valentine,* 1982, for *The True Francine, Arthur's Halloween,* and *Arthur Goes to Camp,* and 1983, for *Arthur's April Fool;* Notable Book citations, American Library Association, 1979, for *Why the Tides Ebb and Flow,* 1982, for *Dinosaurs Beware! A Safety Guide,* and 1984, for *Oh, Kojo! How Could You!; There Goes Feathertop!* included in American Institute of Graphic Arts Book Show, 1980; *Boston Globe/Horn Book* Honor Award for Illustration, 1980, for *Why the Tides Ebb and Flow;* Notable Children's Trade Book in the Field of Social Studies citations, National Council for Social Studies/CBC, 1982, for *The True Francine,* and 1985, for *Oh, Kojo! How Could You!;* Library of Congress Book of the Year citation, 1985, for *Swamp Monsters; Booklist* Children's Editor's Choice and New York Public Library Children's Books citations, both 1985, both for *Hand Rhymes;* Notable Book citation, *New York Times,* 1986, for *Dinosaurs Divorce: A Guide for Changing Families;* Emmy Award, 1999, 2000, and 2001, and Peabody Award, 2001, for *Arthur* television show.

WRITINGS:

SELF-ILLUSTRATED

One Two Three: An Animal Counting Book, Little, Brown (Boston, MA), 1976.

Marc Brown's Full House, Addison-Wesley (Reading, MA), 1977.

Lenny and Lola, Dutton (New York, NY), 1978.

Moose and Goose, Dutton (New York, NY), 1978.

The Cloud over Clarence, Dutton (New York, NY), 1979.

Pickle Things, Parents' Magazine Press (New York, NY), 1980.

Witches Four, Parents' Magazine Press (New York, NY), 1980.

Your First Garden Book, Little, Brown (Boston, MA), 1981.

The True Francine, Little, Brown (Boston, MA), 1981.

Wings on Things, Random House (New York, NY), 1982.

Count to Ten, Golden Press (New York, NY), 1982.

Marc Brown's Boat Book, Golden Press (New York, NY), 1982.

(With Stephen Krensky) *Dinosaurs, Beware! A Safety Guide,* Little, Brown (Boston, MA), 1982, published with teacher's guide, Random House (New York, NY), 1984.

Silly Tail Book, Parents' Magazine Press (New York, NY), 1983.

Spooky Riddles, Random House (New York, NY), 1983.

(With Stephen Krensky) *Perfect Pigs: An Introduction to Manners,* Little, Brown (Boston, MA), 1983.

What Do You Call a Dumb Bunny? And Other Rabbit Riddles, Games, Jokes, and Cartoons, Little, Brown (Boston, MA), 1983.

There's No Place Like Home, Parents' Magazine Press (New York, NY), 1984.

(With wife, Laurene Krasny Brown) *The Bionic Bunny Show,* Little, Brown (Boston, MA), 1984.

(With Laurene Krasny Brown) *Dinosaurs Divorce: A Guide for Changing Families,* Little, Brown (Boston, MA), 1986.

(With Laurene Krasny Brown) *Visiting the Art Museum,* Dutton (New York, NY), 1986, published as *Visiting an Exhibition,* Collins (London, England), 1986.

(With Laurene Krasny Brown) *Dinosaurs Travel: A Guide for Families on the Go,* Little, Brown (Boston, MA), 1988.

(With Laurene Krasny Brown) *Baby Time: A Grownup's Handbook to Use with Baby,* Knopf (New York, NY), 1989.

Dinosaurs Alive and Well!: A Guide to Good Health, Little, Brown (Boston, MA), 1990.

Scared Silly!: A Book for the Brave, Little, Brown (Boston, MA), 1994.

Monster's Lunchbox, Little, Brown (Boston, MA), 1995.

(With Laurene Krasny Brown) *When Dinosaurs Die: A Guide to Understanding Death,* Little, Brown (Boston, MA), 1996.

(With Laurene Krasny Brown) *How to Be a Friend: A Guide to Making Friends and Keeping Them,* Little, Brown (Boston, MA), 1998.

Buster's Dino Dilemma, Little, Brown (Boston, MA), 1998.

"ARTHUR ADVENTURE" SERIES; SELF-ILLUSTRATED

Arthur's Nose, Little, Brown (Boston, MA), 1976.

Arthur's Eyes, Little, Brown (Boston, MA), 1979.

Arthur's Valentine, Little, Brown (Boston, MA), 1980.

Arthur Goes to Camp, Little, Brown (Boston, MA), 1982.

Arthur's Halloween, Little, Brown (Boston, MA), 1982.

Arthur's April Fool, Little, Brown (Boston, MA), 1983.

Arthur's Thanksgiving, Little, Brown (Boston, MA), 1983.

Arthur's Christmas, Little, Brown (Boston, MA), 1984.

Arthur's Tooth: An Arthur Adventure, Little, Brown (Boston, MA), 1985.

Arthur's Teacher Trouble, Little, Brown (Boston, MA), 1986.

Arthur's Baby, Little, Brown (Boston, MA), 1987.

Arthur's Birthday Wish, Little, Brown (Boston, MA), 1988.

Arthur's Pet Business, Little, Brown (Boston, MA), 1990.

Arthur Meets the President, Little, Brown (Boston, MA), 1991.

Arthur Babysits, Joy Street Books (Boston, MA), 1992.

Arthur's New Puppy, Little, Brown (Boston, MA), 1993.

Arthur's Family Vacation, Little, Brown (Boston, MA), 1993.

Arthur's Chicken Pox, Little, Brown (Boston, MA), 1994.

Arthur's First Sleepover, Little, Brown (Boston, MA), 1994.

Arthur Writes a Story, Little, Brown (Boston, MA), 1996.

Arthur's Neighborhood, Little, Brown (Boston, MA), 1996.

Arthur and the True Francine, Little, Brown (Boston, MA), 1996.

Arthur's Really Helpful Word Book, Random House (New York, NY), 1997.

Arthur's Computer Disaster, Little, Brown (Boston, MA), 1997.

Arthur Lost and Found, Little, Brown (Boston, MA), 1998.

Arthur's Valentine Countdown (board book), Random House (New York, NY), 1999

Arthur's New Baby Book: A Lift-the-Flap Guide to Being a Great Big Brother or Sister, Bullseye Books, 1999.

Arthur's Underwear, Little, Brown (Boston, MA), 1999.

Arthur's Teacher Moves In, Little, Brown (Boston, MA), 2000.

Arthur's Truck Adventure (sticker book), Random House (New York, NY), 2000.

Arthur's Really Helpful Bedtime Stories, Random House (New York, NY), 1998.

Arthur's Family Treasury (contains "Arthur's Birthday," "Arthur's Family Vacation" and "Arthur's Baby"), Little, Brown (Boston, MA), 2000.

Arthur's Perfect Christmas, Little, Brown (Boston, MA), 2000.

Arthur, It's Only Rock 'n' Roll, Little, Brown (Boston, MA), 2002.

Arthur's Animal Adventure (sticker book), Random House (New York, NY), 2002.

Arthur's Spookiest Halloween (lift-the-flap book), Random House (New York, NY), 2003.

Arthur's Heart Mix-Up, Little, Brown (Boston, MA), 2004.

"ARTHUR ADVENTURE" SERIES; SELF-ILLUSTRATED CHAPTER BOOKS

Arthur Accused!, Little, Brown (Boston, MA), 1998.

The Mystery of the Stolen Bike, Little, Brown (Boston, MA), 1998.

Arthur and the Crunch Cereal Contest, Little, Brown (Boston, MA), 1998.

Arthur Makes the Team, Little, Brown (Boston, MA), 1998.

Arthur's Mystery Envelope, Little, Brown (Boston, MA), 1998.

Arthur and the Scare-Your-Pants-Off Club, Little, Brown (Boston, MA), 1998.

Locked in the Library!, Little, Brown (Boston, MA), 1998.

Arthur and the Race to Read, Little, Brown (Boston, MA), 2001.

Arthur and the One Thousand-and-one Dads, Little, Brown (Boston, MA), 2003.

"STEP INTO READING" SERIES; SELF-ILLUSTRATED

Arthur's Reading Race, Random House (New York, NY), 1995.

Arthur Goes to School, Random House (New York, NY), 1995.

Arthur Counts!, Random House (New York, NY), 1998.

Arthur Decks the Hall!, Random House (New York, NY), 1998.

Arthur on the Farm, Random House (New York, NY), 1998.

Arthur, Clean Your Room!, Random House (New York, NY), 1999.

Arthur in a Pickle, Random House (New York, NY), 1999.

Arthur's Lost Puppy, Random House (New York, NY), 2000.

Arthur's Fire Drill, Random House (New York, NY), 2000.

Arthur's Hiccups, Random House (New York, NY), 2001.

Arthur's First Kiss, Random House (New York, NY), 2001.

Arthur's Lost Puppy, Random House (New York, NY), 2001.

Arthur's Back-to-School Surprise, Random House (New York, NY), 2002.

Arthur and the School Pet, Random House (New York, NY), 2003.

Arthur's Science Fair Trouble, Random House (New York, NY), 2003.

Arthur and the School Pet, Random House (New York, NY), 2003.

Arthur and the Comet Crisis, Random House (New York, NY), 2003.

Arthur and the No-Brainer, Random House (New York, NY), 2003.

Arthur and the New Kid, Random House (New York, NY), 2004.

Arthur Breaks the Bank, Random House (New York, NY), 2005.

"D. W." SERIES

D. W., the Picky Eater, Little, Brown (Boston, MA), 1995.

Glasses for D.W., Random House (New York, NY), 1995, reprinted, 2003.

D. W.'s Lost Blankie, Little, Brown (Boston, MA), 1997.

D. W. Thinks Big, Joy Street Books (New York, NY), 1993.

D. W. Rides Again, Little, Brown (Boston, MA), 1993.

D. W. Flips!, Little, Brown (Boston, MA), 1987, published as *Roll over D.W.,* Picadilly Press (London, England), 1988.

D. W. All Wet, Little, Brown (Boston, MA), 1988.

D. W., Go to Your Room!, Little, Brown (Boston, MA), 1999.

D. W.'s Library Card, Little, Brown (Boston, MA), 2001.

D. W.'s Guide to Preschool, Little, Brown (Boston, MA), 2003.

ILLUSTRATOR

Isaac Asimov, *What Makes the Sun Shine?,* Little, Brown (Boston, MA), 1970.

Mary Daem, *The Dragon with a Thousand Wrinkles,* Ginn (New York, NY), 1971.

Norma Farber, *I Found Them in the Yellow Pages,* Little, Brown (Boston, MA), 1972.

Peter Dickinson, *The Iron Lion,* Allen & Unwin (London, England), 1972.

Ted Clymer, *The Four Corners of the Sky: Poems, Chants, and Oratory,* Little, Brown (Boston, MA), 1975.

(With Tom Cooke) Doug Morse, *The Little Green Thumb Window Garden,* Storyfold, 1975.

Laurence White, *Science Games/Puzzles/Tricks/Toys* (four books), Addison-Wesley (Reading, MA), 1975, new editions published as *Science Games and Puzzles,* Lippincott (Philadelphia, PA), 1979, and *Science Toys and Tricks,* Lippincott, 1980.

Patty Wolcott, *Super Sam and the Salad Garden,* Addison-Wesley (Reading, MA), 1975.

Louise Moeri, *How the Rabbit Stole the Moon,* Houghton Mifflin (Boston, MA), 1977.

Kathleen Daly, *My Doctor Bag Book,* Golden Press (New York, NY), 1977.

Janwillem Van de Wetering, *Little Owl: An Eight-Fold Buddhist Admonition,* Houghton Mifflin (Boston, MA), 1978.

Joan Chase Bowden, *Why the Tides Ebb and Flow,* Houghton Mifflin (Boston, MA), 1979.

Norma Farber, *There Goes Feathertop!,* Dutton (New York, NY), 1979.

Judy Delton, *Rabbit's New Rug,* Parents' Magazine Press (New York, NY), 1980.

Diane Wolkstein, *The Banza: A Haitian Story,* Dial (New York, NY), 1981.

Verna Aardema, adapter, *What's So Funny, Ketu?,* Dial (New York, NY), 1982.

Mary Blount Christian, *Swamp Monsters,* Dial (New York, NY), 1983.

Deborah Hautzig, *Little Witch's Big Night,* Random House (New York, NY), 1984.

Verna Aardema, *Oh, Kojo! How Could You!,* Dial (New York, NY), 1984.

Deborah Hautzig, *Happy Birthday, Little Witch!,* Random House (New York, NY), 1985.

Mary Blount Christian, *Go West, Swamp Monsters,* Dial (New York, NY), 1985.

Jack Prelutsky, selector, *Read-Aloud Rhymes for the Very Young,* Knopf (New York, NY), 1986.

Laurene Krasny Brown, *Taking Advantage of Media: A Manual for Parents and Teachers,* Routledge, Chapman & Hall (New York, NY), 1986.

John T. McQueen, *A World Full of Monsters,* Crowell (New York, NY), 1986.

Deborah Hautzig, *Little Witch Book and Doll Package,* Random House (New York, NY), 1988.

Alice Low, editor, *The Family Read-Aloud Christmas Treasury,* Little, Brown (Boston, MA), 1989.

Laurene Krasny Brown, *Toddler Time: A Book to Share with Your Toddler,* Little, Brown (Boston, MA), 1990.

Alice Low, editor, *The Family Read-Aloud Holiday Treasury,* Joy Street Books (New York, NY), 1991.

Laurene Krasny Brown, *Dinosaurs to the Rescue: A Guide to Protecting Our Planet,* Little, Brown (Boston, MA), 1992.

Laurene Krasny Brown, *Rex and Lilly Family Time,* Little, Brown (Boston, MA), 1995.

Laurene Kransy Brown, *Rex and Lilly Playtime,* Little, Brown (Boston, MA), 1995.

Laurene Krasny Brown, *Rex and Lilly School Time,* Little, Brown (Boston, MA), 1997.

Judy Sierra, *Wild about Books,* Knopf (New York, NY), 2004.

EDITOR

Finger Rhymes, Dutton (New York, NY), 1980.

Hand Rhymes, Dutton (New York, NY), 1985.

Play Rhymes, Dutton (New York, NY), 1987.

Party Rhymes, Dutton (New York, NY), 1988.

One, Two, Buckle My Shoe, Dutton's Children's Books (New York, NY), 1989.

Can You Jump Like a Frog?, Dutton's Children's Books (New York, NY), 1989.

Teddy Bear, Teddy Bear, Dutton's Children's Books (New York, NY), 1989.

Two Little Monkeys, Dutton's Children's Books (New York, NY), 1989.

Also author of *What's the Big Secret? Talking about Sex with Girls and Boys.*

Several of Brown's books have been translated into Spanish.

ADAPTATIONS: Works that have been adapted for filmstrip with cassette, videocassette, and/or released with an accompanying audiocassette by Random House include *Arthur's Valentine, Arthur's Halloween, Arthur's April Fool, Arthur's Thanksgiving,* and *Arthur Goes to Camp,* all 1983, *Dinosaurs, Beware!,* 1984, *Arthur's Christmas,* 1985, and *Arthur's Tooth,* and *Oh, Kojo! How Could You!,* both 1986. Stories from the "Arthur Adventure" series were adapted for a Public Broadcasting System television program and for multimedia. The "Arthur" characters have also been adapted for chapter books authored by Stephen Krensky.

SIDELIGHTS: When Marc Brown answered his son's request for a bedtime story, little did he know that a quarter-century later he would still be telling the story of his then-created hero, Arthur the aardvark. Third-grader Arthur and his animal friends from Elwood City, with their combination of real-life situations, humor, and appealing watercolor-and-crayon illustrations, have become favorites of generations of children. In book format they have reached more than fifty million readers, and as a popular television series made by the Public Broadcasting Service (PBS) that aired in sixty countries throughout the world they reached millions more. To celebrate Arthur's twenty-fifth birthday, bookstores across the United States threw birthday parties, SFX Family Entertainment created a live theater show "Arthur: A Live Adventure," and the Boston-based PBS affiliate created "Arthur's World and the Art Work of Marc Brown," a museum exhibit that toured ten cities.

Brown spent most of his childhood entertaining himself with pens, pencils, and paper. His grandmother Thora encouraged him to take his drawing seriously, and after a trip to the Chicago Art Institute, he became interested in painting. Nancy Bryan, Brown's high school art teacher, suggested he try working with watercolors and invested her time in his success with them.

The work of other artists continued to influence Brown's choice of a career. He once told an interviewer: "Through art books I discovered the work of Marc Chagall, and was so impressed, I changed my name from Mark to Marc. A light went on with [Maurice] Sendak's *Where the Wild Things Are.*" After high school Brown majored in painting at the Cleveland Institute of Art, where he also studied printmaking, photography, and textile and graphic design. After presenting sample drawings to Boston-based publisher Houghton Mifflin, Brown was offered freelance work in illustration. Having learned more about opportunities in professional illustrating, he decided to make it his career. In 1969 he began part-time teaching at Garland Junior College in Boston and illustrated textbooks.

Because publishers were trying to avoid implying any values about race or gender in their books, each drawing had to fulfill specific instructions. Brown enjoyed the steadiness of the work, but missed using his creativity. By the end of the year he was determined to do more creative drawing. His first illustrations for a fiction book were for Isaac Asimov's *What Makes the Sun Shine?* Children's author Norma Farber and Atlantic Monthly Press editor Emilie McLeod also helped Brown along his way to becoming a published children's author. Upon McLeod's suggestion, he wrote and illustrated *Arthur's Nose,* the first in a series of popular picture books about an aardvark who wears glasses. "I learned so much from her . . . about balancing the elements of words and pictures and using the words to do what pictures can't do, and vice versa," Brown recalled to Kathleen Kernicky of the *Milwaukee Journal Sentinel.* After about five years of illustrating children's books, Brown was confident he could make a living through his art. Brown's animal renderings, particularly the famous Arthur and friends, quickly became the author-illustrator's signature characters. As many readers have noticed, throughout the years Arthur's nose has gotten shorter. The reason: it is easier for Brown to express emotions if Arthur's face is not obscured by an enormous nose.

Brown is most widely known as the creator of Arthur, an aardvark whose day-to-day adventures have become familiar to millions of children. Many bookstores set aside a special area as an "Arthur Room," and the "Arthur" books have continued to be popular, their sales rocketing following broadcast of the *Arthur's World* television show. The "Arthur" books include titles geared to beginning readers, picture-book audiences, and chapter-book readers.

Arthur is a third grader who experiences real-life situations dosed with humor and that end happily. In writing the series, Brown has drawn on his own childhood experiences and those of his three children when they were in the second and third grades. "When I write stories about Arthur and [little sister] D. W., I think about George Burns and Gracie Allen," Brown explained to Ken Hoffman of the *Houston Chronicle.* "That's how I see their relationship. She's always hitting him with zingers." The character D. W. proved to be so popular that Brown created a series of books focusing on Arthur's feisty little sister. As Brown told Jan Crain Rudeen for the *Rocky Mountain News,* D. W. is a "combination of my three younger sisters—that's what makes her triply lethal."

When Brown allowed PBS to use his Arthur character, he retained as much control of the program content as he could, such as the ability to approve scripts. "The show is honest," Brown told Hoffman. "It doesn't talk down to kids. These characters are real to me because they're based on real people." Following its debut in 1997, *Arthur's World* became popular with children from ages two to eleven, and won four Emmy Awards and a Peabody award for outstanding television. Arthur and his friends have appeared in several television specials as well, including a Christmas special and the special *Arthur: It's Only Rock 'n' Roll,* and by 2003 a motion picture featuring Brown's characters was in the planning stages. The author/illustrator's son Tolon served as vice president for onscreen media for the *Arthur Show,* ensuring that Brown's high standards were maintained.

Because of the success of the television program, Brown created the "Arthur's Adventure" series of chapter books. Averaging fifty-four pages in length, these books are geared to third-grade readers. Brown has long known the importance of reading and libraries, and because he supports literacy efforts he has allowed Arthur to act as the "spokes animal" for the U.S. Department of Education's Read*Write*Now Program, the Pizza Hut Book-It! program, and other reading incentive programs. To this end, he has also created books for Random House's "Step into Reading" series for emergent readers, as well as novelty books for toddlers.

Until the mid-1990s, Brown and his wife worked together on a number of book projects, including the trio *Rex and Lilly Family Time, Rex and Lilly Playtime,* and *Rex and Lilly School Time.* Their joint projects have diminished, however, as the popularity of Arthur skyrocketed and Brown needed to devote more time to his star.

Describing his writing process, Brown once explained that he may rewrite a story thirty times before he is satisfied with it. "The two most troublesome parts are staying on a straight line and coming to a satisfying conclusion," he once explained. "If I don't watch it, I can digress and never find my way back. Stories have a way of spawning other stories, which in its way is wonderful." Now that his children are grown, Brown has had to look for inspiration from other sources. "I feel like a professional eavesdropper," he admitted to John Micklos, Jr. in *Reading Today.* "I'm always listening for situations that are important for kids and families."

BIOGRAPHICAL AND CRITICAL SOURCES:

PERIODICALS

American Theatre, December, 2001, Sarah Hart, review of "How the Aardvark Stole Christmas," p. 91.

Atlanta Journal-Constitution, December 3, 2001, "Questions and Answers with the Stars," p. D6.

Booklist, September 15, 1992, p. 159; October 1, 1992, p. 334; May 15, 1993, p. 1695; September 1, 1993, p. 72; November 1, 1993, p. 526; December 1, 1993, p. 696; May 15, 1994, p. 1683; October 1, 1994, pp. 321, 331; February 1, 1995, p. 1008; November 1, 1995, p. 476; September 15, 1996, p. 245.

Books for Keeps, March, 1999, review of *Arthur's Computer Disaster,* p. 20.

Bulletin of the Center for Children's Books, June, 1987; February, 1988; March, 1988; June 1, 1999, review of *D. W., Go to Your Room!,* p. 1838; January 1, 2000, Amy Brandt, review of *Arthur's Underwear,* p. 935; June 1, 2000, Carolyn Phelan, review of *Arthur's Family Treasury,* p. 1904; October 1, 2000, Ilene Cooper, review of *Arthur's Perfect Christmas,* p. 344; November 1, 2000, Carolyn Phelan, review of *Arthur's Teacher Moves In,* p. 546; May 1, 2001, Gillian Engberg, review of *D. W. Thinks Big,* p. 1689; June 1, 2001, Patricia Austin, review of *Marc Brown's Arthur Anniversary Collection,* p. 1906; September 1, 2001, Patricia Austin, review of *Marc Brown's Arthur Chapter Books,* Volume 5 (audio version), p. 125; November 1, 2002, Diane Foote, review of *Arthur, It's Only Rock 'n' Roll,* p. 504.

Children's Bookwatch, February, 1999, review of *D. W., the Picky Eater,* p. 8.

Graphis, number 156, 1979.

Horn Book, September, 1987, p. 597; November, 1987, pp. 721, 751; May, 1988, p. 338; January, 1989, p. 84; September, 1990, p. 588; July, 1991, p. 444; September, 1992, p. 573; May, 1993, p. 311; September, 1993, p. 582; January, 1994, p. 93; May, 1994, p. 338; November, 1994, p. 728; July, 1995, p. 483; March, 1997, p. 219.

Houston Chronicle, March 20, 2001, Ken Hoffman, "Lovable Aardvark Is Coming to Town," p. 1.

Indianapolis Star, November 19, 2000, Marc D. Allan, "*Arthur* Reveals Human Flaws," p. TV03; September 1, 2002, Marc D. Allan, "Boy Band Fits *Arthur's* World," p. TV03.

Kirkus Reviews, May 15, 1987, p. 791; October 15, 1987, p. 1512; November 1, 1987, p. 1571; April 15, 1988, p. 615; May 15, 1989, p. 760; October 15, 1990, p. 1462; May 15, 1991, p. 677; October 1, 1992, p. 1252; May 15, 1993, p. 656; October 1, 1993, p. 1270; November 15, 1994, p. 1523; September 1, 2001, review of *D. W.'s Library Card,* p. 1286.

Los Angeles Times, February 23, 2001, Jon Matsumoto, "The Point Is to Entertain and Educate," p. F29.

Milwaukee Journal Sentinel, May 20, 2001, Kathleen Kernicky, "Creator Details Remarkable History of Arthur Read, Aardvark," p. 16.

New York Times Book Review, March 16, 1986, p. 30; March 12, 1989, p. 35; May 20, 1990, p. 46; June 23, 1991, p. 23; August 8, 1993, p. 22; May 22, 1994, p. 34.

Publishers Weekly, November 29, 1985, p. 49; June 27, 1986, p. 98; November 28, 1986, p. 74; May 8, 1987, p. 68; September 25, 1987, p. 106; November 13, 1987, p. 69; February 26, 1988; April 8, 1988, p. 92; May 19, 1989, p. 82; June 9, 1989,

p. 64; January 19, 1990, p. 112; April 30, 1990, p. 68; February 8, 1991, p. 59; April 5, 1991, p. 146; May 3, 1991, p. 71; April 17, 1992, p. 573; September 21, 1992, p. 96; April 5, 1993, p. 75; August 30, 1993, p. 95; January 10, 1994, p. 63; May 2, 1994, p. 306; July 4, 1994, p. 62; October 24, 1994, p. 61; May 15, 1995, p. 75; August 21, 1995, p. 65; September 11, 1995, p. 87; April 1, 1996, p. 78; April 15, 1996, p. 70; August 12, 1996, p. 85; August 19, 1996, p. 69; March 10, 1997, p. 68; March 24, 1997, p. 85; April 5, 1999, review of *D. W. Thinks Big,* p. 243; November 8, 1999, review of *Arthur's Christmas* (audio version), p. 31; November 15, 1999, review of *Arthur's New Baby Book,* p. 69; January 22, 2001, Karen Raugust, "Happy Birthday, Arthur," p. 182.

Reading Teacher, October, 1999, review of *Arthur's Really Helpful Bedtime Stories,* p. 172.

Reading Today, October, 2000, John Micklos, Jr., "Happy Birthday, Arthur!," p. 17.

Record (Bergen County, NJ), July 20, 2001, Janis Nicolosi-Endo, "Amiable Aardvark; Arthur and Author Are Feted in NYC," p. 18.

Rocky Mountain News (Denver, CO), March 21, 2001, Lisa Bornstein, "Arthur Takes the Stage," p. 15D; January 31, 2003, Jan Crain Rudeen, "Insightful Arthur Draws from Reality," p. 30D.

School Library Journal, May, 1985, p. 68; November, 1985, p. 67; January, 1987, p. 58; June, 1987, p. 78; October, 1987, p. 120; December, 1987, p. 70; March, 1988, p. 158; January, 1989, p. 69; July, 1989, p. 62; November, 1990, p. 86; July, 1991, p. 54; October, 1992, p. 80; May, 1993, p. 81; December, 1993, p. 80; February, 1994, p. 78; June, 1994, p. 96; September, 1994, pp. 175, 206; March, 1995, p. 178; August, 1995, p. 67; February, 1996, p. 81; August, 1996, p. 64; September, 1996, p. 171; January, 1999, Linda Ludke, review of *Arthur Lost and Found,* p. 79; March, 1999, Kimberlie Monteforte, review of *Arthur's Really Helpful Bedtime Book,* p. 190, Marcia Brightman, review of *Marc Brown Reads Arthur! Series,* p. 155; June, 1999, Kirsten Martindale, review of *Arthur's Computer Adventure,* p. 68; July, 1999, review of *Marc Brown's Arthur Chapter Books,* Volume 3, p. 53; July, 1999, Kathy M. Newby, review of *D. W., Go to Your Room!,* p. 61, Mary K. Schecker, review of *Marc Brown's Arthur Chapter Books,* Volume 3, pp. 53-54; December, 1999, Gay Lynn Van Vleck, review of *Arthur's Underwear,* p. 88; February, 2000, Stephanie Bange, review of *Arthur's Valentine*

(sound recording), p. 67; March, 2000, "Brown Is Still Around," p. 109; October, 2000, review of *Arthur's Perfect Christmas,* p. 56; January, 2001, Maryann H. Owen, review of *Arthur's Teacher Moves In,* p. 91; December, 2001, Rachel Fox, review of *D. W.'s Library Card,* p. 90; December, 2002, Kay Bowes, review of *Arthur, It's Only Rock 'n' Roll,* p. 85.

Star-Ledger (Newark, NJ), May 25, 2001, Allison Freeman, "*Arthur's World,* Unfolds for Fans," p. 38.

ONLINE

Arthur Home Page, http://pbskids.org/arthur/ (April 23, 2003).*

*   *   *

BROWNSTEIN, Michael 1943-

PERSONAL: Born August 25, 1943, in Philadelphia, PA; *Education:* Attended Antioch College, 1961-64; New School for Social Research, New York, B.A., 1966. *Hobbies and other interests:* Travel.

ADDRESSES: Home and office—21 East 2nd St., No. 3, New York, NY 10003.

CAREER: Poet and novelist; freelance writer. University of Colorado and Naropa Institute, both Boulder, CO, instructor in creative writing, 1976-77; Columbia University, New York, NY, instructor in creative writing, 1986-87.

AWARDS, HONORS: Poets' Foundation grant, 1966; Fulbright fellowship, Paris, France, 1967-68; Frank O'Hara Award, 1969, for *Highway to the Sky*; National Endowment for the Arts grant, 1979, 1987.

WRITINGS:

POETRY

Behind the Wheel, "C" Press (New York, NY), 1967.
Highway to the Sky, Columbia University Press (New York, NY), 1969.
Three American Tantrums, Angel Hair (New York, NY), 1970.

30 Pictures, Grape Press (Stinson Beach, CA), 1972.

Strange Days Ahead, Z Press (Calais, VT), 1975.

When Nobody's Looking, Rocky Ledge Cottage (Boulder, CO), 1981.

Oracle Night: A Love Poem, Sun & Moon Press (College Park, MD), 1982.

World on Fire, Open City Books (New York, NY), 2002.

FICTION

Brainstorms (short stories), Bobbs-Merrill (Indianapolis, IN), 1971.

Country Cousins (novel), George Braziller (New York, NY), 1974.

Music from the Evening of the World (short stories), Sun & Moon Press (Los Angeles, CA), 1989.

The Touch (novel), Autonomedia (Brooklyn, NY), 1993.

Self-Reliance: A Novel, Coffee House Press (Minneapolis, MN), 1994.

Also editor of *The Dice Cup: Selected Prose Poems of Max Jacob,* Sun (New York, NY), 1980. Contributor to journals and magazines, including *New Yorker, Paris Review, Rolling Stone, Partisan Review, Chelsea Review, Angel Hair, Poetry, Harris Review,* and *Un Poco Loco.*

SIDELIGHTS: Poet and author of novels and short fiction Michael Brownstein has written about his culture and times, from the late 1960s' flower revolution through the mid-1970s, when the New York School of Poets formed at St. Mark's Church in New York City, to the turn of the twenty-first century—a time of globalization, the information age, and the war on terror.

In 1969 he won the Frank O'Hara Award for his first full collection of poetry, *Highway to the Sky.* Brownstein was associated with the poet Anne Waldman, director of the poetry project at St. Mark's, and in 1976 moved to Boulder, Colorado, where he taught writing at the University of Colorado and the Naropa Institute. His collection *Strange Days Ahead* grew out of this period. Influenced by the Beat poets, it "reads like deconstructed ruins of hectic celebration," Andre commented. Brownstein's style is prosy and somewhat deadpan in this collection. In his 1982 prose poem, *Oracle Night,* Brownstein adheres to a single love theme throughout, with one-page stanzas.

Brownstein turned to short stories as early as 1971, with *Brainstorms,* followed in 1974 by the novel *Country Cousins.* His 1993 novel *The Touch* deals with contemporary subjects: New Age characters search for enlightenment and rediscovery of sexuality in the shadow of the AIDS epidemic.

In his 1994 work *Self-Reliance: A Novel,* Brownstein returns to the Manhattan of the mid-1970s. His main character is Roy, a marijuana-smoking freelance journalist who navigates the New York City culture at a time of junkies on the Lower East Side, the psychotic serial killer Son of Sam, the gay revolution, and unruly street people. Desperate to earn enough to take his girlfriend on a vacation, Roy gets an interview with an elderly and reclusive novelist, only to find his apartment broken into and his tapes stolen when he tries to sell the story. Giving up on writing and turning to performance art, Roy falls into a paranoid state in which he believes the elderly novelist is controlling his world. Donna Seaman of *Booklist* found that Brownstein leaves the reader "more than willing to suspend disbelief and soak up this wily and brilliantly created ambience." A *Publishers Weekly* contributor wrote that the author "skillfully re-creates the 1970s setting."

Brownstein's 2002 epic treatise/poem *World on Fire* examines the world at the turn of the twenty-first century. Amid the destruction of rain forests, a globalized society that obliterates cultural diversity, terrorism, breakthroughs in genetic engineering, the drive to produce and consume more fossil fuels, and the dehumanizing effects of mass media, the poet calls on mankind to return to a simpler, more ecologically sustainable lifestyle. Reminiscent of the Beat poets in rhetoric, the book, according to a *Publishers Weekly* contributor, is "one of the most eloquent recent poetic works to cover the downsides of 'progress' and to cry out for a counterpunch against the manipulations of empire."

BIOGRAPHICAL AND CRITICAL SOURCES:

PERIODICALS

American Book Review, September, 1982, review of *Oracle Night: A Love Poem,* p. 4.

Booklist, March 1, 1989, review of *Music from the Evening of the World,* p. 1091; March 15, 1994, Donna Seaman, review of *Self-Reliance: A Novel,* p. 1326

Book World, October 1, 1989, review of *Music from the Evening of the World,* p. 10.

Kirkus Reviews, February 1, 1989, review of *Music from the Evening of the World,* p. 142.

Library Journal, Harold Augenbraum, April 1, 1994, review of *Self-Reliance,* p. 130.

New York Times Book Review, March 8, 1987, review of *Country Cousins,* p. 34; May 22, 1994, Catherine Texier, review of *Self-Reliance,* p. 9

Publishers Weekly, February 3, 1989, review of *Music from the Evening of the World,* p. 93; March 7, 1994, review of *Self-Reliance,* p. 66; April 29, 2002, review of *World on Fire,* p. 66.

Review of Contemporary Fiction, spring, 1990, review of *Music from the Evening of the World,* p. 306.

Village Voice, June 20, 1989, review of *Music from the Evening of the World,* p. 63.*

C

CAMPBELL, Will D(avis) 1924-

PERSONAL: Born July 18, 1924, in Liberty, MS; son of Lee Webb and Hancie Bea (Parker) Campbell; married Brenda Fisher, January 16, 1946; children: Penny Elizabeth, Bonnie Ruth, Lee Webb II. *Education:* Attended Louisiana College, 1941-43; Wake Forest College (now University), A.B., 1948; Tulane University, graduate study, 1948-49; Yale University, B.Div., 1952. *Politics:* Democrat. *Religion:* Baptist. *Hobbies and other interests:* Country music, farming.

ADDRESSES: Home—Vanderbilt Rd., Mt. Juliet, Wilson, TN 37122.

CAREER: Pastor of a Baptist church in Taylor, LA, 1952-54; University of Mississippi, Oxford, director of religious life, 1954-56; National Council of Churches, New York, NY, consultant in race relations, 1956-63; Committee of Southern Churchmen, Nashville, TN, preacher at large and publisher of *Katallagete,* 1963-72. Has also been a civil rights activist, itinerant social worker, farmer, commentator for CNN news and other media stations, and tour bus cook for country singer Waylon Jennings. *Military service:* U.S. Army Medical Department, medic, 1943-46; became sergeant; served in Pacific theater.

AWARDS, HONORS: Lillian Smith Prize, Christopher Award, and National Book Award finalist, all for *Brother to a Dragonfly; Brother to a Dragonfly* was also named one of the best books of 1977 by *New York Times* and one of ten books of the 1970s worthy of surviving by *Time* magazine; Lyndhurst Prize, 1977; first place award for fiction, Friends of American Writers, 1982, for *The Glad River;* Alex Haley Memorial Award for distinguished Tennessee writers, 1992; Tennessee Governor's award for the arts, 1994, and Governor's Humanities award, 1995; Lifetime Achievement Award, American Civil Liberties Union (Tennessee chapter), 1997; Richard Wright Prize, Natchez Literary Celebration, 1998, for *Providence;* first prize in nonfiction, Mississippi Institute of Arts and Letters, for *And Also with You: Duncan Gray and the American Dilemma;* National Humanities Medal, 2000. Litt.D., University of the South, 1993; H.H.D., Mercer University, 1996; D.H.L., University of Southern Mississippi, 1999.

WRITINGS:

NONFICTION

Race and the Renewal of the Church, Westminster (Louisville, KY), 1962.
Brother to a Dragonfly (memoir), Seabury (New York, NY), 1977, twenty-fifth anniversary edition with foreword by Jimmy Carter, Continuum (New York, NY), 2000.
Forty Acres and a Goat: A Memoir, Peachtree Publishers (Atlanta, GA), 1986.
Covenant: Faces, Voices, Places, photographs by Al Clayton, Peachtree Publishers (Atlanta, GA), 1989.
Providence, Longstreet (Atlanta, GA), 1992.
The Stem of Jesse: The Costs of Community at a 1960s Southern School, Mercer University Press (Macon, GA), 1995.
And Also with You: Duncan Gray and the American Dilemma, Hillsboro Press (Franklin, TN), 1997.

Soul among Lions: Musings of a Bootleg Preacher, Westminster John Knox Press (Louisville, KY), 1999.

Robert G. Clark's Journey to the House: A Black Politician's Story, University Press of Mississippi (Jackson, MS), 2003.

EDITOR, WITH JAMES Y. HOLLOWAY

Up to Our Steeples in Politics, Paulist Press (New York, NY), 1970.

The Failure and the Hope: Essays of Southern Churchmen, Eerdmans (Grand Rapids, MI), 1972.

. . . And the Criminals with Him: Luke 23:33: A First-Person Book about Prisons, Paulist Press (New York, NY), 1973.

Callings!, Paulist Press (New York, NY), 1975.

OTHER

The Glad River (novel), Holt (New York, NY), 1982.

Cecelia's Sin (novella), Mercer University Press (Macon, GA), 1983.

Chester and Chun Ling (for children), Abingdon (Nashville, TN), 1989.

The Pear Tree That Bloomed in the Fall (for children), Providence House Publishers (Franklin, TN), 1996.

The Convention: A Parable (novel), Eerdmans (Grand Rapids, MI), 1991.

Also contributor to *God on Earth: The Lord's Prayer for Our Time,* text by Will Campbell, photographs by Will McBride, poetry by Bonnie Campbell, Crossroads (New York, NY), 1983; *Mississippi Writers: Reflections of Childhood and Youth,* University Press of Mississippi (Oxford, MS), 1986; and to *A Life Is More Than a Moment: The Desegregation of Little Rock's Central High,* text and photographs by Will Counts, Indiana University Press (Bloomington, IN), 1999. Contributor to magazines. Columnist, *Christianity and Crisis;* publisher, *Katallabete* (a journal on social issues).

SIDELIGHTS: Will D. Campbell "figures prominently as both an author and a civil rights activist," according to Bob Summers in *Publishers Weekly.* A Baptist minister who was active in the 1960s civil rights movement, Campbell attracted controversy for his rejection of most organized institutions, including churches, in favor of ministering to society's outcasts no matter what their beliefs, ethnic background, or financial means. A Southerner who was the only white person to attend the founding of Martin Luther King, Jr.'s Southern Christian Leadership Conference, Campbell shocked his colleagues with his later willingness to minister even to people such as Ku Klux Klan members. Yet Campbell, who in later life has earned his living as a farmer and writer while continuing to spread God's word as a self-styled "bootleg minister," has maintained the philosophy that "we're all bastards but God loves us anyway," as Knight Ridder/Tribune News Service writer Art Jester quoted him. He feels justified, therefore, in showing no discrimination when talking to people about God.

Campbell came from humble origins. His father was a hard-working farmer who had a difficult time during the Great Depression. The family fell into poverty as his father suffered the indignities of going on welfare. Campbell tells of these early struggles in his award-winning biography *Brother to a Dragonfly,* which also concerns the tragic relationship between Campbell and his brother Joe. In a piece on the book for the *New York Times Book Review,* John Leonard stated that "Joe's slide into madness and Will's attempts to stop or deflect it are the stuff of literature. Brotherhood, sibling caring has seldom been so beautifully portrayed."

This background naturally left Campbell sympathetic to the plight of the poor, and his religious upbringing, which led him to be ordained as a minister at age seventeen, helped set his path in life. Another influence came when he read *Freedom Road* by Howard Fast; this book convinced him that he should work to repair what he called the "tragedy of the South," according to an essay in *Religious Leaders of America.* Enrolling at Louisiana College, Campbell studied there for only a year before enlisting in the army and serving as a medic in World War II's Pacific theater. He later drew on this experience for his award-winning novel *The Glad River,* which is about three southern men who become fast friends and suffer through hell while fighting in the South Pacific. The message in this novel—that we should love one another—becomes crystal clear when one of the soldiers tries to save the life of a Japanese man. The theme that we should love one another as brothers and sisters is a common thread that would appear throughout all of Campbell's writing.

After the war Campbell returned home, started a family, and earned a divinity degree from Yale University. His sympathies for society's outcasts then led him to join the civil rights movement, while working at the University of Mississippi; he later joined the National Council of Churches in 1956 and became involved in a number of civil rights negotiations. He writes about these years in his *Forty Acres and a Goat: A Memoir.*

While involved in this work, he was asked a question that, in essence, demanded why he defended African Americans so stringently—were there not oppressed, poor, white people as well? Campbell realized this was a legitimate question and that he should be applying the gospel to all those who were oppressed. Thus, he began to see that the issue of oppression was not just white against black but, in the main, organized institutions—governments, businesses, and even churches—against the outcasts of society. This realization led him to form the Committee of Southern Churchmen, a group that shared his contempt for organized institutions.

Abandoning the church, he moved to a farm outside of Nashville, Tennessee, and ministered from his house, becoming particularly controversial when it became known in the 1980s that he included Klansmen among those to whom he was willing to preach. The books he has written since then often seem to be about him and his ideals, even when he is writing on other subjects. In *Providence,* for example, Campbell tells the story of members of the Choctaw tribe who are evicted from their land and labeled as lazy and worthless when they cannot adapt to the white man's way of life. This theme echoes the experience of Campbell's own father. Campbell, as *Christian Century* writer Perry H. Biddle, Jr. explained, uses the example of the Choctaws, blacks, and poor whites in rural Holmes County, Mississippi, "as a microcosm of the whole nation and, in a sense, of the rest of the earth." The book, according to Biddle, presents nothing less than "the story of America, of the struggle over race relations and economic justice, and of the search for community."

In *And Also with You: Duncan Gray and the American Dilemma,* Campbell tells the story of Gray, the rector of St. Peter's Episcopal Church in Oxford, Mississippi, who supported the integration of the University of Mississippi in 1962. When Gray argued in front of a large crowd that African American James Meredith should be allowed to enroll at the university, his "speech almost cost the young rector his life," according to Merrill Hawkins, Jr. in *Christian Century.* This event was somewhat reflective of Campbell's experience at the same university, where he lost his job in 1956 when he supported the *Brown vs. Board of Education* decision. "In writing about Gray," continued Hawkins, "Campbell has a forum to express his own ideas—themes that have been with him throughout his writing career. Campbell has long critiqued the evil power structures. The people who perpetuated violence in the name of segregation were themselves victims and symptoms, rather than causes." The author also criticizes churches for allowing secular law to determine their position on race issues and he "calls on religiously oriented social activists to find in the teachings of the church the motivation to address social issues."

More recently, in his *Robert G. Clark's Journey to the House: A Black Politician's Story,* Campbell tells of one African American's struggle up from poverty in Mississippi to become a state legislator. In the process, he was an activist for civil rights, became highly educated, and lost the trust of his fellow activists by working with segregationists in his negotiations to gain more rights for blacks. "This is a unique biography in that it is as much about the author as the subject," observed Vernon Ford in a *Booklist* review in which he saw many parallels between the two men's lives.

Through his writings and lectures around the country—he has become known as an appealing speaker whose wit and humor make his message sound less like preaching and more like storytelling—Campbell has striven to show that we can all be reconciled to God because He loves us all despite our faults. Solutions to social crises reflect not political problems but, as Campbell's colleague the Rev. Dee H. Wade put it in Jester's article, "our failure to be reconciled to God and to one another."

BIOGRAPHICAL AND CRITICAL SOURCES:

BOOKS

Connelly, Thomas L., *Will Campbell and the Soul of the South,* Continuum (New York, NY), 1982.
Contemporary Southern Writers, St. James Press (Detroit, MI), 1999.

Religious Leaders of America, 2nd edition, Gale (Detroit, MI), 1999.

Wright, Lawrence, *Saints & Sinners: Walker Railey, Jimmy Swaggert, Madalyn Murray O'Hair, Anton LaVey, Will Campbell, Matthew Fox,* Knopf (New York, NY), 1993.

PERIODICALS

Booklist, March 1, 2003, Vernon Ford, review of *Robert G. Clark's Journey to the House: A Black Politician's Story,* p. 1128.

Christian Century, May 12, 1982, John McEntyre, review of *The Glad River,* p. 578; May 26, 1982, review of *The Glad River,* p. 638; January 28, 1987, Myron A. Marty, review of *Forty Acres and a Goat: A Memoir,* p. 89; January 25, 1989, Andrew Pratt, review of *The Convention: A Parable,* p. 88; June 16, 1993, Perry H. Biddle, Jr., review of *Providence,* p. 649; June 17, 1998, Merrill Hawkins, Jr., review of *And Also with You: Duncan Gray and the American Dilemma,* p. 621; January 17, 2001, "People," p. 12.

Detroit News, May 16, 1982.

Humanities, January-February, 2001, Katie Towler, Maggie Reichers, and Chrissa Gerard, "Making a Difference: The 2000 National Humanities Medalists," p. 20.

Journal of American History, December, 1995, E. Culpepper Clark, review of *The Stem of Jesse: The Costs of Community at a 1960s Southern School,* p. 1290.

Journal of Southern History, May, 1996, Bill J. Leonard, review of *The Stem of Jesse,* p. 423.

Knight Ridder/Tribune News Service, April 22, 1998, Art Jester, "Maverick Preacher Played Key Role in Civil Rights Movement," p. 422K2968.

Library Journal, May 15, 1982, Grace Jones, review of *The Glad River,* p. 1008; October 15, 1986, Anthony O. Edmonds, review of *Forty Acres and a Goat,* p. 88.

New York Times, November 29, 1977.

New York Times Book Review, November 27, 1977, John Leonard, review of *Brother to a Dragonfly;* April 27, 1980, review of *Brother to a Dragonfly,* p. 39; November 16, 1986, Alison Friesinger, review of *Forty Acres and a Goat,* p. 25.

Publishers Weekly, February 26, 1982, review of *The Glad River,* p. 142; August 29, 1986, review of *Forty Acres and a Goat,* p. 381; October 24, 1986; September 9, 1988, review of *The Convention,* p. 119; October 13, 1989, review of *Covenant: Faces, Voices, Places,* p. 42; January 23, 1995, review of *The Stem of Jesse,* p. 55; March 15, 1999, review of *Soul among Lions: Musings of a Bootleg Preacher,* p. 515; May 17, 1999, "May Publications," p. 73.

OTHER

Here's Will (video), University of Alabama.

*   *   *

CARPENTER, Teresa (Suzanne) 1948-

PERSONAL: Born August 1, 1948, in Independence, MO; daughter of Rawlin Mack and Gloria Lee Harvey (Thompson) Carpenter. *Education:* Graceland College, B.A., 1970; University of Missouri, M.A., 1975. *Politics:* Democrat.

ADDRESSES: Office—Village Voice, 842 Broadway, New York, NY 10003.

CAREER: New Jersey Monthly, Princeton, NJ, senior editor, 1976-79; freelance journalist in New York, NY, 1979-81; *Village Voice,* New York, NY, staff writer, beginning 1981.

AWARDS, HONORS: Fairchild fellowship, University of Missouri, 1975-76; Pulitzer Prize, 1981, for feature articles; Page One Award, New York Newspaper Guild, 1981; Clarion Award, Women in Communications, 1982, 1986; Front Page Award, New York Newspaperwomen's Club, 1981.

WRITINGS:

Missing Beauty: A True Story of Murder and Obsession, Norton (New York, NY), 1988.

Mob Girl: A Woman's Life in the Underworld, Simon & Schuster (New York, NY), 1992.

(With Marcia Clark) *Without a Doubt,* Viking (New York, NY), 1997.

The Miss Stone Affair: America's First Modern Hostage Crisis, Simon & Schuster (New York, NY), 2003.

ADAPTATIONS: Without a Doubt was adapted as an audiocassette.

SIDELIGHTS: While a staff writer for New York City's *Village Voice*, Teresa Carpenter became obsessed with an account that the journalist stumbled across in the *New York Times* in 1983 about a Boston murder case involving a noted college professor and a young artist-turned-prostitute. Carpenter used her skills as a Pulitzer Prize-winning investigative journalist to do hundreds of interviews regarding the professor and his victim over the following four years before writing her first book, *Missing Beauty: A True Story of Murder and Obsession.* In subsequent books, Carpenter has continued to focus on women subjects, including in *Playboy,* which is about Playmate Dorothy Stratten, and 1992's *Mob Girl: A Woman's Life in the Underworld,* in which the author details the life of Mafia moll Arlyne Brickman. More recently, Carpenter delved into history to write about a hostage crisis that occurred back in 1901 in *The Miss Stone Affair: America's First Modern Hostage Crisis.*

In tackling *Missing Beauty,* Carpenter admits "that the lubricous world of the Combat Zone, the porno district not far from Boston Common, was 'foreign and not a little frightening,' but she avoided the temptation to shield herself—or her readers—from the sordid facts necessary to describe the murder case," according to David Black in his review of the work for the *New York Times Book Review.* The murder on which Carpenter based her book is considered bizarre by many experts. Professor William Douglas, a former head of Tufts University Medical School's cell culture research unit, apparently wanted more than sexual relations with Robin Benedict, an intelligent and attractive graphic artist and prostitute. Benedict, described by Sally G. Waters in *Library Journal* as the "dutiful, loving daughter of a middle-class family," was evidently looking for more than money in her relations with Douglas. The basis for anything more than a one-night sexual encounter between Douglas and Benedict is what first intrigued Carpenter, yet she leaves the mystery of the relationship intact for her readers. Wrote David Black in the *New York Times Book Review:* "Together—according to the evidence—they created a third reality that presumably gave both something each lacked." In an interview with Michael Freitag in the *New York Times Book Review,* Carpenter revealed that after the book was completed she was hesitant to tackle a second full-length book: "Four

years immersed in one story was brutalizing in some respects, so I don't know if I want to stay in the water that long again. But I wouldn't rule it out."

In 1992 Carpenter again took the plunge into troubled waters with *Mob Girl: A Woman's Life in the Underworld.* The book's subject, Arlyne Brickman, was a Jewish racketeer's daughter raised on New York's Lower East Side in the days of mobsters Meyer Lansky and Bugsy Siegel. In her teens, Brickman developed an admiration for Siegel's glamorous girlfriend Virginia Hill and kept a scrapbook full of newsclippings related to her. Brickman attempted to emulate Hill's lifestyle as an adult, but never achieved the other woman's status. Instead, Brickman ran numbers games, dealt narcotics, engaged in bookmaking and loan-sharking, and eventually became a mob informant for the government. She never found the respect or admiration of her mob peers as Hill had, and instead found herself the victim of a brutal gang rape and several beatings.

New York Times reviewer Amy Pagnozzi was disgusted, not with the skill of the biography's author, but with Brickman, whom Pagnozzi described as having "the instincts of a hyena—toting her infant daughter, Leslie, on errands because a woman with a baby is less likely to be hurt, later keeping the child home from school for company, ultimately allowing her own hood boyfriend to sell her grown daughter heroin and cocaine that would lead to her addiction and death from AIDS." Pagnozzi added, "This is the story not so much of a mob girl as of a mob groupie, who like any other groupie performed for flunky after flunky to get near the stars." Reviewer Diane Cole assessed *Mob Girl* similarly in the *Chicago Tribune Book World,* maintaining that "Carpenter's complexly detailed characterization of Brickman is powerful, leaving the reader by turns sickened, sad and ultimately drained." "With an individual like Brickman," the critic added, "that is as it should be."

After the infamous O. J. Simpson murder trial, a plethora of books were released by many of the principal players in this drama in which former football star Simpson was acquitted of murdering his wife, Nicole Brown Simpson, and her friend Ronald Goldman. Marcia Clark, a former Los Angeles County district attorney who was one of the prosecutors in the case, wrote her take on this sordid affair with the help of Carpenter in *Without a Doubt.* Although the book focuses on the Simpson trial, it is also a memoir that includes intimate details of Clark's life before and after the court case, including her divorce, child custody battle, and the fact that she was raped at age seventeen. But because the story of the trial has been written about by so many—not to mention that millions of people watched the trial on television—many reviewers of the book shared the opinion of Elizabeth Gleick, who said in her *Time* review that Clark "is not telling us something we did not already know" when she complains about incompetent police work, the inflated egos of the defense team and judge Lance Ito, and the annoying media coverage that intruded into Clark's life. *Billboard* critic Trudi Miller Rosenblum added that the book "offers little but a finger-pointing exercise."

Despite such criticisms, though, some reviewers felt that *Without a Doubt* was one of the better accounts of the Simpson trial. Bill Russell, writing in *Library Journal,* for example, asserted, "This may be one of the best books on the Simpson case available." Gleick, who felt Clark was very sympathetic even though attesting that the book offers no illuminations, declared that *Without a Doubt* "is well written, sometimes moving and occasionally amusing," thanks for the most part to coauthor Teresa Carpenter.

With the concern about terrorism and the dangers Americans face living in political hot spots abroad, Carpenter's 2003 book, *The Miss Stone Affair: America's First Modern Hostage Crisis,* is relevant to today's concerns even though it involves a 1901 hostage case. Ellen Stone, a Congregationalist missionary working in the Balkans, was kidnapped by Macedonian guerillas seeking ransom money to help their cause against the Bulgarian government that ruled them. Although Stone was treated well by her captors, she was still under threat of death if the money was not delivered. Enter the United States government, which Carpenter wastes no time lambasting for incompetence in the situation. The author details how poorly qualified translators and diplomats who knew little about the political situation in the Balkans were of little help in the situation. Were it not for Stone's ability to sympathize with her captors and the fund-raising drive back home, she might have died, especially since the U.S. government hesitated on paying the ransom and was sluggish to respond to any crises after the then-recent assassination of President William McKinley.

Carpenter was praised by critics for her ability to write about the "negotiations [that] involved murky, back-channel dealings and hidden subtexts," as a *Publishers Weekly* reviewer described it. Some critics, however, faulted the author for not better explaining the historical circumstances of the times, which would have helped to put the hostage crisis in perspective. "She might even have indulged the melodramatic potential of the tale more," added the *Publishers Weekly* contributor, who nevertheless declared the book "a gripping yarn." In *Women's Review of Books,* Erika Munk observed that "Carpenter's narrative jumps back and forth without ever shaping a coherent point of view . . . nor does Carpenter examine the obvious questions of gender and patriarchy that leap from the page." *Booklist* writer Roland Green complained of Carpenter's "condescension toward the U.S. Navy and . . . failing to track Stone after 1908," but concluded that the book is "generally well done." In the *New York Times Book Review,* Ben Macintyre called *The Miss Stone Affair* a "worthy account of politics and diplomacy, with a more emotional tale beneath it, itching to break free."

BIOGRAPHICAL AND CRITICAL SOURCES:

PERIODICALS

American Spectator, July, 1997, Joe Queenan, review of *Without a Doubt,* p. 66.

Austin American-Statesman (Austin, Tx), June 15, 2003, Michele Chan Santos, "Hostages and Headlines," p. K5.

Billboard, June 14, 1997, Trudi Miller Rosenblum, review of *Without a Doubt* (sound recording), p. 75.

Booklist, June 15, 1988, p. 1690; January 15, 1992, p. 881; May 1, 2003, Roland Green, review of *The Miss Stone Affair: America's First Modern Hostage Crisis,* p. 1567.

Chicago Tribune Book World, June 12, 1988, p. 6; December 29, 1991, p. 1; March 22, 1992, p. 5.

Esquire, November, 1994, pp. 84-96.

Harper's Bazaar, June, 1994, pp. 62-64.

Kirkus Reviews, May 1, 1988, p. 662; January 15, 1992, p. 87.

Library Journal, October 1, 1988, p. 95; March 1, 1992, pp. 98-99; April 15, 1992, Jodi L. Israel, review of *Mob Girl: A Woman's Life in the Underworld,* p. 138; July, 1997, Bill Russell, review of *Without a Doubt* (sound recording), p. 141.

London Review of Books, January 11, 1990, p. 14.

National Review, July 10, 1981, pp. 764-765.

New Yorker, November 28, 1983, pp. 176-177.

New York Times Book Review, June 26, 1988, p. 9; September 3, 1989, p. 20; July 21, 1991, p. 24; March 15, 1992, pp. 9-10; April 10, 1994, p. 10; January 22, 1995, p. 10; October 13, 1996, p. 10; September 21, 2003, Ben Macintyre, "The Ransom of Battle-Ax," p. 34.

People, November 21, 1983, pp. 12-13.

Publishers Weekly, May 13, 1988, p. 261; January 27, 1992, p. 84; May 31, 1993, p. 47; November 15, 1999, John F. Baker, "Hostage Crisis, 1901," p. 15; April 7, 2003, review of *The Miss Stone Affair,* p. 55.

Redbook, April, 1994, pp. 124-29.

Time, May 12, 1997, Elizabeth Gleick, review of *Without a Doubt,* p. 95.

U.S. News & World Report, April 27, 1981, p. 11.

Vogue, July, 1988, p. 68.

Women's Review of Books, October, 1988, p. 7; June, 2003, Erika Munk, "The Balkans' Balkans," p. 11.*

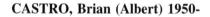

*   *   *

CASTRO, Brian (Albert) 1950-

Brian Castro

PERSONAL: Born January 16, 1950, in Kowloon, Hong Kong, China; immigrated to Australia, 1961; naturalized Australian citizen; son of Alberto Jose and Jessie Maria (Ewing) Castro; married Josephine Mary Gardiner, August 10, 1976 (marriage ended); married Maryanne Elizabeth Dever, December 7, 1997. *Ethnicity:* "Portuguese-Chinese-English." *Education:* University of Sydney, M.A., 1976.

ADDRESSES: Home—Melbourne, Australia. *Agent*—Bettina Keil, Keil & Keil Literatur Agentur, Schulterblatt 58, 20357 Hamburg, Germany.

CAREER: Mount Druitt High School, New South Wales, Australia, teacher, 1972-76; Lycée Technique, Paris, France, assistant in languages, 1976-77; St. Joseph's College, Hunter's Hill, New South Wales, French master, 1978-79; *Asiaweek* magazine, Hong Kong (now in China), literary journalist, 1983-87; Nepean College, Kingswood, New South Wales, visiting fellow, 1988; *All-Asia Review of Books,* Hong Kong, literary journalist, 1989-91; novelist, 1992—. Mitchell College, writer in residence, 1985; University of Western Sydney, tutor in literary studies, 1989-91.

MEMBER: Australian Society of Authors.

AWARDS, HONORS: Shared Australian Vogel Literary Award, Allen & Unwin, 1982, for *Birds of Passage;* Australian Council fellowships, 1983, 1991, 1992-93, 2003; Cité Internationale des Arts, Paris, senior fellow, 1997-98, resident at Keesing Studio, 2000; fiction prize, National Book Council; book of the year award for fiction, *Age,* for *Double-Wolf;* three Victorian Premier's Prizes.

WRITINGS:

NOVELS

Birds of Passage, Allen & Unwin (North Sydney, New South Wales, Australia), 1982.

Pomeroy, Allen & Unwin (North Sydney, New South Wales, Australia), 1990.

Double-Wolf, Allen & Unwin (North Sydney, New South Wales, Australia), 1991.

After China, Allen & Unwin (North Sydney, New South Wales, Australia), 1992.

Drift, Heinemann Australia (Port Melbourne, Victoria, Australia), 1994.

Stepper, Random House RRP (Australia), 1998.

Shanghai Dancing, Giramondo (Sydney, New South Wales, Australia), 2003.

NONFICTION

Writing Asia and Auto/Biography: Two Lectures, Australia Defence Force Academy (Canberra, Australia), 1995.

Looking for Estrellita (essays), International Specialized Book Service (Portland, OR), 1999.

Contributor of fiction to anthologies, including *Picador New Writing,* edited by Helen Daniel and Robert Dessaix, Picador (Chippendale, New South Wales, Australia), 1993; and *Risks: An Anthology,* edited by Brenda Walker, Fremantle Arts Centre Press (Fremantle, Australia), 1996. Contributor of essays and literary criticism to books, including *Writing in Multicultural Australia 1984: An Overview,* edited by Jacques Delaruelle, Alexandra Karakostas-Seda, and Anna Ward, Australia Council for Literature Board (North Sydney, New South Wales, Australia), 1985; and *Striking Cords: Multicultural Literary Interpretations,* edited by Sneja Gunew and Kateryna Longley, Allen & Unwin (North Sydney, New South Wales, Australia), 1992. Contributor to periodicals, including *Australian Book Review, Heat, Meanjin, Australian Literary Studies, Island, Mattoid,* and *Outrider.*

Castro's novels have been translated into French, Chinese, and German.

ADAPTATIONS: After China was adapted for the stage by Peter Copeman and produced in a series of workshops and readings at Queensland University of Technology, 1997-98, and in Sydney, Australia, 1998.

SIDELIGHTS: Brian Castro is "undoubtedly one of the most inventive and original Australian writers," according to *Australian Book Review* contributor Helen

Daniel, reviewing Castro's 1992 novel *After China.* Born in Hong Kong in 1950, the scion on his father's side of a family of Shanghai merchants of Spanish and Portuguese heritage, and on his mother's of Chinese and English ancestry, Castro moved to Australia to pursue his education in 1961. He worked for several years as a schoolteacher, specializing in languages, and briefly taught creative writing on the university level. His 1982 debut novel, *Birds of Passage,* was a cowinner of the Vogel prize given annually by its publisher, Allen & Unwin. Since becoming a prominent novelist Castro he has been writing full-time.

The novel *Double-Wolf* is based on a historical figure in the field of psychoanalysis: Sergei Wespe, better known as Freud's patient "the Wolf-Man." Born in 1876 into the Russian aristocracy, Wespe experienced childhood sexual traumas and grew up to believe himself a werewolf. The novel follows him, not only during the time covered by his psychoanalysis, but into his later life when he married a woman who committed suicide after the Nazi invasion of Vienna. Later still, he was analyzed by a fraudulent psychoanalyst in Australia. The narrative follows events discontinuously, punctuated not only by shifts in setting but by passages that are intended to make the reader question the validity of narrative itself. According to John McLaren in the *Australian Book Review,* "I am not sure what secrets Castro's maze of signs and stories offers, but I am confident its obsessional images will continue to haunt its readers." Daniel, in her review of *After China,* looked back upon *Double-Wolf* as simply "splendid."

In the widely reviewed *After China,* the protagonist is a Chinese architect named You Bok Mun, who, while staying at an Australian hotel that he had designed, meets and becomes symbiotically involved with a dying female writer. Flashbacks not only fill in You's life, but take the reader as far back as the final years of the great Chinese philosopher Lao Tzu (499 B.C.). As in *Double-Wolf,* the narrative structure is fragmented and complex in the postmodernist vein, leaving one reviewer, David Coad in *World Literature Today,* to express disfavor. Daniel, however, applauded this "vast labyrinth of narrative," one which occupied a mere 145 pages. Daniel felt that after some awkwardness at the beginning, the novel grew, "its movement becom[ing] more delicate and poised," until it reached "an ending of brilliant design, resonant with millennial images." In *Meanjin,* Rosemary Sorensen praised the novel's "surface shine and sparkle," which made it, for her, "rewarding reading."

Castro has also written several other novels. *Drift* is a partly imagined, partly researched tale based on the work of a real, though obscure, British novelist, B. S. Johnson, who lived from 1933 to 1973. Taking off from some of Johnson's published and unpublished work, and using Johnson as a character with only the most minimal of name changes—Bryan Stanley, his first two names, became Byron Shelley—Castro constructed a novel on two historical planes, one of them resting in contemporary London and the other in colonial Tasmania. The novel "is a monument to narrative complexity" and an examination of the author's own quandary as a person of a mixture of cultural and ethnic ancestry, according to *Journal of Australian Studies* contributor Miriam Wei Wei Lo, the critic adding that *Drift* "plays with parody on many levels." Writing in the *Australian Book Review,* Katharine England called *Drift* a "funny, fascinating, fabulous book."

Published in 1998, *Stepper* is a psychological novel of espionage set in Tokyo during World War II. Stepper, the protagonist, is a German journalist who is also a spy. Lonely, suspicious, and complex, he has an affair with a modernized Japanese woman named Reiko that prompts his gradual emotional self-exploration during the course of the narrative. Castro described his novel *Shanghai Dancing* as "a mixture of autobiography, history, memoir, and outrageous tales" that "traces the secrets and lies of a cosmopolitan family from Shanghai in the 1920s through to their translation to Australia in the 1960s. In search of a legacy, the narrator discovers all kinds of skeletons, and before too long he is himself drawn into the machinations of families and gangs. Episodic in nature, elegiac in style, the jigsaw chapters" are intended to reveal "a picture of both heroism and shame."

In addition to novels, Castro has published the essay collection *Looking for Estrellita,* a 1999 work that brings together two decades of articles, memoirs, and speeches that follow his development as a writer and his rise to literary luminary status within his native Australia. Noting that Castro remains concerned primarily with "language and the writer's concern for words" in the fourteen works included, *Journal of Australian Studies* contributor Hugh Martin noted that the collection illuminates "the many contradictions and tensions that make up one of Australia's most interesting writers."

BIOGRAPHICAL AND CRITICAL SOURCES:

BOOKS

Contemporary Novelists, St. James Press (Detroit, MI), 1996.

Davis, Geoffrey V., and Hena Maes-Jelinek, *Crisis and Creativity in the New Literature in English,* Rodopi (Amsterdam, Netherlands), 1990.

Heseltine, Harry, editor, *Literature and Psychiatry: Bridging the Divide,* Australia Defence Force Academy (Canberra, Australia), 1992.

Ommundsen, Wenche, and Hazel Rowley, editors, *From a Distance: Australian Writers and Cultural Displacement,* Deakin University Press (Geelong, Australia), 1996.

Proceedings: Association for the Study of Australian Literature, 16th Annual Conference 1994, Australia Defence Force Academy (Canberra, Australia), 1995.

PERIODICALS

Antipodes, December, 2000, Nicholas Birns, review of *Looking for Estrellita,* p. 156.

Australian Book Review, July, 1991, John McLaren, review of *Double-Wolf,* pp. 38-40; July, 1992, Helen Daniel, review of *After China,* pp. 4-8; July, 1994, Katharine England, review of *Drift,* pp. 12-13; May, 1997, pp. 6-10.

Australian Humanities Review, April, 1996.

Australian Literary Studies, Volume 14, number 4, 1990, pp. 464-475; Volume 17, number 2, 1995, pp. 149-156; May, 2002, Karen Barker, "The Artful Man: Theory and Authority in Brian Castro's Fiction," pp. 231-248; May, 2002, Karen Barker, "Theory As Fireworks: An Interview with Brian Castro," p. 241; Volume 20, number 2, 2003, pp. 201-214.

Australian's Review of Books, April, 1997, pp. 3-4.

Eureka Street, Volume 4, number 8, 1994, pp. 41-42.

Independent Monthly, Volume 4, number 7, 1993, pp. 27-28.

Journal of Australian Studies, June, 2000, Peter Copeman and Rebecca Scollen, "Of Training, Tokenism, and Productive Misinterpretation: Reflections on the *After China Project,*" p. 35; June, 2000, Miriam Wei Wei Lo, review of *Drift,* p. 69; June, 2000, Hugh Martin, review of *Looking for Estrellita,* p. 215.

Law Society Journal, August, 2000, Ross Bell, review of *Looking for Estrellita,* p. 95.

Meanjin, summer, 1993, Rosemary Sorensen, review of *After China,* pp. 778-783.

Southerly, Volume 58, number 2, 1998, pp. 59-66; Volume 59, number 2, 1999, pp. 74-84; autumn, 2000, Bernadette Brennan, review of *Drift,* pp. 39-50; winter, 2000, Bernadette Brennan, review of *Stepper,* pp. 168-177.

Tirra Lirra, Volume 5, number 2, 1994, pp. 10-13.

World Literature Today, summer, 1993, David Coad, review of *After China,* p. 667; summer, 1995, David Coad, review of *Drift,* pp. 641-642.

* * *

CHILD, Greg

PERSONAL: Born in Australia.

ADDRESSES: Agent—c/o Author Mail, Mountaineers Books, 1001 Southwest Klickitat Way, Suite 201, Seattle, WA 98134-1162. *E-mail*—gregchild@hotmail.com.

CAREER: Rock and mountain climber and author. Videographer of documentary film *Hitting the Wall.*

AWARDS, HONORS: Emmy Award for videography, for *Hitting the Wall;* National Outdoor Book Award, Outdoor Literature Category, 1998, for *Postcards from the Ledge: Collected Mountaineering Writings of Greg Child.*

WRITINGS:

Thin Air: Encounters in the Himalayas, Peregrine Smith Books (Salt Lake City, UT), 1990, 2nd edition, Mountaineers Books (Seattle WA), 1998.

Mixed Emotions: Mountaineering Writings of Greg Child, Mountaineers Books (Seattle, WA), 1993.

Climbing: The Complete Reference, Facts on File (New York, NY), 1995.

Postcards from the Ledge: Collected Mountaineering Writings of Greg Child, Mountaineers Books (Seattle, WA), 1998.

Over the Edge: The True Story of Four American Climbers' Kidnap and Escape in the Mountains of Central Asia, Villard (New York, NY), 2002.

(With Lynn Hill) *Climbing Free: My Life in the Vertical World,* Norton (New York, NY), 2002.

Child's articles and photographs have also appeared in *Outside, National Geographic, Smithsonian, Climbing* and *Rock and Ice* magazines.

SIDELIGHTS: Greg Child is a rock climber, a mountaineer, and an author of several books on mountaineering. He grew to love climbing in his native Australia, where he established many new climbing routes through rock formations. Child made his name as a top-flight climber in the 1970s when he scaled mountains such as Aurora and Lost in America. Child has made it to the top of Mount Everest and K2, but he now prefers to climb rocks and engage in sport climbing. As he noted to Peter Potterfield in an interview for *Mountain Zone Online,* "Climbing . . . is actually a very primal thing for those who do it. It's true that climbing meets some kind of basic need in me." For Potterfield, "Child's skill as a writer may make his the defining voice of climbing for a generation."

Thin Air: Encounters In the Himalayas, which was published in 1990, is a thorough account of three different climbs taken by Child in 1981, 1983, and 1986. Child takes readers along on each climb, describing in detail the crew mutinies, the financial mistakes, the brushes with death, and actual deaths on the climbs. In addition to the up-and-down journeys, Child describes the history of the politics that have surrounded the Himalayas and makes observations on India's culture, environment, and economy. "Dramatic, detailed, dynamically written," wrote Randy M. Brough in *Kliatt,* "this is the pinnacle of high-altitude adventure." Harry E. Whitmore, writing for *Library Journal,* called *Thin Air* "a worthwhile contribution to the literature of Himalayan climbs."

Child's 1995 volume *Climbing: The Complete Reference* is a fully stocked reference book for mountain, ice, and rock climbing. The book contains entries on geographic regions, mountain groups, techniques for mountain, ice, and rock climbing, climbing equipment and tools, and biographical sketches of past and present climbers. Child also discusses rating systems that gauge the difficulty of particular climbs. Included in the book are appendices with pictures and definitions that are helpful to novice climbers. A *Booklist* contributor assessed *Climbing* as a "unique and authoritative work." A. Spero, writing for *Choice,* advised, "Readers will find this book easy to use and informative. . . . There seems to be no comparable modern publications."

Postcards from the Ledge: Collected Mountaineering Writings of Greg Child is the author's 1998 collection of essays on climbing. The first entry is especially grisly and humorous, featuring as it does vivid descriptions of the difficult task of performing bodily functions while climbing. Child describes in the first chapter other travails awaiting the climber, such as frozen snot, parasites, and bugs. Other essays describe the debris left on high peaks, feats of heroism, tragic mistakes and mishaps, and controversies over historic-but-disputed climbs. A *Publishers Weekly* reviewer credited Child for his "civilized wit" in *Postcards from the Ledge.*

Child attained mainstream publication with his 2002 account of climbing and survival, *Over the Edge: The True Story of Four American Climbers' Kidnap and Escape in the Mountains of Central Asia.* In August, 2000, four young Americans were climbing in the Pamir Alai mountains of Kyrgyzstan. In search of challenging "big wall" climbing, these three men and one woman decided to ignore State Department warnings about the unstable political situation in this former Soviet republic. The region is beset by problems created in part by rampant drug trafficking and by the terrorist activities of Muslim extremists. Taken prisoner at gunpoint by a band of Islamic militants, the four Americans were held for six days and moved from hiding spot to hiding spot in the mountainous terrain. Finally, one of the four managed to push one of the captors over a cliff, and the Americans made a daring escape. Upon their return to the United States, this quartet was greeted by Child, who established an exclusive relationship for their story.

Thus Child had "everything he needs for an Ian Fleming-type mountaineering drama," according to a reviewer for *Publishers Weekly.* This same contributor felt, however, that Child's subsequent tale was "flat," with "wooden" dialogue and motivation and psychological states "overexplain[ed]." Writing on the audio version of the book, John E. Boyd of *Kliatt* was more

praiseworthy, calling Child's book a "gripping story," and further commenting that the author "captured the intensity and drama" of the six-day capture as well as the aftermath. Similarly, Gilbert Taylor, writing in *Booklist,* felt that Child "ably frames the politics as well as the mountaineering lore" in this "excellent rendition." Adam Mazmanian, writing in the *Washington Post Book World,* also found the book "compelling and well-written." Mazmanian did, however, have questions about what he termed "checkbook journalism," as Child shared the money from the book publication and any subsequent film deals with the four climbers in order to get an exclusive on their story. Subsequent articles by other journalists called parts of the climbers' story into question, causing a mini-furor among not only the climbing community but also along publishers row. "This little tempest is all the more unfortunate," thought Mazmanian, "because Child's account is well researched, vivid and more than plausible."

Child assisted climber Lynn Hill with the writing of her memoir *Climbing Free: My Life in the Vertical World.* One of the pioneers of the free climbing movement, in which the mountaineer uses only his or her body to climb without ropes, Hill has been something of a legend since 1975 and participates successfully in World Cup climbing venues. A contributor for *Publishers Weekly* called this a "remarkably entertaining autobiography."

Child, for his part, remains modest about his writing. He admits to no formal creative writing education, but he has "a strong desire to relate stories," as he told Potterfield. "It's something that is as strong a desire in me as the act of going climbing. Since I go climbing a lot, I think about climbing a lot, so it makes sense that I would write about climbing."

BIOGRAPHICAL AND CRITICAL SOURCES:

PERIODICALS

Booklist, February 1, 1996, review of *Climbing: The Complete Reference,* p. 951; April 15, 2002, Gilbert Taylor, review of *Over the Edge: The True Story of Four American Climbers' Kidnap and Escape in the Mountains of Central Asia,* pp. 1373-1374.

Choice, March, 1996, A. Spero, review of *Climbing,* p. 1088.

Climbing, September 15, 2002, Susan Fox Rogers, review of *Climbing Free: My Life in the Vertical World,* p. 120.

Denver Post, April 28, 2002, Claire Martin, review of *Climbing Free,* p. L1.

Kliatt, January, 1994, Randy M. Brough, review of *Thin Air: Encounters in the Himalayas,* p. 40; November 2002, John E. Boyd, review of *Over the Edge* (audiobook), p. 53.

Library Journal, October 1, 1990, Harry E. Whitmore, review of *Thin Air,* p. 95.

Publishers Weekly, August 24, 1998, review of *Postcards from the Ledge: Collected Mountaineering Writings of Greg Child,* p. 41; April 8, 2002, review of *Over the Edge,* p. 223; April 29, 2002, review of *Climbing Free,* p. 54.

Washington Post Book World, June 10, 2002, Adam Mazmanian, review of *Over the Edge,* p. C4.

ONLINE

Mountain Zone Online, http://classic.mountainzone.com/ (October 27, 2003), Peter Potterfield, "Interview with Greg Child."

Smithsonian Online, http://www.smithsonianmag.si.edu/smithsonian/ (October 27, 2003), "Greg Child Image Gallery."*

Arthur C. Clarke

*   *   *

CLARKE, Arthur C(harles) 1917-
(E. G. O' Brian, Charles Willis)

PERSONAL: Born December 16, 1917, in Minehead, Somersetshire, England; son of Charles Wright (a farmer) and Nora (Willis) Clarke; married Marilyn Mayfield, June 15, 1953 (divorced, 1964). *Education:* King's College, London, B.Sc. (first-class honors), 1948. *Hobbies and other interests:* "Observing the equatorial skies with a fourteen-inch telescope," table-tennis, scuba diving, and "playing with his Chihuahua and his six computers."

ADDRESSES: Home—25 Barnes Place, Colombo 7, Sri Lanka; Dene Court, Bishop's Lydeard, Taunton, Somerset TA4 3LT, England; fax (94-1) 698730.

Agent—David Higham Associates, 5-8 Lower John St., Golden Square, London W1R 4HA, England; Scouil, Chichak, Galen Literary Agency, 381 Park Avenue, New York, NY 10016.

CAREER: British Civil Service, His Majesty's Exchequer and Audit Department, London, England, auditor, 1936-41; Institution of Electrical Engineers, *Science Abstracts,* London, assistant editor, 1949-50; freelance writer, 1951—. Underwater explorer and photographer, in partnership with Mike Wilson, on Great Barrier Reef of Australia and coast of Sri Lanka, 1954-64. Has appeared on television and radio numerous times, including as commentator with Walter Cronkite on Apollo missions, CBS-TV, 1968-70, and as host of television series *Arthur C. Clarke's Mysterious World,* 1980, and *Arthur C. Clarke's World of Strange Powers,* 1984. Acted role of Leonard Woolf in Lester James Peries's film *Beddagama* (based on Woolf's *The Village in the Jungle*), 1979. Director of Rocket Publishing Co., United Kingdom; founder, director, and owner, with Hector Ekanayake, of Underwater Safaris (scuba-diving business), Sri Lanka; founder and patron, Arthur C. Clarke Centre for Modern Technologies, Sri Lanka, 1984—. Chancellor of University of Moratuwa, Sri Lanka, 1979—; chancellor, International Space University, 1987—; Vikram Sarabhai Professor, Physical Research Laboratory, Ahmedabad, India, 1980; trustee, Institute of Integral Education, Sri Lanka. Fellow, Franklin Institute, 1971, King's College, 1977, and Carnegie-Mellon University Institute of Robotics, 1981. Lecturer, touring United States and Britain, 1957-74. Board member of National Space Institute, United States, Space Generation Foundation, United States, International Astronomical Union (Search for ExtraTerrestrial Intelligence) Commission 51, and Planetary Society, United States. Chair, Second International Astronautics Congress, London, 1951; moderator, *Space Flight Report to the Nation,* 1961. *Military service:* Royal Air Force, radar instructor, 1941-46; became flight lieutenant.

MEMBER: International Academy of Astronautics (honorary fellow), International Science Writers Association, International Council for Integrative Studies, World Academy of Art and Science (academician), British Interplanetary Society (honorary fellow; chairperson, 1946-47, 1950-53), Royal Astronomical Society (fellow), British Astronomical Association, Association of British Science Writers (life member), British Science Fiction Association (patron), Royal Society of Arts (fellow), Society of Authors (council member), American Institute of Aeronautics and Astronautics (honorary fellow), American Astronautical Society (honorary fellow), American Association for the Advancement of Science, National Academy of Engineering (United States; foreign associate), Science Fiction Writers of America, Science Fiction Foundation, H. G. Wells Society (honorary vice president), Third World Academy of Sciences (associate fellow), Sri Lanka Astronomical Society (patron), Institute of Engineers (Sri Lanka; honorary fellow), Sri Lanka Animal Welfare Association (patron), British Sub-Aqua Club.

AWARDS, HONORS: International Fantasy Award, 1952, for *The Exploration of Space;* Hugo Award, World Science Fiction Convention, 1956, for "The Star"; Kalinga Prize, UNESCO, 1961, for science writing; Junior Book Award, Boys Club of America, 1961; Stuart Ballantine Gold Medal, Franklin Institute, 1963, for originating concept of communications satellites; Robert Ball Award, Aviation-Space Writers Association, 1965, for best aerospace reporting of the year; Westinghouse Science Writing Award, American Association for the Advancement of Science, 1969; Sec-

ond International Film Festival special award, and Academy Award nomination for best screenplay (with Stanley Kubrick), Academy of Motion Picture Arts and Sciences, both 1969, both for *2001: A Space Odyssey; Playboy* editorial award, 1971, 1982; Hon. D.Sc., Beaver College, 1971, University of Moratuwa, 1979; Nebula Award, Science Fiction Writers of America, 1972, for "A Meeting with Medusa"; Nebula Award, 1973, and Hugo Award, John W. Campbell Memorial Award, Science Fiction Research Association, and Jupiter Award, Instructors of Science Fiction in Higher Education, all 1974, all for *Rendezvous with Rama;* Aerospace Communications Award, American Institute of Aeronautics and Astronautics, 1974; Bradford Washburn Award, Boston Museum of Science, 1977, for "contributions to the public understanding of science"; Galaxy Award, 1979; Nebula and Hugo Awards, both 1980, both for *The Fountains of Paradise;* special Emmy Award for engineering, National Academy of Television Arts and Sciences, 1981, for contributions to satellite broadcasting; "Lensman" Award, 1982; Marconi International fellowship, 1982; Centennial Medal, Institute of Electrical and Electronics Engineers, 1984; E. M. Emme Astronautical Literature Award, American Astronautical Society, 1984; Grand Master Award, Science Fiction Writers of America, 1986; Vidya Jyothi Medal (Presidential Science Award), 1986; Charles A. Lindbergh Award, 1987; Third World Academy of Sciences associate fellow, 1987; named to Society of Satellite Professionals Hall of Fame, 1987; D.Litt., University of Bath, 1988; named to International Aerospace Hall of Fame, 1989; named to International Space Hall of Fame, 1989; Special Achievement Award, Space Explorers Association, Riyadh, 1989; R.A. Heinlein Memorial Award, National Space Society, 1990; Freeman of Minehead, 1992; Lord Perry Award for distance education, 1992; Nobel Peace Prize nomination, 1994; Distinguished Public Service Medal, NASA, 1995; Space Achievement Medal and Trophy, BIS, 1995; Mohamed Sahabdeen Award for Science, 1996; Von Karman Award, IAA, 1996; asteroid 4923 named 'Clarke,' IAU, 1996; Presidential Award, University of Illinois, 1997; knighted by Queen Elizabeth, 1998 (invested, 2000); European satellite, launched in April, 2000, named after Clarke in recognition of his contribution to the development of global communication networks. The Arthur C. Clarke Awards bestow annual prizes for writers in fifteen categories and are organized by the Space Frontier Foundation.

WRITINGS:

NONFICTION

Interplanetary Flight: An Introduction to Astronautics, Temple, 1950, Harper (New York, NY), 1951, 2nd edition, 1960.

The Exploration of Space, Harper, 1951, revised edition, Pocket Books (New York, NY), 1979.

The Young Traveller in Space, Phoenix, 1953, published as *Going into Space,* Harper, 1954, revised edition (with Robert Silverberg) published as *Into Space: A Young Person's Guide to Space,* Harper (New York, NY), 1971.

The Exploration of the Moon, illustrated by R. A. Smith, Harper (New York, NY), 1954.

The Coast of Coral, Harper (New York, NY), 1956.

The Reefs of Taprobane: Underwater Adventures around Ceylon, Harper (New York, NY), 1957.

The Scottie Book of Space Travel, Transworld Publishers (London, England), 1957.

The Making of a Moon: The Story of the Earth Satellite Program, Harper (New York, NY), 1957, revised edition, 1958.

Voice across the Sea, Harper (New York, NY), 1958, revised edition, 1974.

(With Mike Wilson) *Boy beneath the Sea,* Harper (New York, NY), 1958.

The Challenge of the Spaceship: Previews of Tomorrow's World, Harper (New York, NY), 1959.

(With Mike Wilson) *The First Five Fathoms: A Guide to Underwater Adventure,* Harper (New York, NY), 1960.

The Challenge of the Sea, Holt (New York, NY), 1960.

(With Mike Wilson) *Indian Ocean Adventure,* Harper (New York, NY), 1961.

Profiles of the Future: An Inquiry into the Limits of the Possible, Harper (New York, NY), 1962, revised edition, Holt (New York, NY), 1984.

The Treasure of the Great Reef, Harper (New York, NY), 1964, new edition, Ballantine (New York, NY), 1974.

(With Mike Wilson) *Indian Ocean Treasure,* Harper (New York, NY), 1964.

(With the editors of *Life*) *Man and Space,* Time-Life (Alexandria, VA), 1964.

Voices from the Sky: Previews of the Coming Space Age, Harper (New York, NY), 1965.

(Editor) *The Coming of the Space Age: Famous Accounts of Man's Probing of the Universe,* Meredith (New York, NY), 1967.

The Promise of Space, Harper (New York, NY), 1968.

(With Neil Armstrong, Michael Collins, Edwin E. Aldrin, Jr., Gene Farmer, and Dora Jane Hamblin) *First on the Moon,* Little, Brown (Boston, MA), 1970.

Report on Planet Three and Other Speculations, Harper (New York, NY), 1972.

(With Chesley Bonestell) *Beyond Jupiter,* Little, Brown (Boston, MA), 1972.

The View from Serendip (autobiography), Random House (New York, NY), 1977.

(With Simon Welfare and John Fairley) *Arthur C. Clarke's Mysterious World* (based on television series), A&W Publishers, 1980.

Ascent to Orbit: A Scientific Autobiography: The Technical Writings of Arthur C. Clarke, Wiley (New York, NY), 1984.

1984: Spring—A Choice of Futures, Del Rey (New York, NY), 1984.

(With Simon Welfare and John Fairley) *Arthur C. Clarke's World of Strange Powers,* Putnam (New York, NY), 1984.

(With Peter Hyams) *The Odyssey File,* Fawcett (New York, NY), 1985.

Arthur C. Clarke's July 20, 2019: Life in the Twenty-first Century, Macmillan (New York, NY), 1986.

Arthur C. Clarke's Chronicles of the Strange and Mysterious, edited by Simon Welfare and John Fairley, Collins (London, England), 1987.

Astounding Days: A Science Fictional Autobiography, Bantam (New York, NY), 1989.

How the World Was One: Beyond the Global Village, Bantam (New York, NY), 1992.

By Space Possessed, Gollancz (London, England), 1993.

Frontline of Discovery: Science on the Brink of Tomorrow, National Geographic Society (Washington, DC), 1994.

The Snows of Olympus: A Garden on Mars, Norton (New York, NY), 1995.

Arthur C. Clarke & Lord Dunsany: A Correspondence, edited by K. A. Daniels, Anamnesis Press (San Francisco, CA), 1998.

Greetings, Carbon-Based Bipeds!: Collected Essays, 1934-1998, edited by I. T. Macauley, St. Martin's Press (New York, NY), 1999.

FICTION

The Sands of Mars, Sidgwick & Jackson (London, England), 1951.

Prelude to Space, World Editions (New York, NY), 1951, published as *Master of Space,* Lancer Books

(New York, NY), 1961, published as *The Space Dreamers,* Lancer Books (New York, NY), 1969.

Islands in the Sky, Winston, 1952, new edition, Penguin Books (New York, NY), 1972.

Childhood's End, Ballantine (New York, NY), 1953.

Against the Fall of Night, Gnome Press (New York, NY), 1953.

Expedition to Earth (short stories), Ballantine (New York, NY), 1953.

Earthlight, Ballantine (New York, NY), 1955.

Reach for Tomorrow (short stories), Ballantine (New York, NY), 1956.

The City and the Stars (based on novel *Against the Fall of Night*), Harcourt (New York, NY), 1956.

The Deep Range (also see below), Harcourt (New York, NY), 1957.

Tales from the White Hart, Ballantine (New York, NY), 1957.

The Other Side of the Sky (short stories), Harcourt (New York, NY), 1958.

Across the Sea of Stars (anthology; includes *Childhood's End* and *Earthlight*), Harcourt (New York, NY), 1959.

A Fall of Moondust, Harcourt, (New York, NY), 1961, abridged edition, University of London Press (London, England), 1964.

From the Oceans, from the Stars (anthology; includes *The Deep Range* and *The City and the Stars*), Harcourt (New York, NY), 1962.

Tales of Ten Worlds (short stories), Harcourt (New York, NY), 1962.

Dolphin Island: A Story of the People of the Sea, Holt (New York, NY), 1963.

Glide Path, Harcourt (New York, NY), 1963.

Prelude to Mars (anthology; includes *Prelude to Space* and *The Sands of Mars*), Harcourt (New York, NY), 1965.

An Arthur C. Clarke Omnibus (contains *Childhood's End, Prelude to Space,* and *Expedition to Earth*), Sidgwick & Jackson (London, England), 1965.

(Editor) *Time Probe: The Science in Science Fiction,* Dial (New York, NY), 1966.

The Nine Billion Names of God (short stories), Harcourt (New York, NY), 1967.

A Second Arthur C. Clarke Omnibus (contains *A Fall of Moondust, Earthlight,* and *The Sands of Mars*), Sidgwick & Jackson (London, England), 1968.

(With Stanley Kubrick) *2001: A Space Odyssey* (screenplay), Metro-Goldwyn-Mayer, 1968.

2001: A Space Odyssey (based on screenplay), New American Library, 1968, published with a new introduction by Clarke, ROC (New York, NY), 1994.

The Lion of Comarre; and, Against the Fall of Night, Harcourt (New York, NY), 1968.

The Lost Worlds of 2001, Gregg Press (Boston, MA), 1972.

The Wind from the Sun (short stories), Harcourt (New York, NY), 1972.

(Editor) *Three for Tomorrow,* Sphere Books (London, England), 1972.

Of Time and Stars: The Worlds of Arthur C. Clarke (short stories), Gollancz (London, England), 1972.

Rendezvous with Rama, Harcourt (New York, NY), 1973, adapted edition, Oxford University Press (Oxford, England), 1979.

The Best of Arthur C. Clarke, edited by Angus Wells, Sidgwick & Jackson (London, England), 1973, published as two volumes, Volume 1: *The Best of Arthur C. Clarke: 1937-1955,* Volume 2: *The Best of Arthur C. Clarke: 1956-1972,* 1977.

Imperial Earth: A Fantasy of Love and Discord, Gollancz (London, England), 1975, Harcourt (New York, NY), 1976.

Four Great Science Fiction Novels (contains *The City and the Stars, The Deep Range, A Fall of Moondust,* and *The Fountains of Paradise*), Harcourt (New York, NY), 1979.

(Editor, with George Proctor) *The Science Fiction Hall of Fame,* Volume 3: *The Nebula Winners,* Avon (New York, NY), 1982.

2010: Odyssey Two, Del Rey (New York, NY), 1982.

The Sentinel: Masterworks of Science Fiction and Fantasy (short stories), Berkeley Publishing (Berkeley, CA), 1983.

Selected Works, Heinemann (London, England), 1985.

The Songs of Distant Earth, Del Rey (New York, NY), 1986.

2061: Odyssey Three, Del Rey (New York, NY), 1988.

(With Gentry Lee) *Cradle,* Warner Books (New York, NY), 1988.

A Meeting with Medusa (bound with *Green Mars* by Kim Stanley Robinson), Tor Books (New York, NY), 1988.

(With Gentry Lee) *Rama II,* Bantam (New York, NY), 1989.

(With Gregory Benford) *Beyond the Fall of Night,* Putnam (New York, NY), 1990.

The Ghost from the Grand Banks, Bantam (New York, NY), 1990.

Tales from the Planet Earth, illustrated by Michael Whelan, Bantam (New York, NY), 1990.

(With Gentry Lee) *The Garden of Rama,* Bantam (New York, NY), 1991.

The Hammer of God, Bantam (New York, NY), 1993.

(With Gentry Lee) *Rama Revealed,* Bantam (New York, NY), 1994.

(With Mike McQuay) *Richter 10,* Bantam (New York, NY), 1996.

3001: The Final Odyssey, Ballantine (New York, NY), 1997.

(With Michael Kube-McDowell) *The Trigger,* Bantam (New York, NY), 1999.

(With Stephen Baxter) *The Light of Other Days,* Tor (New York, NY), 2000.

The Collected Stories of Arthur C. Clarke, Tor (New York, NY), 2001.

OTHER

Opus 700, Gollancz (London, England), 1990.

Rama: The Official Strategy Guide, Prima Pub. (Rocklin, CA), 1996.

Also author of introduction to *Inmarsat History.* Contributor to books, including *Mars and the Mind of Man,* Harper, 1973. Author of foreword for Paul Preuss's books *Breaking Strain,* Avon, 1987, and *Maelstrom,* Avon, 1988. Also author of television series *Arthur C. Clarke's World of Strange Powers* and a movie treatment based on *Cradle.* Contributor of more than 600 articles and short stories, occasionally under pseudonyms E. G. O'Brian and Charles Willis, to numerous magazines, including *Harper's, Playboy, New York Times Magazine, Vogue, Holiday,* and *Horizon.*

Clarke's works have been translated into Polish, Russian, French, German, Spanish, Serbo-Croatian, Greek, Hebrew, Dutch, and over twenty other languages.

ADAPTATIONS: The book *Arthur C. Clarke's Mysterious World* was adapted as a series for television by Yorkshire Television, 1980. The short story "The Star" was adapted for an episode of *The New Twilight Zone* by CBS-TV in 1985. The following works have been optioned for movies: *Childhood's End,* by Universal; *The Songs of Distant Earth,* by Michael Phillips; *The Fountains of Paradise,* by Robert Swarthe; and *Cradle,* by Peter Guber. Sound recordings include *Arthur C. Clarke Reads from his 2001: A Space Odyssey,* 1976; *Transit of Earth*; *The Nine Billion Names of God*; and *The Star,* 1978; *The Fountains of Paradise,* 1979; *Childhood's End,* 1979; and *2010: Odyssey Two.* A full-length recording of *A Fall of Moondust* was made by Harcourt in 1976.

SIDELIGHTS: Renowned not only for his science fiction, which has earned him the title of Grand Master from the Science Fiction Writers of America, Arthur C. Clarke also has a reputation for first-rate scientific and technical writing. Perhaps best known in this field for "Extraterrestrial Relays," the 1945 article in which he first proposed the idea of communications satellites, Clarke has also published works on such diverse topics as underwater diving, space exploration, and scientific extrapolation. Nevertheless, it is Clarke's science fiction which has secured him his reputation, with such novels as *Childhood's End* and *Rendezvous with Rama* acknowledged as classics in their field. In addition, his story "The Nine Billion Names of God" was named to the science fiction "Hall of Fame," while the movie *2001: A Space Odyssey,* written with director Stanley Kubrick, has been called the most important science-fiction film of the twentieth century.

The Exploration of Space, one of Clarke's first novels, broke ground in explaining scientific ideas to a popular audience. As H. H. Holmes described in the *New York Herald Tribune Book Review,* in "the realm of speculative factual writing . . . Clarke's new book will serve as the most important yet in its field. Not that it says much that is new," explained Holmes, but because "it is precisely calculated to bring our present knowledge of space travel before a whole new public." What enables the book to reach such an audience is a "charm and magnetism" that is due to "Clarke's ability to reduce complex subjects to simple language and his steadfast avoidance of fantasy as a substitute for factual narration," observed Roy Gibbons in the *Chicago Sunday Tribune.*

Although most speculative science texts are soon outdated, Clarke's work has withstood years of technical progress. In *The Promise of Space,* published in 1968 to "replace" *The Exploration of Space,* Clarke "is able to show the manner in which many of his predictions have been fulfilled," noted a *Times Literary Supplement* contributor. But rather than simply cataloging recent discoveries, Clarke's work incorporates them into new ideas: "All through the book Clarke not only recounts what has been done during the last two decades," explained Willy Ley in the *New York Times Book Review,* "but has his eye on both the immediate results and the future."

Although much of Clarke's early fiction reinforced the idea that space travel was an eventuality, *Childhood's End,* his first successful novel, is "Clarke's only work—fiction or nonfiction—in which 'The stars are not for Man,'" suggested Thomas D. Clareson in *Voices for the Future: Essays on Major Science Fiction Writers.* The novel relates the appearance of the Overlords, a race of devil-shaped aliens who have come to guide Earth to peace and prosperity. Beginning by eliminating all individual governments and thus ending war, the Overlords use their superior technology to solve the problems of poverty, hunger, and oppression. The cost of this utopia is that most scientific research is set aside as unnecessary, and the exploration of space is forbidden. The motives of the Overlords become clear as the youngest generation of humans develops extrasensory powers; the children of Earth are to join the Overmind, a collective galactic "spirit" that transcends physical form. The need for science, technology, and space is eliminated with humanity's maturation, and the Earth itself is destroyed as her children join the Overmind.

Some critics view *Childhood's End* as the first manifestation of the theme of spiritual evolution that appears throughout Clarke's fiction. John Huntington, writing in the critical anthology *Arthur C. Clarke,* believed the novel to be Clarke's solution to one of the problems posed by technological progress: how spiritual development can keep pace with scientific development when by making man comfortable, science often takes away man's curiosity and drive. *Childhood's End* solves the problem with a stage of "transcendent evolution," and Huntington proposes that "it is its elegant solution to the problem of progress that has rightly earned *Childhood's End* that 'classic' status it now enjoys."

Clarke's best-known work, *2001: A Space Odyssey* was the result of four years' work on both the film version and the subsequent novel. The collaboration between Clarke and director Stanley Kubrick began when the filmmaker sought a suitable basis for making the "proverbial good science fiction movie," as he has frequently described it. The two finally settled upon Clarke's 1951 short story "The Sentinel," and developed it "not [into] a script, which in [Kubrick's] view does not contain enough of the visual and emotional information necessary for filming, but a prose version, rather like a novel," related Michel Ciment in *Focus on the Science Fiction Film.* The result "was of more help to him in creating the right atmosphere because it was more generous in its descriptions," added Ciment.

The film and the novel have the same basic premise: a large black monolith has been sent to Earth to encourage the development of man. First shown assisting in the "dawn of man" four million years ago, a monolith is next uncovered on the moon, and upon its unveiling sends a strong radio signal toward the outer planets. As a result the spaceship *Discovery,* operated by the intelligent computer HAL 9000, is sent in the direction of the signal to investigate. However, while the human crew is kept ignorant of the ship's true assignment, the HAL 9000 begins to eliminate what it sees as obstacles in the way of the mission—including all of the crew. First captain Dave Bowman manages to survive, however, and upon his arrival at a moon of Saturn (Jupiter in the film) encounters yet a third monolith which precipitates a journey through the infinite, "into a world where time and space are relative in ways beyond Einstein," described Penelope Gilliatt in the *New Yorker.* Bowman is transformed during this journey, and subsequently arrives at a higher plane of evolution as the Star Child. "In the final transfiguration," noted Tim Hunter in *Film Heritage,* "director Kubrick and coauthor Arthur Clarke . . . suggest that evolutionary progress may in fact be cyclical, perhaps in the shape of a helix formation." The critic explained, "Man progresses to a certain point in evolution, then begins again from scratch on a higher level."

"Clarke's *2001: A Space Odyssey* was an extraordinary development in fiction, a novel written in collaboration with the director who was simultaneously filming it," wrote Colin Greenland of the *Times Literary Supplement. New Statesman* contributor Brenda Maddox found the book lacking beside the movie. She claimed that the novel "has all the faults of the film and none of its virtues. The characters still have the subtlety of comic-strip men and, lacking the film's spectacular visual gimmickry . . . the story must propel itself with little gusts of scientific explanation." In contrast, Eliot Fremont-Smith asserted in the *New York Times* that "the immense and moving fantasy-idea of *2001* . . . is an idea that can be *dramatically* envisioned only in the free oscillations of the delicately cued and stretched mind." The critic added that the film "is too direct for this, its wonders too unsubtle and, for all their majesty, too confining." And where the movie may have been obscure, "all of it becomes clear and convincing in the novel. It is indeed an odyssey, this story, this exhilarating and rather chilling science fiction fantasy." Nevertheless, in comparing the visual genius of the film with the clarity of the book, Clarke himself admits in *Focus on the Science Fiction Film* that both versions "did something that the other couldn't have done."

Although for several years Clarke—and others—insisted that a sequel to *2001* would be impossible, in 1982 Clarke published *2010: Odyssey Two.* Incorporating elements of both the film and novel versions, as well as new information from the *Voyager* probes of Jupiter, in *2010* "Clarke sensibly steps back down to our level to tell the story of a combined Russian and American expedition to salvage Bowman's deserted ship, the *Discovery,* and find out what happened," related Greenland. Although the expedition finds the remains of the ship and repairs the HAL 9000, the purpose of the black monolith mystifies them. While some critics find this an adequate approach to a sequel, others criticize Clarke for even attempting to follow up a "classic." *Science Fiction Review* writer Gene DeWeese believed a large problem is that *2010* "is not so much a sequel to the original book, which was in many ways superior to the movie, but a sequel to and an explanation of the movie. Unfortunately, many of these explanations already existed [in the novel of *2001*.]" *Washington Post Book World* contributor Michael Bishop similarly noted a tendency to over-explain: "Ponderous expository dialogue alternates with straightforward expository passages in which Heywood Floyd . . . or the author himself lectures the reader." And Gerald Jones of the *New York Times Book Review* complained that *2010* "violates the mystery [of the original] at every turn."

Despite the various criticisms, *2010* still "has its share of that same sense of wonder, which means that it is one of the dozen or so most enjoyable SF books of the year," observed DeWeese. "Clarke deftly blends discovery, philosophy, and a newly acquired sense of play," stated *Time* contributor Peter Stoler, creating a work that will "entertain" readers.

2061: Odyssey Three is the next chapter in the saga of the black monolith. The year 2061 marks the year of the next appearance of Halley's comet; *Odyssey Three* follows Heywood Floyd on a survey of the object. While en route, the survey party is redirected to rescue a ship that has crashed on the Jovian moon of Europa—the one celestial object the monoliths have warned humans against visiting. Some critics have been skeptical of a second sequel, such as the *Time* reviewer who found that "the mix of imagination and anachronism is wearing as thin as the oxygen layer on Mars." Although Jones also observed that "Clarke's heart is obviously not in the obligatory action scenes that advance the plot," he conceded that the author

"remains a master at describing the wonders of the universe in sentences that combine a respect for scientific accuracy with an often startling lyricism." Clarke "is not to be measured by the same standards we apply to a mundane plot-smith," asserted David Brin in the *Los Angeles Times.* "He is, after all, the poet laureate of the Space Age. He is at his best making the reader feel, along with Heywood Floyd," continued Brin, "how fine it might be to stand upon an ancient comet, out under the stars, knowing that it is those dreams that finally come true that are the best dreams of all."

Clarke's faith in the human spirit is evident in his nonfiction book *The Snows of Olympus: A Garden on Mars.* Published in 1995, at a time when NASA struggled with massive budget cutbacks, this book nevertheless looks optimistically toward a future when humans will visit and colonize the planet Mars. Clarke asserts that if money were no object, human beings could walk on Mars early in the twenty-first century. He outlines a three-part mission to Mars, beginning with robot probes, which would locate needed resources on the planet and choose suitable landing sites. Unmanned space freighters would follow with equipment and supplies, intended to support the third part of the mission: the landing of a human crew. Clarke predicts that once a human colony is established, work will begin to alter the environment of Mars to make it habitable by unprotected human beings. He even believes that it is possible to create oceans and large-scale agricultural projects there. *The Snows of Olympus* is illustrated with computer-generated art depicting the transformation of Mars. Clarke created the pictures himself, beginning with maps of the planet generated by NASA's *Voyager* probe.

Clarke told John F. Burns of the *New York Times Book Review* that in the years when he was not writing, he felt like Frank Poole after he had his air supply cut off by HAL. Thus, Clarke has done what he long insisted was impossible: write the fourth installment of his "Odyssey series," *3001: The Final Odyssey.* In *3001* another manned space voyage finds the deep-frozen Poole, long presumed dead, and revives him with fourth-millennium technology. Poole masters the use of the "braincap" and other gadgets, learns about Star City, and studies a thousand years of history he has slept through. During his long sleep, a monolith has exploded Jupiter, turning it and its moons into a secondary solar system. One moon, Europa, has been colonized by a monolith that monitors human behavior and influences the plantlike beings beneath the surface to grow. Poole is alarmed to learn that his old colleague, Dave Bowman, and HAL have both become absorbed by the monolith and that the black slab's superiors are intent on doing something unthinkable to the humans that they have enslaved. Writing in the *New York Times Book Review,* John Allen Paulos found that while the plot hangs together "reasonably well," much of the enjoyment comes from Clarke's ruminations on high technology, Freudian therapy, computer security, terrorism, and religious mania. Ian Watson of the *Times Literary Supplement* suggested that what makes *3001* compelling reading is the way in which he "retrofits" earlier episodes "so that they blend with the new future and the now ex-future."

Clarke released two novels near the turn of the twenty-first century: *The Trigger,* written with Michael Kube-McDowell, and *The Light of Other Days,* written with Stephen Baxter. *The Trigger* depicts a time in the future when weapons using gunpowder are rendered obsolete. A device called the "Trigger" causes them to self-destruct. When the Trigger falls into the wrong hands, questions of ethics arise. According to *Booklist*'s Roland Green, "The discovery's potential for good and evil is enormous." Jackie Cassada of *Library Journal* described the book as a "thought-provoking, suspenseful tale."

Set in the mid-2300s as the last outdated rocket-boosted spaceship is launched in Russia, *The Light of Other Days* tells the tale of scientist Heram Patterson, who unveils wormhole technology, which allows people to view others anywhere in the world. It is soon discovered that this technology can be used to see into the future, and Patterson's son discovers that it can be used to view the past as well. The technology renders privacy nonexistent and reveals the earth's destruction by an asteroid in 500 years. *Booklist*'s Sally Estes noted that "The stories' inter-relationships have a soap-opera quality," but described the book as a "sweeping, mind-boggling read."

The *Collected Stories of Arthur C. Clarke,* published in 2001, contains over 100 science-fiction tales and nearly 1,000 pages. Most stories in the collection date from 1946 to 1970, but a few are earlier and several are more recent. Jackie Cassada of *Library Journal* remarked that the book displays Clarke's "enthusiasm for both good storytelling and impeccable science."

Booklist's Roland Green concluded that *Collected Stories* "may be the single-author science-fiction collection of the decade."

BIOGRAPHICAL AND CRITICAL SOURCES:

BOOKS

Agel, Jerome, editor, *The Making of Kubrick's 2001,* New American Library, 1970.

Aldiss, Brian W., *Trillion Year Spree: The History of Science Fiction,* Atheneum (New York, NY), 1986.

Authors and Artists for Young Adults, Volume 33, Gale (Detroit, MI), 2000.

Bleiler, E. F., editor, *Science Fiction Writers: Critical Studies of the Major Authors from the Early Nineteenth Century to the Present Day,* Scribner (New York, NY), 1982.

Clareson, Thomas D., editor, *Voices for the Future: Essays on Major Science Fiction Writers,* Bowling Green University Press (Bowling Green, OH), 1976.

Contemporary Literary Criticism, Gale (Detroit, MI), Volume 1, 1973, Volume 4, 1975, Volume 13, 1980, Volume 16, 1981, Volume 18, 1981, Volume 35, 1985.

Contemporary Novelists, 7th edition, St. James Press (Detroit, MI), 2001.

Encyclopedia of Occultism and Parapsychology, 5th edition, Gale (Detroit, MI), 2001.

Hollow, John, *Against the Night, the Stars: The Science Fiction of Arthur C. Clarke,* Harcourt, 1983, expanded edition, Ohio University Press (Athens, OH), 1987.

Johnson, William, editor, *Focus on the Science Fiction Film,* Prentice-Hall (Englewood Cliffs, NJ), 1972.

Ketterer, David, *New Worlds for Old: The Apocalyptic Imagination, Science Fiction, and American Literature,* Indiana University Press (Bloomington, IN), 1974, pp. 43-49.

Knight, Damon, *In Search of Wonder: Essays on Modern Science Fiction,* Advent (Chicago, IL), 1967, pp. 177-205.

Magill, Frank N., editor, *Survey of Science Fiction Literature,* Volumes 1-5, Salem Press (Englewood Cliffs, NJ), 1979.

Malik, Rex, editor, *Future Imperfect,* Pinter, 1980.

McAleer, Neil, *Arthur C. Clarke: The Authorized Biography,* Contemporary Books (Chicago, IL), 1992.

Moskowitz, Sam, *Seekers of Tomorrow: Masters of Science Fiction,* World Publishing, 1966.

Of Time and Stars: The Worlds of Arthur C. Clarke, Gollancz (London, England), 1972, pp. 7-10.

Olander, Joseph D., and Martin Harry Greenburg, editors, *Arthur C. Clarke,* Taplinger (New York, NY), 1977.

Platt, Charles, *Dream Makers: The Uncommon Men and Women Who Write Science Fiction,* Volume II, Berkeley Publishing, 1983.

Rabkin, Eric S., *Arthur C. Clarke,* Starmont House, 1979.

Reid, Robin Anne, *Arthur C. Clarke: A Critical Companion,* Greenwood Press (Westport, CT), 1997.

St. James Encyclopedia of Popular Culture, St. James Press (Detroit, MI), 2000.

St. James Guide to Young Adult Writers, St. James Press (Detroit, MI), 1999.

Samuelson, David N., *Arthur C. Clarke: A Primary and Secondary Bibliography,* G. K. Hall (Boston, MA), 1984.

Short Story Criticism, Volume 3, Gale (Detroit, MI), 1989.

Slusser, George Edgar, *The Space Odysseys of Arthur C. Clarke,* Borgo (San Bernadino, CA), 1978.

Wollheim, Donald A., *The Universe Makers,* Harper (New York, NY), 1971.

PERIODICALS

Algol, November, 1974.

Analog Science Fiction and Fact, September, 2000, Tom Easton, review of *The Light of Other Days,* pp. 135-141; May, 2001, Tom Easton, "The Reference Library," pp. 132-138.

Atlantic, July, 1952; April, 1963, p. 152.

Best Sellers, October 1, 1973; May, 1979; May, 1984, pp. 75-76; December 24, 1953, p. 13.

Booklist, October 1, 1995, pp. 239-240; August, 1999, Ray Olson, review of *Greetings, Carbon-Based Bipeds! Collected Essays, 1934-1998,* p. 2003; September 15, 1999, Roland Green, review of *The Trigger,* p. 196; February 1, 2000, Sally Estes, review of *The Light of Other Days,* p. 996; January 1-15, 1997, p. 778; September 15, 2000, Leah Sparks, review of *The Light of Other Days,* p. 259; January 1, 2001, Roland Green, review of "The Collected Stories of Arthur C. Clarke," p. 928.

Book World, June 30, 1968, pp. 1, 3; December 19, 1971, p. 6.

Chicago Sunday Tribune, July 13, 1952.

Chicago Sunday Tribune Magazine of Books, February 16, 1958, p. 7.

Chicago Tribune, December 30, 1990, section 14, p. 6; January 30, 1994, section 14, p. 6.

Christian Science Monitor, February 26, 1963; February 10, 1972, p. 10; August 8, 1973, p. 9; December 3, 1982, p. B3; November 26, 1993, p. 15.

Commonweal, May 3, 1968.

Detroit News, November 28, 1982.

Discover, May, 1997, pp. 68-69.

Economist, April 12, 1997, p. 85.

Extrapolation, winter, 1980, pp. 348-360; summer, 1987, pp. 105-129; spring, 1989, pp. 53-69.

Guardian, January 20, 2001, Andrew Rissik, "Magic among the Stars."

Kirkus Reviews, November 1, 1987.

Library Journal, March 1, 1990, p. 98; November 1, 1995, pp. 101-102; February 15, 1997, p. 164; September 1, 1999, William Baer, review of *Greetings, Carbon-Based Bipeds!,* p. 226; December, 1999, Jackie Cassada, review of *The Trigger,* p. 192; March 15, 2001, Jackie Cassada, review of *The Collected Stories of Arthur C. Clarke,* p. 110; September 15, 2001, Michael Rogers, "The Fountains of Paradise," p. 188; September 15, 2001, Michael Rogers, "The City and the Stars and the Sands of Mars," p. 118.

Locus, February, 1994, p. 75; November, 1993, p. 27.

Los Angeles Times, December 1, 1982; January 24, 1992, pp. E1, E4; February 12, 1995, p. M4; January 29, 1996.

Los Angeles Times Book Review, December 19, 1982; March 4, 1984; December 6, 1987; December 9, 1990, p. 10; February 3, 1991, p. 10; January 24, 1992, p. E1; August 8, 1993, p. 11; March 10, 1996.

Magazine of Fantasy and Science Fiction, September, 1979, pp. 25-26; October, 1999, Robert K. J. Killheffer, review of *Greetings, Carbon-based Bipeds!,* p. 36.

Nation, March 5, 1983.

National Review, November 20, 1962, pp. 403-404; May 14, 1976.

New Republic, May 4, 1968; March 20, 1976; March 24, 1979.

New Scientist, April 12, 1997, p. 44.

Newsday, April 4, 1968; April 20, 1968.

New Statesman, December 20, 1968, pp. 877-878; January 26, 1979.

Newsweek, October 30, 1961.

New Yorker, April 24, 1965; May 27, 1967; April 13, 1968; September 21, 1968; August 9, 1969, pp. 40-65; December 13, 1982; December 20, 1982.

New York Herald Tribune Book Review, July 13, 1952; August 10, 1952; August 23, 1953; March 2, 1958, p. 6.

New York Times, May 29, 1968; July 5, 1968; August 22, 1973, p. 35; February 26, 1985; April 7, 1993, pp. C13, C19; November 28, 1994, p. A4; April 1, 1997; April 11, 1997.

New York Times Book Review, March 14, 1954; July 15, 1956, p. 20; April 14, 1963, pp. 22, 24; August 25, 1968, p. 10; September 23, 1973; January 18, 1976; October 30, 1977, p. 12; March 18, 1979; January 23, 1983, p. 24; March 6, 1983; May 11, 1986; December 20, 1987; May 6, 1990, p. 22; July 8, 1990, p. 22; February 3, 1991, p. 33; September 1, 1991, p. 13; June 13, 1993, p. 22; March 13, 1994, p. 30; January 28, 1996; March 9, 1997; December 26, 1999, Gerald Jones, review of *Greetings! Carbon-based Bipeds!,* p. 14.

New York Times Magazine, March 6, 1966.

Observer, January 21, 2001, Robin McKie, "Master of the Universe."

Omni, March, 1979.

People, December 20, 1982.

Playboy, July, 1986.

Popular Science, October, 2001, Nicole Foulke, "The Banyan Trees of Mars," p. 42.

Publishers Weekly, September 10, 1973; June 14, 1976; January 6, 1984, p. 75; January 27, 1984, p. 72; September 18, 1995, pp. 121-122; January 22, 1996, p. 61; July 26, 1999, review of *Greetings, Carbon-based Bipeds!,* p. 74; December 6, 1999, review of *The Trigger,* p. 58; January 31, 2000, review of *The Light of Other Days,* p. 86.

Reader's Digest, April, 1969.

Saturday Review, July 5, 1952; April 20, 1968.

Science, August 30, 1968, pp. 874-875.

Science Fiction Review, March-April, 1979; August, 1981; February, 1983, p. 15; May, 1984; fall, 1984, p. 26; summer, 1986.

Science-Fiction Studies, July, 1979, pp. 230-231; November, 1997, pp. 441-458.

Scientific American, December, 1999, review of *Greetings, Carbon-based Bipeds!,* p. 143.

Time, July 19, 1968; November 15, 1982; January 11, 1988.

Times (London, England), November 25, 1982.

Times Higher Education Supplement, Andrew Robinson, review of *Greetings, Carbon-based Bipeds!,* p. 21.

Times Literary Supplement, July 15, 1968; January 2, 1969; December 5, 1975; June 16, 1978, p. 662; January 21, 1983; October 31, 1986; March 21, 1997; January 28, 2000, Oliver Morton, review of *Greetings, Carbon-based Bipeds!,* p. 12; March 2, 2001, Edward James, *The Collected Stories,* p. 23.

Tribune Books (Chicago, IL), January 30, 1994, section 14, p. 6.

Virginia Quarterly Review, winter, 1974.

Voice Literary Supplement, November, 1982, pp. 8-9.

Washington Post, February 16, 1982; November 16, 1982.

Washington Post Book World, December 26, 1982, p. 6; March 25, 1984, p. 6; November 25, 1990, p. 8; March 9, 1992, p. B1.

West Coast Review of Books, number 1, 1986.

Western Folklore, number 28, 1969, pp. 230-237.

Wilson Library Bulletin, March, 1990, pp. 110-111.

World Press Review, April, 1985.

ONLINE

Arthur C. Clarke Unauthorized Homepage, http://www.lsi.usp.br/~rbianchi/clarke/ (November 16, 2003).*

*   *   *

CLARKE, I. F.
    See CLARKE, Ignatius (Ian) Frederick

*   *   *

CLARKE, Ian
    See CLARKE, Ignatius (Ian) Frederick

*   *   *

CLARKE, Ignatius (Ian) Frederick 1918-
    (Ian Clarke, I. F. Clarke)

PERSONAL: Born July 10, 1918, in Wallasey, Cheshire, England; son of John Henry (a broker) and Mabel (a homemaker; maiden name, Bradshaw) Clarke; married Margaret Barton (a college lecturer), August 4, 1952; children: Julian, Christopher,

Catherine. *Education:* University of Liverpool, B.A., 1950, M.A., 1953. *Hobbies and other interests:* Baking bread, brewing beer, making wine, walking, painting, and traveling in the United States.

ADDRESSES: Home—Dellwood, Frog Lane, Milton-under-Wychwood, Oxfordshire OX7 6JZ, England. *Agent*—A. P. Watt, 26/28 Bedford Row, London WC 4HL, England.

CAREER: University of Liverpool, Liverpool, England, university fellow, 1950-53; Bedlington Grammar School, Northumberland, England, senior English master, 1953-56; Newcastle College of Commerce, Newcastle-upon-Tyne, Northumberland, director of communication studies, 1956-58; University of Strathclyde, Glasgow, Scotland, professor of English studies, 1958-81. Lecturer on modern English literature for British Council in Thailand and Morocco, 1978. Lecturer on utopian fiction for British Council in Morocco, 1979. *Military service:* Royal Artillery, 1940-42; became second lieutenant. British Army Intelligence, 1942-46; became captain.

MEMBER: Science Fiction Research Association.

AWARDS, HONORS: Pilgrim Award from Science Fiction Research Association of America, 1974, for achievements as bibliographer and historian of future war motif, and 2000, for scholarship; named to the order of Tiroler Adler, 1983, for service to Austrian citizens since 1946.

WRITINGS:

UNDER NAME I. F. CLARKE, EXCEPT AS NOTED

(Compiler, as Ignatius Frederick Clarke) *The Tale of the Future: From the Beginning to the Present Day,* Library Association (London, England), 1961, 2nd enlarged edition (as Ian Clarke), 1972, 3rd enlarged edition, 1978.

Voices Prophesying War, 1763-1984, Oxford University Press (London, England), 1966, revised edition published as *Voices Prophesying War: Future Wars, 1763-3749,* 1992.

The Battle of Dorking Controversy: A Collection of Pamphlets, Cornmarket Reprints (London, England), 1972.

(Editor, with John Butt) *The Victorians and Social Protest: A Symposium,* Archon Books (Hamden, CT), 1973.

The Pattern of Expectation, 1644-2001, Basic Books (New York, NY), 1979.

(Editor) *The Tale of the Next Great War, 1871-1914: Fiction of Future Warfare and of Battles Still-to-Come,* Syracuse University Press (Syracuse, NY), 1995.

(Editor) *The Great War with Germany, 1890-1914: Fictions and Fantasies of the War-to-Come,* Liverpool University Press (Liverpool, England), 1997.

(Editor) *British Future Fiction,* eight volumes, Pickering & Chatto (Brookfield, VT), 2001.

(Translator, with wife, Margaret Clarke) Jean-Baptiste-Francois-Xavier, Cousin de Grainville, *The Last Man,* Wesleyan University Press (Middletown, CT), 2002.

Editor of and contributor to a series of articles on prophecy and prediction, 1968—. Editor of science-fiction reprint program, Cornmarket Press, 1970-73.

SIDELIGHTS: Ignatius Frederick Clarke, a highly regarded historian of ideas, attracted considerable attention with two books published in the 1960s. *The Tale of the Future: From the Beginning to the Present Day* and *Voices Prophesying War, 1763-1984* are both extensive surveys of writings on the future in the past three centuries. In *Voices Prophesying War, 1763-1984,* Clarke traces the significant changes in man's attitude toward war—which ranges from fatalism to a more recent tendency to view war as an abstraction. For example, the author notices that current war fantasies seem to take place in the distant future and in remote corners of the universe. Commenting on Clarke's analyses of the art of prophesying war, Arthur Marwick of the *New Statesman* praised the historian's scholarship, adding that the author's assiduous research yielded "a sparkling study, consistently informed by a clear sense of historical perspective."

Clarke revised *Voices Prophesying War* in 1992, adding a far-futuristic slant in the process. In what is now called *Voices Prophesying War: Future Wars, 1763-3749,* the author includes what Eliot Cohen of *Foreign Affairs* called "a review of the 'Third World War' genre of books that did so well in the 1980s." In the author's reading, Cohen added, "novelists made no greater mistakes than war offices."

As in their assessments of Clarke's earlier books, critics were impressed by the erudition behind his 1979 work, *The Pattern of Expectation, 1644-2001.* According to Bernard Bergonzi of the *Times Literary Supplement,* the author "deals very adroitly with a lot of varied material" in his "immensely readable and well-documented" book. In particular, Thomas Pyne of the *Los Angeles Times Book Review* singled out the author's discussion of the earliest futurologists as the book's "most interesting chapter." Pyne also underscored the crucial link, brought forth by Clarke, between man's thinking about the future and his awareness of the present as a moment in the historical continuum. Clarke himself points out that this awareness resulted in a "vast new literature of expectation" that has been the dominant form of writing about the future since the earliest stages of industrialization.

According to Clarke, man's "idea of the future"—in other words, society's "collective vision" of its future—manifests itself in every aspect of social life. And Clarke's survey of these manifestations, as Henry McDonald of the *Washington Post Book World* observed, is "impressive, sustained by both imagination and scholarship." But Clarke is also interested in tracing the source of man's fascination with the future. "The tale of the future," which he defines as "the dreamtime of industrial society," follows "the mythic roots within human experience to find sources of supreme power, means of transcending all limitations, opportunities for achieving absolute perfection." And like the alphabet, Clarke asserts, it is "a necessary social invention."

In two related volumes from the 1990s, Clarke continued his exploration of future-war narratives. *The Tale of the Next Great War, 1871-1914: Fiction of Future Warfare and of Battles Still-to-Come* and *The Great War with Germany, 1890-1914: Fictions and Fantasies of the War-to-Come* are anthologies of literary works by authors including Jack London, Arthur Conan Doyle, and George Tomkyns Chesney, the latter of whom produced an "1871 literary bombshell," in the words of *Utopian Studies* contributor Paul Alkon. Chesney's short story "The Battle of Dorking," said Clarke in *The Tale of the Next Great War,* "about a rapid German conquest of the United Kingdom was the first tale of the future to attract immediate attention throughout the world." Ian Ousby of the *Times Literary Supplement* commented that "The Battle of Dorking" "set the pattern [for future-war narratives]

by its account of a war that was quick, decisive and cataclysmic: naval engagements followed by a brutally efficient invasion of English soil." "Like Chesney's fable," wrote Alkon, "several of the other stories" in Clarke's anthology "were designed mainly to warn against inadequate military or political measures for defense in a world of dangerously aggressive competing nationalisms."

Clarke "does Anglophone readers a special favor," said Alkon, by including a rare sampling of the futuristic fiction of Albert Robida. "Scattered throughout the anthology, moreover, is a kind of mini-anthology of pictures taken from contemporary illustrations," the critic added, citing illustrations of Martian warriors from a 1906 edition of H. G. Wells's novel *The War of the Worlds.* "We may use this to see how scenes from the stories were imagined at the time of publication."

The eight-volume *British Future Fiction,* published in 2001, includes futuristic fiction both well-known and obscure. In the latter category are the stories "The Reign of George VI, 1900-1923," written by an anonymous author in 1763, and "Under the Red Ensign," a 1912 work that Clarke categorized in the "disasters to come" category. "Many of these pieces . . . are still entertaining reading" centuries after their publication, noted *Utopian Studies* reviewer James Gunn. "Others are useful more as milestones along the road to the story of anticipation, but none are dull. My long-held conviction is that if you wish to know where you are going, it is a good idea to know where you have been. Clarke's collection of hard-to-find stories provides that opportunity."

Clarke once told *CA:* "I came to futures research following a juvenile interest in science fiction and, in particular, because any serving soldier in 1945 had cause to think long and furiously about the future. A major stimulus to my research was the discovery that so little had been written (and most of it partial and ill-informed) about the ways in which the idea of future has developed, first, as a literary mode, and second, as a means of prediction in more recent years.

"The universal interest in the future—science fiction, think tanks, journals, and institutes of futurology—is a general recognition of the rate and the scale of change. In the first century of the now-continuing industrial revolution the steamship and the railroad represented so marvelous a conquest of time and space that the future, perfectly presented in the prophecies of Jules Verne, was the sacramental manifestation of an ideal materialism. Louis Pasteur, Thomas Edison, and the Wright brothers were the high priests of the new religion of progress. For a few brief generations it seemed as if mankind, thanks to technology, would go forward to ever better things.

"That dream was erased in the First World War, when the industrialization of warfare showed the catastrophic difference between expectations and events. The discovery that technological progress does not necessarily equal moral and social progress has been at the core of most radical thinking about the future since 1918 and above all since 1945. The first major statements came from artists, such as authors Karel Capek and Aldous Huxley. Thereafter, there came the sociologists and political scientists who began the first concerted efforts to estimate the probable direction of future developments.

"The gap between today and tomorrow has shortened and we are now experiencing by the decade what our great-grandfathers lived through by the generation. As a consequence, anxieties about the rate and the scale of change have penetrated to the highest levels. As communication technologies make the nations into something like an embryonic world community, the moral and social issues involved in everything from nuclear weapons to very rapid technological development are being raised more and more."

BIOGRAPHICAL AND CRITICAL SOURCES:

PERIODICALS

Air Power History, spring, 1993, review of *Voices Prophesying War: Future Wars, 1763-3749,* p. 60.

Choice, May, 1996, B. Adler, review of *The Tale of the Next Great War, 1871-1914: Fiction of Future Warfare and of Battles Still-to-Come,* p. 1470.

Economist, October 22, 1966.

English Literature in Transition, number 3, 1996, review of *The Tale of the Next Great War, 1871-1914,* p. 406.

Essays in Criticism, July, 1994, David Seed, review of *Voices Prophesying War,* p. 258.

Extrapolation, winter, 1999, pp. 277-283.

Foreign Affairs, September-October, 1993, Eliot Cohen, review of *Voices Prophesying War,* p. 156.

Listener, September 15, 1966.

Los Angeles Times Book Review, August 28, 1979, Thomas Pyne, review of *The Pattern of Expectation, 1644-2001.*

New Statesman, May 26, 1967, Arthur Marwick, review of *Voices Prophesying War,*

Reference & Research Book News, February, 1999, review of *The Great War with Germany, 1890-1914: Fictions and Fantasies of the War-to-Come,* p. 159.

Science Fiction Chronicle, April, 1993, review of *Voices Prophesying War,* p. 31.

Science-Fiction Studies, November, 1993, H. Bruce Franklin, review of *Voices Prophesying War,* p. 476; July, 1996, H. Bruce Franklin, review of *The Tale of the Next Great War, 1871-1914,* p. 287; November, 1997, Charles Gannon, review of *The Great War with Germany, 1890-1914,* p. 508.

Times Literary Supplement, December 7, 1979, Bernard Bergonzi, review of *The Pattern of Expectation, 1644-2001;* May 15, 1998, Ian Ousby, reviews of *The Great War with Germany, 1890-1914* and *The Tale of the Next Great War, 1871-1914,* p. 26.

Utopian Studies, winter, 1997, Paul Alkon, review of *The Tale of the Next Great War, 1871-1914,* p. 147; winter, 2000, Lyman Tower Sargent, review of *The Great War with Germany, 1890-1914,* p. 155; spring, 2001, James Gunn, review of *British Future Fiction,* p. 284.

Washington Post Book World, August 12, 1979, Henry McDonald, review of *The Pattern of Expectation, 1644-2001.*

Wilson Library Bulletin, June, 1993, Elizabeth Shostak, review of *Voices Prophesying War,* p. 133.*

*　　*　　*

CLIFFORD, Christine 1954-

PERSONAL: Born March 13, 1954, in St. Clair Shores, MI; daughter of Frank (a physician) and Mary C. (a homemaker) Meyer; married John Clifford (a stockbroker); children: Tim, Brooks. *Ethnicity:* "Caucasian." *Politics:* Republican. *Religion:* Methodist. *Hobbies and other interests:* Hosting the "Christine Clifford Celebrity Golf Invitational," an event to raise money for breast cancer research.

ADDRESSES: Office—c/o Cancer Club, 6533 Limerick Dr., Edina, MN 55439; fax: 952-941-1229. *E-mail*—christine@cancerclub.com.

CAREER: SPAR Marketing Services (information and merchandising services firm), Minneapolis, MN; served as senior vice president; Cancer Club (marketer of products to cancer-affected individuals), Edina, MN, president and chief executive officer. Producer and director of *One Move at a Time* (exercise videotape for cancer patients). National Speakers Association, certified speaking professional; humorist and inspirational speaker throughout the United States; guest on radio and television programs. Minnesota Oncology Hematology Foundation, member of board of directors, 2001—.

MEMBER: National Speakers Association, Association for Applied and Therapeutic Humor, National Association of Breast Cancer Organizations, Minnesota Speakers Association.

AWARDS, HONORS: Citations for best health book of 1995-96 and best first book of 1996, both National Multiple Sclerosis Society, 1997, and Midwest Independent Publishers Association award, 1997, all for *Not Now . . . I'm Having a No Hair Day;* Benjamin Franklin Award, Publishers Marketing Association, 1998, for *Our Family Has Cancer, Too!;* Council of Excellence Award, American Cancer Society, 2000; Order of Delta Gamma Rose, 2002.

WRITINGS:

Not Now . . . I'm Having a No Hair Day, illustrated by Jack Lindstrom, University of Minnesota Press (Minneapolis, MN), 1996.
Our Family Has Cancer, Too! (juvenile), illustrated by Jack Lindstrom, University of Minnesota Press (Minneapolis, MN), 1997.
Inspiring Breakthrough Secrets to Live Your Dreams, Aviva Publishing (Lake Placid, NY), 2001.
Cancer Has Its Privileges: Stories of Hope and Laughter, Perigee (New York, NY), 2002.

Also author, with Anna Marie Ronning, of *Ask a Woman* (audiocassette) and *Laughter: A New Twist to the Old Illness of Cancer!* (one-hour audiocassette lecture). Contributor to books, including *Chicken Soup for the Survivor's Soul; Chicken Soup for the Golfer's Soul;* and *Chicken Soup for the Writer's Soul.* Publisher and author of *Cancer Club Newsletter.*

SIDELIGHTS: When Christine Clifford was diagnosed with breast cancer at age forty in 1994, it came as a shock but not a complete surprise: her own mother had died of the same disease at age forty-two. Clifford was determined not to repeat her mother's experience, for her mother, as she told *Reporter Interactive* interviewer Cynthia B. Astle, "just gave up—stopped caring for her personal hygiene, got into bed and never got out." A dynamic individual, Clifford was at that time a highly successful salesperson for a Minneapolis information and merchandising firm, with clients that included K-Mart, Procter & Gamble, Toys 'R' Us, and other high-profile corporations. The cancer experience changed her life, but not in a tragic way. After having surgery on December 31, 1994, and going through ten months of chemotherapy, Clifford became the founding president of a company, the Cancer Club, devoted to helping those affected by cancer—both patients and their loved ones—find healing humor in their situation. The firm markets books and tapes by Clifford, a quarterly newspaper with contributions from other cancer patients around the country, and such products as a coffee mug, "attitude" pins, "guardian angel" pins, and a T-shirt. The company has been successful enough to have donated 20,000 dollars to cancer-related charities in 1996 and 1997. As a public speaker, Clifford travels busily around the country giving inspirational, humorous talks.

The humorous approach to cancer came to Clifford in stages and does not exclude grief; she has been capable of crying at any point in the experience, she assured Joyce Terveen in the *Detroit News.* However, she first laughed eight days after her diagnosis, and it was a memorable experience for her. As time went on, following her surgery, she was disappointed at how uncomfortable many of her visitors seemed, how unwilling to say anything humorous. One night only six weeks after her surgery, she had what she calls a "Twilight Zone" experience: waking in the middle of the night, she drew approximately fifty humorous cartoons illustrating the comical side of her experience thus far. She sent cartoons to some of the people who had helped her during the ordeal of chemotherapy, and the response was favorable: her visitors seemed more comfortable after receiving the cartoons. Researching the market for books on cancer-related humor, she found that there was an opening for such a concept. She hired a professional illustrator, Jack Lindstrom, to redraw her cartoons, and wrote her first book, *Not Now. . . I'm Having a No Hair Day,* around them.

The book received a good reception, garnering awards and award nominations within the health-book and motivational fields, and was followed by *Our Family Has Cancer, Too!* This 1997 children's book, which includes eighteen illustrations by Lindstrom, is written by Clifford but narrated in the voice of her elder son, Tim, who tells the reader what it was like to help their mother get through her battle with cancer. The book contains a "Questions to Ask" section that encourages the young reader to write down questions for doctors, teachers, and others; it also includes a glossary of cancer-related terms that are likely to be new to children in cancer-affected families; and it is punctuated by "Stop and Discuss" points that urge parents and children to talk about what they have just read. The overall approach, as with all Clifford's Cancer Club creations, is life-affirming and humor-affirming.

While she admits that having cancer is a very serious trial, Clifford notes that the process of treatment and recovery is at least six months long: "If you don't find some humor during that time, you're going to dry up," she told Terveen. Meanwhile, Clifford's own battle with cancer seemed to be on its way to victory as of late 2002, and she continues gathering the support, not only of a loving family, but of an increasingly large audience of readers and listeners.

Clifford once told *CA:* "Don't forget to laugh."

BIOGRAPHICAL AND CRITICAL SOURCES:

PERIODICALS

American Association for Therapeutic Humor, May, 1997.
American Health for Women, October, 1997.
Better Homes and Gardens, April, 1997.
Breast Cancer Survivor, September, 1997.
Chicago Tribune & Nursing News, January 24, 1996.
Coping, January, 1997; January, 1998.
Detroit News, July 11, 1996; July 30, 1996; November 21, 1996.

Golf Digest, November, 1998.
Healthline, June, 1999.
Journal for Women's Health Research, July, 1998.
Journal of Nursing Jocularity, November, 1997.
Kids Konnected, January, 1998.
Library Journal, October, 1997; January, 1998.
Minneapolis Star & Tribune, December 22, 1995.
Minnesota Monthly, June, 1996.
Minnesota Speaks, March, 1998.
Minnesota Women's Press, October, 1996.
Networking, October, 2002.
Northern Spirit, October, 1998.
Northwest Racquet, Swim & Health, September, 1996.
Professional Speaker, November, 1997; January, 1998.
Publishers Weekly, June 17, 1996.
St. Paul Pioneer Press, July 21, 1996; December 9, 1997.
Sharing Ideas, December, 1997; April, 1998; April, 1999; July, 1999; August, 2000.
Stressfree Living, April, 1999; May, 2002.
Today's Christian Woman, September, 1999.
United Methodist Reporter, October 4, 1996.
Wellness Network, June, 1998.

ONLINE

Cancer Club Online, http://www.cancerclub.com/ (February 28, 2004).
Christine Clifford Enterprises Online, http://www. christineclifford.com/ (February 28, 2004).
Reporter Interactive, http://www.umr.org/ (October 3, 1996), interview by Cynthia B. Astle.

*   *   *

COBBS, Price M(ashaw) 1928-

PERSONAL: Born November 2, 1928, in Los Angeles, CA; son of Peter Price (a physician) and Rosa (Mashaw) Cobbs; married Evadne Priester (a teacher), May 30, 1957 (died, October, 1973); married Frederica Maxwell, May 26, 1985; children: Price Priester, Marion Renata. *Education:* Attended University of California—Los Angeles, 1950-52; University of California—Berkeley, B.A., 1954; Meharry Medical College, M.D., 1958.

ADDRESSES: Office—Pacific Management Systems, 3528 Sacramento St., San Francisco, CA 94118-1847.

CAREER: San Francisco General Hospital, San Francisco, CA, intern, 1958-59; psychiatric resident at Mendocino State Hospital, 1959-61, and Langley Porter Neuropsychiatric Institute, 1961-62; psychiatrist in private practice, 1962—; University of California, San Francisco, assistant clinical professor of psychiatry, 1963—; Pacific Training Associates, San Francisco, codirector, beginning 1967; Pacific Management Systems, San Francisco, founding president and chief executive officer, 1976—; chief executive officer, Cobbs Inc. Chair of Renaissance Books, Inc.; member of board of directors, Foundation for National Progress, and Lucille Packard Foundation for Children's Health; founding member, Diversity Collegium. Consultant to Fortune 500 companies, federal agencies, and community groups. *Military service:* U.S. Army, 1951-53; became corporal.

MEMBER: American Psychiatric Association (life fellow), National Medical Association, American Medical Association, National Urban League (charter member), NAACP (life member), National Academy of Sciences (member of Institute of Medicine), Black Behavioral Scientists, University of California Black Caucus.

AWARDS, HONORS: Named outstanding psychiatrist, *Black Enterprise* magazine, 1988; Pathfinder Award, Association for Humanistic Psychology, 1993.

WRITINGS:

(With William H. Grier) *Black Rage,* Basic Books (New York, NY), 1968.
(With William H. Grier) *The Jesus Bag,* McGraw-Hill (New York, NY), 1971.
(With Judith L. Turnock) *Cracking the Corporate Code: The Revealing Success Stories of 32 African-American Executives,* American Management Association (New York, NY), 2003.

Also wrote text for sound recording *The Scope of Human Potential.* Member of advisory board, *Black Scholar. Black Rage* has been translated into French.

SIDELIGHTS: Price M. Cobbs is a well-known psychiatrist who has focused most of his attention on how racism and other prejudices adversely affect the personal and professional lives of many African Americans. After completing his medical degree, internship, and residency, Cobbs went into private practice in 1962. During these early years, he treated many African-American patients who, he observed, were very angry about American society; interestingly, this anger was present regardless of the patient's social or economic status. This discovery led him to write the groundbreaking book *Black Rage,* with fellow psychiatrist William H. Grier. Here, Cobbs and Grier help explain this rage and to suggest appropriate psychiatric treatment for those who are suffering from its effects. Published in 1968, a time when social unrest from racial tensions was particularly acute in the United States, *Black Rage* became a popular book that is still considered to be a classic in the field. In a *New York Times* review by Christopher Lehmann-Haupt published at the time of its release, the critic called *Black Rage* "among the most important books on the Negro to appear in the last decade."

Three years later, Cobbs and Grier followed their debut with *The Jesus Bag,* which explores the role that religion has played in the psychological welfare of African Americans from the time of slavery to the early 1970s. Religion, the authors explained, actually helped contain black rage for decades by offering comfort to those oppressed by racism. With the Civil Rights movement of the 1960s, however, this rage could be contained no longer, even by a strong faith, and riots and social upheaval were the result. As the authors put it in their book, religion "lost its hold on some of us and the rage-binding conscience was no longer effective." They added, "In a fury we burst into the streets. . . . We looked into ourselves, and, even more, looked deep into white America. Our flaws, which we were taught to hide in shame, were in fact the flaws of this nations. . . . Where once we saw ourselves as deformed and debased, we now see how much more deformed and debased is the white bigotry which has so hurt us."

Despite the hard-earned gains that the Civil Rights movement won for African Americans, many barriers to social equality yet remained—despite such continuing initiatives as affirmative action. An important one has been the barrier to success in the business world, and for this reason Cobbs founded and became president of Pacific Management Systems, a consulting firm that helps businesses come to terms with their own corporate-culture prejudices and to learn how to treat employees as equals regardless of race, gender, or other differences. His work as a consultant for various Fortune 500 companies led him to write 2003's *Cracking the Corporate Code: The Revealing Success Stories of 32 African-American Executives* with Judith L. Turnock. In an interview published on the American Management Association's Web site, Cobbs explained that although blacks were indeed being hired at large corporations, "it was apparent to me that the growing number of blacks in corporate America represented a highly misunderstood and underserved group. They had broken a heretofore impenetrable barrier and gotten in the door, but many hurdles remained."

Cracking the Corporate Code is about the unspoken rules inside a corporate culture that lead to such disservices as management passing up an employee for promotion because he is black or she is a woman. Here, Cobbs and Turnock profile thirty-two minority and women executives who managed to successfully break down this barrier and, although they are not household names, become leaders in their fields. Instead of going into in-depth profiles of each individual, the authors organize their book into subject areas such as "Understanding Power," "Managing Your Demons," and "Fitting In." Using various executives as examples of how to survive in the business world, the book aims to show readers how to not allow themselves to be defeated by corporate barriers, how to know which battles to fight and which to let slide, and how to become part of the team without sacrificing one's sense of self, beliefs, or heritage. "These stories are an inspiration for anyone facing self-doubt and isolation in the competitive world of corporate America," said David Siegfried in his *Booklist* review of *Cracking the Corporate Code*. And a *Publishers Weekly* contributor similarly wrote that "this is a smart, memorable collection of business wisdom that should provide inspirational guidance to young African Americans."

Today, Cobbs is still working to help African Americans and corporate management discard the misunderstandings that have separated them for so long. In the meantime, as he said in his interview, the best advice he could give for minorities in the business world was to "be aware of your personal and cultural history. It is of utmost importance to be aware of your core values. Learn the core values of your organization and figure out where there are gaps between your core values and those of the organization. Learn the difference between 'buying in' and 'selling out.'"

BIOGRAPHICAL AND CRITICAL SOURCES:

PERIODICALS

Black Enterprise, October, 1988, "Prescribing Strong Medicine for the Mind: Dr. Price M. Cobbs," p. 86.
Booklist, May 15, 2003, David Siegfried, review of *Cracking the Corporate Code: The Revealing Success Stories of 32 African-American Executives,* p. 1623.
Book World, September 8, 1968.
Christian Science Monitor, November 14, 1968.
HR Magazine, October, 2003, review of *Cracking the Corporate Code,* p. 141.
Library Journal, April 1, 2003, Carol J. Elsen, review of *Cracking the Corporate Code,* p. 111.
Nation, January 6, 1969.
New Republic, August 17, 1968.
New Yorker, September 28, 1968.
New York Times, August 7, 1968, Christopher Lehmann-Haupt, review of *Black Rage.*
New York Times Book Review, August 17, 1968, September 22, 1968.
Publishers Weekly, March 31, 2003, review of *Cracking the Corporate Code,* p. 52.
Time, July 26, 1968.
Washington Post, August 6, 1968.

ONLINE

American Management Association Web site, http://www.amanet.org/ (October 5, 2003), "An Interview with Price M. Cobbs."
Greater Diversity, http://www.greaterdiversity.com/ (February 12, 2004), review of *Cracking the Corporate Code.**

*   *   *

COFER, Judith Ortiz 1952-

PERSONAL: Born February 24, 1952, in Hormigueros, Puerto Rico; immigrated to United States, 1956; daughter of Jesus Lugo (in U.S. Navy) and Fanny (Morot) Ortiz; married Charles John Cofer (in business), November 13, 1971; children: Tanya. *Education:* Augusta College, B.A., 1974; Florida Atlantic University, M.A., 1977; attended Oxford University, 1977.

Judith Ortiz Cofer

ADDRESSES: Home—P.O. Box 938, Louisville, GA 30434. *Office*—Department of English and Creative Writing, University of Georgia, Athens, GA 30602. *Agent*—Berenice Hoffman Literary Agency, 215 West 75th St., New York, NY 10023. *E-mail*—jcofer@ parallel.park.uga.edu.

CAREER: Bilingual teacher at public schools in Palm Beach County, FL, 1974-75; Broward Community College, Fort Lauderdale, FL, adjunct instructor in English, 1978-80, instructor in Spanish, 1979; University of Miami, Coral Gables, FL, lecturer in English, 1980-84; University of Georgia, Athens, instructor in English, 1984-87, Georgia Center for Continuing Education, instructor in English, 1987-88; Macon College, Macon, GA, instructor in English, 1988-89; Mercer University College, Forsyth, GA, special programs coordinator, 1990; University of Georgia, Athens, associate professor of English and creative writing, 1992-99, Franklin Professor of English and creative writing, 1999—. Adjunct instructor at Palm Beach Junior College, 1978-80. Visiting professor at numerous colleges and universities, including University of Michigan, Arizona University, and University of Minnesota, Duluth. Conducts poetry workshops and gives poetry readings. Member of regular staff of International Conference on the Fantastic in Literature, 1979-82; member of literature panel of Fine Arts Council of Florida, 1982; member of administrative staff of Bread Loaf Writers' Conference, 1983 and 1984.

MEMBER: Poetry Society of America, Poets and Writers, Associated Writing Programs.

AWARDS, HONORS: Scholar of English-Speaking Union at Oxford University, 1977; fellow of Fine Arts Council of Florida, 1980; Bread Loaf Writers' Conference, scholar, 1981, John Atherton Scholar in Poetry, 1982; grant from Witter Bynner Foundation for Poetry, 1988, for *Letters from a Caribbean Island;* National Endowment for the Arts fellowship in poetry, 1989; Pulitzer Prize nomination, 1989, for *The Line of the Sun;* New York Public Library Outstanding Books of the Year, for *The Line of the Sun* and *Silent Dancing;* PEN/Martha Albrand Special Citation for *Silent Dancing;* Pushcart Prize for nonfiction, 1990; O. Henry Prize for short story, 1994; Anisfield Wolf Award in Race Relations, 1994, for *The Latin Deli;* America's Award for Children's and Young Adult Literature honorable mention, 1995, and Best Books of the Year citation, American Library Association (ALA), 1996, both for *An Island Like You: Stories of the Barrio;* Pura Belpre medal, ALA REFORMA, 1996; Georgia Council for the Arts fellowship.

WRITINGS:

Latin Women Pray (chapbook), Florida Arts Gazette Press, 1980.
The Native Dancer (chapbook), Pteranodon Press, 1981.
Among the Ancestors (chapbook), Louisville News Press, 1981.
Latin Women Pray (three-act play), first produced in Atlanta at Georgia State University, 1984.
Peregrina (poems), Riverstone Press (Golden, CO), 1986.
Terms of Survival (poems), Arte Público Press (Houston, TX), 1987.
(With Roberto Durán and Gustavo Pérez Firmat) *Triple Crown: Chicano, Puerto Rican and Cuban American Poetry* (trilogy; contains Cofer's poetry collection *Reaching for the Mainland*), Bilingual Press (Tempe, AZ), 1987.
The Line of the Sun (novel), University of Georgia Press (Athens, GA), 1989.
Silent Dancing: A Partial Remembrance of a Puerto Rican Childhood (personal essays), Arte Público Press (Houston, TX), 1990.
The Latin Deli: Prose and Poetry, University of Georgia Press (Athens, GA), 1993.

An Island Like You: Stories of the Barrio (young adult), Orchard Books (New York, NY), 1995.

The Year of Our Revolution: New and Selected Stories and Poems, Arte Público Press (Houston, TX), 1998.

(Editor, with Marilyn Kallet) *Sleeping with One Eye Open: Women Writers and the Art of Survival,* University of Georgia Press (Athens, GA), 1999.

Woman in Front of the Sun: On Becoming a Writer, University of Georgia Press (Athens, GA), 2000.

The Meaning of Consuelo, Farrar, Straus, & Giroux (New York, NY), 2003.

(Editor and author of introduction) *Riding Low on the Streets of Gold: Latino Literature for Young Adults,* Arte Público Press (Houston, TX), 2003.

Also author of poetry collection *Letters from a Caribbean Island.* Has contributed to many written works, including *Hispanics in the United States,* Bilingual Review/Press, 1982; *Woman of Her Word,* Arte Público, 1983; *The Heath Anthology of Modern American Literature,* Heath, 1990; *Pushcart Prize XV Anthology,* Pushcart Press, 1990; *Puerto Rican Writers at Home in the U.S.A.,* Open Hand, 1991; and *Literature: Reading, Reacting, Writing,* Holt, 1991. Has also contributed poems to magazines, including *Southern Humanities Review, Poem, Prairie Schooner, Apalachee Quarterly, Kansas Quarterly,* and *Kalliope.* Poetry editor of *Florida Arts Gazette,* 1978-81; member of editorial board of *Waves.*

SIDELIGHTS: Judith Ortiz Cofer is a highly regarded poet, essayist, and novelist who has written extensively on the experience of being a Puerto Rican in the United States. Cofer was born in Hormigueros, Puerto Rico, but raised and educated primarily in New Jersey. She grew up attempting to reconcile her parents' traditional values with her experiences stateside, eventually producing work that "focuses on the effect on Puerto Rican Americans of living in a world split between the island culture of their homeland and the teeming tenement life of the United States," to quote Marian C. Gonsior in the *Dictionary of Hispanic Biography.*

Cofer left Puerto Rico as a young child, when her father joined the U.S. Navy and was assigned to a post in the Brooklyn Naval Yard. The family lived in Paterson, New Jersey, but undertook extensive visits back to Puerto Rico whenever the father was sent to sea. Back in New Jersey, it was Cofer who learned English

in order to help her Spanish-speaking mother run the household and make important decisions. In an interview for *MELUS,* the author spoke of reconciling the contradictions in her cultural identity: "I write in English, yet I write obsessively about my Puerto Rican experience. . . . That is how my psyche works. I am a composite of two worlds. . . . I lived with . . . conflictive expectations: the pressures from my father to become very well versed in the English language and the Anglo customs, and from my mother not to forget where we came from. That is something that I deal with in my work all the time."

Trained to be a teacher, Cofer came to creative writing as a graduate student, when she began to craft poems in English about Latina women and their concerns. Her work began to appear in literary periodicals as well as chapbooks and collections by small presses. "I think poetry has made me more disciplined," Cofer observed in *MELUS.* "It taught me how to write, because to write a poem takes so much skill. . . . Poetry contains the essence of language. Every word weighs a ton. . . . Poetry taught me about economizing in language and about the power of language. So I will never stop writing poetry."

Cofer once told *CA:* "The 'infinite variety' and power of language interest me. I never cease to experiment with it. As a native Puerto Rican, my first language was Spanish. It was a challenge, not only to learn English, but to master it enough to teach it and—the ultimate goal—to write poetry in it.

"My family is one of the main topics of my poetry; the ones left behind on the island of Puerto Rico, and the ones who came to the United States. In tracing their lives, I discover more about mine. The place of birth itself becomes a metaphor for the things we all must leave behind; the assimilation of a new culture is the coming into maturity by accepting the terms necessary for survival. My poetry is a study of this process of change, assimilation, and transformation."

Branching out from poetry, Cofer published a well-received novel, *The Line of the Sun,* in 1989, and an essay collection, *Silent Dancing,* in 1990. *The Line of the Sun* was applauded by *New York Times Book Review* contributor Roberto Marquez for the "vigorous elegance" of its language. Marquez called Cofer "a prose writer of evocatively lyrical authority, a novelist of historical compass and sensitivity." The first half of *The Line of the Sun* depicts the poor village of Salud, Puerto Rico, and introduces the characters Rafael Vivente and his wild brother-in-law, Guzman. *Los Angeles Times Book Review* contributor Sonja Bolle noted that the author's eye for detail "brings alive the stifling and magical world of village life." The second part of the novel follows Rafael to Paterson, New Jersey, where his daughter Marisol, the story's narrator, grows up. Marisol's father encourages her to become wholly American, but her mother advises her to adopt the customs and values of Puerto Rico. Marisol learns about her heritage mainly through the stories told by her family, which often focus on her Uncle Guzman, the "demon child"; his arrival at her New Jersey home helps Marisol to balance the American and Puerto Rican aspects of her identity. Though Marquez criticized parts of the plot as contrived, he proclaimed Cofer as "a writer of authentic gifts, with a genuine and important story to tell." *The Line of the Sun* was nominated for a Pulitzer Prize in 1989.

The title of *Silent Dancing* is derived from a home movie of Cofer's parents in their youth. The scene is a New Year's Eve party, and the revelers form a conga line in which each gets a moment of personal attention from the camera. The author uses the film clip as a launching place for a discussion of how her parents' generation—and hers—has responded to the challenge of living between cultures, not wholly comfortable in either.

This theme has been extended into Cofer's volume for young adults, *An Island Like You: Stories of the Barrio.* Set in Paterson, New Jersey, the collection consists of stories about young expatriate Puerto Ricans who live in a tenement building. *Horn Book* contributor Nancy Vasilakis deemed the book "a milestone in multicultural publishing for children," noting: "The Caribbean flavor of the tales gives them their color and freshness, but the narratives have universal resonance in the vitality, the brashness, the self-centered hopefulness, and the angst expressed by the teens as they tell of friendships formed, romances failed, and worries over work, family, and school." In a different *Horn Book* review, Rudine Sims Bishop wrote of *An Island Like You:* "There is humor, and poignancy as well. The voices in these stories ring true, as do the stories themselves. I hope Cofer continues to write for young people." A *Publishers Weekly* reviewer concluded: "This fine collection may draw special attention for its

depictions of an ethnic group underserved by YA writers, but Cofer's strong writing warrants a close look no matter what the topic."

Cofer continued her description of life in the barrio in her 1998 book, *The Year of the Revolution: New and Selected Stories and Poems.* Most of the stories in this collection are told from the perspective of Mary Ellen (Maria Elentia), as she grows up in the barrio during the 1960s. A *Publishers Weekly* reviewer noted that "Cofer further heightens her descriptions of barrio life with a pervasive current of sensuality and rebellion." As Mary Ellen works her way through a mixture of Hispanic and American lifestyles, the reviewer continued, "Readers will likely relate to Mary Ellen's struggle for independence, her idealism and her need for answers."

In *Woman in Front of the Sun: On Becoming a Writer,* Cofer recounts how she became a writer. The mixture of Puerto Rican and American cultures that she grew up with and her love of language contribute to her inspiration to write. "Cofer writes with conviction and power, encouraging all who aspire to writing or creative endeavor to pursue their dream with energy and dedication," wrote Nancy Ives in *Library Journal.*

Sleeping with One Eye Open: Women Writers and the Art of Survival, edited with Marilyn Kallet, is a collection of essays about women writers and writing. The book discusses the many obstacles women writers face, including finding the time to write without interference, searching for inspiration, and the influence of one's world on one's writing. "Quite simply, it suggests that we all need to take time for ourselves," concluded Heather Lee Schroeder on *The Capital Times* Web site.

Cofer's second novel, *The Meaning of Consuelo,* released in 2003, is the story of Consuelo, a girl who lives in the suburbs of San Juan in the 1950s. Consuelo's life is anything but normal—her parents' marriage is falling apart, her sister is developing schizophrenia, and her favorite cousin has moved away. A *Publishers Weekly* reviewer wrote that while these "deeper elements" of the plot "lack originality and are plagued by an overabundance of foreshadowing," the novel "is richly descriptive of the shifting mores of Puerto Rican culture and the historical particularities of the era (especially the growing American presence on the Caribbean island)."

Cofer successfully combines her experiences growing up within a mixture of American and Puerto Rican cultures with her love of language to create essays, poetry, plays, and novels with universal themes. Carmen Faymonville observed in an essay for *MELUS* that Cofer "discovers a complex way to make sense of migrant identity by not exclusively rooting the 'self' in any one home or country." Instead, Cofer combines these two distinct identities and creates powerful, poignant stories about them. A writer for *Contemporary Southern Writers* noted, "Her blurring of traditional genres helps to explain both the realistic detail in her fiction and the interwoven plots and finely developed characters in her essays."

BIOGRAPHICAL AND CRITICAL SOURCES:

BOOKS

American Women Writers, Volume 5, Continuum Publishing (New York, NY), 1994.
Authors and Artists for Young Adults, Volume 30, Gale (Detroit, MI), 1999.
Cofer, Judith Ortiz, *Silent Dancing: A Partial Remembrance of a Puerto Rican Childhood,* Arte Público Press (Houston, TX), 1990.
Contemporary Hispanic Biography, Volume 3, Gale (Detroit, MI), 2003.
Contemporary Southern Writers, St. James Press (Detroit, MI), 1999.
Dictionary of Hispanic Biography, Gale (Detroit, MI), 1996, pp. 235-236.
Iftekharuddin, Farhat, Mary Rohrberger, and Maurice Lee, editors, *Speaking of the Short Story: Interview with Contemporary Writers,* University Press of Mississippi (Jackson, MS), 1997.
Notable Hispanic American Women, Book 2, Gale (Detroit, MI), 1998.
Oxford Companion to Women's Writing in the United States, Oxford University Press (Oxford, England), 1995.
St. James Guide to Young Adult Writers, 2nd edition, St. James Press (Detroit, MI), 1999.

PERIODICALS

Acraa, Volume 18, 1993, Genevieve Fabre, "Liminality, In-Betweeness and Indeterminacy: Notes toward an Anthropological Reading of Judith Ortiz Cofer's *The Line of the Sun.*"

Americas Review, winter, 1991, Juan Bruce-Novoa, "Judith Ortiz Cofer's Rituals of Movement"; fall-winter, 1994, Rafael Ocasio, "An Interview with Judith Ortiz Cofer," pp. 84-90.
Booklist, November 15, 1993, Whitney Scott, review of *The Latin Deli: Prose and Poetry,* p. 609; February 15, 1995, Hazel Rochman, review of *An Island Like You: Stories of the Barrio,* p. 1082; July 19, 1998, Debbie Carton, review of *The Year of Our Revolution: New and Selected Stories and Poems,* p. 1870; May 15, 1999, review of *Bailando en silencio (Silent Dancing),* p. 1685.
Book Report, March, 1999, review of *The Year of Our Revolution,* p. 79.
Bulletin of the Center for Children's Books, April, 1995, p. 267.
Callaloo, summer, 1994, Rafael Ocasio, "The Infinite Variety of the Puerto Rican Reality: An Interview with Judith Ortiz Cofer."
Children's Literature Association Quarterly, spring, 1993, Lucille H. Gregory, "The Puerto Rican 'Rainbow': Distortions vs. Complexities."
Georgia Review, spring-summer, 1990, pp. 51-59.
Horn Book, July-August, 1995, pp. 464-465; September-October, 1995, Rudine Sims Bishop, "Books from Parallel Cultures: Growing Up Is Hard to Do," review of *An Island Like You,* pp. 581-583.
Kirkus Reviews, October 1, 1993, review of *The Latin Deli;* June 15, 1998, p. 892.
Kliatt, September, 1991, p. 5; September, 1996, p. 3; March, 2001, review of *Woman in Front of the Sun: On Becoming a Writer,* p. 28.
Library Journal, May 15, 1989, Starr E. Smith, review of *The Line of the Sun,* p. 88; July 1990, Mary Margaret Benson, review of *Silent Dancing,* pp. 96-97; November 1, 1993, p. 93; February 15, 1996, review of *Reaching for the Mainland,* p. 154; July, 1998, p. 76; September 1, 2000, Nancy R. Ives, review of *Woman in Front of the Sun,* p. 206.
Los Angeles Times Book Review, August 6, 1989, Sonja Bolle, review of *The Line of the Sun,* p. 6.
MELUS, fall, 1993, pp. 83-97; fall, 1997, Kenneth Wishnia, review of *The Latin Deli,* pp. 206-208; summer, 2001, Carmen Faymonville, "New Transnational Identities in Judith Ortiz Cofer's Autobiographical Fiction," p. 129.
New York Times Book Review, September 24, 1989, Roberto Marquez, "Island Heritage," pp. 46-47.
Prairie Schooner, winter, 1994, Marilyn Kallet, "The Art of Not Forgetting: An Interview with Judith Ortiz Cofer."

Publishers Weekly, April 28, 1989, review of *The Line of the Sun,* p. 61; June 8, 1990, review of *Silent Dancing,* p. 609; November 8, 1993, review of *The Latin Deli,* p. 60; April 10, 1995, p. 60; April 17, 1995, review of *An Island Like You,* p. 61; December 2, 1996, p. 62; July 27, 1998, review of *The Year of the Revolution,* p. 78; August 11, 2003, review of *The Meaning of Consuelo,* p. 252.

School Library Journal, July, 1995, Lauren Mayer, review of *An Island Like You,* pp. 92-93.

Social Politics, summer, 1996, Suzanne Oboler, "Narratives of National (Be)longing: Citizenship, Race, and the Creation of Latinas—Ethnicities in Exile in the United States."

Voice of Youth Advocates, August, 1995, p. 155; June, 1999, review of *The Year of Our Revolution,* p. 112.

Wilson Library Journal, October, 1989, Ellen Donohue Warwick, review of *The Line of the Sun,* p. 123.

Women's Review of Books, December, 1990, p. 9.

ONLINE

Capital Times Online (Madison, WI), http://www. madison.com/captimes/ (November 10, 2003), Heather Lee Schroeder, "Lit.: On Recharging, Musing, Writing."

ChelseaForum, http://www.chelseaforum.com/ (November 10, 2003), "Judith Ortiz Cofer."

Online Athens, http://www.onlineathens.com/ (November 10, 2003), "Athens Author Judith Ortiz Cofer Celebrates Her Multicultural Heritage."

University of Georgia Web site, http://parallel.park. uga.edu/ (November 10, 2003), "Judith Ortiz Cofer."*

*   *   *

COLLINS, Ronald K. L. 1949-

PERSONAL: Born July 31, 1949, in Santa Monica, CA; son of LeRoy (self-employed) and Yolanda (self-employed) Collins; married Susan A. Cohen (employed in the field of public interest), May 25, 1986; children: Dylan Lee. *Ethnicity:* "Italian-Irish." *Education:* University of California, Santa Barbara, B.A., 1971; Loyola Marymount University, J.D. *Politics:* "Progressive."

ADDRESSES: Office—School of Law, Seattle University, 950 Broadway Plaza, Tacoma, WA 98402. *E-mail*—collins@seattleu.edu.

CAREER: Temple University, Philadelphia, PA, professor of law, 1988-90; George Washington University, Washington, DC, professor of law, 1992-95; Seattle University, Tacoma, WA, professor of law, 1995—. Center for Science in the Public Interest, member.

MEMBER: Simone Weil Society, Legal Aid Society of Orange County.

WRITINGS:

(Editor) *Constitutional Government in America,* Carolina Academic Press (Durham, NC), 1980.

(Editor) Grant Gilmore, *The Death of Contract,* Ohio State University Press (Columbus, OH), 1995.

(With David M. Skover) *The Death of Discourse,* Westview (Boulder, CO), 1996.

(With David M. Skover) *The Trials of Lenny Bruce: The Fall and Rise of an American Icon,* Sourcebooks (Naperville, IL), 2002.

Contributor to books, including *Simone Weil's Philosophy of Culture,* Cambridge University Press, 1993. Contributor to periodicals.

SIDELIGHTS: Ronald Collins is a First Amendment scholar at the Freedom Forum's First Amendment Center in Arlington, VA, and has written over 150 newspaper op-ed pieces as well as having coauthored two books on the topic of free speech. He, along with coauthor David M. Skover, once discussed some of the details of his writing process and shared some of his ideas about his favorite topic with *CA:* "We have been writing together for a decade. Ron lives in the East, and Dave in the West, yet each word, line, paragraph, section, and chapter of our collaborative works is written together in the same room, with Dave manning the keys and Ron pacing. We thrive on the synergy generated by our different intellects, personalities, and interests.

"We refuse, in Marshall McLuhan's words, to drive into the future with eyes fixed on the rear-view mirror of the past. Thus, we enjoy probing relatively new and unsettled terrains, however uncertain or unruly these efforts may be. In the article 'The Future of Liberal Legal Scholarship,' for example, we urged liberals in 1988 to recognize that Earl Warren is dead and to break out of the mind cells of an era long gone. Similarly, in *The Death of Discourse,* we examined America's free speech as it is, rather than as it should be, and pointed to the pomp and hypocrisy surrounding the First Amendment. We believe in testing Niccolo Machiavelli's claim that it is 'more fitting to go directly to the effectual truth of the thing than to the imagination of it.' Like Antaeus, we need to touch the earth, if only better to appreciate the poetic imagination.

"May our collaboration continue as long as Fortuna smiles. Why? Perhaps it has something to do with the pair principle—the uncanny excitement that comes with mixing two minds in order to communicate with one 'voice.' It is a wondrous experience, this art of re*creation.*

"I enjoy writing, more than most other things. For me, writing is an experiment, as life is. It is a way, both in form and substance, to test new waters, new ways, even new worlds. Part of this experiment is the attempt to make writing mean different things as the reader senses different patterns in the writer's quilt. Hence, style is nearly as important as substance. In the best of writing, the two are blended into one. That is why I have always enjoyed reading Plato's dialogues, Weil's notebooks, Wittgenstein's tracts, McLuhan's anti-books, and yes, Nietzsche's aphorisms, among others. . . . Free speech! Free writing! Free thought! Three maxims in search of a mind. . . . Over the years I have written with several souls, David M. Skover being the best."

Collins's first collaboration, *The Death of Discourse,* "details the dilemma, conundrum, or paradox, between the 'traditional' concept and contemporary applications of the First Amendment," wrote *Journal of Communication* reviewer David R. Allen. In this work, Collins follows the historical development of discourse, beginning with the Greek civilization, in order to create an acceptable and understandable definition of what free speech really is. The result of this is one of the book's main arguments, according to Allen, which is that there is a need in contemporary times for new definitions and a new view of the First Amendment "that will allow us to stem the flood of the new

tyrannical free speech," which has been created by commercial interests. As an example, Allen pointed out that the section of the book called "Commerce and Communication," demonstrates that advertisers, especially via television commercials, use the right of free speech to lure viewers to seek self-gratification rather than to use their minds and make logical decisions about what they need. The question then remains, does the First Amendment protect individual citizens' reason by limiting or defining codes for the kinds of ads that can be shown on television or does it protect the rights of mass advertisers? Allen concluded that despite the fact that readers might have to work hard to make their way through this book, the material and concepts contained within it proved to be "intellectually stimulating."

A slightly more accessible book is Collins's collaboration, again with Skover, about the comedian Lenny Bruce. *The Trials of Lenny Bruce: The Fall and Rise of an American Icon* recounts Bruce's own 1950s struggles with freedom of speech, which included five years' worth of court cases that diminished and then finally extinguished his career as a stand-up comedian. Bruce's comedy routine almost always included very frank comments about sex, race, religion, government, and an assortment of other topics. He said things that other people were afraid to say; and he said them frequently in an effort to tear away the taboos that had been imposed on them. He angered a lot of people, many of whom had the power to see that he was, in turn, harassed through legal cases. The comments that he made may not raise many eyebrows today, but back in the 1950s, many people thought that his language was filthy and his thoughts were depraved. Collins's book takes a look at Bruce as someone who died for the right of freedom of speech.

Bruce did for comedy, wrote *Seattle Times* critic Paul De Barros, "what Bob Dylan would do for pop music." De Barros is referring to the social criticism that both artists employed. "With brutally incisive street humor, he [Bruce] exposed society's hypocrisy about taboo subjects," De Barros wrote.

Critics agree that *The Trials of Lenny Bruce* is highly researched, or as David M. Lisa for *Library Journal* put it, "The book is a literal walking tour of his [Bruce's] time in court." The emphasis of this book is on the many obscenity charges and the subsequent court cases that Bruce had to face, rather than on the biography of the legendary comedian. But it is the legal details that make the book interesting, and that is why a *Kirkus Reviews* writer described it as "detailed, objective, and valuable."

BIOGRAPHICAL AND CRITICAL SOURCES:

PERIODICALS

Booklist, September 1, 2002, Mike Tribby, review of *The Trials of Lenny Bruce: The Fall and Rise of an American Icon*, p. 26.
Discourse and Society, July, 1997, Laurel Sutton, review of *The Death of Discourse*, pp. 428-429.
Journal of Communication, winter, 1997, David R. Allen, review of *The Death of Discourse*, p. 171.
Kirkus Reviews, June 15, 2002, review of *The Trials of Lenny Bruce*, p. 852.
Library Journal, August, 2002, David M. Lisa, review of *The Trials of Lenny Bruce*, p. 97.
Publishers Weekly, July 1, 2002, review of *The Trials of Lenny Bruce*, pp. 49-50.
Reason, January, 2003, Nick Gillespie, review of *The Trials of Lenny Bruce*, p. 55.
Seattle Times, October 7, 2002, Paul De Barros, "Standing Up for Free Speech: New Book Revisits Legal History of Lenny Bruce, First Amendment Warrior," p. F1.

ONLINE

Trials of Lenny Bruce Web site, http://www.trialsoflennybruce.com/ (February 23, 2003), Web site for the book, *The Trials of Lenny Bruce*, containing book reviews and author biographies.*

*   *   *

Douglas Coupland

COUPLAND, Douglas 1961-

PERSONAL: Born December 30, 1961, on a Canadian military base in Baden-Soellingen, Germany; son of Douglas Charles Thomas (a doctor) and C. Janet (Campbell) Coupland. *Education:* Attended Emily Carr College of Art and Design, Vancouver, Canada, 1984; completed a two-year course in Japanese business science, Hawaii, 1986.

ADDRESSES: Home—Vancouver, British Columbia, Canada. *Agent*—c/o Author Mail, HarperCollins, 10 East 53rd St., New York, NY 10022.

CAREER: Writer, sculptor, and editor. Host of *The Search for Generation X* (documentary), PBS, 1991.

WRITINGS:

NOVELS

Generation X: Tales for an Accelerated Culture, St. Martin's Press (New York, NY), 1991.
Shampoo Planet, Pocket Books (New York, NY), 1992.
Microserfs, ReganBooks (New York, NY), 1995.
Girlfriend in a Coma, ReganBooks (New York, NY), 1998.
Miss Wyoming, Pantheon Books (New York, NY), 2000.
God Hates Japan, Kadokawana Shoten (Tokyo, Japan), 2001.

All Families Are Psychotic, Bloomsbury (New York, NY), 2001.

Hey, Nostradamus!, Random House Canada (Toronto, Ontario, Canada), 2003.

OTHER

(Author of introduction) *Slacker* (companion to the Richard Linklater movie), St. Martin's Press (New York, NY), 1992.

Life after God (short fiction), Pocket Books (New York, NY), 1994.

Polaroids from the Dead (essays and short fiction), ReganBooks (New York, NY), 1996.

(With Kip Ward) *Lara's Book: Lara Croft and the Tomb Raider Phenomenon,* Prima Publishers (Rocklin, CA), 1998.

(With others) *Disco 2000* (anthology of stories), edited by Sarah Champion, Sceptre (London, England), 1998.

City of Glass: Douglas Coupland's Vancouver, Douglas & McIntyre (Vancouver, British Columbia, Canada), 2000.

Souvenir of Canada, Douglas & McIntyre (Vancouver, British Columbia, Canada), 2002.

Souvenir of Canada 2, Douglas & McIntyre (Vancouver, British Columbia, Canada), 2004.

Contributor of articles to periodicals, including *New Republic, New York Times, Wired,* and *Saturday Night.*

SIDELIGHTS: Douglas Coupland has become known as the voice of a generation, despite his frequent denials in interviews. According to Andrew Anthony in the *Observer,* "He bristles at the idea of being a spokesman for anyone. . . . To the question of whether he feels like part of a generation, he replies, 'Like I once ever did?'" Nevertheless critics continue to see in him, as does John Fraser in *Saturday Night,* "the self-wrought oracle of our age," and "the Jack Kerouac of his generation." Coupland earned his reputation with his first novel, *Generation X: Tales for an Accelerated Culture,* which originated the term "Generation X" to refer to those Americans born in the 1960s to early 1970s, defining their aggregate interests, concerns, and problems. About Coupland's status as mouthpiece for Generation X-ers, Fraser added that the author achieved it "with a distinctive style and up-market hustle that still leaves me breathless. Not once, so far as I can tell, did he do a sleazy thing to get where he is. He trudged all the way on his talent alone."

Generation X chronicles the story of three "twenty-something" friends living in Palm Springs, California, and mired in "McJobs"—a term coined by Coupland to indicate jobs with low pay, low dignity, and little future. The book, which London *Times* contributor Michael Wright described as "part novel, part manifesto," launched its twenty-nine-year-old author straight to the top of the best-seller lists. Coupland is claimed by some to have written the defining document of his generation, "the new *Catcher in the Rye,*" a book about young people "with too many TVs and too few job opportunities," as a *Newsweek* reviewer commented. In the novel, Andy, Claire, and Dag represent Generation X members and the stories they tell each other in their Palm Springs refuge predict a drab future of "lessness" and an accompanying tedium as the X-ers' fate in life. (One of many neologisms, along with the cartoons and slogans that appear in the book, "lessness" implies the acceptance of lower expectations than those of preceding generations.) "The trio's modern fables of love and death and spacemen and nuclear war sparkle like lumps of quartz amid the granite of their desert life," commented Wright, "each tale offering a small epiphany or moment of spangled optimism amid the prevailing gloom."

Laurel Boone, writing in *Books in Canada,* found fault with Coupland's story and its annotations. She thought "the cartoons, definitions, slogans, and other ephemera running beside the text in a separate column make shallow comments on the slightly less shallow story." John Williams remarked in the *New Statesman* that Coupland's novel is "self-conscious as hell," but he still found *Generation X* "charming" and "a surprisingly endearing read." Describing the book as "funny, colourful and accessible," Wright stated that Coupland's first novel possesses "dizzying sparkle and originality," further lauding it as "a blazing debut."

In *Shampoo Planet,* published a year after *Generation X,* Coupland turns his attention to "the Global Teens," the generation following the X-ers who were raised in the age of information and video stimulation. Tyler Johnson, the youthful narrator and younger brother of *Generation X*'s narrator, has what Sophronia Scott Gregory described in *Time* as "a Smithsonian-class collection of shampoos" (thus the book's title) plus a sister named Daisy—a waif-like, pseudo-hippie sporting blonde dreadlocks—and a twice-divorced mother, Jasmine, a true flower child who seems to Tyler more in need of parenting than he is. "Although the author is almost twice as old as the main characters in *Shampoo Planet*," observed Victor Dwyer in *Maclean's,* "he creates in the book a fictional teenage world that is both convincing and highly entertaining."

Comparisons to Coupland's first novel were to be expected. Some, like Brian Fawcett's in *Books in Canada,* noted a certain heaviness in both books. "Like its predecessor," wrote Fawcett, "*Shampoo Planet* is relentlessly witty and sometimes insistently light-headed without ever quite becoming lighthearted." "Old people will always win," figures *Shampoo*'s narrator; he finds himself in a world experiencing "severe shopping withdrawal and severe goal withdrawal." Still, Tyler remains hopeful about his future. Coupland himself drew attention to this hopefulness as a difference between his two books. He was quoted in *Maclean's* as saying, "I'm not Pollyannaish, but I'm optimistic about the future. I think *Shampoo Planet* has an optimism about it that *Generation X* does not." Dwyer recognized the same distinction: "It is as though the decade that separates him from his latest crop of characters has provided Coupland with a sense of perspective, and levity, that was sometimes lacking in the often bleak, self-absorbed *Generation X*."

Time contributor Gregory complained that Coupland's narrative in *Shampoo Planet* lacks motivation, but she praised the author's quirky descriptive passages, noting that "the book thrives with the energetically bizarre." Gregory further observed, "Fascinating characters abound, but unfortunately they have little to do." Michael Redhill offered a different characterization of the novel in his Toronto *Globe and Mail* review. "Coupland's challenge here was to write about the fascination with surfaces without being superficial himself," he commented. "*Generation X* was a novel filled with an empathetic rage and sadness. In *Shampoo Planet,* Coupland's tears run to jeers." Other critics hailed the book's fresh viewpoint and inventiveness. A *Publishers Weekly* reviewer called the novel "funny, sympathetic, and offhandedly brilliant." Dwyer assessed Coupland as "a maturing author artfully evoking the hopes and dreams of a generation that has good reason to have little of either."

Describing Coupland's 1994 collection of short fiction and essays, *Life after God,* Joe Chidley asserted in *Maclean's* that the book "strips away the paraphernalia of an age-group to investigate the origins of its angst. Unfortunately, he also strips away much of its anger

and wit. What remains is the ennui." Terry Horton drew a similar conclusion in a *Quill & 'Quire* review. "Coupland has a knack for beautiful imagery . . . and each chapter's first page is topped with a lighthearted cartoon," wrote the reviewer. "But, in the end, neither beautiful imagery nor cartoons can sweep away the hopelessness that darkens these tales." Chidley further observed that, "cumulatively, eight stories about the passing of things end up sounding like an extended whine."

Brenda Peterson, reviewing *Life after God* in the *New York Times Book Review,* found that Coupland's effort missed the mark. "Though each of these very short tales has its own narrator, the voice never really varies: it drones where it might delve, it skims where it might seduce, it hoards where it might offer sustenance." Peterson concluded, "Mr. Coupland's vision is as perishable and trendy as the brand names that pass here for characters and story lines." *New Criterion* contributor Jeffrey Bloom explained the collection's shortcomings in the following manner: "Coupland has the eye and the ear of a good reporter, but lacks the vision of a good novelist. He sees the telling detail and hears the revealing bit of dialogue, but he never goes behind or beyond them. The result, *Life after God,* is rather thin gruel. But as such, it is an excellent guide to the thin spiritual life of the first generation raised without religion."

Coupland's 1995 novel, *Microserfs,* again explores the lives of the generation of young men and women in their twenties. However, the characters at the center of this novel are not mourning the hopelessness of their McWorld; they are young computer programmers hyperactively engaged in realizing the hopes of Bill Gates and his MicrosoftWorld. *New Statesman* reviewer Peter Jukes suggested that Coupland has created "perhaps the first great work of *cyberrealism.* Where others are obsessed by pixels and bits, Coupland's subject is the 'biomass' squeezed between the silicon, the 'carbon-based forms' that still sweat, flake away, love, grieve and fail." He added, "*Microserfs* is a tough and raucous celebration of our ability to reinvent and remember ourselves. And it paints a vivid picture of the new geek priesthood, sitting like monks in their VDU-lit cells, embellishing the margins with hieroglyphs, keeping our culture alive."

Microserfs' "main characters are all highly observant, introspective, and almost painfully ironic," noted Dan Bortolotti in *Books in Canada*. "They are, in fact, like most of Coupland's characters: coldly viewing themselves in terms of consumer culture." Daniel, the narrator, and his friends share a house where they pass the few moments they are not working at Microsoft. They eat poorly, sleep rarely, and exercise only their brains. They think and speak in terms of popular culture, defining themselves by their ideal *Jeopardy* categories. "*Microserfs* is entertaining," Nadia Halim commented in *Canadian Forum.* "Coupland's skill at manipulating his pop-culture-reference-laden vocabulary remains as strong as ever. He is capable of producing passages that are funny, provocative and sublime all in the same breath." Even so, Halim found that "Coupland's weaknesses . . . are also on display here. The book's plot is banal: after a few predictable crises, everyone falls in love and lives happily ever after. The characters all talk the same way."

Such reservations notwithstanding, reviewers like *New York* magazine's John Homans pointed out that Coupland is "a journalist . . . and *Microserfs* is a giant, frightening collage, a novel of half-baked ideas about change and technology and obsolescence." Rick Perlstein touched on this quality of the novel and its author's role as a chronicler of social change. He wrote in *Nation,* "Coupland here is mining urgent territory—a new social realism for the dawn of Postindustry and its unholy trinity of data, downsizing and Darwinism. He's investigating a curious sociological quirk of our age: What happens when the very cultural imagination of a society, nay, the very cultural imagination of a planet, is chartered by an elite of preternaturally gifted computer geeks who play with Nerf toys?"

Coupland's 2000 novel *Miss Wyoming* revolves around Susan Colgate. Crowned Miss Wyoming as a teen, Susan rebels against her mother, Marilyn, by refusing the crown. She then makes her way to Hollywood where she has a brief acting career on a television sitcom. After a series of further adventures, including surviving a plane crash, Susan disappears and is sought after by a group including her suitor John Johnson, disappointed that Susan has gone missing before their second date.

"A little edge or satire might have made it more interesting," claimed Marc A. Kloszewski in *Library Journal,* adding "but this is lightweight fun that will find some receptive readers." Though a *Publishers Weekly* critic found the plot twists to be satisfying, the critic

also stated: "Since *Generation X,* Coupland has been read more for his trend-setting insights than his novelistic dexterity. [Here] he loses even that edge by jumping on the already tired beauty-pageant-bashing bandwagon." A *Mother Jones* critic, however, argued that *Miss Wyoming* "presents a refreshingly earnest theme: The shells we create by discarding outdated identities allow 'newer and more wonderful' selves to emerge." Andrew Clark in *Maclean's* was more laudatory, comparing Coupland to F. Scott Fitzgerald, and *Miss Wyoming* to *The Great Gatsby.* Coupland himself described *Miss Wyoming* and the following novel, *All Families Are Psychotic,* as "'experiments' that did not quite work," for *Observer* writer Andrew Anthony.

Miss Wyoming was followed by the novels *All Families Are Psychotic* in 2001, *Hey, Nostradamus!* in 2003, and a first nonfiction work, *City of Glass: Douglas Coupland's Vancouver,* in 2000. *City of Glass,* according to a review by Heather Mallick in Toronto *Globe and Mail,* is a tribute to the entire city of Vancouver: "When people say they like a city, they use its name as a shorthand for the part they like. People say New York, but they mean Manhattan. They say Paris, but they don't mean its suburbs. But Coupland goes everywhere in Vancouver, likes it all, and has mapped it literally and imaginatively. This is urban heresy."

All Families Are Psychotic, described as "a disorientating cacophony of conflicting voices and ricocheting sub-plots" by *Guardian* critic Alfred Hickling, follows the intricate relationships of the Drummond family who are converging on Florida to see their one-armed sister off on a flight into space. Marcel D'Agneau in a *hackwriters* review begins by readying himself to part ways with Coupland over the book but then follows 9/11 and several disastrous contortions within his own family, and *All Families* begins to seem more realistic. "One week of family trauma, hysteria and pain. I came back to 'all families are psychotic' and what a week before was improbable magic realism set in a tawdry Florida backdrop with a classic modern North American family in self destruct and it all seemed well . . . normal." However, D'Agneau still did not find the book riveting or different enough from the two novels that preceded it to satisfy him: "*All Families Are Psychotic* isn't a bad book, it isn't a great book, it is just more of the same and maybe it is my fault for being so familiar with his work I now demand something fresh."

Hey, Nostradamus! was described by *Guardian's* Hickling as "a major shift in Coupland's style." Hickling added, "He has toned down all the arch, ironic posturing and compulsive slew of pop-cultural references, allowing a newly meditative, moral tone to emerge." This 2003 novel is Coupland's look at the lengthy and bitter aftermath of a Columbine High School-type massacre. The *Observer*'s Anthony, in an interview-style review, revealed that Coupland was drawn to contemplate what had happened at Columbine "in December 2001 after a 'nightmarish forty-city tour that began on 10 September.' He talks about the 'collective sorrow' he witnessed and I gather that it was this experience, the fall-out from 11 September, that made him look again at Columbine."

The school that provides the setting for the tragedy is in Vancouver, not in the U.S., but the characters (Coupland focuses on the victims, not the perpetrators) experience similar problems of alienation and dysfunction both before and after the killing. A young student, Cheryl, secretly married and pregnant, is the last victim and the first narrator. She speaks from an ambiguous limbo between earth and the beyond, from a place detached enough that she can meditate and comment on what has happened, and the resulting calmness of description makes for a harrowing beginning to the book. At the point of her death in her seventeen-year-old husband's arms, he takes over the narrative, and the story continues with his inability to escape the trauma until his ultimate disappearance. The depressing realities Coupland confronts have labeled him "increasingly morbid," but Anthony commented, "He's been described as an 'optimist obsessed with apocalypse,' but one might just as easily conclude he's a pessimist preoccupied with redemption."

Hickling pointed out that the cacophony of voices in the two earlier novels is replaced by a clear division between four narrators: Cheryl; her husband, Jason; Heather, the woman who later tries to help him heal; and Reg, Jason's father, "a granite-hard religious fanatic who tortures his family with his twisted strain of spiritual sadism." And Anthony confirmed that the voices of the characters in this novel are more clearly their own, not just a reflection of the author's: "One criticism that might be made of Coupland's work is that there isn't enough delineation between his characters' voices. They often blend into one voice, that of Coupland himself. Notwithstanding some minor lapses, that is not a complaint that could be leveled at *Hey, Nostradamus!*"

Answering Anthony's questions about why he chose to focus on the victims of the shooting rather than the killers, Coupland responded, "To my mind, that was all people talked about. I'm very much a fan of J. G. Ballard, where you have people in this fantastically quotidian situation that goes suddenly wrong, and how people deal with that. Killers get too much press already."

Coupland has been lauded by some as an accurate and keen observer, the voice of his generation, and a seer; by others, he has been faulted as a gloomsayer who only scratches surfaces. Yet, according to Jay McInerney in the *New York Times Book Review*, "Douglas Coupland continues to register the buzz of his generation with a fidelity that should shame most professional *Zeitgeist* chasers."

BIOGRAPHICAL AND CRITICAL SOURCES:

BOOKS

Contemporary Literary Criticism, Volume 85, Gale (Detroit, MI), 1995.

PERIODICALS

Booklist, February 1, 1998, p. 876; October 15, 1999, p. 417.
Books in Canada, September, 1991, pp. 50-51; April, 1992, p. 13; October, 1992; September, 1995, p. 30.
Byte, October, 1995, p. 49.
Canadian Forum, January, 1993, p. 41; June, 1994, p. 44; December, 1995, p. 50.
Christian Century, October 5, 1994, p. 905.
Esquire, March, 1994, pp. 170-171.
Fortune, September 18, 1995, p. 235.
Globe and Mail (Toronto, Ontario, Canada), September 5, 1992, p. C8; October 14, 2000; October 28, 2000.
Guardian, September 8, 2001; September 13, 2003.
Library Journal, May 1, 1998, p. 136; October 1, 1999, p. 132.
Los Angeles Times Book Review, July 6, 2003.
Maclean's, August 24, 1992, p. 60; April 25, 1994, p. 62; June 26, 1995, p. 54; April 20, 1998, p. 61; January 17, 2000, p. 60.
Mother Jones, January, 2000, p. 88.
Nation, June 26, 1995, p. 934.

New Criterion, April, 1994, pp. 79-80.

New Statesman, May 29, 1992, p. 40; July 29, 1994, p. 39; November 10, 1995, p. 37.

Newsweek, January 27, 1992, p. 58; June 19, 1995, p. 12.

New York, June 5, 1995, p. 50.

New York Times Book Review, May 8, 1994, p. 13; June 11, 1995, p. 54.

Observer (London, England), August 7, 1994, p. 22; August 24, 2003.

Paragraph, fall, 1994, pp. 32-33.

People, October 14, 1991, pp. 105-106; April 25, 1994, pp. 31-32; July 10, 1995, p. 30; April 13, 1998, p. 31.

Progressive, January, 1994, p. 42.

Publishers Weekly, February 1, 1991, p. 77; June 15, 1992, p. 82; December 20, 1993, p. 48; May 13, 1996, p. 66; February 1, 1998, p. 127; April 6, 1998, p. 34; October 11, 1999, p. 51.

Quill & Quire, February, 1994, p. 24; June, 1994, p. 38; May, 1995, p. 7; July, 1995, p. 51; May, 1996, p. 1.

San Francisco Chronicle, July 20, 2003.

Saturday Night, March, 1994, pp. 8-9.

Time, October 19, 1992, p. 78; January 17, 2000, p. 93.

Times (London, England), June 4, 1992, p. 6.

Times Literary Supplement, February 19, 1993, p. 23; August 5, 1994, p. 18; November 10, 1995, p. 22.

Toronto Sun, November 23, 1995.

USA Today, March 7, 1994, p. D1.

Vanity Fair, March, 1994, pp. 92, 94.

Voice Literary Supplement, November, 1992, p. 25.

Washington Post, August 3, 2003, p. BW07.

ONLINE

Douglas Coupland Home Page, http://www.coupland.com/ (March 8, 2004).

hackwriters, http://www.hackwriters.com/ (2001).

Spike Magazine, http://www.spikemagazine.com/ (1997), Chris Mitchell, interview with Coupland.

Write Stuff, http://www.altx.com/ (1994), Alexander Laurence, interview with Coupland.

OTHER

Douglas Coupland: Close Personal Friend, TV profile, 1995.*

COWAN, Andrew 1960-

PERSONAL: Born 1960, in Corby, Northamptonshire, England; married Lynne Bryan (a writer); children: Rose. *Education:* Attended Beanfield Comprehensive and University of East Anglia.

ADDRESSES: Home—East Anglia, England. *Agent*—c/o Author Mail, Sceptre/Hodder Headline, 338 Euston Road, London NW1 3BH, England. *E-mail*—cowan.bryan@virgin.net.

CAREER: Novelist. Worked variously as a postal worker, oral historian, cleaner in a cake factory, and chartered librarian.

AWARDS, HONORS: Betty Trask Award, Ruth Hadden Memorial Award, Author's Club First Novel Award, *Sunday Times* Young Writer of the Year Award, Scottish Arts Council Book Award, and John Steinbeck Award shortlist, all for *Pig;* Scottish Arts Council bursary, 1996, for *Common Ground;* Eastern Arts Board bursary, 2000, for *Crustaceans.*

WRITINGS:

NOVELS

Pig, M. Joseph (London, England), 1994, Harcourt (New York, NY), 1996.

Common Ground, M. Joseph (London, England), 1996, Harcourt (New York, NY), 1997.

Crustaceans, Sceptre (London, England), 2000, Picator USA (New York, NY), 2002.

ADAPTATIONS: Film rights to *Pig* were purchased by director Mike Leigh, 1996.

SIDELIGHTS: English novelist Andrew Cowan is acclaimed for his award-winning 1994 debut *Pig,* the winner of a number of major writing awards. Among his other novels are *Common Ground* and *Crustaceans.*

Pig details one summer in the life of fifteen-year-old Danny, whose grandmother dies, leaving an ailing husband—who is promptly moved into a nursing home—and a pig, whose well-being becomes the focus of the boy's life. Making daily visits to the grandparents' abandoned cottage on the edge of a decaying English industrial town, Danny and his Sikh girlfriend, Surinder, care for the animal and escape the stifling atmosphere and racist harassment that characterizes life in town.

Jay A. Fernandez in the *Boston Review* rated *Pig* "a very tender coming-of-age story that reads like a quiet memoir." In a review in the *New York Times Book Review,* James Saynor noted: "On the surface the story is stark and static. But beneath that surface are simmering energies, inklings of the whole rich canvas of life." In particular, Saynor praised Cowan's prose, which he described as "plain as a pikestaff, earnestly fixed on the physical world." However, he continued, "his minimalism is not of the frozen or portentous type. From the title onward, the book's matter-of-factness has an oddly penetrating quality. The author's dispassionate gaze carries with it great compassion." Overall, Saynor found *Pig* to be "a novel about inarticulateness and confusion that could not itself be more direct and sure." In the view of Boyd Tonkin, writing in *New Statesman,* "Cowan writes with a deeply impressive grace and economy. . . . [His] fine brushstrokes broaden the picture to embrace everyday racism, the end of an industrial society, the erosion of family life." David Buckley, who reviewed *Pig* in the *Observer,* appraised the novel as "a wholly satisfying book, quietly beautiful and inescapably ominous." *Publishers Weekly* critic Sybil Steinberg opined that *Pig* is "a simple tale, made moving and memorable by Cowan's beautifully restrained prose."

In *Common Ground* Cowan utilized the epistolary form to combine themes of family life and political activism in the story of Ashley and Jay, a young English couple whose values are challenged through parenthood. The story unfolds through letters from Ashley to his vagabond brother who is traveling around the world. The correspondence details Jay's pregnancy and the first months of the new baby's life along with the couple's growing involvement in the movement to stop development in a local woodland. Phil Baker, critiquing *Common Ground* in the *Times Literary Supplement,* stated that the author's "observation is superb throughout. His ear is also unfailingly good, whether he's catching newer speech patterns . . . or the diction of middle-aged ignorance." Baker maintained, however, that despite these strengths, "*Common Ground* can be dull reading. Ashley's character,

as it comes across in his letters, is marked by an irritating dud wit. . . . He is, to be blunt, a bore." In conclusion, Baker warned that "highly gifted, Cowan risks becoming a prisoner of his own genius for the ordinary." Peter Whittaker, reviewing *Common Ground* in the *New Statesman,* observed that the book was somewhat flawed due to the fact that "both plot and characters falter under the weight of the emblematic and interpretive baggage they are required to carry." But the critic had praise for other aspects of the work, in particular "the freshness and authenticity of the writing; a grounding of accurate observation that underpins even the most mundane detail." Eric Robbins in *Booklist* described the novel as a "quietly intriguing story about finding one's place in the world."

In *Crustaceans* Cowan tells the story of Paul, who is driving to a small seaside English town where his son, Euan, died. Along the way, Paul also journeys through his memories of a suicidal mother, a failed marriage, and the beloved son he has lost. Michael Upchurch in the *New York Times* believed that the novel "with reasonable care but few surprises, pulls (and sometimes drags) the reader through realms of anguished bereavement and rampant family animosity." A critic for *Publishers Weekly* found that "the reader's attention is captured not so much by one significant moment as by the narrative's accumulated force and momentum, which, as in life, overwhelms and makes this book memorable and engrossing." "This novel," Elsa Gaztambide claimed in *Booklist,* "is a journey through sadness, ironically awakening a bittersweet yearning to embrace life."

BIOGRAPHICAL AND CRITICAL SOURCES:

PERIODICALS

Booklist, September 15, 1996, Deanna Larson, review of *Pig,* p. 219; September 1, 1997, Eric Robbins, review of *Common Ground,* p. 56; February 15, 2002, Elsa Gaztambide, review of *Crustaceans,* p. 990.

Boston Review, June 21, 1996, review of *Pig.*

Guardian (London, England), August 10, 2002, Andrew Cowan, "From Flop to Top: How the Fickle Hand of Publishing Finally Gave Andrew Cowan the Thumbs Up," p. 25.

Kirkus Reviews, January 1, 2002, Caroline M. Hallsworth, review of *Crustaceans,* p. 7.

Library Journal, July, 1996, Paul E. Hutchison, review of *Pig,* p. 156; June 15, 1997, review of *Common Ground,* p. 96.

Los Angeles Times, March 24, 2002, Susan Salter Reynolds, review of *Crustaceans,* p. R15.

New Statesman, September 2, 1994, Boyd Tonkin, review of *Pig,* p. 40; May 17, 1996, Peter Whittaker, review of *Common Ground,* pp. 40-41.

New York Times, April 7, 2002, Michael Upchurch, review of *Crustaceans,* p. 16.

New York Times Book Review, December 15, 1996, review of *Pig,* p. 9.

Observer (London, England), August 14, 1994, p. 20.

People, November 25, 1996, Paula Chin, review of *Pig,* p. 31.

Publishers Weekly, August 12, 1996, Sybil Steinberg, review of *Pig,* p. 62; July 21, 1997, review of *Common Ground,* p. 182; January 21, 2002, review of *Crustaceans,* p. 62.

Times Literary Supplement, May 31, 1996, Phil Baker, review of *Common Ground,* p. 23.

ONLINE

Contemporary Writers, http://www.contemporary writers.com/ (November 6, 2003), "Andrew Cowan."*

*   *   *

CUSHMAN, Karen 1941-

PERSONAL: Born October 4, 1941, in Chicago, IL; daughter of Arthur and Loretta (Heller) Lipski; married Philip Cushman (a professor), September 6, 1969; children: Leah. *Education:* Stanford University, B.A., 1963; United States International University (San Diego, CA), M.A. (human behavior), 1977; John F. Kennedy University (Orinda, CA), M.A. (museum studies), 1986. *Religion:* "Secular humanist." *Hobbies and other interests:* Working in the garden—especially growing tomatoes, reading, medieval music.

ADDRESSES: Home—Vashon Island, WA. *Agent*—James Levine, 330 Seventh Ave., New York, NY 10001.

CAREER: Writer, 1990—. John F. Kennedy University, Orinda, CA, adjunct professor in Museum Studies Department, beginning 1986.

AWARDS, HONORS: Carl Sandburg Award for Children's Literature, Golden Kite Award, Society of Children's Book Writers and Illustrators, both 1994, Newbery Honor Book, American Library Association (ALA), Best Books for Young Adults and Recommended Books for Reluctant Readers, ALA/Young Adult Library Services Association (YALSA), and Pick of the Lists selection, American Booksellers' Association, all 1995, and Honour List, International Board on Books for Young People, 1996, all for *Catherine, Called Birdy;* Newbery Medal, ALA, Notable Children's Book selection and Quick Pick for Young Adults selection, ALA, Notable Trade Book in the English Arts, National Council of Teachers of English, and Best Books for Young Adults, ALA/YALSA, 1995, for *The Midwife's Apprentice;* John and Patricia Beatty Award, California Library Association, and Notable Children's Trade Book in the Field of Social Studies, National Council for the Social Studies/Children's Book Council, both 1997, both for *The Ballad of Lucy Whipple.*

WRITINGS:

Catherine, Called Birdy, Clarion (New York, NY), 1994.

The Midwife's Apprentice, Clarion (New York, NY), 1995.

The Ballad of Lucy Whipple, Clarion (New York, NY), 1996.

Matilda Bone, Clarion (New York, NY), 2000.

Rodzina, Clarion (New York, NY), 2003.

SIDELIGHTS: Author Karen Cushman features "strong, spirited, willful, and independent young women" in her novels aimed at the young adult audience, as a critic for the *St. James Guide to Young Adult Writers* noted. Cushman sets these resourceful female protagonists in historical periods as varied as the Middle Ages and the American nineteenth century. "Though centuries distant, they have the same desires as contemporary young women," according to the same contributor. Cushman thus provides readers with compelling coming-of-age tales as well as history primers noted for their accuracy and attention to detail.

The tired adage "better late than never," however, takes on new meaning when applied to this writer. Beginning her writing career at age fifty, she took over three years to write her first young adult novel, *Catherine, Called Birdy*. This story of a thirteen-year-old girl who tries to control her own destiny in the medieval world won numerous awards, including a prestigious Newbery Honor Book. But Cushman is a fast study. Her second published work, *The Midwife's Apprentice*, also set in the Middle Ages and featuring a young female protagonist, took just six months to write and earned her the Newbery Medal. "I've always been a late bloomer," Cushman explained in an interview with *CA*. "But I always eventually bloom. Here I am making a new career late in life and having a wonderful time." Her subsequent novels include *The Ballad of Lucy Whipple*, *Matilda Bone*, and *Rodzina*.

Changing careers and change in general is something Cushman seems quite at home with. Born in a suburb of Chicago in 1941, just before the United States entered World War II, she moved with her family to Tarzana in southern California at age eleven. As she told *Achuka Online*'s Cheryl Bowlan, "I was not thrilled with California. It was too hot. I missed my grandparents, my dog and my public library." The adolescent Cushman soon adapted to her new environment, however. A self-proclaimed avid reader as a child, Cushman found the local library in her new hometown and that helped to make her feel more settled. Soon she was helping herself to the wonders this new library had to offer. "Fiction was my favorite, but I would get these wild passions and read all there was on the Civil War for instance, or on the physiology of the brain. I guess this kind of curiosity explains my later fascination with the Middle Ages." Attending Catholic school through high school, Cushman received an education that "was more controlled than inspired. I remember coming home from the first grade with all the books for the entire year and reading them the first night and then crying all night because I knew I would be stuck with those same books all year long."

Fantasy worlds played an important part in her private education. "I used to hold plays with my neighborhood friends," Cushman once recalled for *CA*. "One time I got hold of a book on ballet, and I had my friends take a ballet class, gripping the car door handles like a ballet bar as I read to them what to do." Her younger brother's homemade scooter provided another outlet: "I used to borrow that scooter and take off and imagine myself going all around the world, which is sort of what I do now, only I travel backwards in time in my writing." Writing was an early avoca-

tion as well, and once her talents for poems and stories were discovered by classmates and teachers, Cushman was in demand for everything from valedictory speeches to writing contests. "I used to write poems and short stories for myself at this time," Cushman once told *CA*. "Recently, I came across a play I wrote in junior high—'Jingle Bagels,' a sort of multicultural Christmas story. I also wrote several possible plots for new Elvis movies."

Upon graduation from high school, Cushman won a scholarship that would allow her to attend any college in the United States, and more by accident than design, she attended Stanford. "I never thought about writing as a profession or as a way to make a living. No one I knew made their living that way. I thought I might want to take creative writing in college, but that's as far as the ambition went." However, Stanford offered no undergraduate creative writing major, so Cushman began with the next best thing, English. "But I liked the wrong kinds of books," she once recalled. Soon she was also studying Greek and began dreaming of a career in archaeology. Her writing, however, stopped for a time. "Writing was a thing I did to ventilate my feelings or to celebrate. But at Stanford there were all these semi-intellectual East Coast types who read [Albert] Camus, and I felt very intimidated about sharing my writing with them. To be honest, the whole experience at Stanford was bit intimidating."

"After graduation, I wanted to dig for treasures on the Acropolis by moonlight," Cushman once told J. Sydney Jones in an interview for *Something about the Author (SATA)*. "Instead, I got a job as a customer service representative for Pacific Bell in Beverly Hills." Several jobs later, she was working at Hebrew Union College in Los Angeles, where she met her future husband, then a rabbinic student. Together, the two packed up for Oregon, where her husband found a job at a small college and "where I wove and made blackberry jam and had a daughter, Leah," Cushman once recalled. After two years, the family returned to California, where both Cushman and her husband earned master's degrees in counseling and human behavior. Her husband went on to get his doctorate in psychology, set up a private practice, and become a professor and respected writer in the field of psychotherapy. Cushman, meanwhile, studied for a second master's—in museum studies—and became an adjunct faculty member at John F. Kennedy University, where she has edited *Museum Studies Journal*, taught classes in museology and material culture, and coordinated the master's project program. "Museum studies was an interesting way for me to put together many of the things that interest me in life. I am fascinated about the concept of what artifacts say about a culture, and also which artifacts are saved and why others are not."

But increasingly her interests focused on writing again. "Over the years, I did a lot of reading of children's books to and with my daughter," Cushman once told *SATA*. "When we got to young adult literature, I just stayed there while she went on to adult books. There is something about the themes of these books that appeal to me—coming of age, the acceptance of responsibility, and development of compassion. I was always coming up with great ideas for books and sharing them with my husband. And finally one day in 1989, when I told him this great idea for a book set in the medieval world, he just told me he didn't want to hear any more about it until it was down on paper." Cushman accepted the challenge and sketched out the book in seven pages. That, however, was the easy part. What followed was another three years of research into the medieval world, discovering "what it might have been like for a girl during the Middle Ages," as she once told *SATA*.

Methodical in her approach, Cushman first read some of the better-known writers of historical fiction for young adults, including Rosemary Sutcliff and Patricia MacLachlan. In an interview with Amy Umland Love for *Publishers Weekly,* she said that she especially admired the "simple and polished prose" of these two. She also attended writers' conferences but got little help from these until the day she heard one speaker who was not dealing out inside tips on marketing or on hot topics, but who simply advised to write from the heart.

For Cushman, this simple piece of advice was a revelation, giving her confidence to follow her own passions and instincts. Her career in museum studies was helpful in giving her access to material on the culture of the medieval world; she also heavily researched the period, using records of the time, including one thirteenth-century book on manners that contained such sage advice as not to blow one's nose on the tablecloth. The distance in time and philosophy afforded by writing about the Middle Ages also allowed Cushman to take a fresh look at the role of women in

society. The transition from the medieval period to the Renaissance with its increased intellectual turmoil is mirrored in the rite of passage of an adolescent girl: in this case, young Catherine, who is nicknamed Birdy. "There was a change toward personal accountability and emphasis on the development of privacy," Cushman said in her *Publishers Weekly* interview. Yet this personal accountability was stymied in the case of young women of the thirteenth century, as it often still is. "Everything I had read about children's books or had heard at conferences told me the child should solve the problem," Cushman once explained to *SATA*. In the case of Birdy, and in most instances involving children, that simply is not true, Cushman believes. "What I wanted to show with Catherine was what a child would do in a situation she could not control and for which she had no options."

The resulting story is told in diary form: "I am bit by fleas and plagued by my family. That is all there is to say." So begins Catherine's personal description of her fourteenth year. She lives in a room full of caged birds and keeps this journal, initially, as a form of discipline for being so self-willed and headstrong. She resists not only her mother's campaign to make her a lady, but also her father's to marry her off to an older landowner she calls Shaggy Beard. Birdy writes that in fact she and her friend Aelis are in "grave danger of being sold like pigs at autumn fair." Her account of her daily adventures takes the reader through an entire year of medieval life in an English manor house in Lincolnshire. There are fairs and feasts, planting and harvesting, difficult births, pitiful deaths, and drunken weddings all described in vivid detail. The harsh realities of life in the Middle Ages are not glossed over: the smells of dung heaps and raw sewage, the bone-strewn floor of the manor, and the total lack of privacy are all minutely presented.

Birdy continues to resist her father's attempts at marrying her off by blacking out her teeth when one suitor comes calling and setting the privy on fire with another suitor still in it. She would much rather marry some swashbuckler like her Uncle George, the Crusader. But Birdy, like the caged birds all around her, ultimately is trapped. In her case, the imprisonment is the marriage—not with Shaggy Beard, but to his somewhat less offensive son. However, by accepting this match, she achieves a new level of maturity and understanding.

At the end of Cushman's three years of writing, she worked with another Oakland writer, Sandy Boucher, to clean up the manuscript and then sent it off to her husband's agent, who quickly found a publisher. If the writing was long and difficult, getting published was something of a cakewalk for Cushman. "I was very lucky," she once told *SATA*. Critical response made the effort all worthwhile. Jane Langton noted in the *New York Times Book Review* that it is the very process of maturation in the protagonist that makes the novel work: "Birdy's progress toward becoming Catherine is the true grist of the story," Langton wrote. *Voice of Youth Advocates* Rebecca Barnhouse praised the novel for its realism: "The novel succeeds because of the attention to detail in both the historical setting and in the development of the delightful character of Catherine." Deborah Stevenson commented in the *Bulletin of the Center for Children's Books* that Birdy seems endowed with a modern sensibility and that Cushman "writes with vigor and craft of a life most young people won't have contemplated but will find fascinating here," while Ann A. Flowers noted in *Horn Book* that Catherine's rebelliousness and curiosity mixed with kindness make her "an amusing and sympathetic figure," concluding that the book is "fascinating and thought-provoking." And *School Library Journal* critic Bruce Anne Shook called Catherine "a feminist far ahead of her time" and summed up the book as a whole as "superb historical fiction."

"I still take that seven-page synopsis of the book with me when talking in the schools," Cushman once told *SATA*. "For me, it's a symbol—it's great to have ideas, but ideas alone are not enough. We have to be willing to act on them." And act on them, Cushman did. The first novel was off in the mail to her agent when she began her second book, also set in the Middle Ages which she knows so well. In this next tale, however, she left the world of the manor house for the life of commoners. "*The Midwife's Apprentice* grew from the title and an image of a nameless, homeless girl sleeping on a dung heap," Cushman once told *SATA*. "I could see this girl crawling out of the warm spot she had created for herself in the heap, sort of exploding out of it like she herself was being born." This Newbery medal-winning book is also considerably shorter than the first. (Cushman had to edit out forty pages of the original manuscript of *Catherine, Called Birdy*.) With *The Midwife's Apprentice,* she wrote a book thinner in secondary characters, but one every bit as rich in period detail. The story opens on a frosty morning early in the fourteenth century in a nameless English village with a preteen girl known as Brat, sleeping on a dung heap for warmth. The girl is described as "un-

washed, unnourished, unloved, and unlovely." A voice awakens her, and Brat sees a formidable looking woman called Jane the Midwife standing over her. Jane takes in this waif and turns her into her apprentice, seeing the girl initially as free labor.

Up to this time, Brat has led a hand-to-mouth existence, a child of the streets in modern jargon. Such a life has given Brat a certain wisdom regarding her fellow humans, but not much hope. Slowly, however, Brat begins to develop a sense of self and of hope. She also acquires her own name: Alyce. "Alyce is every child who is parentless, homeless, and hungry, who lives on the edges of our world, who is mocked or excluded for being different," asserted Cushman in her Newbery Medal acceptance speech, published in *Horn Book*. Through aiding in the delivery of twin calves and her first successful delivery of a baby, Brat/Alyce grows in confidence and spirit. By the end of the book she has learned the powerful lesson that "trying and failing are not the same as failing without ever trying," according to Barnhouse in another *Voice of Youth Advocates* article. Sara Miller wrote in *School Library Journal* that Cushman tells her story with "simplicity, wit, and humor," making *The Midwife's Apprentice* "a delightful introduction to a world seldom seen in children's literature." A reviewer for *Booklist* also commented on Cushman's directness of approach: "Cushman writes with sharp simplicity and a pulsing beat. . . . Kids will be caught up in this short, fast-paced narrative." And a *Kirkus Reviews* critic called the book "a rouser for all times."

Cushman's third book is also historical fiction, though the time period is some five hundred years later. Set during the California Gold Rush, *The Ballad of Lucy Whipple* tells the story of a young girl dragged "like a barrel of lard" from her quiet Massachusetts home to the noise, adventure, and dirt of the California gold country. Twelve-year-old California Morning Whipple is distraught at the move but must help her mother run a boarding house. Morning soon renames herself Lucy and starts a pie business to follow her own dream: she longs to return to her home in the East. However, finally presented with the chance to return, Lucy suddenly learns that home is not a geographical location, but the people she is with and the experiences she has every day. For the time being, home is where Lucy is in California.

Part of the inspiration for this story was a fact Cushman stumbled across in her reading: Some ninety percent of those who came to the Gold Rush were men. "And I asked myself, what about the other ten percent? The women and children? Why did they come? What about their stories?" Another inspiration was Cushman's own removal to California from Chicago as a young girl and the subsequent dislocation she felt. Cushman set the story in the fictional mining camp of Lucky Diggings, which is in the northern mines. "I wanted there to be inclement weather, and I also wanted the miners to be doing wet mining," Cushman once told *SATA*. Two years of research and writing went into the book. "I found it harder to learn about the everyday life of women and children in California of the nineteenth century than I did in thirteenth-century England. Everybody was too busy working, I guess, to keep records." One invaluable source was a set of letters sent back East to a sister by the wife of a miner. *The Ballad of Lucy Whipple* again contained several of Cushman's usual motifs and themes: the spirited adolescent girl, the change of name, the will and dream at the center of things.

Reviewers responded positively to this third novel as they had to the previous two. Linda Perkins, writing in the *New York Times Book Review,* praised Cushman for not simply sticking with her winning formula of following the coming-of-age pains of a girl in medieval England, noting that *The Ballad of Lucy Whipple* is evidence that Cushman's "early honors were not just beginner's luck." Perkins also commended Cushman for "recreat[ing] a time and place in gritty detail," and for "hold[ing] the reader's nose up to the stench of history," something not usually done in young adult historical fiction. A reviewer for *Publishers Weekly* remarked on the author's accuracy in portraying Lucy's emotional turbulence, employing "a voice so heartbreakingly bitter that readers can taste her homesickness." Bruce Anne Shook, writing in *School Library Journal,* also commented that the "historical setting is authentically portrayed" and that the "heroine is a delightful character." A critic for *Kirkus Reviews* found that Cushman's third novel was "less a period piece than a timeless and richly comic coming-of-age story," while the *Publishers Weekly* reviewer concluded that Cushman's novel was "a coming-of-age story rich with historical flavor."

Following dreams is what has allowed Cushman such success with her books. Returning to the Middle Ages for her fourth book, *Matilda Bone*, she found the research into medieval cures with leeches and blood-letting "gross enough for the average seventh grader and me," as she once noted for *SATA*. She is also constantly learning about her craft. "So much of writing is unconscious and intuitive," she once explained. "I have never been plot-conscious. I personally love to read books that have strong plot and strong characters. But when I sit down to write a book, I don't have this structure in mind. I simply want to tell a story about a person's life and how that life changes day to day. I don't consciously think of the audience as I am writing, and I certainly do not wonder if the vocabulary level is correct or not. I just tell a story the way it has to be told. For me, historical fiction is the place where story and setting come together. Historical fiction allows all of us, including kids, to look at today's problems through a prism, to get literal distance on our own problems. I hope my books help kids to see beyond their own experiences, and see themselves as part of the sweep of history instead of an isolated vignette." Speaking with Bowlan, Cushman further elaborated on her craft: "Every time I get an idea for a story, that's what draws me. It's not that I think, oh, it's time for another American book, or it's time for an English book. It's the story and the character I seem to want to get involved with."

Matilda Bone tells the story of a young girl who has been raised by a priest, Father Leufredus, and brought up in the rarefied environment of an English manor house in the Middle Ages. At thirteen, Matilda suddenly finds herself apprenticed to a bone-setter, Red Peg. At first out of her element in Blood and Bone Alley, Matilda priggishly uses Latin in daily conversation and is appalled at the domestic conditions at Peg's. Reared on dreams of saintliness, she at first misunderstands and overlooks the basic goodness in Peg and her cohorts. She longs to return to Randall Manor and her studies. Matilda's abilities in reading and writing come in less handy than skill at hard work and compassion; Peg lets her pious new apprentice slowly come round and follow her own example of helping those less fortunate.

This fourth novel was less well-received critically than Cushman's previous titles. *Booklist*'s Ilene Cooper noted that unlike the author's earlier novels, "setting not character takes precedence" in *Matilda Bone*. Cooper felt that it was "easy to lose track of Matilda's evolution" amidst the array of historical detail served up in the book. A contributor for *Publishers Weekly* had similar reservations, remarking that fans of

Cushman's previous novels "may be disappointed with this historical adventure" because Matilda "is less winning than her supporting cast." Yet other reviewers found the book more laudable. *Horn Book*'s Susan P. Bloom assured readers that Cushman's voluminous research into medieval medical lore "is just as interesting as Matilda's tale." Kit Vaughan, writing in *School Library Journal*, also found *Matilda Bone* praiseworthy, calling it a "fascinating glimpse into the colorful life and times of the fourteenth century." Vaughan concluded that this "humorous, frank look" at medicine as practiced over half a millennium ago "shows readers that love and compassion, laughter, and companionship, are indeed the best medicine."

Cushman once again turns away from medieval themes to deal with the American West in the 2003 *Rodzina*. As a contributor for *Publishers Weekly* noted of the title, Cushman serves up "another feisty heroine," but this time the youthful protagonist, twelve-year-old Rodzina, is being shipped West on an orphan train in the 1880s. Part of a larger project in social engineering in which nineteenth-century orphans and street children were sent out of urban settings to be adopted by rural parents, Rodzina sets out from Chicago in the company of legions of other orphans. Big for her age, she is put in charge of other children on the train. Twice she is sent to homes along the train route, and twice she manages to escape cruel conditions, expected to work nonstop as nursemaid and farmhand or to fill the soon-vacant bed of a settler whose wife is in terminal condition. She finally makes it to Oakland, basking in the sunshine of California, where, as *Horn Book*'s Martha V. Parravano wrote, "readers can bet with confidence on plenty of good things happening for her." *Kliatt*'s Claire Rosser felt that young adult readers "will enjoy this well-written novel." Rosser further commended Cushman for creating a "strong heroine in terrible circumstances, who finds a way to not just survive but to create a life with real possibilities." A critic for *Kirkus Reviews* called the story's ending "agreeable," further commenting that Cushman, "as usual conveys a contemporary feel without anachronism." And *Booklist*'s Hazel Rochman thought that the book was a "natural for American history or social studies classes."

Since earning the Newbery Medal and critical acclaim for her novels, Cushman has spent more time in schools talking with children and is heartened by what she has seen. "It has pleased me to see so many kids still reading and plenty for whom it is a real passion." Among these, there are also aspiring writers, and her advice to these kids is the same as she told *Publishers Weekly*: "Go with your passion." Speaking with another *Publishers Weekly* contributor, Leonard S. Marcus, Cushman shared what she felt was the best part of being a writer. Noting that she dedicated her first book to her daughter and her daughter's friends, whom she had watched grow up, she told Marcus that these young women "taught me a lot about girls—that girls can, for instance, be more independent-minded than I as a girl ever realized." Cushman further explained, "They were an inspiration to me. As a writer, I in turn am glad to have the chance to inspire other girls."

BIOGRAPHICAL AND CRITICAL SOURCES:

BOOKS

Beacham's Guide to Literature for Young Adults, Volume 9, Beacham Publishing (Detroit, MI), 1999.

Children's Literature Review, Volume 55, Gale (Detroit, MI), 1998, pp. 55-75.

Cushman, Karen, *Catherine, Called Birdy,* Clarion (New York, NY), 1994.

Cushman, Karen, *The Midwife's Apprentice,* Clarion (New York, NY), 1995.

Cushman, Karen, *The Ballad of Lucy Whipple,* Clarion (New York, NY), 1996.

St. James Guide to Young Adult Writers, 2nd edition, St. James Press (Detroit, MI), 1999.

Something about the Author, Volume 89, Gale (Detroit, MI), 1996.

PERIODICALS

Booklist, April 15, 1994, p. 1526; March 15, 1995, review of *The Midwife's Apprentice,* p. 1328; April 1, 1995, p. 1399; August, 1997, Barbara Baskin, review of *Catherine, Called Birdy,* p. 1920; December 15, 1997, Jeanette Larson, review of *The Ballad of Lucy Whipple,* p. 711; March 1, 1999, Sally Estes, review of *The Ballad of Lucy Whipple,* p. 1212; April 1, 2000, Ilene Cooper, review of *The Midwife's Apprentice,* p. 1479; June 1, 2000, Stephanie Zvirin, review of *The Midwife's Apprentice,* p. 1875; August, 2000, Ilene Cooper, review of *Matilda Bone,* p. 2131; November 15,

2000, Stephanie Zvirin, review of *Catherine, Called Birdy,* p. 632; March 1, 2003, Hazel Rochman, review of *Rodzina,* p. 1207.

Bulletin of the Center for Children's Books, June, 1994, Deborah Stevenson, review of *Catherine, Called Birdy,* p. 316.

Horn Book, July-August, 1994, Ann A. Flowers, review of *Catherine, Called Birdy,* pp. 457-458; July-August, 1995, p. 465; July-August, 1996, Karen Cushman, "Newbery Medal Acceptance," pp. 413-419; November, 2000, Susan P. Bloom, review of *Matilda Bone,* p. 753; May-June 2003, Martha V. Parravano, review of *Rodzina,* p. 342.

Kirkus Reviews, March 15, 1995, review of *The Midwife's Apprentice,* p. 380; June 15, 1996, review of *The Ballad of Lucy Whipple,* pp. 869-897; March 15, 2003, review of *Rodzina,* p. 464.

Kliatt, July, 2003, Claire Rosser, review of *Rodzina,* pp. 8-9.

New York Times Book Review, August 28, 1994, Jane Langton, review of *Catherine, Called Birdy,* p. 20; September 24, 1995, p. 29; February 16, 1997, Linda Perkins, review of *The Ballad of Lucy Whipple,* p. 25.

Publishers Weekly, April 11, 1994, p. 66; July 4, 1994, Amy Umland Love, "Flying Starts: Seven Talents New to the Children's Book Scene Talk about Their Debuts," pp. 39-40; February 27, 1995, p. 104; May 15, 1995, p. 75; May 18, 1998, review of *The Ballad of Lucy Whipple,* p. 82; February 14, 2000, Leonard S. Marcus, "Talking with Authors," p. 98; September 4, 2000, review of *Matilda Bone,* p. 109; January 13, 2003, review of *Rodzina,* pp. 60-61.

School Library Journal, June, 1994, Bruce Anne Shook, review of *Catherine, Called Birdy,* p. 147; May, 1995, Sara Miller, review of *The Midwife's Apprentice,* p. 118; August, 1996, Bruce Anne Shook, review of *The Ballad of Lucy Whipple,* p. 142; September, 2000, Kit Vaughan, review of *Matilda Bone,* p. 225.

Voice of Youth Advocates, June, 1994, Rebecca Barnhouse, review of *Catherine, Called Birdy,* p. 81; August, 1995, Rebecca Barnhouse, review of *The Midwife's Apprentice,* pp. 156-157.

ONLINE

Achuka Online, http://www.achuka.co.uk/special/cushman.htm/ (September 9, 2003), Cheryl Bowlan, "Interview with Karen Cushman."

Houghton Mifflin Education Place Web site, http://www.eduplace.com/author/ (September 9, 2003).

Houghton Mifflin Web site, http://www.houghtonmifflinbooks.com/ (September 9, 2003).

D

DEAN, Zoey
    See BENNETT, Cherie

*   *   *

dePAOLA, Thomas Anthony 1934-
    (Tomie dePaola)

PERSONAL: Some sources cite surname as de Paola; name pronounced "Tommy de-*pow*la"; born September 15, 1934, in Meriden, CT; son of Joseph N. (a union official) and Florence (Downey) dePaola; married in the 1950s (marriage dissolved). *Education:* Pratt Institute, B.F.A., 1956; California College of Arts and Crafts, M.F.A., 1969; Lone Mountain College, doctoral equivalency, 1970. *Religion:* Roman Catholic.

ADDRESSES: Home—New London, NH. *Agent*—c/o Author Mail, Penguin Putnam, Putnam Juvenile Publicity, 345 Hudson St., New York, NY 10014.

CAREER: Professional artist and designer, and teacher of art, 1956—; writer and illustrator of juvenile books; creative director of Whitebird Books, imprint at G. P. Putnam's Sons. Newton College of the Sacred Heart, Newton, MA, instructor, 1962-63, assistant professor of art, 1963-66; San Francisco College for Women (now Lone Mountain College), San Francisco, CA, assistant professor of art, 1967-70; Chamberlayne Junior College, Boston, MA, instructor in art, 1972-73; Colby-Sawyer College, New London, NH, associate professor, designer, and technical director in speech and theater department, writer and set and costume

Thomas Anthony dePaola

designer for Children's Theatre Project, 1973-76; New England College, Henniker, NH, associate professor of art, 1976-78, artist-in-residence, 1978-79. Painter and muralist; graphic designer and illustrator; designer of theatrical sets. Member of board of directors of Society of Children's Book Writers of Los Angeles. *Exhibitions:* Individual shows at Botolph Group, Boston, MA, 1961, 1964, 1967; Putnam Art Center, Newton College of the Sacred Heart, 1971-72, 1975, 1978; Alliance Corporation, Boston, 1972; Library Arts Center,

Newport, NH, 1975, 1982, 1984; Rizzoli Gallery, New York, NY, 1977; Clark County Library, Las Vegas, NV, 1979; Englewood (NJ) Library, 1980; Louisiana Arts and Science Center, Baton Rouge, LA, 1981; University of Minnesota, Minneapolis, 1981; Children's Theatre, Minneapolis, 1981; Yuma City-County (AZ) Library, 1981; Charles Fenton Gallery, Woodstock, VT, 1984; Arts and Science Center, Nashua, NH, 1985, 1986; Bush Galleries, Norwich, VT, 1987; and Women's Club, Minneapolis, 1988. Work exhibited in group shows at South Vermont Art Center, Manchester, 1958; Grail Festival of the Arts, Brooklyn, 1959; Botolph Group, 1962, 1964, 1969; San Francisco College for Women, 1969; Immaculate Heart College, Los Angeles, 1969; Library Arts Center, Newport, NH, 1975; Everson Museum, Syracuse, NY, 1977; Japan, 1977, 1979, 1981; Children's Book Fair, Bologna, Italy, 1978; Museum of Fine Arts, Houston, 1978; Dayton Art Institute, 1978; Brattleboro Museum and Art Center, 1980; Harley School, Rochester, NY, 1980-88; Port Washington, NY, Public Library, 1981; University of Connecticut Library, Storrs, 1982; Society of Illustrators, New York, 1982, 1983, 1984, 1985; Metropolitan Museum of Art, 1982, 1983; Museum of Fine Art, Houston, 1982; Dog Museum of America, New York, NY, 1983; Boulder Center for Visual Arts, 1983; University of New Hampshire, Durham, 1983; Simmons College, Boston, 1984; Bush Galleries, Norwich, VT, 1985; Congress Square Gallery, Portland, ME, 1985; Denver Public Library, 1986; Colorado Academy, 1986; New London, NH, Historical Society, 1985, 1986, 1988; Aetna Institute Gallery, Hartford, CT, 1986; Miami Youth Museum, 1986; and New Hampshire Historical Society, Concord, 1988. Works are also included in many private collections. Mural installations in Catholic churches and monasteries in New England. Member, National Advisory Council of the Children's Theater Company of Minneapolis; Ballet of the Dolls Dance Company, Minneapolis, member of board of directors.

MEMBER: Society of Children's Book Writers (member of board of directors), Authors Guild.

AWARDS, HONORS: Boston Art Directors' Club awards for typography and illustration, 1968; Child Study Association children's book of the year citations, 1968, for *Poetry for Chuckles and Grins,* 1971, for *John Fisher's Magic Book,* 1974, for *David's Window* and *Charlie Needs a Cloak,* 1975, for *Strega Nona* and *Good Morning to You, Valentine,* 1986, for *Strega*

Nona's Magic Lessons, Tattie's River Journey, Tomie dePaola's Mother Goose, and *The Quilt Story,* 1987, for *Teeny Tiny* and *Tomie dePaola's Favorite Nursery Tales;* Franklin Typographers Silver Award for poster design, 1969; three books included in American Institute of Graphic Arts exhibit of outstanding children's books, *The Journey of the Kiss,* 1970, *Who Needs Holes?,* 1973, and *Helga's Dowry,* 1979; two books included on *School Library Journal's* list of best picture books, *Andy, That's My Name,* 1973, and *Charlie Needs a Cloak,* 1974; Friends of American Writers Award as best illustrator of a children's book, 1973, for *Authorized Autumn Charts of the Upper Red Canoe River Country;* two books chosen as Children's Book Showcase titles, *Authorized Autumn Charts of the Upper Red Canoe River Country,* 1973, and *Charlie Needs a Cloak,* 1975; Brooklyn Art Books for Children Award, Brooklyn Museum and Brooklyn Public Library, 1975, for *Charlie Needs a Cloak,* and 1977, 1978, and 1979, for *Strega Nona,* which also received the Caldecott Honor Book Award, 1976, and the Nakamore Prize (Japan), 1978; *The Quicksand Book* and *Simple Pictures Are Best* were both chosen one of *School Library Journal's* Best Books for Spring, 1977; Chicago Book Clinic Award, 1979, for *The Christmas Pageant; Helga's Dowry* was chosen a Children's Choice by the International Reading Association and the Children's Book Council, 1978, *The Popcorn Book, Pancakes for Breakfast, The Clown of God, Four Scary Stories, Jamie's Tiger,* and *Bill and Pete,* all 1979, *Big Anthony and the Magic Ring* and *Oliver Button Is a Sissy,* both 1980, *The Comic Adventures of Old Mother Hubbard and Her Dog,* 1982, *Strega Nona's Magic Lessons,* 1983, *The Carsick Zebra and other Animal Riddles,* 1984, and *The Mysterious Giant of Barletta,* 1985; Garden State Children's Book Award for Younger Nonfiction, New Jersey Library Association, 1980, for *The Quicksand Book;* Kerlan Award, University of Minnesota, 1981, for "singular attainment in children's literature"; Golden Kite Award for Illustration, Society of Children's Book Writers, 1982, for *Giorgio's Village,* and 1983, for *Marianna May and Nursey; Boston Globe-Horn Book* Award Honor Book for Illustration, 1982, and Critici in Erba commendation from Bologna Biennale, 1983, both for *The Friendly Beasts;* Regina Medal, Catholic Library Association, 1983, for "continued distinguished contribution to children's literature"; *Sing, Pierrot, Sing* was chosen one of *School Library Journal's* Best Books, 1983; *Mary Had a Little Lamb* was chosen as a Notable Book by the Association of Library Service to Children (ALA), 1984; *Clown of God* was selected a Notable Children's Film, 1984; *Sing, Pierrot, Sing* was selected a Notable Children's Trade Book in the Field of Social Studies by the National Council of Social Studies and the Children's Book Council, 1984, and *The Mysterious Giant of Barletta*, 1985; Award from the Bookbuilders West Book Show, 1985, for *Miracle on 34th Street*; *Redbook* Children's Picturebook Award Honorable Mention, 1986, for *Tomie dePaola's Favorite Nursery Tales*; *Horn Book* Honor List citation, 1986, for *Tomie dePaola's Mother Goose*; Golden Kite Honor Book for Illustration, 1987, for *What the Mailman Brought*; *The Art Lesson* was named one of the *New York Times'* best picture books of the year, 1989; American nominee in illustration for the Hans Christian Andersen Award, 1990; Smithsonian Medal, 1990; Helen Keating Ott Award, 1993; University of Southern Mississippi Medallion, 1995; Keene State College Children's Literature Festival Award, 1998; Newbery Award Honor Book, 2000, for *26 Fairmount Avenue*.

WRITINGS:

UNDER NAME TOMIE DEPAOLA

Criss-Cross, Applesauce, illustrations by B. A. King and his children, Addison House (Danbury, NH), 1979.

Strega Nona Takes a Vacation, Putnam (New York, NY), 2000.

Jamie O'Rourke and the Pooka, Putnam (New York, NY), 2000.

Also author of *The Legend of the Persian Carpet*, illustrated by Claire Ewart.

AND ILLUSTRATOR; UNDER NAME TOMIE DEPAOLA

The Wonderful Dragon of Timlin, Bobbs-Merrill (Indianapolis, IN), 1966.

Fight the Night, Lippincott (Philadelphia, PA), 1968.

Joe and the Snow, Hawthorn (New York, NY), 1968.

Parker Pig, Esquire, Hawthorn (New York, NY), 1969.

The Journey of the Kiss, Hawthorn (New York, NY), 1970.

The Monsters' Ball, Hawthorn (New York, NY), 1970.

(Reteller) *The Wind and the Sun*, Ginn (Lexington, MA), 1972.

Andy, That's My Name, Prentice-Hall (New York, NY), 1973.

Charlie Needs a Cloak, Prentice-Hall (New York, NY), 1973.

Nana Upstairs and Nana Downstairs, Putnam (New York, NY), 1973, reissued, 1997.

The Unicorn and the Moon, Ginn (Lexington, MA), 1973.

Watch Out for the Chicken Feet in Your Soup, Prentice-Hall (New York, NY), 1974.

The Cloud Book: Word and Pictures, Holiday House (New York, NY), 1975, translation by Teresa Mlawer, published as *El Libro de las Arenas Movedizas*, Holiday House, 1993.

Michael Bird-Boy, Prentice-Hall (New York, NY), 1975.

(Reteller) *Strega Nona: An Old Tale*, Prentice-Hall (New York, NY), 1975, published as *The Magic Pasta Pot*, Hutchinson (London, England), 1979.

Things to Make and Do for Valentine's Day, F. Watts (New York, NY), 1976.

When Everyone Was Fast Asleep, Holiday House (New York, NY), 1976.

Four Stories for Four Seasons, Prentice-Hall (New York, NY), 1977.

Helga's Dowry: A Troll Love Story, Harcourt (New York, NY), 1977.

The Quicksand Book, Holiday House (New York, NY), 1977, translation by Mlawer, published as *El libro de las nubes*, Holiday House, 1993.

Bill and Pete, Putnam (New York, NY), 1978.

The Christmas Pageant, Winston (Minneapolis, MN), 1978, published as *The Christmas Pageant Cutout Book*, 1980.

(Adapter) *The Clown of God: An Old Story*, Harcourt (New York, NY), 1978.

Pancakes for Breakfast, Harcourt (New York, NY), 1978.

The Popcorn Book, Holiday House (New York, NY), 1978.

Big Anthony and the Magic Ring, Harcourt (New York, NY), 1979.

Flicks, Harcourt (New York, NY), 1979.

The Kids' Cat Book, Holiday House (New York, NY), 1979.

Oliver Button Is a Sissy, Harcourt (New York, NY), 1979.

Songs of the Fog Maiden, Holiday House (New York, NY), 1979.

The Family Christmas Tree Book, Holiday House (New York, NY), 1980.

The Knight and the Dragon, Putnam (New York, NY), 1980.

The Lady of Guadalupe, Holiday House (New York, NY), 1980.

The Legend of the Old Befana: An Italian Christmas Story, Harcourt (New York, NY), 1980.

(Reteller) *The Prince of the Dolomites: An Old Italian Tale,* Harcourt (New York, NY), 1980.

The Comic Adventures of Old Mother Hubbard and Her Dog, Harcourt (New York, NY), 1981.

(Reteller) *Fin M'Coul, the Giant of Knockmany Hill,* Holiday House (New York, NY), 1981.

The Friendly Beasts: An Old English Christmas Carol, Putnam (New York, NY), 1981.

The Hunter and the Animals: A Wordless Picture Book, Holiday House (New York, NY), 1981.

Now One Foot, Now the Other, Putnam (New York, NY), 1981.

Strega Nona's Magic Lessons, Harcourt (New York, NY), 1982.

Francis, the Poor Man of Assisi, Holiday House (New York, NY), 1982.

Giorgio's Village, Putnam (New York, NY), 1982.

(Adapter) *The Legend of the Bluebonnet: An Old Tale of Texas,* Putnam (New York, NY), 1983.

Marianna May and Nursey, Holiday House (New York, NY), 1983.

Noah and the Ark, Winston (Minneapolis, MN), 1983.

Sing, Pierrot, Sing: A Picture Book in Mime, Harcourt (New York, NY), 1983.

(Adapter) *The Story of the Three Wise Kings,* Putnam (New York, NY), 1983.

(Adapter) *David and Goliath,* Winston (Minneapolis, MN), 1984.

Esther Saves Her People, Winston (Minneapolis, MN), 1984.

The First Christmas: A Festive Pop-up Book, Putnam (New York, NY), 1984.

(Adapter) *The Mysterious Giant of Barletta: An Italian Folktale,* Harcourt (New York, NY), 1984.

Tomie dePaola's Country Farm, Putnam (New York, NY), 1984.

Tomie dePaola's Mother Goose Story Streamers, Putnam (New York, NY), 1984.

Tomie dePaola's Mother Goose, Putnam (New York, NY), 1985.

Pajamas for Kit, Simon & Schuster (New York, NY), 1986.

Katie and Kit at the Beach, Simon & Schuster (New York, NY), 1986.

Katie's Good Idea, Simon & Schuster (New York, NY), 1986.

Katie, Kit and Cousin Tom, Simon & Schuster (New York, NY), 1986.

Merry Christmas, Strega Nona, Harcourt (New York, NY), 1986.

(With others) *Once upon a Time: Celebrating the Magic of Children's Books in Honor of the Twentieth Anniversary of Reading Is Fundamental,* Putnam (New York, NY), 1986.

(Adapter) *Queen Esther,* Winston (Minneapolis, MN), 1986, revised edition, Harper (New York, NY), 1987.

Tomie dePaola's Favorite Nursery Tales, Putnam (New York, NY), 1986.

Bill and Pete Go down the Nile, Putnam (New York, NY), 1987.

An Early American Christmas, Holiday House (New York, NY), 1987.

The Legend of the Indian Paintbrush, Putnam (New York, NY), 1987.

The Miracles of Jesus, Holiday House (New York, NY), 1987.

The Parables of Jesus, Holiday House (New York, NY), 1987.

Tomie dePaola's Book of Christmas Carols, Putnam (New York, NY), 1987.

Tomie dePaola's Diddle, Diddle, Dumpling and other Poems and Stories from Mother Goose (selections from *Tomie dePaola's Mother Goose*), Methuen (London, England), 1987.

Tomie dePaola's Three Little Kittens and other Poems and Songs from Mother Goose (selections from *Tomie dePaola's Mother Goose*), Methuen (London, England), 1987.

Baby's First Christmas, Putnam (New York, NY), 1988.

(Reteller) *Hey Diddle Diddle: And other Mother Goose Rhymes* (selections from *Tomie dePaola's Mother Goose*), Putnam (New York, NY), 1988.

Tomie dePaola's Book of Poems, Putnam (New York, NY), 1988.

(With others) *The G.O.S.H. ABC Book,* Aurum Books for Children (London, England), 1988.

The Art Lesson, Putnam (New York, NY), 1989.

Haircuts for the Woolseys, Putnam (New York, NY), 1989.

My First Chanukah, Putnam (New York, NY), 1989.

Tony's Bread: An Italian Folktale, Putnam (New York, NY), 1989.

Too Many Hopkins, Putnam (New York, NY), 1989.

Little Grunt and the Big Egg, Holiday House (New York, NY), 1990.

Tomie dePaola's Book of Bible Stories, Putnam/Zondervan (New York, NY), 1990.

Bonjour, Mr. Satie, Putnam (New York, NY), 1991.

My First Easter, Putnam (New York, NY), 1991.

My First Passover, Putnam (New York, NY), 1991.

My First Halloween, Putnam (New York, NY), 1991.

My First Thanksgiving, Putnam (New York, NY), 1992.

Country Angel Christmas, Putnam (New York, NY), 1995.

Days of the Blackbird: A Tale of Northern Italy, Putnam (New York, NY), 1997.

Tomie's Little Mother Goose, Putnam (New York, NY), 1997.

Big Anthony: His Story, Putnam (New York, NY), 1998.

The Night of Las Posadas, Putnam (New York, NY), 1999.

26 Fairmount Avenue (first book in the "26 Fairmount Avenue" series), Putnam (New York, NY), 1999.

Tomie dePaola's Rhyme Time, Grosset & Dunlap (New York, NY), 2000.

Here We All Are (second book in the "26 Fairmount Avenue" series) Putnam (New York, NY), 2000.

Meet the Barkers: Morgan and Moffat Go to School (first book in the "Barkers" series), Putnam (New York, NY), 2001.

Hide-and-Seek All Week (second book in the "Barkers" series), Grosset & Dunlap (New York, NY), 2001.

On My Way (third book in the "26 Fairmount Avenue" series), Putnam (New York, NY), 2001.

Adelita: A Mexican Cinderella Story, Putnam (New York, NY), 2002.

Four Friends at Christmas, Simon & Schuster (New York, NY), 2002.

Boss for a Day (third book in the "Barkers" series), Grosset & Dunlap (New York, NY), 2002.

A New Barker in the House (fourth book in the "Barkers" series), Putnam (New York, NY), 2002.

T-Rex Is Missing! (fifth book in the "Barkers" series), Grosset & Dunlap (New York, NY), 2002.

What a Year, Putnam (New York, NY), 2002.

Four Friends in Summer, Simon & Schuster (New York, NY), 2003.

Frida Kahlo: The Artist Who Painted Herself, Grosset & Dunlap (New York, NY), 2003.

Marcos Colors: Red, Yellow, Blue, Putnam (New York, NY), 2003.

Marcos Counts: One, Two, Three, Putnam (New York, NY), 2003.

Things Will Never Be the Same, Putnam (New York, NY), 2003.

Trouble in the Barkers' Class (sixth book in the "Barkers" series), Putnam (New York, NY), 2003.

Four Friends in Autumn, Simon & Schuster (New York, NY), 2004.

Pascual and the Kitchen Angels, Putnam (New York, NY), 2004.

Also author and illustrator of *Jingle, the Christmas Clown,* 1992, *Jamie O'Rourke and the Big Potato,* 1992, *Patrick: Patron Saint of Ireland,* 1992, *Tom,* 1993, *Kit and Kat,* 1994, *Christopher: The Holy Giant,* 1994, *The Legend of the Poinsettia,* 1994, *Strega Nona Meets Her Match,* 1995, *Country Angel Christmas,* 1995, *The Baby Sister,* 1996, *Strega Nona: Her Story,* 1996, *Mary: The Mother of Jesus,* 1997, and *Tomie's Little Mother Goose,* 1997.

ILLUSTRATOR; UNDER NAME TOMIE DEPAOLA

Lisa Miller (pseudonym of Bernice Kohn Hunt) *Sound,* Coward (New York, NY), 1965.

Pura Belpre, *The Tiger and the Rabbit and other Tales,* Lippincott (Philadelphia, PA), 1965.

Lisa Miller, *Wheels,* Coward (New York, NY), 1965.

Jeanne B. Hardendorff, editor, *Tricky Peik and Other Picture Tales,* Lippincott (Philadelphia, PA), 1967.

Joan M. Lexau, *Finders Keepers, Losers Weepers,* Lippincott (Philadelphia, PA), 1967.

Melvin L. Alexenberg, *Sound Science,* Prentice-Hall (New York, NY), 1968.

James A. Eichner, *The Cabinet of the President of the United States,* F. Watts (New York, NY), 1968.

Leland Blair Jacobs, compiler, *Poetry for Chuckles and Grins,* Garrard (Champaign, IL), 1968.

Melvin L. Alexenberg, *Light and Sight,* Prentice-Hall (New York, NY), 1969.

Robert Bly, *The Morning Glory,* Kayak (San Francisco, CA), 1969.

Sam and Beryl Epstein, *Take This Hammer,* Hawthorn (New York, NY), 1969.

Mary C. Jane, *The Rocking-Chair Ghost,* Lippincott (Philadelphia, PA), 1969.

Nina Schneider, *Hercules, the Gentle Giant,* Hawthorn (New York, NY), 1969.

Eleanor Boylan, *How to Be a Puppeteer,* McCall (New York, NY), 1970.

Duncan Emrich, editor, *The Folklore of Love and Courtship,* American Heritage Press (New York, NY), 1970.

Duncan Emrich, editor, *The Folklore of Weddings and Marriage,* American Heritage Press (New York, NY), 1970.

Sam and Beryl Epstein, *Who Needs Holes?,* Hawthorn (New York, NY), 1970.

Barbara Rinkoff, *Rutherford T. Finds 21B,* Putnam (New York, NY), 1970.

Philip Balestrino, *Hot As an Ice Cube,* Crowell (New York, NY), 1971.

Sam and Beryl Epstein, *Pick It Up,* Holiday House (New York, NY), 1971.

John Fisher, *John Fisher's Magic Book,* Prentice-Hall (New York, NY), 1971.

William Wise, *Monsters of the Middle Ages,* Putnam (New York, NY), 1971.

Peter Zachary Cohen, *Authorized Autumn Charts of the Upper Red Canoe River Country,* Atheneum (New York, NY), 1972.

Sibyl Hancock, *Mario's Mystery Machine,* Putnam (New York, NY), 1972.

Jean Rosenbaum and Lutie McAuliff, *What Is Fear?,* Prentice-Hall (New York, NY), 1972.

Rubie Saunders, *The Franklin Watts Concise Guide to Babysitting,* F. Watts, 1972, published as *Baby-Sitting: For Fun and Profit,* Archway, 1979.

Sam and Beryl Epstein, *Hold Everything,* Holiday House (New York, NY), 1973.

Sam and Beryl Epstein, *Look in the Mirror,* Holiday House (New York, NY), 1973.

Kathryn F. Ernst, *Danny and His Thumb,* Prentice-Hall (New York, NY), 1973.

Valerie Pitt, *Let's Find Out about Communications,* F. Watts (New York, NY), 1973.

Charles Keller and Richard Baker, compilers, *The Star-Spangled Banana and other Revolutionary Riddles,* Prentice-Hall (New York, NY), 1974.

Alice Low, *David's Window,* Putnam (New York, NY), 1974.

Mary Calhoun, *Old Man Whickutt's Donkey,* Parents' Magazine Press, 1975.

Norma Farber, *This Is the Ambulance Leaving the Zoo,* Dutton (New York, NY), 1975.

Lee Bennett Hopkins, compiler, *Good Morning to You, Valentine* (poems), Harcourt (New York, NY), 1975.

Martha and Charles Shapp, *Let's Find Out about Houses,* F. Watts (New York, NY), 1975.

Eleanor Coerr, *The Mixed-up Mystery Smell,* Putnam (New York, NY), 1976.

John Graham, *I Love You, Mouse,* Harcourt (New York, NY), 1976.

Bernice Kohn Hunt, *The Whatchamacallit Book,* Putnam (New York, NY), 1976.

Steven Kroll, *The Tyrannosaurus Game,* Holiday House (New York, NY), 1976.

Martha and Charles Shapp, *Let's Find Out about Summer,* F. Watts (New York, NY), 1976.

Barbara Williams, *If He's My Brother,* Harvey House, 1976.

Lee Bennett Hopkins, compiler, *Beat the Drum: Independence Day Has Come* (poems), Harcourt (New York, NY), 1977.

Daniel O'Connor, *Images of Jesus,* Winston (Minneapolis, MN), 1977.

Belong, Winston (Minneapolis, MN), 1977.

Journey, Winston (Minneapolis, MN), 1977.

(With others) Norma Farber, *Six Impossible Things before Breakfast,* Addison-Wesley (Reading, MA), 1977.

Jean Fritz, *Can't You Make Them Behave, King George?,* Coward (New York, NY), 1977.

Patricia Lee Gauch, *Once upon a Dinkelsbühl,* Putnam (New York, NY), 1977.

Tony Johnston, *Odd Jobs,* Putnam (New York, NY), 1977, published as *The Dog Wash,* Scholastic (New York, NY), 1977.

Steven Kroll, *Santa's Crash-Bang Christmas,* Holiday House (New York, NY), 1977.

Stephen Mooser, *The Ghost with the Halloween Hiccups,* F. Watts (New York, NY), 1977.

Annabelle Prager, *The Surprise Party,* Pantheon (New York, NY), 1977.

Malcolm E. Weiss, *Solomon Grundy, Born on Oneday: A Finite Arithmetic Puzzle,* Crowell (New York, NY), 1977.

Nancy Willard, *Simple Pictures Are Best* (Junior Literary Guild selection), Harcourt (New York, NY), 1977.

Jane Yolen, *The Giants' Farm,* Seabury (New York, NY), 1977.

Sue Alexander, *Marc, the Magnificent,* Pantheon (New York, NY), 1978.

William Cole, compiler, *Oh, Such Foolishness!* (poems), Lippincott (Philadelphia, PA), 1978.

Tony Johnston, *Four Scary Stories,* Putnam (New York, NY), 1978.

Steven Kroll, *Fat Magic,* Holiday House (New York, NY), 1978.

Naomi Panush Salus, *My Daddy's Moustache,* Doubleday (New York, NY), 1978.

Jan Wahl, *Jamie's Tiger,* Harcourt (New York, NY), 1978.

The Cat on the Dovrefell: A Christmas Tale, translation from the Norse by George Webbe Dasent, Putnam (New York, NY), 1979.

Lee Bennett Hopkins, compiler, *Easter Buds Are Springing: Poems for Easter* (poems), Harcourt (New York, NY), 1979.

Anne Rose, *The Triumphs of Fuzzy Fogtop,* Dial (New York, NY), 1979.

Daisy Wallace, compiler, *Ghost Poems,* Holiday House (New York, NY), 1979.

Jane Yolen, *The Giants Go Camping,* Seabury (New York, NY), 1979.

Patricia L. Gauch, *The Little Friar Who Flew,* Putnam (New York, NY), 1980.

Patricia MacLachlan, *Moon, Stars, Frogs, and Friends,* Pantheon (New York, NY), 1980.

Clement Moore, *The Night before Christmas,* Holiday House (New York, NY), 1980.

Daniel M. Pinkwater, *The Wuggie Norple Story,* Four Winds (New York, NY), 1980.

Pauline Watson, *The Walking Coat,* Walker (New York, NY), 1980.

Malcolm Hall, *Edward, Benjamin and Butter,* Coward (New York, NY), 1981.

Michael Jennings, *Robin Goodfellow and the Giant Dwarf,* McGraw-Hill (New York, NY), 1981.

Stephen Mooser, *Funnyman's First Case,* F. Watts (New York, NY), 1981.

Annabelle Prager, *The Spooky Halloween Party,* Pantheon (New York, NY), 1981.

Jeanne Fritz, adapter, *The Good Giants and the Bad Pukwudgies,* Putnam (New York, NY), 1982.

Tony Johnston, *Odd Jobs and Friends,* Putnam (New York, NY), 1982.

Ann McGovern, *Nicholas Bentley Stoningpot III,* Holiday House (New York, NY), 1982.

David A. Adler, *The Carsick Zebra and other Animal Riddles,* Holiday House (New York, NY), 1983.

Tony Johnston, *The Vanishing Pumpkin,* Putnam (New York, NY), 1983.

Shirley Rousseau Murphy, *Tattie's River Journey,* Dial (New York, NY), 1983.

Valentine Davies, *Miracle on 34th Street,* Harcourt (New York, NY), 1984.

Sarah Josepha Hale, *Mary Had a Little Lamb,* Holiday House (New York, NY), 1984.

Stephen Mooser, *Funnyman and the Penny Dodo,* F. Watts (New York, NY), 1984.

Tony Johnston, *The Quilt Story,* Putnam (New York, NY), 1985.

(With others) Hans Christian Andersen, *The Flying Trunk and other Stories by Andersen,* new English version by Naomi Lewis, Andersen Press (Atlanta, GA), 1986.

Jill Bennett, reteller, *Teeny Tiny,* Putnam (New York, NY), 1986.

Tom Yeomans, *For Every Child a Star: A Christmas Story,* Holiday House (New York, NY), 1986.

Sanna Anderson Baker, *Who's a Friend of the Water-Spurting Whale?,* Chariot (Elgin, IL), 1987.

Carolyn Craven, *What the Mailman Brought* (Junior Literary Guild selection), Putnam (New York, NY), 1987.

Jeanne Fritz, *Shh! We're Writing the Constitution,* Putnam (New York, NY), 1987.

Nancy Willard, *The Mountains of Quilt,* Harcourt (New York, NY), 1987.

Elizabeth Winthrop, *Maggie and the Monster,* Holiday House (New York, NY), 1987.

Caryll Houselander, *Petook: An Easter Story,* Holiday House (New York, NY), 1988.

Tony Johnston, *Pages of Music,* Putnam (New York, NY), 1988.

Cindy Ward, *Cookie's Week,* Putnam (New York, NY), 1988.

Tony Johnston, adapter, *The Badger and the Magic Fan: A Japanese Folktale,* Putnam (New York, NY), 1990.

Jane Yolen, *Hark! A Christmas Sampler,* Putnam (New York, NY), 1991.

Mice Squeak, We Speak, Putnam (New York, NY), 1997.

Benny's Big Bubble, Grosset & Dunlap (New York, NY), 1997.

Erandi's Braids, Putnam (New York, NY), 1999.

The Holy Twins: Benedict and Scholastica, Putnam (New York, NY), 2001.

Annabelle Prager, *The Surprise Party,* Random House (New York, NY), 2003.

Also illustrator of *I Love You Sun, I Love You Moon,* 1994, *The Tale of Rabbit & Coyote,* 1994, *The Bubble Factory,* 1996, and *Get Dressed Santa,* 1996.

DePaola's books have been published in many countries, including Denmark, Germany, Netherlands, Sweden, Norway, Japan, Italy, France and South Africa. His work is represented at the Kerlan Collection at the University of Minnesota and at the Osborne Collection, Toronto, Ontario, Canada.

ADAPTATIONS: Wind and the Sun (sound filmstrip), Xerox Films/Lumin Films, 1973; *Andy* (sound filmstrip), Random House, 1977; *Charlie Needs a Cloak* (filmstrip with cassette), Weston Woods, 1977; *Strega Nona* (filmstrip with cassette), Weston Woods, 1978, (musical, adapted by Dennis Rosa, based on *Strega Nona, Big Anthony and the Magic Ring,* and *Strega*

Nona's Magic Lessons), first produced in Minneapolis, MN, by the Children's Theatre Company, 1987, (videocassette), CC Studios, 1985; *Clown of God* (play; adapted by Thomas Olson), first produced in Minneapolis by the Children's Theatre Company, 1981, (16mm film; videocassette), Weston Woods, 1984; *Strega Nona's Magic Lessons and other Stories* (record and cassette; includes *Strega Nona's Magic Lessons, Strega Nona, Big Anthony and the Magic Ring, Helga's Dowry, Oliver Button Is a Sissy, Now One Foot, Now the Other, Nana Upstairs and Nana Downstairs*), read by Tammy Grimes, Caedmon, 1984; *Big Anthony and Helga's Dowry,* Children's Radio Theatre, 1984; *The Night before Christmas* (cassette), Live Oak Media, 1984; *The Vanishing Pumpkin* (filmstrip with cassette), Random House; *The Legend of the Bluebonnet: An Old Tale of Texas* (filmstrip with cassette), Random House, 1985; *The Mysterious Giant of Barletta* (cassette), Random House, 1985; *Mary Had a Little Lamb* (filmstrip with cassette), Weston Woods, 1985; *The Legend of the Indian Paintbrush* (filmstrip with cassette), Listening Library, 1988; *Tomie dePaola's Christmas Carols* (cassette), Listening Library, 1988; *Merry Christmas, Strega Nona* (cassette), Listening Library, (play; adapted by Thomas Olson), first produced in Minneapolis by the Children's Theatre Company, 1988; *Tomie dePaola's Mother Goose* (play; adapted by Constance Congdon), first produced in Minneapolis by the Children's Theatre Company, 1990. *Charlie Needs a Cloak* has been adapted into Braille and *Strega Nona* has been produced as a talking book. Filmstrips of *Let's Find Out about Houses, Let's Find Out about Summer, The Surprise Party, Pancakes for Breakfast, Sing, Pierrot, Sing,* and *Tattie's River Journey* have been produced.

SIDELIGHTS: "Tomie dePaola is one of the most popular creators of picture books for children in America today," state Richard F. Abrahamson and Marilyn Colvin in the *Reading Teacher.* Calling dePaola "an artist and writer of seemingly boundless energy," Anne Sherrill noted in an essay for the *Dictionary of Literary Biography* that he "has worked in several areas of children's literature." In addition to the scores of books he has written himself, dePaola's gently drawn, brightly colored illustrations fill the pages of many books written by other authors. Several critics, such as Abrahamson and Colvin, observed that dePaola is at his best, though, "when he both illustrates and writes a picture book," and considered his retold folk tales to "represent some of the most beautiful picture storybooks available today."

DePaola was born in 1934, near the end of the Great Depression, to Irish and Italian parents in Meriden, Connecticut. This talented and prolific author and illustrator grew up during World War II, before television deposed radio in American homes, in a family that appreciated books and creativity. He has frequently said that he decided to become an artist when he was only four. "I must have been a stubborn child," he once commented, "because I never swayed from that decision." By the time he was a sophomore in high school, dePaola knew that he wanted to attend Pratt Institute in New York and wrote to them to find out what classes he should be taking to prepare for his studies there. In 1952 he entered Pratt, earning a degree in 1956.

After graduation from Pratt, dePaola entered a Benedictine Monastery in Vermont where he stayed for six months. He has stated that he used the time there to solidify some deep spiritual values. Because the Benedictines are involved in the arts, he also learned the value of culture. DePaola maintained his association with the monastery when he returned to the secular life. In addition to crafting liturgical art, he designed fabric for their weaving studio and designed Christmas cards. Living in the monastery influenced the subject matter of his writing as well. Several of his children's books draw upon religious stories or themes, often from the perspective of legend. *The Clown of God: An Old Story,* for example, is a retelling of the story about the rise and fall of a juggler and the miracle that occurs at his final astonishing performance before a statue of the Virgin Mary and Christ Child. Sherrill remarked that dePaola's tale "was inspired by Anatole France's version of the legend about a juggler who offers his talent as a gift to the Christ Child. DePaola retells it with an Italian Renaissance setting."

Beginning his career as a teacher of art at Newton College of the Sacred Heart in Massachusetts in 1962, dePaola first illustrated Lisa Miller's science book, *Sound,* in 1965. The following year, he illustrated the first of his own books, *The Wonderful Dragon of Timlin.* In 1967, he traveled west to teach at San Francisco College for Women, which became Lone Mountain College. While in California, he earned a master of fine arts degree from the California College of Arts and Crafts in 1969, and a doctoral equivalency a year later at Lone Mountain College. "The time I spent in San Francisco also helped raise my consciousness—about women's issues especially—and to realign my thinking about antiwar and peace organizations," dePaola told Lisa Lane in a *Chicago Tribune* interview. Following his graduate work, he returned to New England where he continued to teach art, adding theatrical writing, technical direction, and set design to his professorial tasks. DePaola has also exhibited his work extensively in numerous one-man and group shows, both nationally and internationally. He is the recipient of numerous awards and honors as well as high praise from reviewers for his appealing retellings of religious and ethnic folktales, realistic fiction with elements of fantasy, and concept books that combine fiction with educational topics. But as Abrahamson and Colvin remarked, "Can there be a higher honor for a creator of children's books than to be selected by children as a favorite? In 1978, children across the United States chose four of Tomie dePaola's works among their favorites. No other creator of children's books during that year was given such an honor."

DePaola's family was a closely connected one and some of his stories for children focus upon relationships among family members. One of dePaola's first books, *Nana Upstairs and Nana Downstairs,* is "based upon the death of his grandmother," noted Lane, adding that he admitted that "it was a highly personal and challenging book to write." It is the story of Tommy, whose grandmother and great-grandmother both live in the same house with him. When he is very young, his great-grandmother dies; several years later, his grandmother passes away also. Remarking that "years later when the grandmother dies, he thinks of them both as Nana Upstairs," Sherrill added that "though the book deals with the death of loved ones, the focus is on affection and fond memories."

A companion piece to *Nana Upstairs and Nana Downstairs* is *Now One Foot, Now the Other,* which involves young Bobby and his grandfather, Bob, who enjoy doing many things together. When the grandfather suffers a stroke, though, Bobby helps him to learn to walk again. Indicating that the "explanations are forthright and appropriate to readers' level of understanding," Karen Harris added in *School Library Journal,* "The tone is gentle and low-key and the illustrations are, as usual, first-rate." Natalie Babbitt remarked in the *New York Times Book Review* that although "this is a big and difficult story compressed into a small and simple story," dePaola omits nothing and is able to "present a warm and positive picture of the power of love." She also found that "the illustrations are exactly

right. In calm browns and blues, with figures that are just realistic enough, they reinforce the straightforward tone of the prose."

Strega Nona: An Old Tale, which was named a Caldecott Honor Book and received the Nakamore Prize in Japan, is a traditional tale about a magic pot that, upon the recitation of a verse, produces food and ceases only with the recitation of another verse. In *Strega Nona* ("Grandmother Witch") has hired a helper, Anthony, who secretly observes her and believes that he too can make the pot perform magically. What Anthony has missed is that Strega Nona also blows three kisses to the pot to get it to stop. Chaos ensues, threatening the entire town. Strega Nona sets things right and chooses to punish Anthony not by hanging him, as the townspeople suggest, but by forcing him to eat all the pasta he has created—"an ending children will probably enjoy tremendously," remarked Zena Sutherland in *Bulletin of the Center for Children's Books.*

In *Helga's Dowry: A Troll Love Story,* the story of a beautiful but poor troll who accumulates a dowry and attracts the handsome king of the trolls as her suitor but discards him for another of her own choice, dePaola invents his own tale in the folktale tradition. According to Jennifer Dunning in the *New York Times Book Review,* dePaola's inspiration often comes from faculty-meeting doodles. "A troll appeared on the doodle pad," Mr. dePaola recalled. "I thought, 'Gee, must be a troll story inside me.' So I did a lot of research on trolls and found the women are condemned to wander the face of the earth if they have no dowry." DePaola's troll acquires her dowry from doing enormous tasks for others—cows for laundry, land for clearing trees; and, according to Sutherland in *Bulletin of the Center for Children's Books,* "Most of the fun is in Helga's magical despatch of loot-producing tasks." DePaola also has some very definite ideas about the presence of sexual stereotyping in children's books. According to Sherrill, dePaola has frequently said that he "consciously tries to avoid presenting sexual stereotypes, and certainly the independent Helga underscores that."

In *Fin M'Coul: The Giant of Knockmany Hill,* Celtic motifs frame the half-page illustrations and text involving the legendary Irish hero Cu Chulainn. M'Coul is huge and powerful good giant who is afraid of being beaten by Cucullin, who is larger than he is. M'Coul's clever wife comes to his rescue, and he appears dressed as a baby stuffed into a real cradle. Cucullin retreats fearing that if the giant M'Coul could produce a child the size of the baby before him, what must the father be like? "Fin M'Coul comes alive through Tomie dePaola's comic illustrating and retelling of this tale," wrote Fellis L. Jordan in *Children's Book Review Service*. "You can almost hear Fin's Irish brogue as you read the story." "Much as we may admire the sheer cleverness of the book it is the humour that lives longest in the mind," stated a reviewer in the *Junior Bookshelf*. "This is the perfect version of the immemorial theme of the triumph of cunning over force, and Mr. dePaola tells it for all it is worth."

Critics have repeatedly praised dePaola's illustrations, noting that he has an almost primitive style reminiscent of folk art. "Although colored inks and watercolors on handmade watercolor paper are used most frequently as a base for dePaola's books, he also uses pencil drawings, etchings, charcoal drawings, and other techniques," wrote Sherrill, adding that his "characters in the stories are made distinctive through dePaola's treatment of eyes, facial expressions, noses, hair, and mouths. Tousle-haired children have become an identifying characteristic of his work." Considering his use of color "distinctive," dePaola added, "I think my style of illustration has been refined over the years. Style has to do with the kinds of things you are drawn to personally, and I'm drawn to Romanesque and folk art. I think that my style is very close to those—very simple and direct. I simplify."

"The child dePaola once was shines through all his works, captivating readers and enriching the field of children's books," remarked Barbara Elleman in *Twentieth-Century Children's Writers*. This is especially true in dePaola's autobiographical series of chapter books. In the Newbery Honor winner *26 Fairmount Avenue*, the first in the series, five-year-old Tomie tells about moving from an apartment to his family's new and only house. Tomie also details his first day of kindergarten and "an unfortunate but funny episode with a laxative," noted *Booklist*'s Linda Perkins. "DePaola successfully evokes the voice of a precocious, inquisitive five-year-old everyone would want to befriend," concluded a *Publishers Weekly* contributor. Perkins also praised dePaola's writing, noting "the colloquial narrative gently meanders, introducing family, friends, and neighbors, noting holidays, and anticipating moving day."

Young Tomie continues his tales in *Here We All Are*, and *On My Way*, both of which are sequels to *26 Fairmount Avenue*. In *Here We All Are* the family is settled in their new house and Tomie continues kindergarten. Tomi begins tap-dancing lessons and takes a stand against his tough Italian grandmother. *On My Own* focuses on change as Tomie graduates kindergarten and enters first grade. The narrator also vividly describes his fears as his sister battles pneumonia. Noted a *Horn Book* reviewer about *On My Own*: "DePaola's writing and recollective skills are so fresh that kids will feel like he's sitting right next to them, telling his tales in and out of school with disarming charisma and not a hint of nostalgia."

In *Meet the Barkers: Morgan and Moffat Go to School*, dePaola introduces readers to two dogs dressed as elementary students, who are starting school. In *School Library Journal*, reviewer Wanda Meyers-Hines observed, "Moffie is smart, outspoken, and always has to be first." Moffie is proud of her elementary school accomplishments, especially her gold stars and ability to count to ten. Morgie, on the other hand, is most proud of his new friendship with a classmate who also likes dinosaurs. After the teacher talks to Moffie about always having to answer first in class, Moffie realizes that she has no friends, a situation that is quickly resolved. "Although never stated, the concept of complementary talents is very clear, and children will get the point," contended Perkins. A *Publishers Weekly* reviewer praised that "many of the situations here will strike a cord with young children and their parents, and dePaola's sunny, gently humorous acrylic paintings are as winning as ever."

DePaola continued the "Barkers" series with *Hide-and-Seek All Week*, *Boss for a Day*, *A New Barker in the House*, *T-Rex Is Missing*, and *Trouble in the Barkers' Class*. Of these, *A New Barker in the House* received the most critical attention because of the international adoption featured in the book. Moffie and Morgie learn that their parents are adopting Marcos, a Spanish-speaking three-year-old. When Marcos arrives, they teach him English and he, in turn, teaches them Spanish. "With Spanish words woven into the narrative, the bicultural intent of the story is obvious, but never didactic," noted Perkins. She added that the book is "brimming with dePaola's characterization, charm, and clarity." A contributor to *Kirkus Reviews* explained, "While the children's adjustment to the adoption may be a bit unrealistically smooth, their feelings of excitement will be familiar and contagious to readers."

"Of all the zillions of things that could be said about Tomie dePaola," observed Robert D. Hale in *Horn Book,* "the one that comes most strongly to mind is his exuberance. He is joyful, ebullient. His exhilaration fills all the spaces around him, wrapping everyone present in rare high spirits. The books he creates radiate this quality of good cheer, even when they have serious messages to impart. . . . Everything Tomie does is done with gusto and zest—which is why his work appeals to all generations. Tomie's softly colorful illustrations invite tots, while at the other end of the cycle adults appreciate his sharing of feelings." "For me," dePaola once remarked, "my expression is always the sum total of my personal experience with people. Not that it shows consciously or conspicuously, but it is the inner support that makes the terrifying experience of starting a new project less frightening."

BIOGRAPHICAL AND CRITICAL SOURCES:

BOOKS

Dictionary of Literary Biography, Volume 61, *American Writers for Children since 1960: Poets, Illustrators, and Nonfiction Authors,* Gale (Detroit, MI), 1987, pp. 15-26.

Kingman, Lee, and others, compilers, *Illustrators of Children's Books: 1957-1966,* Horn Book (Boston, MA), 1968.

Marquardt, Dorothy A., and Martha E. Ward, *Illustrators of Books for Young People,* Scarecrow Press (Metuchen, NJ), 1975.

Roginski, Jim, compiler, *Newbery and Caldecott Medalists and Honor Book Winners,* Libraries Unlimited (Littleton, CO), 1982.

Twentieth-Century Children's Writers, 3rd edition, St. James Press (Detroit, MI), 1989, pp. 279-281.

PERIODICALS

Booklist, February 15, 1992, Carolyn Phelan, review of *Jamie O'Rourke and the Big Potato: An Irish Folktale,* p. 1108; March 15, 1992, Hazel Rochman, review of *Patrick: Patron Saint of Ireland,* p. 1382; October 1, 1992, Ilene Cooper, review of *Jingle, the Christmas Clown,* p. 328; November 1, 1993, Carolyn Phelan, review of *Strega Nona Meets Her Match,* p. 730; May 1, 1994, Ilene Cooper, review of *Christopher: The Holy Giant,* p. 1603; May 15, 1994, Karen Harvey, review of *The Tale of Rabbit and Coyote,* p. 1678; August, 1994, Ilene Cooper, review of *The Legend of Poinsettia,* p. 2050; January 1, 1995, Carolyn Phelan, review of *The Unicorn and the Moon,* pp. 824-826, Ilene Cooper, review of *Kit and Kat,* p. 827; March 15, 1995, Ilene Cooper, review of *Alice Nizzy Nazzy: The Witch of Sante Fe,* p. 1334; September 1, 1995, Carolyn Phelan, review of *Mary: The Mother of Jesus,* p. 56; September 15, 1995, Carolyn Phelan, review of *Country Angel Christmas,* p. 169; March 15, 1996, Hazel Rochman, review of *The Baby Sister,* p. 1268; October 1, 1996, Ilene Cooper, review of *Mary,* p. 338; March 15, 1997, Susan Dove Lempke, review of *Days of the Blackbird: A Tale of Northern Italy,* p. 1247; July, 1997, Annie Ayres, review of *The Eagle and the Rainbow: Timeless Tales from Mexico,* pp. 1815-1817; September 15, 1997, Hazel Rochman, review of *Mice Squeak, We Speak,* p. 231; February 15, 1998, Michael Cart, review of *Nana Upstairs and Nana Downstairs,* p. 1020; May 15, 1998, Carolyn Phelan, review of *Bill and Pete to the Rescue,* p. 1629; November 15, 1998, Michael Cart, review of *Big Anthony: His Story,* p. 595, Isabel Schon, review of *La Leyenda de la flor de Nochebuena (The Legend of Poinsettia),* p. 599; January 1, 1999, Hazel Rochman, review of *Erandi's Braids,* p. 861; September 1, 1999, Ilene Cooper, review of *The Night of Las Posadas,* p. 147; August 9, 1999, review of *Andy: That's My Name,* p. 355; August, 1999, Linda Perkins, review of *26 Fairmount Avenue,* p. 2048; June, 2001, Linda Perkins, review of *Meet the Barkers: Morgan and Moffat Go to School,* p. 1890; February 1, 2002, Carolyn Phelan, review of *Boss for a Day,* p. 949, review of *Hide-and-Seek All Week,* p. 949; July, 2002, Linda Perkins, review of *A New Barker in the House,* pp. 1856-1858; August, 2002, Ilene Cooper, review of *Adelita: A Mexican Cinderella Story,* pp. 1967-1969; March, 2003, John Peters, review of *Things Will Never Be the Same,* pp. 1193-1195; April 1, 2003, Ilene Cooper, review of *Marcos Colors: Red, Yellow, Blue,* p. 1401, and review of *Adelita: A Mexican Cinderella Story,* pp. 1967-1969; John Peters, review of *Things Will Never Be the Same,* pp. 1193-1195.

Books for Your Children, summer, 1980, pp. 2-3.

Bulletin of the Center for Children's Books, October, 1973, pp. 24-25; November, 1975, p. 42; October, 1995, review of *Country Angel Christmas,* p. 14.

Chicago Tribune, February 13, 1989.

Children's Book Review Service, May, 1981, p. 81.

Children's Playmate, December, 1996, Samantha Hill, review of *Country Angel Christmas,* p. 13.

Entertainment Weekly, December 11, 1992, Michele Landsberg, review of *Jingle at Christmas,* p. 82; April 30, 1993, Leonard S. Marcus, review of *Tom,* p. 70.

Family Life, May 1, 2001, Sara Nelson, "Books," p. 89.

Hartford Courant (Hartford, CT), September 13, 1985.

Horn Book, April, 1974; August, 1975; October, 1975; November-December, 1985, pp. 770-772; January 15, 1993, Deborah Abbott, review of *Tom,* p. 898; July-August, 1993, Hanna B. Zeiger, review of *Tom,* p. 441; November-December, 1993, Hanna B. Zeiger, review of *Strega Nona Meets Her Match,* p. 730; May-June, 1994, Margaret M. Burns, review of *Christopher,* pp. 333-335, May-June, 1994, Elizabeth S. Watson, review of *The Tale of Rabbit and Coyote,* pp. 340-342; November-December, 1994, Hanna B. Zeiger, review of *The Legend of Poinsettia,* pp. 710-712; September 15, 1996, Carolyn Phelan, review of *Strega Nona: Her Story,* p. 246; January-February, Mary M. Burns, review of *Mary,* p. 89; November-December, 1996, Maria B. Salvadore, *Strega Nona: Her Story,* p. 722; March-April, 1997, Margaret A. Bush, review of *Days of the Blackbird,* p. 205; May, 1999, review of *26 Fairmount Avenue,* p. 351; March, 2001, review of *On My Way,* p. 228; March-April, 2002, Roger Sutton, review of *What a Year,* p. 228.

Instructor, April, 2003, Judy Freeman, review of *Adelita,* p. 55.

Junior Bookshelf, August, 1981, p. 144.

Kirkus Reviews, January 1, 2002, review of *What a Year,* p. 43; September 1, 2002, review of *Adelita,* pp. 1307-1309; November 1, 2002, review of *Four Friends at Christmas,* p. 1617; January 15, 2003, review of *Things Will Never Be the Same,* p. 141.

Language Arts, March, 1979.

New York Times Book Review, November 13, 1977, pp, 42, 45; September 20, 1981, p. 30.

Publishers Weekly, July 19, 1976; July 23, 1982; September 7, 1992, Elizabeth Devereaux, review of *My First Thanksgiving,* p. 62, and *Jingle, the Christmas Clown,* p. 67; January 25, 1993, review of *Tom,* p. 86; July 19, 1993, review of *Strega Nona Meets Her Match,* p. 251; November 1, 1993, review of *The Legend of the Persian Carpet,* p. 78; April 18, 1994, review of *The Tale of Rab-*bit and Coyote, p. 60; February 27, 1995, review of *Alice Nizzy Nazzy,* p. 103; September 18, 1995, review of *Country Angel Christmas,* p. 100; February 19, 1996, review of *The Baby Sister,* p. 214; July 26, 1996, review of *Strega Nona: Her Story,* p. 241; December 16, 1996, review of *Days of the Blackbird,* p. 59; April 18, 1997, review of *Mice Sqeak, We Speak,* p. 91; April 20, 1998, review of *Bill and Pete to the Rescue,* pp. 65-67; September 7, 1998, review of *Big Anthony,* p. 94; March 29, 1999, review of *26 Fairmount Avenue,* p. 105; April 12, 1999, review of *The Next Best Thing,* p. 29; September, 1999, review of *The Night of Las Posadas,* p. 60; April 16, 2001, review of *Bill and Pete to the Rescue,* p. 67; July 2, 2001, review of *Meet the Barkers,* p. 75; July 11, 2001, review of *Big Anthony,* p. 87; July 16, 2001, p. 150; August 27, 2001, review of *The Holy Twins: Benedict and Scholastica,* p. 82; February 4, 2002, p. 78; March 25, 2002, "Beginning Reader Buddies," p. 66; June 3, 2002, review of *On My Way,* p. 91; July 1, 2002, review of *Adelita,* p. 79.

Reading Teacher, December, 1979, pp. 264-269; November, 1995, review of *The Legend of the Poinsettia,* p. 253.

School Library Journal, September, 1973, p. 56; November, 1974, pp. 46-47; September, 1981, pp. 105-106; February, 1992, Jacqueline Elsner, review of *My First Halloween,* p. 72, and Jean H. Zimmerman, review of *The Great Adventure of Christopher Columbus,* p. 81; April, 1992, Lisa Dennis, review of *Jamie O'Rourke and the Big Potato,* p. 104; May, 1992, Lisa S. Murphy, review of *Patrick,* pp. 98-100; April, 1993, Karen James, review of *Tom,* p. 95; November, 1993, Rose Zertuch Trevino, review of *El Libro de las Arenas Movedizas,* p. 138, review of *El Libro de las nubes,* p. 138D; March, 1994, Joy Fleishhacker, review of *Christopher,* p. 60; October, 1994, Jane Marino, review of *The Legend of Poinsettia,* p. 30; May, 1996, Susan Hepler, review of *The Baby Sitter,* p. 91; March, 1997, Heide Piehler, review of *Days of the Blackbird,* p. 150; May, 1997, Teresa Bateman, "A Visit with Tomie dePaola," p. 81; October, 1997, Susan Garland, review of *Mice Squeak, We Speak,* p. 110; November 1, 1998, Sue Sherif, review of *Big Anthony,* p. 83; January, 1995, Emily Kutler, review of *I Love You, Sun; I Love You Moon,* p. 91; December, 1995, Patricia Pearl Dole, review of *Mary,* p. 96; October, 1995, review of *Country Angel Christmas,* p. 36; December, 1995, review of *Mary,* p. 96; October, 1996, Jane

Marino, review of *Get Dressed, Santa,* p. 34; October, 1996, Karen MacDonald, review of *Strega Nona: Her Story,* p. 91; May, 1998, Heide Piehler, review of *Bill and Pete to the Rescue,* p. 113; February, 1999, Ann Welton, review of *Erandi's Braids,* p. 87; June, 1999, Heide Piehler, review of *26 Fairmount Avenue,* p. 112; August, 2001, Coop Renner, review of *The Baby Sister,* p. S60, Wanda Meyers-Hines, review of *Meet the Barkers,* p. 146; September, 2001, Coop Renner, review of *The Baby Sister,* p. S60, Patricia Pearl Dole, review of *The Holy Twins: Benedict and Scholastica,* p. 220; February, 2002, Debbie Stewart, review of *Boss for a Day,* p. 98; March, 2002, Alice Casey Smith, review of *What a Year,* p. 209; April 8, 2002, "Ongoing Series," pp. 229-231; June, 2002, Shara Alpern, review of *A New Barker in the House,* p. 92; September, 2002, Ann Welton, review of *Adelita,* pp. 210-212; February, 2003, Patricia Manning, review of *T-Rex Is Missing,* p. 104.

Top of the News, April, 1976.

Wilson Library Bulletin, October, 1977; February, 1992, Donnarae McCann and Olga Richard, review of *The Great Adventure of Christopher Columbus: A Pop-Up Book,* p. 82; January, 1995, Donnarae McCann and Olga Richard, review of *I Love You, Sun; I Love You, Moon,* p. 120.

World of Children's Books, spring, 1978, pp. 38-39.*

* * *

dePAOLA, Tomie
See dePAOLA, Thomas Anthony

* * *

DICKSON, Athol 1955-

PERSONAL: First name is pronounced "ay-thole"; born 1955, in Tulsa, OK; son of a traveling salesman, and a homemaker; married; wife's name Sue. *Religion:* Christian. *Hobbies and other interests:* Travel in Mexico, flatbottom boating.

ADDRESSES: Home—Dallas, TX. *Agent*—c/o Author Mail, Tyndale House Publishers, 351 Executive Dr., Carol Stream, IL 60188.

CAREER: Writer, architect, entrepreneur. Has worked as salesman, boxer, carpenter, bartender; teaches Sunday School.

WRITINGS:

Whom Shall I Fear?, Zondervan Publishing (Grand Rapids, MI), 1996.
Every Hidden Thing, Zondervan Publishing (Grand Rapids, MI), 1998.
Kate and Ruth: A Novel, Zondervan Publishing (Grand Rapids, MI), 1999.
They Shall See God, Tyndale House Publishers (Wheaton, IL), 2002.
The Gospel according to Moses: What My Jewish Friends Taught Me about Jesus, Brazos Press (Grand Rapids, MI), 2003.

Contributor of short story "Hannah's Home" to anthology *The Storytellers' Collection: Tales of Faraway Places,* edited by Melody Carson, Multnomah (Sisters, OR), 2000.

ADAPTATIONS: Whom Shall I Fear? has been adapted for audio cassette.

SIDELIGHTS: Athol Dickson is a Christian writer and an architect who has designed hundreds of restaurants throughout the United States. His first novel is the Southern gothic murder mystery *Whom Shall I Fear?,* which he calls "a murder mystery with a spiritual subtheme." Dickson's protagonist, Garrison ("Garr") Reed, owner of a family construction business in the Deep South, discovers the body of his former partner and friend and becomes the prime suspect in the murder. As these circumstances unfold, Reed begins to doubt his belief in God. A significant part of the plot of *Whom Shall I Fear?* revolves around Reed's spiritual dilemma. John Mort, reviewing the novel for *Booklist,* described the plot as one in which the "trials that come with [Reed's] being a [murder] suspect force him to rely on God." He also commented that Dickson's "charm" lies in his characters.

Melissa Hudak, writing for *Library Journal,* called the book "a dark, Gothic tale of old hatreds and . . . vengeance." She commented that the character Reed's "need for Christian life" at times sets aside the mystery but makes it "an engrossing novel." A writer for the *Homer Public Library New Book List* described the story as one that "ends with not only justice but also redemption."

Garr Reed returns in Dickson's novel *Every Hidden Thing*. When Garr accompanies his mild-mannered wife, Mary Jo, to a Christian demonstration at an abortion clinic, the peaceful rally turns violent. A priest is fatally shot and the doctor wounded. Mary Jo arouses Reed's suspicion when she runs away from the protest and later begins acting strangely. Melissa Hudak, in a review for *Library Journal,* called the book a "taut, fast-paced mystery" that gives a "nonpreachy" voice to the debate over abortion.

Dickson's *They Shall See God* is another murder mystery, this time involving two women, Rabbi Ruth Gold and Protestant Kate Flint, who as children witnessed a brutal murder and helped put its perpetrator behind bars for twenty-five years. When the killer is released from prison, strange events seemingly taken from the biblical book of Genesis begin occurring in Ruth's Jewish community in New Orleans. Her boyfriend dies from eating a poisoned apple, zoo animals are released into the city, and a man kills his brother. At the same time, a radical group of Christians begins to picket Ruth's synagogue in hopes of converting the Jews to Christianity. A *Publishers Weekly* contributor thought the story was told from too many points of view and perhaps had more Jewish terms than the average reader would understand. However, the reviewer praised the original writing, humor, and plot twists, calling the novel a "highly entertaining nail-biter" that could "promote greater understanding between people of both faiths." A contributor to *Today's Christian Woman* found the book "a page-turning story of bitter prejudice and the hope of reconciliation."

Published in 2003, Dickson's *The Gospel according to Moses: What My Jewish Friends Taught Me about Jesus* is a nonfiction book taken from Dickson's experiences as an evangelical Christian participating in a Reform Jewish Bible study group, or Chever Torah, at the invitation of a friend. The author's years in the group helped him to develop the character of Rabbi Ruth Gold in *They Shall See God.* It also helped him to understand the tensions between Christians and Jews as each group clings to its preconceived notions about the other. Richard S. Watts, in a review for *Library Journal,* said the lengthy description of the study

group's discussions "make this book more scholarly than personal." However, Watts found that Dickson had learned to "ask questions and face difficult paradoxes" within Christianity. At the end of the book, the author states his strong faith in Christianity but does not preach, said Watts.

In an interview for *Today's Christian Woman,* Dickson said he continues to write his Christian-based novels because it gives him a chance to reach readers who are looking for an escape from everyday life. He told the interviewer: "Encountering a well-written novel with a Christian point of view, the doubter who trusts no sermon may willingly lift the veil from his imagination and peek beyond, thereby drawing near to the indescribable joy of knowing God."

BIOGRAPHICAL AND CRITICAL SOURCES:

PERIODICALS

Booklist, November, 1996, John Mort, review of *Whom Shall I Fear?,* p. 571; October 1, 2000, John Mort, review of *The Storytellers' Collection: Tales of Faraway Places.*
Christianity Today, May, 2003, review of *The Gospel according to Moses: What My Jewish Friends Taught Me about Jesus,* p.70.
Library Journal, November 1, 1996, Melissa Hudak, review of *Whom Shall I Fear?*; June 1, 1998, Melissa Hudak, review of *Every Hidden Thing,* p. 94; June 1, 2002, Melanie C. Duncan, review of *They Shall See God,* p. 122; February 1, 2003, Richard S. Watts, review of *The Gospel according to Moses,* p. 96.
Marriage Partnership, summer, 2002, review of *They Shall See God,* p. S5.
Publishers Weekly, April 29, 2002, review of *They Shall See God,* p. 42; March 4, 2003, review of *The Gospel according to Moses:,* p. S16.
Today's Christian Woman, May-June, 2002, review of *They Shall See God* and "An Author Speaks: Athol Dickson Explains Why He Takes Time to Write 'Mere Stories,'" p. 63.

ONLINE

Homer Library New Book List Web site, http://www.xyz.net/ (July 1, 1997), review of *Whom Shall I Fear?*

Tyndale House Publishers Web site, http://www. tyndale.com/ (March 7, 2003), "Athol Dickson."

Zondervan Publishing House Web site, http://www. zondervan.com/ (1998).*

*   *   *

DUBNER, Stephen J. 1963-

PERSONAL: Born August 26, 1963, in Schenectady, NY; son of Paul (a newspaperman) and Florence Veronica (Greenglass) Dubner; married Ellen Binder (a photographer). *Education:* Appalachian State University, graduate, 1984; Columbia University, M.F.A., 1990.

ADDRESSES: Agent—Suzanne Gluck, International Creative Management, 40 West 57th St., New York, NY 10019. *E-mail*—sdubner@mindspring.com.

CAREER: Journalist. *New York Times Magazine,* New York, NY, editor, 1994-99.

WRITINGS:

Turbulent Souls: A Catholic Son's Return to His Jewish Family, Morrow (New York, NY), 1998.
Confessions of a Hero Worshiper, Morrow (New York, NY), 2003.

SIDELIGHTS: The youngest of eight children in his Roman Catholic family, journalist Stephen J. Dubner decided to investigate his family history. In 1996 he published an article in the *New York Times Magazine* in which he recounted the discovery of his family's Jewish origins, his parents' conversion to Roman Catholicism, and his own return to the Jewish faith. When the article garnered interest, both positive and negative, Dubner expanded it into the memoir *Turbulent Souls: A Catholic Son's Return to His Jewish Family.* By using two narrative voices—telling his parents' story in the third person and his own in the first person—Dubner was able to include the viewpoints of other relatives, such as grandparents and siblings, as well.

Turbulent Souls captured reviewers' attention. John Moryl, writing in *Library Journal,* remarked that the memoir "reads like a novel," and predicted that most readers "would find the story fascinating." Likewise, a *Publishers Weekly* critic found the work to be "searching," "poignant," and "captivating." Writing in the *New York Times Book Review,* contributor Jonathan Wilson praised Dubner for his "intense" and acute observations as well as his "splendidly evoked" scenes of life in the family's ramshackle farmhouse in upstate New York. Wilson also found it interesting that, compared with his parents' radical Catholicism, Dubner's practicing of his Jewish faith was much less devout. Charles Colson, writing for *Good News,* saw Dubner's experience as typical of many Americans who "shop for faith" rather than believing in a religion because it is true.

Dubner followed up with another very personal book on the quest for self-awareness, this time focusing on the intense bond that can develop between a fan and a star athlete. Since the age of ten, when his father died, Dubner had idolized Pittsburgh Steelers running back Franco Harris, whose "Immaculate Reception" in 1972 lives on in football lore. In *Confessions of a Hero Worshiper* Dubner recounts that boyhood fascination and his efforts to track down Harris in adulthood. While Dubner does get to meet his idol, his hope of getting Harris to collaborate on a book about the relationship between hero and worshiper ultimately proves futile. Instead, Dubner provides a "veritable *Searching for Bobby Fisher* for sports fans," wrote *Booklist* reviewer Gilbert Taylor, as Harris cancels or simply misses subsequent interviews and Dubner finds himself placing frantic calls to Harris's acquaintances in an effort to understand the man behind the football legend. Frustrated in his attempt at a true collaboration, Dubner instead tries to illuminate the mysterious hold that this substitute father-figure had on his adolescence. The result is "primarily a psychological memoir," according to a *Kirkus Reviews* contributor. While finding this approach "somewhat disjointed," a *Publishers Weekly* reviewer concluded that "Dubner's elegant, deeply honest writing will keep readers engaged."

BIOGRAPHICAL AND CRITICAL SOURCES:

PERIODICALS

Booklist, February 15, 2003, Gilbert Taylor, review of *Confessions of a Hero Worshiper,* p. 1031.
Kirkus Reviews, December 1, 2002, review of *Confessions of a Hero Worshiper,* p. 1747.

Library Journal, January, 1999, John Moryl, review of *Turbulent Souls: A Catholic Son's Return to His Jewish Family,* p. 105.

New York Times Book Review, November 8, 1998, Jonathan Wilson, review of *Turbulent Souls,* p. 10.

Publishers Weekly, October 26, 1998, review of *Turbulent Souls,* p. 61; December 16, 2002, review of *Confessions of a Hero Worshiper,* p. 54.

ONLINE

Good News, http://www.goodnewsmag.com/jan98/colson.htm/ (February 2, 1999), Charles Colson.

Stephen J. Dubner Web site, http://www.stephenjdubner.com/ (November 15, 2003).*

*   *   *

DURANG, Christopher (Ferdinand) 1949-

PERSONAL: Born January 2, 1949, in Montclair, NJ; son of Francis Ferdinand and Patricia Elizabeth Durang. *Education:* Harvard University, B.A., 1971; Yale University, M.F.A., 1974. *Religion:* "Raised Roman Catholic."

ADDRESSES: Office—Creative Artists Agency, 9830 Wilshire Blvd., Beverly Hills, CA 90212-1804. *Agent*—Helen Merrill, Helen Merrill Agency, 337 West 22nd St., New York, NY 10011-2607.

CAREER: Yale Repertory Theatre, New Haven, CT, actor, 1974; Southern Connecticut College, New Haven, teacher of drama, 1975; Yale University, New Haven, teacher of playwriting, 1975-76; playwright, 1976-. Actor in plays, including *The Idiots Karamazov* and *Das Lusitania Songspiel;* actor in film and television, including *The Secret of My Success, Joe's Apartment, Mr. North, Housesitter, The Butcher's Wife, The Cowboy Way, Penn and Teller Get Killed,* and *Fraiser;* director of plays. Currently cochair of the playwriting program at Juilliard.

MEMBER: Dramatists Guild, Writers Guild, Actors Equity Association, American Society of Composers, Authors, and Publishers.

Christopher Durang

AWARDS, HONORS: Fellow of Columbia Broadcasting System (CBS), 1975-76; Rockefeller Foundation grant, 1976-77; Guggenheim fellow, 1978-79; Antoinette Perry Award (Tony) nomination for best book of a musical, League of New York Theatres and Producers, 1978, for *A History of the American Film;* grant from Lecomte du Nouy Foundation, 1980-81; off-Broadway Award (Obie), *Village Voice,* 1980, for *Sister Mary Ignatius Explains It All for You,* and 1999, for *Betty's Summer Vacation;* Kenyon Festival Playwriting award, 1983; Hull-Warriner Award, Dramatists Guild, 1985; Lila Wallace-*Reader's Digest* Fund Writer's Award, 1994-96.

WRITINGS:

PLAYS

The Nature and Purpose of the Universe (first produced in Northampton, MA, 1971; produced in New York, NY, 1975), Dramatists Play Service (New York, NY), 1979.

Robert, first produced in Cambridge, MA, 1971; produced as *'dentity Crisis* in New Haven, CT, 1975.

Better Dead Than Sorry, first produced in New Haven, CT, 1972; produced in New York, NY, 1973.

(With Albert Innaurato) *I Don't Generally Like Poetry, But Have You Read "Trees"?,* first produced in New Haven, CT, 1972; produced in New York, NY, 1973.

(With Albert Innaurato) *The Life Story of Mitzi Gaynor; or, Gyp,* first produced in New Haven, CT, 1973.

The Marriage of Betty and Boo (first produced in New Haven, CT, 1973; revised version produced in New York, NY, 1979), Dramatists Play Service, 1985.

(With Albert Innaurato) *The Idiots Karamazov* (first produced in New Haven at Yale Repertory Theatre, October 10, 1974), Dramatists Play Service (New York, NY), 1980.

Titanic (first produced in New Haven, CT, 1974; produced off-Broadway at Van Dam Theatre, May 10, 1976), Dramatists Play Service (New York, NY), 1983.

Death Comes to Us All, Mary Agnes, first produced in New Haven, CT, 1975.

(With Wendy Wasserstein) *When Dinah Shore Ruled the Earth,* first produced in New Haven, CT, 1975.

(With Sigourney Weaver) *Das Lusitania Songspiel,* first produced off-Broadway at Van Dam Theatre, May 10, 1976.

A History of the American Film (first produced in Hartford, CT, at Eugene O'Neill Playwrights Conference, summer, 1976; produced on Broadway at American National Theatre, March 30, 1978), Avon (New York, NY), 1978.

The Vietnamization of New Jersey (first produced in New Haven, CT, at Yale Repertory Theatre, October 1, 1976), Dramatists Play Service (New York, NY), 1978.

Sister Mary Ignatius Explains It All for You (first produced in New York City at Ensemble Studio Theatre, December, 1979), Dramatists Play Service (New York, NY), 1980; adapted for film as *Sister Mary Explains It All,* Showtime, 2001.

The Nature and Purpose of the Universe, Death Comes to Us All, Mary Agnes, 'dentity Crisis: Three Short Plays, Dramatists Play Service (New York, NY), 1979.

Beyond Therapy (first produced off-Broadway at Phoenix Theatre, January 5, 1981), Samuel French (New York, NY), 1983.

The Actor's Nightmare (first produced in New York at Playwrights Horizons, October 21, 1981), Dramatists Play Service (New York, NY), 1982.

Christopher Durang Explains It All for You (contains *The Nature and Purpose of the Universe, 'dentity Crisis, Titanic, The Actor's Nightmare, Sister Mary Ignatius Explains It All for You,* and *Beyond Therapy,*) Avon (New York, NY), 1982.

Baby with the Bathwater (first produced in Cambridge, MA, 1983; produced in New York, NY, 1983), Dramatists Play Service (New York, NY), 1984.

Sloth, first produced in Princeton, NJ, 1985.

Laughing Wild, first produced in New York, NY, 1987; Dramatists Play Service (New York, NY), 1996.

Cardinal O'Connor [and] *Woman Stand-Up,* first produced as part of musical revue *Urban Blight,* New York, NY, 1988.

Chris Durang and Dawne (cabaret), first produced in New York, NY, 1990.

Naomi in the Living Room, first produced in New York, NY, 1991.

Media Amok, first produced in Boston, MA, 1992.

Putting It Together, first produced in New York, NY, 1993.

Shaken, Not Stirred, first produced at Fountainhead Theater in Los Angeles, CA, 1993.

For Whom the Southern Belle Tolls, first produced in New York, NY, 1994.

Durang Durang (six short plays, including *For Whom the Southern Belle Tolls* and *A Stye in the Eye*), first produced in New York, NY, 1994.

Twenty-seven Short Plays, Smith & Kraus (Lyme, NH), 1995.

Collected Works, Smith & Kraus (Lyme, NH), 1995.

Sister Mary Ignatius Explains It All for You; and The Actor's Nightmare: Two Plays, Dramatists Play Service (New York, NY), 1995.

Complete Full-Length Plays, Smith & Kraus (Lyme, NH), 1996.

Sex and Longing, first produced at Cort Theater, 1996.

Betty's Summer Vacation, Grove Press (New York, NY), 1999.

Wanda's Visit, first produced at Blue Heron Arts Center, New York, NY, 2001.

Monologues, edited by Erick Kraus, Smith & Kraus (Hanover, NH), 2002.

Also author, with Robert Altman, of screenplay *Beyond Therapy,* 1987. Writer for television series *Comedy Zone* and for the *Carol Burnett Special.* Lyricist of songs for plays.

SIDELIGHTS: Early in Christopher Durang's career, a *New York Times* reviewer included him in the constellation of "new American playwrights," dramatists such as Michael Cristofer, Albert Innaurato, David Mamet, and Sam Shepard who follow in the footsteps of Tennessee Williams, Arthur Miller, and Edward Albee. Writers like Durang, the reviewer explained, "are not one-play writers—a home run and back to the dugout—but artists with staying power and growing bodies of work."

Stylistically, Durang specializes in collegiate humor. He deals in cartoons and stereotypes, employing mechanical dialogue and brand names to exploit clichés. In his works for the stage, Durang has parodied drama, literature, movies, families, the Catholic church, show business, and society. But his lampoons are not vicious or hostile; they are controlled comedies. He "is a parodist without venom," wrote *Horizon* magazine contributor Antonio Chemasi. "At the moment he fixes his pen on a target, he also falls in love with it. His work brims with an unlikely mix of acerbity and affection and at its best spills into a compassionate criticism of life."

Durang's first target as a professional playwright was literature. In 1974 the Yale Repertory Theatre produced *The Idiots Karamazov,* a satire of Dostoyevsky's *The Brothers Karamazov.* The play, featuring Durang in a leading role, was praised by critics for its "moments of comic inspiration." "I was . . . impressed—with their [Durang's and coauthor Albert Innaurato's] wit as well as their scholarship," Mel Gussow stated in the *New York Times.* The playwright followed *The Idiots Karamazov* by collaborating with well-known actress Sigourney Weaver on *Das Lusitania Songspiel,* a musical travesty that met with critical and popular success.

Durang's major success of the 1970s was *A History of the American Film,* for which he was nominated for a Tony Award in 1978. A tribute to movie mania, the play illustrates America's perceptions of Hollywood from 1930 to the present. *A History of the American Film* parodies some two hundred motion pictures and chronicles the evolution of movie stereotypes in American culture. There are five characters: a tough gangster typified by James Cagney, an innocent Loretta Young type, a sincere guy, a temptress, and a girl who never gets the man of her dreams. The production parodies movies such as *The Grapes of Wrath, Citizen*

Kane, and *Casablanca.* Show girls dressed up like vegetables satirize the razzmatazz of big Hollywood productions by singing "We're in a Salad." And the character portraying Paul Henreid's role in *Now, Voyager* is forced to smoke two cigarettes when Bette Davis's character refuses one because she does not smoke. "In Durang's hands," wrote *Time* critic Gerald Clarke, "the familiar images always take an unexpected turn, however, and he proves that there is nothing so funny as a cliché of a different color."

After the success of *A History of the American Film,* Durang wrote two satires of suburban families: *The Vietnamization of New Jersey* and *The Nature and Purpose of the Universe,* as well as a parody of the Catholic church, *Sister Mary Ignatius Explains It All for You.* Called a "savage cartoon" by Mel Gussow, *Sister Mary Ignatius Explains It All for You* uses the character of an elderly nun to expose the hypocrisies of Catholicism. The nun, Gussow observed, is "a self-mocking sister [who] flips pictures of hell, purgatory and heaven as if they are stops on a religious package tour." Her list of the damned includes David Bowie, Betty Comden, and Adolph Green, and she lists hijacking planes alongside murder as a mortal sin. "Anyone can write an angry play—all it takes is an active spleen," observed Rich. "But only a writer of real talent can write an angry play that remains funny and controlled even in its most savage moments. *Sister Mary Ignatius Explains It All for You* confirms that Christopher Durang is just such a writer." The play was also adapted as a film for Showtime Television.

In October, 1981, the Obie-winning *Sister Mary Ignatius* was presented on the same playbill as *The Actor's Nightmare,* a satire of show business and the theater. Using the play-within-a-play technique for *The Actor's Nightmare,* Durang illustrates the comedy that ensues when an actor is forced to appear in a production he has never rehearsed. Earlier in 1981 the Phoenix Theatre produced Durang's *Beyond Therapy,* a parody in which a traditional woman, Prudence, and a bisexual man, Bruce, meet through a personal ad, only to have their relationship confounded by their psychiatrists. Hers is a lecherous, he-man Freudian; his is an absent-minded comforter. "Some of Durang's satire . . . is sidesplitting," commented a *New York* reviewer, "and there are many magisterial digs at our general mores, amores, and immores."

A writer heaped with honors early in his career may begin to feel the weight of the mantle later on. *Daily*

News reviewer Douglas Watt wrote of Durang's 1983 drama, *Baby with the Bathwater,* Durang "continues to write like a fiendishly clever undergrad with some fresh slants but an inability to make them coalesce into a fully sustained evening of theater." Frank Rich, writing in the *New York Times,* commented: "We can't ignore that Act I of *Baby with the Bathwater* is a strained variation on past Durang riffs. We're so inured by now to this writer's angry view of parental authority figures that at intermission we feel like shaking him and shouting: 'Enough already! Move on!'" *New York Magazine* contributor John Simon sounded a similar theme: "Christopher Durang is such a funny fellow that his plays cannot help being funny; now, if they could only help being so undisciplined. . . . Free-floating satire and rampant absurdism are all very well, but even the wildest play must let its characters grow in wildness and match up mouth with jokes." But *Nation* reviewer Eliot Sirkin stated that Durang "is, at heart, a writer who divides humanity into the humiliators and the humiliated." Sirkin compared Durang's methods to those of Tennessee Williams: "When Williams created an overwhelming woman, he didn't create a psychopathic fiend—at least not always. . . . Durang's witches are *just* witches."

Durang's next play, *The Marriage of Bette and Boo,* draws from the playwright's own childhood. *New York Post* reviewer Clive Barnes summarized the characters: "The father was a drunk, the mother rendered an emotional cripple largely by her tragic succession of still-born children, the grandparents were certifiably nutty, the family background stained with the oppression of the Roman Catholic Church, and the son himself is primarily absorbed in a scholarly enquiry into the novels of Thomas Hardy. Just plain folks!" *New York Times* critic Frank Rich explained, "*Bette and Boo* is sporadically funny and has been conceived with a structural inventiveness new to the writer's work. . . . But at the same time, Mr. Durang's jokemaking is becoming more mannered and repetitive. . . . *Bette and Boo* has a strangely airless atmosphere." *New York Magazine* critic John Simon wrote, "Christopher Durang's latest, *The Marriage of Bette and Boo,* is more recycling than writing. Here again, the quasi-autobiographical boy-hero growing up absurd." A *Contemporary Dramatists* writer was more complimentary about this play, calling *The Marriage of Bette and Boo* "a trenchantly amusing dissection of the contemporary Catholic family. . . . The playwright gives an outrageously satiric view of society that characterizes his best work."

In a 1990 *Chicago Tribune* interview with Richard Christiansen, Durang revealed that he felt "burned out on New York, and that includes its theater." For a time Durang left the theater to tour with a one-hour cabaret act, *Chris Durang and Dawne.* Durang explained his "premise" to Christiansen: "I was fed up with being a playwright and had decided to form my own lounge act with two back-up singers and go on a tour of Ramada Inns across the country."

In 1992 Durang returned to the theater with *Media Amok,* a lampoon of the characters and obsessions of television talk shows. Noting its content, Durang told *Boston Globe* critic Kevin Kelly that he had become "more political." The play features an elderly couple watching television talk shows which assault them constantly with the same three topics: abortion, gay rights, and racial tension. All of the topics are handled in a flippant and inflammatory fashion.

In 1994 *Durang Durang,* a series of six sketches taking swipes at fellow playwrights Tennessee Williams, Sam Shepard and David Mamet, debuted in New York City. One section, the one-act play titled *For Whom the Southern Belle Tolls,* is a parody of *The Glass Menagerie,* while *A Stye in the Eye* focuses on Shepard's typical cowboy characters. In a *New Yorker* review, Nancy Franklin called the play "Beckett with a joy buzzer. . . . Sitting through *Durang Durang* is a little like going on the bumper cars at an amusement park: you're so caught up in the exhilarating hysteria that it doesn't matter to you that you're not actually going anywhere except—momentarily, blissfully—outside yourself." In a *New York Times* review, Ben Brantley described *Durang Durang* as "endearing and exasperating . . . juvenile and predictable."

Lulu, a nymphomaniac, and Justin, a nearly as insatiable homosexual, share an apartment in the play *Sex and Longing.* A philandering and drunkard senator and his puritanical wife, as well as a reverend from the political right, also figure into the plot. *Newsweek* critic Marc Peyser remarked: "This intersection of sex, religion, hypocrisy and spiritual emptiness was bracing two decades ago . . . now it's trite and labored and, worst of all, almost devoid of humor." *New York* critic John Simon, who thought the play's humorlessness stems from its silliness bordering on the ridiculous, wrote that the play "is strictly anti-realistic absurdist farce, but even as such it ought to know where it is going. . . . It is all rather like automatic writing with a glitch in the automation." *Variety* contributor Greg Evans noted that Durang "can mine any laughs at all from such perversity," noting that the "characters [are] so broadly drawn that to call them stereotypes would be an understatement." Still, Evans observed, "Despite his misstep here, the playwright retains a distinctive voice—one that finds its way even through the indulgences of this play."

Durang's 1999 effort, *Betty's Summer Vacation,* is "a summer sandstorm of horrifying fun," according to Everett Evans in the *Houston Chronicle.* The critic explained, "Sensible, normal Betty has come to a seaside 'summer share' with a simple wish for rest and quiet. As soon as we meet the fellow tenants to which fate has subjected her, we realize this is to be a comedy of excruciating frustration." These characters include a very talkative victim of childhood incest, a serial killer, and a flasher. Steven Winn, reviewing a local production of the play for the *San Francisco Chronicle,* mentioned the chorus of voices that Durang included in the script. "These offstage voices are the American public," wrote Winn, and "the whole thing's a kind of tabloid catharsis, like waking up from a bad dream and finding yourself in the studio audience of *The Jerry Springer Show.*" As Holly Hildebrand explained in *Back Stage West,* "Who better to take a poke—not to mention quite a number of stabs—at this bizarre entertainment business than Durang, who's never shrunk from satirizing American society and culture." Durang premiered a briefer effort, *Wanda's Visit,* in 2001. Laura Weinert, also reviewing for *Back Stage West,* summed it up as "the lighter side of Durang, an uproarious glimpse at what happens when the world of tired, static marrieds Marsha and Jim is upset by a surprise knock on the door by Jim's high school sweetheart Wanda."

BIOGRAPHICAL AND CRITICAL SOURCES:

BOOKS

American Theatre Annual, 1979-1980, Gale (Detroit, MI), 1981.

Contemporary Dramatists, 6th edition, St. James Press (Detroit, MI), 1999.

Contemporary Literary Criticism, Gale (Detroit, MI), Volume 27, 1984, Volume 38, 1986.

PERIODICALS

Advocate, April 27, 1999, Don Shewey, review of *Betty's Summer Vacation,* p. 79.

American Theatre, December, 1999, Christopher Durang, "An Interview with the Playwright by Himself," review of *Betty's Summer Vacation,* p. 37.

Atlanta Constitution, March 18, 1994, p. P17.

Back Stage West, April 7, 2000, Karl Levett, "Durang, Durang and More Durang," p. 42; July 27, 2000, Brad Schreiber, review of *The Marriage of Bette and Boo,* p. 18; February 15, 2001, Madeleine Shaner, review of *Baby with the Bathwater,* p. 13; May 24, 2001, Holly Hildebrand, "Durang Delivers," p. 11; August 15, 2002, Kristina Mannion, "*Sister Mary Ignatius Explains It All for You* and *The Nature and Purpose of the Universe* at the Empire Theater," p. 23; September 19, 2002, Laura Weinert, "Durang, Make It a Double! at the Complex," p. 13, and Gi-Gi Downs, "*Beyond Therapy* at the Cassius Carter Centre Stage," p. 13.

Boston Globe, March 22, 1992, p. B25.

Chicago Tribune, January 21, 1990.

Daily News (New York, NY), March 31, 1978; November 9, 1983.

Entertainment Weekly, April 16, 1993, p. 31.

Horizon, March, 1978.

Houston Chronicle, May 7, 2001, Everett Evans, "Pack Your Bags for Comic *Betty's Summer Vacation,*" p. 5.

Library Journal, August, 1997, Howard E. Miller, "Complete Full-Length Plays," p. 86.

Los Angeles Times, August 11, 1989, p. 8; November 25, 1994, p. 1.

Nation, April 15, 1978; February 18, 1984, pp. 202-204.

New Leader, October 7, 1996, Stefan Kanfer, review of *Sex and Longing,* p. 23.

New Republic, April 22, 1978.

Newsweek, April 10, 1978; October 21, 1996, Marc Peyser, review of *Sex and Longing,* p. 89.

New York, April 17, 1978; January 19, 1981; October 23, 1989, p. 166; November 28, 1994, p. 76; October 21, 1996, pp. 76-77; March 29, 1999, John Simon, review of *Betty's Summer Vacation,* p. 46.

New Yorker, May 24, 1976; April 10, 1978; January 19, 1981; November 28, 1994, pp. 153-55.

New York Magazine, November 21, 1983, pp. 65-68; June 3, 1985, pp. 83-84.

New York Post, March 31, 1978; November 9, 1983; December 12, 1983, p. 80; May 17, 1985, pp. 268-269.

New York Times, November 11, 1974; February 13, 1977; March 17, 1977; May 11, 1977; August 21, 1977; June 23, 1978; December 27, 1978; February 24, 1979; December 21, 1979; February 8,

1980; August 6, 1980; January 6, 1981; October 22, 1981; November 9, 1983, p. C21; May 17, 1985, p. 3; June 27, 1994, p. C13; November 14, 1994, p. 11; March 14, 1999, Bob Morris, review of *Betty's Summer Vacation,* p. AR7; March 15, 1999, Ben Brantley, review of *Betty's Summer Vacation,* p. E1; January 15, 2001, Sarah Boxer, review of *The Idiots Karamazov,* p. B9; May 25, 2001, Caryn James, review of *Sister Mary Ignatius Explains It All for You,* p. E23.

San Francisco Chronicle, May 22, 2001, Steven Winn, "*Vacation* Feeds on Craving for Sex and Gore; Actors Theatre Takes on Durang's Biting Satire," p. B5.

Saturday Review, May 27, 1978.

Time, May 23, 1977.

USA Today, May 17, 1985.

Variety, November 14, 1994, p. 54; October 14-20, 1996, p. 72; March 22, 1999, Charles Isherwood, review of *Betty's Summer Vacation,* p. 46; May 28, 2001, Steven Oxman, review of *Sister Mary Ignatius Explains It All for You,* p. 29.

Washington Post, December 11, 1994, p. 4.

Women's Wear Daily, May 20, 1985.

World Literature Today, summer, 1991, p. 487.

ONLINE

Moonstruck Web site, http://www.imagi-nation.com/moonstruck/ (May 1, 2003), author profile.*

*   *   *

DURRANT, Lynda 1954-

PERSONAL: Born December 17, 1954, in Cleveland, OH; daughter of Oliver (an engineer) and Shirley (a teacher; maiden name, Petersen) Durrant; married Wesley Lemmon (an executive), May 27, 1989; children: Jonathan. *Education:* University of Washington—Seattle, B.A., 1979, M.A., 1982, M.A.T. *Politics:* "Moderate." *Religion:* Congregationalist. *Hobbies and other interests:* Horses.

ADDRESSES: Home and office—P.O. Box 123, Bath, OH 44210.

CAREER: Writer and teacher.

MEMBER: Society of Children's Book Writers and Illustrators.

AWARDS, HONORS: Young Adult Choice Award, International Reading Association, and Books for the Teenage selection, New York Public Library (NYPL), both for *Echohawk;* Notable Children's Trade Book in the Field of Social Studies selection, National Council for the Social Studies/Children's Book Council, 1998, Ohioana Book Award (juvenile category), Ohioana Library Association (OLA), 1999, and Books for the Teenage selection, NYPL, all for *The Beaded Moccasins: The Story of Mary Campbell;* Ohioana Book Award (juvenile category), OLA, 2001, Quick Picks selection, American Library Association, 2001, and Books for the Teenage selection, NYPL, all for *Betsy Zane, the Rose of Fort Henry.*

WRITINGS:

Echohawk, Clarion Books (New York, NY), 1996.

The Beaded Moccasins: The Story of Mary Campbell, Clarion Books (New York, NY), 1998.

Turtle Clan Journey, Clarion Books (New York, NY), 1999.

Betsy Zane, the Rose of Fort Henry, Clarion Books (New York, NY), 2000.

The Sun, the Rain, and the Apple Seed: A Novel of Johnny Appleseed's Life, Clarion Books (New York, NY), 2003.

Contributor to periodicals such as *Jack and Jill* and *Beehive.*

SIDELIGHTS: "Even when I was a young reader, I knew that I wanted to write for young readers," Lynda Durrant once told *CA.* "I write to a child's enthusiasm, curiosity, and more than anything else, a child's willingness to suspend his disbelief. A children's book could seem outlandish, even repulsive, in any other medium. Children give the writer the benefit of the doubt. That's what makes children's books so special."

Durrant's historical young adult novels focus on pioneer days and on the lives, legends, and hardships of the many U.S. settlers and the Native Americans who encountered them. In *Echohawk,* Durrant's first novel, Jonathan is kidnapped and his family slain by Mohicans, who fully adopt him and teach him their language and their ways. Having become more a Mohican than a white settler, Jonathan, or Echohawk as he is known, strives to reconcile the two worlds that harbor significant parts of his life.

In *Turtle Clan Journey,* the stand-alone sequel to *Echohawk,* young Jonathan/Echohawk is on the cusp of adulthood as he, his adopted father, and his brother are forced to flee from the Ohio Territory. The last of their clan, the trio must keep ahead of the government-sponsored hunters seeking to reclaim any white captives from Native-American bands. Inevitably, Echohawk is ambushed by soldiers and sent to live with his Aunt Ruth in a white settlement in Albany, New York, but he quickly learns that the trivial comforts of the white man's village are no substitute for the freedom and independence found as a member of the Mohican clan. During Echohawk's scenes in the settlement, "Durrant does what she does best, sympathetically balancing the differences between Mohican and colonial attitudes," thought a *Kirkus Reviews* critic. Roger Helmer, writing in *Book Report,* thought that the book's plot, detailed characterization, and "wonderful attention to historic detail take this tale to a level beyond the traditional captivity story." The young teenager "remains a sympathetic protagonist," wrote Michael Cart in *Booklist,* noting that "readers who enjoyed Durrant's first novel will want to read the sequel."

The Beaded Moccasins: The Story of Mary Campbell is a "strong fictionalization" of the real-life kidnapping of twelve-year-old Mary Campbell by Delaware Indians in 1759 Pennsylvania, wrote Hazel Rochman in *Booklist.* Intended to replace the deceased granddaughter of the Delaware chief, Mary is snatched from her family farm in Connecticut and taken on a grueling trip across Pennsylvania, New York, and Ohio into Delaware territory. Mary, along with neighbor Mary Stewart and her toddler son, are forced to walk for miles to the Dakota reservation. Along the way, the fussy child is killed and scalped because he slows the party's progress, and Mary Stewart is traded to a French merchant near Lake Erie. Mary Campbell is fully adopted into the Dakota family, and she struggles to adjust to the difficult life and physical hardships shared by the Dakota. Although she yearns for the comforts of her previous life and early on looks for ways to escape, she eventually learns and accepts the Dakota lifestyle. "In fact, she loves her new family as much as she ever loved her old one," observed Claire Rosser in *Kliatt.* "She was treated at all times as a member of the family, but of course that meant sharing the hard work and hardships" faced by everyone in the tribe, Rosser added. Elizabeth Bush, writing in the *Bulletin of the Center for Children's Books,* remarked that "Durrant's exceptionally graceful prose and nonjudgmental description of the cultural chasm between the colonists' and Delawares' worlds set this novel apart" from other novels addressing similar subjects. "The abundant details of the daily habits of the tribe will be beneficial for students," commented Joyce Sparrow in *Voice of Youth Advocates,* adding, "The story of an adolescent forced to adapt to a different culture is fascinating." Durrant's audience "will be moved by the psychological truth of [Mary's] adjustment and her yearning to prove herself and belong," concluded Hazel Rochman in *Booklist.*

Another brave frontier girl is the central character in *Betsy Zane, the Rose of Fort Henry,* a book that reviewer Catherine T. Quattlebaum, writing in *School Library Journal,* called "a compelling work of period fiction strongly rooted in fact." Twelve-year-old Betsy Zane lives with her Great Aunt Elizabeth in Revolutionary War-era Philadelphia, a town that Betsy finds barely tolerable. Her brothers had sent her there to avoid the dangers of war in their home state of Virginia, but when her aunt dies, Betsy is left alone and has little choice but to rejoin her family. She arranges her aunt's funeral, takes care of necessary business affairs, and heads off to join her brothers near Fort Henry. Her brothers are initially angry at her sudden appearance in a war zone, but Betsy soon proves herself and single-handedly delivers a critical shipment of gunpowder to the soldiers at Fort Henry, sustaining the fort during the siege that became the final battle of the Revolutionary War. Afterward, Betsy encounters cultural prejudices against women, reconsiders her own ideas about slavery, and learns more about herself, her family, and her country. Durrant "has delved deeply into the complex, shifting relations between European settlers and native populations, and she depicts a wide range of attitudes among the Zane family," observed John Peters in *Booklist.* "Exhaustively researched, Durrant's story successfully brings the remarkable Zane family members to life," Quattlebaum remarked.

The Sun, the Rain, and the Appleseed: A Novel of Johnny Appleseed's Life is Durrant's fictionalized biography of John Chapman, the famed historical figure whose sometimes bizarre behavior and single-minded determination gave life to the legend of Johnny Appleseed. Chapman's early childhood experiences of planting apple seeds with his father and watching the apple trees grow and bear fruit led to his adult mission in life, when he decided in 1799 that he would travel the frontiers in Illinois, Indiana, and Ohio, planting apple seeds and ensuring a supply of fruit for later settlers. Chapman's goals were admirable, but sometimes his behavior was odd. He occasionally wore a stew pot for a hat; he talked to angels and spirits; he claimed to be married to a pair of stars he called his spirit-wives; and even his casual conversation with other people was filled with Biblical quotations and verses. However, Chapman was also known to be brave and concerned for others, reportedly once running nonstop for three days and nights to warn some settlers of an impending native attack. Eventually, his sincerity and charm won over many people worried about his odd behaviors. In an afterword, Durrant expands on the historical details of Chapman's life. Gillian Engberg, writing in *Booklist,* remarked that "Durrant creates a vivid portrayal of a historical legend with a powerful vision," and Kristen Oravec noted in *School Library Journal* that Durrant's Chapman "is well delineated."

BIOGRAPHICAL AND CRITICAL SOURCES:

PERIODICALS

Booklist, September 1, 1996, p. 118; March 15, 1998, Hazel Rochman, review of *The Beaded Mocca-sins: The Story of Mary Campbell,* pp. 1233-1234; May 1, 1999, Michael Cart, review of *Turtle Clan Journey,* p. 1585; September 15, 2000, John Peters, review of *Betsy Zane, the Rose of Fort Henry,* p. 240; May 15, 2003, Gillian Engberg, review of *The Sun, the Rain, and the Appleseed: A Novel of Johnny Appleseed's Life,* p. 1665.

Book Report, November, 1999, Roger Helmer, review of *Turtle Clan Journey,* p. 60.

Bulletin of the Center for Children's Books, October, 1996, p. 56; May, 1998, Elizabeth Bush, review of *The Beaded Moccasins,* p. 319; April, 1999, Elizabeth Bush, review of *Turtle Clan Journey,* p. 277.

Kirkus Reviews, April 1, 1999, review of *Turtle Clan Journey,* p. 532; March 15, 2003, review of *The Sun, the Rain, and the Appleseed,* p. 465.

Kliatt, July, 1998, Claire Rosser, review of *The Beaded Moccasins,* p. 6.

Publishers Weekly, September 9, 1996, p. 84; February 24, 2003, review of *The Sun, the Rain, and the Appleseed,* p. 73.

School Library Journal, September, 1996, p. 201; June, 1998, Gerry Larson, review of *The Beaded Moccasins,* p. 145; June, 1999, Renee Steinberg, review of *Turtle Clan Journey,* p. 129; April, 2001, Catherine T. Quattlebaum, review of *Betsy Zane, the Rose of Fort Henry,* p. 140; May, 2003, Kristen Oravec, review of *The Sun, the Rain, and the Appleseed,* p. 150.

Voice of Youth Advocates, December, 1998, Joyce Sparrow, review of *The Beaded Moccasins,* p. 353.*

E

ESPOSITO, Mary Ann 1942-

PERSONAL: Born August 3, 1942, in Buffalo, NY; daughter of Roy J. (a chemist) and Louise (a dietician; maiden name, Galasso) Saporito; married Guy M. Esposito (a physician), 1968; children: Elizabeth, Christopher. *Education:* Daeman College, B.A., 1964; University of New Hampshire, M.A. 1991; graduate of Cucina della Campania (Sorrento, Italy) and Italianissimo (Perugia, Italy). *Politics:* Independent. *Religion:* Roman Catholic. *Hobbies and other interests:* Travel, foreign-language study.

ADDRESSES: Office—Mary Ann Esposito, Inc., P.O. Box 891, Durham, NH 03824. *Agent*—Michael Jones, P.O. Box 397, Pelham, NH 03807. *E-mail*—maesposito@attbi.com.

CAREER: Public Broadcasting Service (PBS), host and creator of "Ciao Italia" (televised cooking show), 1989—; Mary Ann Esposito, Inc. (production company), Durham, president, 1996—. University of New Hampshire, Portsmouth, instructor in Italian cooking, 1985-90; European Heritage Institute, Richmond, VA, lecturer and cook, 1990-91. Visiting and guest chef to numerous culinary institutes, including Boston University; guest cook at Tre Vaselle, Torgiano, Italy, and La Cucina d'Edgardo, Montalcino, Tuscany; Strawberry Banke, Portsmouth, NH, president of board of trustees, 1980-84.

MEMBER: International Association of Cooking Professionals.

AWARDS, HONORS: Columbus Foundation Literary Award, 1993, for *Ciao Italia;* Pirandello Lyceum Award, 1995, for educational and entertainment contributions made by an Italian American.

WRITINGS:

COOKBOOKS

Ciao Italia: Traditional Italian Recipes from Family Kitchens, Morrow (New York, NY), 1991.

Nella Cucina: More Italian Cooking from the Host of "Ciao Italia," Morrow (New York, NY), 1993.

Celebrations, Italian Style: Recipes and Menus for Special Occasions and Seasons of the Year, illustrated by Tomie de Paola, Morrow (New York, NY), 1995.

Easy Book of Yeast Dough, Morrow (New York, NY), 1997.

What You Knead, Morrow (New York, NY), 1997.

Mangia Pasta!: Easy-to-Make Recipes for Company and Every Day, Morrow (New York, NY), 1998.

Ciao Italia—Bringing Italy Home: Regional Recipes, Flavors, and Traditions As Seen on the Public Television Series "Ciao Italia," St. Martin's Press (New York, NY), 2001.

Ciao Italia in Umbria: Recipes and Reflections from the Heart of Italy, St. Martin's Press (New York, NY), 2002.

Ciao Italia in Tuscany: Traditional Recipes from One of Italy's Most Famous Regions, St. Martin's Press (New York, NY), 2003.

SIDELIGHTS: Beginning in 1989, Mary Ann Esposito has hosted the weekly PBS cooking show "Ciao Italia," on which she instructs viewers in preparing a variety of authentic Italian dishes, and educates them about Italian history and folklore. "Ciao Italia" has been carried by over 250 public television stations, and in the wake of its popularity Esposito has written several best- selling cookbooks containing Italian regional recipes.

Esposito learned a great deal about Italian cooking from her Sicilian and Neapolitan-born grandmothers, but she also attended cooking schools in Italy and earned a master's degree in Italian Renaissance history from the University of New Hampshire. Michael Schrader in *Nation's Restaurant News* recounted: "As a child, Esposito wished her extended family would cook more American meals, and she embarked on a career in teaching that had no relationship to the cookery that surrounded her in her youth. With the passage of years, she turned back to the food of her heritage with an enthusiasm that would lead her to make cooking her vocation and the rediscovery of forgotten dishes the object of many trips to Italy."

In her first cookbook, *Ciao Italia: Traditional Italian Recipes from Family Kitchens,* Esposito "concentrates equally on technique and history," according to a critic for *Publishers Weekly.* She has continued this approach in all of her later books as well, mixing traditional Italian recipes with information about Italian history, her own travels, and family stories. Speaking of *Mangia Pasta!: Easy-to-Make Recipes for Company and Every Day,* Judith C. Sutton in *Library Journal* explained that Esposito's book "features favorite pasta dishes, both classic and contemporary, along with chatty reminiscences about her culinary travels throughout Italy." Reviewing *Ciao Italia: Bringing Italy Home,* a critic for *Publishers Weekly* noted that "Esposito's travel stories, family memories and tips . . . infuse the recipes with a warm and personal touch." Mark Knoblauch in *Booklist* summed up her popularity: "Esposito's personality and enthusiasm for her subject shine through her work."

Esposito's cookbooks are also known for introducing Italian regional recipes not widely known in America. Her *Ciao Italia in Umbria: Recipes and Reflections from the Heart of Italy,* featuring recipes from the mid-section of the Italian peninsula, for example, contains "simple, rustic fare not overexposed in other Italian cookbooks," as a critic for *Publishers Weekly* explained. *Celebrations, Italian Style: Recipes and Menus for Special Occasions and Seasons of the Year*

contains recipes for all the major holidays and family celebrations, as well as for local festivals found throughout Italy.

On the *Ciao Italia* Web site, Esposito explained what she hoped to accomplish through her television series and her cookbooks. She noted: "I try to share my love for my heritage with all of you. I feel like I am really accomplishing my goal when I get wonderful comments and letters from you. Of course, like a good teacher, I learn so much from you as well."

BIOGRAPHICAL AND CRITICAL SOURCES:

PERIODICALS

Booklist, November 15, 1995, Barbara Jacobs, review of *Celebrations, Italian Style: Recipes and Menus for Special Occasions and Seasons of the Year,* p. 524; November 15, 1998, Barbara Jacobs, review of *Mangia Pasta!: Easy-to-Make Recipes for Company and Every Day,* p. 555; May 15, 2001, Mark Knoblauch, review of *Ciao Italia—Bringing Italy Home: Regional Recipes, Flavors, and Traditions As Seen on the Public Television Series "Ciao Italia,"* p. 1720.

Entertainment Weekly, January 24, 1992, Sada Fretz, review of *Ciao Italia: Traditional Italian Recipes from Family Kitchens,* p. 53.

Library Journal, May 15, 1993, Judith C. Sutton, review of *Nella Cucina: More Italian Cooking from the Host of "Ciao Italia,"* p. 92; December, 1995, Judith C. Sutton, review of *Celebrations, Italian Style,* p. 150; October 15, 1998, review of *Mangia Pasta!,* p. 91; April 15, 2001, Judith Sutton, review of *Ciao Italia—Bringing Italy Home,* p. 127; November 15, 2002, Judith Sutton, review of *Ciao Italia in Umbria: Recipes and Reflections from the Heart of Italy,* p. 95.

Nation's Restaurant News, February 12, 1996, Michael Schrader, review of *Celebrations, Italian Style,* p. 76.

Publishers Weekly, August 23, 1991, review of *Ciao Italia,* p. 58; December 4, 1995, review of *Celebrations, Italian Style,* p. 59; April 2, 2001, review of *Ciao Italia—Bringing Italy Home,* p. 59; October 7, 2002, review of *Ciao Italia in Umbria,* p. 69.

Yankee, December, 1987, Stephen O. Muskie, "Overlooking the Oyster River," p. 122; April, 2000, Kelly Horan, "*Ciao Italia*'s Recipe for Success," p. 102.

ONLINE

Ciao Italia Web site, http://ciaoitalia.com/ (March 20, 2003).*

*   *   *

EVANS, Walker 1903-1975

PERSONAL: Born November 3, 1903, in St. Louis, MO; died April 10, 1975, in New Haven, CT; son of Walker II (an advertising executive) and Jessie Beach (Crane) Evans; married Jane Smith Ninas (divorced, 1955); married Isabelle Böschenstein von Steiger, 1960 (divorced, 1972). *Education:* Attended Williams College, Williamstown, MA, 1922-23, and the Sorbonne, Paris, France, 1926-27.

CAREER: Photographer. Worked in New York City Public Library, 1923-25; freelance photographer, 1928-65; staff photographer, Farm Security Administration, 1935-37; *Fortune* magazine, New York, NY, associate editor and photographer, 1945-65; Yale University, New Haven, CT, professor of graphic arts, 1964-74, professor emeritus, 1974-75. Artist in residence, Dartmouth College, 1972. Exhibitions of Evans's work have been held in North America and Europe, beginning in 1932, and include showings at the Museum of Modern Art, New York, NY; National Gallery of Canada, Ottawa; Robert Schoelkopf Gallery, New York, NY; Galerie Baudoin Lebon, Paris, France; Bibliothéque Royale, Brussels, Belgium; Cronin Gallery, Houston, TX; Grand Central Palace, New York, NY; Art Institute of Chicago, IL; Centre Georges Pompidou, Paris; Ferens Art Gallery, Hull, Yorkshire, England; Museum Ludwig, Cologne, Germany; Kluuvin Galleria, Helsinki, Finland; Yale University, New Haven, CT; and other locations.

MEMBER: American Academy of Arts and Sciences (fellow), National Institute of Arts and Letters.

AWARDS, HONORS: Guggenheim fellowships, 1940, 1941, 1959; Carnegie Corporation award, 1962; D.Litt., Williams College, 1968; Mark Rothko Foundation grant, 1973.

Walker Evans

WRITINGS:

PHOTOGRAPHER

Hart Crane, *The Bridge,* Black Sun Press (New York, NY), 1930.

Carleton Beals, *The Crime of Cuba,* [Philadelphia, PA], 1933.

James Johnson Sweeney, *African Negro Art,* Museum of Modern Art (New York, NY), 1935.

Lincoln Kirstein, *Walker Evans: American Photographs,* Museum of Modern Art (New York, NY), 1938.

James Agee, *Let Us Now Praise Famous Men,* Houghton Mifflin (Boston, MA), 1941.

J. Edgar Park, *Wheaton College Photographs,* [Norton, MA], 1941.

Karl Bickel, *The Mangrove Coast,* [New York, NY], 1942.

Paul Radin and James Johnson Sweeney, *African Folk Tales and Sculptures,* Bollington Foundation (New York, NY), 1953, revised in two volumes as *African Folktales,* by Paul Radin, and *African Sculpture,* by James Johnson Sweeney, Princeton University Press (Princeton, NJ), 1970.

Many Are Called, introduction by James Agee, Houghton Mifflin (Boston, MA), 1966.

Message from the Interior, afterword by John Szarkowsky, Eakins Press (Boston, MA), 1966.

Walker Evans, introduction by Robert Penn Warren, Yale University Press (New Haven, CT), 1971.

Walker Evans' Photographs for the Farm Security Administration, 1935-1938, edited by Jerald C. Maddox, Da Capo Press (New York, NY), 1973.

Selected Photographs, introduction by Lionel Trilling, [New York, NY], 1974.

I, [New Haven, CT, and Washington, DC], 1978.

Walker Evans: First and Last, Harper & Row (New York, NY), 1978.

Jerry L. Thompson, *Walker Evans at Work,* Harper & Row (New York, NY), 1978.

Lloyd Fonvielle, *Walker Evans,* Aperture (New York, NY), 1979.

Walker Evans: Havana, 1933, Pantheon (New York, NY), 1989.

Walker Evans: Amerika, Rizzoli (New York, NY), 1991.

Giles Mora and John T. Hill, *Walker Evans: The Hungry Eye,* Abrams (New York, NY), 1993.

Cynthia Rylant, *Something Permanent* (poems), Harcourt (New York, NY), 1994.

Walker Evans: The Brooklyn Bridge, Eakins Press (Boston, MA), 1994.

Judith Keller, *Walker Evans: The Getty Museum Collection,* J. Paul Getty Museum (Los Angeles, CA), 1995.

Simple Secrets: Photographs from the Collection of Marian and Benjamin Hill, High Museum of Art (Atlanta, GA), 1998.

Andre Codrescu, *Walker Evans: Signs,* J. Paul Getty Museum (Los Angeles, CA), 1998.

Maria Morris Hambourg and others, *Walker Evans,* Metropolitan Museum of Art (New York, NY), 2000.

Walker Evans: The Lost Work, Arena Editions (Santa Fe, NM), 2000.

Virginia-Lee Webb, *Perfect Documents: Walker Evans and African Art, 1935,* Metropolitan Museum of Art (New York, NY), 2000.

Andre Codrescu, *Walker Evans: Cuba,* introduction by Judith Keller, J. Paul Getty Museum (Los Angeles, CA), 2001.

Luc Sante, *Walker Evans,* Phaidon (London, England), 2001.

Christian A. Peterson, *Walker Evans: The Collection of the Minneapolis Institute of Arts,* Minneapolis Institute of Arts (Minneapolis, MN), 2003.

Contributor to *Quality:, Its Image in the Arts,* edited by Louis Kronenberger, Atheneum (New York, NY), 1969; and *Wooden Churches: A Celebration,* by Rick Bragg, Algonquin, 1999. Collections of Evans's work are maintained at the Modern Museum of Art, New York, NY; Metropolitan Museum of Art, New York, NY; Yale University, New Haven, CT; Wadsworth Atheneum, Hartford, CT; Fogg Art Museum, Harvard University, Cambridge, MA; Library of Congress, Washington, DC; New Orleans Museum of Art; University of New Mexico, Albuquerque; Smithsonian Institute; San Francisco Museum of Modern Art; and National Gallery of Canada, Ottawa, Ontario.

SIDELIGHTS: Most often remembered for his black-and-white photographs taken of poor families in America during the Great Depression, and collected in the book *Let Us Now Praise Famous Men* with text by James Agee, Walker Evans remains today one of the most important documentary photographers of the twentieth century. Also well known for his series of photos taken of commuters in New York City's subways, Evans was a longtime editor and photographer for *Fortune* magazine. But although he continued to produce pictures professionally through the 1960s, many critics feel that Evans never again equaled his Depression-Era work; yet even if that had been all he had accomplished in his lifetime, his place as an influential photographer would remain assured. Evans found beauty, interest, irony, and even humor in what most people would consider to be the ordinary, even ugly, aspects of everyday life. As he was quoted by Malcolm Jones in *Newsweek* as saying, "A garbage can, occasionally, to me at least, can be beautiful. . . . I lean toward the enchantment, the visual power, of the esthetically rejected object." As Jed Perl described Evans in a *New Republic* article, "Evans is a master at getting at the classicism of commonness. He is also a master when it comes to the classicism of kitsch. Evans is enraptured by ordinary images. Perhaps even more importantly, he is obsessed with a quotidian way of representing reality."

Evans's first aspiration, however, was to become a novelist, and some critics would later describe the photographer as a storyteller of sorts. For example, Leo Rubinfien, writing in *Art in America,* called his pictures "literary . . . in that they are much interested in character—in what kind of person it is that has come into the area of their concern." Evans was drawn to literature as a way of rebelling against his parents and their values; he admired the bohemian lifestyle of certain authors and the characters they depicted, which contrasted with the values of his parents. His father, an advertising executive, was more concerned with his career than with his son, and his mother was also preoccupied with being upwardly mobile socially. Thus left largely to his own devices, his first experience with photography came after the family moved to Toledo, Ohio, in 1916, and Evans began to fiddle with a Kodak Brownie camera. He enjoyed taking pictures of people without their knowing it, and thus began a fascination with catching people in real-life situations. However, by the time he was set to enter Williams College in 1922, his mind was on becoming a writer. Evans was especially interested in French authors such as Gustave Flaubert, Charles Baudelaire, Andre Gide, and Arthur Rimbaud. After dropping out of Williams College he moved to Paris, where he hoped to find some spiritual camaraderie in the American expatriate community. While in Paris, he attended the Sorbonne, and eventually decided that his talents lay more with photography than in writing.

Moving from Paris to New York City in the late 1920s, Evans worked on his photography while earning a paycheck working nights for a brokerage firm. His first publication, titled *The Bridge,* a collaboration with poet Hart Crane whom he had met in Paris, was released in 1930. Though many young artists struggled to achieve recognition and earn a living, Evans's gifts as a photographer were soon recognized, and in 1931 art patron Lincoln Kirstein gave him an assignment to photograph Victorian architecture in the New York City area. The next year, Evans had his first exhibition at the Julien Levy Gallery in New York City; and in 1933 he was commissioned to photograph historic buildings in New Orleans. His photos commanded a fee of $125 per picture, a huge sum at the time, and he soon traveled on assignments to foreign locales such as Cuba and Tahiti. In 1935, Evans was hired by the federal government's Farm Security Administration to document the struggles of the working class in America. He complemented this work with a 1936 project for *Fortune* magazine about the country's poor to be written by James Agee; thus began the work on Evans's most acclaimed photographic pieces.

Depicting what would later become regarded as the most striking and enduring images of the Great Depression, Evans and Agee completed a record of the downtrodden that was rejected by the editors at *For-*

tune for being too lengthy for the magazine's needs. Instead, their work was released in 1941's *Let Us Now Praise Famous Men.* But because this book came out just before the United States entered World War II, it did not receive considerable attention at the time. Today, however, it is considered by many to be Evans's masterpiece. As Perl observed, "What is extraordinary about *Let Us Now Praise Famous Men* is the extent to which Agee and Evans present the hopeless poverty of these families in all its grinding everydayness. The book's enduring power rests with their insistence that the world that they are chronicling is too complex to be described as anything but a collage, a scrapbook; this is a tragedy without conclusion or catharsis." Despite this, Perl added that the photographs in the earlier *Walker Evans: American Photographs* are more accomplished: "Taken together, the photographs in *Let Us Now Praise Famous Men* are by no means the most sustained demonstration of Evans's gifts as a photographer; I would give that honor to *American Photographs.*"

Evans had left the Farm Security Administration by 1937, and during World War II he wrote book reviews for *Time,* a job he enjoyed because it gave him the chance to exercise his still-lingering love for writing. From 1938 to 1941, he also embarked on what is perhaps his second-most-famous endeavor: a series of photographs taken in New York City's subways. Echoing his childhood love of taking photographs of people surreptitiously, Evans concealed his camera in his coat as he snapped pictures of subway passengers. This work was later published in his 1966 book *Many Are Called.*

After the war, Evans was hired by *Fortune* to be a photographer and associate editor. He remained at *Fortune* for the next twenty years, and here was given considerable leeway in choosing his assignments. "Evans's *Fortune* projects reflected his intensifying interest in the discarded object," commented *Afterimage* writer Melissa Rachleff. "Evans was interested in the aesthetic possibilities of juxtaposing the past with the present. In several photo essays he recorded specific objects that were becoming increasingly anachronistic in the era of mass production." Rachleff further observed, "To some, Evans's interest in these topics might have seemed nostalgic. Upon further consideration, they may represent his interest in the effects of current cultural transition."

Evans joined the faculty at Yale University to teach graphic arts during the last decade of his life. Meanwhile, he continued to take photographs, even taking color photos on assignment for *Fortune*, something he had shunned for most of his career as being vulgar compared to black-and-white photography. He became interested, too, in collecting such items as old postcards and rusty street signs, which he also photographed along with kitchen utensils and other ordinary objects. During the last years of his life, he resorted to using a Polaroid camera when illness made it too difficult for him to operate a professional-quality camera.

Though Evans's later photographs are generally considered less important than his earlier works, his reputation increased after his death in 1974. In 2000 a retrospective of his work at the Metropolitan Museum of Art in New York City confirmed his stature as one of the leading photographers of the twentieth century. "By declining to beautify or dramatize," wrote Rubinfien, "each of Evans's best photographs forces its subject to speak for itself, even to talk too much, until its vulgarity, pathos, tawdriness, hysteria—whatever its essential qualities are—begin to yell from the page."

BIOGRAPHICAL AND CRITICAL SOURCES:

BOOKS

Authors and Artists for Young Adults, Volume 44, Gale (Detroit, MI). 2002.

Contemporary Photographers, 3rd edition, St. James Press (Detroit, MI), 1996.

Encyclopedia of World Biography, 2nd edition, Gale (Detroit, MI), 1998.

Mora, Gilles, *Walker Evans: The Hungry Eye,* Abrams (New York, NY), 1993.

Rathbone, Belinda, *Walker Evans: A Biography,* Houghton Mifflin (Boston, MA), 1995.

Thompson, Jerry L., *The Last Years of Walker Evans,* Thames & Hudson (New York, NY), 1997.

PERIODICALS

Afterimage, January-February, 1996, Melissa Rachleff, "Scavenging the Landscape: Walker Evans and American Life," p. 7; January-February, 2002, "Command CV: A Legend by Default," p. 6; winter, 2002, Roberto Tejada, "Documentary and Anti-Graphic: Three at the Julien Levy Gallery, 1935," p. 15.

American Heritage, December, 1994, review of *Something Permanent,* p. 126.

Art in America, December, 2000, Leo Rubinfien, "The Poetry of Plain Seeing," p. 74.

Economist, January 29, 2000, "Against Nature," p. 98.

Library Journal, September 15, 1998, Nathan Ward, review of *Simple Secrets: Photographs from the Collection of Marian and Benjamin A. Hill,* p. 71; April 1, 2000, Michael Rogers, review of *Let Us Now Praise Famous Men,* p. 136; June 1, 2000, David Bryant, review of *Walker Evans,* p. 120.

Los Angeles Magazine, September, 2001, "Democratic Eye," p. 140.

New Criterion, March, 2000, Daniel Mark Epstein, "The Passion of Walker Evans," p. 14.

New Republic, February 14, 2000, Jed Perl, "On Art—In the American Grain," p. 31.

Newsweek, July 5, 1999, "Dilettante, Documentarian, Genius," p. 59; January 31, 2000, Malcolm Jones, "An American Eye: New Exhibits Celebrate the Austere Beauty of Photographer Walker Evans's World," p. 62.

Publishers Weekly, January 24, 2000, "Let Us Now Praise Evans and Agee," p. 307; August 27, 2001, review of *Walker Evans: Cuba,* p. 75.*

F

FARBER, Thomas (David) 1944-

PERSONAL: Born April 26, 1944, in Boston, MA; son of Sidney (a professor and cancer researcher) and Norma (an opera singer, poet, novelist, and children's book writer; maiden name, Holzman) Farber. *Education:* Harvard University, B.A., 1965. *Hobbies and other interests:* Surfing, diving.

ADDRESSES: Home—1827 Virginia St., Berkeley, CA 94703. *Office*—Box #2, 1678 Shattuck Ave., Berkeley, CA 94709. *Agent*—Ellen Levine, 370 Lexington Ave., Suite 906, New York, NY 10017. *E-mail*—tfarber@ tfarber.org.

CAREER: Writer. Commentator for National Public Radio; University of Hawaii, visiting distinguished writer; University of California, Berkeley, Rockefeller Foundation resident scholar at Bellagio; currently visiting senior lecturer.

AWARDS, HONORS: Guggenheim fellow; National Endowment for the Arts fellow; Fulbright scholar for Pacific Islands Studies; Dorothea Lange-Paul Taylor Prize.

WRITINGS:

Tales for the Son of My Unborn Child, Dutton (New York, NY), 1971.

(With Nacio Brown) *Rag Theatre,* Great Star Press (Berkeley CA), 1975.

Who Wrote the Book of Love?, Norton (New York, NY), 1977.

Whatever the Cost, Creative Arts Books (Berkeley, CA), 1979.

Hazards to the Human Heart, Dutton (New York, NY), 1980.

The Material Plane, Dutton (New York, NY), 1980.

Too Soon to Tell, Ten Mile River Press (Fort Bragg, CA), 1981.

Curves of Pursuit, Putnam (New York, NY), 1984.

Compared to What?: On Writing and the Writer's Life, Norton (New York, NY), 1988.

On Water, Okeanos (Oakland, CA), 1991.

Learning to Love It: Seven Stories and a Novella, Capra Press (Santa Barbara, CA), 1993.

The Price of the Ride, Creative Arts Book (Berkeley, CA), 1996.

(Author of introduction) Wayne Levin, *Through a Liquid Mirror: Photographs,* Editions Limited (Honolulu, HI), 1997.

Compressions: A Second Helping, Serendipity Books (Berkeley, CA), 1998.

The Face of the Deep, Mercury House (San Francisco, CA), 1998.

A Lover's Question: Selected Stories, Creative Arts Books (Berkeley, CA), 2000.

The Beholder: A Novel, Metropolitan Books (New York, NY), 2002.

SIDELIGHTS: For over a quarter century, Thomas Farber has meditated on life and love, publishing short and long fiction and creative nonfiction written in economical yet poetic prose. Although Farber was born and raised in Boston and graduated from Harvard University, shortly after earning his degree he relocated to

California, where he has retained a residence ever since. "I came out to California in the summer of 1964," he once told a *San Diego Reader* reporter. "And with great ambivalence I've ended up for many years, staying in California and making my home in Northern California, in particular, Berkeley." After publishing several collections of essays and stories during the 1970s and 1980s, Farber made his debut as a novelist with *Curves of Pursuit,* a novel that is "venturesome to an almost foolhardy degree," to quote Anatole Broyard in the *New York Times.* Farber stretches the bounds of narrative as he portrays the relationships among two unnamed brothers and the narrator's wife, using the physics of motion, represented by the flight of a football pass. According to *Houston Chronicle* reviewer Emily Vincent, "Each chapter is a neatly shaped, pithy anecdote—almost a parable—about fraternal love and exasperation, childhood, the joys of sex and the pitfalls of marriage. . . . Separate and unique, they join seamlessly in a beautifully textured fabric." Describing the novel as "worrying, but not depressing," Broyard continued, "It's one of those new novels whose structure appeals not only to your sense of order, but to your sense of humor. . . . Some of his chapters are head fakes, some are probes, some run interference for others." "When it works," Broyard concluded, "when you make the catch, it's a beautiful feeling of everything coming together in space and time."

By the 1970s, Farber had discovered Hawaii, and he has spent much time there, though always keeping his home in Berkeley. Several of his books express and expand on the allure water has for Farber: *On Water,* a collection of "lyrical, broadly cast essays," to quote a *Publishers Weekly* reviewer, *Through a Liquid Mirror,* the literary foreword to photographs by Wayne Levin, and *The Face of the Deep,* a reflection on the mythology and literature of Oceania. "Part of the reason I became a writer was to say, 'This is what happened, this is what otherwise would be missed, unmentioned,'" Farber explains in *The Face of the Deep.* He discusses visiting, surfing, and diving in the Pacific, and reflects on the literature of the indigenous writers as well as the Western colonizers. Minal Hajratwala pointed to the chapter titled "The Literary Pacific" for special praise, calling it an "excellent survey of indigenous literature in the island nations of the Pacific" in her *San Jose Mercury News* review. Not only does Farber say "what happened," but according to a number of critics, he says it with style. For ex-

ample, a *Kirkus Reviews* contributor likened the chapters to "epigrams—witty; paradoxical riffs" written in "evocative and keen" prose and laced with "amusing asides." In her *Boston Globe* review, Amanda Heller remarked, "There is nothing earthbound about his prose, which spreads a descriptive *joie de vivre* over all its touches," and "at its best, *The Face of the Deep,* dropping in and cutting back in time, reads rather like the spiraling of a wave, where the surfer/reader planes on a rail, or line of prose," concluded *Nation* reviewer Mindy Pennybacker.

Farber's 2002 title, *The Beholder,* returns to questions of love and sex. In this novel a married twenty-something female art historian has an affair with a single, middle-aged male writer. Although *Booklist* contributor Carol Haggas decided that Farber's "terse, minimalist prose . . . mordantly conveys the raw, emotive tension" in the situation, several reviewers expressed reservations about Farber's style. These include a contributor to *Kirkus Reviews,* who found the characters unsympathetic and the portrayal of sexual relations fraught with "missteps and affectations." Jonathan Shipley, reviewing the novel for *Book Reporter,* found it "in parts . . . heated and visual, using the sparest of words and the shortest of sentences. At times it's like a poem, sharp and exact, meanings dripping from the words." Despite believing this elliptical style loses effectiveness over time, Shipley dubbed the novel as a whole a "scintillating examination of love and art, passions and the human form."

BIOGRAPHICAL AND CRITICAL SOURCES:

BOOKS

Farber, Thomas, *The Face of the Deep,* Mercury House (San Francisco, CA), 1998.

PERIODICALS

Best Sellers, March, 1984, review of *Curves of Pursuit,* p. 436.
Booklist, October 15, 1988, review of *Compared to What?: On Writing and the Writer's Life,* p. 358; August, 2002, Carol Haggas, review of *The Beholder,* p. 1918.

Boston Globe, September 29, 1998, Amanda Heller, review of *The Face of the Deep.*

Houston Chronicle, February 12, 1984, Emily Vincent, "Fraternal Love in the Arc of a Pass," review of *Curves of Pursuit.*

Hungry Mind Review, winter, 1994, review of *On Water,* p. 8.

Kirkus Reviews, November 1, 1983, review of *Curves of Pursuit,* p. 1138; August 15, 1988, review of *Compared to What?,* p. 1209; May 26, 1998, review of *The Face of the Deep*; June 1, 1998, review of *The Face of the Deep,* pp. 789-790; May 15, 2002, review of *The Beholder,* p. 683.

Kliatt Paperback Book Guide, fall, 1985, review of *Curves of Pursuit,* p. 6.

Library Journal, November 15, 1983, review of *Curves of Pursuit,* p. 2171; July, 1994, Tim Markus, review of *On Water,* p. 121; June 15, 2002, Marc Kloszewski, review of *The Beholder,* p. 93.

Los Angeles Times, January 25, 1984, Richard Eder, review of *Curves of Pursuit,* p. 6; September 19, 1993, review of *Learning to Love It: Seven Stories and a Novella,* p. 11; July 17, 1994, review of *On Water,* p. 3; August 4, 2002, Susan Salter Reynolds, review of *The Beholder,* p. R-15.

Nation, September 7, 1998, Mindy Pennybacker, review of *The Face of the Deep,* pp. 38-41.

New York Times, January 14, 1984, Anatole Broyard, review of *Curves of Pursuit,* p. 14.

New York Times Book Review, January 8, 1984, Richard Elman, review of *Curves of Pursuit,* p. 18; October 23, 1988, Monroe Engel, review of *Compared to What?,* p. 39; November 28, 1993, David Galef, review of *Learning to Love It,* p. 26.

Publishers Weekly, November 18, 1983, review of *Curves of Pursuit,* p. 60; May 3, 1985, review of *Curves of Pursuit,* p. 72; April 18, 1994, review of *On Water,* p. 56; July 13, 1998, review of *The Face of the Deep,* p. 71; July 8, 2002, review of *The Beholder,* p. 29.

San Diego Reader, August 6, 1998, review of *The Face of the Deep.*

San Jose Mercury News, September 20, 1998, Minal Hajratwala, review of *The Face of the Deep.*

Sewanee Review, July, 1990, review of *Compared to What?,* p. 515.

Studies in Short Fiction, spring, 1995, Leigh Block, review of *Learning to Love It,* pp. 247-248.

West Coast Review of Books, July, 1984, review of *Curves of Pursuit,* p. 32; Volume 14, number 4, 1989, review of *Compared to What?,* p. 48.

ONLINE

Book Reporter Web site, http://www.bookreporter.com/ (May 17, 2003), Jonathan Shipley, review of *The Beholder.*

Thomas Farber Web site, http://www.thomasfarber.org/ (May 19, 2003).*

*　　*　　*

FELDMAN, Egal 1925-

PERSONAL: Born April 9, 1925, in New York, NY; son of Moshe and Chaya (Fishman) Feldman; married Mary Kalman (an insurance agent), June 30, 1959 (divorced, 1991); married Joan Bischoff (a professor of English), June 14, 1992; children: (first marriage) Tyla Feldman Portnoy, Auora Feldman Goldfine, Naomi Feldman Gauthier. *Ethnicity:* "Jewish." *Education:* Brooklyn College (now of the City University of New York), B.A., 1950; New York University, M.A., 1954; University of Pennsylvania, Ph.D., 1959. *Religion:* Jewish.

ADDRESSES: Home—2019 Weeks Ave., Superior, WI 54880. *Office*—Department of History, Sundquist 230, University of Wisconsin—Superior, Superior, WI 54880. *E-mail*—egal@cpinternet.com.

CAREER: University of Texas—Arlington, assistant professor of history, 1960-66; University of Wisconsin—Superior, associate professor, 1966-67, professor of history, 1968-94, director of Area Research Center, 1970-74, department chair, 1973-77, 1982-94, dean of College of Letters and Science, 1977-81, professor emeritus, 1994—.

MEMBER: American Historical Association, Organization of American Historians, American Jewish Historical Society.

AWARDS, HONORS: Essay award, YIVO-Institute for Jewish Research, 1954, for "The Impact of the American Revolution on the Jewish Community in America"; University of Wisconsin—Superior, teacher of the year award, 1968, several travel and research grants, between 1971 and 1990, Chancellor's Award for scholarly interpretations, 1982, Max H. Lavine Award for scholarly contribution to contemporary concerns, 1975, 1982, 1985, 1992; grants from Wisconsin Humanities Committee, 1977, 1980; travel grant, National Endowment for the Humanities, 1984; Faculty Achievement Award for Research, Burlington Northern Foundation, 1992; Kingery Award, best scholarly book published in Wisconsin, Council of Wisconsin Writers, 2002.

WRITINGS:

Fit for Men: A History of New York's Clothing Trade, Public Affairs Press (Washington, DC), 1960.
The Dreyfus Affair and the American Conscience, 1895-1906, Wayne State University Press (Detroit, MI), 1981.
Dual Destinies: The Jewish Encounter with Protestant America, University of Illinois Press (Urbana, IL), 1990.
Catholics and Jews in Twentieth-Century America, University of Illinois Press (Urbana, IL), 2001.

Contributor to books, including *American Vistas,* Volume II, edited by Leonard Dinnerstein and Kenneth T. Jackson, Oxford University Press (New York, NY), 1971; *Documentary History of the Jews in the United States,* edited by Lloyd Gartner, University of Tel Aviv Press (Tel Aviv, Israel), 1975; *Anti-Semitism in American History,* edited by David A. Gerber, University of Illinois Press (Urbana, IL), 1986; and *Studies in Contemporary Judaism,* Volume 21, edited by Eli Lederhendler; author of introduction, *The Dreyfus Affair: The Ben Shahn Prints,* Crossroads Books (Cincinnati, OH), 1984. Contributor of articles and reviews to periodicals, including *American Jewish Archives, Journal of Church and State, Cimarron Review, Societas: Review of Social History, Judaism: Quarterly Journal, Middle East Review, Jewish Social Studies,* and *Revue de la Bibliotheque Nationale de France.*

SIDELIGHTS: Egal Feldman once told *CA:* "The Dreyfus Affair, the subject of my 1981 book, was too important an event to be left to the French. The false conviction of the Jewish French Army officer, Captain Alfred Dreyfus, was the first conspicuous sign that Jews could not rely upon Western liberal institutions at the end of the nineteenth century for their safety. Its impact was broad and deep, affecting Catholics, Prot-

estants, and Jews in the United States and abroad, and it touched and shaped the lives of a generation. As a classic moment in human affairs, it should be remembered and reflected upon for years to come.

"Being aware of the cosmic importance of the Dreyfus event, I was surprised to learn that despite the countless books written about it, not a single publication existed that examined America's reaction to it. By the mid-1970s I was well on my way to correcting this situation.

"Actually, my interest in the Dreyfus Affair was an outgrowth of a wider pursuit—a desire to understand the evolution of Jewish-Christian relations in the United States. This interest began many years ago, during the 'ecumenical revolution' of the mid-sixties. Here, too, I was surprised to discover how little attention American historians have devoted to this important subject. I decided to devote my spare time to the history of the history of Jewish-Christian relations in the United States."

More recently Feldman added: "When I left graduate school in 1959, it was clear that the area of writing that I was to pursue, the history of Christian-Jewish relations, was not a fruitful one. It held little academic interest among scholars of American history; few opportunities in teaching and writing in this area existed in public universities. In subsequent years, despite growth of the interfaith movement, its historiography remained small, and historians paid only scant attention to it. Even so, it remained the area which for the past thirty years has continued to dominate my historical interest.

"My decision to follow this area of study was reinforced by a major event, the meeting of the Second Vatican Council (1962-1965), in which the Roman Catholic church resolved to alter its thinking about Jews. This event produced one of the most remarkable transformations during the past 2,000 years of Christian attitudes toward Jews. It convinced me that a vast field of the history of Christian-Jewish relations was ready for cultivation.

"My early writing dealt with American Protestant-Jewish relations. I examined the life and work of a number of Protestant theologians of a variety of denominations and religious ideologies. Most of these individuals paid only scant attention to Jews and Judaism, but the work of those who were concerned with Judaism, such as Reinhold Niebuhr, A. Roy Eckardt, and Franklin H. Littell, I found particularly helpful. Generally, Jews, like Protestants, did not produce any comprehensive study of Jewish-Protestant relations. After writing a number of articles and a book, *The Dreyfus Affair and the American Conscience, 1895-1906,* which also dealt in large part with American Christian-Jewish relations, I wrote the first comprehensive account of Protestant-Jewish relations, *Dual Destinies: The Jewish Encounter with Protestant America.*

"At this time I concluded that with respect to the interfaith movement, for the reader to better understand Christian attitudes toward Jews, all Christians ought not to be put into one package. It is especially important that American Roman Catholics should be separated from the numerous denominations and ideologies of Protestantism. Besides, it was the Vatican II endorsement of the 'Statement on the Jews' of *Nostra Aetate* of 1965 which promulgated a new relationship with Jews and which has had a profound effect on all of Christendom.

"What is more, the relationship of Catholics and Jews has been a much longer one than that of Jews and Protestants. Its hostilities were inherited from biblical and patristic times. The Middle Ages added to the legacy of bitterness between the two groups. The Church's questionable behavior during the Holocaust has also lingered. Unpalatable memories had been first transported to the New World by both groups. For many centuries, the gulf between the two ancient faiths seemed unbridgeable. How Roman Catholics and Jews in the United States managed to transform their relationship to one of accommodation and friendship is the subject of my book, *Catholics and Jews in Twentieth-Century America.*

"Most important in this last work is the suggestion that anti-Semitism is not an outgrowth of social and economic forces but of deeply rooted theological and religious ones. It is the religious foundations of Christianity that have enabled anti-Semitism to metamorphose into its modern grotesqueness; only by uprooting its foundation can a new edifice, free of Jew-hatred, be built. In *Catholics and Jews in Twentieth-Century America* I suggest that a small but significant step toward this goal was taken in the latter half of the last century."

BIOGRAPHICAL AND CRITICAL SOURCES:

PERIODICALS

American Historical Review, June, 1982.
Gazette (Montreal, Quebec, Canada), August 21, 1982.
History: Review of New Books, May, 1982.
Journal of American History, fall, 1982.
Reform Judaism, September, 1981.*

* * *

FRANK, Andre Gunder 1929-

PERSONAL: Born February 24, 1929, in Berlin, Germany; son of Lenhard and Elena (Pevsner) Frank; married Marta Fuentes Enberg (a librarian), December 21, 1962 (died, 1993); married second wife, Nancy Howell (divorced); children: Paulo Rene, Miguel Leonardo. *Education:* Swarthmore College, B.A. (with honors), 1950; University of Michigan, graduate study, 1951; University of Chicago, M.A., 1952, Ph.D., 1957; University of Paris, Doctorat d'Etat, 1978.

ADDRESSES: Home—One Longfellow Place, Apt. 3411, Boston, MA 02114. *Office*—World History Center, Northeastern University, 270 Holmes Hall, Boston, MA 02115. *E-mail*—agfrank@neu.edu.

CAREER: Educator and economist. Iowa State University, Ames, instructor, 1956-57; Michigan State University, East Lansing, began as lecturer, became assistant professor, 1957-61; University of Brasilia, Brasilia, Brazil, associate professor, 1963; UNESCO Latin American Center for Research in the Social Sciences, Rio de Janeiro, Brazil, visiting research fellow, 1963-64; National Autonomous University of Mexico, Obregon, professor extraordinario, 1965; Sir George Williams University, Montreal, Quebec, Canada, visiting professor, 1966-68; University of Chile, Santiago, professor, 1968-73, research professor, 1970-73; Max Planck Institute, visiting research associate and fellow of German Society for Peace and Conflict Research, 1974-78; University of East Anglia, Norwich, England, professor of development studies, 1978-83; University of Amsterdam, Amsterdam, Netherlands, professor of development economics, 1981-94, director of Institute for Socio-Economic Studies of Developing

Regions, 1981-94; University of Toronto, Toronto, Ontario, Canada, professor of sociology, 1996-98; Northeastern University, Boston, MA, senior fellow at World History Center, 2002—. Visiting professor to colleges and universities, including Catholic University of Louvain, 1971, Free University of Berlin, 1973, Boston University, 1979, New School for Social Research, 1981, Florida International University, 1999-2000, University of Miami, FL, 1999-2000, and University of Nebraska at Lincoln, 2001. Consultant, United Nations Economic Commission for Latin America, 1964; worked in field office for United Nations International Labour Organization, 1968.

MEMBER: International Studies Association, International Political Science Association, International Sociological Association, International Society of Comparative Study of Civilizations, World Futures Society, Prehistoric Society, World Association of International Relations (member of board of directors), World History Association, American Political Science Association, Political Economy of World Systems Section of the American Sociological Association, American Anthropological Association, Social Science History Association, New England Historical Association.

AWARDS, HONORS: Distinguished Scholar Selectee, International Studies Association, 1989; MacArthur Foundation grant, 1990; World Society Foundation grant, 1996-97; Political Economy of World Systems Section of American Sociological Association, Career of Distinguished Scholarship Award, 1997, and Book Award, 2000, for *ReOrient: Global Economy in the Asian Age;* First Book Prize, World History Association, 1999.

WRITINGS:

Hugo Blanco Must Not Die: An Address to a Meeting in Solidarity with the Imperilled Peruvian Leader and the Freedom Struggle in Latin America, R. McCarthy, 1967.

Capitalism and Underdevelopment in Latin America: Historical Essays of Chile and Brazil, Monthly Review Press (New York, NY), 1967, revised edition, 1969.

Latin America: Underdevelopment or Revolution, Monthly Review Press (New York, NY), 1969.

Sociology of Development and Underdevelopment of Sociology, Zenit (Stockholm, Sweden), 1969.

La Sociologia subdesarrollante, Aportes, 1969.

Sociologia del desarrollo y subdesarrollo de la sociologia. El desarrollo del subdesarrollo, Anagrama (Barcelona, Spain), 1971.

Lumpenbourgeoisie: Lumpendevelopment; Dependency, Class, and Politics in Latin America, Monthly Review Press (New York, NY), 1972.

(With R. Puiggros and E. Laclau) *America Latina: Feudalismo o capitalismo?,* Oveja Negra (Bogota, Colombia), 1972.

(With D. Johnson and J. Cockcroft) *Dependence and Underdevelopment: Latin America's Political Economy,* Doubleday (New York, NY), 1972.

(With O. Caputo, R. Pizarro, and A. Quijano) *Aspectos de la realidad Latinoamericana,* Quimantu (Santiago, Chile), 1973.

Carta abierta en el aniversario del Golpe militar en Chile, edited by Alberto Corazon, [Madrid, Spain], 1974.

Raices del desarrollo y del subdesarrollo en el nuevo mundo, Universidad Central de Venezuela Facultad de Ciencias Economicas y Sociales (Caracas, Venezuela), 1974.

?Quien es el enemigo inmediato?: America Latina, subdesarrollo capitalista o revolucion socialista, Centro de Estudios Politicos, 1974.

On Capitalist Underdevelopment, Oxford University Press (Bombay, India), 1975.

Capitalismo y genocidio economico: Carta abierta a la escuela de cconomia de Chicago a proposito de su intervencion en Chile, Zero (Madrid, Spain), 1976.

La Inversion extranjera en el subdesarrollo latinoamericano, Causachun (Lima, Peru), 1976.

Economic Genocide in Chile, Spokesman Books (Nottingham, England), 1976.

(With S. Amin and H. Jaffe) *Quale 1983/no esperar a 1984,* Zero (Madrid, Spain), 1976.

Critica y anti-critica, Zero (Madrid, Spain), 1978, translation published as *Critique and Anti-Critique,* Macmillan (New York, NY), 1984.

World Accumulation, 1492-1789, Monthly Review Press (New York, NY), 1978.

Dependent Accumulation and Underdevelopment, Macmillan (London, England), 1978, Monthly Review Press (New York, NY), 1979.

Mexican Agriculture, 1521-1630: Transformation of the Mode of Production, Cambridge University Press (Cambridge, England), 1979.

(With S. Amin) *Pa Vei Mot 1984,* Gyldendal (Oslo, Norway), 1979.

Crisis: In the World Economy, Holmes & Meier (New York, NY), 1980.

Crisis: In the Third World, Holmes & Meier (New York, NY), 1981.

Reflections on the World Economic Crisis, Monthly Review Press (New York, NY), 1981.

The European Challenge, Spokesman Books (Nottingham, England), 1983, published as *The European Challenge: From Atlantic Alliance to Pan-European Entente for Peace and Jobs,* foreword by Richard J. Barnet, L. Hill (Westport, CT), 1984.

El Desafío de la crisis, Nueva Sociedad (Caracas, Venezuela), 1988.

(Coauthor) *Widerstand im Weltsystem,* Promedia (Vienna, Austria), 1990.

The Underdevelopment of Development, Bethany Books (Santa Cruz, CA), 1991.

The Centrality of Central Asia, VU University Press (Amsterdam, Netherlands), 1992.

(Editor and contributor, with Barry Gills) *The World System: Five Hundred Years or Five Thousand?,* Routledge (New York, NY), 1993.

ReOrient: Global Economy in the Asian Age, University of California Press (Berkeley, CA), 1998.

Contributor to books, including *The European Workers' Movement,* Synthesis Publications, 1981; *Dynamics of Global Crisis,* Monthly Review Press, 1982; and *Der Sozialismus an der Schwelle zum 21. Jahrhundert,* Argument, 1985; contributor to professional journals and magazines. Member of editorial board, *Review of International Political Economy, Third World Quarterly, Society and Nature, Dialectical Anthropology, Scandinavian Journal of Development Alternatives, Journal of Social Studies, Social Identities, Passages,* and *Inner Asia.*

SIDELIGHTS: Historical economist Andre Gunder Frank has repeatedly challenged generally accepted ideas of how economies and societies evolve and interrelate. In an article for *Social Justice,* writers Pat Lauderdale, Ken Kyle, and Annamarie Oliverio explained that in much of Frank's work he argues that crises that occur in economies populated by marginalized societies are largely the result of the West's hoarding of resources and capitalism's attempts to standardize and homogenize cultures for the sake of efficiency. "For thirty years," noted the *Social Justice* writers, "he has objected to attempts to develop peoples, nations, states, or even nature under any particular homogeneous model—monolithic models tolerating no de-

viation, no diversity. His objections to the dynamics of dependency, marginalization, and the over-accumulation of capital by the core nations also exemplify his concern with injustice. Despite major backlashes in the past, Frank . . . continues to protest both legally and philosophically against the unjust distribution of benefits and burdens, including rights, responsibilities, . . . and needs."

In such books as *Crisis: In the World Economy* and *World Accumulation, 1492-1789,* Frank maintains that "Capital over-accumulation is identified as the source of numerous crises and reactions," noted the *Social Justice* contributors. "Efficiency has not led to equality, but rather to more inequality, to greater injustice." The economist views the economic development of North America, in particular, to have come at the cost of development in Latin America, as well as the economic disadvantage of indigenous Americans. Not only are these people at an economic disadvantage, but their cultural identities have also been suppressed. The reason: the concept of what "development" entails in a Western culture is diametrically opposed to what many indigenous people view as development. In his books Frank asserts that, in accordance with the Enlightenment ideology that inspired Rousseau, Locke, and Hobbes, with its imperative that civil societies must strive to counteract the chaos inherent in the "state of nature," homogenous societies bound by Locke's "social contract" became the ideal.

Part of the response to Frank's theories has not only been to stimulate debate among economists and sociologists but also to fuel the liberation theology movement prevalent in underdeveloped, predominately Catholic countries. Liberation theology is concerned with the inequities that exist between the economically elite and those who have been marginalized and denied such things as land ownership. In addition, Frank's work has impacted the field of archaeology and the understanding of the divergence by indigenous peoples of their use of the land following colonization by Western powers.

An important aspect of Frank's work is how it considers economies in terms of world systems, rather than simply how business and trade works within a state or group of states. In *The World System: Five Hundred Years or Five Thousand?* and *ReOrient: Global Economy in the Asian Age,* for example, the author challenges Eurocentric ideas of economic and technological development. In *The World System,* which Frank edited with Barry Gills, as well as writing many of the book's chapters, he posits that the development of a country or region cannot be fully understood without looking at the entire world system. In the case of the West, which benefitted from trade from Asian and Arabic regions of the world for centuries, the main reason for its prosperity beginning in the 1500s was the discovery of resources in the New World and the later decline of a dynamic economy in the East in the 1800s, due to a large population and consequentially cheap labor. The Europeans, in contrast, did not have as easy access to cheap labor, which spurred the creation of time- and labor-saving technologies, as Frank further explains in *ReOrient.* In *ReOrient* the author also speculates that the West's current dominance in the world is only a temporary phenomenon and that Asia will soon regain the ascendancy. Writing in the *Journal of Interdisciplinary History,* David Ludden further summarized Frank's theses: "First, long economic cycles influencing the global economy (from ancient times) also affected modern change; the rise and fall of each world region derives significantly from its position within global cycles. Second, within the global economy, the rise of the West occurred as Europe 'climbed up on Asian shoulders' to take advantage of Asia's old strength."

"Frank's *ReOrient* has caused great waves of anxiety among social scientists because of his claim that this new perspective on the rise of the West invalidates all our theories of development," reported Christopher Chase-Dunn in the *American Journal of Sociology.* "The great contribution of the book, and its predecessor, *The World System . . . ,* is that it forces us to focus on the significant economic and political/military continuities that have characterized the rise and fall of powerful regions for millennia." But while Chase-Dunn agreed with many of Frank's arguments, including the importance of China in the world economy and the belief that Europe was actually "a peripheral region" that with the exception of the period of the Roman Empire was less well developed than the East, the critic still held that the economist's "claim that the European rise to hegemony was a short-term and conjunctural outcome that had no implications for developmental logic is most probably mistaken." Nevertheless, despite such occasional objections, many critics have hailed Frank's fresh perspectives on the development of world civilizations and cultures. As *Pacific Affairs* contributor Marta Rohatynskyj concluded, "Frank calls for a restructuring of the social sciences

on a non-Eurocentric basis. Here! Here! *ReOrient* challenges readers to reconsider the importance of Europe in world history and in doing so touches upon important contemporary questions about how and what we can know."

BIOGRAPHICAL AND CRITICAL SOURCES:

PERIODICALS

American Journal of Sociology, January, 2000, Christopher Chase-Dunn, review of *ReOrient: Global Economy in the Asian Age,* p. 1196.

Antiquity, September, 1995, Andrew Sherratt, review of *The World System: Five Hundred Years or Five Thousand?,* p. 633.

Foreign Affairs, fall, 1984, review of *Critique and Anti-Critique: Essays on Dependence and Reformism,* p. 191.

Journal of Interdisciplinary History, winter, 1999, David Ludden, review of *ReOrient,* p. 564.

Journal of World History, spring, 2000, Janet L. Abu-Lughod, review of *ReOrient,* p. 111.

Library Journal, November 1, 1980, M. Balachandran, review of *Crisis: In the World Economy,* p. 2323; March 1, 1981, M. Balachandran, review of *Crisis: In the Third World,* p. 564.

Nation, June 6, 1981, Wendy Cooper, review of *Reflections on the World Economic Crisis,* p. 707, and *Crisis: In the Third World,* p. 708.

Pacific Affairs, spring, 2000, Marta Rohatynskyj, review of *ReOrient,* p. 98.

Pacific Historical Review, August, 2000, Akira Iriye, review of *ReOrient,* p. 471.

Social Forces, September, 1991, Michael S. Kimmel, review of *Transforming the Revolution: Social Movements and the World System,* p. 253.

Social Justice, winter, 1994, Pat Lauderdale, Ken Kyle, and Annamarie Oliviero, "Millennia and Injustice from the View of Andre Gunder Frank," p. 5.*

*   *   *

FULLER, Mary Lou 1929-

PERSONAL: Born January 31, 1929, in Bryn Mawr, PA; daughter of Guy and Corinne (Wood) Jordan; first marriage ended; married Enoch D. Fuller (an innkeeper), 1963 (died, May, 1973); children: (second marriage; adopted) Joshua, Amey Fuller Cole. *Ethnic-*

Mary Lou Fuller

ity: "White Protestant." *Education:* University of Pennsylvania, associate's degree, 1956. *Politics:* Republican. *Religion:* Protestant. *Hobbies and other interests:* Reading, gardening, hiking.

ADDRESSES: Home—39 Cherokee Way, Rochester, NH 03867. *Office*—KALM Publishing, P.O. Box 522, Durham, NH 03824. *E-mail*—uniqueyankee@ metrocast.net.

CAREER: First Pennsylvania Banking and Trust, assistant director of training, 1946-1961; Guaranty Bank and Trust, Worcester, MA, assistant director of training, 1961-1963; Fitzwilliam Inn, Fitzwilliam, NH, owner and innkeeper (with husband), 1963-1973; National Grange Mutual, Keene, NH, assistant director of training, 1975-1980; University of New Hampshire, Durham, business manager for student dining, 1980-1989; KALM Publishing, Durham, partner, beginning 1989. Also worked as manager of John Hancock Inn, Hancock, NH.

MEMBER: Fitzwilliam Historical Society (president, 1970-72; member of board of directors, 1993-97).

WRITINGS:

A Horse in the Ladies' Room, illustrated by Jim Dugan, KALM Publishing (Durham, NH), 1997.
(And illustrator) *Where Lame Donkeys Lie,* KALM Publishing (Durham, NH), 1998.
On the Wings of a Unicorn, KALM Publishing (Durham, NH), 1999.
Sisters by Heart: Partners in Aging, illustrated by Jim Dugan, KALM Publishing (Durham, NH), 2001.

SIDELIGHTS: Mary Lou Fuller had yearnings to become a writer from an early age, and satisfied them to the extent of writing occasional poems and stories for local periodicals or for important social gatherings. Feeling, however, that she needed to make a living at a more stable occupation, she studied industrial psychology at the University of Pennsylvania during the evenings and pursued a career writing and conducting personnel training programs for banks. A first marriage unhappily led to what Fuller once told *CA* was an emotional crisis. She began a new life in New England in the early 1960s, when she met Enoch "Red" Fuller, a New Hampshire native whose father had once been secretary of that state. Fuller, a diabetic from childhood, had learned to live with his ailment and had established a career in hotel management. After a romance that led to a loving marriage, the couple decided to work together, first in managing the John Hancock Inn in Hancock, New Hampshire, and after a few months, as owners and managers of the equally historic Fitzwilliam Inn in Fitzwilliam. Ten of the best years of the Fullers' lives followed, as they worked hard and harmoniously, sharing their lives fully and adopting two children.

Sadly, Red Fuller died in a diabetic coma in May, 1973, at the age of forty-eight. Mary Lou Fuller continued running the inn herself for a brief period, but when the chef died soon afterward, she decided to sell, and reentered the field of bank personnel training. From there, she accepted a position as business manager of student dining for the University of New Hampshire. Finally, at age sixty, she felt it was time to devote herself to writing. She retired from her university position and became a partner in KALM Publishing.

Fuller's first book, *A Horse in the Ladies' Room,* was a memoir of innkeeping, largely based on the detailed records her late husband kept of the day-to-day life and business of the Fitzwilliam Inn. To these, Fuller added her own recollections and considerable raconteurial skill. *A Horse in the Ladies Room* was widely publicized in Fuller's local area and was declared the number-one best-seller by a writer for the *Keene Sentinel* of Keene, New Hampshire.

A follow-up, *Where Lame Donkeys Lie,* is also a memoir. Fuller's third book, *On the Wings of a Unicorn,* was described by the author, while in progress, as being "largely autobiographical"; it also, Fuller added, "pays tribute to the women who have 'passed me from hand-to-hand' sharing their strength and helping me survive spousal abuse in my first marriage and its ensuing emotional breakdown."

Fuller once told *CA:* "At the age of sixty, I finally succumbed to the writing 'itch' I had been nurturing for decades. Abandoning a successful career, I purchased a word processor and wallowed in the sheer glory of putting words on paper.

"I had studied creative writing in school and even though several poems and a short story had been published in newspapers and local periodicals, I was convinced no one would take my writings seriously; much less, pay to read them. Instead, I dutifully pursued the dry subject of industrial psychology because it would further my chances in the personnel work in which I was involved at the time.

"However, whenever an occasion warranted—Christmas, retirement party, et cetera—I wrote a poem or story to commemorate the event or to extol the virtues of the retiree. This kept the writing 'bug' at bay until finally I simply challenged myself to quit my day job, stop my complaining and 'write, damn it, write!'

"I had a perfect place to start: with the notes my husband had kept during the ten years we owned and operated one of New Hampshire's oldest early American inns, the 200-year-old Fitzwilliam Inn. Although my husband passed away many years ago, his daily records of meals served and popular entrees were intact and each was accompanied by his notations describing the unusual events, guests, or staff members.

"Knowing I should start writing about something I knew, I organized the records into outline form and from this wrote *A Horse in the Ladies' Room,* which, much to my amazement, became an overnight best-seller in New England. I elected to self-publish because I was impatient to get going at my now seventy years.

"I do my best writing early in the morning—occasionally in the middle of the night as well; particularly if I am lying awake. I snap on the light and jot down thoughts on the pad I keep nearby. I write in longhand first, sometimes only a page or two, and then put it on the computer, print it out, and do a quick rewrite. By whittling away at a chapter or thought in small bits, I find my word choices are easier, more profound or more humorous.

"Writing has always been a spiritual adventure: cleansing, healing and cathartic. I kept journals for many years and these have become source materials for *On the Wings of a Unicorn.*"

Recently Fuller added: "My fourth book, *Sisters by Heart: Partners in Aging,* is the story of two women in their fifties who met purely by chance. Now, over twenty years later and despite the differences in our backgrounds, we are still moving forward together. The story, a memoir, moves from a difficult transition period following the merging of our households to a series of humorous adventures and misadventures that drew us closer together. I wrote this book to carry forward the theme of my third book, *On the Wings of a Unicorn,* in which I speak at great length about the importance of the sharing of women's strength. In *Sisters,* I found the words to describe the emotional attachment my partner and I have discovered: pride in our relationship and accomplishments, how good it is to be a woman, and the importance to share our experiences."

BIOGRAPHICAL AND CRITICAL SOURCES:

PERIODICALS

New Hampshire Sunday News (Manchester, NH), February 8, 1998.
Yankee, March, 1998.

FURUTANI, Dale 1946-

PERSONAL: Born December 1, 1946, in Hilo, HI; adopted by John Flanagan, c. 1951; married; wife's name Sharon. *Education:* California State University, Long Beach, B.A.; University of California, Los Angeles, M.B.A.

ADDRESSES: Home—Los Angeles, CA. *Agent*—Neeti Madan, Sterling Lord Literistic, 65 Bleecker St., New York, NY 10012. *E-mail*—dfurutani@aol.com.

CAREER: Owner of private consulting company for automotive industry; president of a software company; Yamaha Motorcycles, parts marketing manager; Nissan Motor Corporation USA, director of information technology; writer.

AWARDS, HONORS: Macavity Award for Best First Mystery Novel, and Anthony Award for Best First Novel, both 1997, both for *Death in Little Tokyo;* several awards for poetry.

WRITINGS:

MYSTERY NOVELS

Death in Little Tokyo, St. Martin's Press (New York, NY), 1996.
The Toyotomi Blades, St. Martin's Press (New York, NY), 1997.
Death at the Crossroads (first part of trilogy), Morrow (New York, NY), 1998.
Jade Palace Vendetta (second part of trilogy), Morrow (New York, NY), 1999.
Kill the Shogun (third part of trilogy), Morrow (New York, NY), 2000.

Author of three nonfiction books; contributor of numerous articles to periodicals.

WORK IN PROGRESS: Blood on the Pacific Rim (working title), a "Ken Tanaka" mystery.

SIDELIGHTS: Mystery writer Dale Furutani has paved the way to success for Asian-American crime novelists, being the first to win a major mystery award. A sansei—third-generation Japanese American—Furutani, whose mother was Japanese, was born in Hawaii in 1946 and moved to California at age five when he was adopted by John Flanagan. There, Furutani found himself a minority; sometimes he was the only Asian student in his school, and he frequently experienced racial prejudice. "This was the early fifties," he noted in an online interview with Claire E. White for *Writers Write,* "so the war wasn't that far away, and some kids thought I was personally responsible for Pearl Harbor." As a boy, Furutani absorbed the stories of the "camp generation" of Japanese Americans—those interned during World War II—and when he began writing fiction he was determined to preserve as much as possible of this legacy in his work.

Furutani worked his way through California State University in Long Beach by writing articles and serving as contributing editor for several magazines. After earning a degree in creative writing, he attended the University of California, Los Angeles, where he received an M.B.A. in marketing and information systems and began a successful career as a consultant in the automotive industry, owning his own consulting company for nineteen years. Furutani also served as president of a software company and as parts marketing manager for Yamaha Motorcycles before becoming director of information technology for Nissan Motor Corporation, USA—a position he still holds. During his career he has written three nonfiction books and has won prizes for his poetry.

In 1993 Furutani's friend, mystery writer Michael Nava, suggested he try a mystery, and *Death in Little Tokyo* was the result. The novel features the debut of Ken Tanaka, a Japanese-American amateur sleuth who, at the novel's start, is hosting an L.A. Mystery Club weekend. Playing the role of a private eye, Tanaka is hired by a woman who thinks he's the real thing; soon he finds himself a suspect in a murder plot that touches on blackmail and Japanese mobsters.

Furutani was intent on making Tanaka an authentic character. "Most of the Asian-American detectives I read didn't have the right 'aji' [taste]—they didn't resonate with me and I couldn't identify with them," the author explained to White. But Tanaka resonates with readers; reportedly, both Asians and non-Asians have told Furutani that they find Tanaka a very sympathetic character. Although *Death in Little Tokyo* received only lukewarm praise from reviewers, who found the book contrived and sometimes pedantic, it was nominated for an Agatha award and won a Macavity award and an Anthony Award for Best First Mystery Novel.

Furutani followed this popular success with another "Ken Tanaka" mystery, *The Toyotomi Blades.* In this book Tanaka is invited to visit Japan, where he is soon caught in a tangled web involving the possession of a seventeenth-century sword and the Yakuza, the Japanese mafia. To his surprise, Tanaka feels a bit alienated in the country of his ancestry—he doesn't speak the language or understand all of the customs. Placing his detective in Japan, Furutani explained, enabled him to explore a theme of great interest: racial versus cultural identity.

Taking a vacation from his fictional protagonist Tanaka, Furutani completed a trilogy set in seventeenth-century Japan comprised of *Death at the Crossroads, Jade Palace Vendetta,* and *Kill the Shogun.* The series, inspired by one of Furutani's many visits to Japan, focuses on the masterless samurai Matsuyama Kaze and his attempts to find the kidnapped daughter of his murdered master and mistress. Drawing upon extensive research, the three books synthesize historical detail about everyday life during the period while providing adventurous and violent plots. "It occurred to me that most of the historical fiction about ancient Japan dealt with the nobility," Furutani commented in his *Writers Write* interview. "My protagonist comes in contact with the peasants, merchants and entertainers which formed the common classes of ancient Japan."

Death at the Crossroads concerns the events leading to Kaze's status as a *ronin* or masterless samurai. In *Jade Palace Vendetta* Kaze discovers that the wealthy merchant whose life he has saved harbors deadly secrets. The trilogy's finale, *Kill the Shogun,* finds Kaze in Edo with the dual purposes of saving his late master's daughter from a brothel and eluding those who think he has plotted to kill the local Shogun. Although bearing no resemblance to the "Ken Tanaka" books, these historical novels received warm reviews and attracted an audience of their own.

Some critics were particularly enthusiastic about *Jade Palace Vendetta.* A *Publishers Weekly* reviewer declared that Furutani writes with "the unhurried care of a master craftsman . . . visual poetry, horror and

beauty nightmarishly juxtaposed." Jenny McLarin in *Booklist* found the novel to be an "entertaining story full of heart-stopping sword fights," and *Library Journal* correspondent Rex E. Klett deemed it "essential reading for historical mystery fans." With the publication of *Kill the Shogun,* several reviewers expressed hope that Furutani would continue to write historical mysteries, with or without his mystical and mercurial Kaze as the hero. Klett described *Kill the Shogun* as a "colorful adventure," and McLarin called it "compelling fiction." A *Publishers Weekly* contributor concluded that, despite its position as the last volume of a trilogy, the work "stand[s] alone as a complete and entertaining period mystery."

By 2002 Furutani, who lives in Los Angeles with his wife and Labrador retriever and still holds his position at Nissan, was busy working on a third "Ken Tanaka" mystery; this one deals more straightforwardly with interracial marriage and features the disappearance of a sumo wrestler.

BIOGRAPHICAL AND CRITICAL SOURCES:

PERIODICALS

Booklist, May 15, 1999, Jenny McLarin, review of *Jade Palace Vendetta,* p. 1673; August, 2000, Jenny McLarin, review of *Kill the Shogun,* p. 2119.
Kirkus Reviews, August 15, 1996, p. 1189.
Library Journal, October 1, 1997, Rex E. Klett, review of *The Toyotomi Blades,* p. 129; July, 1999, Rex E. Klett, review of *Jade Palace Vendetta,* p. 140; August, 2000, Rex E. Klett, review of *Kill the Shogun,* p. 166.
Los Angeles Times, July 26, 1998.
Publishers Weekly, September 2, 1996, review of *Death in Little Tokyo,* p. 117; August 25, 1997, review of *The Toyotomi Blades,* p. 49; June 28, 1999, review of *Jade Palace Vendetta,* p. 57; July 31, 2000, review of *Kill the Shogun,* p. 75.
Washington Post, October 10, 1999.

ONLINE

BookBrowser, http://www.bookbrowser.com/ (November 6, 2003).
Dale Furutani Web site, http://members.aol.com/ Dfurutani/ (November 6, 2003).
Writers Write, http://www.writerswrite.com/ (January, 1998), interview with Furutani.*

G

GALLAGHER, Gary W(illiam) 1950-

PERSONAL: Born October 8, 1950, in Glendale, CA; son of William (a farmer) and Shirley (a homemaker; maiden name, Gray) Gallagher; children: William Paul. *Education:* Adams State College, B.A., 1972; University of Texas at Austin, M.A., 1977, Ph.D., 1982.

ADDRESSES: Office—Corcoran Department of History, 227 Randall Hall, University of Virginia, Charlottesville, VA 22903-3284. *E-mail*—gallagher@virginia.edu.

CAREER: National Archives and Records Administration, Washington, DC, archivist at Lyndon Baines Johnson Library, 1977-86; Pennsylvania State University, University Park, assistant professor, 1986-89, associate professor, 1989-91, professor of history, 1991-98, and head of department, 1991-95; University of Virginia, Charlottesville, professor of history, 1998-99, John L. Nau III Professor of the History of the American Civil War, 1999—. University of Texas at Austin, visiting lecturer, spring, 1986, George W. Littlefield lecturer, 1995-96. American Battlefield Protection Foundation, member of board of trustees, 1991—.

MEMBER: Organization of American Historians, Society of Civil War Historians, Association for the Preservation of Civil War Sites (president, 1987-94, 1998—, trustee, 1994-96), Southern Historical Association.

AWARDS, HONORS: Grant from National Endowment for the Humanities, 1985; Mellon fellow, Virginia Historical Society, 1988 and 1989; grant from American Council of Learned Societies, 1989-90; Daniel Harvey Hill Award, 1990; Douglas Southall Freeman Prize, 1990, and Founder's Award, 1991, both for *Fighting for the Confederacy*; Nevins-Freeman Award, 1991; Society of American Historians citation, 1996; Lincoln Prize honorable mention, 1998, for *The Confederate War;* Fletcher Pratt Award, 1998; Times-Mirror Foundation distinguished fellow at Huntington Library, San Marino, CA, 2001-02; Organization of American Historians Lecturer, 2002—.

WRITINGS:

(Editor and contributor) *Essays on Southern History: Written in Honor of Barnes F. Lathrop,* General Libraries, University of Texas at Austin (Austin, TX), 1980.

Stephen Dodson Ramseur: Lee's Gallant General, University of North Carolina Press (Chapel Hill, NC), 1985.

(Editor and contributor) *Antietam: Essays on the 1862 Maryland Campaign,* Kent State University Press (Kent, OH), 1989.

(Editor) *Fighting for the Confederacy: The Personal Recollections of General Edward Porter Alexander,* University of North Carolina Press (Chapel Hill, NC), 1989.

(Editor and contributor) *Struggle for the Shenandoah: Essays on the 1864 Valley Campaign,* Kent State University Press (Kent, OH), 1991.

(Editor and contributor) *The First Day at Gettysburg: Essays on Confederate and Union Leadership,* Kent State University Press (Kent, OH), 1992.

(Editor and contributor) *The Second Day at Gettysburg: Essays on Confederate and Union Leadership,* Kent State University Press (Kent, OH), 1993.

(Editor and contributor) *The Third Day at Gettysburg and Beyond,* University of North Carolina Press (Chapel Hill, NC), 1994.

(Editor and contributor) *The Fredericksburg Campaign: Decision on the Rappahannock,* University of North Carolina Press (Chapel Hill, NC), 1995.

Jubal A. Early, the Lost Cause, and Civil War History: A Persistent Legacy, Marquette University Press (Milwaukee, WI), 1995.

(Editor and contributor) *Lee the Soldier,* University of Nebraska Press (Lincoln, NE), 1996.

(Editor and contributor) *Chancellorsville: The Battle and Its Aftermath,* University of North Carolina Press (Chapel Hill, NC), 1996.

The Confederate War: How Popular Will, Nationalism, and Military Strategy Could Not Stave Off Defeat, Harvard University Press (Cambridge, MA), 1997.

(Editor and contributor) *The Wilderness Campaign,* University of North Carolina Press (Chapel Hill, NC), 1997.

(Editor and contributor) *The Spotsylvania Campaign,* University of North Carolina Press (Chapel Hill, NC), 1998.

Lee and His Generals in War and Memory, Louisiana State University Press (Baton Rouge, LA), 1998.

(Editor and contributor) *The Antietam Campaign,* University of North Carolina Press (Chapel Hill, NC), 1999.

(Editor and contributor) *Three Days at Gettysburg: Essays on Confederate and Union Leadership,* Kent State University Press (Kent, OH), 1999.

(Editor and contributor, with Alan T. Nolan) *The Myth of the Lost Cause and Civil War History,* Indiana University Press (Bloomington, IN), 2001.

Lee and His Army in Confederate History, University of North Carolina Press (Chapel Hill, NC), 2001.

The American Civil War: The War in the East, 1861-May 1863, Fitzroy Dearborn Publishers (Chicago, IL), 2001.

(Editor, with Margaret E. Wagner and Paul Finkelman) *The Library of Congress Civil War Desk Reference,* Simon & Schuster (New York, NY), 2002.

(Editor and contributor) *The Richmond Campaign of 1862: The Peninsula and the Seven Days,* University of North Carolina Press (Chapel Hill, NC), 2002.

(Editor and contributor) *The Shenandoah Valley Campaign of 1862,* University of North Carolina Press (Chapel Hill, NC), 2003.

Work represented in anthologies, including *The Civil War Battlefield Guide,* edited by Frances H. Kennedy, Houghton Mifflin, 1990; *The Confederate General,* edited by William C. Davis, six volumes, National Historical Society, 1991—; *Why the Confederacy Lost,* edited by Gabor S. Boritt, Oxford University Press, 1991; *Ken Burns's "The Civil War": Historians Respond,* edited by Robert Brent Toplin, Oxford University Press, 1996; *New Perspectives on the Civil War: Myths and Realities of the National Conflict,* edited by John Y. Simon and Michael E. Stevens, Madison House, 1998; *Writing the Civil War: The Quest to Understand,* edited by James M. McPherson and William J. Cooper, Jr., University of South Carolina Press, 1998. Contributor of articles and reviews to history and military journals.

WORK IN PROGRESS: An assessment of Confederate general Jubal A. Early and his role in shaping perceptions about the war; an interpretive study of Civil War military history that emphasizes connections between the home front and the battlefield.

SIDELIGHTS: Gary W. Gallagher is a prolific and prominent historian of the U.S. Civil War, dealing with both the actual events of the war and the mythology that has developed around them. *Chicago Tribune* contributor James A. Ramage has described Gallagher as "one of today's foremost Civil War historians," and *Washington Times* commentator Mackubin Thomas Owens has called him "one of the best of a new generation of Civil War scholars." His work, as both writer and editor, has emphasized the importance of military history at a time when it had fallen out of favor among some academics. He has chronicled many of the major campaigns of the war's eastern theater, dissected both romantic and revisionist views of the Confederacy, and scrutinized the generalship and postwar reputation of Southern commander Robert E. Lee.

In *The Confederate War: How Popular Will, Nationalism, and Military Strategy Could Not Stave Off Defeat,* Gallagher disputes the idea held by many late-twentieth-century historians that the Southern war effort was fatally undermined by dissension within the Confederacy, including resentment of economic inequities, distrust of centralized government, and perhaps an unconscious distaste for defending the institution of slavery. On the contrary, he asserts, there was deep and wide support for the war; more than three-quarters of Southern white men of military age served in the army, as opposed to half of the North's available fighters, and civilians had great loyalty to their young country and reverence for Lee. It was only the North's greater military might, not any lack of Southern resolve, that brought the Union victory, he contends. He draws on hundreds of Civil War letters and diary entries to provide examples of this resolve.

Gallagher "argues that the current emphasis on class, race and gender on the home front exaggerates tensions in Southern society and distorts the picture," related Ramage in the *Chicago Tribune*. His case, Ramage added, is "well-organized and well-presented." Jonathan Yardley, writing in the *Washington Post Book World,* deemed Gallagher's evidence "impressive if limited," but thought the author failed to address "a central and well-founded tenet of the conventional wisdom: that the South was doomed from the outset by an agrarian economy" with little heavy industry. Yardley allowed, however, that the South "prolonged the conflict to an almost unimaginable extent precisely for the reasons Gallagher cites: its puissant nationalism, its devotion to its 'cause,' the genius of its chief military leaders and the dogged bravery of its soldiers." *Civil War History* reviewer Christopher Phillips described *The Confederate War* as "an extremely satisfying book" that demonstrates the importance of studying military history, and Ramage concluded that Gallagher's "bold revisions make this one of the most significant works in this generation of Civil War literature."

Gallagher returns to this theme in *Lee and His Army in Confederate History,* a collection of essays on the Southern military leader and key battles. "Gallagher revives the overwhelming numbers and resources explanation for Confederate defeat, shorn of its false aura of inevitability," commented James M. McPherson in the *New York Review of Books.* McPherson continued that Gallagher argues "forcefully and convincingly" that the South's "white unity and strength of purpose," even with its army outnumbered and outgunned, made it a tenacious foe for the Union throughout the conflict.

In *Lee and His Generals in War and Memory,* Gallagher makes a "persuasive" case that Lee himself was "a significant factor in prolonging the life of the Confederacy," observed Joseph L. Harsh in *Civil War History.* This book, according to *Washington Times*

contributor Owens, "provides a balanced assessment of Lee the soldier—avoiding the dual pitfalls of Lost Cause hagiography and the Lee bashing that too often characterizes the work of revisionists." Gallagher's work, Owens continued, offers a picture of "Lee's great qualities, including most of all his ability to compensate for weak subordinates," as well as discussion of instances where his strategies went wrong, such as at Gettysburg.

Gallagher devotes space to several of Lee's subordinate commanders, both the weak and the strong, and shows how one of them, Jubal A. Early, helped develop and popularize the romanticized Lost Cause view of the Confederacy. Early crafted "for future generations a written record that celebrated the Confederacy's hopeless but heroic military resistance against the overwhelming power of the Union," Owens remarked. This view also idealized Lee, downplayed slavery, and portrayed the South as fighting primarily for independence. It gained many adherents in the late nineteenth century and far into the twentieth, even though modern academic historians have put forth some decidedly different views. "Gallagher illustrates how even today, the Lost Cause interpretation dominates both historiography and popular images of the war," commented Owens. Willard Carl Klunder, reviewing the book for the *Historian,* noted that Gallagher "cogently argues that the romantic image of the 'Lost Cause' is based as much on perception as fact." *Lee and His Generals,* Klunder added, "augments Gallagher's reputation as a thoughtful interpreter of Civil War military history."

The Myth of the Lost Cause and Civil War History, which Gallagher edited with Alan T. Nolan, further addresses the growth and persistence of the Lost Cause viewpoint, with Gallagher contributing an essay on Early's role. Gallagher's work as an editor and contributor to volumes of essays also includes anthologies on Lee and on major battles including Gettysburg, Antietam, Fredericksburg, Chancellorsville, Spotsylvania, and the Virginia Peninsula campaign. Critiquing *The Richmond Campaign of 1862: The Peninsula and the Seven Days* for *Civil War History,* Richard J. Sommers praised Gallagher's "graceful and learned editorship." *The Spotsylvania Campaign,* George C. Rable wrote in *History: Review of New Books,* is "a fine piece of work," gathering varied perspectives and challenging conventional viewpoints. In *Chancellorsville: The Battle and Its Aftermath,* with historians emphasizing new interpretations and including first-hand observations from, among others, children and military doctors, Gallagher "has again shown why he is a master editor-historian," in the opinion of *Civil War History* contributor Ervin L. Jordan, Jr. With both his writing and editing work, as Phillips reported in that same journal, Gallagher "has become one of the most well-regarded of our Civil War scholars."

BIOGRAPHICAL AND CRITICAL SOURCES:

PERIODICALS

Booklist, October 15, 2000, Jay Freeman, review of *The Myth of the Lost Cause and Civil War History,* p. 415.

Chicago Tribune, October 1, 1997, James A. Ramage, "A Well-Reasoned View of What Kept the South Going," Tempo section, p. 3.

Civil War History, September, 1997, Ervin L. Jordan, Jr., review of *Chancellorsville: The Battle and Its Aftermath,* pp. 250-251; March, 1998, Arthur W. Bergeron, Jr., review of *The Wilderness Campaign,* p. 62; September, 1998, Christopher Phillips, review of *The Confederate War: How Popular Will, Nationalism, and Military Strategy Could Not Stave Off Defeat,* p. 221; June, 1999, Joseph M. Priest, review of *The Spotsylvania Campaign,* p. 163; September 1, 1999, Joseph L. Harsh, review of *Lee and His Generals in War and Memory,* p. 271; December 1, 1999, Arthur W. Bergeron, Jr., review of *The Antietam Campaign,* p. 357, Jeffry D. Wert, review of *Three Days at Gettysburg: Essays on Confederate and Union Leadership,* p. 363; December 1, 2001, James Tice Moore, review of *The Myth of the Lost Cause and Civil War History,* p. 354; June, 2002, Richard J. Sommers, review of *The Richmond Campaign of 1862: The Peninsula and the Seven Days,* p. 172.

Historian, spring, 2000, Willard Carl Klunder, review of *Lee and His Generals in War and Memory,* p. 655; fall, 2000, Daniel E. Sutherland, review of *The Antietam Campaign,* p. 148.

History: Review of New Books, spring, 1999, George C. Rable, review of *The Spotsylvania Campaign,* p. 105.

Journal of Southern History, May, 2002, James M. Morris, review of *The Richmond Campaign of 1862,* p. 575.

Library Journal, June 15, 1998, Brooks D. Simpson, review of *Lee and His Generals in War and Memory,* p. 91; October 15, 2000, Jim Doyle, review of *The Myth of the Lost Cause and Civil War History,* p. 84.

New York Review of Books, June 13, 2001, James M. McPherson, "Could the South Have Won?," pp. 23-25.

Washington Post Book World, September 24, 1997, Jonathan Yardley, "A New Perspective on a Lost Cause," p. D2.

Washington Times, September 27, 1997, Kevin Levin, "'Lack of Will' Theory Takes a Beating," p. B3; December 16, 2000, Kevin Levin, "Finding the Truth about 'Lost Cause,'" p. B3; September 25, 1999, Mackubin Thomas Owens, "Lee, Flaws and Genius Intact," p. B3.

ONLINE

University of Virginia, http://www.virginia.edu/ (November 8, 2003), author profile.

*   *   *

GAMBRELL, Jamey

PERSONAL: Born in New York, NY. *Education:* University of Texas, B.A., 1975; graduate work at Columbia University.

ADDRESSES: Office—Art in America, 575 Broadway, New York, NY 10012. *Agent*—Deborah Karl, Wylie, Aitken & Stone, 250 West 57th St., New York, NY 10107.

CAREER: Art in America, New York, NY, contributing editor and staff writer, 1983—; freelance art critic, essayist, and translator from Russian.

AWARDS, HONORS: Translation fellowship, National Endowment for the Arts, 1993.

WRITINGS:

TRANSLATOR

(And editor and author of introduction) Andrei Honchalovsky and Alexander Lipkov, *The Inner Circle: An Inside View of Soviet Life under Stalin,* Newmarket (New York, NY), 1991.

Tatyana Tolstaya, *Sleepwalker in a Fog,* Knopf (New York, NY), 1992.

Daniil Kharms, *The Story of a Boy Named Will, Who Went Sledding down a Hill,* North-South (Lanham, MD), 1993.

(With Margaret Wettlin and Walter Arndt) Boris Pasternak, *Letters, Summer 1926,* edited by Yegevny Pasternak, Yelena Pasternak, and Konstantin M. Azadovsky, New York Review Books (New York, NY), 2001.

(And editor and author of introduction) Marina Tsvetaeva, *Earthly Signs: Moscow Diaries, 1917-1922* Yale University Press (New Haven, CT), 2002.

Tatyana Tolstaya, *The Slynx,* Houghton Mifflin (Boston, MA), 2003.

Tatyana Tolstaya, *Pushkin's Children: Writings on Russia and Russians,* Mariner/Houghton Mifflin (Boston, MA), 2003.

OTHER

Telephone, translated and adapted from *Telefon* by Kornei Chukovskii, illustrated by Vladimir Radunsky, North-South Books (New York, NY), 1996.

Also author of essays on Russian art, literature, media, and culture in *New York Review of Books* and *Harper's.*

SIDELIGHTS: Jamey Gambrell is known for his skill and dedication in translating modern Russian literature. Since 1990 he has been translating the work of Tatyana Tolstaya, a great-grandniece of literary great Leo Tolstoy and an essayist and fiction writer in her own right. Her first novel, *The Slynx,* is a futuristic dystopia "heroically translated by Jamey Gambrell," according to *Women's Review of Books* contributor Helena Goscilo. A *Publishers Weekly* reviewer similarly praised how "Gambrell ably translates the mix of neologisms and plain speech with which Tolstaya describes this devastated world."

Gambrell has also edited and translated the diaries and essays of Russian poet Marina Tsvetaeva, who committed suicide in 1941. In *Earthly Signs: Moscow Diaries, 1917-1922,* he brings together many of the poet's political writings that could not be published under the Soviet regime. "Gambrell's excellently translated edition, with its well-researched and informative introduction, graciously fulfils Tsvetaeva's desire to see these

pieces of diaristic prose bound in a single volume," Rachel Polonsky commented in the *Times Literary Supplement.* While noting the work "would have benefited from more extensive gloss and annotation," *New Statesman* critic Robert Potts likewise observed that Gambrell's organization and translation gives Tsvetaeva's writing "a fine sense of urgency and exhilaration."

Gambrell has also turned his translating efforts into producing picture books for children. In 1993 he translated a poem by Daniil Kharms into *The Story of a Boy Named Will, Who Went Sledding down a Hill,* while in 1996 he translated and adapted a poem by Kornei Chukovskii into *Telephone.* This nonsensical story shows a man answering a series of increasingly bizarre phone calls, with each animal caller making an unusual request. A *Publishers Weekly* critic observed Gambrell's use of "tongue twisters and involved rhyme schemes," while *Booklist* contributor Michael Cart concluded, "No youngster will want to put this hilarious call on hold."

BIOGRAPHICAL AND CRITICAL SOURCES:

PERIODICALS

Booklist, December 15, 1996, Michael Cart, review of *Telephone,* p. 729.

New Statesman, January 20, 2003, Robert Potts, "Faithful Only to Poetry," p. 50.

Publishers Weekly, November 18, 1996, review of *Telephone,* p. 74; November 25, 2002, review of *The Slynx,* p. 41.

Times Literary Supplement, February 28, 2003, Rachel Polonsky, "A Terrible Intimacy," February 28, 2003, pp. 3-4.

Women's Review of Books, May, 2003, Helena Goscilo, "Dystopian Dreams," p. 10.*

*   *   *

GARCEAU, Dee 1955-

PERSONAL: Born October 8, 1955, in Boston, MA; daughter of Arthur J. (a physician) and Davida G. (a horticulturist; maiden name, Gordon) Garceau; married second husband, Ron Hagen, 2003. *Ethnicity:* "Caucasian." *Education:* Brown University, Ph.D.,

1995. *Politics:* Democrat. *Hobbies and other interests:* Hiking, rafting, canoeing in the Rocky Mountain West, interior decoration.

ADDRESSES: Home—Memphis, TN. *Office*—Department of History, Rhodes College, Memphis, TN 38122. *E-mail*—garceau@rhodes.edu.

CAREER: Canyonlands Field Institute, Moab, UT, program coordinator and director of Desert Writer's Workshop, 1986-89; University of Montana, Missoula, visiting instructor in history, 1991-95; Rhodes College, Memphis, TN, began as assistant professor, became associate professor of history, 1995—. Producer of the film *A Capital Beat,* at Center for Documentary Film, George Washington University, 2002.

MEMBER: Organization of American Historians, Western Historical Association, Organization of Western Women's Historians.

WRITINGS:

The Important Things of Life: Women, Work, and Family in Sweetwater County, Wyoming, 1880-1929, University of Nebraska Press (Lincoln, NE), 1995. (Editor, with Matthew Basso and Laura McCall) *Across the Great Divide: Cultures of Manhood in the American West,* Routledge (New York, NY), 2000.

Contributor to books, including *Writing the Range: Race, Class, and Culture in the Women's West,* edited by Susan Armitage and Elizabeth Jameson, University of Oklahoma Press (Norman, OK), 1997; and *Sifters: Native American Women's Lives,* edited by Theda Purdue, Oxford University Press (New York, NY), 2001.

WORK IN PROGRESS: Editing a collection of biographical essays on women of the Rocky Mountain West, including her own essay on Mary Fields, an African-American settler in turn-of-the-century Montana.

*   *   *

GARCIA, Cristina 1958-

PERSONAL: Born July 4, 1958, in Havana, Cuba; immigrated to the United States, c. 1960; daughter of Frank M. and Hope Lois Garcia; married Scott Brown, December 8, 1990; children: Pilar Akiko. *Education:* Barnard College, B.A., 1979; Johns Hopkins Univer-

Cristina Garcia

sity, M.A., 1981. *Politics:* "Registered Democrat." *Hobbies and other interests:* Contemporary dance, music, travel, foreign languages.

ADDRESSES: Agent—Ellen Levine, 15 East 26th St., Suite 1801, New York, NY 10010.

CAREER: Journalist and author. *Time* (magazine), New York, NY, reporter and researcher, 1983-85, correspondent, 1985-90, bureau chief in Miami, FL, 1987-88.

MEMBER: Amnesty International, PEN American Center.

AWARDS, HONORS: National Book Award finalist, National Book Foundation, 1992, for *Dreaming in Cuban;* Hodder fellowship, Princeton University, 1992-93; Cintas fellowship, 1992-93; Whiting Writers Award, 1996.

WRITINGS:

Dreaming in Cuban (novel), Knopf (New York, NY), 1992.

Cars of Cuba (essay), created by D. D. Allen, photographs by Joshua Greene, Abrams (New York, NY), 1995.

The Aguero Sisters (novel), Knopf (New York, NY), 1997.

Monkey Hunting (novel), Knopf (New York, NY), 2003.

(Editor and author of introduction) *Cubanismo!: The Vintage Book of Contemporary Cuban Literature,* Vintage (New York, NY), 2003.

Dreaming in Cuban and *The Aguero Sisters* have been translated into Spanish.

WORK IN PROGRESS: Poems and novels.

SIDELIGHTS: A reporter and correspondent for *Time* magazine during the 1980s, Cristina Garcia published her first novel, *Dreaming in Cuban,* in 1992. Inspired by Garcia's Cuban heritage, the book was highly acclaimed and became a finalist for the National Book Award. Reviewer Michiko Kakutani remarked in the *New York Times:* "Fierce, visionary, and at the same time oddly beguiling and funny, *Dreaming in Cuban* is a completely original novel. It announces the debut of a writer, blessed with a poet's ear for language, a historian's fascination with the past and a musician's intuitive understanding of the ebb and flow of emotion."

Dreaming in Cuban chronicles three generations of a Cuban family. The matriarch, Celia, falls in love with a married Spaniard and writes him letters for twenty-five years. Despite this long-distance affair, Celia marries a man she does not love, and the couple has two daughters, Lourdes and Felicia, and a son, Javier. Celia also becomes enamored of the Cuban Revolution and its leader, Fidel Castro. Lourdes, however, is raped by a revolutionary, and carries her hatred of the revolution with her when she moves to New York with her husband and opens two successful bakeries. Felicia stays in Cuba with her mother, but she marries a sailor who gives her syphilis, and she eventually meets a tragic end. Javier becomes a scientist and immigrates to Czechoslovakia, only to return a bitter alcoholic. As for the next generation, Thulani Davis explained in *New York Times Book Review,* "Celia's grandchildren can only be described as lost and abandoned by the obsessions of the parents. Of these, Lourdes's daughter, Pilar Puente del Pino, a would-be painter and stu-

dent in New York, becomes the secret sharer, a distant repository of the family's stories and some of its demons." Pilar is also the one who reunites the family, dragging her mother along with her on a trip to Cuba to see her grandmother.

In detailing this family history, Alan West observed in *Washington Post Book World,* "Garcia deftly shifts the narrative from third to first person, mixing in a series of Celia's letters to her long-lost Spanish lover, Gustavo. Likewise, she shifts from the past to the present, from Brooklyn to Havana, from character to character caught in the web that blood and history have set up for them, often with cruel irony." Richard Eder, writing in the *Los Angeles Times,* called *Dreaming in Cuban* "poignant and perceptive," noting that "the realism is exquisite." Davis concluded in *New York Times Book Review:* "I have no complaints to make. Cristina Garcia has written a jewel of a first novel."

Garcia's second novel, *The Aguero Sisters,* tells of two Cuban sisters, Constancia and Reina, who have been separated for thirty years. Constancia and her husband, who has recently retired from his cigar business, have moved from New York to Key Biscayne, Florida, and she has become a successful businesswoman and entrepreneur with her own line of homemade, natural body and face creams made from such ingredients as overripe peaches and avocado pits. Heberto, though, disappears from the main plot as he embarks on a new career as a counterrevolutionary, embroiled in a Bay of Pigs-like plot to overthrow the Cuban government.

Reina still lives in Cuba as a traveling electrician, and she has been nicknamed "Companera Amazonas" for her voluptuousness and free-spirited sexuality. While Constancia is somewhat prudish and has only had two lovers in her entire life—her two husbands—the uninhibited libertine Reina relishes the pleasure men provide her. As Garcia describes her, "Often, Reina selects the smallest, shiest electrician in a given town for her special favors, leaving him weak and inconsolable for months. After she departs, black owls are frequently sighted in the Ceiba trees." *Washington Post Book World* editor Nina King noted, "The sudden appearance of those ominous black owls is typical of Garcia's stylistic shifts from reality to myth to the heightened reality of 'magic realism.'"

According to *Time* reviewer Pico Iyer, "Both Aguero sisters share something deep as blood: a matter-of-fact commitment to the magic of their island of honey and rum. Constancia makes spells for women in the form of the 'luscious unguents' she markets; Reina casts spells over men." This is typical of a mystical parallelism that runs throughout the novel; for example, at approximately the same time Constancia elects cosmetic surgery that inadvertently leaves her with her mother's face, Reina is struck by lightning and must undergo experimental skin grafts—her skin becomes a patchwork contributed by friends and family.

As Kakutani commented in a *New York Times* review, "In Cristina Garcia's haunting new novel, *The Aguero Sisters,* a strange scar is handed down generation to generation. Blanca Aguero, the clan's ill-fated matriarch, receives the mysterious mark on her heel while swimming in Las Casas river during her honeymoon. Years later, while escaping from Cuba to the United States, Blanca's daughter Constancia leaves a similar mark on the foot of *her* daughter, Isabel, while trying to revive her from heatstroke. Isabel, in turn, eventually has a boy named Raku, who is born with a red birthmark on his foot in the same place as his mother's wound."

When the two sisters are reunited in Miami, they work to strip away the lies that constitute their lives. By the novel's denouement, their respective daughters, the artist, Isabel, and former volleyball coach-turned-prostitute, Dulce, are united, as well. The primary element that connects all four women, aside from their kinship per se, is the quest to learn the truth about the death of Constancia and Reina's mother, Blanca Mestre de Aguero. Blanca and her husband were both ornithologists, documenting the endangered wildlife of Cuba when her estranged husband, Ignacio, brutally murdered her. The reader is told, early on, the nature of her fate, but the protagonists must untwist truth from lies.

Ruth Behar noted in Chicago's *Tribune Books* that "Garcia offers an even more gorgeously written, even more flamboyant feminist vision of Cuban and American history, women's lives, memory and desire" than her previous novel, *Dreaming in Cuban.* The critic added, "Constancia and Reina, the feisty and rebellious Aguero sisters, are strong female protagonists whose meditations on men, sex, power and longing are among the great joys of Garcia's novel." Kakutani noted "the force of Ms. Garcia's powerfully imagined characters" and "the magic of her prose." In *Nation,* Ilan Stavans mentioned Garcia's "astonishing literary

style and dazzling attention to telling detail," and deemed her "an immensely talented writer, whose work ... is renewing American fiction." And, describing Garcia as "a wise and generous storyteller," Iyer praised the novelist. "Garcia has crafted a beautifully rounded work of art," the reviewer noted, "as warm and wry and sensuous as the island she clearly loves."

With 2003's *Monkey Hunting,* Garcia tackles another multigenerational saga with a twist: this time, the family she follows is of mixed Chinese and Cuban descent. The story begins with Chen Pan, who travels from his homeland in China to Cuba in the 1850s, where he is at first enslaved and forced to work in the sugarcane fields. However, Chen surmounts this challenge to become a successful Havana businessman who falls in love with a mulata named Lucrecia and finds happiness as a family man. The story then follows his descendants, whose experiences vary widely: their son Lorenzo becomes a physician; his daughter Chen Fang lives in China, where she becomes a teacher and counterrevolutionary; and, finally, her son Domingo Chen, ends up in New York City, where he encounters racism and ends up a soldier fighting in Vietnam. Critics delighted in Garcia's deft handling of shifts in time and point of view in a novel that is relatively short, given the expanse of years it covers. For example, Mary Margaret Benson, writing in *Library Journal,* called *Monkey Hunting* "a brilliantly conceived work—and it's also delightful reading." And although a *Publishers Weekly* reviewer wished that Garcia had taken more time in her story to develop the characters further, the critic praised the author's third novel as "a richly patterned mini-epic, a moving chorus of distinct voices." *New York Times* critic Michiko Kakutani, however, felt that *Monkey Hunting* "lacks the fierce magic and unexpected humor of Ms. Garcia's remarkable debut novel." Jennifer Schuessler, in *New York Times Book Review,* expressed a similar judgment, noting that, though the novel "leaps sure-footedly between the branches of a bushy and far-flung family tree," it does not convey the "spark of life that allows the Chen family to survive and transcend its forced march through endless war and revolution." Margot Livesey, on the other hand, observed in *Atlantic Monthly* that the novel combines "gorgeous writing" with extraordinary empathy and understanding.

BIOGRAPHICAL AND CRITICAL SOURCES:

BOOKS

Contemporary Literary Criticism, Volume 76, Gale (Detroit, MI), 1993.

Contemporary Novelists, 7th edition, St. James (Detroit, MI), 2001.

Notable Hispanic American Women, 2nd edition, Gale (Detroit, MI), 1998.

PERIODICALS

Atlantic Monthly, May, 2003, Margot Livesey, "Time Travel," p. 123.

Boston Globe, May 25, 1997, p. N15.

Entertainment Weekly, March 27, 1992, p. 68; March 26, 1993, p. 74.

Globe and Mail (Toronto, Ontario, Canada), March 21, 1992, p. C9.

Library Journal, March 15, 1997, Barbara Hoffert, review of *The Aguero Sisters,* p. 88; April 1, 2003, Mary Margaret Benson, review of *Monkey Hunting,* p. 128; June 15, 2003, Ron Ratliff, review of *Cubanismo!: The Vintage Book of Contemporary Cuban Literature,* p. 71.

Los Angeles Times, March 12, 1992, p. E10.

Los Angeles Times Book Review, November 19, 1995, p. 11; June 8, 1997, p. 8.

MELUS, fall, 2000, Katherine Payant, "From Alienation to Reconciliation in the Novels of Cristina Garcia," p. 163.

Nation, May 19, 1997, p. 32.

Newsweek, April 20, 1992, p. 78-79; April 28, 1997, p. 79.

New Yorker, June 1, 1992, p. 86.

New York Times, February 25, 1992, p. C17; May 27, 1997, p. C16; June 24, 2003, Michiko Kakutani, review of *Monkey Hunting,* p. E6.

New York Times Book Review, May 17, 1992, p. 14; June 15, 1997, p. 38; May 18, 2003, Jennifer Schuessler, "Fantasy Island," p. 11.

Observer, August 10, 1997, p. 15.

Publishers Weekly, January 13, 1992, review of *Dreaming in Cuban,* p. 46; March 10, 1997, review of *The Aguero Sisters,* p. 48; April 7, 2003, review of *Monkey Hunting,* p. 48.

Review of Contemporary Fiction, fall, 1997, Jane Juffer, review of *The Aguero Sisters,* p. 243.

Time, March 23, 1992, p. 67; May 12, 1997, Pico Ayer, review of *The Aguero Sisters,* p. 88.

Tribune Books (Chicago, IL), June 8, 1997, section 14, p. 1.

Washington Post Book World, March 1, 1992, p. 9; July 13, 1997, p. 1.

World Literature Today, winter, 1998, Ana Maria Hernandez, review of *The Aguero Sisters,* p. 134; winter, 2000, Rocio G. Davis, "Back to the Future: Mothers, Languages, and Homes in Cristina Garcia's *Dreaming in Cuban,*" p. 60.*

*　　*　　*

GEORGE, Anne Carroll (?)-2001

PERSONAL: Died March 14, 2001, during cardiac surgery; married; husband's name Earl; children: Buster. *Education:* Attended Samford University.

CAREER: Writer, editor, and former school teacher. Cofounder of Druid Press.

AWARDS, HONORS: Named Alabama Poet of the Year, 1994; Agatha Award for Best First Mystery for *Murder on a Girls' Night Out,* 1997; former Alabama State Poet; nominated for the Pulitzer Prize for *Some of It Is True;* Alumna of the Year, 1999, Samford University; *The Map That Lies between Us* was named Book of the Year, Alabama State Poet's Society, 2001; recipient of other writing awards, including the Hackney Award, for poetry.

WRITINGS:

"SOUTHERN SISTERS" SERIES

Murder on a Girls' Night Out, Avon (New York, NY), 1996.

Murder on a Bad Hair Day, Avon (New York, NY), 1996.

Murder Runs in the Family, Avon (New York, NY), 1997.

Murder Makes Waves, Avon (New York, NY), 1997.

Murder Gets a Life, Avon (New York, NY), 1998.

Murder Shoots the Bull, Morrow (New York, NY), 1999.

Murder Carries a Torch, Morrow (New York, NY), 2000.

Murder Boogies with Elvis, Morrow (New York, NY), 2001.

OTHER

Wild Goose Chase, Druid Press (Birmingham, AL), 1982.

(Editor, with Jerri Beck) *A Baker's Dozen: Contemporary Women Poets of Alabama* (anthology), Druid Press (Birmingham, AL), 1988.

This One and Magic Life: A Novel of a Southern Family, Avon (New York, NY), 1999.

The Map That Lies between Us: New and Collected Poems, 1980-2000, Black Belt Press (Montgomery, AL), 2000.

Also a contributor to literary journals.

SIDELIGHTS: One-time school teacher Anne George began her writing career with a book entitled *Wild Goose Chase,* published in 1982 by the small Alabama publishing house Druid Press, which she cofounded. Over two decades she contributed short stories and poems to literary magazines, coedited an anthology of poetry by Alabama women, and wrote seven mysteries featuring the irascible "Southern Sisters" Patricia Anne and Mary Alice. Readers know George's mysteries for their middle-aged sleuths, humorous dialogue, and comic situations rather than their plots, which have variously been called fragile or derivative. Shortly before her death in 2001 due to complications of cardiac surgery, George saw the publication of a collection of her verse, entitled *The Map That Lies between Us: New and Collected Poems, 1980-2000.*

In 1996 George made her debut as a mystery writer with *Murder on a Girls' Night Out,* which features unlikely sleuth Patricia Anne Hollowell, a retired teacher suddenly drawn into the world of murder investigation when her flamboyant sister, Mary Alice, becomes proprietor of a country-music nightclub. George constructs a plot that centers around the slaying of the club's former owner and the prime suspect in the deed—coincidentally, one of Hollowell's favorite students from her classroom days. A review of *Murder on a Girls' Night Out* in *Publishers Weekly* offered a mixed assessment: as a crime novel, its solution involved too many flimsy links and long-dormant secrets, but the reviewer praised George for her "sprightly dialogue and a humorous eye for detail."

Patricia Anne and Mary Alice return in *Murder Runs in the Family,* which begins with the wedding of Mary Alice's daughter. At the festivities, the sisters strike up a friendship with genealogist Meg Ryan, but they are later shocked to learn that she has committed suicide. The Hollowells suspect foul play in Ryan's improb-

able jump from a courthouse window. The more the sisters dig, the more intrigue they uncover, and eventually they learn that Ryan was not the person she seemed. A contributor to *Publishers Weekly* found that the story line of *Murder Runs in the Family* "spins out of control" but granted that George creates "wonderful dialogue," exceptional characterizations of even minor players, and an engaging party scene that opens the novel.

Clearly, the "effervescent" sisters, as *Library Journal*'s Rex E. Klett dubbed them, are the stars of these mysteries, rather than the plots. Additional "Southern Sisters" mysteries include *Murder on a Bad Hair Day,* in which the sisters discover a victim dead, without a hair out of place, and *Murder Makes Waves,* in which they investigate the death of a new friend while vacationing at a Florida condominium. Asserting that the "enjoyable characters and light humor" of the latter novel compensate for its unoriginal plot, Klett added that it is the first title of the "Southern Sisters" series to debut in hardcover. In *Murder Gets a Life,* the duo discovers a corpse in the family trailer of Patricia's son's fiancée, while in *Murder Shoots the Bull* they find the murderer of their neighbor Arthur's wife. Writing about the latter, a *Publishers Weekly* critic praised the humorous dialogue, "nifty web of subplots and . . . complications," and true-to-life characters.

George's 2000 offering, *Murder Carries a Torch,* which a *Publishers Weekly* reviewer dubbed "another genuinely funny mystery," revolves around the sisters' discovery of a the dead body of a renegade preacher while looking for their cousin Luke's wife, who has supposedly deserted him to run off with a painter. The critic also complimented George's ability to write humorous dialogue, a view shared by Klett, who commented about the "loads of excitement" in the narrative. Remarking on the development of Mary Alice and Patricia as the series has progressed, *Booklist*'s GraceAnne A. DeCandido remarked: "They make great company." *Murder Boogies with Elvis* was George's last "Southern Sisters" publication, though not her last published work. This novel recounts the adventures of the sisters as they investigate the murder of an Elvis Presley impersonator who was one of a group of such impersonators at a benefit. Like the real Elvis, George will likely linger through her poetry and the colorful characters that she brought to life in her mysteries. "Thanks for all the sweet tea," concluded DeCandido.

BIOGRAPHICAL AND CRITICAL SOURCES:

PERIODICALS

Booklist, April 15, 1998, GraceAnne A. DeCandido, review of *Murder Gets a Life,* pp. 1382-1383; May 15, 1999, GraceAnne A. DeCandido, review of *Murder Shoots the Bull,* p. 1673; May 1, 2000, GraceAnne A. DeCandido, review of *Murder Carries a Torch,* p. 1616; July, 2001, GraceAnne A. DeCandido, review of *Murder Boogies with Elvis,* p. 1987.

Kirkus Reviews, June 1, 2001, review of *Murder Boogies with Elvis,* p. 774.

Library Journal, July, 1997, Rex E. Klett, review of *Murder Makes Waves,* p. 130; December, 1997, Dean James and Shirley E. Havens, review of *Murder Makes Waves,* p. 184; May, 1998, Rex E. Klett, review of *Murder Gets a Life,* p. 143; August, 2000, Rex E. Klett, review of *Murder Carries a Torch,* p. 165; August, 2001, Rex E. Klett, review of *Murder Boogies with Elvis,* p. 170.

Publishers Weekly, January 22, 1996, review of *Murder on a Girls' Night Out,* p. 66; March 14, 1997, Sybil S. Steinberg and Jeff Zaleski, review of *Murder Runs in the Family,* p. 71; January 22, 1996, p. 66; April 14, 1997, review of *Murder Runs in the Family,* p. 71; March 23, 1998, review of *Murder Gets a Life,* p. 81; May 24, 1999, review of *Murder Shoots the Bull,* p. 71; June 19, 2000, review of *Murder Carries a Torch,* p. 63; July 9, 2001, review of *Murder Boogies with Elvis,* p. 51.

References Services Review, summer 1995.

Southern Living, October, 2000, Charly Porter, review of *Murder Carries a Torch,* p. 124; December, 2001, Nancy Dorman-Hickson, review of *Murder Boogies with Elvis,* p. 100.

ONLINE

Avon Books, http://www.avonbooks.com/ (November 11, 1999).

Books 'n' Bytes, http://www.booksnbytes.com/ (May 7, 2003), Harriet Klausner, reviews of *Murder Carries a Torch* and *Murder Boogies with Elvis.**

*   *   *

GILL, LaVerne McCain 1947-

PERSONAL: Born October 13, 1947, in Washington, DC; daughter of Paul McCain and Mary Williams; married Tepper Gill (a mathematician), February 9, 1977; children: Dylan McDuffie, Tepper Gill. *Ethnic-*

LaVerne McCain Gill

ity: "African American." *Education:* Howard University, B.A., 1969; Rutgers University, M.B.A., 1976; Princeton Theological Seminary, M.Div., 1997, Th.M., 1998. *Religion:* United Church of Christ.

ADDRESSES: Home—Fax: 734-426-1219. *Agent*—Natasha Kern, A. Kern Agency, P.O. Box 2908; Portland, OR 99728. *E-mail*—lgill@ic.net.

CAREER: Writer and minister of United Church of Christ.

WRITINGS:

African American Women in Congress: Forming and Transforming History, Rutgers University Press (New Brunswick, NJ), 1997.

Daughters of Dignity: African Women in the Bible and the Virtues of Black Womanhood, Pilgrim Press (Cleveland, OH), 2000.

My Mother Prayed for Me: Faith Journaling for African American Women, United Church Press (Cleveland, OH), 2000.

Vashti's Victory and Other Biblical Women Resisting Injustice, Pilgrim Press (Cleveland, OH), 2003.

BIOGRAPHICAL AND CRITICAL SOURCES:

PERIODICALS

Booklist, February 15, 1997, Lillian Lewis, review of *African American Women in Congress: Forming and Transforming History,* p. 979.

Library Journal, December, 1996, Jill Ortner, review of *African American Women in Congress,* p. 122.

Women's Review of Books, June, 1997, Leora Tanenbaum, review of *African American Women in Congress,* p. 7.

*   *   *

GIOVANNI, Nikki 1943-

PERSONAL: Born Yolande Cornelia Giovanni, Jr., June 7, 1943, in Knoxville, TN; daughter of Gus Jones (a probation officer) and Yolande Cornelia (a social worker; maiden name, Watson) Giovanni; children: Thomas Watson. *Education:* Fisk University, B.A. (with honors), 1967; postgraduate studies at University of Pennsylvania School of Social Work and Columbia University School of Fine Arts, 1968.

ADDRESSES: Office—English Department, Virginia Tech, Blacksburg, VA 24061.

CAREER: Poet, writer, and lecturer. Queens College of the City University of New York, Flushing, assistant professor of black studies, 1968; Rutgers University, Livingston College, New Brunswick, NJ, associate professor of English, 1968-72; Ohio State University, Columbus, visiting professor of English, 1984; College of Mount St. Joseph on the Ohio, Mount St. Joseph, Ohio, professor of creative writing, 1985-87; Virginia Tech, Blacksburg, VA, professor, 1987—, and Gloria D. Smith Professor of Black Studies; Texas Christian University, visiting professor in humanities, 1991. Founder of publishing firm, NikTom Ltd., 1970;

Nikki Giovanni

participated in "Soul at the Center," Lincoln Center for the Performing Arts, 1972; Duncanson Artist-in-Residence, Taft Museum, Cincinnati, 1986; Cochair, Literary Arts Festival for State of Tennessee Homecoming, 1986; director, Warm Hearth Writer's Workshop, 1988—; appointed to Ohio Humanities Council, 1987; member of board of directors, Virginia Foundation for Humanities and Public Policy, 1990-93; participant in Appalachian Community Fund, 1991-93, and Volunteer Action Center, 1991-94; featured poet, International Poetry Festival, Utrecht, Holland, 1991. Has given numerous poetry readings and lectures worldwide and appeared on numerous television talk shows.

MEMBER: National Council of Negro Women, Society of Magazine Writers, National Black Heroines for PUSH, Winnie Mandela Children's Fund Committee, Delta Sigma Theta (honorary member).

AWARDS, HONORS: Grants from Ford Foundation, 1967, National Endowment for the Arts, 1968, and Harlem Cultural Council, 1969; named one of ten "Most Admired Black Women,"*Amsterdam News,* 1969; outstanding achievement award, *Mademoiselle,*

1971; Omega Psi Phi Fraternity Award, 1971, for outstanding contribution to arts and letters; Meritorious Plaque for Service, Cook County Jail, 1971; Prince Matchabelli Sun Shower Award, 1971; life membership and scroll, National Council of Negro Women, 1972; National Association of Radio and Television Announcers Award, 1972, for recording *Truth Is on Its Way;* Woman of the Year Youth Leadership Award, *Ladies' Home Journal,* 1972; National Book Award nomination, 1973, for *Gemini: An Extended Autobiographical Statement on My First Twenty-five Years of Being a Black Poet;* Best Books for Young Adults citation, American Library Association, 1973, for *My House;* Woman of the Year citation, Cincinnati Chapter of YWCA, 1983; elected to Ohio Women's Hall of Fame, 1985; Outstanding Woman of Tennessee citation, 1985; Post-Corbett Award, 1986; *Spirit to Spirit* received the Silver Apple Award from Oakland Museum Film Festival; Woman of the Year, National Association for the Advancement of Colored People (Lynchburg chapter), 1989. Honorary Doctorate of Humanities, Wilberforce University, 1972, and Fisk University, 1988; Honorary Doctorate of Literature, University of Maryland (Princess Anne Campus), 1974, Ripon University, 1974, and Smith College, 1975; Honorary Doctorate of Humane Letters, College of Mount St. Joseph on the Ohio, 1985, Indiana University, 1991, Otterbein College, 1992, Widener University, 1993, Albright College, 1995, Cabrini College, 1995, and Allegheny College, 1997; Honorary Doctor of Humane Letters, Manhattanville College, 2000; Honorary Doctorate of Humane Letters, Central State University, 2001. Keys to numerous cities, including Dallas, TX, New York, NY, Cincinnati, OH, Miami, FL, New Orleans, LA, and Los Angeles, CA; Ohioana Book Award, 1988; Jeanine Rae Award for the Advancement of Women's Culture, 1995; Langston Hughes Award, 1996; NAACP Image award, 1998; Tennessee Governor's award, 1998; Virginia Governor's Award for the Arts 2000; the first Rosa Parks Woman of Courage Award, 2002.

WRITINGS:

POETRY

Black Feeling, Black Talk, Broadside Press (Detroit, MI), 1968, 3rd edition, 1970.

Black Judgement, Broadside Press (Detroit, MI), 1968.

Black Feeling, Black Talk/Black Judgement (contains *Black Feeling, Black Talk,* and *Black Judgement*),

Morrow (New York, NY), 1970, selection published as *Knoxville, Tennessee,* illustrated by Larry Johnson, Scholastic (New York, NY), 1994.

Re: Creation, Broadside Press (Detroit, MI), 1970.

Poem of Angela Yvonne Davis, Afro Arts (New York, NY), 1970.

Spin a Soft Black Song: Poems for Children, illustrated by Charles Bible, Hill & Wang (New York, NY), 1971, illustrated by George Martins, Lawrence Hill (Westport, CT), 1985, revised edition, Farrar, Straus (New York, NY), 1987.

My House, foreword by Ida Lewis, Morrow (New York, NY), 1972.

Ego-Tripping and Other Poems for Young People, illustrated by George Ford, Lawrence Hill (Chicago, IL), 1973.

The Women and the Men, Morrow (New York, NY), 1975.

Cotton Candy on a Rainy Day, introduction by Paula Giddings, Morrow (New York, NY), 1978.

Vacation Time: Poems for Children, illustrated by Marisabina Russo, Morrow (New York, NY), 1980.

Those Who Ride the Night Winds, Morrow (New York, NY), 1983.

The Genie in the Jar, illustrated by Chris Raschka, Holt, 1996.

The Selected Poems of Nikki Giovanni, 1968-1995, Morrow (New York, NY), 1996.

The Sun Is So Quiet, illustrated by Ashley Bryant, Holt (New York, NY), 1996.

Love Poems, Morrow (New York, NY), 1997.

Blues: For All the Changes: New Poems, Morrow (New York, NY), 1999.

Quilting the Black-Eyed Pea: Poems and Not Quite Poems, Morrow (New York, NY), 2002.

Prosaic Soul of Nikki Giovanni, HarperCollins (New York, NY), 2003.

The Collected Poetry of Nikki Giovanni: 1968-1998, Morrow (New York, NY), 2003.

Girls in the Circle, illustrated by Cathy Ann Johnson, Scholastic (New York, NY), 2004.

OTHER

(Editor) *Night Comes Softly: An Anthology of Black Female Voices,* Medic Press (Newark, NJ), 1970.

Gemini: An Extended Autobiographical Statement on My First Twenty-five Years of Being a Black Poet, Bobbs-Merrill (Indianapolis, IN), 1971.

Truth Is on Its Way (album), Atlantis, 1971.

(With James Baldwin) *A Dialogue: James Baldwin and Nikki Giovanni*, Lippincott (Philadelphia, PA), 1973.

Like a Ripple on a Pond (album), Collectibles, 1973.

(With Margaret Walker) *A Poetic Equation: Conversations between Nikki Giovanni and Margaret Walker*, Howard University Press (Washington, DC), 1974.

The Way I Feel (album), Atlantic, 1975.

Legacies—The Poetry Of Nikki Giovanni—Read By Nikki Giovanni (album), Folkways, 1976.

The Reason I Like Chocolate (And Other Children's Poems) (album), Folkways, 1976.

Cotton Candy on a Rainy Day (album), Folkways, 1978.

(Author of introduction) *Adele Sebastian: Intro to Fine* (poems), Woman in the Moon, 1985.

Sacred Cows . . . and Other Edibles (essays), Morrow (New York, NY), 1988.

(Editor, with C. Dennison) *Appalachian Elders: A Warm Hearth Sampler*, Pocahontas Press (Blacksburg, VA), 1991.

(Author of foreword) *The Abandoned Baobob: The Autobiography of a Woman*, Chicago Review Press (Chicago, IL), 1991.

Nikki Giovanni and the New York Community Choir (album), Collectibles, 1993.

Racism 101 (essays), Morrow (New York, NY), 1994.

(Editor) *Grand Mothers: Poems, Reminiscences, and Short Stories about the Keepers of Our Traditions*, Holt (New York, NY), 1994.

(Editor) *Shimmy Shimmy Shimmy Like My Sister Kate: Looking at the Harlem Renaissance through Poems*, Holt (New York, NY), 1995.

In Philadelphia (album), Collectibles, 1997.

Stealing Home: For Jack Robinson (album), Sony, 1997.

(Editor) *Grand Fathers: Reminiscences, Poems, Recipes, and Photos of the Keepers of Our Traditions*, Holt (New York, NY), 1999.

Our Souls Have Grown Deep Like the Rivers (compilation), Rhino, 2000.

(Author of foreword) Margaret Ann Reid, *Black Protest Poetry: Polemics from the Harlem Renaissance and the Sixties*, Peter Lang (New York, NY), 2001.

The Nikki Giovanni Poetry Collection (CD), Harper-Audio, 2002.

Contributor to *Voices of Diversity: The Power of Book Publishing*, a videotape produced by the Diversity Committee of the Association of American Publishers and Kaufman Films, 2002. Contributor to numerous anthologies. Contributor of columns to newspapers. Contributor to periodicals, including *Black Creation, Black World, Ebony, Essence, Freedom Ways, Journal of Black Poetry, Negro Digest,* and *Umbra.* Editorial consultant, Encore American and Worldwide News.

A selection of Giovanni's public papers is housed at Mugar Memorial Library, Boston University.

ADAPTATIONS: Spirit to Spirit: The Poetry of Nikki Giovanni (television film), 1986, produced by Corporation for Public Broadcasting and Ohio Council on the Arts.

SIDELIGHTS: One of the best-known African-American poets to reach prominence during the late 1960s and early 1970s, Nikki Giovanni has continued to create poems that encompass a life fully experienced. Her unique and insightful verses testify to her own evolving awareness and experiences as a woman of color: from child to young woman, from naive college freshman to seasoned civil rights activist, and from daughter to mother. Frequently anthologized, Giovanni's poetry expresses strong racial pride and respect for family. Her informal style makes her work accessible to both adults and children. In addition to collections such as *Re: Creation, Spin a Soft Black Song,* and *Those Who Ride the Night Winds,* Giovanni has published several works of nonfiction, including *Racism 101* and the anthology *Grand Mothers: Poems, Reminiscences, and Short Stories about the Keepers of Our Traditions.* A frequent lecturer and reader, Giovanni has also taught at Rutgers University, Ohio State University, and Virginia Tech.

Giovanni was born in Knoxville, Tennessee, in 1943, the younger of two daughters in a close-knit family, and had a reputation for being strong-willed even as a child. She gained an intense appreciation for her African-American heritage from her outspoken grandmother, Louvenia Terrell Watson, Giovanni. "I come from a long line of storytellers," she once explained in an interview, describing how her family influenced her poetry through oral traditions. "My grandfather was a Latin scholar and he loved the myths, and my mother is a big romanticist, so we heard a lot of stories growing up." This early exposure to the power of spoken language would influence Giovanni's career as a poet, particularly her tendency to sprinkle her verses with colloquialisms, including curse words. "I appreciated the quality and the rhythm of the telling of the stories," she once commented, "and I know when I started to write that I wanted to retain that—I didn't want to become the kind of writer that was stilted or that used language in ways that could not be spoken. I use a very natural rhythm; I want my writing to sound like I talk."

When Giovanni was a young child, she moved with her parents from Knoxville to a predominantly black suburb of Cincinnati, Ohio. She remained close to her grandmother, however, spending both her sophomore and junior years of high school at the family home in Knoxville. Encouraged by several schoolteachers, Giovanni enrolled early at Fisk University, a prestigious, all-black college in Nashville, Tennessee. Unaccustomed to Fisk's traditions, the outspoken young woman came into conflict with the school's dean of women and was asked to leave. She returned to Fisk in 1964, however, determined to be an ideal student. She accomplished her goal, becoming a leader in political and literary activities on campus during what would prove to be an important era in black history.

Giovanni had experienced racism firsthand during her childhood in the South. Random violence that erupted in and near Knoxville "was frightening," she later recalled in an autobiographical essay for *CA.* "You always felt someone was trying to kill you." Yet when Giovanni re-entered the freshman class at Fisk she had not yet found her later radical stance. She was decidedly conservative in political outlook: during high school she had been a supporter of Republican presidential candidate Barry Goldwater, as well as an avid reader of books by Ayn Rand, famous for her philosophy of "objectivism" (based on self-assertion, individualism, and competition). The poet credits a Fisk roommate named Bertha with successfully persuading her to embrace revolutionary ideals. In the wake of the civil rights movement and demonstrations against U.S. involvement in the Vietnam conflict, demands for social and political change were sweeping college campuses around the country. "Bertha kept asking, 'how could Black people be conservative?', " Giovanni wrote in *Gemini: An Extended Autobiographical Statement on My First Twenty-five Years.* "'What have they got to conserve?' And after a while (realizing that I had absolutely nothing, period) I came around."

While Giovanni was at Fisk, a black renaissance was emerging as writers and other artists of color were finding new ways of expressing their distinct culture to an increasingly interested public. As Chauncey Mabe put it in a November, 2002, *Knight Ridder* article, "The Black Arts Movement [was] a loosely organized aesthetic and political movement that rejected European concepts of art for its own sake, insisting instead that art must benefit and uplift blacks." In addition to serving as editor of the campus literary magazine, *Elan,* and participating in the Fisk Writers Workshop, Giovanni worked to restore the Fisk chapter of the Student Non-Violent Coordinating Committee (SNCC). At that time, the organization was pressing the concept of "black power" to bring about social and economic reform. Giovanni's political activism ultimately led to her planning and directing the first Black Arts Festival in Cincinnati, held in 1967.

Later that year, Giovanni graduated magna cum laude with a degree in history. She decided to continue her studies at the University of Pennsylvania School of Social Work under a grant from the Ford Foundation, and then took classes at Columbia University's School of Fine Arts. This period was darkened, however, when Giovanni's beloved grandmother died. The loss "stirred in her a sense of guilt and shame both for the way in which society had dealt with this strong, sensitive woman, to whom she had been so close and who had deeply influenced her life, as well as for the way she herself had left her alone to die," according to Mozella G. Mitchell in the *Dictionary of Literary Biography.*

Giovanni's first published volumes of poetry grew out of her response to the assassinations of such figures as Martin Luther King, Jr., Malcolm X, Medgar Evers, and Robert Kennedy, and the pressing need she saw to raise awareness of the plight and the rights of black people. *Black Feeling, Black Talk* (which she borrowed money to publish) and *Black Judgement* (with a grant from Harlem Council of the Arts) display a strong, militant African-American perspective as Giovanni explores her growing political and spiritual awareness. "Poem (No Name No. 2)," from the first volume shows the simple forcefulness of her voice: "Bitter Black Bitterness / Black Bitter Bitterness / Bitterness Black Brothers / Bitter Black Get / Blacker Get Bitter / Get Black Bitterness / NOW." "These were the years," as Calvin Reid in a 1999 *Publishers Weekly* article observed, "she published such poems as 'Great Pax Whitie' (1968), with its intermingling of classical history, irony and antiracist outrage, and

'Woman Poem,' which considered the social and sexual limits imposed on black women."

These early books, which were followed by *Re: Creation,* quickly established Giovanni as a prominent new African-American voice. *Black Feeling, Black Talk,* "sold more than ten thousand copies in its first year alone, making the author an increasingly visible and popular figure on the reading and speaking circuit. Because of Giovanni's overt activism, her fame as a personality almost preceded her critical acclaim as a poet. She gave the first public reading of her work at Birdland, a trendy New York City jazz club, to a standing-room-only audience." Mitchell described the poems Giovanni produced between 1968 and 1970 as "a kind of ritualistic exorcism of former nonblack ways of thinking and an immersion in blackness. Not only are they directed at other black people whom [Giovanni] wanted to awaken to the beauty of blackness, but also at herself as a means of saturating her own consciousness." *Dictionary of Literary Biography* contributor Alex Batman heard in Giovanni's verse the echoes of blues music. "Indeed the rhythms of her verse correspond so directly to the syncopations of black music that her poems begin to show a potential for becoming songs without accompaniment," Batman noted.

Critical reaction to Giovanni's early work focused on her more revolutionary poetry. Some reviewers found her political and social positions to be unsophisticated, while others were threatened by her rebelliousness. "Nikki writes about the familiar: what she knows, sees, experiences," Don L. Lee observed in *Dynamite Voices I: Black Poets of the 1960s.* "It is clear why she conveys such urgency in expressing the need for Black awareness, unity, solidarity. . . . What is perhaps more important is that when the Black poet chooses to serve as political seer, he must display a keen sophistication. Sometimes Nikki oversimplifies and therefore sounds rather naive politically." A contributor to the Web site *Voices from the Gaps: Women Writers of Color* added, however, "In *A Poetic Equation: Conversations between Nikki Giovanni and Margaret Walker,* she again raises the issue of revolution. When Walker says to Giovanni, 'I don't believe individual defiant acts like these will make for the revolution you want,' Giovanni replies, 'No, don't ever misunderstand me and my use of the term "revolution." I could never believe that having an organization was going to cause a revolution'. Throughout *A Poetic Equation,* the two talk about issues from how to raise a child to the Vietnam War to how to save the African-American race that white America is trying to destroy."

Giovanni's first three volumes of poetry were enormously successful, answering as they did a need for inspiration, anger, and solidarity in those who read them. She was among those who publicly expressed the feelings of people who had felt voiceless, vaulting beyond the usual relatively low public demand for modern poetry. *Black Judgement* alone sold six thousand copies in three months, almost six times the sales level expected of a book of its type. As she traveled to speaking engagements at colleges around the country, Giovanni was often hailed as one of the leading black poets of the new black renaissance. The prose poem "Nikki-Rosa," Giovanni's reminiscence of her childhood in a close-knit African-American home, was first published in *Black Judgement.* In becoming her most beloved and most anthologized work, "Nikki-Rosa" also expanded her appeal to an audience well beyond followers of her more activist poetry. During this time, she also made television appearances, out of which the published conversation with Margaret Walker and one with James Baldwin emerged.

In 1969, Giovanni took a teaching position at Rutgers University. That year she also gave birth to her son, Thomas. Her decision to have a child out of wedlock was understandable to anyone who knew her. Even as a young girl she had determined that the institution of marriage was not hospitable to women and would never play a role in her life. "I had a baby at twenty-five because I *wanted* to have a baby and I could *afford* to have a baby," she told an *Ebony* interviewer. "I did not get married because I didn't *want* to get married and I could *afford* not to get married."

Following her success as a poet of the black revolution, Giovanni's work exhibited a shift in focus after the birth of her son. Her priorities had shifted to encompass providing her child with the security of a stable home life. As she remarked to an interviewer for *Harper's Bazaar,* "To protect Tommy there is no question I would give my life. I just cannot imagine living without him. But I can live without the revolution." During this period Giovanni produced a collection of autobiographical essays, two books of poetry for children, and two poetry collections for adults. She also made several recordings of her poetry set against a gospel or jazz backdrop. Martha Cook, in an article in *Southern Women Writers,* explained, "'Truth Is on Its Way' includes a number of poems from Giovanni's Broadside volumes, with music by the New York Community Choir under the direction of Benny Diggs. According to *Harper's Bazaar,* Giovanni introduced the album at a free concert in a church in Harlem. Following her performance, 'the audience shouted its appreciation'." Reviewing these works, Mitchell noticed "evidence of a more developed individualism and greater introspection, and a sharpening of her creative and moral powers, as well as of her social and political focus and understanding."

In addition to writing her own poetry, Giovanni used her boundless energy to offer exposure for other African-American women writers through NikTom, Ltd., a publishing cooperative she founded in 1970. Gwendolyn Brooks, Margaret Walker, Carolyn Rodgers, and Mari Evans were among those who benefited from Giovanni's work in the cooperative. Travels to other parts of the world, including the Caribbean, also filled much of the poet's time and contributed to the evolution of her work. As she broadened her perspective, Giovanni began to review her own life. Her introspection led to *Gemini: An Extended Autobiographical Statement on My First Twenty-five Years of Being a Black Poet,* which earned a nomination for the National Book Award.

Gemini is a combination of prose, poetry, and other "bits and pieces." In the words of a critic writing in *Kirkus Reviews,* it is a work in which "the contradictions are brought together by sheer force of personality." From sun-soaked childhood memories of a supportive family to an adult acceptance of revolutionary ideology and solo motherhood, the work reflected Giovanni's internal conflict and self-questioning. "I think all autobiography is fiction," Giovanni once observed in an interview, expressing amazement that readers feel they will learn something personal about an author by reading a creative work. "The least factual of anything is autobiography, because half the stuff is forgotten," she added. "Even if you [write] about something terribly painful, you have removed yourself from it. . . . What you have not come to terms with you do not write." While she subtitled *Gemini* an autobiography, Giovanni denied that it offered a key to her inner self. But the essays contained in the volume—particularly one about her grandmother—were personal in subject matter and "as true as I could make it," she commented. But, as Giovanni noted in an interview several decades later, "I also recognize that there are [parts of] the book in which I'm simply trying to deal with ideas. I didn't want it to be considered *the definitive.* It's far from that. It's very selective and how I looked at myself when I was twenty-five."

In addition to writing for adults in *Gemini* and other works during the early 1970s, Giovanni began to compose verse for children. Among her published volumes for young readers are *Spin a Soft Black Song, Ego-Tripping and Other Poems for Young People,* and *Vacation Time.* Written for children of all ages, Giovanni's poems are unrhymed incantations of childhood images and feelings. *Spin a Soft Black Song,* which she dedicated to her son, Tommy, covers a wealth of childhood interests, such as basketball games, close friends, moms, and the coming of spring. "Poem for Rodney" finds a young man contemplating what he wants to be when he grows up. "If" reflects a young man's daydreams about what it might have been like to participate in a historic event. In a *New York Times Book Review* article on *Spin a Soft Black Song,* Nancy Klein noted, "Nikki Giovanni's poems for children, like her adult works, exhibit a combination of casual energy and sudden wit. No cheek-pinching auntie, she explores the contours of childhood with honest affection, sidestepping both nostalgia and condescension."

Ego-Tripping and Other Poems for Young People contains several poems previously published in *Black Feeling, Black Talk.* Focusing on African-American history, the collection explores issues and concerns specific to black youngsters. In "Poem for Black Boys," for example, Giovanni wonders why young boys of color do not play runaway slave or Mau-Mau, identifying with the brave heroes of their own race rather than the white cowboys of the Wild West. "Revolutionary Dreams" and "Revolutionary Music" speak to the racial strife of the 1960s and 1970s and look toward an end to racial tension. Commenting on *Ego-Tripping,* a *Kirkus Reviews* contributor claimed: "When [Giovanni] grabs hold . . . it's a rare kid, certainly a rare black kid, who could resist being picked right up."

Vacation Time contrasts with Giovanni's two earlier poetry collections for children by being "a much more relaxed and joyous collection which portrays the world of children as full of wonder and delight," according to Kay E. Vandergrift in *Twentieth-Century Children's Writers*. In *Vacation Time* Giovanni uses more traditional rhyme patterns than in *Spin a Soft Black Song*. Reviewing the work for the *Bulletin of the Center for Children's Books*, Zena Sutherland argued that the rhythms often seem forced and that Giovanni uses "an occasional contrivance to achieve scansion." But other critics praised the poet's themes. "In her singing lines, Giovanni shows she hadn't forgotten childhood adventures in . . . exploring the world with a small person's sense of discovery," wrote a *Publishers Weekly* reviewer. Mitchell, too, claimed: "One may be dazzled by the smooth way [Giovanni] drops all political and personal concerns [in *Vacation Time*] and completely enters the world of the child and brings to it all the fanciful beauty, wonder, and lollipopping."

Giovanni's later works for children, include *Knoxville, Tennessee* and *The Sun Is So Quiet*. The first work, a free-verse poem originally published in *Black Feeling, Black Talk, Black Judgement*, celebrates the pleasures of summer. Many of the warm images presented in the picture book came directly from the author's childhood memories. Ellen Fader, writing in *Horn Book*, called *The Sun Is So Quiet* "a celebration of African-American family life for all families." Published in 1996, *The Sun Is So Quiet* is a collection of thirteen poems, ranging in topics from snowflakes to bedtime to missing teeth. "The poems," wrote a *Publishers Weekly* reviewer, "hover like butterflies, darting in to make their point and then fluttering off."

Giovanni says she has found writing for children particularly fulfilling because she is a mother who reads to her son. "Mostly I'm aware, as the mother of a reader, that I read to him," she once observed in an interview. "I think all of us know that your first line to the child is going to be his parent, so you want to write something that the parent likes and can share." According to Mitchell, the children's poems have "essentially the same impulse" as Giovanni's adult poetry—namely, "the creation of racial pride and the communication of individual love. These are the goals of all of Giovanni's poetry, here directed toward a younger and more impressionable audience." Love is not excluded by outrage.

Throughout the 1970s and 1980s Giovanni's popularity as a speaker and lecturer increased along with her success as a poet and children's author. She received numerous awards for her work, including honors from the National Council of Negro Women and the National Association of Radio and Television Announcers. She was featured in articles for such magazines as *Ebony, Jet,* and *Harper's Bazaar.* She also continued to travel, making trips to Europe and Africa.

Giovanni's sophistication and maturity continue to grow in *My House*. Her viewpoint, still firmly seated in black revolutionary consciousness, expanded further, balancing a wide range of social concerns. Her rhymes became more pronounced, more lyrical, more gentle. The themes of family love, loneliness, and frustration, which Giovanni had raged over in her earlier works, find softer expression in *My House*. "*My House* is not just poems," commented Kalumu Ya Salaam in *Black World*. "*My House* is how it is, what it is to be a young, single, intelligent Black woman with a son and no man. It is what it is to be a woman who has failed and is now sentimental about some things, bitter about some things, and generally always frustrated, always feeling frustrated on one of various levels or another." In a review for *Contemporary Women Poets*, Jay S. Paul called the book "a poetic tour through . . . a place rich with family remembrance, distinctive personalities, and prevailing love." And in the foreword to *My House*, Ida Lewis observed that Giovanni "has reached a simple philosophy more or less to the effect that a good family spirit is what produces healthy communities, which is what produces a strong (Black) nation." Noting the continued focus on self-discovery and the connectedness of self to community throughout *My House,* critic John W. Conner suggested in *English Journal* that Giovanni "sees her world as an extension of herself . . . sees problems in the world as an extension of her problems, and . . . sees herself existing amidst tensions, heartache, and marvelous expressions of love." *My House* contained the revelations of a woman coming to terms with her life. *The Women and the Men* continued this trend.

When Giovanni published *Cotton Candy on a Rainy Day,* critics viewed it as one of her most somber works, singing a note of grief. They noted the focus on emotional ups and downs, fear and insecurity, and the weight of everyday responsibilities. Batman also observed the poet's frustration at aims unmet. "What distinguishes *Cotton Candy on a Rainy Day* is its poignancy," the critic maintained. "One feels throughout that here is a child of the 1960s mourning the passing of a decade of conflict, of violence, but most of all, of hope."

During the year *Cotton Candy* was published, Giovanni's father suffered a stroke. She and her son immediately left their apartment in New York City and returned to the family home in Cincinnati to help her mother cope with her father's failing health. After her father's death, Giovanni and her son continued to stay in Cincinnati with her mother. Giovanni thus ensured the same secure, supportive, multigenerational environment for Tommy that she had enjoyed as a child.

The poems in *Vacation Time* turn again to reflect, perhaps, the poet's growing lightness of spirit and inner stability as she enjoys her family. Similarly, *Those Who Ride the Night Winds* reveals "a new and innovative form," according to Mitchell, who added that "the poetry reflects her heightened self-knowledge and imagination." *Those Who Ride the Night Winds* echoes the political activism of Giovanni's early verse as she dedicates various pieces to Phillis Wheatley, Martin Luther King, Jr., and Rosa Parks. In *Sacred Cows . . . and Other Edibles* she presents essays on a wide range of topics: African-American political leaders, national holidays, and termites all come under her insightful and humorous scrutiny. Such essays as "Reflections on My Profession," "Four Introductions," and "An Answer to Some Questions on How I Write" were described by *Washington Post Book World* critic Marita Golden as "quintessential Nikki Giovanni—sometimes funny, nervy and unnerving with flashes of wisdom."

As Giovanni moved through her middle years, her works continued to reflect her changing concerns and perspectives. *The Selected Poems of Nikki Giovanni, 1968-1995,* which spans the first three decades of her career, was heralded by *Booklist* critic Donna Seaman as a "rich synthesis [that] reveals the evolution of Giovanni's voice and charts the course of the social issues that are her muses, issues of gender and race." Twenty of the fifty-three works collected in *Love Poems* find the writer musing on subjects as diverse as friendship, sexual desire, motherhood, and loneliness, while the remainder of the volume includes relevant earlier works. "Funny yet thoughtful, Giovanni celebrates creative energy and the family spirit of African-American communities," Frank Allen wrote of *Love Poems* in a *Library Journal* review.

Giovanni continues to supplement her poetry with occasional volumes of nonfiction. In *Racism 101* she looks back over the past thirty years as one who influenced the civil rights movement and its aftermath.

Characterized by a *Publishers Weekly* reviewer as "fluid, often perceptive musings that beg for more substance," this collection of essays touches on diverse topics. Giovanni gives advice to young African-American scholars who are just starting an academic career, and she reflects on her own experiences as a teacher. She also provides a few glimpses into her personal life—for instance, she admits to being a confirmed "Trekkie." The book is a rich source of impressions of other black intellectuals, including writer and activist W. E. B. DuBois, writers Henry Louis Gates, Jr. and Toni Morrison, Supreme Court Justice Clarence Thomas, and filmmaker Spike Lee. "Giovanni is a shrewd observer and an exhilarating essayist," maintained Seaman in *Booklist,* "modulating her tone from chummy to lethal, hilarious to sagacious as smoothly as a race-car driver shifts gears." She does not believe in padding black realities in cotton wool and rainbows, admiring Native American writer Sherman Alexie for his honesty about "warts and all" depictions of Indian life. In addition to publishing original writings, Giovanni has edited poetry collections like the highly praised *Shimmy Shimmy Shimmy Like My Sister Kate.* A compilation of works composed by African-American writers during the Harlem Renaissance of the early twentieth century, *Shimmy* helps students of black writing to gain an understanding of the past.

Giovanni told Mabe that the Black Arts movement wasn't about presenting black culture as "Hallmark" perfect, and she feels that "the hip-hop movement took that from us, as we took it from the Harlem Renaissance before us." She is an avid supporter of hip-hop, "calling it," as she said to Mabe, "the modern equivalent of what spirituals meant to earlier generations of blacks. She admires OutKast, Arrested Development, Queen Latifah, and above all, Tupac Shakur. 'We're missing Tupac like my generation missed Malcolm X,' she said. 'It's been six years and people feel like he was just here. He brought truth and we're still trying to learn what he was trying to teach us.'" Rather than trying to imitate black culture, "White rappers, Giovanni noted, could get at the heart of racialism in America. 'It would be great to learn from whites why white supremacy is so prevalent. Most people have rejected it, but they still know something about it they aren't saying. I want them to jump into hip-hop and address it'."

Two new volumes, *Blues: For All the Changes* and *Quilting the Black-Eyed Pea: Poems and Not Quite Poems* mark the crossover from the twentieth to the twenty-first century with poetry that is "socially conscious, outspoken, and roguishly funny," according to Donna Seaman in *Booklist*. "Giovanni makes supple use of the irony inherent in the blues, writing tough, sly, and penetrating monologues that both hammer away at racism and praise the good things in life." *Blues,* published after a battle with lung cancer and her first volume of poetry in five years, "offers thoughts on her battle with illness, on nature, and on the everyday—all laced with doses of harsh reality, a mix of socio-political viewpoints, and personal memories of loss," wrote Denolynn Carroll of *American Visions* who quotes from "The Faith of a Mustard Seed (In the Power of a Poem)": "I like my generation for trying to hold these truths to be self-evident. I like us for using the weapons we had. I like us for holding on and even now we continue to share what we hope and know what we wish." In an interview with *Publishers Weekly*'s Calvin Reid, Giovanni "described *Blues* as 'my environmental piece,' and there are impressions of the land around her home in Virginia, but this collection also salutes the late blues singer Alberta Hunter; it reveals her love of sports as well as her love of Betty Shabazz; jazz riffs mingle with memories of going to the ballpark with her father to see the Cincinnati Reds." *Quilting* includes, as the title already tells, "anecdotes, musings, and praise songs," according to Tara Betts of *Black Issues Book Review*. There is a prose poem honoring Rosa Parks, reflecting the honor recently bestowed on Giovanni when she was recognized with the first Rosa Parks Woman of Courage Award in 2002. Mabe noted that "single motherhood, a bout with lung cancer, showers of literary awards and an academic career have enriched but not blunted her edge," in the volume, though, she adds wryly, "being radical today has sometimes meant being reduced to voting for Ralph Nader." But as Tara Betts pointed out, Giovanni continues to fight against racism with her words wherever it crops up, as "revealed in 'The Self-Evident Poem': 'We just can't keep bomb / -ing the same people over and over again because we don't want / to admit the craziness is home grown.'" In an interview at the time of *Quilt*'s publication, Samiya Bashir of *Black Issues Book Review* felt Giovanni has maintained a "broad fan base, perhaps because she has always put love at the forefront of her life and work," a love that sometimes sparks protective rage, which still comes out in her writing.

In 2003, Giovanni published *The Nikki Giovanni Poetry Collection,* an audio compilation. Spanning her poetry from 1968 to the present and ranging in content from "from racism and Rosa Parks and Emmett Till to love and motherhood to boxes of yummy chicken," according to Sandy Bauers of *Knight Ridder,* the collection brings the poet's voice to life. "On the page, much of Giovanni's writing seems rhetorical," claimed Rochelle Ratner in *Library Journal,* but "hearing her read, dogma is replaced by passion." Bauers praised the production: "The poems are worth the price all by themselves. Giovanni reads with gobs of energy and enthusiasm. Hers is the poetry of plainspeak. None of the metaphorical mumbo jumbo that baffles so many of us. Her hopeful view of the future: 'Maybe one day the whole community will no longer be vested in who sleeps with whom. Maybe one day the Jewish community will be at rest, the Christian community will be content, the Moslem community will be at peace, and all the rest of us will get great meals on holy days and learn new songs and sing in harmony.'"

"Most writers spend too much time alone; it is a lonely profession," Giovanni once explained. "I'm not the only poet to point that out. Unless we make ourselves get out and see people, we miss a lot." Teaching, lecturing, sustaining close family ties, and remaining active in her community have allowed the poet to balance the loneliness of writing with a myriad of life experiences. "[Teaching] enriches my life, I mean it keeps reminding all of us that there are other concerns out there," Giovanni said. "It widens your world. . . . I have certain skills that I am able to impart and that I want to, and it keeps me involved in my community and in a community of writers who are not professional but who are interested. I think that's good."

"Writing is . . . what I do to justify the air I breathe," Giovanni wrote, explaining her choice of a vocation in *CA*. "I have been considered a writer who writes from rage and it confuses me. What else do writers write from? A poem has to say something. It has to make some sort of sense; be lyrical; to the point; and still able to be read by whatever reader is kind enough to pick up the book." Giovanni believes one of her most important qualities is to have experienced life and to have been able to translate those experiences into her work—"apply the lessons learned," as she termed it in *CA*. "Isn't that the purpose of people living and sharing? So that others will at least not make the same mistake, since we seldom are able to recreate the positive things in life." She continues to look back on her contributions to American poetry with pride. "I think that I have grown; I feel that my work has grown a lot," she once told an interviewer. "What I've always wanted to do is something different, and I think each book has made a change. I hope that the next book continues like that. Like all writers, I guess, I keep looking for the heart." She concluded, "human beings fascinate me. You just keep trying to dissect them poetically to see what's there." To Mabe, she added, "People say writers need experience. You don't need experience, you need empathy. It's so limiting to think that you have to go do something in order to write about it. It's important to raise our ability to empathize and listen. I don't need to be enslaved to write about it."

BIOGRAPHICAL AND CRITICAL SOURCES:

BOOKS

Contemporary Literary Criticism, Volume 64, Gale (Detroit, MI), 1991.

Contemporary Poets, St. James Press (Detroit, MI), 1996, pp. 390-391.

Dictionary of Literary Biography, Gale (Detroit, MI), Volume 5: *American Poets since World War II,* 1980, Volume 41: *Afro-American Poets since 1955,* 1985, pp. 135-151.

Evans, Mari, editor, *Black Women Writers, 1950-1980: A Critical Evaluation,* Doubleday (New York, NY), 1984.

Fowler, Virginia, *Nikki Giovanni,* Twayne (Boston, MA), 1992.

Fowler, Virginia, editor, *Conversations with Nikki Giovanni,* University Press of Mississippi (Jackson, MS), 1992.

Georgoudaki, Ekaterini, and Domna Pastourmatzi, editors, *Women: Creators of Culture.* Hellenic Association of American Studies (Thessaloníki, Greece), 1997.

Giovanni, Nikki, *Gemini: An Extended Autobiographical Statement on My First Twenty-five Years of Being a Black Poet,* Bobbs-Merrill (Indianapolis, IN), 1971.

Inge, Tonette Bond, editor, *Southern Women Writers: The New Generation,* University of Alabama Press (Tuscaloosa, AL), 1990.

Josephson, Judith P., *Nikki Giovanni: Poet of the People,* Enslow Publishers, 2003.

Lee, Don L., *Dynamite Voices I: Black Poets of the 1960s,* Broadside Press (Detroit, MI), 1971, pp. 68-73.

Lewis, Ida, introduction to *My House,* Morrow (New York, NY), 1972.

Mitchel, Felicia, editor, *Her Words: Diverse Voices in Contemporary Appalachian Women's Poetry,* University of Tennessee Press (Knoxville, TN), 2002.

Tate, Claudia, editor, *Black Women Writers at Work,* Crossroads Publishing, 1983.

Twentieth-Century Children's Writers, 4th edition, St. James Press (Detroit, MI), 1995, p. 388.

Twentieth-Century Young Adult Writers, St. James Press (Detroit, MI), 1994, pp. 245-246.

Weixlmann, Joe, and Chester J. Fontenot, editors, *Studies in Black American Literature,* Volume II: *Belief vs. Theory in Black American Literary Criticism,* Penkevill Publishing, 1986.

PERIODICALS

American Visions, February-March, 1998, p. 30; October 1999, p. 34.

Black Issues Book Review, November-December 2002, pp. 1, 32; March-April 2003, p. 31.

Black World, July, 1974.

Booklist, December 1, 1993, p. 658; September 15, 1994, p. 122; December 15, 1995, p. 682; October 15, 1996, p. 426; January 1, 1997, p. 809; August 1998, p. 2029; March 15, 1999, p. 1276; June 1, 1999, p. 1807; February 15, 2001, p. 1102; December 15, 2002, p. 727; December 15, 2003, Donna Seaman, review of *The Collected Poems of Nikki Giovanni: 1968-1998,* p. 721.

Bulletin of the Center for Children's Books, October, 1980, p. 31; June, 1996, p. 334.

Capital Times (Madison, WI), February 7, 1997, p. 13A.

Christian Science Monitor, March 20, 1996, p. 13.

Cimarron Review, April 1988, p. 94.

Cincinnati Enquirer (Cincinnati, OH), June 3, 1999, p. B01.

Ebony, February, 1972, pp. 48-50.

English Journal, April, 1973, p. 650.

Essence, May, 1999, p. 122.

Griot, spring, 1995, p. 18.

Harper's Bazaar, July, 1972, p. 50.

Horn Book, September-October, 1994, p. 575.

Jet, April 4, 1994, p. 29.

Kirkus Reviews, September 15, 1971, p. 1051; January 1, 1974, p. 11; March 15, 1996, p. 447.

Knight Ridder/Tribune News Service, February 16, 1994, p. 0216K0139; July 3, 1996, p. 703K4426; January 24, 2001, p. K3551; November 20, 2002, p. K1262; January 7, 2003, p. K5130.

Library Journal, January, 1996, p. 103; February 1, 1997, p. 84; May 1 1999, p. 84; November 1, 2002, p. 114; November 15, 2002, p. 76; February 1, 2003, p. 136.

New York Times, August 1, 1996, p. C9; May 14, 2000, p. A40.

New York Times Book Review, November 28, 1971, p. 8.

Publishers Weekly, May 23, 1980, p. 77; December 13, 1993, p. 54; December 18, 1995, pp. 51-52; October 21, 1996, p. 83; June 28, 1999, p. 46; July 12, 1999, p. 96; December 19, 1999, p. 51; March 11, 2002, p. 14.

School Library Journal, April, 1994, p. 119; October, 1994, p. 152; May, 1996, p. 103; January 1997, p. 100; July 1999, p. 107; November 17, 2003, review of *The Collected Poems of Nikki Giovanni,* p. 59.

Virginian Pilot, March 2, 1997 p. J2.

Voice of Youth Advocates, December, 1994, p. 298; October, 1996, pp. 229-230.

Washington Post Book Review, February 14, 1988, p. 3.

Washington Post Book World, February 13, 1994, p. 4.

ONLINE

African-American Literature Book Club, http://authors.aalbc.com/ (March 9, 2004), author profile.

BlackEngineer, http://www.blackengineer.com/ (January 14, 2003), discussion with Giovanni.

Horizon Magazine, http://www.horizonmag.com/ (2000), "Black Is Black."

Nikki Giovanni Home Page, http://nikki-giovanni.com (March 9, 2004).

Paula Gordon Show, http://www.paulagordon.com/ (January 22, 2003), interview with Giovanni.

Poets, http://www.poets.org/ (March 9, 2004), "Nikki Giovanni."

Voices from the Gaps: Women Writers of Color, http://voices.cla.umn.edu/ (March 9, 2004).

Writers Write, http://www.writerswrite.com/ (July-August 2000), interview with Nikki Giovanni.

OTHER

Spirit to Spirit: The Poetry of Nikki Giovanni, a PBS special, 1987.*

GOLDBERG, Leonard S. 1936-

PERSONAL: Born March 19, 1936, in Charleston, SC. *Education:* Attended the Citadel, 1953-54, and College of Charleston, 1954-56; Medical College of South Carolina, M.D., 1959.

ADDRESSES: Home—Los Angeles, CA. *Agent*—Jane Jordan Browne, Multimedia Product Development, Inc., 410 South Michigan Ave., Suite 724, Chicago, IL 60605.

CAREER: St. Louis City Hospital, St. Louis, MO, intern and resident in medicine, 1960-61; Medical College of Virginia, Richmond, resident in medicine, 1963-64; Jackson Memorial Hospital, Miami, FL, resident in medicine, 1964-65; University of California—Los Angeles, fellow in hematology, 1965-66, research fellow in immunology, 1966-67; University of California—San Francisco, research fellow in immunology, 1967-68; University of California—Los Angeles, assistant professor, 1968-71, associate professor, 1971-75, professor, 1975-79, clinical professor of medicine, 1979—. Veterans Administration, clinical investigator 1968-71; Wadsworth Veterans Hospital, consultant in rheumatology, 1971—. American Board of Internal Medicine, diplomate in internal medicine, hematology, and rheumatology. *Military service:* U.S. Air Force, physician, 1961-63; served in Japan; became captain.

MEMBER: International Society of Hematology, American Association of Immunologists, American Federation for Clinical Research, American Rheumatism Association, American Society of Hematology, American College of Physicians (fellow), British Society for Immunology, Western Society for Clinical Research.

WRITINGS:

MEDICAL SUSPENSE NOVELS

Transplant, Signet (New York, NY), 1980.
Deadly Medicine, Signet (New York, NY), 1992.
A Deadly Practice, Signet (New York, NY), 1994.
Deadly Care, Dutton (New York, NY), 1996.
Deadly Harvest, Dutton (New York, NY), 1997.
Deadly Exposure, Dutton (New York, NY), 1998.

Lethal Measures, Dutton (New York, NY), 2000.
Fatal Care, Signet (New York, NY), 2001.
Brainwaves, Signet (New York, NY), 2002.

Contributor of reviews to medical journals, including *Journal of Clinical Investigation, Clinical Immunology and Immunopathology, Journal of Laboratory and Clinical Medicine,* and *Annals of Internal Medicine.* Member of editorial advisory board, *Journal of the Life Sciences.*

SIDELIGHTS: Leonard S. Goldberg is one of the leading forensic doctors in the United States. In addition to acting as a consultant and an expert witness in medical malpractice trials, he uses his specialized knowledge in his medical thriller novels. The lead character in most of his books—which include *Deadly Medicine, Deadly Care,* and *Deadly Harvest*—is Dr. Joanna Blalock, a beautiful, brilliant Los Angeles forensic pathologist. Working with her lover, police detective Jake Sinclair, Blalock investigates suspicious hospital deaths, black-market organ transplants, and the like.

Deadly Care was described as a "brainy nailbiter" by Pam Lambert in *People* magazine. The plot concerns mysterious deaths at a prestigious Los Angeles hospital. Blalock suspects foul play either by agents of the hospital or from the patients' insurance company. While following the trail of clues, Blalock's car is forced off a hillside road, leaving her with amnesia. She is protected by a homeless woman who hides her in a deserted building. A *Publishers Weekly* reviewer dismissed Goldberg's characters as "largely two-dimensional," but found that "a plethora of technical forensic detail adds much-needed gloss" to the book. And while calling the author's writing "at best serviceable," the critic added that "Goldberg . . . engages us with enough convincing and engaging shop talk to keep this thriller off the coroner's table." Lambert offered more wholehearted praise, declaring that Goldberg had "clearly hit his stride" with this, his fourth book. "*Deadly Care* offers not only fascinating forensics and insider insights into the health-care system but plenty of intriguing characters and a devilish plot—the perfect Rx for curing those reading blahs." *Booklist* contributor William Beatty went so far as to call *Deadly Care* "thought-provoking," thanks to its commentary on the dangers of managed medical care.

In *Deadly Harvest,* Blalock's younger sister Kate returns from an archeological expedition with a deadly Ebola-like virus. When Kate requires a liver transplant, Blalock discovers an international organization that sells organs to the highest bidders after harvesting them from unwilling "donors." Jo Ann Vicarel in *Library Journal* credited Goldberg with writing "a solid story" but felt that he "fails to allow enough time for character development and abruptly catapults the reader into a shockingly stark climax." She noted, however, that Goldberg "certainly knows how to bring authenticity to his novels." William Beatty endorsed *Deadly Harvest* in a *Booklist* review: "Thanks to his clear style and storytelling ability, this is another bell ringer for Goldberg, who, teaching and practicing physician that he is, appends to his yarn a note pointing out how desperate the real organ-transplant situation currently is."

BIOGRAPHICAL AND CRITICAL SOURCES:

PERIODICALS

Booklist, March 1, 1996, William Beatty, review of *Deadly Care,* p. 1120; March 15, 1997, William Beatty, review of *Deadly Harvest,* p. 1224.
Library Journal, March 15, 1997, Jo Ann Vicarel, review of *Deadly Harvest,* p. 90; February 1, 2000, Linda M. G. Katz, review of *Lethal Measures,* p. 116.
People, April 22, 1996, Pam Lambert, review of *Deadly Care,* p. 36.
Publishers Weekly, January 29, 1996, review of *Deadly Care,* p. 86; April 7, 1997, p. 75; October 8, 2001, review of *Fatal Care,* p. 50; November 18, 2002, review of *Brainwaves,* p. 47.

*   *   *

GORE, Mary Elizabeth 1948-
(Tipper Gore)

PERSONAL: Born Mary Elizabeth Aitcheson, August 19, 1948, in Washington, DC; married Albert Gore, Jr. (a politician and former U.S. vice president), May 19, 1970; children: Karenna, Kristin, Sarah, Albert III. *Education:* Boston University, B.A., 1970; George Peabody College for Teachers of Vanderbilt University, M.A., 1976. *Politics:* Democrat. *Religion:* Baptist.

ADDRESSES: Agent—c/o Author Mail, Henry Holt Inc., 115 West 18th St., New York, NY 10011.

Mary Elizabeth Gore

CAREER: Tennessean (daily newspaper), Nashville, TN, affiliated with photography department, 1971-76; chair of congressional task force, Washington, DC, 1978-79; Parents' Music Resource Center, Arlington, VA, cofounder and vice president, beginning 1985; freelance photographer. Member of board of directors, Capital Children's Museum and Center for Science in the Public Interest; served on American Academy of Pediatrics Task Force on Children and Television.

WRITINGS:

AS TIPPER GORE

Raising PG Kids in an X-Rated Society, Abingdon Press (Nashville, TN), 1987.
Picture This: A Visual Diary, Diane Publishing, 1996.
(With husband, Al Gore, Gail Buckland, and Katy Homans) *The Spirit of Family,* Holt (New York, NY), 2002.
(With Al Gore) *Joined at the Heart: The Transformation of the American Family,* Holt (New York, NY), 2002.

SIDELIGHTS: Mary Elizabeth "Tipper" Gore, wife of former U.S. Vice President Albert Gore, Jr., is the author of the 1987 book *Raising PG Kids in an X-Rated Society.* The book is an outgrowth of Gore's activism against the violence, misogynism, and graphic sexuality in television programs, movies, music videos, and popular music aimed at young people. She and her husband have also written *Joined at the Heart.*

Gore was born in Arlington, Virginia. Her unusual nickname came from a lullaby, "Tippy Tippy Tin," her mother often sang her. After her parents divorced, she and her mother moved in with her grandparents. She excelled in school, especially as an athlete, and was the drummer in an all-girl band called the Wildcats. She met Al Gore, Jr., in Washington, D.C., and followed him to the Boston area during his studies at Harvard University. She earned a psychology degree from Boston University in 1970, and the Gores were wed in May of that year. The couple relocated to Tennessee, which Albert Gore, Sr. had represented in Congress for many years, and Gore worked in journalism for a time as a news photographer for the Nashville *Tennessean.* Gore eventually earned a master's degree in her field in 1975 from Vanderbilt University; the following year she became a political spouse when Tennessee voters sent her husband to the U.S. House of Representatives. He was elected to the Senate in 1984.

In the late 1970s Gore served as chair of the Congressional Wives Task Force. In 1984, at the request of her eleven-year-old daughter, she purchased a copy of the Prince recording *Purple Rain,* and became frustrated that she had no way of knowing beforehand the unsuitableness of the music's adult-themed lyrics. A year later she formed the Parents' Music Resource Center (PMRC) as a means of forcing the record industry to label albums containing explicit lyrics. The Center's first action was to propose to the Recording Industry of America (RIAA) a rating system for records similar to the one already in use for films, but the RIAA counterproposed a simpler, blanket warning label. The matter attracted media attention after the Parent-Teacher Association (PTA) joined forces with the PMRC and a hearing on the issue was scheduled by the Senate Committee on Commerce, Science, and Transportation. Gore was deemed a reactionary right-wing crusader for censorship by some in the press; in response she vehemently denied any desire to truncate First Amendment rights, stating that her objective was to protect

America's children from easily accessible images of sex, violence, and death.

Many in the recording industry feared that the 1985 senate hearings might lead to the governmental legislation of artistic license and viewed them as another facet of the conservative tide that seemed to be sweeping the nation. Ultimately, eighty percent of U.S. record companies voluntarily agreed to tag products with a label and to make explicit lyrics visible to the purchaser.

In a similar vein to her activism, Gore's book *Raising PG Kids in an X-Rated Society* is a guide for parents who wish to become aware of the potentially negative media images that are accessible to children through cable television, movies, and recorded music. In the book Gore reiterates the arguments she presented at the Senate hearings. She contends that the major media conglomerates exploit teenagers and children by providing sensationalistic music and videos that are naturally attractive to youth culture. Gore also argues that alcoholic-beverage companies, often the sponsors of concert tours, manipulate youths by exposing them to advertising at concert venues, leading teenagers to substance abuse. She marshals statistics detailing the rising rates of alcohol and drug addiction, as well as climbing figures for teenage suicide and violent crime, to present her case, calling for parents to keep abreast of what their children are watching and hearing. She stresses that this behavior does not resemble censorship since it promotes more information and not less. *Raising PG Kids in an X-Rated Society* received mixed reviews from conservative and liberal quarters alike. Fred Barnes in the *American Spectator* described Gore as "a leaden writer," and deemed the book "repetitive." However, *Chicago Tribune* contributor Stephen Chapman noted: "In a society that cherishes freedom enough to tolerate its offensive manifestations, all adults have an obligation to help preserve the sanctity of childhood. Tipper Gore, who has not been deterred by the abuse of rock musicians or the scorn of journalists, deserves the gratitude of both parents and children for trying to awaken Americans to that duty."

After Al Gore became vice president during the Clinton Administration, Gore began a period of renewed political activism. She became an advocate for the homeless, for disenfranchised children, and for mental-health issues. She served as special advisor to Clinton's Interagency Council on the Homeless and organized a nonpartisan group of Washingtonians called Families for the Homeless. In 1996 she authored *Picture This: A Visual Diary,* documenting her life as the wife of the vice president with her own photography. Revenues from the book were donated to the National Health Care for the Homeless Council. She has also coauthored another work that features her images, *The Way Home: Ending Homelessness in America.*

During her eight years in Washington, Gore worked to eradicate the stigma associated with mental-health issues and provide affordable help for all Americans. She won praise for speaking candidly about her own experiences after admitting in 1999 that she had been treated for depression during the time her six-year-old son was recuperating from a serious accident.

In 2002 Gore and her husband published *Joined at the Heart: The Transformation of the American Family,* a look at the variety of groupings many Americans call families. Among those profiled are couples with children from several previous marriages, mixed-race families, a gay white couple that adopted black children, and other such examples. A critic for *Publishers Weekly* remarked that the Gores employ "a holistic approach to the underlying problems affecting today's families." Beth Kephart in *Book* called the title a "homey, accessible volume whose authors' commitment to their family and to the lives of others feels genuine and absolute."

In 2002's *The Spirit of Family* the Gores collect some 250 photographs depicting contemporary American families. Organized by theme, the photographs range from the touching to the tragic, covering a whole array of family types and possibilities. A critic for *Publishers Weekly* called the book an "impressive collection," and Raymond Bial, in a review for *Library Journal,* concluded that "the Gores did a fine job of selecting and arranging an outstanding collection of photographs."

BIOGRAPHICAL AND CRITICAL SOURCES:

BOOKS

Contemporary Newsmakers, 1985, Gale (Detroit, MI), 1986.

PERIODICALS

American Spectator, September, 1987, p. 42.
Book, November-December, 2002, review of *Joined at the Heart: The Transformation of the American Family,* p. 84.
Chicago Tribune, May 22, 1987, p. 27.
Christian Science Monitor, June 10, 1999.
Insight on the News, January 7, 2003, Janice Shaw Crouse, review of *Joined at the Heart,* p. 52.
Kirkus Reviews, October 1, 2002, review of *Joined at the Heart,* p. 1444.
Library Journal, December, 2002, Raymond Bial, review of *The Spirit of Family,* p. 117.
Life, March, 1994.
Nation, July 18, 1987, pp. 61-63; June 28, 1999.
New York Times, November 6, 1987, p. A19; January 4, 1988, p. C18; September 6, 1992; May 19, 2000; June 1, 2000.
Publishers Weekly, October 7, 2002, review of *Joined at the Heart,* p. 63; October 21, 2002, review of *The Spirit of Family,* p. 66.
Rolling Stone, April 15, 1993.*

*　　*　　*

GORE, Tipper
See GORE, Mary Elizabeth

*　　*　　*

GRAHAM, Robert
See HALDEMAN, Joe (William)

*　　*　　*

GRANT, Cynthia D. 1950-

PERSONAL: Born November 23, 1950, in Brockton, MA; daughter of Robert C. and Jacqueline (Ford) Grant; married Daniel Heatley (divorced); married Eric Neel, 1988; children: (first marriage) Morgan; (second marriage) Forest.

ADDRESSES: Home—Box 95, Cloverdale, CA 95425.

CAREER: Writer, 1974—.

AWARDS, HONORS: Woodward Park School book award, 1981, for *Joshua Fortune;* Best Book of the Year, Michigan Library Association Young-Adult Caucus, 1990, PEN/Norma Klein award, 1991, and Detroit Public Library Author Day Award, 1992, all for *Phoenix Rising; or, How to Survive Your Life;* several of Grant's books have been selected as American Library Association's Best Book for Young Adults.

WRITINGS:

Joshua Fortune, Atheneum (New York, NY), 1980.
Summer Home, Atheneum (New York, NY), 1981.
Big Time, Atheneum (New York, NY), 1982.
Hard Love, Atheneum (New York, NY), 1983.
Kumquat May, I'll Always Love You, Atheneum (New York, NY), 1986.
Phoenix Rising; or, How to Survive Your Life, Atheneum (New York, NY), 1989.
Keep Laughing, Atheneum (New York, NY), 1991.
Shadow Man, Atheneum (New York, NY), 1992.
Uncle Vampire, Atheneum (New York, NY), 1993.
Mary Wolf, Atheneum (New York, NY), 1995.
The White Horse, Atheneum (New York, NY), 1998.
The Cannibals: Starring Tiffany Sprat, As Told to Cynthia D. Grant, Roaring Brook Press (Brookfield, CT), 2002.

SIDELIGHTS: Cynthia D. Grant has won admiration for her highly perceptive treatment of adolescent struggles, convincing young characters, and unsparing truthfulness. Her novels, which include *Shadow Man, The White Horse,* and *Keep Laughing,* often deal directly with painful loss—through death, divorce, neglect, or the bittersweet process of growing-up itself—and her teen protagonists rely on the support of imperfect families and friends. Humor also finds its way into many of her novels, none more fully than Grant's 2002 novel *The Cannibals: Starring Tiffany Sprat, As Told to Cynthia D. Grant,* a purported diary of a California cheerleader whose views on life, love, and high school bring new meaning to the word "superficial."

Born in 1950, Grant grew up in Palo Alto, California, and still makes her home in that state. "One reason I write for teenagers is those years remain so vivid in my mind," she once told *CA.* "Junior high and high school were difficult times. The kids were so mean to each other! If you stuck out in any way, by being especially smart, or handicapped, or saddled with a hideous home permanent, you were picked on until you bled to death of a thousand tiny cuts. Kids who were picked on took it out on smaller kids. Hurt people hurt people—and themselves. Is this a system?"

In her books for young readers, Grant lets teens know that their adolescent angst is shared by many others, that their loneliness, fear, and uncertainties are universal. Many of her characters are misfits of one sort or another. In *Summer Home,* Grant introduces readers to Baby Boris Schmaltzman, a lumpish, friendless fifteen-year-old bully. Popular Gabriel McCloud in *Shadow Man* is an alcoholic high-school drop-out, burdened by a dysfunctional family. *Kumquat May, I'll Always Love You* finds Livvy abandoned by her mother and trying to keep up appearances while finishing high school, while grief-stricken Jesse is tormented by bad dreams until she finds solace in the diary of her dead sister in *Phoenix Rising; or, How to Survive Your Life.*

Grant's 1992 young adult novel *Shadow Man* begins as its main character, high-school dropout Gabe McCloud, wraps his pickup truck around a tree and is killed. As the plot develops, interior monologues by the survivors, in addition to excerpts from Gabe's high school journal, show readers a bright student, the victim of an abusive family background, who might have overcome the consequences of his past had he been given the chance. Gary Young noted in a *Booklist* review that, despite the novel's tragic core, Gabe's suicide is transformative to those he leaves behind, changing the "mood from sadness to strength." Dubbing the book "impressive," *Books for Keeps* contributor Robert Dunbar went on to praise Grant for her poignant treatment of a small-town tragedy, adding that she imbues her work with "a powerful and distinctive imagination."

Uncle Vampire confronts a difficult topic in a unique way, as Grant's young teen protagonist equates the devastation caused by sexual abuse with the ravages of the undead. Sixteen-year-old Carolyn was once a good student and an energetic friend; however, when her mother's unemployed brother comes to live with the family, her grades begin to slump and she starts to withdraw from friends and family—except for her twin, Honey, who knows Carolyn's secret. Praising the novel for retaining its suspense until the final pages,

Voice of Youth Advocates contributor Beverly Youree commented that *Uncle Vampire* "is a terrific novel about a very serious and all too prevalent problem." "Grant's plot and character development are flawless," added *Horn Book* contributor Maeve Visser Knoth; "she never loses the limited perspective of a young woman struggling with a terrifying and damaging situation." In *Book Report,* contributor Sherry York praised Grant's fiction for its "surprising but optimistic" conclusion, as well as for the author's inclusion of suggestions for teens in need of aid in dealing with abusive situations.

Despite her family's misfortune—her father is chronically unemployed and her mother is a childish dreamer who hides from reality and responsibility—the mature teen protagonist of *Mary Wolf* has something that many of Grant's protagonists go without: a close family. However, love is not enough, and Mary soon finds that the responsibility for the welfare of her four siblings rests solely on her young shoulders. After living a peripatetic life in an RV for two years, the Wolfs link up with a squatter's camp and engage in petty thievery to make ends meet. When the youngest child becomes sick, Mary's despairing father succumbs to mental illness. In a story that quickly becomes tragic, "Grant establishes the desperation of lives ruled by nightmare," explained a *Publishers Weekly* reviewer. *Mary Wolf* ends in a manner that "is disturbing but not sensationalized," continued *Horn Book* contributor Nancy Vasilakis, explaining that the family's "story is so sad precisely because it is so convincing." Praising the book as a "stunning family drama," *Booklist* reviewer Anne O'Malley called the novel "a riveting look at poverty and homelessness, told from the heart."

The White Horse focuses on a homeless teen who, like several other Grant protagonists, has a knack for expressing herself through writing. A budding poet, Raina writes verse for school assignments that revolves around her problems with her heroin-addled boyfriend, her lack of a place to live, and her eventual pregnancy. Through her school work, the student gains a confidante, forty-something writing teacher, Ms. Johnson. For her own part, single and childless Ms. Johnson finds a sense of purpose through her friendship with the young teen, and she gains confidence in her ability to teach as she helps show Raina the means to gain stability in her life. "Realistic dialogue . . . and vivid descriptions make this book heartbreakingly believable," noted *Voice of Youth Advocates* contributor Colleen Harris, adding that in *The White Horse,* Grant has penned a novel that "makes for compelling reading." In a *Booklist* review of *The White Horse,* Shelle Rosenfeld noted that Grant's book—"brutal, heartbreaking, occasionally shocking, yet beautifully written"—provides readers with an insight into lives of those people who slip through the cracks of modern society, while a *Publishers Weekly* contributor called the 1998 novel "an understated and deeply poignant portrayal of a troubled teen."

In addition to "problem" fiction, Grant has authored several novels in which humor is a major ingredient. In *Kumquat May, I'll Always Love You,* humor and pathos are equally mixed as abandoned teen Livvy, living alone after her mother's disappearance, goes to sometimes funny lengths to make people believe her mother still lives there. One of the schemes Livvy employs is buying her mother's Harlequin romances and favorite lipsticks. A contributor to the *Bulletin of the Center for Children's Books* noted: "The plot is preposterous but rendered totally entertaining by a humorous sense of itself: a witty style . . . and plenty of quirky caricatures to lift the underlying sadness of Livvy's loss of family."

In a change of pace for Grant, the 2002 novel *The Cannibals* is a comic send-up of the life of a stereotypical, flaky, airheaded teen. Blonde cheerleader Tiffany Spratt, who cares more about the state of her hair than the state of the world, videotapes and narrates in hyperbolic fashion the events of her terribly un-fun senior year at high school, sure that her film will one day be viewed by millions. From Tiffany's superficial crush on a cute new student to the daily spats among the carefully coiffed members of the top school clique to Tiffany's energetic efforts to allow in-school filming of a movie she is certain will make her a star, *The Cannibals* "points the finger at . . . a culture of consumption," according to a *Publishers Weekly* reviewer. Reflecting the personality of its teen narrator, the novel's narrative "is air-headed, vacuous, and relentlessly upbeat," commented *Bulletin of the Center for Children's Books* contributor Janice M. Del Negro. Calling the book "a hoot" despite its heavy satire, Cindy Darling Codell added in her *School Library Journal* review that *The Cannibals* effectively "razzes lots of different social agendas."

Grant once told *CA:* "As a child, I was in love with the magic of words; their power to create worlds on paper. Childhood is a vivid time of intensely held emotions and experiences. Now I write what I feel strongly about."

In Grant's 1989 novel *Phoenix Rising; or, How to Survive Your Life,* one of the characters, a teen writer, says: "I'd like to be able to make readers laugh and cry; to reach across the page and say, Hey, we're alive! I want to show the courage of fathers and mothers who bring forth babies who brave the maze of childhood; learning to crawl, standing up, oops, falling, starting over, getting up, going on, finding love, losing hope, enduring pain and disappointment; believing that happiness is just around the corner, if we don't give up, if we keep moving forward—There is so much I want to say." As Grant explained: "She speaks for me."

BIOGRAPHICAL AND CRITICAL SOURCES:

BOOKS

Authors and Artist for Young Adults, Volume 23, Gale (Detroit, MI), 1998.
Grant, Cynthia D., *Phoenix Rising; or, How to Survive Your Life,* Atheneum (New York, NY), 1989.
St. James Guide to Young Adult Writers, 2nd edition, St. James Press (Detroit, MI), 1999.

PERIODICALS

Booklist, November 1, 1992, Gary Young, review of *Shadow Man,* p. 504; August, 1983, p. 1457; March 15, 1994, p. 1358; October 15, 1994, p. 413; October 1, 1995, Anne O'Malley, review of *Mary Wolf,* p. 303; March 15, 1996, p. 1282; October 15, 1998, Shelle Rosenfeld, review of *The White Horse,* p. 413; October 1, 2002, Anne O'Malley, review of *The Cannibals: Starring Tiffany Spratt, As Told to Cynthia D. Grant,* p. 313.
Book Report, March-April, 1996, Carol Fox, review of *Mary Wolf,* p. 35; November, 1999, Sherry York, review of *Uncle Vampire,* p. 30.
Books for Keeps, May, 1996, David Bennett, review of *Shadow Man,* p. 17; July, 1999, Robert Dunbar, review of *Shadow Man,* p. 25.
Bulletin of the Center for Children's Books, April, 1982, p. 148; September, 1986, review of *Kumquat May, I'll Always Love You,* p. 7; February, 1989,

p. 147; December, 1998, Deborah Stevenson, review of *The White Horse,* p. 132; December, 2002, Janice M. Del Negro, review of *The Cannibals,* p. 157.

Horn Book, December, 1980, p. 641; July-August, 1989, p. 488; January, 1994, Maeve Visser Knoth, review of *Uncle Vampire,* p. 73; March-April, 1996, Nancy Vasilakis, review of *Mary Wolf,* p. 206.

Kirkus Reviews, November 1, 1992, p. 1375; September 15, 1995, p. 1351.

Publishers Weekly, June 27, 1986, p. 95; February 10, 1989, p. 73; October 11, 1991, p. 64; November 1, 1991, p. 1402; October 12, 1992, p. 80; October 16, 1995, review of *Mary Wolf,* p. 62; November 2, 1998, review of *The White Horse,* p. 84; August 26, 2002, review of *The Cannibals,* p. 70.

School Library Journal, September, 1981, p. 125; April, 1982, p. 82; October, 1983, p. 168; February, 1989, p. 100; October, 1992, p. 140; November, 1993, p. 122; December, 1998, Marilyn Payne Phillips, review of *The White Horse,* p. 124; September, 2002, Cindy Darling Codell, review of *The Cannibals,* p. 225.

Times Educational Supplement, March 26, 1999, Adèle Geras, review of *Uncle Vampire* and *Shadow Man,* p. 23.

Voice of Youth Advocates, April, 1982, p. 34; August-October, 1986, pp. 142, 144; December, 1992, p. 278; February, 1994, Beverly Youree, review of *Uncle Vampire,* p. 381; December, 1995, p. 300; December, 1998, Colleen Harris, review of *The White Horse,* p. 355.*

H

HAKIM, Catherine 1948-

PERSONAL: Born May 30, 1948. *Education:* University of Sussex, B.A. (with honors), 1969; University of Essex, Ph.D., 1974.

ADDRESSES: Office—Department of Sociology, London School of Economics and Political Science, University of London, Houghton St., London WC2A 2AE, England; fax: 01-71-955-7405. *E-mail*—c.hakim@lse.ac.uk.

CAREER: Conducted field research in Caracas, Venezuela, 1969-72; Tavistock Institute, London, England, research officer, 1972-74; British Office of Population Censuses and Surveys (now Office of National Statistics), London, senior research officer, 1974-78; British Department of Employment, London, principal research officer, 1978-89; University of Essex, Colchester, Essex, England, professor of sociology and director of ESRC Data Archive, 1989-90; University of London, London School of Economics and Political Science, London, began as Morris Ginsberg fellow, became senior research fellow in sociology, 1993—.

MEMBER: Royal Statistical Society (fellow), British Sociological Association, Social Policy Association.

WRITINGS:

(With W. R. Hawes) *Labour Force Statistics,* Open University Press (Milton Keynes, England), 1982.

Catherine Hakim

Secondary Analysis in Social Research: A Guide to Data Sources and Methods with Examples, Allen & Unwin (London, England), 1982.
Research Design: Strategies and Choices in the Design of Social Research, Allen & Unwin (London, England), 1987.
Key Issues in Women's Work: Female Heterogeneity and the Polarisation of Women's Employment, Athlone Press/Continuum (London, England), 1996.

(Editor, with H.-P. Blossfeld, and contributor) *Between Equalization and Marginalization: Women Working Part-time in Europe and the USA,* Oxford University Press (Oxford, England), 1997.

Social Change and Innovation in the Labour Market: Evidence from the Census SARs on Occupational Segregation and Labour Mobility, Part-time Work and Student Jobs, Homework and Self-Employment, Oxford University Press (Oxford, England), 1998.

Research Design: Successful Designs for Social and Economic Research, Routledge (New York, NY), 2000.

Work-Lifestyle Choices in the 21st Century: Preference Theory, Oxford University Press (New York, NY), 2000.

Models of the Family in Modern Societies: Ideals and Realities, Ashgate Publishing (Aldershot, England), 2003.

Contributor to books, including *Censuses, Surveys, and Privacy,* edited by M. Bulmer, Macmillan (London, England), 1979; *Essays on the History of British Sociological Research,* edited by M. Bulmer, Cambridge University Press (Cambridge, England), 1985; *Understanding Unemployment: New Perspectives on Active Labour Market Policies,* edited by E. McLaughlin, Routledge (London, England), 1992; and *Rewriting the Sexual Contract,* edited by G. Dench, Transaction Publishers (New Brunswick, NJ), 1999. Contributor of about forty articles to professional journals, including *European Societies, British Journal of Sociology, European Sociological Review, Work, Employment, and Society, Journal of Historical Sociology,* and *International Journal of Comparative Labour Law and Industrial Relations.*

*   *   *

HALDEMAN, Joe (William) 1943-
(Robert Graham, a pseudonym)

PERSONAL: Born June 9, 1943, in Oklahoma City, OK; son of Jack Carroll (a hospital administrator) and Lorena (Spivey) Haldeman; married Mary Gay Potter (a teacher), August 21, 1965. *Education:* University of Maryland, B.S., 1967; University of Iowa, M.F.A., 1975; also attended American University and University of Oklahoma; participated in the Milford Writer's

Joe Haldeman

Workshop. *Politics:* "Skeptic." *Religion:* "Skeptic." *Hobbies and other interests:* Classical guitar, bicycling, woolgathering, strong drink, travel, gardening, astronomy, painting.

ADDRESSES: Home and office—5412 Northwest 14th Ave., Gainesville, FL 32605; and, Cambridge, MA. *Agent*—Ralph Vicinanza, 111 Eighth Ave., #1501, New York, NY 10011. *E-mail*—haldeman@mit.edu.

CAREER: Freelance writer, 1970—. University of Iowa, teaching assistant, 1975; former editor of *Astronomy;* has taught writing at University of North Florida and other schools; Massachusetts Institute of Technology, adjunct professor, 1983—. Author of screen story "I of Newton," *The Twilight Zone,* Columbia Broadcasting System (CBS), 1985. Screenwriter for film *Robot Jox,* Empire, 1990. *Military service:* Served with U.S. Army, 1967-69; became combat engineer; served in Vietnam; wounded in combat; received Purple Heart and other medals.

MEMBER: Authors Guild, Science Fiction Writers of America (treasurer, 1970-73; chair of Grievance Committee, 1977-79; president, 1992-94), National Space Society, Writers Guild, Poets and Writers.

AWARDS, HONORS: Hugo Award, World Science Fiction Convention, 1975, Nebula Award, Science Fiction Writers of America, 1975, and Locus Award, *Locus* magazine, 1975, all for *The Forever War;* Hugo Award, World Science Fiction Convention, 1976, and Locus Award, *Locus* magazine, 1976, both for best short story, for "Tricentennial"; Ditmar Award, 1976; Galaxy Award, 1978, for *Mindbridge;* Rhysling Award, Science Fiction Poetry Association, 1984, 1990; Nebula Award for Best Novella, Science Fiction and Fantasy Writers, 1990, for *The Hemingway Hoax;* Hugo Award, World Science Fiction Convention, 1991, for *The Hemingway Hoax;* Nebula Award, Science Fiction Writers of America, 1993, and World Fantasy Award, World Fantasy Convention, 1993, both for "Graves"; Hugo Award, World Science Fiction Convention, 1995, Nebula Award, Science Fiction Writers of America, 1995, and Locus Award, *Locus* magazine, 1995, all for "None So Blind"; Homer Award, 1995; Hugo Award, World Science Fiction Convention, 1998, and Campbell Award, University of Kansas, 1998, and Nebula Award for Best Novel, Science Fiction and Fantasy Writers, 1998, all for *Forever Peace.*

WRITINGS:

SCIENCE FICTION NOVELS

The Forever War, St. Martin's Press (New York, NY), 1974.

Mindbridge, St. Martin's Press (New York, NY), 1976.

Planet of Judgment (a "Star Trek" novel), Bantam (New York, NY), 1977.

All My Sins Remembered, St. Martin's Press (New York, NY), 1977.

(Author of introduction) Robert A. Heinlein, *Double Star,* Gregg (Boston, MA), 1978.

World without End (a "Star Trek" novel), Bantam (New York, NY), 1979.

(With brother, Jack C. Haldeman) *There Is No Darkness,* Ace (New York, NY), 1983.

Tool of the Trade, Morrow (New York, NY), 1987.

Buying Time, Morrow (New York, NY), 1989, reprinted, with an introduction by James Gunn, illustrated by Bryn Barnard, Easton Press (Norwalk, CT), 1989, published as *The Long Habit of Living,* New English Library (London, England).

The Hemingway Hoax (novella), Morrow (New York, NY), 1990.

Forever Peace, Ace (New York, NY), 1997.

Forever Free, Ace (New York, NY), 1999.

The Coming, Ace (New York, NY), 2000.

Guardian, Ace (New York, NY), 2002.

"WORLDS" TRILOGY; SCIENCE FICTION NOVELS

Worlds: A Novel of the Near Future, Viking (New York, NY), 1981, reprinted, Gollancz (London, England), 2002.

Worlds Apart, Viking (New York, NY), 1983.

Worlds Enough and Time: The Conclusion of the Worlds Trilogy, Morrow (New York, NY), 1992.

ADVENTURE NOVELS; UNDER PSEUDONYM ROBERT GRAHAM

Attar's Revenge, Pocket Books (New York, NY), 1975.

War of Nerves, Pocket Books (New York, NY), 1975.

WAR NOVELS

War Year, Holt Reinhart (New York, NY), 1972, Pocket Books (New York, NY), 1978.

1968: A Novel, Hodder & Stoughton (London, England), 1994, Morrow (New York, NY), 1995.

SHORT STORY COLLECTIONS

Infinite Dreams, St. Martin's Press (New York, NY), 1978.

Dealing in Futures: Stories, Viking (New York, NY), 1985.

More Than the Sum of His Parts, Pulphouse (Eugene, WA), 1991.

Vietnam and Other Alien Worlds (with essays and poetry), New England Science Fiction Association Press (Framingham, MA), 1993.

None So Blind, Morrow (New York, NY), 1996.

POETRY

Saul's Death and Other Poems, Anamnesis Press (San Francisco, CA), 1996.

PLAYS

The Devil His Due (produced at the University of Iowa Film Workshop), published in *Fantastic* (New York, NY), August, 1974.

The Moon and Marcek, published in *Vertex* (Los Angeles, CA), August, 1974.

The Forever War, produced by Organic Theater Company, Chicago, IL, 1983.

SCREENPLAYS

Robot Jox, Empire, 1990.

(Author of screen story) "I of Newton," *The Twilight Zone,* Columbia Broadcasting System (CBS), 1985.

EDITOR

Cosmic Laughter: Science Fiction for the Fun of It, Holt Reinhart (New York, NY), 1974.

Study War No More: A Selection of Alternatives, St. Martin's Press (New York, NY), 1977.

Nebula Award Stories 17, Holt Reinhart (New York, NY), 1983.

(With Martin H. Greenberg and Charles G. Waugh) *Body Armor: 2000,* Ace (New York, NY), 1986.

(With Martin H. Greenberg and Charles G. Waugh) *Supertanks,* Ace (New York, NY), 1987.

(Author of introduction) *The Best of John Brunner,* Ballantine (New York, NY), 1988.

(With Martin H. Greenberg and Charles G. Waugh) *Spacefighters,* Ace (New York, NY), 1988.

Work included in numerous "best of" anthologies, including *The Best from Galaxy,* edited by Ejler Jakobbsen, Universal-Award, 1972; *Best SF: 1972,* edited by Harry Harrison and Brian Aldiss, Putnam, 1973; *The Best Science Fiction of the Year—1972,* edited by Terry Carr, Ballantine, 1973; *Best SF: 1973,* edited by Harry Harrison and Brian Aldiss, Putnam, 1974; *The Best from Galaxy,* Volume 3, Award, 1975; *Nebula Award Stories 11,* Harper, 1975; *Best Science Fiction Stories,* Dutton, 1977; *Nebula Award Stories XII,* Harper, 1977; *Annual World's Best SF,* DAW, 1978; *The Best of Destinies,* Ace, 1981; *Best SF Stories of the Year,* Dutton, 1980; *Best of OMNI Science Fiction,* 1980; *Vicious Circles: The Best Modern Sesti-*

nas, 1994; *The Year's Best Science Fiction, Eleventh Annual,* St. Martin's Press, 1994; and *Year's Best Science Fiction,* edited by David Hartwell, HarperPrism, 1996.

Contributor to science fiction anthologies, including *Orbit Eleven,* edited by Damon Knight, Putnam, 1971; *Showcase,* edited by Roger Elwood, Harper, 1973; *Analog 9,* edited by Ben Bova, Doubleday, 1973; *Combat SF,* edited by Gordon Dickson, Doubleday, 1975; *Frights,* edited by Kirby McCauley, St. Martin's Press, 1976; *Close Up: New Worlds,* St. Martin's Press, 1977; *Time of Passage,* Taplinger, 1978; *The Endless Frontier,* Ace, 1979; *The Road to SF 3,* Mentor, 1979; *Thieve's World,* edited by Robert Asprin, Ace, 1979; *The Future at War,* Ace, 1980; *Dark Forces,* edited by Kirby McCauley, Viking, 1980; and *Dogs of War,* edited by David Drake, Warner, 2002.

Contributor of numerous short stories and articles to *Analog, Galaxy, Isaac Asimov's SF Adventures, Magazine of Fantasy and Science Fiction, Omni, Playboy,* and other publications.

Haldeman's novels have been translated into French, Italian, German, Dutch, Japanese, Hebrew, Spanish, Swedish, Russian, Greek, Czech, Bulgarian, and Korean.

ADAPTATIONS: Movie rights to *The Forever War* have been purchased by the Sci-Fi Channel, and it is set to run as a miniseries in 2004.

SIDELIGHTS: In his award-winning science fiction novel *The Forever War,* Joe Haldeman combines his experiences as a soldier during the Vietnam War, in which he was severely wounded, with a realistic, scientifically accurate presentation. The novel tells of a war that stretches across intergalactic distances and long periods of time, the soldiers involved traveling to remote battlefields via black holes. Because the soldiers travel at faster-than-light speeds, they age far slower than the civilians for whom they fight. This difference in relative age—the soldiers a few years older, their society centuries older—results in an alienation between the soldiers and the people they defend.

"Haldeman exercises his literary license," James Scott Hicks wrote in the *Dictionary of Literary Biography,* "to comment on, and ultimately to expunge from his memory, America's last ground war [Vietnam]." Hicks pointed out that Haldeman's first novel, *War Year,* based on his army diaries, deals with the Vietnam fighting directly. "But the demon of Vietnam," Hicks continued, "was not exorcised from Haldeman's soul by writing [*War Year*], and frontline combat became the subject of . . . *The Forever War.*" Haldeman, Hicks believed, is particularly adept at presenting his "theme of quiet resentment felt by those waging war." Because of his scientific training in physics and astronomy, Haldeman is particularly careful to present *The Forever War* as realistically and accurately as possible. "The technology involved in this interplanetary campaign," Martin Levin of the *New York Times Book Review* noted in his review of *The Forever War,* "is so sophisticated that the book might well have been accompanied by an operator's manual. But then, all the futuristic mayhem is plugged into human situations that help keep the extraterrestrial activity on a warm and even witty plane."

Among newer novelists in the field, Haldeman, Richard Geis of *Science Fiction Review* believed, "is one of the best realistic science fiction writers going; maybe *the* best." Hicks found that "Haldeman confronts his readers with painful questions, but he asks them with no small literary skill and with careful attention to scientific credibility." "It's comforting to know," wrote Algis Budrys of the *Magazine of Fantasy and Science Fiction,* "that the cadre of impressive talent among younger writers is not diminishing, and to think that people like Haldeman will be around for a long time to set high standards."

Haldeman's "Worlds" trilogy, published over a span of a dozen years, follows the exploits of Marianne O'Hara, who is, summarized Michael Pavese in *Best Sellers,* "an intelligent, promiscuous (in space promiscuity is encouraged) New New York citizen." Born in space, she travels from her orbiting, manmade world to Earth, to engage in postgraduate studies at N.Y.U. in the first book, *Worlds: A Novel of the Near Future.* It details her adventures and misadventures on Twenty-second-century Earth, a far poorer, more decadent, chaotic, and dangerous extension of contemporary society. It is a society rapidly nearing a total breakdown—which, by the denouement, it indeed has, with Marianne's space ship veritably riding the shockwave of nuclear devastation home to New New York. *Worlds Apart* details Marianne's career as an ambitious politician of the orbital worlds, who, thinking her former

lover, Jeff Hawkings, is dead (he isn't) from the nuclear holocaust, takes a pair of husbands. In addition, the book not only tracks Jeff's career, now peddling medications to devolved Earth tribes, it includes, noted Charles Platt in the *Washington Post,* "a grab-bag of extraneous notions in between: a Manson-worshipping death cult, a starship with an anti-matter drive, a formalized menage-a-trois, a hijacked space shuttle, an expedition into regressed Florida, a new science of behavioral conditioning, and more." In the final book, *Worlds Enough and Time,* Marianne, her two husbands and her cybernetic "twin sister," along with 10,000 other would-be colonists, venture forth in the starship *Newhome* to seek their destinies on an Earth-like planet in the Epsilon Eridani system. A *Publishers Weekly* reviewer concluded, "Haldeman shows his strengths here: the workings of *Newhome* are believably complex, the novel's scientific background is neither strained nor especially complicated, and the reader's attention is focused on O'Hara's character, her inner life and her interpersonal relationships."

In addition to the obvious recurring theme of war—both real and imagined—in many of Haldeman's books, essayist Duncan Lunan noted another theme in the *St. James Guide to Science Fiction Writers.* Referring back to *The Forever War,* where the enemy aliens are controlled by a hive-mind, Lunan said, "*Mindbridge* was another examination of human contact with a hive-mind, while *All My Sins Remembered* was a damning indictment not merely of big government but also of the standard SF attitude toward individuality. SF used to be full of people who find out that they're really someone else (usually someone more powerful), and part of the problem in identifying with central characters is often they lack individuality." Explained Lunan, "McGavin in *All My Sins Remembered* is a government agent, repeatedly given new identities through psychological conditioning and plastic surgery." Lunan added, "He is an individual moved and controlled by an organisation which commands his loyalty but is beyond his control." The theme of individuals preyed upon and controlled by ultra-powerful agencies or corporate entities is also central to Haldeman's "Worlds" trilogy, as with the CIA and KGB in *Tool of the Trade,* and by the wealthy in *Buying Time.* A *Publishers Weekly* contributor wrote, "Evoking painful nostalgia, . . . Haldeman uses bold language, powerful images and a graphic style to tell his emotional tale, in which concentrated, diary-like entries intensify the drama and despair."

Sue Martin, writing in the *Los Angeles Times,* termed *The Hemingway Hoax* "a bright, short science fiction novel, . . . [this] quirky effort offers a unique solution to one of the enduring literary mysteries of our time: Just what DID happen to Ernest Hemingway's missing manuscripts, lost in 1922 at the Gare de Lyon in Paris?" She continued, "For Hemingway fans, Haldeman's answer is a hoot, and as different a theory as you can find." Marc Leepson, in a *Book World* review, described Haldeman's fictionalized but largely autobiographical *1968* as "a well-crafted, biting novel set in Vietnam."

Forever Peace is a follow-up novel to the problems raised in Haldeman's acclaimed *Forever War*. In 2043, an American-led alliance has been battling with the third-world Ngumi confederation, primarily, on the alliance's part, with "soldierboys"—killing machines controlled by brain-linked "mechanics," among them, the protagonist, physicist Julian Class. Meanwhile, the Jupiter Project, the most ambitious scientific experiment of all time, circles Jupiter, and Julian's lover, Amelia, discovers it may endanger not only our solar system, but the universe, in a new "Big Bang." Among other complications, their attempt to stop the disaster runs afoul of an influential Christian cult, the Hammer of God, dedicated to bringing on the Endtime. A *Publishers Weekly* reviewer concluded, "As always, Haldeman, a Vietnam vet, writes with intelligence and power about the horrors of war, and about humanity's seeming inability to overcome its violent tendencies."

While *Forever Peace* quenched the thirst of many of Haldeman's devoted readers, fans still clamored for a sequel to *The Forever War*, which the author provided in *Forever Free*. According to Jackie Cassada of *Library Journal*, Haldeman "continues his exploration of the essential nature of humanity in a deceptively simple story that questions the foundations of human belief." Haldeman describes life after the war, focusing on William and Margay Mandella, two retired soldiers banished to the frozen planet of Middle Finger by the highly evolved species of humans who took over when the war ended. Cassada recommended the book, crediting Haldeman with "clear, concise storytelling" and an "understanding of human behavior." A *Publishers Weekly* contributor called *Forever Free* "a well-written and worthy sequel to one of SF's enduring classics."

Following *Forever Free,* Haldeman wrote *The Coming,* a first-contact type story about a professor named Aurora Bell, who gets a message from an alien popu-

lation announcing their upcoming visit to Earth. Bell attempts to warn officials by telling them about the message she's received, but no once cares to listen. *Library Journal*'s Cassada noted, Haldeman "demonstrates an uncanny ability to tell a large-scale story with a minimum of words" and commented that the book "provides food for thought as well as fast-paced action." The protagonist of Haldeman's next book, *Guardian,* is another courageous woman. The story follows Rosa Coleman, a woman from the late nineteenth century who leaves her abusive husband. Rosa believes she has an important destiny and a mystical raven verifies her belief. Cassada remarked that Haldeman "delivers an elegant parable of many worlds and multiple possibilities while telling the tale of a courageous woman whose life spans most of a century." Roland Green of *Booklist* noted, "Many may prefer the historical traits of the novel to its SF aspect. They also may admit that Haldeman couldn't write a bad book to win a bet."

BIOGRAPHICAL AND CRITICAL SOURCES:

BOOKS

Authors and Artists for Young Adults, Volume 38, Gale (Detroit, MI), 2001.
Contemporary Literary Criticism, Volume 61, Gale (Detroit, MI), 1990.
Dictionary of Literary Biography, Volume 7: *Twentieth-Century American Science Fiction Writers,* Gale (Detroit, MI), 1981.
Encyclopedia of Science Fiction, St. Martin's Press (New York, NY), 1993.
Gordon, Joan, *Joe Haldeman,* Starmont House (Mercer Island, WA), 1980.
St. James Guide to Science Fiction Writers, St. James Press (Detroit, MI), 1996.
Science Fiction and Fantasy Literature, 1975-1991, Gale (Detroit, MI), 1992.
Science Fiction Writers: Critical Studies of the Major Authors from the Early Nineteenth Century to the Present Day, 2nd edition, Scribner (New York, NY), 1999.
Twentieth-Century Science-Fiction Writers, 3rd edition, St. James Press (Detroit, MI), 1991.

PERIODICALS

Algol, summer-fall, 1977; summer-fall, 1978.
Analog, March, 1978; September, 1978; July, 1979; November, 1982, pp. 164-165; September, 1983,

p. 164; March, 1984, p. 168; February, 1986, p. 182; December, 1986, p. 182; January, 1990, pp. 308-309.

Analog Science Fiction and Fact, May, 2000, Tom Easton, review of *Forever Free,* p. 132.

Best Sellers, June 15, 1972; December, 1976; February, 1978.

Bloomsbury Review, January-February, 1996, pp. 3, 20.

Booklist, June 1, 1975; June 1995; September 15, 1997; November 1, 2000, Ray Olson, review of *The Coming,* p. 492; January 1, 2002, review of *Forever Free,* p. 832; November 1, 2002, Roland Green, review of *Guardian,* p. 480.

Book World, July 2, 1995, p. C95; February 4, 2001, review of *The Coming,* p. 10.

Chicago Tribune, September 26, 1976; September 2, 1991, p. 10.

Chicago Tribune Book World, June 14, 1981.

Commonweal, October 27, 1972.

Destinies, November-December, 1978.

Foundation, May, 1978.

Futures, June, 1975.

Galaxy, December, 1976; March, 1978.

Kirkus Reviews, November 1, 1999, review of *Forever Free,* p. 1690.

Library Journal, September 15, 1972; October 15, 1997, p. 97; December, 1999, Jackie Cassada, review of *Forever Free,* p. 192; December, 2000, Jackie Cassada, review of *The Coming,* p. 196; December, 2002, Jackie Cassada, review of *Guardian,* p. 185.

Los Angeles Times Book Review, October 30, 1983, p. 4; July 8, 1990, p. 9.

Magazine of Fantasy and Science Fiction, May, 1975; October, 1975; April, 1977; September, 1979; August, 1981, pp. 55-56; March, 1984, pp. 43-45; October, 2000, Charles De Lint, review of *Forever Free,* p. 41.

New Republic, November 26, 1977.

New Scientist, April 10, 1999, review of *The Forever War,* p. 48.

New York Times Book Review, May 21, 1972; March 23, 1975; February 27, 1977; January 15, 1984, p. 29; February 10, 1985, p. 40; June 7, 1987, p. 18; July 2, 1989, p. 15; June 14, 1992, p. 24.

Observer (London, England), May 8, 1977.

Publishers Weekly, March 13, 1987, p. 70; December 7, 1990, p. 78; April 6, 1992, p. 54; April 17, 1995, p. 38; April 22, 1996, p. 64; August 25, 1997, p. 49; November 15, 1999, review of *Forever Free,* p. 59; November 20, 2000, review of *The Coming,* p. 51; December 2, 2002, review of *Guardian,* p. 39.

Science Fiction Review, August, 1976; February, 1977; February, 1978.

Science Fiction Studies, Volume 21, 1994, pp. 238-240.

Starlog, Volume 17, 1978.

Thrust, summer, 1979.

Times Literary Supplement, July 8, 1977.

Voice of Youth Advocates, April, 2001, review of *The Coming,* p. 52.

Washington Post Book World, April 26, 1981; May 13, 1990, p. 8; May 31, 1992, p. 6; July 2, 1995, p. 4.

ONLINE

Joe Haldeman's Tangled Web site, http://home.earthlink.net/˜haldeman/ (February 19, 2004), Joe Haldeman home page.

Mostly Fiction, http://www.mostlyfiction.com/ (March 17, 2003), Cindy Lynn Speer, review of *Guardian.*

RebeccasReads, http://rebeccasreads.com/ (February 19, 2004), David Brown, review of *Dogs of War.*

Science Fiction and Fantasy Books, http://www.sfandf.com/ (February 19, 2004), description of *Dogs of War.*

Steve and Marta's Web site (part of "The Ring of Vintage TV" Web ring), http://www.steveandmarta.com/ (February 19, 2004), *The Twilight Zone:* "I of Newton."*

*　　*　　*

HALE, John (Barry) 1926-

PERSONAL: Born February 5, 1926, in Woolwich, England; son of Alfred John (a soldier) and Ethel (Barr) Hale; married Valerie June Bryan (an artist), August, 1950; children: Simon John, Felicity Joanna. *Education:* Attended Royal Naval College, Greenwich, England.

ADDRESSES: Home—Margate, Kent, England. *Agent*—Stephen Durbridge, Harvey Unna & Stephen Durbridge Ltd., 14 Beaumont Mews, Marylebone High St., London W1N 4HE, England.

CAREER: Stage hand, stage manager, and electrician in variety, touring, and repertory companies, 1952-55; Lincoln Repertory Theatre, Lincoln, England, founder and artistic director, 1955-58; Arts Theatre, Ipswich, England, artistic director, 1958-59; Bristol Old Vic Theatre, Bristol, England, artistic director, 1959-61; freelance director, 1961—; freelance writer, 1965—. Director of television dramas for independent television companies, 1961-64; directed Shakespearean plays on record for EMI, 1962-64. Greenwich Theatre, London, member of board of governors, 1963-71, associate artistic director, 1968-71, 1975-76, resident playwright, 1975-76. *Military service:* Royal Navy, 1941-51.

WRITINGS:

NOVELS

Kissed the Girls and Made Them Cry, Collins (London, England), 1963, Prentice-Hall (Englewood Cliffs, NJ), 1966.

The Grudge Fight, Collins (London, England), 1964, Prentice-Hall (Englewood Cliffs, NJ), 1967.

A Fool at the Feast, Collins (London, England), 1966.

The Paradise Man, Bobbs-Merrill (Indianapolis, IN), 1969.

The Fort, Quartet (London, England), 1973.

The Love School, BBC Publications (London, England), 1974, St. Martin's Press (New York, NY), 1975.

Lovers and Heretics, Gollancz (London, England) 1976, Dial (New York, NY), 1978.

The Whistle Blower, J. Cape (London, England), 1984, Atheneum (New York, NY), 1985.

PLAYS

The Black Swan Winter (two-act; first produced in Hampstead, England, at Hampstead Theatre Club, 1968), published in *Plays of the Year,* Volume 37, edited by J. C. Trewin, Elek (London, England), 1970.

It's All in the Mind (two-act), first produced at Hampstead Theatre Club, 1968.

Decibels (one-act; first produced in Liverpool, England, at Liverpool Everyman Theatre, 1969), published in *Prompt Three,* edited by Alan Burband, Hutchinson (London, England), 1976.

Here Is the News (one-act), first produced in Beaufort, England, at Beaufort Theatre, 1970.

Lorna and Ted (two-act), first produced in Greenwich, England, at Greenwich Theatre, 1970.

Spithead (three-act; first produced in Greenwich, England, at Greenwich Theatre, 1969), published in *Plays of the Year,* Volume 38, edited by J. C. Trewin, Elek (London, England), 1971.

The Lion's Cub (one-act; first broadcast by British Broadcasting Corp., 1971), published in *Elizabeth R,* Elek (London, England), 1971.

In Memory of . . . Carmen Miranda (one-act), first produced in Greenwich, England, at Greenwich Theatre, 1975.

Love's Old Sweet Song (two-act), first produced at Greenwich Theatre, 1976.

The Case of David Anderson Q. C. (two-act), first produced in Manchester, England, at Library Theatre, 1980.

SCREENPLAYS

The Rules That Jack Made, 1965.

The Noise Stopped, 1966.

Light the Blue Touch Paper, 1966.

The Queen's Traitor (five-part series), 1967.

Retreat, 1968.

(With Bridget Boland) *Anne of the Thousand Days* (adapted from the play by Maxwell Anderson), Universal, 1969.

The Picnic, 1969.

The Distracted Preacher, 1969.

(With Edward Simpson) *The Mind of Mr. Soames* (adapted from a novel by Charles Eric Maine), Columbia, 1970.

Mary, Queen of Scots, Universal, 1971.

The Lion's Cub, 1971 (also see above).

The Bristol Entertainment, 1971.

Anywhere but England, 1972.

Ego Hugo: A Romantic Entertainment, 1973.

The Brotherhood, 1975.

An Impeccable Elopement, 1975.

Good-bye America, 1976.

The Whistle Blower, 1986.

Also writer for *Thirteen against Fate* (television series) and *Micah Clarke* (radio series). Has directed sound recordings of thirteen Shakespeare plays for FCM Productions.

SIDELIGHTS: Although John Hale has written a number of novels and plays, he has perhaps received most attention in America for his television script *The Lion's Cub* (first in the "Elizabeth R." series), his screenplay for *Mary, Queen of Scots,* his contribution to the screenplay for *Anne of the Thousand Days,* and his novel *The Whistle Blower,* which was made into a motion picture of the same name. Regarding his plays and screenplays, critics have praised Hale's ability to portray the complexities of Elizabethan England and to present a coherent plot and an engaging drama. For example, in a review of *Mary, Queen of Scots,* a *Variety* writer said Hale "has fashioned a good original screenplay which alternates dramatically between the quirks and fortunes of Mary Stuart in Scotland and the well-organized court of Elizabeth." *Punch* writer Richard Mallett found the dialogue of *Anne of the Thousand Days* to be "unobtrusively modern, without being out of key."

The Lion's Cub tells the story of Elizabeth I in the years before she assumed the throne. James Preston of *Stage and Television Today* praised Hale's "ability to untangle the intricacies of Tudor politics, underscore the religious faith and fervour of the age and characterise dead names from history books." A *Variety* reviewer also noted that the "path to the throne was a tortuous one for Elizabeth the girl and John Hale's script gave . . . [Glenda] Jackson ample opportunities to reveal how intrigues, environment and eventual imprisonment were the crucible that formed her character in those early days."

Hale's play *Lorna and Ted* is a drastic departure from the majestic courts of Elizabethan England. Set in rural Suffolk, it is the story of a lonely, aging bachelor and his equally lonely housekeeper. Through a series of various comic maneuverings Ted persuades Lorna to marry him, but once they are married, their relationship decays rapidly. Although Robert Cushman of *Plays and Players* praised Hale for writing with "insight, intelligence, [and] a mournful humour," he wrote that the "long duologues punctuated by blackouts during which the actors visibly rearranged themselves, are really the stuff of television." *Stage* contributor R. B. Marriott commented that the "success of the play . . . is in the effect of everyday detail, personal and domestic, and the creation of an air of relentless aloneness."

The Black Swan Winter, which Hale wrote as a requiem for his father, is about a man who, though he is a "success," senses that something vital is missing from his life. He journeys to his childhood home in an effort to learn what he can from his father, who counsels his son that the only way he can hope to avoid disappointment is to give up his dreams and adhere to a strict course of duty and discipline. The dialogue, wrote Jeremy Kingston of *Punch,* is "at its best in the heart-to-heart talks."

Kingston called *It's All in the Mind* an "alert, suspenseful play" and observed that Hale "has a keen ear for the edgy, slightly kidding talk that goes on between friends." This play, like *The Black Swan Winter,* deals with disillusionment as its heroine is confronted with the knowledge that both her husband and an old friend have been manipulating her for their own (in her eyes, dishonorable) ends.

The principal characters in Hale's novel *The Grudge Fight* are two teenage apprentices in the Royal Navy who, in an attempt to settle their multiple disputes, stage a "grudge fight." Hale, a Royal Navy veteran and the son of a career soldier, drew on his military background to create what David Sharpe of *Best Sellers* called a "confusing yet compelling story about the life of a young apprentice during the first hectic months of naval training." A *New York Times Book Review* critic described *The Grudge Fight* as "an action story that concentrates effectively on the immediate moment." Sharpe also praised Hale's ability to "get into the mind of a boy, his thoughts, his feelings, his language, and his ambitions."

Over a two-decade period, Hale also wrote a "handful" of novels. In his 1973 offering, *The Fort,* he employs another military setting. This novel is set on the Mediterranean island of Dragut, "which, in the best traditions of fiction, is anywhere and everywhere," wrote Peter Ackroyd in the *Spectator* In 1807 the island had been the scene of a mutiny; over a century and a half later the descendants of those original mutineers attempt to avenge the unjust execution of their ancestors. A *Times Literary Supplement* reviewer praised Hale for allowing his characters to develop fully: "None of the characters is trotted out for the convenience of the plot; each one comes with its own cloud of existence about it, a felt and complex past." Ackroyd called the novel "innovative" and went on to say that "this is no naive forward narrative, but the continual spinning of past and present into . . . a web."

Nearly a decade later, Hale published what is likely his most popular novel, *The Whistle Blower,* a "startling spy thriller rife with bracing political and psychological truths," wrote a *Publishers Weekly* critic. Following in the literary footsteps of George Orwell and Arthur Koestler, Hale makes his subject the intrigue within British and American secret governmental security organizations. Thus when protagonist Frank Jones listens to his son tell how he will soon resign from the British intelligence service, and the son is killed in a suspicious accident, Jones feels compelled to investigate. Reviewer Paxton Davis complimented Hale for his characterization of Jones, which he dubbed a "solid creation," and his "crisp and competent" prose, yet he wrote in the *New York Times* that the author "does not lift his novel above the ordinary." *Library Journal* contributor Brian Alley also praised Hale's writing as "sensitive and thought-provoking" and his characters as "realistically portrayed"; yet Peter Lewis of the *Times Literary Supplement* went even further, seeing more in *The Whistle Blower* than pure entertainment. "For Hale," Lewis wrote, "Britain may present the illusion of an open society, but under it he locates creeping totalitarianism, layers of conspiratorial secrecy within the Establishment, and officially sanctioned machiavellianism devoted to preserving the status quo at any cost." Therefore Lewis saw the work as one man's struggle against the State and as a "kind of *Bildungsroman* of middle age, a novel of moral and political wakening."

The novel *The Whistle Blower* formed the basis of a motion picture of the same name, for which Hale wrote the screenplay. Starring Michael Caine, this "bleak, believable, and very English espionage thriller" as a *Mystery Guide* reviewer described it, appeared in 1987. "The English have always been fascinated with treachery and espionage," actor Caine told *Boston Globe* writer Jay Carr. *The Whistle Blower* is as "an angry film . . . [with] much of its anger . . . directed at the futility of Britain's global position." Although this anger make Americans its target, in Carr's view the film also criticizes the British class system, and because this anger disrupts the movie's focus, it robs it of any power. Nevertheless Carr thought *The Whistle Blower* worth seeing, if only for Caine's performance.

When asked to comment on his writing, Hale once told *CA,* "I don't want to address my readers directly, I want to speak to them through my work!"

BIOGRAPHICAL AND CRITICAL SOURCES:

PERIODICALS

Best Sellers, October 1, 1967; November, 1985, review of *The Whistle Blower,* p. 296.

Booklist, September 1, 1985, review of *The Whistle Blower,* p. 31.

Books and Bookmen, December, 1984, review of *The Whistle Blower,* p. 35.

Boston Globe, August 7, 1987, Jay Carr, "*Whistle Blower* Rages at British Bureaucracy"; August 16, 1987, Jay Carr, "Britain's Troubles, Told with Gusto," p. A1; August 26, 1987, "Michael Caine: Actor with a Lot to Say," p. 25.

British Book News, November, 1984, review of *The Whistle Blower,* p. 688.

Kirkus Reviews, July 15, 1985, review of *The Whistle Blower,* p. 655.

Library Journal, October 1, 1985, Brian Alley, review of *The Whistle Blower,* p. 112.

Listener, January 10, 1985, review of *The Whistle Blower,* p. 25.

New York Times Book Review, September 10, 1967; November 10, 1985, Paxton Davis, *The Whistle Blower,* p. 28.

Plays and Players, October, 1970.

Publishers Weekly, July 26, 1985, review of *The Whistle Blower,* p. 155; July 22, 1988, review of *The Whistle Blower,* p. 56.

Punch, October 16, 1968, May 21, 1969; March 4, 1970; November 21, 1984, review of *The Whistle Blower,* p.74; January 16, 1985, review of *The Whistle Blower,* p. 83.

Spectator, September 29, 1973.

Stage, September 10, 1970.

Stage and Television Today, February 25, 1971.

Times Literary Supplement, November 23, 1973; October 12, 1984, Peter Lewis, review of *The Whistle Blower,* p. 1167.

Variety, December 22, 1971; February 23, 1972.

Washington Post Book World, October 6, 1985, review of *The Whistle Blower,* p. 6.

ONLINE

Mystery Guide, http://www.mysteryguide.com/ (August 8, 2003), review of *The Whistle Blower.**

HARVEY, Steven 1949-

PERSONAL: Born June 9, 1949, in Dodge City, KS; son of Max J. and Roberta (Reinhardt) Harvey; married Barbara Hupfer, May 8, 1971; children: Matthew, Nessa, Samuel, Alice. *Ethnicity:* "White." *Education:* Wake Forest University, B.A., 1971; Johns Hopkins University, M.A., 1973; Middlebury College, M.A., 1984; University of Virginia, Ph.D., 1989. *Politics:* Democrat. *Religion:* "Not affiliated with any church." *Hobbies and other interests:* Banjo, guitar, folk music.

ADDRESSES: Home—P.O. Box 356, Young Harris, GA 30582. *Office*—Humanities Division, Young Harris College, Young Harris, GA 30582. *E-mail*—sharvey@ yhc.edu.

CAREER: English teacher at a day school in Charlotte, NC, 1974-76; Young Harris College, Young Harris, GA, professor of English, 1976—. John C. Campbell Folk School, writing instructor, 1995—; Butternut Creek and Friend (folk music group), performer. Georgia Humanities Council, member, 1999-2002.

MEMBER: Associated Writing Programs.

AWARDS, HONORS: Essay award, Augusta Writers Conference, 1990, for "Kid Talk"; fellow, MacDowell Colony, 1994.

WRITINGS:

Powerlines (poetry), Aleph Press, 1976.
A Geometry of Lilies (nonfiction), University of South Carolina Press (Columbia, SC), 1993.
Lost in Translation (nonfiction), University of Georgia Press (Athens, GA), 1997.
(Editor) *In a Dark Wood: Personal Essays by Men on Middle Age,* University of Georgia Press (Athens, GA), 1997.
Bound for Shady Grove, University of Georgia Press (Athens, GA), 2000.

Work represented in anthologies, including *Best American Essays 1992,* edited by Robert Atwan. Contributor of essays, poetry, and reviews to periodicals, including

Steven Harvey

Doubletake, Harper's, Beloit Poetry Journal, Creative Nonfiction, Southern Humanities Review, Shenandoah, and *Iowa Review.*

WORK IN PROGRESS: A series of personal essays.

SIDELIGHTS: Steven Harvey once told *CA:* "'Much is in little,' Roman poet and satirist Horace wrote. Essayists like me keep the job manageable by thinking for a long, long time about hardly anything at all, the essay forcing us to pay attention to all that we take for granted. It helps to have a dull life, a simple life like mine of family and friends and time to think, one in which 'what is' is more important than 'what happens.'

"Since I write essays exclusively, the form says a great deal about who I am and why I write. Essays like mine are not arranged by plot or form, but by anxieties. They don't wonder 'what next?' Instead, like a worried parent, they ask 'now what?' with a groan. The anxieties are relieved not so much by the telling, like confessions, but by the arranging, the way some of us fix a problem at work by cleaning up the desk.

"As a result, 'getting it right' for me is not a matter of being true to events or details. It is a matter of putting events and details into a revealing—a revelatory—relationship with each other. That is the lesson I have learned from the writers who have influenced me the most: Michel de Montaigne, Henry David Thoreau, William Hazlitt, E. B. White, Loren Eiseley, James Baldwin, Annie Dillard, Scott Russell Sanders, Franklin Burroughs, James Kilgo, and Sam Pickering. Strolling through the museum of love and change I try to do what these other writers do so well: rearrange for all to see the treasures we cannot keep."

*   *   *

HARWELL, Ernie
     See HARWELL, William Earnest

*   *   *

HARWELL, William Earnest 1918-
     (Ernie Harwell)

PERSONAL: Born January 25, 1918, in Washington, GA; son of Davis Gray (a furniture salesperson) and Helen (a homemaker; maiden name, Barksdale) Harwell; married Lulu Tankersley (a homemaker), August 30, 1941; children: William Earnest, Jr., Gray Neville, Carolyn, Julie. *Education:* Emory University, A.B., 1940. *Religion:* "A believer in Christ." *Hobbies and other interests:* Reading fiction and the classics; crossword puzzles.

ADDRESSES: Home—25387 Witherspoon, Farmington Hills, MI 48335.

CAREER: Sporting News, Atlanta, GA, correspondent, 1934-48; *Atlanta Constitution,* Atlanta, sportswriter, 1936-40; WSB Atlanta (radio station), Atlanta, sports director, 1940-42; Atlanta Crackers (baseball team), Atlanta, radio announcer, 1940-42; Brooklyn Dodgers (baseball team), Brooklyn, NY, radio and television announcer, 1948-49; New York Giants (baseball team), New York, NY, radio and television announcer, 1950-53; Baltimore Orioles (baseball team), Baltimore, MD, radio and television announcer, 1954-59; Detroit Tigers (baseball team), Detroit, MI, radio announcer, 1960-91 and 1993-2002; retired, 2002. Guest national radio

broadcaster for post-season professional baseball and football games. Appeared in feature films, including *One Flew over the Cuckoo's Nest, Paper Lion,* and *Tigertown.* Spokesperson for American Lung Association in Detroit and for Detroit Rescue Mission. *Military service:* U.S. Marine Corps, sports editor and human interest story writer for *Leatherneck* magazine, 1942-46; became sergeant.

MEMBER: American Society of Composers, Authors, and Publishers, Sigma Alpha Epsilon.

AWARDS, HONORS: Ford C. Frick Award, Major League Baseball Hall of Fame, 1981, for excellence in baseball broadcasting; inducted into National Baseball Hall of Fame, 1981; named Michiganian of the Year, 1981; Lowell Thomas Award, 1985, for national distinguished achievement; Litt.D., Adrian College, 1985; Al Foon Award, Michigan Jewish Hall of Fame, 1988; National Sportscasters and Sportswriters Association, inducted into Hall of Fame, 1989, and named best broadcaster in Michigan twenty times; Big Mac Award, *Detroit News,* 1989; Golden Compass Award, Campfire, Inc., 1989; Life Directions Enrichment Award, 1989; L.H.D., Northern Michigan College, 1990; National Lifetime Achievement Award, March of Dimes, 1991; Joe Louis Award, 1991; Ken Hubbs Memorial Award, 1991; Stanley Kresge Award, 1994; Jesuit Magis Award, University of Detroit, 1995; inducted into National Radio Hall of Fame, 1998, and SAE Leadership Hall of Fame, 2001; Neal Shine Award, Operation Able, 2002, for lifetime achievements; also inducted into Michigan Sports Hall of Fame, Emory University Hall of Fame, American Sportscasters Hall of Fame, Catch Hall of Fame, and Georgia Broadcasters Hall of Fame.

WRITINGS:

UNDER NAME ERNIE HARWELL

(With Fred Smith) *Tiger Trivia,* privately printed, 1978.
Tuned to Baseball, foreword by wife, Lulu Harwell, Diamond Communications (Notre Dame, IN), 1985.
Ernie Harwell's Diamond Gems, Momentum (Ann Arbor, MI), 1991.

The Babe Signed My Shoe: Baseball As It Was—and Will Always Be; Tales of the Grand Old Game, Diamond Communications (Notre Dame, IN), 1994.

Stories from My Life in Baseball, edited by Alison Boyce and Carlos Monarrez, Detroit Free Press (Detroit, MI), 2001.

(With Tom Keegan) *Ernie Harwell: My Sixty Years in Baseball,* Triumph (Chicago, IL), 2002.

Also author of *Ernie Harwell's Tiger Fan Calendar,* 1988 and 1989. Author of lyrics to more than fifty recorded songs, including "I Don't Know Any Better," "Maestro of the Mound," "Move Over Babe, Here Comes Henry," "One Room World," "Wake Up Wiser," and "Why Did It Take You So Long." Contributor to books, including *Baseball Is Their Business,* Random House (New York, NY), 1952; and *Voices of Sport,* edited by Marv Albert and others, Grosset (New York, NY), 1971; author of introduction, *A Picture Postcard History of Baseball,* by Ron Menchine, Rowman & Littlefield (Lanham, MD), 1993; author of foreword, *The Great Chase: The Dodger-Giants Pennant Race of 1951,* by Harvey Rosenfeld, iUniverse, 2001. Contributor to newspapers and magazines, including *Sports Illustrated, Sporting News, Reader's Digest, Collier's, Esquire, Saturday Evening Post,* and *Catholic Digest.*

SIDELIGHTS: For more than forty years, beginning in 1960, William Earnest "Ernie" Harwell was the radio voice of the Detroit Tigers baseball team. The first active radio announcer to be inducted into the Major League Baseball Hall of Fame, Harwell broadcast professional baseball games longer than any other major league announcer on the air. Best known for his relaxed voice, methodical reporting, and notably impartial style of play-by-play description, Harwell is also the author of several baseball books which contain stories and reminiscences about his long career.

"For baseball fans, Ernie Harwell's voice is like crickets humming through a screen door: one of summer's most familiar and soothing sounds," wrote Michael Betzold in *Newsmakers: The People behind Today's Headlines.* "Harwell's articulate, melodious Georgia drawl is like a smooth ride on the river of baseball's heritage."

A native of Georgia, Harwell has loved baseball since his childhood, despite his admitted lack of great athletic talent. "I wanted to play baseball in the worst way, and that's the way I did play it," the announcer quipped in a *Chicago Tribune* interview by Bruce Buursma. Nor did the prospects of a broadcasting career seem bright. As a child Harwell was tongue-tied and inarticulate to the point of drawing ridicule from his classmates. Speech teachers and his own dogged persistence helped him to overcome the disability by the time he entered his teens.

While attending high school and, later, Emory University, Harwell worked as a correspondent for the *Sporting News* and as a sports reporter for the *Atlanta Constitution* newspaper. As a college senior he landed a job as sports director at Atlanta radio station WSB, where he aired a fifteen-minute sports program. He longed to broadcast baseball games like his heroes Red Barber and Mel Allen, and he spent hours each evening practicing play-calling for imaginary games.

After serving in the Marines during World War II, Harwell returned to Atlanta and station WSB, where he got his start in play-by-play announcing for the Atlanta Crackers minor league baseball team. He continued there until early in the 1948 season, when Brooklyn Dodgers' radio commentator Red Barber developed a bleeding ulcer. Dodger owner Branch Rickey subsequently expressed an interest in hiring Harwell to call the Brooklyn games. After some negotiation—in the only known transaction in baseball history involving both a broadcaster and a player—Harwell replaced Barber and became a major league announcer when the Crackers traded Harwell to the Dodgers for catcher-manager Cliff Dapper. "The Crackers were willing to give me up, alright, but they wanted something in return," Harwell recounted to Buursma, adding, "I thought it was a great deal."

Harwell remained with the Dodgers through the end of the following season and then worked as the New York Giants' television broadcaster until 1953. His tenure with the club included the telecast of the famous 1951 playoff series between the Giants and the Dodgers in which the Giants, having overtaken the opposing team's thirteen-game lead during the final weeks of the season, went on to defeat them in a three-game series that ended with Bobby Thomson's dramatic bottom-of-the-ninth-inning home run in the final game. Ironically, it is not Harwell's call of the Thomson homer that is remembered today, but rather that of his partner, Russ Hodges, who drew the radio assignment that day and coined the phrase "shot heard 'round the world." Nevertheless, Harwell recalled that particular game as "the biggest thrill of my career. It was such a great rivalry between the Giants and the Dodgers." Buursma quoted Harwell in the *Grand Rapids Press:* "So much hung on that one pitch—the pennant, the whole season." Harwell's account of the historic pennant-clinching game was published in *Voices of Sport,* a 1973 collection of essays written by sportscasters about memorable events in sports history.

Harwell left the Giants in 1954 to give the radio play-by-play for the Baltimore Orioles, where he worked until the 1960 season, his first as broadcaster for the Detroit Tigers. Since then the announcer has been admired, in the words of Buursma, for his "straightforward and remarkably nonpartisan accounts" of each game. "I'm a reporter first and foremost," Harwell told the sportswriter, explaining that "most people tune in for the game. I bring the play-by-play report to people. All the rest is trappings—salt and pepper. And you don't want the seasoning to overwhelm the food." His philosophy has also earned him the respect of his colleagues. In the *Grand Rapids Press,* Buursma quoted Paul Carey, Harwell's longtime Tiger broadcasting partner: "I knew he was a good baseball broadcaster, but I didn't know HOW good he was until I sat next to him shoulder to shoulder every day. . . . I now realize how accurate he is. He can conjure up the mental imagery for the listener. You know, there are those in this business who want to be overly colorful. But with a minimum of words, Ernie can describe a maximum of action." Nonetheless, Harwell does have his own broadcasting trademarks. He intersperses the play-by-play with his formidable knowledge of baseball trivia and anecdotes, and his stock phrases such as "He stood there like a house by the side of the road and watched that one go by," for a called third strike. Fans throughout the Tiger baseball network's listening area are familiar with Harwell's pretending to know the name of the hometown of any fan who catches a foul fly ball in Tiger Stadium.

During his off seasons, Harwell wrote numerous articles for magazines and has composed dozens of songs, some of which have been recorded by such artists as B. J. Thomas, Barbara Lewis, and Merrilee Rush. He has also written songs about baseball, most notably "Move Over Babe, Here Comes Henry," about Hank Aaron's 1973 surpassing of baseball legend Babe Ruth's career home-run record, and "Maestro of the Mound," which lauded former Tiger pitcher Denny McLain, the thirty-game winner who led his team to victory in the 1968 World Series.

In 1985 Harwell wrote *Tuned to Baseball,* a book containing memories of his associations with his colleagues, including Red Barber, Mel Allen, and Russ Hodges, his reminiscences of pregame interviews with major league players, managers, umpires, and owners, and his observations about his long career as a baseball broadcaster. His other books include *Ernie Harwell's Diamond Gems* and *The Babe Signed My Shoe: Baseball As It Was—and Will Always Be; Tales of the Grand Old Game.* The latter title includes more reminiscences and interviews with such baseball luminaries as Joe DiMaggio, Ted Williams, and award-winning sportswriter Fred Lieb. Betzold commented that Harwell's "books are filled with straightforward, charming accounts of the game's big and little people, from famous managers and star players to clubhouse attendants, groundskeepers, and traveling secretaries."

Later books are *Stories from My Life in Baseball,* a selection of Harwell's columns published in the *Detroit Free Press,* and *Ernie Harwell: My Sixty Years in Baseball,* another collection of stories and reminiscences.

It is safe to say that Harwell is an institution in Michigan. When he was released at the end of the 1991 season, the uproar was so great that it contributed to then-owner Tom Monaghan's decision to sell the Tigers. Just two years later, new owner Mike Ilitch re-hired Harwell, and the hardy announcer remained at his post until his retirement in 2002. Betzold described Harwell as a dedicated broadcaster who believes his job is "reporting, not commentary. . . . Unlike most modern announcers who feel they must fill every second with chatter, Harwell [is] unafraid to pause and let listeners soak up the summertime buzz of the crowd."

Harwell was the first active announcer to be inducted into the National Baseball Hall of Fame. A devout Christian who spends part of his spare time helping charitable causes in the Detroit area, he has also been known to conduct chapel services in baseball clubhouses. Betzold concluded of the popular broadcaster: "In the insular, backbiting world of major league baseball, Harwell is one of the few longtimers with no enemies and thousands of friends."

BIOGRAPHICAL AND CRITICAL SOURCES:

BOOKS

Harwell, Ernie, *Tuned to Baseball,* Diamond Communications (Notre Dame, IN), 1985.

Harwell, Ernie, *The Babe Signed My Shoe: Baseball As It Was—and Will Always Be; Tales of the Grand Old Game,* Diamond Communications (Notre Dame, IN), 1994.

Harwell, Ernie, *Stories from My Life in Baseball,* edited by Alison Boyce and Carlos Monarrez, Detroit Free Press (Detroit, MI), 2001.

Harwell, Ernie, and Tom Keegan, *Ernie Harwell: My Sixty Years in Baseball,* Triumph (Chicago, IL), 2002.

PERIODICALS

Chicago Tribune, June 1, 1988, interview by Bruce Buursma.

Detroit Free Press, September 30, 1993; September 15, 2002, Heath J. Meriwether, "The Importance of Being Ernie: 42 Years As Tigers Broadcaster, Harwell Ends His Career with Class."

Grand Rapids Press, July 28, 1974, article by Bruce Buursma.

Los Angeles Times, August 15, 2002, Mike Penner, "Last Call," pp. D1, D7.

Newsmakers: The People behind Today's Headlines, 1997, Issue 3, pp. 67-69.

New York Daily News, March 22, 2002, Bill Madden, "At 84, Harwell Springs Ahead."

New York Times, February 26, 2002, "Last Season for Harwell," p. D7; September 30, 2002, Richard Sandomir, "Ernie Harwell Signs Off; As Promised, Voice of the Tigers Retires at Age 84 after Decades on the Job," p. D3.

People, May 23, 1983.

Sports Illustrated, April 13, 1987; December 31, 1990, p. 19.

Tampa Tribune, March 31, 2002, Steve Kornacki, "Last Call for Tigers' No. 1 Star," p. S9.

TV Guide, September 21-27, 2002, Jon Miller, "The Harwell Way: Thanks to Ernie, Detroit Always Knew the Score—and More," p. 53.

Wall Street Journal, September 26, 2002, Bryan Gruley, "A Big Tiger Goodby to Ernie Harwell," p. D10; October 21, 2003, Jeffrey Zaslow, "Working Past Retirement . . . Way Past: An Octogenarian Scores a 10-Year Deal," p. D1.

Washington Post, August 18, 2004, William Gildea, "Harwell's Small Talk Will Be Sorely Missed," p. D10.

*   *   *

HASLUCK, Nicholas 1942-

PERSONAL: Born October 17, 1942, in Canberra, Australia; son of Paul (a historian) and Alexandra (a historian; maiden name, Darker) Hasluck; married Sally Anne Bolton (a museum curator), April 16, 1966; children: Anthony Guy, Lindsay Robert. *Ethnicity:* "Australian." *Education:* University of Western Australia, LL.B., 1964; Oxford University, B.C.L., 1966.

ADDRESSES: Home—14 Reserve St., Claremont, Western Australia 6010, Australia. *E-mail*—hasluck@iinet.net.au.

CAREER: Keal Brinsden (law firm), Perth, Australia, partner, 1970-84; barrister in private practice, 1985—. Australia Council, deputy chair, 1978-82.

MEMBER: Order of Australia.

AWARDS, HONORS: Award for book of the year, *Age Monthly,* 1984, for *The Bellarmine Jug;* Premier's Fiction Prize, 1991, for *The Country without Music.*

WRITINGS:

NOVELS

Quarantine, Macmillan (London, England), 1978, Holt (New York, NY), 1979.

The Blue Guitar, Macmillan (London, England), 1980, Holt (New York, NY), 1981.

The Hand That Feeds You: A Satiric Nightmare, Fremantle Arts Centre Press (Fremantle, Western Australia, Australia), 1982.

The Bellarmine Jug, Penguin (Ringwood, Victoria, Australia), 1984.

Truant State, Penguin (Ringwood, Victoria, Australia), 1987, Penguin (New York, NY), 1988.

The Country without Music, Viking (Ringwood, Victoria, Australia), 1990.

The Blosseville File, Penguin (Ringwood, Victoria, Australia), 1992.

A Grain of Truth, Penguin (Ringwood, Victoria, Australia), 1994.

Our Man K, Penguin (Ringwood, Victoria, Australia), 1999.

OTHER

Anchor and Other Poems, Fremantle Arts Centre Press (Fremantle, Western Australia, Australia), 1976.

The Hat on the Letter O and Other Stories, Fremantle Arts Centre Press (Fremantle, Western Australia, Australia), 1978.

(With William Grono) *On the Edge* (poetry), Freshwater Bay Press (Claremont, Western Australia, Australia), 1981.

(With C. J. Koch) *Chinese Journey* (poetry), Fremantle Arts Centre Press (Fremantle, Western Australia, Australia), 1985.

Collage: Recollections and Images of the University of Western Australia, Fremantle Arts Centre Press (Fremantle, Western Australia, Australi), 1987.

Offcuts: From a Legal Literary Life, University of Western Australia Press (Nedlands, Western Australia, Australia), 1993.

(Editor and author of introduction) Paul Hasluck, *The Chance of Politics,* Text Publishing (Melbourne, Australia), 1997.

The Legal Labyrinth: The Kisch Case and Other Reflections on Law and Literature, Freshwater Bay Press (Claremont, Western Australia, Australia), 2003.

SIDELIGHTS: Australian writer Nicholas Hasluck has gained particular renown for his fiction. Louis James in *Contemporary Novelists* found a "combination of intrigue, dark humour, and fable" to be "characteristic of Hasluck's style."

Hasluck's first novel, *Quarantine,* concerns a group of passengers who are subjected to unspecified quarantine while attempting to pass through the Suez Canal. The novel's hero, an unnamed law student, eventually surmises that the travelers are victims of obscure bureaucratic complications, and he preoccupies himself with observations and considerations of the group's peculiar plight. As days become weeks, however, the various passengers, who have been detained at a filthy station situated in a bleak and barren area, grow restless and

plot to negotiate their way to freedom. But this scheme, engineered by one of the group's more opportunistic members, fails to bring about their release and leads, instead, to violence and the further degeneration of the hapless band's already precarious situation. Martin Lebowitz, in his review for the *Chicago Tribune Book World,* compared *Quarantine* to both Albert Camus's *The Plague* and Samuel Beckett's *Waiting for Godot,* and he pronounced Hasluck's account "a fascinating first novel." James concluded that *Quarantine* displays a "brand of mordant absurdism."

Hasluck's next novel, *The Blue Guitar,* is a concentrated depiction of thirty-four-year-old entrepreneur Dyson Garrick during a few pivotal days. Garrick hopes to market a mechanical guitar invented by his German friend Hermann. Already deep in debt, Garrick dodges his creditors and federal investigators while pitching his unlikely commodity to potential investors, including both financiers and loan sharks. While he futilely hustles about the city, an industrial center in Australia, Garrick also manages to lose his mistress and further infuriate his ex-wife, from whom he steals at one point. Eventually, Garrick's desperation compels him to execute an unethical business maneuver, one that causes him to lose Hermann's friendship even as it stabilizes—at least temporarily—his own finances. Garrick's "quest is idealistic (the title directs us to Wallace Stevens's poem 'Things as they are are changed by the blue guitar') but also tangled in the temptations of commercial exploitation, and this conflict leads to Garrick's own moral disintegration as he finally betrays his friend," wrote James.

Among the enthusiasts of *The Blue Guitar* was *New York Times Book Review* contributor Jeffrey Burke, who reported that with this novel Hasluck had produced a "character study [that] is entertaining and insightful." Tom Clark declared in his review for the *Los Angeles Times* that Hasluck's novel "is a vivid account of life in the contemporary hells of getting and spending." Clark added that *The Blue Guitar* is evidence that Hasluck possesses both "a fine novelist's narrative skills and complexity of vision."

The Bellarmine Jug concerns the discovery of a historical manuscript that undermines long-held perceptions of Dutch activities in Indonesia. Cold War intrigue ensues, with authorities determined to expose a British spy, one who allegedly revealed nuclear test sites to the Soviets in the 1940s. *Times Literary Supple-*

ment contributor Jim Crace called *The Bellarmine Jug* an "entertaining and provoking novel." According to James, "*The Bellarmine Jug* explores the roots of Australian identity on both personal and social levels, using techniques from the spy thriller and a legal examination that probes each layer of truth to reveal alternative realities. . . . The novel rates amongst the finest Australian novels of the 1980s."

Hasluck's novel *Truant State* relates a British family's experiences after relocating to Australia following World War I. The Travernes settle next to the Guys, whose patriarch, Romney, is an ingratiating con artist. Soon the Travernes' patriarch, Henry, is lured into one of Romney's schemes, one that leads to ruin. Narrating these and other events is Henry's son, Jack, who courts Romney's daughter, Diana, and involves himself in politics during the Great Depression. "The novel," wrote James, "which shows Hasluck's characteristic interweaving of personal, social, and metaphysical issues, with detective intrigue, is remarkable for its regional evocation of the fictional Butler's Swamp and Western Australia between the wars."

The Country without Music, *The Blosseville File*, and *A Grain of Truth* chronicle the history of a fictional French colony in the southwest corner of Western Australia which, in the course of time, develops into a separate country within the larger land mass. Hasluck uses this fictional setting to comment on contemporary Australian society and to explore the evolution of national identity. *The Country without Music* focuses on the islands of Baie de Baudin, whose history is retold through various narrators associated with its past. Helen Daniel, in her book *Liars*, called the novel "a work of imaginative energy and intellectual elegance."

The Blosseville File spotlights Lucien Chabot, a freelance journalist commenting on various aspects of life in the former French colony of Blosseville. His observations are fueled by collected clippings and photographs about the people and places of the community. In his musings he offers opinions on subjects such as computer technology, discrimination against minorities, and the undependable nature of writing. In addition to praising the satirical tone of the work, reviewers admired the poignancy of one of the novel's final sketches—a farewell scene between father and son. Regarding *The Blosseville File*, Rod Moran of the *West Australian* stated: "It has the shrewdness of observation, eloquence, humour, and delicate sensi-

tivity to the currents and textures of human reality that are hallmarks of both his fiction and poetry."

In *A Grain of Truth* Hasluck tells of "the lawyer Michael Cheyne, [who] finds himself standing for human rights against the weight of apparent justice within the legal system," wrote James. "The novel, which has an optimistic ending, underlines Hasluck's conviction that life is a conflict between the structures of social order—exemplified by the law—and the anarchy that lies at the core of human experience."

Hasluck once described his novels to *CA* as "moral thrillers, the plots taut and intricate. Caught up in events which work in collusion to obscure moral choices, the characteristic figure struggles to construct his own ethical framework."

BIOGRAPHICAL AND CRITICAL SOURCES:

BOOKS

Contemporary Novelists, 6th edition, St. James Press (Detroit, MI), 1996.
Daniel, Helen, *Liars*, Penguin (Ringwood, Victoria, Australia), 1988.
Hasluck, Nicholas, *Offcuts: From a Legal Literary Life*, University of Western Australia Press (Nedlands, Western Australia, Australia), 1993.

PERIODICALS

Age Monthly Review, December, 1984.
Chicago Tribune Book World, June 17, 1979, Martin Lebowitz, review of *Quarantine*, p. 3.
Financial Times, June 15, 1978.
Los Angeles Times, September 11, 1980, Tom Clark, review of *The Blue Guitar*.
Newsweek, April 6, 1979.
New York Times Book Review, August 5, 1979, p. 10; September 28, 1980, Jeffrey Burke, review of *The Blue Guitar*, p. 14.
Times Literary Supplement, April 18, 1980, p. 430; January 29, 1982, p. 114; March 8, 1985, Jim Crace, review of *The Bellarmine Jug*, p. 266.
West Australian, April 18, 1992, Rod Moran, review of *The Blosseville File*.

HECK, Alfons 1928-

PERSONAL: Born November 3, 1928, in Wittlich, Germany; immigrated to Canada, 1951; immigrated to the United States, 1963, naturalized citizen, 1969; son of Jakob Johann (a farmer) and Maria Anna (a housewife; maiden name, Wambach) Heck; married Berniece June Appleby, November 3, 1965. *Education:* Attended University of Victoria, 1958. *Politics:* Independent. *Religion:* Roman Catholic.

ADDRESSES: Home and office—San Diego, CA. *Agent*—Loma Lectures, 4444 West Point Loma Blvd., Suite 95, San Diego, CA 92107. *E-mail*—alfonsheck@attglobal.net.

CAREER: Rhein Zeitung, Wittlich, Germany, newspaper reporter, 1949-50; worked in Canada as lumber inspector, owner of a taxicab business, and restaurant manager, 1952-63; Greyhound Lines, supervisor, 1964-72; freelance writer, 1975—. Converse School of Languages, San Diego, CA, German teacher,1974-77; teacher of German and registered court interpreter for U.S. and California courts, beginning 1975. Lecturer on Hitler and the Holocaust; guest speaker at more than 300 colleges and universities; narrator and subject of the television special *Heil Hitler! Confessions of a Hitler Youth,* broadcast by Home Box Office, 1991; guest on television documentary "The Fatal Attraction of Adolf Hitler," aired by British Broadcasting Corp., 1989; and several other television programs, including "Today Show," "Hour," and "Good Morning America." *Wartime service:* Hitler Youth, 1938-45; became district leader; captured by U.S. Army, 1945; received War Service Cross, first class, from Adolf Hitler.

MEMBER: San Diego Press Club.

AWARDS, HONORS: Awards from San Diego Press Club, 1978, 1979, 1981, 1982, 1983, and 1985; Annual Cable Excellence Award, National Cable Television Association, George Foster Peabody Broadcasting Award, Henry W. Grady School of Journalism and Mass Communications, University of Georgia, Emmy Award, outstanding historical programming, Academy of Television arts and Sciences, and International Cindy Award, all 1991, for *Heil Hitler! Confessions of a Hitler Youth;* Christopher Award, best young adult book, 1995, for *Parallel Journeys.*

WRITINGS:

A Child of Hitler: Germany in the Days When God Wore a Swastika (autobiography), Renaissance House (Frederick, CO), 1985.
The Burden of Hitler's Legacy (autobiography), Renaissance House (Frederick, CO), 1988.
(With Eleanor H. Ayer and Helen Waterford) *Parallel Journeys* (young adult), Atheneum (New York, NY), 1995.

Contributor of more than 200 articles on the Nazi era to magazines and newspapers, including *Worldview* and *Europe.*

ADAPTATIONS: The television special *Heil Hitler: Confessions of a Hitler Youth* is based on Heck's book *A Child of Hitler: Germany in the Days When God Wore a Swastika.*

SIDELIGHTS: Alfons Heck once told *CA:* "I was born in 1928 in Wittlich, a small town in the Rhineland of Germany. I joined the Hitler Youth in 1938 and attended the Nuremberg Nazi Party Congress that year as a ten-year-old delegate. At the age of fourteen I was selected for the Flying Hitler Youth, and in 1944 I was (briefly) Germany's youngest top-rated sailplane pilot. I was accepted as an officer cadet for the Luftwaffe but was not drafted. As a captain of the Hitler Youth, I was sent to the Siegfried Line, where I later commanded 3,000 Hitler Youth engaged in defense projects. I met Armaments Minister Albert Speer and Hitler himself. By 1945 I had reached the rank of acting *bannführer,* a district leader comparable to brigadier general, and I organized units of the Volksturm in the last-ditch defense of Germany. I was captured by the American Third Army and later arrested by French occupation officials. After a 'de-Nazification' hearing, I was sentenced to one month of hard labor and restricted to the town limits for two years.

"Although *A Child of Hitler: Germany in the Days When God Wore a Swastika* is an autobiography, it is also the only book in English which provides insight on the Hitler Youth. My aim is to present the German tragedy of World War II fairly and also as a warning to young Americans. That is one reason why I joined Helen Waterford, a Jewish survivor of Auschwitz, to lecture at universities, colleges, and high schools. I believe both perspectives ought to be heard. Although Helen Waterford died in 1997, I continue to lecture about the Nazi era.

"I wrote *The Burden of Hitler's Legacy* to answer a number of inquiries readers had about my postwar life as well as a reply to questions I received from many students when I gave lectures at universities across the country. Just as in my first book, my principal aim was to present a unique personal view into the Nazi era and its legacy."

BIOGRAPHICAL AND CRITICAL SOURCES:

BOOKS

Heck, Alfons, *A Child of Hitler: Germany in the Days When God Wore a Swastika,* Renaissance House (Frederick, CO), 1985.
Heck, Alfons, *The Burden of Hitler's Legacy,* Renaissance House (Frederick, CO), 1988.

PERIODICALS

Boston Globe, March 29, 1985.
Los Angeles Times, March 7, 1985.
People, June 17, 1991.
St. Louis Globe-Democrat, May 4, 1985.

*　　*　　*

HERMES, Patricia (Mary) 1936-

PERSONAL: Born February 21, 1936, in Brooklyn, NY; daughter of Frederick Joseph (a bank vice president) and Jessie (Gould) Martin; married Matthew E. Hermes (a research and development director for a chemical company), August 24, 1957 (divorced, 1984); children: Paul, Mark, Timothy, Matthew, Jr., Jennifer. *Education:* St. John's University, B.A., 1957.

ADDRESSES: Home—1414 Melville Ave., Fairfield, CT 06430. *Agent*—Dorothy Markinko (juvenile books) and Julie Fallowfield (adult books), McIntosh & Otis, Inc., 310 Madison Ave., New York, NY 10017.

CAREER: Rollingcrest Junior High School, Takoma Park, MD, teacher of English and social studies, 1957-58; Delcastle Technical High School, Delcastle, DE, teacher of homebound children, 1972-73; Norfolk Public School System, Norfolk, VA, writer-in-residence, beginning 1981; Sacred Heart University, Fairfield, CT, teacher of English and writing, 1986-87. Gives numerous talks and workshops in elementary schools.

MEMBER: Authors Guild, Authors League of America, Society of Children's Book Writers.

AWARDS, HONORS: Best Book for Young Adults designation, American Library Association, 1985, for *A Solitary Secret,* and 1992, for *Mama, Let's Dance;* Hodge-Podger Award, 1993, for *Mama, Let's Dance; Someone to Count On* named among Best Books for the Teen Age, New York Library, 1993; California Young Reader Medal, Hawaii Nene Award, Pine Tree Book Award, and Iowa Young Reader Medal, all for *You Shouldn't Have to Say Goodbye;* several Children's Choice awards.

WRITINGS:

YOUNG ADULT NOVELS

What If They Knew?, Harcourt (New York, NY), 1980.
Nobody's Fault?, Harcourt (New York, NY), 1981.
You Shouldn't Have to Say Goodbye, Harcourt (New York, NY), 1982.
Who Will Take Care of ME?, Harcourt (New York, NY), 1983.
Friends Are Like That, Harcourt (New York, NY), 1984.
A Solitary Secret, Harcourt (New York, NY), 1985.
Kevin Corbett Eats Flies, illustrated by Carol Newsom, Harcourt (New York, NY), 1986.
A Place for Jeremy, Harcourt (New York, NY), 1987.
Heads I Win, Harcourt (San Diego, CA), 1988.
Be Still My Heart, Putnam (New York, NY), 1989.
I Hate Being Gifted, Putnam (New York, NY), 1990.
Mama, Let's Dance, Little, Brown (Boston, MA), 1991.
My Girl (movie novelization), Simon & Schuster (New York, NY), 1991.
Take Care of My Girl, Little, Brown (Boston, MA), 1992.

Someone to Count On, Little, Brown (Boston, MA), 1993.

My Girl II (movie novelization), Pocket Books (New York, NY), 1994.

On Winter's Wind, Little, Brown (Boston, MA), 1995.

Zeus and Roxanne, Pocket Books (New York, NY), 1996.

Fly Away Home, Newmarket Press (New York, NY), 1996.

Christmas Magic, Scholastic (New York, NY), 1996.

Calling Me Home, Avon (New York, NY), 1998.

Cheat the Moon, Little, Brown (Boston, MA), 1998.

Our Strange New Land: Elizabeth's Diary, Scholastic (New York, NY), 2000.

In God's Novel, Marshall Cavendish (Tarrytown, NY), 2000.

Westward to Home: Joshua's Journal, Scholastic (New York, NY), 2001.

A Perfect Place: Joshua's Oregon Trail Diary, Book Two, Scholastic (New York, NY), 2001.

The Starving Time: Elizabeth's Diary, Book Two, Jamestown, Virginia, 1609, Scholastic (New York, NY), 2001.

Season of Promise: Elizabeth's Jamestown Colony Diary, Book Three, Scholastic (New York, NY), 2002.

Sweet By and By, HarperCollins (New York, NY), 2002.

The Wild Year: Joshua's Oregon Trail Diary, Book Three, Scholastic (New York, NY), 2003.

JUVENILES

Nothing but Trouble, Trouble, Trouble, Scholastic (New York, NY), 1994.

I'll Pulverize You, William, Minstrel, 1994.

Everything Stinks, Minstrel, 1995.

Thirteen Things Not to Tell a Parent, Minstrel, 1995.

Boys Are Even Worse Than I Thought, Pocket Books (New York, NY), 1996.

Christmas Magic, illustrated by John S. Gurney, Scholastic (New York, NY), 1996.

Turkey Trouble, illustrated by John S. Gurney, Scholastic (New York, NY), 1996.

Something Scary, Scholastic (New York, NY), 1996.

When Snow Lay Soft on the Mountain, Little, Brown (Boston, MA), 1996.

My Secret Valentine, Scholastic (New York, NY), 1997.

Summer Secrets, Marshall Cavendish (Tarrytown, NY), 2004.

OTHER

A Time to Listen: Preventing Youth Suicide, Harcourt (New York, NY), 1987.

Contributor to periodicals, including *Woman's Day, Life and Health, Connecticut, County, American Baby,* and *Mother's Day.*

Some of Hermes's books have been translated into French, Italian, Japanese, Danish, and Portuguese.

ADAPTATIONS: Fly Away Home was made into a feature film starring Jeff Daniels.

SIDELIGHTS: The author of such juvenile novels as *Fly Away Home* and *A Place for Jeremy,* Patricia Hermes writes candidly about the most difficult events that a child can face. Whether her protagonists are enduring famine in colonial Jamestown or the erratic behavior of a modern-day alcoholic parent, they are thrust into demanding situations and forced by fate to make choices beyond their years. Hermes's books are often somber in tone and rarely resolve themselves with fairytale endings. Instead her first-person narrators grow stronger through adversity and learn to depend upon themselves despite their tender years. As a contributor to the *St. James Guide to Young Adult Writers* put it, "Problem novels such as these tend to condescend to readers, focusing on a specific issue at the expense of plot and character development, and offering solutions where sometimes none can be reached. Hermes attempts to avoid these foibles by implementing a first-person narrative voice. . . . Allowing a character to tell his or her own story adds dimension and complexity to the character."

A former school teacher, Hermes began to write novels when her own children were young. She forged her early plots from her own memories of childhood as well as from her children's adventures amongst themselves and with their friends. Now that her children have grown and started families of their own, Hermes makes frequent visits to elementary schools to take the pulse of a new generation of students. Unlike other authors who have followed trends toward more realistic fiction, Hermes has always addressed serious issues such as child abuse, fatal illness, and moral dilemmas. While she leavens her work with humor, she writes with serious intent. The *St. James Guide to Young Adult Writers* contributor observed that the author's books "explore the idea of hidden shame. Most young people do not want to be different; conformity becomes almost an obsession. A step toward maturity comes with the realization that everyone has secrets, problems they will not tell even their 'best friend.'"

A recurring theme in Hermes's novels is the fallibility of parents or guardians. In *A Solitary Secret,* one of the characters is the victim of incest. In *Take Care of My Girl,* the award-winning *Mama, Let's Dance, Someone to Count On,* and *Cheat the Moon,* the problem is parental abandonment, which forces the young-teen narrators to step into a position of responsibility and care for home and siblings. Such works as *You Shouldn't Have to Say Goodbye* and *The Sweet By and By* deal with the grief children feel when a parent or grandparent dies. Sometimes the most difficult lesson these young narrators must learn is to have the faith to place their trust in another adult. In an interview with *Authors and Artists for Young Adults,* Hermes said, "I think children know everything there is to know about emotions by the time they are three or four. As parents we sometimes want to protect our children from anything that is painful, but what we're really trying to do is protect ourselves, and in doing so, we harm them. When you're dealing with these things in a book—if it gets too scary or too painful—you can close it, or go talk to someone about it."

Many reviewers have praised Hermes not only for the subject matter of her novels but for their subdued presentation as well. Vicki Hardesty in, *Voice of Youth Advocates,* called *You Shouldn't Have to Say Goodbye* "an excellent portrayal of a teenager adjusting to the terminal illness of a parent." *Booklist* reviewer Karen Stang Hanley commended *Who Will Take Care of ME?* as "an affecting story that is especially moving in its portrayal of the complex, tender relationship between two brothers." In *School Library Journal,* Barbara Auerbach noted that *Sweet By and By* "is filled with memorable characters and heart." And a *Publishers Weekly* correspondent felt that *Calling Me Home* is "a cut above" most juvenile historical fiction. The critic concluded that the novel is "a solid story, neatly told."

Hermes once told *CA:* "Children live in the world and are part of the world, and they need books that reflect their world. Adults often forget this. And in trying to present a sanitized version of life, we cheat children.

Kids are gutsier and more courageous than we give them credit for. They need honest books. So many good books are removed from libraries because *adults* fear their content. And the content is often not threatening, but something as harmless as slang or normal kids' speech." In the *St. James Guide to Young Adult Writers,* she concluded: "I can do things in a book that I wouldn't dare do in real life. . . . But best of all, I can sometimes—in a very small way—make a difference in the life of a young reader, as authors made a difference in my life when I was a young adult—as they continue to do today."

BIOGRAPHICAL AND CRITICAL SOURCES:

BOOKS

Authors and Artists for Young Adults, Volume 15, Gale (Detroit, MI), 1995.
St. James Guide to Young Adult Writers, 2nd edition, St. James Press (Detroit, MI), 1999.

PERIODICALS

Booklist, September 15, 1983, Karen Stang Hanley, review of *Who Will Take Care of ME?,* p. 171; August, 1986, Ilene Cooper, review of *Kevin Corbett Eats Flies,* p. 1688; October 1, 1995, Chris Sherman, review of *On Winter's Wind,* p. 314; June 1, 1998, Debbie Carton, review of *Cheat the Moon,* p. 1766; January 1, 1999, Kay Weisman, review of *Calling Me Home,* p. 876; February 1, 2001, Ellen Mandel, review of *Westward to Home: Joshua's Diary,* p. 1053; October 1, 2002, Kay Weisman, review of *Sweet By and By,* p. 341; January 1, 2003, Todd Morning, review of *A Perfect Place,* p. 890.
Bulletin of the Center for Children's Books, November, 1995, Elizabeth Bush, review of *On Winter's Wind,* p. 92.
Horn Book, September-October, 1998, Susan P. Bloom, review of *Cheat the Moon,* p. 608.
Publishers Weekly, October 30, 1995, review of *On Winter's Wind,* p. 62; October 21, 1996, review of *When Snow Lay Soft on the Mountain,* p. 82; December 4, 1998, review of *Calling Me Home,* p. 76; November 11, 2002, review of *Sweet By and By,* p. 64.

School Library Journal, May, 1984, Donna S. Rodda, review of *Friends Are Like That,* p. 80; April, 1994, Susan Hepler, review of *Nothing but Trouble, Trouble, Trouble,* p. 128; January, 1997, Mollie Bynum, review of *When Snow Lay Soft on the Mountain,* p. 83; June, 1998, Connie Tyrrell Burns, review of *Cheat the Moon,* p. 146; August, 2000, Shawn Brommer, review of *Our Strange New Land,* p. 156; June, 2001, Kristen Oravec, review of *The Starving Time: Elizabeth's Diary, Book Two, Jamestown, Virginia, 1609,* p. 118; October, 2002, Barbara Auerbach, review of *Sweet By and By,* p. 164; November, 2002, Sally Bates Goodroe, review of *A Perfect Place: Joshua's Oregon Trail Diary, Book Two,* p. 124; February, 2003, Leslie Barban, review of *Season of Promise: Elizabeth's Jamestown Colony Diary, Book Three,* p. 112.

Voice of Youth Advocates, October, 1993, Vicki Hardesty, review of *You Shouldn't Have to Say Goodbye,* p. 203; December, 1993, Kathleen Beck, review of *Someone to Count On,* pp. 291-292.*

*   *   *

HOFMANN, Paul Leopold 1912-

PERSONAL: Born November 20, 1912, in Vienna, Austria; came to the United States in 1959; naturalized U.S. citizen, 1968; son of Joseph Martin (a civil servant) and Ida Anna (Pirkmayr) Hofmann; married Maria A. Tratter, December 18, 1940; children: Ernest, Alexander. *Education:* University of Vienna, Dr. Jur., 1936.

ADDRESSES: Home—94 Via della Dataria, 00187 Rome, Italy. *Office*—c/o *New York Times,* 229 West 43rd St., New York, NY 10036. *Agent*—Georges Borchardt, Inc., 136 East 57th St., New York, NY 10022.

CAREER: Berner Tagblatt, Berne, Switzerland, correspondent from Rome, Italy, and Vienna, Austria, 1936-45; *New York Times,* New York, NY, editorial assistant in Rome, 1945-56, foreign correspondent in Italy, France, Nigeria, Spain, Algeria, Cuba, and Zaire, 1956-74, chief of United Nations Bureau, 1974-76, correspondent from Vienna, 1976-78, roving correspondent in Rome, 1978-80, bureau chief and writer for magazine, beginning 1980.

WRITINGS:

Rome: The Sweet, Tempestuous Life, Congdon & Lattes (New York, NY), 1982.

O Vatican! A Slightly Wicked View of the Holy See, Congdon & Weed (New York, NY), 1984.

The Viennese: Splendor, Twilight, and Exile, Anchor Press (New York, NY), 1988.

Cento Citta: A Guide to the 'Hundred Cities and Towns' of Italy, Holt (New York, NY), 1988.

That Fine Italian Hand, Holt (New York, NY), 1990.

Roma: The Smart Traveler's Guide to the Eternal City, Holt (New York, NY), 1993.

Switzerland: The Smart Traveler's Guide to Zurich, Basel, and Geneva, Holt (New York, NY), 1994.

The Spell of the Vienna Woods: Inspiration and Influence from Beethoven to Kafka, Holt (New York, NY), 1994.

The Sunny Side of the Alps: Year-Round Delights in South Tyrol and the Dolomites, Holt (New York, NY), 1995.

The Seasons of Rome: A Journal, Holt (New York, NY), 1997.

Umbria: Italy's Timeless Heart, Holt (New York, NY), 1999.

The Vatican's Women: Female Influence at the Holy See, St. Martin's Press (New York, NY), 2002.

SIDELIGHTS: Paul Leopold Hofmann has parlayed his longtime position as *New York Times* Rome correspondent and bureau chief into several books on Italy's landmarks and culture. Reviewing *Rome: The Sweet, Tempestuous Life* in the *Los Angeles Times,* Elaine Kendall called this book "the ideal way to enjoy a Roman holiday without coping with strikes, parking problems or the bother of converting thousands of deflated dollars into millions of inflated lire." More than a travelogue, Hofmann's work is "a subtle fascinating character study of the city and its people," according to Kendall. "Hofmann's book strikes a delicate balance between the apparently trivial and the deceptively serious. By concentrating upon the paradoxes and contradictions, he uncovers the essence of a city unlike any other."

Hofmann's two books on the Vatican take an off-the-wall look at the spiritual landmark. *O Vatican! A Slightly Wicked View of the Holy See* was followed by *The Vatican's Women: Female Influence at the Holy See.* The latter volume, according to *Booklist* reviewer

Ray Olson, is an "entertaining" analysis of "the scope of women's sway in the Vatican." Indeed, about a tenth of the Vatican's contemporary employees are women, whose job titles include nun, housekeeper, lawyer, and art curator; although *Library Journal* reviewer Anna Donnelly mentioned that *The Vatican's Women* is "peppered with innuendo, conjecture, and hearsay, as interviewed sources chose to remain anonymous." While writing about today's Vatican women, Hofmann also looks at the female presence of the past, including "Pope Joan," a German (some sources say English) woman of the ninth century. "Disguised as a man," a *Kirkus Reviews* contributor wrote, Joan "so impressed the papal city with her learning that she was made a cardinal and eventually elected pope until an untimely pregnancy revealed her true gender."

Departing Italy, Hofmann tours his native land of Austria in such volumes as *The Viennese: Splendor, Twilight, and Exile* and *The Spell of the Vienna Woods: Inspiration and Influence from Beethoven to Kafka.* The latter title has the author revisiting the woods fifty years after the scourge of World War II. In doing so, Hofmann recounts "what it was like to grow up in this forest-encircled, romantic city," remarked a *Publishers Weekly* critic. As much a guide as a memoir, *The Spell of the Vienna Woods* "tells us what to see and do," said John Shreffler of *Booklist,* in what he called "an exemplary work beautifully written."

BIOGRAPHICAL AND CRITICAL SOURCES:

PERIODICALS

Booklist, May 1, 1994, John Shreffler, review of *The Spell of the Vienna Woods: Inspiration and Influence from Beethoven to Kafka,* p. 1580; December 15, 1996, Brad Hooper, review of *The Seasons of Rome: A Journal,* p. 706; March 15, 1999, Bill Ott, review of *Umbria: Italy's Timeless Heart,* p. 1286; October 1, 2002, Ray Olson, review of *The Vatican's Women: Female Influence at the Holy See,* p. 290.

Kirkus Reviews, August 15, 2002, review of *The Vatican's Women,* p. 1196.

Library Journal, April 15, 1988, Ann Cohen, review of *Cento Citta: A Guide to the 'Hundred Cities and Towns' of Italy,* p. 79; April 15, 1988, Benny Kraut, review of *The Viennese: Splendor, Twilight, and Exile,* p. 88; May 15, 1990, David Nudo, review of *The Viennese,* p. 88; May 15, 1990, David Nudo, review of *That Fine Italian Hand,* p. 88; January, 1993, Melinda Stivers Leach, review of *Roma: The Smart Traveler's Guide to the Eternal City,* p. 150; January, 1994, William Smith, review of *Switzerland: The Smart Traveler's Guide to Zurich, Basel, and Geneva,* p. 146; April 15, 1994, Jo-Anne Mary Benson, review of *The Spell of the Vienna Woods,* p. 100; July, 1995, Martin Kalfatovic, review of *The Sunny Side of the Alps: Year-Round Delights in South Tyrol and the Dolomites,* p. 108; November 15, 1996, David Nudo, review of *The Seasons of Rome,* p. 78; January, 1999, David Nudo, review of *Umbria,* p. 137; September 15, 2002, Anna Donnelly, review of *The Vatican's Women,* p. 67.

Los Angeles Times, May 27, 1982, Elaine Kendall, review of *Rome: The Sweet, Tempestuous Life;* February 13, 1984, Elaine Kendall, review of *O Vatican! A Slightly Wicked View of the Holy See,* p. 8.

Mademoiselle, February, 1984, Elin Schoen, review of *O Vatican!,* p. 220.

New Yorker, July 11, 1994, review of *The Spell of the Vienna Woods,* p. 91.

New York Review of Books, June 29, 1989, Michael Ignatieff, review of *The Viennese,* p. 21.

New York Times, November 13, 1988, Henry Kamm, review of *Cento Citta.*

New York Times Book Review, February 19, 1984, Peter Hebblethwaite, review of *O Vatican!,* p. 17; October 30, 1988, Mark Anderson, review of *The Viennese,* p. 13; June 17, 1990, Michael Mewshaw, review of *That Fine Italian Hand,* p. 10; September 11, 1994, Erik Burns, review of *The Spell of the Vienna Woods,* p. 33.

Publishers Weekly, November 25, 1983, review of *O Vatican!,* p. 55; April 8, 1988, Genevieve Stuttaford, review of *Cento Citta,* p. 81; April 26, 1988, Genevieve Stuttaford, review of *The Viennese,* p. 70; April 4, 1994, review of *The Spell of the Vienna Woods,* p. 63; May 29, 1995, review of *The Sunny Side of the Alps,* p. 72; November 4, 1996, review of *The Seasons of Rome,* p. 58; February 8, 1999, review of *Umbria,* p. 208.

Travel-Holiday, December-January, 1994, Peter Lewis, review of *The Spell of the Vienna Woods,* p. 93.

U.S. Catholic, May, 1984, Michael Christopher, review of *O Vatican!,* p. 48.

Wall Street Journal, January 12, 1984, Ellen Wilson, review of *O Vatican!,* p. 22.

Washington Monthly, April, 1984, Joseph Nocera, review of *O Vatican!,* p. 56.*

HUNT, David
   See BAYER, William

*   *   *

HUTCHEON, Michael 1945-

PERSONAL: Born July 29, 1945, in Toronto, Ontario, Canada; son of Alexander J. (a solicitor) and Kathleen M. (a homemaker) Hutcheon; married, 1970; wife's name Linda. *Education:* University of Toronto, M.D.

ADDRESSES: Home—8 High Park Gardens, Toronto, Ontario M6R 1S9, Canada. *Office*—Toronto Lung Transplant Program, 10-236EN, Toronto General Hospital, 200 Elizabeth St., Toronto, Ontario M5G 2C4, Canada.

CAREER: University of Toronto, Toronto, Ontario, Canada, head of Respirology Division, Department of Medicine, 1976-99, medical director of Toronto Lung Transplant Program at Toronto General Hospital, 1996—.

MEMBER: Royal College of Physicians of Canada (fellow), Toronto Wagner Society (cochair).

WRITINGS:

(With wife, Linda Hutcheon) *Opera: Desire, Disease, Death,* University of Nebraska Press (Lincoln, NE), 1996.

(With Linda Hutcheon) *Bodily Charm: Living Opera,* University of Nebraska Press (Lincoln, NE), 2000.

(With Linda Hutcheon) *Opera: The Art of Dying,* Harvard University Press (Cambridge, MA), 2004.

SIDELIGHTS: Michael Hutcheon once told *CA:* "I work with my collaborator, Linda Hutcheon, to bring the expertise of medicine together with that of literary theory in a project that views medical practice and meaning in a large social structure. We use opera as a cultural vehicle to explore this concept. The major motivation for both of us is intellectual pleasure."

I

IHIMAERA, Witi (Tame) 1944-

PERSONAL: Born February 7, 1944, in Gisborne, New Zealand; son of Tame Czar, Jr. (a farmer) and Julia (Keelan) Ihimaera; married Jane Cleghorn, May 9, 1970; children: Jessica Kiri, Olivia Ata. *Ethnicity:* "Maori." *Education:* Attended University of Auckland, 1962-66; Victoria University of Wellington, B.A., 1970.

ADDRESSES: Home—2 Bella Vista Rd., Herne Bay, Auckland, New Zealand.

CAREER: Author. Post Office, Headquarters, Wellington, New Zealand, postman, 1969-72; Ministry of Foreign Affairs, Wellington, New Zealand, diplomatic officer and writer, 1973-89; Auckland University, Auckland, New Zealand, lecturer in the English department, 1990—. Member of Queen Elizabeth II Arts Council of New Zealand.

MEMBER: International PEN, Maori Writers and Artists Society of New Zealand.

AWARDS, HONORS: Wattie Award, 1974, for *Tangi,* and 1986, for *The Matriarch;* Burns Fellow at University of Otago, 1975; Katherine Mansfield Memorial Fellow, 1993.

WRITINGS:

Pounamu, Pounamu (short stories; title means "Greenstone, Greenstone"; also see below), Heinemann (Auckland, New Zealand), 1972.

Tangi (novel; title means "Mourning"), Heinemann (Auckland, New Zealand), 1973.

Whanau (novel; title means "Family"), Heinemann (Auckland, New Zealand), 1974.

Maori (nonfiction), New Zealand Government Printer (Wellington, New Zealand), 1975.

The New Net Goes Fishing (short stories; also see below), Heinemann (Auckland, New Zealand), 1977.

The Matriarch, Heinemann (Auckland, New Zealand), 1986.

Dear Miss Mansfield: A Tribute to Kathleen Mansfield Beauchamp, Heinemann (Auckland, New Zealand), 1987, Viking (New York, NY), 1989.

The Whale Rider, illustrated by John Hovell, Mandarin (Auckland, New Zealand), 1992, reprinted with movie stills, Reed (Auckland, New Zealand), 2002, Harcourt (Orlando, FL), 2003.

Land, Sea, and Sky, with photographs by Holger Leue, Reed Books (Auckland, New Zealand), 1994.

Bulibasha: King of the Gypsies, Penguin (Auckland, New Zealand), 1994.

The Legendary Land, photographed by Holger Leue, Reed (Auckland, New Zealand), 1994.

Kingfisher Come Home: The Complete Maori Stories, Secker & Warburg (Auckland, New Zealand), 1995.

Aotearoa = New Zealand: Faces of the Land, with photographs by Holger Leue, Reed Books (Auckland, New Zealand), 1995.

Nights in the Gardens of Spain, Secker & Warburg (Auckland, New Zealand), 1995.

Kingfisher Come Home: The Complete Maori Stories (contains *Pounamu, Pounamu* and *The New Net Goes Fishing*), Secker & Warburg (Auckland, New Zealand), 1995.

The Kaieke Tohora, Reed Books (Auckland, New Zealand), 1995.

The Dream Swimmer (sequel to *The Matriarch*), Penguin (Auckland, New Zealand), 1997.

(With Tim Plant) *New Zealand: Land of Adventure,* photographed by Holger Leue, Reed (Auckland, New Zealand), 1997.

On Top/Down Under, photographed by Sally Tagg, HarperCollins (Auckland, New Zealand), 1998.

(With Tim Plant) *This Is New Zealand,* photographed by Holger Leue, Reed (Auckland, New Zealand), 1998.

New Zealand: First to See Dawn, photographed by Holger Leue, Reed (Auckland, New Zealand), 1999.

The Uncle's Story, University of Hawaii Press (Honolulu, HI), 2000.

Woman Far Walking (play), Huia (Wellington, New Zealand), 2000.

Out There: Portraits of the Hero Parade, photographed by Murray Savidan, Savidan Productions (Auckland, New Zealand), 2001.

The Little Kowhai Tree (for children), illustrated by Henry Campbell, Huia (Wellington, New Zealand), 2002.

Ihimaera: His Best Stories, Reed (Auckland, New Zealand), 2003.

Sky Dancer, Penguin (Auckland, New Zealand), 2003.

Also author of short stories, including "Big Brother, Little Sister" and "Truth of the Matter." Contributor of lecture to *New Zealand through the Arts: Past and Present,* Friends of Turnbull Library (Wellington, New Zealand), 1982.

EDITOR

(With D. S. Long) *Into the World of Light* (collection of contemporary Maori writing), Heinemann (Exeter, NH), 1982.

Te Ao Marama: Contemporary Maori Writing, five volumes, Reed Books (Auckland, New Zealand), 1992-96.

Vision Aotearoa: Kaupapa New Zealand, Bridget Williams (Wellington, New Zealand), 1994.

(Coeditor) *Mataora: The Living Face: Contemporary Maori Art,* D. Bateman (Auckland, New Zealand), 1996.

Growing Up Maori, Tandem Press (Auckland, New Zealand), 1998.

Where's Waari? A History of the Maori through the Short Story, Reed (Auckland, New Zealand), 2000.

(With Ngarino Ellis) *Te Ata: Maori Art from the East Coast, New Zealand,* Reed (Auckland, New Zealand), 2002.

Auckland: The City in Literature, Exisle (Auckland, New Zealand), 2003.

ADAPTATIONS: "Big Brother, Little Sister" was adapted to video by Aardvark Films (New Zealand), 1976; "Truth of the Matter" was adapted to video as *Against the Lights* by Sam Pillsbury Film Productions (New Zealand), 1980; *The Whale Rider* was made into a motion picture of the same name, written and directed by Niki Caro, by South Pacific Pictures (Auckland, New Zealand), 2002.

SIDELIGHTS: Witi Ihimaera "has the distinction of being the first Maori writer to publish both a book of short stories and a novel," wrote a contributor on the New Zealand Book Council Web site. The Maori people were the native culture in New Zealand before the Europeans arrived. Ihimaera has written many books for adults, as well as some for children and young adults, that help to illuminate the world of the Maori.

Perhaps Ihimaera's most famous children's book is *The Whale Rider,* written in three weeks in New York and on Cape Cod. It relates the story of a Maori girl, her relationship with a whale, and how that relationship saves her village. The story is told from the viewpoint of her uncle and of the whales. Originally written in 1987, the book gained prominence in 2003, with the worldwide release of an award-winning movie version. Reviewing the 2003 edition, A *Kirkus Reviews* contributor wrote, "Dazzling ocean descriptions from the whales' perspective highlight the poetic writing," while *Booklist*'s Gillian Engberg called it "a haunting story." Calling the work "a poetic blend of reality and myth," *School Library Journal* critic Susan Oliver found *The Whale Rider* "a tale rich in intense drama and sociological and cultural information."

Ihimaera once said, "There are two landscapes to New Zealand, the Maori and the Pakeha (European). I began writing and continue writing to ensure that the Maori landscape of New Zealand is taken into account. I am Maori. I write about Maori people. They are my commitment—and I am committed not only in my writing, but also in my career and my whole life."

BIOGRAPHICAL AND CRITICAL SOURCES:

BOOKS

Contemporary Novelists, 7th edition, St. James Press (Detroit, MI), 2001.

PERIODICALS

Booklist, July, 2003, Gillian Engberg, review of *The Whale Rider,* p. 1881.

Choice, June, 1990, review of *Dear Miss Mansfield: A Tribute to Kathleen Mansfield Beauchamp,* p. 1678.

Contemporary Pacific, spring, 1998, Paul Lyons, review of *Nights in the Gardens of Spain,* p. 280.

Encounter, May, 1987, Michael Thorpe, review of *The Matriarch,* p. 45.

Gay & Lesbian Review Worldwide, January-February, 2003, Margaret Meklin, "A Maori Writer in Two Worlds," p. 30.

Journal of Commonwealth Literature, spring, 1999, Juniper Ellis, interview with Witi Ihimaera, p. 169.

Kirkus Reviews, December 1, 1989, review of *Dear Miss Mansfield,* p. 1698; May 1, 2003, review of *The Whale Rider,* p. 678.

Landfall, November, 1998, Peter Beatson, review of *The Dream Swimmer,* p. 308.

London Review of Books, December 18, 1986, review of *The Matriarch,* p. 20.

Modern Fiction Studies, winter, 1990, review of *The Matriarch,* pp. 483-498.

Publishers Weekly, December 8, 1989, review of *Dear Miss Mansfield,* p. 42.

School Library Journal, September, 2003, Susan Oliver, review of *The Whale Rider,* p. 214.

Times Literary Supplement, February 9, 1973, review of *Pounamu, Pounamu,* p. 141; July 12, 1974, review of *Tangi,* p. 741; March 7, 1975, Martha Miller, review of *Whanau,* p. 260.

World Literature Today, spring, 1978, Charles R. Larson, review of *The New Net Goes Fishing,* p. 247; autumn, 1978, Norman Simms, review of *The New Net Goes Fishing,* p. 696; spring, 1987, Reed Way Daenbrock, review of *The Matriarch,* p. 351.

ONLINE

New Zealand Book Council Web site, http://www.bookcouncil.org.nz/ (September 23, 2003), biographical information on Ihimaera.*

IKE, (Vincent) Chukwuemeka 1931-

PERSONAL: Born April 28, 1931, in Ndikelionwu, Anambra, Nigeria; son of Charles and Dinah (Ezeani) Ike; married Adebimpe Olurinsola Abimbolu (a librarian, professor of library science, and educational administrator), December 13, 1959; children: Osita Naanyelugo Adeolu Olusanya (son). *Ethnicity:* "Igbo." *Education:* Attended Government College, Umuahia, Nigeria; University College, Ibadan, Nigeria, B.A., 1955; Stanford University, M.A., 1966.

ADDRESSES: Office—Chinwuba House, Ndikelionwu Postal Agency, Via Awka, Anambra State 420001, Nigeria. *E-mail*—nbkfound@infoweb.abs.net.

CAREER: Teacher at a primary school in Amichi, Nigeria, 1950-51; teacher at a girls' secondary school, Nkwerre, Nigeria, 1955-56; University College, Ibadan, Nigeria, administrative assistant and assistant registrar, 1957-60; University of Nigeria, Nsukka, deputy registrar, 1960-63, registrar and secretary to council, 1963-71; West African Examinations Council, Accra, Ghana, registrar and chief executive, 1971-79; Emekike and Co., executive chair, 1979—. *Daily Times of Nigeria Ltd.,* director, 1971-87; Times Leisure Services Ltd., chair, 1977-1979; University Press Ltd., director, 1978-2002; Nigerian Book Foundation, chair, 1991-93, president and chief executive, 1993—. Nigerian Universities Joint Superannuation Scheme, trustee, 1964-71; University of Nigeria, chair of planning and management committee, 1970; University of Jos, visiting professor, 1983-85; University of Benin, pro-chancellor and chair of governing council, 1990-91; Anambra State University of Science and Technology, pro-chancellor and chair of governing council, 2001—. Nigerian National Commission for UNESCO, chair of culture sector, 1986-91; Nigerian Copyright Council, member of governing board and chair of technical committee, 1989-94; National Anti-Piracy Committee, chair, 1991-94. Republic of Biafra, provincial refugee officer in charge of Umuahia Province, 1968-69; headquarters scout commander in charge of Nsukka Province, 1970-71. Anglican Communion, member of General Synod of the Church of Nigeria, 1995-2002.

MEMBER: International PEN (vice president of Nigerian Centre, 1989-91), International Association for Educational Assessment (member of executive committee from Africa, 1975-78), Association of Nigerian

Chukwuemeka Ike

Authors (member of executive committee, 1982-83), Nigerian Institute of Management (fellow), Bible Society of Nigeria (life member), University of Ibadan Alumni Association (life member).

AWARDS, HONORS: UNESCO travel grant, 1954; fellow, U.S. Agency for International Development, 1962; Ford Foundation grant, 1966; honorary fellow, City and Guilds of London Institute of Publishers, 1978; honorary fellow, University of Iowa, 1987; named distinguished friend of the council, West African Examinations Council, 1994; D.Litt., University of Nigeria, 1998, and University of Lagos, 2000; distinguished alumnus award, University of Ibadan Alumni Association, 2000; decorated officer, Order of the Federal Republic (Nigeria), 2001.

WRITINGS:

FICTION

Toads for Supper, Harvill Press (London, England), 1965.
The Naked Gods, Harvill Press (London, England), 1970.

The Potter's Wheel, Harvill Press (London, England), 1973.
Sunset at Dawn: A Novel about Biafra, Harvill Press (London, England), 1976, reprinted, University Press (Ibadan, Nigeria), 1993.
The Chicken Chasers, Fontana (Douglas, Isle of Man), 1980.
Expo '77, Fontana (London, England), 1980.
The Bottled Leopard, University Press (Ibadan, Nigeria), 1985.
Our Children Are Coming!, Spectrum Books (Ibadan, Nigeria), 1990.
The Search, Heinemann Educational Books Nigeria (Ibadan, Nigeria), 1991.
To My Husband from Iowa, Malthouse Press (Ikeja, Lagos, Nigeria), 1996.
Conspiracy of Silence (novel), Longman Nigeria (Lagos, Nigeria), 2001.
The Accra Riviera (short stories), Oyster St. Iyke (Lagos, Nigeria), 2001.

NONFICTION

University Development in Africa: The Nigerian Experience, Oxford University Press (Ibadan, Nigeria), 1976.
(Editor, with Emmanuel Obiechina and John Anenechukwu Umeh) *The University of Nigeria, 1960-1985: An Experiment in Higher Education,* University of Nigeria Press (Nsukka, Nigeria), 1986.
How to Become a Published Writer, Heinemann Educational Books Nigeria (Ibadan, Nigeria), 1991.
(Editor) *Creating a Conducive Environment for Book Publishing: Proceedings of the Second Annual National Conference on Book Development,* Nigerian Book Foundation (Awka, Nigeria), 1996.
(Editor) *Meeting the Books Needs of the Rural Family,* Nigerian Book Foundation (Awka, Nigeria), 1997.
(Editor) *Directory of Nigerian Book Development,* Nigerian Book Foundation (Awka, Nigeria), 1998.
(Editor) *Ndikelionwu and the Spread of Christianity,* privately printed (Ndikelionwu, Nigeria), 2000.
(Editor) *The Book in 21st Century Nigeria and Universal Basic Education,* Nigerian Book Foundation (Awka, Nigeria), 2000.
(Editor) *Creating and Sustaining a Reading Culture,* Nigerian Book Foundation (Awka, Nigeria), 2000.

Contributor to books and to periodicals. Member of editorial committee, *African Writer,* 1961-62; founding member of editorial committee, *Okike,* 1970-71.

ADAPTATIONS: The Potter's Wheel was adapted as a textbook for foreign speakers of English, abridged by Lewis Jones, illustrated by Anthea Eames, and published by Collins (Glasgow, Scotland), 1986.

SIDELIGHTS: Chukwuemeka Ike has been a successful novelist both within Nigeria and beyond its borders since the release of his first novel, *Toads for Supper,* in 1965. That debut was a comedy with strongly realistic elements, about a young man from a village who goes to the University of Nigeria and finds his head turned. Protagonist Amobi has been groomed and financed by his whole village to become its first university-educated resident; the village has even built him a special hut to study in, and the girl to whom he has been betrothed since childhood has been sent to a teacher-training college in order to be a better match for him. Once at the university, however, Amobi decides to change his major from English and medicine to history; worse, in the view of his Ibo family, he falls in love with, and betroths himself to, a pretty Yoruba girl he meets on campus. Complicating matters is the fact that a Lagos prostitute named Sweetie accuses him of fathering her child.

Returning to his village, Amobi encounters the displeasure of the entire village, especially in the person of his father, an uneducated but wise and powerful figure who bombards Amobi with what a London *Times Literary Supplement* reviewer called "paternal homilies." The trouble with the prostitute is easily smoothed out since Amobi is in fact not the father of the child; his romantic entanglements, however, require a more difficult resolution that did not satisfy either the *Times Literary Supplement* reviewer or another British critic, Edwin Morgan of the *New Statesman.* Nevertheless, the last page was, for Morgan, the only flaw in the otherwise "unassuming, humorous," and "well-observed" novel, in which satirical insights blended neatly with "warm feeling for the realities of village life."

The critic for the *Times Literary Supplement,* appreciating the "wry poetry" with which Ike illustrated generational conflict, called the "unpretentious" novel "a pleasing comedy, animated by a fluent, good-humoured intelligence." The preeminent flaw pointed out by the *Times Literary Supplement* reviewer was an unevenness and a rushed quality in parts of the book, particularly the ending. Novelist Shiva Naipaul, reviewing

Toads for Supper for *Books and Bookmen,* enjoyed its "steadying realism" and its "fine writing," noting that the latter was to be found in the descriptions of village life and in the "moving" characterizations of Amodi's father, mother, and friends. Like the other two reviewers, Naipaul had reservations about the ending, which he termed a "plunge . . . into sudden tragedy and melodrama." Naipaul had words of praise, however, for Ike's cataloguing of "the dissonances in modern Nigerian society": tensions between tribes, between villagers and university graduates, between Christianity and native religion, between white professors and black students, and even between "the girls who can dance the high life and the girls who can't."

After his reputation had been made by *Toads for Supper,* Ike continued in his already-established career in educational administration, which had begun with his first teaching experiences in the early 1950s. In the 1970s he branched out into newspaper publishing and other businesses while continuing to produce a steady stream of novels, short stories, and occasional nonfiction books. The latter genre includes a study of Nigerian higher education, in 1976, and a book on how to become a published writer, in 1991.

BIOGRAPHICAL AND CRITICAL SOURCES:

BOOKS

Ugbabe, Kanchana, editor, *Chukwuemeka Ike: A Critical Reader,* Malthorse Press (Ikeja, Lagos, Nigeria), 2001.

PERIODICALS

Books and Bookmen, February, 1971, p. 41, Shiva Naipaul, review of *Toads for Supper.*

Journal of Modern African Studies, December, 2000, Charles Armour, review of *Directory of Nigerian Book Development,* p. 723.

Law Society Journal, July, 2003, Stephen Booth, review of *The Chicken Chasers,* p. 85.

New Statesman, May 14, 1965, Edwin Morgan, review of *Toads for Supper,* p. 772.

Times Literary Supplement, April 8, 1965, review of *Toads for Supper,* p. 269.

J

JEN, Gish
See JEN, Lillian

*   *   *

JEN, Lillian 1956(?)-
(Gish Jen)

PERSONAL: Born c. 1956; married David O'Connor; children: Luke, Paloma (daughter). *Education:* Harvard University, B.A., 1977; attended Stanford University, 1979-80; University of Iowa, M.F.A., 1983.

ADDRESSES: Home—Cambridge, MA. *Agent*— Maxine Groffsky, Maxine Groffsky Literary Agency, 2 Fifth Ave., New York, NY 10011.

CAREER: Writer. Tufts University, lecturer in fiction writing, 1986; University of Massachusetts, visiting writer, 1990-91; Radcliffe writer-in-residence, Institute's fellowship program; advanced creative writing seminar in women's studies, Harvard, 2001.

MEMBER: Massachusetts Artists Foundation (fellow, 1988), Radcliffe Bunting Institute and James A. Michener Foundation/Corpernicus Society (fellow, 1986).

AWARDS, HONORS: Henfield Foundation/ *Transatlantic Review* Award, 1983; resident, MacDowell Colony, 1985 and 1987; fellow, National Endowment for the Arts, 1988; prize from Katherine Anne Porter Contest, *Nimrod,* 1987; Bunting Institute fellowship, 1987; prize from Boston MBTA UrbanArts Project, 1988; grants from James Michener/Copernicus Society and the Massachusetts Artist's Foundation; stories published in *Best American Short Stories of the Century,* 1988, 1995; Lannan Foundation Literary Award, 1999; American Academy of Arts and Sciences Strauss Living Award, 2002-2007.

WRITINGS:

UNDER NAME GISH JEN

Typical American (novel), Houghton Mifflin (Boston, MA), 1991.
Mona in the Promised Land (novel), Knopf (New York, NY), 1996.
Who's Irish? (short stories), Knopf (New York, NY), 1999.
The Love Wife, Knopf (New York, NY), 2004.

Work represented in anthologies, including *Best American Short Stories of 1988,* Houghton Mifflin (Boston, MA), 1988; *New Worlds of Literature,* Norton (New York, NY), 1989; and *Home to Stay: Asian American Women's Fiction,* Greenfield Review Press (Greenfield Center, NY), 1990. Contributor to periodicals, including *New Yorker, Atlantic Monthly, Yale Review, Fiction International,* and *Iowa Review.*

ADAPTATIONS: The story "The Water Faucet Vision" has been adapted for audio by OtherWorld Media, 1995.

SIDELIGHTS: Lillian Jen, who writes under the name Gish Jen, is a writer of lively fiction filled with keenly observed moments and gestures. Though she dislikes being categorized as an "Asian-American writer," her novels and stories do provide an insightful look into what it means to be Asian in contemporary America, but it is a very different look from that offered by her predecessors Maxine Hong Kingston and Amy Tan, whose prototypes she had to break through to make a witty and sardonic entrance of her own. Greg Changnon of the *Atlanta Journal-Constitution* considered, "Amy Tan, in her three novels of the Chinese-American experience, gently nudged readers toward ethnic awareness, offering a taste test of her culture's exotic fables. But Jen, with her dazzling prose and wicked point of view, shoves readers past sightseeing and into the territory of self-discovery." To Calvin Liu of *AsianWeek* Jen "maintains that her intention is never to reflect any certain ethnic experience, though she admits that her heritage and her writing are unconsciously inseparable."

Her first novel, *Typical American,* "examines the disorienting freedom and often illusory promises of the New World" through the story of Ralph and Helen Chang, according to Wendy Smith in *Publishers Weekly.* As the Changs struggle with poverty, an insensitive landlord, and the machinations of a slick huckster, Jen produces a "tragic-comic" tale, as she told Ron Hogan in a *Beatrice* interview. Their story, which *People* reviewer Sara Nelson called "wise but sweet, hopeful yet knowing," ends with their financial success through a fast-food chicken restaurant. *Boston Herald*'s Judith Wynn quipped, "Are Chinese-Americans really as debt-ridden and volatile as the rest of us?" and answered that the novel "debunked the notion of Chinese-Americans as a 'model minority,' naturally inclined to modesty and workaholism."

The story of the Changs continues in Jen's next novel, *Mona in the Promised Land,* a book more on the comic side, as Jen told Hogan in the same interview. This novel focuses on Mona, the Chang's younger daughter, and the cultural confusion she experiences—and causes—when the family moves to the upscale, mostly Jewish area of Scarshill (a reflection of the real-life New York area known as Scarsdale, where Jen grew up in circumstances similar to those sketched out for Mona). The novel is a sort of testing ground for the idea that being "American means being whatever you want" to quote Mona. Renouncing her Chinese heritage, converting to Judaism, and changing her name to Changowitz, Mona seems to change ethnicities as easily as she would change her clothes. Other characters in the book behave similarly, trying on black, Jewish, and Oriental philosophies and mannerisms as the mood takes them. "Ms. Jen is good at capturing different voices, which is fortunate because the one thing all these people have in common is that they talk constantly about who they are," noted *New York Times book Review* contributor Jacqueline Carey. "[*Mona in the Promised Land*] has a wide-ranging exuberance that's unusual in what is still—to its credit—a realistic novel. . . . The book is both hopeful and smart, a rare combination. All the characters are basically good; they remind you that the optimism of the late 60's and early 70's was real. Ms. Jen even persuaded me for hours at a time that it doesn't matter whether you choose to become more or less 'Chinese'; that the forces that are binding us together have just as much strength as the ones that are pulling us apart."

The Changs again feature prominently in *Who's Irish?,* Jen's first collection of short stories, one of which, "Birthmates," was chosen by John Updike for *Best American Short Stories of the Century.* An *Entertainment Weekly* reviewer credited it with chronicling "the Chinese-American experience with tart realism and sometimes guffaw-inducing humor," and further noted: "Jen's stories are amazingly compressed, and she studs them with perversely funny social disasters that explode like skillfully placed narrative land mines." In "The Water Faucet Vision," narrated by Mona's elder sister Callie, the Chang parents argue violently in a dialect the girls don't understand. "In the American Society" traces Ralph's misadventures in assimilation. *Time International*'s Hilary Roxe assessed "House, House, Home": "Pammie wants to live outside the American Dream her Chinese parents strived to attain, but she recognizes the differences between herself and other social rebels. Wondering at her nonconformist husband, she asks, 'Could an elective outsider ever know what it feels like to be the other kind of outsider?' Though Jen broaches such issues, she declines to provide answers, saving the stories from becoming didactic diatribes and allowing humor to outshine analysis." Other stories in the book deal with immigrants, their children, and Chinese Americans visiting the ancient homeland for the first time. The collection was solidly praised by Jean Thompson in the *New York Times Book Review;* she wrote: "Jen's gift is for comedy that resonates, and sadnesses that arise with perfect timing from absurdities. Her subject matter is so appealing, it almost obscures the power and suppleness of her language. 'Who's Irish?,' at its considerable best, finds words for all the high and low notes of the raucous American anthem."

Jen has been recognized with two "living" awards: a Lannen Award in 1999 and an American Academy of Arts and Sciences Strauss Award in 2003. The latter pays $50,000 a year for five years to a writer, who may not be employed elsewhere during that time. Jen joked to *University Wire* interviewer Hana R. Alberts, "The danger of this award is that one develops the largest case of writer's block one ever had." Jen intends to return to teaching at the end of the award term. She was teaching at Harvard when the news came but has also enjoyed teaching in literacy programs. A student at Harvard commented, "She was quick and witty. At the end of two hours, we wished we had two more." "She laughs all the time during class," said a seminar member. "She's pushing us. We're doing graduate level writing theory. I'm glad I got to catch her while she was here." Jen told the interviewer that she planned to "head for China for six months, and . . . to come back with plenty of material." Alberts added that "Jen said with the money provided by the award she will continue work on a novel . . . about a Chinese-American family with biological and adopted children." *Newsweek* interviewer Malcolm Jones asked, "How will this money change your life?" Jen answered, "Writing was becoming a luxury I couldn't quite afford. I had to have a job. So I have gone from someone who perhaps couldn't afford to write for some years to someone who needs to write" and "there are all these temptations, like writing for the movies—all these auxiliary activities which are related to artistic expression but are not artistic expression. Also, when you're young, you can live on very little with very little security. You never think about how much it costs to get a tooth crowned. And then suddenly you're older, and you've got kids and your teeth are falling apart. It's a tremendous gift, the ultimate *deus ex machina*."

In an interview with *Powell's City of Books*' Dave Weich, Jen addressed the simultaneous sadness and happiness of her writing: "Early on in my career people would say, 'Is this supposed to be funny or it supposed to be sad?' . . . I was somebody who simultaneously sees things as happy and sad. I am the kind of person who would make a joke on someone's deathbed, tacky as it may seem. It could be seen an Asian

part of my sensibility, in the sense that it's a very Asian thing to imagine that opposites go together. . . . I don't know if that's completely true, but in any case that ying-yang quality certainly embodies a lot of these stories." To Weich's comment that the connections she makes are not heavyhanded, she responded, "I do hope there will be layers and layers of things for people to find. There are references and jokes along the way. Did you get the Oscar Wilde reference?" She concluded the interview, "Of course I'm interested in the Asian-American experience. But I'm also interested in architecture; I'm interested in religion. I'm very interested in the different realities, not just my own ethnic group."

BIOGRAPHICAL AND CRITICAL SOURCES:

BOOKS

Cheung, King-Kok, editor, *Words Matter: Conversations with Asian-American Writers,* University of Hawaii Press, with UCLA Asian-American Studies Center (Honolulu, HI), 2000.
Kaylor, Noel Harold, Jr., editor, *Creative and Critical Approaches to the Short Story,* Mellen (Lewiston, NY), 1997.
Lee, Rachel C., *The Americas of Asian-American Literature: Gendered Fictions of Nation and Transnation,* Princeton University Press (Princeton, NJ), 1999.

PERIODICALS

American Journal of Psychiatry, December, 1999, p. 2001.
AsiaWeek, Friday, December 31, 1999.
Atlanta Journal-Constitution, June 20, 1999, p. L12.
Atlantic, April, 1991, p. 108.
Atlantic Monthly, September, 1996, p. 114.
Austin American-Statesman, June 23, 1996, p. G7; July 18, 1999, p. K6.
Booklist, April 15, 1996, p. 1421; June 1, 2001, p. 1837.
Boston Globe, June 25, 2000, p. N6.
Boston Herald, May 16, 1999, p. 071; June 25, 1999, p. 064.
Boston Magazine, June, 1999, p. 145.

Christian Science Monitor, March 25, 1991, p. 13; June 27, 1996, p. B2; March 24, 1998, interview with Jen, p. B8.

Daily News (Los Angeles, CA), July 11, 1999, p. V5.

Entertainment Weekly, July 9, 1999, p. 70.

EurAmerica: A Journal of European and American Studies, December, 2002, pp. 641, 675.

Far Eastern Economic Review, November 14, 1991, p. 56A; October 31, 1996, p. 47.

Fresno Bee (Fresno, CA), October 3, 1999, p. E3.

Glamour, April, 1991, p. 228.

Harper's Bazaar, May, 1996, p. 94.

Hitting Critical Mass: A Journal of Asian-American Cultural Criticism, fall, 1996, p. 103; summer, 1997, p. 61.

Houston Chronicle, August 18, 1996, p. 20.

Independent (London, England), May 14, 1998, p. 2.

Kirkus Reviews, March 15, 1996.

Library Journal, March 15, 1996, p. 95; September 15, 2000, p. 144.

Long Beach Press-Telegram, September 18, 2000, "The Bashing of the Asian-American Dream," p. A13.

Los Angeles Times, April 29, 1991, p. E1.

Mademoiselle, June, 1996, p. 106.

MELUS: The Journal of the Society for the Study of the Multi-Ethnic Literature of the United States, winter, 1993-1994, interview with Jen, p. 111; summer, 2003, p. 47.

Ms., November-December, 1991, p. 76.

Nation, June 17, 1996, p. 35.

New Perspectives Quarterly, summer, 1991, p. 56.

Newsweek, July 15, 1996, p. 56; June 7, 1999, p. 75; January 13, 2003, interview with Jen, p. 71.

New Yorker, July 8, 1996, p. 78.

New York Review of Books, August 15, 1991, p. 9.

New York Times, June 4, 1999, p. E40; September 15, 2000, "For Wen Ho Lee, a Tarnished Freedom," p. 35; December 4, 2000, "Writers on Writing," p. 11.

New York Times Book Review, February 15, 1991, p. 221; March 31, 1991, pp. 9-10; June 9, 1996, p. 16; June 27, 1999, p. 13.

NTU Studies in Language and Literature, December 2002, p. 71.

Parnassus: Poetry in Review, 1992, p. 88.

People, April 29, 1991, p. 25; January 15, 1996, p. 35.

Philippine-American Studies Journal, 1991, p. 1.

Philippine Daily Inquirer, June 20, 2001, p. 2.

Ploughshares, fall, 2000, p. 217.

Proteus: A Journal of Ideas, fall, 1994, p. 21.

Publishers Weekly, January 18, 1991, p. 46; February 8, 1991, p. 25; March 11, 1996, p.40; April 26, 1999, p. 52; June 7, 1999, p. 59.

San Francisco Chronicle, May 19, 1996, p. 5; May 26, 1996, p. 11.

School Library Journal, December, 1999, p. 164.

Scotsman (Edinburgh, Scotland), August 28, 1999, p. 10.

Seattle Post-Intelligencer, June 12, 1999, p. C2.

Seattle Times, August 18, 1996, p. M2; February 3, 1998, p. D5; June 10, 1999, p. G24.

Southwest Review, winter, 1993, interview with Jen, p. 132.

Sun Yat-sen Journal of Humanities, October, 2001, p. 103.

Time, June 3, 1991, p. 66.

Time International, August 9, 1999, p. 48.

University Wire, January 9, 2002.

Virginian Pilot, June 30, 1996, p. J2.

Wasafiri: Journal of Caribbean, African, Asian and Associated Literatures and Film, autumn, 1995, p. 25.

Washington Times, May 19, 1996, p. 6.

Winston-Salem Journal, November 21, 1999, p. A24.

Yearbook of English Studies, 1994, p. 263.

ONLINE

AsianWeek, http://www.asianweek.com/ (September 27-October 3, 1996), "American As Apple Pie"; (June 24, 1999), "Who's Chinese American?."

Beatrice, http://www.beatrice.com/ (March 11, 2004), Ron Hogan, "Gish Jen: 'So Aren't You Going to Ask Me If I'm Jewish?.'"

Harvard University Gazette, http://www.news.harvard.edu/ (January 24, 2002), "Gish Jen: American."

Polkonline.com, http://www.polkonline.com/ (September 9, 1999), "Author Gish Jen Explores America's Immigrant Experience."

Powell's City of Books, http://www.powells.com/ (June 17, 1999), interview with Jen.

Public Affairs Television: Personal Journeys, http://www.pbs.org/ (2003), Bill Moyers, "Becoming American: The Chinese Experience."*

*　　*　　*

JIN, Ha
See JIN, Xuefei

JIN, Xuefei 1956-
(Ha Jin)

PERSONAL: Born February 21, 1956, in Liaoning, China; son of Danlin (an officer) and Yuanfen (a worker; maiden name, Zhao) Jin; married Lisah Bian, July 6, 1982; children: Wen. *Education:* Heilongjian g University, B.A., 1981; Shangdong University, M.A., 1984; Brandeis University, Ph.D., 1992.

ADDRESSES: Office—Department of English, Callaway Memorial Center, 302 North Callaway, Emory University, Atlanta, GA 30322; fax: 404-727-2605. *Agent*—Christina Ward, P.O. Box 515, North Scituate, MA 02060.

CAREER: Emory University, Atlanta, GA, assistant professor of creative writing, 1993-2002; Boston University, 2002—. *Military service:* Chinese People's Army, 1987-95.

AWARDS, HONORS: Three Pushcart Prizes for fiction; prize from *Kenyon Review;* Agni Best Fiction Prize; PEN Hemingway Award for first fiction, 1998, for *Ocean of Words;* Flannery O'Connor Award, 1998, and 34th Georgia Author of the Year Awards for *Under the Red Flag;* National Book Award, 1999, and PEN/Faulkner Award for Fiction, 2000, both for *Waiting;* Townsend Prize for Fiction for *The Bridegroom.*

WRITINGS:

UNDER NAME HA JIN

Between Silences: A Voice from China (poems), University of Chicago Press (Chicago, IL), 1990.

Facing Shadows (poems), Hanging Loose Press (Brooklyn, NY), 1996.

Ocean of Words: Army Stories, Zoland Books (Cambridge, MA), 1996, Vintage (New York, NY), 1998.

Under the Red Flag (stories), University of Georgia Press (Athens, GA), 1997, Zoland Books (Cambridge, MA), 1999.

In the Pond (novel), Zoland Books (Cambridge, MA), 1998.

Waiting (novel), Pantheon (New York, NY), 1999.

Quiet Desperation (stories), Pantheon (New York, NY), 2000.

The Bridegroom (stories), Pantheon (New York, NY), 2000.

Wreckage (poetry), Hanging Loose (Brooklyn, NY), 2001.

The Crazed, Pantheon (New York, NY), 2002.

War Trash, Pantheon (New York, NY), 2004.

ADAPTATIONS: Waiting has been adapted by Brilliance for audiotape and is being produced as a film.

WORK IN PROGRESS: Man to Be: Country Stories, short fiction.

SIDELIGHTS: In 1986 thirty-year-old Xuefei Jin, who writes under the name Ha Jin, came to the U.S. on a student visa from his native China to begin working on a Ph.D. in English at Brandeis University in Waltham, Massachusetts. His dissertation was on high Modernist poets Pound, Eliot, Auden, and Yeats because, as he told Dave Weich of *Powell's City of Books,* "Those four have poems which are related to Chinese texts and poems that reference the culture. My dissertation was aimed at a Chinese job market. I planned to return to China." Jin and his wife decided to stay in the U.S. after seeing what happened at Tiananmen Square on television. Before taking his degree in 1992, Jin had already published his first book of poems in English, *Between Silences.* The next year he began teaching at Emory University in Atlanta, Georgia, and another book of poetry, *Facing Shadows,* appeared a few years later in 1996. As Weich pointed out, it wasn't an easy beginning: "Taking odd jobs (a night watchman, a busboy) until eventually his publishing success convinced Emory University to hire him to teach and write, Jin was arguably one of the most prolific literary writers of the nineties." In the next three years Jin published two story collections and two novels, all written in English, all set in the People's Republic of China. Jin's work has received nearly universal acclaim from American critics and garnered numerous awards.

Jin's second collection of stories, *Under the Red Flag,* won the Flannery O'Connor Award for Short Fiction. The book is set in a rural town, Dismount Fort, during the Cultural Revolution that swept across China in 1966. This was a time when fanatical beliefs gained sway and those who did not embrace them were often persecuted. In what Paul Gray of *Time* singled out as the best story in the book, "Winds and Clouds over a Funeral," a communist official is torn between conflicting loyalties. His mother's last request upon her death bed was that she not be cremated. However, it is the official policy of the Communist Party that all dead bodies should be cremated in order to conserve arable land. In another story, the Communist Party has arrested a woman accused of being a whore and are planning a public humiliation and punishment for her. A young boy, the narrator of the story, looks forward to the event. In another, a man castrates himself to gain admission to the Communist Party. Gray noted: "Ha Jin is not a preachy author. He offers his characters choices that are incompatible and potentially destructive and then dispassionately records what they do next." Frank Caso of *Booklist* found *Under the Red Flag* to be a "powerful" collection, but also remarked "there is . . . an undisguised cynicism, in . . . many of the . . . tales, that the truth must first be shaped to a political purpose." A *Publishers Weekly* reviewer though, stating of Jin that "sometimes his allegories are too simple," maintained that the stories are used by Jin "to explore larger themes about human relationships and the effect of government on individual lives."

Jin's first novel, *In the Pond,* is the tale of a talented artist, Shao Bin, who must spend his time working at a fertilizer plant to support his family. After being assigned inferior housing, Bin protests by drawing a series of cartoons that criticize his supervisors at work, the villains of the story. After a series of conflicts with the supervisors, spurred on by more cartoons, Bin eventually receives a promotion to the propaganda office. A writer reviewing *In the Pond* for *Publishers Weekly* found that Jin "offers a wise and funny first novel that gathers meticulously observed images into a seething yet restrained tale of social injustice in modern China." The reviewer also applauded the complexity of the book's characters, such as the supervisors, and concluded by stating that the novel goes beyond its setting of Communist China to "engagingly illustrat[e] a universal conundrum."

A National Book and PEN/Faulkner Award winner, *Waiting,* which Jin told Weich was based on a true story, generated considerable critical attention. "[A] deliciously comic novel . . . [told] . . . in an impeccably deadpan manner," exclaimed Gray, again writing in *Time.* One *Publishers Weekly* reviewer deemed *Waiting* "quiet but absorbing . . . powerful," while another

remarked that besides its "affecting love story," *Waiting* "presents a trenchant picture of Chinese life under communism." According to Shirley N. Quan of *Library Journal:* "This touching story about love, honor, duty, and family speaks feelingly to readers on matters of the heart." The plot of *Waiting* centers on three individuals: Lin, a medical student who later becomes a doctor; Shuyu, the woman his ailing parents force him to marry so they will have someone to care for them; and Manna Wu, a nurse with whom Lin falls in love. According to communist law, a couple must be separated for eighteen years before they can legally divorce. The novel covers twenty years, including the eighteen during which Lin and Manna maintain their relationship but decide to wait until they can marry before they will consummate it. Assessing the strengths and weaknesses of the book for *Entertainment Weekly,* Megan Harlan stated: "Jin overexplains the story's background. But the lengthy finale . . . resounds with elegant irony." Francine Prose of the *New York Times Book Review* noted: "Character is fate, or at least some part of fate, and Ha Jin's achievement is to reveal the ways in which character and society conspire."

Since the success of *Waiting,* Jin has produced two volumes of short stories, one of poetry, and another novel, *The Crazed.* Of the 2002 novel, *Commonweal's* Valerie Sayers found, "In an age when so many critics have declared the death of literary realism, Ha Jin's depiction of real absurdity and absurd reality is a good argument against realism's premature burial." Neil Freudenberger in the *New Yorker* commented, "Ha Jin explores an intimate subject with a surgeon's combination of detachment and depth." Sayers added, "*The Crazed* . . . is also a compelling read, more directly political than *Waiting,* more focused on an inevitable plot march that will end in Tiananmen Square." The narrator is a young man, Jian Wan, studying for his Ph.D. exams and waiting to marry the daughter of his professor, Dr. Yang. The professor, however, suffers a stroke and while Jian and another student wait in the hospital for his wife to arrive home from a trip to Tibet, Yang raves and sings in hallucinations that take him wandering back to days of persecution during the Cultural Revolution, to sexual liaisons, and to his early ambitions. He also talks about spiritual matters. As Freudenberger noted, "Professor Yang slowly goes mad—conducting imaginary conversations, spilling his own secrets, and giving his student an education he's not sure he wants." Sayers considered "many of the professor's monologues and spoken dreams, which are designed to unveil his biography as well as to move the plot along . . . ridiculously contrived in dramatic terms, yet their language is so direct that they remain strangely compelling." Yang's words move Jian to abandon his studies and join the students marching on Tiananmen Square. "The novel's climax is utterly realistic and utterly involving—its movement out of the sickroom and into the streets of Beijing provides just the right change of perception and scale," Sayers concluded.

The *Spectator*'s Jonathan Mirsky, however, found the novel plodding. He experienced Yang's ranting and singing, the slow unfolding of Jian's understanding through the confusing and hazy words of his professor as frustrating: "None of this is clear and after a while one ceases to care. The sordid dreariness, petty politicking and general hopelessness of Chinese academic life are well shown, but without a story it palls." Patrick Ness in the London *Daily Telegraph* maintained, "For these potentially incendiary materials, Ha Jin has adopted a curiously grey, meditative style. The pace is slow, and the prose tends toward the obvious ('I felt confused and upset'), draining colour and drama from the story." Mark Schechner of the *Buffalo News* suggested that Jin, in "the least subtle" of his books, may be using the "hoariest cliche of socialist writing, the general strike, and use it against the keepers of socialist myth. Only instead of the people triumphant, we have the carnage of Tiananmen and a baffled hero." But many critics, while they also had difficulty with linguistic and timing aspects of the work, held that the "hyperrealism" and attention to detail that Jin employed, together with the interest of the story and the movement to action at the end of the novel combined to create another compelling work. As Sarah A. Smith wrote in the *Guardian,* "At first glance Ha Jin appears to have lost some of his lightness of touch. There is a depressing, communism-by-numbers feel about the way he drops background detail into the plot," but, she continued, "Ha Jin's talent is narrative, however, and when he has dispensed with scene-setting *The Crazed* becomes a compelling book." She concluded, "If this novel fails to live up to the promise of its predecessor, it is perhaps because it falls prey to the problem that faces much diaspora literature—the need to explain the motherland, rather than just to write. But this shouldn't overshadow what Ha Jin has achieved in his tragi-comic portrayal of Yang and the naive Jian. This novelist has a fine sense of the human scale of history and an eye for the absurd."

Irene Wanner of the *Seattle Times* credited the success of Jin's work to its "skill, compassion and enlighten-ing aspects." Gray felt Jin's success is in part due to the "accident of his birth." Having been born in another country, Gray explained, Jin was "protected from the homogenizing and potentially trivializing influences that afflict so many U.S.-born aspiring authors." However, Gray concluded that although "exotic subject matter" has helped Jin's career, his "narrative talent proves victorious."

Jin once told *CA:* "Because I failed to do something else, writing in English became my means of survival, of spending or wasting my life, of retrieving losses, mine and those of others. Because my life has been a constant struggle, I feel close in my heart to the great Russian masters, including Chekhov, Gogol, and Babel. As for poetry, some ancient Chinese influences are Tu Fu, Li Po, and Po Chu-I.

"Since I teach full time, my writing process has been adapted to my teaching. When I have a large piece of time, I write drafts of stories, or a draft of a novel, which I revise and edit when I teach. Each draft is revised thirty times before it is finished.

"If I am inspired, it is from within. Very often I feel that the stories have been inside me for a long time, and that I am no more than an instrument for their manifestation. As for the subject matter, I guess we are compelled to write about what has hurt us most."

Asked by Weich whether he would eventually write about the immigrant experience, Jin answered, "I haven't returned to China since I've been here. China is distant. I don't know what contemporary Chinese life is like now. I follow the news, but I don't have the mature sensation—I can't hear the noise, I can't smell the place. I'm not attached to it anymore. What's meaningful to me is the immigrant experience, the American life." The most important work of immigrant literature for him was Nabokov's *Pnin,* which, as he said, "deals with the question of language, and I think that's at the core of the immigrant experience: how to learn the language—or give up learning the language!—but without the absolute mastery of the language, which is impossible for an immigrant. Your life is always affected by the insufficiency."

BIOGRAPHICAL AND CRITICAL SOURCES:

PERIODICALS

Associated Press, October 1, 2003.
Atlanta Journal-Constitution, January 10, 1999, p. L11; October 31, 1999, p. L15; June 23, 2000, p. E5; October 8, 2000, p. D3; October 27, 2002, p. Q4.

Australian (Sydney, New South Wales, Australia), July 3, 2000, p. 013.

Booklist, November 1, 1997, Frank Caso, review of *Under the Red Flag,* p. 454; September 15, 2000, p. 216; April 1, 2002, p. 1314; September 1, 2002, p. 6; January 1, 2003, p. 792; March 15, 2003, p. 1338.

Boston Herald, November 17, 2002, p. 065.

Buffalo News (Buffalo, NY), December 8, 2002, p. F6.

Capital Times (Madison, WI), January 28, 2000, p. 9A; September 28, 2001, p. 9A; January 3, 2003, p. 11A.

Chicago Tribune Books, December 24, 1996, p. 6.

Christian Science Monitor, November 2, 2000, p. 21.

Commonweal, February 14, 2003, p. 17.

Courier-Mail (Brisbane, Australia), April 1, 2000, p. W09.

Daily Telegraph (London, England), January 6, 2001; May 12, 2001; October 19, 2002; September 27, 2003, p. 12.

Daily Telegraph (Surry Hills, Australia), June 10, 2000, p116.

Denver Post, October 27, 2002, p. EE-02.

Entertainment Weekly, October 29, 1999, Megan Harlan, review of *Waiting,* p. 106; December 3, 1999, Lori Tharps and Clarissa Cruz, "Between the Lines," p. 93; November 15, 2002, p. 140.

Guardian (London, England), October 7, 2000, p. 11; November 30, 2002, p. 27; October 04, 2003.

Herald (Glasgow, Scotland), June 22, 2000, p. 18.

Herald Sun (Melbourne, Australia), November 20, 1999, p. 023; June 3, 2000, p. W18.

Hindu, February 2, 2003.

Houston Chronicle (Houston, TX), December 5, 1999, p. 15; September 17, 2000, p. 24; December 17, 2000, p. 14; November 10, 2002, p. 18.

Independent (London, England), May 27, 2000, p. 10; October 10, 2003.

Indianapolis Star, November 28, 1999, p. D06; October 18, 2003, p. A15.

Knight Ridder/Tribune News Service, November 13, 2002, p. K4516.

Library Journal, October 15, 1999, Shirley N. Quan, review of *Waiting,* p. 105; September 1, 2000, p. 254; June 1, 2001, p. 170; September 15, 2002, p. 91.

Los Angeles Times, June 6, 2000, p. A1; June 24, 2000, p. A4; October 3, 2000, p. E-3; October 11, 2000, p. E-3.

Milwaukee Journal Sentinel, November 14, 1999, p. 8E; June 23, 2000, p. 08; October 8, 2000, p. 06.

New Straits Times, October 1 2003, p. 6.

Newsweek International, November 29, 1999, p.73.

New Yorker, November 4, 2002.

New York Review of Books, March 23, 2000, p. 29; March 13, 2003, p. 25.

New York Times, November 19, 1999, p. B44; June 24, 2000, p. A17, B9; October 21, 2002, p. B7.

New York Times Book Review, June 2, 1996, p. 21; January 11, 1998; January 31, 1999, p. 16; October 24, 1999, p. 9; October 22, 2000, p. 9; September 30, 2001, p. 24; October 27, 2002, p. 7.

New York Times Magazine, February 6, 2000, p. 38.

Plain Dealer (Cleveland, OH), November 2, 2002, p. E1.

Progressive, March, 2000, John McNally, review of *Waiting,* p. 44.

Publishers Weekly, February 26, 1996, review of *Ocean of Words: Army Stories,* p. 98; October 3, 1997, review of *Under the Red Flag,* p. 58; October 12, 1998, review of *In the Pond,* p. 58; August 23, 1999, review of *Waiting,* p. 42; November 1, 1999, review of *Waiting,* p. 46; March 20, 2000, p. 20; September 4, 2000, p. 81; June 4, 2001, p. 78; July 9, 2001, p. 13; September 30, 2002, p. 47.

Rocky Mountain News (Denver, CO), October 25, 2002, p. 26D.

St. Louis Post-Dispatch, October 31, 1999, p. F12.

St. Petersburg Times (St. Petersburg, FL), June 23, 2000, p. 10A; November 10, 2002, p. 4D.

Seattle Post-Intelligencer, November 18, 1999, p. D6.

Seattle Times, October 31, 1999, Irene Wanner, review of *Waiting;* November 18, 1999, p. A9; June 23, 2000, p. E3; October 15, 2000, p. M14; November 3, 2002, p. K12.

Spectator, June 3, 2000, p. 42; September 21, 2002, p. 45.

Star-Ledger (Newark, NJ), April 16, 2000, p. 005.

Star Tribune (Minneapolis, MN), January 24, 2000, p. 01E; November 10, 2002, p. 15F.

Sunday Mail (Brisbane, Australia), July 9, 2000, p. 023.

Sunday Times (London, England), June 24, 2001, p. 48.

Tampa Tribune, November 10, 2002, p. 4.

Time, December 1, 1997, Paul Gray, review of *Under the Red Flag,* p. 94; November 8, 1999, Paul Gray, "Divorce, Chinese-Style," p. 144.

Times (London, England), June 14, 2000, p. 19; December 16, 2000, p. 6; May 2, 2001, p. 15; January 26, 2002, p. 14; October 5, 2002, p. 15; November 2, 2002, p. 16.

Virginian Pilot, January 14, 2001, p. E3.

Wall Street Journal, October 22, 1999, p. W8; October 27, 2000, p. W12.

Washington Post, October 6, 2000, p. C03.

Washington Times, May 15, 2000, p. 8; December 15, 2002, p. B06.

Weekend Australian (Sydney, Australia), May 27, 2000, p. R13.

Winston-Salem Journal (Winston-Salem, NC), June 11, 2000, p. A20; January 26, 2003, p. A20.

World and I, May, 2000, p. 247.

World Englishes: Journal of English As an International and Intranational Language, July, 2002, p. 305.

World Literature Today, autumn, 1997, Timothy C. Wong, review of *Ocean of Words: Army Stories,* p. 862; autumn, 1997, K. C. Leung, review of *Facing Shadows,* p. 861; spring, 1998, Fatima Wu, review of *Under the Red Flag,* p. 454; spring, 1999, Jeffrey C. Kinkley, review of *In the Pond,* p. 389.

ONLINE

AsianWeek, http://www.asianweek.com/ (December 16, 1999), interview with Ha Jin.

AsiaSource, http://www.asiasource.org/ (November 17, 2000), interview with Ha Jin.

Austin Chronicle, http://www.austinchronicle.com/ (November 10, 2000), article on Ha Jin.

Boldtype, http://www.randomhouse.com/ (December 1999), "Ha Jin."

Book, http://www.bookmagazine.com/ (January, 2000), "Ha Jin of America,"

BookReporter, http://www.bookreporter.com/ (October 13, 2000), interview with Ha Jin.

BostonReview, http://www.bostonreview.net/ (August, 1988), "Ha Jin."

DesiJournal, http://www.desijournal.com/ (October 26, 2002), review of *The Crazed.*

Emory Magazine, http://www.emory.edu/ (spring, 1998), "Ha Jin."

MostlyFiction, http://mostlyfiction.com/ (October 12, 2002), review of *The Crazed.*

Powell's City of Books, http://www.powells.com/ (February 2, 2000), Dave Weich, interview with Ha Jin.

World and I, http://www.worldandi.com/ (May, 2000), review of *Waiting.**

*   *   *

JUNGER, Sebastian 1962-

PERSONAL: Born January 17, 1962, in Boston, MA; son of Miguel (a physicist) and Ellen (an artist; maiden name, Sinclair) Junger. *Education:* Concord Academy, graduated 1980; Wesleyan University, B.A., 1984. *Politics:* Democrat. *Religion:* Atheist.

Sebastian Junger

ADDRESSES: Home—88 East Third #7, New York, NY 10003. *Office*—83 Rivington St., Apt. 3C, New York, NY 10002. *Agent*—Stuart Krichevsky, 212-725-5288.

CAREER: Freelance writer.

WRITINGS:

The Perfect Storm: A True Story of Men against the Sea, Norton (New York, NY), 1997.

Frontline Diaries: Into the Forbidden Zone (documentary film), National Geographic Channel, 2001.

Fire, Norton (New York, NY), 2001.

Contributor to periodicals, including *Men's Journal, Outside, American Heritage,* and *New York Times Magazine.*

ADAPTATIONS: The Perfect Storm was produced as an audiobook (read by Stanley Tucci) and released by Random House Audio, 1997; *The Perfect Storm* was also adapted for film and released by Warner Brothers, 2000; *Fire* was produced as an audiobook, 2002.

SIDELIGHTS: With his first book, *The Perfect Storm*, Sebastian Junger quickly established himself as a best-selling writer of literary nonfiction, combining the journalist's clarity and eye for detail with the novelist's sense of narrative and drama. *The Perfect Storm* tells the story of a commercial swordfishing boat caught in the grip of a killer storm. The *Andrea Gail*, out of Gloucester, Massachusetts, was fishing the Great Banks of the North Atlantic in October, 1991, when the convergence of three storms from north, south, and west created a tempest of unmatched severity—in meteorological terms, a "perfect storm." Buffeted by one-hundred-foot waves and winds in excess of eighty-five m.p.h., the seventy-two-foot vessel was destroyed and her crew drowned. Drawing on interviews, radio dialogues, court depositions, and various other sources, Junger depicts a New England fishing community and the dangerous lives of the fishermen with gritty realism, and even recreates what the final harrowing hours of the *Andrea Gail* must have been like. The author also recounts tales of the storm's survivors, including Air National Guard rescue workers forced to abandon their helicopter and ride out the storm at sea.

In addition to exploring the human interest of the events surrounding the sinking of the *Andrea Gail*, Junger offers a great deal of historical and technical information on such topics as the commercial swordfishing industry, the formation of storms, fluid mechanics, naval architecture, and the experience of drowning. Junger's method of fusing large bodies of factual material with the elements of high drama left him open to criticism from a number of perspectives. *New York Observer* critic Warren St. John pointed to what he considered to be errors and omissions in *The Perfect Storm*, accusing the author of distorting the record to make a better story. Junger himself, on the other hand, feared the book would hold little interest for readers more concerned with plot and action than historical accuracy. "I didn't want to invent dialogue or fictionalize or do any of the stuff that readers love," he explained in an interview with Ellen Barry in the *Boston Phoenix*. "I was sure I was condemned to write a journalistically interesting book that just wouldn't fly. It would be too heavy. The topic is too weird and idiosyncratic. It's all the things that kill books."

Nonetheless, *The Perfect Storm* became a best-seller, with movie and paperback rights selling for hefty sums. Junger's desire to write about the fishermen's fate stemmed from having witnessed the 1991 storm firsthand and from having prior experience working a

dangerous job, as a high-climber for tree-removal companies. The same love of adventure drew him to a writing career. "I write because it thrills me," he once told *CA*. "I write journalism—not fiction—because it thrusts me out there into the world and I'm so awed by what I find." Junger, who credits Barry Lopez, Joan Didion, Pete Matthiessen, Norman Maclean, and Michael Herr as his primary literary influences, continues to work as a freelance contributor to magazines. "I sit down in the morning with a cup of coffee, edit what I wrote the day before, start in on the next section, stop writing, go running and have lunch, take a nap on the floor (so I don't sleep too long), get up and write for another couple of hours and then go out to a bar and play pool or sit there and just think about what I wrote that day. If it went well I'll have a cigarette, too."

After the publication of *A Perfect Storm*, Junger traveled with Iranian photographer, Reza, into Afghanistan in order to meet Ahmad Shah Massoud, a Taliban resistance leader. The result of their journey was a documentary entitled *Frontline Diaries: Into the Forbidden Zone*. "I'd always wanted to make the pilgrimage into [his] territory to do a profile of him," Junger stated in a *NationalGeographic* online article by Ted Chamberlain. Both journalists spent a month in Afghanistan as guests of the Northern Alliance leader, Massoud, and "visited a refugee camp inhabited by thousands of Afghans who had fled the Taliban regime." *Los Angeles Times* writer Hugh Hart commented that "surreal touches abound" in *Frontline Diaries*, a documentary which "offers sobering footage detailing the hazards of war, Afghan-style." *Hollywood Reporter* contributor Marilyn Moss called it a "fascinating, well-documented and well-mounted look" at the ongoing struggle in Afghanistan. She also noted the "first-rate journalism" that permeates the documentary.

"Junger is an excellent storyteller. . . .[and] observer," said Justin Marozzi in a London *Sunday Telegraph* review of *Fire*, Junger's second book, which is a compilation of previously published magazine articles. Only the first two pieces are actually devoted to firefighting and the personalities engaged in controlling a forceful blaze in the canyons of Idaho. Other articles feature Kashmir terrorists, the war in Kosovo, the last person who harpoons whales by hand, and Ahmed Shah Massoud, the Afghan resistance fighter—and subject of the documentary, *Frontline Diaries*—who was assassinated in September, 2001.

"The essays are short, punchy, full of fascinating factual research and altogether very readable," remarked *New Republic* contributor David Thomson. Thomson's chief criticism of the work was what he viewed as a quality of over-simplification present in Junger's work. *Book* reviewer Chris Barsanti noted that the stories in *Fire* "are marked with a generous humanity and sharpness of eye." Iain Finlayson of the London *Times* wrote that the author's work "is frontline reporting of the highest order from the dangerous, blade-sharp edge of things." "[Junger's] stories . . . hold our interest" even when they are no longer present in the daily news, stated Anthony Brandt in *National Geographic Adventure*. "The jewel [of the book] is the profile of Massoud," wrote a *Business Week* reviewer. In a *Booklist* article, Joanne Wilkinson commented that the book's "topics are compelling." *Library Journal* contributor Rachel Collins observed the author's "unfailing eye for detail" and for the fact that Junger tries to write his articles in such a way that he includes as many different perspectives as he possibly can. "The prose is clean and hard," said *Guardian* reviewer Steven Poole. London *Sunday Telegraph* critic Marozzi praised Junger's writing style in these words: "He understands, as too many of his colleagues do not, that his surroundings . . . are of more interest to the reader than his reactions to them."

BIOGRAPHICAL AND CRITICAL SOURCES:

PERIODICALS

Book, December 1, 1999, review of audiobook version of *The Perfect Storm: A True Story of Men against the Sea,* p. 718; November-December 2001, Chris Barsanti, review of *Fire,* p. 70.

Booklist, September 1, 2001, Joanne Wilkinson, review of *Fire,* p. 22; March 15, 2002, review of audiobook version of *Fire,* p. 1270.

BookPage, October, 2001, review of *Fire,* p. 2.

Business Week, October 22, 2001, review of *Fire,* p. 22E4.

Detroit Free Press, November 4, 2001, review of *Fire,* p. 4E.

Entertainment Weekly, July 14, 2000, Owen Gleiberman, review of the movie version of *The Perfect Storm,* p. 51; September 28, 2001, review of *Fire,* p. 68.

Globe and Mail (Toronto, Ontario, Canada), October 13, 2001, review of *Fire,* p. D12.

Guardian (London, England), October 19, 2002, Steven Poole, review of *Fire,* p. 30.

Harper's, November, 2001, review of *Fire,* p. 73.

Hollywood Reporter, September 25, 2001, Marilyn Moss, review of *Frontline Diaries: Into the Forbidden Zone,* p. 15.

Kirkus Reviews, August 1, 2001, review of *Fire,* p. 1092.

Kliatt Young Adult Paperback Book Guide, May, 1999, review of *The Perfect Storm,* p. 68.

Library Journal, September 1, 2001, Rachel Collins, review of *Fire,* p. 220; April 1, 2002, Mark Pumphrey, review of audiobook version of *Fire,* p. 160.

Los Angeles Times, September 24, 2001, Hugh Hart, review of *Frontline Diaries,* p. F-11.

National Geographic Adventure, November-December, 2001, Anthony Brandt, review of *Fire,* p. 59.

New Republic, November 5, 2001, David Thomson, review of *Fire,* p. 35.

New Yorker, August 11, 1997, p. 79.

New York Observer, August, 1997.

New York Review of Books, December 20, 2001, William McNeill, review of *Fire,* p. 86.

New York Times, October 6, 2001, Caryn James, review of *Frontline Diaries,* p. A13; October 17, 2001, Michiko Kakutani, review of Fire.

New York Times Book Review, June 18, 1997, p. 8; September 29, 2002, Scott Veale, review of *Fire,* p. 32; October 14, 2001, Paula Friedman, review of *Fire,* p. 28.

People, November 5, 2001, review of *Fire,* p. 52.

Publishers Weekly, April 7, 1997, p. 83; September 24, 2001, review of *Fire,* p. 79; September 24, 2001, interview with Sebastian Junger, p. 80.

Sunday Telegraph (London, England), November 11, 2001, Justin Marozzi, review of *Fire.*

Time, July 3, 2000, Richard Corliss, review of the movie version of *The Perfect Storm,* p. 56.

Times (London, England), November 14, 2001, Iain Finlayson, review of *Fire,* p. 12.

Times Literary Supplement, July 18, 1997, p. 8.

Underwater Naturalist, January, 1999, review of *The Perfect Storm,* p. 46.

Us Weekly, July 24, 2000, Oliver Jones, p. 54.

Washington Post, October 12, 2001, Carolyn See, review of *Fire,* p. C04.

Yankee, September, 2000, Robert Pushkar, review of *The Perfect Storm,* pp.66-75.

ONLINE

Boston Phoenix Online, http://www.bostonphoenix. com/ (October 11-18, 2001), Tamara Wieder, interview with Sebastian Junger.

Literati Web site, http://literati.net/ (May 12, 2003), reviews of *Fire* and *The Perfect Storm.*

National Geographic Web site, http://www.national geographic.com/ (May 12, 2003), Ted Chamberlain, review of *Frontline Diaries.**

K

KATZ, William Loren 1927-

PERSONAL: Born June 2, 1927, in New York, NY; son of Bernard (a researcher) and Madeline (Simon) Katz. *Education:* Syracuse University, B.A., 1950; New York University, M.A., 1952.

ADDRESSES: Home—231 West 13th St., New York, NY 10011. *Agent*—c/o Author Mail, Atheneum/Simon & Schuster, 1230 Avenue of the Americas, New York, NY 10020.

CAREER: Writer. New York City public schools, New York, NY, teacher of American history, 1955-60; Greenburgh District 8 School System, Hartsdale, NY, high school teacher of American history, 1960-68; New School for Social Research (now New School University), New York, NY, instructor in U.S. history, beginning 1977. Scholar-in-residence and research fellow, Columbia University, 1971-73; lecturer on American Negro history at teacher institutes; teacher of black history at Tombs Prison; producer of audio-visual materials on minorities for classrooms. Has testified before U.S. Senate on Negro history; has appeared on television and radio programs, including *Today Show.* Consultant to President Kennedy's Committee on Juvenile Delinquency and Youth Development, Smithsonian Institution, U.S. Air Force schools in England, Belgium, and Holland, 1974-75, Inner London Educational Authority, 1982, British House of Commons, *Life* magazine, *New York Times,* and Columbia Broadcast System (CBS-TV). *Military service:* U.S. Navy, 1945-46.

MEMBER: United Federation of Teachers.

AWARDS, HONORS: Gold Medal Award for nonfiction, National Conference of Christians and Jews, and Brotherhood Award, both 1968, both for *Eyewitness: The Negro in American History;* Oppie Award, 1971, for *The Black West: A Documentary and Pictorial History;* White Dove Peace Award, White Dove-Imani-Rainbow Lodge, 2000.

WRITINGS:

Eyewitness: The Negro in American History, Pitman (New York, NY), 1967, 3rd edition, 1974.

Five Slave Narratives, Arno/New York Times (New York, NY), 1968.

Teachers' Guide to American Negro History, Quadrangle (New York, NY), 1968, revised edition, 1971.

(With Warren J. Halliburton) *American Minorities and Majorities: A Syllabus of United States History for Secondary Schools,* Arno (New York, NY), 1970.

The Black West: A Documentary and Pictorial History of the African-American Role in the Westward Expansion of the United States, Doubleday (New York, NY), 1971, revised edition, 1973, reprinted, Harlem Moon (New York, NY), 2003.

(With Warren J. Halliburton) *A History of Black Americans,* Harcourt (New York, NY), 1973.

An Album of Reconstruction, F. Watts (New York, NY), 1974.

An Album of the Civil War, F. Watts (New York, NY), 1974.

(With Bernard Gaughran) *The Constitutional Amendments,* F. Watts (New York, NY), 1974.

Minorities in American History, six volumes, F. Watts (New York, NY), 1974-75.

(With Jacqueline Hunt) *Making Our Way,* Dial (New York, NY), 1975.

Black People Who Made the Old West, Crowell (New York, NY), 1977.

The Great Depression, F. Watts (New York, NY), 1978.

An Album of Nazism, F. Watts (New York, NY), 1979.

Flight from the Devil: Six Slave Narratives, Africa World Press, 1986.

The Invisible Empire: The Ku Klux Klan Impact on History, Open Hand Publishing, 1986.

The Lincoln Brigade: A Picture History, Atheneum (New York, NY), 1989.

Breaking the Chains: African-American Slave Resistance, Atheneum (New York, NY), 1990.

The Civil War to the Last Frontier, 1850-1880s, Raintree Steck-Vaughn (New York, NY), 1993.

Minorities Today, Raintree Steck-Vaughn (New York, NY), 1993.

The New Freedom to the New Deal, 1913-1939, Raintree Steck-Vaughn (New York, NY), 1993.

Proudly Red and Black: Stories of African and Native Americans, Atheneum (New York, NY), 1993.

The Westward Movement and Abolitionism, 1815-1850, Raintree Steck-Vaughn (New York, NY), 1993.

World War II to the New Frontier, 1940-1963, Raintree Steck-Vaughn (New York, NY), 1993.

The Great Migrations, 1880s-1912, Raintree Steck-Vaughn (New York, NY), 1993.

The Great Society to the Reagan Era, 1964-1990, Raintree Steck-Vaughn (New York, NY), 1993.

Exploration to the War of 1812, 1492-1814, Raintree Steck-Vaughn (New York, NY), 1993.

Eyewitness: A Living Documentary of the African-American Contribution to American History, Simon & Schuster (New York, NY), 1995.

Black Women of the Old West, Atheneum (New York, NY), 1995.

Black Legacy: A History of New York's African Americans, Atheneum (New York, NY), 1997.

Black Indians: A Hidden Heritage, Alladin (New York, NY), 1997.

Black Pioneers: An Untold Story, Atheneum (New York, NY), 1999.

I Demand Justice: Black Settlers of the West, Atheneum (New York, NY), 2001.

(Editor, with Laurie R. Lehman) *The Cruel Years: American Voices at the Dawn of the Twentieth Century,* Apex Press, 2002.

General editor, "The American Negro: His History and Literature" series, 147 volumes, Arno (New York, NY), 1968-71, "Minorities in America: Picture Histo-

ries" series, 1972—, "Teaching Approaches to Black History in the Classroom," 1973; editor, "The Anti-Slavery Crusade in America" series, 70 volumes, Arno/New York Times (New York, NY), "Pamphlets in American History" series, Microfilm Corp. of America/New York Times (New York, NY), 1978-82, and "Vital Sources in American History for High School Students" series, 179 volumes, 1980. Contributor of articles to periodicals and professional journals, including *Reader's Digest, Journal of Negro History, Journal of Black Studies, Teachers College Record, Freedomways,* and *Southern Education Report.* Member of editorial board, *Black Studies,* 1970—.

ADAPTATIONS: Breaking the Chains was adapted as an audiobook.

SIDELIGHTS: William Loren Katz specializes in writing black history for a young audience. As a writer for *Black Child* explained: "African-American parents are on the prowl for children's books with positive Black images. In the field of nonfiction, many will probably find what they want in the carefully researched, exciting works of William Loren Katz," whose books contain "an abundance of stirring women and men pioneers and daring doers. This author is a master of simple, no-nonsense prose and his books are crammed with powerful antique prints and vintage photographs from his historic collection." Brad Hooper, in his *Booklist* review of *The Black West: A Documentary and Pictorial History of the African-American Role in the Westward Expansion of the United States,* noted that "Katz is extremely comprehensive, very readable, and peppers his text with abundant and edifying illustrations."

Especially focusing on the history of black Americans in the settling of the Old West, Katz has written a number of titles chronicling the achievements of black pioneers. *Black Women of the Old West,* for example, tells of the many women who were pioneers, settlers, farmers, business owners, and army wives throughout the American West. Margaret A. Bush in *Horn Book* found that Katz's book provides "well-organized explanations of many aspects of black history." Chris Sherman in *Booklist* concluded that "this very readable book is likely to be an eye-opener for many readers."

Katz's *Black Pioneers: An Untold Story* describes the efforts of black settlers in the Ohio and Mississippi river valleys. In addition to settling the land and establishing farms and businesses, black Americans were also obliged to fight moves to legalize slavery in the sparsely settled territories. They also worked to set up the Underground Railroad to assist escaped slaves from the South to reach safety. Deborah Taylor in *Horn Book* noted that "the narration is clear, fluid, and enlivened with quotes from the pioneers themselves." Anne O'Malley in *Booklist* judged *Black Pioneers* to be "an excellent source for reports and a rich supplement to the U.S. history curriculum."

Katz once told *CA:* "Since I agree with the idea that the historian who condoned a crime was perpetuating it throughout history—his guilt was greater than that of the original perpetrator of the crime, not only because the effect of his sin was more enduring, but also because his motive was less pressing—I have attempted to offer a history that enables us to look at the past intelligently and shape our future with the knowledge of the past in mind. My concentration on minorities has been pursued because I believe that society is only as strong as its weakest members, and that the responsibility of our nation is to spread justice to all within its borders. The first line of defense of all of us is protection for the least of us."

BIOGRAPHICAL AND CRITICAL SOURCES:

PERIODICALS

Black Child, February-March, 1997, "Black History As It Really Was."
Booklist, December 15, 1995, Chris Sherman, review of *Black Women of the Old West,* p. 695; February 15, 1997, Ilene Cooper, review of *Black Legacy: A History of New York's African Americans,* p. 1012; February 15, 1999, Brad Hooper, review of *The Black West: A Documentary and Pictorial History of the African-American Role in the Westward Expansion of the United States,* p. 1012; June 1, 1999, Barbara Baskin, review of *Breaking the Chains: African-American Slave Resistance* (audiobook), p. 1857; July, 1999, Anne O'Malley, review of *Black Pioneers: An Untold Story,* p. 1936; February 15, 2002, Patricia Austin, review of *Breaking the Chains* (audiobook), p. 1038.
Horn Book, January-February, 1996, Margaret A. Bush, review of *Black Women of the Old West,* p. 92; May, 1999, Kristi Beavin, review of *Breaking the Chains* (audiobook), p. 356; July, 1999, Deborah Taylor, review of *Black Pioneers,* p. 484.

Reader's Digest, July, 1969.
School Library Journal, September, 1999, Debbie Feulner, review of *Black Pioneers,* p. 236.
Village Voice, May 13, 2002, Robin D. G. Kelley, "Shirtwaist Tales."

ONLINE

William Loren Katz Web site, http://www.williamlkatz.com/ (November 13, 2003).*

* * *

KAVASCH, E(lizabeth) Barrie 1942-

PERSONAL: Surname is accented on second syllable; born December 31, 1942, in Springfield, OH; daughter of Herschel M. (a musician) and Vera E. (a nurse; maiden name, Ferguson) McLemore; divorced, 1982; children: Christopher Jon, Kimberlee Beth. *Education:* "Principally self-taught."

ADDRESSES: Home and office—Bayberry Meadow, R.R. 1, Bridgewater, CT 06752.

CAREER: American Museum of Natural History, New York, NY, lecturer in ethnobotany, 1981—. Guest curator at Smithsonian Institution, 1982-86; lecturer at New York Botanical Garden, 1982-83, and New School for Social Research, 1983. Chairman of board of directors of *Eagle Wing Press.* Secretary of board of trustees of Brookfield Craft Center. Consultant to U.S. National Arboretum.

MEMBER: National Audubon Society (member of local board of trustees), Herb Society of America (member of board of trustees of Connecticut unit), Connecticut Botanical Society (CBS), Connecticut Mycological Association (COMA), Connecticut Valley Mycological Society (CVMS).

WRITINGS:

(And illustrator) *Native Harvests: Recipes and Botanicals of the American Indians,* Random House (New York, NY), 1979.

(And illustrator) *Botanical Tapestry,* Gunn Historical Museum, 1979.

(And photographer) *Wild Edibles of the Northeast,* Hancock House (Blaine, WA), 1981.

(And photographer) *Wildflowers of the Northeast,* Hancock House (Blaine, WA), 1982.

(And photographer) *Guide to Eastern Mushrooms,* Hancock House (Blaine, WA), 1982.

(And photographer) *Guide to Eastern Roadside Wildflowers,* Hancock House (Blaine, WA), 1983.

Enduring Harvests: Native American Foods and Festivals for Every Season, Globe Pequot Press (Old Saybrook, CT), 1995.

A Student's Guide to Native American Geneology, Oryx Press (Phoenix, AZ), 1996.

(With Karen Barr) *American Indian Healing Arts: Herbs, Rituals, and Remedies for Every Season of Life,* Bantam Books (New York, NY), 1999.

Apache Children and Elders Talk Together, PowerKids Press (New York, NY), 1999.

Blackfoot Children and Elders Talk Together, PowerKids Press (New York, NY), 1999.

Crow Children and Elders Talk Together, PowerKids Press (New York, NY), 1999.

Lakota Sioux Children and Elders Talk Together, PowerKids Press (New York, NY), 1999.

Seminole Children and Elders Talk Together, PowerKids Press (New York, NY), 1999.

Zuni Children and Elders Talk Together, PowerKids Press (New York, NY), 1999.

The Seminoles, Raintree Steck-Vaughn (Austin, TX), 2000.

Hands of Time: Select Poetry and Haiku in Five Seasons (self-published), 2000.

The Medicine Wheel Garden: Creating Sacred Space for Healing, Celebration and Tranquility, Random House (New York, NY), 2002.

The Mound Builders of Ancient America, 21st Century Books (Breckenridge, CO), 2003.

Author of "Native Harvests," a column in *Eagle Wing Press,* and "Herbaria," a column in *Artifacts,* both self-illustrated. Contributor of articles and photographs to magazines, including *National Geographic, Garden, Cook's,* and *Yankee.*

SIDELIGHTS: E. Barrie Kavasch is an authority on Native Americans and their wisdom and traditions. She has penned several books for young people about many different Native American nations, including the Apaches, the Zuni, the Crow, and the Seminoles. For adult audiences, Kavasch has authored titles such as *American Indian Healing Arts: Herbs, Rituals, and Remedies for Every Season of Life* and *The Medicine Wheel Garden: Creating Sacred Space for Healing, Celebration, and Tranquility.* She has also authored a self-published volume of poetry, *Hands of Time.*

Reviewing Kavasch's collaboration with Karen Barr, *American Indian Arts,* for the *New Living* Web site, Barbara Sabatino praised the inclusion of Native American ritual ceremonies for healing and peace of mind, natural remedies for wounds and illnesses, and recipes for attracting love. "Rituals of puberty and marriage of various Indian tribes are also discussed in this book," Sabatino noted. "These rites address the passage of becoming an adult and what it means to be a member of the tribe. Children's games had a deeper symbolic meaning to help adolescents understand their roles in life. Marriage ceremonies," the critic continued, "would reflect the road of life, or path, the couple should take." Sabatino concluded that "these philosophies are just as relevant today and this book offers thoughtful spiritual contemplation along with Native American healing arts." Of Kavasch's *The Medicine Wheel Garden,* Carol Haggas reported in *Booklist* that it is "a comprehensive, step-by-step guide to how primitive traditions can have modern applications."

Kavasch told *CA:* "I am principally self-taught, having taken the rich opportunities to study with various scientists, specialists, artists, and photographers in the areas of natural sciences, literature, and anthropology. After traveling in other parts of the world, I've directed the focus of my interest, research, and writing on the primal peoples and native plants of North America. Years of prehistoric research have brought me full circle into historic and contemporary ethnobotany and social development.

"I teach and lecture throughout the northeast and have traveled extensively to different geographical locations, reservations, preserves, and other Amerindian areas. I am also a camera naturalist with an extensive color photograph collection and research library."

BIOGRAPHICAL AND CRITICAL SOURCES:

PERIODICALS

Booklist, December 15, 1995, Iva Freeman, review of *Enduring Harvests: Native American Foods and Festivals for Every Season,* p. 677; January 1,

2000, Dona Helmer, review of *A Student's Guide to Native American Geneology,* p. 962; June 1, 2002, Carol Haggas, review of *The Medicine Wheel Garden: Creating Sacred Space for Healing, Celebration, and Tranquility,* p. 1661.

Library Journal, March 15, 1996, Judith C. Sutton, review of *Enduring Harvests,* p. 92.

Publishers Weekly, October 2, 1995, review of *Enduring Harvests,* p. 1661.

School Library Journal, April, 2000, Darcy Schild, review of *The Seminoles,* p. 1661.

ONLINE

E. Barrie Kavasch Home Page, http://ebarriekavasch. hypermart.net/ (October 7, 2002).

New Living, http://www.newliving.com/ (October 7, 2002).*

*   *   *

KELMAN, James 1946-

PERSONAL: Born June 9, 1946, in Glasgow, Scotland; married Marie Connors (a social worker), 1969; children: two daughters. *Education:* Attended University of Strathclyde, 1975-78, 1981-82.

ADDRESSES: Home—244 West Princess St., Glasgow G4 9DP, Scotland. *Agent*—Cathie Thomson, 23 Hillhead St., Glasgow G12, Scotland.

CAREER: Novelist and author of short fiction. Worked various semiskilled and laboring jobs. Scottish Arts Council writing fellowship, 1978-80, 1982-85.

AWARDS, HONORS: Scottish Arts Council bursary, 1973 and 1980, writing fellowship, 1978-80 and 1982-85, and book award, 1983, 1987, and 1989; Cheltenham Prize, 1987; James Tait Black Memorial Prize, 1990, for *A Disaffection;* Booker Prize, and Writers' Guild Award, both 1994, both for *How Late It Was, How Late; Sunday*/Glenfiddich Spirit of Scotland Award, Stakis Prize for Scottish Writer of the Year, Saltire Scottish Book of the Year designation, and Scottish Arts Council Autumn Book Award, all 1998, all for *The Good Times;* Booker Prize nomination, 2001, for *Translated Accounts.*

WRITINGS:

NOVELS

The Busconductor Hines, Polygon Press (Edinburgh, Scotland), 1984.

A Chancer, Polygon Press (Edinburgh, Scotland), 1985.

A Disaffection, Farrar, Straus (New York, NY), 1989.

How Late It Was, How Late, Norton (New York, NY), 1994.

Translated Accounts, Secker & Warburg (London, England), 2001.

You Have to Be Careful in the Land of the Free, Harcourt (Orlando, FL), 2004.

SHORT STORIES

An Old Pub near the Angel, Puckerbrush Press (Orono, ME), 1973.

(With Tom Leonard and Alex Hamilton) *Three Glasgow Writers,* Molendinar Press (Glasgow, Scotland), 1976.

Short Tales from the Nightshift, Print Studio Press (Glasgow, Scotland), 1978.

Not Not While the Giro and Other Stories, Polygon Press (Edinburgh, Scotland), 1983.

(With Alasdair Gray and Agnes Owens) *Lean Tales,* J. Cape (London, England), 1985.

Greyhound for Breakfast, Farrar, Straus (New York, NY), 1987.

(Editor) *An East-End Anthology,* Clydeside Press (Glasgow, Scotland), 1988.

The Burn, Secker & Warburg (London, England), 1991.

Busted Scotch: Selected Stories, Norton (New York, NY), 1997.

Seven Stories (audiobook), AK Press (Stirling, Scotland), 1997.

The Good Times, Random House (New York, NY), 1999.

PLAYS

Hardie and Baird: The Last Days (radio play broadcast 1978; stage play produced in Edinburgh, 1990), Secker & Warburg (London, England), 1991.

The Busker, produced in Edingurgh, 1985.

Le Rodeur (adaptation of a play by Enzo Cormann), produced in Edinburgh, 1987.

In the Night, produced in Stirling, Scotland, 1988.

One Two-Hey (musical), produced 1994.

The Art of the Big Bass Drum (radio play), Radio 3, 1998.

OTHER

Some Recent Attacks: Essays Clutural and Political, AK Press (Stirling, Scotland), 1992.

(With Benjamin Zephaniah) *Inna Liverpool,* AK Press (Stirling, Scotland), 1993.

Ten Guitars (short film), BBC Drama, 1995.

(With Ken Grant) *The Close Season,* Dewi Lewis (Stockport, England), 2002.

And the Judges Said . . . : Essays, Secker & Warburg, (London, England), 2002.

Also author of screenplay *The Return,* 1990.

ADAPTATIONS: How Late It Was, How Late was adapted for the stage by Kirk Lynn and produced in Austin, TX, 2003.

SIDELIGHTS: Scottish novelist and short-story writer James Kelman is the author of *How Late It Was, How Late,* winner of the prestigious Booker Prize in 1994. In Kelman's fiction the working class of Glasgow endure a bleak existence, living among urban decay and laboring at menial, unfulfilling jobs. Full of black humor, raw language, and Scottish dialect, Kelman's prose has earned the author a reputation as one of Great Britain's finest authors, while also frustrating those who want an easy read. Kelman, according to *Times Literary Supplement* contributor James Campbell, "conveys to the reader, as no other writer does, the feeling of Glasgow, the smell and sight and sound of pubs and betting shops, working-men's cafes, the texture of the streets."

Kelman's *Not Not While the Giro and Other Stories* contains twenty-six tales that employ the author's penchant for black humor; most also explore various social and economic aspects of the poor in London and Glasgow. As they cut corners to live from day to day, Kelman's ambitionless characters have little hope of rising above their dreary circumstances and are resigned to their lowly positions in life. The protagonist

in the title story, for example, contemplates suicide, but dismisses the idea when he remembers his welfare check is soon to arrive. Other stories in the collection include "Away in Airdrie," about a boy's trip to a football game with his drunken uncle, and "The Block," in which a milkman is downed by a falling corpse. Writing in *British Book News,* reviewer Donald Campbell declared that "Kelman's ability to re-create" the squalor of contemporary urban Scotland "is a major achievement," and praised the author's "satisfying insight, an economic eye for detail and a telling accuracy in the evocation of atmosphere." Also applauding *Not Not While the Giro* was Gerald Mangan who, in the *Times Literary Supplement,* praised Kelman's "humour and pathos" and ability to keep "the prose readable as well as authentic. Speaking the same voice as his characters, yet avoiding all the pitfalls of condescension and nostalgia, he mines a rich ore from many unexplored seams of working-class life."

Kelman followed *Not Not While the Giro* with the novel *The Busconductor Hines,* a portrait of a bus conductor who hates his job, is bored with life, and dreams, without much hope, that things could be better one day. This first novel earned praise from several reviewers, among them *Times Literary Supplement* critic Edwin Morgan, who deemed it "an intelligent, exploratory, and sometimes very touching novel," and *British Book News* contributor Jim Miller, who stated: "With Kelman, and other writers such as Alasdair Gray, the great city of Glasgow and urban Scotland in general are finding the literary voices they deserve."

Kelman furthered his reputation as one of Scotland's most promising authors with the release of *Greyhound for Breakfast,* a book of forty-seven stories ranging in length from the eight-line "Leader from a Quality Newspaper" to the much longer title story about a despondent, unemployed man who spends his last eighty dollars on a dog. As he walks the dog around town, the man realizes how foolish he was to purchase the animal, which he cannot afford to feed. He also reflects on the misery in his life and pines for his son, who left without a word to find work in London. In *Greyhound for Breakfast,* as in his previous works, Kelman explores the psyche of Glasgow's down-and-out. *New York Times* critic Michiko Kakutani faulted the work, citing the author's "decidedly limited image bank—his inability to come up with more than half a dozen situations. By the time most readers have finished this volume," Kakutani opined, "they will never want to hear about another person bumming a cigarette, placing a bet or drinking a beer. They will feel nearly as suffocated as Mr. Kelman's characters do."

Other critics, however, applauded *Greyhound for Breakfast,* among them Arnold Weinstein, who wrote in the *New York Times Book Review* that Kelman has "rightly been dubbed the crown prince of the Scottish avant-garde." Weinstein also praised Kelman's "hilarious genius for detail, his casual social subtext, his unique refreshing burr that echoes the shivering slums." Similar comments were issued by William Grimes in his *Voice Literary Supplement* assessment of *Greyhound for Breakfast.* Grimes concluded his review with a plea to the book's publisher: "Memo to Roger Straus: Please, sir, can we have some more?"

The 1990 James Tait Black Memorial Prize was awarded to Kelman for his third novel, *A Disaffection,* the story of a week in the life of a Glaswegian school teacher. Overtaken with boredom and loneliness, Patrick Doyle is depressed by his elderly parents, at times burdened by his brother, and hopelessly infatuated with and sexually frustrated by a married colleague who flirts with him yet insists she wants no relationship. Caught in the gloom of Glasgow, Doyle finds comfort, oddly, in the tones he produces by blowing on a couple of industrial pipes he found discarded in an alley. As *London Review of Books* critic Karl Miller observed of the novel's protagonist: "For a man of twenty-nine he seems to have grabbed hold of very little of anything except a glass and a book. Drink figures in the novel, in precisely rendered scenes, as a bastion of the culture which is also a slow death. And yet this man is very far from useless. What we are reading is the Book of Patrick Doyle. . . . the portrait of an artist." Miller judged *A Disaffection* "pretty terrific, both truly challenging and nearly always very diverting." On the other hand, *Times Literary Supplement* reviewer Mangan found Doyle "the same restless and sardonic day-dreamer" featured in Kelman's earlier stories. *A Disaffection,* Mangan observed, "can be read as a fuller orchestration of its solipsistic lament." Although noting that Kelman has perfectly captured the sights and sounds of Glasgow in his writings, Mangan suggested: "It may be time for Kelman to direct his formidable capacities beyond this subject, and break new ground."

While some critics have advised Kelman to seek new subjects, others express admiration for his work and yearn for more. *Times Literary Supplement* contributor

Angela McRobbie defended Kelman in a review of his story collection *The Burn,* writing: "He has been seen as a working-class writer working in the realist tradition, and this has prompted critics to complain that Kelman merely records what anyone could just as easily overhear in a Glasgow pub on any night of the week. . . . The realist label is a misunderstanding of Kelman's work, which takes aspects of working-class life as its raw material but which quickly moves inwards to explore a kind of psychic pain and paralysis." A London *Times* reviewer, discussing *The Burn,* also expressed appreciation for Kelman's tales: "Elegance in machinery, as in mathematics or storytelling, consists in employing the least means to the greatest effect, and so the first thing to be said about *The Burn* . . . is that it's a very elegant machine. As a writer, Kelman has the remarkable ability to synthesize deep emotion and routine behaviour." He reproduces the sources and consequences of so many people's stuckness in "civilized" society.

The 1994 Booker Prize was Kelman's reward for writing *How Late It Was, How Late.* In the novel Sammy goes on a drinking binge, wakes up beaten, shoeless, and blind in a police cell unable to recall how he got there, and stumbles home to discover his girlfriend has left him. Much of the story consists of Sammy's interior monologue, explained critic Andrew O'Hagan, who observed in the *London Review of Books:* "This stuff is close to perfect: Kelman identifies with characters like Sammy . . . and he can slip first-person perceptions and psychological tics into a third-person narrative in an astonishing way. For someone who's made such a palaver about ways of talking, about speech . . . , he's actually not so very good at dialogue. . . . It's the way people talk to themselves that he gets so brilliantly, so matchlessly."

After winning the Booker Prize, Kelman became the target of criticism due to the profusion of obscenities that appear in *How Late It Was, How Late.* In Kelman's defense, Richard Bausch wrote in the *New York Times Book Review:* "Objections to the language in which this good book is couched seem to me to be so far beside the point as to be rather ridiculous. *How Late It Was, How Late* is a book constructed out of the vernacular speech of a time and place, exactly as, once, Chaucer's tales were. . . . It is a work of marvelous vibrance and richness of character [and] . . . deserves every accolade it gets."

Kelman addressed his use of profanity in the *New York Times.* "The dictionary would use the term 'debased,'" he told interviewer Sarah Lyall, referring to his dialogue as "living language." "In order to fight against the house style," the author continued, "you have to justify every single comma. . . . You have to revise and revise and proof at every bloody stage to insure that everything's spot on, especially because you're working in what other people regard as inconsistent ways, so you have to be really sure. . . . You have to trust the fact that you're a writer."

Busted Scotch: Selected Stories, published in 1997, is a collection of thirty-five short stories. Most of the characters are saddened or pained, and the stories follow them through private healing processes whereby they come to terms with their situations. Richard Burgin, in the *New York Times Book Review,* noted, "In addition to his vivid language and sense of comedy, [it] is the masterly internal monologues of his characters, which often lead them to surprising discoveries." Burgin added that Kelman "has fashioned a vision of the world so tormented and despairing that he has had to work hard to make it not only palatable but entertaining. His solution is twofold: exquisitely precise (although frequently obscene) language and a humor that is by turns dry, fanciful, slapstick and savage." Barbara A. MacAdam, in the *Los Angeles Times Book Review,* likened reading *Busted Scotch* to entering an unfamiliar neighborhood bar full of unknown people with unknown stories: "You listen to their stories, first with sympathy, then with empathy, and finally, when the bar closes, you're reluctant to leave." MacAdam attributed her affinity for the stories to their universality, noting, "While being regional and class-conscious, the work is really about basic issues of human nature."

Salon contributor Todd Pruzan described Kelman's short-story collection *The Good Times* as not "a collection of twenty stories so much as a twenty fragments, twenty arguments, twenty interviews with hideous men. These aural folktales, seemingly overheard from the next table in the pub or through thin apartment walls, assume a participatory familiarity as Kelman isolates the throwaway thoughts and insignifica of our daily lives. We're conditioned to ignore our quotidian habits; Kelman stares them in the face." An *Eye Weekly* contributor mused over the fact that Kelman chose to follow his Booker-winning novel with a collection of short stories, opining that "Kelman always has a political bent, and is sometimes overly fond of big ideas—passages from novels or philosophy

that free-float into some of the stories like intriguing but alien spores. But all is outshone by the writer's great gift—an ability to drive stories solely with emotion and character."

Critiquing Kelman's essay collection *And the Judges Said . . . ,* Alan Marshall wrote in the London *Daily Telegraph* that the author focuses on "the scandal of exposure to asbestos on Clydeside, the destruction of the steel industry in Scotland, racism in Britain and the Turkish persecution of the Kurds. In writing about these issues in the angry, frank, straightforward way he does, Kelman is true to one of the beliefs that runs through the book: the confrontation with chronic specialisation, incapacitating expertise. . . . When an artist addresses himself so artlessly to the world we live in, he reaches beyond his own specialisation: he lands in the street. The street is where the action is, where ordinary people live and come together." Kelman doesn't just write about such issues; he has also become personally involved: He has signed letters and raised money in support of a Kurdish writer imprisoned in Turkey, and taken part in public events, such as Writers against War on the eve of the U.S.-led invasion of Iraq in 2003. As Tim Conley noted for *ModernWorld:* "Unlike CNN, Kelman has not abdicated his responsibility as a witness."

Reviewing Kelman's 2001 novel *Translated Accounts,* London *Sunday Telegraph* contributor Dave Robson remarked, "Giving voice to the inarticulate has become something of a crusade for James Kelman. . . . With *Translated Accounts,* he goes a stage further." While Robson experienced the book's intent as "an honourable ambition," the author's writing style "is so cumbersome, so unsuitable, so downright weird, that I would have to describe *Translated Accounts* . . . as the most unreadable novel I have ever had to wade my way through." London *Sunday Times* contributor Sean O'Brien held a different opinion however, writing that the novel "doesn't give an inch to simplification." "For one thing," O'Brien commented, "this is a political novel. It offers a set of fifty-four translations, by various administrative hands, of the testimony of an uncertain number of speakers following incidents during what appears to be a civil war in a police state. The translators' grasp of English idioms is not perfect. . . . Chronology is by no means certain: the past has ceased to be a resource and become an allegation." Finding parallels with the work of Franz Kafka and Samuel Beckett, and noting that reading the novel "requires a certain commitment," O'Brien nonetheless found *Translated Accounts* worth the effort: "There is considerable imaginative reward—a sense of having somehow seen the world with its labels taken off."

BIOGRAPHICAL AND CRITICAL SOURCES:

BOOKS

Contemporary Literary Criticism, Volume 58, Gale (Detroit, MI), 1990.

Contemporary Novelists, 6th edition, St. James Press (Detroit, MI), 1996.

Hagemann, Susanne, editor, *Studies in Scottish Fiction: 1945 to the Present,* Peter Lang (Frankfurt, Germany), 1996.

Lane, Richard J., Rod Mengham, and Philip Tew, editors, *Contemporary British Fiction,* Polity Press (Cambridge, England), 2003.

Mengham, Rod, editor, *An Introduction to Contemporary Fiction: International Writing in English since 1970,* Polity (Cambridge, England), 1999.

Wallace, Gavin, and Randall Stevenson, editors, *The Scottish Novel since the Seventies: New Visions, Old Dreams,* Edinburgh University Press (Edinburgh, Scotland), 1993.

PERIODICALS

Austin American-Statesman, September 7, 2003. p. K2.

Booklist, May 1, 1997, p. 1480; June 1, 1999, p. 1790; September 15, 2001, p. 192.

British Book News, August, 1983, pp. 517-518; June, 1984, p. 365; November, 1985, pp. 684-685.

Bucknell Review, 2000, p. 150.

Christian Science Monitor, January 11, 1995, p. 13.

Contemporary Literature, winter, 2000, p. 693; spring, 2002, p. 50.

Daily Telegraph (London, England), June 9, 2001; April 13, 2002.

Economist (U.K.), April 26, 1997, p. 113.

English, summer, 1999, p. 101.

Evening Times (Glasgow, Scotland), July 24, 1998, p. 26; May 22, 2001, p. 2; March 11, 2002, p. 17; June 3, 2002, p. 3; November 21, 2002, p. 3; March 26, 2003, p. 15.

Financial Times, October 12, 1994, p. 12.

Guardian (London, England), July 18, 1998, pp. 10, 26; November 28, 1998, p. 16; October 30, 1999, p. 11; June 2, 2001, p. 6; July 25, 2001, p. 19; July 28, 2001, p. 8.

Herald (Glasgow, Scotland), March 1, 2001, p. 7; May 22, 2001, pp. 1, 3; May 23, 2001, p. 3; May 24, 2001, p. 19; June 1, 2001,7 p. 6; June 2, 2001, p. 12; August 16, 2001, p. 7; April 6, 2002, p. 12; August 28, 2003, p. 5.

Independent (London, England), July 11, 1998, p. 16; July 18, 1998, p. 10; May 26, 2001, p. 10.

Independent on Sunday (London, England), July 19, 1998, p. 30; June 10, 2001, p. 51.

Insight on the News, January 23, 1995, p. 30.

Library Journal, April 15, 1989, p. 99; May 1, 1997, p. 142; July, 1999, p. 139; October 1, 2001, p. 141.

Listener, March 9, 1989, p. 31.

Literature and History, autumn, 1999, p. 44.

London Review of Books, May 2, 1985, pp. 22-23; April 2, 1987, p. 23; March 2, 1989, p. 13; May 26, 1994, p. 8.

Los Angeles Times Book Review, April 10, 1988, p. 11; April 6, 1995, p. E1; June 8, 1997, p. 13.

New Republic, December 8, 1997, p. 46.

New Statesman, May 24, 1985, p. 30; April 17, 1987, p. 30; May 10, 1991, p. 39; March 18, 1994, p. 56; June 11, 2001, p. 73.

Newsweek, January 23, 1995, p. 68.

New Yorker, January 9, 1995, p. 80.

New York Review of Books, April 25, 1991, pp. 12-18; June 8, 1995, p. 45.

New York Times, January 16, 1988, p. 16; October 12, 1994; November 29, 1994, pp. B1-B2; December 16, 1994, p. B8; October 16, 2003, p. E1.

New York Times Book Review, March 20, 1988, p. 19; June 18, 1989, p. 14; February 5, 1995, p. 8; May 18, 1997, p. 16; July 11, 1999, p. 22.

Observer (London, England), April 19, 1987, p. 22; November 15, 1987, p. 25; February 19, 1989, p. 44; February 4, 1990, p. 60; April 28, 1991, p. 59; March 27, 1994, p. 16; April 3, 1994, p. 19; July 19, 1998, p. 15; June 10, 2001, p. 15; October 20, 2002, p. 18.

Publishers Weekly, December 25, 1987, p. 63; December 5, 1994, p. 68; April 21, 1997, p. 59; June 14, 1999, p. 49; September 10, 2001, p. 59.

Rain Taxi, fall, 1997.

Review of Contemporary Fiction, fall, 2000, p. 42.

San Francisco Chronicle, May 2, 1997, p. C2; July 13, 1997, p. 6.

Scotsman (Edinburgh, Scotland), February 23, 1998, p. 13; July 18, 1998, p. 16; July 24, 1998, p. 19;

December 5, 1998, p. 17; September 27, 2000, p. 16; February 14, 2001, p. 9; June 1, 2001, p. 5; June 2, 2001, pp. 5, 10; August 23, 2001, p. 12; August 27, 2001, p. 7; April 27, 2002, p. 10; May 11, 2002, p. 8; May 19, 2003, p. 16; August 27, 2003, p. 16.

Scottish Literary Journal, spring, 2000, p. 105.

Spectator, April 2, 1994, p. 33; July 18, 1998, p. 34; June 9, 2001, p. 33.

Sunday Herald (Glasgow, Scotland), June 3, 2001, p. 10.

Sunday Telegraph (London, England), June 3, 2001.

Sunday Times (London, England), April 26, 1998, p. 3; July 12, 1998, p. 8; July 26, 1998, p. 2; June 3, 2001, p. 45; August 19, 2001, p. 13; April 14, 2002, p. 12; August 4, 2002, p. 44.

Swansea Review, 1994, p. 393.

Times (London, England), April 16, 1987, p. 397; May 2, 1991, p. 16; October 24, 1997, p. 19; July 16, 1998, p. 39; May 30, 2001, p. 9; May 1, 2002, p. 19; May 18, 2002, p. 16.

Times Literary Supplement, December 30, 1983, p. 1462; April 13, 1984, p. 397; May 10, 1985, p. 529; December 6, 1985, p. 1407; May 8, 1987, p. 488; February 24-March 2, 1989, p. 191; April 26, 1991, p. 18; January 1, 1993, p. 5; April 1, 1994, p. 20.

Tribune Books (Chicago, IL), January 1, 1995, p. 3.

Variant, August, 2000.

Voice Literary Supplement, February, 1988, p. 3.

Wall Street Journal, October 12, 1994, p. A15.

Washington Post, October 12, 1994, p. C1; November 25, 2001, p. T06.

ONLINE

Barcelona Review, http://www.barcelonareview.com/ (2002), author interview.

Between the Lines, http://www.thei.aust.com/ (March 26, 2004), author interview.

Eye Weekly, http://www.eye.net/ (March 18, 1999).

ModernWorld, http://www.themodernword.com/ (March 26, 2004).

Salon, http://www.salon.com/ (July 6, 1999).*

*   *   *

KEMP, Kenny 1955-

PERSONAL: Born May 9, 1955, in San Diego, CA; son of Omer C. (a pharmacist) and Virginia T. (a homemaker) Kemp. *Ethnicity:* "White." *Education:* Brigham Young University, B.A., 1980, J.D., 1984.

Religion: Church of Jesus Christ of Latter-day Saints (Mormon). *Hobbies and other interests:* Filmmaking, composing music, flying, travel, art.

ADDRESSES: Home—3292 East Bengal Blvd., Salt Lake City, UT 84121; fax 801-943-7227. *E-mail*—kk@kennykemp.com.

CAREER: Attorney and author. Law Office of Kenneth O. Kemp, Salt Lake City, UT, attorney, 1984—. Also works as a building contractor.

AWARDS, HONORS: CINE Gold Eagle, Council on International Non-theatrical Events, 1995, Best of Fest, Breckenridge Film, 1995, NEMN Silver Apple, National Educational Media Network, 1996, Togetherness Award, Family Favorite Film Festival, 2000, and Children's Choice, American Library Association, 2000, all for short film *Fedora;* essay award, 1996, for *3/4 Inch Marine Ply;* Inspirational Fiction award, Independent Publisher, 1998, for *I Hated Heaven;* Grand Prize National Self-Published Book Awards, *Writer's Digest,* 1999, Best Nonfiction Audio Book, Independent Publisher's Association, 2000, and Best Memoir, Independent Publisher, 2000, all for *Dad Was a Carpenter.*

WRITINGS:

(And director) *Wildest Dreams* (short film), Alta Films Press (Salt Lake City, UT), 1987.

(And director) *Fedora* (short film), Alta Films Press (Salt Lake City, UT), 1995.

3/4 Inch Marine Ply (essay), Alta Films Press (Salt Lake City, UT), 1996.

I Hated Heaven (romance fiction), Alta Films Press, (Salt Lake City, UT), 1998.

Dad Was a Carpenter: A Memoir, Alta Films Press, (Salt Lake City, UT), 1999, published as *Dad Was a Carpenter: Blueprints for a Meaningful Life,* HarperSanFrancisco (San Francisco, CA), 2001.

The Welcoming Door: Parables of the Carpenter, HarperSanFrancisco (San Francisco, CA), 2002.

WORK IN PROGRESS: Hell Is 10,000 Cable Channels, a sequel to *I Hated Heaven;* second historical fiction in series of three, *City on a Hill.*

SIDELIGHTS: When asked about his beginnings as a writer, Kenny Kemp commented, "I took the long way around to finding a career in writing, though I've always been a storyteller. In college, I majored in film, but when it came time to go to Los Angeles, reason got the best of me and I opted for law school, which was fine if all I wanted to do was get an education, but once I was out, being a hired hand still didn't suit me."

Kemp's writing career began in 1987 with the production of *Wildest Dreams,* a short film that he both wrote and directed. While the film was nominated for a student Academy Award, it did not provide Kemp with the opportunity to break into the film industry. He decided to turn to writing instead, and self-published his first novel, *I Hated Heaven.* The book sold over twenty-thousand copies and was described as an "original, comic novel" by *Booklist* reviewer John Mort. *I Hated Heaven*'s success prompted Kemp to produce a memoir about his father called *Dad Was a Carpenter.* The book was awarded the Grand Prize in the 1999 *Writer's Digest* National Self-Published Book Awards. Kemp was offered a deal with HarperCollins and his book was reprinted in 2001.

Dad Was a Carpenter was lauded by critics for its inspirational story of a son reminiscing about his father. Writing for *Word Weaving,* Cindy Penn said, "This beautifully written story of father, a son, and the meaning of life must be read." She believed that "the subtle life lessons shared within will remain with the reader for a lifetime." *Library Journal* reviewer Douglas C. Lord described the novel as "a brief but beautiful love letter" written in "a frankly inspirational style."

Kemp's original vision for his next project was a picture book containing imagined stories about Jesus Christ as an adolescent experiencing the events that he later teaches about in the parables. The idea was reworked and published as *The Welcoming Door: Parables of the Carpenter,* the first novel in a series of three. Kemp considered this novel to be "the best work he's ever done." Critics also praised the novel. Shawna Saavedra Thorup of *Library Journal* compared the novel to Joseph Girzone's *Joshua,* commenting that readers who enjoyed *Joshua* "will appreciate the powerful storytelling and exceptional look at Jesus and His world." Although a reviewer for *Publishers Weekly,* remarked, "Turning these parables into actual stories anchors them to details, perhaps diluting their power as compact, versatile teaching tools," the reviewer maintained that Kemp's "far greater accomplishment is his characterization of a young Jesus. . . . Kemp creates a Jeshua who is human, who sometimes doubts himself, who becomes exhausted and frustrated, but who is the kind of man readers will wish they could work alongside of or have as a brother."

To aspiring writers and dreamers alike, Kemp offered the advice, "Lucky people are those who put themselves in luck's path; those who stay home are never lucky. Never give up. No one knows how far you'll need to go to succeed. The key to your dreams might be right around the next corner."

BIOGRAPHICAL AND CRITICAL SOURCES:

PERIODICALS

Booklist, August, 1998, John Mort, review of *I Hated Heaven,* p. 1965.
Library Journal, June 1, 2002, Douglas C. Lord, review of *Dad Was a Carpenter: Blueprints for a Meaningful Life,* p. 193; November 1, 2002, Shawna Saavedra Thorup, review of *The Welcoming Door: Parables of the Carpenter,* p. 74.
Publishers Weekly, September 30, 2002, review of *The Welcoming Door,* p. 49.
School Library Journal, December, 1998, Carol DeAngelo, review of *I Hated Heaven,* pp. 146-147.

ONLINE

Alta Films Web site, http://www.alta-films.com/ (March 10, 2003), reviews and description of *The Welcoming Door.*
Kenny's Studio (author's Web site), http://www.kennykemp.com/ (November 8, 2003).
WordWeaving, http://www.wordweaving.com/ (March 10,2003), Cindy Penn, review of *Dad Was a Carpenter,* and interview with Kemp.*

*　　*　　*

KENEALLY, Thomas (Michael) 1935-

PERSONAL: Born October 7, 1935, in Sydney, Australia; son of Edmund Thomas and Elsie Margaret (Coyle) Keneally; married Judith Martin, August 15, 1965; children: Margaret Ann, Jane Rebecca. *Education:* Attended St. Patrick's College, New South Wales.

Thomas Keneally

ADDRESSES: Agent—Curtis Brown, P.O. Box 19, Paddington, New South Wales 2021, Australia.

CAREER: Writer and journalist. Trained for priesthood (never ordained); high school teacher in Sydney, Australia, 1960-64; University of New England, New South Wales, Australia, lecturer in drama, 1968-70; New York University, New York, NY, inaugural Berg Professor, 1988; University of California, Irvine, School of Writing, visiting professor, 1985, distinguished professor 1991-95. Member of Australia-China Council, 1978-88; Australian Constitutional Committee, advisor, 1985-88; Literary Arts Board of Australia, member, 1985-88; Australian Republican Movement, chair, 1991-93, director, 1994—. Actor in films, including *The Devil's Playground,* 1976, and *The Chant of Jimmie Blacksmith,* 1978. *Military service:* Served in Australian Citizens Military Forces.

MEMBER: Australian Society of Authors (chair, 1987-90), National Book Council of Australia (president, 1985-90), PEN, Royal Society of Literature (fellow), American Academy of Arts and Sciences (fellow).

AWARDS, HONORS: Commonwealth Literary Fund fellowship, 1966, 1968, 1972; Miles Franklin Award, 1968, 1969; Captain Cook Bi-Centenary Prize, 1970; Heinemann Award, Royal Society of Literature, 1973, for *The Chant of Jimmie Blacksmith;* notable book citation, American Library Association, 1980, for *Confederates;* Booker McConnell Prize for Fiction, and fiction prize, *Los Angeles Times,* both 1982, both for *Schindler's List;* named Officer, Order of Australia, 1983.

WRITINGS:

NOVELS

The Place at Whitton, Cassell (London, England), 1964, Walker (New York, NY), 1965.
The Fear, Cassell (London, England), 1965.
Bring Larks and Heroes, Cassell (Melbourne, Australia), 1967, Viking Press (New York, NY), 1968.
Three Cheers for the Paraclete, Angus & Robertson (London, England), 1968, Viking Press (New York, NY), 1969.
The Survivor, Angus & Robertson (London, England), 1969, Viking Press (New York, NY), 1970.
A Dutiful Daughter, Viking Press (New York, NY), 1971.
The Chant of Jimmie Blacksmith, Viking Press (New York, NY), 1972.
Blood Red, Sister Rose: A Novel of the Maid of Orleans, Viking Press (New York, NY), 1974, published as *Blood Red, Sister Rose,* Collins (London, England), 1974.
Gossip from the Forest, Collins (London, England), 1975, Harcourt Brace (New York, NY), 1976.
Moses the Lawgiver, Harper (New York, NY), 1975.
Season in Purgatory, Collins (London, England), 1976, Harcourt Brace (New York, NY), 1977.
A Victim of the Aurora, Collins (London, England), 1977, Harcourt Brace (New York, NY), 1978.
Ned Kelly and the City of the Bees (juvenile), J. Cape (London, England), 1978, Penguin (New York, NY), 1980.
Passenger, Harcourt Brace (New York, NY), 1979.
Confederates, Collins (London, England), 1979, Harper (New York, NY), 1980.
The Cut-Rate Kingdom, Wildcat Press (Sydney, Australia), 1980.
Bullie's House, Currency Press (Sydney), 1981.
Schindler's List, Simon & Schuster (New York, NY), 1982, published as *Schindler's Ark,* Hodder & Stoughton (London, England), 1982.

A Family Madness, Hodder & Stoughton, 1985, Simon & Schuster (New York, NY), 1986.

The Playmaker, Simon & Schuster (New York, NY), 1987.

To Asmara: A Novel of Africa, Warner Books (New York, NY), 1989, published as *Towards Asmara,* Hodder & Stoughton (London, England), 1989.

By the Line, University of Queensland Press (St. Lucia, Queensland, Australia), 1989.

Flying Hero Class, Warner Books (New York, NY), 1991.

Woman of the Inner Sea, Hodder & Stoughton (London, England), 1992, Doubleday (Garden City, New York), 1993.

Jacko the Great Intruder, Hodder & Stoughton (London, England), 1994.

A River Town, Nan A. Talese (New York, NY), 1995.

Bettany's Book, Bantam (New York, NY), 1999.

An Angel in Australia, Doubleday (Sydney, Australia), 2002.

Office of Innocence: A Novel, Sceptre (London, England), 2002, Nan A. Talese (New York, NY), 2003.

NONFICTION

Outback, photographs by Gary Hansen and Mark Lang, Hodder & Stoughton (London, England and Sydney, Australia), 1983, Rand McNally (Chicago, IL), 1984.

(With Patsy Adam-Smith and Robyn Davidson) *Australia: Beyond the Dreamtime,* BBC Publications (London, England), 1987, Facts on File (New York, NY), 1989.

With Yellow Shoes, Prentice-Hall, 1992.

Now and in Time to Be: Ireland and the Irish, Norton (New York, NY), 1992.

The Place Where Souls Are Born: A Journey into the Southwest, Simon & Schuster (New York, NY), 1992, published as *The Place Where Souls Are Born: A Journey into the American Southwest,* Hodder & Stoughton (London, England), 1992.

Memoirs from a Young Republic, Heinemann (London, England), 1993.

Homebush Boy: A Memoir, Heinemann (London, England), 1995.

The Great Shame: A Story of the Irish in the Old World and the New, Random House (Milsons Point, New South Wales, Australia), 1998, published as *The Great Shame: And the Triumph of the Irish in the English-Speaking World,* Nan A. Talese (New York, NY), 1999.

American Scoundrel: The Life of the Notorious Civil War General Dan Sickles, Nan A. Talese (New York, NY), 2002, published as *American Scoundrel: Love, War and Politics in Civil War America,* Chatto & Windus (London, England), 2002.

Abraham Lincoln ("Penguin Lives" series), Lipper/Viking (New York, NY), 2003.

PLAYS

Halloran's Little Boat (produced in Sydney, 1966), published in *Penguin Australian Drama 2,* Penguin (Melbourne, Australia), 1975.

Childermass, produced in Sydney, 1968.

An Awful Rose, produced in Sydney, 1972.

Bullie's House (produced in Sydney, 1980; New Haven, CT, 1985), Currency Press (Sydney, Australia), 1981.

Writer for television, including *Essington* (play), 1974; *The World's Wrong End* (play), 1981; and *Australia* (series), 1987; contributor to screenplays, including *The Priest,* 1973, and *Silver City,* 1985; and to periodicals, including the *New York Times Book Review.*

Keneally's manuscripts are collected at the Mitchell Library, Sydney, and the Australian National Library, Canberra.

ADAPTATIONS: Schindler's List was adapted for film by Steven Zaillian for Amblin Entertainment, 1993.

SIDELIGHTS: Well known for his novel *Schindler's List,* which served as the basis for an award-winning motion picture in 1993, Thomas Keneally has become one of Australia's most distinguished authors. In works characterized by their sensitivity to style, their objectivity, their suspense, and diversity, this "honest workman"—as Raymond Sokolev called Keneally in the *New York Times*—has explored subjects as diverse as the history of his native Australia and war-torn Ethiopia.

While discussions of Keneally often emphasize his years spent as a seminary student, only one of his novels focuses directly on the subject. In *Three Cheers for the Paraclete,* his protagonist is a "doubting priest," Father James Maitland, who "runs afoul of the local taboos" in a Sydney seminary. As in many of his novels, Keneally presents his characters objectively and compassionately; priests and bishops are seen in the fullness of their humanity. Richard Sullivan wrote in the *Washington Post Book World,* "Though this admirably sustained novel makes it clear that some structures are too rigid, that the Church is not unflawed in its members, both clerical and lay, and that more windows need opening, at the same time it reveals with fine objectivity that it is human beings who are at fault, each in his own way, Maitland as much as any."

A similar example of Keneally's desire for objectivity is evident in his account of the St. Joan of Arc story *Blood Red, Sister Rose.* Bruce Cook of the *Washington Post Book World* claimed Keneally's "intent, in fact, seems to be to reduce her and her legend to recognizably human dimensions." Placing Keneally's Joan of Arc in a historical perspective, *Time*'s Melvin Maddocks saw her standing between the "Joan-too-spiritual" of the original legend and the "Joan-too-earthy" of George Bernard Shaw. She is "less spectacular than the first two but decidedly more convincing and perhaps, at last, more moving."

Perhaps Keneally's most ambitious historical novel is *Confederates,* set during the American Civil War and told from a Southern perspective. The book has no central character, but rather focuses on a group of characters who are involved in the preparations for the Second Battle of Antietam, fought in 1862. Keneally "keeps his canvas as vast as possible," wrote John Higgins in the *Times Literary Supplement,* "and his concern is as much with the conscripts as with the captains; the volunteers get just as large a show as the likes of Robert E. Lee and Stonewall Jackson."

Several critics found that Keneally's portrayal of the American South is surprisingly realistic. Jeffrey Burke of the *New York Times Book Review,* for example, wrote that it "is almost necessary to remind oneself that the author is Australian, so naturally, intrinsically Southern is the narrative voice." Robert Ostermann of the *Detroit News* stated that Keneally's account of the Second Battle of Antietam "deserves comparison . . . to Tolstoy's rendering of the Russian defeat and retreat at Borodino and to Hemingway's of the retreat from Caporetto in *Farewell to Arms,*" and added that "the fact that this massive, absorbing narrative is the work of an Australian—not a Southerner, not even a native American—testifies even further to the stature of his achievement."

With the publication of *Schindler's List,* published in England as *Schindler's Ark,* Keneally found himself embroiled in a controversy over whether his book was fiction or nonfiction, an important point since the book was nominated for England's prestigious Booker McConnell Prize for fiction. Although the story of Oskar Schindler, a German industrialist during World War II who saved the Jews assigned to work in his factory from Nazi gas chambers, is historical truth, Keneally wrote the book as a novel. "The craft of the novelist," Keneally explained in the London *Times,* "is the only craft to which I can lay claim, and . . . the novel's techniques seem suited for a character of such ambiguity and magnitude as Oskar [Schindler.]" After deliberation, the judges deemed the work a novel and awarded it the Booker Prize in 1982.

The controversy over *Schindler's List* is understandable. As Richard F. Shepard pointed out in the *New York Times,* the real-life story of Oskar Schindler "is indeed stranger than fiction." The owner of a German armaments factory staffed with forced Jewish laborers from nearby concentration camps, Schindler made a fortune during the war by supplying the German army with war materials. But when the Nazi regime decided to solve the "Jewish question" through mass extermination of Jewish prisoners, Schindler acted to save as many of his workers as possible. He convinced the local S.S. chief to allow him to house his Jewish workers in a compound built on his factory grounds rather than at a concentration camp "so that their labor [could] be more fully exploited," as Schindler explained it. Through the use of bribes and favors, Schindler worked to reunite his workers with their families, provided them with adequate food and medical care, and even managed to get a particularly murderous S.S. officer transferred to the Russian front. When the Russian army threatened to capture the area of southern Poland where Schindler's factory was located—and the German army made plans to execute the Jewish workers before retreating—Schindler moved his company and his workers to safety in German-held Czechoslovakia. By the end of the war, Schindler had some thirteen hundred Jewish workers under his protection—far more than he needed to operate his factory—and had spent his entire fortune on bribes and favors.

Critical reaction to *Schindler's List* was generally favorable. Keneally, wrote Christopher Lehmann-Haupt in the *New York Times,* "does not attempt to analyze in detail whatever made Oskar Schindler tick," which the reviewer found "a little disconcerting, considering the novelistic technique he employs to tell his story. But this restraint increases the book's narrative integrity. Because the story doesn't try to do what it can't honestly do, we trust all the more what it does do." Jonathan Yardley of the *Washington Post Book World* felt that the book's major flaw is "the author's insistence on employing devices of the 'new' journalism. . . . But *Schindler's List* has about it a strong, persuasive air of authenticity, and as an act of homage it is a most emphatic and powerful document." Phillip Howard of the London *Times* agreed, saying that "the book is a brilliantly detailed piece of historical reporting. It is moving, it is powerful, it is gripping."

In *A Family Madness,* Keneally again returns to World War II, this time exploring its repercussions upon later generations. The book was inspired by a real-life tragedy in Sydney during the summer of 1984, in which a family of five willingly ended their lives. The author's rugby-playing protagonist, Terry Delaney, goes to work for a security firm owned by a Byelorussian named Rudi Kabbel. Haunted by traumatic memories of his childhood in Russia during the war and his father's wartime journals, which reveal countless horrors inflicted upon his family, Kabbel is mentally unstable. When Delaney, who is married, falls in love with Kabbel's daughter and fathers her child, the Kabbel family closes ranks—not only against Delaney but against the world. As Blake Morrison explained in the London *Observer,* "They sell up the business, surround themselves with heavy weaponry, and wait for the new dawn."

Writing in the *Times Literary Supplement,* Michael Wood said, *A Family Madness* conveys the idea that "even here, in this comfort-loaded and forward-looking Australia, history will get you one way or another." Wood praised the novel, calling it "an ambitious and successful book that makes connections we need to think about." John Sutherland of the *London Review of Books,* lauded the novel as "better than its applauded predecessor [*Schindler's List*]" and noted that the nobility of the characters makes a genuine claim on the reader. However, in a review for the *New York Times Book Review,* Robert Towers criticized Keneally's characterization, writing that "the lack of an adequately realized psychological dimension" in the character of Rudi Kabbel "is . . . crippling to the novel's aspirations."

With the publication of *To Asmara: A Novel of Africa,* as with *Schindler's List,* Keneally found himself once again accused of writing, not a novel, but an impassioned journalistic tribute. A fictionalized portrayal of the brutal African guerilla warfare of the 1980s, *To Asmara* focuses on the Eritrean Peoples Liberation Front's struggle to break free from an Ethiopia dominated by tyrants. Assisted by Russian military aid, the Ethiopian army was permitted to commit a form of genocide against the Eritreans, in the course of which Ethiopian troops destroyed the beautiful ancient city of Asmara.

Protagonist and narrator Tim Darcy is an Australian freelance journalist on "loose assignment" from the London *Times,* "one of those tentative, self-despising dreamers drawn to the empty quarters and violent margins of the West's known world," according to Robert Stone in the *New York Times Book Review.* Stone had high praise for both the character of Darcy and the novel as a whole: "Not since *For Whom the Bell Tolls* has a book of such sophistication, the work of a major international novelist, spoken out so unambiguously on behalf of an armed struggle." In contrast, Andrew Jaffe, reviewing the book for the *Los Angeles Times Book Review,* took issue with Keneally's advocacy of the Eritrean cause. Jaffe wrote, "The nobility of the rebels shouldn't be the concern of the novelist. His job is to sketch an intriguing story against an exotic backdrop. Keneally forgot to leave his commitment to the cause behind in Port Sudan."

Keneally uncharacteristically moves away from the sweeping panoramas of his earlier fiction and limits the action to the confines of one airplane in *Flying Hero Class.* Frank McCloud, tour manager for a troupe of Australian aboriginal dancers, finds himself involved in a hijacking on a flight from New York to Frankfurt following the troupe's performance. Describing *Flying Hero Class* as a "thoughtful and exciting novel," Richard Lipez pointed out in the *Washington Post Book World* that Keneally examines with ease two complex issues: the issue of Israeli security versus Palestinian justice and the issue of the territorial rights of the Australian aboriginal tribe versus U.S. and international mining interests. Although finding some fault with the novel, Edward Hower of the *New York Times Book Review* shared Lipez's positive opinion. "Keneally's people are fascinating, and so are the ideas his plot generates, making the hijacking a metaphor for the complex relationship between the West and the third world peoples deprived of land and dignity," Hower stated, ending his review with the conclusion that "*Flying Hero Class* gives original insights into the way one man learns to reclaim responsibility for his own fate."

With *Woman of the Inner Sea,* Keneally returns to his native Australian turf and bases his plot on a real-life incident. In the work, Kate Gaffney-Kozinski, wife of a wealthy construction-empire scion, loses her husband to another woman, and her two precious children to the fire that levels the family's expensive beach home near Sydney. In an effort to forget, Kate boards a train for the interior. The place Kate chooses for her "self-annihilation" is Myambagh, a town built on the hard, flat rock of what was once an immense inland sea. Donna Rifkind, in the *Los Angeles Times Book Review,* wrote that the Australian outback, "with its miles of empty red earth, stringybark and eucalyptus, savage storms and eccentric wildlife, represents more than just external landscape . . . the fluid unpredictability of the land also mirrors Kate's transformation."

In commending the novel, Rifkind wrote that in "the tragedy of her dead children and her subsequent pilgrimage, Kate represents a nation on a perpetual search for reinvention, a nation hardened by countless histories of hunger, tough luck and untimely death." Susan Fromberg Schaeffer echoed Rifkind's praise in the *New York Times Book Review,* commenting that "*Woman of the Inner Sea* succeeds on many fronts. It is a picaresque and often hilarious adventure story, recounting one woman's unforgettable if improbable travels. It is a series of love stories . . . and it is a mystery story as well. But the novel is also very much an exploration of ethics."

Drawing on his family background again, Keneally's novel *River Town* is based on his Irish grandparents' immigration to Australia. In *River Town,* Keneally relates the experiences of a turn-of-the-century Irishman, Tim Shea, who immigrates to Australia when he tires of the confining mores of his own country. While happy to be rid of the restraints he experienced in Ireland, Tim discovers through a series of adverse events many of the same problems with the social conventions of the Australian frontier. In his new hometown of Kempsey, New South Wales, Tim becomes a community hero when he rescues two children from a cart accident. Shortly after, he finds himself being ostracized by the same community for his opposi-

tion to the Boer War—a position which ends in near economic disaster for Tim and his family when town members boycott his general store. As unfortunate events continue to plague Tim, he uncovers more of the very same social conventions he had hoped to leave behind in Ireland.

In general, critics were impressed with *River Town.* "This is truly a compassionate novel, full of vividly portrayed outcasts," wrote reviewer David Willis McCullough in the *New York Times Book Review,* noting the characters are "outsiders in a nation of outsiders who are only beginning to define themselves in their new home, people who thought that 'if they traveled 12,000 miles, they might outrun original sin.'" Also finding the novel full of compassion and featuring a well-depicted historical background, a *Publishers Weekly* contributor concluded that "the story is haunting because it is both commonplace and universal. Keneally looks clearly at moral rot, but he is cautiously optimistic about the survival of good people and the uplifting heritage they bequeath." "Keneally has marvelous descriptive powers," said *Detroit News* reviewer Barbara Holiday, who praised the author's ability to "[bring] the community alive." Holiday summarized, "Keneally has written an absorbing homespun account of ordinary people who are heroic in spite of themselves."

While reviews of his fiction have been generally favorable, several of Keneally's works of nonfiction have been received with less enthusiasm. In *Now and in Time to Be: Ireland and the Irish,* for example, the author attempts to describe the land of his grandparents. In the *New York Times Book Review* Katharine Weber wrote that "dazzled by his adventure" in Ireland, Keneally fails to discern what is significant and what is not. Reviewing Keneally's study of Australian independence, titled *Memoirs from a Young Republic,* for the *Observer,* Peter Conrad cited the author's carelessness, writing that, "Grammar and syntax frequently slump out of control." Many critics would agree that the novel is Keneally's forte. His impressive body of fiction, as Schaffer wrote in the *New York Times Book Review,* "makes convincing the very serious belief that each of us has a necessary place—and that our most important task is to find it."

Keneally's later nonfiction works received considerable praise, however. *The Great Shame: A Story of the Irish in the Old World and the New,* published in the

United States as *The Great Shame: And the Triumph of the Irish in the English-Speaking World,* was praised by Mary Elizabeth Williams in a review for *Salon. com.* Williams considered the book compelling because of "the smoothness with which the author moves around the globe. Observing both the rooted and the scattered, he shows not just how the outside world affected the Irish, but also how the Irish changed the world." Williams called Keneally's "greatest gift . . . his flair for molding real events into memorable narratives, in the smart turns of phrase that draw the reader into the action."

One of the figures in *The Great Shame* gets his own book with *American Scoundrel: The Life of the Notorious Civil War General Dan Sickles. Times Literary Supplement* reviewer Benjamin Markovits called Sickles "a characteristic object of Keneally's curiosity, a man, like Oskar Schindler, who exhibited the often uneasy relation between public and private virtues. Sickles, again like Schindler, excelled at the particulars of political life, at details and connections—like Keneally himself, whose talents as a writer reflect the qualities that draw him to his subjects."

Biographies of Abraham Lincoln abound, but in Keneally's *Abraham Lincoln* he touches on undocumented moments, and as *New York Times Book Review* contributor David Walton noted, "the droll and unusual image." Walton called this an "excellent brief biography."

A *Kirkus Reviews* contributor called Keneally's look at Lincoln "so fresh that one wishes only that the 'Penguin Lives' format afforded Keneally room to say more about this iconic leader. Exemplary and illuminating, even for readers well-versed in Lincolniana."

BIOGRAPHICAL AND CRITICAL SOURCES:

BOOKS

Contemporary Literary Criticism, Gale (Detroit), Volume 27, 1984, pp. 231-234, Volume 43, 1987, pp. 229-237, Volume 117, 1999, pp. 207-252.

Contemporary Novelists, St. James Press (Detroit, MI), 2001.

Encyclopedia of World Literature in the Twentieth Century, St. James Press (Detroit, MI), 1999.

Keneally, Thomas, *Homebush Boy: A Memoir,* Heinemann (London, England), 1995.

Pierce, Peter, *Australian Melodramas: Thomas Keneally's Fiction,* University of Queensland Press (Queensland, Australia), 1995.

Quartermaine, Peter, *Thomas Keneally,* Edward Arnold (London, England), 1992.

PERIODICALS

Chicago Tribune Book World, December 20, 1980; November 14, 1982.

Detroit News, September 28, 1980; November 21, 1982; May 21, 1995, p. 8J.

Kirkus Reviews, March 15, 1971; July 1, 1972; February 1, 1976; November 1, 1976; November 1, 2002, review of *Abraham Lincoln,* p. 1591.

Library Journal, February 15, 1995, pp. 122-124; March 1, 1997, p. 87.

London Review of Books, November 7, 1985, pp. 24-26.

Los Angeles Times Book Review, October 15, 1989, pp. 2, 13; May 16, 1993, p. 7.

Nation, November 6, 1972.

National Review, April 29, 1977.

New Statesman, September 1, 1972; October 26, 1973; October 11, 1974; September 19, 1975; September 3, 1976; September 9, 1978; January 19, 1979; November 2, 1979; September 29, 1985; September 12, 1993.

Newsweek, April 19, 1976; February 7, 1977; June 18, 1979.

New Yorker, February 10, 1975; August 23, 1976; May 23, 1977; May 8, 1978; May 19, 1986, pp. 118-119.

New York Times, April 4, 1970; September 9, 1972; October 18, 1982; November 22, 1982.

New York Times Book Review, September 27, 1970; September 12, 1971; January 16, 1972; August 27, 1972; December 3, 1972; February 9, 1975; April 11, 1976; February 27, 1977; October 14, 1977; March 26, 1978; July 8, 1979; October 5, 1980; September 20, 1987, pp. 7, 9; October 1, 1989, pp. 1, 42; April 7, 1991, p. 9; April 26, 1992, p. 12; April 18, 1993, p. 9; March 16, 1986; April 19, 1992; April 26, 1992, p. 22; May 14, 1995, p. 12; April 14, 2002, Kevin Baker, review of *American Scoundrel: Love, War and Politics in Civil War America,* p. 11; January 19, 2003, David Walton, review of *Abraham Lincoln,* p. 21.

Observer, April 25, 1971; September 10, 1971; November 24, 1974; September 21, 1975; December 14, 1975; September 5, 1976; September 4, 1977; January 21, 1979; October 21, 1979; September 29, 1985, p. 23; September 6, 1987, p. 25; March 10, 1991, p. 60; July 19, 1992, p. 58; September 12, 1993, p. 53.

Publishers Weekly, January 18, 1983, p. 447; August 7, 1987, p. 434; January 6, 1992, p. 60; January 30, 1995, p. 84; April 3, 1995, p. 40.

Spectator, March 1, 1968; November 25, 1972; September 7, 1974; November 15, 1975; September 4, 1976; September 3, 1977.

Time, May 15, 1995, p. 80.

Times (London, England), August 16, 1968; June 7, 1971; August 28, 1972; February 10, 1975; March 7, 1981; October 20, 1982; October 21, 1982.

Times Literary Supplement, May 7, 1970; April 23, 1971; September 15, 1972; October 26, 1973; October 11, 1974; September 19, 1975; September 3, 1976; October 14, 1977; November 2, 1979; November 23, 1979; October 18, 1985, p. 1169; October 20, 1989, p. 1147; January 29, 1993, p. 28; March 18, 1994, p. 13; May 24, 2002, Benjamin Markovits, review of *American Scoundrel.*

Washington Post Book World, April 27, 1969; April 19, 1970; August 29, 1971; August 13, 1972; January 26, 1975; February 20, 1977; March 26, 1978; August 31, 1980; October 4, 1981; October 20, 1982; March 24, 1991, p. 8.

West Coast Review of Books, July, 1978.

World Literature Today, winter, 1977; autumn, 1978; spring, 1980; autumn, 1996, p. 1025.

ONLINE

Salon.com, http://www.salon.com/ (September 13, 1999), Mary Elizabeth Williams, review of *The Great Shame: And the Triumph of the Irish in the English-Speaking World.*

*   *   *

KNELMAN, Martin 1943-

PERSONAL: Born June 17, 1943, in Winnipeg, Manitoba, Canada; son of John M. (an insurance executive) and Marion (Medovy) Knelman; married Bernadette Sulgit (managing editor of *Saturday Night*), June 12, 1975; children: Joshua Medovy, Sara. *Education:* University of Manitoba, B.A., 1964, B.A. (with honors), 1967; University of Toronto, M.A., 1972.

ADDRESSES: Home and office—224 Robert St., Toronto, Ontario M5S 2K7, Canada. *E-mail*—martknel@ idirect.com.

CAREER: Manitoban, Winnipeg, Manitoba, Canada, editor, 1963-64; *Globe & Mail,* Toronto, Ontario, copy editor and reporter, 1964-66; *Toronto Star,* Toronto, Ontario, film critic, 1967-69; entertainment columnist, 1999—; *Globe & Mail,* film critic, 1969-76; freelance writer, 1973—; lecturer at York University, 1970-73.

MEMBER: Periodical Writers Association of Canada.

AWARDS, HONORS: Senior arts fellowship from Canada Council, 1973-74; Nathan Cohen Award for Drama Criticism, 1982, 1989, 1995; Imperial Oil Award for Arts Journalism, 1992; White Award for Journalism, 1993.

WRITINGS:

This Is Where We Came In: The Career and Character of Canadian Film, McClelland & Stewart (Toronto, Ontario, Canada), 1977.

A Stratford Tempest, McClelland & Stewart (Toronto, Ontario, Canada), 1982.

Laughing on the Outside: The Life of John Candy, St. Martin's Press (New York, NY), 1997.

The Joker Is Wild: The Trials and Triumphs of Jim Carrey, Penguin Putnam (New York, NY), 1999.

Mike's World: The Life of Mike Myers, Penguin (Toronto, Ontario, Canada), 2002, Firefly Books (Buffalo, NY), 2003.

Author of columns, including a theatre column in *Saturday Night,* 1975—, a film column in *Toronto Life,* 1976-94, and "O Canada" in *Weekend,* 1976-77. Frequent contributor to *Financial Post,* 1989-99. Contributor to magazines, including *Weekend, Atlantic Monthly,* and *Maclean's.*

SIDELIGHTS: Canadian journalist and author Martin Knelman has made a successful career writing about Canadian film and biographies of Canada's funniest men. With his background as a film critic and arts and entertainment columnist for the *Toronto Star* and *Globe & Mail*, Knelman has been able to draw on a wide array of materials to assist him in writing about Canada's cinematic history in *This Is Where We Came In: The Career and Character of Canadian Film*. Following his general studies on film, Knelman has written several unauthorized biographies of Canadian funnymen, including John Candy, Jim Carrey, and Mike Myers.

John Candy, the SCTV comedian who appeared in over forty films and died an untimely death at age forty-three, is the subject of Knelman's *Laughing on the Outside: The Life of John Candy*. *Booklist* reviewer Mike Tribby commented that though Knelman found many sad and dark elements in Candy's life, "he focuses on the comedy." He added that Knelman made what is ultimately a sad story "sympathetic and memorable, too." *Maclean's* contributor Morton Ritts also felt *Laughing on the Outside* is a sympathetic biography, but he concluded that ultimately, "the reader is left with a two-dimensional impression of a three-dimensional man."

The career of actor Jim Carrey is the subject of Knelman's *The Joker Is Wild: The Trials and Triumphs of Jim Carrey*. The book chronicles Carrey's rise from his humble and often difficult childhood, to his time as a stand-up comic in Toronto, to his meteoric star status in Hollywood. *Winston-Salem Journal* reviewer Mark Burger noted that Knelman relied primarily on "a seemingly endless collection" of published interviews for his information, and that he "can't be accused of not doing his homework." Knelman explores how the young, misfit Carrey felt out of place dragged onto the Toronto nightclub scene as a boy by his father. *Toronto Sun* critic Jim Slotek suggested "that alienation may have laid the groundwork for the eventual sea-change in [Carrey's] career, where he began to explore darker comic impulses."

Mike's World: The Life of Mike Myers is Knelman's unauthorized biography of a Canadian comic who hit the big time in Hollywood with such films as *Wayne's World* and the Austin Powers series. *Quill & Quire* reviewer Keith Garebian observed that the book's title is somewhat misleading as the narrative offers a "hasty introduction to Myers's Scarborough upbringing and comedy apprenticeship," then "focuses almost exclusively on the films." Knelman does argue that Myers's reputation for being difficult is unwarranted.

BIOGRAPHICAL AND CRITICAL SOURCES:

PERIODICALS

Booklist, September 1, 1997, Mike Tribby, review of *Laughing on the Outside: The Life of John Candy,* p. 49.

Entertainment Weekly, October 17, 1997, Katherine Hazelwood, review of *Laughing on the Outside,* p. 68.

Library Journal, June 15, 2000, Kelli Perkins, review of *The Joker Is Wild: The Trials and Triumphs of Jim Carrey,* p. 85.

Maclean's, December 23, 1996, Morton Ritts, review of *Laughing on the Outside,* p. 79.

Quill & Quire, September, 2002, Keith Garebian, review of *Mike's World: The Life of Mike Myers,* p. 55.

Winston-Salem Journal, October 1, 2000, Mark Burger, review of *The Joker Is Wild,* p. A20.

ONLINE

Jam! Showbiz Web site, http://Jam.canoe.ca/ (December 19, 1999), Jim Slotek, review of *The Joker Is Wild.*

*   *   *

KREMER, Marcie
   See SORENSON, Margo

*   *   *

KRETZMER, Herbert 1925-

PERSONAL: Born October 5, 1925, in Kroonstad, South Africa; son of William and Tilly Kretzmer; married Elisabeth Margaret Wilson, December 20, 1960 (divorced, 1973); married Sybil Sever, 1988; children: Danielle, Matthew. *Education:* Attended Rhodes University, Grahamstown, South Africa.

ADDRESSES: Home—Flat 55, Lincoln House, Basil St., London SW3 1AW, England. *Office*—Daily Mail, Tudor St., London EC4, England. *Agent*—London Management, Noel House, 2/4 Noel St., London W1V 3RB, England.

Herbert Kretzmer

CAREER: African Film Productions, Johannesburg, South Africa, wrote weekly cinema newsreel commentaries and documentary films, 1946; *Sunday Express,* Johannesburg, journalist, 1951-54; *Daily Sketch,* London, England, feature writer and columnist, 1954-59; *Sunday Dispatch,* London, columnist, 1959-61; *Daily Express,* London, journalist, 1960-62, drama critic and feature writer, 1962-78; *Daily Mail,* London, television critic, 1979-87.

MEMBER: Royal Automobile Club.

AWARDS, HONORS: Ivor Novello Award, 1960, for song "Goodness Gracious Me"; award from American Society of Composers, Authors and Publishers (AS-CAP), 1969, for song "Yesterday When I Was Young"; gold record, 1974, for "She"; Tony Award, 1987, and Grammy Award, 1988, for *Les Misérables*; television critic of the year award from Phillips Industries, 1980; Honorary Doctorate of Letters, Richmond College, American International University, London, England, 1996; Jimmy Kennedy Award, British Academy of Songwriters, Composers, and Authors, 1989.

WRITINGS:

Our Man Crichton (play; first produced on the West End at Shaftesbury Theatre, December, 1964), Hodder & Stoughton, 1965.
(With Milton Shulman) *Every Home Should Have One* (novel), Hodder & Stoughton, 1980.

Author of song lyrics for plays, including English version of *Les Misérables,* 1985, and *The Four Musketeers.* Also author of lyrics for films, including *Hieronymus Merkin.* and *Les Misérables.* Writer for television programs, including *That Was the Week That Was.*

SIDELIGHTS: Herbert Kretzmer is a former drama critic for British newspapers who turned to writing adaptations and lyrics later in life. He is best known for writing the lyrics to the English version of *Les Misérables.*

Kretzmer began his journalism career writing a commentary for a weekly cinema newsreel. He also worked as a feature writer before moving to London in 1954. He joined the London *Daily Express* in 1960 and later became the drama critic, a position he held for eighteen years. Kretzmer covered more than three thousand first nights and garnered many awards for his work. He turned to television criticism in 1979 when he accepted a job for the *Daily Mail.* For this criticism, he was awarded two national press awards.

Kretzmer wrote the book and lyrics to adaptations for the musical stage. His first was *The Admirable Crichton.* He wrote both the lyrics and the play for *Our Man Crichton,* performed in the Shaftesbury Theatre in 1964 and starring Millicent Martin and Kenneth More and the lyrics for *The Four Muskateers,* featuring Harry Secombe and performed in Drury Lane in 1967. During this time, Kretzmer also wrote many songs for stars, including "Goodness Gracious Me," which won the Ivor Novello Award and was sung by Peter Sellers and Sophia Loren.

Kretzmer's thirty-year partnership with French sensation Charles Aznavour resulted in songs such as "Yesterday When I Was Young," "Happy Anniversary," and the very popular, "She," which first topped the charts in 1974. In a confession to a reporter for the *Evening Chronicle,* Kretzmer admitted a past romance inspired him to write the song. "In the summer of 1973 I enjoyed what you might call a luminous romance with a delightful woman, a Geordie," he recalled. "When we split up, I remember saying to her in a pub on the Kings Road: 'There'll be a song in this one day.' Six months later, when I was offered 'She,' she was very much in my mind when I was describing the personal attributes of a woman." Kretzmer has never revealed the identity of the woman, but noted that both he and the woman are now married to other people. "She" enjoyed renewed success when it was re-recorded by Elvis Costello for the movie *Notting Hill,* released in 1999, starring Julia Roberts and Hugh Grant. Writing for the *Independent on Sunday,* Stuart Husband noted that Kretzmer "wasn't invited to mingle with Hugh, Julia, Liz and Co." Husband considered this "an astonishing oversight, given that he wrote the lyrics for the movie's theme song." Kretzmer told Husband he was pleased with the remake of "She." "They haven't messed with it. It's a heartfelt song, and Costello plays it straight," he said.

It was Kretzmer's collaborations with Aznavour that caught the attention of Carmeron Mackintosh, who invited Kretzmer to write an English version of the French musical *Les Misérables,* based on the novel by Victor Hugo. *Les Misérables* was Kretzmer's greatest success. *Les Misérables* tells the story of Jean Valjean, who steals a loaf of bread and is then condemned to prison and life on the run. In time Valjean is forgiven of his crimes and becomes the mayor of a poor town, which he transforms into a prosperous community. He falls in love with a beautiful, but poverty-stricken woman in the town. After her death, he raises her daughter, Cosette, and devotes his life to keeping her out of harm's way. In a *NYTheatre.com* review, Martin Denton said this about the prologue: "In ten deft, remarkable minutes, Nunn & Card and authors Claude-Michel Schonger, Alain Boublil, and Herbert Kretzmer provide economical exposition and set forth the major themes of their show; they also introduce their simple epic story theatre format and all of the important musical motifs that define *Les Misérables.*" Kretzmer extended the original musical from two to three hours. It opened in the Barbican Theatre, London, England, in 1985. Since then, it has been seen by more then forty-three million people.

BIOGRAPHICAL AND CRITICAL SOURCES:

BOOKS

Encyclopedia of the Musical Theatre 2nd edition, Schirmer Books (New York, NY), 2001.

PERIODICALS

Evening Chronicle, October 18, 2003, "She Was a Geordie," p. 13.
Guardian, "The Guide: Sound Bites," p. 67.
Independent on Sunday, Stuart Husband, "The Real Heroine of *Notting Hill* the Film's Soundtrack, 'She,' Could Be This Summer's Hit, but Who Inspired It?," May 2, 1999, p.4.
South Wales Echo, October 15, 2002, "Amazing Story of Musical: Do You Hear the Students Sing?," p. 11.
Sunday Telegraph, December 8, 2002, "Black Notes."

ONLINE

NYTheatre.com, http://www.Nytheatre.com/ (February 19, 2004).*

* * *

KUSHNER, Tony 1956-

PERSONAL: Born July 16, 1956, in New York, NY. *Education:* Columbia University, B.A., 1978; New York University, M.F.A., 1984.

ADDRESSES: Office—Walter Kerr Theatre, 225 West 48th St., New York, NY 10036. *Agent*—Joyce Ketay Agency, 1501 Broadway, Ste. 1908, New York, NY 10036.

CAREER: United Nations Plaza Hotel, New York, NY, switchboard operator, 1979-85; St. Louis Repertory Theatre, St. Louis, MO, assistant director, 1985-86; New York Theatre Workshop, New York, artistic director, 1987-88; Theatre Communication Group, New York, director of literary services, 1990-91; Juilliard School of Drama, New York, playwright-in-residence, 1990-92. Guest artist at New York University Graduate Theatre Program, Yale University, and Princeton University, beginning 1989.

MEMBER: AIDS Coalition to Unleash Power (ACT UP).

Tony Kushner

AWARDS, HONORS: Directing fellowship, National Endowment for the Arts, 1985, 1987, and 1993; Princess Grace Award, 1986; playwriting fellowship, New York State Council for the Arts, 1987; John Whiting Award, Arts Council of Great Britain, 1990; Kennedy Center/American Express Fund for New American Plays Awards, 1990 and 1992; Kesserling Award, National Arts Club, 1992; Will Glickman playwriting prize, 1992; London *Evening Standard* Award, 1992; Pulitzer Prize for drama, Antoinette Perry Award ("Tony") for best play, and New York Drama Critics Circle Award for Best New Play, all 1993, all for *Millennium Approaches*, Part One of *Angels in America*; American Academy of Arts and Letters Award, 1994; Tony Award for best play, 1994, for *Perestroika*, Part Two of *Angels in America*; Lambda Literary Award, Drama, 1994, for *Angels in America;* Lambda Literary Award, Lesbian and Gay Drama, 1996, for *Thinking about the Longstanding Problems of Virtue and Happiness: Essays, a Play, Two Poems, and a Prayer; Village Voice* Obie Award, 2002, for *Homebody/Kabul.*

WRITINGS:

PLAYS

Yes, Yes, No, No (juvenile; produced in St. Louis, MO, 1985), published in *Plays in Process,* 1987.

Stella (adapted from the play by Johann Wolfgang von Goethe), produced in New York, NY, 1987.

A Bright Room Called Day (produced in San Francisco, CA, 1987), Broadway Play Publishing, 1991.

Hydriotaphia, produced in New York, NY, 1987.

The Illusion (adapted from Pierre Corneille's play *L'Illusion comique;* produced in New York, NY, 1988, revised version produced in Hartford, CT, 1990), Broadway Play Publishing, 1991.

(With Ariel Dorfman) *Widows* (adapted from a book by Ariel Dorfman), produced in Los Angeles, CA, 1991.

Angels in America: A Gay Fantasia on National Themes, Part One: *Millennium Approaches* (produced in San Francisco, 1991), Hern, 1992, Part Two: *Perestroika,* produced in New York, NY, 1992.

A Bright Room Called Day, Theatre Communications Group (New York, NY), 1994.

Angels in America: A Gay Fantasia on National Themes (includes both parts; produced as two-part television film on Home Box Office, 2003), Theatre Communications Group (New York, NY), 1995.

Slavs! Thinking about the Longstanding Problems of Virtue and Happiness, Theatre Communications Group (New York, NY), 1995.

A Dybbuk; or, Between Two Worlds (adapted from Joachim Neugroschel's translation of the original play by S. Ansky; produced in New York, NY, at Joseph Papp Public Theater, 1997), Theatre Communications Group (New York, NY), 1997.

The Good Person of Szechuan (adapted from the original play by Bertolt Brecht), Arcade, 1997.

(With Eric Bogosian and others) *Love's Fire: Seven New Plays Inspired by Seven Shakespearean Sonnets,* Morrow (New York, NY), 1998.

Henry Box Brown, or the Mirror of Slavery, performed at Royal National Theatre, London, 1998.

Homebody/Kabul, (produced in New York, NY, 2001), Theatre Communications Group (New York, NY), 2002.

Caroline or Change (musical), produced in New York, NY, at Joseph Papp Public Theater, 2002.

OTHER

A Meditation from Angels in America, HarperSanFrancisco (San Francisco, CA), 1994.

Tony Kushner in Conversation, edited by Robert Vorlicky, University of Michigan Press (Ann Arbor, MI), 1997.

Death and Taxes: Hydriotaphia, and Other Plays, Theatre Communications Group (New York, NY), 2000.

Brundibar, illustrated by Maurice Sendak, Michael di Capua/Hyperion Books for Children (New York, NY), 2002.

SIDELIGHTS: Playwright Tony Kushner took the theater world by storm in the early 1990s with his epic drama, *Angels in America: A Gay Fantasia on National Themes.* A seven-hour play in two separate parts, *Millennium Approaches* and *Perestroika, Angels in America* explores in uncompromising terms what it was like to be gay and affected by AIDS (acquired immunodeficiency syndrome) during the 1980s and 1990s. Despite its grim subject matter and open attacks on the administration of former U.S. President Ronald Reagan, the play has proved quite popular with mainstream audiences from Broadway to Los Angeles and London. It has also won great acclaim from drama critics, garnering both the Pulitzer Prize for drama and two Antoinette Perry ("Tony") awards for best play in 1993 and 1994.

Kushner was born in New York City in 1956, but his parents, who were classical musicians, moved to Lake Charles, Louisiana, shortly after his birth. His parents encouraged Kushner and his siblings to explore literature and the arts; the children were given a dollar whenever they had memorized a poem to recite. His mother was also an actress, and Kushner confided to Susan Cheever in the *New York Times* that "that's the major reason I went into the theater. I saw some of her performances when I was four or five years old and they were so powerful. I had vivid dreams afterwards." Kushner realized he was different from most other children in yet another significant way, however. "I have fairly clear memories of being gay since I was six," the playwright told Richard Stayton in the *Los Angeles Times.* "I knew that I felt slightly different than most of the boys I was growing up with. By the time I was eleven there was no doubt. But I was completely in the closet."

He continued to keep his sexuality a secret throughout his undergraduate years at Columbia University, during which time he underwent psychotherapy trying to become heterosexual, even though his therapist told him at the beginning of treatment that psychotherapy did not change people's sexual orientation. Kushner eventually accepted this and "came out," meaning he told his family and friends that he was gay.

Kushner's early plays, however, did not focus on gay themes. *A Bright Room Called Day,* perhaps the best-known of his pre-*Angels* works, concerns a group of liberal-minded acquaintances in the Weimar Republic of Germany, just before the establishment of Adolf Hitler's Nazi regime. M. Elizabeth Osborn described the plot in *Contemporary Dramatists,* saying, this "circle of friends disintegrates under the pressures of Hitler's rise to power, one after another forced into hiding or exile until just one woman, Agnes, is left cowering in her apartment." This main story is entwined, however, with the commentary of Zillah Katz, a contemporary young American woman, who draws parallels—sometimes extreme—between Hitler's regime and the administrations of U.S. Presidents Reagan and George Bush, Sr. Osborn quoted Kushner as explaining that he continues to rewrite Zillah's lines because he "will cheerfully supply new material, drawing appropriate parallels between contemporary and historical monsters and their monstrous acts, regardless of how superficially outrageous such comparisons may seem. To refuse to compare is to rob history of its power to inform present action."

When *A Bright Room Called Day* was performed in New York City in 1991, it received less than enthusiastic reviews. A somewhat neutral Gerald Weales in *Commonweal* labeled it "ambitious," but observed that he felt it was "a more despairing play than it probably intended to be." Less ambiguous was the response of Frank Rich in the *New York Times,* who took exception to Kushner's linking of Nazi Germany with the United States during the 1980s. "Is the time ever right for a political work in which the National Socialism of the Third Reich is trivialized by being equated with the 'national senility' of the Reagan era?" he demanded. Rich also called the work "fatuous" and "an early front-runner for the most infuriating play of 1991." *A Bright Room Called Day* did, however, impress Oskar Eustis, then artistic director of the Eureka Theater in San Francisco, California. He commissioned Kushner to write a comic play for his theater. This was the play that would become *Angels in America,* though the Eureka would no longer exist by the time the entire play was ready for production.

Though *Angels in America* is filled with many different characters, it is meant to be performed by eight persons who each play several roles. In *Millennium Approaches,* the story focuses on two couples—two gay men named Louis and Prior dealing with Prior's AIDS, and Harper and Joe, a nominally straight couple—although the married Mormon man, Joe, is trying to suppress his secret homosexuality. Also central to the play is the figure of lawyer Roy Cohn—based on the real Cohn who helped Senator Joseph McCarthy persecute suspected communists during the 1950s. Cohn also persecuted gays, although he himself was a closet homosexual and died of AIDS. The play's Cohn, whom Joe works for, is true to the somewhat rapacious image of the historical figure. Lloyd Rose in the *Washington Post* explained that "Cohn is clearly meant to be the Devil of the piece: the man who lies to himself, who abuses his power, who has sacrificed his moral self for success. Yet the play jolts with energy whenever he's onstage, because his self-hatred turns splendidly and splenetically outward. . . . Cohn rages against the definitions society would force on him. He destroys his own soul in satanic spite, and he goes down raging and in flames." In one scene, for example, after his doctor has told him that he has AIDS, Cohn declaims against labels: "They tell you one thing and one thing only: where does an individual so identified fit in the food chain, in the pecking order? Not ideology, or sexual taste, but something much simpler: clout. . . . Now to someone who does not understand this, homosexual is what I am because I have sex with men. But really this is wrong. Homosexuals are not men who sleep with other men. Homosexuals are men who in fifteen years of trying cannot get a pissant antidiscrimination bill through City Council. Homosexuals are men who know nobody and who nobody knows. Who have zero clout. Does this sound like me, Henry?"

Yet, while "the play is a political call to arms for the age of AIDS," as Rich noted in the *New York Times,* "it is no polemic." Critics of *Millennium Approaches* in its various performances greeted it with high praise. Rich himself first reviewed the London staging of *Angels in America's* first part, and at that time hailed it in the *New York Times* as "a searching and radical rethinking of the whole esthetic of American political drama in which far-flung hallucinations, explicit sexual encounters and camp humor are given as much weight as erudite ideological argument." John Lahr in the *New Yorker* noted that Kushner, "with immense good humor and accessible characters . . . honors the gay community by telling a story that sets its concerns in the larger historical context of American political life."

Millennium Approaches takes its name from the sense of apocalypse the character Prior feels while dealing with his deadly disease. At the end, an angel descends dramatically to visit him, and he is declared a prophet, temporarily, at least, saved from death by AIDS. *Perestroika,* by contrast, is a somewhat quieter piece, getting its title from the Russian word ex-Soviet leader Mikhail Gorbachev used for his proposals for "restructuring" economic and social policies. As Lahr reported, *Perestroika* "is the messier but more interesting of the two plays, skillfully steering its characters from the sins of separation in the eighties to a new sense of community in the embattled nineties." In the second part of *Angels,* the glorious being that visited Prior at the end of the first part turns out to represent stasis or death, and Prior decides to reject it. Cohn dies, but this does not prevent his ghost from reappearing later in the play—in the role of God's lawyer, no less. The comedy of *Millennium* continues; in *Perestroika,* according to Lahr, "Kushner uses laughter carefully, to deflate the maudlin and to build a complex tapestry of ironic emotion." Lahr concluded that Kushner's work is "a victory . . . for the transforming power of the imagination to turn devastation into beauty."

In 1995 Kushner wrote and produced what he terms a "coda" to *Angels in America, Slavs! Thinking about the Longstanding Problems of Virtue and Happiness,* which Christopher Hawthorne of *Salon.com* called "a compact, quirky exploration of the collapse of the Soviet Union and the ruin, both philosophical and environmental, left in its wake." *Slavs!* resembles the *Angels in America* plays because, according to Kushner in an interview with Andrea Bernstein of *Mother Jones,* the play proceeds from the problem that if you do not know where you are heading, it is difficult to move or make choices. In *Slavs!,* the character Prelapsarianov, "the world's oldest living Bolshevik," asks, "How are we to proceed without theory? Is it enough to reject the past, is it wise to move forward in this blind fashion? . . . You who live in this sour little age cannot imagine the sheer grandeur of the prospect we gazed upon." *Slavs!,* Kushner told *Mother Jones,* answers the conundrum of whether we make history or are made by history by arguing that socialists need to stop looking to the past for an appropriate antecedent upon which to model the present revolutionary response. Kushner also remarked that in the United States it is easier to come out as a gay man than it is as a socialist. Reviews of *Slavs!* were somewhat lukewarm, and Kushner suspects it is because "people have been promised over and over by the media . . . that we don't have to think about these issues" anymore.

Continuing Kushner's search for how the past informs people's present choices and shapes the choices they make about the future is his play, *A Dybbuk; or Between Two Worlds,* an adaptation of S. Ansky's 1920 Yiddish play. *A Dybbuk* concerns the marriage of a young woman, Leah, the daughter of a wealthy man who has broken off negotiations with three prospective husbands because he is displeased with the financial terms of the engagements. A poor Yeshiva student loves Leah, and she secretly returns his passion. When the father announces that he has finally settled on an appropriate husband for Leah, the student, Khonen, turns to dark spiritual forces to prevent the marriage. Khonen returns as a dybbuk, a spirit that takes possession of Leah's body. When the father turns to a Hasidic rabbi for assistance, he finds himself under judgment. It seems that long ago, the father promised Leah to Khonen, but greed for a wealthy match had blinded him to Leah's fate. In the end, he pays for his transgression by donating half his wealth to the poor. Commenting on the play in *Variety,* Charles Isherwood suggested that the play's central truth "is the idea that even the smallest, most unintended immoral act can have profound social and even metaphysical consequences."

Writing in *New York* magazine, John Simon observed, "In *A Dybbuk* . . . Kushner's adaptation of S. Ansky's old chestnut, the work comes funnily, furiously, crochetily alive, as it links the two worlds of the living and the dead, the musty past and the lively present." Isherwood further commented, "The strange flavor of the play defies easy description," but overall he commended the closing speech and the ways in which the play finds connections with the evil of the Holocaust. Ben Brantley of the *New York Times* noted that there are "lovely touches" throughout the production, "not least the hauntingly atmospheric music of the Klezmatics." Brantley lamented the play's "analytical

detachment," but found that "Kushner and Neugroschel have imbued much of their adaptation's language with an exquisite sense of poetry."

Homebody/Kabul, Kushner's play about Afghanistan, opens with an hour-long monologue by a British housewife on the meaning of life, the universe, and everything in it, and the remaining two hours and forty minutes are taken up with a murder committed in Kabul. The first hour, in which the woman reveals her empty marriage and encounter with an Afghan shopkeeper, has been performed by itself. James Reston, Jr. wrote in *American Theatre* that "the Homebody's confrontation with the terrible emptiness of her life leads to her disappearance. The playwright has her act on her romance, even if it means going to an unimaginably awful place, where she can take on the burqua, submit to a husband as his second or third wife, devote herself, unthinking like a teenager in a madrassa, to committing the entire Koran to memory. She acts on romance, and she sticks to it. She has rejected the values of her home, of her life, of her society, of the West. In the act is the whiff of metaphysical treason."

Toby Young reviewed the play in the *Spectator,* saying that the central focus "is the clash between the militant fundamentalism of the East and the moribund humanism of the West, yet it also touches on other, equally big subjects, such as the limits of scientific knowledge and the roles played by language and history in exacerbating international conflicts."

Robert Brustein noted in the *New Republic* that the play opened in December, 2000, prior to the attack on the World Trade Towers on September 11, 2001, after which Brustein felt it "was crying out for revision." Brustein felt that although the play is set in 1998, "it is now impossible to imagine these Western characters circulating among the Taliban without thinking of abductions, corpses, bomb craters, detention camps, and the recent terrorist attacks." He continued, "On second thought, instead of trying to update his play, Kushner might better have employed his energies trying to find some unity for it, or at least settling on what it was supposed to be about in the first place. I say this with profound respect for Kushner's talents. He is one of the very few dramatists now writing whose works are contributions to literature as well as to theater."

BIOGRAPHICAL AND CRITICAL SOURCES:

BOOKS

American Writers, Supplement IX, Scribner (New York, NY), 2001, pp. 131-149.

Completely Queer: The Gay and Lesbian Encyclopedia, Holt (New York, NY), 1998.

Contemporary Dramatists, St. James Press (Detroit, MI), 1999.

Contemporary Literary Criticism, Volume 81, Gale (Detroit, MI), 1994.

Dictionary of Literary Biography, Volume 228: *Twentieth-Century American Dramatists,* Gale (Detroit, MI), pp. 144-160.

Drama Criticism, Volume 10, Gale (Detroit, MI), pp. 212-283.

Drama for Students, Volume 5, Gale (Detroit, MI), 1999, pp. 1-33.

Geis, Deborah R., and Steven F. Kruger, *Approaching the Millennium: Essays on "Angels in America,"* University of Michigan Press (Ann Arbor, MI), 1997.

Savran, David, *Speaking on Stage: Interviews with Contemporary American Playwrights,* University of Alabama Press (Tuscaloosa, AL), 1996.

Vorlicky, Robert, editor, *Tony Kushner in Conversation,* University of Michigan Press (Ann Arbor, MI), 1997.

PERIODICALS

Advocate, November 17, 1992; December 14, 1993; December 28, 1993; February 5, 2002, Don Shewey, review of *Homebody/Kabul,* p. 49.

America, May 29, 1993; March 5, 1994, p. 12.

American Theatre, April, 1999, "Tony Kushner in Conversation," p. 45; September, 2000, Irene Oppenheim, "Shedding More Light on *Bright Room,*" p. 75; March, 2002, James Reston, Jr., review of *Homebody/Kabul,* p. 28.

Back Stage, January 28, 1994, Irene Backalenick, review of *The Illusion,* p. 60; January 11, 2002, David A. Rosenberg, review of *Homebody/Kabul,* p. 43.

Back Stage West, September 21, 2001, John Angell Grant, review of *The Illusion,* p. 24.

Booklist, September 1, 1993; April 15, 1994; January, 1, 1995, review of *A Bright Room Called Day,* p. 795; April 1, 1995, p. 1372; July, 1998, Ray Olson, review of *A Dybbuk* pp. 1851-1874.

Chicago, September, 1994, p. 37.

Chicago Tribune, May 5, 1993.

Choice, September, 1994, review of *Angels in America,* p. 198.

Chronicle of Higher Education, September 14, 1994, review of *Millennium Approaches,* p. A63.

Commentary, January, 1995, p. 51.

Commonweal, February 22, 1991, p. 132; July 16, 1993.

Daily Variety, August 27, 2002, Robert L. Daniels, review of *The Illusion,* p. 12.

Detroit News, June 1, 1993, p. 3D.

Economist, February 22, 1992; December 4, 1993.

Entertainment Weekly, November 26, 1993.

Europe Intelligence Wire, October 14, 2002, review of *Angels in America.*

Interview, February, 1994.

Lambda Book Report, May, 1994, review of *Angels in America,* p. 24; January, 1995, review of *A Bright Room Called Day,* p. 47.

Library Journal, July, 1994, review of *Angels in America,* p. 94; January, 1998, "Tony Kushner in Conversation," p. 101; September 15, 1999, review of *Refugees in an Age of Genocide,* p. 99.

London Review of Books, August 18, 1994, review of *The Jewish Heritage in British History,* p. 23.

Los Angeles Times, May 13, 1990, pp. 45-46, 48; May 6, 1993, pp. F1, F7; December 24, 1995, review of *Slavs! Thinking about the Longstanding Problems of Virtue and Happiness,* p. 11.

Mother Jones, July-August, 1995, p. 59.

Nation, March 18, 1991; February 22, 1993; July 4, 1994; February 6, 1995, p. 177.

Los Angeles Times Book Review, April 24, 1994, review of *Angels in America,* p. 12.

National Review, June 7, 1993; January 24, 1994, p. 71.

New Leader, June 14, 1993; December 13, 1993.

New Republic, May 24, 1993; June 14, 1993; December 27, 1993, p. 25; January 30, 1995, p. 30; March 18, 2002, Robert Brustein, review of *Homebody/Kabul,* p. 27.

Newsweek, May 10, 1993; May 17, 1993; December 6, 1993, p. 83; June 27, 1994, p. 46; December 17, 2001, Marc Peyser, review of *Homebody/Kabul,* p. 68.

New York, January 21, 1991; April 12, 1993; May 17, 1993; December 6, 1993, p. 130; April 4, 1994, p. 74; January 31, 1994, p. 69; December 1, 1997, p. 110.

New Yorker, November 23, 1992, pp. 126-130; May 31, 1993; June 21, 1993; December 13, 1993, p. 129; January 9, 1995, p. 85.

New York Times, January 18, 1990; January 8, 1991, p. C11, C14; March 5, 1992, C1, C21; September 13, 1992; April 14, 1993, p. B6; May 5, 1993; June 7, 1993; November 21, 1993; December 4,

1994; November 17, 1997, p. B2, B5; November 23, 1997, p. AR20; March 1, 1998.

New York Times Magazine, April 25, 1993, pp. 29-30, 48, 56.

Publishers Weekly, June 26, 1995, review of *Slavs!,* p. 105.

Spectator, June 1, 2002, Toby Young, review of *Homebody/Kabul,* p. 48.

Time, November 23, 1992; May 17, 1993; December 6, 1993.

Translation Review Supplement, December, 1999, review of *A Dybbuk,* p. 35.

Vanity Fair, March, 1993.

Variety, January 17, 1990; January 14, 1991; July 29, 1991; August 12, 1991; November 16, 1992; May 10, 1993; December 6, 1993; January 24, 1994; May 9, 1994; August 8, 1994; October 17, 1994; October 31, 1994; December 19, 1994, p. 86; February 27, 1995, p. 83; March 6, 1995, p. 71; November 18, 1997; September 2, 2002, Robert L. Daniels, review of *The Illusion,* p. 33.

Village Voice December 7, 1993; April 18, 1995.

Vogue, November, 1992.

Wall Street Journal, November 26, 1997, p. A12.

Washington Post, November 7, 1992, pp. G1, G4; May 5, 1993, B1, B10.

World Literature Today, winter, 1995, review of *Angels in America,* p. 144; summer, 1996, review of *Slavs!,* p. 695.

ONLINE

Metro Active Stage, http://www.metroactive.com/ (February 11, 2003), "Earth Angel: Tony Kushner Speaks on Art and Politics."

Playbill Web site, http://www.playbill.com/ (October 23, 2003), "Kushner's *Angels in America* Film Debuts in Two Parts on HBO, December 7 and 14."

Salon.com, http://www.salon.com/ (September, 1997), Christopher Hawthorne, review of *Slavs!.*

Steven Barclay Agency Web site, http://www.barclay agency.com/ (February 11, 2003), "Tony Kushner."*

L

LABRIE, Ross (E.) 1936-

PERSONAL: Born October 17, 1936, in Montreal, Quebec, Canada; son of Ernest (a purchasing manager) and Helen (McCarthy) Labrie; married, 1966; wife's name Gisela (a translator and legal secretary); children: Mark, Steven. *Education:* Loyola College, B.A., 1957; McGill University, M.A., 1960; University of Toronto, Ph.D., 1966.

ADDRESSES: Home—592 Carisbrooke Rd., North Vancouver, British Columbia V7N 1N5, Canada. *Office*—Arts One, University of British Columbia, Vancouver, British Columbia V6T 1Z4, Canada. *E-mail*—labrie@interchange.ubc.ca.

CAREER: University of Saskatchewan, Saskatoon, Saskatchewan, Canada, instructor in English, 1962-63; University of British Columbia, Vancouver, British Columbia, Canada, professor of English, 1963-2001, professor of Arts One, 2002—.

MEMBER: International Thomas Merton Society, American Studies Association, Christianity and Literature Association.

AWARDS, HONORS: Fellow, Social Science and Humanities Research Council of Canada, 1980-81; "outstanding book" citation, *Choice,* 1979, for *The Art of Thomas Merton.*

WRITINGS:

The Art of Thomas Merton, Texas Christian University Press (Fort Worth, TX), 1979.

Ross Labrie

Howard Nemerov, G. K. Hall (Boston, MA), 1980.
James Merrill, G. K. Hall (Boston, MA), 1982.
The Writings of Daniel Berrigan, University Press of America (Lanham, MD), 1989.
The Catholic Imagination in American Literature, University of Missouri Press (Columbia, MO), 1997.
Thomas Merton and the Inclusive Imagination, University of Missouri Press (Columbia, MO), 2001.

Contributor to periodicals. Member of advisory board, *Merton Annual.*

SIDELIGHTS: Ross Labrie is a professor of English whose specialties include the writings of Thomas Merton and other Catholic Americans. Among Labrie's works is *The Catholic Imagination in American Literature,* in which he examines the writings of thirteen prominent Catholic Americans, including poets Robert Lowell and Daniel Berrigan and short-story writer Flannery O'Connor. In these writers, Labrie traces a shared perspective that he did not find in more contemporary Catholic writers. According to Labrie, the perception of being part of a cultural minority in America has influenced the work of the various writers discussed in *The Catholic Imagination.*

Library Journal reviewer Denise J. Stankovics deemed Labrie's study "well documented," while William F. McInerny, writing for the *National Catholic Reporter* Web site, called Labrie's work "a scholarly, extensively researched, incisive, probing, intellectually and spiritually stimulating analysis." McInerny concluded that the book is "exquisitely written, masterfully composed, comprehensive in scope, rich [in] insight." Patricia Dunlavy Valenti wrote in *America* that Labrie's book "examines how the Catholic Church's sacramental vision of a world flawed yet charged with redemptive energy infuses the poetry and fiction of selected American writers." Valenti also affirmed that Labrie's volume "will gratify those who desire broader critical attention for writers whose orbit has been predominantly Catholic or whose public acclaim has been in response to their nonliterary works." At the University of Missouri Press Web site, *The Catholic Imagination in American Literature* was described as a "well-written and comprehensive volume," one that "fills a distinctive place in the study of American literature."

Labrie once told *CA:* "How circuitous a business writing can be. I began writing about Henry James and especially about James's interest in consciousness. Somehow, this led in time to an interest in Thomas Merton, whose evocative autobiography, *The Seven Storey Mountain,* had such an influence on me as a student (I can still remember turning the pages in the bus as I crossed town every day toward my university). Merton was also interested in consciousness, as his voluminous, now fully published journals attest. Merton led me to Daniel Berrigan, a Catholic poet with

whom he corresponded and who, like Merton, was an anti-Vietnam War protester. Then I realized that, although some useful work had already been done, a book that explained exactly what Catholic American literature *was* needed to be written, one that included writers like Merton and Berrigan, Robert Lowell, and Flannery O'Connor, Allen Tate, and Caroline Gordon, Walker Percy, and Mary Gordon. The study, published as *The Catholic Imagination in American Literature,* focused on writers who were practicing Catholics, whose writing was of high quality, and whose works dealt with Catholic themes. In attempting to lay out a field for study, I looked at ore with a high concentration of Catholic metal in it so that others might be able to use the book as a point of departure in dealing with American authors who might exhibit Catholic consciousness in a more attenuated form."

BIOGRAPHICAL AND CRITICAL SOURCES:

PERIODICALS

America, May 30, 1998, Patricia Dunlavy Valenti, review of *The Catholic Imagination in American Literature,* pp. 26-27.

American Literature, June, 2000, James Emmett Ryan, review of *The Catholic Imagination in American Literature,* p. 445.

Choice, June, 2002, D. A. Brown, review of *Thomas Merton and the Inclusive Imagination,* p. 1786.

Journal of American Studies, April, 1999, review of *The Catholic Imagination in American Literature,* p. 141.

Library Journal, March 15, 1997, Denise J. Stankovics, review of *The Catholic Imagination in American Literature,* p. 64.

ONLINE

National Catholic Reporter, http://www.natcath.com/ (March 4, 1999), William F. McInerny, review of *The Catholic Imagination in American Literature.*

University of Missouri Press, http://www.system. missouri.edu/ (November 4, 1998), publisher's description of *The Catholic Imagination in American Literature;* (April 17, 2003), description of *Thomas Merton and the Inclusive Imagination.*

LACKMANN, Ron(ald) 1934-

PERSONAL: Born May 8, 1934, in New York, NY; son of Frederick and Minerva (Morlock) Lackmann. *Education:* Hofstra College (now University), B.A., 1959, M.A., 1962; University of Hull, drama certificate, 1967-71.

ADDRESSES: Home—18 East Beverly Pkwy., Valley Stream, NY 11580.

CAREER: Writer and actor. Central High School, Valley Stream, NY, 1960—, began as speech and drama consultant, currently instructor in English, speech, and drama. Hofstra University, Hempstead, NY, drama instructor in adult education program, 1970-71. Host-moderator, "Education in Action," WHLI-Radio, 1974-75; narrator, Pan Am's "Music in the Air." Actor on radio, television, and stage; playwright. *Military service:* U.S. Army, 1957-59; served as personnel and broadcast specialist.

MEMBER: Actors Equity Association, Screen Actors Guild.

WRITINGS:

Under the Angel's Wing (play), first produced at Hofstra College, 1958.
(With Barbara Gelman) *Bonnie and Clyde Scrapbook,* Personality Posters, 1968.
Remember Radio, Putnam (New York, NY), 1970.
Hadrian's Wall (play), first produced at Showcase Theatre, May, 1970.
Remember Television, Putnam (New York, NY), 1971.
TV Soap Opera Almanac, Berkley Publishing (New York, NY), 1976.
TV Superstars 1978, Xerox Education Publications (Middletown, CT), 1978.
TV Superstars 1979, Xerox Education Publications (Middletown, CT), 1979.
Super Vans, Xerox Education Publications (Middletown, CT), 1979.
Disco, Disco, Disco, Xerox Education Publications (Middletown, CT), 1980.
TV Superstars 1980, Xerox Education Publications (Middletown, CT), 1980.
TV Superstars 1981, Xerox Education Publications (Middletown, CT), 1981.
Animal Superstars, Xerox Education Publications (Middletown, CT), 1981.
TV Superstars 1982, Xerox Education Publications (Middletown, CT), 1982.
TV Superstars 1983, Xerox Education Publications (Middletown, CT), 1983.
Kids Video Game Guide, Xerox Education Publications (Middletown, CT), 1983.
Video Game Joke and Puzzle Book, Xerox Education Publications (Middletown, CT), 1983.
TV Superstars Scrapbook, Xerox Education Publications (Middletown, CT), 1984.
Same Time, Same Station: An A-Z Guide to Radio from Jack Benny to Howard Stern, Facts on File (New York, NY), 1996, published as *The Encyclopedia of American Radio: An A-Z Guide to Radio from Jack Benny to Howard Stern,* Facts on File (New York, NY), 2000.
Women of the Western Frontier in Fact, Fiction, and Film, McFarland (Jefferson, NC), 1997.
The Encyclopedia of American Television: Broadcast Programming Post-World War II to 2000, Facts on File (New York, NY), 2002.
The Encyclopedia of Twentieth-Century American Television, Checkmark Books (New York, NY), 2003.

Author of several short stories and children's plays. Contributor of articles to various periodicals. Editor-in-chief, *Vid-Kid* (video game players newsletter), 1983.

SIDELIGHTS: Writer and actor Ron Lackmann has been active in the film and television industry since the 1950s. As a college student at Hofstra University in the 1950s, Lackmann portrayed Bud on the NBC radio soap opera *Pepper Young's Family.* During his U.S. Army stint in the late 1950s, he served as a personnel and radio broadcast specialist at WFDH radio, the Fort Dix radio station. While serving at Fort Dix, he was producer and narrator for radio shows, and an actor in more than fifty dramatic productions on radio. Following his military service, he toured in stage productions of several well-known plays, including *My Fair Lady, Oklahoma, Death of a Salesman,* and *Auntie Mame.* Lackmann has also taught high school speech and drama, cohosted the *Joe Franklin Show,* and lent his voice to cartoon characters.

Lackmann brings his insider's knowledge of film and television to bear in his numerous books on broadcast arts and history. In *The Encyclopedia of American Radio: An A-Z Guide to Radio from Jack Benny to Howard Stern* (previously published as *Same Time, Same Station: An A-Z guide to Radio from Jack Benny to Howard Stern*), Lackmann offers a concise history of radio programming, both as entertainment and as a resource for news and information. "Ambitious in design but limited in execution, this eminently browsable guide to major North American network radio programming from the 1920s to the present will delight some readers while disappointing others," wrote David Ettinger in *RQ*. The book provides synopses of hundreds of radio shows from the 1920s to the talk radio of the present day, with longer features on more popular programs and personalities. The entries provide data on show stars, writers, producers, date and year the show aired, network on which it appeared, and major sponsor. Coverage includes legendary radio personalities such as Walter Winchell and Edward R. Murrow, and programming such as Franklin Roosevelt's fireside chats, the "War of the Worlds" broadcast, and genre programs in areas of mystery, soap opera, and adventure. Black-and-white photographs provide faces for famous voices, and a number of appendices provide information on related areas such as museums, newsletters, Canadian radio, lists of radio program sponsor, birth and death dates of radio personalities, lists of current radio stations running vintage radio shows, and more. However, Ettinger remarked that "the treatment of topics is uneven and seems capricious, raising questions of editorial judgment and priorities." Despite its flaws, "The work is still a useful resource for research on radio because Lackmann, like every radio history buff, has stories, tidbits, and information to add to the growing body of knowledge about the subject," wrote a reviewer on the *Booknews* Web site.

Lackmann also wrote *The Encyclopedia of American Television: Broadcast Programming Post-World War II to 2000*, which "is just as valuable [as its radio counterpart], in addition to being fun to read and use," commented David M. Lisa in *Library Journal*. The book includes more than 1,000 descriptions of major network and syndicated television shows that appeared on the airwaves from 1947 through 2000 (cable television programming is excluded). Entries include biographies of notable television personalities from the time period. Details provided in the capsule entries include broadcast schedules and network data, and a number of listings include photographs. Lackmann also provides bits of trivia and interesting facts in the

descriptions. "Lackmann offers two excellent appendixes," Lisa noted, a list of top-rated programs from 1952 to 1999 and a listing of Emmy Award winners from 1948 to 1999. A reviewer in *Booklist* called *The Encyclopedia of American Television* "worthwhile" and "a readable, popular guide."

Lackmann's 1997 book *Women of the Western Frontier in Fact, Fiction, and Film* collects biographical information from newspaper clippings, novels, fictional accounts, and tall tales to provide a collection of biographies of notable women from the American West. Lackmann divides the book into four sections, according to Candy Moulton in *Wild West:* gunfighters' wives and lovers, and female outlaws; female entertainers; prostitutes, madams, and gambling ladies; and "respectable" women of the frontier. Although Moulton noted that the mixing of fact and fiction in the book would likely keep it out of the category of serious history, it is still "entertaining." A reviewer in the *Journal of Women's History* called it "a handy resource for western lore in American memory and media."

BIOGRAPHICAL AND CRITICAL SOURCES:

PERIODICALS

Booklist, February 15, 1996, review of *Same Time, Same Station: An A-Z Guide to Radio from Jack Benny to Howard Stern,* p. 1044; June 1, 2003, review of *The Encyclopedia of American Television: Broadcast Programming Post-World War II to 2000,* p. 1828.
Journal of Women's History, winter, 2000, review of *Women of the Western Frontier in Fact, Fiction, and Film,* p. 215.
Library Journal, February 15, 2003, David M. Lisa, review of *The Encyclopedia of American Television,* pp. 128-129.
RQ, summer, 1996, David Ettinger, review of *Same Time, Same Station,* p. 565.
Wild West, June, 1998, Candy Moulton, review of *Women of the Western Frontier in Fact, Fiction, and Film,* p. 68.

ONLINE

Booknews Web site, http://www.booknews.com/ (November 14, 2003), review of *The Encyclopedia of American Radio: An A-Z Guide to Radio from Jack Benny to Howard Stern.*

Internet Movie Database Web site, http://www.imdb. com/ (November 14, 2000), biography of Ron Lackmann.*

*   *   *

LEE, Andrew
    See AUCHINCLOSS, Louis (Stanton)

*   *   *

LERNER, Gerda 1920-

PERSONAL: Born April 30, 1920, in Vienna, Austria; immigrated to United States, 1939; naturalized U.S. citizen, 1943; daughter of Robert and Ilona (Neumann) Kronstein; married Carl Lerner (a filmmaker), 1941 (died, 1973); children: Stephanie, Daniel. *Education:* New School for Social Research, B.A., 1963; Columbia University, M.A., 1965, Ph.D., 1966. *Hobbies and other interests:* Music, gardening, backpacking.

ADDRESSES: Home—6005 Hammersley Rd., Madison, WI 53711-3113. *Agent*—c/o Author Mail, Temple University Press, 1601 North Broad St., Philadelphia, PA 19122.

CAREER: Professional writer and translator, 1941—; New School for Social Research, New York, NY, lecturer and historian, 1963-65; Long Island University, Brooklyn, NY, assistant professor, 1965-67, associate professor of American history, 1967-68; Sarah Lawrence College, Bronxville, NY, member of history faculty, 1968-80, director of graduate program in women's history, 1972-76, 1978-79; University of Wisconsin, Madison, Robinson-Edwards Professor of history, beginning 1980, director and codirector of graduate program in women's history, 1981-90, Robinson-Edwards Professor of History Emerita. Member of Columbia University Seminar on American Civilization, and Seminar on Women and Society, 1972. FIPSE grant for Promoting Black Women's History, codirector, 1980-83; Sarah Lawrence College, educational director of summer institutes in women's history, 1976 and 1979; project director for "Documenting the Midwest Origins of Twentieth-Century Feminism," 1990-93.

MEMBER: National Organization for Women (founding member), Organization of American Historians (president, 1981-82), American Historical Association, American Association of University Women, American Studies Association, Authors League of America, Wisconsin Academy of Science, Arts, and Letters (fellow), American Academy of Arts.

AWARDS, HONORS: American Association of University Women fellow, 1968-69; Social Science Research Council research fellow, 1970-71; Robert H. Lord Award, Emmanuel College, 1974; Rockefeller Foundation fellow, 1975, 77, 91, grantee, 1972-76; National Endowment for the Humanities fellow, 1976; Ford Foundation fellow, 1978-79; Lilly Foundation fellow, 1979; Special Book award, Berkshire Conference of Women Historians, 1980, for *The Majority Finds Its Past: Placing Women in History;* Guggenheim fellow, 1980-81; Organization of American Historians grant, 1980-83; Senior Distinguished Research Professor, University of Wisconsin Alumni Research Foundation, 1984-1990; Educational Foundation Achievement Award, American Association of University Women, 1986; Joan Kelly Award, American Historical Association, 1986, for best book in women's history, for *Women and History;* Lucretia Mott Award, 1988; award for scholarly distinction, American Historical Association, 1992; Kathe Leichter-Preis, Austrian State Prize for Women's History and the History of the Labor Movement, both 1995; Austrian Cross for Science and Art, 1996; recipient of ten honorary degrees.

WRITINGS:

No Farewell (novel), Associated Authors (New York, NY), 1955.
(With husband, Carl Lerner) *Black Like Me* (screenplay; based on book of same title by John Howard Griffin), Walter Reade Distributors, 1964.
The Grimke Sisters from South Carolina: Rebels against Slavery, Houghton Mifflin (Boston, MA), 1967, published as *The Grimke Sisters from South Carolina: Pioneers for Woman's Rights and Abolition,* Oxford University Press (New York, NY), 1998, revised and expanded edition, University of North Carolina Press (Chapel Hill, NC), 2004.
The Woman in American History (textbook), Addison-Wesley (Reading, MA), 1971.
(Editor) *Black Women in White America: A Documentary History,* Pantheon (New York, NY), 1972.
Women Are History: A Bibliography in the History of American Women, Sarah Lawrence College (New

York, NY), 1975, 4th revised edition (with Marie Laberge), University of Wisconsin Press (Madison, WI), 1986.

(Editor) *The Female Experience: An American Documentary,* Bobbs-Merrill (Indianapolis, IN), 1976.

A Death of One's Own, Simon & Schuster (New York, NY), 1978.

The Majority Finds Its Past: Placing Women in History, Oxford University Press (New York, NY), 1979.

Teaching Women's History, American Historical Association (Washington, DC), 1981.

Women and History, Oxford University Press (New York, NY), Volume 1: *The Creation of Patriarchy,* 1986, Volume 2: *The Creation of Feminist Consciousness, from the Middle Ages to 1870,* 1997.

Why History Matters: Life and Thought, Oxford University Press (New York, NY), 1997.

The Feminist Thought of Sarah Grimke, Oxford University Press (New York, NY), 1998.

Fireweed: A Political Autobiography, Temple University Press (Philadelphia, PA), 2002.

Also author of *Dorothea Dix* and *Elizabeth Cady Stanton and Susan B. Anthony,* sound recordings, Pacifica Tape Library. Coauthor, with Eve Merriam, of the musical, *Singing of Women,* 1956. Contributor of short stories to various literary magazines, and of articles and reviews to professional journals. Author of numerous professional translations.

SIDELIGHTS: A pioneer in the field of women's studies, Gerda Lerner has written extensively about the role of women in history and how traditional histories have failed to address specifically female issues. Using a variety of sources, Lerner frequently compares issues of race, class, and gender in her studies of women. Believed to have taught the first postwar college course in women's history, she has also helped establish several graduate programs in the field.

Anne Lewis Osler in *Feminist Writers* explained that "Lerner's research, combined with her commitment to organize programs designed to train future generations of feminist scholars, helped establish women's history as an essential component of contemporary history curriculums in colleges and universities both in the United States and abroad." As Elizabeth Fox-Genovese described her in the *New Republic,* Lerner "has played a unique role in making women's history the thriving

field it has become; she has delineated its appropriate contours; searched for a method and a theory appropriate to its practice; unearthed the sources necessary to its writing; insisted not merely on its autonomy and integrity, but on its inescapable centrality to any worthy history of humankind."

Lerner's *Black Women in White America: A Documentary History* chronicles 350 years of suffering by individuals who were often considered property not only by reason of their race, but of their gender. Reviewer Joyce Jenkins commented in the *Saturday Review* that this "superb" book is "the first, to my knowledge, to treat in depth the grossly neglected segment of American history staked out by the book's title." Lerner uses numerous documents as well as newspaper items to report the troubles of these women from their own perspective, not that of a distanced observer. While Jenkins disputed some of the author's assertions, such as the supposedly recurrent theme of racial solidarity, she remarked that overall it "displays sharp insight into the long-range effects of this slave past."

Adrienne Rich observed in the *New York Times Book Review* that, although as a white historian Lerner is "scrupulously restrained in her theorizing," in *Black Women in White America* she provides "a thorough historical framework in which the documents could be read and interpreted." Moreover, Rich described the documentary as an "indispensable complement" to Lerner's next work, *The Female Experience: An American Documentary.* Rich explained that this second documentary "expands [Lerner's] vision of history, while keeping the form begun earlier." As with *Black Women in White America,* the book presents letters, diaries, newspaper clips, speeches, and other documents that had not been published previously.

"More than any other compilation," remarked Eve Merriam in *Ms.,* "all the many strands needed for comprehending the female experience are successfully interwoven." More notable, however, is the author's presentation of her material; instead of following traditional divisions of history, which she claims do not represent important milestones for women, Lerner attempts to establish an order according to women's issues known as "historical periodization." As Rich explained, the author recognizes that "periods of history regarded as progressive for men have often been regressive for women. . . . 'Progress' has been defined from a male point of view." Merriam offered similar praise, saying that "in *The Female Experience,* Lerner has lifted history out of its iron rigidity, out of its chronological framework—what a daring concept and how inexorable it seems now that she has done so."

The Majority Finds Its Past: Placing Women in History compiles many of Lerner's essays and speeches, including those of her theories of historical periodization, into one book. "By bringing these pieces together," commented June Sochen in the *Washington Post Book World,* "Lerner gives us a good opportunity to see the development of her thought as she participated in the shaping of the discipline." Sochen criticized some of Lerner's ideas, however, such as her tendency to see women's history and culture as independent from mainstream events. "Does the existence of a female culture operate outside history? . . . The temptation of some women historians to portray all examples of female culture as subversive, alternative value-systems is questionable at best."

Fox-Genovese, while praising Lerner's work as groundbreaking, still faulted the author's failure to consider religious and class issues as notable influences in women's history. These reservations aside, the critic found that "committed to recreating the female perspective, Lerner nonetheless never sacrifices the specificities of income and race to an all-inclusive feminism."

In *The Creation of Patriarchy,* Volume One of *Women and History,* Lerner ventures into prehistory, attempting to trace the roots of patriarchal dominance. Kamarck Minnich claimed in *Ms.* that in doing so, Lerner "gives us a grand historical framework that was impossible even to imagine before the enlightenment about women's place in the world provided by her earlier work." In this volume, Lerner cites "historical, archeological, literary, and artistic evidence for the idea that patriarchy is a cultural invention," noted Glenn Collins in the *New York Times.* Although the author herself acknowledges that this kind of evidence is "fragile," Sarah B. Pomeroy still criticized her use of these sources. "To construct a grandiose paradigm demonstrating the continually deteriorating position of women," the critic wrote in the *New York Times Book Review,* "Mrs. Lerner considers societies as different as the Sumerians, Babylonians . . . Hebrews, and Greeks as though they existed on a historical continuum and evolved directly from one another." This kind of evidence, remarked Pomeroy, "does not permit

definitive conclusions." Contrarily, Minnich found that Lerner uses "careful scholarship and ever more carefully refined theoretical concepts" to present her ideas about women and the evolution of patriarchy.

The Creation of Feminist Consciousness: From the Middle Ages to 1870 is the second volume of *Women and History.* In this book, the author reviews European culture from the seventh century through the nineteenth century, showing the limitations imposed by a male-dominated culture and the sporadic attempt to resist that domination. She examines in detail the educational deprivation of women, their isolation from many of the traditions of their societies, and the expressive outlet many women have found through writing. "Interwoven with the multitudes of fascinating examples that Lerner provides is, of course, the broader argument," advised Susan E. Henking in *America.* "Mysticism, motherhood, and creativity have been available—and utilized—as routes to self-authorization for centuries. Glimmers of feminist consciousness appeared and disappeared in the interstices of patriarchal culture; feminism's lineage thus reaches much further back than has been traditionally understood. Yet it did not linger. Why?"

Lerner examines the many reasons for this, and gives her thoughts on what is needed to continue the social progress for women. Lynn Hunt, a contributor to the *Journal of Social History,* said of *The Creation of Feminist Consciousness:* "Its range and sympathetic detail make this an excellent one-volume overview of women writing about women's consciousness in the centuries before the organization of an explicit feminist movement." Evaluating both volumes of *Women and History,* Londa L. Schiebinger stated in the *Journal of Interdisciplinary History* that "together they provide a powerful history of the insidious workings of patriarchy and the toll that being left out of history has taken on women and their creativity."

Although it is a personal narrative rather than a historical study, *A Death of One's Own* contains the same humanist perspective and development of ideas as the rest of Lerner's work. Written six years after her husband's death, the work recounts Gerda and Carl Lerner's attempts to deal with the knowledge that Carl was dying of a brain tumor. The two decide on a policy of openness and honesty, sharing their feelings as the cancer progresses, even if this policy conflicts with their individual needs. "There's little melodrama or self-pity in this," observed Alex Raksin in the *Los Angeles Times Book Review,* "only an extraordinarily personal evocation of [Lerner's] struggle to achieve peace of mind through realism rather than nihilism."

In writing the book, Lerner takes an approach similar to that of her other work; she uses various sources, such as diary entries, poems, and straight narrative to present her story. "In her deeply moving book," commented Joan Kron in *Ms.,* Lerner "has woven a tapestry: recollections of Carl's illness, her conflicting diary entries from the same period, and 'fragments' of her life in Europe before she became a refugee from the Nazis." In doing so, she "strives to connect past and present, living and dead in a continuum of meaning," said Helen Yglesias in the *New York Times Book Review.*

Many reviewers expressed similar praise for *A Death of One's Own.* Yglesias commented that it is "a book that heartens and breaks the heart at the same time," even though Lerner "is no sentimentalist, and does not sensationally display the grim details." Anne Tyler wrote in the *Washington Post Book World,* "Gerda Lerner's simple ability to cope—her endurance, her strength, her willingness to fight whenever fighting will help—is admirable. . . . But what I found awe-inspiring is the fact that through it all, she never loses the capacity to feel." Tyler also found the book to be a "page-turner," and Kron similarly found it involving. "When Carl Lerner finally dies," Kron wrote, "one not only weeps for him, but for oneself with envy for such a relationship."

In *Why History Matters: Life and Thought,* Lerner fuses memoir and scholarly thought. This collection of essays begins with her recollections of life in post-World War I Austria and describes her family's flight from the advance of the Nazis and their subsequent relocation to the United States. Lerner relates how, as a teenager, she questioned the exclusion of women from full participation in synagogue, and eventually abandoned organized Judaism for over fifty years. She reflects on her experiences with anti-Semitism, her path to scholarly eminence, and all the things she lost when she rejected her Jewish heritage and her German background.

"The result is an intensely moving and intellectually satisfying collection," wrote Eleanor J. Bader in the *Progressive.* Bader concluded, "*Why History Matters*

underscores the importance of knowing our familial, ethnic, and societal histories. These are starting points toward a world without hierarchies, war, or economic inequity." Catharine R. Stimpson in the *Nation* wrote, "As survivor and historian, Lerner warns us that we cannot survive and grow—as individuals or as a species—unless we have a full, accurate, enabling sense of the past. This triple sense of loss, pain and responsibility pervades her work. . . . *Why History Matters* records her heroic quest to respect differences among women, to work hard, if not always successfully, to avoid the false universal, and to offer a unifying vision of women's history and of America."

Fireweed: A Political Autobiography is Lerner's detailed documentation of her years from childhood to 1958 when she first began her studies at the New School for Social Research in New York. She recalls in "Beginnings" starvation and imprisonment in Austria and her family's survival, due in part to the fact that her father had opened a branch of the family business in Liechtenstein, where he stayed. Her mother moved to France, and Lerner's sister relocated to Israel. Lerner came to the United States at the age of eighteen under the sponsorship of the family of the young man she would marry. The marriage failed, and Lerner survived as a typical immigrant, working for minimum wage. She met Carl, and they both obtained divorces in Reno so that they could marry, then moved from New York to Hollywood, where Carl's career in film blossomed.

Carl Lerner was a member of the Communist Party, and in 1946, Lerner, who had become a citizen several years earlier, also joined and became active in progressive politics. During the era of McCarthyism, they were swept up in the anti-Communist hysteria, and Carl was unable to secure work. He returned to New York, leaving Lerner to cope with caring for their two sons with few resources. Lerner joined her husband after six months, and once in New York, she worked for education, integration, women's rights, and international peace. *New York Times Book Review* contributor Inga Clendinnen noted that "the protection from deportation of aliens suspected of Communist sympathies was especially dear to her: she cites a pamphlet she wrote on one tragic case, and it's a dazzler." The Lerners left the Party and wrote a documentary that was instrumental in bringing Martin Luther King to prominence, but they were excluded from the campaign for racial equality, possibly because of their radical past.

Women's Review of Books writer Karen Offen wrote, "What I find especially important is precisely that this is a life told by a woman who is deeply aware of and concerned about world and national events and their impact on the lives of ordinary people. Yet, as a woman historian devoted to women's history and recognition of the female experience, she also fully acknowledges the importance of the 'private' side—the men and women in her life, her two American-born children, and the irreplaceable gifts of love, friendship, genuine human sympathy, generosity, hard work—and uncommon good luck."

BIOGRAPHICAL AND CRITICAL SOURCES:

BOOKS

American Women Writers, 2nd edition, St. James Press (Detroit, MI), 2000.
Feminist Writers, St. James Press (Detroit, MI), 1996.
Lerner, Gerda, *A Death of One's Own,* Simon & Schuster (New York, NY), 1978.
Lerner, Gerda, *Fireweed: A Political Autobiography,* Temple University Press (Philadelphia, PA), 2002.

PERIODICALS

America, December 4, 1993, p. 17; September 16, 1995, pp. 3-5.
Booklist, June 1, 1996, p. 1744; April 1, 1997, p. 1279; April 15, 2002, Vanessa Bush, review of *Fireweed,* p. 1378.
Boston Globe, April 6, 1997, p. N17.
Journal of Interdisciplinary History, spring, 1995, pp. 671-672.
Journal of Social History, spring, 1995, pp. 675-77.
Kirkus Reviews, February 1, 1997, p. 202; February 15, 2002, review of *Fireweed,* p. 238.
Library Journal, March 15, 1997, p. 74; May 1, 2002, Elaine Machleder, review of *Fireweed,* p. 112.
Life, May 5, 1972.
Los Angeles Times Book Review, November 17, 1985.
Ms., May, 1977; October, 1978; September, 1980; May, 1986.
Nation, May 12, 1997, p. 34; October 14, 2002, Nancy MacLean, review of *Fireweed,* p. 28.
New Republic, December 1, 1979.
New Yorker, March 25, 1972.
New York Times, April 28, 1986; July 27, 1997, p. 20.

New York Times Book Review, March 20, 1977; August 6, 1978; April 20, 1986; May 2, 1993; December 4, 1994, p. 88; July 27, 1997, p. 20; August 11, 2002, Inga Clendinnen, review of *Fireweed,* p. 14.
Progressive, March, 1994, pp. 18-22; May, 1997, p. 39.
Publishers Weekly, February 3, 1997, p. 83.
Saturday Review, May 6, 1972.
Voice Literary Supplement, November, 1995, p. 24.
Washington Post Book World, August 13, 1978; January 27, 1980.
Women's Review of Books, October, 2002, Karen Offen, review of *Fireweed,* pp. 3-5.

ONLINE

Independent Weekly, http://www.indyweek.com/ (April 24, 2003), "The Personal Is Historical."
National Woman's History Project Web site, http://www.nwhp.org/ (March 10, 2003), "Gerda Lerner: A Pioneer in Woman's History."
University of Wisconsin, Madison Web site, http://www.news.wisc.edu/ (April 30, 2002), "Emeria's Autobiography Places Personal History in Political Context."*

*　　　*　　　*

LEWIS, Bernard 1916-

PERSONAL: Born May 31, 1916, in London, England; immigrated to United States, 1974, naturalized citizen, 1982; son of Harry (in business) and Jane (a housewife; maiden name, Levy) Lewis; married Ruth Helene Oppenhejm, 1947 (divorced, 1974); children: Melanie, Michael. *Education:* University of London, B.A. (with first-class honors), 1936, Ph.D., 1939; University of Paris, diplome des etudes semitiques, 1937.

ADDRESSES: Home—Princeton, NJ. *Office*—Department of Near Eastern Studies, 110 Jones Hall, Princeton University, Princeton, NJ 08544; Institute for Advanced Study, Olden Lane, Princeton, NJ 08540.

CAREER: University of London, London School of Oriental and African Studies, London, England, professor of history of the Near and Middle East, 1949-74; Princeton University, Princeton, NJ, Cleveland E. Dodge Professor of Near Eastern Studies, 1974-86,

Bernard Lewis

professor emeritus, 1986—; Cornell University, A. D. White Professor at Large, 1984-90; Annenberg Research Institute, Philadelphia, PA, director, 1986-90. Institute for Advanced Study, Princeton, visiting member, 1969, long-term member, 1974—. Visiting professor at University of California, Los Angeles, 1955-56, Columbia University, 1960, Indiana University, 1963, University of California, Berkeley, 1965, College de France, 1980, Ecole des Hautes Etudes en Sciences Sociales, Paris, 1983, and University of Chicago, 1985. Class of 1932 lecturer at Princeton University, 1964; Gottesman lecturer at Yeshiva University, 1974; Douglas Robb Foundation lecturer at University of Auckland, New Zealand, 1982. Testified before U.S. Senate committees on several occasions. *Military service:* British Army, 1940-41; served in Royal Armoured Corps and Intelligence Corps; attached to Foreign Office, 1941-45.

MEMBER: American Academy of Arts and Sciences, American Historical Society, American Oriental Society, American Philosophical Society, Council on Foreign Relations, Royal Historical Society, Royal Asiatic Society, Royal Institute of International Affairs, British Academy (fellow, 1963—), Institut d'Egypte (associate member, 1969—), Turkish Historical Society (honorary member, 1972—), Ataturk Academy of History, Language, and Culture (honorary member, 1984—), Societe Asiatique (honorary member, 1984—), Athenaeum Club, Princeton Club (New York City).

AWARDS, HONORS: Honorary doctorates from Hebrew University of Jerusalem, 1973, and Tel Aviv University, 1979; citation of honor, Turkish Ministry of Culture, 1973; named fellow of University College, London, 1976; Harvey Prize, Technion-Israel Institute of Technology, 1978; National Endowment for the Humanities fellow, 1990; Ataturk Peace Prize, 1998; George Polk Award, 2001.

WRITINGS:

The Origins of Ismailism: A Study of the Historical Background of the Fatimid Caliphate, W. Heffer, 1940.

Turkey Today, Hutchinson (London, England), 1940.

(Collector) *Child Heroes of South Africa,* illustrated by Joyce Ordbrown, Unie-volkspers Beperk (Cape Town, South Africa), 1940.

(Translator, with Elize D. Lewis) *Tales from the Malay Quarter,* M. Miller (Cape Town, South Africa), 1945.

A Handbook of Diplomatic and Political Arabic, Luzac (London, England), 1947.

(Editor) *Land of Enchanters: Egyptian Short Stories from the Earliest Times to the Present Day,* illustrated by Ali Nur, Harvill Press, 1948, reprinted, Marcus Weiner Publications (Princeton, NJ), 2001.

The Arabs in History, Hutchinson University Library, 1950, Harper (New York, NY), 1960, 6th edition, Oxford University Press (New York, NY), 1993.

Notes and Documents from the Turkish Archives: A Contribution to the History of the Jews in the Ottoman Empire, Israel Oriental Society (Jerusalem, Israel), 1952.

The Emergence of Modern Turkey, Oxford University Press (New York, NY), 1961, 2nd revised edition, 1968.

(Translator and author of introduction and notes) Solomon ben Judah Ibn Gabirol, *The Kingly Crown* (poem), Vallentine, Mitchell, 1961.

(Editor, with P. M. Holt) *Historians of the Middle East,* Oxford University Press (New York, NY), 1962.

Istanbul and the Civilization of the Ottoman Empire, University of Oklahoma Press (Norman, OK), 1963.

The Middle East and the West, Indiana University Press (Bloomington, IN), 1964.

The Assassins: A Radical Sect in Islam, Weidenfeld & Nicolson (London, England), 1967, Basic Books (New York, NY), 1968.

(Editor, with P. M. Holt and Ann K. S. Lambton) *The Cambridge History of Islam,* Volume 1: *The Central Islamic Lands,* Volume 2: *The Further Islamic Lands, Islamic Society, and Civilization,* Cambridge University Press (New York, NY), 1970.

Race and Color in Islam, Harper (New York, NY), 1971.

Islam in History: Ideas, Men, and Events in the Middle East, Library Press, 1973, revised and expanded edition, Open Court (Chicago, IL), 1993.

(Editor and translator) *Islam: From the Prophet Muhammad to the Capture of Constantinople,* Volume 1: *Politics and War,* Volume 2: *Religion and Society,* Harper (New York, NY), 1974.

History—Remembered, Recovered, Invented, Princeton University Press (Princeton, NJ), 1975.

Studies in Classical and Ottoman Islam: Seventh to Sixteenth Centuries, Valorium Reprints (London, England), 1976.

(Editor and contributor) *The World of Islam: Faith, People, Culture,* Thames & Hudson (London, England), 1976, published as *Islam and the Arab World: Faith, People, Culture,* Knopf (New York, NY), 1976.

(With Amnon Cohen) *Population and Revenue in the Towns of Palestine in the Sixteenth Century,* Princeton University Press (Princeton, NJ), 1978.

(Author of introduction and additional notes) Ignaz Goldziher, *Introduction to Islamic Theology and Law,* translated by Andras and Ruth Hamori, Princeton University Press (Princeton, NJ), 1981.

(Editor and translator) *Diwan, Poems in Arabic, Persian, Turkish, and Hebrew: Eighth to Eighteenth Centuries,* Holmes & Meier (New York, NY), 1981.

The Muslim Discovery of Europe, W. W. Norton (New York, NY), 1982, reprinted, 2002.

(Editor, with Benjamin Braude) *Christians and Jews in the Ottoman Empire: The Functioning of a Plural Society,* Volume 1: *The Central Lands,* Volume 2: *The Arabic-Speaking Lands,* Holmes & Meier (New York, NY), 1982.

The Jews of Islam, Princeton University Press (Princeton, NJ), 1985.

Semites and Anti-Semites: An Inquiry into Conflict and Prejudice, W. W. Norton (New York, NY), 1986.

The Political Language of Islam, University of Chicago Press (Chicago, IL), 1988, reprinted, Oxford University Press (New York, NY), 2002.

Race and Slavery in the Middle East: An Historical Enquiry, Oxford University Press (New York, NY), 1990.

Islam and the West, Oxford University Press (New York, NY), 1993.

The Shaping of the Modern Middle East, Oxford University Press (New York, NY), 1994.

(Editor, with Dominique Schnapper) *Muslims in Europe,* Pinter (New York, NY), 1994.

The Middle East: Two Thousand Years of History from the Rise of Christianity to the Present Day, Weidenfeld & Nicolson (London, England), 1995, published as *The Middle East: A Brief History of the Last Two Thousand Years,* Scribner (New York, NY), 1995.

Cultures in Conflict: Christians, Muslims, and Jews in the Age of Discovery, Oxford University Press (New York, NY), 1995.

(Editor) *A Middle East Mosaic: Fragments of Life, Letters, and History,* Random House (New York, NY), 1999.

The Multiple Identities of the Middle East, Schocken Books (New York, NY), 1999.

(Translator and author of introduction) *Music of a Distant Drum: Classical Arabic, Persian, Turkish, and Hebrew Poems,* Princeton University Press (Princeton, NJ), 2001.

What Went Wrong? Western Impact and Middle Eastern Response, Oxford University Press (New York, NY), 2002.

(Translator and author of introduction) Keter Malkhut, *The Kingly Crown,* University of Notre Dame (Notre Dame, IN), 2003.

The Crisis of Islam: Holy War and Unholy Terror, Modern Library (New York, NY), 2003.

Coeditor of *The Encyclopaedia of Islam,* E. J. Brill, 1956—. Contributor to periodicals, including *Foreign Affairs, Daedalus, Commentary, New Republic, New York Review of Books, American Scholar,* and the *New York Times Book Review.*

Contributor to volumes such as *The Legacy of Islam,* 2nd edition, 1974, published as *Politics and War in Islam,* Program in Near Eastern Studies, Princeton University, 1975, and *Wirtschaftsgeschichte des Vorderen Orients in islamischer Zeit,* E. J. Brill, 1977.

WORK IN PROGRESS: "A history of the Holy Land and a book on Islam and democracy."

SIDELIGHTS: In the course of his lengthy career as a scholar and professor of Near and Middle Eastern history, Bernard Lewis has written, translated, and edited numerous articles and books, several of which have come to be considered Orientalist classics. Lewis first attracted the attention of fellow Orientalists with his doctoral thesis, *The Origins of Ismailism,* which was published with revisions in 1940; he proceeded to gain prestige when he spent a year among the Turkish archives—a rare opportunity for a Westerner—and has since sustained a reputation for innovative perspective, thorough research, and clear, informative prose.

Among Lewis's most acclaimed publications is the 1961 book *The Emergence of Modern Turkey.* In this work he studies the revolutionary changes that have occurred since the seventeenth century in Turkey's cultural, religious, social, economic, and political attitudes, beliefs, and practices. "Based on both Turkish and other sources," H. N. Howard explained in *Annals of the American Academy of Political and Social Science,* Lewis's *Emergence of Modern Turkey* "is a model study of the development of nationalism in the Near East and should be read because of its wider implications as well." Moreover, Howard noted, "it has some excellent illustrations of both the old and the new in Turkey." An *American Historical Review* critic also praised the book, deeming it an "authoritative contribution by a distinguished English historian, which fills a long-existing need for an interpretive study of developments in Turkey during the last two centuries." And a *Times Literary Supplement* reviewer concluded, "No book, until the present one by Professor Lewis, has enabled us to see the emergence of modern Turkey in full historical perspective."

Lewis again drew critics' accolades for editing the 1976 book *Islam and the Arab World: Faith, People, Culture,* published in Britain as *The World of Islam.* He also contributed two essays and an epilogue to the volume, which is comprised of pieces by scholars specializing in Islamic and Arabic cultures. According to Charles Issawi, reviewing *The World of Islam* in the *Times Literary Supplement,* "Bernard Lewis, one of the foremost Islamicists, has put together a first-class team gathered from four continents, who between them cover Islamic history and culture in a comprehensive

and authoritative way. All but the most advanced experts in any given field can learn much from it." Yet, the critic continued, "This is a book not for specialists but for the general reader, . . . who will find here much information, lucidly and interestingly presented, and many insights into one of the world's major civilizations." Reviewing *Islam and the Arab World* in the *New York Times,* Alden Whitman described the collection as "a thinking man's guide to the faith, customs, culture and history of a large segment of the civilized world." Explained Whitman, "With the help of some thirteen ranking Islamicists and Arabists in the West, Professor Lewis has produced a splendid survey that is agreeably enriched by almost 500 photographs, reproductions, drawings and maps, 160 of them in color." Furthermore, observed David Pryce-Jones in the *New Republic:* "The general reader for once is not being solicited to vote for or against the Arabs, or indeed anyone. On the contrary, here is a free-for-all invitation to accompany a baker's dozen of professors on a tour of their subjects—though it is not for easy-riders or slackers."

Several critics commented on the range of topics covered by *Islam and the Arab World* as a whole, and on the depth and breadth of each individual essay, made especially remarkable by the complexity of a religion and culture that spans some twelve hundred years and several continents. As Whitman observed, "The basics of Islam as a religion are similar wherever it put down its roots," so it "is a culture of many common features." But, the critic remarked, Islam is "also of great diversity as a result of disparate geographic, ethnic and historical forces." Nonetheless, reviewers of *Islam and the Arab World* agreed that the essayists competently and informatively compress their vast topics into their allotted space and, as Whitman expressed it, together "manage to impose an order of sorts on the multinational constituents of Islamic culture."

Lewis also garnered praise aimed specifically at his contributions to *Islam and the Arab World.* Describing Lewis's introductory essay as "a brisk and compact history" of Islam "that is virtually a primer," Whitman noted that "Lewis employs to excellent effect his lucidity of style in explaining the Islamic faith and those who profess it." Pryce-Jones judged the essay to be "as masterly a survey of the rise of the great Muslim empires as is possible in a few thousand words." Issawi commended Lewis for his epilogue in which he brings modern-day Islam and its renewed wealth and power—based largely on the Middle East's vast petroleum resources—into focus. Lewis observes in his epilogue: "For the first time in centuries the Muslims have, in some measure, the power to choose their own form of government and to decide their own fate. The choices that they have made and are continuing to make will affect the course of history, for themselves and for many others, for a long time to come." Remarked Issawi, "This is a fitting note on which to conclude this informative, absorbing, lucidly written and beautifully illustrated book."

In his 1982 book *The Muslim Discovery of Europe*, Lewis presents the history of Muslim and European societies' knowledge of one another and their attitudes toward acquiring this knowledge, focusing in particular on the often-neglected Muslim perspective. R. W. Southern explained in his *New York Review of Books* critique of the book: Lewis "was prompted to write it when he observed that, while much had been written about the discovery of Islam by Europeans, there was no connected account of the parallel process of Muslim discovery of Europe. He has now provided one with precision and authority. . . . The book covers every side of Muslim life in its bearing on attitudes to Europe, and an extraordinarily wide range of Muslim historians, geographers, diplomats, administrators, and writers on trade and government is used to complete the picture." David Williams similarly remarked in *Newsweek* that *The Muslim Discovery of Europe* "is an attempt to cover more than a thousand years of East-West relations from the Muslim point of view and, predictably, it's filled with the rude shocks and occasional pleasant surprises that come with seeing ourselves as others see us." And according to Williams, "The rudest shock of all" rendered by Lewis's book "may be to learn how little the Muslims did see of 'the infidel' and how even less they cared."

Lewis speculates on the reasons for this Islamic indifference, as opposed to the European, and thus largely Christian, interest in Islamic culture, in *The Muslim Discovery of Europe*. For many years, as J. D. Gurney explained in the *Times Literary Supplement,* "It was, as Lewis recognizes, Christians who had greater need and also greater opportunity for understanding their neighbors." Their fear of Islam's military prowess and potential threat to Christianity in its claims to more recent and therefore more perfect divine revelation, and their desire to improve European standards of learning and living, led the Europeans to seek contact with Muslim society in order to meet its challenges and profit by its superior stores of scholarly and material riches. Moreover, the Muslims' very indifference allowed Europeans to travel and inhabit Islamic lands more freely than Muslims could European lands. As Lewis remarks: "The Christian attitude toward Islam was far more bigoted and intolerant than that of the Muslims to Christianity." But, Southern commented, it "should be added that the reasons for this intolerance, namely hatred of any kind of heresy or schism and the fear of Islam's strength, are the reasons also why Europeans were more interested in the nature of Islam than Muslims in the nature of Christendom."

European Christians thought that understanding the nature of Islam would enable them to defuse Islam's power by exposing its inadequacies as a religion. Islam, on the other hand, succeeded Christianity in its inception and therefore considered the Christian faith an inferior predecessor. Moreover, as Gurney explained, "Muslim civilization had been established through conquest and developed so rapidly that it could afford to feel arrogant towards the backward barbarians of Europe." But, Gurney continued, "as Lewis rightly points out, this explanation cannot hold good for the whole period" of history treated in *The Muslim Discovery of Europe.* "From the late fifteenth century onwards, the Ottomans shared a common frontier with an increasingly powerful enemy [Europe]. They had both the need and the opportunity for closer study; they failed to respond and their attitudes," which had been "assimilated into the Islamic heritage [and had] survived into a period when its earlier vigour had been sapped," became "dangerously obsolete."

Eventually, Lewis explains, Islam realized that significant technological developments, and with them increased military power, had made Europe a neighbor both to respect and to fear. Islamic interest in Europe grew, and by the eighteenth century, as Europe became increasingly secularized (i.e., as Europeans began to rely more on reason, logic, and scientific method as opposed to faith in divine revelation and tradition), studying European society and its resources became more acceptable. As Lewis observed: "Secularism as such had, of course, no special attraction for Muslims, quite the reverse; but an ideology which was non-Christian could be considered by Muslims with a detachment that was not possible for doctrines tainted with a rival religion. In such a secular or, rather, religiously neutral ideology, Muslims might even hope to find the talisman that would give them the secrets of Western knowledge and progress without endangering their own traditions and way of life."

In time, as some reviewers of *The Muslim Discovery of Europe* observed, adopting secular ways of thinking would prove a challenge to the religious authority of Islamic society and provoke Islamic theologians to resist Western influences. Lewis, however, takes his subject only as far as the Muslims' recognition of the West as a potential power with which to be reckoned. "When this was grasped, the real Muslim discovery of Europe starts," remarked Gurney. But, he concluded, "at this point the book disappointingly ends." Southern likewise commented that the unfolding of the attitudes of Islam toward Western thought after 1840 "deserves another volume," but he concluded that "no one is better qualified to write it than the author of this distinguished work." The critic also praised Lewis for the amount of "rare and exact information" that *The Muslim Discovery of Europe* provides within its roughly one-thousand-year scope and commented: "No doubt many more details can be added, but it is hard to believe that the general picture will be greatly altered by any future work. . . . What we are given is a remarkable collection of new information, which will be of deep interest to students of European history."

In 1985's *The Jews of Islam* Lewis studies Islamic attitudes toward another cultural group as he recounts the history of the Jewish minority in Islam-dominated lands of the Middle East and North Africa from about the sixth century onward. Lawrence Rosen explained in the *Times Literary Supplement:* "In a masterful synthesis [Lewis] argues that until quite recent times there existed a symbiosis of Muslims and Jews quite unlike anything that ever developed in the West. Indeed, he suggests, we can speak of a Judaeo-Islamic tradition which may well have been stronger and deeper than the more familiar Judaeo-Christian." In setting forth this argument, Lewis cites observations written by Muslim and Jewish poets, scholars, and politicians on the often humiliating and discriminatory but nonviolent tolerance to which the Jews were subject. He also, according to Alain Silvera, who critiqued *The Jews of Islam* for the *New York Times Book Review,* examines various "interpretations of the Jewish experience under Moslem domination," giving them "greater relevance" by looking at the evolution of this experience "in terms of Islam's own distinctive chronology," rather than in

terms of the corresponding European periods of history. "By doing this," continued Silvera, "he makes the shifting relations between Jews and Moslems more intelligible." One shift in particular that Lewis discusses in *The Jews of Islam* is the breakdown of the Judaeo-Islamic symbiosis in modern times, and he links this deterioration to the disruption of traditional Islamic society by the introduction, since the eighteenth century, of Western ideas and attitudes. As Rosen noted: "Muslims may have held their Jewish neighbors in contempt, Lewis concludes, but it was only when the pattern of tolerated protection was broken and Western theories of racial and religious hostility were introduced that the Judaeo-Islamic tradition was finally undermined and its history brought to an end." Silvera commented of Lewis's treatment of the later stages of Jewish-Muslim interaction: "The details for this more recent period, made familiar by an abundance of sources, are given shape and meaning by Mr. Lewis's emphasis on people's attitudes and perceptions. The Jews of Islam are no more, but their story over fourteen centuries is recounted here with sympathy, wit and authority." The critic concluded that *The Jews of Islam* "is an elegant and masterly survey. It is a measure of Mr. Lewis's gift for synthesis that all the many findings of recent scholarship, including his own in the Turkish archives, are made to fit into a coherent and plausible pattern."

In 1986 Lewis left his full-time teaching career at Princeton University to devote more time to his writing. While maintaining contact with students of the Near and Middle East through his post as A. D. White Professor at Large at Cornell University from 1986 to 1990, he went on to publish a number of other books, including *Semites and Anti-Semites: An Inquiry into Conflict and Prejudice, Race and Slavery in the Middle East, Islam and the West,* and *The Political Language of Islam.* Based on a series of lectures given in 1986, *The Political Language of Islam* delves into the meaning of such terms as *jihad* ("holy war") and *faqih* (legal scholar), which often refer to concepts alien to Westerner students of Eastern cultures. Covering the Arabic, Persian, and Turkish languages spoken in the more highly politicizes regions of the Middle East, the volume does not include the lesser-known languages spoken by inhabitants of the area's more remote regions. Lewis, instead, concentrates his study on the semantics and etymology of the written language of urban politics. In her critique of the volume for the *American Historical Review,* Marilyn Robinson Waldman took issue with the historian's relatively narrow approach, noting that Lewis's "reliance on textualized language raises a problem not limited to the Orientalist but in fact common to many historians of ideas," as the interconnectedness of texts from differing provenances or political persuasions must be assumed for comparisons between terms to be made at all. While noting that the volume contains "limitations and dead-ends," P. Edward Haley maintained in his review for the *Los Angeles Times Book Review* that "The Islamic political tradition emerges as far more complex, diverse, humane, and, therefore, worthy of respect than one would have imagined before reading [Lewis's] book."

Islam and the West, published in 1993, is an anthology of essays reprinted from scholarly journals and other periodicals that reflects what *New York Times Book Review* commentator Ira M. Lapidus referred to as Lewis's "great learning, his deep knowledge of Arabic philology, his masterly acquaintance with the history and culture of the Middle East, and his intimate familiarity with the relations of East and West." The collection is divided into three sections: encounters between East and West, the evolving European view of Islam, and the responses to that evolving viewpoint by Middle Eastern leaders. Within *Islam and the West*—particularly in the essay titled "The Question of Orientalism"—Lewis stages a counterattack on the anti-Orientalist movement that grew in U.S. academic circles during the 1980s and that views "Orientalists" in a derogatory light as what Lapidus called "agents of intellectual and political imperialism, scholars dedicated to a discourse that fosters oppression of Eastern peoples by Western." Although Lapidus acknowledged that Lewis's view of the Middle East was indeed "antagonistic," "he is correct in many of responses," diminishing the academic criticism against his approach by noting that scholarly study of the region began long before the rise of Western imperialism. "In examining the broader, Orientalist scholarly position, Lewis, unlike his critics, does not take a monolithic view," concluded *New York Review of Books* contributor Shaul Bakhash. "He does not conclude that because there was scholarship and there was empire, the two must converge. . . . He avoids dogmatic positions himself and sees dogma as something to be analyzed. It is this sense of nuance, of historical setting, of honesty to [historic] texts, that informs the essays in *Islam and the West.*"

With 2003's *The Crisis of Islam: Holy War and Unholy Terror,* Lewis offers a detailed analysis of "the violence [and] hostility to the West in the modern Islamic world," wrote Jasper Griffin in the *Spectator.* Lewis's book is aimed at those Americans who wondered in the wake of the September 11, 2001, terrorist attacks on the United States by Islamic fundamentalists, "Why do the Muslims hate us?," wrote Harry Levins in the *St. Louis Post-Dispatch.* "His answer: A lot of them don't, and those who do have motives that bear some looking at," Levins observed. *"The Crisis of Islam* examines these motives—some zany, some entirely rational. If the book offers no easy answers, it at least gives the general reader some easy-to-grasp insights into the nature of the problem," Levins remarked.

Lewis traces the origins and early history of Islam, "stressing the amazing early successes of the new faith from the deserts of Arabia," Griffin wrote. "A creed which was warlike from the beginning, founded by a prophet who was himself a conqueror and a statesman, it came from nowhere, and in 100 years it destroyed the Persian empire and conquered great parts of the empire of Byzantium," sweeping through North Africa, Egypt, Tunisia, and into France, Griffin remarked. In addition to martial prowess, "Islamic science and scholarship kept more of the legacy of Greece and were for centuries ahead of those of Europe," Griffin wrote.

During the last 300 years, however, Christianity resurged, "and the Christians, the despised Unbelievers, came back from apparent defeat and irrelevance to dominate the Middle East," remaking it to reflect their attitudes and desires, bringing in Western ways and foreign thought, creating new political states and dividing old ones, Griffin wrote. "Islam as such is not an enemy of the West, and there are growing numbers of Muslims, both here and there, who desire nothing better than a closer and more friendly relationship with the west and the development of democratic institutions in their own countries," observed Michael Potemra in the *National Review.* Lewis finds "no justification in Islamic doctrine and no precedent in Islamic history" for such radicalism as the September 11 attacks and the subsequent continued terrorism, Potemra stated.

Some critics expressed harsh views towards *The Crisis of Islam.* Siddhartha Deb, writing in the *Boston Globe,* called the notion that Islam is angry for losing its dominance in the world "an old and pernicious argument," and commented on the "stale rhetoric emanating from" Lewis's basic arguments. An *Economist* reviewer stated that the book "does little to help the reader to form even a rough view about how many Muslims are sympathetic to this bleak bin Ladenesque interpretation of Islam." Others, such as Potemra, found much more to appreciate about Lewis's volume. "Lewis provides an excellent brief summary for the nonspecialist of how what was once 'the leading civilization in the world' came to be seen by many as synonymous with all that is most sinister in the human heart," Potemra wrote. "And he does so with an intellectual sensitivity that makes his book a source of remarkable insights, and a joy to read."

Solving the problem will require direct contact between the West and the Islamic world, Lewis observes. Without deliberate and meaningful attempts by the West to cooperate with forward-looking Muslims, Lewis believes "the reactionaries could make dangerous demographic strides," Levins wrote. "*Crisis* is more than a good primer," Levins concluded. "It's also fair warning."

In a *Wall Street Journal* profile of Lewis, Tunku Varadarajan remarked that "Of all the scholars of Islam, Mr. Lewis is the one whom Muslims would do best to heed." Lewis, Varadarajan wrote, "will always be encyclopedic, original, and as near to irrefutable as a man can get in a field that is so combustible."

For a previously published interview, see entry in *Contemporary Authors*, Volume 118, 1986, pp. 282-288.

BIOGRAPHICAL AND CRITICAL SOURCES:

BOOKS

Bosworth, C. E., *The Islamic World from Classical to Modern Times: Essays in Honor of Bernard Lewis*, Darwin Press (Princeton, NJ), 1989.
Lewis, Bernard, *Islam and the Arab World: Faith, People, Culture*, Knopf, 1976.
Lewis, Bernard, *The Muslim Discovery of Europe*, Norton, 1982.

PERIODICALS

American Historical Review, April, 1962, review of *The Emergence of Modern Turkey;* December, 1991, Marilyn Robinson Waldman, review of *The Political Language of Islam*, pp. 1586-1587.

Annals of the American Academy of Political and Social Science, March, 1962, H. N. Howard, review of *The Emergence of Modern Turkey.*
Boston Globe, June 8, 2003, Siddhartha Deb, "An Archaic View of the Making of Modern Islam," p. H8.
Economist, May 3, 2003, "How Many bin Ladens? Islam and the West," pp. 77-78.
Guardian (Manchester, England), April 19, 2003, "Faith, Hope, Not Much Charity," p. 3; September 6, 2003, Terry Eagleton, "September 11: Radical Islam's Fusion of the Primitive and the Progressive Is a Typically Modern Phenomenon," p. 14.
International Social Science Review, spring-summer, 2003, Charles W. McClellan, review of *What Went Wrong? Western Impact and Middle Eastern Response*, p. 59.
Los Angeles Times Book Review, June 12, 1988, P. Edward Haley, review of *The Political Language of Islam*, p. 15.
National Review April 7, 2003, Michael Potemra, "The War for Islam," pp. 53-54.
New Republic, November 27, 1976, David Pryce-Jones, review of *Islam and the Arab World;* August 16-23, 1982.
Newsweek, July 5, 1982, David Williams, review of *The Muslim Discovery of Europe*, p. 70.
New York Review of Books, November 4, 1982, R. W. Southern, review of *The Muslim Discovery of Europe*, p. 23; October 7, 1993, Shaul Bakhash, review of *Islam and the West*, pp. 42-45.
New York Times, September 18, 1976, Alden Whitman, review of *Islam and the Arab World.*
New York Times Book Review, July 21, 1985, Alain Silvera, review of *The Jews of Islam*, p. 20; May 30, 1993, Ira M. Lapidus, review of *Islam and the West*, pp. 8-9.
St. Louis Post-Dispatch, May 4, 2003, Harry Levins, review of *The Crisis of Islam: Holy War and Unholy Terror*, p. F12.
Spectator, April 12, 2003, Jasper Griffin, "Why Do They Hate Us?," pp. 35-36.
Times Literary Supplement, September 29, 1961, review of *The Emergence of Modern Turkey;* April 30, 1976, Charles Issawi, review of *The World of Islam: Faith, People, Culture;* March 11, 1983, J. D. Gurney, review of *The Muslim Discovery of Europe;* June 7, 1985, Lawrence Rosen, review of *The Jews of Islam*, p. 648; April 11, 2003, Francis Robinson, "Thoroughly Modern Muslims," p. 26.
Wall Street Journal, September 23, 2003, Tunku Varadarajan, "Lewis of Arabia," p. A24.

ONLINE

Barnes & Noble Web site, http://www.barnesandnoble. com/ (November 14, 2003), interview with Bernard Lewis.

Princeton University Web site, http://www.princeton. edu/ (November 14, 2003), biography of Bernard Lewis.*

*   *   *

LIND, Michael 1962-

PERSONAL: Born 1962. *Education:* Attended Yale University and University of Texas. *Religion:* Methodist.

*ADDRESSES: Home—*Washington, DC. *Office—*New America Foundation, 1630 Connecticut Ave. NW, 7th Floor, Washington, DC 20009. *E-mail—*lind@ newamerica.net.

CAREER: Journalist and author. *National Interest,* executive editor, 1991-94; *Harper's,* New York, NY, senior editor, beginning 1994; New America Foundation, director of American Strategy Project and Whitehead Senior Fellow.

WRITINGS:

The Next American Nation: The New Nationalism and the Fourth American Revolution, Free Press (New York, NY), 1995.

(Author of introduction) *The New Republic Guide to the Issues: The 1996 Campaign,* Basic Books (New York, NY), 1996.

Powertown, HarperCollins (New York, NY), 1996.

Up from Conservatism: Why the Right Is Wrong for America, Free Press (New York, NY), 1996.

The Alamo: An Epic, Houghton Mifflin (Boston, MA), 1997.

(Editor and author of introduction) *Hamilton's Republic: Readings in the American Democratic Nationalist Tradition,* Free Press (New York, NY), 1997.

Vietnam, the Necessary War: A Reinterpretation of America's Most Disastrous Military Conflict, Free Press (New York, NY), 1999.

(With Ted Halstead) *The Radical Center: The Future of American Politics,* Doubleday (New York, NY), 2001.

Made in Texas: George W. Bush and the Southern Takeover of American Politics, New America/ Basic Books (New York, NY), 2003.

What Lincoln Believed: The Values and Convictions of America's Greatest President, Doubleday (New York, NY), 2004.

Contributor to periodicals such as *Dissent, Atlantic Monthly, Financial Times, Washington Post,* and *Wall Street Journal.*

SIDELIGHTS: Michael Lind was the editor of the conservative journal *National Interest* and a protege of columnist William F. Buckley, Jr., until the changing tide of Republican politics caused him to re-evaluate his right-of-center stance. The rising popularity of archconservative, fundamentalist Christian politics as embodied by Pat Robertson and Pat Buchanan, and the incorporation of some of their ideology into more mainstream Republican thought, was the impetus behind Lind's defection. Leaving both the *National Interest* and the flock, he took a job as a senior editor at *Harper's* and wrote his first book, *The Next American Nation: The New Nationalism and the Fourth American Revolution.* In the 1995 work, Lind presents the theory that the history of American national identity can be divided into three epochs: the "Anglo-America," when the country's first settlers were mostly emigrants from the British Isles; the "Euro-America," from the Civil War until World War II; and finally, "Multicultural America," from about 1950 until the present.

In *The Next American Nation,* Lind finds great fault with the idea of enforced multiculturalism during this latest phase, and posits that its actual strategy is to keep Americans divided and resentful of other ethnic groups, even though they may have common interests. As a remedy, Lind proposes numerous and dramatic changes. He advises abolishing certain class-perpetuating prerogatives, such as the M.D. and J.D. titles and the favoring of children of alumni in Ivy League admissions policies, suggests relocating inner-city families to more positive suburban environments, and finally, argues a case for the nullification of all affirmative action policies and quota systems. Lind and his theories attracted widespread attention in the media, much of it positive. "Lind is a pleasure to read because he is so manifestly intelligent and because he has done a great deal of hard and consistent work," noted Christopher Hitchens in the *New York Times Book Review.* "Sacred cows are slaughtered at the rate of one a paragraph," remarked Alan Ryan of the *New York Review of Books.* "Lind turns upside down every platitude of orthodox American history and political science." In the *New York Times,* Richard Bernstein faulted the book, describing it as "both tendentious and dreamy, based too much on pure thought and not enough on any experience with the way the world actually works," but the critic conceded that "Lind saves himself by his obvious intelligence. His book is one of the best—certainly it is the most visionary, the most forward-looking—in the growing library of works on the American identity, multiculturalism and the future."

In *The Radical Center: The Future of American Politics,* written with Ted Halstead, Lind offers up the political concept of the radical center. "Beyond the familiar concepts of left and right, untold numbers of Americans are somewhere in the middle," remarked Richard D. Kahlenberg in *American Prospect.* "They are centrist in the sense that they represent a broad part of the American mainstream. But some are radical, too, in that they are deeply disapproving of the untrammeled privilege and unbalanced power that mars American democracy," Kahlenberg wrote. Based on work with Lind and Halstead's political think tank, the New America Foundation, the book provides a detailed elaboration on the politics and thinking of the "alienated majority" that makes up the political center. "In the authors' eyes, the radical center is not the equivalent of the so-called Reagan Democrats of the 1980s; Halstead and Lind find radical centrists among all Americans who feel disengaged from the Republican and Democratic parties," Kahlenberg commented.

If no other lesson emerged from the effect of Ralph Nader's candidacy on the 2000 presidential elections, there was "the notion that American politics is desperately in need of reform," wrote Daniel Casse in *Commentary.* The two-party adversarial system is no longer relevant in the current technologically savvy age. "Independent voters are the new majority," Casse remarked. In response to this position, *The Radical Center* "sets forth a new philosophy for American political life and specific, far-reaching proposals for changing the role and shape of government," Casse observed. Among Lind and Halstead's proposed re-

forms are elimination of the current tax code; abandoning the reliance on employer-sponsored health care in favor of mandatory private individual insurance, supported with assistance for those who cannot afford it; adoption of a federal funding system for schools; ending race-based preferences; and offering improved tax advantages for charitable contributions made to help the poor. They support a ranking system for elections that would allow voters to numerically order their choices according to preference.

The authors' "arguments are quite persuasive and, to their credit, they write in a clear, succinct prose style and employ a McCainesque straight-talk sensibility that will help them attract the independent, centrist-minded voters at whom the book is aimed," wrote Heath Madom in *Library Journal.* Other critics noted that the authors offer an interesting selection of policy ideas but little concrete information on how to impose them. "Despite overextending themselves in the sheer volume of reforms they propose, Halstead and Lind have nevertheless crafted an intriguing collection of public policy reforms, sure to be debated in years to come," observed Paul McCleary in *Social Policy.* "All in all," Kahlenberg concluded, "Halstead and Lind have done a superb job of outlining a provocative starting point for the radical center."

Lind analyzes the political structure and "delves deep into the heart of George W. Bush's Texas" in *Made in Texas: George W. Bush and the Southern Takeover of American Politics,* wrote a *Publishers Weekly* critic. Lind reports that the politics of western Texas are rife with racism, exploitation of the environment, "jingoistic militarism, crony capitalism," a bias against public education, and "a fundamentalist evangelicism inconsistent with the separation of church and state," the *Publishers Weekly* reviewer wrote. A Texan himself, Lind warns against a "southern takeover of American politics," wrote Gary Rosen in *Commentary.* "Mr. Lind treats Texas as a southern state masquerading as a western one, and believes Mr. Bush is involved in a similar disguise," wrote a reviewer in the *Economist.* Bush is considered the first southern conservative to hold the office of president since James Polk in 1844. "Worse," the *Economist* reviewer commented, Bush has "set about reordering the world in a similarly reactionary way, pushing religion into domestic policy and militarism back into diplomacy." *Made in Texas* "offers a trenchant intellectual analysis of the reactionary, right-wing roots of Bush in the Lone Star State," wrote an interviewer on the *Buzzflash* Web site.

BIOGRAPHICAL AND CRITICAL SOURCES:

PERIODICALS

American Prospect, December 3, 2001, Richard D. Kahlenberg, review of *The Radical Center: The Future of American Politics,* pp. 41-44.

Booklist, September 1, 2001, Mary Carroll, review of *The Radical Center,* p. 22.

Commentary, October, 2001, Daniel Casse, review of *The Radical Center,* p. 86; February, 2003, Gary Rosen, "Lone Star," pp. 59-61.

Commonweal, January 11, 2002, Julia Vitullo-Martin, "Are the Parties Over?," p. 23.

Economist, January 18, 2003, "The Sphinx in the White House; George Bush."

Kirkus Reviews, August 1, 2001, review of *The Radical Center,* p. 1089.

Library Journal, August, 2001, Heath Madom, review of *The Radical Center,* p. 137.

New York Review of Books, October 5, 1995, Alan Ryan, *The Next American Nation: The New Nationalism and the Fourth American Revolution,* pp. 30-34.

New York Times, July 5, 1995, Richard Bernstein, review of *The Next American Nation,* p. C14.

New York Times Book Review, June 25, 1995, Christopher Hitchens, review of *The Next American Nation,* p. 7.

Publishers Weekly, January 6, 2003, review of *Made in Texas: George W. Bush and the Southern Takeover of American Politics,* p. 54.

Social Policy, summer, 2002, Paul McCleary, "Politics, Policy, & Paranoia," pp. 60-65.

Washington Monthly, September, 2001, Bruce Reed, review of *The Radical Center,* p. 45.

ONLINE

Buzzflash Web site, http://www.buzzflash.com/ (March 20, 2003), interview with Michael Lind.

New America Foundation Web site, http://www. newamerica.net/ (November 14, 2003), biography of Michael Lind.*

M

MacLACHLAN, Patricia 1938-

PERSONAL: Born March 3, 1938, in Cheyenne, WY; daughter of Philo (a teacher) and Madonna (a teacher; maiden name, Moss) Pritzkau; married Robert MacLachlan (a clinical psychologist), April 14, 1962; children: John, Jamie, Emily. *Education:* University of Connecticut, B.A., 1962.

ADDRESSES: Home—Williamsburg, MA. *Office*—Department of Education, Smith College, Northampton, MA 01063. *Agent*—c/o Author Mail, HarperCollins, 10 East 53rd St., New York, NY 10022.

CAREER: Writer and educator. Bennett Junior High School, Manchester, CT, English teacher, 1963-79; Smith College, Northampton, MA, visiting lecturer, 1986—; writer. Lecturer; social worker; teacher of creative writing workshops for adults and children. Children's Aid Family Service Agency, board member, 1970-80.

AWARDS, HONORS: Golden Kite Award, Society of Children's Book Writers 1980, for *Arthur, for the Very First Time;* Notable Book Citation, American Library Association, 1980, for *Arthur, for the Very First Time,* 1984, for *Unclaimed Treasures,* 1984, for *Sarah, Plain and Tall,* and 1988, for *The Facts and Fictions of Minna Pratt;* Notable Children's Trade Book, National Council for Social Studies and the Children's Book Council, 1980, for *Through Grandpa's Eyes,* 1982, for *Mama One, Mama Two,* and 1985, for *Sarah, Plain and Tall; Boston Globe-Horn Book* Award, 1984, for

Patricia MacLachlan

Unclaimed Treasures; Horn Book Honor List citation, 1984, for *Unclaimed Treasures,* and 1985, for *Sarah, Plain and Tall;* Golden Kite Award, Scott O'Dell Historical Fiction Award, one of *School Library Journal*'s Best Books of the Year, and one of the *New York Times* Notable Children's Books of the Year, all 1985, Newbery Medal, American Library Association, Jefferson Cup Award, Virginia Library Association, Christopher Award, and one of Child Study Association of

America's Children's Books of the Year, all 1986, Garden State Children's Book Award, New Jersey Library Association, Charlie May Simon Book Award, Elementary Council of the Arkansas Department of Education, and International Board on Books for Young People Honor List nominee, both 1988, all for *Sarah, Plain and Tall; Parents' Choice* Award, Parents' Choice Foundation, 1988, and *Horn Book* Fanfare citation, 1989, for *The Facts and Fictions of Minna Pratt.*

WRITINGS:

FOR CHILDREN

The Sick Day (picture book), illustrated by William Pene Du Bois, Pantheon (New York, NY), 1979.

Arthur, for the Very First Time (novel), illustrated by Lloyd Bloom, Harper (New York, NY), 1980.

Moon, Stars, Frogs, and Friends, illustrated by Tomie de Paola, Pantheon (New York, NY), 1980.

Through Grandpa's Eyes (picture book), illustrated by Deborah Ray, Harper (New York, NY), 1980.

Cassie Binegar (novel), Harper (New York, NY), 1982.

Mama One, Mama Two (picture book), illustrated by Ruth Lercher Bornstein, Harper (New York, NY), 1982.

Tomorrow's Wizard, illustrated by Kathy Jacobi, Harper (New York, NY), 1982.

Seven Kisses in a Row (picture book), illustrated by Maria Pia Marrella, Harper (New York, NY), 1983.

Unclaimed Treasures (novel), Harper (New York, NY), 1984.

Sarah, Plain and Tall (novel), Harper (New York, NY), 1985.

The Facts and Fictions of Minna Pratt (novel), Harper (New York, NY), 1988.

Journey, Delacorte Press (New York, NY), 1991.

Three Names, illustrated by Alexander Pertzoff, HarperCollins (New York, NY), 1991.

Baby, Delacorte Press (New York, NY), 1993.

All the Places to Love, paintings by Mike Wimmer, HarperCollins (New York, NY), 1994.

Skylark, HarperCollins (New York, NY), 1994.

What You Know First, engravings by Barry Moser, HarperCollins (New York, NY), 1995.

Caleb's Story, Joanna Cotler Books (New York, NY), 2001.

(With daughter, Emily MacLachlan) *Painting the Wind,* illustrated by Katy Schneider, Joanna Cotler Books, (New York, NY), 2003.

(With Emily MacLachlan) *Bittle,* illustrated by Dan Yaccarino, Joanna Cotler Books (New York, NY), 2004.

Author of *Skylark* (teleplay), CBS-TV, 1993; author of teleplay for *Sarah, Plain and Tall* broadcast as a *Hallmark Hall of Fame* presentation, starring Glenn Close, 1991. Short fiction has appeared in anthologies such as *Newbery Award Library II,* edited by Joseph Krumgold, Harper (New York, NY), 1988.

ADAPTATIONS: Arthur, for the Very First Time was adapted as a filmstrip with cassette, Pied Piper, 1984; *Sarah, Plain and Tall* was adapted as a filmstrip with cassette, Random House, 1986, and as a television film starring Glenn Close; *Mama One, Mama Two, Through Grandpa's Eyes,* and *The Sick Day* were adapted as an audiocassette, Caedmon, 1987; *Sarah, Plain and Tall* was adapted as a musical by Julia Jordan, Nell Benjamin, and Laurence O'Keefe. The play opened at the Lucille Lortel Theater in Manhattan and is directed by Joe Calarco.

SIDELIGHTS: Patricia MacLachlan is known for her award-winning picture books and novels for children, which include *The Sick Day; Arthur, for the Very First Time; Sarah, Plain and Tall;* and *The Facts and Fictions of Minna Pratt.* Populated by eccentric, endearing characters and often focusing on family relationships, MacLachlan's works are considered to be tender, humorous, and perceptive. Though she usually concentrates on the realities of everyday life in her books, MacLachlan has also penned more fanciful tales such as *Tomorrow's Wizard* and *Moon, Stars, Frogs, and Friends.* Reviewers generally praise MacLachlan's work, indicating that her graceful, lucid prose is particularly suitable for reading aloud and that her warm, optimistic stories both enlighten and entertain young readers. "MacLachlan is the critically acclaimed author of the kind of children's stories so compelling that readers clasp the book to their chest and sigh when the last page is turned," wrote Catherine Keefe in the *Orange County Register.*

Born in Wyoming and reared in Minnesota, MacLachlan was an only child. Her lack of siblings was offset by a strong relationship with her parents and an active imagination. MacLachlan's parents were teachers and encouraged her to read; her mother urged her to "read a book and find out who you are," the author related in *Horn Book.* She did read voraciously, sometimes discussing and acting out scenes in books with her parents. She wrote in *Horn Book,* "I can still feel the goose bumps as I, in the fur of Peter Rabbit, fled from the garden and Mr. McGregor—played with great ferocity by my father—to the coat closet. . . . Some days I would talk my father into acting out the book a dozen times in a row, with minor changes here and there or major differences that reversed the plot."

MacLachlan was also kept company by her imaginary friend, Mary, "who was real enough for me to insist that my parents set a place for her at the table," the author recalled in *Horn Book.* "Mary was a free spirit. She talked me into drawing a snail on the living room wall, larger and larger, so that the room had to be repainted. . . . My parents tolerated Mary with good humor, though I'm sure it was trying. Mary was ever present. 'Don't sit there,' I'd cry with alarm. 'Mary's there!' One of my early memories is of my father, negotiating with Mary for the couch after dinner."

Though she was creative enough to invent a friend and concoct elaborate fantasies, MacLachlan did not write stories as a child. The author remembers being intimidated by the intensely personal nature of writing. In an autobiographical essay in *Authors and Adults for Young Adults,* she confessed: "I was afraid of putting my own feelings and thoughts on a page for everyone to read. This is still a scary part of writing." She also noted in *Horn Book* that she believed "writers had all the answers." She continued, remembering a school assignment: "I wrote a story on a three by five card. I still have it: 'My cats have names and seem happy. Often they play. The end.' My teacher was not impressed. I was discouraged, and I wrote in my diary: 'I shall try not to be a writer.'"

Indeed, MacLachlan did not begin to write until years later, at the age of thirty-five. Married with children of her own, she kept busy by working with foster mothers at a family services agency and spending time with her family. As her children grew older, though, she "felt a need to do something else—go to graduate school or go back to teaching, perhaps," she once noted. "It dawned on me that what I really wanted to do was to write. How would I ever have the courage, I wondered. It was very scary to find myself in the role of student again, trying to learn something entirely new."

MacLachlan started her successful writing career by creating picture books. Her first, *The Sick Day,* details how a little girl with a cold is cared for by her father. Another work, *Through Grandpa's Eyes,* explores how a young boy is taught by his blind grandfather to "see" the world through his other senses. *Mama One, Mama Two,* a somewhat later book, takes a frank yet comforting look at mental illness and foster parenting. In it a girl is taken in by "Mama Two" while waiting for her natural mother, "Mama One," to recover from psychological problems. MacLachlan, praised for the simplicity and sensitivity she brings to these stories, is especially noted for her deft handling of unconventional subject matter.

Encouraged by her editor, MacLachlan also started to write novels, which are intended for a slightly older audience than her picture books. She once commented on the differences between the two genres: "It is more difficult to write a picture book than a novel. A good picture book is much like a poem: concise, rich, bare-boned, and multileveled. . . . When I want to stretch into greater self-indulgence, I write a novel." MacLachlan's first novel, *Arthur, for the Very First Time,* tells of a young boy's emotional growth during the summer he spends with his great-uncle and great-aunt. Reviews of the work were laudatory; critics particularly praised MacLachlan's realistic characters and her sincere yet entertaining look at childhood problems.

A character in *Arthur, for the Very First Time* provided the seed for MacLachlan's best-known work, *Sarah, Plain and Tall.* Aunt Mag in *Arthur* was a mail-order bride (a woman who meets her husband by answering a newspaper advertisement) as was a distant relative of MacLachlan's. In *Sarah, Plain and Tall* the title character answers a newspaper advertisement and as a result goes to visit a lonely widower and his children on a midwestern prairie. When Sarah arrives, the children take to her immediately and hope she'll stay and marry their father. Considered a poignant and finely wrought tale, *Sarah, Plain and Tall* garnered widespread critical acclaim; MacLachlan received a Newbery Medal for the novel in 1986. Margery Fisher, a *Growing Point* contributor, deemed the book a "small masterpiece."

Skylark, which first appeared in 1994, is the sequel to *Sarah, Plain and Tall,* and invites inevitable comparison to the original, wrote Mary M. Burns in *Horn*

Book. Skylark, however, "does not suffer in such a pairing [with the original], for it has its own center and momentum," Burns concluded. A terrible drought has overwhelmed Sarah and Jacob Witting's farm. The crops wither and die, drinking water is scarce, neighbors leave for better conditions elsewhere, and the barn is burned in a freak rainless lightning strike. "Sarah is increasingly on edge, not so firmly rooted as her husband, Jacob," wrote a *Publishers Weekly* critic. "She cries out that Jacob 'once said his name was written in this land, but mine isn't. It isn't!'" To alleviate their problems, Sarah, along with children Anna and Caleb, go to visit her aunts in coastal Maine, where water is plentiful and life is easier than on a hardscrabble farm in the plains. The only connection Sarah and the children have with the farm is letters from Jacob, until one day he appears in Maine to collect his family. Rain has come to the farm, and Sarah is expecting a new baby. With renewed hope, the family returns to the farm, where Sarah symbolically writes her own name in the land. "*Skylark* is one sequel that is as successful as the original," Burns wrote. "This stirring novel's flawlessly crafted dialogue and imagery linger long after the final, hopeful message is delivered" by young Caleb, "who looks forward to arrival of spring and of his new sibling," wrote the *Publishers Weekly* reviewer.

In *Caleb's Story,* young Caleb from *Sarah, Plain and Tall* and *Skylark* narrates the continuing story of the Witting family. Anna has moved to town to attend school and work for the area doctor, while the newest arrival to the family, Cassie, grows up on the farm. One day, Jacob's father, who had abandoned his farm and his family and who Jacob thought was dead, returns, creating a difficult conflict between Jacob and his father. Jacob struggles with his bitter anger toward his father. Clues emerge, however, that Jacob's father is illiterate, which may have contributed to his past actions. Caleb takes on the task of teaching his grandfather to read, and Sarah urges Jacob to find the courage to forgive. In the book, "the relationships are believable, the emotions ring true, and MacLachlan has an unabated gift for clean, well-honed dialogue that carries its resonant meanings with unusual grace," wrote a *Horn Book* reviewer. A *Kirkus Reviews* critic remarked that "MacLachlan's appreciative readers will savor this new addition to the chronicle of a delightful family" while hoping for more volumes in the ever-growing series. In a *Publishers Weekly* review, critic Jason Britton noted that MacLachlan undertook *Caleb's Story* in response to a phone call from a worried little boy who was concerned that she might not continue writing after the September 11 terrorist attacks on the United States. "And I thought, 'By God, I owe it to him,'" MacLachlan is quoted as saying. "It is that characteristic spark that fans of MacLachlan and her writing—and specifically, of the collection of books that began with *Sarah, Plan and Tall*—have come to expect," Britton remarked.

Echoing the unwilling separation from home found in *Skylark,* MacLachlan's *What You Know First* tells the story of a girl whose parents have been forced to sell their farm and move elsewhere. Heartbroken, she begins to catalogue the things about the farm and the country that she will miss, and even tries to come up with reasons for not moving. In the end, she cannot avoid the inevitable, but she takes a tangible reminder with her: a bag of prairie dirt, and cuttings from a beloved cottonwood tree. The book "touches the heart," wrote a *Publishers Weekly* reviewer. MacLachlan is a real-life example of the character in the story: she also carries a bag of prairie dirt with her wherever she goes, to remind her of where she came from. "It is the prairie dirt—clutched in a plastic sandwich bag, dusty and twiggy and brown, toted everywhere that MacLachlan goes—that speaks volumes about the connection between her own life and her work," Keefe observed.

MacLachlan has also undertaken collaborations with her daughter, Emily. In *Painting the Wind,* a young painter finds inspiration from the dozens of other painters who migrate to his island and work at their easels every summer. At summer's end, an exhibition from all the artists lets the narrator find new ways to look at his work and appreciate the work of others. *Painting the Wind* "bears insights into how artists look at their world, and their work, and will broaden children's understanding of how and why art is made," a *Kirkus Reviews* critic remarked.

The entire body of MacLachlan's work has been consistently well-regarded by reviewers as well as readers. MacLachlan's "simple, compassionate stories, including *Sarah, Plain and Tall* and *the Facts and Fictions of Minna Pratt,* portray a cast of individualistic children on the brink of adolescence," wrote a critic in *Authors and Artists for Young Adults.* "And it is the graceful, lyrical style of MacLachlan's writing that makes these characters so real and so full of life as they experience the entire range of emotions associated with growing up."

As with the mail-order bride in *Sarah, Plain and Tall,* MacLachlan often gleans elements of her stories from personal experience. As she once explained, "My books derive chiefly from my family life, both as a child with my own parents as well as with my husband and kids. *The Sick Day* . . . could happen in almost any family. *Mama One, Mama Two* comes from my experiences with foster mothers and the children they cared for." MacLachlan also noted in *Horn Book* that "the issues of a book are the same issues of life each day. What is real and what is not? How do you look at the world? How do I?" Sometimes the influence of the author's life on her work is unconscious; scenes from her childhood appear on her pages, episodes that she thought she had invented but that had actually happened. Once, she described an unusual tablecloth in one of her books, thinking she had made up the cloth's design; she later discovered that her mother had used a virtually identical tablecloth when MacLachlan was a child. Referring to such a instance in the *Junior Literary Guild Catalog,* MacLachlan commented, "I realized that this is the magic. When you write you reach back somewhere in your mind or your heart and pull out things that you never even knew were there."

MacLachlan is heartened by children's reactions to her work; she once noted that "it's hugely gratifying to know that kids all over read what I write." Affirming the importance of encouraging young writers, the author visits schools to speak with students and give writing workshops. "In my experience, children believe that writers are like movie stars. I am often asked if I arrived in a limousine," MacLachlan remarked. "I admit that sometimes I'm a little flattered at the exalted idea kids have about writers. But more importantly, I feel it's crucial that kids who aspire to write understand that I have to rewrite and revise as they do. Ours is such a perfectionist society—I see too many kids who believe that if they don't get it right the first time, they aren't writers."

"I think the children often think they don't have very exciting lives that are worth writing about," MacLachlan commented on the Random House Web site. "I just tell them that that's what we write about—we make them more interesting by writing about them. We change our lives in our books in a way, and that's the most exciting thing about writing about your own life. Kids get very excited when they hear that because they can change their own lives in their stories."

When asked what advice she would have for beginning writers, MacLachlan commented in *Language Arts,* "I would certainly say only write books for children if you really love children's books and want to do it. Writing for children is special because I think children read with a great true belief in what they're reading. The other thing is to read. One must understand the far reaches of children's books because they're really about many of the same subjects as adults are concerned with. Don't be condescending. I hate the didacticism that sometimes comes through in children's books. I would read and read and read. There is no better model than a good book."

BIOGRAPHICAL AND CRITICAL SOURCES:

BOOKS

Authors and Artists for Young Adults, Volume 18, Gale (Detroit, MI), 1996.
Children's Literature Review, Volume 14, Gale (Detroit, MI), 1988, pp. 177-186.
Russell, David L., *Patricia MacLachlan,* Twayne (New York, NY), 1997.
Twentieth-Century Children's Writers, 4th edition, St. James Press (Detroit, MI), 1995.

PERIODICALS

Booklist, October 15, 1980, Judith Goldberger, review of *Arthur, for the Very First Time,* pp. 328-329; April 1, 1982, Denise M. Wilms, review of *Mama One, Mama Two,* pp. 1019-1020; May 1, 1985, Betsy Hearne, review of *Sarah, Plain and Tall,* p. 1254, 1256; August, 1991, p. 2157; March 15, 1992, review of *Journey,* p. 1364; May 1, 1992, review of *Sarah, Plain and Tall,* p. 1612; September 1, 1993, review of *Baby,* p. 51; January 1, 1994, review of *Skylark,* p. 827; March 15, 1994, review of *Baby,* p. 1355; March 15, 1994, review of *Baby,* p. 1358; May 15, 1994, Nancy McCray, review of *Baby,* p. 1701; June 1, 1994, Stephanie Zvirin, review of *All the Places to Love,* p. 1810; June 1, 1997, review of *Sarah, Plain and Tall,* p. 1701; March 1, 1999, review of *Sarah, Plain and Tall,* p. 1212; February 15, 2001, review of *The Sick Day,* p. 1141; September 1, 2001, review of *Caleb's Story,* p. 107; December 15, 2001, review of *The Sick Day,* p. 728.

Books for Keeps, May, 1993, review of *Journey,* p. 15; July, 1994, review of *Skylark,* p. 11; September, 1998, review of *Sarah, Plain and Tall,* p. 22.

Books for Your Children, autumn, 1994, review of *Baby,* p. 21.

Bulletin of the Center for Children's Books, September, 1979, Zena Sutherland, review of *The Sick Day,* pp. 11-12; September, 1980, Zena Sutherland, review of *Arthur, for the Very First Time,* pp. 15-16; April, 1982, Zena Sutherland, review of *Mama One, Mama Two,* pp. 153-154; January, 1992, review of *Three Names,* p. 132; September, 1993, review of *Baby,* p. 16; February, 1994, review of *Skylark,* p. 194; July, 1994, review of *All the Places to Love,* p. 367; December, 1995, review of *What You Know First,* p. 132; October, 2001, review of *Caleb's Story,* p. 68.

Changing Men, winter, 1994, review of *Through Grandpa's Eyes,* p. 40.

Childhood Education, summer, 1992, review of *Three Names,* p. 245.

Children's Book Review Service, April, 1980, Ruth W. Bauer, review of *Through Grandpa's Eyes,* p. 84; June, 1994, review of *All the Places to Love,* p. 126; September, 1995, review of *What You Know First,* p. 7.

Children's Book Watch, January, 1992, review of *Three Names,* p. 2; March, 1994, review of *Baby,* p. 3; March, 1994, review of *Baby* (audio version), p. 6; July, 1995, review of *Sarah, Plain and Tall* (audio version), p. 4; November, 1995, review of *What You Know First,* p. 8; May, 2001, review of *The Sick Day,* p. 7.

Children's Literature, March, 1995, review of *Unclaimed Treasures,* p. 202.

Children's Literature Association Quarterly, spring, 1993, review of *Arthur, for the Very First Time,* p. 23; spring, 1994, review of *The Facts and Fictions of Minna Pratt,* p. 23; spring, 1993, review of *Unclaimed Treasures,* p. 23; spring, 1993, review of *Sarah, Plain and Tall,* p. 23; spring, 1993, review of *Journey,* p. 23.

Christian Science Monitor, November 5, 1993, review of *Baby,* p. 10; May 6, 1994, review of *Skylark,* p. 12.

Day Care & Early Education, summer, 1995, review of *All the Places to Love,* p. 42.

Emergency Librarian, January, 1992, review of *Journey,* p. 50; January, 1992, review of *Three Names,* p. 50; November, 1993, review of *Baby,* p. 46; May, 1994, review of *Skylark,* p. 45.

Entertainment Weekly, April 8, 1994, review of *Skylark,* p. 69.

Five Owls, November, 1993, review of *Sarah, Plain and Tall,* pp. 29-30; November, 1994, review of *All the Places to Love,* p. 25, 28; May, 1995, review of *Skylark,* p. 95, 100.

Growing Point, March, 1987, Margery Fisher, review of *Sarah, Plain and Tall,* p. 4750.

Horn Book, February, 1983, Ann A. Flowers, review of *Cassie Binegar,* pp. 45-46; January-February, 1986, pp. 19-26; July-August, 1986, "Newbery Medal Acceptance," pp. 407-413; July-August, 1986, Robert MacLachlan, "A Hypothetical Dilemma," pp. 416-419; July-August, 1988, review of *The Facts and Fictions of Minna Pratt,* pp. 495-496; November-December, 1989, Charlotte Zolotow, "Dialogue between Charlotte Zolotow and Patricia MacLachlan," pp. 736-745; September, 1991, p. 592; July, 1994, p. 453; November-December, 1993, Mary M. Burns, review of *Baby* pp. 746-747; July-August, 1994, Mary M. Burns, review of *Skylark,* pp. 453-454; January-February, 1996, Nancy Vasilakis, review of *What You Know First,* pp. 66-67; January, 1998, review of *Sarah, Plain and Tall,* p. 26; September, 2001, review of *Caleb's Story,* p. 590.

Horn Book Guide, spring, 1992, review of *Three Names,* p. 60; spring, 1992, review of *Journey,* p. 69; spring, 1994, review of *Baby,* p. 80; fall, 1994, review of *All the Places to Love,* p. 282; fall, 1994, review of *Skylark,* p. 313; spring, 1996, review of *What You Know First,* p. 15; fall, 2001, review of *The Sick Day,* p. 266; spring, 2002, review of *Caleb's Story,* p. 75.

Hungry Mind Review, summer, 1994, review of *Skylark,* p. 55.

Instructor, January, 1993, review of *Through Grandpa's Eyes,* p. 51; October, 1993, review of *Journey,* p. 68.

Journal of Adult Reading, March, 1994, review of *Baby,* p. 519.

Journal of Reading, March, 1992, review of *Journey,* p. 501; November, 1992, review of *Sarah, Plain and Tall,* p. 174.

Junior Bookshelf, April, 1992, review of *Journey,* p. 75.

Junior Literary Guild Catalog, September, 1980.

Kirkus Reviews, August 15, 1991, p. 1091; January 1, 1994, review of *Skylark,* p. 71; June 15, 1994, review of *All the Places to Love,* p. 848; August, 15, 1995, review of *What You Know First,* p. 1190; October 1, 2001, review of *Caleb's Story,* p. 1428; April 15, 2003, review of *Painting the Wind,* p. 609.

Kliatt Young Adult Paperback Book Guide, March, 1994, review of *Journey,* p. 54; March, 1994, review of *Baby,* p. 54.

Language Arts, November, 1985, Ann Courtney, interview with Patricia MacLachlan, pp. 783-787; March, 1992, review of *Three Names,* p. 218; November, 1992, review of *Journey,* p. 516; November, 1992, review of *Journey,* p. 541; October, 1994, review of *Baby,* p. 460; February, 1995, review of *Skylark,* p. 142; October, 1995, review of *All the Places to Love,* p. 435; April, 1996, review of *What You Know First,* p. 263; September, 1996, review of *All the Places to Love,* p. 352.

Learning, October, 1995, review of *Journey,* p. 83.

Library Talk, January, 1992, review of *Journey,* p. 33; September, 1992, review of *Three Names,* p. 46; May, 1994, review of *Baby,* p. 44; September, 1994, review of *Skylark,* p. 42; September, 1994, review of *All the Places to Love,* p. 11.

Los Angeles Times Book Review, December 17, 1995, review of *What You Know First,* p. 15.

Magpies, July, 1993, review of *Journey,* p. 39.

Newsweek, December 28, 1992, review of *Through Grandpa's Eyes,* p. 54.

New York Times Book Review, September 28, 1980, Natalie Babbitt, review of *Through Grandpa's Eyes,* p. 36; May 19, 1985, Martha Saxton, review of *Sarah, Plain and Tall,* p. 20; June 29, 1986, p. 31; January 8, 1989, Heather Vogel Frederick, review of *The Facts and Fictions of Minna Pratt,* p. 36; March 22, 1992, Nancy Bray Cardozo, review of *Journey,* p. 25; November 14, 1993, review of *Baby,* p. 34; June 5, 1994, review of *All the Places to Love,* p. 30; November 16, 1996, review of *Sarah, Plain and Tall,* p. 26; January 20, 2002, review of *Caleb's Story,* p. 15.

Orange County Register, September 21, 1994, Catherine Keefe, "Patricia MacLachlan Remains Connected with Her Childhood" (interview).

Parents, December, 1994, review of *Skylark,* p. 24.

Plays, March, 1997, review of *Tomorrow's Wizard,* p. 64.

Publishers Weekly, May 9, 1980, review of *Through Grandpa's Eyes,* p. 57; December 26, 1980, review of *Arthur, for the Very First Time,* p. 59; July 25, 1991, p. 53; April 16, 1993, review of *Baby,* p. 104; August 16, 1993, Diane Roback and Elizabeth Devereaux, review of *Baby,* p. 104; November 29, 1993, review of *Skylark,* p. 65; March 21, 1994, review of *All the Places to Love,* p. 70; July 31, 1995, review of *What You Know First,* p. 79; April 25, 1994, review of *Three Names,* p. 81;

July 31, 1995, review of *What You Know First,* p. 79; September 11, 1995, review of *Baby,* p. 87; February 3, 1997, review of *Skylark,* p. 108; March 23, 1998, review of *What You Know First,* p. 102; May 28, 2001, review of *The Sick Day,* p. 990; September 24, 2001, review of *Caleb's Story,* p. 94; October 22, 2001, Jason Britton, review of *Caleb's Story,* p. 26.

Quill & Quire, November, 1993, review of *Baby,* p. 40; February, 1996, review of *What You Know First,* p. 43.

Reading Teacher, December, 1992, review of *Three Names,* p. 333; May, 1993, review of *Journey,* p. 692; September, 1994, review of *Skylark,* p. 71; November, 1994, review of *Baby,* p. 241; March, 1995, review of *All the Places to Love,* p. 510; November, 1995, review of *All the Places to Love,* p. 238; October, 1996, review of *What You Know First,* p. 153; April, 2002, review of *Caleb's Story,* p. 697.

San Francisco Review of Books, September, 1995, review of *Baby,* p. 46.

School Librarian, May, 1992, review of *Journey,* p. 71.

School Library Journal, September, 1982, Wendy Dellett, review of *Cassie Binegar,* p. 124; May, 1985, Trev Jones, review of *Sarah, Plain and Tall,* p. 93-93; July, 1991, p. 60; April, 1992, review of *Journey,* p. 44; November, 1993, review of *Baby,* p. 109; March, 1994, review of *Skylark,* p. 222; June, 1994, review of *All the Places to Love,* p. 110; June, 1996, review of *Arthur, for the Very First Time,* p. 55; January, 1998, review of *Journey,* p. 43; August, 1998, review of *Baby,* p. 27; September, 2001, review of *Caleb's Story,* p. 230; May, 2002, review of *Sarah, Plain and Tall* (audio version), p. 71; May, 2002, review of *Caleb's Story,* (audio version), p. 71; May, 2002, review of *Skylark* (audio version), p. 71.

Smithsonian, November, 1994, review of *All the Places to Love,* p. 34.

Social Education, April, 1992, review of *Journey,* p. 262; April, 1995, review of *All the Places to Love,* p. 217.

Social Studies, March, 1995, review of *Through Grandpa's Eyes,* p. 92.

Times Educational Supplement, February 14, 1992, review of *Journey,* p. 30; September 16, 1994, review of *Baby,* p. 20; June 26, 1998, review of *Sarah, Plain and Tall,* p. 10.

Times Literary Supplement, November 28, 1986, p. 1344.

Tribune Books (Chicago, IL), November 14, 1993, review of *Baby,* p. 7; April 10, 1994, review of *All the Places to Love,* p. 8; March 13, 1994, review of *Skylark,* p. 7; January 14, 1996, review of *What You Know First,* p. 7; October 21, 2001, review of *Caleb's Story,* p. 4.

Variety, July 29, 2002, Marilyn Stasio, review of *Sarah, Plain and Tall* (musical production), p. 30.

Voice of Youth Advocates, October, 1993, p. 216.

Wilson Library Bulletin, May, 1992, review of *Journey,* p. S5; January, 1994, review of *Baby,* p. 119.

ONLINE

Baisusu Picture Book Reviews Web site, http://members/tripod.com/baisusu/ (May 28, 2003), David Bartholomew, review of *All the Places to Love.*

Eduplace.com, http://www.eduplace.com/ (May 28, 2003), Katy Smith, review of *All the Places to Love.*

HarperChildrens Web site, http://www.harperchildrens.com/ (May 28, 2003), "Patricia MacLachlan."

Random House Web site, http://www.randomhouse.com/ (May 28, 2003), "Patricia MacLachlan."*

* * *

MAILER, Norman (Kinsley) 1923-

PERSONAL: Born January 31, 1923, in Long Branch, NJ; son of Isaac Barnett (an accountant) and Fanny (owner of a small business; maiden name, Schneider) Mailer; married Beatrice Silverman, 1944 (divorced, 1952); married Adele Morales (an artist), 1954 (divorced, 1962); married Lady Jeanne Campbell, 1962 (divorced, 1963); married Beverly Rentz Bentley (an actress), 1963 (divorced, 1980); married Carol Stevens, 1980 (divorced, 1980); married Norris Church (an artist), 1980; children: (first marriage) Susan; (second marriage) Danielle, Elizabeth Anne; (third marriage) Kate; (fourth marriage) Michael Burks, Stephen McLeod; (fifth marriage) Maggie Alexandra; (sixth marriage) John Buffalo. *Education:* Harvard University, S.B. (cum laude), 1943; graduate studies at Sorbonne, University of Paris, 1947-48. *Politics:* "Left Conservative." *Hobbies and other interests:* Skiing, sailing, boxing, hiking.

ADDRESSES: Office—c/o Author Mail, Random House, 201 East 50th St., New York, NY 10022-7703.

Norman Mailer

CAREER: Writer. Producer, director, and actor in films, including *Wild 90,* 1967, and *Maidstone: A Mystery,* 1968; producer, *Beyond the Law,* 1967; actor, *Ragtime,* 1981; director, *Tough Guys Don't Dance,* 1987. Lecturer at colleges and universities; University of Pennsylvania Pappas fellow, 1983. Candidate for democratic nomination in mayoral race, New York City, 1960 and 1969. Cofounding editor of *Village Voice,* 1955; founder, Fifth Estate (merged with Committee for Action Research on the Intelligence Community), 1973. *Military service:* U.S. Army, 1944-46, field artillery observer; became infantry rifleman serving in the Philippines and Japan.

MEMBER: PEN (president of American Center, 1984-86), American Academy and Institute of Arts and Letters, National Institute of Arts and Letters.

AWARDS, HONORS: Story magazine college fiction prize, 1941, for "The Greatest Thing in the World"; National Institute and American Academy grant in literature, 1960; elected to National Institute of Arts and Letters, 1967; National Book Award nomination, 1967, for *Why Are We in Vietnam?;* National Book Award for nonfiction, 1968, for *Miami and the Siege* of Chicago; National Book Award for nonfiction, Pulitzer prize in letters, general nonfiction, and George Polk Award, all 1969, all for *Armies of the Night;* Edward MacDowell Medal, MacDowell Colony, 1973, for outstanding service to arts; National Arts Club Gold Medal, 1976; National Book Critics Circle nomination, Notable Book citation from the American Library Association, and Pulitzer prize in letters, all 1979, and American Book Award nomination, 1980, all for *The Executioner's Song;* Emmy nomination for best adaptation, for screenplay of *The Executioner's Song;* University of Pennsylvania Pappas fellow; Rose Award, Lord and Taylor, 1985, for public accomplishment; Emerson-Thoreau Medal for lifetime literary achievement from American Academy of Arts and Sciences, 1989.

WRITINGS:

NOVELS

The Naked and the Dead, Rinehart (New York, NY), 1948, reprinted, Holt (Orlando, FL), 1980.
Barbary Shore, Rinehart (New York, NY), 1951.
The Deer Park, Putnam (New York, NY), 1955, new edition, with preface and notes by Mailer, Berkley (New York, NY), 1976.
An American Dream (first published in serial form for *Esquire,* January-August, 1964), Dial (New York, NY), 1965.
Why Are We in Vietnam?, Putnam (New York, NY), 1967.
A Transit to Narcissus: A Facsimile of the Original Typescript with an Introduction by the Author, H. Fertig (New York, NY), 1978.
The Executioner's Song (excerpted in *Playboy* in 1979), Little, Brown (New York, NY), 1979.
Ancient Evenings, Little, Brown (New York, NY), 1983.
Tough Guys Don't Dance, Random House (New York, NY), 1984.
Harlot's Ghost, Random House (New York, NY), 1991.
The Gospel according to the Son, Random House (New York, NY), 1997.

NONFICTION NARRATIVES

The Armies of the Night: History As a Novel, the Novel As History, New American Library (New York, NY), 1968.

Miami and the Siege of Chicago, New American Library (New York, NY), 1968, published as *Miami and the Siege of Chicago: An Informal History of the American Political Conventions of 1968,* Weidenfeld & Nicolson (London, England), 1969.
Of a Fire on the Moon (first appeared in *Life* magazine), Little, Brown (Boston, MA), 1970, published as *A Fire on the Moon,* Weidenfeld & Nicolson (London, England), 1970.
King of the Hill: On the Fight of the Century, New American Library (New York, NY), 1971.
St. George and the Godfather, New American Library (New York, NY), 1972.
The Fight, Little, Brown (Boston, MA), 1975.
How the Wimp Won the War, Lord John Press (London, England), 1991.

NONFICTION

The Bullfight: A Photographic Narrative with Text by Norman Mailer (with recording of Mailer reading from text), CBS Legacy Collection/Macmillan (New York, NY), 1967.
The Prisoner of Sex (first published in *Harper's* magazine), Little, Brown (Boston, MA), 1971.
Marilyn: A Biography, Grosset & Dunlap (New York, NY), 1973, new edition, with new chapter, Warner Books (New York, NY), 1975.
The Faith of Graffiti, photographs by Jon Naar, Praeger (New York, NY), 1974, published as *Watching My Name Go By,* Mathews Miller Dunbar (London, England), 1974.
(Editor and author of introductions) *Genius and Lust: A Journey through the Major Writings of Henry Miller,* Grove (New York, NY), 1976.
Of a Small and Modest Malignancy, Wicked and Bristling with Dots (essay), Lord John Press (London, England), 1980.
Huckleberry Finn: Alive at One Hundred (booklet; criticism), limited edition, Caliban Press (Montclair, NJ), 1985.
Pablo and Fernande: Portrait of Picasso As a Young Man: An Interpretive Biography, Doubleday (Garden City, NY), 1994, published as *Portrait of Picasso As a Young Man: An Interpretive Biography,* Atlantic Monthly Press (New York, NY), 1995.
Oswald's Tale: An American Mystery, Random House (New York, NY), 1995.
The Spooky Art: Some Thoughts on Writing, Random House (New York, NY), 2003.
Why Are We At War?, Random House (New York, NY), 2003.

PLAYS

The Deer Park: A Play (two acts; adaptation of novel *The Deer Park*; produced Off-Broadway at Theater De Lys, 1967), Dell (New York, NY), 1967, adapted as *Wild 90* (screenplay), Supreme Mix, 1967.

Beyond the Law (screenplay), Supreme Mix/Evergreen Films, 1968.

Maidstone: A Mystery (screenplay; includes essay "A Course in Filmmaking"), New American Library (New York, NY), 1971.

The Executioner's Song (screenplay), Film Communication Productions, 1982.

Tough Guys Don't Dance (screenplay), Zoetrope, 1987.

Strawhead (play), first produced at Actors Studio, January 3, 1985.

COLLECTIONS

The White Negro: Superficial Reflections on the Hipster (essays; includes "Communications: Reflections on Hipsterism"; "The White Negro" first published in *Dissent* magazine, summer, 1957), City Lights (San Francisco, CA), 1957.

Advertisements for Myself (short stories, verse, articles, and essays, with narrative; includes "The White Negro," "The Man Who Studied Yoga," and "The Time of Her Time"), Putnam (New York, NY), 1959, new edition, with preface by Mailer, Berkley (New York, NY), 1976.

The Presidential Papers, Putnam (New York, NY), 1963.

Cannibals and Christians, Dial (New York, NY), 1966, abridged edition, Panther, 1979.

The Short Fiction of Norman Mailer, Dell (New York, NY), 1967.

The Idol and the Octopus: Political Writings on the Kennedy and Johnson Administrations (includes selections from *The Presidential Papers* and *Cannibals and Christians*), Dell (New York, NY), 1968.

The Long Patrol: Twenty-five Years of Writing from the Work of Norman Mailer, edited by Robert F. Lucid, World (New York, NY), 1971.

Existential Errands (includes *The Bullfight: A Photographic Narrative with Text by Norman Mailer,* "A Course in Filmmaking," and *King of the Hill*; also see below), Little, Brown (Boston, MA), 1972.

Some Honorable Men: Political Conventions 1960-1972 (narratives), Little, Brown (Boston, MA), 1976.

The Essential Mailer (includes *The Short Fiction of Norman Mailer* and *Existential Errands*), New English Library (Kent, England), 1982.

Pieces and Pontifications (essays and interviews; includes *The Faith of Graffiti* and *Of a Small and Modest Malignancy, Wicked and Bristling with Dots*), edited by Michael Lennon, Little, Brown (Boston, MA), 1982, published as *Pieces*, 1982, published as *Pontifications: Interviews*, 1982.

The Time of Our Time, Random House (New York, NY), 1998.

OTHER

Deaths for the Ladies and Other Disasters: Being a Run of Poems, Short Poems, Very Short Poems, and Turns of Prose, Putnam (New York, NY), 1962, new edition, with introduction by Mailer, New American Library (New York, NY), 1971.

Gargoyle, Guignol, False Closets (booklet; first published in *Architectural Forum*, April, 1964), privately printed, 1964.

The Pulitzer Prize for Fiction, Little, Brown (Boston, MA), 1967.

Of Women and Their Elegance (fictional interview), photographs by Milton H. Greene, Simon & Schuster (New York, NY), 1980.

The Last Night: A Story (first published in *Esquire*, 1962), limited, signed edition, Targ Editions (New York, NY), 1984.

Also author of novel *No Percentage*, 1941, and of screenplay for a modern version of *King Lear*. Contributor to anthologies. Author of column for *Esquire*, "The Big Bite," 1962-63; columnist for *Village Voice*, January-May, 1956, and for *Commentary*, 1962-63. Contributor to numerous periodicals, including *Harper's, Rolling Stone, New Republic, Playboy, New York Times Book Review,* and *Parade*. Contributing editor of *Dissent*, 1953-69; cofounding editor of *Village Voice*, 1955.

ADAPTATIONS: The Naked and the Dead was made into a film by Warner Bros. in 1958; *An American Dream* was adapted for film as *See You in Hell, Darling,* produced by Warner Bros. in 1966.

SIDELIGHTS: When *The Naked and the Dead,* drawing on writer Norman Mailer's experiences in the Pacific theater during World War II, was published in 1948, *New York Times* critic Orville Prescott called it "the most impressive novel about the Second World War that I have ever read." The large, ambitious book was number one on the *New York Times* best-seller list for eleven consecutive weeks and was the object of continuing critical admiration. Mailer, then a twenty-five-year-old literary novice, was suddenly famous and at the dawn of a prolific career in which he would loom as one of the major U.S. writers of the twentieth century. He would also continue to be measured by others as well as by himself against his 1948 success. "I had the freak of luck to start high on the mountain, and go down sharp while others were passing me," Mailer would later write in the autobiographical *Advertisements for Myself,* published in 1959.

After publishing his second book, *Barbary Shore,* to generally unenthusiastic reviews, Mailer conceived an ambitious cycle of eight novels centering on a universal mythical hero he named Sergius O'Shaugnessy. The short story "The Man Who Studied Yoga" was designed as a prologue to the series, and *The Deer Park,* published in 1955, was to be its first installment. Three years in the making, *The Deer Park,* which Mailer later adapted for the stage, also proved to be the cycle's only volume. Primarily because of the work's overt sexuality, Mailer's original publisher refused to publish the novel, which is a study in the powers of art, sex, and money in a hedonist resort in southern California. Eventually, the work was accepted by Putnam. Reviews of *The Deer Park* were mixed, with Brendan Gill asserting in the *New Yorker,* "Only a writer of the greatest and most reckless talent could have flung it between covers."

Mailer published *An American Dream* in 1965. The story of a prominent professor of existential psychology who murders his wealthy wife, the novel was a great commercial success, albeit the object of intense critical controversy. Elizabeth Hardwick described it in the *Partisan Review* as "a very dirty book, dirty and extremely ugly," while John Aldridge's review in *Life* called the novel "a major creative breakthrough." The protagonist of *An American Dream,* Stephen Rojack, was loosely modeled after Mailer himself, reflecting the novelist's tendency to incorporate autobiographical elements within his fiction.

Another self-portrait appears in *The Armies of the Night,* a literary triumph that redeemed Mailer in the eyes of critics and won both the Pulitzer prize and the National Book Award. Richard Gilman's review in the *New Republic* applauded "the central, rather wonderful achievement of the book, that in it history and personality confront each other with a new sense of liberation."

In 1970 Mailer found himself portrayed as the archetypal male chauvinist pig in Kate Millett's groundbreaking feminist study *Sexual Politics.* In response, he participated in a debate on feminism at New York's Town Hall and authored *The Prisoner of Sex,* which, when first published in *Harper's,* resulted in the largest sales of any issue in the magazine's history, as well as in the departure of the magazine's editorial staff, who took objection to the work's offensive language. *The Prisoner of Sex* is one of several chapters in Mailer's continuous obsession with sexuality, along with his meditation on Marilyn Monroe in *Marilyn* and *Of Women and Their Elegance.* Praising *The Prisoner of Sex* as "Mailer's best book," *New York Times* critic Anatole Broyard asserted, "What Mailer has tried to do here is write a love poem." But Gore Vidal disagreed in the *New York Review of Books,* writing, "There has been from Henry Miller to Norman Mailer to Charles Manson a logical progression." Vidal's cutting remark not surprisingly ignited a sensational public feud between the two rival novelists.

Mailer attracted further public controversy when he successfully petitioned the Utah State Prison parole board to release Jack Henry Abbott, for whose book, *In the Belly of the Beast,* he had helped find a publisher. One month after leaving prison, Abbott killed another man, and Mailer was again sparring with the press. Mailer had first met Abbott while conducting exhaustive research for *The Executioner's Song,* a self-described "true life novel" about the life and death of Gary Gilmore, who, on January 17, 1977, became the first convict to be executed in the United States in more than a decade. Perhaps the most surprising aspect of the work is the patient self-effacement of its author. Gone from *The Executioner's Song* are the familiar "Mailerisms": the baroque syntax, the hectoring tone, the outrageous epigrams, the startling bravura imagery, the political/metaphysical digressions, the self-conscious presence of the author in every line. Instead, Mailer's prose assumes the coloration of its huge cast of characters lawyers, policemen, doctors, journalists, as well as relatives, friends, and victims of Gary Gilmore and immerses the reader in the alarmingly ordinary world of its main character. *The Executioner's Song* was an extraordinary triumph, the second Mailer work to win a Pulitzer prize.

Mailer's characteristic intoxication with grandiose ideas, his delight in stylistic flourishes, and his preoccupation with sex and violence are again on display in *Ancient Evenings.* George Stade in the *New Republic* called *Ancient Evenings* "a new and permanent contribution to the possibilities of fiction and our communal efforts of self-discovery," while Benjamin DeMott dismissed it in the *New York Times Book Review* as "pitiably foolish in conception" and "a disaster." Mailer characteristically taunted his critics with a full-page advertisement for *Ancient Evenings,* juxtaposing scathing reviews of his novel with similar attacks on Herman Melville's *Moby Dick,* Leo Tolstoy's *Anna Karenina,* Walt Whitman's *Leaves of Grass,* and Charles-Pierre Baudelaire's *Les Fleurs du mal.*

During the 1980s Mailer positioned himself in the role of elder statesman of American letters. The feistiness was still there, but the aging *enfant terrible* was growing perceptibly more mellow and even courtly. Active in the writers' organization PEN, he became president of its American Center in 1984 and hosted the 1986 international PEN Congress in New York City. The gathering of some seven hundred authors from throughout the world proved to be a tumultuous event, and while fulfilling his presidential responsibilities, Mailer was again the lightning rod for public controversy. His decision to invite Secretary of State George Schultz to address the assembly of writers provoked fierce opposition. Mailer was also angrily attacked for his alleged sexism in assigning men a dominant position in the Congress program.

After seven years in the making, Mailer's 1,310-page novel *Harlot's Ghost* was published in 1991. A study of the U.S. Central Intelligence Agency (CIA) and its function within U.S. Cold War society, the novel was called by *New York Times* reporter Elaine Sciolino "a glorification of the godless, life-and-death struggle against Communism from the mid-1950s to the mid-1960s and the men and women who waged it."

Critical reception to *Harlot's Ghost* was generally favorable, except with regard to the novel's length. Suggesting that the work should have ended in 1961, with a description of CIA operations during President John

F. Kennedy's Bay of Pigs invasion, Wilfred Sheed added in his review for the *New York Review of Books:* "No doubt to end the book here would be false to the facts. . . . Still, it would be good for the novel, which after all, is not a perpetual motion machine, but is designed from the outset to go a certain distance, and not a heck of a lot farther. Even a novel about the Hundred Years' War has to end sometime, but *Harlot's Ghost* runs right over the sides of the frame as the author tries to cram more and more history into a manifestly finite picture." Louis Menand was more critical of the lengthy work, writing in the *New Yorker* that Mailer's ambition has destroyed his art. While praising the author's fearless examination of the Establishment during the 1960s and 1970s, Menand noted that "he has never written a book so flaccid or so unwilling to challenge and provoke as [*Harlot's Ghost.*]. He has set the bar at the highest level, taken a long look, and then walked underneath it." However, reviewer Thomas R. Edwards viewed the work from a different perspective in the *New Republic,* opining that *Harlot's Ghost* "advances a very imposing ideal of itself as being something like a religious epic, Mailer's *Paradise Lost,* as it were, in which the cold war would figure as the War in Heaven, the Creation, and the Fall."

Reflective of Mailer's interest in human sexuality as it relates to creativity, 1994's *Portrait of Picasso As a Young Man* sets out to uncover the inner life of the noted Spanish painter during the first thirty-five years of his life. The work, illustrated with numerous examples of Picasso's artwork, focuses on the erotic aspects of the artist's life, particularly his relationships with female and, Mailer contends, male lovers.

Portrait of Picasso was met by a strong critical backlash upon its publication. Foremost among the criticism was the author's indulgence in artistic criticism that was either derivative or deemed to be ill-founded. "What is most disturbing about *Portrait of Picasso,* however, is not its awkward assessment of Picasso's work," contended critic Michiko Kakutani in the *New York Times,* "but its even more awkward attempt to promote the notion that art redeems, that the cruelties and sins of a great artist can be rationalized, excused or glossed over." And, characteristically, Mailer's egotism enters into much of the criticism of the work. "Might Mailer be plumbing the mystery of Picasso's legendary sexual magnetism to measure, for the umpteenth time, the dynamics of his own 'phallitude'?"

queried Francine du Plessix Gray in the *Los Angeles Times*. Commenting on the author's relative disregard for Picasso's artistic development in favor of an almost voyeuristic obsession with his personal relationships, Gray dubbed *Portrait of Picasso* "an impassioned, well-meaning, but curiously tentative and wobbly work." Robert Storr went further in his review of the work in the *Washington Post Book World*: "Though the clash of temperaments between Norman Mailer and his subject could not be more obvious, . . . the result reads like a big, shapeless first draft that . . . blatantly rehashes the ideas of just about everybody who has written about [Picasso] in the past while failing to bring anything fresh to our understanding."

Mailer's fascination with violence, which was given full reign in his earlier writing, resurfaces in 1995's *Oswald's Tale: An American Mystery*. The nonfiction work, Mailer's twenty-eighth published book, is a journalistic rather than quasi-fictional examination of the life of Lee Harvey Oswald, the assumed assassin of President John F. Kennedy. With characteristic obsessiveness, Mailer threw himself into the task of uncovering the truth about Oswald, a figure who has remained something of a mystery despite all the research into his 1963 crime. With the help of investigative reporter Lawrence Schiller, Mailer went to Russia to interview those who had known Oswald for the two years he resided in that country and examine KGB files in the city of Minsk, where Oswald lived between 1959 and 1962.

While praising the workmanlike quality of *Oswald's Tale*, Thomas Powers contended in the *New York Times Book Review* that by the end of the book, he was unable to be moved by Mailer's portrait of Oswald. "I admire Mailer for his effort to understand Oswald," wrote Powers, "but at some level I feel invited to place a sympathetic arm around the killer's shoulder, and I'm not about to do it. . . . He brought pain to many and happiness to none. Anger is what this makes me feel." However, John W. Aldridge cited *Oswald's Tale* as "the greatest body of information on the Oswalds yet attempted." While noting that Mailer's characteristic "sprawling" style might prove off-putting to some readers, Aldridge added that the work presents a clear, well-researched case and leaves the conclusions up to the reader. "That is the primary mission of journalism at its best, and Mailer performs it with all his customary skill and thoroughness, and a quite uncharacteristic determination to keep himself out of the story."

In 1997 Mailer published *Gospel according to the Son*, a first-person account of the life of Jesus, closely based on the events described in the New Testament. Mailer said in an interview with the *New York Times Book Review*'s Bruce Weber that he considered the project "the largest dare of all" for a writer. Michiko Kakutani assessed the novel as just another installment in Mailer's self-centered exploration of fame and infamy. In the *New York Times*, Kakutani compared Mailer's Jesus to Luke Skywalker and a guest on *Oprah*, elaborating that Mailer had turned both Jesus and God "into familiar contemporary types: he has knocked them off their celestial thrones and turned them into what he knows best, celebrities." However, as always, the opinion on Mailer is sharply divided. A writer for *Kirkus Reviews* assessed the novel as "generally plainspoken and sometimes plodding," but found its "occasional flashes of Mailer's pugnacious intellectual gamesmanship" praiseworthy. A *Booklist* critic lauded *Gospel* for "[escaping] Mailer's own image" and called the book "limpid" and "nonflamboyant," "a provocatively imagined historical novel."

The Spooky Art: Thoughts on Writing was released on Mailer's eightieth birthday and was warmly received by critics. In it, Mailer reflects on the writer's craft using interviews, essays, lectures, and other pieces he has written spanning his tumultuous career. Writing for Knight Ridder/Tribune News Service, William McKeen commented, "Just when most discriminating readers in the Western World have come to the conclusion that Norman Mailer is an insufferable blowhard, he publishes this book. *The Spooky Art* is a charming book, alternately egomaniacal (it is Norman Mailer, after all) and self-deprecating." Anne Larson in *Kirkus Reviews* shared similar opinions, asking rhetorically, "Will we ever hear such a thing again, in our pale and sheepish publishing age of today—such a good, strong, straight, fearless talk from an ambitious writer? Not often."

With his later books, as with his earlier ones, Mailer has by turns fascinated and angered his critics, who contend that his fame has been as much the result of his own self-aggrandizement as his writing talent. Though finding that much of his writing has quickly become dated due to its focus on current events, biographer and critic Harold Bloom characterized Mailer as "a historian of the moral consciousness of his era, and as the representative writer of his generation," in his foreword to the critical anthology *Norman Mailer*.

And in the *London Review of Books,* Andrew O'Hagan praised the author for his courage and originality. "Norman Mailer has been as compulsive a literary character as we've had this half-century, but he has also been among the most compelling on the page," O'Hagan contended. "He has wasted much of his talent on money-spinning inelegance, and fruitless meanderings and quests into the mysteries of sex and destiny, but he has also risked and emboldened his talent by imagining himself at the core of things."

BIOGRAPHICAL AND CRITICAL SOURCES:

BOOKS

Adams, Laura, *Mailer: A Comprehensive Bibliography,* Scarecrow Press (Metuchen, NJ), 1974.

Adams, Laura, *Will the Real Norman Mailer Please Stand Up?,* Kennikat Press (Port Washington, NY), 1974.

Adams, Laura, *Existential Battles: The Growth of Norman Mailer,* Ohio University Press (Athens, OH), 1976.

Algeo, Ann M., *The Courtroom As Forum: Homicide Trials by Dreiser, Wright, Capote, and Mailer,* P. Lang (New York, NY), 1996.

Alter, Robert, *Motives for Fiction,* Harvard University Press (Cambridge, MA), 1984, pp. 46-60.

Amis, Martin, *The Moronic Inferno and Other Visits to America,* J. Cape (London, England), 1986, pp. 57-73.

Anderson, Chris, *Style As Argument: Contemporary American Nonfiction,* Southern Illinois University Press (Carbondale, IL), 1987, pp. 83-132.

Arlett, Robert, *Epic Voices: Inner and Global Impulse in the Contemporary American and British Novel,* Susquehanna University Press (Selingsgrove, PA), 1996.

Bailey, Jennifer, *Norman Mailer: Quick-Change Artist,* Harper (New York, NY), 1979.

Begiebing, Robert J., *Acts of Regeneration: Allegory and Archetype in the Works of Norman Mailer,* University of Missouri Press (Columbia, MO), 1980.

Bloom, Harold, editor, *Norman Mailer,* Chelsea House (New York, NY), 1986.

Braudy, Leo Beal, editor, *Norman Mailer: A Collection of Critical Essays,* Prentice Hall (Englewood Cliffs, NJ), 1972.

Bufithis, Philip, *Norman Mailer,* Ungar (New York, NY), 1978.

Cohen, Sandy, *Norman Mailer's Novels,* Rodopi (Amsterdam, Netherlands), 1979.

Concise Dictionary of American Literary Biography: Broadening Views, 1968-1988, Gale (Detroit, MI), 1989.

Contemporaries, Little, Brown (Boston, MA), 1962.

Contemporary Literary Criticism, Gale (Detroit, MI), Volume 1, 1979, Volume 2, 1974, Volume 3, 1975, Volume 4, 1975, Volume 5, 1976, Volume 8, 1978, Volume 11, 1979, Volume 14, 1980, Volume 28, 1984, Volume 39, 1986, Volume 74, 1993.

Contemporary Novelists, 6th edition, St. James Press (Detroit, MI), 1996.

Contemporary Popular Writers, St. James Press (Detroit, MI), 1995.

Dictionary of Literary Biography, Gale (Detroit, MI), Volume 2: *American Novelists since World War II,* 1978, Volume 16: *The Beats: Literary Bohemians in Postwar America,* 1983, Volume 28: *Twentieth-Century American-Jewish Fiction Writers,* 1984.

Dictionary of Literary Biography Documentary Series, Volume 3, Gale (Detroit, MI), 1983.

Dictionary of Literary Biography Yearbook, Gale (Detroit, MI), 1980, 1981, 1983, 1984.

Ehrlich, Robert, *Norman Mailer: The Radical As Hipster,* Scarecrow Press (Metuchen, NJ), 1978.

Foster, Richard, *Norman Mailer,* University of Minnesota Press (Rochester, MN), 1968.

Friedman, Melvin, and Ben Siegel, editors, *Traditions, Voices and Dreams: The American Novel since the 1960s,* University of Delaware Press (Newark, DE), 1995.

Girgus, Sam B., *The New Covenant: Jewish Writers and the American Idea,* University of North Carolina Press (Chapel Hill, NC), 1984, pp. 135-159.

Glenday, Michael K., *Norman Mailer,* St. Martin's Press (New York, NY), 1995.

Gordon, Andrew, *An American Dreamer: A Psychoanalytic Study of the Fiction of Norman Mailer,* Fairleigh Dickinson University Press (Rutherford, NJ), 1980.

Guest, David, *Sentenced to Death: The American Novel and Capital Punishment,* University Press of Mississippi (Jackson, MS), 1997.

Gutman, Stanley T., *Mankind in Barbary: The Individual and Society in the Novels of Norman Mailer,* University Press of New England (Hanover, NH), 1976.

Jackson, Richard, *Norman Mailer,* University of Minnesota Press (Rochester, MN), 1968.

Kazin, Alfred, *Bright Book of Life: American Novelists and Storytellers from Hemingway to Mailer,* Little Brown (Boston, MA), 1973.

Kellman, Steven G., *Loving Reading: Erotics of the Text,* Archon (Hamden, CT), 1985.

Kernan, Alvin B., *The Imaginary Library: An Essay on Literature and Society,* Princeton University Press (Princeton, NJ), 1982.

Leeds, Barry H., *The Structured Vision of Normal Mailer,* New York University Press (New York, NY), 1969.

Leigh, Nigel, *Radical Fictions and the Novels of Norman Mailer,* St. Martin's Press (New York, NY), 1990.

Lennon, J. Michael, editor, *Critical Essays on Norman Mailer,* G. K. Hall (Boston, MA), 1986.

Lennon, J. Michael, editor, *Conversations with Norman Mailer,* University Press of Mississippi (Jackson, MS), 1988.

Lounsberry, Barbara, *The Art of Fact: Contemporary Artists of Nonfiction,* Greenwood Press (Westport, CT), 1990, pp. 139-189.

Lucid, Robert F., editor, *Norman Mailer: The Man and his Work,* Little Brown (Boston, MA), 1971.

Mailer, Adele, *The Last Party: Scenes from My Life with Norman Mailer,* Barricade Books (New York, NY), 1997.

Manso, Peter, *Mailer: His Life and Times,* Simon & Schuster (New York, NY), 1985.

Merrill, Robert, *Norman Mailer,* Twayne (New York, NY), 1978.

Merrill, Robert, *Norman Mailer Revisited,* Twayne (New York, NY), 1992.

Middlebrook, Jonathan, *Mailer and the Times of His Time,* Bay Books (San Francisco, CA), 1976.

Millett, Kate, *Sexual Politics,* Doubleday (New York, NY), 1970.

Mills, Hilary, *Mailer: A Biography,* Empire (New York, NY), 1982.

Morton, Brian, *Norman Mailer,* Arnold (London, England), 1991.

Podhoretz, Norman, *Ex-Friends: Falling Out with Allen Ginsberg, Lionel and Diana Trilling, Lillian Hellman, Hannah Arendt, and Norman Mailer,* Free Pres (New York, NY), 1999.

Poirier, Richard, *Norman Mailer,* Viking (New York, NY), 1972.

Radford, Jean, *Norman Mailer: A Critical Study,* Barnes & Noble (New York, NY), 1975.

Rollyson, Carl, *The Lives of Norman Mailer: A Biography,* Paragon House (New York, NY), 1991.

Sokoloff, B. A., *A Biography of Norman Mailer,* Darby Books (Darby, PA), 1969.

Solotaroff, Robert, *Down Mailer's Way,* University of Illinois Press (Urbana, IL), 1974.

Sorkin, Adam J., editor, *Politics and the Muse: Studies in the Politics of Recent American Literature,* Bowling Green State University Popular Press (Bowling Green, OH), 1989, pp. 79-92.

Weatherby, William J., *Squaring Off: Mailer vs. Baldwin,* Mason/Charter (New York, NY), 1977.

Wenke, Joseph, *Mailer's America,* University Press of New England (Hanover, NH), 1987.

PERIODICALS

American Spectator, April, 1992, p. 78.

Atlantic, July, 1971; September, 1984; May, 1995, pp. 120-125.

Booklist, November 15, 1999, review of *The Time of Our Time,* p. 601.

Business Wire, April 9, 2003, review of *Why Are We at War?* p. 5228.

Chicago Tribune, December 20, 1982; September 21, 1987.

Commentary, April, 2003, Thomas L. Jeffers, "Down for the Count?," review of *The Spooky Art: Some Thoughts on Writing,* p. K2081.

Contemporary Review, January, 1999, review of *The Time of Our Time,* p. 56.

Esquire, June, 1966; December, 1968; June, 1986; May, 1995, p. 142.

Gentlemen's Quarterly, November, 1996, p. 332.

Harper's, June, 1999, review of *The Executioner's Song,* p. 76.

Journal of American Studies, December, 1987; December, 1990.

Kirkus Reviews, March 15, 1997; November 15, 2002, review of *The Spooky Art,* p. 1678; February 3, 2003, "The Spookiest Art," p. 1709.

Knight Ridder/Tribune News Service, January 29, 2003, William McKeen, review of *The Spooky Art,* p. K2081; March 5, 2003, Douglas Perry, review of *The Spooky Art,* p. K6979

Library Journal, March 1, 2003, Nathan Ward, review of *The Spooky Art,* p. 90.

Life, March 19, 1965, John Aldridge, review of *An American Dream,* p. 12; September 24, 1965; February 24, 1967; September 15, 1967.

London Review of Books, November 7, 1991; December 14, 1995, Andrew O'Hagan, review of *Oswald's Tale,* pp. 7-9; April 1, 1999, review of *The Time of Our Time,* p. 18.

Los Angeles Times, September 23, 1984; May 24, 1995, p. E1; May 12, 1997, p. E1; February 26, 2003, Scott Timberg, "Mailer, 80, hasn't lost his bite; The Controversial Author Displays His Pugnacious Wit during a Largely Genial Writers Bloc Appearance," p. E3.

Los Angeles Times Book Review, December 14, 1980; July 11, 1982; April 24, 1983; August 19, 1984; October 15, 1995, pp. 2, 15.

Maclean's, December 2, 1991, p. 90; June 5, 1995, p. 69.

Modern Fiction Studies, spring, 1987.

Nation, May 27, 1968; June 25, 1983; September 15, 1984; November 6, 1995, p. 543.

National Review, April 20, 1965; November 4, 1991, p. 54; August 28, 1995, p. 42; February 12, 1996, p. 50; June 23, 1997, pp. 27-29; July 28, 1997, pp. 55-56.

New Criterion, January, 1992; April, 2003, "Notes and Comments: Junk Mailer," p. 1.

New Republic, February 9, 1959; February 8, 1964; April 17, 1965, Richard Gilman, review of *An American Dream,* p. 22; June 8, 1968; January 23, 1971; May 2, 1983; August 27, 1984; November 25, 1991, p. 42; July 17, 1995, p. 46; March 31, 2003, "Notebook: Why Are We in Iraq?" (editorial), p. 8.

New Statesman, September 29, 1961.

Newsweek, December 9, 1968; April 18, 1983; August 6, 1984; April 24, 1995, p. 60; April 14, 2003, David Gates, "Stormin' Norman: Mailer on Saddam, Bush, and Post 9-11 America," review of *Why Are We at War?,* p. 58.

Newsweek International, February 3, 2003, Malcolm Jones, "More Craft, Less Smoke," review of *The Spooky Art,* p. 58.

New York, September 28, 1987; September 11, 1995, p. 80; October 16, 1995, p. 28.

New Yorker, October 23, 1948; October 22, 1955, Brendan Gill, review of *The Deer Park;* November 4, 1991, Louis Menand, review of *Harlot's Ghost,* pp. 113-119; April 10, 1995, p. 56; December 11, 1995, p. 42.

New York Review of Books, May 6, 1971; June 15, 1972; December 5, 1991, pp. 41-48; May 11, 1995, p. 52; June 22, 1995, p. 7; January 11, 1996, pp. 4-8; March 13, 2003, John Leonard, "Don Quixote at Eighty," review of *The Spooky Art,* p. 10.

New York Times, October 27, 1968; April 28, 1983; December 23, 1985; September 22, 1991, p. 28;

April 25, 1995, p. B2; February 4, 1997, p. B7; April 14, 1997, p. B7; April 24, 1997, p. A21.

New York Times Book Review, May 7, 1948, Orville Prescott, review of *The Naked and the Dead;* September 17, 1967; May 5, 1968; October 27, 1968; January 10, 1971; February 18, 1972; October 7, 1979; September 20, 1980; December 7, 1980; June 6, 1982; January 30, 1983; April 10, 1983, Benjamin DeMott, review of *Ancient Evenings;* July 20, 1984; July 29, 1984; April 11, 1985; September 29, 1991; April 30, 1995, pp. 1, 32; October 15, 1995, p. 16; October 6, 1996, p. 94; April 14, 1997; April 24, 1997; May 4, 1997, p. 9; November 28, 1999, review of *The Time of Our Time,* p. 32; December 5, 1999, review of *The Time of Our Time,* p. 105.

New York Times Sunday Magazine, September, 1979.

Observer, July 11, 1999, review of *The Time of Our Time,* p. 18.

Parameters, autumn, 1999, review of *The Naked and the Dead,* p. 147.

Partisan Review, spring, 1965, Elizabeth Hardwick, review of *An American Dream,* p. 291; fall, 1965; summer, 1967; July, 1980.

People, May 30, 1983; October 5, 1987.

PR Newswire, January 19, 2003, Naomi Starkman, "Norman Mailer Talks about Writing, Aging, and Crossword Puzzles: Says 'What I Have Is . . . More Craft and Less Smoke.'"

Publishers Weekly, March 22, 1965; October 8, 1979; March 20, 1995, p. 48; June 5, 1995, p. 34; September 11, 1995, p. 69; March 31, 2003, John F. Baker, "Mailer on the War (Hot Deals)," p. 16.

Saturday Review, January, 1981.

Time, May 28, 1951; June 28, 1982; April 18, 1983; January 27, 1986; September 30, 1991, p. 70; May 1, 1995, p. 94; April 28, 1997, p. 75; September 29, 1997, p. 46; December 9, 2002, review of *The Spooky Art,* p. 75.

Times (London, England), June 10, 1983.

Times Literary Supplement, October 3, 1968; January 11, 1980; March 6, 1981; December 10, 1982; June 10, 1983; October 19, 1984.

Tribune Books (Chicago, IL), October 7, 1979; November 30, 1980; June 13, 1982; April 10, 1983; August 5, 1984; July 14, 1985.

Village Voice, February 18, 1965; January 21, 1971.

Wall Street Journal, May 17, 1995, p. A16; October 2, 1995, p. A13; April 18, 1997, p. A16.

Washington Post, August 22, 1989.

Washington Post Book World, July 11, 1970; October 14, 1979; November 30, 1980; July 11, 1982; April

10, 1983; August 12, 1984; November 24, 1985; November 5, 1995, pp. 1, 10.
Yale Review, February, 1986.

ONLINE

Rake Online, http://www.rakemag.com/ November 22, 2003) review of *The Spooky Art.**

*   *   *

MANDELBROT, Benoit B. 1924-

PERSONAL: Born November 20, 1924, in Warsaw, Poland; immigrated to France, 1936; immigrated to the United States, 1958; son of Charles (in the clothing business) and Belle (a doctor and dentist; maiden name, Lurie) Mandelbrot; married Aliette Kagan (a biologist), November 5, 1955; children: Laurent, Didier. *Education:* École Polytechnique, Paris, France, diploma, 1947; California Institute of Technology, M.S., 1948; University of Paris, Ph.D., 1952.

ADDRESSES: Office—Department of Mathematics, Yale University, P.O. Box 208283, New Haven, CT 06520-8283; International Business Machines, P.O. Box 218, Yorktown Heights, NY 10598-0218.

CAREER: Philips Electronics, Paris, France, mathematician, 1950-53; Institute for Advanced Study, Princeton, NJ, junior member and Rockefeller scholar, 1953-54; University of Geneva, Geneva, Switzerland, junior professor of mathematics, 1955-57; University of Lille, Lille, France, junior professor of mathematics, 1957-58; École Polytechnique, Paris, junior professor of mathematics, 1957-58; International Business Machines Co., Thomas J. Watson Research Center, Yorktown Heights, NY, member of research staff, 1958-74, fellow, 1974-93, fellow emeritus, 1993—, member of IBM Academy of Technology, 1989-93. Yale University, Abraham Robinson Professor of Mathematical Sciences, 1987-99, Sterling Professor of Mathematical Sciences, 1999—. Harvard University, visiting professor, 1962-64, 1979-80, professor, 1984-87; Yale University, visiting professor, 1970; Yeshiva University, visiting professor at Albert Einstein College of Medicine, 1970; University of California—Berkeley, Charles M. and Martha Hitchcock Professor, 1992;

L'Académie des Sciences, Paris, associate 1995; visiting institute lecturer at Massachusetts Institute of Technology, 1953, University of Paris-Sud, 1966, Collège de France, 1973, Institut des Hautes Études Scientifiques, 1980, Mittag-Leffler Institute, 1984, 2001, and Max Planck Institute for Mathematics, 1988; lecturer at Cambridge University, 1990, Oxford University, 1990, Imperial College of Science and Technology, London, 1991; Sigma Xi, national lecturer, 1980-82; also associate at Institut Henri Poincaré, Paris, 1950s. American Academy of Arts and Sciences, fellow, 1982; National Academy of Sciences, foreign associate, 1987, member, 2001; European Academy of Arts, Sciences, and Humanities, member, 1987; Norwegian academy of Science and Letters, foreign member, 1998. Also worked as apprentice toolmaker and horse caretaker. *Military service:* French Air Force, 1949-50.

MEMBER: International Statistics Institute, American Physical Society, Institute for Mathematics and Statistics, Econometric Society, American Geophysicists Union, American Statistical Association, American Mathematical Society, Institute of Electronics and Electrical Engineers, American Association for the Advancement of Science (fellow), French Mathematical Society.

AWARDS, HONORS: Guggenheim fellow, 1968; Bernard Medal for Meritorious Service in Science, National Academy of Sciences, 1985; Franklin Medal, Franklin Institute, 1986; Alexander von Humboldt Prize, 1987; Charles Proteus Steinmetz Medal, 1988; Caltech Distinguished Service Award, 1988; Moet-Hennessy Prize, 1988; decorated chevalier, French Legion of Honor, 1989; Harvey Prize, 1989; Nevada Prize, University of Nevada system, 1991; Wolf Prize for physics, 1993; Honda Prize, 1994; Médaille de Vermeil, Ville de Paris, 1996; John Scott Award, John Scott Fund, 1999; Lewis Fry Richardson Medal, European Geophysical Society, 1999; Sven Berggren Priset, Kungliga Fysiografika Sällskapet, Lund, Sweden, 2002; Medal of the President of the Republic of Italy, 2002; William Procter Prize for Scientific Achievement, Sigma Xi, 2002; Japan Prize for Science and Technology, Science and Technology Foundation of Japan, 2003; honorary degrees from Syracuse University, 1986, Laurentian University, 1986, Boston University, 1987, State University of New York, 1988, University of Bremen, 1988, University of Guelph, 1989, Pace University, 1989, University of Dallas, 1992, Union College, Schenectady, NY, 1993, University of Buenos Aires, 1993, University of Tel Aviv, 1995, Open University, Milton Keynes, England, 1998, University of Business and Commerce, Athens, Greece, 1998, University of St. Andrews, 1999, and Emory University, 2002.

WRITINGS:

Logique, langage et theorie de l'information, [France], 1957.

Les Objets fractals: forme, hasard et dimension, Flammarion (Paris, France), 1975, 3rd edition, 1989, translation published as *Fractals: Form, Chance, and Dimension,* W. H. Freeman (San Francisco, CA), 1977, expanded edition published as *The Fractal Geometry of Nature,* W. H. Freeman (San Francisco, CA), 1982.

(With Christopher H. Scholz) *Fractals in Geophysics,* Birkauser Verlag (Boston, MA), 1989.

Fractals in Physics: Essays in Honour of Benoit B. Mandelbrot, Elsevier Science (New York, NY), 1990.

Fractals and Scaling in Finance: Discontinuity, Concentration, Risk, Springer (New York, NY), 1997.

Gaussian Self-Affinity and Fractals: Globality, the Earth, 1/f Noise and R/S, Springer (New York, NY), 2003.

(With Michael L. Frame) *Fractals, Graphics, and Mathematical Education,* Mathematical Association of America (Washington, DC), 2002.

(With C. J. G. Evertsz and M. C. Gutzwiller) *Fractals and Chaos: The Mandelbrot Set and Beyond,* Springer (New York, NY), 2004.

Contributor to books, including *Multifractals and 1/f Noise: Wild Self-Affinity in Physics (1963-1976),* Springer (New York, NY), 1999. Contributor of articles to professional journals.

ADAPTATIONS: Mandelbrot's work on fractals inspired the symphonic work *The Mandelbrot Echoes,* created by Harri Vuori, published by Edition Love (Helsinki, Finland) in 1998.

SIDELIGHTS: Benoit B. Mandelbrot is the mathematician who conceived, developed, and named the field of fractal geometry. This field is devoted to the study of roughness in nature and culture. Thus it describes the everyday forms of nature—such as mountains,

clouds, and the path traveled by lightning—that do not fit into the world of straight lines, circles, and smooth curves known as Euclidean geometry. It also describes the charts of the variation of financial prices. Therefore, Mandelbrot also recognized the value of fractal geometry as a tool for analyzing a variety of physical, social, and biological phenomena.

Mandelbrot was born in 1924 to a Lithuanian Jewish family in Warsaw, Poland. His father, the descendant of a long line of scholars, was a manufacturer and wholesaler of children's clothing. His mother, trained as a doctor and dentist, feared exposing her children to epidemics, so instead of sending her son to school, she arranged for him to be tutored at home by his Uncle Loterman. Mandelbrot and his uncle played chess and read maps; he learned to read, but not the whole alphabet. He first attended elementary school in Warsaw. When he was eleven years old, his family moved to France, first to Paris and then to Tulle, in south central France. When Mandelbrot entered secondary school, he was thirteen years old instead of the usual eleven, but he gradually caught up with his age group. His uncle Szolem Mandelbrojt, a mathematician, was a university professor, and Mandelbrot became acquainted with his uncle's mathematician colleagues. Mandelbrot's teenage years were disrupted by World War II, which rendered his school attendance irregular. From 1942 to 1944, he and his younger brother wandered from place to place. He found work as an apprentice toolmaker for the railroad, and for a time he took care of horses at a chateau near Lyon. He carried books with him and tried to study on his own.

After the war, at the age of twenty, Mandelbrot took the month-long entrance exams for the leading science schools. Although he had not received the usual two years of preparation, he did very well. He had not received much formal training in algebra or complicated integrals, but he remembered all kinds of geometric shapes. Faced with an analytic problem, he would make a drawing, and this would often lead him to the solution. He enrolled in École Polytechnique. Graduating two years later, he earned a scholarship to study at the California Institute of Technology. After two years there, he returned to France with a master's degree in aeronautics and spent a year in the French Air Force.

Mandelbrot next found himself in Paris, looking for a topic for his doctoral thesis. One day his uncle, rummaging through his wastebasket for something for

Mandelbrot to read on the subway, pulled out a book review of *Human Behavior and the Principle of Least Effort* by George Zipf. The reviewer discussed examples of frequency distributions in the social sciences that did not follow the Gaussian "bell-shaped curve," the so-called normal distribution according to which statistical data cluster around the average. Mandelbrot wrote part of his doctoral thesis on Zipf's claims about word frequencies; the second half was on statistical thermodynamics. Much later, Mandelbrot commented that the book review greatly influenced his early thinking; he saw in Zipf's work flashes of genius, projected in many directions yet nearly overwhelmed by wild notions and extravagance, and he cited Zipf's career as an example of the extraordinary difficulties of doing scientific work that is not limited to one field. At the time, Mandelbrot had read Norbert Wiener on cybernetics and John von Neumann on game theory, and he was inspired to follow their example in using mathematical approaches to solve long-standing problems in other fields.

In the 1960s Mandelbrot studied stock market and commodity price variations and the mathematical models used to predict prices. A Harvard professor had observed that the daily changes in the price of cotton over many years did not follow the Gaussian bell-shaped distribution. Existing statistical models assumed that the rise and fall of stock-market prices was continuous, but Mandelbrot noted that prices may jump or drop suddenly. This showed that a model that assumes continuous prices is wrong. Working at the International Business Machines (IBM) Company's Thomas J. Watson Research Center in Yorktown Heights, New York, using IBM computers to analyze the data, he found that the pattern for daily and monthly price changes are matched. Statistically, the choice of time scale made no difference; the patterns were self-similar. Using this concept, he was able to account for a great part of the observed price variations, where earlier statistical techniques had not succeeded.

Shortly thereafter, IBM scientists asked Mandelbrot to help on a practical problem. In sending computer signals along electric wires, they found occasional random mistakes, or "noise." They suspected that some of the noise was being caused by other technicians tinkering with the equipment. Mandelbrot studied the times when the noise occurred. He found long periods of error-free transmission separated by bursts of noise.

When he looked at a burst of noise in detail, he saw that it, in turn, consisted of smaller error-free periods interspersed with smaller noisy chunks. As he continued to examine chunks at smaller and smaller scales, he found that the pattern noise occurring was statistically the same, regardless of the level of detail he was looking at. He described the probability distribution of the noise pattern as self-similar, or scaling—that is, at every time scale the ratio of noisy to clean transmission remained the same. The noise need not be due to technicians tinkering with screwdrivers; it may be spontaneous—that is, due to physics. In understanding the noise phenomenon, Mandelbrot used as a model the Cantor set, an abstract geometric construction of Georg Cantor, a nineteenth-century German mathematician. The model changed the way engineers viewed and addressed the noise problem.

For centuries humankind has tried to predict the water level of rivers like the Nile in order to prevent floods and crop damage. Engineers have relied on such predictions in building dams and hydroelectric projects. In the 1960s Mandelbrot studied the records of the Nile River level and found that existing statistical models did not fit the long periods of drought and that the longer a drought period, the more likely the drought was to continue. The resulting picture looked like random noise superimposed on a background of random noise. Mandelbrot showed unlabeled graphs of the river's actual fluctuations to a noted hydrologist, along with graphs drawn from the existing statistical models and other graphs based on Mandelbrot's statistical theories. The hydrologist dismissed the graphs from the old models as unrealistic, but he could not distinguish Mandelbrot's graphs from the real ones. For Mandelbrot, this experience illustrated the value of using visual representations to gain insight into natural and social phenomena. Other researchers found support for Mandelbrot's statistical model when they showed fake stock charts to a stockbroker; the stockbroker rejected some of the fakes as unrealistic, but not Mandelbrot's.

Early in the twentieth century, mathematicians and geometers created curves that were infinitely wrinkled and solids that were full of holes. Much later, Mandelbrot found their abstract mathematics indispensable in modeling shapes and phenomena found in nature. He had read an article about the length of coastlines in which Lewis Fry Richardson reported that encyclopedias in Spain and Portugal differed on the length of the border between the two countries; Richardson found similar discrepancies—up to twenty percent—for the border between Belgium and the Netherlands. Mandelbrot took up the question in a paper he called "How Long Is the Coast of Britain?" The answer, he said, depends on the length of the ruler you use. Measuring a rocky shoreline with a foot ruler would produce a longer answer than measuring it with a yardstick. As the scale of measurement becomes smaller, the measured length becomes infinitely large. Mandelbrot also investigated ways of measuring the degree of "wiggliness" of a curve. He worked with programmers to develop computer programs to draw fake coastlines. By changing a number in the program, he could produce relatively smooth or rough coastlines that resembled New Zealand or those of the Aegean Sea. The number determined the degree of wiggliness and came to be identified as the curve's fractal dimension.

Fascinated with this approach, Mandelbrot looked at other patterns in nature, such as the shapes of clouds and mountains, the meanderings of rivers, the patterns of moon craters, the frequency of heartbeats, the structure of human lungs, and the patterns of blood vessels. He found that many shapes in nature—even those of ferns and broccoli and the holes in Swiss cheese—could be described and replicated on the computer screen using fractal formulas.

Mandelbrot's reports and research papers during this period made clear that his methods were part of a more general approach to irregularity and chaos that was applicable to physics as well. Editors, however, usually preferred a more narrowly technical discussion. But then he was invited to give a talk at the Collège de France in 1973. Rather than selecting one of his many areas of research, he decided to explain how his many different interests fit together. A name was needed for this new family of geometric shapes, which typically involved statistical irregularities and scaling. Looking through his son's Latin dictionary, he found the adjective *fractus,* meaning "fragmented, irregular," and the verb *frangere,* "to break," and he came up with "fractal." His lecture aroused considerable interest and was published in expanded form in 1975 in French as *Les Objets fractals: forme, hasard et dimension.* Revised and expanded versions were published later in English in the United States as *The Fractal Geometry of Nature.* The book, which Mandelbrot called a manifesto and a casebook, attracted inter-

est from researchers in fields from mathematics and engineering to economics and physiology.

Using fractal formulas, computer programmers could produce artificial landscapes that were remarkably realistic. This technology could be used in movies and computer games. Among the first films to use fractal landscapes were George Lucas's *Return of the Jedi,* for the surface of the Moons of Endor, *Star Trek II: The Wrath of Khan,* and *The Last Starfighter.* Some fractal formulas produced fantastic abstract designs and strange dragon-like shapes. Mathematicians of the early twentieth century had done research in this area, but they did not have the advantage of seeing visual representations. The formulas were studied as abstract mathematical objects and, because of their strange properties, were called "pathological."

In the 1970s Mandelbrot became interested in a topic he had glimpsed around 1950—investigations carried out during World War I by French mathematicians Pierre Fatou and Gaston Julia, the latter having been one of his teachers years before at the Polytechnique. Julia had worked with mathematical expressions involving complex numbers, which have as a component the square root of negative one. Instead of graphing the solutions of equations in the familiar method of Descartes, Julia used a different approach; he fed a number into an equation, calculated the answer, and then fed the answer back into the equation, recycling again and again, noting what was happening to the answer. Mandelbrot used the computer to explore the patterns generated by this approach. For one set, he used a relatively simple calculation in which he took a complex number, squared it, added the original number, squared the result, continuing again and again; he plotted the original number on the graph only if its answers did not run away to infinity. The figure generated by this procedure turned out to contain a strange cardioid shape with circles and filaments attached. As Mandelbrot made more detailed calculations, he discovered that the outline of the figure contained tiny copies of the larger elements, as well as strange new shapes resembling fantastic seahorses, flames, and spirals. The figure came to be known as the Mandelbrot set. Representations of the Mandelbrot set and the related sets studied by Julia, some in psychedelic colors, soon appeared in books and magazines—some even in exhibits of computer art.

Through his work with fractals and computer projections of various equations, Mandelbrot had discovered tools that could be used by scientists and engineers for strengthening steel, creating polymers, locating underground oil deposits, building dams, and understanding protein structure, corrosion, acid rain, earthquakes, and hurricanes. Physicists studying dynamical systems and fractal basin boundaries could use Mandelbrot's model to better understand phenomena such as the breaking of materials or the making of decisions. If images could be reduced to fractal codes, the amount of data necessary to transmit or store images could be greatly reduced.

Fractal geometry showed that highly complex shapes could be generated by repeating simple instructions, and small changes in the instructions could produce very different shapes. For Mandelbrot, the striking resemblance of some fractal shapes to living organisms raised the possibility that only a limited inventory of genetic coding is needed to obtain the diversity and richness of shapes in plants and animals.

BIOGRAPHICAL AND CRITICAL SOURCES:

BOOKS

Aharony, Amnon, and Jens Feder, editors, *Fractals in Physics: Essays in Honour of Benoit B. Mandelbrot,* North-Holland (New York, NY), 1990.

Albers, Donald J., and G. L. Anderson, editors, *Mathematical People: Profiles and Interviews,* Birkhauser Verlag (Boston, MA), 1985.

Briggs, John, *Fractals, the Patterns of Chaos: A New Aesthetic of Art, Science, and Nature,* Simon & Schuster (New York, NY), 1992.

Gardner, Martin, *Penrose Tiles to Trapdoor Ciphers,* W. H. Freeman (San Francisco, CA), 1989.

Gleick, James, *Chaos: Making a New Science,* Viking Penguin (New York, NY), 1987.

Peitgen, Heinz-Otto, and C. J. G. Evertsz, editors, *Fractal Geometry and Analysis: The Mandelbrot Festschrift, Curaçao 1995,* World Scientific (River Edge, NJ), 1996.

Peitgen, Heinz-Otto, and Dietmar Saupe, editors, *The Science of Fractal Images,* Springer-Verlag (New York, NY), 1988.

Peitgen, Heinz-Otto, and P. H. Richter, *The Beauty of Fractals,* Springer-Verlag (New York, NY), 1986.

PERIODICALS

American Scientist, May, 2002, "Benoit Mandelbrot Receives 2002 William Procter Prize," p. 293.

Choice, February, 2003, H. P. Koirala, review of *Fractals, Graphics, and Mathematics Education,* p. 1034.

Economist, December 26, 1987, pp. 99-103; December 6, 2003, "The Father of Fractals: Last Word," p. 36US.

Java Developer's Journal, February, 2002, Blair Wyman, "Brushes with Greatness," p. 114.

Journal of Economic Literature, June, 2001, Philip Mirowski, review of *Fractals and Scaling in Finance: Discontinuity, Concentration, Risk,* p. 585.

Mathematics Teacher, November, 2000, Dane R. Camp, "Benoit Mandelbrot: The Euclid of Fractal Geometry," p. 708.

New York Times Magazine, December 8, 1985, p. 64.

Omni, February, 1984, pp. 65-66, 102-107.

Physics Today, April, 1987, pp. 101-102.

Scientific American, August, 1990, pp. 60-67.

Skeptic, winter, 2001, "Chaos Forum," p. 26.

* * *

MARTINSON, Harry (Edmund) 1904-1978

PERSONAL: Born May 6, 1904, in Jämshög, Blekinge, Sweden; died, February 11, 1978, in Stockholm, Sweden; son of Martin (a sea captain) and Bengta Svensdotter Olofsson; married Moa Swartz, 1929 (divorced, 1940); married Ingrid Lindcrantz, 1942.

CAREER: Worked as a seaman and a stoker throughout the world from the end of World War I until 1927; writer, 1927-78.

MEMBER: Swedish Academy.

AWARDS, HONORS: Henrik Steffins Prize, 1972; Nobel Prize for Literature, 1974.

WRITINGS:

(With Artur Lundkvist, Erik Asklund, Josef Kjellgren, and Gustav Sandgren) *Fem unga: Unglitterär antologi,* Bonnier (Stockholm, Sweden), 1929.

Spökskepp (poems; title means "Ghost Ship"), Bonnier (Stockholm, Sweden), 1929.

Nomad (poems; title means "Nomad"), Bonnier (Stockholm, Sweden), 1931.

Modern lyrik (poems; title means "Modern Poems"), Bonnier (Stockholm, Sweden), 1931.

Resor utan mål, Bonnier (Stockholm, Sweden), 1932.

Natur, Bonnier (Stockholm, Sweden), 1934.

Vägen ut (novel; title means "The Way Out"), Bonnier (Stockholm, Sweden), 1936, reprinted, 1974.

Svärmare och harkrank, Bonnier (Stockholm, Sweden), 1937.

Midsommardalen (also see below), Bonnier (Stockholm, Sweden), 1938.

Det enkla och det svåra (also see below), Bonnier (Stockholm, Sweden), 1939.

Verklighet till döds (title means "Realism unto Death"), Norstedt (Stockholm, Sweden), 1940.

Den förlorade jaguaren, Norstedt (Stockholm, Sweden), 1940.

Passad (poems; title means "Trade Wind"), Bonnier (Stockholm, Sweden), 1945, reprinted, 1966.

Cikada (poems, title means "Cicada"), Bonnier (Stockholm, Sweden), 1953.

Gäsen i Thule (poems; title means "The Grasses in Thule"), Bonnier (Stockholm, Sweden), 1958.

Dikter (poems; also see below), Bonnier (Stockholm, Sweden), 1959.

Vagnen (poems; title means "The Wagon"), Bonnier (Stockholm, Sweden), 1960.

(Editor) *Vishetens ord i öster,* Bokförlaget Piccolo (Stockholm, Sweden), 1962.

Utsikt från en grästuva (title means "View from a Tussock"; also see below), Bonnier (Stockholm, Sweden), 1963.

Lotsan från Moluckas: En radiospel om den portugisiske sjö fararen Magellans världsomsegling, 1519-1522, Bonnier (Stockholm, Sweden), 1964.

(With Björn von Rosen) *Bestiarium: Omfattande djur och fåglar från alla jordens länder och historiens åldrar infångade med tankens snaror vid stranden av sjön Sillen sommaren 1963,* Bonnier (Stockholm, Sweden), 1964, reprinted as *Harry Martinsons och Björn von Rosens nya bestiarium: Omfattande djur och fåglar från alla jordens länder och historiens åldrar,* Bra bok (Stockholm, Sweden), 1984.

Tre knivar från Wei (play; title means "Three Knives from Wei"), Bonnier (Stockholm, Sweden), 1964.

Vildbukettan: Naturdikter i urval av Ake Runnquist, Bonnier (Stockholm, Sweden), 1965.

Dikter om ljus och mörker (poems), Bonnier (Stockholm, Sweden), 1971.

Keemia Instituudi tänpaeev, Eesti NSV Teaduste Akadeemia, 1973.

Tuvor (poems), Bonnier (Stockholm, Sweden), 1973.

Dikter, 1929-1953 (poems), Bonnier (Stockholm, Sweden), 1974.

Dikter, 1958-1973 (poems), Bonnier (Stockholm, Sweden), 1974.

Längs ekots stigar: Ett urval efterlämnade dikter (poems), Bonnier (Stockholm, Sweden), 1978.

Doriderna: Efterlämnade dikter och prosastycken, selected by Tord Hall Bonnier (Stockholm, Sweden), 1980.

Bollesagor: Ur det efterlämnade materialet till Vägen till Klockrike, Bonnier (Stockholm, Sweden), 1983.

Kåserier på allvar, Bokvännerna (Stockholm, Sweden), 1984.

Gyro, Jord-eco (Stockholm, Sweden), 1986.

Ur de tusen dikternas bok, Ellerström (Lund, Sweden), 1986.

Kring Aniara, compiled by Stefan Sandelin, Vekerum (Södra Sandby, Sweden), 1989.

Hav och resor, compiled by Stefan Sandelin, Vekerum (Södra Sandby, Sweden), 1992.

Skillingtrycket och Vildgåsresan, compiled by Stefan Sandelin, Vekerum (Södra Sandby, Sweden), 1994.

Dramatik: Gringo, Salvation, Lotsen från Moluckas, Tre knivar från Wei, Bonnier (Stockholm, Sweden), 1999.

IN ENGLISH TRANSLATION

Kap Färval! (also see below), Bonnier (Stockholm, Sweden), 1933, translation by Naomi Walford published as *Cape Farewell,* Putnam (New York, NY), 1934.

Nässlorna blomma (novel), Bonnier (Stockholm, Sweden), 1935, reprinted, 1966, translation by Naomi Walford published as *Flowering Nettle,* Cresset (London, England), 1935.

Vägen till Klockrike (novel; also see below), Bonnier (Stockholm, Sweden), 1948, translation by M. A. Michael published as *The Road,* J. Cape (London, England), 1955, Reynal (New York, NY), 1956.

Aniara: En revy om människan i tid och rum (epic poem), Bonnier (Stockholm, Sweden), 1956, adaptation by Hugh McDiarmid and Elspeth Harley Shubert published as *Aniara: A Review of Man in Time and Space,* Knopf (New York, NY), 1963, reprinted, Avon (New York, NY), 1976.

(Contributor) Robert Bly, compiler and translator, *Friends, You Drank Some Darkness,* Beacon Press (Boston, MA), 1975.

Wild Bouquet: Nature Poems, translation and introduction by William Jay Smith and Leif sjoberg, BKMK Press (Kansas City, MO), 1985.

OMNIBUS VOLUMES

Vildbukettan: Naturdikter i urval Åke Runnquist, Bonnier (Stockholm, Sweden), 1965.

Dikter, Ur Kap Färval, Naturstycken, Kalender, [and] *Vägen till Klockrike,* Bonnier (Stockholm, Sweden), 1974.

Midsommardalen, Det enkla och det svåra, Utsikt från en grästuva, Bonnier (Stockholm, Sweden), 1974.

Resor utan mål [and] *Kap Färval!* (titles mean "Journeys without a Goal" [and] "Cape Farewell"), Bonnier (Stockholm, Sweden), 1974.

OTHER

Lotsen från Moluckas (radio script), broadcast January 10, 1937.

The main collection of Harry Martinson's papers is housed at the University of Uppsala. Smaller collections are housed at the Royal Library, Albert Bonniers Förlags arkiv, and the Archives of the Labor Movement, Stockholm.

ADAPTATIONS: Aniara was adapted as an opera in 1959 by Swedish composer Karl-Birger Blomdahl.

SIDELIGHTS: "Harry Martinson is widely regarded as one of the leading figures in twentieth-century Swedish literature," Paul Norlén noted in the *Dictionary of Literary Biography.* "When he began publishing his works, critics and fellow writers alike quickly recognized his lyric gifts; in particular, his collection *Nomad* contributed greatly to the introduction of literary modernism in Sweden. Innovative without being obscure, Martinson was an extremely popular writer as well, and his verse epic, *Aniara: En revy om människan i tid och rum* (translated as *Aniara: A Review of Man in Time and Space*), is one of the most important works of the postwar generation. His country officially recognized him with such honors as his election to the Swedish Academy in 1949 and a Nobel Prize for literature in 1974."

Born in southern Sweden, Martinson was named according to "the old Swedish tradition in giving names; Harry, as the son of Martin, was thus given the surname Martinson," Norlén recounted. "Martin, who had lived for a time in North America and Australia, was an unsuccessful store owner with a penchant for storytelling, fighting, and drinking, and Bengta, whom Martin liked to call 'Betty,' was the parish beauty. After Olofsson's store went bankrupt in 1904, Betty took over the business in her own name. In 1905 Olofsson was sentenced to a month in prison for assault, but while appealing the conviction he left for the United States and stayed there for three years. He returned home when he was diagnosed with tuberculosis. The appeal of his sentence, which had been delayed during his absence, ultimately failed, and he served the prison term. Upon his release, however, another case of assault led to a term of hard labor for nine months in 1909, the same year that his and Betty's seventh child was born. She sold the store and moved with the children further south to the province of Skåne, where she opened another store. The following year, however, this store also went bankrupt, and Martin died of tuberculosis. In 1910, one year before Martinson's oldest sister, Edit, died of the same disease that took their father, Betty left her children for the United States—ostensibly to collect a life-insurance policy taken out by her husband—and remained there until her death in 1946."

In 1912, when Martinson was almost eight years old, the children were made wards of the parish and placed in foster homes. Over the next few years he was housed at a series of farms in the area. One bright spot in the boy's environment, however, was school, and reading—newspapers, adventure novels, and popular-science magazines—soon became one of his most enjoyable pastimes. He also performed a variety of chores on the farms where he was sent to live, experiencing a rural way of life that soon thereafter disappeared in Sweden. While Martinson's early years were spent in a mostly traditional, rural landscape, he became in his youth a part of the industrialized world—first as a seaman and then as a luffare, a tramp. In 1915 he ran away for the first time, an attempt he repeated often throughout his youth. Instead of returning to farm life, however, he was sent to live at the old people's home in Jämshög in 1916 and 1917. A couple of years later he enrolled in the 'skeppsgossekår' (cabin-boy corps) in Karlskrona but again ran away and was then dismissed. After working as a laborer, he finally took the decisive step of going to sea aboard the schooner Willy in Göteborg in 1920. He was sixteen years old at the time, and for the next seven years he was either working at sea or unemployed and drifting as a luffare. In the years after World War I, employment among seamen fluctuated widely and periods of unemployment were common. A reconstruction of Martinson's travels indicates that he was in Europe and Sweden from 1920 to 1922 and then at sea and en route to ports in North and South America, Africa, and Asia; between 1922 and 1925 he also embarked on a journey by foot from Brazil to Uruguay. In 1925 he performed compulsory military service in Sweden, after which he again went to sea. He abandoned the seaman's life on his birthday in 1927 at the French port of Bordeaux and returned to Sweden to become a writer.

Among his novels, *Vägen till Klockrike,* later translated as *The Road,* was one of Martinson's most popular novels in Sweden, prompting the writer's election to the Swedish Academy. A rambling account of the travels of a vagabond in Sweden, *The Road* was not successful in its English translation. *Books Abroad* contributor Leif sjoberg hypothesized that the book's mediocre reception outside of Sweden was due to "Martinson's poetic language. He is a stylistic innovator comparable to [August] Strindberg and an imaginative coiner of words. . . . Martinson's assertion that translation is impossible is not entirely an exaggeration." Few of the author's works, therefore, have been translated into other languages.

Martinson became the corecipient of the 1974 Nobel Prize for Literature along with Eyvind Johnson. The author won the award largely for his work on the epic poem, *Aniara: A Review of Man in Time and Space.* The poem is a science fiction tale about a group of colonists who have left Earth after it has been destroyed by war. Intending to build a new life on Mars, a malfunction instead causes the ship, the Aniara, to go off course, taking the colonists on an endless journey into deep space. The author once said, according to a *Books Abroad* article, that *Aniara* is an allegorical story that "offers . . . a vision of our own time, of the life journey through our own emptiness." The doom of the colonists is determined by their over-dependence on technology, which blinds them to science's drawbacks. Shortsightedness and greed, Martinson warns, has made us similarly blind to technology's liabilities. Alan Swanson, writing in *Scandinavian Studies,* argued that "when the peculiar charm of its invented vocabulary has faded and become the stuff of literary history, when its apocalyptic imagery has paled in the face of everyday atrocity, and when its Buck Rogers characters have collapsed into their postures, there yet remains the force of its language, the virtuosity of its invention, and the urgency of its message."

"Direct inspiration for *Aniara,*" according to Norlén, "can be traced to a summer evening in 1953 when Martinson aimed his telescope on the spiral galaxy Andromeda, the most distant entity in the universe that is visible to the naked eye, and received an unusually clear view. This experience of cosmic distance so overwhelmed and affected the writer that for the next fourteen days—while lying prostrate on his sofa at home—Martinson dictated to his wife the material that became the initial twenty-nine songs of *Aniara.* He completed the remaining poems—103 in all—during the next two years."

"Almost since the atom bomb was exploded over Hiroshima and Nagasaki in 1945," Sjoberg related in the *American Scandinavian Review,* "Martinson has warned us of man's capacity for destruction." Although his books never reached a large international audience, Sjöberg concluded in *Books Abroad* that Martinson "has been of great importance to the Swedish (and Scandinavian) literary world. Indeed, he has helped form a specific consciousness for an entire generation of his compatriots at large and not just the literary gourmets."

BIOGRAPHICAL AND CRITICAL SOURCES:

BOOKS

Barnie, John, *No Hiding Place: Essays on the New Nature and Poetry,* University of Wales Press, 1996.

Bayerschmidt, Carl F. and Erik J. Friis, editors, *Scandinavian Studies: Essays Presented to Dr. Henry Goddard Leach on the Occasion of His Eighty-fifth Birthday,* American-Scandinavian Foundation and University of Washington Press (Seattle, WA), 1965.

Contemporary Literary Criticism, Volume 14, Gale (Detroit, MI), 1980.

Dictionary of Literary Biography, Volume 259: *Twentieth-Century Swedish Writers before World War II,* Gale (Detroit, MI), 2002.

Erfurth, Sonja, *Harry Martinsons barndomsvärld,* Bonnier (Stockholm, Sweden), 1980.

Erfurth, Sonja, *Harry Martinson och vägen ut,* Bonnier (Stockholm, Sweden), 1981.

Erfurth, Sonja, *Harry Martinson och Moa,* Bonnier (Stockholm, Sweden), 1987.

Erfurth, Sonja, *Harry Martinsons 30-tal,* Bonnier (Stockholm, Sweden), 1989.

Espmark, Kjell, *Harry Martinson erövrar sitt språk: En studie i hans lyriska metod, 1927-1934,* Bonnier (Stockholm, Sweden), 1970.

Hall, Tord, *Vår tids stjärnsång: En naturvetenskaplig studie omkring Harry Martinsons "Aniara,"* Bonnier (Stockholm, Sweden), 1958.

Holm, Ingvar, *Harry Martinson: Myter Målningar Motiv,* Aldus/Bonnier (Stockholm, Sweden), 1965.

Lönnroth, Lars and Sven Delblanc, editors, *Den svenska litteraturen: Modernister och arbetardiktare, 1920-1950,* Bonnier (Stockholm, Sweden), 1989.

Lundberg, Johan, *Den andra enkelheten: Studier i Harry Martinsons lyrik, 1935-1945,* Vekerum (Revingeby, Sweden), 1992.

Ramnefalk, Marie Louise, *Tre lärodiktare: Studier i Harry Martinsons, Gunnar Ekelöfs och Karl Vennbergs lyrik,* Cavefors (Staffanstorp, Sweden), 1974.

Söderblom, Staffan, *Harry Martinson,* Natur och kultur (Stockholm, Sweden), 1994.

PERIODICALS

American Scandinavian Review, December, 1972.

Books Abroad, summer, 1974.

Extrapolation: A Journal of Science Fiction and Fantasy, winter, 1998, Scott Andrew Smith, "The Role of the Emersonian 'Poet' in Harry Martinson's *Aniara: A Review of Man in Time and Space,"* pp. 326-327.

Moons and Lion Tailes, Volume 2, number 1, 1976.

Scandinavian Studies, summer, 1994, Alan Swanson, review of *Aniara,* p. 421.

Scandinavica: An International Journal of Scandinavian Studies, May, 1997, Brita Green, "Foregrounding and Prominence: Finding Patterns in Harry Martinson's Poetry," pp. 43-57.

Swedish Book Review, number 2, 1991, Brita Green, "Harry Martinson's *Aniara* in a New Translation," pp. 23-27, and Sven Arne Bergmann, "Rhyme and Reason in Harry Martinson's *Aniara,"* pp. 28-30.

Times Literary Supplement, October 31, 1975.*

*　　*　　*

McCAFFERTY, Barbara Taylor 1946-
(Taylor McCafferty and Tierney McClellan, pseudonyms)

PERSONAL: Born September 15, 1946, in Louisville, KY; daughter of Charles Allen (a foundry foreman) and Marjorie (a homemaker; maiden name, Meador) Taylor; married Richard Clark Taylor, October 15, 1966 (divorced, 1979); married John McCafferty (an owner of an advertising agency), November 15, 1982; children: (first marriage) Geoffrey Richard, Christopher Allen, Rachael Emily. *Education:* University of Louisville, B.A. (magna cum laude), 1980.

ADDRESSES: Home and office—Estero, FL 33928. *Agent*—Richard Parks, Richard Parks Agency, 138 East 16th St., Suite 5B, New York, NY 10003. *E-mail*—mysterytwin1@comcast.net.

CAREER: Writer. Schneider, DeMuth Advertising, Louisville, KY, art director, 1980-88.

MEMBER: Mystery Writers of America, Sisters in Crime.

WRITINGS:

WITH SISTER, BEVERLY TAYLOR HERALD

Double Murder, Kensington Books (New York, NY), 1997.

Double Exposure, Kensington Books (New York, NY), 1997.

Double Cross, Kensington Books (New York, NY), 1998.

Double Dealer, Kensington Books (New York, NY), 2000.

Double Date, Kensington Books (New York, NY), 2001.

UNDER PSEUDONYM TIERNEY MCCLELLAN

Heir Condition, Signet (New York, NY), 1994.
Closing Statement, Signet (New York, NY), 1995.
A Killing in Real Estate, Signet (New York, NY), 1996.
Two Story Frame, Signet (New York, NY), 1997.

UNDER PSEUDONYM TAYLOR MCCAFFERTY; "HASKELL BLEVINS" MYSTERIES

Pet Peeves, Pocket Books (New York, NY), 1990.
Ruffled Feathers, Pocket Books (New York, NY), 1992.
Bed Bugs, Pocket Books (New York, NY), 1993.
Thin Skins, Pocket Books (New York, NY), 1994.
Funny Money, Pocket Books (New York, NY), 2000.

Contributor of short stories to periodicals, including *Alfred Hitchcock's Mystery Magazine* and *Redbook.*

SIDELIGHTS: Barbara Taylor McCafferty and her twin sister, Beverly Taylor Herald, wrote a mystery series featuring the identical twin sisters Nan and Bert Tatum of Louisville, Kentucky. The pair, named for the Bobbsey Twins (although the Bobbseys were brother and sister), find themselves involved in criminal investigations when, as often happens, they are confused for one another.

In *Double Murder,* Bert is asked on a date by a stranger she assumes has mistaken her for her sister, Nan. But Nan does not know the man either. When he turns up dead, the sisters begin receiving threatening phone calls and must solve the dead man's murder before his killer strikes again. A critic for *Publishers Weekly* dubbed the novel a "quirky story of revenge and long-held secrets."

Double Exposure is told in alternating chapters by the two sisters and deals with a pair of identical twin brothers, one of whom may have committed suicide after the murder of his fiancee. Calling the novel a "fluffy little cozy" and "a nice little twinset," GraceAnne A. DeCandido in *Booklist* believed that the twins share "a remarkable bond and sympathy" and "the exploration of that relationship is the most engag-ing part of the book." A critic for *Publishers Weekly* termed the novel "easy, breezy fun" and found that the "story bounces along even if it's twice as cute as it needs to be."

Double Cross finds the twins investigating the murder of Bert's employer, a female attorney specializing in divorce settlements. "The prose," wrote a critic for *Publishers Weekly,* "is airy and entertaining." Rex. E. Klett in *Library Journal* noted that "the use of twins as alternating narrators, the humorous differences in their attitudes, and the police detective boyfriend they seem to have in common should keep reader interest high." According to DeCandido of *Booklist,* "The novel makes a good, fast read, complete with appeal-ing touches of local Louisville color."

BIOGRAPHICAL AND CRITICAL SOURCES:

PERIODICALS

Booklist, September 1, 1997, GraceAnne A. DeCan-dido, review of *Double Exposure,* p. 66; July 19, 1998, GraceAnne A. DeCandido, review of *Double Cross.*
Kirkus Reviews, August 1, 1996; August 15, 1997.
Library Journal, August, 1998, Rex E. Klett, review of *Double Cross,* p. 138.
Publishers Weekly, August 5, 1996, review of *Double Murder,* p. 434; August 4, 1997, review of *Double Exposure,* p. 69; July 27, 1998, review of *Double Cross,* p. 56.

*   *   *

McCAFFERTY, Taylor
    See McCAFFERTY, Barbara Taylor

*   *   *

McCLELLAN, Tierney
    See McCAFFERTY, Barbara Taylor

*   *   *

McDONELL, J(oan) M.

PERSONAL: Born March 3, in Springfield, MA; mar-ried; husband's name Terry. *Education:* Johns Hopkins University, M.A.

ADDRESSES: Agent—Ed Victor, 6 Bayley, St. Bedford Sq., London W4B 3HB, England. *E-mail*—joanie mcdonell@aol.com.

CAREER: Writer.

WRITINGS:

Half Crazy, Little, Brown (Boston, MA), 1995.
(Compiler) *The Little Book of Hope,* New Millennium Press (Beverly Hills, CA), 2001.

WORK IN PROGRESS: Time and Chance, a novel.

*   *   *

McLAREN, Clemence 1938-

PERSONAL: Born November 3, 1938, in NJ; daughter of Edward (an engineer) and Grayce (Berg) Dobson; married Robert McLaren, August, 1960; children: Kevin, Heather. *Ethnicity:* "Caucasian/Native American." *Education:* Rutgers University, A.B., 1960; University of Hawaii—Manoa, Ed.D., 1994. *Religion:* Society of Friends (Quakers).

ADDRESSES: Home—2009 McKinley St., Honolulu, HI 96822. *Agent*—Linda Allen, 1949 Green St., No. 5, San Francisco, CA 94123. *E-mail*—clmclare@ksbe. edu.

CAREER: Kamehameha Secondary Schools, Honolulu, HI, administrator.

MEMBER: Phi Beta Kappa.

AWARDS, HONORS: Best Books of the Year citation, American Library Association Award, and for, Best Books about Diversity citation, International Reading Association, both 1997, for *Inside the Walls of Troy: A Novel of the Women Who Lived the Trojan War;* Bank Street Book Store award for *Dance for the Land;* Library Guild Award for *Aphrodite's Blessings: Love Stories from the Greek Myths.*

WRITINGS:

Inside the Walls of Troy: A Novel of the Women Who Lived the Trojan War, illustrated by Joel Peter Johnson, Simon & Schuster (New York, NY), 1996.

Dance for the Land, Atheneum (New York, NY), 1999.
Waiting for Odysseus: A Novel, illustrated by Robert Goldstrom, Atheneum (New York, NY), 2000.
Aphrodite's Blessings: Love Stories from the Greek Myths, illustrated by Robert Goldstrom, Atheneum Books for Young Readers (New York, NY), 2001.
Dance for the Aina, Bess Press (Honolulu, HI), 2003.

WORK IN PROGRESS: Achilles' War, the story of the Trojan War, told by the greatest warrior in the world, and the woman who caused him to stop fighting.

SIDELIGHTS: Clemence McLaren once told *CA:* "As a child I was hooked on the myths. I always wondered how the mythological characters felt about what happened to them. In writing my retellings, I am addressing these same questions."

In *Achilles' War,* McLaren recently commented, "I explore the fierce, teenage Achilles (bursting with testosterone) and how he feels when his mother disguises him as a girl to keep him from going to war."

BIOGRAPHICAL AND CRITICAL SOURCES:

PERIODICALS

Booklist, March 1, 2000, Gillian Engberg, review of *Waiting for Odysseus: A Novel,* p. 1236.
Kirkus Reviews, December 1, 2001, review of *Aphrodite's Blessings: Love Stories from the Greek Myths,* p. 1688.
Publishers Weekly, March 27, 2000, review of *Waiting for Odysseus,* p. 82; December 17, 2001, review of *Aphrodite's Blessings,* p. 92.
School Library Journal, January, 2002, Patricia Lothrop-Green, review of *Aphrodite's Blessings,* p. 137.

*   *   *

MILLER, Jason 1939(?)-2001

PERSONAL: Born c. 1939, in Long Island, NY; died of a heart attack, May 13, 2001, in Scranton, PA; son of John (an electrician) and Mary (a special education teacher) Miller; married Linda Gleason, 1963 (marriage ended); married Ruth Josem (separated); chil-

Jason Miller

dren: (first marriage) Jennifer, Jason Patric, Jordan; (with actress Susan Bernard) Joshua. *Education:* University of Scranton, B.A., 1961; attended Catholic University of America, 1962-63.

CAREER: Playwright and actor. Worked as messenger, waiter, truck driver, welfare investigator, and actor in New York City. Film and television actor appearing in such films as *The Exorcist,* 1973, and *Nickel Ride,* 1975, also on television in *Bell System Family Theater,* 1975. Scranton Public Theater, actor and director, late 1980s-2001.

AWARDS, HONORS: New York Drama Critics Circle Award, 1972, and Best Play citation, both 1972, and Antoinette Perry ("Tony") Award, and Pulitzer Prize in Drama, both 1973, all for *That Championship Season;* Academy Award nomination for best supporting actor, 1973, for *The Exorcist.*

WRITINGS:

PLAYS

Lou Gehrig Did Not Die of Cancer (one-act play), first produced in New York, NY, at Equity Theater, March 2, 1970.

Nobody Hears a Broken Drum (three-act play; first produced Off-Broadway at Fortune Theater, March 19, 1970), Dramatists Play Service (New York, NY), 1971.

That Championship Season (first produced Off-Broadway at New York Shakespeare Festival Theatre, May 2, 1972; produced on Broadway at Booth Theatre, September 14, 1972; adapted as a screenplay by Miller for a movie of the same name, Cannon, 1982), Atheneum (New York, NY), 1972.

Barrymore's Ghost (solo show; produced in U.S. cities, 1997), Dramatists Play Service (New York, NY), 1997.

Also author of one-act plays *Perfect Son* and *The Circus Lady.*

OTHER

Stone Step (poetry), privately printed, 1968.

SIDELIGHTS: Award-winning playwright Jason Miller achieved his greatest success with the play *That Championship Season* in 1973. The story of a basketball team that reunites each year to celebrate their past glory as state champions, the play was welcomed by critics as a traditional well-made play with a flair for realistic dialogue and characterization.

Miller once told Glen Loney of *After Dark:* "I'm not committed to any one style or vision—or one concept of the theater." The playwright did, however, have definite ideas about theatrical form. "For an audience psyche—if there is such a thing as a collective audience psyche—story or plot is necessary," he commented to Loney. "Perhaps that feeling stems from an instinct for design, for an ordering of experience. Roughly, that's what Aristotle said. Perhaps he's right. Again, I don't know. But it's absolutely imperative that other forms of theater flourish. Old-fashioned plays and derivative European Absurdism—anything. I think the theater should never strap itself down to one definition, one style or one type of performance. As for the well-made play idea, I prefer to write that way. In terms of 'well-made' having the connotations of 'craft,' I believe in craftsmanship."

Set in Miller's hometown of Scranton, Pennsylvania, *That Championship Season* is about George Sikowski, James Daley, Tom Daley, and Phil Romano, four middle-aged men, once members of a championship high school basketball team, who gather in an annual reunion to honor their coach and relive their memories. They are now grown men, with layers of betrayal and deceit that have turned them bitter and unhappy, unable to recapture the glory of being state champs. As secrets are exposed and lies are uncovered, it is up to Coach to bring the men back together. His pep talk reminds them of the champions they once were.

"That Championship Season was born out of my own sense of personal failure," Miller once told the *New York Times*. "When an Off-Off Broadway play of mine, *Nobody Hears a Broken Drum,* lasted exactly two and one-half hours and I had to watch the crew members auctioning off pieces of the set, I started examining the nature of failure. I had to ask myself what type of men would harbor a sense of failure. In the process, I was also forced to account for my own values."

That Championship Season received an Antoinette Perry ("Tony") Award and a Pulitzer Prize after its first run on Broadway in 1973. The play was revived in 1999 at the Second Stage Theatre in New York. "Though fairly conventional in its construction, the work is unsparing in its exposure of the corruption, ruthlessness and denial permeating these disappointed men," said *Variety* reviewer Charles McNulty. "That it's also fiercely entertaining suggests how well the playwright's cunning observations are comically deployed." David Sheward of *Back Stage* said that while the play has "not aged well," when Miller wrote *That Championship Season* in the early 1970s, he gave it "a spin of political and social relevance" by addressing such topics as the Vietnam War and the corruption of President Nixon. He called the play "a psychic strip show as layers of illusion are removed and the lives of the five characters are exposed for the mediocre messes they are." Miller later adapted *That Championship Season* to a screenplay, and the film rights were acquired by Playboy Productions.

A talented writer for stage and screen, Miller was an exceptional actor as well. After the success of *That Championship Season,* Miller concentrated on acting. His portrayal of Father Damien Karras in *The Exorcist* won him an Academy Award nomination for Best Supporting Actor in 1973. Miller appeared in other films, playing the title character in *F. Scott Fitzgerald in Hollywood,* and portraying Notre Dame coach Ara Parseghian in *Rudy.*

"When I'm acting," Miller once told the *New York Times,* "I'm not on an ego trip, so I try to enter into a close collaboration with the writer. And the same applies vice versa. Most good actors have a sense of character and dialogue. The trick is to create it on paper and to live with the discipline. Acting is a communal experience, whereas writing is a solitary one."

In 1997, Miller traveled to cities throughout the United States producing his one-man show, *Barrymore's Ghost.* The show also appeared on stage at the Philadelphia Fringe Festival in September, 2000. The solo show is told from the perspective of John Barrymore. The festival billed the play as "a one man tour de force that explores the mythology of the Barrymore Family in all its wit, terror, agony and hope."

At the end of his career, Miller served the Scranton Public Theater as an actor and director. Miller passed away from a heart attack in 2001. He had been working on a film script about Jackie Gleason, and he and his son, Joshua, were writing a play titled *Me and My Old Man.* Miller once told *People* that he was always writing. "I'm still searching, still looking for a story I can put onstage that will have universal implications. I haven't made my mark yet—only a scratch."

BIOGRAPHICAL AND CRITICAL SOURCES:

BOOKS

Contemporary Literary Criticism, Volume 2, Gale (Detroit, MI), 1974.
Dictionary of Literary Biography, Volume 7: *Twentieth-Century American Dramatists,* Gale (Detroit, MI), 1981.

PERIODICALS

After Dark, January, 1972.
Back Stage, April 30, 1999, David Sheward, theater review of *That Championship Season,* p. 56; May 18, 2001, p. 49.
Newsweek, September 25, 1972.
New Yorker, March 28, 1970; May 20, 1972.
New York Post, September 23, 1972.
New York Times, March 20, 1970; September 15, 1972; May 8, 1973; February 10, 1974.

People, February 7, 1983, movie review of *That Championship Season*, p. 18.

Variety, April 26, 1999, Charles McNulty, theater review of *That Championship Season*, p. 56; May 28, 2001, p. 63.

OBITUARIES:

BOOKS

Dictionary of Literary Biography Yearbook, Gale (Detroit, MI), 2001, p. 469.

PERIODICALS

Back Stage, May 18, 2002, p. 49.
Chicago Tribune, May 16, 2001, section 2, p. 11.
Los Angeles Times, May 15, 2001, p. B10.
New York Times, May 15, 2001, p. A20.
Variety, May 28, 2001, p. 63.
Washington Post, May 16, 2001, p. B7.*

* * *

MOSS, Marissa 1959-

PERSONAL: Born September 29, 1959; daughter of Robert (a engineer) and Harriet Moss; married Harvey Stahl (a professor; died, 2002); children: Simon, Elias, Asa. *Education:* University of California—Berkeley, B.A.; attended California College of Arts and Crafts.

ADDRESSES: Agent—c/o Author Mail, Scholastic Inc., 555 Broadway, New York, NY 10012.

CAREER: Author and illustrator.

MEMBER: Authors Guild, PEN West, Society of Children's Book Writers and Illustrators, Screenwriters Guild.

WRITINGS:

SELF-ILLUSTRATED PICTURE BOOKS

Who Was It?, Houghton Mifflin (Boston, MA), 1989.
Regina's Big Mistake, Houghton Mifflin (Boston, MA), 1990.

Want to Play?, Houghton Mifflin (Boston, MA), 1990.
After-School Monster, Lothrop (New York, NY), 1991.
Knick Knack Paddywack, Houghton Mifflin (Boston, MA), 1992.
But Not Kate, Lothrop (New York, NY), 1992.
In America, Dutton (New York, NY), 1994.
Mel's Diner, BridgeWater Books (Mahwah, NJ), 1994.
The Ugly Menorah, Farrar, Straus & Giroux (New York, NY), 1996.

"AMELIA'S NOTEBOOK" SERIES; SELF-ILLUSTRATED

Amelia's Notebook, Tricycle Press (Berkeley, CA), 1995.
Amelia Writes Again, Tricycle Press (Berkeley, CA), 1996.
My Notebook with Help from Amelia, Tricycle Press (Berkeley, CA), 1997.
Amelia Hits the Road, Tricycle Press (Berkeley, CA), 1997.
Amelia Takes Command, Tricycle Press (Berkeley, CA), 1998.
Dr. Amelia's Boredom Survival Guide: First Aid for Rainy Days, Boring Errands, Waiting Rooms, Whatever!, Pleasant Co. (Middleton, WI), 1999.
Luv Amelia, Luv Nadia, Pleasant Co. (Middleton, WI), 1999.
The All-New Amelia, Pleasant Co. (Middleton, WI), 1999.
Amelia Works It Out, Pleasant Co. (Middleton, WI), 2000.
Amelia's Family Ties, Pleasant Co. (Middleton, WI), 2000.
Amelia's Easy-as-Pie Drawing Guide, Pleasant Co. (Middleton, WI), 2000.
Madame Amelia Tells All, Pleasant Co. (Middleton, WI), 2001.
Amelia Lends a Hand, Pleasant Co. (Middleton, WI), 2001.
Oh Boy, Amelia!, Pleasant Co. (Middleton, WI), 2001.
Amelia's School Survival Guide, Pleasant Co. (Middleton, WI), 2002.
Amelia's Best Year Ever: Favorite Amelia Stories from American Girl Magazine, Pleasant Co. (Middleton, WI), 2003.

OTHER CHILDREN'S BOOKS

True Heart, illustrated by Chris F. Payne, Silver Whistle (New York, NY), 1998.
(And illustrator) *Rachel's Journal: The Story of a Pioneer Girl*, Harcourt (New York, NY), 1998.

(And illustrator) *Emma's Journal: The Story of a Colonial Girl,* Harcourt (New York, NY), 1999.

(And illustrator) *Hannah's Journal: The Story of an Immigrant Girl,* Silver Whistle (New York, NY), 2000.

(And illustrator) *Brave Harriet: The First Woman to Fly the English Channel,* Silver Whistle (New York, NY), 2001.

(And illustrator) *Rose's Journal: The Story of a Girl in the Great Depression,* Silver Whistle (New York, NY), 2001.

(And illustrator) *Galen: My Life in Imperial Rome: An Ancient World Journal,* Silver Whistle (New York, NY), 2002.

Mighty Jackie: The Strike-Out Queen, illustrated by C. F. Payne, Silver Whistle (New York, NY), 2002.

(And illustrator) *Max's Logbook,* Scholastic Press (New York, NY), 2003.

(And illustrator) *Max's Mystical Logbook,* Scholastic Press (New York, NY), 2004.

ILLUSTRATOR

Catherine Gray, *One, Two, Three, and Four—No More?,* Houghton Mifflin (Boston, MA), 1988.

Dr. Hickey, adapter, *Mother Goose and More: Classic Rhymes with Added Lines,* Additions Press (Oakland, CA), 1990.

Bruce Coville, *The Lapsnatcher,* BridgeWater Books (Mahwah, NJ), 1997.

David Schwartz, *G Is for Googol,* Tricycle Press (Berkeley, CA), 1998.

WORK IN PROGRESS: Writing and illustrating *Amelia's Sixth-Grade Notebook,* publication by Simon & Schuster Books for Young Readers (New York, NY) expected in 2005.

SIDELIGHTS: Author and illustrator Marissa Moss has produced several popular picture books, as well as a series of beginning readers featuring a young writer named Amelia. Beginning with *Amelia's Notebook,* Moss follows her eponymous heroine through her daily adventures in the fourth grade, as the young protagonist changes schools, makes new friends, and copes with an annoying older sister. Moss has captured the imagination of primary graders with the adventures of her spunky character, and has tempted them with the opportunity to "read the secrets a peer records in her journal," according to *Publishers Weekly* writer Sally

Lodge. Hand-lettered and bound in a manner that resembles a black-and-white school composition book, *Amelia's Notebook* and its companion volumes *Amelia Writes Again* and *Amelia Hits the Road* are "chock-full of personal asides and tiny spot drawings" and contain a "narrative [that] rings true with third-grade authenticity," according to *School Library Journal* contributor Carolyn Noah.

Moss earned a degree in art history from the University of California at Berkeley. She related, "I could say I never thought I'd be a writer, only an illustrator and writing was forced upon me by a lack of other writers' stories to illustrate. Or I could say I always wanted to be a writer, but I never thought it was really possible. As a voracious reader, it seemed too much of a grown up thing to do, and I'd never be mature enough to do it. Or I could say I've been writing and illustrating childrens' books since I was nine. It just took me longer than most to get published. All these stories are true, each in their own way."

Moss began her career as a picture-book illustrator, working with author Catherine Gray as well as composing her own simple texts. One of her first published efforts as both writer and illustrator, *Who Was It?,* depicts young Isabelle's quandary after she breaks the cookie jar while attempting to sneak a between-meals snack. Praising Moss's watercolor illustrations, *Booklist* reviewer Denise Wilms also noted that the book's "moral about telling the truth is delivered with wry, quiet humor." In *Regina's Big Mistake,* a young artist's frustration with her own inability compared to the rest of her classmates is counteracted by a sensitive art teacher, as Regina is shown how to "draw around" a lumpy sun, transforming it into a moon. Readers "will enjoy the solace of having another child struggling to achieve, and succeeding," maintained Zena Sutherland of the *Bulletin of the Center for Children's Books. School Library Journal* contributor Ruth Semrau noted that "Moss's crayon cartoons are exactly what is needed to depict the artistic endeavors of very young children."

In *After-School Monster,* Luisa returns home from school one day to find a sharp-toothed creature waiting in her kitchen. Although scared, she stands up to the monster, turning the tables on the creature and evicting him from the house before Mom gets home. While noting that the theme could frighten very small children contemplating being left alone, a *Junior Book-*

shelf contributor praised Moss's "striking" full-page illustrations, which feature "an imaginative use of changing sizes." And in an equally imaginative picture-book offering, Moss updates the traditional nursery rhyme "Knick Knack Paddywack" with what Sheilamae O'Hara of *Booklist* described as "rollicking, irreverent verse" and "colorful, action-filled" pictures. The author-illustrator's "use of language will tickle all but the tongue tied," added Jody McCoy in an appraisal of *Knick Knack Paddywack* for *School Library Journal.*

"The character of Amelia came to me when I opened a black and white mottled composition book and started to write and draw the way I remembered I wrote and drew when I was nine," Moss said in commenting on the beginnings of her popular "Amelia's Notebook" series. "By that age I was already a pretty good artist, winner of drugstore coloring contests and determined to grow up to be another Leonardo da Vinci." The age of nine was also significant for Moss because that was when she had grown confident enough to send her first illustrated children's book to a publisher. "I don't remember the title, but the story involved an owl's tea party and was in rhymed couplets—bad rhyme I'm sure, as I never got a response from the publisher whose name I mercifully don't recall." Lacking encouragement, Moss left writing for several years, although she continued to tell stories.

The power of storytelling is one of the key themes Moss endeavors to express through her young protagonist, Amelia. "When you write or tell about something," she explained, "you have a kind of control over it, you shape the events, you sort them through, you emphasize some aspects, omit others. . . . Besides the flights of pure fancy, the imaginative leaps that storytelling allows, it was this sense of control, of finding order and meaning that mattered most to me as a child."

In the Amelia books, the spunky young chronicler dives into activities in a new school after leaving her old friends behind during a family move. "Amelia is droll and funny and not too sophisticated for her years," noted *Booklist* reviewer Stephanie Zvirin, who added that the diarist has a more emotional side too, missing her old friends and full of childhood aspirations about her future. In *Amelia Writes Again,* the heroine has turned ten and has begun a new notebook. In doodles, sketches, and snippets of thoughts Amelia

comments on such things as a fire at school and her inability to pay attention during math class. Everything Moss includes in Amelia's notebooks is true, "or," as Moss tells the groups of students she visits, "is based on the truth. Names have all been changed, because my older sister is mad enough at me already, and some details are altered to make for a better story. So, yes, there really was a fire in my school, but the idea of putting treasures in the newly poured pavement didn't occur to me at the time." Moss wishes it had; instead, she was able to let Amelia do so in *Amelia Writes Again.*

Moss enjoys writing in Amelia's voice because it allows her a flexibility that conventional picture-book writing does not. "I can go back and forth between different kinds of writing—the pure invention of storytelling, the thoughtful searching of describing people and events, and the explorations Amelia takes when she writes about noses or numbers, things she notices and writes down to figure out what it is that she's noticing. In the same way that I can go from describing a new teacher to making a story about clouds, Amelia allows me to move freely between words and pictures. I can draw as Amelia draws or I can use *trompe l'oeil* for the objects she tapes into her notebook. I can play with the art as much as I play with the text. The notebook format allows me to leap from words to images and this free-flowing back and forth is how I work best. It reflects the way I think— sometimes visually, sometimes verbally—with the pictures not there just to illustrate the text, but to replace it, telling their own story. Often the art allows me a kind of graphic shorthand, a way of conveying what I mean that is much more immediate than words. Kids often ask me which comes first, the words or the pictures. With Amelia, it can be either, and I love that fluidity.

"Amelia is headed in a new direction under her new publisher, American Girl. Besides various Amelia products (including, of course, a journaling kit), there are plans for an Amelia CD-ROM (an electronic journal naturally) and an Amelia video, which will expand Amelia's world—and journal—into animation."

In addition to Amelia's notebooks, Moss has begun a new series, this time focusing on young writers from different historical periods. "Like Amelia's notebooks, the pages will seem like real notebook pages," Moss explained, "with drawings and inserted objects on every page, only the main character will be someone from the past." The first book in the series, *Rachel's Journal: The Story of a Pioneer Girl*, introduces readers to a girl accompanying her family to California in 1850 along the Oregon Trail. Unlike the Amelia books, which were drawn from the author's own memories, Moss had to spend many hours doing research, reading histories, exploring library archives, and pouring over the actual letters and diaries of people who traversed the United States by covered wagon. "It was, for the most part, rivetting reading and I was impressed with what an enormous undertaking, what a leap of faith it was for pioneers to come here," Moss noted. "It was a dangerous trip. Indians, river crossings, storms, and especially sickness were all feared. But I was struck by the difference between how men and women viewed the journey and how children saw it. To kids, it was a great adventure, troublesome at times, tedious and terrifying at others, but ultimately exciting. These children showed tremendous courage and strength of character, and I tried to capture some of that, as well as the exhilaration of travelling into the unknown, in Rachel's journal."

Critics have praised Moss's books for leading younger readers into the art of journal writing. And Moss couldn't be happier. "The many letters I get from kids show that, inspired by Amelia, they, too, are discovering the magic of writing," she commented. "When readers respond to Amelia by starting their own journals, I feel I've gotten the highest compliment possible—I've made writing cool."

Moss recently added: "*Max's Logbook* is my latest foray into the world of journal, this time a boy's logbook of his inventions and experiments, with his life written in between."

BIOGRAPHICAL AND CRITICAL SOURCES:

PERIODICALS

Booklist, November 1, 1989, Denise Wilms, review of *Who Was It?,* p. 555; March 1, 1992, p. 1287; July, 1992, Sheilamae O'Hara, review of *Knick Knack Paddywack,* p. 1941; October 1, 1994, p. 333; April 1, 1995, Stephanie Zvirin, review of *Amelia's Notebook,* p. 1391; June 1, 1997, p. 1716; November 15, 1997, p. 561; August, 2001, Susan Dove Lempke, review of *Madame Amelia Tells All,* p. 2121; January 1, 2002, Carolyn Phelan, review of *Oh Boy, Amelia!,* p. 859; March 1, 2002, Ilene Cooper, review of *Brave Harriet: The First Woman to Fly the English Channel,* p. 1146; December 15, 2002, GraceAnne A. DeCandido, review of *Galen: My Life in Imperial Rome: An Ancient World Journal,* p. 760; October 15, 2003, Todd Morning, review of *Max's Logbook,* p. 412; January 1, 2004, GraceAnne A. DeCandido, review of *Mighty Jackie: The Strike-Out Queen,* p. 868.

Bulletin of the Center for Children's Books, October, 1990, Zena Sutherland, review of *Regina's Big Mistake,* p. 40; November, 1996, p. 108.

Junior Bookshelf, April, 1993, review of *After-School Monster,* p. 62.

Kirkus Reviews, August 15, 1989, p. 1248; August 15, 1990, p. 1171; July 1, 1991, p. 865; July 1, 1996, p. 972; September 15, 2002, review of *Galen,* p. 1396; January 15, 2004, review of *Mighty Jackie,* p. 87.

Publishers Weekly, June 14, 1991, p. 57; September 30, 1996, Sally Lodge, review of *Amelia's Notebook,* p. 87; June 16, 1997, p. 61; July 28, 1997, p. 77; August 31, 1998, p. 20; October 21, 2002, review of *Galen,* p. 76; July 14, 2003, review of *Max's Logbook,* p. 76; January 19, 2004, review of *Mighty Jackie,* p. 76.

Reading Today, August, 2001, Lynne T. Burke, review of *Amelia Works It Out,* p. 30.

School Library Journal, January, 1991, Ruth Semrau, review of *Regina's Big Mistake,* p. 79; May, 1992, Jody McCoy, review of *Knick Knack Paddywack,* p. 92; June, 1992, p. 100; December, 1994, p. 79; July, 1995, Carolyn Noah, review of *Amelia's Notebook,* p. 79; July, 1997, p. 60; November, 1997, p. 95; September, 2001, Ann Chapman Callaghan, review of *Brave Harriet,* p. 220; October, 2001, Debbie Stewart, review of *Oh Boy, Amelia!,* p. 126; December, 2001, Roxanne Burg, review of *Rose's Journal: The Story of a Girl in the Great Depression,* p. 108; October, 2002, Lynda S. Poling, review of *Galen,* p. 168; October, 2003, Elaine Lesh Morgan, review of *Max's Logbook,* p. 132; February, 2004, Grace Oliff, review of *Mighty Jackie,* p. 134.

N

NAYLOR, Gloria 1950-

PERSONAL: Born January 25, 1950, in New York, NY; daughter of Roosevelt (a transit worker) and Alberta (a telephone operator; maiden name, McAlpin) Naylor; divorced. *Education:* Brooklyn College of the City University of New York, B.A., 1981; Yale University, M.A., 1983.

ADDRESSES: Office—One Way Productions, 638 Second St., Brooklyn, NY 11215. *Agent*—Sterling Lord Literistic, 65 Bleecker St., New York, NY 10012-2420.

CAREER: Missionary for Jehovah's Witnesses in New York, North Carolina, and Florida, 1968-75; worked for various hotels in New York, NY, including Sheraton City Squire, as telephone operator, 1975-81; writer, 1981—; One Way Productions, New York, NY, president, 1990—. Writer in residence, Cummington Community of the Arts, 1983; visiting lecturer, George Washington University, 1983-84, and Princeton University, 1986-87; cultural exchange lecturer, United States Information Agency, India, 1985; scholar in residence, University of Pennsylvania, 1986; visiting professor, New York University, 1986, and Boston University, 1987; Fannie Hurst Visiting Professor, Brandeis University, 1988. Senior fellow, Society for the Humanities, Cornell University, 1988; executive board, Book of the Month Club, 1989-94; producer, One Ways Productions, 1990; visiting scholar, University of Kent, 1992; playwright, Hartford Stage Company, 1994.

MEMBER: PEN, Authors Guild, National Writers Union, Book of the Month Club (executive board member, 1989-94).

Gloria Naylor

AWARDS, HONORS: American Book Award for best first novel, 1983, for *The Women of Brewster Place;* Distinguished Writer Award, Mid-Atlantic Writers Association, 1983; National Endowment for the Arts fellowship, 1985; Candace Award, National Coalition of 100 Black Women, 1986; Guggenheim fellowship, 1988; Lillian Smith Book Award, Southern Regional Council, 1989, for *Mama Day;* New York Foundation for the Arts fellowship, 1991; Brooklyn College President's Medal, 1993; D.H.L., Sacred Heart University, 1994; American Book Award, New Columbus Foundation, 1998, for *The Men of Brewster Place.*

WRITINGS:

The Women of Brewster Place (novel), Viking (New York, NY), 1982.

Linden Hills (novel), Ticknor & Fields (New York, NY), 1985.

Mama Day (novel), Ticknor & Fields (New York, NY), 1988.

Bailey's Cafe (novel), Harcourt (New York, NY), 1992.

(Editor) *Children of the Night: The Best Short Stories by Black Writers, 1967 to the Present,* Little, Brown (Boston, MA), 1995.

The Men of Brewster Place (novel), Hyperion (New York, NY), 1998.

Gloria Naylor Reads "The Women of Brewster Place" and "Mama Day" (sound recording), American Audio Prose Library (Columbia, MO), 1988.

Maxine Montgomery, editor, *Conversations with Gloria Naylor,* University Press of Mississippi (Jackson, MS), 2004.

Also author of stage adaptation of *Bailey's Cafe,* produced in Hartford, CT, 1994, and of a children's play, *Candy.* Author of unproduced screenplay adaptation of *The Women of Brewster Place,* for American Playhouse, 1984, and of an unproduced original screenplay for Public Broadcasting System's "In Our Own Words," 1985.

Contributor of essays and articles to periodicals, including *Southern Review, Essence, Ms., Life, Ontario Review,* and *People.* Contributing editor, *Callaloo,* 1984—. "Hers" columnist for *New York Times,* 1986.

ADAPTATIONS: The Women of Brewster Place was adapted as a miniseries, produced by Oprah Winfrey and Carole Isenberg, and broadcast by American Broadcasting Co. (ABC-TV) in 1989; it became a weekly ABC series in 1990, produced by Oprah Winfrey, Earl Hamner, and Donald Sipes.

WORK IN PROGRESS: A sequel to *Mama Day,* about Cocoa and Saphira Wade.

SIDELIGHTS: Gloria Naylor won critical and popular acclaim for her first published novel, *The Women of Brewster Place.* In that book, as in her successive novels, including *Linden Hills, Mama Day,* and *The Men of Brewster Place,* Naylor gave an intense and vivid depiction of many social issues, including poverty, racism, homophobia, discrimination against women, and the social stratification of African Americans. Vashti Crutcher Lewis, a contributor to the *Dictionary of Literary Biography,* commented on the "brilliance" of Naylor's first novel, derived from "her rich prose, her lyrical portrayals of African Americans, and her illumination of the meaning of being a black woman in America." In *The Women of Brewster Place* and her other novels, Naylor focuses on "themes of deferred dreams of love (familial and sexual), marriage, respectability, and economic stability, while observing the recurring messages that poverty breeds violence, that true friendship and affection are not dependent on gender, and that women in the black ghettos of America bear their burdens with grace and courage," stated Lewis.

Naylor's parents left Mississippi, where they worked as sharecroppers, to seek new opportunities in New York City. Gloria was born there in 1950. A quiet, precocious child who loved to read, she began writing prodigiously even before her teen years, filling many notebooks with observations, poems, and short stories. After graduating from high school, she worked as a missionary for the Jehovah's Witnesses in the city and in the South. In 1981, she entered Brooklyn College, majoring in English. It was at that time that she read Toni Morrison's novel *The Bluest Eye,* which was a pivotal experience for her. She began to avidly read the work of Zora Neale Hurston, Alice Walker, and other black women novelists, none of which she had been exposed to previously. She went on to earn an M.A. in African-American studies at Yale University; her thesis eventually became her second published novel, *Linden Hills.*

Publication of some short fiction in *Essence* magazine led to her first book contract. *The Women of Brewster Place* is made up of seven interconnected stories, involving seven black women who live in a dreary apartment complex that is isolated from the rest of the city. Though they are from widely varying age groups and social backgrounds, and have very different outlooks and approaches to life, the women become a strong support group for each other as they struggle with the pain and frustration of finding their dreams constantly thwarted by the forces of racism and sexism. Naylor's work won the prestigious American Book Award for the best first novel in 1983.

Reviewing *The Women of Brewster Place* in the *Washington Post*, Deirdre Donahue wrote: "Naylor is not afraid to grapple with life's big subjects: sex, birth, love, death, grief. Her women feel deeply, and she unflinchingly transcribes their emotions. . . . Naylor's potency wells up from her language. With prose as rich as poetry, a passage will suddenly take off and sing like a spiritual. . . .Vibrating with undisguised emotion, *The Women of Brewster Place* springs from the same roots that produced the blues. Like them, her book sings of sorrows proudly borne by black women in America." Lewis described *The Women of Brewster Place* as "a tightly focused novel peopled with well-delineated, realistically portrayed African-American women. Naylor's use of authentic African-American vernacular and precise metaphors are hallmarks."

One of the characters in *Brewster Place* is a refugee from Linden Hills, an exclusive black suburb. Naylor's second novel spotlights that affluent community, revealing the material corruption and moral decay that would prompt an idealistic young woman to abandon her home for a derelict urban neighborhood. Though *Linden Hills,* as the book is called, approaches the Afro-American experience from the upper end of the socioeconomic spectrum, it is also a black microcosm. This book "forms the second panel of that picture of contemporary urban black life which Naylor started with in *Women of Brewster Place,*" wrote *Times Literary Supplement* contributor Roz Kaveney. "Where that book described the faults, passions, and culture of the good poor, this shows the nullity of black lives that are led in imitation of suburban whites."

Naylor was more ambitious in structuring her second novel. *Linden Hills* has been described as a contemporary allegory with gothic overtones, structurally modeled after Dante's *Inferno*. Among its many accomplishments, Dante's Italian masterpiece describes the nine circles of hell, Satan's imprisonment in their depths, and the lost souls condemned to suffer with him. In Naylor's modern version, "souls are damned not because they have offended God or have violated a religious system but because they have offended themselves. In their single-minded pursuit of upward mobility, the inhabitants of Linden Hill, a black,

middle-class suburb, have turned away from their past and from their deepest sense of who they are," wrote Catherine C. Ward in *Contemporary Literature*. To correspond to Dante's circles, Naylor uses a series of crescent-shaped drives that ring the suburban development. Her heroes are two young street poets—outsiders from a neighboring community who hire themselves out to do odd jobs so they can earn Christmas money. "As they move down the hill, what they encounter are people who have 'moved up' in American society . . . until eventually they will hit the center of their community and the home of my equivalent of Satan," Naylor told *Publishers Weekly* interviewer William Goldstein. Naylor's Satan is one Luther Nedeed, a combination mortician and real estate tycoon, who preys on the residents' baser ambitions to keep them in his sway.

Naylor's third novel, *Mama Day,* is named for its main character—a wise old woman with magical powers whose name is Miranda Day, but whom everyone refers to as Mama Day. This ninety-year-old conjurer made a walk-on appearance in *Linden Hills* as the illiterate, toothless aunt who hauls about cheap cardboard suitcases and leaky jars of preserves. But it is in *Mama Day* that this "caster of hoodoo spells . . . comes into her own," according to *New York Times Book Review* contributor Bharati Mukherjee. "The portrait of Mama Day is magnificent," Mukherjee wrote. Mama Day lives on Willow Springs, a wondrous island off the coast of Georgia and South Carolina that has been owned by her family since before the Civil War. The fact that slaves are portrayed as property owners demonstrates one of the ways that Naylor turns the world upside down, according to Rita Mae Brown. Another, Brown stated in the *Los Angeles Times Book Review,* is "that the women possess the real power, and are acknowledged as having it." When Mama Day's grandniece Cocoa brings George, her citified new husband, to Willow Springs, he learns the importance of accepting mystery. "George is the linchpin of *Mama Day,*" Brown said. "His rational mind allows the reader to experience the island as George experiences it. Mama Day and Cocoa are of the island and therefore less immediately accessible to the reader." The critical point in the story is the moment when George is asked not only to believe in Mama Day's power, but to act on it. A hurricane has made it impossible to summon a doctor from the mainland, but Cocoa is critically ill. Mama Day gives George a task to do in order to help save Cocoa's life, but he fails to do it because he only uses his rational thinking. George does ultimately save Cocoa, but doing so demands a great personal sacrifice.

The plot twists and thematic concerns of *Mama Day* have led several reviewers to compare the work to that of Shakespeare. "Whereas *Linden Hills* was Dantesque, *Mama Day* is Shakespearean, with allusions, however oblique and tangential, to *Hamlet, King Lear,* and, especially, *The Tempest,*" wrote Chicago's *Tribune Books* critic John Blades. "Like Shakespeare's fantasy, Naylor's book takes place on an enchanted island. . . . Naylor reinforces her Shakespearean connection by naming her heroine Miranda." Mukherjee also believed that *Mama Day* "has its roots in *The Tempest.* The theme is reconciliation, the title character is Miranda (also the name of Prospero's daughter), and Willow Springs is an isolated island where, as on Prospero's isle, magical and mysterious events come to pass."

Naylor's ambitious attempt to elevate a modern love story to Shakespearean heights "is more bewildering than bewitching," according to Blades. "Naylor has populated her magic kingdom with some appealingly offbeat characters, Mama Day foremost among them. But she's failed to give them anything very original or interesting to do." Mukherjee also acknowledged the shortcomings of Naylor's mythical love story, but added, "I'd rather dwell on *Mama Day*'s strengths. Gloria Naylor has written a big, strong, dense, admirable novel; spacious, sometimes a little drafty like all public monuments, designed to last and intended for many levels of use."

Naylor's fourth novel, *Bailey's Cafe,* also had its inspiration in a literature classic, Edith Wharton's *The House of Mirth.* Like Wharton's novel, *Bailey's Cafe* focuses on women's sexuality and the ways women are defined by society's perceptions of them. With this book, Naylor hoped to deconstruct the Judeo-Christian thinking about women. To achieve this, she took women characters from the Bible and placed them in the twentieth century to relate their stories. Eve runs a boardinghouse and has a reputation for healing troubled women. Eve was banished naked from her father's house, and her place now is suspected by many of being a bordello. Eve's boarders include Sadie, Sweet Esther, Mary, and Jesse Bell, modern women whose stories parallel those in the Bible. "The novel sings the blues of the socially rejected," stated Lewis, "who arrive at Bailey's struggling to find some measure of solace from a brutal American environ-

ment filled with racial and sexual stereotypes." The book was a critical success, and was adapted by Naylor as a stage play.

Naylor revisited her first success in 2000 with *The Men of Brewster Place.* Male characters were very marginal in her first novel, functioning mainly as people who wreaked havoc upon the lives of the women of Brewster Place. In *The Men of Brewster Place,* the author fills in the background of those characters, giving insight into their actions. The ten chapters in the book discuss seven individuals known as the sons of Brewster Place: Basil, Eugene, Maxine Lavon Montgomery, Ben, Brother Jerome, Moreland T. Woods, C. C. Baker, and Abshu. Ben, a character who died in the earlier book, is brought back in creative and magical ways. He functions as a sort of Greek chorus, overseeing the events and giving otherworldly perspective.

African American Review writer Maxine Lavon Montgomery called Naylor "a skillful writer adept at creating a range of uniquely individual characters." The author's look at the plight of the black man is rendered "in such a way as to render a compelling fictional expose of his dilemma." *Black Issues in Higher Education* reviewer Jackie Thomas praised *The Men of Brewster Place* as "a profound work that explores the other side of the gender issue." He approved of Naylor's depiction of them as rational beings who "are able to think for themselves and who realize that they have problems they must solve" and concluded: "It is refreshing to see someone address the Black male character and explore him realistically. Certainly, this work should be an inspiration to all who read it, and it should also encourage other writers to explore Black male characters from similar vantage points." But *Booklist* contributor Donna Seaman felt "these characters remain flat, and their stories are cautionary tales, intriguing in terms of the issues they raise yet a touch too facile and melodramatic." Yet, Seaman added, "there are flashes of genuine insight, tragedy, and great warmth." A *Publishers Weekly* writer allowed that the stories "feature the familiar ills of the inner city," but added that "Naylor lends these archetypal situations complexity and depth."

BIOGRAPHICAL AND CRITICAL SOURCES:

BOOKS

African-American Writers, Scribner (New York, NY), 1991.

Black Literature Criticism, Gale (Detroit, MI), 1992.

Contemporary Literary Criticism, Gale (Detroit, MI), Volume 28, 1984, Volume 52, 1989.

Contemporary Novelists, 7th edition, St. James Press (Detroit, MI), 2001.

Contemporary Popular Writers, St. James Press (Detroit, MI), 1997.

Dictionary of Literary Biography, Volume 173: *American Novelists since World War II, Fifth Series,* Gale (Detroit, MI), 1996.

Encyclopedia of World Biography, 2nd edition, Gale (Detroit, MI), 1998.

Feminist Writers, St. James Press (Detroit, MI), 1996.

Fowler, Virginia C., *Gloria Naylor: In Search of Sanctuary,* Prentice-Hall, 1996.

Hall, Chekita T., *Gloria Naylor's Feminist Blues Aesthetic,* Garland, 1998.

Harris, Trudier, *The Power of the Porch: The Storyteller's Craft in Zora Neale Hurston, Gloria Naylor, and Randall Kenan,* University of Georgia Press (Athens, GA), 1996.

PERIODICALS

Advocate, April 14, 1998, review of *The Men of Brewster Place,* p. 73.

African American Review, summer, 1994, p. 173; spring, 1995, pp. 27, 35; spring, 2000, Maxine Lavon Montgomery, review of *The Men of Brewster Place,* p. 176; spring, 2001, Christopher N. Okonkwo, "Suicide or Messianic Self-Sacrifice?: Exhuming Willa's Body in Gloria Naylor's *Linden Hills,*" p. 117.

American Visions, April, 1996, Dale Edwyna Smith, review of *Children of the Night: The Best Short Stories by Black Writers, 1967 to the Present,* p. 26.

Antioch Review, summer, 1996, Ed Peaco, review of *Children of the Night,* p. 365.

Black Issues in Higher Education, December 10, 1998, Jackie Thomas, review of *The Men of Brewster Place,* p. 31.

Booklist, December 1, 1995; January 1, 1996; March 1, 1998, Donna Seaman, review of *The Men of Brewster Place,* p. 1045; January 1, 1999, Barbara Baskin, review of *The Men of Brewster Place,* p. 900; November 1, 2001, Nancy Spillman, review of *The Men of Brewster Place* (audio version), p. 494.

Boston Herald, April 19, 1998, Judith Wynn, review of *The Men of Brewster Place,* p. 71.

Chicago Tribune Book World, February 23, 1983.

Christian Science Monitor, March 1, 1985.

Commonweal, May 3, 1985.

Contemporary Literature, Volume 28, number 1, 1987.

Detroit News, March 3, 1985; February 21, 1988.

Ebony, May, 1998, p. 14.

Emerge, May, 1998, Valerie Boyd, review of *The Men of Brewster Place,* p. 76.

English Journal, January, 1994, p. 81; March, 1994, p. 95.

Essence, June, 1998, p. 70; August, 2001, review of *Mama Day,* p. 62.

Houston Chronicle, June 9, 1998, Carol Rust, review of *The Men of Brewster Place,* p. 1.

Library Journal, June 1, 1998, p. 187.

London Review of Books, August 1, 1985.

Los Angeles Times, December 2, 1982.

Los Angeles Times Book Review, February 24, 1985; March 6, 1988.

Ms., June, 1985.

New Republic, September 6, 1982.

New York Times, February 9, 1985; May 1, 1990.

New York Times Book Review, August 22, 1982; March 3, 1985; February 21, 1988; April 19, 1998, Roy Hoffman, review of *The Men of Brewster Place,* p. 19.

People, June 22, 1998, p. 39.

Publishers Weekly, September 9, 1983; December 11, 1995, review of *Children of the Night,* p. 56; February 23, 1998, p. 49.

St. Louis Post-Dispatch, July 3, 1998, Andrea M. Wren, review of *The Men of Brewster Place,* p. E7.

San Francisco Review of Books, May, 1985.

Seattle Times, June 2, 1998, review of *The Men of Brewster Place,* p. E1.

Tampa Tribune, May 31, 1998, review of *The Men of Brewster Place,* p. 4.

Times (London, England), April 21, 1983.

Times Literary Supplement, May 24, 1985.

Tribune Books (Chicago, IL), January 31, 1988.

Twentieth Century Literature, fall, 2002, Robin Blyn, "The Ethnographer's Story: Mama Day and the Specter of Relativism," p. 239.

Washington Post, October 21, 1983; May 1, 1990.

Washington Post Book World, March 24, 1985; February 28, 1988.

Women's Review of Books, August, 1985.

Writer, December, 1994, p. 21.

ONLINE

Unofficial Gloria Naylor Web site, http://www.lytha studios.com/gnaylor/ (January 21, 2004).*

NELSON, Sharlene (P.) 1933-

PERSONAL: Born August 27, 1933, in Los Angeles, CA; daughter of William O. (a coach and teacher) and Katherine (an office manager; maiden name, Bailey) Patten; married Ted William Nelson (a forester), July 17, 1955; children: Gregg, Janise Nelson Gates. *Ethnicity:* "Caucasian." *Education:* University of California—Berkeley, B.A., 1955. *Politics:* Republican. *Religion:* Congregationalist. *Hobbies and other interests:* Sailing, backpacking with her grandchildren, skiing, writing.

ADDRESSES: Home and office—824 South Marine Hills Way, Federal Way, WA 98003.

CAREER: Freelance writer, 1956—. *Pacific Search,* staff writer, 1966-72; *Oregonian,* correspondent, 1973-82. Lewis and Clark Trail Heritage Foundation, member.

MEMBER: Society of Children's Book Writers and Illustrators, U.S. Lighthouse Society, Pacific Northwest Writers Conference, Oregon Historical Society, Washington State Historical Society, Washington Trail Association, Washington County Historical Society of North Carolina (president, 1969-70), Tacoma Yacht Club, Tacoma Women's Sailing Association.

AWARDS, HONORS: Second-place award, children's nonfiction book category, Pacific Northwest Writers Conference, 1972, for *Gray Whale.*

WRITINGS:

WITH HUSBAND, TED NELSON

(And with Joan LeMieux) *Cruising the Columbia and Snake Rivers: Eleven Cruises in the Inland Waterway,* Pacific Search Press (Seattle, WA), 1981, revised edition, 1986.
The Umbrella Guide to Washington Lighthouses, Umbrella Books (Friday Harbor, WA), 1990, revised edition, 1998.
The Umbrella Guide to California Lighthouses, Epicenter Press (Seattle, WA), 1993, revised edition, 1999.

The Umbrella Guide to Oregon Lighthouses, Epicenter Press (Seattle, WA), 1994.
Bull Whackers to Whistle Punks: Logging in the Old West, Franklin Watts (Danbury, CT), 1996.
The Umbrella Guide to Exploring the Columbia-Snake River Inland Waterway, Epicenter Press (Seattle, WA), 1997.
Mount St. Helens National Volcanic Monument, Children's Press (Danbury, CT), 1997.
Olympic National Park, Children's Press (Danbury, CT), 1997.
Hawaii Volcanoes National Park, Children's Press (New York, NY), 1998.
Mount Rainier National Park, Children's Press (New York, NY), 1998.
William Boeing: Builder of Planes, Children's Press (New York, NY), 1999.
The Golden Gate Bridge, Children's Press (New York, NY), 2001.
Brett Favre, Capstone Books (Mankato, MN), 2001.
The Makah, Franklin Watts (Danbury, CT), 2003.
The Nez Percé, Franklin Watts (Danbury, CT), 2002.
Jedediah S. Smith, Franklin Watts (Danbury, CT), 2004.

Author of booklets about forestry. Author of the children's book *Gray Whale.*

WORK IN PROGRESS: Nonfiction articles for children.

SIDELIGHTS: Sharlene and Ted Nelson once commented: "Little did we suspect that a college assignment would lead to our working together as coauthors many years later. In 1953 Sharlene was given a course assignment to write a children's story or review 100 children's books. She chose to write a story about Smokey Bear, a then well-known symbol for forest fire prevention. Her fiance, Ted, agreed to do the illustrations. We produced the hand-printed book with watercolor illustrations and had it bound in hardcover. The assignment yielded an 'A.' The story was submitted later to publishers, and Sharlene received her first rejection slip. Now and then, we pull the original from the bookshelf and read it to our grandchildren, who ask, 'Who is Smokey Bear?'

"After our marriage, Ted pursued a career in forestry, and we developed an affinity for the outdoors, an interest in local history, and an enjoyment of research. Sharlene patiently pursued her interest in writing, despite numerous rejection slips.

"In 1977 we moved from the Oregon coast to Longview, Washington, and began sailing on the nearby Columbia River. Sharlene learned of a publisher who wanted to produce a boaters' guide to the Columbia River, and she volunteered. When Ted heard of the project, he exclaimed, 'That river is 1,200 miles long, and we've only sailed thirty miles of it!' We got busy. The publisher agreed to a book covering only the 465-mile-long inland waterway, a navigable portion of the lower Snake and Columbia Rivers that follows the western end of the Lewis and Clark Trail. After traveling every mile by water, doing interviews and research, our first book, *Cruising the Columbia and Snake Rivers: Eleven Cruises in the Inland Waterway,* was published in 1981.

"In 1989, then living on Washington's Puget Sound, we had an urge to write another book. Learning of a publisher who was looking for regional guidebooks, we began brainstorming ideas. One morning Ted looked out of the window and across the sound at the flashing light of a lighthouse. 'How about a book about lighthouses?' he asked. We knew little about lighthouses, but we had enjoyed seeing them when sailing. *The Umbrella Guide to Washington Lighthouses* was published in 1990.

"For *Bull Whackers to Whistle Punks: Logging in the Old West,* we drew on our experiences living in a remote logging camp in northern California. While the other books used mostly photographs taken by Ted, this book used mostly historic photographs. Ted was able, however, to provide drawings for the chapter art.

"The bull whackers book led to an assignment for books on three national parks and the Mount St. Helens National Volcanic Monument. We had backpacked the trails of Olympic and Mount Rainier National Parks and hiked trails at the Hawaii Volcanoes National Park. When Mount St. Helens erupted, we were living in Longview, only thirty-five miles away.

"We have an ability to work closely together. Our shared experiences and mutual interests have gotten us through the times when there were writing commitments and only a blank page before us. Sharlene likes the quotation, 'When you want to know a subject, write a book about it.'"

BIOGRAPHICAL AND CRITICAL SOURCES:

PERIODICALS

Booklist, August, 1996, p. 1899.

Library Journal, June 1, 1990, p. 158.
School Library Journal, July, 1996, p. 94.

*   *   *

NOONAN, Tom 1951-
(Richmond Arrley, Ludovico Sorret)

PERSONAL: Born April 12, 1951, in Greenwich, CT; son of a dentist and jazz musician; married Karen Young (an actress), c. 1988 (divorced); children: Wanda, one son. *Education:* Attended Yale University.

ADDRESSES: Office—Paradise Theatre Company, Genre Pictures, 64 East 4th St., New York, NY 10003-8903. *Agent*—HWA Talent Representatives, 220 East 3rd St., Suite 400, New York, NY 10010.

CAREER: Actor, director, producer, music composer, film editor, and writer. Columbia University, New York, NY, faculty of graduate film department, 2001-02. Paradise Theatre, New York, NY, executive director and instructor in acting, writing, and directing.

Actor in stage productions, including Michael Weller's *Split* (off-Broadway production), 1977; (as Tilden) Sam Shephard's *Buried Child,* Theatre for a New City, Theatre De Lys (now Lucille Lortel Theatre), 1978-79, Circle Repertory Theatre, New York, NY, 1979; (as Sepp) F. X. Kroetz's *Farmyard,* Theatre for a New City, New York, NY, 1981; (as Rube Januk) Harvey Fierstein's *Spookhouse,* Playhouse 91, New York, NY, 1984; (as Michael) *What Happened Was . . . ,* Paradise Theatre, New York, NY, 1992; (as Mickey Hounsell) *Wang Dang,* Paradise Theatre, 1999; and (as man in video) *Intrigue with Faye,* Acorn Theatre, New York, NY, 2003. Also appeared in the stage productions (as Jack) *Wifey* (also known as *The Wife*), *The Breakers,* Len Jenkins's *Five of Us, The Invitational,* and *Marathon '88,* all produced in New York, NY, and Lanford Wilson's *A Poster of the Cosmos.* Actor in motion pictures, including (as gangster and second man) *Gloria,* Columbia, 1980; (as Jake) *Heaven's Gate* (also known as *Johnson County Wars*), United Artists, 1980; *Rage* (made for television), 1980; (as man in park) *Willie and Phil,* Twentieth Century-Fox, 1980; (as Ferguson) *Wolfen,* Warner Bros., 1981; (as Paddy) *Easy Money,* Orion, 1983; (as Daryl Potts) *Eddie*

Macon's Run, Universal, 1983; (as Frank Holtzman) *Best Defense,* Paramount, 1984; (as Varrick) *F/X* (also known as *F/X—Murder by Illusion* and *Murder by Illusion*), Orion, 1986; (as Reese) *The Man with One Red Shoe,* Twentieth Century-Fox, 1985; (as Francis Dollarhyde) *Manhunter* (also known as *Red Dragon: The Pursuit of Hannibal Lecter*), De Laurentiis Entertainment Group, 1986; *Tom Goes to the Bar* (short film), Cinecom International, 1986; (as Frankenstein) *The Monster Squad,* TriStar, 1987; (as Scully) *Collison Course* (also known as *East/West Cop*), Recording Releasing/Rich International, 1989; (as man in diner) "A Ghost," *Mystery Train,* Orion Classics, 1989; (as Cain) *Robocop 2,* Orion, 1990; *BoneDaddy,* Sundance workshop, 1991; (as Ripper and himself) *The Last Action Hero,* Columbia, 1993; (as Michael) *What Happened Was . . . ,* Samuel Goldwyn Company, 1994; (as Jack) *The Wife,* Artistic License, 1995; (as Kelson; some sources cite Kelso) *Heat,* Warner Bros., 1996; (as Chicago) *Phoenix,* Trimark Pictures, 1998; (as Mickey Hounsell) *Wang Dang,* 1999; (as Jackson McLaren) *The Astronaut's Wife,* New Line Cinema, 1999; (as Mort Stein) *The Opportunists,* First Look Pictures Releasing, 2000; (as Butler) *The Photographer,* HBO, 2000; (as Gary Jackson) *The Pledge,* Warner Bros., 2001; (as Anders) *A Bullet in the Brain* (short film), 2001; (as Sheriff Decker) *Knockaround Guys,* New Line Cinema, 2001; (as himself) *A Constant Forge: The Life and Art of John Cassavetes,* 2001; (uncredited; as Joshua Taft) *Eight-Legged Freaks,* Warner Bros., 2002; (as Byron Bradley) *The Egoists,* April Films, 2003; and (as Frank Donovan) *Madness and Genius,* 2003. Also appeared in the independent short film *Doris and Inez* (also known as *Doris and Inez Speak the Truth*). Voice appears in the motion picture *High Hair,* 2004.

Actor in television movies, including (as Bo) *Rage!,* NBC, 1980; (as Mr. Y) *The 10 Million-Dollar Getaway,* USA Network, 1991; and (as Chicago) *Phoenix,* HBO, 1998.

Actor in episodes of television programs, including (as Lacey) "The Odds," *Tales from the Darkside,* Laurel, 1984; (as Brandon Thornton) "The Making of a Martyr," *The Equalizer,* CBS, 1989; "The Moving Finger," *Monsters,* Laurel, 1991; (as John Lee Roche) "Paper Hearts," *The X-Files,* Fox, 1996; (as Frank Price) *Early Edition* (pilot), CBS, 1996; (as Howard Schmidt) "The Beat Goes On," *The Beat,* UPN, 2000; (as Zephyr Dillinger) "Abra Cadaver," *C.S.I.: Crime Scene Inves-* *tigation,* CBS, 2002; and (as Malcolm Bruce) "Graansha," *Law and Order: Criminal Intent,* NBC, 2003. Also appeared in *Midtown* (Metro Media). Also actor in the television miniseries (as Willard Fenway) *John Jakes' Heaven and Hell: North and South, Book III* (also known as *John Jakes' Heaven and Hell: North and South, Book III* and *North and South III*), ABC, 1994.

Director of stage productions, including (and producer) *What Happened Was . . . ,* Paradise Theatre, New York, NY, 1992; (and producer) *Wifey,* Paradise Theatre, 1994; *Wang Dang,* Paradise Theatre, 1999; and *What the Hell's Your Problem? An Evening with "Dr. Bob" Nathelson,* Paradise Theatre, 2002. Also producer of *Hitting Town, Hoover, Queer and Alone, Two by Bose,* and *X-mas Concert '92,* all Paradise Theatre. Director of motion pictures, including *BoneDaddy,* Sundance Workshop, 1991; *What Happened Was . . . ,* Samuel Goldwyn Company, 1994; (and sound designer) *The Wife,* Artistic License, 1996; and *Wang Dang,* 1999. Director of television episodes, including "The Bargain" and "Malcolm," both *Monsters,* 1990. Also director and producer of the television episode "The Eternal Sideman."

Producer of television movie *Red Wind,* USA Network, 1991. Producer of motion pictures, including *Wang Dang, The Wife, The Pesky Suitor,* and *What Happened Was . . . .*

Editor, under pseudonym Richmond Arrley, of motion pictures, including *BoneDaddy,* Sundance Workshop, 1991; *What Happened Was . . . ,* Samuel Goldwyn Company, 1994; *The Pesky Suitor,* 1995; *The Wife,* Artistic License, 1996; *Wang Dang,* 1999; and *The Eternal Sideman.* Editor of television episodes, including "Malcolm" and "The Bargain," both *Monsters,* and "The Eternal Sideman."

AWARDS, HONORS: OBIE Award for play *Wifey,* 1994; Grand Jury Prize, Sundance Film Festival, and Waldo Salt Award/Screenwriting Prize, Sundance Film Festival, both 1994, for *What Happened Was . . . ;* Silver Hugo, Chicago International Film Festival, 1994, for *What Happened Was . . . ;* National Endowment for the Arts Media Award, 1994, 1995; New York Foundation for the Arts screenwriting/playwriting fellow, 1998. Guggenheim fellowship for film making, 1998. *What Happened Was . . .* was nominated for two Independent Spirit Awards.

WRITINGS:

PLAYS

(And director) *What Happened Was . . . ,* produced at the Paradise Theater in New York, NY, 1992.

(And director) *Wifey* (also known as *The Wife*), produced at the Paradise Theater in New York, NY, 1993.

What the Hell's Your Problem?: An Evening with "Dr. Bob" Nathelson, produced at the Paradise Theater in New York, NY, 2002.

Wang Dang, 1999.

What Happened Was . . . was published in *Scenario* magazine.

SCREENPLAYS

(And editor) *BoneDaddy,* Sundance Workshop, 1991.

(And producer and editor) *Red Wind* (teleplay), USA Network, 1991.

(And director and editor) *What Happened Was . . . ,* Samuel Goldwyn Company, 1994.

(And director and editor) *The Wife,* Artistic License Films, 1996.

Wang Dang, 1999.

Also author of the unpublished novel *Must Have* and the short-story collection *Agog and Amygdala.*

Author of plays, including *Weekend at Bob's,* 1998; *Wunderkinder,* 1999; *When We Fall,* 1999; *Wake Up and Go to Sleep,* 2000; *Waiting,* 2001; *Waltz,* 2002; and *Whoopee,* 2002. Also author of plays *Starring Beck Falcone* and *Swallow.* Author of unproduced screenplays, including *Zing!, Dam, Deaf and Dumb, The Psychic Dentist, The Dark, P.A.N.I.C., Bagdad,* and *Fast and Loose.*

Author of the television episodes "The Bargain" and "Malcom," both *Monsters,* 1990, and "The Eternal Sideman." Also music composer under own name, for television miniseries, *Heaven and Hell.* Also author of several unproduced works for television, including "First Fly of Spring," "Baby's Driving Me Crazy," "Elevator Man," "Anybody Out There?," "Narcissus," "Dr. Flowerw," "Obscura," "What's Got into You?,"

"Troll," "Tattoo," "Black and White," "Incredibly Moving," and "Not Fade Away." Author, under pseudonym Ludovico Sorret, of television episodes, including "The Odds," *Tales from the Dark Side,* 1984; "The Bargain," *Monsters,* 1990; and "Malcolm," *Monsters,* 1990.

Music composer, under pseudonym Ludovico Sorret, for motion pictures, including *BoneDaddy,* Sundance Workshop, 1991; *What Happened Was . . . ,* Samuel Goldwyn Company, 1994; *The Wife,* Artistic License, 1996; and *Wang Dang,* 1999. Also music composer, under pseudonym Ludovico Sorret, for stage scores, including those for *What Happened Was . . . ,* Paradise Theatre, New York, NY, 1992; *Wifey,* Paradise Theatre, 1994; and *Wang Dang,* 1999. Also music composer, under pseudonymn Ludovico Sorret, for the plays *The Breakers,* produced in New York, NY, *Flow My Tears, Good-bye and Keep Cold,* and *My Hollywood Uncle.* Also music composer, under pseudonym Ludovico Sorret, for the television miniseries *John Jakes' Heaven and Hell: North and South: Book III,* ABC, 1994. Also music composer, under own name, for motion picture *Romance.*

SIDELIGHTS: Tom Noonan is a multitalented artist who has won particular recognition as an actor, playwright, and filmmaker. Noonan has appeared as a supporting player in numerous motion pictures, including Michael Cimino's maligned western *Heaven's Gate,* the freewheeling Rodney Dangerfield comedy *Easy Money,* John Cassavetes's feminist gangster work *Gloria,* and the extravagant Arnold Schwarzenegger action film *The Last Action Hero.* He also received much attention for his portrayal of psychopathic killer Francis Dollarhyde in Michael Mann's 1986 Hannibal Lecter film *Manhunter*—one of a number of noted sinister roles in his career—a character whom *Entertainment Weekly* contributor Ty Burr described as "one of the freakiest madmen Hollywood has ever given us." In recent years, Noonan has stepped into more prominent movie roles. In addition to his many cinema roles, Noonan has graced the television screen numerous times throughout his career, with guest appearances on television shows, including *The X-Files, C.S. I.: Crime Scene Investigation,* and *Law and Order: Criminal Intent.* Noonan has written three major stage plays, which he then adapted and produced as films, also occupying the lead roles: *What Happened Was . . . , The Wife,* and *Wang Dang.*

Noonan applied the profits from his acting into the funding of *What Happened Was . . . ,* his own venture into writing and directing. This film, which was derived from Noonan's stage production of the same title, chronicles—in painstaking detail—an awkward first date between coworkers at a law office. The film couple, secretary Jackie and paralegal Michael, meet at the latter's apartment and share an unsettling evening. *Newsweek* reviewer David Ansen remarked on the "painful comedy" captured in the film and reported that the work "acknowledges the terror behind the phrase 'getting acquainted.'" A *Rolling Stone* reviewer described Noonan's work as having "an edgy hothouse quality." Since the piece is filmed in real-time, the critic noted, the film depicts "the agony of getting to know someone . . . in every awkward gesture and excruciating pause." An *Entertainment Weekly* contributor termed *What Happened Was . . .* "an unsettling glimpse into the feelings that all our faces hide." Noonan, in addition to writing and directing *What Happened Was . . .,* also directed, edited, and produced the film. He also occupied the role of Michael in both the stage and film productions.

After the critical success of *What Happened Was . . .* in 1994, Noonan wrote and directed his second film, *The Wife,* which he adapted from his 1993 play *Wifey,* also known as *The Wife.* In the movie, husband and wife, Cosmo and Arlie, unexpectedly drop by the home of another married couple, Jack and Rita, both of whom are therapists. Cosmo is Jack and Rita's patient, and hopes to convince his therapists that he hasn't fabricated the things he's said about his wife. As the awkward evening progresses, Cosmo grows increasingly uncomfortable as Arlie's behavior becomes more flamboyant. A *Variety* reviewer described *The Wife* as "a bizarre, often provocative seriocomic dissection of marriage as a fragile yet almost universal institution." Noonan played Jack in the stage production and the motion picture, which he also directed and edited.

In 1999, Noonan again adapted an original stage work for film. *Wang Dang* introduces audiences to Mickey Hounsell, a has-been movie director who visits a college campus to give a lecture on filmmaking. It becomes clear, however, that he has a different agenda when film student Deana Icksty comes to his off-campus motel room. Deana is awed by the movie director, who has agreed to view a film project she is working on, and the two appear to be in for a cozy night when another student, Kim Procthkow, arrives at the door. Kim, however, is more interested in Deana than she is Mickey. The audience watches with gritted teeth as the awkward, taciturn, and sleazy Mickey, played by Noonan, tries to seduce the two young women.

"The character Noonan has supplied for himself is richly woven," wrote Les Gutman in a review of *Wang Dang* for *Curtain Up.* "Nervous, uncomfortable, lonesome, goofy, defeated. . . . Every nuance resonates in his portrayal." *New York Times* contributor Peter Marks wrote of the character's "anti-charm," stating, "Mickey may not be the type of guy you'd want to be stuck with in an empty room. But Noonan, in his intimate style of theater, makes him seem so real that you can almost feel his unpleasant breath on your neck." Gutman also commended Noonan's style, referring to the play's authentic, sordid motel room set, lack of stage lighting or music, and real-time atmosphere. "Also distinctive is Noonan's dialogue, which is sometimes jarringly real," Gutman maintained. "Speech is tentative—there are no glib, well-considered statements. . . . This is a mixed blessing: as effective and intriguing as it can be, it can also be tedious. Such is reality." Marks wrote of the play that "watching it is an almost clinical experience," dubbing *Wang Dang* a "discursive drama played as if a documentary camera had been left running." Marks went on to reflect that the play is "enjoyable in the way that experimental theater makes you aware of new applications for old formulas." In 1999, Noonan began filming the play for the screen—in Liberty, New York, near his home in the Catskill Mountains—with the assistance of fellowships from the Guggenheim Foundation and the New York Foundation for the Arts. Although Noonan's films have been financed on modest budgets, especially in comparison to those films in which he has acted, he scarcely sees this limited funding as a disadvantage. "That's the great thing about no-budget moviemaking," he told *Entertainment Weekly.* "You have no money, but you have all the time in the world."

Since the production of *Wang Dang,* Noonan has written numerous unpublished plays. In 2001 he put playwriting on hold to take a lead role in the film *Knockaround Guys,* written, directed, and produced by Brian Koppelman and David Levien, and starring Barry Pepper, Dennis Hopper, John Malkovich, Vin Diesel, and Seth Green. In *Knockaround Guys,* young Brooklyn mobster Matty (Barry Pepper) wants to prove his talent for illicit activities to his big-time boss father (Dennis Hopper). While the movie itself received mixed reactions from critics, even the most jaded had positive comments to make about Noonan's acting. "Tom Noonan, as Andy Griffith with a big stick and attitude, carries his scenes smoothly, and really makes you believe that he hasn't had a facial expression in twenty odd years," commented Marc Eastman on the *Movie Gurus* Web site. In a review for *Film Freak Central*, contributor Walter Chaw stated that "*Knockaround Guys* demonstrates what it could be when Noonan struts on the screen with his careful reptilian gait." Chaw went on to say that "the real failures of this film are . . . its uncontrollable glee with its veteran cast, too much faith in its freshman players . . . and not enough time spent in the company of Noonan."

Noonan returned to the screen the following year with the movie *Eight-Legged Freaks*, written by Jesse Alexander and Ellory Elkayem, and starring David Arquette and Kari Wuhrer. Noonan plays Joshua Taft, a recluse and owner of an exotic spider farm who collects bugs for his spiders from an area undisclosed as a nuclear waste spill site. Joshua's spiders grow to astronomical sizes and begin eating the citizens of the desert town. *Eight- Legged Freaks* was a hit with movie fans who enjoy the classically cheesy thrills of the 1950s monster movies. In a review for *Reel Movie Critic*, reviewer Brenda Sexton praised Noonan for his "fabulously played role" as Joshua. The next year, Noonan played the lead role in *Madness and Genius*.

"I've realized that the experience of the moment on a film set that was of value—not the deal, not the press, not the power," revealed Noonan in an article on his Web site titled "Why I Make Movies." "Making a movie with that kind of understanding has made me a better person. That's why I make movies. I feel lucky that I found a way to be alive, if only for those brief moments. It's like they turn the lights on for a minute and I can see the world. And that's enough for me. Life's become that simple, and I pray to God it stays that simple."

BIOGRAPHICAL AND CRITICAL SOURCES:

BOOKS

Contemporary Theatre, Film, and Television, Volume 53, Gale (Detroit, MI), 2004.

PERIODICALS

Entertainment Weekly, September 23, 1994, p. 46; April 19, 1996, Melissa Pierson, movie review of *What Happened Was . . . ,* p. 86; June 21, 1996, Ty Burr, movie review of *Manhunter,* p. 73.

Film Comment, November-December, 1995, Dan Gribbin, movie review of *Mystery Train,* pp. 80-83.
Newsweek, September 12, 1994, pp. 59-60.
New York Times, August 11, 1996, p. B12; August 16, 1996, p. C5.
People, March 20, 2000, "Tube," television review of *The Beat,* p. 27.
Quadrant, April, 2001, Neil MacDonald, "Dr. Lecter, I Presume," movie review of *Manhunter,* p. 59.
Rolling Stone, September 22, 1994, p. 106.
Variety, January 30, 1995, p. 48.

ONLINE

Curtain Up Web site, http://www.curtainup.com/ (February 18, 2004), Les Gutman, "A *Curtain Up* Review: *Wang Dang.*"
Film Bug Web site, http://www.filmbug.com/ (May 30, 2003), "Tom Noonan."
Film Freak Central Web site, http://www.filmfreak central.net/ (February 18, 2004), Walter Chaw, review of *Knockaround Guys.*
Filmmaker Magazine Web site, http://www.filmmaker magazine.com/ (February 18, 2004), "Production Update: *Wang Dang.*"
IndieWire Web site, http://www.indiewire.com/ (February 18, 2004), Eugene Hernandez, "Festival Discovery: Introducing Ryan Eslinger."
Internet Movie Database Web site, http://www.imdb.com/ (February 17, 2004), "Tom Noonan."
Microsoft Network Entertainment Web site, http://entertainment.msn.com/ (May 30, 2003), "Tom Noonan: Biography."
Movie Gurus Web site, http://www.movie-gurus.com/ (February 18, 2004), Marc Eastman, review of *Knockaround Guys.*
Reel Movie Critic Web site, http://www.reelmoviecritic.com/ (February 18, 2004), Brenda Sexton, review of *Eight-Legged Freaks.*
Slam Dance Film Festival Web site, http://www.slam dance.com/ (February 18,2004), description of *Madness and Genius.*
Tom Noonan Web site, http://www.tomnoonan.com/ (February 17, 2004), author biography and resume; Peter Marks, "*Wang Dang*: A Seducer with a Whiff of Genius (or Pizza)."
TV Guide Web site, http://www.tvguide.com/ (February 18, 2004), Maitland McDonagh, review of *Eight-Legged Freaks.**

NORMAN, Marc 1941-

PERSONAL: Born February 10, 1941, in Los Angeles, CA; son of Harry Fisher and Molly (Gillis) Norman; married Dale Moore (a psychotherapist), 1967; children: Zachary, Alexander (twins). *Education:* University of California, Berkeley, M.A., 1964.

ADDRESSES: Office—c/o WGA West Inc., 7000 West Third St., Los Angeles, CA 90048. *Agent*—Robert Lescher, 155 East 71st St., New York, NY 10021.

CAREER: Author, screenwriter, and producer. Screenwriter for films, including *Oklahoma Crude,* Columbia, 1973; *Zandy's Bride,* Warner Bros., 1974; *The Killer Elite,* MGM/UA, 1975; *Breakout,* Columbia/Tristar, 1975; *The Challenge,* Embassy, 1982; *The Aviator,* MGM/UA, 1985; *Bat 21,* Anchor Bay, 1988; *Cutthroat Island,* Artisan, 1995. Screenwriter and producer for film *Shakespeare in Love,* Miramax, 1998.

Screenwriter for television movies, including *Five Desperate Women,* American Broadcasting Companies, Inc. (ABC), 1971, and *The Challenge,* 1970.

Author of screen story for "The Innocent," *Mission: Impossible,* Columbia Broadcasting System (CBS), 1970.

MEMBER: Phi Beta Kappa.

AWARDS, HONORS: Academy Award, best screenplay written directly for the screen and best picture, L.A. Film Critics Association Award, best screenplay, Golden Globe Award, best screenplay and best picture, Broadcast Film Critics Association Award, best original screenplay, Golden Satellite Award, best picture, Writers Guild of America Award, best screenplay written directly for the screen, Fennecus Award, best screenplay, Apex Scroll Award, best picture and best original screenplay for a comedy, all 1998, all for *Shakespeare in Love;* Berlin Film Festival Award, best single achievement (for the screenplay), British Academy Award, both 1999, both for *Shakespeare in Love.*

WRITINGS:

Bike Riding in Los Angeles (nonfiction), Dutton (New York, NY), 1973.
Fool's Errand (novel), Holt, Rinehart, & Winston (New York, NY), 1978.

Marc Norman

SCREENPLAYS FOR TELEVISION

"The Innocent," *Mission: Impossible,* CBS, 1970.
Five Desperate Women, ABC, 1971.

SCREENPLAYS FOR CINEMA

Oklahoma Crude, Columbia, 1973, published by Dutton (New York, NY), 1973.
Zandy's Bride (adapted from the novel *The Stranger* by Lillian Bos Ross), Warner Bros., 1974.
The Killer Elite, MGM/UA, 1975.
Breakout, Columbia/Tristar, 1975.
The Challenge, Embassy, 1982.
The Aviator (based on a novel by Ernest Gann), MGM/UA, 1985.
Bat 21, Anchor Bay, 1988.
Cutthroat Island, Artisan, 1995.
(With Tom Stoppard) *Shakespeare in Love* (Miramax, 1998), Hyperion (New York, NY), 1998.

Also screenwriter for the television movie *The Challenge,* 1970.

SIDELIGHTS: Marc Norman is the screenwriter and producer of the Oscar-winning film *Shakespeare in Love,* a romantic comedy set in Elizabethan England that attempts to answer the question, "What inspired William Shakespeare?" Prior to the overwhelming success of *Shakespeare in Love* and Norman's own award-winning writing, he worked as a screenwriter on a number of films for cinema and television, including an episode of the *Mission: Impossible* television series.

One of Norman's earliest films, *Oklahoma Crude,* stars Faye Dunaway as a woman intent on drilling for oil on her Oklahoma property. She hires a man played by George C. Scott to drill for the oil, and the two find themselves battling large oil firms to keep control of the land. They manage to hold on to the land, finally striking oil and earning bids from several oil companies wishing to pump oil. Norman penned both the dramatic screenplay for the movie and the book by the same name. Also set in the dusty ranches of the West is *Zandy's Bride.* Norman wrote the screenplay based on the Lillian Bos Ross novel, *The Stranger.* The movie stars Gene Hackman as rancher Zandy Allan, who is in search of extra help on his land, which he receives by ordering a bride from Sweden. When the headstrong Hannah arrives, Zandy is not prepared for her forceful ways. The odd couple works its way through some difficult times, eventually falling in love.

Norman's next movie, *The Killer Elite,* stars James Caan as a retired CIA agent who was injured by his former partner but returns to the line of duty to protect a political leader named Yuen Chung. Robert Duvall plays Caan's old partner, the man hired to assassinate Chung. The final battle pits the ex-partners against one another. Duvall also appears in another Norman movie, *Breakout.* In the film, Duvall plays a prisoner in a South American country, and Charles Bronson stars as the pilot attempting to rescue him. Norman, who is an acrobatic pilot, demonstrated his knowledge of aviation in both *Breakout* and *The Aviator.* Christopher Reeve stars in *The Aviator* as a pilot whose facial scar is a constant reminder of his recent crash. Rosanna Arquette stars as a rich, spoiled woman whom the pilot agrees to carry with him on one of his flights. When the plane crashes, the two must put aside their petty arguments and fend for their lives in the dangerous mountains.

Norman's next screenplay, *Bat 21,* starring Gene Hackman as Lt. Colonel Iceal Hambleton, is based on a true story and takes place during the Vietnam War.

Hambleton crashes his plane in the midst of Vietnamese military forces and must struggle for survival. In his screenplay for the film *Cutthroat Island,* Norman tells the story of a female pirate named Morgan Adams, played by Geena Davis, who is in search of the rest of a treasure map left behind by her father. Morgan battles her uncle and other pirates with the help of a slave named William Shaw, all while under the watchful eye of a British newspaper reporter.

While Norman has many film credits to his name, none have garnered the attention or the critical acclaim of his most celebrated work, *Shakespeare in Love.* As coauthor of the screenplay, Norman helps tell the fictional story of a young Will Shakespeare (played by Joseph Fiennes), a playwright struggling to write a play that will gain him recognition. Gwyneth Paltrow plays Viola De Lesseps, the beautiful woman who dreams of acting in a play, very much against the rules of the Elizabethan era. Viola, however, dresses as a man named Thomas Kent and auditions for Will's newest play titled "Romeo and Ethel, The Pirate's Daughter." As Will and Viola gradually grow closer, Will's play is enlivened with new passion. Will knows that he and Viola cannot be together when the play ends, but their affair helps him transform his work into the tragic love story of the star-crossed lovers, *Romeo and Juliet.*

According to Timothy Dykstal of the *National Forum,* Norman conceived of the idea for *Shakespeare in Love* while his son was studying Elizabethan drama in school. Norman paired with screenwriter Tom Stoppard to work on the script. Together, they combined the general storyline with some traditional Shakespearean themes and several excerpts from Shakespeare's original works. They added the few facts actually known about Shakespeare and sprinkled in some of the myths as well. *ReelViews* critic James Berardinelli commented, "Numerous aspects of the script are peppered with elements from the Bard's plays: mistaken identities, transvestites, ghosts, poetry, and significant chunks of dialogue from *Romeo and Juliet.*" Berardinelli continued, "Stoppard and Norman's script seamlessly blends comedy, romance, and light drama." Roger Ebert of the *Chicago Sun-Times* noted in his review, "I was carried along by the wit, the energy, and a surprising sweetness." According to Rob Blackwelder of the *SPLICEDwire* Web site, *Shakespeare in Love* is "a comedic and romantic masterpiece that would make Shakespeare proud."

Shakespeare in Love won Academy Awards for best picture and best screenplay written directly for the screen. A reviewer for *New Straits Times* called *Shakespeare in Love* "a wonderfully conceived and brilliantly executed romantic comedy," noting that Norman and Stoppard "cleverly tie in literary allusions and many of the fiercely debated facts surrounding [Shakespeare's] life into the narrative." Norman told Robert Elisberg in an interview on the *Absolute Write* Web site, that he "like[s] to make up worlds and populate them." Norman said, "I like inventing people and putting them in settings so finely drawn that the viewer, for some short period of time, forgets he or she is looking at an artifice and thinks it's real. That's my performance. That's my, for lack of a better word, magic."

BIOGRAPHICAL AND CRITICAL SOURCES:

PERIODICALS

Best Sellers, August, 1978, review of *Fool's Errand,* p. 145.

Christian Science Monitor, May 24, 1978, review of *Fool's Errand,* p. 23.

Kirkus Reviews, February 15, 1978, review of *Fool's Errand,* p. 197.

Library Journal, May 15, 1978, review of *Fool's Errand,* p. 1082.

National Forum, summer, 1999, Timothy Dykstal, review of *Shakespeare in Love,* p. 41.

New Statesman, January 29, 1999, David Jays, review of *Shakespeare in Love,* p. 39.

New Straits Times, January 2, 2001, "Endearing Tale of the Bard's Muse."

Observer (London, England), September 3, 1978, review of *Fool's Errand,* p. 26.

Publishers Weekly, March 27, 1978, review of *Fool's Errand,* p. 67.

Variety, December 7, 1998, Lael Loewenstein, review of *Shakespeare in Love,* p. 53.

West Coast Review of Books, May, 1978, review of *Fool's Errand,* p. 36.

ONLINE

Absolute Write Web site, http://www.absolutewrite.com/ (June 2, 2003), Robert J. Elisberg, "Interview with Marc Norman."

Chicago Sun-Times Web site, http://www.suntimes.com/ (June 2, 2003), Roger Ebert, review of *Shakespeare in Love.*

Fennec Awards Database, http://awards.fennec.org/ (February 18, 2004), list of Academy, Golden Globe, Satellite, Guild, Fennecus, and Apex awards for Marc Norman.

Filmtracks Web site, http://www.filmtracks.com/ (June 2, 2003), review of music in *Shakespeare in Love.*

Movie Club Web site, http://www.movieclub.com/ (December 25, 1998), Joe Baltake, "*Shakespeare* Has Fun with the Bard in Love."

Movies.com Web site, http://movies.go.com/ (February 18, 2004), *Oklahoma Crude* and *The Challenge.*

MSN Entertainment Web site, http://entertainment.msn.com/ (February 18, 2004).

ReelViews: Movie Review Web site, http://moviereviews.colossus.net/ (June 2, 2003), James Berardinelli, review of *Shakespeare in Love.*

SLICEDwire Web site, http://www.splicedonline.com/ (1998), Rob Blackwelder, "Rosencrantz and Juliet: Tom Stoppard Helps Pen Another Mock Shakespearean Masterpiece."

TV Tome Web site, http://www.tvtome.com/ (February 18, 2004), *Mission: Impossible.**

O-P

O'BRIAN, E. G.
  See CLARKE, Arthur C(harles)

*   *   *

PAULY, Louis W. 1952-

PERSONAL: Born 1952, in Erie, PA; son of Louis W. and Elizabeth Ann (Barrett) Pauly; married Caryl Clark, August 26, 1978; children: Tessa, Reid. *Education:* Fordham University, B.A., 1974; London School of Economics and Political Science, M.Sc., 1977; Cornell University, Ph.D., 1987.

ADDRESSES: Home—10 Boswell Ave., Toronto, Ontario, Canada. *Office*—Centre for International Studies, University of Toronto, Toronto, Ontario M5S 3K7, Canada. *E-mail*—lpauly@chass.utoronto.ca.

CAREER: Royal Bank of Canada, in management, 1978-82; University of Toronto, Toronto, Ontario, Canada, professor of political science, 1987—.

MEMBER: American Political Science Association, International Studies Association, Canadian Political Science Association.

WRITINGS:

Foreign Banks in Australia: The Politics of Deregulation, Centre for Money, Banking, and Finance, Macquarie University (Mosman, Australia), 1987.

Regulatory Politics in Japan: The Case of Foreign Banking, China-Japan Program, Cornell University Press (Ithaca, NY), 1987.

Opening Financial Markets: Banking Politics on the Pacific Rim, Cornell University Press (Ithaca, NY), 1988.

(Editor, with Janice Gross Stein) *Choosing to Cooperate: How States Avoid Loss,* Johns Hopkins University Press (Baltimore, MD), 1993.

The League of Nations and the Foreshadowing of the International Monetary Fund, International Finance Section (Princeton, NJ), 1996.

Who Elected the Bankers? Surveillance and Control in the World Economy, Cornell University Press (Ithaca, NY), 1997.

(With Paul N. Doremus, William W. Keller, and Simon Reich) *The Myth of the Global Corporation,* Princeton University Press (Princeton, NJ), 1998.

(Editor, with Michael Th. Greven) *Democracy beyond the State? The European Dilemma and the Emerging Global Order,* Rowman & Littlefield (Lanham, MD), 2000.

(Editor, with David Andrews and C. Randall Henning) *Governing the World: Money,* Cornell University Press (Ithaca, NY), 2002.

WORK IN PROGRESS: Studies on industrial innovation, the political management of the global economy, and adaptation within international organizations.

SIDELIGHTS: Drawing on his experience both as a banker and as an academic, author Louis W. Pauly has published several books, most dealing with connections between international politics and global finance. In *Who Elected the Bankers? Surveillance and Control in the World Economy,* Pauly outlines the evolution of the global economy and the presence and growth of institutions such as the International Monetary Fund (IMF), which were created to enhance global financial cooperation. The book traces the roots of key roles played by the IMF to the economic and financial work of the League of Nations in the 1920s. Pauly makes the point that the evolution of entities like the IMF was not accidental, but the result of deliberate decisions by public authorities.

Foreign Affairs reviewer Richard N. Cooper called Pauly's treatment "skillful," but criticized the author's claim that global finance raises fundamental legitimacy problems for the nation-state. According to Cooper, economic problems in countries are usually the result of internal influences. Richard Drezen of *Library Journal* wondered why Pauly focused on the IMF to the exclusion of the World Bank and the United Nations. Timothy Sinclair, writing for the *American Political Science Review,* called the book "an excellent contribution to the literature on international capital mobility and multilateral economic surveillance."

Opening Financial Markets: Banking Politics on the Pacific Rim examines the regulatory policies in the banking systems of four industrialized nations—Japan, Canada, Australia, and the United States. Pauly focuses on how and why government and business across the globe have worked to establish common standards in international banking. According to William Diebold, Jr. of *Foreign Affairs,* "This excellent book stands out as a study of the dynamics of global interdependence." Diebold commented that Pauly's book is "clearly and succinctly" written, and called it a "valuable" book for readers of many knowledge levels. Reviewer D. E. Bond of *Choice* noted small faults in some use of details (a mistaken date for the founding of the Canadian Bankers Association, for example) but declared the work "a worthwhile addition to any collection on money and banking," noting that it offers "a concise review of the reasons for and methods of achieving the basic aims of banking regulation."

BIOGRAPHICAL AND CRITICAL SOURCES:

PERIODICALS

American Political Studies Review, September, 1989, p. 1090; December, 1997, Timothy Sinclair, review of *Who Elected the Bankers? Surveillance and Control in the World Economy,* pp. 1010-1011.

Annals of the American Academy of Political and Social Science, January, 2001, Jonathan D. Aronson, review of *The Myth of the Global Corporation,* p. 205.
Booklist, March 15, 1997, p. 1210.
Choice, February, 1989, D. E. Bond, review of *Opening Financial Markets: Banking Politics on the Pacific Rim,* p. 982; September, 1997, p. 180.
Foreign Affairs, summer, 1989, William Diebold, Jr., review of *Opening Financial Markets,* p. 166; May-June, 1997, Richard N. Cooper, review of *Who Elected the Bankers?,* pp. 125-126.
International Journal, fall, 2000, review of *Democracy beyond the State? The European Dilemma and the Emerging Global Order,* pp. 685-686.
Journal of Economic Literature, March, 1989, pp. 175-176.
Journal of Interamerican Studies and World Affairs, summer, 2000, Bryan R. Daves, review of *The Myth of the Global Corporation,* p. 109.
Library Journal, April 15, 1997, Richard Drezen, review of *Who Elected the Bankers?,* p. 93.

* * *

PEPLOE, Mark

PERSONAL: Born in Kenya; immigrated to England. *Education:* Attended Magdalen College, Oxford.

ADDRESSES: Home—England. *Agent*—Anthony Jones, PFD, Drury House, 34-43 Russell Street, London, WC2B 5HA.

CAREER: Screenwriter and motion picture director. BBC-TV, researcher for documentary department; researcher, writer, and director for television series *Creative Persons.* Screenwriter, 1971—; motion picture director, 1991—. Director of the films *Afraid of the Dark* (1991; also known as *Double Vue*) and *Victory* (1995). Served as a script consultant for *The Triumph of Love* (2001), written and directed by Clare Peploe.

AWARDS, HONORS: Academy Award for screenplay based on material from another medium, and Golden Globe for best screenplay, both with Bernardo Bertolucci, both 1987, both for *The Last Emperor.*

WRITINGS:

SCREENPLAYS

(With Andrew Birken and Jacques Demy) *The Pied Piper of Hamlin,* 1972.

Mark Peploe

(With Peter Wollen and Michelangelo Antonioni) *The Passenger* (also known as *Profession: Reporter*), Metro-Goldwyn-Mayer/United Artists, 1975.

(With Bernardo Bertolucci) *The Last Emperor,* Columbia, 1987.

(With sister, Clare Peploe) *High Season,* Hemdale, 1988.

(With Bernardo Bertolucci) *The Sheltering Sky* (based on a novel by Paul Bowles), Warner Bros., 1990.

(With Frederick Seidel; and director) *Afraid of the Dark* (also known as *Double Vue*), Fine Line Features/New Line Cinema, 1992.

(With Bernardo Bertolucci and Rudy Wurlitzer) *Little Buddha,* Miramax, 1994.

(And director) *Victory* (based on a novel by Joseph Conrad), Miramax, 1995.

Also coauthor of psychological thriller screenplay *La Baby-Sitter* (1975; also known as *La Jeune fille libre le soir, The Babysitter,* and *Wanted: Babysitter*) with Luciano Vincenzoni, Nicola Badalucco, and Rene Clement. Also coauthor of screenplay *Out of the Blue* with Gary Jules Jouvenat, Leonard Yakir, and Brenda Nielson. Also author and director of the short film *Samson & Delilah.* Also worked on screenplay *Heaven and Hell* (RPC/Jermey Thomas) with Bernardo Bertolucci, based on a biography by Giovanni Ludica.

SIDELIGHTS: Mark Peploe has been writing screenplays since the early 1970s. He has collaborated on screenplays with others, including Italian director Bernardo Bertolucci and Clare Peploe, his sister. In the early 1990s, Peploe turned to directing in addition to screenwriting. He and Bertolucci were awarded the 1987 Academy Award for their screenplay *The Last Emperor.*

Peploe's first produced screenplay, an adaptation of the Brothers Grimm fairy tale and the poem by Robert Browning, *The Pied Piper of Hamlin,* was written with Andrew Birkin and Jacques Demy, who also directed the film. Set in the Middle Ages, *The Pied Piper of Hamlin* opens on bubonic plague-ridden and rat-infested England. Donovan stars in the role of the pied piper, who ultimately entrances the rats—and the children of Hamlin—with his flute. The rats march into the river and drown, while the children of Hamlin follow the pied piper wherever he leads them. Peploe next wrote the screenplay *The Passenger* (1975) with Peter Wollen and Michelangelo Antonioni, who also directed the film. Jack Nicholson starred with Maria Schneider as television reporter David Locke, who is sent to Africa to write about African guerilla freedom fighters. Upon returning to his hotel room after one day's exhausting desert excursion, he discovers that the hotel patron in the next room has died. Unhappy with his own life, Locke switches identities with the dead man, whom he resembles, and leaves Africa with the deceased's appointment book in the hope that he will discover a more interesting life. In the same year, Peploe was also one of four writers to collaborate on a film titled *The Babysitter.*

The Last Emperor, Peploe's next screenwriting project and the first of many collaborations with Bertolucci, won Academy Awards in several categories, including best picture and best screenplay. *The Last Emperor* tells the true story—in flashbacks—of the life of Pu Yi, a boy who in 1908, at age three, was installed in China's Forbidden City and elevated to the status of emperor. He was honored as a god, the Lord of Ten Thousand Years, and was titular ruler of one-third of all people on Earth. Pu Yi became the last emperor in 1912, when the Ch'ing dynasty's 268-year reign was ended by the establishment of a republic. Pu Yi remained in the Forbidden City until he was exiled to a coastal city, from there becoming Japan's puppet emperor of Manchuria from the 1930s through 1945. Pu Yi spent the last half of the 1940s in Soviet custody, followed by ten years in prisons in China, where he was "re-educated." From 1959 until his death in 1967, the "last emperor" worked as a gardener in Peking's Botanical Gardens.

In 1988, Peploe wrote a screenplay with his sister Clare, who was also the film's director, titled *High Season*. The story is set on the Greek island of Rhodes, the location of the 120-foot-high statue known as the Colossus of Rhodes, one of the Seven Wonders of the World, which was constructed during the third century B.C. The film's concern is a sculpture dedicated to the Unknown Tourist—the brainchild of a shopkeeper's son who also wants to turn the ancient family store into a T-shirt shop. The shopkeeper, however, wants nothing to do with tourists. The Peploes' characters in this film include a well-known British photographer (played by Jacqueline Bisset) who lives on the island, a visiting sculptor who turns out to be the photographer's ex-husband, an art expert from England who turns out to be a spy for the Soviets, and a young and confused British couple. Roger Ebert, reviewing the work for the *Chicago Sun-Times,* called the film "a light-footed social satire," stating, "The ingeniousness with which [the Peploes] weave their tangled plot created real questions in my mind, which were resolved in one of those deeply satisfying endings in which everything has an answer and yet nobody turns out to have been blameless." Ebert concluded his review by calling *High Season* "an example of a rare species: the intelligent silly movie." On the *Apollo Movie Guide* Web site, reviewer Kurt Dahlke determined that "*High Season* has so much going on for it that it breaks the mould for romantic summer comedies," pointing out, "Even if you don't like [romantic summer comedies], you'll enjoy this one."

Released in 1990, *The Sheltering Sky* is based on Paul Bowles's 1949 novel about a troubled American couple who travels to North Africa in an effort to rekindle the romance of their dull marriage. Kit and Port Moresby, played by John Malkovich and Debra Winger, soon find themselves in the confines of a love triangle as steamy and taxing as the African desert itself, each seeking personal shelter from life and one another. Peploe wrote the script with Bertolucci, who directed the film. Peploe again collaborated with Bertolucci to create *Little Buddha,* also written with Rudy Wurlitzer and starring Keanu Reeves, Bridget Fonda, and Chris Isaak. *Little Buddha* tells the story of a Seattle boy taken voluntarily to Bhutan by Tibetan Buddhist

monks who think he might be the reincarnation of an important lama named Dorje. The boy (and two others, also candidates for the reincarnation role) are given a book about the youth of Prince Siddhartha, whose life is interwoven within the contemporary story. *Little Buddha* received less than favorable reviews. In the *National Review* John Simon called the movie "a pure abomination" and "a crashing bore." Stanley Kauffmann in the *New Republic* deemed the screenplay "flaccid" and pointed out that although it was based on true stories, he felt "art needs to be better managed than life."

In 1991, Peploe turned his cinematic efforts toward both screenwriting and directing with the horror movie *Afraid of the Dark,* written with Frederick Seidel. A psychological thriller, the story involves a young boy's visions of a razor slasher who attacks blind women in his neighborhood. The visions turn out to be the child's fears of his own impending blindness and of the surgery necessary to prevent it. Peploe's second screenwriting and directing venture was 1995's *Victory,* which he based on a novel by Joseph Conrad. The story is set in 1913 in the Dutch East Indies, in a hotel owned by an anti-Semitic German. The owner of an all-woman orchestra that plays there nightly tries to "sell" one of the women to the hotel owner. When she escapes with a local resident to a remote island, the hotel owner has them pursued by three bandits under the pretext that fortune awaits them on the island.

BIOGRAPHICAL AND CRITICAL SOURCES:

BOOKS

Writers Directory, 19th edition, St. James Press (Detroit, MI), 2003.

PERIODICALS

Chicago Sun-Times, June 24, 1988.
Maclean's, December 14, 1987, p. 66.
National Review, June 27, 1994, John Simon, review of *Little Buddha,* pp. 59-60.
New Republic, December 14, 1987, pp. 22-23; June 13, 1994, Stanley Kauffmann, review of *Little Buddha,* p. 32.

New Yorker, November 30, 1987, pp. 98-101; August 24, 1992, pp. 77-79.

People, December 17, 1987, p. 12; August 3, 1992, pp. 10-11.

Playboy, February, 1991, p. 16; August, 1992, p. 18.

Rolling Stone, January 10, 1991, p. 58.

Time, November 23, 1987, p. 100.

Variety, December 13, 1993, p. 37.

Washington Post, June 24, 1988.

ONLINE

Apollo Movie Guide's Review, http://apolloguide.com/ (1987), Kurt Dahlke, review of *High Season.*

Chicago Sun-Times Web site, http://www.suntimes.com/ (February 27, 2004), Roger Ebert, review of *High Season.*

Golden Globes Web site, http://www.thegoldenglobes.com/ (June 2, 2003), "Mark Peploe."

Internet Movie Database Web site, http://www.us.imdb.com/ (February 27, 2004), "Mark Peploe."

Microsoft Network Entertainment Web site, http://entertainment.msn.com/ (June 2, 2003), "Mark Peploe."

PFD Agency Web site, http://www.pfd.co.uk/ (February 27, 2004), "Mark Peploe (Writer)."*

*   *   *

PERELMAN, Michael 1939-

PERSONAL: Born 1939, in New Castle, PA. *Education:* Attended University of Michigan, 1961, graduate study, 1963-64; University of California—Berkeley, Ph.D., 1971.

ADDRESSES: Home—Route 3, Box 295, Chico, CA 95926. *Office*—Department of Economics, California State University, Chico, CA 95929. *E-mail*—michael@ecst.csuchico.edu.

CAREER: California State University, Chico, professor of economics, 1971—. Visiting scholar at University of Paris X, 1978. Member of U.S. Department of Agriculture task force on spatial heterogeneity in agricultural landscapes and enterprises, 1973; member of California governor's small farm viability project task force, 1977; member of editorial board of *Review of Radical Political Economy,* 1981-83; workshop leader.

WRITINGS:

Farming for Profit in a Hungry World: Capital and the Crisis in Agriculture, Allanheld, Osmun (Montclair, NJ), 1977.

Classical Political Economy, Primitive Accumulation, and the Social Division of Labor, Allanheld, Osmun (Montclair, NJ), 1982, revised edition published as *The Invention of Capitalism: Classical Political Economy and the Secret History of Primitive Accumulation,* Duke University Press (Durham, NC), 2000.

Marx's Crises Theory: Scarcity, Labor, and Finance, Praeger (New York, NY), 1987.

Keynes, Investment Theory, and the Economic Slowdown: The Role of Replacement Investment and Q-Ratios, St. Martin's Press (New York, NY), 1989.

Information, Social Relations, and the Economics of High Technology, St. Martin's Press (New York, NY), 1991.

The Pathology of the U. S. Economy: The Costs of a Low-Wage System, St. Martin's Press (New York, NY), 1993.

The End of Economics, Routledge (New York, NY), 1996.

Class Warfare in the Information Age, St. Martin's Press (New York, NY), 1998.

The Natural Instability of Markets: Expectations, Increasing Returns, and the Collapse of Capitalism, St. Martin's Press (New York, NY), 1999.

Transcending the Economy: On the Potential of Passionate Labor and the Wastes of the Market, St. Martin's Press (New York, NY), 2000.

The Pathology of the U.S. Economy Revisited: The Intractable Contradictions of Economic Policy, Palgrave (New York, NY), 2002.

Steal This Idea: The Corporate Confiscation of Creativity, Palgrave (New York, NY), 2002.

CONTRIBUTOR

Huey Johnson, editor, *No Deposit—No Return,* Addison-Wesley (Reading, MA), 1970.

Ira Winn, editor, *Basic Issues in Environment,* C. E. Merrill, 1971.

Peter Barnes, editor, *The People's Land*, Rodale Press (New York, NY), 1974.

Patterns of Civilization: Asia; Changes in Asian Society, Cambridge Book Co., 1974.

William J. Jewell, editor, *Energy, Agriculture, and Waste Management*, Ann Arbor Science Publishers, 1975.

Norman Chigier and Edward Stern, editors, *Proceedings of the International Seminar on Collective Phenomena and the Applications of Physics to Other Fields of Science*, Brian Publications, 1975.

Barry Commoner and others, editors, *Energy and Human Welfare: A Critical Analysis*, Volume III: *Human Welfare: The End Use of Power*, Macmillan (New York, NY), 1975.

Richard Merrill, editor, *Radical Agriculture*, Harper (New York, NY), 1976.

Richard D. Rodefeld, Jan Flora, and other editors, *Change in Rural America: Causes, Consequences, and Alternatives*, Mosby (St. Louis, MO), 1978.

Louis Junker, editor, *The Political Economy of Food and Energy: Lectures Given at Western Michigan University*, Division of Research, Graduate School of Business Administration, 1977.

R. S. Ganapathy, editor, *Agriculture, Rural Energy, and Development*, Division of Research, Graduate School of Business Administration, University of Michigan (Ann Arbor, MI), 1981.

Also contributor of articles and reviews to economic journals.

SIDELIGHTS: Michael Perelman has had a long career as a professor of economics at California State University in Chico. He has penned several books about his area of study, and contributed to many others. Among his titles is the 1993 title *The Pathology of the U.S. Economy: The Cost of a Low-Wage System*. In it Perelman suggests raising wages to reanimate what was then a sluggish U.S. economy. Critiquing the volume in the *Journal of Economic Issues*, Brent McClintock praised the author's "survey of economic history and the history of economic thought on a high-wage strategy," and further noted that "the book is written with a clarity of style that makes it highly accessible to both undergraduate and graduate student audiences."

The Invention of Capitalism: Classical Political Economy and the Secret History of Primitive Accumulation, published in 2000, is a revision of his previous *Classical Political Economy, Primitive Accumulation, and the Social Division of Labor*, which puts forth Perelman's support for Karl Marx's theory that the exodus of British workers from the countryside to the cities during the Industrial Revolution was not so much a voluntary change as a forced one because gaming laws and other restrictions made it impossible for rural commoners to supplement their subsistence farming by hunting. Perelman takes to task classical economists such as Adam Smith for portraying this sociological phenomenon as one of increasing freedom from serfdom. Jay Carlander, reviewing *The Invention of Capitalism* in *Labor History*, felt that "Perelman does a service to call attention to the darker side of classical economic theory." He went on to praise the work as "a clearly written, vigorously argued book."

Perelman takes on the issue of intellectual property rights in his 2002 volume, *Steal This Idea: The Corporate Confiscation of Creativity*. He maintains that remedying the problems associated with intellectual property rights will require "a complete overhaul of the institutions that handle ideas and information," wrote Joan Pedzich in *Library Journal*. Pedzich concluded that *Steal This Idea* is a "timely, thoughtful work."

Perelman told *CA:* "For me, economics provides a window to the inner workings of society. It appears to relate to abstract quantities. In reality, it deals with the full complex of social relations."

BIOGRAPHICAL AND CRITICAL SOURCES:

PERIODICALS

Journal of Economic Issues, September, 1995, Brent McClintock, review of *The Pathology of the U.S. Economy: The Costs of a Low-Wage System*, p. 963.

Labor History, August, 2001, Jay Carlander, review of *The Invention of Capitalism: Classical Political Economy and the Secret History of Primitive Accumulation*, p. 297.

Library Journal, April 15, 2002, Joan Pedzich, review of *Steal This Idea: The Corporate Confiscation of Creativity*, pp. 106-107.*

*   *   *

PHILLIPS, Roger 1932-

PERSONAL: Born 1932. *Education:* Trained at Chelsea School of Art.

ADDRESSES: Office—RogersPlants Ltd., 12 Eccleston Square, London SW1V 1NP, England. *E-mail*—Roger. Phillips@rogersroses.com.

CAREER: Botanist and writer. RogersRoses.com, London, England, managing director, 2001—. Also worked at Ogilvy & Mather Advertising. Freelance photographer; host of gardening television programs for BBC and other networks.

WRITINGS:

(With others) *Trees of North America and Europe,* Random House (New York, NY), 1978.

(With others) *Grasses, Ferns, Mosses, and Lichens of Great Britain and Ireland,* Ward Lock (London, England), 1980.

Mushrooms and Other Fungi of Great Britain and Europe, Pan (London, England), 1981.

Sources and Applications of Ultraviolet Radiation, Academic Press (London, England), 1983.

(With others) *Herbs and Medicinal Plants,* Elm Tree Books (London, England), 1987.

(With Martyn Rix) *Roses,* Random House (New York, NY), 1988.

(With Martyn Rix) *Shrubs,* Pan (London, England), 1989.

(With Martyn Rix) *The Random House Book of Bulbs,* Random House (New York, NY), 1989.

(With Nicky Foy) *The Random House Book of Herbs,* Random House (New York, NY), 1990.

Mushrooms of North America, Little, Brown (Boston, MA), 1991.

(With Martyn Rix) *Perennials,* Pan (London, England), 1991.

(With Martyn Rix) *The Random House Book of Perennials* (two volumes), Random House (New York, NY), 1992.

(With Martyn Rix) *The Quest for the Rose,* Random House (New York, NY), 1993.

(With Martyn Rix) *Vegetables,* Random House (New York, NY), 1994.

Grasses, Ferns, Mosses, and Lichens of Great Britain and Ireland, Trans-Atlantic (London, England), 1994.

(With Nicky Foy) *A Photographic Garden History,* Macmillan (London, England), 1995, Random House (New York, NY), 1996.

(With Martyn Rix and others) *Perfect Plants,* Macmillan (London, England), 1996.

(With Martyn Rix) *Conservatory and Indoor Plants,* Macmillan (London, England), 1997.

(With Martyn Rix) *The Indoor and Greenhouse Plants,* two volumes, Random House (New York, NY), 1997.

(With Leslie Land) *The Three Thousand Mile Garden: An Exchange of Letters on Gardening, Food, and the Good Life,* Viking/Penguin (New York, NY), 1997.

Trees of North America, Random House (New York, NY), 1997.

(With Martyn Rix) *The Best Scented Plants,* Pan (London, England), 1998.

(With Martyn Rix) *Climbers for Walls and Arbours,* Pan (London, England), 1998.

(With Martyn Rix) *Herbs for Cooking,* Pan (London, England), 1998.

(With Martyn Rix) *Plants for Pots and Patios,* Pan (London, England), 1998.

(With Martyn Rix) *Plants for Shade and How to Grow Them,* Pan (London, England), 1998.

(With Martyn Rix) *Salad Plants for Your Vegetable Garden,* Pan (London, England), 1998.

(With Martyn Rix) *Summer Annuals,* Pan (London, England), 1998.

(With Martyn Rix) *Traditional Old Roses,* Pan (London, England) 1998.

(With Martyn Rix) *The Random House Book of Salad Plants,* Random House (New York, NY), 1999.

(With Martyn Rix) *The Random House Book of Scented Plants,* Random House (New York, NY), 1999.

(With Martyn Rix) *Old Roses,* Random House (New York, NY), 1999.

(With Martyn Rix) *The Random House Book of Climbers for Walls and Arbors,* Random House (New York, NY), 2000.

(With Martyn Rix and others) *Annuals and Biennials: The Definitive Reference with Over 1,000 Photographs,* Firefly Books (Buffalo, NY), 2002.

(With Martyn Rix) *The Botanical Garden,* Firefly Books (Buffalo, NY), 2002.

(With Martyn Rix) *Perennials: The Definitive Reference with Over 2,500 Photographs,* Firefly Books (Buffalo, NY), 2002.

SIDELIGHTS: Although he began his career in advertising, eventually making his way to art director of the British firm Ogilvy & Mather, Roger Phillips is most renowned for his collection of lavishly illustrated garden guide books. Whether depicting roses or edible plants, Phillips brings the natural world to life using vivid photographs and makes his topic both accessible for novice readers and interesting for more knowledgeable ones. Librarians have commented upon the usefulness of Phillips's books for their gardening collections, and general reviewers have admired their quality, making the books suitable for coffee-table display.

The critically acclaimed "Random House" gardening series to which Phillips contributes comprises volumes titled *Roses, Shrubs, Bulbs, Herbs,* and *Perennials.* All of the books have numerous, full-color photographs accompanied by descriptions about the plants' physical appearances, natural habitats, and growth cycles, among other pertinent characteristics. A reviewer in *Horticulture* magazine admired the "superb color photographs of more than 1,400 roses—old roses, species roses, hybrid teas, floribundas, climbers, ramblers, and miniature roses, with a chapter on hips for good measure."

Likewise, *Shrubs* features almost two thousand common shrubs. In a large, reference-book format, *Shrubs* is broken into chapters according to flowering season. The pictures were taken both in the studio, to focus on detail, and in the field, to put the shrubs into context for gardeners. *Library Journal* reviewer Peter C. Leonard contended that the book "should become the definitive book on shrubs for American libraries."

Perennials encompasses two separate volumes: *Early Perennials,* featuring plants that grow in late winter, spring and early summer, and *Late Perennials,* depicting those that bloom in late summer and autumn. *Horticulture* reviewer Ann Lovejoy praised Phillips's comprehensive treatment of the topic and admired the "evocative pictures" in the volumes. Over three thousand photographs show perennials in garden settings, but some photos feature the plants in the wild, "providing an armchair overview of the exotic jungles and bleak mountain passes frequented by plant hunters," noted Lovejoy.

Phillips's volume *Herbs* contains useful information about the plants' various purposes, including culinary, medicinal, and cosmetic. By their very nature, "most herbs are decidedly weedy in appearance," explained a reviewer in *Horticulture,* so the book presents a tougher sell than the book about roses. But Phillips rises to the challenge and supplies excellent content

and an able discussion of herbs, remarked the *Horticulture* reviewer. *Herbs* is organized into nine sections, each containing detailed, informative entries about the various botanical features of herbs, including appearance, habitat, origin, growth, history, uses, modern scientific research, and directions for preparation. *Library Journal* reviewer Marilyn Rosenthal considered the book "well written," and believed it merits special attention "because of the hundreds of beautiful, colored photographs." A *New York Times* critic admired the book's "crisply informative text, describing the geographical range, culture and history of some 400 plants, accompanied by detailed photographs of each, with close-ups of leaves, flowers and—in vintage herbal style—roots."

In *Mushrooms of North America,* Phillips depicts the fungi world with similarly meticulous attention. Over one thousand color pictures were mostly shot in the studio in order to "capture both the external features of the mushrooms as well as their internal anatomy," according to *Library Journal* reviewer Paul C. Radich. Both amateur and professional mycologists will find this book an invaluable guide, Radich believed. In *American Libraries,* a reviewer admired the volume's "stunning" pictures that show the "external features, internal anatomy, and various stages of growth" of mushrooms.

The Botanical Garden contains two volumes: one describing trees and shrubs and the other describing perennials and annuals. These volumes serve as encyclopedias that are organized in evolutionary order and contain details about plants and their origin, common names, dates of discovery, cultivation methods, and a variety of other facts. A reviewer for *Science News* declared, "This amazingly comprehensive guide to plants bridges the gap gardening between books and scientific texts." The reviewer added that the strongest element of the book is the photographs, which the reviewer described as "brilliant." A *Booklist* reviewer described the photographs as "pure art." A reviewer for *Publishers Weekly* observed, "Some of the listings also include advice on cultivation." The same reviewer cautioned that readers may not be helped by these listings because they may not be able to "tear their eyes away from the four thousand-some color photographs, which show remarkable detail and are carefully arranged so that seed, fruit, and important identifying parts can be seen up close."

BIOGRAPHICAL AND CRITICAL SOURCES:

PERIODICALS

American Libraries, May, 1992, pp. 398, 400.

Booklist, August, 2002, review of *Annuals and Biannuals,* p. 2006; December 1, 2002, review of *The Botanical Garden,* Volume 1: *Trees and Shrubs,* p. 696.

Conservationist, November-December, 1990, p. 50.

Gourmet, February, 1992, John Bainbridge, "A Gardener's Vision," pp. 50-54.

Horticulture, December, 1988, pp. 66-67; June, 1989, p. 59; August-September, 1991, p. 85; August-September, 1992, p. 59.

Library Journal, April 15, 1989; January, 1991, p. 134; June 15, 1991; October 15, 2002, Sue O'Brien, review of *The Botanical Garden Series,* p. 64.

Nation's Restaurant News, August 29, 1994, Michael Schrader, review of *The Random House Book of Vegetables,* p. 18.

New York Times, January 9, 1992, Linda Yang, review of *The Random House Book of Perennials,* p. C7; December 2, 1990, Linda Yang, review of *The Random House Book of Herbs,* p. 21; December 3, 1995, Allen Lacey, review of *The Three Thousand Mile Garden: An Exchange of Letters on Gardening, Food, and the Good Life,* p. 45; December 8, 1996, Michael Pollan, review of *A Photographic Garden History,* p. 42; December 2, 1990, p. 21; June 2, 2002, Verlyn Klinkenborg, review of *Perennials: The Definitive Reference with Over 2,500 Photographs,* pp. 13-15; September 29, 2002, Anne Raver, "Botanical Books for Eye and Intellect," p. SP13.

Publishers Weekly, July 29, 2002, review of *The Botanical Garden,* p. 69.

Revolution, November 12, 2002, "Gardening Gurus to Launch Paid-for Site," p. 10.

Science News, August 17, 2002, review of *The Botanical Garden,* p. 111.

Wall Street Journal, January 7, 1993, Patti Hagan, review of *The Random House Book of Perennials,* p. A12; December 13, 1994, Patti Hagan, review of *The Quest for the Rose,* p. A16; December 21, 1995, Patti Hagan, review of *The Three Thousand Mile Garden,* p. A10.

ONLINE

Guardian Unlimited, http://www.books.guardian.co.uk/ (January 11, 2003), Claire Armistead, review of *The Botanical Garden.*

RogersRoses.com, http://www.rogersroses.com/ (November 10, 2003).*

PINN, Anthony B(ernard) 1964-

PERSONAL: Born May 2, 1964, in Buffalo, NY; son of Raymond and Anne H. (a minister) Pinn; married Cheryl Johnson. *Ethnicity:* "African-American." *Education:* Columbia University, B.A., 1986; Harvard University, M.Div., 1989, M.A., 1991, Ph.D., 1994. *Religion:* "Humanism."

ADDRESSES: Office—Department of Religious Studies, Macalester College, 1600 Grand Ave., St. Paul, MN 55105; fax 612-696-6008. *E-mail*—Pinn@ macalester.edu.

CAREER: Gordon-Conwell Theological Seminary, Boston, MA, instructor at Center for Urban Ministerial Education, 1993, 1994; Macalester College, St. Paul, MN, assistant professor 1994-1999, associate professor, 1999-2002, professor of religious studies, 2002—, and director of African-American Studies Program, professor, 2002. Suffolk University, senior lecturer, 1993, 1994; University of New Mexico, visiting professor, 1995; speaker at colleges and universities, including Tufts University and Boston University, 1990, Shaw University, 1991, Bates College, 1994, North Hennepin Community College, 1995, 1996, Carleton College, 1996, and State University of Bahia, 1997; guest on television programs.

MEMBER: American Academy of Religion, Society for the Study of Black Religion, Association for Religion and Intellectual Life, American Association of University Professors, Committee for the Scientific Examination of Religion, African Americans for Humanism.

AWARDS, HONORS: Coolidge fellow, Research Colloquium, Association for Religion and Intellectual Life, 1997; African American Humanist Award, Council for Secular Humanism, 1999.

WRITINGS:

Why, Lord? Suffering and Evil in Black Theology, Continuum (New York, NY), 1995.

Varieties of African-American Religious Experience: A Theological Introduction, Fortress (Minneapolis, MN), 1998.

(With mother, Anne Pinn) *Fortress Introduction to Black Church History,* Fortress Press (Minneapolis, MN), 2002.

The Black Church in the Post-Civil Rights Era, Orbis Books (Maryknoll, NY), 2002.

Terror and Triumph: The Nature of Black Religion, Fortress (Minneapolis, MN), 2003.

African American Humanist Principles: Living and Thinking Like the Children of Nimrod, Palegrave (New York, NY), 2004.

EDITOR

Making the Gospel Plain: The Writings of Bishop Reverdy C. Ransom, Trinity Press International (Harrisburg, PA), 1999.

(With Stephen W. Angell) *Social Protest Thought in the African Methodist Episcopal Church, 1862-1939,* University of Tennessee Press (Knoxville, TN), 2000.

By These Hands: A Documentary History of African-American Humanism, New York University Press (New York, NY), 2001.

(With Benjamin Valentin) *The Ties That Bind: African American and Hispanic American/Latino: A Theology in Dialogue,* Continuum (New York, NY), 2001.

Moral Evil and Redemptive Suffering: A History of Theodicy in African-American Religious Thought, University Press of Florida (Gainesville, FL), 2002.

Noise and Spirit: The Religious and Spiritual Sensibilities of Rap Music, New York University Press (New York, NY), 2003.

Contributor to *Voices on the Future: Black Religion after the Million Man March,* edited by G. Kasimu Baker-Fletcher, Orbis Books (Maryknoll, NY). General coeditor of the series "Studies in African-American Religious Thought and Life," Trinity Press International, and "Studies in the History of African-American Religions," University Presses of Florida (Gainesville, FL). Contributor of articles and reviews to periodicals, including *American Journal of Theology and Philosophy, Religious Studies News, African American Review, Journal of Religious Thought, Journal of African-American Men,* and *Free Inquiry.*

WORK IN PROGRESS: Earth Bound: Toward a Theology of Fragile Cultural Memory and Religious Diversity (tentative title), for Fortress.

SIDELIGHTS: Anthony Pinn, who teaches religious studies at Macalester College, writes on topics of the African-American religious experience. His *Why, Lord? Suffering and Evil in Black Theology* drew the attention of *African American Review* contributor Dwight Hopkins, who noted that the author presents views counter to two established tenets of black faith in America: The first being that "God is all-powerful, good, and just," and second, that "evil and suffering exist." Traditionally, Hopkins continued, "black believers never blame God for racial oppression. Furthermore, black churches have preached fervently a gospel advocating how suffering for the black race has built strong positive character." Pinn, noted Hopkins, "problematizes this cornerstone of black Christianity and rejects the reality of God in the process. Specifically, he argues that the Christian doctrine of redemptive suffering is fundamentally and irreparably flawed."

Hopkins questioned Pinn's thesis, saying that the author's own explanation of "enslaved Africans and African Americans created and deployed the redemptive suffering in the spirituals reveals, in practice, how some forms of suffering enabled enslaved ebony bodies to endure, hope, and struggle." In Hopkins's view, "Many black Christians believe in redemptive suffering . . . because life has shown them that their black race would have undergone possible genocide without such an understanding of evil." Still, the critic found *Why, Lord?* a "positive contribution to the discourse of black theology in particular, and the debate over suffering and freedom in the African-American community in general."

In *Varieties of African-American Religious Experience,* Pinn covers a spectrum that includes Christianity, Islam, Humanism, Voodoo, and Yoruba—but Willie James Jennings of *Interpretation* saw even this list as "too narrow a canon of resources." In this work Pinn contends that religious scholars should consider the great range of faith to more fully grasp what the reviewer called the "widest possible picture of black cultural reality." But to Jennings, "The central drawback of the text is that it bypasses a number of pressing issues in theology," including "the relation of personal identity to essentialist definitions of culture, race, and gender." More positive notices greeted *Social Protest Thought in the African Methodist Episcopal Church.* The place of the AME church in African-American life has been well documented in the past; but reviewer Lewis Baldwin wrote in the *Journal of*

Church and State that Pinn and coeditor Stephen Angell "skillfully selected documents that reflected the vitality and range of social and political ideas" in the church, particularly during the turbulent times of the eighteenth and nineteenth centuries.

Pinn and his mother, minister Anne Pinn, produced *Fortress Introduction to Black Church History* in 2001. "I wanted to develop a text that provided the rough outline of black church development," he told Jacqueline Trussell in a *Black and Christian* interview. "And I wanted to base this study on one central question: What are the roots of the Black Church Tradition celebrated in the twenty-first century?" A *Publishers Weekly* reviewer felt that the Pinns were to be "commended for consistently paying attention to women" in their volume, such as AME preacher Mary Evans. While *Fortress Introduction* "is not terrifically analytical," the critic concluded, the book nonetheless "provides a fact-packed, handy introduction to African-American Christian history."

BIOGRAPHICAL AND CRITICAL SOURCES:

PERIODICALS

African American Review, fall, 1997, Dwight Hopkins, review of *Why, Lord? Suffering and Evil in Black Theology,* p. 514.
Interpretation, October, 1999, Willie James Jennings, review of *Varieties of African-American Religious Experience: A Theological Introduction,* p. 436.
Journal of Church and State, summer, 2000, Lewis Baldwin, review of *Social Protest Thought in the African Methodist Episcopal Church,* p. 589.
Publishers Weekly, November 12, 2001, review of *Fortress Introduction to Black Church History,* p. 56.

ONLINE

Black and Christian, http://www.blackandchristian. com/ (September 19, 2002), Jacqueline Trussell, "BNC Academy Exclusive: An E-Interview with Anthony Pinn."

*   *   *

PORTER, Laurence M(inot) 1936-

PERSONAL: Born January 17, 1936, in Ossining, NY; son of Fairfield (an artist and art critic) and Anne Elizabeth (a poet; maiden name, Channing) Porter; married Elizabeth Johnson Hart (an architect), June 9, 1960 (divorced, 1979); married Laurel Melinda Cline (a social worker and writer), January 17, 1980 (divorced, 1992); married Marjorie Risser (a fundraiser), May 29, 1993; children: Leon Fairfield, Sarah Elizabeth, John Carl Fairfield. *Ethnicity:* "Caucasian." *Education:* Harvard University, A.B. (cum laude), 1957, A.M., 1959, Ph.D., 1965. *Politics:* Independent. *Religion:* "Agnostic." *Hobbies and other interests:* Tennis, backpacking, competitive running (including the Boston Marathon), music.

ADDRESSES: Home—723 Collingwood Dr., East Lansing, MI 48823-3416. *Office*—Department of Romance and Classical Languages and Literatures, Michigan State University, 256 Old Horticulture Building, East Lansing, MI 48824-1112; fax: 517-432-3844. *E-mail*—porter@msu.edu.

CAREER: Michigan State University, East Lansing, instructor, 1963-65, assistant professor, 1965-69, associate professor, 1969-73, professor of French and comparative literature, African studies, Canadian studies, and West European studies, 1973—. University of Pittsburgh, Andrew W. Mellon Distinguished Visiting Professor of Comparative Literature, 1980. National Colloquium on Nineteenth-Century French Studies, codirector, 1978. *Military service:* U.S. Army Reserve, Corps of Engineers, 1957-63.

MEMBER: International Comparative Literature Association, International Society of Dix-Neuvièmistes, Modern Language Association of America (life member), American Association of University Professors, American Comparative Literature Association, American Association of Teachers of French, Women in French, Phi Kappa Phi, Sierra Club, Appalachian Mountain Club.

AWARDS, HONORS: Ford Foundation fellowship, 1966; National Endowment for the Humanities, travel grant, 1989, senior fellowship, 1998; United States Information Agency grant for Senegal, 1991.

WRITINGS:

(Translator) Joseph de Maistre, *On God and Society: Essay on the Generative Principle of Constitutions and Other Human Institutions,* edited by Elisha Greifer, Regnery (Chicago, IL), 1959.

The Renaissance of the Lyric in French Romanticism: Elegy, Ode, and "Poëme," French Forum Monographs (Lexington, KY), 1978.

The Literary Dream in French Romanticism: A Psychoanalytical Interpretation, Wayne State University Press (Detroit, MI), 1979.

(Editor, with Laurel Melinda Porter) *Aging in Literature,* International Book Publishers (Troy, MI), 1984.

(Editor) *Critical Essays on Gustave Flaubert,* G. K. Hall (Boston, MA), 1986.

The Interpretation of Dreams: Freud's Theories Revisited, Twayne (Boston, MA), 1987.

The Crisis of French Symbolism, Cornell University Press (Ithaca, NY), 1990.

(Editor, with Eugene F. Gray) *Approaches to Teaching Flaubert's "Madame Bovary,"* Modern Language Association of America (New York, NY), 1995.

Victor Hugo, Twayne (Boston, MA), 1999.

(Editor) *Approaches to Teaching Baudelaire's "Flowers of Evil,"* Modern Language Association of America (New York, NY), 2000.

(Editor) *A Gustave Flaubert Encyclopedia,* Greenwood Press (Westport, CT), 2001.

(With Eugene F. Gray) *Gustave Flaubert's "Madame Bovary": A Reference Guide,* Greenwood Press (Westport, CT), 2002.

Contributor to books, including *A Critical and Selective Bibliography of French Literature,* Volume 5: *The Nineteenth Century,* Syracuse University Press (Syracuse, NY), 1994. Contributor to professional journals. Member of editorial board, *Degré Second,* 1976-92, *Nineteenth-Century French Studies,* 1982—, *Studies in Twentieth-Century Literature,* 1990—, and *Women in French Studies,* 2002—.

WORK IN PROGRESS: Reading Great Women Authors beyond Gender: The Autonomous Imagination, for Greenwood Press (Westport, CT); "Happening, Knowing, and Telling: How Stories Work in Life and Art," to be included in *Characterization in Flaubert,* Cambridge University Press (New York, NY).

SIDELIGHTS: Laurence M. Porter once told *CA:* "As a critic and professor, I try to teach people to read and write better. To me, this means helping people to overcome the unreasoning prejudices that impoverish their experience and to recognize the nuance, hidden coherence, and significant detail which disclose the richness of artistic creation. I encourage people to articulate their own perceptions in a way which allows them to discover the wealth of their own individualities and to profit from the unlimited second chances which reading and writing, unlike life, can offer.

"My primary motivations for writing have been to serve as a bridge between French literature and culture, and the United States, so as to foster a deeper understanding and a keener enjoyment of a great civilization among Americans; to improve my teaching, which I feel must always be grounded in ongoing research; and to honor creative artists, to whom we owe so much—in particular, my late father (a painter, critic and poet); my mother (a poet and finalist for the National Book Award); my daughter (an artist and writer of fiction); and many others whom I have had the pleasure of knowing and admiring. Finally, I would like to contribute to a heightened awareness of the value, rights, and sufferings of others, so that the world might become a better place, freed from brutality and from the tyranny of ideologies.

"The major influences on my work have been eclectic. Deconstruction has influenced my open-ended use of provisional binary opposites, posited only to demonstrate that the rigid systems of thought that they define always prove incomplete and inadequate. The lucidity and rigorous argumentation of thinkers such as Stanley Fish and Jean-Luc Nancy has provided a model to emulate. The skepticism of writers such as Sigmund Freud and Frederic Jameson has encouraged me to look beneath the surface of texts, and to explore the emotional, political, and religious 'unconscious' (usually, in fact, the 'preconscious,' suppressed but still accessible). As a pedagogical technique, in my writings I often posit an hypothetical 'organic unity' of texts, meaning that often, an individual part can help one understand the whole, as the DNA in a single cell may allow scientists to identify the organism of which that cell was part. The linguistic concept of 'marked choice' strongly influences my thinking, as do many positions in feminist thought.

"When I write about an author, I first read and reread the text, meditating on the dynamic interrelationships of forces that I observe there. I then alternate between sketches, rough drafts, outlines, and more sketches, trying always to be in a position where I need to prune my essays down to the essentials, and to be sparing of words. I may return to a topic at intervals over a decade or more, until my experiences have become rich enough to share. I often pause to psychoanalyze the emotional needs and drives that have led me to choose certain subjects.

"Probably my main inspiration for writing most often on nineteenth-century French literature was the influence of the late Rene Jasinski and Paul Benichou, who left the Sorbonne to teach at Harvard beacuse they found the French system too stuffy and hidebound. Their gentle warmth and kindness were priceless gifts. Shortly after Paul Benichou came to the states, we were exchanging French for English lessons. One evening in his apartment, as he warmed his dinner, he looked over toward me from the stove, grinned, and observed, 'In France, it would be unthinkable for a professor to allow his student to see him cooking.' To their influence and erudition was added that of two young, temporary faculty who tutored each for a year during my last two undergraduate years—Roger Shattuck and Serge Doubrovsky. When one discussed literature with them, they trembled with excitement, and their eyes glowed with pleasure. Modeling enjoyment may be the most important thing a teacher can do."

BIOGRAPHICAL AND CRITICAL SOURCES:

PERIODICALS

Booklist, September 1, 2001, Mary Ellen Quinn, review of *A Gustave Flaubert Encyclopedia,* p. 150.
Nineteenth-Century French Studies, spring-summer, 2001, Stamos Metzidakis, review of *Victor Hugo,* p. 358.

*   *   *

PROTHERO, Stephen (Richard) 1960-

PERSONAL: Born November 13, 1960, in Cooperstown, NY. *Ethnicity:* "White." *Education:* Yale University, B.A. (summa cum laude), 1982; Harvard University, M.A., 1986, Ph.D., 1990.

ADDRESSES: Office—Department of Religion, Boston University, 745 Commonwealth Ave., Boston, MA 02215. *E-mail*—prothero@bu.edu.

CAREER: Harvard University, Cambridge, MA, instructor in religion, 1988; Yale University, New Haven, CT, visiting lecturer in religious studies and American studies, 1990; Georgia State University, Atlanta, assistant professor of religious studies, 1990-95; Boston University, Boston, MA, assistant professor and director of undergraduate studies, 1996-2000, associate professor of religion, 2000—.

MEMBER: American Academy of Religion, American Historical Association, American Society of Church History, American Studies Association, Phi Beta Kappa.

AWARDS, HONORS: Lyndon Baines Johnson legislative intern, U.S. House of Representatives, 1981; Sinclair Kennedy traveling fellow in India and Frederick Sheldon traveling fellow in India, both Harvard University, 1988-89; American Academy of Religion, grants, 1992-93, 1996, 2002, award for best first book in the history of religions, 1997, for *The White Buddhist: The Asian Odyssey of Henry Steel Olcott;* Young Scholars in American Religion fellow, Center for the Study of Religion and American Culture, Indiana University-Purdue University—Indianapolis, 1992-94.

WRITINGS:

(With Gardiner Shattuck, Edward Queen II, and others) *The Encyclopedia of American Religious History,* Facts on File (New York, NY), 1996, revised edition, 2002.
The White Buddhist: The Asian Odyssey of Henry Steel Olcott, Indiana University Press (Bloomington, IN), 1996.
(Editor, with Thomas Tweed) *Asian Religions in America: A Documentary History,* Oxford University Press (New York, NY), 1999.
Purified by Fire: A History of Cremation in America, University of California Press (Berkeley, CA), 2001.
American Jesus: How the Son of God Became a National Icon, Farrar, Straus & Giroux (New York, NY), 2004.

Author of introduction to *Big Sky Mind: Buddhism and the Beat Generation,* edited by Carole Tonkinson, Riverhead (New York, NY), 1995; contributor to other books, including *Practicing the Religious: Lived Reli-*

gion in America, edited by David Hall, Princeton University Press (Princeton, NJ), 1997. Contributor of articles and reviews to scholarly journals, including *Theosophical History, Tricycle: Buddhist Review, Quest, Religion and American Culture: Journal of Interpretation, Wall Street Journal,* and *Harvard Theological Review.*

BIOGRAPHICAL AND CRITICAL SOURCES:

PERIODICALS

Booklist, January 1, 2001, Mary Carroll, review of *Purified by Fire: A History of Cremation in America,* p. 887; November 15, 2003, Bryce Christensen, review of *American Jesus: How the Son of God Became a National Icon,* p. 551.

Books and Culture, January-February, 2004, Philip Jenkins, review of *American Jesus,* p. 8.

Choice, June, 2001, P. Harvey, review of *Purified by Fire,* p. 1829; April, 2002, W. Fontaine, review of *The Encyclopedia of American Religious History,* p. 1394.

Economist (U.S.), March 10, 2001, review of *Purified by Fire,* p. 6.

First Things: Monthly Journal of Religion and Public Life, December, 2003, review of *American Jesus,* p. 59.

Journal of American History, March, 2002, David C. Sloane, review of *Purified by Fire,* p. 1545.

Journal of Religion, April, 2002, Bradford Verter, review of *Purified by Fire,* p. 288.

Kirkus Reviews, October 1, 2003, review of *American Jesus,* p. 1213.

Library Journal, January 1, 2001, Jay Stephens, review of *Purified by Fire,* p. 115; October 1, 2003, Gary P. Gillum, review of *American Jesus,* p. 83.

New York Times, January 8, 2004, R. Scott Appleby, review of *American Jesus,* p. E9.

New York Times Book Review, December 28, 2003, Michael Massing, review of *American Jesus,* p. 7.

Psychology Today, November-December, 2003, Kathleen McGowan, review of *American Jesus,* p. 83.

Publishers Weekly, November 20, 2000, Jana Riess, review of *Purified by Fire,* p. S14; October 13, 2003, review of *American Jesus,* p. 73; October 13, 2003, Andy Crouch, "Mom, Baseball, Apple Pie, and Jesus" (interview), p. 75.

R

RAPHAEL, Dan (Ambrose) 1952-

PERSONAL: Born June 7, 1952, in Fargo, ND; son of Raymond John (a journalist) and Cecelia Agnes (a tailor; maiden name, Banaszek) Raphael; married Melba Joyce Jones (a botanist), October 31, 1984; children: Orion S. *Education:* Cornell University, B.A., 1973; Bowling Green State University, M.F.A., 1975; Western Washington University, M.A. *Politics:* Green. *Religion:* Buddhist.

ADDRESSES: Home—6735 Southeast 78th St., Portland, OR 97206. *Office*—Oregon Department of Motor Vehicles, 3 Monroe Parkway, Lake Oswego, OR 97035. *E-mail*—raphael@aracnet.com.

CAREER: Poet. Oregon Department of Transportation, Medford, weigh-master, 1977-78; U.S. Postal Service, Portland, OR, mail carrier, 1978-81; Oregon Department of Motor Vehicles, Sandy office manager, 1981-95, Lake Oswego customer service manager, 1995—. Northwest Artists Workshop, organizer of readings, beginning 1980; Portland Poetry Festival, project coordinator, beginning 1985. Metropolitan Crisis Service, volunteer, beginning 1979. Also worked as a substitute teacher, 1975-76, radio record announcer, 1976-77, and meat carver, 1977-78.

MEMBER: Coordinating Council of Literary Magazines, Committee of Small Magazine Editors and Publishers.

AWARDS, HONORS: Rhysling Award, SFPA, 1995, for the poem "Sking of Glass."

WRITINGS:

POETRY

Truck, Pisspoor Press, 1973.
Energumen, Cherry Valley, 1976.
Polymerge, Skydog Press, 1979.
Dawn Patrol, Contraband Press, 1979.
Zone du Jour, Potes and Poets Press, 1981.
To Taste, 1983.
Attention Spotcheck, 1983.
The Matter What Is, 1984.
Bop Grit Storm Cafe, 1985.
Rain Away, 1987.
Here the Meat Turns to the Audience, Shattered Wig, 1991.
The Bones Begin to Sing, 26 Books, 1993.
Molecular Jam, Jazz Police, 1996.
Trees through the Road, Nine Muses, 1997.
Playing with a Ful Deck, 26 Books, 1998.
Showing Light a Good Time, Jazz Police, 2001.

Also author of *Isn't How We Got Here.* Work represented in chapbook series "Greatest Hits," Pudding House Writers Innovation Center (Johnstown, OH), 2001. Contributor to periodicals, including *Antenym, Asylum, Caliban, First Intensity, Haven Bone, Plazm, Temple,* and *Tinfish.* Editor of *NRG,* c. 1975-90.

SIDELIGHTS: Dan Raphael once told *CA:* "All my comments are postfactum. I do not make money with my writing nor do I expect to, but language hence thought, knowledge, and perception must be explored and not de-liberated. My poems work best in performance, and it is my hope to tour nationally, as well as to work more with cassette-books and eventually videotapes."

He later added several additional comments: "Don't read much contemporary poetry, fail to reach to understand to have the patience and/or desire to probe the nuances. feel too outside this world of 'professional writers,' even the level of state grants and medium press prizes, what does this have to do with writing? Seems like writers always say they write 'coz they have to. I guess many are lucky that what they have to do is vendable, accessible, in fashion.

"Seems all the art forms made acceptable transition into nonrepresentational a while back but poetry continues the most anachronistic, precious, hung up in expectations and traditions like a private club clinging dearly to its tiny outmoded magic.

"Where does language come from? It is not a pure medium like music or painting, words are both heard and seen and more importantly processed, or how much of language is learned and what is there in a deeper, universal, cosmic, etc. sense? Language is this energy that taps into me—is the base of my work, a flow I do not understand & highly respect.

"It's damned frustrating to build a body of polished work, work that can speak to many people in different voices, and have no way of getting it out, have no channels that will accept it for distribution or even for itself. Yet this is the way I am committed to, and must accept others for what they're doing and believe they have as much integrity as I do, and vision, and skill—we are just walking different paths.

"To talk more makes no difference. The more ideas I formulate the more they may block the free unassuming flow of language, which though dependent on my circumstances, exposures etc., my instrumentality, must be given open rein (craft, in relation to my work, is a fine tuning, just whacking the words and going for the right tone; newness is important; not repeating nor taking an easy path, though I begin to realize the potential of recognizable structures & linkages within the work, how repetition w/variation can be highly dimensional.)

"The channel that works best for me in presenting my work is reading, as I've some dramatic training and experience, and the aural (I seem to have a natural though eccentric ear for rhythm and interrelation of sound) underpinnings of my poetry, coupled with the works lack of syntax, of recognizable clues to how to read—people don't know what to do with it when seen on the page, but reactions in public are always strong, in all parts of the country I've read, and the couple times I've read to older and nonpoetry audience. Since books are becoming a thing of the past, it may be time for poetry to become multi-media, and I hope to eventually tour more as a reader, to make tapes to accompany written texts (for I feel the poems work well as written, and with angles that can't be perceived through hearing, that poetry can fill both aural and visual spaces and unite these in the mind and deeper) as well as eventual appearances in radio and video."

More recently Raphael added: "I write because it's the thing I do with the most energy, creativity, and uniqueness. My poems happen when enough language energy builds in me through what I've seen, heard, read, and thought. So I can't just sit down and write, the built-up energy needs a spark (usually a few words, whether from inside or outside of me). My writing is not like most other poets—I am not representational, narrative, confessional, or intentional. My poetry is visionary, energized, and needs readers more receptive than analytical. One source of inspirational material is science-fiction novels. I often write after seeing movies, though I am not writing about the movie."

BIOGRAPHICAL AND CRITICAL SOURCES:

PERIODICALS

Heaven Bone, spring, 1994, review of *The Bones Begin to Sing,* p. 80.

*   *   *

RAPP, Adam 1968(?)-

PERSONAL: Born c. 1968, in Chicago, IL; son of a prison nurse. *Education:* Clark College (Dubuque, IA), B.A.

ADDRESSES: Home—New York, NY. *Agent*—c/o Author Mail, Front Street Books, 20 Battery Park Ave., Asheville, NC 28801. *E-mail*—rapp@frontstreetbooks. com.

CAREER: Playwright and novelist. Artist-in-residence at Vassar College and Dartmouth College; playwright-in-residence at Juilliard School of Music, New York, NY, 2000—.

AWARDS, HONORS: Best Books for Young Adults and Best Books for Reluctant Readers citations, American Library Association, both 1995, both for *Missing the Piano;* Brodkin scholarship, National Playwright's Conference, and Camargo Foundation fellowship to France, both 1997, both for *Trueblinka;* Princess Grace fellowship for playwriting, 1999; Roger L. Stevens Award from the Kennedy Center Fund for New American Plays, 2000; Suite Residency with Mabou Mines, 2000; two Lincoln Center LeComte du Nouy Awards; Elliott Norton Award for Best New Script, Best New Play selection, Independent Reviewers of New England, and selected as one of the ten best plays of 2000-2001, *Chronicle* of U.S. theater, all for *Nocturne;* Helen Merrill Award, 2001.

WRITINGS:

YOUNG ADULT NOVELS

Missing the Piano, Viking (New York, NY), 1994.
The Buffalo Tree, Front Street (Asheville, NC), 1997.
The Copper Elephant, Front Street (Asheville, NC), 1999.
Little Chicago, Front Street (Ashville, NC), 2002.
Thirty-three Snowfish, illustrated by Timothy Basil Ering, Candlewick Press (Cambridge, MA), 2003.

PLAYS

Netherbones, produced at Steppenwolf Theatre, Chicago, IL, 1995.
Ghosts in the Cottonwood, produced at New York Shakespeare Festival, 1996.
Trueblinka, produced at New York Shakespeare Festival, 1997.
Blackfrost, produced at New York Shakespeare Festival, 1997.
Night of the Whitefish, produced at New York Shakespeare Festival, 1998.
Finer Noble Gases (also see below), produced at Ojai Playwrights Conference, 2000.

Nocturne (produced by American Repertory Theater, Cambridge, MA, 2000), Faber & Faber (New York, NY), 2002.
Faster (also see below), produced in New York, 2000.
Dreams of the Salthorse, produced at Juilliard School of Music, 2000.
Animals and Plants, produced by American Repertory Theater, Cambridge, MA, 2001.
Blackbird, produced at Bush Theater, London, England, 2001.
Stone Cold Dead Serious (also see below), produced by American Repertory Theater, Cambridge, MA, 2002.
Stone Cold Dead Serious and Other Plays (contains *Finer Noble Gases, Faster,* and *Stone Cold Dead Serious*), Faber & Faber (New York, NY), 2004.

SIDELIGHTS: Adam Rapp has written critically acclaimed novels for young adults that address tough issues of peer abuse and dysfunctional families. Reviews of Rapp's *Missing the Piano* and *The Copper Elephant* have commended the author for his ability to create believable characters whose triumphs over adversity are not easily won. "Rapp writes about naively innocent adolescents caught in violent and emotionally isolated places," stated Ann Angel in the *ALAN Review.* An accomplished playwright whose works have been produced by the prestigious American Repertory Theatre, Rapp is pleased that his novels seemed to have struck a chord with young readers. "I think kids are incredibly resilient and much smarter than we think they are," he told Angel in an *ALAN Review* interview. "I hate the idea of sheltering kids from challenging books. It's just another form of conservative fear that promotes ignorance more than anything else."

Rapp's own difficult childhood has served as the basis for much of his work. He grew up in Joliet, Illinois, and his family included an older sister and younger brother. Their mother supported them by working as a prison nurse, but his brother Anthony was a talented stage prodigy, even at an early age. At one point, Anthony was cast in a Broadway production of *The Little Prince,* so the family moved to the New York City borough of Staten Island. The stage project was abandoned by its producers, however, and the family found themselves stranded in a cheap rental unit that did not even have a refrigerator. It took two months for Rapp's mother to save up enough funds to get the family back to Illinois.

Later, Rapp's brother was cast in a national tour for a popular stage musical, and their mother arranged for

Rapp to live with his father and stepmother while she accompanied Anthony on tour. The situation was unpleasant for Rapp, and he became involved in so much delinquent activity that he landed in a reform school; afterward, he was sent to a military academy in Wisconsin. "I was a troubled youth," Rapp admitted in an interview with *American Theatre* writer Karen Fricker. "There were a lot of problems." Despite the worries, Anthony's success was a bright spot in all their lives. "We had nothing," Rapp told Fricker, noting that even for the mother, living in hotel rooms on the road with her son was a unique experience. "There was nothing to look forward to. Joliet is a dismal, sad little town. Every time I go back there, there is this sense that I am never going to leave."

Reading became Rapp's salvation, he admitted to *ALAN Review* interviewer Angel. As a teen, he discovered the novels of J. D. Salinger, and Salinger's *Catcher in the Rye,* the classic novel of disenchanted youth, in particular. "I started making all of these great friends that I would have otherwise never met," he recalled of his favorite books. "I feel like I know [*Catcher in the Rye* narrator] Holden Caulfield better than many of the guys I played basketball with in college." For Rapp, athletics became a ticket out of Joliet. He earned a scholarship to play for Clarke College in Dubuque, Iowa, where he took his first writing class and found his calling. "I knew right then that was what I wanted to do," he told Fricker. His early literary output also forged a more mature relationship with Anthony, who was still living at home. The two had fallen out, but Rapp began sharing his short stories with his little brother. "When I told him that I had started writing," Rapp recounted to the *American Theatre* interviewer, "he sent me some of his own stories—and that's how we started hanging out again."

At Clarke College, Rapp captained the basketball team and graduated with a degree in fiction writing. He then moved to New York City, where he could divide his time between his two passions: playing street basketball and writing. Anthony eventually moved there, too, finding early success on Broadway and in some feature-film roles. Between parts, he began directing off-Broadway plays, and Rapp began assisting him, which led to an attempt at writing for the stage. His play *Ghosts in the Cottonwoods* was selected for the New Work Now! series of the prestigious New York Shakespeare Festival in 1996. Set in rural Appalachia, the play revolves around a tremendously dysfunctional family whose members are based in part on the family of one of Rapp's college friends. "They had beautiful music in their voices," Rapp recalled to Fricker in *American Theatre.* "I became obsessed by the way they said things and made up words—it was a strange form of poetry for me."

Living in New York, Rapp became an avid eavesdropper, which gave his imagination unlimited fodder, and much of his work has evolved from this habit. "It always starts with the voice," he told Angel. "I have never successfully written in the third person. If there's a rhythm or a musicality that interests me, I become obsessed with the character and just have this need to spend time with him or her. Sometimes I'll be in the park playing ball and I'll hear a kid say something that I've never heard before. Sometimes one word can set me off."

Rapp's next play, *Trueblinka,* won its creator two awards—a scholarship from the National Playwright's Conference and a Camargo Foundation to Cassis, France. The success also helped *Ghosts in the Cottonwoods,* which went on to premier at Chicago's Victory Gardens and be produced in Los Angeles. Rapp has continued to pen works for the stage, including *Netherbones, Blackfrost,* and *Finer Noble Gases,* all of which have enjoyed successful productions. However, it would be Rapp's first novel for young adults, *Missing the Piano,* that firmly launched his career as a writer. Published in 1994, *Missing the Piano* was named a "Best Book for Young Adults" and "Best Book for Reluctant Readers" by the American Library Association.

Missing the Piano is the story of Mike Tegroff, a talented basketball player whose life is disrupted when his younger sister is cast in *Les Misérables.* Since their mother must accompany her daughter on the road, Mike is sent to live with his father and stepmother, whom he detests. Once his mother and sister have departed, the stepmother refuses to shelter him, so his father takes him to a military academy. Mike finds the place more than just a harsh change from his normal teenage routine; it is a brutal, insulated world whose code of honor seems farcical. The older students beat and taunt the younger cadets, and racial prejudice is rampant. Mike's African-American roommate is the victim of cruel slurs, and after he is beaten by other students and expelled, Mike feels guilty for not coming to his rescue. *Publishers Weekly* called *Missing the*

Piano a "promising but not entirely successful debut novel," faulting its conclusion but noted that "the main characters' voices are authentic and generally engaging." *Booklist* reviewer Stephanie Zvirin admitted that some passages were disturbing, but felt that "the novel's harsh language fits the intensity of the story, which Rapp successfully moderates with some flashes of irreverent humor and the actions of a caring teacher."

Rapp's second novel for young adults, *The Buffalo Tree,* was published in 1997. Like *Missing the Piano,* it too draws upon his own experiences in a reform school, introducing readers to the Hamstock Boys Center, where twelve-year-old Sura has been sent for stealing hood ornaments from automobiles. As Rapp remarked to Angel, "One of the things that concerns me is the lack of adult supervision, and more specifically, caring adult supervision at various reform schools and juvenile detention centers. I think there's a kind of Darwinian brutality that can run rampant when kids are given power, and if you're on the wrong end of the pecking order things can be very scary."

In *The Buffalo Tree,* Sura finds himself the only detainee at Hamstock who is not African American or Hispanic, and he recounts the brutal atmosphere which works to criminalize the boys further. Even with strict rules and regulations, abuse from other teens makes life at Hamstock a daily nightmare. Guards at the detention facility ignore potentially harmful situations, or even become involved in them. Sura is tough enough to survive, but he witnesses more timid boys, like his roommate, Coly Jo, become targets of the worst bullies. Coly Jo has been sent to Hamstock for breaking and entering people's homes, where he watched them sleep. Picked on by the others, Coly Jo dies after being forced to climb a dead tree in one of the center's sadistic rituals. Sura's next roommate escapes with the intention of murdering his father. Sura himself finds salvation in running. "Although the brutality is unremitting, the book is hard to put down," thought *Horn Book* contributor Nancy Vasilakis, going on to state that Sura's "tone of bravado relieves the harshness without resorting to sentimentality." *Booklist* reviewer Susan Dove Lempke called Rapp's prose "challenging, demanding that readers become immersed in the richly realized, dark look at an American subculture," while a *Publishers Weekly* reviewer of *The Buffalo Tree* asserted that the author's "graphic images and use of first-person, present-tense narrative makes Sura's hellish story all the more real and immediate."

Rapp's first two novels found an appreciative audience among teens and educators alike, and in 1999, he was invited to spend a week as an author-in-residence at a suburban Chicago high school. As he told *ALAN Review* interviewer Penny Blubaugh, it "was one of the most surprisingly important events of my career as an author." He met with the student staff of Ridgewood High's literary magazine and school newspaper, and spoke to groups of students who came to visit from other high schools. He recalled being shocked when he visited an English class one day and saw eighty students all holding a copy of *The Buffalo Tree,* ready to talk about it with him. "With novels, there's this built-in disappearing act," he told Blubaugh. "I can write the story, but there is no immediate public culpability. The book is a thing on its own. At Norridge, this romantic idea I had of novelist-as-escape-artist was instantly proven false, and for all the right reasons." This particular ninth-grade class was designed to improve the English skills of those for whom English was as a second language, or who had encountered other difficulties. The teacher had students illustrate a book cover with favorite scenes from *The Buffalo Tree* to show Rapp. "Somehow, this almost moved me to tears," he told Blubaugh. "I'm still not sure why. I guess it's because they actually took the time."

Rapp's third novel for young adults, *The Copper Elephant,* appeared in 1999. It is set in a nightmarish, post-apocalyptic world, where the environment has been decimated by acid rain. Children are housed in brutal orphanages, and even taken as slave labor to work in lime pits. The novel's protagonist is eleven-year-old Whensday Bluenose, whose best friend dies in the dangerous underground mines. An elderly man saves Whensday from a similar fate, but not before she is sexually assaulted by an authority figure from the omnipotent Syndicate. Her rescuer then lands in trouble with the Syndicate and is falsely accused of murder, but Whensday knows who the true culprit is: a developmentally disabled teenager. In the end, a pregnant Whensday comes across a renegade group of women determined to reproduce in an effort to save their world. A *Horn Book* reviewer found the novel "compelling despite the unrelenting cruelty; Whensday's gripping narration describes the hellish landscape so skillfully that readers will find themselves gasping for air." *Booklist* contributor Debbie Carton asserted that "this raw-voiced story is both distinctive and unique, with Rapp's grim vision brilliantly executed."

Rapp discussed the portrayal of brutality in his works with *ALAN Review* interviewer Angel, asserting: "I am not interested in romanticizing or sensationalizing violence. I am interested in honoring what I know to be true. I've seen and lived through certain things that no one should be exposed to. . . . I think violence can become gratuitous when it's not serving the story. I try to steer clear of this as much as possible. In general I feel that my responsibility as an artist is to tell the truth, and it's as simple as that."

In the late 1990s, Rapp was living in New York City's East Village with his brother Anthony, who had attained fame in the hit Broadway musical *Rent*. A third roommate served to inspire Rapp's play *Nocturne,* which debuted in October of 2000 as part of the American Repertory Theatre's New Stages Series. *Nocturne*'s story is a family tale which the unnamed narrator, once a piano prodigy, recounts in a first-act monologue. He reveals that fifteen years earlier, he was a seventeen-year-old in Joliet driving a car whose brakes suddenly failed and struck his young sister, beheading her. The play's second act follows the aftermath of the tragedy: their parents' marriage dissolves, the narrator's father spends time in a psychiatric facility, and even threatens to kill his son at one point. The narrator recounts his move to New York City, where he gives up music entirely, and instead becomes obsessed with books and literature. He returns to Joliet at the request of his estranged father, who has been diagnosed with cancer. *Variety* contributor Markland Taylor called *Nocturne* "an unremittingly dark play," and noted that "the playwright edits himself much more ruthlessly in act two, cutting much closer to the blood and bone of his central character." Taylor concluded that Rapp was "a playwright . . . to watch with keen interest." And theatergoers had several more opportunities to see Rapp's work that year; in 2000, he premiered three other plays: *Faster, Dreams of the Salthorse,* and *Finer Noble Gases.*

Yet more plays were to come. In 2001, Rapp's *Animals and Plants* was produced in Cambridge under the auspices of the American Repertory Theatre. The two-act work revolves around two drug couriers from North Carolina who are waylaid by a snowstorm. As they sit the storm out in a motel room, tensions mount. Taylor, writing in *Variety,* called *Animals and Plants* "a lurid comedic phantasmagoria of life on the underside of Middle America," finding its dialogue "rough-spoken, raunchy, and sometimes guffawingly funny. . . . Rapp

relishes language." The playwright also had a two-act drama premiere in London. *Blackbird* visits an ailing and abusive Gulf War Veteran and his girlfriend, a former stripper with a heroin addiction, on Christmas Eve. According to Matt Wolf in a *Variety* review, Rapp strayed from the "grave austere beauty" of *Nocturne,* with a play that, despite its subject matter, "suffers from a dismaying case of the cutes." The next year, *Stone Cold Dead Serious* was produced by the American Repertory Theatre. Taylor, writing for *Variety* said the play "mixes blackly comic moments with sentimental ones" and missed the "individual voice" Rapp showed in previous plays.

Rapp confesses that he is drawn to writing for the stage because of the camaraderie inherent in a production. As he told *Boston Phoenix* writer Carolyn Clay: "When you have a play in rehearsal, you have a family. The novelist part of me has always felt solitary and secluded. I'm not very good at parties. . . . Theater became a great excuse to talk to people." Novels, he noted, seem to take him much longer to write. "But the playwriting is this fever thing," he explained to Clay. "The plays kind of burst out of me, and I don't know why. The stuff I write about in plays tends to be the stuff that keeps me up at night, and the stuff I write about in novels tends to be the things I think about during the day."

The plot of Rapp's next novel for young adults, *Little Chicago,* continued in the same dark vein of his earlier fiction, concentrating on the effects of child abuse. Blacky Brown is an eleven-year-old boy who has been molested by his mother's boyfriend. He finds he has no one but himself to rely on, after his mother, siblings, friends, and social services fail to support or shield him. The only friendship he finds is from a girl who has also been rejected by the others at school, another "freak." The book's choppy first-person narrative reflects Blacky's inability to cope with his life, a horrifying existence filled with pain, neglect, poverty, filth, and fear. In his desperation, Blacky gets a gun. In the end, after throwing the gun away, the boy departs into the woods looking to escape. According to *School Library Journal* writer Connie Tyrrell Burns, it was the "bleakest yet" of Rapp's novels. She commented, "The sense of hopelessness in this disturbing novel is almost physically painful." The book prompted other warnings. A *Publishers Weekly* contributor said that it "contains metaphors and vocabulary that, more sophisticated than the messenger, reveal the hand of the author at work." Writing for *Booklist,* Gillian Engberg advised that "some of the scenes' repellent details verge on the gratuitous and occasionally the sensational." However, Lauren Adams remarked in *Horn Book* that "Rapp's portrayal of the abused child is sensitive, sympathetic, and honest."

Four runaway children with backgrounds even more gruesome than Blacky's populate *Thirty-three Snowfish.* In this novel, Rapp explores the desperation of young teens who were introduced to sex, drugs, and violence long ago. Boobie is on the run with his infant brother after killing his parents. Curl is fifteen, a drug addict and prostitute. Custis has escaped from the control of a man who produces child pornography and snuff films. Together they flee in a stolen car into rural Illinois, where two of the teens die. Custis and the baby are rescued by an elderly black man named Seldom, who takes them into his home. Despite the boy's racist attitude, it is the first healthy relationship with an adult that he has known. The story both shocked and stimulated reviewers. A *Publishers Weekly* reviewer responded that "readers may have trouble stomaching the language . . . as well as the horrors so flatly depicted and, in the end, so handily overcome." In *School Library Journal,* Joel Shoemaker judged that "spare descriptions and stellar characterization reel readers into the dark and violent world" and concluded that the book "invites both an emotional and intellectual response and begs to be discussed." And a *Kirkus Reviews* contributor found that "with his customary ear for the language of the marginalized teen, Rapp . . . allows his characters to present themselves in total unselfconsciousness, frankly and powerfully laying out the squalor of their existence."

BIOGRAPHICAL AND CRITICAL SOURCES:

PERIODICALS

ALAN Review, fall, 2000, Ann Angel, "The Bad Boys of YA," pp. 7-9, and "E-View with Adam Rapp," pp. 10-13, and Penny Blubaugh, "An Author in Residence?," pp. 14-15.

American Theatre, January, 1997, Karen Fricker, "Adam and Anthony Rapp: Genuine Bohemia," p. 50; January, 2004, review of *Stone Cold Dead Serious,* p. 126.

Booklist, June 1, 1994, Stephanie Zvirin, review of *Missing the Piano,* p. 1804; September 1, 1997, Susan Dove Lempke, review of *The Buffalo Tree,*

p. 107; November 15, 1999, Debbie Carton, review of *The Copper Elephant,* p. 615; August, 2002, Gillian Engberg, review of *Little Chicago,* p. 1947.

Boston Herald, October 18, 2000, Terry Byrne, review of *Nocturne.*

Boston Phoenix, October 12, 2000, Carolyn Clay, "Night Music."

Horn Book, July-August, 1997, Nancy Vasilakis, review of *The Buffalo Tree,* p. 461; January, 2000, review of *The Copper Elephant,* p. 83; September-October, 2002, Lauren Adams, review of *Little Chicago,* p. 580.

Kirkus Reviews, February 1, 2003, review of *Thirty-three Snowfish,* p. 237.

Publishers Weekly, May 23, 1994, review of *Missing the Piano,* p. 90; April 7, 1997, review of *The Buffalo Tree,* p. 93; March 11, 2002, review of *Little Chicago,* p. 73; January 13, 2003, review of *Thirty-three Snowfish,* p. 61.

School Library Journal, April, 2002, Connie Tyrrell Burns, review of *Little Chicago,* p. 196; April, 2003, Joel Shoemaker, review of *Thirty-three Snowfish,* p. 166.

Variety, November 6, 2000, Markland Taylor, review of *Nocturne,* p. 29; April 16, 2001, Markland Taylor, review of *Animals and Plants,* p. 38; June 18, 2001, Matt Wolf, review of *Blackbird,* p. 26; February 18, 2002, Markland Taylor, review of *Stone Cold Dead Serious,* p. 43.

ONLINE

Front Street Books Web Site, http://www.frontstreetbooks.com/ (March 13, 2004), biography of Adam Rapp.*

*   *   *

RAZON, Felix
 See SAN JUAN, E(pifanio), Jr.

*   *   *

RHUE, Morton
 See STRASSER, Todd

RICCI, Nino (Pio) 1959-

PERSONAL: Surname is pronounced "*ree*-chee"; born August 23, 1959, in Leamington, Ontario, Canada; son of Virginio (a farmer) and Amelia (a farmer; maiden name, Ingratta) Ricci. *Education:* York University, B.A., 1981; Concordia University, M.A., 1987; attended University of Florence, 1988-89.

ADDRESSES: Home—139 Wolseley St., Toronto, Ontario M6J 1K3, Canada. *Office*—c/o Writers' Union of Canada, 40 Wellington St. E, Toronto, Ontario M5E 1C7, Canada. *Agent*—Anne McDermid & Associates, 92 Wilcocks St., Toronto, Ontario M5S 1C8, Canada.

CAREER: Writer. Ogun State Education Board, Nigeria, secondary school teacher, 1981-83; Concordia University, Montreal, Quebec, instructor in creative writing, composition, and Canadian literature, 1986-88; Berlitz Language Schools, Montreal, English and Italian instructor, 1987.

MEMBER: PEN, Canadian PEN Center (member of board of directors, 1990-97; president, 1995-97), Amnesty International (coordinator of human rights education committee, 1987-88).

AWARDS, HONORS: F. G. Bressani Prize from Italian Cultural Center Society, Governor-General's Literary Award from Canada Treasury Board of Canada Secretariat, Winifred Holtby Memorial Prize from Royal Society of Literature, W. H. Smith/*Books in Canada* First Novel Award, and Betty Trask Award from Society of Authors, all 1990, all for *Lives of the Saints;* short list, QSPELL award for fiction, 1990, Los Angeles Book Prize, 1991, Giller Prize for Fiction, 1997; Trillium Book Award, 2003, for *Testament.*

WRITINGS:

Lives of the Saints, Cormorant Books (Dunvegan, Ontario, Canada), 1990, published as *The Book of Saints,* Knopf (New York, NY), 1991.
In a Glass House: A Novel, McClelland & Stewart (Toronto, Ontario, Canada), 1993, Picador (New York, NY), 1995.
Where She Has Gone, McClelland & Stewart (Toronto, Ontario, Canada), 1997, Picador (New York, NY), 1998.

Testament, Doubleday Canada (Toronto, Ontario, Canada), 2002, Houghton Mifflin (Boston, MA), 2003.

Contributor to books, including *The Moosehead Anthology: A Collection of Contemporary Writing,* DC Books, 1989; *Ricordi: Things Remembered,* edited by C. D. Minni, Guernica Editions, 1989. Contributor to many periodicals, including *Saturday Night, Canadian Journal of Political and Social Theory, Fiddlehead,* and *Toronto Life.*

Lives of the Saints has been translated into seven languages.

SIDELIGHTS: First-generation Canadian Nino Ricci, author of the award-winning novel *Lives of the Saints,* told *New York Times Book Review* critic Richard E. Nicholls that in his writing he wants to portray "the experience of being an immigrant in the modern world." Ricci's parents emigrated from Italy to Canada, but regaled their son with stories of their native village and faithfully observed Italian culture. During his interview with Nicholls, Ricci explained that "being raised in a tight-knit Italian community in Canada, I grew up with a sense of village dynamics." As a secondary school teacher in Nigeria for two years, Ricci found further inspiration for his novel. He told Nicholls that living in this "energetic and flamboyant land" was "like going back to an older Italy. In its strong mix of religion and folk beliefs it gave me a sense of how life might transpire in the small world of a village. My image of life in [the fictional Italian village of] Valle del Sole had at least part of its origins in Africa."

Lives of the Saints, which earned Canada's prestigious Governor-General's Literary Award, is set in a small, theistic Italian village in 1960. Seven-year-old narrator Vittorio Innocente and his mother Cristina Innocente live alone in Valle del Sole while Vittorio's father prepares a home for them in Canada. Lonely and unhappy with her marriage, Cristina finds comfort with a non-Italian, but their affair is revealed when she is bitten by a snake during a rendezvous. Outraged by her debauchery, Cristina's fellow villagers believe the snake bite signals her disfavour with God; mother and son become outcasts in the village. Cristina fights the vicious insults in a brazen manner, but naive Vittorio is harassed and beaten by his peers. Because of their neighbors' unforgiving attitudes, they are eventually forced to flee to Canada. *Listener* contributor Steven Amidon commented that the novel's "pagan atmosphere adds drama and poignancy both to Cristina's transgression and Vittorio's fall from grace, showing them to be innocents in a world which long ago lost any resemblance to Eden. Their flight from this weedy garden is as fraught and terrifying as expulsion from paradise must be." Barbara Grizzuti Harrison concluded in the *New York Times Book Review* that *Lives of the Saints* is "an extraordinary story—brooding and ironic, suffused with yearning, tender and lucid and gritty."

In a Glass House, Ricci's next novel, is the second installment in what Ricci plans will be a trilogy about Vittorio Innocente. The novel begins with Vittorio's arrival in Canada with his baby half-sister—the product of his mother's illicit affair in Italy. His mother has died in childbirth on the passage to Canada, and his father is revealed as a bitter and angry man, part of an immigrant farming community. In an attempt to grow things in the harsh Canadian climate, he is forever building greenhouses, which become the metaphorical glass houses of the title.

Vittorio struggles to fit in and to love his father and his sister (who is rejected by his father and eventually adopted by a Canadian family). He teaches for a while in Africa, returns to Canada, and, at the end of the novel, confronts his father's death. John Melmoth's review in the *Times Literary Supplement* noted that "Vittorio's experience is, in part, representative of the 'subtle' embitterment of the migrant, forever out of place. He is trapped between antithesis: between . . . self-conscious aloofness and the need to belong . . . between Italy and Canada; resistance and acquiescence; dark and light."

Maclean's critic Lawrence Scanlan wrote, "The operative word in the novel is 'humiliation'" and noted that the novel "explores an immigrant's pain as a doctor explores a wound. It is far more personal, even autobiographical than its predecessor." Melmoth felt that "*In a Glass House* is a novel of great power, but it is almost entirely devoid of any lighter moments." Yet Scanlan observed, "Ricci's great gift is to capture, sometimes in exquisite prose, the texture of people and place," and *Quill & Quire* reviewer David Prosser commented: "Vittorio's self-discovery is one in which we all share: it is as if, in focusing a microscope on an unpromising slide, we had caught a glimpse of the human soul."

Ricci completed his immigrant trilogy in 1997 with the publication of *Where She Has Gone.* In this novel, Vittorio, now known as Victor, attempts to establish a relationship with his illegitimate half-sister, Rita, who is studying in Toronto. Brother and sister get somewhat too close as Victor becomes obsessed with Rita, causing her to flee to Europe to avoid the situation. Haunted by the tragedies in his mother's life and death, Victor returns to his ancestral village in Italy, searching for a glimpse into his family's history. *Time* reviewer Pico Iyer commented: "Ricci has spun out a delicate and soulful novel, tiptoeing around silences and respecting those secrets that are guessed at, as well as those that are best left untouched." *Maclean's* critic John Bemrose commented that Ricci "has a great gift for evoking the nuances of human relationship: those loaded silences and gestures that say more than words ever can," but he also noted that "too much of the novel has fallen prey to a narrative meagerness, a thinness of character and situation."

Ricci's fourth novel, *Testament,* a fictionalized biography of Jesus from the perspective of four people who knew him, emerged in a hailstorm of debate over its treatment of the life of Jesus. *Maclean's* contributor Brian Bethune explained, "Ricci's Jesus is not divine, but he is a moral visionary whose illegitimacy—he's the bastard child of Mary and the Roman officer who raped her—leads him to embrace the cause of the outcast." *Books in Canada* critic Donald Akeson wrote, "Ricci is trying to accomplish on an artistic level what scholarly searchers for the historical Jesus are doing: telling what Jesus of Nazareth might have done as a human being, and then explaining how this man somehow was transformed by his followers and their descendants into a god or, maybe, the God." Because of its subject matter, *Testament* was as controversial as it was critically acclaimed. A *Catholic Insight* reviewer called it "extremely offensive." In 2003 the government of Ontario, Canada, awarded Ricci the Trillium Book Award for *Testament.*

BIOGRAPHICAL AND CRITICAL SOURCES:

PERIODICALS

Booklist, October 1, 1995, Kathy Broderick, review of *In A Glass House: A Novel,* p. 252.
Books in Canada, December, 1992, review of *Lives of the Saints,* pp. 10-12; October, 1993, review of *In A Glass House,* p. 34; December, 1997, reviews of

Where She Has Gone, Lives of the Saints, and *In a Glass House,* p. 4; August, 2002, Donald Akenson, review of *Testament,* pp. 6-7.

Canadian Book Review Annual, Volume 3, 1997, review of *Where She Has Gone,* p. 195.

Canadian Literature, spring, 1992, review of *Lives of the Saints,* p. 176.

Catholic Insight, July-August, 2002, review of *Testament,* p. 30.

CM: A Reviewing Journal of Canadian Materials for Young People, March, 1994, review of *In A Glass House,* p. 40.

Dalhousie Review, spring, 1992, review of *Lives of the Saints,* p. 38.

Essays on Canadian Writing, fall, 1992, review of *Lives of the Saints,* p. 69.

Kirkus Reviews, August 15, 1995, review of *In A Glass House,* p. 1138; May 15, 1998, review of *Where She Has Gone,* p. 684.

Library Journal, May 1, 1998, Joshua Cohen, review of *Where She Has Gone,* p. 140; May 15, 2003, Patrick Sullivan, review of *Testament,* p. 126.

Listener, September 27, 1990, p. 33; October 4, 1993, p. 52.

Los Angeles Times Book Review, October 12, 1995, review of *In a Glass House,* p. 10.

Maclean's, February 4, 1991, p. 63; October 4, 1993, review of *In a Glass House,* p. 52; October 20, 1997, John Bemrose, review of *Where She Has Gone,* p. 98; May 13, 2002, Brian Bethune, review of *Testament,* p. 75.

New York Times Book Review, June 2, 1991, p. 7; October 8, 1995, review of *In a Glass House,* p. 42; October 22, 1995, review of *The Book of Saints,* p. 44; October 11, 1998, review of *In a Glass House,* p. 32; October 27, 1998, Allen Lincoln, review of *Where She Has Gone,* p. 23.

Observer (London, England), August 7, 1994, review of *In A Glass House,* p. 22; February 22, 1998, review of *Where She Has Gone,* p. 16.

Publishers Weekly, September 11, 1995, review of *In a Glass House,* p. 74, and *The Book of Saints,* p. 82; May 18, 1998, review of *Where She Has Gone,* p. 69; April 21, 2003, review of *Testament,* p. 38.

Quill & Quire, October, 1993, p. 26; August, 1997, review of *Where She Has Gone,* p. 22.

Spectator, July 30, 1994, review of *In A Glass House,* p. 28.

Studies in Canadian Literature, Volume 18, number 2, 1993, pp. 168-184.

Sun (Edmonton, Alberta, Canada), April 12, 1998, Vanna Tessier, review of *Where She Has Gone.*

Time, August 10, 1998, Pico Iyer, review of *Where She Has Gone,* p. 86.

Times Literary Supplement, August 12, 1994, review of *In A Glass House,* p. 22; March 20, 1998, review of *Where She Has Gone,* p. 22.

ONLINE

Random House Web site, http://www.randomhouse.ca/ (November 23, 2002), review of *Testament.**

*   *   *

RIGDEN, John S. 1934-

PERSONAL: Born January 10, 1934, in Painesville, OH; son of William P. (a water company employee) and Eltheda X. (a homemaker; maiden name, Weaver) Rigden; married Dorothy Takala, 1953 (divorced, 1983); married Diana E. Wyllie (a consultant in education), 1985; children: Jeffrey W., Gregory J., Jonathan R., Keith D., Karen R. Montes de Oca, L. Brick. *Education:* Eastern Nazarene College, B.S., 1956; Johns Hopkins University, Ph.D., 1960. *Politics:* "Moderate-liberal." *Hobbies and other interests:* Gardening, Hudson steam locomotives.

ADDRESSES: Office—c/o Department of Physics, Washington University, St. Louis, MO 63130. *E-mail*—jrigden@aip.org.

CAREER: Eastern Nazarene College, Quincy, MA, assistant professor, 1961-64, associate professor of physics, 1964-67; Middlebury College, Middlebury, VT, associate professor of physics, 1967-68; University of Missouri—St. Louis, associate professor, 1968-78, professor of physics, 1978-87; American Institute of Physics, College Park, MD, director of physics programs, 1987-97. International Science Exhibition, U.S. representative.

MEMBER: American Physical Society (fellow), History of Science Society, American Association for the Advancement of Science (fellow).

AWARDS, HONORS: Fulbright fellow in Burma and Uruguay; honorary D.Sc., Denison University.

WRITINGS:

Physics and the Sound of Music, Wiley (New York, NY), 1977, 2nd edition, 1985.

Rabi: Scientist and Citizen, Basic Books (New York, NY), 1987.

(Editor, with Laurie M. Brown) *Most of the Good Stuff: Memories of Richard Feynman,* American Institute of Physics (New York, NY), 1993.

(Editor) *Macmillan Encyclopedia of Physics,* five volumes, Simon & Schuster (New York, NY), 1996.

(Editor, with Judy R. Franz) *Physics in the Twentieth Century,* Harry N. Abrams (New York, NY), 1999.

Hydrogen: The Essential Element, Harvard University Press (Cambridge, MA), 2002.

Contributor to books. Contributor of more than 100 articles and reviews to scientific journals. Editor, *American Journal of Physics,* 1977-87; coeditor, *Physics in Perspective,* 1999—.

WORK IN PROGRESS: Einstein: The Standard of Greatness.

SIDELIGHTS: John S. Rigden once told *CA:* "I have had a long fascination for I. I. Rabi, one of the twentieth century's foremost physicists. Rabi was not only an outstanding physicist (he won the Nobel Prize in physics in 1944), but also a statesman of science. He saw in physics a cultural force, a means to bridge cultural, ideological, and nationalistic differences. Rabi, along with J. Robert Oppenheimer, was behind the Baruch Plan presented to the United Nations in June, 1946. He also organized the first International Conference on the Peaceful Uses of Atomic Energy in 1955."

Recently Rigden added: "Science is dependent on the support of the general public. If that support is to be sustained, citizens must understand and accept the values that undergird the quest for new knowledge. Thus it is crucial that communication between scientists and the general public be maintained. My writing has been motivated by my desire to edify the general reader about physics."

BIOGRAPHICAL AND CRITICAL SOURCES:

PERIODICALS

Los Angeles Times Book Review, July 14, 1987.
New York Times Book Review, May 10, 1987.

ROSS, Andrew 1956-

PERSONAL: Born 1956; immigrated to United States, 1982. *Education:* Aberdeen University, Scotland, M.A., 1978; University of Kent, England, Ph.D., 1984.

ADDRESSES: Office—New York University, American Studies Program, 285 Mercer St., 8th Floor, New York, NY 10003.

CAREER: Princeton University, Princeton, NJ, professor of English, 1985-93; New York University, New York, NY, director of American Studies Program, 1993—, professor of comparative literature.

MEMBER: American Association of University Professors, Modern Language Association, Society for Cinema Studies, Society for Critical Exchange, American Studies Association, Society for Literature and Science, Teachers for a Democratic Culture, Union of Democratic Intellectuals.

AWARDS, HONORS: Unit for Criticism and Theory, University of Illinois, Urbana—Champaign, fellow, 1983-84; Stauffer Bicentennial fellow, Princeton University, 1989-92; Society for the Humanities, Cornell University, fellow, 1989-90; Guggenheim fellow, 2002- 03.

WRITINGS:

The Failure of Modernism: Symptoms of American Poetry, Columbia University Press (New York, NY), 1986.

(Editor) *Universal Abandon? The Politics of Postmodernism,* University of Minnesota Press (Minneapolis, MN), 1988.

No Respect: Intellectuals and Popular Culture, Routledge (New York, NY), 1989.

Strange Weather: Culture, Science, and Technology in the Age of Limits, Verso (New York, NY), 1991.

(Editor, with Constance Penley) *Technoculture,* University of Minnesota Press (Minneapolis, MN), 1991.

The Chicago Gangster Theory of Life: Nature's Debt to Society, Verso (New York, NY), 1994.

(Editor, with Tricia Rose) *Microphone Fiends: Youth Music and Youth Culture,* Routledge (New York, NY), 1994.

(Editor) *Science Wars,* Duke University Press (Durham, NC), 1996.

(Editor) *No Sweat: Fashion, Free Trade, and the Rights of Garment Workers,* Verso (New York, NY), 1997.

Real Love: In Pursuit of Cultural Justice, New York University Press (New York, NY), 1998.

The Celebration Chronicles: Life, Liberty, and the Pursuit of Property Value in Disney's New Town, Ballantine (New York, NY), 1999.

No-Collar: The Humane Workplace and Its Hidden Costs, Basic Books (New York, NY). 2003.

Low Pay, High Profile: The Global Fight for Fair Labor, New Press (New York, NY), 2004.

Contributor to periodicals, including *Nation, Village Voice,* and *Artforum;* editor, *Social Text.*

SIDELIGHTS: Professor and author Andrew Ross focuses on a wide range of social issues in both his teaching and writing. Such subjects include intellectual history, labor and work, sub/urban policies, cultural studies, ecology, and science and technology as they interact with society. Ross has brought his own definition to cultural studies through his writing and teaching. After receiving his Ph.D. in English and American literature from the University of Kent, Ross taught literary theory at Princeton University in a deliberate attempt to influence those he called the "children of the ruling classes." Later he taught at New York University, where he redefined American studies to focus not necessarily on literature but on issues of race, gender, and sexuality in American society. Ross's interpretation of American studies met with resistance, and some of his peers felt that his approach was too glib and emphasized facile over traditional aspects of culture. However, Ross's approach appealed to many of his students, who he hoped would use their education in American studies in activist positions or in involvement with social causes.

Ross published *The Failure of Modernism: Symptoms of American Poetry* in 1986. Reviewer B. Galvin of *Choice* assessed the work as laced with jargon and language hard to pin down. The critic warned that those unfamiliar with Ross's thought processes might have difficulty with the work. A *Virginia Quarterly*

Review contributor responded favorably to *The Failure of Modernism,* praising Ross's look at modernism through the filters of language, psychology, and history.

The author continued his examination of the topic of postmodernism as editor of a 1988 collection of twelve essays titled *Universal Abandon? The Politics of Postmodernism.* While reviewer Bruce Robbins of *Modern Fiction Studies* noted that the book is presented to inspire questions rather than promote answers for readers, this reviewer also remarked on the focus on consumerism and popular culture. Among the cultural phenomena discussed are the movie *Crocodile Dundee,* the "Banana Republic" clothing line, and the singer Bruce Springsteen. To Robbins the essays are presented in a manner that secures an equal place for the study of popular culture alongside other aspects of postmodern studies. David Leon Higdon of *Rocky Mountain Review* noted that, jargon aside, the essays in *Universal Abandon?* are presented in a depth sufficient to challenge the reader.

Ross examined the role of technology in popular U.S. culture in his 1991 book *Strange Weather: Culture, Science, and Technology in the Age of Limits.* According to reviewer James T. Fisher of *Commonweal,* Ross goes beyond an interpretation of technological sprawl as "irrelevant." Instead, the author makes a case that technological trends are closely indicative of popular culture. In a study of the New Age movement, Ross argues against its division between technology and nature, claiming instead that technology merely represents a type of organization forced on people by society. While the author calls for readers to look at technology in a different light, he also acknowledges the chasm that continues to exist between science and the liberal arts. Ross also addresses technological issues in *Technoculture,* a collection of essays he coedited with Constance Penley in 1991. The collection, according to R. L. Rutsky of *Film Quarterly,* goes beyond defining the title and looks instead at technology's impact on society.

In *The Chicago Gangster Theory of Life: Nature's Debt to Society,* which was published in 1994, Ross proposes that the environmental movement is self-serving and compromises the civil rights of Americans. In line with the book's main premise, Ross claims that resource scarcity is caused by inequality in ownership of resources rather than a lack of natural resources themselves. P. D. Travis of *Choice* asserted that the arguments in Ross's essays are hard to follow yet acknowledged that the book has an important message. Harold Fromm of the *Hudson Review* responded less favorably, calling the work "almost unreadable." Fromm faulted the author's example of ecotourism in Hawaii, which Ross presented as a capitalist venture facilitated by interest and sympathies toward the environmental movement. The reviewer maintained that Ross uses a haphazard approach and plucks examples randomly from pop culture to support his thesis.

Microphone Fiends: Youth Music and Youth Culture, a 1994 volume that Ross edited with Tricia Rose, covers topics ranging from the disco phenomenon and its connection to the gay community to the relationship between hard rock and feminism. Essays examine the Latino influence on rap music, the presence of women in rock music, and the role of rebellion in modern music. A *Publishers Weekly* critic noted that the collection would appeal to those outside of academic settings. Ross includes interviews with popular musicians, and to reviewer Timothy D. Taylor in *Drama Review,* the interview material goes beyond that usually found in fan magazines. "No musicologist of popular music can afford to pass this up," Taylor declared.

Ross published two additional works in the late 1990s. *No Sweat: Fashion, Free Trade, and the Rights of Garment Workers,* which appeared in 1997, treats the exploitation of human resources in the fashion industry and such issues as the use of sweat shops, dangerous working conditions, and starvation faced by garment industry workers. Ross uses specific examples in the essays, including a close look at the industry in New York City and Los Angeles, and newsworthy cases of human abuse in the industry. Ross's 1998 volume *Real Love: In Pursuit of Cultural Justice* offers nine formerly published essays by the author on a range of topics, including opposition to DNA testing for court use, cyberspace, gangsta rap, and the O. J. Simpson case. Brooke Allen of the *New York Times Book Review* argued that the connection between the essays is tenuous, and that Ross's idea of cultural justice is never truly defined. The quality of the collection is compromised, in Allen's opinion, by Ross's attempt to advance a political agenda.

Ross's cultural critique continued in his 1999 book, *The Celebration Chronicles: Life, Liberty, and the Pursuit of Property Values in Disney's New Town.* In this work, Ross examines the new town created by the Disney Company in Celebration, Florida, an attempt, as David L. Kirp noted in the *New York Times Book Review,* at the "revival of Norman Rockwell's America." The town of Celebration consciously set out to create such a wholesome atmosphere from whole cloth, and its achievements have been mixed at best: crime, neglected children, and spousal abuse are present in Celebration just as in other towns. Ross details the underside of this supposed idyllic community: the mosquitoes that keep inhabitants off their front porches at night, the vacuuming of the main street each night. He also provides a brief history of such attempts at creating new towns and ideal communities, from Brook Farm to Levittown. Kirp felt that Ross's chronicle of the town was "entertaining and . . . insightful." The same reviewer further praised Ross as a "raconteur with delicious—and telling—anecdotes." Ross, who spent over a year living in Celebration researching his topic, "is good at striking a balance between observer and participant" in the writing of his book, according to John E. Czarnecki in *Architectural Record.* However, Sam Staley, writing in *Reason,* felt that Ross had a tendency to see "power relationships as the almost exclusive source of the new town's conflicts." For Staley, such "quasi-Marxist interpretations" are "incomplete." Peter Whoriskey, reviewing the *Celebration Chronicles* in the *Boston Globe,* similarly found Ross's account "impressionistic," an approach that allowed the author to tackle topics including the "nature of American values, the history of city design, and even the moral choices imposed by world trade." A contributor for the *Economist,* however, commented on Ross's "detached and analytical look." And Peter Mandler, reviewing the same work in the *Times Literary Supplement,* called it a "reflective, penetrating and personal account." For Mandler, "There can be few books in recent years that have probed so directly and devastatingly at the heart of what (white, middle-class) Americans mean today by 'community.'"

In his 2003 book *No-Collar: The Humane Workplace and Its Hidden Costs,* Ross investigates the new economy of technology workers. To research the topic, he spent more than a year-and-a-half with two such Internet media companies in New York City. Ross began working with Razorfish.com in 2000 and stayed on until 2002; at the same time, he also devoted a half-year to 360Hiphop.com. This span of time took in the Internet bubble and resulting crash. Such research was intended to provide Ross with insights into aspects of the modern workplace, in particular the notion that the new technologies have a more informal environment, a nonhierarchical "no collar" atmosphere, where input from all levels is valued. However, for *Library Journal*'s Susan Hurst, the resulting book "reads more like a corporate chronology than the broader social work it was intended to be." A critic for *Publishers Weekly* found more to like in Ross's book, praising the author for his "insights into the upheavals and heartbreak" that came with the bursting of the dot-com bubble. The same reviewer also mentioned Ross's "chilling assessment" of what happens to New Economy workers in hard times. According to Ross, the seemingly egalitarian workplace ethos at such firms convinced the workers to make their work their lives; after the crash, these same "valued" employees later learned of their impending dismissals through Web chat rooms. For Joseph A. McCartin, writing in the *Washington Post Book World*, Ross's account was a "self-consciously hip, impressionistic examination of the New Economy workplaces." In contrast, William Wolman, writing in the *Los Angeles Times*, praised Ross's book as a "balanced, richly textured and, in the end, chilling account of work in the high-tech digitized world."

BIOGRAPHICAL AND CRITICAL SOURCES:

PERIODICALS

Across the Board, March-April, 2003, Matthew Budman, review of *No-Collar: The Humane Workplace and Its Hidden Costs*, pp. 13-14.

Architectural Record, December, 1999, John E. Czarnecki, review of *The Celebration Chronicles: Life, Liberty, and the Pursuit of Property Value in Disney's New Town*, p. 47.

Boston Globe, October 23, 1999, Peter Whoriskey, review of *The Celebration Chronicles*, p. D5.

Business Week, October 4, 1999, David Rocks, review of *The Celebration Chronicles*, p. J18.

Choice, March, 1987, B. Galvin, review of *The Failure of Modernism: Symptoms of American Poetry*, p. 1064; April, 1995, P. D. Travis, review of *The Chicago Gangster Theory of Life: Nature's Debt to Society*, p. 1369.

Commonweal, February 28, 1992, James T. Fisher, review of *Strange Weather: Culture, Science, and Technology in the Age of Limits*, pp. 26-27.

Drama Review, summer, 1997, Timothy D. Taylor, review of *Microphone Fiends: Youth Music and Youth Culture*, pp. 163-169.

Economist, June 10, 2000, review of *The Celebration Chronicles*, pp. 92-93.

Film Quarterly, fall, 1992, R. L. Rutsky, review of *Strange Weather*, pp. 53-54.

Harvard Business Review, January, 2003, John T. Landry, review of *No-Collar*, p. 22.

HR Magzine, April, 2003, review of *No-Collar*, pp. 126-127.

Hudson Review, summer, 1996, Harold Fromm, review of *The Chicago Gangster Theory of Life*, pp. 323-330.

Journal of American History, September, 1990, p. 731; March, 1993, p. 1695.

Library Journal, March 15, 2003, Susan Hurst, review of *No-Collar*, p. 92.

Los Angeles Times Book Review, March 2, 2003, William Wolman, review of *No-Collar*, p. R5.

Modern Fiction Studies, winter, 1989, Bruce Robbins, review of *Universal Abandon? The Politics of Postmodernism*, pp. 856-858.

New York Times Book Review, July 12, 1998, Brooke Allen, review of *Real Love: In Pursuit of Cultural Justice;* September 19, 1999, David L. Kirp, review of *The Celebration Chronicles*, pp. 22-23.

Publishers Weekly, May 16, 1994, review of *Microphone Fiends*, p. 61; November 18, 2002, review of *No-Collar*, p. 51.

Reason, February, 2001, Sam Staley, review of *The Celebration Chronicles*, pp. 48-54.

Rocky Mountain Review, 1992, David Leon Higdon, review of *Universal Abandon?*, pp. 103-104.

Times Literary Supplement, December 8, 2000, Peter Mandler, review of *The Celebration Chronicles*, p. 3.

Virginia Quarterly Review, summer, 1987, review of *The Failure of Modernism*, p. 102.

Washington Post Book World, March 9, 2003, Joseph A. McCartin, review of *No-Collar*, p. WBK13.

ONLINE

New York University, http://www.nyu.edu/ (November 1, 2003), "Andrew Ross."*

*   *   *

RUSH, Norman 1933-

PERSONAL: Born October 24, 1933, in San Francisco, CA; son of Roger and Leslie (Chesse) Rush; married Elsa Scheidt; children: Jason, Liza. *Education:* Swarthmore College, B.A., 1956.

ADDRESSES: Agent—Andrew Wylie, Wylie, Aitken & Stone, Inc., 250 West 57th St., Suite 2114, New York, NY 10107.

CAREER: Part-time writer and dealer of antiquarian books, 1958-73; College instructor, 1978-83; full-time writer, 1983—.

MEMBER: PEN American Center.

AWARDS, HONORS: Short fiction selected for *Best American Short Stories,* 1971, 1984, and 1985; *Paris Review* Aga Khan Award, 1985, for "Instruments of Seduction"; New York Foundation for the Arts fellowship, 1985; Grant from National Endowment for the Arts and finalist for American Book Award, both 1986, nominated for Pulitzer Prize and recipient of annual literary award from the Academy and Institute of Arts and Letters, both 1987, all for *Whites;* Guggenheim fellowship, 1987; Rockefeller Foundation Bellagio Residency, 1990; National Book Award for fiction, 1991, for *Mating;* National Book Critics Circle Fiction Award finalist, 1991; Aer Lingus/*Irish Times* International Fiction Prize, 1991; selected as one of 100 best books of the twentieth century by *New York Times.*

WRITINGS:

Whites: Stories, Knopf (New York, NY), 1986.
Mating (novel), Knopf (New York, NY), 1991.
(With Philip Levine and Orlando Patterson), *Earth, Stars, and Writers,* Library of Congress (Washington, DC), 1992.
Mortals (novel), Knopf (New York, NY), 2003.

Contributor of short stories to anthologies, including *Best American Short Stories,* and to periodicals, including *New Yorker, Paris Review, Grand Street,* and *Massachusetts Review.* Contributor of articles and reviews to periodicals, including *New York Review of Books, New York Times Book Review, New Yorker, Nation, Transition, Village Voice, Grand Street,* and *Gentleman's Quarterly.*

WORK IN PROGRESS: Subtle Bodies (novel).

SIDELIGHTS: In his highly acclaimed collection of six short stories, *Whites,* Norman Rush explores what *Nation* reviewer George Packer described as the

"moral and spiritual quandaries of middle-class foreigners who happen to be stuck out in [the African country of] Botswana." While living in Botswana for five years as codirector of the Peace Corps, the author became familiar with the political and racial difficulties existing in a country bordering the controversial apartheid nation of South Africa. Herbert Mitgang quoted Rush in the *New York Times:* "'In these stories I concentrate on whites, especially American whites, as they define themselves against the contours of African life and encounter the limits and contradictions of the Western undertaking in that part of the world.'" The characters in Rush's "low-keyed yet forceful" stories exist under unique circumstances, explained Jonathan Yardley in the *Los Angeles Times Book Review* (review also published in *Washington Post Book World*), because for them "Africa is a place where the ordinary rules do not apply. They are in a country that is not their own, in a civilization they do not understand, cannot really connect to, and feel no obligation toward." As missionaries in a country plagued by drought and poverty, "they are at a distance . . . because they are white and because, of course, they can always go home."

With what Packer labeled "intricate structures and ironic themes," Rush presents a variety of situations involving sexual and power struggles, inequity, disillusionment, and political apathy. A story in the collection illustrating some responses of whites to the plight of Africans is "Near Pala." Two white couples driving through the desert discuss race; one of the women, Nan, is sensitive to racial injustice, the other is oblivious to it, and the men are obviously impatient with the issue. In a heated part of the conversation and in a particularly rough part of the journey, the group passes three African women and an infant pleading for water. Nan begs her husband, Gareth, to stop. When he doesn't, she frantically, though too late, throws their water bottle from the vehicle. Relating the author's message in this story, Yardley commented, "Rush has presented in Nan and Gareth opposing white attitudes toward Africa, and by placing them inside a single marriage has shown how intimately connected they are."

Another story—"Instruments of Seduction," which received the Aga Khan Fiction Prize after its original appearance in the *Paris Review*—depicts a middle-aged American dentist's wife, Ione, in one episode of her secret career of seducing men. Ione believes that skillfully manipulated allusions to death and danger are erotic, and she finds the atmosphere of expatriate life in Botswana conducive to satisfying her desires. Assessing Ione's acclimation to Botswana's climate, Leslie Marmon Silko in the *New York Times Book Review* remarked that ironically Ione is one of few foreigners able "to grasp the possibilities for personal salvation Africa offers them despite all its contradictions and ugly colonial legacies. . . . She not only fashions a sense of self and identity that keeps her humanity intact, she also manages to realize how the terrifying atmosphere of Botswana can actually be used to deliver her from isolation and loneliness."

Ione also appears in the stories "Official Americans" and "Alone in Africa." In the former she persuades an American agency bureaucrat, Carl, to seek a local medicine man to cure him of insomnia caused by a neighbor's barking dog. When the prescribed witchcraft results in permanent injury to Carl, he is nevertheless overjoyed, believing that the price of white life in black Africa makes any cost a bargain. In "Alone in Africa" Ione's husband, Frank, is visited by the seductive young daughter of a neighbor's maid. Described by Christopher Lehmann-Haupt in the *New York Times* as "a perfect little sexual psychodrama," the story reveals Frank's weakness and propensity for self-delusion and delineates the girl's victory, achieved by her drive and cunning, as well as by her youth, strength, and poverty.

The remaining stories in the collection—"Bruns" and "Thieving"—render, according to Packer, a vision of political futility: "Simply put, any effort at change does more harm than good, though vanity and naivete will delude us into trying." In "Bruns" a Dutch pacifist volunteer is unable to free a tribe from its violent injustices and ends up killing himself out of revenge. And in "Thieving" a christianized African boy, Paul Ojang, interprets the various injustices and temptations to which he is subjected as comprehensible only if God desires that he, an honest boy, become a thief. Paul's effort to retain his personal integrity while satisfying God's injunction to steal is doomed to tragic failure.

Asserting that Rush is "a master at plot," Packer observed that "his stories often end with an ironic inversion on a nearly farcical chain of events that exposes the self-deception his characters use to detach themselves from any meaningful connection to other lives. . . . Their lack of conviction haunts them without initiating deep change." Critic Silko concurred: "The failure of American idealism and technical resources that Mr. Rush describes in these stories, and the subsequent disillusionment—both national and personal—are second only to the Vietnam War in their continuing impact on the direction of American foreign and domestic policy today."

Rush, in *Whites,* has been further hailed for not offering simplistic analyses of the political and economic crises in southern Africa. Silko, for example, stated that "Rush attempts to articulate what Americans or whites in general may be able to salvage where the legacies of apartheid and colonialism make it almost impossible to live and remain decent human beings." The author seems to be saying, Silko suggested, that "it isn't just whites who must face up to moral and political failures in the third world today." Deeming Rush "an effective political writer," Steve Katz in the *American Book Review* noted that the author "has the experience and talent to give us the political forces operating in the lives of ordinary, imperfect people." "If we are honest with ourselves," added the reviewer, "we have no trouble isolating the contradictions and ironies in the attitudes of Carl, Ione, Frank, etc., in our own hearts. We can be grateful to Norman Rush for identifying them with so much wit and compassion, so that the healing might begin."

Lehmann-Haupt noted minor difficulties in the conceptions and structures of Rush's stories, criticizing that "here and there, [Rush's] endings are a trifle abrupt or heavy-handed" and that "there are passages where the characters' behavior is psychologically fuzzy." He qualified those remarks, however, with the observation that the author may be doing this intentionally in order to heighten the unreal and hallucinatory feel of some of the stories. Comments like Katz's, though, were more common: "*Whites* is a terrific book, important for our understanding of white people in the world, particularly of the roles of whites in Botswana. Everyone should read it. . . . Rush is an extraordinary writer."

Rush's first novel, *Mating,* follows a young, female American anthropologist in Botswana as she sets out in search of Nelson Denoon, the American man who has set up a utopian society called Tsau, run by and for poor African women. Verlyn Klinkenborg wrote in the *New Republic,* "*Mating* is not a fairy tale or a chivalric romance. It's an extremely sophisticated dramatic monologue, one of whose many theses is that only a woman has heart enough to search for heroic love." *Nation* reviewer David Kaufman noted, "Although far from obvious at first, *Mating* is a satirical con of sorts, a delicious comedy of manners that toys with its all-wise narrator." Kaufman continued, Rush "emerges as a puppeteer pulling strings by inverting sexist roles, letting his readers draw the comparisons implicit in his characters' movements." A *Publishers Weekly* reviewer, "Even readers who remember the luminous stories in Rush's debut, *Whites*, may not be prepared for the cleverness, humor, insight into human nature, and intellectual acuity demonstrated in this accomplished novel."

Mortals, Rush's second novel is also set in Botswana. The book tells the story of Ray, a CIA agent who works undercover as a teacher. Ray is deeply in love with his beautiful wife, Iris, who is having an affair with Davis Morel, a black American holistic healer. Ray suspects that something is amiss in their relationship. His suspicions are confirmed when, during a mission for the CIA, he is caught and imprisoned with Morel, who speaks the truth about his relationship with Iris. A reviewer in the *Economist* noted, "At its heart, *Mortals* isn't about political intrigue, but a marriage. . . . . Mr. Rush is a master at parsing the seemingly casual exchange between true inmates. And although much of the novel is bitterly funny, he also captures the genuine agony of his cuckold." The reviewer also observed that Rush "has a canny understanding of Africa, a profound appreciation for the fine points of romantic love, a muscular style of description, and an eye for character so frighteningly sharp that it argues against running across the man at parties." A *Publishers Weekly* critic explained that *Mortals* is both a "textured, erotic portrait of a disintegrating marriage and a society in flux" and "a political thriller infused with violence." The same critic concluded that "the richness of Rush's vision," and his "stringent moral clarity, sweep the reader into his brilliantly observed world." A *Kirkus Reviews* writer pointed out that "*Mortals* isn't easy going," but felt that "Rush's authoritative grasp of his subject, rich characterizations, and complex handling of social issues of sexual and political fidelity, morality, and mortality make it a reading experience not to be missed." Writing in the *New Republic*, reviewer James Wood declared "*Mortals* to be many things, but said the book's central achievement has to be the fidelity with which it represents consciousness, the way in which it

traces the mind's own language. This concern with the insides of our minds makes Rush almost an original in contemporary American writing."

BIOGRAPHICAL AND CRITICAL SOURCES:

BOOKS

Contemporary Literary Criticism, Volume 44, Gale (Detroit, MI), 1986.

PERIODICALS

Africa Today, winter, 1993, Sheldon G. Weeks, review of *Mating,* p. 79.
American Book Review, March-April, 1987; December 1992, review of *Mating,* p. 15.
Antioch Review, summer, 1992, review of *Mating,* p. 594.
Booklist, July 1, 1991, review of *Mating,* p. 2012; January 15, 1992, review of *Mating,* p. 870; April 1, 2003, Hazel Rochman, review of *Mortals,* p. 1355.
Economist, May 31, 2003, "Number One Detective Agent; New American Fiction," p. 84.
Esquire, September 1991, review of *Mating,* p. 68.
Fortune, May 26, 2003, Erik Torkells, review of *Mortals,* p. 178.
Guardian, September 12, 1993, review of *Mating,* p. 28; October 24, 1993, review of *Whites,* p. 28.
Kirkus Reviews, July 1, 1991, review of *Mating,* p. 820; May 1, 2003, review of *Mortals,* p. 638.
Kliatt Young Adult Paperback Book Guide, November, 1992, review of *Mating,* p. 11.
Library Journal, September 1, 1991, review of *Mating,* p. 232; Barbara Hoffert, May 15, 2003, review of *Mortals,* p. 127.
Los Angeles Times Book Review, March 9, 1986.
Nation, May 24, 1986; November 18, 1991, David Kaufman, review of *Mating,* p. 638; December 30, 1991, review of *Mating,* p. 856; August 24, 1998, review of *Mating,* p. 25.
New Republic, December 23, 1991, Verlyn Klinkenborg, review of *Mating,* p. 44; June 23, 2003, James Wood, "Thinking," p. 34.
Newsweek, September 16, 1991, review of *Mating,* p. 62; October 21, 1991, review of *Mating,* p. 66.

New Yorker, October 21, 1991, review of *Mating,* p. 129; June 2, 2003, John Updike, "Botswana Blues," p. 97.

New York Review of Books, October 10, 1991, review of *Mating,* p. 33.

New York Times, February 27, 1986; April 19, 1986; September 12, 1991, review of *Mating,* p. C17.

New York Times Book Review, March 23, 1986; September 22, 1991, review of *Mating,* p. 3; October 11, 1992, review of *Whites,* p. 36.

Observer (London, England), November 22, 1992, review of *Mating,* p. 63; August 22, 1993, review of *Mating,* p. 48.

Partisan Review, February, 1992, review of *Mating,* p. 282.

Publishers Weekly, June 21, 1991, review of *Mating,* p. 52; November 1, 1991, review of *Mating,* p. 20; June 29, 1992, review of *Mating,* p. 58; April 21, 2003, review of *Mortals,* p. 35.

Time, July 7, 1986; January 6, 1992, review of *Mating,* p. 74.

Times Literary Supplement, September 18, 1992, review of *Mating,* p. 24.

Tribune Books (Chicago, IL), September 1, 1991, review of *Mating,* p. 1; December 8, 1991, review of *Mating,* p. 10; September 20, 1992, review of *Mating,* p. 2.

Virginia Quarterly Review, winter, 1992, review of *Mating,* p. 24.

Wall Street Journal, September 17, 1991, review of *Mating,* p. A14.

Washington Post Book World, March 23, 1986; September 8, 1991, review of *Mating,* p. 3.

World & I, November, 1991, review of *Mating,* p. 402.

ONLINE

Alfred A. Knopf Web site, http://www.randomhouse. com/knopf/ (November 5, 2003).

Christian Science Monitor Online, http://www. csmonitor.com/ (June 5, 2003), Ron Charles, "One Man's Paradise, Lost in Africa."

LA Weekly Online, http://www.laweekly.com/ (November 5, 2003), "Botswana Blues."

National Book Foundation Web site, http://www. nationalbook.org/ (November 5, 2003), "Interview with Norm Rush."

Newsday Online, http://www.newsday.com/ (November 5, 2003), Dan Cryer, "Puffs of Wind around an African Desert."

New York Magazine Online, http://www.newyorkmetro. com/ (May 26, 2003), John Homans, "Mortal Splendor."

New York Observer Online, http://www.observer.com/ (November 5, 2003), Jennifer Egan, "A Man Who Loves His Mate: Rush's Post-coital Comedy."

Peace Corps Writers Web site, http://www. peacecorpswriters.org/ (November 5, 2003), "Talking with Norm Rush."

Time Online, http://www.time.com/ (November 5, 2003), Lev Grossman, "A Spy in the House of Love."

*　　*　　*

RUSSELL, Dick
   See RUSSELL, Richard B.

*　　*　　*

RUSSELL, Richard B. 1947-
  (Dick Russell)

PERSONAL: Born August 19, 1947, in Minneapolis, MN; son of Clarence H. (an advertising executive) and Olive (a piano instructor and composer; maiden name, Nelson) Russell; married Etta Green; children: Franklin D. *Education:* University of Kansas, B.A., 1969. *Hobbies and other interests:* Fishing, music.

ADDRESSES: Office—8118 Hollywood Blvd., Los Angeles, CA 90069. *Agent*—Sarah Jane Freymann, Stepping Stone Literary Agency, 59 West 71st St., New York, NY 10023. *E-mail*—dickrussell@dickrussell.org.

CAREER: Journalist and author. *Topeka Capital-Journal* (newspaper), Topeka, KS, sports and feature writer, columnist, 1965-72; *Sports Illustrated* (magazine), New York, NY, reporter, 1969-70; *TV Guide* (magazine), Los Angeles, CA, writer, 1977-79; freelance journalist, 1980—. President of Striped Bass Emergency Council, 1984—; clerk for Menemsha Pond Preservation Trust, 1995-96.

MEMBER: Society of Environmental Journalists, PEN USA West.

AWARDS, HONORS: Golden Swordfish Award, National Coalition for Marine Conservation, 1984; Chevron Conservation Award, 1988, for exceptional service to the cause of conservation; *Los Angeles Times* and *Washington Post* Best Book of the Year designations, both 2001, both for *Eye of the Whale.*

WRITINGS:

UNDER NAME DICK RUSSELL

The Man Who Knew Too Much (nonfiction), Carroll & Graf (New York, NY), 1992, revised edition, 2003.

Black Genius and the American Experience, Carroll & Graf (New York, NY), 1998.

Eye of the Whale; Epic Passage from Baja to Siberia, Simon & Schuster (New York, NY), 2001.

Contributor to periodicals, including *Village Voice, Nation, In These Times, New Times, Harper's Weekly, True, Boston Globe Magazine, Today's Health, Family Health, E, Parenting, New Age, Mother Jones, Ecologist, Los Angeles Times Book Review,* and *Saltwater Sportsman.* Contributing editor to *Argosy,* 1975-76; *Boston,* 1981-83; and *Amicus Journal* (now *Onearth*), 1986—.

WORK IN PROGRESS: A children's book on gray whales; a book about the Fort Hill community; research on environmental subjects.

SIDELIGHTS: During the 1970s and 1980s, Richard "Dick" Russell built a career as a journalist, specializing in sports and environmental issues. At the same time, however, he was investigating the controversy and mystery surrounding the 1963 assassination of U.S. President John F. Kennedy. In a *Los Angeles Times Book Review* article about his 1992 book, *The Man Who Knew Too Much,* Russell revealed that it "became, by the spring of 1978, a curious kind of journalistic double life. The day passed inside my then-office at *TV Guide*'s Hollywood bureau, writing about taking a road trip with [comedian] Bob Hope. At twilight I found myself in a dimly lit Irish bar, sitting across from a tall, scarred man who kept a wary eye on the other patrons. Once, he had been an agent of the CIA—and the KGB."

The double-agent of whom Russell writes in *The Man Who Knew Too Much* is Richard Case Nagell, who claimed, according to the author-reporter, to have had orders from the KGB to kill Lee Harvey Oswald in order to prevent Oswald from assassinating President Kennedy. Nagell alleged that the U.S. Central Intelligence Agency (CIA) and Federal Bureau of Investigation (FBI) both knew about the assassination plot—which also sought to place the blame for the president's death upon communist Cuba—but did nothing to stop it. Nagell maintained that he got cold feet about killing Oswald. He was supposed to do it in Mexico in September, 1963, but he purposely got himself put in federal custody for firing shots inside a Texas bank. He was in prison when President Kennedy was murdered in Dallas, Texas, on November 22, 1963.

In his *Los Angeles Times Book Review* article, Russell commented on the fate of three individuals he interviewed for *The Man Who Knew Too Much.* "Shortly after we met [two interviewees] ended up dead; another survived a gunshot to the head. It was, to say the least, an unsettling pursuit." Of his own fascination with the subject of the Kennedy assassination, Russell remarked: "I cannot exclude myself from the legion of private-citizen detectives who pursue new clues about the tragedy of Dallas with indefatigable perseverance (or, some observers might say, with a monomania that makes Captain Ahab look like a well-rounded man)."

The Man Who Knew Too Much received favorable attention from some critics. A *Publishers Weekly* reviewer concluded: "No praise can be too high for Russell's mastery of a massive quantity of detail, for his determination to seek out primary sources and for his refusal to over-dramatize. This is a model work of historical reconstruction."

Russell compiled his 1998 book, *Black Genius and the American Experience,* to provide inspiration for his biracial son. The book's theme is the interconnectedness throughout the generations; Russell focuses on thirty-three African-American men and women, weaving their stories together "in a refreshingly atypical narrative style of juxtapositions rather than linearity," as Susan Hamburger put it in her *Library Journal* review. Some of the portraits are of famous persons; others are "black innovators often omitted from white America's history books," as a *Publishers Weekly* contributor explained.

Russell undertakes an investigation of a different sort in 2001's *Eye of the Whale: Epic Passage from Baja to Siberia.* The book follows the trek of the gray whale, a species that inhabited both the Atlantic and Pacific for centuries before being nearly rendered extinct through harvesting. Conservation efforts have helped bring back some of their numbers, but, as Russell points out in his book, the future of the gray whale is still threatened by hunting. As one of the case studies from the book notes, the Native American Makah tribe of the Olympic Peninsula off the coast of Washington successfully lobbied to hunt a gray whale as part of their native tradition. The event attracted advocates from both sides of the hunting issue: environmentalists, the U.S. Coast Guard, tribal police, and the International Whaling Commission. The hunting party killed one gray whale with a harpoon, amid a media storm of protest. "Though the ensuing struggle between Indians and ecologists wound up being portrayed as a culture war," Sally Eckhoff wrote in *Newsday* that "we learn from Russell's elaborate and painstaking explanation that the situation was vastly more complicated. He shows that any simple accounting of the conflict remains in doubt, even while the idea that the payoff could be strictly spiritual is effectively deep-sixed." Meanwhile, with international concerns, "the most alarming aspect of Russell's tidal wave of information is how close the gray whale is to being put back on the menu in countries that can do a lot more damage to it than the Makah ever could," as Eckhoff stated.

Because of its tendency to feed near shorelines, the gray whale has become a favorite of tourists who gather for whale-watching expeditions. *Eye of the Whale* tracks the animals' annual migration from the Baja region of Mexico to the Bering Strait. The author follows the route "up the coast to Alaska and then around to Siberia, including the remote Sakhalin Island . . . , interviewing scientists and naturalists as he goes, and this is the backbone of his book," reported *Washington Post* contributor Nicols Fox. *Eye of the Whale* also chronicles the work of nineteenth-century whale expert Captain Charles Melville Scammon. Scammon, who began his career as a commercial whaler, was responsible for the killing of countless gray whales; later he became a noted authority on the animal, and his writings are still respected as scientific literature. "When Scammon is on the page the book soars, especially when Russell artfully arranges excerpts from Scammon's own papers and scrapbooks," stated Neal Matthews in a *San Diego Union Tribune* article.

Russell's inclusion of whale husbandry, whaling lore, and modern controversy makes for a large—688

pages—and sometimes unwieldy volume, in the opinion of some reviewers. "With so many stories to tell, Russell's compelling challenge must have been weaving them together into a seamless whole," Fox continued. "He doesn't entirely achieve that goal." "It's impossible not to say it: This is a whale of a book—massive, shapely, surprisingly agile and overblessed with blubber," commented Matthews. "Five hundred pages would have been more than enough; 400 might have made it a classic."

Still, *Eye of the Whale* was warmly received by critics, Matthews concluding that Russell has compiled "an engaging, highly readable account that mostly succeeds in melding history, culture and science." While "big and heavy, with a complex construction and a maddingly confusing cast of characters," commented Fox, the book is nonetheless "worth every minute devoted to it." "Better than anyone else to date," Nathaniel Philbrick commented in the *New York Times Book Review,* "Russell has documented the historical and cultural importance of the gray whale to the peoples, past and present, of the Pacific Coast." And to *Los Angeles Times Book Review* critic Richard Ellis, Russell's book is nothing less than the last word on gray whales: "Once in a while, a book comes along that redefines its subject to the extent that most previous works immediately become obsolete." *Eye of the Whale,* Ellis noted, "is such a book."

Russell once told *CA:* "Writing has been my primary interest since I was in grade school and used to read my short stories and epic novel (*sans* paragraphs) aloud to my classmates. I was a sportswriter in high school and college, and later achieved my dream of going to work for *Sports Illustrated.* But, I suddenly found that my interests had broadened considerably during the turmoil of the late 1960s. I was greatly influenced during my formative years by, among others, Henry Miller and Norman Mailer—both of whom I later had the marvelous opportunity to get to know. My fascination with uncovering more of the truth behind the assassination of President Kennedy began in the early 1970s, a long odyssey into the dark side of recent history which preoccupied me off and on for nearly twenty years. What I hoped to achieve by setting down the results of my quest was a greater consciousness of the tragedy from which I believe the country has never recovered. Until the full truth is known about the forces behind the murders of all four great leaders of the 1960s—John and Robert Kennedy, Martin Luther King, Jr., and Malcolm X—we cannot honestly move forward as a nation. In authoring articles about environmental concerns, and in writing a book about the genius of African Americans who remain largely unknown in our history, my goal is the same: to achieve a heightened understanding, one which might inspire young people in particular to become more involved in fighting for a stronger democracy.

"My latest book took me by surprise," Russell later added. "In March of 1998, my wife and I traveled to San Ignacio Lagoon along Mexico's Baja California peninsula, where I had a magazine assignment to write about plans to build the world's largest salt factory within the last pristine breeding ground of the gray whale. In venturing out among these majestic animals in a small boat, I experienced what scientists have called 'the friendly whale phenomenon.' Numerous whales came over, mothers introducing their newborns, each seeking a human touch. The whales simply captured my heart and I resolved to tell their story.

"I ended up following their nearly 6,000-mile-long migration—the longest made by any mammal—from Mexico to the remote reaches of northern Alaska and the Russian Far East. My adventures were many, including traveling by an old Russian tank across snow-covered mountainsides and river valleys to reach a remote Eskimo village. I followed the historical path taken by a renowned whaling captain, Charles Melville Scammon, who underwent a metamorphosis from whale killer to naturalist and author of a definitive book on the marine mammals of the Pacific northwest.

"So the book became a combination of personal travel odyssey, history, and science—based upon interviews with numerous marine biologists—as well as addressing the environmental problems still faced by whales despite a moratorium on the sale of whale products worldwide. The question I was left with is, can we humans survive what whales cannot?—global warming, toxic contamination and noise pollution, carelessness about our habitats in general? By telling the story of the eventually successful fight against the saltworks, I hoped again to offer inspiration to others involved in their own battles to preserve our planetary home."

Russell considers himself "a writer/activist," and explained: "When writing, I follow a basic pattern. I gather far more research than I will ever be able to use, then home in on the essentials. If I have prepared well, often I find that my material almost writes itself. My advice to young writers is to read as many diverse types of authors as possible, having faith that one's own style will eventually emerge. Also, keep a daily journal and seek a wide range of interests. Explore relationships, and one's own being as it unfolds through these relationships, as deeply as you can. A writer needs to experience life to the fullest extent, and be willing to face one's own limitations at the same time."

BIOGRAPHICAL AND CRITICAL SOURCES:

PERIODICALS

Baltimore Sun, August 18, 2001, John Muncie, review of *Eye of the Whale: Epic Journey from Baja to Siberia.*

Booklist, February 15, 1998, review of *Black Genius and the American Experience,* p. 974; June 1, 2001, Nancy Bent, review of *Eye of the Whale,* p. 1810.

Choice, July, 1999, review of *Black Genius and the American Experience,* p. 1953.

Kirkus Reviews, February 15, 1998, review of *Black Genius and the American Experience,* p. 260; May 1, 2001, review of *Eye of the Whale.*

Kliatt Young Adult Paperback Book Guide, May, 1999, review of *Black Genius and the American Experience,* p. 35.

Library Journal, January, 1998, Susan Hamburger, review of *Black Genius and the American Experience,* p. 117; June 1, 2001, Judith B. Barnett, review of *Eye of the Whale,* p. 206.

Los Angeles Times Book Review, February 7, 1993, pp. 1, 5; August 5, 2002, Richard Ellis, review of *Eye of the Whale.*

Milwaukee Journal Sentinel, August 11, 2001, Curt Schleier, "Eye-Catching."

Newsday (New York, NY), August 12, 2001, Sally Eckhoff, review of *Eye of the Whale.*

New York Times Book Review, August 12, 2001, Nathaniel Philbrick, "The Jolly Gray Giant," p. 6.

Publishers Weekly, November 16, 1992, p. 51; December 22, 1997, review of *Black Genius and the American Experience,* p. 48; June 18, 2001, review of *Eye of the Whale,* p. 70.

St. Louis Post-Dispatch, August 19, 2001, Patricia Corrigan, review of *Eye of the Whale.*

San Diego Union Tribune, July 15, 2001, Neal Matthews, "Thar He Blows."

Virginia Quarterly Review, spring, 2002, review of *Eye of the Whale,* p. 68.

Wall Street Journal, August 10, 2001, Adam Goodheart, "Gentle Leviathans," p. W14.

Washington Post, August 5, 2001, Nicols Fox, "Living Large," p. T5.

ONLINE

Dick Russell Web site, http://www.dickrussell.org/ (February 15, 2004).

S

SANDERS, Scott Russell 1945-

PERSONAL: Born October 26, 1945, in Memphis, TN; son of Greeley Ray (in farming and industrial relations) and Eva (Solomon) Sanders; married Ruth Ann McClure (a medical researcher), August 27, 1967; children: Eva Rachel, Jesse Solomon. *Education:* Brown University, B.A. (summa cum laude), 1967; Cambridge University, Ph.D., 1971. *Hobbies and other interests:* Carpentry, hiking, bicycling, canoeing, gardening.

ADDRESSES: Home—1113 East Wylie St., Bloomington, IN 47401. *Office*—Department of English, Indiana University, Bloomington, IN 47405; fax: 812-855-3780. *E-mail*—sanders1@indiana.edu.

CAREER: Indiana University, Bloomington, assistant professor, 1971-74, associate professor, 1975-80, professor of English, 1980-96, distinguished professor, 1996—, director of the Wells Scholars Program, 1997—.

MEMBER: Phi Beta Kappa, Land Institute, Orion Society, Nature Conservancy, Audubon Society, Wilderness Society.

AWARDS, HONORS: Marshall scholarship, 1967-71; Bennett fellowship in creative writing, 1974-75; fellowship, National Endowment for the Arts, 1983-84; Editor's Choice, *Booklist,* 1985, for *Hear the Wind Blow: American Folksongs Retold;* Penrod Award,

Scott Russell Sanders

1986, for *Stone Country;* award for creative nonfiction, Associated Writing Programs, 1987, for *The Paradise of Bombs;* PEN Syndicated Fiction Award, 1988; award for literacy excellence, *Kenyon Review,* 1991; Frederick Bachman Lieber Award for Distinguished Teaching, Indiana University, 1992; Ohioana

Book Award in Nonfiction, 1994, for *Staying Put;* Lannan Literary Award in Nonfiction, 1995; Great Lakes Book Award, 1996, for *Writing from the Center;* John Burroughs Award, for best natural history essay, 2000.

WRITINGS:

D. H. Lawrence: The World of the Major Novels, Viking (New York, NY), 1974.

Wilderness Plots: Tales about the Settlement of the American Land, Morrow (New York, NY), 1983.

Fetching the Dead: Stories, University of Illinois Press (Urbana, IL), 1984.

Wonders Hidden: Audubon's Early Years, Capra (Santa Barbara, CA), 1984.

Terrarium, Tor Books (New York, NY), 1985.

Stone Country, Indiana University Press (Bloomington, IN), 1985, revised edition published as *In Limestone Country,* Beacon Press (Boston, MA), 1991.

Hear the Wind Blow: American Folksongs Retold, Bradbury Press (Scarsdale, NY), 1985.

Audubon Reader: The Best Writings of John James Audubon, Indiana University Press (Bloomington, IN), 1986.

Bad Man Ballad, Bradbury Press (New York, NY), 1986.

The Paradise of Bombs, University of Georgia Press (Athens, GA), 1987.

The Engineer of Beasts, Orchard (New York, NY), 1988.

The Invisible Company, Tor Books (New York, NY), 1989.

Aurora Means Dawn, Bradbury Press (Scarsdale, NY), 1989.

Secrets of the Universe: Scenes from the Journey Home, Beacon Press (Boston, MA), 1991.

Warm As Wool, Atheneum/Simon & Schuster (New York, NY), 1992.

Staying Put: Making a Home in a Restless World, Beacon Press (Boston, MA), 1993.

Here Comes the Mystery Man, Macmillan (New York, NY), 1994.

Writing from the Center, Indiana University Press (Bloomington, IN), 1995.

The Floating House, Atheneum/Simon & Schuster (New York, NY), 1995.

A Place Called Freedom, Atheneum/Simon & Schuster (New York, NY), 1997.

Meeting Trees, National Geographic Society (Washington, DC), 1997.

Hunting for Hope, Beacon Press (Boston, MA), 1998.

The Country of Language, Milkweed Editions (Minneapolis, MN), 1999.

Crawdad Creek, National Geographic Society (Washington, DC), 1999.

The Force of Spirit, Beacon Press (Boston, MA), 2000.

(With Will Counts and James H. Madison) *Bloomington Past and Present,* Indiana University Press (Bloomington, IN), 2002.

Contributor to books, including *Openings: Original Essays by Contemporary Soviet and American Writers,* edited by Robert Atwan and Valeri Vinokurov, University of Washington Press (Seattle, WA), 1990; *Communion: Contemporary Writers Reveal the Bible in Their Lives,* edited by David Rosenberg, Anchor Books (New York, NY), 1996; *Fathering Daughters: Reflections by Men,* edited by DeWitt Henry and James Alan McPherson, Beacon Press (Boston, MA), 1998; *Falling toward Grace: Images of Religion and Culture from the Heartland,* edited by J. Kent Calder and Susan Neville, Indiana University Press (Bloomington, IN), 1998; and *Our Fathers: Reflections by Sons,* edited by Steven L. Shepherd, Beacon Press (Boston, MA), 2001. Contributor to anthologies. Author of column, "One Man's Fiction,"*Chicago Sun-Times,* 1977-83. Contributor to literary journals and popular magazines, including *Audubon, Orion, North American Review, Georgia Review, Omni, Harper's, Kenyon Review, Sewanee Review, Michigan Quarterly Review, Seattle Review, Northern Lights, Wild Earth* and *Utne Reader.*

SIDELIGHTS: Scott Russell Sanders is the author of books for children and nonfiction for adults. No matter what the genre, his work evinces a concern for and appreciation of nature. He grew up near the Ravenna Arsenal in northeastern Ohio, "a landscape and community that seem unlikely to produce a nature writer," as an essayist for *American Nature Writers* stated. Yet it was pondering the weapons of death housed in the arsenal that inspired his love of nature, as Sanders has made clear in his writings. His essays, stories, and novels all seek to understand how mankind created such a violent world, and how it could be transformed into something better. Sanders studied physics at Brown University, then changed his focus to literature, doing graduate work at Cambridge University. He lived in England for four years, writing some short stories that were published in periodicals and later collected in book form, in *Fetching the Dead.* He also did extensive study of the work of D. H. Lawrence and his writings on love. In 1974, he published *D. H. Lawrence: The World of the Major Novels.*

His next book, *Stone Country,* describes the limestone quarries in Indiana, and the men who worked in them. He explores the source of the stone that makes up many of America's most important buildings, including the Empire State Building and the Pentagon. *A Paradise of Bombs,* published two years later, offers essays "crafted so beautifully that they have been mistaken for short stories," according to an *American Nature Writers* contributor. "These essays often teeter on the edge of despair, as though Sanders were unsure of finding enough light to counter the darkness he describes."

Secrets of the Universe: Scenes from the Journey Home is a highly personal collection of essays. Sanders's childhood, which was marked with pain and guilt due to his father's alcoholism, is the basis of many of the narratives, yet his recollections lead into larger musings on family relations, neighborhood, region, and the world. It is "an engaging sampling of intellect enlivened by imagination," recommended a reviewer for *Publishers Weekly.* In *Staying Put: Making a Home in a Restless World,* the writer reflects on the necessity of, and difficulty in, finding a sense of community in a world that has become increasingly rootless. He believes that remaining loyal to a place, and trying to learn about it, can awaken a sense of self and of the inherent order in nature. Incorporating biology, physics, poetry, Taoism, and more, it is "a wise and beautifully written book," stated a *Publishers Weekly* writer. Similar themes were the basis of *Writing from the Center.*

Sanders has written several books for young readers, incorporating themes of history and nature. In *Crawdad Creek,* a girl visits a creek near her home in the company of her brother. In her reflections on the water and the land and life around it, "many concrete sensory images help keep the poetic text grounded in reality and accessible to young children," advised Carolyn Phelan in *Booklist.* In *A Place Called Freedom,* a young boy named James Starman is freed from slavery in 1832, and then travels to Indiana with his family to start a new life there. James's father travels back to Tennessee whenever he can to bring more freed blacks with him, and eventually a village named Freedom grows up around this little community. The book is "a

lyrical intertwining of fact and fiction," according to a *Publishers Weekly* critic, who further recommended it as a "concise and eloquent story."

Sanders returned to the essay form with *The Country of Language* and *The Force of the Spirit.* In *The Country of Language,* he goes back to his childhood and college years, his involvement in the civil rights and antiwar movements, and the origin of his "determinedly positive way of thinking about our relationship with the world around us," explained Donna Seaman in *Booklist.* Nancy Patterson Shires, reviewing the book for *Library Journal,* also recommended it for the author's "usual articulate and well-crafted prose." In *The Force of Spirit,* Sanders took on what he considered the ultimate questions of life: "the death of parents and marriage of children, the valuable lessons of the natural world, and the sacredness of good work and good writing," stated Shires. The fourteen essays in the book discuss subjects from sustainable agriculture to literature to carpentry, but all are written in "simple, clean prose," wrote a *Publishers Weekly* reviewer, in which "Sanders finds his critical truths."

Sanders once told *CA:* "I have long been divided, in my life and in my work, between science and the arts. Early on, in graduate school, this took the form of choosing literary studies rather than theoretical physics. When I began writing fiction in my late twenties, I wanted to ask, through literature, many of the fundamental questions that scientists ask. In particular, I wanted to understand our place in nature, trace the sources of our violence, and speculate about the future evolution of our species. My writing might seem diverse in form—realistic fiction, science fiction, folktales, stories for children, personal essays, historical novels—yet it is bound together by this web of questions. In all of my work, regardless of period or style, I am concerned with the ways in which human beings come to terms with the practical problems of living on a small planet, in nature and in communities. I am concerned with the life people make together, in marriages and families and towns, more than with the life of isolated individuals.

"I do not much value experimentation in form and style, if it is not inspired by new insights into human experience. I do value clarity of language and vision. Much of my writing deals with the lives of rural people, with children, with the elderly, with outcasts, with figures who are neither literary nor intellectual;

and I would like the real-life counterparts of those people to be engaged and moved by my fiction and essays.

"I have worked on several literary magazines, and I feel their health is a good gauge of the health of literature at any given time. I have also worked against the Vietnam War, nuclear weapons, and the militarization of America, and in favor of protecting wild lands, other creatures, and the habitability of earth. Marriage and child-rearing are two of the most important influences on the shaping of my imagination."

Sanders later added: "In recent years, my impulse toward realism and social commentary has been expressed mainly in nonfiction, personal essays and fact-based narratives. My fiction, meanwhile, has become increasingly speculative, playing with our notions of reality, transforming the familiar into the fabulous.

"I believe that a writer should be a servant of language, community, and nature. Language is the creation and sustenance of community; and any community, if it is to be healthy and durable, must be respectful of the natural order which makes life possible. Because there is no true human existence apart from family and community, I feel a deep commitment to my region, to the land, to the people and all other living things with which I share this place. My writing is driven by a deep regard for particular places and voices, persons and tools, plants and animals, for human skills and stories, for the small change of daily life—a regard compounded of grief and curiosity and love. If my writing does not help my neighbors to live more alertly, pleasurably, or wisely, then it is worth little.

"I wish to convey through my work an awareness that existence itself is miraculous, and that the earth is bountiful beyond our deserving or reckoning."

BIOGRAPHICAL AND CRITICAL SOURCES:

BOOKS

American Nature Writers, Scribner (New York, NY), 2002.

PERIODICALS

Arts Indiana, December, 1987; October, 1993; October, 1995.

Booklist, November 15, 1992, Kathryn Broderick, review of *Warm As Wool,* p. 611; June 1, 1993, Angus Trimnel, review of *Staying Put: Making a* *Home in a Restless World,* p. 1772; June 1, 1997, Kay Weisman, review of *A Place Called Freedom,* p. 1721; September 1, 1998, GraceAnne A. DeCandido, review of *Hunting for Hope,* p. 56; November 15, 1999, Donna Seaman, review of *The Country of Language,* p. 595; December 1, 1999, Carolyn Phelan, review of *Crawdad Creek,* p. 714.

Boston Globe, October 6, 1998.

Chronicle of Higher Education, October 2, 1998.

Detroit News, June 14, 1987.

Fourth Genre, spring, 1999.

Georgia Review, winter, 1992; summer, 1994.

Horn Book Magazine, September-October, 1988; September-October, 1989, Mary M. Burns, review of *Aurora Means Dawn,* p. 616.

Indianapolis Star, October 11, 1998.

Journal of Kentucky Studies, 1994.

Kenyon Review, summer-fall, 1996; winter, 2000.

Library Journal, November 1, 1991, Lynn Randall, review of *Secrets of the Universe: Scenes from the Journey Home,* p. 99; May 15, 1993, Tim Markus, review of *Staying Put,* p. 86; September 1, 1995, Nancy Patterson Shires, review of *Writing from the Center,* p. 177; November 1, 1999, Nancy Patterson Shires, review of *The Country of Language,* p. 82; October 1, 2000, Nancy Patterson Shires, review of *The Force of Spirit,* p. 98.

Los Angeles Times, January 10, 1987.

Los Angeles Times Book Review, May 26, 1985; April 13, 1986; October 29, 1995.

New York Times Book Review, January 26, 1986; November 9, 1986; May 24, 1987; June 27, 1997, Christopher Paul Curtis, review of *A Place Called Freedom,* p. 22.

Ohioana Quarterly, spring, 1996.

Publishers Weekly, October 14, 1988, review of *The Engineer of Beasts,* p. 78; June 30, 1989, review of *Aurora Means Dawn,* p. 104; October 4, 1991, review of *Secrets of the Universe,* p. 74; April 26, 1993, review of *Staying Put,* p. 63; July 26, 1993, review of *Here Comes the Mystery Man,* p. 72; August 21, 1995, review of *Writing from the Center,* p. 54; May 19, 1997, review of *A Place Called Freedom,* p. 76; August 10, 1998; January 4, 1999, review of *Warm As Wool,* p. 92; August 9, 1999, review of *Natural Wonders,* p. 354; December 13, 1999, review of *The Floating House,* p. 85; September 11, 2000, review of *The Force of Spirit,* p. 75; December 18, 2000, review of *A Place Called Freedom,* p. 80.

School Library Journal, November, 1989, Eleanor K. MacDonald, review of *Aurora Means Dawn,* p. 93;

December, 1992, Patricia Pearl Dole, review of *Warm As Wool,* p. 90; October, 1993, Beth Tegart, review of *Here Comes the Mystery Man,* p. 111; February, 1996, Molly Connally, review of *Writing from the Center,* p. 134; July, 1997, Lucinda Snyder Whitehurst, review of *Meeting Trees,* p. 74; August, 1997, Wendy Lukehart, review of *A Place Called Freedom,* p. 141.

Southern Review, spring, 1992; Edward Lueders, review of *Secrets of the Universe,* p. 412.

Sun, February, 2000.

Traces: Indiana Historical Society, spring, 1996.

Tribune Books (Chicago, IL), July 12, 1987.

Washington Post Book World, April 30, 1989.

Water-Stone, fall, 2000.

Wilson Library Bulletin, September, 1989, Lesley S. J. Farmer, review of *The Engineers of the Beasts,* p. S5; September, 1993, Patty Campbell, review of *Staying Put,* p. 106.

ONLINE

Indiana State University, http://www.indiana.edu/ (March 13, 2004), Sanders biography.*

*   *   *

SAN JUAN, E(pifanio), Jr. 1938-
(Felix Razon)

PERSONAL: Born December 29, 1938, in Manila, Philippines; son of Epifanio and Loreto (Samia) San Juan; married Delia Aguilar, August 3, 1960; children: Karin, Eric. *Ethnicity:* "Filipino." *Education:* University of the Philippines, B.A. (magna cum laude), 1958; Harvard University, A.M., 1962, Ph.D., 1965.

ADDRESSES: Office—Philippines Cultural Studies Center, 117 Davis Rd., Storrs, CT 06268. *E-mail*—philcsc@earthlink.net.

CAREER: University of the Philippines, Quezon City, instructor, 1959-60, assistant professor of English and comparative literature, 1960-61; San Francisco State College (now University), San Francisco, CA, Peace Corps language instructor, 1962; University of California—Davis, assistant professor, 1965-66; University of the Philippines, associate professor of English and comparative literature, 1966-67; University of Connecticut, Storrs, associate professor of English, 1967-77; Brooklyn College of the City University of New York, visiting professor, 1977-79; University of Connecticut, professor of English and comparative literature, beginning 1979; Philippines Cultural Studies Center, Storrs, CT, director, 2001—. Zagreb University, visiting professor at Inter-University Center of Postgraduate Studies, 1981; Wesleyan University, Middletown, CT, visiting professor and fellow of Center for the Humanities, 2002; Catholic University of Louvain, Fulbright lecturer in American studies, 2003.

MEMBER: International Brecht Society, PEN, Modern Language Association of America, American Studies Association, College English Association, Phi Kappa Phi.

AWARDS, HONORS: Fulbright/Smith Mundt fellowship, 1960-63; Rockefeller Foundation fellowship, 1963-65; Palanca Memorial Award for poetry, 1965, and for fiction, 1968; Catholic Mass Media Award and National Book Award, Manila Critics Circle, both 1985, for *Toward a People's Literature: Essays in the Dialectics of Praxis and Contradiction in Philippine Writing;* Fulbright exchange scholar, University of the Philippines and Ateneo de Manila University, 1987-88; Centennial Award for Literature, Cultural Center of the Philippines, 1999; Outstanding Book Award, Gustavus Myers Human Rights Center, 2002, for *After Postcolonialism: Remapping Philippines-United States Confrontations.*

WRITINGS:

Godkissing Carrion: Selected Poems, 1954-1964, Concord Press (Seal Beach, CA), 1965.

(Compiler and translator) Amado V. Hernández, *Rice Grains: Selected Poems,* International Publishers (New York, NY), 1966.

The Art of Oscar Wilde, Princeton University Press (Princeton, NJ), 1967.

The Exorcism and Other Poems, Panitikan Publications, 1967.

Balagtas: Art and Revolution; A Critical Study of Florante at Laura, Manlapaz Publishing (Quezon City, Philippines), 1969.

Maliwalu, mga bagong tula, Manlapaz Publishing (Quezon City, Philippines), 1969.

(Editor) T. S. Eliot, *A Casebook on "Gerontion,"* C. E. Merrill (Columbus, OH), 1970.

The Radical Tradition in Philippine Literature, Manlapaz Publishing (Quezon City, Philippines), 1971.

(Editor) *Critics on Ezra Pound,* University of Miami Press (Coral Gables, FL), 1971.

A Preface to Pilipino Literature, Alemar-Phoenix (Quezon City, Philippines), 1972.

Carlos Bulosan and the Imagination of the Class Struggle, University of the Philippines Press (Quezon City, Philippines), 1972.

James Joyce and the Craft of Fiction: An Interpretation of "Dubliners," Farleigh Dickinson University Press (Rutherford, NJ), 1972.

Mayo 1971: At iba pang tula, Manlapaz Publishing (Quezon City, Philippines), 1972.

Marxism and Human Liberation: Selected Essays by Georg Lukacs, Dell (New York, NY), 1972.

(Editor) *Introduction to Modern Pilipino Literature,* Twayne Publishers (New York, NY), 1974.

Ang sining ng tula: Mga sanaysay sa panunuring pampanitikian, Alemar-Phoenix (Quezon City, Philippines), 1975.

Ang mga mangwawasak: At iba pang maikling katha (short stories in Tagalog), New Day Publishers (Quezon City, Philippines), 1976.

(Under pseudonym Felix Razon; with Richard Hensman) *The Oppression of the Indigenous Peoples of the Philippines,* International Work Group for Indigenous Affairs (Copenhagen, Denmark), 1976.

(Translator from Tagalog) Francisco Balagtas, *Florante/Laura,* illustrated by Rodolfo Paras-Perez, Art Multiples (Manila, Philippines), 1978.

(Editor and author of introduction) Carlos Bulosan, *The Philippines Is in the Heart: Selected Stories,* New Day Publishers (Quezon City, Philippines), 1978.

Poetics: The Imitation of Action; Essays in Interpretation, Fairleigh Dickinson University Press (Rutherford, NJ), 1979.

Only by Struggle: Literature and Revolution in the Philippines, Philippines Research Center (Mansfield Depot, CT), 1980, new edition published as *Only by Struggle: Reflections on Philippine Culture, Society and History in a Time of Civil War,* Kalikasan Press (Quezon City, Philippines), 1988, revised edition, Giraffe Books (Quezon City, Philippines), 2002.

(With Luis V. Teodoro, Jr.) *Two Perspectives on Philippine Literature and Society,* Center for Asian and Pacific Studies, University of Hawaii (Honolulu, HI), 1981.

Toward a People's Literature: Essays in the Dialectics of Praxis and Contradiction in Philippine Writing, University of the Philippines Press (Quezon City, Philippines), 1983.

Toward Rizal: A Reading of Rizal's Novels "Noli Me Tangere" and "El Filibusterismo," Philippines Research Center (Mansfield Depot, CT), 1983.

(Compiler) *Bulosan: An Introduction with Selections,* National Book Store (Manila, Philippines), 1983.

(Editor) *If You Want to Know What We Are: A Carlos Bulosan Reader,* introduction by Leigh Bristol-Kagan, West End Press (Minneapolis, MN), 1983.

Kung ikaw ay inaapi, bakit hindi ka magbalikwas?, or, Kung ikaw ay inaalipin, bumangon ka at lumaban!: At iba pang tula, Makibaka Publications (Manila, Philippines), 1984.

The Ashes of Pedro Abad Santos and Other Poems, Philippines Research Center (Mansfield Depot, CT), 1985.

Crisis in the Philippines: The Making of a Revolution, Bergin & Garvey (South Hadley, MA), 1986.

Subversions of Desire: Prolegomena to Nick Joaquin, University of Hawaii Press (Honolulu, HI), 1988.

Transcending the Hero, Reinventing the Heroic: An Essay on André Gide's Theater, University Press of America (Lanham, MD), 1988.

Ruptures, Schisms, Interventions: Cultural Revolution in the Third World, De La Salle University Press (Manila, Philippines), 1988.

From People to Nation: Essays in Cultural Politics, Asian Social Institute (Manila, Philippines), 1990.

Writing and National Liberation: Essays in Critical Practice, University of the Philippines Press (Quezon City, Philippines), 1991.

Racial Formations/Critical Transformations: Articulations of Power in Ethnic and Racial Studies in the United States, Humanities Press (Atlantic Highlands, NJ), 1992.

Reading the West/Writing the East: Studies in Comparative Literature and Culture, Peter Lang (New York, NY), 1992.

Pakikibaka tungo sa mapagpalayang kultura, Kalikasan Press (Manila, Philippines), 1993.

Smile of the Medusa (short stories), Anvil Publishing (Pasig, Philippines), 1994.

From the Masses, to the Masses: Third World Literature and Revolution, MEP Publications (Minneapolis, MN), 1994.

Allegories of Resistance: The Philippines at the Threshold of the Twenty-first Century, University of Philippines Press (Quezon City, Philippines), 1994.

(Editor and author of introduction) Carlos Bulosan, *The Cry and the Dedication*, Temple University Press (Philadelphia, PA), 1995.

Hegemony and Strategies of Transgression: Essays in Cultural Studies and Comparative Literature, State University of New York Press (Albany, NY), 1995.

(Editor and author of introduction) *On Becoming Filipino: Selected Writings of Carlos Bulosan*, Temple University Press (Philadelphia, PA), 1995.

History and Form: Selected Essays, Ateneo de Manila University Press (Quezon City, Philippines), 1996.

The Philippine Temptation: Dialectics of Philippines-U.S. Literary Relations, Temple University Press (Philadelphia, PA), 1996.

Mediations from a Filipino Perspective, Anvil Publishing (Pasig City, Philippines), 1996.

Rizal in Our Time: Essays in Interpretation, Anvil (Pasig City, Philippines), 1997.

Beyond Postcolonial Theory, St. Martin's Press (New York, NY), 1998.

Filipina Insurgency: Writing against Patriarchy in the Philippines: Selected Essays, Giraffe Books (Quezon City, Philippines), 1998.

From Exile to Diaspora: Versions of the Filipino Experience in the United States, Westview Press (Boulder, CO), 1998.

After Postcolonialism: Remapping Philippines-United States Confrontations, Rowman & Littlefield Publishers (Lanham, MD), 2000.

Alay sa paglikha ng bukang-liwayway (poetry in Tagalog), Ateneo de Manila University Press (Quezon City, Philippines), 2000.

Racism and Cultural Studies: Critiques of Multiculturalist Ideology and the Politics of Difference, Duke University Press (Durham, NC), 2002.

Working through the Contradictions: From Cultural Theory to Critical Practice, Bucknell University Press (Lewisburg, PA), 2004.

Editor of "Makibaka! Revolutionary Literature from the Philippines," Philippines Research Center (Mansfield Depot, CT), 1979. Contributor to books, including *"Winesburg, Ohio": Text and Criticism*, edited by John H. Ferres, Viking (New York, NY), 1967; *Oedipus: Myth and Dramatic Form*, edited by J. L. Sanderson and Everett Zimmerman, Houghton-Mifflin (Boston, MA), 1967; *Revaluations of Victorian Literature*, edited by Shiv Kumar, New York University Press (New York, NY), 1968; and *The Weapons of Criticism*, edited by Norman Rudich, Ramparts Publishing (Palo Alto, CA), 1975. Contributor of articles on literary topics to journals, including *Asian Studies, Personalist,* and *University of Toronto Quarterly.*

WORK IN PROGRESS: *Marx and Spinoza: A Comparative Study; Dialectics of National Liberation.*

BIOGRAPHICAL AND CRITICAL SOURCES:

BOOKS

Makata, Makata, Inc., 1967.

Manghas, R., editor, *Manlilikha*, Kadipan, Inc., 1967.

San Juan, E., Jr., *The Exorcism and Other Poems*, Panitikan Publications, 1967.

PERIODICALS

Canadian Literature, summer, 2000, Laura Moss, review of *Beyond Postcolonial Theory*, p. 167.

Choice, December, 2000, M. P. Onorato, review of *After Postcolonialism: Remapping Philippines-United States Confrontations*, p. 760.

Contemporary Sociology, January, 2003, review of *Racism and Cultural Studies: Critiques of Multiculturalist Ideology and the Politics of Difference*, p. 132.

International Migration Review, summer, 2000, Ann D. Bagchi, review of *From Exile to Diaspora: Versions of the Filipino Experience in the United States*, p. 575.

Journal of American Ethnic History, spring, 2002, Martin F. Manalansan IV, review of *From Exile to Diaspora*, p. 100.

Journal of Contemporary Asia, August, 2003, Joel Wendland, review of *Racism and Cultural Studies*, p. 427.

Journal of Southeast Asian Studies, October, 2001, Millard O. Lim, review of *After Postcolonialism*, p. 486.

Research in African Literatures, fall, 2000, Chadwick Allen, review of *Beyond Postcolonial Theory*, p. 187.

*   *   *

SANTIAGO, Esmeralda 1948-

PERSONAL: Born May 17, 1948, in San Juan, Puerto Rico; daughter of Pablo Santiago Diaz (a poet and carpenter) and Ramona Santiago (a factory worker); married Frank Cantor (a filmmaker), June 11, 1978; children: Lucas David, Ila. *Ethnicity:* "Puerto Rican."

Esmeralda Santiago

Education: Harvard University, B.A. (magna cum laude), 1976; Sarah Lawrence College, M.F.A., 1992. *Hobbies and other interests:* Reading, opera, theater, long walks, regional and local history museums and exhibits, the paintings of Francisco Goya, world and classical music, salsa dancing, yoga.

ADDRESSES: Home—P.O. Box 679, Amawalk, NY 10501. *Agent*—Molly Friedrich, Aaron Priest Literary Agency, 708 Third Ave., New York, NY 10017. *E-mail*—list@EsmeraldaSantiago.com.

CAREER: Journalist, memoirist, and novelist. ACCION/AITEC, Cambridge, MA, bilingual secretary, 1974-76; H/M Multi Media Co., Boston, MA, producer, 1975-76; Cantomedia Corp., Boston, cofounder and president, 1977—. Advisor, Massachusetts Film Bureau, Boston, 1984-89, and Massachusetts Cultural Alliance, Boston, 1986-90; Massachusetts Small Business Advice Council, Boston, advisor and appointed member, 1985-89. *Radcliffe Quarterly* advisory board, 1986-2000; Alianza Hispana, member, board of directors, 1978

AWARDS, HONORS: Silver Award, International Film and TV Festival, 1980; Gold Award, Houston Interna-tional Film Festival, 1984; New England Minority Businesswoman of the Year, and Minority Small Business of the Year, U.S. Department of Commerce, both 1988; Leadership Award, Massachusetts Latino Democratic Committee, 1989; achievement award, Westchester Hispanic Democrats, 1994; award from Coalition of Hispanic American Women, 1995; Guanín award, Sales and Marketing Executives International, and achievement award, Latin American Confederation of Marketing Executives, both 1996; Best Book about Puerto Rico Life and Culture, Club Civico, for *When I Was Puerto Rican,* 1996; WomenRise! Award, Wider Opportunities for Women, 1998; fellowship, National Hispana Leadership Institute, 1990; American Library Association Alex Award, and Westchester Library System Best Books selection, both 1999, both for *Almost a Woman;* Latina of the Year in literature, *Latina,* 1999; Literary Arts Award, Teatro Circulo, 1999; Orgullo Hispano, Univision Network, 2001; Radcliffe Association Alumnae Recognition Award, 2001; Women of Distinction Award, Girl Scouts of America, and All Star Award, Women in Communications, both 2002; Artist award, Westchester Arts Council, 2003; honorary degrees from Trinity College, 1994, Pace University, 1999, and Metropolitan College, 2004.

WRITINGS:

When I Was Puerto Rican (memoir), Addison-Wesley (Reading, MA), 1993.
América's Dream (novel), HarperCollins (New York, NY), 1996.
(Editor, with Joie Davidow) *Las Christmas: Favorite Latino Authors Share Their Holiday Memories,* illustrated by José Ortega, Knopf (New York, NY), 1998.
Almost a Woman (memoir), Perseus (Reading, MA), 1998.
(Editor, with Joie Davidow) *Las Mamis: Favorite Latino Authors Remember Their Mothers,* Knopf (New York, NY), 1999.

Also author of screenplays *Beverly Hills Supper Club,* 1980, and *Button, Button,* 1982. Contributor to anthologies, including *Home: American Writers Remember Rooms of Their Own,* edited by Steve and Sharon Fiffer, Pantheon (New York, NY), 1995; *Perspectivas Sobre Puerto Rico en Homenaje a Muñoz Rivera y Muñoz Marín,* Fundacíon Luis Muñoz Marín, 1997; *Body,* edited by Steve and Sharon Fiffer, Avon, 1999;

Metropolis Found, Crown, 2003. Contributor of articles and short stories to periodicals including, *Boston Globe, Christian Science Monitor, New York Times, Los Angeles Times, Latina, Metropolitan Home, House & Garden, Good Housekeeping* and have been published in Spanish-language publications; books have been published into seven different languages.

ADAPTATIONS: Almost a Woman was filmed for Exxon Masterpiece Theater's American Collection, 2002.

WORK IN PROGRESS: The Turkish Lover (memoir); *A Baby Doll Like Jenny's* (illustrated children's book), publication expected in 2005.

SIDELIGHTS: The oldest of eleven children, Esmeralda Santiago moved with her mother and siblings to New York City from Puerto Rico in 1961. Her memoirs, which include 1998's *Almost a Woman*, chronicle her experiences of growing up in a large, turbulent, and mobile household in Puerto Rico before relocating to New York when Santiago was thirteen. Santiago has also published a full-length novel, *América's Dream*, as well as two screenplays and various short stories.

Together with 1993's *When I Was Puerto Rican, Almost a Woman* focuses on Santiago's youth; the first volume concentrates on her childhood in Puerto Rico and treats the move to New York City briefly, while the second volume completes the story of the family's move and Santiago's struggles with American culture and language, and her drive to success, first at the High School for Performing Arts in New York City and at various jobs and part-time study at community colleges. *When I Was Puerto Rican* not only tells the story of Santiago's life but looks at the tensions that Americanization brings, both in the new land and on return trips to the homeland.

When I Was Puerto Rican begins with Santiago's description of growing up in many different households, one centered in the rural barrio of Macun and the others closer to her mother's family in a town called Santurce. In Macun the family lived in a "home [that] was a giant version of the lard cans used to haul water from the public fountain. Its windows and doors were also metal, and as we stepped in, I touched the wall and burned my fingers." Macun was the home of Santiago's father, Papi, a laborer and poet who was father to Esmeralda and all of her siblings, but who, after vacillating through nine pregnancies, finally refused to marry her mother. Mami and Papi's relationship was a "sometimes passionate, sometimes turbulent common-law marriage," according to Yvonne V. Sapia in the *Los Angeles Times*. Esmeralda, called "Negi" ("little dark one"), likes the country life, the "crude yet intoxicating world of fruity perfume, fish-head soup, *pan de agua* and the poetry of Don Luis Llorens Torres, who began the Modernismo movement in Puerto Rico that followed World War I," according to Sapia.

It is only during the times when, after one of many serious quarrels with Papi, Mami moves the family to Santurce that Esmeralda finds out that she and her siblings are considered *jibaros*, or peasants, the lowest tier in Puerto Rican society. The increasingly long and frequent stays in town are painful, as Santiago must tolerate the ridicule of her more affluent fellow students. Mami ultimately moves the entire family to Brooklyn, New York, where her own mother lives. While the transition was terrifying at first, Santiago manages to impress her teachers and win their help gaining admittance to the New York High School of Performing Arts.

Santiago's visits back to Puerto Rico open her eyes to alterations in her identity. As she wrote in *When I Was Puerto Rican*, "I was told I was no longer Puerto Rican because my Spanish was rusty, my gaze too direct, my personality too assertive. . . . Yet in the United States, my darkness, my accented speech, my frequent lapses into confused silence between English and Spanish identified me as foreign, non-American. In writing the book I wanted to get back to that feeling of Puertoricanness I had before I came here."

Critics were much taken with Santiago's first memoir. Sapia called it "stylistically fluid and finely detailed" and deserving "a unique place in contemporary Latino storytelling," while a contributor to *Publishers Weekly* commented that "Santiago's portraits are clear-sighted, the Puerto Rican ambience rich, and her immigrant experience is artfully and movingly told." And a *Kirkus* reviewer praised *When I Was Puerto Rican* as "clear eyed, quietly powerful, and often lyrical: a story of true grit."

Santiago's next memoir, *Almost a Woman*, picks up her experience upon coming to New York and extends it. At age thirteen, the eldest of her mother's then eight children, she helps her younger siblings negotiate their way through their new environs in Brooklyn; they have their poverty in common with most of their new neighbors, but as new immigrants they face challenges beyond their income level. Quick to begin learning English, Santiago accompanies her mother to the welfare office to translate for her, ensuring the family's survival. Mami's attempts to keep her children safe and in-line with her culture's traditions come through clearly; she forbids her eldest daughter to go out with boys until she is seventeen, but while Santiago tries to be obedient, her independent spirit and quickness to assimilate make for conflicts. *Almost a Woman* chronicles the author's experiences at the New York School of Performing Arts, where she trains as an actress and achieves a small role in the film *Up the Down Staircase*. It also, despite Mami's rules, "details several romantic involvements, including an affair with a Turkish filmmaker," according to a reviewer for *Publishers Weekly*.

Donna Seaman, reviewing *Almost a Woman* for *Booklist,* appreciated its depiction of Santiago's relationship with Mami as "the fulcrum of Santiago's balancing act between life in their brimming barrio apartment and life in the wider world, where she discovers the joy and frustrations of artistic pursuits and the puzzlements of love." And a *Library Journal* contributor noted that "Santiago's descriptive prose and lively dialog draw the reader in; we are reminded of the pains and pleasures of adolescence and wonder what happens next in her life."

Published between the two memoirs, Santiago's *América's Dream* tells the story of a Puerto Rican woman who is trying to break the cycle of early pregnancy and domestic violence in which she is caught, as her mother was, and as she fears her daughter will be. América works on the Puerto Rican resort island of Vieques, cleaning hotel rooms; she lives with the abusive Correa, the father of her teenage daughter. In a chapter called "Correa's Gifts" the reader discovers that all of his gifts have followed assaults: "The size and expense of the gifts is usually in proportion to the severity of the beating. Electronics typically means he knows he's really hurt her, but chocolates always mean she deserved it." When the hotel manager recommends América for a nanny position for some wealthy American guests, she recognizes that if she leaves, it must be for good; Correa will kill her if she ever returns.

But she takes her chances, hoping to be able to bring her daughter with her and to show her a new life free of violence and fear. Her time in New York City increases her critical consciousness and her savvy. When Correa tracks América down in New York City, prepared to do his worst, she is better able to face him than ever before.

Respectful reviews greeted Santiago's first full-length novel. Elizabeth Coonrod Martinez wrote in the *Women's Review of Books* that *América's Dream* "takes its place alongside other major works by Latina writers such as [Sandra] Cisneros, [Denise] Chavez, Ana Castillo and Julia Alvarez. Like other contemporary novels, this one begins in adult life and looks back, an artistic strategy that pulls the reader in to acknowledge the destructive violence that many women still endure." A contributor to *Kirkus Reviews* noted that "Santiago's acute eye and feel for the telling detail make this a work of fine reportage, as well as an engrossing if often somber tale with a quiet but always tenacious heroine." And Sylvia Brownrigg wrote in the *Times Literary Supplement* that "what begins as a bleak study of a beaten, hapless woman evolves into a detailed portrayal of the life of a Latina *empleada* working for New York's wealthy elite. The subtlety of Santiago's writing reveals itself, as she describes the fear of violence and the indignities of domestic employment on the mainland."

In addition to her memoirs and novel, Santiago has edited two books with Joie Davidow, *Las Christmas: Favorite Latino Authors Share Their Holiday Memories,* and *Las Mamis: Favorite Latino Authors Remember Their Mothers*. In *Las Mamis* Latino authors describe their fondest holiday memories, depicting a wide variety of thoughts and emotions. Some describe special traditions and holiday meals (with recipes included). Others describe how traditions changed when they moved to the United States. *Booklist* reviewer Toni Hyde observed, "As diverse as the authors themselves, every story is richly fulfilling and offers many variations on a common theme. Despite its Latin focus, *Las Christmas,* does not discriminate, but rather captivates readers regardless of their heritage."

Las Mamis is a collection of fourteen essays by Latin American authors, such as Marjorie Agosin and Jose Vasconcelos, and includes photographs of each author's mother. The true stories vividly capture the experiences of the authors as they related to their mothers. A *Publishers Weekly* reviewer wrote, "From rich mamis to poor ones, loving to relentless, this collection of essays eloquently captures the diversity of Latino culture, while paying tribute to its most enduring characteristic: amor a madre." "The voices are so personal that you keep turning back while you're reading to look at the photo at the start of each story," wrote *Booklist* reviewer Hazel Rochman. Rochman concluded, "It's that combination of family, folklore, and self-discovery that makes these stories universal."

BIOGRAPHICAL AND CRITICAL SOURCES:

BOOKS

Authors and Artists for Young Adults, Volume 43, Gale (Detroit, MI), 2002.
Notable Hispanic American Women, 2nd edition, Gale (Detroit, MI), 1998.

PERIODICALS

Booklist, August, 1998, p. 1957; October 15, 1998, Toni Hyde, review of *Las Christmas: Favorite Latino Authors Share Their Holiday Memories,* p. 374; March 15, 2000, Hazel Rochman, review of *Las Mamis: Favorite Latino Authors Remember Their Mothers,* p. 1299.
Kirkus Reviews, August 15, 1993, p. 1058; March 1, 1996, p. 327.
Library Journal, October 1, 1998, pp. 105-106; May 1, 2000, Rene Perez-Lopez, review of *Las Mamis,* p. 112.
Los Angeles Times, December 26, 1993, p. 9.
Publishers Weekly, September 13, 1993, p. 114; June 15, 1998, p. 47; April 3, 2000, review of *Las Mamis,* p. 74.
Times Literary Supplement, June 27, 1997, p. 21.
Women's Review of Books, January 1997, p. 22.

ONLINE

Esmeralda Santiago Official Web site, http://www.esmeraldasantiago.com/ (November 6, 2003).
LaGuardia Community College Web site, http://faculty.lagcc.cuny.edu/ (November 6, 2003).

Puerto Rico Herald Online, http://www.puertorico-herald.org/ (November 6, 2003), "Esmeralda Santiago."
Vintage Books Web site, http://www.randomhouse.com/vintage/ (November 6, 2003).
Voices from the Gaps Web site, http://voices.cla.umn.edu/ (November 6, 2003), "Esmeralda Santiago."

*   *   *

SAUNDERS, Max 1957-

PERSONAL: Born June 24, 1957, in London, England; son of Alfred (an artist) and Diana (an art dealer; maiden name, Snow) Cohen; companion of Alfred Saunders. *Ethnicity:* "Caucasian." *Education:* Queen's College, Cambridge, B.A. (with honors), 1979. *Politics:* "Left/Green."

ADDRESSES: Office—Department of English, King's College, University of London, The Strand, London WC2R 2LS, England. *E-mail*—max.saunders@kcl.ac.uk.

CAREER: Cambridge University, Cambridge, England, research fellow at Selwyn College, 1983-88, lecturer, 1988-89; University of London, King's College, London, England, lecturer, 1989-97, reader in English, 1997-2000, professor of English, 2000—.

MEMBER: Ford Madox Ford Society (chair, 1997—).

AWARDS, HONORS: Le Bas Prize, Cambridge University, 1985.

WRITINGS:

Ford Madox Ford: A Dual Life (biography), Volume 1: *The World before the War;* Volume 2: *The After-War World,* Oxford University Press (Oxford, England), 1996.
(Editor and author of introduction) *Selected Poems: Ford Madox Ford,* Carcanet Press (Manchester, England), 1997.
(Editor) *War Prose: Ford Madox Ford,* Carcanet (Manchester, England), 1999.

(Editor, with Richard Stang) *Critical Essays of Ford Madox Ford,* Carcanet (Manchester, England), 2002.

SIDELIGHTS: "Literature," wrote the twentieth-century novelist, critic, and essayist Ford Madox Ford, "exists for the Reader and by the Reader." As a specialist on Ford's life and letters, Max Saunders paints his subject as a complex man who was something of a liar. Born Ford Hermann Hueffer in 1873, Ford was the son of a music critic and an artist; the boy was subsequently "raised in the hothouse of late-nineteeth-century intellectualism and radicalism," as critic Martin Stannard noted in the *New York Times Book Review.* Changing his name to Ford Madox Ford (after his maternal grandfather, painter Ford Madox Brown), the young man was frequently, as Saunders put it, "dishonest in matters of large change." He claimed to be descended from German aristocracy, to have attended Eton, to have met Lord Byron. "None of it was true," stated Stannard. "He made up his life as he went along." What was true about Ford's life is his influence on contemporary letters: He founded the *English Review,* published James Joyce, Gertrude Stein, and e. e. cummings, and counted among his friends Henry James and H. G. Wells.

In Volume 1 of Saunders's two-part *Ford Madox Ford: A Dual Life,* the author examines his subject's life prior to World War I. "Rather than worry about whether Ford was a liar," Stannard remarked, "Mr. Saunders turns the difficulty into a literary question. Ford's characteristic style is based on 'reminiscential anecdote,' on desiring 'remembrance now': 'In all Ford's writing, make-believe is inseparable from reminiscence.'"

Saunders contributed thorough research into Ford's private life, which included extramarital affairs, and examined how such behavior affected his and others' literary work. "One single example," said Giovanni Cianci of *Prolepsis,* "may suffice as an instance of the exhaustiveness of [the author's] biographical method: His reconstruction (aided, it should be noted, by the prior research carried out by Carole Angier) of the affair between Ford, Stella Bowen and Jean Rhys. He traces their triangular relationship not only in Bowen's accounts, but also in the fictionalised elaboration of the other two partners (*Postures* by Rhys, and Ford's *When the Wicked Man*), not forgetting the novel by Jean Lenglet (Rhys' Dutch husband), *Sous le verrous.*"

By 1915, Ford's affair with novelist Viola Hunt was on the wane; his marriage had ended, his father had died, and his signature book *The Good Soldier* "had met with enough critical hostility to insure low sales," as Stannard noted. To the despondent writer, World War I "beckoned as a form of legitimate suicide." But his war experiences led to the novel *Parade's End,* which Saunders sees as "not only an exemplary, essential text of 1920s modernism, but also the most important and complex English novel on the First World War," according to Cianci. "As a critic with the simultaneous task of unraveling the complex web of his subject's life," Cianci continued, "Saunders must have been sorely tempted to highlight biographical coincidence and motivation, limiting his interpretation of the texts to subservient transcriptions. . . . On the contrary, however, once he has exorcised the 'biographical sourcery' which he rightly shuns, Saunders makes intelligently elastic use of biographical data."

As editors of Ford's *Critical Essays,* Saunders and Richard Stang turn their focus toward the writer's interpretation of the works of such peers as Joseph Conrad and James Joyce. Ford's "aesthetic doctrine came down, in essence to a single tenet," wrote *Times Literary Supplement* critic P. N. Furbank. "The writer must eschew verbiage and abstraction, must aim at the exact rendering of the concrete." To Furbank, "It was a doctrine that the age was in need of, and he preached it with such persistence and good humour . . . that it bore fruit." *Critical Essays* "brings together essays which, for the most part, have never been republished in book form. Since Ford made a practice of republishing his longer pieces, it means that it is something of a ragbag, but for a reader coming fresh to Ford it might be just the right introduction."

Saunders once told *CA:* "I am a literary critic first. My biography of Ford grew out of an interest in his writing. His novels and memoirs are some of the most engaging pieces of English prose I know. He has attracted many champions, often novelists or poets themselves, but the strengths of his writing had never been persuasively demonstrated. Ford said he was perfectly conscious of how he got his effects. His imagination was permeated by a stringent critical sensibility, which is manifest not just in his appreciations of other writers, but in his fiction, too—in the ways he attends to the experiences of writing and reading. I suppose what predisposed me toward such interests was being brought up in a home where art—particularly visual art—was always being discussed. My stepfather, the American painter Alfred Cohen, has a gift for making one see a painter's technique, and the strengths and weaknesses of a composition."

BIOGRAPHICAL AND CRITICAL SOURCES:

PERIODICALS

Guardian (London, England), March 23, 2002, Nicholas Lezard, review of *Critical Essays of Ford Madox Ford*, p. 11.

Hudson Review, summer, 1998, review of *Ford Madox Ford: A Dual Life*, p. 425.

New York Times Book Review, June 30, 1996, Martin Stannard, "The Art of Lying," review of *Ford Madox Ford: A Dual Life*.

Times Literary Supplement, May 10, 2002, P. N. Furbank, review of *Critical Essays of Ford Madox Ford*, p. 36.

ONLINE

Prolepsis Web site, http://www.uni-tuebingen.de/uni/nes/ (October 30, 2001), Giovanni Cianci, review of *Ford Madox Ford: A Dual Life.**

*   *   *

SCHWARTZ, Amy 1954-

PERSONAL: Born April 2, 1954, in San Diego, CA; daughter of I. Henry (a writer and newspaper columnist) and Eva (a professor of chemistry; maiden name, Herzberg) Schwartz; married Leonard Marcus (a historian and critic); children: Jacob. *Education:* Attended Antioch College, 1972-73; California College of Arts and Crafts, B.F.A., 1976.

ADDRESSES: Agent—Jane Feder, 305 East 24th St., New York, NY 10010.

CAREER: Author and illustrator of books for children.

AWARDS, HONORS: Parents' Choice Award, Parents' Choice Foundation, 1989, for *The Crack-of-Dawn Walkers* and *The Lady Who Put Salt in Her Coffee;*
Sydney Taylor Award, Association of Jewish Libraries for *Mrs. Moskowitz and the Sabbath Candlesticks; Parents'* Certificate of Excellence for *Annabelle Swift, Kindergartner;* Christopher Award for *The Purple Coat;* Ten Best Illustrated Children's Books designation, *New York Times Book Review,* for *A Teeny Tiny Baby;* Best Children's Books of the Year citation, *School Library Journal,* and 100 Best Children's Books citation, New York Public Library, both 1982, both for *Bea and Mr. Jones;* National Jewish Book Award for *Mrs. Moskowitz and the Sabbath Candlesticks.*

WRITINGS:

SELF-ILLUSTRATED

Bea and Mr. Jones, Bradbury Press (Scarsdale, NY), 1982.

Begin at the Beginning, Harper (New York, NY), 1983.

Mrs. Moskowitz and the Sabbath Candlesticks, Jewish Publication Society, 1983 (Philadelphia, PA).

Her Majesty, Aunt Essie, Bradbury Press (Scarsdale, NY), 1984.

Yossel Zissel and the Wisdom of Chelm, Jewish Publication Society (Philadelphia, PA), 1986.

Oma and Bobo, Bradbury Press (Scarsdale, NY), 1987.

Annabelle Swift, Kindergartner, Orchard (New York, NY), 1988.

(Compiler) *The Lady Who Put Salt in Her Coffee: From the Peterkin Papers,* Harcourt Brace (San Diego, CA), 1989.

(Editor, with Leonard S. Marcus) *Mother Goose's Little Misfortunes,* Bradbury Press (Scarsdale, NY), 1990.

Camper of the Week, Orchard (New York, NY), 1991.

(With Henry Schwartz) *Make a Face,* Scholastic (New York, NY), 1994.

A Teeny Tiny Baby, Orchard (New York, NY), 1994.

Old MacDonald, Scholastic (New York, NY), 1999.

How to Catch an Elephant, DK Publishing (New York, NY), 1999.

Some Babies, Orchard (New York, NY), 2000.

The Boys Team, Atheneum Books for Young Readers (New York NY), 2001.

What James Likes Best, Atheneum Books for Young Readers (New York, NY), 2003.

A Glorious Day, Atheneum Books for Young Readers (New York, NY), 2004.

Things I Learned in Second Grade, Harper (New York, NY), 2005.

ILLUSTRATOR

Amy Hest, *The Crack-of-Dawn Walkers*, Macmillan (New York, NY), 1984.

Eve Bunting, *Jane Martin, Dog Detective*, Harcourt Brace (San Diego, CA), 1984.

Joanne Ryder, *The Night Flight*, Four Winds Press (Bristol, FL), 1985.

Donna Guthrie, *The Witch Who Lives down the Hall* (Junior Literary Guild selection), Harcourt Brace (San Diego, CA), 1985.

Amy Hest, *The Purple Coat*, Four Winds Press (New York, NY), 1986.

Elizabeth Lee O'Donnell, *Maggie Doesn't Want to Move*, Four Winds Press (New York, NY), 1987.

Mary Stolz, *The Scarecrows and Their Child*, Harper (New York, NY), 1987.

Larry King, *Because of Lozo Brown*, Viking (New York, NY), 1988.

I. Henry Schwartz, *How I Captured a Dinosaur*, Orchard (New York, NY), 1989.

Lucretia Hale, *The Lady Who Put Salt in Her Coffee*, Harcourt Brace (San Diego, CA), 1989.

Amy Hest, *Fancy Aunt Jess*, Morrow (New York, NY), 1990.

Nancy White Carlstrom, *Blow Me a Kiss, Miss Lillie*, Harper (New York, NY), 1990.

Stephanie Calmenson, *Wanted: Warm Furry Friend*, Macmillan (New York, NY), 1990.

Pat Brisson, *Magic Carpet*, Bradbury Press (Scarsdale, NY), 1991.

I. Henry Schwartz, *Albert Goes Hollywood*, Orchard (New York, NY), 1992.

David Gale, editor, *Funny You Should Ask*, Delacorte (New York, NY), 1992.

Kathryn Lasky, *My Island Grandma*, Morrow (New York, NY), 1993.

Amy Hest, *Nana's Birthday Party*, Morrow (New York, NY), 1993.

Kathleen Krull, *Wish You Were Here: Emily Emerson's Guide to the 50 States*, Doubleday (New York, NY), 1997.

Amy Hest, *Gabby Growing Up*, Simon & Schuster Books for Young Readers (New York, NY), 1998.

ADAPTATIONS: Bea and Mr. Jones was adapted for television and broadcast on "Reading Rainbow," PBS, 1983, and *The Purple Coat* was adapted for the same series in 1989.

SIDELIGHTS: Amy Schwartz has been recognized by many reviewers as a talented writer and gifted illustrator of children's books. Her stories have been praised for their realistic, yet sensitive portrayal of childhood experiences. She explained to *CA:* "I often pick these rather stubborn and determined types as main characters—both in little girls and grandmotherly figures. I think it's a part of me, a part of the people in my family."

Schwartz described her early love of books to *CA:* "Looking back on my childhood, I can easily see a progression of interests that led to my writing and illustrating children's books. Some of my strongest memories from my childhood involve books. I always had the most number of stars in the class for 'Books Read' on the elementary school book awards. I remember looking forward each year to the annual ritual of receiving a book from my grandmother on my birthday.

"I wrote stories and plays in elementary school, and adapted my favorite picture books for school theater productions. I was shy and awkward in real life, but I had an active fantasy life. I was also a real ham on stage. I also loved to draw and paint when I was young, as I still do. I would draw after school, either with friends or on my own. I was usually enrolled in an art class on Saturday mornings. This interest in drawing and painting has been continuous throughout my life."

Schwartz's first children's book, *Bea and Mr. Jones*, in which a creative kindergartner and an advertising-executive father trade daily routines, was adapted for the popular children's television show *Reading Rainbow.*

Schwartz published many other award-winning children's books after *Bea and Mr. Jones*, all of which display her signature brightly colored gouache illustrations. Her rendition of the classic *Old MacDonald* garnered much critical acclaim. A reviewer in *Publishers Weekly* described it as a "refreshing departure from the traditional lyrics" with "an uplifting storyline." Mary M. Burns in *Horn Book* praised Schwartz's characterization. She maintained that "the various characters are definitely but not overwhelmingly in a manner calculated to appeal to the youngest readers."

A *Publishers Weekly* critic praised Schwartz's *How to Catch an Elephant,* in which a young girl concludes that the only supplies needed to accomplish the feat are three cakes, two raisins, one telescope, and a pair of tweezers. "With playful repetition and shrewdly kid-targeted visual humor, the author chronicles the capturing of a temperamental, brightly hued yellow pachyderm," the reviewer explained. Writing in *Book* online, Kathleen Odean considered the book "a captivating story with a fresh look."

In *Some Babies,* a sequel to *A Teeny, Tiny Baby,* a toddler puts off going to bed by pleading with his tired mother to tell him stories about "some babies." She patiently tells him about children in the park, who are sliding down slides, splashing in sprinklers, having a snack in their strollers, and digging the dirt. Her storytelling amuses the toddler, but keeps him focused and awake. In the end, it's the mother, not the toddler, who falls asleep. In *School Library Journal,* reviewer Joy Fleishhacker noted that the illustrations in the book alternate between the toddler in his crib and the children the mother is describing. "The bright hues and cheerful patterns of the children's clothing make a nice contrast to the grainy gray sidewalks and rusty colored bricks of the city-park setting," she concluded. In *Horn Book,* a reviewer praised *Some Babies,* saying "It is sure to engage both the sippy-cup set and the adults reading to them."

Also writing in *Horn Book,* critic Lauren Adams described Schwartz's *The Boys Team,* published in 2001, as a "spot-on portrayal of kindergarten boys." The book is about a loyal friendship between three boys who are so close they wear identical Darth Vader costumes on Halloween. Adams described it as a tale where "loyalty is fierce and distractions are many" and noted that the "illustrations depict the protected world of play in a diverse, urban neighborhood." Adams concluded, "Any first grader worth his salt will dismiss this kindergarten kingdom, but four- and five-year old boys will see themselves in every picture and phrase." A critic in the *Kirkus Reviews* criticized *The Boys Team* for its portrayal of girls: "Both the text and art reinforce some unfortunate stereotypes: boys chasing girls with a worm, all three little girls in dresses, exclusively female teachers, all wearing dresses, and boys treating girls like second-class citizens, with girls accepting this status meekly." The same reviewer concluded that while boys will like the book, it might leave "little girls feeling like the last person to be picked for the softball game."

Schwartz's *What James Likes Best,* published in 2003, contains four short stories targeted toward preschoolers. A reviewer in *Kirkus Reviews* explained that the book provides "a wonderful introduction to chapter form in chronicling James's travels on a bus to visit twins, in a taxi to visit Auntie, in the car to go to the fair, and walking to a play date." The same reviewer described the book as "unique" because Schwartz employs a "simple, repetitive narrative, emphasizing the colors, toys, sounds, foods, places, and animals that young children find remarkable." Each story in the book ends with the question, "And what do you think James likes best?" Writing in *Booklist* reviewer Ilene Cooper felt such questioning "invites children to figure out what the characters are thinking about." Cooper described Schwartz's dialogue as "simplicity itself," and remarked that "Schwartz knows just what children will find interesting."

In addition to writing and illustrating her own books, Schwartz has illustrated books for children's author Amy Hest. Among these are *The Purple Coat* and its sequel *Gabby Growing Up.* In *The Purple Coat,* a young girl, Gabby, asks her tailor grandfather to make her a purple coat, a switch from the navy coat she wears each winter. Gabby and her loving grandfather return in *Gabby Growing Up.* This time Gabby sets out in quest of the perfect birthday gift from her grandfather and gets a grown-up haircut along the way. Both stories take place in 1950s in New York City. Cooper suggested that "the setting may evoke nostalgia for adults," but "Gabby's story of universal hopes and worries will easily appeal to today's children."

Commenting on whether she thinks of herself more as an artist than a writer, Schwartz once told *CA:* "I actually think of myself as an illustrator first, I suppose because I do more illustrating than writing. And I've drawn and painted since I was a child, whereas the writing still feels fairly new to me."

Schwartz also explained how she became successful. "With me it mainly took sticking with it, being persistent. I'm very glad that I did stick with it, that I didn't give up early and drop the whole thing. Also, before I started doing this, I had the idea—especially with writing—that it was something you did all on your own. With practically all my writing I've gotten help from somebody: a teacher, a friend, my agent, an editor. I think that's also good to know, that it's not something you have to do from start to finish all on your own without getting advice from someone else, an outside reader."

BIOGRAPHICAL AND CRITICAL SOURCES:

BOOKS

Continuum Encyclopedia of Children's Literature, Continuum (New York, NY), 2001, p. 698.

PERIODICALS

Booklist, January 1, 1998, Ilene Cooper, review of *Gabby Growing Up,* p. 822-24; May 15, 1999, review of *Old MacDonald,* p. 1700; November 15, 1999, Shelle Rosenfeld, review of *How to Catch an Elephant,* p. 639; November 1, 2001, review of *The Boys Team,* p. 485; March 1, 2003, Ilene Cooper, review of *What James Likes Best,* p. 1196.

Children's Bookwatch, June, 1999, review of *Old MacDonald,* p. 4.

Horn Book, January, 2002, review of *The Boys Team,* p. 72; March, 1999, Mary M. Burns, review of *Old MacDonald,* p. 200; September, 2000, review of *Some Babies,* p. 555; January-February, 2002, Lauren Adams, review of *The Boys Team,* pp. 72-74.

Instructor, May, 1999, review of *A Teeny Tiny Baby,* p. 14.

Kirkus Reviews, July 1, 1999, review of *How to Catch an Elephant,* p. 1059; October 1, 2001, review of *The Boys Team,* p. 1433; March 15, 2003, review of *What James Likes Best,* p. 478; October 1, 2001, review of *The Boys Team,* p. 1433.

New York Times Book Review, March 10, 2002, review of *The Boys Team,* p. 21; May 17, 1987; December 1, 1997, review of *Gabby Growing Up,* p. 53; July 13, 1998, review of *Oma and Bobo,* p. 79; February 26, 1988; July 26, 1999, review of *How to Catch an Elephant,* p. 90; May 24, 1999, review of *Old MacDonald,* p. 77; July 31, 2000, review of *Some Babies,* p. 93; November 5, 2001, review of *The Boys Team,* p. 66; February 24, 2003, review of *What James Likes Best,* p. 70; November 5, 2001, review of *The Boys Team,* p. 66.

Publishers Weekly, May 24, 1999, review of *Old MacDonald,* p. 77; July 26, 1999, review of *How to Catch an Elehant,* p. 90.

Riverbank Review, winter, 2001, review of *The Boys Team,* p. 26.

School Library Journal, February, 1997, review of *Annabelle Swift, Kindergartner,* p. 70; June, 1999, review of *Old MacDonald,* p. 122; October, 2000, Joy Fleishhacker, review of *Some Babies,* p. 136; January, 2002, review of *The Boys Team,* p. 110.

ONLINE

Book Online, http://www.bookmagazine.com/ (October 28, 2003), review of *How to Catch an Elephant.*

Chicago Parent Web site, http://www.chicagoparent.com/ (February, 2003), Stephanie Zvirin, "Kid Culture Books."

Jewish Publication Society Web site, http://www.jewishpub.org/ (November 10, 2003), *Mrs. Moskowitz and the Sabbath Candlesticks.**

*   *   *

SEABROOKE, Brenda 1941-

PERSONAL: Born May 23, 1941, in FL; married James Seabrooke (an oceanographer); children: Kevin, Kerria. *Education:* Newcomb College of Tulane University, B.A., 1963. *Hobbies and other interests:* Traveling, gardening, painting.

ADDRESSES: Agent—c/o Author Mail, Dutton, 345 Hudson St., New York, NY 10014. *E-mail*—seabrooke@ewol.com.

CAREER: Freelance writer. High school teacher of history in Fitzgerald, GA, 1967-68; substitute teacher in schools in New York and Maryland, 1968-70; Jayland Nursery School, Governor's Island, NY, teacher, 1973.

MEMBER: Coast Guard Officer's Wives Association, Petaluma Ballet Guild (director, 1980-81), Children's Book Guild of Washington, D.C.

AWARDS, HONORS: Boston Globe-Horn Book Honor Book for Fiction, 1991, for *Judy Scuppernong;* Notable Children's Trade Book in the Field of Social Studies, National Council for the Social Studies/

Children's Book Council, for *The Bridges of Summer*. Recipient of the Robie MacCauley Fellowship, Emerson College, and of a grant from the National Endowment for the Arts.

WRITINGS:

The Best Burglar Alarm, illustrated by Loretta Lustig, Morrow (New York, NY), 1978.

Home Is Where They Take You In, Morrow (New York, NY), 1980.

The Boy Who Saved the Town, illustrated by Howard M. Burns, Tidewater Publications (Centreville, MD), 1990.

Judy Scuppernong, illustrated by Ted Lewin, Cobblehill Books (New York, NY), 1990.

The Chester Town Tea Party, illustrated by Nancy Coates Smith, Tidewater Publications (Centreville, MD), 1991.

The Bridges of Summer, Cobblehill Books (New York, NY), 1992.

The Dragon That Ate Summer, Putnam (New York, NY), 1992.

Jerry on the Line, Puffin Books (New York, NY), 1992.

The Haunting of Holroyd Hill, Cobblehill Books (New York, NY), 1995.

Looking for Diamonds, Cobblehill Books (New York, NY), 1995.

The Swan's Gift, Candlewick Press (Cambridge, MA), 1995.

Under the Pear Tree, illustrated by Roger Essley, Cobblehill Books (New York, NY), 1997.

The Care and Feeding of Dragons, Cobblehill Books (New York, NY), 1998.

The Vampire in My Bathtub, Holiday House (New York, NY), 1999.

The Haunting at Stratton Falls, Dutton (New York, NY), 2000.

The Haunting of Swain's Fancy, Dutton (New York, NY), 2003.

Stonewolf, Holiday House (New York, NY), 2004.

Contributor of stories to periodicals, including *Redbook, Humpty Dumpty,* and *Jack and Jill.* Contributor of poem, "Wash Day," to *Heart to Heart,* Abrams (New York, NY), 2002.

SIDELIGHTS: Brenda Seabrooke grew up surrounded by storytellers in a rural part of Georgia and became a dedicated reader at a young age. When reading as a child, "I always hated to let go of the characters in the end," she wrote in a profile published on the Children's Book Guild of Washington, D.C. Web site. "So after I finished a book, I continued the stories, making up further adventures that went on and on." She added, "As soon as I figured out that books had authors, I knew that was what I wanted to be." This desire to create stories meshed with the inspiration she found later in memories of her childhood, in her son and daughter, and in the children she taught. Moving often because of her husband's career in the Coast Guard, the author has used this experience as well in several of her books that focus on young people adjusting to life in unfamiliar places.

The Bridges of Summer tells a story of cross-cultural interactions in a distinctive place, an island off the coast of South Carolina. Zarah, a fourteen-year-old New Yorker with dancing and acting ambitions, comes to spend the summer on the island with her grandmother Quanamina while Zarah's mother, a nightclub singer, is on tour. Quanamina is a Gullah, a descendant of former slaves who settled the island after the Civil War. She is superstitious and dedicated to traditional ways of living, which causes conflict between her and Zarah. Zarah must also learn to get along with Quanamina's young great-grandson, Loomis, who lives with her. Zarah misses modern conveniences—her grandmother's home is without electricity or running water—and longs for city life. Meanwhile, Zarah becomes friends with a white girl, Benicia, who is visiting her own grandparents, and the girls find themselves constrained by their respective grandmothers' ideas about race. Zarah finally comes to appreciate Gullah culture, but then, when Quanamina dies, the young girl must find a way to get herself and Loomis to New York.

A *Publishers Weekly* reviewer thought readers may be disappointed with this conclusion and wonder whether Zarah "really had to burn those bridges she crossed in going to her grandmother." *Kliatt* critic Dean E. Lyons allowed that some "controversy" might arise from the ending, but he praised the book overall. A *Kirkus Reviews* contributor commented that "past and present mores are contrasted in an absorbing story . . . with acumen and sympathy." The issues the book deals with, remarked Sylvia V. Meisner in *School Library Journal,* "are not only those of black and white, but also of old and new and the fear of change."

Like *The Bridges of Summer, The Haunting of Holroyd Hill* also portrays a displaced character and is set in the American South. What's more, it is one of several Seabrooke works to deal with the supernatural. Melinda and her brother, Kevin, have moved with their parents from the suburbs of Washington, D.C., to a rural part of Virginia, and Melinda is unhappy with the change. Eventually, she finds that her new home is haunted, and her brother and a neighborhood friend join with her to learn why the ghost walks through the house. Their research connects the ghost to happenings in the Civil War. "Seabrooke believably weaves the supernatural elements into the story," observed Elaine Fort Weischedel in *School Library Journal.*

A ghost and the Civil War also figure in *The Haunting at Stratton Falls.* In 1944, with World War II raging, eleven-year-old Abby and her mother relocate from Florida to live with relatives in the small town of Stratton Falls in upstate New York. Abby's father has been fighting in Europe and has been declared missing in action. She feels his absence deeply, and she dislikes her new home. She finds the home more interesting, though, after she discovers it is haunted by the ghost of a young girl, Felicia, who died eighty years earlier, when her father was away serving in the Civil War. Local residents say that Felicia's visitations come when someone is going to die. With the help of her cousin, Chad, Abby learns more about the ghost, who goes on to make one appearance that is life-saving rather than death-predicting. *School Library Journal* reviewer Connie Tyrrell Burns thought the novel "formulaic but diverting," with a "fastpaced and suspenseful" plot. While she praised the book's detailed World War II-era background, Burns found the characters underdeveloped. *Booklist* contributor Shelle Rosenfeld, however, liked its "diverse characters" as well as its "well-paced suspense, period detail, and descriptive, expressive prose."

In *The Vampire in My Bathtub,* thirteen-year-old Jeff has settled in a new and very small town in West Virginia with his mother after his parents' divorce. Initially, he finds the town boring, but he begins to enjoy life more after he accidentally frees a vampire, Eugene, who has been locked in a trunk for more than 100 years. Eugene is a "good" vampire—he does not drink blood—and also a funny and likable one, who loves television and sleeps in Jeff's bathtub. He longs to be reunited with Carlotta, the female vampire he loves, but he must do battle for her with his evil vampire cousin, Vennard. Jeff and a friend, Alison, end up assisting Eugene in this effort. A *Publishers Weekly* critic

found the novel marred by "stilted" language and lacking in suspense, though offering a few "humorous moments." *Booklist's* Rosenfeld, on the other hand, thought it both funny and suspenseful, with well-developed characters and creative plotting making it a "delightful read."

Also set in West Virginia is *The Haunting of Swain's Fancy.* Taylor, an eleven-year-old girl, is visiting her father and her new stepmother and stepsiblings at their West Virginia home, which dates to the eighteenth century. She is wary at first of her stepsister, Nicole, and stepbrother, Pete, but eventually they all join forces, along with a friend, to find out why there are ghosts in their house. What they discover is a Civil War-era rivalry between brothers who fought on different sides in the war while also battling over the family fortune and the woman they both loved; their struggle culminated in murder. "Seabrooke ably combines a ghost story with stepsibling rivalry," commented Diane Foote in *Booklist,* while *School Library Journal* reviewer Terrie Dorio observed that the novel has "suspenseful pacing that will draw readers in." A *Kirkus Reviews* contributor added, "The ghostly drama's source in the Civil War lends the whole an historical frisson entirely appropriate to the setting."

Seabrooke's rural Georgia childhood inspired her prize-winning *Judy Scuppernong* and its follow-up, *Under the Pear Tree.* In *Judy Scuppernong,* the author uses a series of prose poems to relate the summer a new girl moves into a small Southern town. *School Library Journal* critic Sally T. Margolis found the work "a delightful, delicate book, full of color and light and feelings of childhood." In *Under the Pear Tree,* set in the early 1950s, three girls, all age eleven, spend a lovely, lazy summer discovering their growing interest in boys and dealing with other coming-of-age issues. "These poems are gentle, quiet, insightful, and timeless," Sharon Korbeck remarked in *School Library Journal,* and a *Kirkus Reviews* critic wrote that "the emotions are genuine, powerful, and sweet."

Many of Seabrooke's books are written for students in the middle grades, but some are aimed at younger readers. These include *The Dragon That Ate Summer,* about a boy who finds a dragon in his garden and decides to make it his pet, and its sequel, *The Care and Feeding of Dragons,* in which the dragon must be saved from would-be thieves. Discussing the sequel in *School Library Journal,* Beth Wright reported that it "will keep readers smiling." Other Seabrooke works include the picture book *Looking for Diamonds,* inspired by her walks with her grandfather, and the original fairy tale *The Swan's Gift,* about a swan who assists the boy who has spared its life.

Seabrooke has remained not only a respected writer but also a devoted reader, commenting in her online piece for the Children's Book Guild of Washington, D.C., "I'd still rather read a good book than anything but write one!"

BIOGRAPHICAL AND CRITICAL SOURCES:

PERIODICALS

Booklist, January 1, 2000, Shelle Rosenfeld, review of *The Vampire in My Bathtub,* p. 927; July, 2000, Shelle Rosenfeld, review of *The Haunting at Stratton Falls,* p. 2030; May 15, 2003, Diane Foote, review of *The Haunting of Swain's Fancy,* p. 1662.

Kirkus Reviews, July 15, 1992, review of *The Bridges of Summer,* p. 924; June 1, 1997, review of *Under the Pear Tree,* p. 879; June 15, 2003, review of *The Haunting of Swain's Fancy,* p. 864.

Kliatt, January, 1995, Dean E. Lyons, review of *The Bridges of Summer,* p. 12.

Publishers Weekly, October 12, 1992, review of *The Bridges of Summer,* p. 80; January 3, 2000, review of *The Vampire in My Bathtub,* p. 76.

School Library Journal, November, 1990, Sally T. Margolis, review of *Judy Scuppernong,* p. 117; September, 1992, Sylvia V. Meisner, review of *The Bridges of Summer,* p. 279; April, 1995, Elaine Fort Weischedel, review of *The Haunting of Holroyd Hill;* September, 1997, Sharon Korbeck, review of *Under the Pear Tree,* p. 236; February, 1998, Beth Wright, review of *The Care and Feeding of Dragons,* p. 91; August, 2000, Connie Tyrrell Burns, review of *The Haunting at Stratton Falls,* p. 189; August, 2003, Terrie Dorio, review of *The Haunting of Swain's Fancy,* p. 166.

ONLINE

Children's Book Guild of Washington, D.C. Web Site, http://www.childrensbookguild.org/ (January 28, 2004), biography of Brenda Seabrooke.

SENNA, Danzy 1970-

PERSONAL: Born September 13, 1970, in Boston, MA; daughter of Carl Senna (a journalist) and Fanny Howe (a poet and novelist). *Education:* Stanford University, B.A. (with honors), 1992; University of California at Irvine, M.F.A., 1996. *Politics:* Democrat.

ADDRESSES: Agent—Amanda Urban, International Creative Management, 40 West 57th St., New York, NY 10019.

CAREER: Newsweek, New York, NY, researcher and reporter, 1992-94; *American Benefactor,* New York, NY, contributing editor, 1996-97. Also taught writing and literature at the College of the Holy Cross.

AWARDS, HONORS: MacDowell Colony fellow, 1997; Stephen Crane First Fiction Award, Book-of-the-Month Club, 1998, for *Caucasia;* American Whiting Writers' Award, 2002.

WRITINGS:

Caucasia (novel), Riverhead Press (New York, NY), 1998, published as *From Caucasia with Love,* Bloomsbury (London, England), 2000.

Also author of the novel *Schnee in Alabama,* 2001. Contributor of essays to books, including *To Be Real: Telling the Truth and Changing the Face of Feminism,* edited by Rebecca Walker, Doubleday (New York, NY), 1995, *Half and Half,* edited by Claudine O'Hearn, Pantheon (New York, NY), 1998, and *Giant Steps: The New Generation of African-American Writers.*

SIDELIGHTS: Danzy Senna's first novel, *Caucasia,* traces the imposed separation of Birdie Lee, the light-skinned daughter in a mixed-race family, from her older sister, Cole, the darker of the two mulatto siblings, when racial politics rip apart their family. The sisters desperately seek a coming-of-age in 1970s Boston, while their white mother and black father stage protests for racial equity. Birdie is the younger of the two, and her skin is so pale that people often assume she is white. Cole has dark skin, and her black hair hangs in braids. Despite their contrasting appearances,

Birdie and Cole are incredibly close, often speaking in a secret language they call Elemeno. Together their family experiences racism at each end of the spectrum. At one point in the story, when Birdie and her father are lounging together in the park, they are approached by police officers who have assumed that Birdie has been abducted. Birdie is enraged at the white community's perception of black people, but she learns that ignorance exists in any race when she goes to a predominantly black school and is ostracized because she is different. *Caucasia* "explores life in the middle of America's racial chasm," reported Ellen Flexman in *Library Journal. Newsweek* contributor Laura Shapiro called *Caucasia* "remarkable," noting that "Senna . . . knows racial politics first-hand, but she's more interested in their real-life consequences." Senna's knowledge of racial politics comes from her own childhood. The daughter of a white mother and a black father herself, Senna drew Birdie's character from her own childhood struggle with what she called "the experience of 'looking white' and identifying as black."

Writing in the first person, Senna uses Birdie to draw conclusions from the telling incongruities in her childhood world. June Unjoo Yang praised Senna's eye for detail in the *Hungry Mind Review.* "Working within the novel's episodic structure," Yang wrote, "Senna has a knack for plumping up scenes of political significance with attention to small gestures and details that evoke an immediate emotional response." Yang cited an example: "It struck me as odd that my mother hadn't warned Cole not to go to the park, just me," Senna's protagonist observes in *Caucasia.* "There are perverts, crazies, dirty old men, and they want little girls just like you. Girls like you. When [Mum] was gone, Cole looked up from her *Jet* magazine and watched me from behind her braids, which hung like bars across her face, dividing her features into sections." The tension in Birdie's family intensifies with the racial and political tension of the time, and when their mother takes their cause to great extremes, the family is separated down color lines. Cole and her father leave in search of a more diverse atmosphere, while Birdie and her mother reinvent themselves in white suburbia. Birdie feels more estranged than ever, attending an all-white high school and mourning the loss of her sister's companionship. Birdie's diversity is stifled as she wanders through a world to which she seems to belong, yet remains isolated from. "What Ms. Senna gets so painfully well is how the standard-issue cruelties of adolescence . . . are revitalized when they encounter race," wrote Margo Jefferson for the *New York Times Book Review.*

While most reviewers praised *Caucasia,* even some who liked the novel criticized Senna's treatment of the topic of race. Most critics agreed that Senna is dead-on in her biting assessments of everything from Waspish behavior to women's communes. However, Yang concluded that Senna is sometimes so unrelenting in her approach that she "runs the risk of sounding shrill and thereby undermining a frank and often thought-provoking meditation on race and identity." Others found her prose to lack such complexity. "In spite of some elegant descriptions and moments of metaphorical precision . . . Senna seems uncomfortable writing with emotional depth," stated Kathryn Heyman in the *New Statesman.* "Passages that should be moving are merely sentimental or coy. As a result, politics, not emotions, are engaged." However, *Booklist*'s Donna Seaman thought Senna's first novel was "as thematically and dramatically rich as fiction can be, infused, as it is, with emotional truth." Since the work's publication, Senna has continued to explore those emotional truths, and always celebrates her ethnicity. Speaking of her childhood, Senna once recalled, "At home, it was clear to me which tribe I belonged to: that of my own eccentric family. It was when I left home that I had to navigate the color-coded world. Without my kin surrounding me, reminding me who I was, I had to find other ways to feel at home." She then reveals the power behind her craft: "Writing became this home—black words against white paper—the space where I could both make sense of and escape from the problems of my everyday existence."

Caucasia "avoids the usual extremes in its depiction of racial tension," pointed out a *Publishers Weekly* critic. Writing in the *Women's Review of Books,* Marilyn Richardson described *Caucasia* as anything but overly pedantic or moralistic. Senna "has perfect pitch for all sorts of dialogue, the technical sleight of hand to place the reader deftly in the landscapes and mindscapes of her characters, laugh-out-loud wit, and a racial political consciousness so integral to her storytelling that it is never didactic." Further, Richardson praised the young writer's respect for her cultural heritage: "With a bow of acknowledgment to her elders—you'll recognize her homage to and commentary upon writing by the likes of Harriet Jacobs, Nella Larsen, Zora Neale Hurston, and Alice Walker—Senna sets in motion a brilliant, beautifully crafted work that continues to challenge the reader's mind and spirit long after the last page is turned." Reflecting on her experiences, it seems Senna has challenged her own mind as well. "What has become clear to me through my racial trials and tribulations, is that at some point you do make a choice—not between white and black, but between silence and speech. . . . Through fiction, I have found a way to speak for myself—and to embrace the contradictions that define my world."

BIOGRAPHICAL AND CRITICAL SOURCES:

BOOKS

Senna, Danzy, *Caucasia*, Riverhead (New York, NY), 1998.

PERIODICALS

Booklist, February 15, 1998, Donna Seaman, review of *Caucasia*, p. 985; November 15, 1998, Bonnie Smothers, review of *Caucasia*, p. 571; April 1, 1999, Stephanie Zvirin, review of *Caucasia*, p. 1401; February 15, 2000, Deborah Taylor, review of *Caucasia*, p. 1096.
Entertainment Weekly, April 3, 1998, Megan Harlan, review of *Caucasia*, p. 89.
Essence, March, 1998, Lise Funderberg, review of *Caucasia*, p. 66.
Hungry Mind Review, spring, 1998, June Unjoo Yang, "Watching the Canary," p. 34.
Kirkus Reviews, December 1, 1997, p. 1733.
Library Journal, January 1998, Ellen Flexman, review of *Caucasia*, p. 145.
Los Angeles Times, March 25, 1998, Susie Linfield, "Writing about More Than Listless Youth," p. E3.
New Statesman, December 18, 2000, Kathryn Heyman, review of *From Caucasia with Love*, p. 55.
Newsweek, February 16, 1998, Laura Shapiro, review of *Caucasia*, p. 71.
New York Times Book Review, March 15, 1998, Elizabeth Schmidt, "Soul Mates," p. 22; May 4, 1998, Margo Jefferson, "Seeing Race As a Costume That Everyone Wears," p. E2.
Publishers Weekly, December 8, 1997, review of *Caucasia*, p. 54.
School Library Journal, September, 1998, Frances Reiher, review of *Caucasia*, pp. 230-231.
Utne Reader, September-October, 1998, pp. 31-34.
Women's Review of Books, July, 1998, Marilyn Richardson, review of *Caucasia*, pp. 24-25.

ONLINE

AgBlog, http://www.agblog.com/ (November 14, 2003), "Searching for Danzy Senna."
Bloomsbury Online, http://www.blommsburymagazine.com/ (November 14, 2003).
Intermix.org, http://www.intermix.org.uk/ (November 14, 2003), review of *From Caucasia with Love*.
Ms. Online, http://www.msmagazine.com/ (November 14, 2003).
Salon.com, http://www.salon.com/ (November 14, 2003), Danzy Senna, "Mulatto Millennium: Since When Did Being the Daughter of a WASP and a Black-Mexican Become Cool?."
University of Wisconsin-Stevens Point Web site, http://www.uwsp.edu/ (November 14, 2003), "News Release: Novelist Senna Visits UWSP."
UppityWomen.com, http://www.uppitywomen.com/ (November 14, 2003), Heidi Johnston, review of *Caucasia*.
WithItGirl.com, http://www.withitgirl.com/ (November 14, 2003), Eric Appleton, review of *Caucasia*.*

*   *   *

SILLIPHANT, Stirling (Dale) 1918-1996

PERSONAL: Born January 16, 1918, in Detroit, MI; died of prostate cancer, April 26, 1996, in Bangkok, Thailand; son of Leigh Lemuel (a sales director) and Ethel May (Noaker) Silliphant; married Tiana du Long (an actress under name Tiana Alexandra), July 4, 1974; children: Stirling, Dayle, Loren (deceased). *Education:* University of Southern California, B.A. (magna cum laude), 1938.

CAREER: Screenwriter, producer, and novelist. Walt Disney Studios, Burbank, CA, publicist, 1938-41; Twentieth Century-Fox Film Corp., New York, NY, publicist, 1942, publicity director, 1946-53; screenwriter and independent producer, Hollywood, CA, 1953-96. President of Pingree Productions. Producer of film *Joe Louis Story*, United Artists, 1953; executive producer of films *Shaft*, Metro-Goldwyn-Mayer, 1971, and *Shaft's Big Score*, Metro-Goldwyn Mayer, 1972. *Military service:* U.S. Navy, 1942-46.

MEMBER: California Yacht Club, Writers Guild of America West, Mystery Writers of America, Authors League, Foreign Correspondents' Club (Thailand), Phi Beta Kappa.

Stirling Silliphant

AWARDS, HONORS: Academy Award, Academy of Motion Picture Arts and Sciences, 1967, Edgar Award, Mystery Writers of America, and Golden Globe Award, Hollywood Foreign Press Association, both 1968, all for screenplay *In the Heat of the Night;* Golden Globe Award, Foreign Press Association, 1969, for screenplay *Charly;* Image Award, National Association for the Advancement of Colored People, 1972, for production of *Shaft;* Box Office Writer of the Year Award, National Association of Theater Owners, 1972, for *The Poseidon Adventure,* and 1974, for *The Towering Inferno.*

WRITINGS:

NOVELS

Maracaibo, Farrar, Straus (New York, NY), 1955, reprinted, Ballantine (New York, NY), 1985.
The Slender Thread, Signet (Greenock, Scotland), 1966.

(With Neil D. Isaacs and Rachel Maddux) *Fiction into Film: A Walk in the Spring Rain* (includes the screenplay for *A Walk in the Spring Rain*), University of Tennessee Press (Knoxville, TN), 1970.
Pearl, Dell (New York, NY), 1978, reprinted, Mutual Publishing (New York, NY), 1991.
Steel Tiger, Ballantine (New York, NY), 1983.
Bronze Bell, Ballantine (New York, NY), 1985.
Silver Star, Ballantine (New York, NY), 1986.

SCREENPLAYS

(With William Bowers and John Barnwell; and co-producer) *Five against the House* (adapted from a story by Jack Finney), Columbia, 1955.
Huk! (adapted from a novel by Silliphant), United Artists, 1956.
Nightfall (adapted from the novel *The Dark Chase* by David Goodis), Columbia, 1957.
Damn Citizen, Universal, 1958.
The Lineup (adapted from the television series of the same title), Columbia, 1958.
(With Wolf Rilla, Ronald Kinnoch, and George Barclay) *Village of the Damned* (adapted from the novel *The Midwich Cuckoos* by John Wyndham), Metro-Goldwyn-Mayer, 1960.
(And executive producer) *The Slender Thread* (adapted from the novel by Silliphant), Paramount, 1965.
In the Heat of the Night (adapted from the novel by John Ball), United Artists, 1967.
Charly (adapted from the short story "Flowers for Algernon" by Daniel Keyes), Cinerama, 1968.
(And producer) *Marlowe* (adapted from the novel *The Little Sister* by Raymond Chandler), Metro-Goldwyn-Mayer, 1969.
(With Jesse Hill Ford) *The Liberation of Lord Byron Jones* (adapted from the novel by Ford), Columbia, 1970.
(And producer) *A Walk in the Spring Rain* (adapted from the novel by Rachel Maddux), Columbia, 1970.
Murphy's War (adapted from the novel by Max Catto), Paramount, 1971.
The New Centurions (adapted from the novel by Joseph Wambaugh; also known as *Precinct 45: Los Angeles Police*), Columbia, 1972.
(With Wendell Mayes) *The Poseidon Adventure* (adapted from the novel by Paul Gallico), Twentieth Century-Fox, 1972.

(And executive producer) *Shaft in Africa*, Metro-Goldwyn-Mayer, 1973.

The Towering Inferno (based on the novels *The Tower*, by Richard Martin Stern, and *The Glass Inferno*, by Thomas N. Scortia and Frank M. Robinson), Twentieth Century-Fox, 1974.

Killer Elite (adapted from the novel by Robert Rostand), United Artists, 1974.

(With Dean Reisner) *The Enforcer*, Warner Bros., 1976.

(With Peter Hyams) *Telefon*, Metro-Goldwyn-Mayer/United Artists, 1977.

The Swarm (adapted from a novel by Arthur Herzog), Warner Bros., 1978.

(With Stanley Mann) *Circle of Iron* (also released as *The Silent Flute;* adapted from a story by Silliphant, Bruce Lee, and James Coburn), Avco Embassy, 1979.

(With Carl Foreman) *When Time Ran Out* (adapted from the novel *The Day the World Ended* by Gordon Thomas; also known as *Earth's Final Fury*), Warner Bros., 1980.

(With Sylvester Stallone) *Over the Top* (also known as *Meet Me Half Way*), Cannon, 1987.

(And executive producer) *Catch the Heat* (also released as *Feel the Heat*), TransWorld, 1987.

TELEVISION SHOWS

(With others) *Mickey Mouse Club* (series), American Broadcasting Co. (ABC), 1955-59.

Brock Callahan (also broadcast as *The Silent Kill*), Columbia Broadcasting System, Inc. (CBS), August 11, 1959.

(With others) *Tightrope* (series; also known as *The Unnamed Agent* and *The Undercover Agent*), CBS, 1959-60.

(Contributor of scripts and cocreator) *Naked City* (series), ABC, 1958-63.

(Contributor of scripts and cocreator) *Route 66* (series), CBS, 1960-64.

(And producer) *New Healers*, ABC, March 27, 1972.

(And creator) *Movin' On*, National Broadcasting Co., Inc. (NBC), July 24, 1972.

(Contributor of scripts, creator, and executive producer) *Longstreet* (series), ABC, 1972-74.

(And executive producer) *A Time for Love*, NBC, 1973.

Death Scream (also known as *Streetkill* and *The Woman Who Cried Murder*), ABC, 1975.

(And executive producer) *The First Thirty-six Hours of Dr. Durant*, ABC, 1975.

(And executive producer) *Pearl* (mini-series; adapted from the novel by Silliphant), ABC, 1978.

(And executive producer) *Salem's Lot* (also known as *Blood Thirst*), CBS, 1979.

(And executive producer) *Fly Away Home* (pilot), ABC, 1981.

Golden Gate (pilot), ABC, 1981.

Hardcase, NBC, 1981.

Travis McGee (pilot; based upon the stories by John D. MacDonald; also known as *Travis McGee: The Empty Copper Sea*), ABC, 1982.

(And executive producer) *Welcome to Paradise*, CBS, 1984.

(And producer) *Mussolini: The Untold Story* (mini-series), NBC, 1985.

(With Dick Berg) *Space* (mini-series; adapted from the novel by James A. Michener), CBS, 1985.

(And producer with Mel Damski) *The Three Kings* (mini-series), ABC, 1987.

A Stranger in the Mirror, (teleplay; adapted from the novel by Sidney Sheldon), 1993.

Also author of scripts for the television shows *The Sands of Time* (mini-series), *Maya* (miniseries; 1967), *Suspicion, Mr. Novak, Rawhide, Mr. Lucky, Markham* (crime series), *Tightrope* (crime series), *Wings of Fire* (also known as *The Cloudburst*), 1967, and two episodes of *Perry Mason.* Also wrote television scripts for *Schlitz Playhouse; G. E. Theatre*, ABC, 1953-62; *Alfred Hitchcock Presents*, NBC, 1955-65; *Alcoa-Goodyear Theater*, 1957-60; *Chrysler Theatre*, NBC, 1963-67; and *CBS Playhouse.*

Also author of the screenplays *The Grass Harp* (1995; also coproduced) and *Day of Reckoning* (1994).

Silliphant's novel *Pearl* was translated into Spanish.

ADAPTATIONS: Maracaibo was adapted for film by Ted Sherdeman and released by Paramount in 1958.

SIDELIGHTS: Stirling Silliphant was working as the Eastern publicity manager for Twentieth Century-Fox in 1950 when he heard that a rival studio was looking for a script for actress Joan Crawford. Hoping to supply that script, he wrote *Maracaibo.* Set in the Venezuelan town of the same name, *Maracaibo*'s hero is Vic

Scott. In the story, Scott saves the town from fiery consumption when an oil well sets ablaze and captures the love of writer Laura Kingsley. *Maracaibo* was flatly rejected by the studio, but Silliphant reworked it into a novel, and, when published in 1955, his first book received excellent reviews. "Characterized by both taut and poignant writing, *Maracaibo* is off-beat adventure handled in a gripping off-beat way," wrote Rex Lardner in the *New York Times*. Ironically, film rights to the book were later purchased by Paramount, but when Silliphant applied for the job of screenwriter for that project, he was turned down. Instead, writer Ted Sherderman adapted the novel, and Paramount released it in 1958. Cornell Wilde directed, produced, and starred in the movie as Vic Scott. His wife, Jean Wallace, was cast as Laura Kingsley.

In 1953, Silliphant produced *The Joe Louis Story,* a biographical tale of the boxer who overcame several obstacles, including racial prejudice, to become a 1930s heavyweight champion. Unhappy with the script, Silliphant rewrote several sections of it. He told Catherine A. Peters in the *Chicago Tribune:* "When I saw the film, the only scenes I liked in it were the ones I had written. I said, 'Hey, maybe I'm a scriptwriter.'" Despite his extensive work on the script, Silliphant received credit only for producing the film, which he did on a very small budget. Though writer Robert Sylvester was credited as the sole author of the screenplay, the project proved important for Silliphant as it reinforced his desire for a career in screenwriting.

Encouraged by his work on *The Joe Louis Story,* Silliphant bought the rights to a story by Jack Finney, *Five against the House.* Silliphant wrote an adapted screenplay of the story and coproduced the film. *Five against the House* presents five college students who find themselves performing an unintentional heist on a big-time Nevada casino. The movie was praised by A. H. Weiler in the *New York Times* as a "suspenseful diversion" with "crisp, idiomatic and truly comic dialogue and a story line that suffers only from surface characterizations." The following year, Silliphant adapted his own novel *Huk,* about a plantation owner fighting to protect his property from violent advocates of social revolt. Silliphant then wrote and produced what Peters terms a trio of film-noir classics: *Nightfall, Damn Citizen,* and *The Lineup.*

Nightfall's plot is based on David Goodis's novel *The Dark Chase.* In the film, friends James Vanning (played by Aldo Ray) and Dr. Edward Gurston (played by Frank Albertson) are hunting in the woods when they are attacked by bank robbers and left for dead. Vanning survives, finds the bank robbers' money, and hides it. Realizing that he has been charged with his friend's murder, Vanning spends the rest of the movie running from both the police and the bank robbers, making the acquaintance of model Marie Gardner (played by Anne Bancroft) along the way. *Damn Citizen,* Silliphant's next film noir is based on the true story of a WWII army colonel who tries to rid Louisiana—and its government—of crime and corruption. *The Lineup* was based on a televisions series about policemen; however, Silliphant chose to base the movie on two criminals, Dancer (Eli Wallach) and Julian (Robert Keith), who are trying to smuggle heroin across the Mexican border. The movie was directed by Don Siegel.

In 1958, Silliphant turned to television, creating and writing scripts for two classic series: *Naked City* and *Route 66. Naked City* was a documentary-style police show, set and filmed in New York City at a time when most filming was done on Hollywood sets. Its two main characters were Lieutenant Dan Muldoon (John McIntire) and Detective Jim Halloran (James Franciscus). The series was inspired by Jules Dassin's 1948 feature film of the same title. Producer Herbert Leonard hired Silliphant to write the pilot script, which saw its ABC debut on September 30, 1958. Silliphant wrote thirty-one of the first season's thirty-nine half-hour episodes. *The Naked City* quickly became a favorite of American television viewers in the 1960s.

Route 66 also conceived and produced by Leonard, chronicled the adventures of two American drifters driving a Corvette. Like *The Naked City, Route 66* was filmed on location, but as the series followed its two main characters around the country, the concept of filming "on location" took on a new meaning as the cast and crew took to the road as well. Dedicated viewers tuned into CBS weekly to become lost in the personal dramas of the series' two main characters, Buz Murdock (George Maharis) and Tod Stiles (Martin Milner), as they traveled the 1960s American landscape. "Those were probably the most exciting, absorbing four years of my life," Silliphant told Peters. "I lived on the road, traveled all over the U.S. looking for ideas. Then I'd go to New York to work on *Naked City.* That's how I learned to meet deadlines. We'd have crews waiting for pages from my typewriter. Never missed a deadline." Silliphant wrote seventy-one scripts for *Route 66.* The high productivity demanded by television gave Silliphant an increased feeling of autonomy as a writer. He told Jay Stuller in *Writer's Digest:* "There's not as much time or money to waste [as there is in films] and so the writer's vision comes through stronger. I'm a defender of television and what can be done on it."

In between the filming of these two series, Silliphant wrote *The Village of the Damned,* a script based on John Wyndham's science-fiction novel *The Midwich Cuckoos* about an English town visited by aliens that cause the townspeople to sleep. When they awaken, many of the women are unjustifiably pregnant. These women then give birth to look-alike children with unsettling telekinetic powers. The script was revised by Wolf Rilla (director), Ronald Kinnoch (producer), and George Barclay before production, and upon release in the United States and Canada, it made over 1.5 million dollars.

When *The Naked City* and *Route 66* were canceled, Silliphant devoted more time to screenwriting. His next movie was *The Slender Thread,* a Seattle-based drama starring Anne Bancroft and Sidney Poitier. Based on a true event, and originally a novel written by Silliphant, the film's main characters are a suicide-prevention clinic volunteer (Poitier) and a woman who calls the clinic after taking an overdose of sleeping pills (Bancroft). *The Slender Thread,* which was directed by Sydney Pollack and produced by Silliphant, attracted a lot of attention because of its interracial costars, an unconventional practice at the time. Silliphant's next film, *In the Heat of the Night,* won an Academy Award, a Golden Globe, and the Mystery Writers of America's Edgar, all for best screenplay. This murder mystery, based on the novel by John Ball, also starred Poitier, again introducing the controversial topic of race relations.

Charly, Silliphant's next big movie, also earned him a Golden Globe for best screenplay. Based on Daniel Keyes's short story *Flowers for Algernon,* the film stars Cliff Robertson as a retarded man who undergoes experimental surgery, becomes a genius, then loses his newfound intelligence. After *Charly,* Silliphant wrote screenplays for a number of different films: *Marlowe* (adapted from the novel *The Little Sister* by Raymond Chandler), *The Liberation of L. B. Jones* (adapted from the novel by Jesse Hill Ford), *A Walk in the Spring Rain* (adapted from the novel by Rachel Mad-

dux), and *Murphy's War* (a WWII adventure adapted from the novel by Max Catto).

Silliphant's 1971 movie *Shaft,* for which he served as executive producer, earned him an Image Award from the NAACP. Silliphant produced the sequel to this movie, *Shaft's Big Score* and wrote the third Shaft movie, *Shaft in Africa,* in 1973. Silliphant's later work included a string of disaster films for producer Irwin Allen: *The Poseidon Adventure, The Towering Inferno, The Swarm,* and *When Time Ran Out.* In *The Poseidon Adventure,* an earthquake causes a tidal wave to overtake a cruise ship and its passengers. *The Towering Inferno* involves a fire engulfing the world's largest skyscraper. In *The Swarm,* a town in Texas is attacked by a massive swarm of killer bees. *When Time Ran Out* takes place on an island resort. Disaster strikes this time when a volcano erupts and threatens to consume the island. Though generally dismissed by critics, these disaster films were successes at the box office, and Silliphant was much in demand. "When producers call and want you to write a script from an idea, or write a screenplay from a novel, then you tend to feel satisfied, successful, wanted, and admired. More than money, writing films was an ego thing. I could have been secure, at the top of my field, and gone on writing movies until the day I died. But I was not growing and developing," Silliphant told Stuller.

After his series of disaster films, Silliphant returned to fiction with the 1983 publication of *Steel Tiger,* the first in a planned series of twelve novels detailing the adventures of John Locke, soldier of fortune. "The characters in this novel are lively and eccentric, . . . and the plot's complex action is fast paced," a *Publishers Weekly* reviewer wrote.

"Once you leave [Hollywood], the studios often won't let you back in," Silliphant once told Stuller. Despite this and the fact that writing the novels "represented a major financial change," it is something the author said he "had to do . . . I have some freedom and am finally released from committee- and group-thinking. . . . Most writing is pretty automatic for me. I like the emotional preparation of research; that's perhaps the best part. But in all 85,000 to 90,000 words of *Steel Tiger,* there are only about 5,000 words that are to me a mystery. Where I read back and feel a kind of magic, that third wind where you're in another place. . . . Those passages are what make you want to keep writing." Silliphant followed *Steel Tiger* with two other novels, *Bronze Bell* and *Silver Star.*

In 1987 Silliphant and his family moved to Bangkok, where he began to research a long novel about American exports in Thailand, concentrate on original screenplays, and study Buddhism with his wife. While in Bangkok, Silliphant became ill, and it was revealed that he had prostate cancer. He died in 1996 at the age of seventy-eight.

BIOGRAPHICAL AND CRITICAL SOURCES:

BOOKS

Contemporary Theatre, Film, and Television, Volume 16, Gale (Detroit, MI), 1997.
Dictionary of Literary Biography, Volume 26: *American Screenwriters,* Gale (Detroit, MI), 1984.
Pickard, Roy, *A Companion to the Movies: From 1903 to the Present Day,* Hippocrene Books (New York, NY), 1972.
Von Gunden, Kenneth, and Stuart H. Stock, *Twenty All-Time Great Science Fiction Films,* Arlington House (New York, NY), 1982, pp. 150-158.

PERIODICALS

American Film, March, 1988, pp. 13-15.
Chicago Tribune, April 3, 1980; August 23, 1983; February 15, 1987.
Christian Science Monitor, July 9, 1969.
Los Angeles Times, February 13, 1987.
Newsweek, January 31, 1972.
New Yorker, December 20, 1974.
New York Post, January 6, 1975.
New York Times, March 13, 1955; June 22, 1955; January 24, 1957; September 24, 1968; October 23, 1969; January 18, 1970; July 2, 1971; August 4, 1972; December 13, 1972; January 14, 1973; June 21, 1973; December 20, 1974; December 18, 1975; April 12, 1976; December 23, 1976; December 17, 1977; July 23, 1978; January 19, 1979; March 29, 1980; February 12, 1987.
Publishers Weekly, April 29, 1983.
Time, January 6, 1975.
Women's Wear Daily, December 18, 1974.
Writer's Digest, March, 1984.

ONLINE

American Movie Classics Web site, http://www.amctv. com/ (October 27, 2003), "Stirling Silliphant."

Bruce Lee and Stirling Silliphant, http://www.geocities. com/ (October 27, 2003), "Part II: Up Close and Personal with Stirling Silliphant: The *Towering* Writer Who Helped Launch Bruce Lee's Career."
Hollywood.com, http://www.hollywood.com/ (October 27, 2003), "Stirling Silliphant."
Museum of Broadcast Communications Web site, http://www.museum.tv/ (October 29, 2003) "Silliphant, Stirling: U.S. Writer."

OBITUARIES:

PERIODICALS

Entertainment Weekly, May 10, 1996, p. 20.
Los Angeles Times, April 27, 1996, p. A22.
New York Times, April 27, 1996, p. 30.
Time, May 6, 1996, p. 27.
Times (London, England), April 27, 1996, p. 21.*

*   *   *

SIMON, Uriel 1929-

PERSONAL: Born July 29, 1929, in Jerusalem, Palestine (now Israel); son of Ernst Akibah (a professor of education) and Toni (Rappaport) Simon; married Shulamith Munk, 1960; children: Itamar, Michal Simon Genack. *Ethnicity:* "Jewish." *Education:* Attended City University of New York, 1947; Hebrew University of Jerusalem, M.A., 1953, Ph.D., 1961. *Religion:* Jewish.

ADDRESSES: Home—17 Hatayassim St., Jerusalem 92507, Israel.

CAREER: Educator of new immigrants in the transitional camps Har-Tuv and Beer-Sheva, Israel, 1954-58; Bar-Ilan University, Ramat-Gan, Israel, lecturer, 1962-73, associate professor, 1973-82, professor of Bible, 1982-98, professor emeritus, 1999—, head of department, 1964-75, director of Institute for the History of Jewish Bible Research, 1974-98. Jewish Theological Seminary, New York, NY, visiting associate professor, 1970-71; Tel-Aviv University, visiting senior lecturer, 1972-73; Hebrew University of Jerusalem, fellow of Institute for Advanced Studies, 1982-83,

1988-89; Yale University, visiting professor, 1991-92, 1996-97; Harvard University, visiting professor, 1994-95. *Military service:* Israeli Army, 1948-49.

WRITINGS:

Arba' gishot le-Sefer Tehilim, Bar-Ilan University Press (Ramat-Gan, Israel), 1982, translation of revised edition by Lenn J. Schramm published as *Four Approaches to the Book of Psalms: From Saadiah Gaon to Abraham Ibn-Ezra,* State University of New York Press (Albany, NY), 1991.

(Author of commentary) *Yonah,* Magnes Press (Tel-Aviv, Israel), 1992, translation by Lenn J. Schramm published as *Jonah: The Traditional Hebrew Text with the New JPS Translation,* Jewish Publication Society (Philadelphia, PA), 1999.

Reading Prophetic Narratives, translation by Lenn J. Schramm, Indiana University Press (Bloomington, IN), 1997.

Yosef ve-ehav, sipur shel hishtanut, translation by David Louvish published as *Joseph and His Brothers: A Story of Change,* Lookstein Center (Ramat-Gan, Israel), 2002.

BOOKS PUBLISHED IN HEBREW

(Editor) *The Bible and Us,* Devir (Tel-Aviv, Israel), 1979.

(Editor, with others) *'Iyune Mikra u-farshanut* (title means "Studies in Bible and Exegesis"), six volumes, Bar-Ilan University Press (Ramat-Gan, Israel), 1980-2002.

Shene perushe R. Abraham Ibn 'Ezra le-Tere-'a´sar: Ha-perush ha-mekubal 'al-pi ketav-yad Montifyori ve-'shitah aheret' she-'adayin lo ra'atah or; Be-livyat hilufe girsa'ot mi-kol kitve-ha-yad veha-defus ha-rishon, mar'e-mekomot, be'ur u-mavo (title means "Abraham Ibn Ezra's Two Commentaries on the Minor Prophets: An Annotated Critical Edition"), Volume 1: *Hosea, Joel, Amos,* Bar-Ilan University Press (Ramat-Gan, Israel), 1989.

(Editor, with Yosef Kohen) Abraham ben Meïr Ibn Ezra, *Yesod mora ve-sod Torah* (title means "The Foundation of Piety and the Secret of the Torah"), University of Bar-Ilan Press (Ramat-Gan, Israel), 2002.

Bakesh shalom ve-rodfehu: She'elot ha-sha'ah be-or ha-Mikra, ha-Mikra be-or she'elot ha-sha'ah (title means "Seek Peace and Pursue It: Topical Issues in the Light of the Bible, the Bible in the Light of Topical Issues"), Sifre hemed (Tel-Aviv, Israel), 2002.

BIOGRAPHICAL AND CRITICAL SOURCES:

PERIODICALS

Catholic Biblical Quarterly, April, 2000, Roland E. Murphy, review of *Jonah: The Traditional Hebrew Text with the New JPS Translation,* p. 340.

Interpretation, October, 2000, Irene Nowell, review of *Jonah,* p. 431.

Journal of Law and Religion, winter-summer, 2002, David L. Lieber, review of *Four Approaches to the Book of Psalms: From Saadiah Gaon to Abraham Ibn-Ezra,* pp. 167-170.

*   *   *

SORENSON, Margo 1946-
   (Marcie Kremer)

PERSONAL: Born 1946; married James Sorenson (a retired investment manager); children: Jane, Jill. *Education:* University of California—Los Angeles, B.A., 1967. *Religion:* Lutheran. *Hobbies and other interests:* Golf, reading, travel.

ADDRESSES: Home and office—56-895 Jack Nicklaus Blvd., La Quinta, CA 92253. *E-mail*—MSorensoaol.com.

CAREER: Teacher in California and Hawaii, 1967-85; writer. Johns Hopkins University, fellow, beginning 1988. A Better Chance (ABC) Foundation, volunteer tutor.

MEMBER: Society of Children's Book Writers and Illustrators, Junior League of Minneapolis.

AWARDS, HONORS: Excellence in Teaching Award, Center for Academically Talented Youth, Johns Hopkins University, 1988, 1994; California Educator of the Year Award, Milken Family Foundation and California State Department of Education, 1991; Global Teaching Award, Xerox Corp., Allstate, Anheuser-Busch Co., and Immaculate Heart College Center for International and Multicultural Studies, 1992.

WRITINGS:

CHILDREN'S BOOKS

(Under pseudonym Marcie Kremer) *Aloha, Love* (romance novel), Bantam (New York, NY), 1995.

Danger Canyon (novel), Perfection Learning (Logan, IA), 1996.

The Hidden Dagger (novel), Perfection Learning (Logan, IA), 1996.

Soccer Blaster (novel), Perfection Learning (Logan, IA), 1996.

Kimo and the Secret Waves (novel), Perfection Learning (Logan, IA), 1996.

Nothing Is for Free (novel), Perfection Learning (Logan, IA), 1996.

The Gotcha Plot (novel), Perfection Learning (Logan, IA), 1996.

Firewatch (novel), Perfection Learning (Logan, IA), 1996.

Time Trap (novel), Perfection Learning (Logan, IA), 1996.

Who Stole the Bases? (novel), Perfection Learning (Logan, IA), 1996.

Don't Bug Me (novel), Perfection Learning (Logan, IA), 1996.

Tsunami! (nonfiction), Perfection Learning (Logan, IA), 1997.

Hurricane (nonfiction), Perfection Learning (Logan, IA), 1997.

Fight in the Fields: The Story of Cesar Chavez, Perfection Learning (Logan, IA), 1998.

Leap into the Unknown: The Story of Albert Einstein, Perfection Learning (Logan, IA), 1998.

Danger Marches to the Palace: The Story of Queen Lili'uokalani, Perfection Learning (Logan, IA), 1998.

Death of Lies: The Story of Socrates, Perfection Learning (Logan, IA), 1998.

Shatter with Words: The Story of Langston Hughes, Perfection Learning (Logan, IA), 1998.

Clubhouse Threat, Perfection Learning (Logan, IA), 2001.

Funny Man, Perfection Learning (Logan, IA), 2002.

Tori and the Sleigh of Midnight Blue, North Dakota Institute for Regional Studies, North Dakota State University Press (Fargo, ND), 2002.

Soccer Battle, Perfection Learning (Logan, IA), 2002.

Secret Heroes, Perfection Learning (Logan, IA), 2003.

Armando's Backpack, Brookfield Reader (Sterling, VA), 2004.

Funny Man Gets Rolling, Perfection Learning (Logan, IA), in press.

Work represented in anthologies, including *The Will to Survive,* Steck-Vaughn (Austin, TX), 2003.

SIDELIGHTS: Margo Sorenson once commented to *CA*: "Most kids today would rather turn on the television or a video game than read a book. The competition for readers is tough, and I try to keep that in mind when I write. For my ideas, I draw on my experiences from teaching middle school for many years, from raising my own family, and from author visits in schools. I hope in this way I can 'hook' kids into reading by packing in lots of action that will keep them turning the pages and, even more important, by tapping into feelings and emotions they really know about."

BIOGRAPHICAL AND CRITICAL SOURCES:

ONLINE

Aloha! Dear Readers. Margo Sorenson, Author of Books for Young Readers, http://www.members. aol.com/msorenso/sorenson.html/ (April 8, 2004).

*   *   *

SORRET, Ludovico
    See NOONAN, Tom

*   *   *

SPIVEY, Richard L. 1937-

PERSONAL: Born April 2, 1937, in San Jose, CA; son of Thomas S. (a restaurateur) and Sylvia (a homemaker; maiden name, Rhoten) Spivey; married Leora Scattini, August, 1963 (divorced, 1970); married Lynne Plant (a housewife), November 24, 1978. *Education:* Stanford University, B.A. 1958.

ADDRESSES: Home and office—Carmel, CA. *Agent*—c/o Author Mail, Museum of New Mexico, P.O. Box 2087, Santa Fe, NM 87504-2087.

CAREER: Spivey's Coffee Shops, San Jose, CA, general manager, 1959-62, president, 1962-69; Indian Trader (dealers in Pueblo pottery), Santa Fe, NM, owner, 1969-81; American Indian art consultant and farmer, beginning 1981. Judge of Pueblo Indian pottery for Southwestern Association on Indian Affairs, Heard Museum, and Gallup Inter-Tribal Indian Ceremonial; Wheelwright Museum of the American Indian, vice president of board of trustees, guest curator, 1980. *Military service:* U.S. Army Reserve, 1959-65.

MEMBER: Southwestern Association on Indian Affairs (past president), California State Restaurant Association (member of board of directors), Old Santa Fe Association (member of board of directors).

WRITINGS:

Maria, Northland Press (Flagstaff, AZ), 1979, revised edition, 1981.
The Legacy of Maria Poveka Martinez, photographs by Herbert Lotz, Museum of New Mexico (Santa Fe, NM), 2003.

Contributor to books, including *Arizona Highways: Indian Arts and Crafts,* edited by Clara Lee Tanner, Arizona Highways (Phoenix, AZ), 1976; author of foreword, Susan Brown McGreevy, *Maria: The Legend, the Legacy,* Sunstone Press (Santa Fe, NM), 1982. Contributor to *American Craft* and *El Palacio.* Member of editorial advisory board, *American Indian Art.*

SIDELIGHTS: Richard L. Spivey once told *CA:* "In regard to my career with Pueblo Indian pottery, I have to give considerable credit to Popovi Da, the son of Maria Martinez, who was my mentor until his death in 1971. Without his guidance and support, it would have been difficult to obtain the depth of knowledge and the degree of success that I achieved in this field. Popovi Da provided a compelling reason for writing the book on Maria.

"A subject of vital importance to Pueblo Indian pottery is the disturbing recent and growing use of nontraditional methods and materials in the manufacture of what is represented as traditionally made pottery. I will deal with this subject in a future book on Pueblo potters.

"I have a broad interest in ceramics in general, but especially (other than Pueblo Indian pottery) I am interested in early Japanese and Chinese wares, and the contemporary folk-craft pottery wares of Japan."

BIOGRAPHICAL AND CRITICAL SOURCES:

PERIODICALS

Arizona Highways, May, 1974.
Arizona Republic, March 12, 1972.
Library Journal, June 15, 2003, Sylvia Andrews, review of *The Legacy of Maria Poveka Martinez,* p. 69.
Los Angeles Times, October 5, 1971.
Santa Fean, December, 1973-January, 1974.
Santa Fe Reporter, August 14, 1980.*

*   *   *

STEWART, Mary (Florence Elinor) 1916-

PERSONAL: Born September 17, 1916, in Sunderland, Durham, England; daughter of Frederick Albert (a Church of England clergyman) and Mary Edith (Matthews) Rainbow; married Sir Frederick Henry Stewart, September 24, 1945 (died, 2001). *Education:* University of Durham, B.A., 1938, M.A., 1941. *Hobbies and other interests:* Music, painting, the theatre, gardening, crossword puzzles, playing the piano.

ADDRESSES: Office—338 Euston Rd., London NW1 3BH, England. *Agent*—c/o Author Mail, William Morrow & Co., 105 Madison Ave., New York, NY 10016.

CAREER: University of Durham, Durham, England, lecturer, 1941-45, part-time lecturer, 1948-55; writer, beginning 1954. *Military service:* Royal Observer Corps, World War II.

MEMBER: PEN, Royal Society of Arts (fellow).

AWARDS, HONORS: British Crime Writers Association Silver Dagger Award, 1961, for *My Brother Michael;* Mystery Writers of America Edgar Award, 1964, for *This Rough Magic;* Frederick Niven Literary

Mary Stewart

Award, 1971, for *The Crystal Cave;* Scottish Arts Council Award, 1975, for *Ludo and the Star Horse;* fellow, Newnham College, Cambridge, 1986.

WRITINGS:

Madam, Will You Talk? (also see below), Hodder & Stoughton (London, England), 1955, Mill (New York, NY), 1956.

Wildfire at Midnight (also see below), Appleton (New York, NY), 1956.

Thunder on the Right, Hodder & Stoughton (London, England), 1957, Mill (New York, NY), 1958.

Nine Coaches Waiting (also see below), Hodder & Stoughton (London, England), 1958, Mill (New York, NY), 1959.

My Brother Michael (also see below), Mill (New York, NY), 1960.

The Ivy Tree (also see below), Hodder & Stoughton, 1961, Mill (New York, NY), 1962.

The Moon-Spinners (also see below), Hodder & Stoughton (London, England), 1962, Mill (New York, NY), 1963.

Three Novels of Suspense (contains *Madam, Will You Talk?, Nine Coaches Waiting,* and *My Brother Michael*), Mill (New York, NY), 1963.

This Rough Magic (also see below), Mill (New York, NY), 1964.

Airs above the Ground (also see below), Mill (New York, NY), 1965.

The Gabriel Hounds (also see below), Mill (New York, NY), 1967.

The Wind off the Small Isles, illustrated by Laurence Irving, Hodder & Stoughton (London, England), 1968.

The Spell of Mary Stewart (contains *This Rough Magic, The Ivy Tree,* and *Wildfire at Midnight*), Doubleday (New York, NY), 1968.

Mary Stewart Omnibus (contains *Madam, Will You Talk?, Wildfire at Midnight,* and *Nine Coaches Waiting*), Hodder & Stoughton (London, England), 1969.

The Crystal Cave (also see below), Morrow (New York, NY), 1970, Ballantine (New York, NY), 1996.

The Little Broomstick (for children), illustrated by Shirley Hughes, Brockhampton Press (Leicester, England), 1971, Morrow (New York, NY), 1972.

The Hollow Hills (also see below), Morrow (New York, NY), 1973, Ballantine (New York, NY), 1996.

Ludo and the Star Horse (juvenile), illustrated by Gino D'Achille, Brockhampton Press (Leicester, England), 1974.

Touch Not the Cat (also see below), Morrow (New York, NY), 1976.

Triple Jeopardy (contains *My Brother Michael, The Moon-Spinners,* and *This Rough Magic*), Hodder & Stoughton (London, England), 1978.

Selected Works (contains *The Crystal Cave, The Hollow Hills, Wildfire at Midnight,* and *Airs above the Ground*), Heinemann (London, England), 1978.

The Last Enchantment (also see below), Morrow (New York, NY), 1979, Ballantine (New York, NY), 1996.

A Walk in Wolf Wood: A Tale of Fantasy and Magic, illustrated by Emanuel Schongut, Morrow (New York, NY), 1980.

Mary Stewart's Merlin Trilogy (contains *The Crystal Cave, The Hollow Hills,* and *The Last Enchantment*), Morrow (New York, NY), 1980.

The Wicked Day, Morrow (New York, NY), 1983, Ballantine (New York, NY), 1996.

Mary Stewart—Four Complete Novels (contains *Touch Not the Cat, The Gabriel Hounds, This Rough*

Magic, and *My Brother Michael*), Avenel Books (New York, NY), 1983.

Thornyhold, Morrow (New York, NY), 1988.

Frost on the Window: Poems, Morrow (New York, NY), 1990.

The Stormy Petrel, Morrow (New York, NY), 1991.

The Prince and the Pilgrim, Morrow (New York, NY), 1995.

Rose Cottage, Morrow (New York, NY), 1997.

Also author of radio plays, *Lift from a Stranger, Call Me at Ten-Thirty, The Crime of Mr. Merry,* and *The Lord of Langdale,* produced by British Broadcasting Corporation, 1957-58. Stewart's works have been translated into sixteen languages, including Hebrew, Icelandic, and Slovak. The National Library of Scotland houses Stewart's manuscript collection.

ADAPTATIONS: The Moon-Spinners was filmed by Walt Disney in 1964. *Frost on the Window: Poems* was adapted for audiocassette by Dove (Beverly Hills, CA), 1991.

SIDELIGHTS: Mary Stewart's writing career is divided into two distinct parts. In her first period, according to Kay Mussell in the *St. James Guide to Crime and Mystery Writers,* Stewart "wrote a remarkable series of ten popular novels of romantic suspense. . . . In her later phase, beginning in the late 1960s, Stewart's novels have been concerned with history and frequently with the occult. Her best-known work from this period was her four-volume series about King Arthur and Merlin." In the words of a *National Observer* critic, "Like a magician, she conjures exotic moods and mysteries from mere words, her only aim to entertain."

Stewart explained in an article for *Writer* magazine: "I am first and foremost a teller of tales, but I am also a serious-minded woman who accepts the responsibilities of her job, and that job, if I am to be true to what is in me, is to say with every voice at my command: 'We must love and imitate the beautiful and the good.' It is a comment on our age that one hesitates to stand up and say this aloud."

While "predictability" is not a quality most authors would strive for, a *Christian Science Monitor* reviewer felt that this trait has been the secret of Stewart's

success. Prior to 1970, for example, her plots followed a fairly consistent pattern of romance and suspense set in vividly depicted locales such as Provence, the Isle of Skye, the Pyrenees, Delphi, and Lebanon. Furthermore, noted the *Christian Science Monitor* reviewer, "Mrs. Stewart doesn't pull any tricks or introduce uncomfortable issues. Attractive, well-brought-up girls pair off with clean, confident young men, always on the side of the angels. And when the villains are finally rounded up, no doubts disturb us—it is clear that the best men have won again." The heroine of these stories is always "a girl displaying just the right combination of strengths and weaknesses. She may blunder into traps and misread most of the signals, but she will—feminine intuition being what it is—stumble onto something important. She will also need rescuing in a cliff-hanging finale." In short, the reviewer concluded, "It all makes excellent escape fiction."

"One of Stewart's finest qualities as a writer," Mussell wrote, "is her extraordinary descriptive prose. Stewart's ability to evoke a highly specific time and place, through sensuous descriptions of locale, character, and food, provides an immediacy that is often lacking in mystery fiction. Her academic background in English literature lends thematic and dramatic elements in the epigrams to her chapters and the literary allusions within the works."

New York Times Book Review critic Anthony Boucher defined Stewart's fiction as belonging to "that special subspecies of mystery one might call the Cinderella-suspense novel." This subspecies, Boucher believed, "is designed by feminine authors for feminine readers; yet a male can relish such highpoints as *Jane Eyre* or *Rebecca.* Of current practitioners, I can't think of anyone (aside from du Maurier herself) who tells such stories quite as well as Mary Stewart."

Other critics have noted the same qualities in Stewart's writing. *New York Herald Tribune Book Review* critic James Sandoe called *Madam, Will You Talk?* "a distinctly charming, romantic thriller. . . [that is] intelligently soft-boiled, pittypat and a good deal of fun." *My Brother Michael,* according to Francis Iles of the *Guardian,* was "the contemporary thriller at its very best." Speaking of the same novel, a *Publishers Weekly* contributor wrote that the novel "oozes Southern authenticity like honey over a hot biscuit . . . her fine writing and the ring of her natural voice will carry readers along like a tale told on a porch on a sultry

Southern night." Boucher, too, found the book worthy of praise: "If the delightfully entertaining novels of Mary Stewart . . . have had a fault, it is that their plots are (in James Sandoe's useful term) Eurydicean—they cannot survive a backward glance. But in *My Brother Michael* even this flaw vanishes . . . . This detective adventure, rich in action and suspense, is seen through the eyes of a characteristic Stewart heroine; and surely there are few more attractive young women in today's popular fiction. . . .These girls are as far removed as you can imagine from the Idiot Heroine who disfigures (at least for men) so much romantic fiction."

In 1970, Stewart turned to historical fiction. The main focus of this new interest was Arthurian England, especially as seen through the eyes of Merlin the magician. Liz Holliday in the *St. James Guide to Fantasy Writers* believed Stewart's Merlin character "is an intriguing mixture of pragmatist and fey, believer and agnostic. He has visions, true dreams in which he sees what is and what is to come. These, he believes, come from a god: but he refuses to identify this god as being Christian, Mithraditic or of the Druidic, goddess-worshipping Old Faith. At the same time he is portrayed as a polymath, dedicated to understanding the world through scholarship in the fields of science, mathematics and engineering."

Unlike most other authors who have written about the legends of Camelot in terms of the Middle Ages, Stewart placed her story in more historically accurate fifth-century Britain. Reviewing *The Crystal Cave,* the first of three books on Merlin, a *Best Sellers* critic wrote: "Fifth-century Britain and Brittany come to life in Miss Stewart's vigorous imagination. . . . Those who have read and enjoyed the many novels of Mary Stewart will not need to be told this is an expertly fashioned continually absorbing story, with a facile imagination fleshing out the legend of the parentage of the future King Arthur—and, too, of Merlin himself." A *Books and Bookmen* critic called it "a highly plotted and rattling good yarn. Mary Stewart's evocation of an era of magic, as well as of bloodletting, is magnificently done. Her writing is virile, and of a very high quality indeed. Her descriptions of the countryside are often moving, also poetical."

New York Times Book Review critic Martin Levin, after reminding readers that little is actually known of Merlin's life, noted that "the author obligingly expands [Merlin's] myth into a first-person history. . . . Cheerfully disclaiming authenticity, Miss Stewart . . . lightens the Dark Ages with legend, pure invention and a lively sense of history." A *Christian Science Monitor* reviewer, however, found this type of "history" to be somewhat compromised by the author's emphasis on Merlin's magical powers. "There really is little 'magic' in the story," the reviewer explained, "and what there is rarely exceeds the familiar 'knowing before the event.' But the very uncertainty of its inclusion lends a certain falseness to an otherwise absorbing story, which has been carefully researched historically so that it is peripherally authentic." But the reviewer concluded, "*The Crystal Cave* evokes an England long gone and could prove an interesting guidebook to some of the less touristy attractions of the Cornish and Welsh countryside."

The Hollow Hills is a continuation of Merlin's story. A *Publishers Weekly* critic called it "romantic, refreshing and most pleasant reading. . . . Mrs. Stewart has steeped herself well in the folklore and known history of fifth-century Britain and she makes of her feuding, fighting warlords lively and intriguing subjects." A *Best Sellers* critic wrote: "All in all, this makes a smashing good tale. The suspense is superb and the reader is kept involved in the unwinding of the plot. Miss Stewart has taken the main lines of the Arthurian legend and has developed the basic elements in a plausible way."

Joseph McLellan of the *Washington Post Book World* found the third Merlin book, *The Last Enchantment,* to be somewhat anticlimactic. "Having used two long, exciting novels to get Arthur on the throne," he concluded, "Miss Stewart has reached the final volume of her trilogy and we can settle back expecting to hear the old stories told again with her unique touch. There is only one trouble with this expectation: Mary Stewart does not fulfill it, and she quite clearly never had any intentions of fulfilling it. Her story is not strictly about Arthur but about Merlin. . . . Strictly speaking, once Arthur is safely on the throne . . . Merlin's life work is over. He spends most of *The Last Enchantment* fading away as gracefully as he can manage. . . . [As a result of this shift in emphasis,] the role of Arthur in this volume is fitful and erratic; he is a powerful presence but not the central character."

Very much aware of the difficulties involved in gathering and making sense out of the confusing source material available on Merlin's life, McLellan praised

Stewart for "the ingenuity of [her] effort," though he felt that the story's ultimate plausibility was somewhat in doubt. "She gives us . . . traditional materials," he noted, "but the treatment is her own, the emphasis shifted for her purpose, which is not simply to recast old material but to bring alive a long-dead historical epoch—not the Middle Ages of Malory but the Dark Ages of the original Arthur. This she does splendidly. Fifth-century Britain is caught in these pages, and while it may lack some of the exotic glitter of the imaginary twelfth-century Britain that Arthur usually inhabits, it is a fascinating place."

Stewart followed her Merlin Trilogy with one last book based on the Arthurian legends, *The Wicked Day,* a tale told by Arthur's bastard son Mordred. According to Arthurian tradition, Mordred is the cause of Arthur's eventual downfall. He has a "bad reputation as Arthur's mean-spirited, traitorous, regicidal son," as Roy Hoffman explained in the *New York Times Book Review.*

But in Stewart's version of the story, Mordred is more a tragic figure in the drama than a conscious agent of destruction. "Stewart," Hoffman wrote, "attempts to resurrect him as a compassionate young man who is helpless before fate." *Journal of Reading* contributor M. Jean Greenlaw found that "Stewart shapes a sense of the inevitable doom of Camelot, not by Mordred's desire but by the fateful actions of many men and women." *School Library Journal* writer Mary Mills concluded that "Stewart has created flesh and blood characters out of legends, and in doing so has crafted a well-plotted and passionate drama." Holliday believed that "telling the tale from Mordred's point of view works splendidly. It allows his character to emerge as much more complex and sympathetic than it might otherwise have done. Here, Mordred is clearly as much a victim . . . as Arthur ever was, and his attempts to overcome the weakness of character that leads him to his final clash with his father make him an engaging, if not wholly likeable, character." A *School Library Journal* reviewer noted that Stewart demonstrated "how average people can be manipulated by their destiny toward . . . far-reaching consequences."

In an article for *Philological Quarterly,* Maureen Fries compared Stewart's treatment of Arthurian legend with that of T. H. White, the author of *The Once and Future King.* "Of all literary genres," Fries began, "romance is perhaps the most irrational, focusing as it does upon the strange, the marvelous, and the supernatural. And of all the 'matters' of romance, that of Britain contains the most irrationalities." But Fries concluded that "in making over medieval romance into modern novels, T. H. White and Mary Stewart have not only coped, mostly successfully, with the irrationality of the Matter of Britain. They have also grasped and translated into a convincing modern, if diverse, idiom that rational core of truth about human psychology, and the human condition, which constitutes not only the greatness of the Arthurian legend but also its enduring appeal to readers of all centuries and all countries, and to writers of every time and every literary persuasion."

In the early 1980s Stewart continued writing medieval tales. *A Walk in Wolf Wood* concerns two modern-day children who are thrust backwards in time to the Middle Ages. "The eerie events that overtake [the children] become the vehicle for an incisive exploration of magic, savagery and the mis-uses of power," observed *Times Literary Supplement* contributor Mary Cadogan. "The trappings of another time like jousts and hunts, terraces and towers, are vivid and atmospheric but not overdone."

Explaining her decision to switch from writing thrillers to historical fiction, Mary Stewart once told *CA:* "I always planned that some day I would write a historical novel, and I intended to use Roman Britain as the setting. This is a period that I have studied over many years. But then, quite by chance, I came across a passage in Geoffrey of Monmouth's *History of the Kings of Britain,* which described the first appearance of Merlin, the Arthurian 'enchanter.' Here was a new story, offering a new approach to a dark and difficult period, with nothing known about the 'hero' except scraps of legend. The story would have to come purely from imagination, pitched somewhere between legend and truth and fairy-tale and known history. The setting would be imaginary, too, a Dark Age Britain in the unrecorded aftermath of the Roman withdrawal. I had originally no intention of writing more than one volume, but the story seized my imagination. . . . It has been a tough job and a rewarding one. I have learned a lot, not least that the powerful themes of the Arthurian 'Matter of Britain' are as cogent and real today as they were fourteen centuries ago. And Merlin's story has allowed me to return to my first avocation of all, that of poet."

BIOGRAPHICAL AND CRITICAL SOURCES:

BOOKS

Contemporary Literary Criticism, Gale (Detroit, MI), Volume 7, 1977, Volume 35, 1985.

Continuum Encyclopedia of Children's Literature, Continuum (New York, NY), 2001.

Friedman, Lenemaja, *Mary Stewart,* Twayne (Boston, MA), 1990.

Newquist, Roy, *Counterpoint,* Rand McNally (New York, NY), 1964.

St. James Guide to Crime and Mystery Writers, 4th edition, St. James Press (Detroit, MI), 1996.

St. James Guide to Fantasy Writers, St. James Press (Detroit, MI), 1996.

PERIODICALS

Arthurian Interpretations, spring, 1987, pp. 70-83.

Best Sellers, October 1, 1967; July 15, 1970; July 15, 1973; November, 1976, p. 250.

Booklist, April 15, 1992, p. 1547; April 1, 1998, p. 1314; June 1, 1998, p. 1723.

Books and Bookmen, August, 1970.

Book Week, November 21, 1965.

Christian Science Monitor, September 28, 1967; September 3, 1970.

Guardian, February 26, 1960.

Harper's, September, 1970.

Journal of Reading, May, 1984, p. 741.

Kirkus Reviews, August 1, 1983, p. 840; July 15, 1991, p. 887.

Library Journal, June 15, 1973; March 1, 2002, review of *Mary Stewart's Merlin Trilogy* and *The Wicked Day,* p. 172.

National Observer, October 23, 1967.

New Statesman, November 5, 1965.

New York Herald Tribune Book Review, May 27, 1956; October 5, 1958; March 8, 1959; March 4, 1962.

New York Times, March 18, 1956; September 9, 1956; May 18, 1958; January 18, 1959.

New York Times Book Review, April 10, 1960; January 7, 1962; October 24, 1965; October 15, 1967; August 9, 1970; July 29, 1973; September 2, 1979; January 1, 1984, p. 20.

Philological Quarterly, spring, 1977, pp. 259-265.

Publishers Weekly, September 16, 1988; July 12, 1991; January 20, 1997.

San Francisco Chronicle, October 21, 1956; May 22, 1960.

School Library Journal, March, 1984, p. 178.

Sunday Times Colour Supplement, June 13, 1976.

Time, January 5, 1968.

Times Educational Supplement, February 5, 1982, p. 28.

Times Literary Supplement, July 18, 1980, p. 806.

Washington Post Book World, March 31, 1968; September 15, 1976; July 22, 1979.

Writer, May, 1970, pp. 9-12, 46.*

*   *   *

ST. JOHN, Leonie
See BAYER, William

*   *   *

STRASSER, Todd 1950-
(Morton Rhue)

PERSONAL: Born May 5, 1950, in New York, NY; son of Chester S. (a manufacturer of dresses) and Sheila (a copyeditor; maiden name, Reisner) Strasser; children: Lia, Geoff. *Education:* Beloit College, B.A., 1974. *Hobbies and other interests:* Fishing, skiing, and tennis.

ADDRESSES: Office—P. O. Box 859, Larchmont, NY 10538. *E-mail*—todd@toddstrasser.com.

CAREER: Freelance writer, 1975—. Beloit College, Beloit, WI, worked in public relations, 1973-74; *Times Herald Record,* Middletown, NY, reporter, 1974-76; Compton Advertising, New York, NY, copywriter, 1976-77; *Esquire,* New York, NY, researcher, 1977-78; Toggle, Inc. (fortune cookie company), New York, NY, owner, 1978-89. Speaker at upper elementary schools, middle schools, and at junior and senior high schools, teachers' and librarians' conferences. Lectures and conducts writing workshops for adults and teenagers.

MEMBER: International Reading Association, Writers Guild of America, Authors Guild, Freedom to Read Foundation, PEN.

Todd Strasser

AWARDS, HONORS: American Library Association's Best Books for Young Adults citations, 1981, for *Friends till the End: A Novel,* and 1982, for *Rock 'n' Roll Nights: A Novel;* New York Public Library's Books for the Teen Age citations, 1981, for *Angel Dust Blues,* 1982, for *The Wave* and *Friends till the End,* 1983, for *Rock 'n' Roll Nights,* and 1984, for *Workin' for Peanuts; Friends till the End* was chosen a Notable Children's Trade Book in the Field of Social Studies by the National Council for Social Studies and the Children's Book Council, 1982; *Rock 'n' Roll Nights* was chosen for the Acton Public Library's CRABbery Award List, 1983; Young Reader Medal nomination from the California Reading Association, 1983, for *Friends till the End;* Book Award from the Federation of Children's Books (Great Britain), 1983, for *The Wave,* and 1984, for *Turn It Up!;* Outstanding Book Award from the Iowa Books for Young Adult Program, 1985, for *Turn It Up!;* Colorado Blue Spruce Award nomination, 1987, for *Angel Dust Blues;* Edgar Award nomination, Mystery Writers of America, 1998, for *The Accident;* Washington Irving Award, 1998, for

Abe Lincoln for Class President; Volunteer State Book Award, 1998; New York State Charlotte Award, Rhode Island Teen Book Award, and Washington Irving Children's Choice Book Award, all 2002, all for *Give a Boy a Gun.*

WRITINGS:

YOUNG ADULT FICTION

Angel Dust Blues, Coward, McCann (New York, NY), 1979.

Friends till the End: A Novel, Delacorte (New York, NY), 1981.

(Under pseudonym Morton Rhue) *The Wave* (novelization based on the television drama of the same title by Johnny Dawkins), Delacorte (New York, NY), 1981.

Rock 'n' Roll Nights: A Novel, Delacorte (New York, NY), 1982.

Workin' for Peanuts, Delacorte (New York, NY), 1983.

Turn It Up! (sequel to *Rock 'n' Roll Nights*), Delacorte (New York, NY), 1984.

A Very Touchy Subject, Delacorte (New York, NY), 1985.

Ferris Bueller's Day Off (novelization based on film of the same title by John Hughes), New American Library (New York, NY), 1986.

Wildlife (sequel to *Turn It Up!*), Delacorte (New York, NY), 1987.

The Accident (also see below), Delacorte (New York, NY), 1988.

Cookie (novelization based on film of the same title by Nora Ephron), New American Library (New York, NY), 1989.

Moving Target, Fawcett (New York, NY), 1989.

Beyond the Reef, illustrations by Debbie Heller, Delacorte (New York, NY), 1989.

Home Alone (novelization based on film of the same title), Scholastic (New York, NY), 1991.

The Diving Bell, illustrated by Debbie Heller, Scholastic (New York, NY), 1992.

Honey, I Blew Up the Kids, Disney Press (New York, NY), 1992.

Hocus Pocus, Disney Press (New York, NY), 1993.

Disney's "The Villains" Collection, poems by Mark Rifkin, illustrated by Gil DiCicco, Disney Press (New York, NY), 1993.

The Three Musketeers, Disney Press (New York, NY), 1993.

Free Willy, Scholastic (New York, NY), 1993.

Disney's "It's Magic": Stories from the Films, with poems by Richard Duke, illustrated by Philippe Harchy, Disney Press (New York, NY), 1994.

(Adapter) *Walt Disney's "Lady and the Tramp,"* illustrated by Franc Mateu, Disney Press (New York, NY), 1994.

(Adapter) *Walt Disney's Peter Pan,* illustrated by Jose Cardona and Fred Marvin, Disney Press (New York, NY), 1994.

Tall Tale: The Unbelievable Adventures of Pecos Bill, Disney Press (New York, NY), 1994.

Street Fighter, Newmarket Press (New York, NY), 1994.

Man of the House, Disney Press (New York, NY), 1995.

How I Changed My Life, Simon & Schuster (New York, NY), 1995.

Girl Gives Birth to Own Prom Date, Simon & Schuster (New York, NY), 1996.

Hey Dad, Get a Life!, Holiday House (New York, NY), 1996.

How I Spent My Last Night on Earth, Simon & Schuster (New York, NY), 1998.

Kidnap Kids, Putnam (New York, NY), 1998.

Kids' Book of Gross Facts and Feats, Watermill Press, 1998.

Star Wars Episode One, Journal, Anakin Skywalker, Scholastic (New York, NY), 1999.

Give a Boy a Gun, Simon & Schuster (New York, NY), 2000.

Con-Fidence, Holiday House (New York, NY), 2002.

Thief of Dreams, Putnam (New York, NY), 2003.

Can't Get There From Here, Simon & Schuster (New York, NY), 2004.

"HELP! I'M TRAPPED" SERIES

Help! I'm Trapped in the First Day of School, Scholastic (New York, NY), 1994.

Help! I'm Trapped in My Teacher's Body, Scholastic (New York, NY), 1994.

Help! I'm Trapped in Obedience School, Scholastic (New York, NY), 1995.

Help! I'm Trapped in Santa's Body, Scholastic (New York, NY), 1997.

Help! I'm Trapped in My Sister's Body, Scholastic (New York, NY), 1997.

Help! I'm Trapped in My Gym Teacher's Body, Scholastic (New York, NY), 1997.

Help! I'm Trapped in the President's Body, Scholastic (New York, NY), 1997.

Help! I'm Trapped in Obedience School Again, Scholastic (New York, NY), 1997.

Help! I'm Trapped in the First Day of Summer Camp, Scholastic (New York, NY), 1998.

Help! I'm Trapped in an Alien's Body, Scholastic (New York, NY), 1998.

Help! I'm Trapped in a Movie Star's Body, Scholastic (New York, NY), 1999.

Help! I'm Trapped in the Principal's Body, Scholastic (New York, NY), 1999.

Help! I'm Trapped in My Lunch Lady's Body, Scholastic (New York, NY), 1999.

Help! I'm Trapped in the Camp Counselor's Body, Scholastic (New York, NY), 1999.

Help! I'm Trapped in a Professional Wrestler's Body, Scholastic (New York, NY), 2000.

Help! I'm Trapped in a Vampire's Body, Scholastic (New York, NY), 2000.

Help! I'm Trapped in a Supermodel's Body, Scholastic (New York, NY), 2001.

"WORDSWORTH" SERIES

Wordsworth and the Cold Cut Catastrophe, illustrated by Leif Peng, HarperCollins (New York, NY), 1995.

Wordsworth and the Kibble Kidnapping, HarperCollins (New York, NY), 1995.

Wordsworth and the Roast Beef Romance, HarperCollins (New York, NY), 1995.

Wordsworth and the Mail-Order Meatloaf Mess, HarperCollins (New York, NY), 1995.

Wordsworth and the Tasty Treat Trick, HarperCollins (New York, NY), 1995.

The Lip-Smacking Licorice Love Affair, HarperCollins (New York, NY), 1996.

"CAMP RUN-A-MUCK" SERIES

Greasy Grimy Gopher Guts, Scholastic (New York, NY), 1997.

Mutilated Monkey Meat, Scholastic (New York, NY), 1997.

Chopped-Up Birdy's Feet, Scholastic (New York, NY), 1997.

"AGAINST THE ODDS" SERIES

Shark Bite, Pocket Books (New York, NY), 1998.

Grizzly Attack, Pocket Books (New York, NY), 1998.

Buzzards' Feast, Pocket Books (New York, NY), 1999.
Gator Prey, Pocket Books (New York, NY), 1999.

"HERE COMES HEAVENLY" SERIES

Here Comes Heavenly Litebody, Pocket (New York, NY), 1999.
Dance Magic, Pocket (New York, NY), 1999.
Pastabilities, Pocket (New York, NY), 1999.
Spell Danger, Pocket (New York, NY), 1999.

"DON'T GET CAUGHT" SERIES

Driving the School Bus, Scholastic (New York, NY), 2001.
In the Teacher's Lounge, Scholastic (New York, NY), 2001.
Wearing a Lunch Lady's Hairnet, Scholastic (New York, NY), 2001.
In the Girl's Locker Room, Scholastic (New York, NY), 2001.

"IMPACT ZONE" SERIES

Take Off, Simon & Schuster (New York, NY), 2004.
Cut Back, Simon & Schuster (New York, NY), 2004.
Close Out, Simon & Schuster (New York, NY), 2004.

OTHER

The Complete Computer Popularity Program, Delacorte (New York, NY), 1984.
The Mall from Outer Space, Scholastic (New York, NY), 1987.
The Family Man (novel for adults), St. Martin's Press (New York, NY), 1988.
Over the Limit (teleplay based on Strasser's *The Accident*), ABC Afterschool Special, American Broadcasting Company (New York, NY), 1990.
Super Mario Bros., Hyperion (New York, NY), 1993.

Also contributor to periodicals, including *New Yorker, Esquire, New York Times*, and *Village Voice*.

ADAPTATIONS: Workin' for Peanuts was adapted for cable television as a Home Box Office "Family Showcase" presentation, 1985; *A Very Touchy Subject* was adapted for television as an "ABC After-School Special" titled *Can a Guy Say No?*, 1986. *The Accident* was adapted for television as an ABC After-School special called *Over the Limit. How I Created My Perfect Prom Date* was released as a Twentieth Century-Fox major motion picture called *Drive Me Crazy.*

WORK IN PROGRESS: Series about teenage surfers.

SIDELIGHTS: Todd Strasser writes critically recognized realistic fiction for preteens and teenagers. In works ranging from *Friends till the End*, the story of a young man stricken with leukemia, to *Wildlife*, a study of the breakup of a successful rock group, Strasser blends humor and romance with timely subjects to address various concerns of teens: drugs, sex, illness, popularity, music. Lacing his work for younger readers with a vein of humor, Strasser has also tantalized even the most reluctant reader to open books with titles like *Hey Dad, Get a Life!, Help! I'm Trapped in My Gym Teacher's Body*, and *Greasy Grimy Gopher Guts.* In addition to his many original works of fiction, Strasser has also written novelizations of many popular motion pictures, including some from the Disney Studios. His understanding of the feelings of children and adolescents has made his works popular with young people.

Angel Dust Blues appeared in 1979 and won Strasser critical acclaim. The story itself is about, Strasser told Nina Piwoz in *Media and Methods*, "a group of fairly well-to-do, suburban teenagers who get into trouble with drugs." It was based on actual events Strasser had witnessed when he was growing up. Two years later, he published another young-adult novel, again based on his own experiences. "My second book, *Friends till the End*, is about a healthy teenager who has a friend who becomes extremely ill with leukemia," he explained to Piwoz. "When I moved to New York, I had a roommate . . . an old friend of mine. Within a few weeks, he became very ill. I spent a year visiting him in the hospital, not knowing whether he was going to live or die."

Rock 'n' Roll Nights, Strasser's third novel under his own name, was a change of pace from the serious themes of his first two works. "It's about a teenage rock and roll band—something with which I had absolutely no direct experience," he told Piwoz. "However, I grew up in the 1960s when rock and roll was really our 'national anthem.' I relate much better to rock stars than to politicians. I always wanted to be in a rock band, as did just about everybody I knew." "I think the kind of music teens listen to may change, or what they wear may change," Strasser continued, "but dealing with being popular, friends or the opposite sex, or questions of morality and decency . . . [I don't think] those things really ever change. I hate to say this, but I think authors tell the same stories—just in today's language and in today's settings." Strasser continued the story of the band "Coming Attractions" in two sequels, *Turn It Up!* and *Wildlife.*

In his more recent works, Strasser continues to write hard-hitting, realistic stories about teenagers and their problems. For example, *The Accident,* which Strasser adapted for ABC-TV's After-School Special under the title *Over the Limit,* deals with a drunken-driving incident in which three of four high-school swimming stars are killed. The surviving teen commits himself to understanding what actually happened the night of the accident, in a novel that, in the opinion of *Horn Book* reviewer Margaret A. Bush, "reads well and competently uses the troublesome occurrence of drunk driving and teenage death to provoke thought and discussion on multifaceted issues."

Strasser has also produced a large number of light-hearted books for middle graders. *The Mall from Outer Space* is about aliens who have chosen, for mysterious reasons of their own, to construct shopping centers on Earth. *Hey Dad, Get a Life!* finds twelve-year-old Kelly and younger sister Sasha haunted by their deceased father. Ghostly Dad proves to be a great help around the house—he makes the girls' beds, tidies their room, does their homework, and even helps out on the soccer field. *Booklist* contributor Debbie Carton called the work a "lighthearted and occasionally poignant ghost story" that features "appealing, believable characters and a satisfying plot." Equally laudatory in *Bulletin of the Center for Children's Books,* Deborah Stevenson described *Hey, Dad, Get a Life!* as "touchingly yet surprisingly cheerful," and called it "a compassionate and accessible tale of a family's adjustment to loss."

Several novels reveal Strasser's more quirky, humorous side. *Girl Gives Birth to Own Prom Date* finds ardent environmentalist Nicole taking time off from saving the world to transform her grungy next-door neighbor Chase into the perfect prom date. Praising

the novel's "goofy plot twists" and "effervescent dialogue," a *Kirkus Reviews* critic noted that Strasser's "high humor doesn't detract" from his "understated message about nonconformity and self-acceptance." The author's "Help! I'm Trapped . . ." books position their young protagonists in everything from the unwieldy body of Santa Claus to the summer camp from hell. In *Help! I'm Trapped in Obedience School,* for example, Jake's dog, Lance, switches bodies with Jake's friend Andy, and while Andy excels at most things doggy—although he never quite acquires a taste for dog food—Jake spends his time in human form chasing squirrels and barking during school. Calling Strasser's tale "briskly paced," *Booklist* contributor Chris Sherman wrote that the "easy, breezy" story would appeal to reluctant readers. *School Library Journal* contributor Cheryl Cufari predicted that readers will relate to the "predicaments in which Strasser's energetic boys find themselves and enjoy this light entertaining read."

Strasser once told *CA:* "Since I've written [many] books about teenagers, people often ask me how I know what today's teens are like. It's true that almost twenty years have passed since I qualified for that age group, so I suppose the question has some merit. I think the single most important thing I do to keep up with teens is accept invitations to speak at junior high and high schools all over the country. This year, for instance, I visited schools in Alaska, Iowa, Massachusetts, Pennsylvania, Ohio, and Colorado. Thus I'm not only able to keep up with teens, but with teens from all over the country.

"Another question I'm often asked is why I concentrate solely on books for teens. Well, actually, I don't. In the next few months I will publish a juvenile as well as an adult novel. I guess I originally wrote a lot of books for teens because that was where I had my first success and felt the most confident. But as I grow older, I find my interests widening not only towards writing books for older people, but for younger ones as well. I'd like to think that the day will come when I will write books for people of all ages, from three to eighty-three.

"The other day, someone who didn't know me well said that because I was a writer I must be a 'free spirit' and lead a wonderful life. At first I wanted to tell him he was completely wrong, but then I thought about it and decided he was only half wrong. In a way I am a free spirit, in that I am free to pick any idea or topic and write about it. That, indeed, is a wonderful freedom and I am grateful to have it. Along with that freedom, however, comes an awful lot of hard work. Unless you are fortunate enough to be one of the handful of perpetual best-selling writers in this world, you really cannot make a living writing a book every two or three years. My work is about as close to 'nine-to-five' as my schedule allows. Being a writer is great, but I can't say it's easy."

More recently, Strasser told *CA:* "Writing has basically become the default activity of my life. If the waves aren't rideable, and I'm not doing something with a friend or loved one, then I'm probably writing. I feel as if I have many more ideas for books than I will ever have time to write. I hope the overall contribution of my books will be to encourage, in some very small way, people to love and tolerate each other."

"Two summers ago, at the age of fifty-two, I went surfing for the first time. It is now the great passion of my life, and something both my teenage children love to do as well. This past year we surfed in Hawaii, California, and up and down the East coast from New York to Florida. I am currently writing a series about teenage surfers as well as an adult mystery starring a detective who surfs."

BIOGRAPHICAL AND CRITICAL SOURCES:

BOOKS

Children's Literature Review, Volume 11, Gale (Detroit, MI), 1986.

Nilsen, Alleen Pace, and Kenneth L. Donelson, *Literature for Today's Young Adults,* 2nd edition, Scott, Foresman (Glenview, IL), 1985.

Roginski, Jim, *Behind the Covers: Interviews with Authors and Illustrators of Books for Children and Young Adults,* Libraries Unlimited (Littleton, CO), 1985.

St. James Guide to Young Adult Writers, 2nd edition, St. James Press (Detroit, MI), 1999.

PERIODICALS

Best Sellers, May, 1983, p. 75; June, 1984, p. 118.

Booklist, May 1, 1995, p. 1564; October 1, 1996, p. 344; October 1, 2000, Michael Cart, review of *Give a Boy a Gun,* p. 337.

Book Report, November, 1993, Annette Thorson, "Author Profile: Todd Strasser," p. 30.

Bulletin of the Center for Children's Books, February, 1980, p. 120; June, 1995, p. 361; February, 1999, p. 219.

English Journal, September, 1982, p. 87; January, 1985; December, 1985; December, 1986; November, 1987, p. 93; March, 1988, p. 85.

Horn Book, April, 1980, p. 178; April, 1983, p. 175; May-June, 1985, p. 321; March/April, 1986, Todd Strasser, "Stalking the Teen," pp. 236-239; January, 1990, p. 90.

Journal of Adolescent and Adult Literacy, March, 2002, Devon Clancy Sanner, review of *Give a Boy a Gun,* p. 547.

Journal of Youth Services in Libraries, fall, 1988, pp. 64-70.

Kirkus Reviews, May 15, 1992, p. 676; September 1, 1998, p. 1293; December 1, 2002, review of *Con-Fidence,* p. 1775; March 1, 2003, review of *Thief of Dreams,* p. 399.

Library Journal, January, 1988, p. 100.

Media and Methods, February, 1983.

New Yorker, January 24, 1977, p. 28.

New York Times, October 2, 1983; June 19, 1985.

Publishers Weekly, November 27, 1981, p. 88; April 24, 1987, p. 73; December 4, 1987, p. 63; November 25, 2002, review of *Con-Fidence,* p. 69; February 24, 2003, review of *Thief of Dreams,* p. 73.

School Library Journal, January, 1980, p. 81; March, 1982, p. 160; August, 1983, p. 80; August, 1984, p. 87; April, 1985, p. 100; February, 1988, p. 75; June-July, 1988, p. 59; September, 1989, p. 278; January 1, 2000, Shelle Rosenfeld, review of *Here Comes Heavenly,* p. 906; August, 2000, Jane Halsall, review of *Pastabilities,* p. 190; September, 2000, Vicki Reutter, review of *Give a Boy a Gun,* p. 237; February, 2002, Francisca Goldsmith, review of *Give a Boy a Gun,* p. 75.

Teacher Librarian, February, 2003, Teri S. Lesesne, "Surfing for Readers: An Interview with Todd Strasser," p. 48.

Variety, March 22, 1990, p. 14.

Voice of Youth Advocates, June, 1981, p. 32; December, 1982, p. 36; October, 1983, p. 209; June, 1984, p. 98; June, 1985, p. 136; December, 1986; December, 1988, p. 242; October, 1989, p. 217; October, 1995, p. 224; April, 1997, pp. 22, 33.

Wilson Library Bulletin, May, 1981, p. 691; April, 1983, p. 692; March, 1985, p. 485.

Writer's Digest, December, 1979.

ONLINE

Todd Strasser's Home Page, http://www.toddstrasser.com/ (April 10, 2003).

*   *   *

SULLIVAN, George (Edward) 1927-

PERSONAL: Born August 11, 1927, in Lowell, MA; son of Timothy J. (a salesman) and Cecilia (a registered nurse; maiden name, Shea) Sullivan; married Muriel Moran, May 24, 1952; children: Timothy. *Education:* Fordham University, B.S., 1952. *Religion:* Roman Catholic. *Hobbies and other interests:* Photography, photographs, tennis.

ADDRESSES: Home—330 East 33rd St., New York, NY 10016. *Agent*—Eleanor Wood, Spectrum Literary Agency, 111 Eighth Ave., New York, NY 10011. *E-mail*—gjsbooks@aol.com.

CAREER: Popular Library (publishing house), New York, NY, public relations director, 1952-55; American Machine and Foundry Co., Inc., New York, NY, publicity manager, 1955-61; freelance writer, 1962—. Fordham University, Bronx, NY, adjunct professor of nonfiction writing, 1969-72, 1979-81. *Military service:* U.S. Navy, 1945-48.

MEMBER: PEN, Authors Guild, Authors League of America, Society of Children's Book Writers and Illustrators.

WRITINGS:

NONFICTION

(With Frank Clause) *How to Win at Bowling,* Fleet (New York, NY), 1961.
(With Frank Clause and Patty McBride) *Junior Guide to Bowling,* Fleet (New York, NY), 1963.
The Story of Cassius Clay, Fleet (New York, NY), 1964.
Harness Racing, foreword by Walter J. Michael, Fleet (New York, NY), 1964.

George Sullivan

(With Irving Crane) *The Young Sportsman's Guide to Pocket Billiards,* Nelson (New York, NY), 1964.
The Story of the Peace Corps, introduction by Sargent Shriver, Fleet (New York, NY), 1964, revised edition, 1965.
Boats: A Guidebook to Boating Procedures, Maintenance, and Fun!, Maco (New York, NY), 1965.
(With Luther Lassiter) *Billiards for Everyone,* Grosset & Dunlap (New York, NY), 1965.
Camping Guidebook: Outdoor Living, from Luxury to Roughing It, Maco (New York, NY), 1965.
The Complete Guide to Softball, introduction by Don E. Porter, Fleet (New York, NY), 1965.
(With Larry Scott) *Fell's Teen-Age Guide to Skin and Scuba Diving,* Fell (New York, NY), 1965, revised edition, 1975.
How Do They Make It?, Westminster (Philadelphia, PA), 1965.
Better Boxing for Boys, Dodd, Mead (New York, NY), 1966.
Camping: Skills, Places, Pleasures, Maco (New York, NY), 1966.
The Champions' Guide to Golf, introduction by Mike Turnesa, Fleet (New York, NY), 1966.

How Do They Grow It?, Westminster (Philadelphia, PA), 1966.

The Personal Story of Lynda and Luci Johnson, Popular Library (New York, NY), 1966.

Philip Vampatella, Fighter Pilot: The Complete Life Story of a College Dropout Who Became One of the First Aircraft Carrier Pilots to Fly over Vietnam, Nelson (New York, NY), 1966.

(With Finn Eddy Larsen) *Skiing for Boys and Girls*, Follett (Chicago IL), 1966.

(With Harry Kramp) *Swimming for Boys and Girls*, Follett (Chicago IL), 1966.

Tennis, Follett (Chicago IL), 1966.

Wilt Chamberlain, Grosset & Dunlap (New York, NY), 1966, revised edition, 1971.

(With Wes Ellis) *All-Weather Golf*, foreword by Tommy Bolt, Van Nostrand (Princeton, NJ), 1967.

Better Swimming and Diving for Boys and Girls, Dodd, Mead (New York, NY), 1967, revised edition, 1982.

Better Track and Field Events for Boys, Dodd, Mead (New York, NY), 1967, revised edition published as *Better Track for Boys*, 1985.

The Complete Book of Family Skiing, Coward, McCann (New York, NY), 1967.

The Modern Guide to Skin and Scuba Diving, Coward, McCann (New York, NY), 1967.

Pro Football's Unforgettable Games, Putnam (New York, NY), 1967.

Touchdown! The Picture History of the American Football League, Putnam (New York, NY), 1967.

The Boom in Going Bust: The Threat of a National Scandal in Consumer Bankruptcy, Macmillan (New York, NY), 1968.

The Complete Book of Family Bowling, Coward, McCann (New York, NY), 1968.

Face-Off: A Guide to Modern Ice Hockey, Van Nostrand (Princeton, NJ), 1968.

Guide to Badminton, introduction by Waldo W. Lyon, Fleet (New York, NY), 1968.

The New World of Construction Engineering, Dodd, Mead (New York, NY), 1968.

Pass to Win: Pro Football Greats, illustrated by Pers Crowell, Garrard (Champaign, IL), 1968.

Pro Football's All-Time Greats: The Immortals in Pro Football's Hall of Fame, Putnam (New York, NY), 1968.

Seven Modern Wonders of the World, Putnam (New York, NY), 1968.

(With George L. Seewagen) *Tennis*, Follett (Chicago IL), 1968.

Better Horseback Riding for Boys and Girls, Dodd, Mead (New York, NY), 1969.

The Complete Book of Skin and Scuba Diving, Coward, McCann (New York, NY), 1969.

Hockey Heroes: The Game's Greatest Players, illustrated by Dom Lupo, Garrard (Champaign, IL), 1969.

(With Earl Morrall) *In the Pocket: My Life As a Quarterback*, Grosset & Dunlap (New York, NY), 1969.

More How Do They Make It?, Westminster (Philadelphia, PA), 1969.

The New World of Communications, Dodd, Mead (New York, NY), 1969.

Plants to Grow Indoors, illustrated by Bill Barss, Follett (Chicago IL), 1969.

They Flew Alone, illustrated by Serge Hollerback, Warne (New York, NY), 1969.

(With John Fanning) *Work When You Want to Work: The Complete Guide for the Temporary Worker— From the President of Uniforce*, Macmillan (New York, NY), 1969, revised edition, 1985.

Bart Starr, the Cool Quarterback, Putnam (New York, NY), 1970.

Better Archery for Boys and Girls, Dodd, Mead (New York, NY), 1970.

The Dollar Squeeze and How to Beat It, Macmillan (New York, NY), 1970.

Knute Rockne: Notre Dame's Football Great, illustrated by Dom Lupo, Garrard (Champaign, IL), 1970.

This Is Pro Football, Dodd, Mead (New York, NY), 1970, revised edition, 1975.

Trees, illustrated by Norman Adams, Follett (Chicago IL), 1970.

(With Earl Morrall) *Comeback Quarterback: The Earl Morrall Story*, Grosset & Dunlap (New York, NY), 1971.

The Complete Book of Autograph Collecting, Dodd, Mead (New York, NY), 1971.

The Gamemakers: Pro Football's Great Quarterbacks—From Baugh to Namath, Putnam (New York, NY), 1971.

Jim Thorpe, All-Around Athlete, illustrated by Herman B. Vestal, Garrard (Champaign, IL), 1971.

How Do They Run It?, Westminster (Philadelphia, PA), 1971.

(With Edward J. Zegarowicz) *Inflation-Proof Your Future*, Walker (New York, NY), 1971.

Pro Football Plays in Pictures, Grosset & Dunlap (New York, NY), 1971.

Rise of the Robots, Dodd, Mead (New York, NY), 1971.

(With George Kirby) *Soccer,* Follett (Chicago IL), 1971.

(With Harry Kramp) *Swimming,* Follett (Chicago IL), 1971.

Tom Seaver of the Mets, Putnam (New York, NY), 1971.

Understanding Architecture, Warne (New York, NY), 1971.

The Backpacker's Handbook, Grosset & Dunlap (New York, NY), 1972.

Better Table Tennis for Boys and Girls, Dodd, Mead (New York, NY), 1972.

By Chance a Winner: The History of Lotteries, Dodd, Mead (New York, NY), 1972.

Football, Follett (Chicago IL), 1972.

The Great Running Backs, Putnam (New York, NY), 1972.

How Do They Build It?, Westminster (Philadelphia, PA), 1972.

Pitchers and Pitching, Dodd, Mead (New York, NY), 1972.

Pro Football's Great Upsets, Garrard (Champaign, IL), 1972.

Pro Football's Passing Game, Dodd, Mead (New York, NY), 1972.

Understanding Photography, Warne (New York, NY), 1972.

Do-It-Yourself Moving, Macmillan (New York, NY), 1973.

How Does It Get There?, Westminster (Philadelphia, PA), 1973.

Pro Football's Kicking Game, Dodd, Mead (New York, NY), 1973.

Sports for Your Child, Winchester Press (Tulsa, OK), 1973.

Willie Mays, illustrated by David Brown, Putnam (New York, NY), 1973.

Baseball's Art of Hitting, Dodd, Mead (New York, NY), 1974.

Better Bicycling for Boys and Girls, Dodd, Mead (New York, NY), 1974, revised edition, 1984.

Linebacker!, Dodd, Mead (New York, NY), 1974.

Queens of the Court, Dodd, Mead (New York, NY), 1974.

Roger Staubach: A Special Kind of Quarterback, Putnam (New York, NY), 1974.

Better Softball for Boys and Girls, Dodd, Mead (New York, NY), 1974.

Hank Aaron, illustrated by George Young, Putnam (New York, NY), 1975.

How Do They Find It?, Westminster (Philadelphia, PA), 1975.

Larry Csonka, Power and Pride, Putnam (New York, NY), 1975.

The Modern Treasure Finder's Manual, Chilton (Radnor, PA), 1975.

Paddle: The Beginner's Guide to Platform Tennis, Coward, McCann (New York, NY), 1975.

Pro Football A to Z: A Fully Illustrated Guide to America's Favorite Sport, Scribner (New York, NY), 1975.

Winning Plays in Pro Football, Dodd, Mead (New York, NY), 1975.

Additives in Your Food, Cornerstone Library (New York, NY), 1976.

Better Ice Skating for Boys and Girls, Dodd, Mead (New York, NY), 1976.

Bobby Bonds, Rising Superstar, Putnam (New York, NY), 1976.

The Catcher, Baseball's Man in Charge, Dodd, Mead (New York, NY), 1976.

How Do They Package It?, Westminster (Philadelphia, PA), 1976.

On the Run, Franco Harris, Children's Press (Chicago, IL), 1976.

Pro Football and the Running Back, Dodd, Mead (New York, NY), 1976.

This Is Pro Hockey, Dodd, Mead (New York, NY), 1976.

Understanding Hydroponics: Growing Plants without Soil, Warne (New York, NY), 1976.

Winning Basketball, McKay (New York, NY), 1976.

Bert Jones: Born to Play Football, Putnam (New York, NY), 1977.

Better Gymnastics for Girls, Dodd, Mead (New York, NY), 1977.

Dave Cowens: A Biography, Doubleday (New York, NY), 1977.

Home Run!, Dodd, Mead (New York, NY), 1977.

Making Money in Autographs, Coward, McCann (New York, NY), 1977.

The Picture Story of Catfish Hunter, Messner (New York, NY), 1977.

The Picture Story of Nadia Comaneci, Messner (New York, NY), 1977.

The Picture Story of Reggie Jackson, Messner (New York, NY), 1977.

This Is Pro Basketball, Dodd, Mead (New York, NY), 1977.

Better Basketball for Girls, Dodd, Mead (New York, NY), 1977.

Amazing Sports Facts, Scholastic (New York, NY), 1978.

Better Soccer for Boys and Girls, Dodd, Mead (New York, NY), 1978.

Sports Superstitions, Coward, McCann (New York, NY), 1978.

Supertanker! The Story of the World's Biggest Ships, Dodd, Mead (New York, NY), 1978.

Wind Power for Your Home: The First Complete Guide That Tells How to Make the Wind's Energy Work for You, Cornerstone Library (New York, NY), 1978.

Wood-Burning Stoves, Cornerstone Library (New York, NY), 1978.

Better Volleyball for Girls, Dodd, Mead (New York, NY), 1979.

The Complete Beginner's Guide to Pool and Other Billiard Games, Doubleday (New York, NY), 1979.

The Complete Sports Dictionary, Scholastic (New York, NY), 1979, revised edition, 1993.

Modern Olympic Superstars, Dodd, Mead (New York, NY), 1979.

This Is Pro Soccer, Dodd, Mead (New York, NY), 1979.

The All-Sports Puzzle and Quiz Book, Scholastic (New York, NY), 1980.

Better Basketball for Boys, Dodd, Mead (New York, NY), 1980.

Better Football for Boys, Dodd, Mead (New York, NY), 1980.

Better Roller Skating for Boys and Girls, Dodd, Mead (New York, NY), 1980.

Charms and Spells, Witches, and Demons, Scholastic (New York, NY), 1980.

Cross-Country Skiing: A Complete Beginner's Book, Messner (New York, NY), 1980.

Discover Archaeology: An Introduction to the Tools and Techniques of Archaeological Fieldwork, Doubleday (New York, NY), 1980.

(With Gary Player) *Gary Player's Golf Book For Young People,* Simon & Schuster (New York, NY), 1980.

Marathon—The Longest Race, Westminster (Philadelphia, PA), 1980.

Run, Run Fast!, illustrated by Don Madden, Crowell (New York, NY), 1980.

The Supercarriers, Dodd, Mead (New York, NY), 1980.

Track and Field: Secrets of the Champions, Doubleday (New York, NY), 1980.

Better Baseball for Boys, revised edition, Dodd, Mead (New York, NY), 1981.

Better Field Hockey for Girls, Dodd, Mead (New York, NY), 1981.

Better Track for Girls, Dodd, Mead (New York, NY), 1981.

The Gold Hunter's Handbook, Stein & Day (New York, NY), 1981.

Sadat: The Man Who Changed Mid-East History, Walker (New York, NY), 1981.

Superstars of Women's Track, Dodd, Mead (New York, NY), 1981.

The Art of Base-Stealing, Dodd, Mead (New York, NY), 1981.

Better Field Events for Girls, Dodd, Mead (New York, NY), 1982.

Famous Firsts, Scholastic (New York, NY), 1982.

Great Impostors, Scholastic (New York, NY), 1982.

Inside Nuclear Submarines, Dodd, Mead (New York, NY), 1982.

Picture Story of George Brett, Messner (New York, NY), 1982.

Quarterback, illustrated by Don Madden, Crowell (New York, NY), 1982.

Better Cross-Country Running for Boys and Girls, Dodd, Mead (New York, NY), 1983.

The Complete Book of Baseball Collectibles, Arco (New York, NY), 1983.

The Complete Car Book, Scholastic (New York, NY), 1983.

Computer Puzzles and Quizzes, Scholastic (New York, NY), 1983.

Great Sports Hoaxes, Scholastic (New York, NY), 1983.

Return of the Battleship, Dodd, Mead (New York, NY), 1983.

Screen Play: The Story of Video Games, Warne (New York, NY), 1983.

Strange but True Stories of World War II, Walker (New York, NY), 1983, revised edition, 1991.

(With Tim Sullivan) *Stunt People,* Beaufort Books (New York, NY), 1983.

Video Games, Puzzles, and Quizzes, Scholastic (New York, NY), 1983.

Baseball's Wacky Players, Dodd, Mead (New York, NY), 1984.

Better Weight Training for Boys, photographs by Ann Hagen Griffiths, Dodd, Mead (New York, NY), 1984.

Better BMX Riding and Racing for Boys and Girls, Dodd, Mead (New York, NY), 1984.

Computer Kids, Dodd, Mead (New York, NY), 1984.

Mr. President: A Book of U.S. Presidents, Dodd, Mead (New York, NY), 1984, revised edition, 1993.

Pope John Paul II: The People's Pope, Walker (New York, NY), 1984.

Famous Air Force Bombers, Dodd, Mead (New York, NY), 1985.

Famous Air Force Fighters, Dodd, Mead (New York, NY), 1985.

Mary Lou Retton: A Biography, Wanderer Books (New York, NY), 1985.

Ronald Reagan, Messner (New York, NY), 1985.

Baseball Backstage, Holt (New York, NY), 1986.

Better Wrestling for Boys, Dodd, Mead (New York, NY), 1986.

Famous Navy Attack Planes, Dodd, Mead (New York, NY), 1986.

Famous Navy Fighter Planes, Dodd, Mead (New York, NY), 1986.

Pitcher, illustrated by Don Madden, Crowell (New York, NY), 1986.

The Thunderbirds, Dodd, Mead (New York, NY), 1986.

All about Football, Dodd, Mead (New York, NY), 1987.

Better Tennis for Boys and Girls, Dodd, Mead (New York, NY), 1987.

Facts and Fun about the Presidents, Scholastic (New York, NY), 1987, revised edition, 1993.

Famous U.S. Spy Planes, Dodd, Mead (New York, NY), 1987.

Great Racing Cars, Dodd, Mead (New York, NY), 1987.

Treasure Hunt: The Sixteen-Year Search for the Lost Treasure Ship "Atocha," Holt (New York, NY), 1987.

Work Smart, Not Hard, Facts on File (New York, NY), 1987.

All about Baseball, Putnam (New York, NY), 1988.

Center, illustrations by Don Madden, Crowell (New York, NY), 1988.

Famous Blimps and Airships, Dodd, Mead (New York, NY), 1988.

Great Escapes of World War II, Scholastic (New York, NY), 1988.

Great Lives: Sports, Scribner (New York, NY), 1988.

Mikhail Gorbachev, Messner (New York, NY), 1988, revised edition, 1990.

Big League Spring Training, Holt (New York, NY), 1989.

Cars, Doubleday (New York, NY), 1989.

George Bush, Messner (New York, NY), 1989.

Here Come the Monster Trucks, Cobblehill (New York, NY), 1989.

How the White House Really Works, Lodestar (New York, NY), 1989.

Any Number Can Play, illustrated by John Caldwell, Crowell (New York, NY), 1990, reprinted as *Any Number Can Play: The Numbers Athletes Wear,* with illustrations by Anne Canevari Green, Millbrook Press (Brookfield, CT), 2000.

Baseball Kids, Cobblehill (New York, NY), 1990.

The Day We Walked on the Moon, Scholastic (New York, NY), 1990.

Football Kids, Cobblehill (New York, NY), 1990.

All about Basketball, Putnam (New York, NY), 1990.

Campaigns and Elections, Silver Burdett (Morristown, NJ), 1991.

Choosing the Candidates, Silver Burdett (Morristown, NJ), 1991.

The Day They Bombed Pearl Harbor, Scholastic (New York, NY), 1991.

Sluggers!: Twenty-seven of Baseball's Greatest, Atheneum (New York, NY), 1991.

Disaster! The Destruction of Our Planet, Scholastic (New York, NY), 1992.

Modern Bombers and Attack Planes, Facts on File (New York, NY), 1992.

Racing Indy Cars, Cobblehill (New York, NY), 1992.

Unsolved Famous Real-Life Mysteries, Scholastic (New York, NY), 1992.

How an Airport Really Works, Lodestar (New York, NY), 1993.

Blading for Beginners: A Compete Guide to In-Line Skating, Cobblehill (New York, NY), 1993.

Modern Combat Helicopters, Facts on File (New York, NY), 1993.

The Official Price Guide to American Stoneware, Random House (New York, NY), 1993.

They Shot the President: Ten True Stories, Scholastic (New York, NY), 1993.

The Day Women Got the Vote: A Photo History of the Women's Rights Movement, Scholastic (New York, NY), 1994.

Mathew Brady: His Life and Photographs, Cobblehill (New York, NY), 1994.

Slave Ship: The Story of the Henrietta Marie, Cobblehill (New York, NY), 1994.

Great Impostors, Scholastic (New York, NY), 1994.

Unsolved II: More Famous Real-Life Mysteries, Scholastic (New York, NY), 1994.

Elite Warriors: The Special Forces of the United States and Its Allies, Facts on File (New York, NY), 1995.

Presidents at Play, Walker & Co. (New York, NY), 1995.

Glovemen: Twenty-seven of Baseball's Greatest, Atheneum (New York, NY), 1996.

Women War Spies, Scholastic (New York, NY), 1996.

Alamo!, Scholastic (New York, NY), 1996.

Black Artists in Photography, 1840-1940, Cobblehill (New York, NY), 1996.

(With John Powers) *The Yankees: An Illustrated History,* Temple University Press (Philadelphia, PA), 1997.

Not Guilty: Six Times when Justice Failed, Scholastic (New York, NY), 1997.

Snowboarding: A Complete Guide for Beginners, Cobblehill Books (New York, NY), 1997.

The Yankees Fan's Little Book of Wisdom: 101 Truths Learned the Hard Way, Diamond Communications (South Bend, IN), 1998.

Trapped, Scholastic (New York, NY), 1998.

All about Hockey, Putnam (New York, NY), 1998.

Burnin' Rubber: Behind the Scenes in Stock Car Racing, Millbrook Press (Brookfield, CT), 1998.

Portraits of War: Civil War Photographers and Their Work, Twenty-First Century Books (Brookfield, CT), 1998.

Quarterbacks!: Eighteen of Football's Greatest, Atheneum (New York, NY), 1998.

100 Years in Photographs, Scholastic (New York, NY), 1999.

Lewis and Clark, Scholastic (New York, NY), 1999.

Paul Revere, Scholastic (New York, NY), 1999.

To the Bottom of the Sea: The Exploration of Exotic Life, the "Titanic," and Other Secrets of the Oceans, Twenty-First Century Books (Brookfield, CT), 1999.

Picturing Lincoln: Famous Photographs That Popularized the President, Clarion Books (New York, NY), 2000.

Helen Keller, Scholastic (New York, NY), 2000.

Abraham Lincoln, Scholastic Reference (New York, NY), 2000.

Don't Step on the Foul Line: Sports Superstitions, Millbrook Press (Brookfield, CT), 2000.

All about Soccer, Putnam (New York, NY), 2001.

The Civil War at Sea, Twenty-First Century Books (Brookfield, CT), 2001.

Power Football: The Greatest Running Backs, Atheneum (New York, NY), 2001.

Davy Crockett, Scholastic (New York, NY), 2001.

Harriet Tubman, Scholastic (New York, NY), 2001.

Pocahontas, Scholastic (New York, NY), 2001.

The Wright Brothers, Scholastic (New York, NY), 2002.

Thomas Edison, Scholastic (New York, NY), 2003.

Baseball's Boneheads, Bad Boys, and Just Plain Crazy Guys, illustrated by Anne Canevari Green, Millbrook Press (Brookfield, CT), 2003.

Journalists at Risk: Reporting America's Wars, Twenty-First Century Books (Brookfield, CT), 2004.

In the Wake of Battle: The Civil War Images of Matthew Brady, Prestel (New York, NY), 2004.

EDITOR

Dick Weber, *The Champion's Guide to Bowling,* Fleet (New York, NY), 1964.

Luther Lassiter, *The Modern Guide to Pocket Billiards,* Fleet (New York, NY), 1964.

Bowling Secrets of the Pros, illustrated by Dom Lupo, Doubleday (New York, NY), 1968.

Charles Fellows, *Baseball Rules Illustrated,* Cornerstone Library (New York, NY), 1981.

Charles Fellows, *Football Rules Illustrated,* Cornerstone Library (New York, NY), 1981.

Charles Fellows, *Soccer Rules Illustrated,* Cornerstone Library (New York, NY), 1981.

Charles Fellows, *Tennis Rules Illustrated,* Cornerstone Library (New York, NY), 1981.

Lawrence P. Konopka, *Racquetball Rules and Techniques Illustrated,* illustrated by Konopka and Madelon Skoogfors, Cornerstone Library (New York, NY), 1982.

WORK IN PROGRESS: Built to Last, for Scholastic (New York, NY), publication expected in 2006.

SIDELIGHTS: In a career spanning more than four decades, George Sullivan has written over 200 adult and juvenile nonfiction books on a wide array of topics. Sullivan has been fortunate to be able to follow his natural curiosity wherever it has led. From the excitement and challenge of the sports arena to the high-powered plays of politics, from fascinating true-life stories hidden in the web of history to the technological breakthroughs that are changing the future, Sullivan's many books continue to open the minds and fire the imaginations of thousands of young readers.

Born in Lowell, Massachusetts, and raised in Springfield, Sullivan worked as a journalist for the Navy prior to going to college. Writing every day, beginning at four or five o'clock in the morning, for at least four or five hours, Sullivan has maintained the disciplined habits he developed in the Navy. In addition to writing his books, he often illustrates them as well, using his skills as an amateur photographer. Because many of Sullivan's books concern sports—professional football in particular—he once spent most of his fall and winter weekends taking football action photos, both at practice sessions and at games. "In the summer, I do the same with baseball," he once told *CA*, "but it's mostly to keep me proficient with my cameras until fall and football arrive."

Football has indeed been a favorite subject for Sullivan. From fact-filled histories that include *Pro Football's All-Time Greats* and *Touchdown! The Picture History of the American Football League*, to instructional books such as *Pro Football's Passing Game*, he has shared his enthusiasm for the game with his readers. Sullivan also covers the world of baseball in *The Catcher, Baseball's Man in Charge*. *All about Baseball* and *Baseball Backstage* provide overviews of the game, while beginning players can hone their skills and understanding of the game with *Baseball Rules Illustrated* and *Better Softball for Boys and Girls*. Sullivan trades his bat for a racquet in *Better Tennis for Boys and Girls*, in which he provides beginners with encouragement: "Learning to play tennis is something like learning to swim or bake a cake. Just about anyone can do it with the right instruction and determination to practice."

In *Snowboarding: A Complete Guide for Beginners*, Sullivan turns his attention to this alternative sport. Describing the history, equipment, and basic techniques, the author presents "solid" information accompanied by full-color photos, according to Tom S. Hurlburt in *School Library Journal*. Hurlburt went on to call *Snowboarding* "an easy-to-read, eye-pleasing book." NASCAR takes the spotlight in the 1998 *Burnin' Rubber: Behind the Scenes in Stock Car Racing*. Sullivan traces the sport from its beginnings in the 1930s, introducing young readers "to the astonishing range of material, manpower, and money" needed to put a racing car on the track, as Patricia Manning noted in a *School Library Journal* review. Ice sports get the Sullivan treatment in *All about Hockey*, featuring the author's "efficient, workmanlike prose," according to Richard Luzer in *School Library Journal*. In *Quarterbacks!: Eighteen of Football's Greatest*, Sullivan looks again at one of his favorite team sports in an "excellent introduction" to the

game's key player, as Kate Kohlbeck noted in *School Library Journal*. Sullivan provides biographical details about players both historical and contemporary, including Sammy Baugh, Sid Luckman, Troy Aikman, and Brett Favre. Backs get the same treatment in *Power Football: The Greatest Running Backs*, a book characterized by "lively writing," according to Michael McCullough in *School Library Journal*. Here Sullivan provides brief profiles of running backs from Eric Dickerson to Emmitt Smith.

In *Don't Step on the Foul Line: Sports Superstitions* and *Any Number Can Play: The Numbers Athletes Wear*, Sullivan focuses on some unusual aspects of sports. In *Don't Step on the Foul Line*, he looks at strange rituals and beliefs athletes indulge in, from lucky socks to favorite pregame foods. Similar anecdotes sprinkle the pages of *Any Number Can Play*, in which Sullivan tells the stories and history of numbers that athletes wear. Chris Crowe, writing in *Voice of Youth Advocates*, praised the "wealth of minutia sure to engage any sports fan" that appears in both titles. *Booklist*'s Denia Hester similarly wrote, "Here are a couple of sure bets for trivia nuts, or anyone who wants a good chuckle." *School Library Journal*'s Steve Clancy also commended the books for being "well researched and loaded with detail." A similar title, the 2003 *Baseball's Boneheads, Bad Boys, and Just Plain Crazy Guys*, takes a look at baseball players famous for their humor, superstitions, and odd behavior. A *Booklist* reviewer praised these "funny, offbeat, true stories," including the one about a New York Mets pitcher who had a fixation on the number nine.

In addition to sports, Sullivan has written about the game of politics, presenting both the complexities of the political process and the major players in a way that make them both interesting and accessible for young students of government. *Choosing the Candidates* and *Campaigns and Elections* describe the history of our electoral system and discuss some of the latest issues, including the debate over the role of television within the election process. Profiles of influential twentieth-century political figures are presented in *Ronald Reagan, George Bush, Sadat: The Man Who Changed Mid-East History*, and *Mikhail Gorbachev*, the latter a profile of the leader of the former U.S.S.R. set within his rise to power in the Communist party. *How the White House Really Works*—which President Clinton is reported to have read as entertainment during the last days before the 1992 elections—is a behind-the-scenes look at the building that not only houses the president and his family, but also serves as an office for both president and staff, a museum, and a tourist attraction as well. On the lighter side, Sullivan illuminates the personalities of several U.S. leaders in *Presidents at Play* by revealing how each of them chose to spend their time away from the stresses of political office.

Sullivan's years of Navy service have provided him with both an interest and insight into U.S. military history; from the high-flying exploits of the Thunderbirds to the pivotal Civil War battle between the *Monitor* and the *Merrimac,* he shares his enthusiasm for military history in several volumes. In *Famous Blimps and Airships,* he provides an in-depth survey of twenty different airships, from the German Zeppelin LZ-1 first manufactured in 1900, to the "Spirit of Akron," the Goodyear superblimp that took quietly to the airways in 1988. On a faster track, *Famous U.S. Spy Planes* follows the attempt to infiltrate enemy airspace to gain top-secret information by taking to the skies in such "birds" as the Curtiss JN and Lockheed's SR-71 "Blackbird."

Further forays into military history include the 2001 title *The Civil War at Sea,* an album of archival photos of some of the ships that fought in that war, accompanied by "an engrossing account of the war's progress" on water, as a critic for *Kirkus Reviews* noted. Sullivan describes how the North's superior sea power allowed it to close off Southern ports despite the hard-fought efforts of the Confederates. *Booklist*'s Carolyn Phelan found the book to be a "clearly written account [that] broadens students' knowledge." Similarly, *School Library Journal*'s Elizabeth M. Reardon felt the same book would "appeal to every Civil War buff" with its illustrations and "lively text."

Introducing children to both the past and the future is crucial, and Sullivan has directed many of his books to accomplishing just that. In his "How Do They" series, he covers the stages of manufacturing: locating resources; constructing power stations, bridges, skyscrapers, and highways; packaging goods; and transporting everything from zoo reptiles to launch-bound rocket ships. *Understanding Hydroponics: Growing Plants without Soil* examines the futuristic technology of increasing the earth's agricultural production and offsetting future food shortages.

While hydroponics may be the agriculture of the future, the agriculture of the distant past is revealed through archeology, as Sullivan notes in his *Discover Archaeology: An Introduction to the Tools and Techniques of Archaeologic Fieldwork.* The exploration of a sunken ship provides the excitement in *Treasure Hunt: The Sixteen-Year Search for the Lost Treasure Ship "Atocha,"* a true story about the work of marine archaeologists, historians, and divers to recover a sunken galleon off the Florida Keys. And in *Mathew Brady: His Life and Photographs,* Sullivan combines technology and history in a discussion of the famous photographer's decision to document the Civil War with his camera during an era when advances in photographic technology were occurring at a rapid rate. Other historic events covered by Sullivan range from the slave trade to man's first walk on the moon, the women's movement, and the beginning of U.S. involvement in World War II.

History of a different sort is served up in other books from Sullivan. In *Black Artists in Photography, 1840-1940,* he explores the life and works of eight little-known African-American pioneers in photography. "Each of the men Sullivan has profiled played a significant part in advancing photography as a force in American culture," wrote Jabarl Asim in a *Washington Post Book World* review. Asim went on to conclude that Sullivan's book was "an excellent beginning" to a full documentation of the black achievement in photographic arts. Sullivan also looks at the frailties of the judicial system in *Not Guilty: Six Times when Justice Failed.* Sullivan examines miscarriages of justice ranging from a teen wrongly convicted of killing his mother to the case of a Native American activist, Leonard Peltier, and a union activist, Joe Hill. Barbara Schepp, writing in *Kliatt,* found the book "simplistic," yet "a worthwhile examination of something that is often swept under the rug: justice denied." Writing in *Canadian Materials,* Ian Stewart remarked that Sullivan relates "the sad and tragic stories of what happens when police, the courts, media, and volatile public opinion disregard [the] fundamental premise" that a person is innocent until proven guilty. In *Trapped,* Sullivan tells six real tales of "courage and survival," as Sister Bernadette Marie Ondus noted in *Kliatt.* These deal with a toddler who fell down a Texas well, kindergarten students caught in World Trade Center elevators during a bombing, and other stories of true heroism and resilience in the face of desperate situations.

Sullivan has also produced numerous biographies that highlight the lives and times of some prominent

Americans; many of these books are easy readers. His *Lewis and Clark* follows that expedition westward to the Pacific Ocean in the early 1800s. *School Library Journal* contributor Nancy Collins-Warner felt that Sullivan provides "the drama of history well told" in this book. President Abraham Lincoln is featured in other books from Sullivan. In *Picturing Lincoln: Famous Photographs That Popularized the President,* Sullivan produces "a curious mix of biography, media literacy, and the history of photography," according to *Booklist's* Randy Meyer. Sullivan chooses five often-used pictures of the president and demonstrates how these were employed to project an image of Lincoln both in life and in death. Betty Carter, writing in *Horn Book Guide,* found this book a "fascinating historical footnote," while Patricia Ann Owens of *School Library Journal* dubbed it a "unique and sharply focused volume."

Sullivan again deals with the same president in *Abraham Lincoln* for the Scholastic series "In Their Own Words." *Helen Keller* was also written for that series. Both books contain primary and secondary sources. As Catherine Andronik commented in *Booklist* about both titles, "Sullivan seamlessly interweaves information about his subjects with excerpts from primary sources." In Keller's case, this primary source is her autobiography; in Lincoln's case, Sullivan drew from speeches and letters. Todd Morning, reviewing both titles in *School Library Journal,* called these works "well written, fast moving, and highly readable." Both books, according to *Horn Book Guide* reviewer Cyrisse Jaffee, "read smoothly and will be accessible" for children. In *Harriet Tubman,* Sullivan features the life of the woman who was born a slave and became the leader of the Underground Railroad, seeing other slaves to safety in the North. *Pocahontas* likewise details the life of that Native-American woman who helped John Smith and the settlers at Jamestown. According to Shauna Yusko, writing in *School Library Journal,* "Both titles are highly readable and well organized." In time for the 2003 Wright Centennial was *The Wright Brothers,* a biography of those pioneers in flight. Harriet Fargnoli of *School Library Journal* found this book "a good choice for reports."

"I'm always being asked where I get the ideas for my books," Sullivan once revealed. "That's never been a problem for me. The ideas spring from my curiosity about people, places, and events. *How the White House Really Works* is a signature book of mine. What I tried to do in this and many of my other books is to convey to young readers the exciting facts and information brought to light by my inquiring mind." Although he has written several books for adults, Sullivan prefers to illuminate young minds. "Adult books . . . are a nice change of pace for me," he told Chuck Lawliss in *Publishers Weekly,* "but if I had to pick one or the other I'd stick to young adult books. I don't enjoy going into a subject too exhaustively. The text length of young adult books—10,000 words for a sports instructional book, 25,000 or a bit more for general books— suits my temperament."

BIOGRAPHICAL AND CRITICAL SOURCES:

BOOKS

Sullivan, George, *Better Tennis for Boys and Girls,* Dodd, Mead (New York, NY), 1987.

PERIODICALS

Aethlon: The Journal of Sport Literature, fall, 1999, S. Michael Dewey, review of *The Yankees: An Illustrated History,* pp. 180-181.

Booklist, July, 1992, p. 1934; November 15, 1998, Randy Meyer, review of *Portraits of War,* p. 579; March 1, 1999, Carolyn Phelan, review of *All about Hockey,* p. 1211; October 1, 1999, John Peters, review of *To the Bottom of the Sea,* p. 356; December 15, 2000, Denia Hester, review of *Don't Step on the Foul Line: Sports Superstitions* and *Any Number Can Play: The Numbers Athletes Wear,* p. 818; February 1, 2001, Carolyn Phelan, review of *The Civil War at Sea,* p. 1052; February 1, 2001, Randy Meyer, review of *Picturing Lincoln: Famous Photographs That Popularized the President,* p. 1048; April 1, 2001, Catherine Andronik, review of *Abraham Lincoln* and *Helen Keller,* p. 1463; June 1, 2001, Carolyn Phelan, review of *All about Soccer,* p. 1876; July, 2003, Ed Sullivan, review of *Baseball's Boneheads, Bad Boys, and Just Plain Crazy Guys,* p. 1888.

Bulletin of the Center for Children's Books, May, 1973, p. 146; October, 1975, p. 35; July-August, 1986, p. 218; December, 1987, p. 78; September, 1997, Elizabeth Bush, review of *Alamo!,* p. 25.

Canadian Materials, October 15, 1999, Ian Stewart, review of *Not Guilty: Six Times when Justice Failed.*

Choice, February, 1998, R. Browning, review of *The Yankees*, p. 1030.

Horn Book, March, 2001, review of *Picturing Lincoln*, p. 234.

Horn Book Guide, spring, 1997, Peter D. Sieruta, review of *Black Artists in Photography, 1840-1940*, p. 139; spring, 1999, Jack Forman, review of *Burnin' Rubber: Behind the Scenes in Stock Car Racing* and *All about Hockey*, p. 126; spring, 1999, Carrie Harasimowicz, review of *Quarterbacks!: Eighteen of Football's Greatest*, p. 126; spring, 1999, Tanya Auger, review of *Portraits of War*, p. 154; spring, 2001, Carrie Harasimowicz, review of *Don't Step on the Foul Line* and *Any Number Can Play*, p. 138; fall, 2001, Tanya Auger, review of *All about Soccer*, p. 339; fall, 2001, Cyrisse Jaffee, review of *Abraham Lincoln* and *Helen Keller*, p. 417; fall, 2001, Jack Forman, review of *The Civil War at Sea*, p. 438; fall, 2001, Betty Carter, review of *Picturing Lincoln*, p. 438; spring, 2002, Carolyn Shute, review of *Power Football: The Greatest Running Backs*, p. 169; fall, 2002, review of *Harriet Tubman* and *Pocahontas*, p. 469.

Kirkus Reviews, February 1, 2001, review of *The Civil War at Sea*, p. 189; January 15, 2002, review of *Helen Keller*, p. 110.

Kliatt, May, 1998, Barbara Schepp, review of *Not Guilty*, p. 31; September, 1998, Sister Bernadette Marie Ondus, review of *Trapped*, p. 38; March, 1999, Deane A. Beverly, review of *100 Years in Photographs*, p. 38.

New York Times Book Review, November 23, 1971; February 19, 1978, p. 36; June 11, 1978, p. 30; November 13, 1983, p. 48; May 10, 1987.

Publishers Weekly, January 1, 1982, Chuck Lawliss, interview with Sullivan, pp. 10-11; January 11, 1999, review of *100 Years in Photographs*, p. 74.

Reading Teacher, October, 1998, review of *Snowboarding: A Complete Guide for Beginners*, p. 160.

School Library Journal, February, 1976, p. 49; August, 1987, p. 88; November, 1989, p. 133; February, 1991, p. 92; January, 1992, pp. 133-134; March, 1997, Tom S. Hurlburt, review of *Snowboarding*, p. 209; September, 1998, Kate Kohlbeck, review of *Quarterbacks!*, p. 227; January, 1999, Patricia Manning, review of *Burnin' Rubber*, p. 155; March, 1999, Richard Luzer, review of *All about Hockey*, p. 228; January, 2001, Nancy Collins-Warner, review of *Lewis and Clark*, p. 156; February, 2001, Steve Clancy, review of *Don't Step on the Foul Line* and *Any Number Can Play*, p. 140; March, 2001, Patricia Ann Owens, review of *Pic-turing Lincoln*, p. 279; March, 2001, Elizabeth M. Reardon, review of *The Civil War at Sea*, p. 279; April, 2001, Todd Morning, review of *Abraham Lincoln* and *Helen Keller*, pp. 169-170; May, 2001, Blair Christolon, review of *All about Soccer*, p. 171; November, 2001, Michael McCullough, review of *Power Football*, p. 186; November, 2002, Shauna Yusko, review of *Harriet Tubman* and *Pocahontas*, p. 192; July, 2003, Harriet Fargnoli, review of *The Wright Brothers*, p. 150; November, 2003, Julie Webb, review of *Baseball's Boneheads, Bad Boys, and Just Plain Crazy Guys*, p. 168.

Voice of Youth Advocates, August, 1981, p. 41; June, 1992, p. 133; February, 2001, Chris Crowe, review of *Don't Step on the Foul Line* and *Any Number Can Play*, p. 448.

Washington Post Book World, August 14, 1983, p. 13; May 11, 1986, p. 21; March 6, 1994, p. 11; April 6, 1997, Jabarl Asim, review of *Black Artists in Photography, 1840-1940*, p. 8.

ONLINE

Scholastic Web site, http://www2.scholastic.com/ (October 1, 2003).

*   *   *

SWEET, Jeffrey 1950-

PERSONAL: Born May 3, 1950, in Boston, MA; son of James Stouder (a writer) and Vivian (a violinist; maiden name, Roe) Sweet; children: Jonathan Brian. *Education:* New York University, B.F.A., 1971. *Hobbies and other interests:* Reading, playing piano, plays and movies, and "having endless conversations."

ADDRESSES: Home—250 West 90th St., No. 15G, New York, NY 10024.

CAREER: Writer, critic, and educator, 1967—. New Dramatists, alumnus; Ensemble Studio Theater, member of company; Victory Gardens Theater, resident playwright. Scholastic Magazines, editorial assistant, 1970-71; W. W. Norton and Co., Inc., editorial assistant, 1974-75; Russell Sage Foundation, librarian, 1977-78; *Another World* (television series), associate writer, 1981-82; Embassy Television, writer, 1983-84; American Broadcasting Companies, executive story editor for the television series *Hothouse*, 1987; *One Life to Live* (television series), script editor, 1991-92. State University of New York College at Purchase, professor of playwriting, 2002—.

MEMBER: Writers Guild of America, Dramatists Guild (member of council), Drama Desk, New York Writer's Bloc (founder).

AWARDS, HONORS: Award for best drama, Society of Midland Authors, 1978, for *Porch*, and 1982, for *The Value of Names;* playwriting fellowship, National Endowment for the Arts, 1989, for *Porch;* Heideman Award, best one-act play, 1983, for *The Value of Names;* Outer Critics Circle Award, 1984, for *Love;* Joseph Jefferson Award, outstanding new work, 1998, for *Flyovers;* playwriting prize, American Theater Critics Association, 1991, for *American Enterprise,* and 2001, for *The Action against Sol Schumann;* Kennedy Center-American Express Prize and citation in *The Best Plays of . . .* (annual), both for *American Enterprise.*

WRITINGS:

PLAYS

Porch (one-act; produced in Washington, DC, 1977), published in *Best Short Plays, 1976,* edited by Stanley Richards, Chilton Book Co. (Radnor, PA), 1976, revised edition, Samuel French (New York, NY), 1985.

Responsible Parties (three-act; produced in New York, NY at Actors Studio, 1978), Dramatists Play Service (New York, NY), 1985.

After the Fact (produced in New Haven, CT, 1980), Samuel French (New York, NY), 1981.

Stops along the Way (one-act; produced in Evanston, IL, 1980) published in *Best Short Plays, 1981,* edited by Stanley Richards, Chilton Book Co. (Radnor, PA), 1976, revised edition, Dramatists Play Service (New York, NY), 1981.

Holding Patterns, produced in Chicago, IL, 1981.

Ties (two-act; produced in Chicago, IL, at Victory Gardens Theater, 1981, produced on television by WTTW-TV), Dramatists Play Service (New York, NY), 1982.

Routed (produced in Chicago, IL, at Victory Gardens Theater, 1981), Dramatists Play Service (New York, NY), 1982.

The Value of Names (produced in Louisville, KY, at Humana Festival of New American Plays, 1982), Dramatists Play Service (New York, NY), 1986.

Love (musical adaptation of the play *Luv* by Murray Schisgal), composed by Howard Marren, lyrics by Susan Birkenhead (produced in New York, NY at Audrey Wood Theater, 1984; produced as *What about Luv?* in New York, NY, by York Theater Company, 1992), Music Theater International (New York, NY), 1984.

With and Without (produced in Chicago, IL, at Victory Gardens Theater, 1977), Dramatists Play Service (New York, NY), 1997.

American Enterprise (originally produced in Chicago, IL, at Organic Theater), produced in New York, NY, at St. Clement's Church Theater, 1994.

I Sent a Letter to My Love (musical), composed by Melissa Manchester, produced in New York, NY, at Primary Stages, 1995.

Flyovers (produced in Chicago, IL, at Victory Gardens Theater, 1998), Samuel French (New York, NY), 2004.

Bluff (produced in Chicago, IL, at Victory Gardens Theater, 1999), Samuel French (New York, NY), 2004.

The Action against Sol Schumann (first produced in Chicago, IL, at Victory Gardens Theater, 2000), Dramatists Play Service (New York, NY), 2003.

Immoral Imperatives, produced in Chicago, IL, at Victory Gardens Theater, 2001.

OTHER

Something Wonderful Right Away: An Oral History of the Second City and the Compass Players, Limelight Editions (New York, NY), 1978, revised edition, 1987.

(Editor, with Otis L. Gurnsey) *The Best Plays of . . . ,* (annual), Dodd, Mead (New York, NY), 1986-97.

The Dramatist's Toolkit, Heinemann (Portsmouth, NH), 1993.

Solving Your Script: Tools and Techniques for the Playwright, Heinemann (Portsmouth, NH), 2001.

Contributor of articles and stories to periodicals, including *Chicago Tribune, Los Angeles Times, News-*

day, Ellery Queen's Mystery, and *Dramatists Guild Quarterly.* Columnist for *Back Stage,* 1989—, and *Dramatics,* 1996—.

SIDELIGHTS: Though primarily a playwright, Jeffrey Sweet first made his mark with an account of the improvisational theater movement in 1950s Chicago. *Something Wonderful Right Away: An Oral History of the Second City and the Compass Players* includes interviews with the original performers. Sweet once told *CA,* "The greatest single influence on my work is the improvisational theater movement, as developed by such figures as Viola Spolin, Paul Sills, David Shepherd, Alan Myerson, Mike Nichols, Elaine May, Del Close, Sheldon Patinkin and others. Watching and/or workshopping with these people over the years has taught me a great deal about the structure and purposes of theater. I cannot recommend any better preparation for a career as a writer, director or actor than to study in an improvisational workshop."

Several of Sweet's early one-act plays take place in small-town, middle America and examine family strife and unmet expectations. *Porch,* a one-act play first produced in 1977, concerns a woman's return from New York City to her Ohio hometown and the strained relationship with her father due to their conflicting lifestyles and values. *New York Times* critic Richard Eder said that *Porch* is "written with subtlety and an increasingly compelling emotion." Similarly, *Ties,* a two-act play that presents a college theater director's involvement in a doomed romantic triangle, "grabs hold of an audience with a quietly played story about real human beings in a truly delineated setting," according to *Chicago Times* critic Richard Christiansen. However, in trying to achieve a balance of comedy and drama, "its funny lines sometimes are a little too flip, and [Sweet's] sentimental nature gets the best of him in a pat ending that . . . is just too good to be true," Christiansen commented.

Similar ideas are explored in *The Value of Names,* in which an aging comedian comes to terms with the people and events that resulted in his blacklisting during the McCarthy era. In *Responsible Parties,* Sweet creates two characters whose philosophical debate concerning the extent of one's responsibility for others is played out against the backdrop of a rundown motel full of somewhat desperate characters.

Sweet once told *CA:* "I see the primary business of the playwright being not the writing of dialogue but the creation of opportunities for actors to create compelling behavior on stage. Sometimes spoken language is a part of this behavior, sometimes not. (For instance, the part of Helen Keller in William Gibson's *The Miracle Worker* affords the actress playing the role brilliant opportunities even though she speaks only a few syllables.) The theater depicts behavior for an audience's evaluation. Of course, as soon as you talk about evaluating behavior, you're talking about ethics. I think that the theater is, by its very nature, an ethical medium. To deal with ethical questions without being didactic is one of the key challenges facing serious dramatic writing today.

"I have a great love for musical theater (I'm a composer-lyricist and have studied with Lehman Engel and Paul Simon), but, Stephen Sondheim and a handful of others aside, see little to be cheery about in the field these days. I hope to get more deeply involved in musical projects in the future."

BIOGRAPHICAL AND CRITICAL SOURCES:

PERIODICALS

Back Stage, January 24, 1992, Martin Schaeffer, review of *What about Luv?,* p. 46; April 15, 1994, Ira J. Bilowit, review of *American Enterprise,* p. 19; February 17, 1995, William Stevenson, review of *I Sent a Letter to My Love,* p. 44; October 8, 1999, Jonathan Abarbanel, review of *Bluff,* p. 23; October 19, 2001, Elias Stimac, review of *Solving Your Script: Tools and Techniques for the Playwright,* p. 40.

Chicago Times, January 30, 1981, Richard Christiansen, review of *Ties;* April 1, 1983; June 17, 1983.

Indianapolis Star, July 26, 2002, Marion Garmel, "Phoenix Stages Drama of Suspected Nazi Collaborator," p. G19; August 7, 2002, Marion Garmel, review of *The Action against Sol Schumann,* p. E2.

Los Angeles Times, February 20, 1984.

New York Times, November 15, 1978, Richard Eder, review of *Porch;* March 6, 1981; April 16, 1984; October 18, 1984; March 24, 1985.

TCI, May, 1995, David Barbour, review of *The Best Plays of 1993-94: 75th Anniversary Edition; The Otis Guernsey/Burns Mantle Theatre Yearbook,* p. 59.

Time, April 11, 1983, Richard Corliss, review of *The Value of Names,* p. 99.

Variety, June 1, 1998, Chris Jones, review of *Flyovers,* p. 52.

ONLINE

Jeffrey Sweet's Home Page, http://www.jeffreysweet. com/ (April 9, 2004).

T

TALBERT, Marc (Alan) 1953-

PERSONAL: Born July 21, 1953, in Boulder, CO; son of Willard L. (a physicist) and Mary A. Talbert; married Moo Thorpe (a real estate broker and contractor); children: Molly. *Education:* Attended Grinnell College, 1971-73; Iowa State University, B.S., 1976. *Hobbies and other interests:* Running, cooking.

ADDRESSES: Home—Route 4, Box 1B, Santa Fe, NM 87501. *Agent*—Rosemary Sandberg at rosemary@ sandberg.demon.co.uk. *E-mail*—moot@ix.netcom.com.

CAREER: Marshalltown Public Schools, Marshalltown, IA, teacher of fifth and sixth grade, 1976-77; Ames Public Schools, Ames, IA, teacher of fifth grade, 1977-81; Los Alamos National Laboratory, Los Alamos, NM, writer and editor, 1981-86; National Science Foundation, Washington, DC, speech writer for director, 1984-85; writer. University of New Mexico, instructor in children's literature, 1989-90. College of Santa Fe, instructor, writing for children, 2000-01.

MEMBER: PEN, Society of Children's Book Writers, Authors Guild.

AWARDS, HONORS: Best Books for Young Adults citation, American Library Association, 1985, short-listed for British Children's Book Group award, 1986, West Australian Young Readers' Book Award, Library Association of Australia, 1988, all for *Dead Birds Singing; Toby* was named a Notable Children's Book in the Field of Social Studies, National Council on Social Studies, 1987; Owl of the Month Prize, *Bulletin of Youth and Literature,* 1989, for *The Paper Knife.*

WRITINGS:

FOR CHILDREN

Dead Birds Singing, Little, Brown (Boston, MA), 1985.

Thin Ice, Little, Brown (Boston, MA), 1986.

Toby, Dial Books (New York, NY), 1987.

The Paper Knife, Dial Books (New York, NY), 1988.

Rabbit in the Rock, Dial Books (New York, NY), 1989.

Double or Nothing, Dial Books (New York, NY), 1990.

Pillow of Clouds, Dial Books (New York, NY), 1991.

The Purple Heart, HarperCollins (New York, NY), 1992.

A Sunburned Prayer, Simon & Schuster (New York, NY), 1995.

Heart of a Jaguar, Simon & Schuster (New York, NY), 1995.

Star of Luis, Clarion (New York, NY), 1999.

The Trap, DK Publishing (New York, NY), 1999.

Small Change, DK Publishing (New York, NY), 2000.

Holding the Reins (nonfiction; for children and adults), HarperCollins (New York, NY), 2003.

Contributor of short stories "Fountain of Youth" to *Trapped,* edited by Lois Duncan, Simon & Schuster (New York, NY), 1998; and "Books Don't Cry" to *When I Went to the Library,* edited by Debora Pearson, Groundwood (Toronto, Ontario, Canada), 2001. Also author of *Dictator of the World,* a serialized novel for newspapers, published by Breakfast Serials.

Contributor of adult short story "Will McBride's Show Me" to *Censored Books II,* edited by Nicholas Karolides, Scarecrow Press (Lanham, MD), 2002. Author of foreword to *Lost Masterworks of Young Adult Literature,* edited by Connie Zitlow, Scarecrow Press (Lanham, MD), 2002. Columnist for *Daily Tribune,* Ames, IA, *Cedar Valley Times,* Vinton, IA, and *Iowa State Daily.*

SIDELIGHTS: Marc Talbert follows a unique philosophy in writing books for children and young adults. Whereas many authors create stories for a specific age group and others focus on a popular type of fiction, Talbert writes for his characters. The writer once explained: "My stories have to remain true to the characters I've created. If they don't, then I feel I've betrayed the characters and I haven't fulfilled my purpose as a novelist." In keeping with this perception of his role, Talbert conducts meticulous research for all of his books. He reads extensively, talks with experts, observes human behavior, and even tries new and unusual experiences to gain insight into his characters. Talbert's approach clearly has worked. He currently ranks among the foremost writers of social-issue novels for younger readers, and critics consistently praise his complex, realistically drawn characters.

"If you are the kind of reader who enjoys books that focus on serious issues and that let you empathize with characters who must make difficult choices," Bonnie O. Ericson noted in *Writers for Young Adults,* "then it is likely that you will enjoy Marc Talbert's books. Maybe you will count your blessings at the end of a story, maybe you will approve or disapprove of how a particular character acts, or maybe you will feel less alone knowing that others have similarly serious problems. However you respond, most readers will appreciate the honesty of this writer's unique characters and their stories."

Talbert wrote his first book in reaction to a tragic incident that happened while he was teaching fifth grade in Ames, Iowa: One of his students died in an automobile accident. Finding few books that could help young people cope with the death of a friend, Talbert decided he would someday write a book to fill that gap. He finished the book, *Dead Birds Singing,* while he was living in Washington and working as a speech writer at the National Science Foundation. Within two weeks of submitting the manuscript to Little, Brown and Company, he received a contract. The book, which earned Talbert immediate recognition as a serious novelist for young adults, went on to win several prestigious awards.

Dead Birds Singing features seventh-grader Matt Smythe, whose mother and sister are killed in an automobile accident by a drunken driver. Now an orphan, Matt is adopted by the Fletchers, the family of his best friend. The story takes place during the four months following the crash as Matt confronts questions about life and death. In a review for the *New York Times Book Review,* Otto R. Salassi observed that this "seriously intense first novel" effectively portrays Matt's struggle. Yet the reader can only give the boy "a pat on the shoulder and wish him good luck," Salassi noted. "There's not much else we feel we can say or do, and maybe there's not supposed to be."

Moving back to New Mexico, his wife's native state, Talbert began working on *Thin Ice,* a book about a young boy whose parents are separated. Like *Dead Birds Singing, Thin Ice* was inspired by Talbert's students. The author explained: "When I was a teacher I was astonished to learn that a quarter to a third of all the kids in every class I taught came from divorced, remarried or redefined families. In an upper-middle-class, highly educated community like Ames, Iowa, I thought that was astonishing. It was something that as a teacher I addressed every single day in one way or another. . . . Frannie, the girl in that book, was diabetic, and that was inspired by working with diabetic kids at Camp Ho Mita Koda, outside Cleveland, Ohio."

Ten-year-old Martin Enders, the main character in *Thin Ice,* is confused about his place in the world. He is "skating on thin ice" as he tries to adjust to his parents' recent divorce while his life spins out of control. Not only does he have the stress of helping care for his diabetic sister, Frannie, but he also loses his best friend, Barney, and his school work goes into a steady decline. Martin reaches a crisis point when his mother starts dating his fifth-grade teacher, Mr. Raven—a development that Martin considers to be a profound betrayal. Commenting on the character of Mr. Raven, Talbert said, "The idea of the mother dating the teacher was pure whimsy, it was almost a challenge to the audience—What would you do in this situation?" *Voice of Youth Advocates* reviewer Jane Van Wiemokly called *Thin Ice* "a thought provoking, touching story" that has "added relevance" for young adults facing similar family problems today. A *Publishers Weekly* reviewer described it as a "beautifully written book," and a critic in the *Junior Bookshelf* praised the novel's "freedom from exaggeration," further noting that "we get to know [Martin] intimately, warts and all."

Talbert's third novel is *Toby,* which is based on the experiences of one of Talbert's former students. "Toby was inspired by a student in my class the first year I taught, whose parents were retarded," Talbert said. "He was a very bright boy, he was a very clever boy. He was my favorite student." The novel depicts the prejudices, conflicts, and misunderstandings encountered by the title character, whose parents are illiterate and mentally slow. *Toby* was named a Notable Children's Book in the Field of Social Studies by the National Council of Social Studies.

Although *The Paper Knife* could be considered "controversial," Talbert has never received adverse reactions from young readers, teachers, or librarians. In fact, he has explained, when he visits schools students thank him for the honest portrayal of a painful topic that mirrors their own experiences. *The Paper Knife* is the story of Jeremy Johnson, whose mother, Ginny, has been mistreated by her boyfriend, George. As the book opens, Ginny has taken Jeremy to live with George's parents, the Hayeses, in the small town of Clifton. Although Ginny has found a safe haven, Jeremy fears that George will find them. Soon it becomes apparent that Jeremy has been sexually abused by George, who made him swear not to tell anyone. When George calls to remind Jeremy about the vow of silence, the boy realizes he can use the truth as a weapon. So he decides to "write those things down." He tells himself, "I'll write them down on a piece of paper, and I'll carry that paper around with me like my knife." Then in a chaotic series of events the paper knife is stolen, and Ginny and Mrs. Hayes wrongly accuse Jeremy's teacher of abusing the boy. After being transferred to a new school, Jeremy must confront the consequences of his silence. In a riveting conclusion, he is finally able to tell the truth to Mr. Hayes.

In *Bulletin of the Center for Children's Books* Zena Sutherland praised Talbert for taking *The Paper Knife* beyond the "problem novel." The author deals "perceptively with . . . other facets of Jeremy's life," Sutherland stated, for "he sees children as people, avoiding either condescension or evasion in depicting them." Denise Wilms noted in *Booklist* that *The Paper Knife* succeeds in "showing how to get help if one is a victim."

Reviewers frequently label Talbert a "problem novelist" because of the subjects he portrays in his books. Yet the writer refuses to accept such a narrow interpre-

tation of his work. "Sometimes I cringe when people say I have written problem novels," he has revealed. "We all have problems, and there are always problems in novels. You don't write a novel about a world that is perfect—you portray a problem that needs to be solved or overcome. I would like to think that if there are problems in my books that they're more than just the surface problem that is being dealt with." Talbert went on to point out that in *The Paper Knife,* for instance, "the problem, from a 'problem novel' point of view, is sexual abuse. But I think it's more universal than that. I think it has to do with deep, dark, horrible secrets," he asserted. "I think it has to do with injuries to the part of you that is deep and inaccessible, not only to other people but even to yourself. Sexual abuse is an example of that, which can be made more universal. So it's not just a book for kids who have been sexually abused, or for adults who work with them," Talbert concluded. "It's for anybody who has a deep, dark, horrible secret, or some grinding kind of guilt or some huge fear."

Talbert described his next novel, *Rabbit in the Rock,* as his "fun book." A distinct departure in subject matter from *The Paper Knife,* it tells the story of Bernie, a teenager who lives on her family's dude ranch in New Mexico. Talbert explained that the character of Bernie is based on his wife, whose family once owned a resort ranch in New Mexico. "And there really is a rabbit in the rock," he announced. "There is a rock formation in the canyon on the resort that looks exactly like a rabbit, and when it rains it disappears. It's peeking out from a little canopy of rock. The first time it was ever noticed was when a seven- or eight-year-old girl came back from horseback riding and went to the chef at the restaurant and asked for carrots. He asked, 'Why do you want carrots?' and she said, 'For the rabbit in that canyon over there.' So she took the carrots and was amazed to find it wasn't a real rabbit but a rock." Talbert added that the rabbit is not visible to most observers, "but it's perfect from the perspective of a seven-year-old on a horse."

Rabbit in the Rock opens as Bernie is riding her horse in the hills near her parents' ranch. She happens upon Sean Raven, a rock star and former member of a successful band called the Supersonics. Tired of the music business, he is seeking refuge in the hills. Bernie begins sneaking food and clothing to Sean, and soon they concoct a bogus kidnaping plot that involves sending ransom notes to his father—also a member of the Supersonics—whom he hates. But the scheme backfires when the FBI intercepts the notes and, as they always do in such cases, set out in search of the pair. After spending several days and nights roaming the area, Bernie and Sean are discovered by Bernie's brother, Carlton. When Carlton breaks his leg, Sean and Bernie rescue him, an act that forces them to turn themselves in.

Talbert returned to family relationships in *Pillow of Clouds*. Chester, the main character, is faced with a difficult dilemma: According to his parents' divorce settlement, he must choose a permanent home with one of them when he turns thirteen. After he decides to join his father in Santa Fe, his alcoholic mother, who lives alone in a small Iowa town, attempts suicide. A private and sensitive young boy, Chester writes poetry in an effort to come to terms with his guilt over hurting his mother. Critics unanimously praised *Pillow of Clouds*. Susan Oliver described it as a "moving, thought-provoking novel" in *School Library Journal*, and *Voice of Youth Advocates* reviewer James E. Cook found the book to be "first-rate." Cook noted especially the "positively portrayed" Hispanic family as well as the realistic ending, which does not conveniently resolve Chester's problems. Randy Meyer concluded in *Booklist*, "In a society nearly as quick to divorce as it is to marry, [Chester's] search for friendship and stability will be familiar and rewarding."

Equally well received was *The Purple Heart*, which *School Library Journal* reviewer Gerry Larson described as a portrayal of "believable characters" and "a positive statement on the healing power of family love." When Luke Canvin's father comes home from the Vietnam war, Luke is puzzled to see a brooding, worn-out shell of a man instead of a triumphant hero. Finally learning that his father won a Purple Heart but had concealed it in a trunk, Luke sneaks the medal into his pocket and carries it around with him. As a tornado hovers over the Canvins' midwestern town, the boy loses the Purple Heart in a silly prank. Through a culminating rush of events that mirror the storm, Luke learns the true facts of his father's injury and gains a deeper understanding of genuine courage. A *Publishers Weekly* reviewer stated that Talbert "creates a compelling, resonant tale." A critic in *Kirkus Reviews* noted that the author effectively presents an "ironic contrast" between war games Luke plays with a friend and the "heavy reality and evident cost of his father's experience."

Two other Talbert novels, *A Sunburned Prayer* and *Heart of a Jaguar,* are both products of the author's extensive research into Mexican and Hispanic culture. Set in contemporary New Mexico, *A Sunburned Prayer* portrays the story of a boy named Eloy who goes on a Good Friday pilgrimage to the shrine of the Santaurio de Chimayó. Talbert explained that, in preparation for writing the book, he walked the route himself not once but twice. The first time he wanted to learn how Eloy would feel as he traveled the seventeen miles to the church on foot with hundreds of other pilgrims. Talbert made the second trip after completing the novel, to make sure he had the details right. The author went on to say that not only did he gain insight into the character he was creating but he was also able to immerse himself more deeply in New Mexican traditions. He noted that, as one of the few blond Anglo-Americans in the group, on each pilgrimage he had the curious sensation of being both an insider and an outsider.

Talbert said he got the idea for *A Sunburned Prayer* when he saw people walking toward Chimayó on Good Friday as he drove to work at Los Alamos. "Many of them looked like they had no business walking a distance any longer than from their house to the mailbox," he noted. "Some of them were carrying heavy wooden crosses, some of them were using crutches, and there were some wheelchairs. It was always very moving and it would bring tears to my eyes as I was driving. Having grown up white Anglo-Saxon Protestant middle-class in Iowa, I just wondered at the faith people must have that would compel them to walk sometimes as far away as from Albuquerque, which would be seventy-five miles to Chimayó. The seed for the story, then, was what kind of faith would compel people to do this. When, finally, I couldn't stand it any longer, I decided I would have to do the pilgrimage myself and find out from observing people and observing myself to find out exactly what went on during a pilgrimage."

Talbert also did research at the archdiocese offices in Santa Fe, and he spent considerable time with the priest at the Santaurio de Chimayó. "There I got a feel for the historical perspective as well as the current perspective," the author said. Next, he took the pilgrimage from his house, a distance of seventeen miles. Although Talbert is a long-distance runner, he found "it was torture to walk." He did discover, however, that "the physical journey almost perfectly matched the emotional journey, and that when you're the most physically tired the terrain gets the most austere, most difficult to walk. Usually that time of the day is the hottest. That part of it was a wonderful coincidence." For the first time in his writing career, Talbert recalled, he "began the book not knowing how it was going to end. . . . So I wrote this book about faith on faith that it would work its way out." He took the second walk in memory of his father-in-law, who had recently died and to whom he dedicated *A Sunburned Prayer.*

In the book Talbert again portrays complex family dynamics, depicting eleven-year-old Eloy who has disobeyed his parents by going to Chimayó. The boy believes that if he can taste some of the Santuario's holy soil, his dying grandmother will be cured of cancer. Tired and hungry from fasting on Good Friday, Eloy meets a stray dog who accompanies him the rest of the way. When they reach Chimayó, Eloy discovers that his brother, Benito, has already taken their grandmother to the church in his car. She assures Eloy, however, that he has brought her peace by making the pilgrimage.

After they return home, Eloy is forgiven by his parents and is allowed to keep the dog as a pet. His grandmother's words help him come to terms with her death, making him understand that "sometimes we ask God for one thing and He gives us some other things we might need instead. And sometimes He takes things away. He knows what He's doing." *A Sunburned Prayer* received tremendous praise from critics. In *School Library Journal* Jack Forman asserted that it is "one of Talbert's most moving and meaningful novels to date." He also also commended the author for including a glossary of Spanish words at the end of the book. *Booklist* reviewer Mary Harris Veeder noted Talbert's success in telling an engrossing story through interior monologues that explore Eloy's feelings. And, she added, "readers will find the portrait of [Benito], who is certainly no saint, rich in realistic detail."

Heart of a Jaguar is set in a village near Chichén Itzá during the thirteenth century. Fourteen-year-old Balam is approaching manhood as villagers try to cope with a serious drought. Hoping to receive rain so they can plant the corn they need for survival, leaders make blood sacrifices to the gods. With exquisite attention to detail, Talbert traces the sights, smells, sounds, and sensations of Balam's daily life among the villagers. *School Library Journal* David N. Pauli called the book a "fascinating and worthwhile read." Patty Campbell was even more laudatory in her *Horn Book* review, hailing *Heart of a Jaguar* as a "tour de force." She noted that Talbert immerses the reader in Mayan culture through Balam's daily experiences while at the same time making the boy "an adolescent recognizable in contemporary terms, with all his poignant striving for the dignity of adulthood." But, Campbell continued, "Talbert plays tricks with this, lulling the reader into perceiving him as a familiar young adult protagonist, and then jarring us with the shock of cultural difference."

The author uses this technique throughout the novel, building to a conclusion that the reader may find shocking. Yet it is consistent with Mayan traditions—and with the character of Balam as Talbert has created him. According to Campbell, "*Heart of a Jaguar* is a breakthrough novel, but not because it contains . . . unprecedented scenes. While many historical novels for young adults settle for fancy dress and a protagonist who moves through past times with a twentieth-century mindset, Marc Talbert has had the courage to anatomize a profoundly exotic physicality and mentality without sentimentalizing it for easy consumption." Talbert revealed that Balam is still with him almost daily. He added that he feels he has been true to Balam if *Heart of a Jaguar* moves the reader to think of the character as a living, breathing person. On the evidence of critical response to the novel, Talbert has clearly achieved this goal.

Star of Luis is set during World War II. When a young Mexican-American boy's father goes off to war with the army, his mother takes the family to her hometown in New Mexico. There, Luis discovers a family secret: he finds out that the family is not Catholic but Jewish. During the Inquisition in Spain, many Jews left the country for the Spanish colony in Mexico. There, they converted to Catholicism to avoid discrimination. When his family return to Los Angeles, Luis tries to come to terms with the knowledge that his religious background is different from what he has always believed it to be. Hazel Rochman in *Booklist* believed that "readers will be caught up in the astonishing revelations about Luis's identity and his new awareness of diversity in religion, family, and friends." A critic for *Publishers Weekly* noted a "lack of resolution" to an otherwise "engrossing tale about a little-known subject."

In *The Trap* Ellie loses her cat to local coyotes. When a classmate suggests setting a trap near the coyotes' den, she agrees. But a harmless stray dog sets off the trap instead, and Ellie feels guilt for what she has done. The critic for *Publishers Weekly* noted Talbert's "characteristic insight into human nature" and found that "Ellie's ruminations are carried along by a plot that includes more than one brush with danger."

Talbert creates a portrait of modern Mexican rural life in *Small Change*. In this novel, American teenagers become separated from their families during a guerrilla attack in the Mexican countryside. They escape from kidnappers and find refuge with a friendly farm family. John Peters in *Booklist* concluded that *Small Change* was "a vivid, ultimately sympathetic snapshot of a segment of Mexican life and politics."

In his first nonfiction book for children and adults, *Holding the Reins*, Talbert profiled (with noted western photographer Barbara Van Cleve) four young women who live and work on their families' ranches. Each girl is described in one of four seasons of the year, and each ranch has its own focus—cattle, sheep, horses, or combinations. This book took Talbert to Montana, Wyoming (where he spent time as a boy at the ranch of relatives), Utah, Colorado, and New Mexico. Talbert told *CA:* "The young women I wrote about are great role models for young women today: female and proud and capable. I wanted my daughters to see young women like them, and be inspired," Talbert said. "They were."

"What will Talbert's next books be like?," Ericson asked in *Writers for Young Adults.* "Given that he has two daughters, perhaps he will write a book featuring a main character who is female. Whatever his future directions, readers can be assured that Talbert will draw on his own experiences to develop realistic and honest characters and stories."

Talbert once commented to *CA:* "I was always torn between wanting to work with children and wanting to write. I feel lucky to be able to combine these loves in children's books."

BIOGRAPHICAL AND CRITICAL SOURCES:

BOOKS

Writers for Young Adults, Scribner (New York, NY), 1997.

PERIODICALS

ALAN Review, spring, 1990, Sharon Chinn, "Modern Fairy Tales: Archetypal Structure in the Novels of Marc Talbert," pp. 35-37.
Booklist, March 1, 1989, Denise Wilms, review of *The Paper Knife,* p. 1197; November 15, 1989, p. 653; March 1, 1991, Randy Meyer, review of *Pillow of Clouds,* p. 1378; August, 1995, Mary Harris Veeder, review of *A Sunburned Prayer,* p. 1950; September 15, 1995, p. 154; March 1, 1999, Hazel Rochman, review of *Star of Luis,* p. 1203; November 15, 1999, John Peters, review of *The Trap,* p. 628; April 1, 2000, John Peters, review of *Small Change,* p. 1451.
Bulletin of the Center for Children's Books, January, 1989, Zena Sutherland, review of *The Paper Knife,* p. 137.
Children's Book Review Service, August, 1991, p. 168.
English Journal, September, 1992, p. 95.
Horn Book, July-August, 1985, p. 459; January-February, 1991, pp. 71-72; January-February, 1996, Patty Campbell, review of *Heart of a Jaguar,* pp. 110-114.
Junior Bookshelf, December, 1987, review of *Thin Ice,* pp. 289-290.
Kirkus Reviews, September 1, 1989, pp. 1333-1334; December 15, 1991, review of *The Purple Heart,* p. 1599.
New York Times Book Review, May 12, 1985, Otto R. Salassi, review of *Dead Birds Singing,* p. 16.
Publishers Weekly, December 12, 1986, review of *Thin Ice,* p. 54; September 9, 1988, p. 138; October 13, 1989, p. 55; August 31, 1990, p. 68; March 15, 1991, p. 218; December 6, 1991, review of *The Purple Heart,* pp. 73-74; April 17, 1995, p. 61; September 18, 1995, review of *Heart Like a Jaguar,* p. 133; February 22, 1999, review of *Star of Luis,* p. 96.
School Library Journal, January, 1987, p. 80; November 27, 1987, pp. 82-83; January, 1988, p. 77; October, 1988, pp. 148-149; January, 1990, p. 108; November, 1990, p. 119; March, 1991, Susan Oliver, review of *Pillow of Clouds,* p. 218; February, 1992, Gerry Larson, review of *The Purple Heart,* pp. 89-90; July, 1995, Jack Forman, review of *A Sunburned Prayer,* p. 82; November, 1995, David N. Pauli, review of *Heart of a Jaguar,* p. 122.
Voice of Youth Advocates, August, 1985, p. 190; February, 1987, Jane Van Wiemokly, review of *Thin Ice,* p. 287; April, 1991, James E. Cook, review of *Pillow of Clouds,* p. 37.

Wilson Library Bulletin, December, 1988, Frances Bradburn, review of *The Paper Knife*, pp. 90-91; November, 1989, p. S11.

*   *   *

TATTERSALL, Ian (Michael) 1945-

PERSONAL: Born May 10, 1945, in Paignton, Devon, England; immigrated to United States, 1967. *Education:* Cambridge University, B.A., 1967, M.A., 1970; Yale University, M.Phil., Ph.D., 1971.

ADDRESSES: Office—Department of Anthropology, American Museum of Natural History, Central Park at 79th St., New York, N.Y. 10024. *E-mail*—iant@amnh. org.

CAREER: New School for Social Research, New York, NY, visiting lecturer, 1971-72; Lehman College, City University of New York, New York, NY, adjunct assistant professor, 1971-74, adjunct professor of anthropology; American Museum of Natural History, New York, NY, assistant curator, 1971-76, associate curator, 1976-81, curator of physical anthropology, 1981—.

MEMBER: American Association for the Advancement of Science, American Anthropological Association, American Association of Physical Anthropologists, Society of Systematic Zoology, Society of Vertebrate Paleontology.

WRITINGS:

Man's Ancestors: An Introduction to Primate and Human Evolution, Murray, 1970.
(Editor, with R. W. Sussman) *Lemur Biology*, Plenum, 1975.
The Primates of Madagascar, Columbia University Press (New York, NY), 1982.
(With Niles Eldredge) *The Myths of Human Evolution*, Columbia University Press (New York, NY), 1982.
The Human Odyssey: Four Million Years of Human Evolution, Prentice Hall General Reference (New York, NY), 1993.
Primates: Lemurs, Monkeys, and You, Millbrook Press (Brookfield, CT), 1995.
The Fossil Trail: How We Know What We Think We Know about Human Evolution, Oxford University Press (New York, NY), 1995.
Becoming Human: Evolution and Human Uniqueness, Harcourt (New York, NY), 1998.
The Last Neanderthal: The Rise, Success and Mysterious Extinction of Our Closest Human Relatives, Westview (Boulder, CO), new edition, 1999.
(With Jeffrey H. Schwartz) *Extinct Humans*, Westview (Boulder, CO), 2000.
The Monkey in the Mirror: Essays on the Science of What Makes Us Human, Harcourt (New York, NY), 2002.
(With Jeffrey H. Schwartz) *The Human Fossil Record*, Volume 1: *Terminology, and Craniodental Morphology of Genus Homo*, Wiley (New York, NY), 2002.

Contributor to numerous scientific journals and popular magazines.

SIDELIGHTS: English paleontologist Ian Tattersall has written several popular books about human evolution. In *The Myths of Human Evolution*, he examines certain misconceptions the public has about the theory of evolution. *Becoming Human: Evolution and Human Uniqueness* is a study of early human behavior in psychological terms. In *Extinct Humans* Tattersall argues that the history of human evolution is not one of a single continuous development but rather of various branches, some of which failed and one of which resulted in contemporary human beings.

Tattersall believes that scientists are influenced by their culture. A case in point, according to Tattersall, is nineteenth-century British naturalist Charles Darwin's theory that evolution is a slow, gradual process. Darwin's "gradualism," as Tattersall and coauthor Niles Eldredge point out in their 1982 book *The Myths of Human Evolution*, is one of the "myths" that became incorporated into the theory of evolution in spite of insufficient evidence. The authors themselves are proponents of "punctuationism," a hypothesis that the life of species consists of long periods of stagnation interrupted by brusque transformations, and, as J. R. Durant recounted in the *Times Literary Supplement*, Tattersall and Eldredge "attribute the general tendency among Darwinian biologists to explain evolution in terms of constant, adaptive change to the pernicious influence of the Victorian idea of social progress." While critics found the argument for punctuationism convincing, they were skeptical about the authors' attempt to apply this hypothesis to social history. As David Graber of the *Los Angeles Times* asserted, this approach may be valid, "but it's hardly a new idea." However, Graber praised *The Myths of Human Evolution* as "better balanced" than other books on the same topic, such as Richard E. Leakey's *The Making of Mankind* or Donald C. Johanson and Maitland A. Edey's *Lucy.*

In *The Myths of Human Evolution*, Tattersall and Eldredge also challenge the notion of creationism, a religious explanation of natural history. According to the book's authors, creationism is another "myth of human evolution," and should be approached as a cultural phenomenon, an "aspect of American populism." *Washington Post Book World*'s Edwin M. Yoder, Jr. concurred with this analysis of creationism, observing that "the validity of a scientific proposition cannot be tested by majority opinion or vote." Furthermore, critics maintained that the book's discussion of myths, both within and outside the realm of science, dispels much of the confusion surrounding the conflict between creationists and the scientific community. As Yoder concluded, Tattersall and Eldredge show "that the creationist controversy is as much a social and pedagogical crisis as a crisis in science."

In *Becoming Human: Evolution and Human Uniqueness*, Tattersall attempts to delineate "the cognitive difference between humans, their ancestral species, and their closest living relatives, the great apes," as Gilbert Taylor recounted in *Booklist*. As Shaun Calhoun noted in *Library Journal*, Tattersall "reveals our species' unique characteristics, including language, symbolic thought, art, and innovation." In making his case, the critic for *Publishers Weekly* remarked, Tattersall consults "the fossil record for corroboration of the innovations he takes to be significant." "A felicitous writer," Taylor concluded, "Tattersall gracefully summarizes what science knows for certain about human origins and indicates areas, such as language development, where debate rages."

In *Extinct Humans*, written with Jeffrey H. Schwartz, Tattersall traces the evolution of human beings in a manner far different than that usually taught in school. He finds that existing fossil evidence can be best explained not as a single line of human development leading from the early apes to modern humans but as a number of different branches. Some of these

branches died out while other branches flourished. "Hominid history," wrote the critic for *Publishers Weekly*, "ought to look less like a queue than like a tree." The book explains, according to Taylor, "why the idea of the one-track, lineal descent of human beings is obsolete." H. James Birx in *Library Journal* called *Extinct Humans* "a clear and detailed overview of fossil hominid evidence and its various interpretations" and concluded that "this impressive and indispensable book is a very important contribution to modern paleoanthropology."

Speaking to Amy Otchet in the *UNESCO Courier,* Tattersall explained: "Somehow we believe it is normal and natural for us to be alone in the world. Yet in fact, if you look at the fossil record, you find that this is totally unusual—this may be the first time that we have ever had just one species of humans in the world. We have a history of diversity and competition among human species which began some five million years ago and came to an end with the emergence of modern humans. Two million years ago, for example, there were at least four human species on the same landscape."

BIOGRAPHICAL AND CRITICAL SOURCES:

PERIODICALS

Booklist, September 1, 2001, Gilbert Taylor, review of *The Monkey in the Mirror*, p. 27.

Library Journal, February 1, 1998, Shaun Calhoun, review of *Becoming Human: Evolution and Human Uniquenss*, p. 95; June 1, 2000, H. James Birx, review of *Extinct Humans*, p. 188; September 15, 2001, H. James Birx, review of *The Monkey in the Mirror*, p. 107.

Los Angeles Times, December 26, 1982, David Graber, review of *The Myths of Human Evolution*.

Natural History, December, 2001, review of *The Monkey in the Mirror*, p. 82.

New Scientist, March 9, 2002, Bernard Wood, review of *The Monkey in the Mirror*, p. 52.

Publishers Weekly, January 19, 1998, review of *Becoming Human*, p. 363; July 2, 2001, p. 59.

Times Literary Supplement, February 18, 1983, J. R. Durant, review of *The Myths of Human Evolution*.

UNESCO Courier, December, 2000, Amy Otchet, "Ian Tattersall: The Humans We Left Behind," p. 47.

Washington Post Book World, December 26, 1982, Edwin M. Yoder, Jr., review of *The Myths of Human Evolution.*

ONLINE

City University of New York Graduate Center Web site, http://web.gc.cuny.edu/anthropology/fac_tattersall.html/ (December 11, 2002).*

*   *   *

TAUBMAN, William 1941-

PERSONAL: Born November 13, 1941, in New York, NY; son of Howard (a critic for the *New York Times*) and Nora (Stern) Taubman; married Jane Andelman (an assistant professor of Russian), 1969; children: Alexander James. *Education:* Harvard University, B.A., 1962; Columbia University, M.A. and Certificate of Russian Institute, 1965, Ph.D., 1969; attended Moscow State University, 1965-66.

ADDRESSES: Home—46 Orchard St., Amherst, MA. *Office*—Political Science Department, Amherst College, 104 Clark House, Amherst, MA 01002-5000. *E-mail*—wctaubman@amherst.edu.

CAREER: Amherst College, Amherst, MA, instructor, 1967-69, assistant professor, 1969-73, associate professor, beginning 1973, currently Bertrand Snell Professor of Political Science.

MEMBER: American Political Science Association, American Association for the Advancement of Slavic Studies, American Association of University Professors, Council on Foreign Relations.

AWARDS, HONORS: Woodrow Wilson fellowship, 1962; Fulbright Hays fellowship, 1965-66; International Affairs fellowship, Council on Foreign Relations, 1970-71.

WRITINGS:

The View from Lenin Hills: Soviet Youth in Ferment, Coward, McCann (New York, NY), 1967.
Governing Soviet Cities: Bureaucratic Politics and Urban Development in the USSR, Praeger (New York, NY), 1973.

(Editor) *Globalism and Its Cities: The American Foreign Policy Debate of the 1960's,* Heath (Lexington, MA), 1973.
Stalin's American Policy, Norton, (New York, NY), 1982.
Moscow Spring, Summit Books (New York, NY), 1989.
(Editor) Sergei Khrushchev, *Khrushchev on Khrushchev: An Inside Account of the Man and His Era,* Little, Brown (Boston, MA), 1991.
(Editor, with Sergei Khrushchev and Abbott Gleason) *Nikita Khrushchev,* Yale University Press (New Haven, CT), 2000.
Khrushchev: The Man and His Era, Norton (New York, NY), 2003.

SIDELIGHTS: William Taubman has written extensively on the Soviet Union and, in particular, on Soviet leader Nikita Khrushchev. He is the editor of *Khrushchev on Khrushchev: An Inside Account of the Man and His Era,* a memoir written by Khrushchev's son, Sergei, and editor with Sergei and Abbott Gleason of *Nikita Khrushchev,* a collection of essays based on previously unavailable information on the Soviet premier. *Khrushchev: The Man and His Era* is Taubman's own full-length biography of the controversial leader of the former Soviet Union.

Taubman's year as an exchange student in the Soviet Union in 1965 is the subject of his first book, *The View from Lenin Hills.* Fred M. Hechinger of the *New York Times* found that "the Taubman view from Lenin Hills is clear, fresh and entertaining. The conclusion that many young Russians are not anticapitalist in the way many Americans are anti-Communist is shrewdly accurate and worth thinking about." In the same year he visited the Soviet Union, Taubman also served as one of the interpreters for the Soviet National Basketball Team on its American tour.

In *Khrushchev on Khrushchev,* the premier's son, Sergei, remembers his influential father's long career as a Soviet official, his eventual ouster in the 1960s, and the painful years of forced retirement. Khrushchev began as a henchman of Soviet dictator Joseph Stalin, played a role in the bloody purges of the 1930s, and oversaw a period of relative calm and stability before leading the world to the brink of nuclear war during the Cuban Missile Crisis of the early 1960s. Genevieve Stuttaford in *Publishers Weekly* found the book to be "astute, wrenching, brimming with disclosures," although she believed that Sergei "attempts to rehabilitate his father."

In *Nikita Khrushchev*, Taubman, Sergei Khrushchev, and Abbott Gleason present newly released documents about the life and career of the former Soviet leader. After Khrushchev was declared a "non-person" by the Soviet government after his ouster as premier in 1964, information about his life and career was strictly controlled. Only when Soviet premier Mikhail Gorbachev allowed government archives to be opened to the public in the 1980s did details about Khrushchev's reign become available. These documents, along with Khrushchev's own memoirs and the memoirs of those who served under him, are drawn upon in the essays gathered in *Nikita Khrushchev*. Harry Willems of *Library Journal* noted that "this book fills a void in Soviet studies." "Overall," Christopher Read in *History Today* found, "the collection advances the study of the Khrushchev years very considerably, throwing light on almost all the key issues."

Taubman's 2003 title *Khrushchev: The Man and His Era* is a massive, 700-page biography of the Soviet premier and the first to be written by an American. Taubman argues that Khrushchev's paradoxical career—beginning as a murderous underling to Joseph Stalin but eventually becoming the premier himself and denouncing Stalin—can be seen "as a mirror of the entire Soviet experience," as Gilbert Taylor in *Booklist* noted. A critic for *Publishers Weekly* believed that "Taubman has pieced together a remarkably detailed chronicle, complete with riveting scenes of Kremlin intrigue and acute psychological analysis that further illuminates some of the nightmarish episodes of Soviet history." Similarly, Willems described Taubman's book as "a massive biography that is both psychologically and politically revealing." Taylor concluded that *Khrushchev: The Man and His Era* is an "outstandingly composed work, assuredly the reference point for future writings on Khrushchev."

BIOGRAPHICAL AND CRITICAL SOURCES:

PERIODICALS

Biography, summer, 2003, Leon Aron, review of *Khrushchev: The Man and His Era,* p. 539.

Booklist, November 1, 2002, Gilbert Taylor, review of *Khrushchev: The Man and His Era,* p. 472.

Bulletin of the Atomic Scientists, May, 1991, Richard Ned Lebow, review of *Khrushchev on Khrushchev,* p. 43.

Current History, October, 1989, R. Scott Bomboy, review of *Moscow Spring,* p. 345.

Foreign Affairs, winter, 1990, John D. Campbell, review of *Khrushchev on Khrushchev,* p. 198.

History Today, May, 2001, Christopher Read, review of *Nikita Khrushchev,* p. 55; January, 2004, Sergei Kudryashov, review of *Khrushchev: The Man and His Era,* p. 57.

Library Journal, March 1, 1982, review of *Stalin's American Policy,* p. 549; March 15, 1989, R. H. Johnston, review of *Moscow Spring,* p. 79; April 15, 2000, Harry Willems, review of *Nikita Khrushchev,* p. 100; October 15, 2002, Harry Willems, review of *Khrushchev: The Man and His Era,* p. 80.

Nation, May 26, 2003, Robert D. English, review of *Khrushchev: The Man and His Era,* p. 29.

New Leader, February 22, 1982, Robert Taylor, review of *Stalin's American Policy,* p. 18.

New Statesman and Society, August 10, 1990, Lawrence Freddman, review of *Khrushchev on Khrushchev,* p. 33.

Newsweek, June 26, 1989, Carroll Bogert, review of *Moscow Spring,* p. 68.

New York Review of Books, December 19, 1991, David Remnick, review of *Khrushchev on Khrushchev,* p. 72.

New York Times, January 22, 1968, Fred M. Hechinger, review of *The View from Lenin Hills.*

New York Times Book Review, January 17, 1982, Joseph S. Nye, review of *Stalin's American Policy,* p. 8; April 23, 1989, Abraham Brumberg, review of *Moscow Spring,* p. 15; July 29, 1990, George W. Breslauer, review of *Khrushchev on Khrushchev,* p. 10.

Publishers Weekly, November 27, 1981, William Stuttaford, review of *Stalin's American Policy,* p. 78; February 10, 1989, Genevieve Stuttaford, review of *Moscow Spring,* p. 59; April 13, 1990, Genevieve Stuttaford, review of *Khrushchev on Khrushchev,* p. 50; November 11, 2002, review of *Khrushchev: The Man and His Era,* p. 47.

Spectator, April 19, 2003, Simon Heffer, review of *Khrushchev: The Man and His Era,* p. 39.

Times Higher Education Supplement, December 5, 2003, Catherine Andreyev, review of *Khrushchev: The Man and His Era,* p. 31.

ONLINE

Amherst College Web site, http://www.amherst.edu/
(December 11, 2002).*

* * *

TAYLOR, Joan E(lizabeth) 1958-

PERSONAL: Born September 13, 1958, in Horsell, Surrey, England; daughter of Robert Glenville and Birgit Elisabeth (Norlev) Taylor; married Paul Hunt (an international human rights lawyer), December 30, 1988; children: Emily, Robert. *Ethnicity:* "European." *Education:* University of Auckland, B.A., 1979; University of Otago, B.D., 1985; University of Edinburgh, Ph.D., 1989.

ADDRESSES: Office—Department of Religious Studies, University of Waikato, P.O. Box 3105, Hamilton, New Zealand. *E-mail*—joan_far@btinternet.com.

CAREER: University of Waikato, Hamilton, New Zealand, fellow, 1992-93, lecturer, 1994-97, senior lecturer in religious studies, 1998-2000, research associate, 2000-01, adjunct senior lecturer, 2002—. Harvard University, visiting lecturer and research associate in women's studies in religion, 1996-97; University of London, honorary research fellow of University College, 2002—. Palestine Exploration Fund, member of executive committee.

MEMBER: Royal Asiatic Society (fellow).

AWARDS, HONORS: Irene Levi-Sala Award, 1995, for *Christians and the Holy Places: The Myth of Jewish-Christian Origins.*

WRITINGS:

Christians and the Holy Places: The Myth of Jewish-Christian Origins, Clarendon Press (Oxford, England), 1993.
(With Shimon Gibson) *Beneath the Church of the Holy Sepulchre, Jerusalem,* Palestine Exploration Fund (London, England), 1994.

The Immerser: John the Baptist within Second Temple Judaism, Eerdmans (Grand Rapids, MI), 1997, published as *John the Baptist within Second Temple Judaism: A Historical Study,* Society for the Promotion of Christian Knowledge (London, England), 1997.
Jewish Women Philosophers of First-Century Alexandria: The "Therapeutae" Reconsidered, Clarendon Press (Oxford, England), 2003.
Palestine in the Fourth Century A.D.: The "Onomasticon" of Eusebius of Caesarea, Carta (Jerusalem, Israel), 2003.

WORK IN PROGRESS: The Englishman and the Moor.

BIOGRAPHICAL AND CRITICAL SOURCES:

PERIODICALS

Journal of Religion, April, 2000, Brenda J. Shaver, review of *The Immerser: John the Baptist within Second Temple Judaism,* p. 306.

* * *

THOM, James Alexander 1933-

PERSONAL: Born May 28, 1933, in Gosport, IN; son of Jay Webb (a physician) and Julia (a physician; maiden name, Swain) Thom; married Cody Sweet (an international platform lecturer), May 16, 1975; married second wife, Mari Silveus (a writer), May 28, 1984. *Education:* Butler University, B.A., 1960. *Hobbies and other interests:* Sculpture, outdoor activities.

ADDRESSES: Office—10061 West Stogsdill Rd., Bloomington, IN 47401. *E-mail*—phd@intelos.net.

CAREER: Indianapolis Star, Indianapolis, IN, business editor, 1961-67; *Saturday Evening Post,* Indianapolis, senior editor, 1967-94; communications director for state trade association, 1971-73; freelance writer, 1973—. Lecturer at Indiana University, 1977-81. *Military service:* U.S. Marine Corps, 1953-56; served in Korea; became sergeant.

AWARDS, HONORS: Golden Spur Award, Western Writers of America, 1989.

WRITINGS:

Let the Sun Shine In (inspirational essays), C. R. Gibson (Norwalk, CT), 1976.
Spectator Sport, Avon (New York, NY), 1978.
Long Knife, Avon (New York, NY), 1979.
Follow the River, Ballantine (New York, NY), 1981.
From Sea to Shining Sea, Ballantine (New York, NY), 1984.
Panther in the Sky, Ballantine (New York, NY), 1989.
The Children of First Man, Ballantine (New York, NY), 1994.
The Spirit of the Place: Indiana Hill Country, photographs by Darryl L. Jones, Indiana University Press (Bloomington, IN), 1995.
Indiana II, Graphic Arts Center (Portland, OR), 1996.
The Red Heart, Ballantine (New York, NY), 1997.
Sign-Talker: The Adventure of George Drouillard on the Lewis and Clark Expedition, Ballantine (New York, NY), 2001.

Contributor to periodicals, including *Reader's Digest, National Geographic,* and *Country Gentleman.* Editor and contributing writer, *Nuggets* magazine, 1967—.

SIDELIGHTS: James Alexander Thom has published a number of novels set in the early days of American history. Among his most popular books are *The Children of First Man, The Red Heart,* and *Sign-Talker: The Adventure of George Drouillard on the Lewis and Clark Expedition.*

In *The Children of First Man,* Thom spins a story based on an old Welsh legend of Madoc, a twelfth-century king who sailed to the west with a band of followers and never returned. In Thom's version, the Welsh adventurers land in America and intermarry with Indians, creating the Mandan tribe, who survived until the arrival of European colonists centuries later. The Mandans were said to possess such European characteristics as blonde hair. Joe Collins of *Booklist* thought that "Thom's use of the language is masterful" and concluded that *The Children of First Man* was "a terrifically entertaining novel."

In *The Red Heart* Thom draws on historical fact for his story. In 1778, five-year-old Frances Slocum was kidnapped from her Pennsylvania Quaker family by Delaware Indians. The girl was raised among Indians, who named her Maconakwa, Little Bear Woman. She eventually became a mother and raised a family of her own. In Thom's story, when Maconakwa's tribe is ordered to move west after losing a battle with the Americans, she must make a choice as to which people she will join. A critic for *Publishers Weekly* called *The Red Heart* "an ambitious, epic novel" and concluded that "the scope of [Thom's] tale will draw in readers undaunted by his natural expansiveness."

Thom chronicles the famous voyage of Lewis and Clark across the unexplored West in his novel *Sign-Talker.* George Drouillard, hired as translator by the exploration party, is the narrator of the story. Through his comments on the internal frictions between party members, the attempts to make friends with the Indian tribes encountered, and their efforts to overcome rough weather and harsh terrain, Drouillard "emerges as genuine and credible," as a critic for *Publishers Weekly* noted. In addition, the critic believed that "Thom's research, mechanics and execution are impeccable in almost every regard."

Thom once told *CA:* "No book or article is begun until some concept has asserted itself *irresistibly* in my mind. The idea is always the primary motivation, but the idea must be conveyed by clear imagery and strong narrative. I learned early that the reading public wants storytelling, not philosophizing. As my historical novels are about heroes and heroines who really lived, I slave over my research. *From Sea to Shining Sea,* for example, required research and field trips in forty states, and I've become proficient in the use of many eighteenth-century tools and weapons."

BIOGRAPHICAL AND CRITICAL SOURCES:

PERIODICALS

Booklist, April 15, 1994, Joe Collins, review of *The Children of First Man,* p. 1485; July, 2000, Margaret Flanagan, review of *Sign-Talker: The Adventure of George Drouillard on the Lewis and Clark Expedition,* p. 2010.
Chicago Tribune, July 4, 1979.
Library Journal, March 1, 1989, Andrea Lee Shuey, review of *Panther in the Sky,* p. 90; June 1, 1994, Scott H. Silverman, review of *The Children of First Man,* p. 164; July, 2000, review of *Sign-Talker,* p. 143.

New York Times Book Review, October 7, 1984, D. G. Myers, review of *From Sea to Shining Sea,* p. 22.

Publishers Weekly, June 26, 1981, Sally A. Lodge, review of *Follow the River,* p. 58; November 4, 1983, Michael Barson, "The Frontiers of Western Fiction: Territory Still to Be Won," p. 43; February 10, 1989, Sybil Steinberg, review of *Panther in the Sky,* p. 53; September 8, 1997, review of *The Red Heart,* p. 60; June 5, 2000, review of *Sign-Talker,* p. 74.

Writer's Digest, March, 1998, Sherita Campbell, "The Research Time Machine," p. 29.*

* * *

TOPLIN, Robert Brent 1940-

PERSONAL: Born September 26, 1940, in Philadelphia, PA; son of Maurice C. (a businessman) and Janet (a commodities manager) Toplin; married Aida Zukowski (a college instructor in Spanish), September 3, 1962; children: Cassandra, Jennifer. *Education:* Pennsylvania State University, B.S., 1962; Rutgers University, M.A., 1965, Ph.D., 1968.

ADDRESSES: Home—6324 Marywood Dr., Wilmington, NC 28403. *Office*—Department of History, University of North Carolina at Wilmington, Morton 224, 601 South College Rd., Wilmington, NC 28403-3297. *Agent*—Scott Meredith Literary Agency, 845 Third Ave., New York, NY 10022. *E-mail*—toplinrb@uncwil.edu.

CAREER: Denison University, Granville, OH, assistant professor of history, 1968-74; University of Houston, Clear Lake City, TX, associate professor of history, 1974-75; Denison University, associate professor of history, 1976-78; University of North Carolina at Wilmington, professor of history, 1978—. Project director for several Public Broadcasting system dramatic films, 1982-85. Organization of American Historians Lecturer in Japan, 1999.

MEMBER: American Historical Association, Organization of American Historians, Southern Historical Association, Conference on Latin American Historians.

AWARDS, HONORS: Ford Foundation fellow, 1967, 1971; Organization of American States fellow, 1967, 1970; National Endowment for the Humanities younger humanist fellow, 1970, production grant, 1991; American Philosophical Society fellow, 1970; American Council of Learned Societies fellow, 1970, 1991; Denison University Research Foundation fellow, 1972; Mellon Foundation Award for teaching merit, Denison University, 1972; grants from National Endowment for the Humanities, 1977, 1978, 1979-80, 1982-83, American Philosophical Society, 1981, and Annenberg Foundation and Corporation for Public Broadcasting, 1983-84; Virginia Center for the Humanities fellow, 1994; University of North Carolina-Wilmington summer research initiative, 1996.

WRITINGS:

The Abolition of Slavery in Brazil, Atheneum (New York, NY), 1972.

(Editor) *Slavery and Race Relations in Latin America,* Greenwood Press (Westport, CT), 1974.

Unchallenged Violence: An American Ordeal, Greenwood Press (Westport, CT), 1975.

Freedom and Prejudice: The Legacy of Slavery in the United States and Brazil, Greenwood Press (Westport, CT), 1982.

(Editor) *American History through Film* (articles previously published in *OAH Newsletter*), Organization of American Historians, 1983.

(Editor) *Hollywood As Mirror: Changing Views of "Outsiders" and "Enemies" in American Movies,* Greenwood Press (Westport, CT), 1993.

(Editor) *Ken Burns's "The Civil War": Historians Respond,* Oxford University Press (New York, NY), 1996.

History by Hollywood: The Use and Abuse of the American Past, University of Illinois Press (Urbana, IL), 1996.

(Editor) *Oliver Stone's USA: Film, History, and Controversy,* University Press of Kansas (Lawrence, KS), 2000.

Reel History: In Defense of Hollywood, University Press of Kansas (Lawrence, KS), 2002.

Contributor of articles and book reviews to history and Latin American studies journals, including *American Historical Review, New York Times, Chronicle of Higher Education, Journal of Southern History, Journal of Black Studies, Hispanic American Historical Review, Civil War History*, and *Societas.* Film review editor, *Journal of American History;* former film and media editor, *Perspectives.*

SIDELIGHTS: Robert Brent Toplin has written several books examining how history is presented in film: *History by Hollywood: The Use and Abuse of the American Past, Oliver Stone's USA: Film, History, and Controversy,* and *Reel History: In Defense of Hollywood.*

In *History by Hollywood* Toplin looks at how Hollywood filmmakers have presented stories about real historical events, asking particularly if they strayed too far from the truth in order to create an entertaining work of art. Although a filmmaker must be concerned with the artistic side of his craft, Toplin argues that "artistic interpretation is not synonymous with fabrication—that the film artist can use the devices at his or her disposal to penetrate below the surfaces of history, thereby bringing history to life," according to Peter C. Rollins in the *Historical Journal of Film, Radio and Television.* Thomas Winter in the *Historian* found that "Toplin's book challenges historians to see their field and the profession in new and potentially exciting ways."

In *Oliver Stone's USA* Toplin gathers essays written by a number of historians and other interested parties about controversial film director Oliver Stone. Stone himself is among the contributors, as are former Democrat Party presidential candidate George McGovern and esteemed historian Stephen Ambrose. As Peter Augustine Lawler noted in *American Enterprise,* "Stone's films are full of obvious and overwhelming errors of fact and interpretation." Toplin's book, Lawler continued, "presents a showdown between Stone and some leading historians. They evaluate his films, and he responds."

Toplin calls for restraint when criticizing Hollywood's portrayal of historical events in his 2002 book *Reel History: In Defense of Hollywood.* While acknowledging the distortions of historical personalities, timelines, and events which are often found in films, Toplin argues that such changes are inevitable in filmmaking and that Hollywood nonetheless creates dramas which accurately give the feel of a period. Andrea Slonosky, reviewing the book for *Library Journal,* found that "Toplin makes his point eloquently, if somewhat repetitively, and builds a strong case for Hollywood's overall success in bringing certain aspects of history to life."

Toplin once told *CA:* "In recent years I have been exploring ways to communicate ideas about American history through the media of film and television. My work led to the creation of a docu-drama series about slavery in America called 'A House Divided' and a documentary series entitled 'USA,' which covers American history from 1865 to the present. Both of these series were designed for broadcast nationally on the PBS television network."

BIOGRAPHICAL AND CRITICAL SOURCES:

PERIODICALS

American Enterprise, January, 2001, Peter Augustine Lawler, review of *Oliver Stone's USA: Film, History, and Controversy,* p. 56.

American Quarterly, March, 1998, J. David Slocum, review of *History by Hollywood: The Use and Abuse of the American Past,* p. 175.

American Studies International, October, 2001, James Deutsch, review of *Oliver Stone's USA,* p. 98.

Choice, December, 2000, R. C. Cottrell, review of *Oliver Stone's USA,* p. 766.

Chronicle of Higher Education, October 4, 2002, Nina C. Ayoub, review of *Reel History: In Defense of Hollywood,* p. A22.

Film Quarterly, winter, 1997, Richard Maltby, review of *History by Hollywood,* p. 60.

Historian, summer, 1998, Thomas Winter, review of *History by Hollywood,* p. 879.

Historical Journal of Film, Radio and Television, March, 1998, Peter C. Rollins, review of *History by Hollywood,* p. 147.

Journalism History, autumn, 2000, Douglass K. Daniel, review of *Oliver Stone's USA,* p. 131.

Journal of American History, September, 1998, review of *History by Hollywood,* p. 765; September, 2001, Paul Ruhle, review of *Oliver Stone's USA,* p. 747.

Journal of Southern History, February, 1998, Daniel Blake Smith, review of *History by Hollywood,* p. 175.

Library Journal, October 1, 2002, Andrea Slonosky, review of *Reel History,* p. 99.

Literature-Film Quarterly, January, 2001, Don Kunz, review of *Oliver Stone's USA,* p. 71.

New Republic, July 24, 2000, Stanley Kauffmann, "On Films—Telling One's Truth," p. 28.

Publishers Weekly, May 8, 2000, review of *Oliver Stone's USA,* p. 214.

Reviews in American History, September, 2002, John Bodnar, review of *Reel History,* p. 492.

Southern Communication Journal, summer, 1999, Rise Jane Samra, review of *History by Hollywood,* p. 357.

Teaching History: A Journal of Methods, spring, 2001, Tom Pynn, review of *Oliver Stone's USA,* p. 45.

Variety, July 17, 2000, Dade Hayes, review of *Oliver Stone's USA,* p. 34.

ONLINE

Robert Brent Toplin's Home Page, http://www.uncwil. edu/hst/homepage/faculty/Toplin.htm/ (December 11, 2002).*

*　　*　　*

TRIPP, Valerie 1951-

PERSONAL: Born September 12, 1951, in Mount Kisco, NY; daughter of Granger (an advertising executive) and Kathleen (a teacher; maiden name, Martin) Tripp; married Michael Petty (a teacher), June 25, 1983; children: Katherine. *Education:* Yale University, B.A. (with honors), 1973; Harvard University, M.Ed., 1981. *Hobbies and other interests:* Reading, hiking, conversation.

ADDRESSES: Home—1007 McCeney Ave., Silver Spring, MD 20901.

CAREER: Little, Brown, Boston, MA, staff member, 1973; Addison-Wesley, Menlo Park, CA, writer in language arts program, 1974-80; freelance writer, 1981—.

AWARDS, HONORS: Children's Choice Award, International Reading Association, 1987, for *Meet Molly: An American Girl.*

WRITINGS:

"AMERICAN GIRLS COLLECTION" SERIES

Meet Molly: An American Girl, illustrated by C. F. Payne, vignettes by Keith Skeen and Renee Graef, Pleasant Co. (Middleton, WI), 1986.

Molly Learns a Lesson: A School Story, illustrated by C. F. Payne, vignettes by Keith Skeen and Renee Graef, Pleasant Co. (Middleton, WI), 1986.

Molly's Surprise: A Christmas Story, illustrated by C. F. Payne, vignettes by Keith Skeen, Pleasant Co. (Middleton, WI), 1986.

Happy Birthday, Molly!: A Springtime Story, illustrated by Nick Backes, vignettes by Keith Skeen, Pleasant Co. (Middleton, WI), 1987.

Happy Birthday, Samantha!: A Springtime Story, illustrated by Robert Grace and Nancy Niles, vignettes by Jana Fothergill, Pleasant Co. (Middleton, WI), 1987.

Changes for Samantha: A Winter Story, illustrated by Luann Roberts, Pleasant Co. (Middleton, WI), 1988.

Changes for Molly: A Winter Story, illustrated by Nick Backes, vignettes by Keith Skeen, Pleasant Co. (Middleton, WI), 1988.

Molly Saves the Day: A Summer Story, illustrated by Nick Backes, vignettes by Keith Skeen, Pleasant Co. (Middleton, WI), 1988.

Samantha Saves the Day: A Summer Story, illustrated by Robert Grace and Niles, vignettes by Luann Roberts, Pleasant Co. (Middleton, WI), 1988.

Felicity's Surprise: A Christmas Story, illustrated by Dan Andreasen, vignettes by Luann Roberts and Keith Skeen, Pleasant Co. (Middleton, WI), 1991.

Felicity Learns a Lesson: A School Story, illustrated by Dan Andreasen, vignettes by Luann Roberts and Keith Skeen, Pleasant Co. (Middleton, WI), 1991.

Meet Felicity: An American Girl, illustrated by Dan Andreasen, vignettes by Luann Roberts and Keith Skeen, Pleasant Co. (Middleton, WI), 1991.

Changes for Felicity: A Winter Story, illustrated by Dan Andreasen, vignettes by Luann Roberts and Keith Skeen, Pleasant Co. (Middleton, WI), 1992.

Felicity Saves the Day: A Summer Story, illustrations by Dan Andreasen, vignettes by Luann Roberts and Keith Skeen, Pleasant Co. (Middleton, WI), 1992.

Happy Birthday, Felicity!: A Springtime Story, illustrated by Dan Andreasen, vignettes by Luann Roberts and Keith Skeen, Pleasant Co. (Middleton, WI), 1992.

War on the Home Front: A Play about Molly, Pleasant Co. (Middleton, WI), 1994.

Addy's Theater Kit: A Play about Addy for You and Your Friends, Pleasant Co. (Middleton, WI), 1994.

Kirsten's Theater Kit: A Play about Kirsten for You and Your Friends, Pleasant Co. (Middleton, WI), 1994.

Molly's Theater Kit: A Play about Molly for You and Your Friends, Pleasant Co. (Middleton, WI), 1994.

Felicity's Theater Kit: A Play about Felicity for You and Your Friends, Pleasant Co. (Middleton, WI), 1994.

Samantha's Theater Kit: A Play about Samantha for You and Your Friends, Pleasant Co. (Middleton, WI), 1994.

Actions Speak Louder Than Words: A Play about Samantha, Pleasant Co. (Middleton, WI), 1994.

Five Plays for Girls and Boys to Perform: Teacher's Guide and Scripts, Pleasant Co. (Middleton, WI), 1995.

Josefina Learns a Lesson: A School Story, Pleasant Co. (Middleton, WI), 1997.

Meet Josefina, An American Girl, Pleasant Co. (Middleton, WI), 1997.

Josefina's Surprise: A Christmas Story, Pleasant Co. (Middleton, WI), 1997.

Josefina's Theater Kit: A Play about Josefina for You and Your Friends, Pleasant Co. (Middleton, WI), 1998.

Josefina Saves the Day: A Summer Story, Pleasant Co. (Middleton, WI), 1998.

Happy Birthday, Josefina! A Springtime Story, Pleasant Co. (Middleton, WI), 1998.

Changes for Josefina: A Winter Story, Pleasant Co. (Middleton, WI), 1998.

Changes for Samantha: A Winter Story, Pleasant Co. (Middleton, WI), 1998.

Six Plays for Girls and Boys to Perform: Teacher's Guide and Scripts, Pleasant Co. (Middleton, WI), 1998.

Felicity's New Sister, Pleasant Co. (Middleton, WI), 1999.

Molly Takes Flight, Pleasant Co. (Middleton, WI), 1999.

A Reward for Josefina, Pleasant Co. (Middleton, WI), 1999.

Samantha's Winter Party, Pleasant Co. (Middleton, WI), 1999.

Kit's Surprise: A Christmas Story, Pleasant Co. (Middleton, WI), 2000.

Kit Learns a Lesson: A School Story, Pleasant Co. (Middleton, WI), 2000.

Again, Josefina! Pleasant Co. (Middleton, WI), 2000.

Felicity's Dancing Shoes, Pleasant Co. (Middleton, WI), 2000.

Meet Kit, An American Girl, Pleasant Co. (Middleton, WI), 2000.

Molly and the Movie Star, Pleasant Co. (Middleton, WI), 2000.

Samantha Saves the Wedding, Pleasant Co. (Middleton, WI), 2000.

Molly Marches On, Pleasant Co. (Middleton, WI), 2001.

Felicity Takes a Dare, Pleasant Co. (Middleton, WI), 2001.

Happy Birthday, Kit! A Springtime Story, 1934, Pleasant Co. (Middleton, WI), 2001.

Josefina's Song, Pleasant Co. (Middleton, WI), 2001.

Samantha and the Missing Pearls, Pleasant Co. (Middleton, WI), 2001.

(With Susan S. Adler and MaxineRose Schur) *Samantha's Story Collection,* Pleasant Co. (Middleton, WI), 2001.

Felicity's Story Collection, Pleasant Co. (Middleton, WI), 2001.

Kit's Story Collection, Pleasant Co. (Middleton, WI), 2001.

Molly's Story Collection, Pleasant Co. (Middleton, WI), 2001.

Changes for Kit!: A Winter Story, 1934, Pleasant Co. (Middleton, WI), 2001.

Felicity Discovers a Secret, Pleasant Co. (Middleton, WI), 2002.

Just Josefina, Pleasant Co. (Middleton, WI), 2002.

Kit's Home Run, Pleasant Co. (Middleton, WI), 2002.

Molly's A+ Partner, Pleasant Co. (Middleton, WI), 2002.

Samantha's Blue Bicycle, Pleasant Co. (Middleton, WI), 2002.

Kit's Tree House, Pleasant Co. (Middleton, WI), 2003.

Molly's Puppy Tale, Pleasant Co. (Middleton, WI), 2003.

Thanks to Josefina, Pleasant Co. (Middleton, WI), 2003.

Bright, Shiny Skylar, illustrated by Joy Allen, Pleasant Co. (Middleton, WI), 2003.

Hallie's Horrible Handwriting, illustrated by Joy Allen, Pleasant Co. (Middleton, WI), 2003.

Thank You Again, Logan, illustrated by Joy Allen, Pleasant Co. (Middleton, WI), 2003.

"JUST ONE MORE STORIES" SERIES

The Singing Dog, illustrated by Sandra Kalthoff Martin, Children's Press (New York, NY), 1986.

Baby Koala Finds a Home, illustrated by Sandra Kalthoff Martin, Children's Press (New York, NY), 1987.

The Penguins Paint, illustrated by Sandra Kalthoff Martin, Children's Press (New York, NY), 1987.

Squirrel's Thanksgiving Surprise, illustrated by Sandra Kalthoff Martin, Children's Press (New York, NY), 1988.

Sillyhen's Big Surprise, illustrated by Sandra Kalthoff Martin, Children's Press (New York, NY), 1989.

Happy, Happy Mother's Day!, illustrated by Sandra Kalthoff Martin, Children's Press (New York, NY), 1989.

OTHER

An Introduction to Williamsburg (nonfiction), Pleasant Co. (Middleton, WI), 1985.

Home Is Where the Heart Is (play), Pleasant Co. (Middleton, WI), 1990.

Actions Speak Louder Than Words (play), Pleasant Co. (Middleton, WI), 1990.

War on the Homefront (play), Pleasant Co. (Middleton, WI), 1990.

Baby Koala Finds a Home has been translated into Spanish.

SIDELIGHTS: Valerie Tripp has written a number of books in the popular "American Girls Collection," published by the Pleasant Company. These books feature girls living in different periods of American history and realistically depict the day-to-day activities, problems, and pastimes of the era. Each book also includes a section of factual information about the time period of the story.

Tripp grew up in a large family, sandwiched between two older sisters and one younger sister and brother. The Tripp children were a close-knit group, spending their free time playing games, riding bikes, and, when winter came, sledding and ice skating. "We were a noisy, rambunctious, rag-taggle bunch," she explained in a publicity brochure issued by one of her publishers, the Pleasant Company. But their favorite activity was reading. Tripp learned to read while playing school with her older sisters, and she, in turn, taught her younger siblings. Tripp's parents encouraged the family's love of books.

Tripp has vivid and mostly fond memories of school: "I liked school, especially reading. I was like [my character] Molly in that I loved the teachers and al-

ways wanted to be the star of the school play. . . . Also, unfortunately, just like Molly, I was terrible at multiplication."

Tripp was one of the first women to be admitted to Yale University; she graduated with honors in 1973. After college, she worked in publishing, first at Little, Brown, and Co., and later at Addison-Wesley, where she wrote educational materials, such as songs, stories, and skills exercises for the language arts division.

In 1981, she received her Masters of Education degree from Harvard University. Since then, she has developed educational programs for such companies as Houghton Mifflin, Macmillan, and Harcourt. While working on the editorial staff of the Addison-Wesley publishing company, Tripp befriended Pleasant Rowland. The two women shared a belief that young girls were rushed out of childhood. Just when they reach the age when they can read independently, and can fantasize themselves acting in a variety of situations and settings, girls are too often discouraged from reading. Tripp and Rowland wanted to create a series of books for girls set in historical settings of the American past. Darci Glass-Royal, in an article for the *Washington Parent Magazine* Web site, explained that "Pleasant Company was created to portray history from the perspective of a young heroine the same age as their readers."

Pleasant Company's "American Girls" books focus on young women growing up during different periods in American History. Carolyn Phelan in *Booklist* noted that the series books are "short, fast-moving, and involving stories." Among the girls Tripp has written about are Molly, a nine-year-old whose father serves in England during World War II; Samantha, an orphan who lives with her aunt and uncle in turn-of-the-century New York City; Felicity, who lives in Williamsburg, Virginia, during colonial times, and whose life changes drastically during the outbreak of the American Revolution; and Kit, who lives in Cincinnati during the Great Depression of the 1930s.

Tripp draws on events from her own childhood experiences when writing. Samantha's adventures in New York City are based on Tripp's own visits to the city. "Sometimes my whole family would go into the city to see a Broadway show, or go to a museum or a concert or the ballet," she remarked. "When I was writing

Happy Birthday, Samantha!, I remembered the feeling of exhilaration of being in the busy, fast-moving, enormous city. I knew just how Samantha felt."

Felicity's adventures reflect Tripp's fascination with colonial history. When the author was ten, she visited Williamsburg with her family. She uses her experience of attending a concert at the Governor's Palace as the basis for Felicity's night of dance at the same facility. For both writer and character, their respective evenings are among their most memorable ones.

Speaking in an interview posted at the *Children's Literature* Web site, Tripp discussed her books concerning Depression-era Kit: "Kit's story is about one family, a family that used its energy, creativity, ingenuity, resilience, and love for one another to not only survive the Depression but to learn and grow. During the course of her story, because of the Depression, Kit's circle of concern widens from herself, to her family, to her friends, to her community, to the world at large. I'd like young readers to widen their circles of concern, too, and realize that they are part of a world community and that they have a responsibility beyond their own happiness and comfort."

"Asked to choose a favorite among her characters," Glass-Royal recounted, "[Tripp] responded diplomatically. 'I am like a mother with many daughters,' she replied. 'They are all different and, at times, difficult, but I love them all.'" Tripp, according to Glass-Royal, "maintains a low public profile. She prefers to be known through her books and through the correspondence she maintains with the hundreds of girls who write to her every year and whose letters never go unanswered."

BIOGRAPHICAL AND CRITICAL SOURCES:

PERIODICALS

Booklist, November 1, 1991, p. 523; April 15, 1992, Candace Smith, "Meet Valerie Tripp: An American Girls Author," p. 1544; May 1, 1992, Carolyn Phelan, reviews of *Changes for Felicity: A Winter Story, Felicity Saves the Day: A Summer Story,* and *Happy Birthday, Felicity! A Springtime Story,* p. 1603; October 1, 1997, Carolyn Phelan, reviews of *Meet Josefina: An American Girl* and *Josefina Learns a Lesson,* p. 333; August, 1998, Carolyn Phelan, reviews of *Happy Birthday, Josefina! A Springtime Story* and *Josefina Saves the Day: A Summer Story,* p. 2009; September 1, 2000, Carolyn Phelan, reviews of *Meet Kit: An American Girl* and *Kit Learns a Lesson: A School Story,* p. 119; August, 2001, Carolyn Phelan, review of *Kit Saves the Day,* p. 2122; December 1, 2001, Carolyn Phelan, review of *Changes for Kit: A Winter Story,* p. 644; July, 2003, Hazel Rochman, review of *Thank You Again, Logan* and *Hallie's Horrible Handwriting,* p. 1903.

Bulletin of the Center for Children's Books, October, 1991, p. 51.

Publishers Weekly, February 14, 2000, "More Pleasant Than Ever," p. 203; October 13, 2003, review of *Bright, Shiny Skylar,* p. 80.

School Library Journal, January, 1992, p. 116; February, 1992, p. 90; December, 1997, Ann Welton, reviews of *Meet Josefina: An American Girl* and *Josefina Learns a Lesson,* p. 102; December, 2000, Debbie Feulner, reviews of *Meet Kit: An American Girl* and *Kit Learns a Lesson: A School Story,* p. 126.

ONLINE

Children's Literature Web site, http://www.childrenslit.com/home.htm/ (December 11, 2002).

Washington Parent Magazine Web site, http://www.washingtonparent.com/ (November, 1997), Darci Glass-Royal, "Meet Valerie Tripp."*

W-Y

WALCOTT, Derek (Alton) 1930-

PERSONAL: Born January 23, 1930, in Castries, St. Lucia, West Indies; son of Warwick (a civil servant, poet, and visual artist) and Alix (a teacher) Walcott; married Fay Moston, 1954 (divorced, 1959); married Margaret Ruth Maillard, 1962 (divorced); married Norline Metivier (an actress and dancer), 1982 (divorced); children: (first marriage) Peter, (second marriage) two daughters. *Education:* Attended St. Mary's College (St. Lucia); University of the West Indies (Kingston, Jamaica), B.A. 1953.

ADDRESSES: Home—(summer) 165 Duke of Edinburgh Ave., Diego Martin, Trinidad and Tobago; (winter) 71 St. Mary's, Boston, MA 02215. *Office*—Creative Writing Department, Boston University, 236 Bay State Rd., Boston, MA 02215. *Agent*—Bridget Aschenberg, International Famous Agency, 1301 Avenue of the Americas, New York, NY 10019.

CAREER: Poet and playwright. Teacher at St. Mary's College, Castries, St. Lucia, West Indies, 1947-50 and 1954, Grenada Boys' Secondary School, St. George's, Grenada, West Indies, 1953-54, and at Jamaica College, Kingston, 1955. Feature writer, 1960-62, and drama critic, 1963-68, for *Trinidad Guardian* (Port-of-Spain, Trinidad); feature writer for *Public Opinion* (Kingston), 1956-57. Cofounder of St. Lucia Arts Guild, 1950, and Basement Theatre, Port-of-Spain, Trinidad; founding director of Little Carib Theatre Workshop (later Trinidad Theatre Workshop), 1959-76; Boston University, assistant professor of creative writing, 1981, visiting professor, 1985, currently pro-

Derek Walcott

fessor of English. Visiting professor at Columbia University, 1981, and Harvard University, 1982 and 1987. Also lecturer at Rutgers University and Yale University.

AWARDS, HONORS: Rockefeller grant, 1957, 1966, and fellowship, 1958; Jamaica Drama Festival prize, 1958, for *Drums and Colours: An Epic Drama;* Arts

Advisory Council of Jamaica prize, 1960; Guinness Award, 1961, for "A Sea-Chantey"; Borestone Mountain poetry awards, 1964, for "Tarpon," and 1977, for "Midsummer, England"; Ingram Merrill Foundation grant, 1962; named fellow of the Royal Society of Literature, 1966; Heinemann Award, Royal Society of Literature, 1966, for *The Castaway,* and 1983, for *The Fortunate Traveller;* Cholmondeley Award, 1969, for *The Gulf;* Eugene O'Neill Foundation-Wesleyan University fellowship, 1969; Gold Hummingbird Medal, Order of the Hummingbird, Trinidad and Tobago, 1969 (one source says 1979); Obie Award, 1971, for *Dream on Monkey Mountain;* honorary doctorate of letters, University of the West Indies, Mona, Jamaica, 1972; O.B.E. (Officer, Order of British Empire), 1972; Jock Campbell/*New Statesman* Prize, 1974, for *Another Life;* Guggenheim fellowship, 1977; named honorary member of the American Academy and Institute of Arts and Letters, 1979; *American Poetry Review* Award, 1979; International Writer's Prize, Welsh Arts Council, 1980; John D. and Catherine T. MacArthur Foundation grant, 1981; Los Angeles *Times* Prize in poetry, 1986, for *Collected Poems, 1948-1984;* Queen Elizabeth II Gold Medal for Poetry, 1988; Nobel Prize for literature, 1992; St. Lucia Cross, 1993.

WRITINGS:

POETRY

25 Poems, Guardian Commercial Printery (Port-of-Spain, Trinidad), 1948.

Epitaph for the Young: XII Cantos, Barbados Advocate (Bridgetown, Barbados), 1949.

Poems, Kingston City Printery (Kingston, Jamaica), 1953.

In a Green Night: Poems, J. Cape (London, England), 1962, published as *In a Green Night: Poems, 1948-1960,* J. Cape (London, England), 1969.

Selected Poems, Farrar, Straus (New York, NY), 1964.

The Castaway, J. Cape (London, England), 1965.

The Gulf and Other Poems, J. Cape (London, England), 1969, published with selections from *The Castaway* as *The Gulf: Poems,* Farrar, Straus (New York, NY), 1970.

Another Life (long poem), Farrar, Straus (New York, NY), 1973, 2nd edition published with introduction, chronology and selected bibliography by Robert D. Hammer, Three Continents Press (Washington, DC), 1982.

Sea Grapes, Farrar, Straus (New York, NY), 1976.

Selected Verse, Heinemann (London, England), 1976.

The Star-Apple Kingdom, Farrar, Straus (New York, NY), 1979.

The Fortunate Traveller, Farrar, Straus (New York, NY), 1981.

Selected Poetry, selected, annotated, and introduced by Wayne Brown, Heinemann (London, England), 1981, revised edition, 1993.

The Caribbean Poetry of Derek Walcott and the Art of Romare Beardon, Limited Editions Club (New York, NY), 1983.

Midsummer, Farrar, Straus (New York, NY), 1984.

Collected Poems, 1948-1984, Farrar, Straus (New York, NY), 1986.

The Arkansas Testament, Farrar, Straus (New York, NY), 1987.

Omeros, Farrar, Straus (New York, NY), 1990.

Collected Poems, Faber (London, England), 1990.

Poems, 1965-1980, J. Cape (London, England), 1992.

Derek Walcott: Selected Poems, Longman (London, England), 1993.

The Bounty, Farrar, Straus (New York, NY), 1997.

Tiepolo's Hound, Farrar, Straus (New York, NY), 2000.

Contributor of poems to numerous periodicals, including *New Statesman, London Magazine, Encounter, Evergreen Review, Caribbean Quarterly, Tamarack Review,* and *Bim.*

PLAYS

Cry for a Leader, produced in St. Lucia, 1950.

Senza Alcum Sospetto (radio play), broadcast 1950, produced as *Paolo and Francesca,* in St. Lucia, 1951.

(And director) *Henri Christophe: A Chronicle in Seven Scenes* (first produced in Castries, West Indies, 1950; produced in London, England, 1952), Barbados Advocate (Bridgetown, Barbados), 1950.

Robin and Andrea, published in *Bim* (Christ Church, Barados), 1950.

Three Assassins, produced in St. Lucia, West Indies, 1951.

The Price of Mercy, produced in St. Lucia, West Indies, 1951.

(And director) *Harry Dernier: A Play for Radio Production* (produced in Mona, Jamaica, 1952; radio play broadcast as *Dernier,* 1952), Barbados Advocate (Bridgetown, Barbados), 1952.

(And director) *The Wine of the Country* (produced in Mona, Jamaica, 1956), University College of the West Indies (Mona, Jamaica), 1953.

The Sea at Dauphin: A Play in One Act (first produced in Mona, Jamaica, 1953; produced in Trinidad, 1954, London, England, 1960, New York, NY, 1978), Extra-Mural Department, University College of the West Indies (Mona, Jamaica), 1954, also included in *Dream on Monkey Mountain and Other Plays* (also see below).

Crossroads, produced in Jamaica, 1954.

(And director) *The Charlatan,* Walcott directed first production in Mona, Jamaica, 1954; revised version with music by Fred Hope and Rupert Dennison produced in Port-of-Spain, Trinidad, 1973; revised version with music by Galt MacDermot produced in Los Angeles, 1974; revised version produced in Port-of-Spain, Trinidad, 1977.

Ione: A Play with Music (first produced in Kingston, 1957), Extra-Mural Department, University College of the West Indies (Mona, Jamaica), 1957.

Drums and Colours: An Epic Drama (first produced in Port-of-Spain, Trinidad, 1958), published in *Caribbean Quarterly,* March-June, 1961.

(And director) *Ti-Jean and His Brothers* (first produced in Castries, St. Lucia, 1957; Walcott directed a revised version produced in Port-of-Spain, Trinidad, 1958; produced in Hanover, NH, 1971; Walcott directed a production Off-Broadway at Delacorte Theatre, 1972; produced in London, 1986), included in *Dream on Monkey Mountain and Other Plays* (also see below).

Malcauchon; or, The Six in the Rain (sometimes "Malcauchon" transliterated as "Malcochon"; one-act; first produced as *Malcauchon* in Castries, St. Lucia, 1959; produced as *Six in the Rain,* in London, England, 1960; produced Off-Broadway at St. Mark's Playhouse, 1969), Extra-Mural Department, University of West Indies (Port-of-Spain, Trinidad), 1966, also included in *Dream on Monkey Mountain and Other Plays* (also see below).

Journard; or, A Comedy till the Last Minute, first produced in St. Lucia, 1959; produced in New York, NY, 1962.

(And director) *Batai* (carnival show), produced in Port-of-Spain, Trinidad, 1965.

(And director) *Dream on Monkey Mountain* (first produced in Toronto, Ontario, Canada, 1967; produced in Waterford, CT, 1969; and Off-Broadway at St. Mark's Playhouse, 1970), included in *Dream on Monkey Mountain and Other Plays* (also see below).

(And director) *Franklin: A Tale of the Islands,* first produced in Georgetown, Guyana, 1969; Walcott directed a revised version produced in Port-of-Spain, Trinidad, 1973.

Dream on Monkey Mountain and Other Plays (contains *Dream on Monkey Mountain, The Sea at Dauphin, Malcauchon; or, The Six in the Rain, Ti-Jean and His Brothers,* and the essay "What the Twilight Says: An Overture"), Farrar, Straus (New York, NY), 1970.

(And director) *In a Fine Castle,* (Walcott directed first production in Mona, Jamaica, 1970; produced in Los Angeles, CA, 1972), excerpt as *Conscience of a Revolution* published in *Express* (Port-of-Spain, Trinidad), October 24, 1971.

The Joker of Seville (musical; music by Galt MacDermot; adaptation of the play by Tirso de Molina; first produced in Port-of-Spain, Trinidad, 1974), included in *The Joker of Seville and O Babylon!: Two Plays* (also see below).

(And director) *O Babylon!* (music by Galt MacDermot; Walcott directed first production in Port-of-Spain, Trinidad, 1976; produced in London, England, 1988), included in *The Joker of Seville and O Babylon!: Two Plays* (also see below).

(And director) *Remembrance* (three-act; Walcott directed first production in St. Croix, Virgin Islands, December, 1977; produced Off-Broadway at The Other Stage, 1979; and London, England, 1980), included in *Remembrance & Pantomime: Two Plays* (also see below).

The Snow Queen (television play), excerpt published in *People* (Port-of-Spain, Trinidad), April, 1977.

Pantomime (first produced in Port-of-Spain, Trinidad, 1978; produced London, England, 1979, Washington, DC, 1981, and Off-Broadway at the Hudson Guild Theater, 1986), included in *Remembrance & Pantomime: Two Plays* (also see below).

The Joker of Seville and O Babylon!: Two Plays, Farrar, Straus (New York, NY), 1978.

(And director) *Marie Laveau* (music by Galt MacDermot; first produced in St. Thomas, U.S. Virgin Islands, 1979), excerpts published in *Trinidad and Tobago Review* (Tunapuna), 1979.

Remembrance & Pantomime: Two Plays, Farrar, Straus (New York, NY), 1980.

Beef, No Chicken (Walcott directed first production in New Haven, CT, 1982; produced in London, England, 1989), included in *Three Plays* (also see below).

The Isle Is Full of Noises, first produced at the John W. Huntington Theater, Hartford, CT, 1982.

Three Plays (contains *The Last Carnival, Beef, No Chicken,* and *A Branch of the Blue Nile*), Farrar, Straus (New York, NY), 1986.

Steel, first produced at the American Repertory Theatre, Cambridge, MA, 1991.

The Odyssey: A Stage Version, Farrar, Straus (New York, NY), 1993.

(With Paul Simon) *The Capeman: A Musical* (produced on Broadway at the Marquis Theater, December, 1997), Farrar, Straus (New York, NY), 1998.

The Haitian Trilogy, Farrar, Straus and Giroux (New York, NY), 2002.

Also author of the play *To Die for Grenada.*

OTHER

Henri Christophe: A Chronicle in Seven Scenes, Barbados Advocate (Bridgetown, Barbados), 1950.

Another Life: Fully Annotated, Lynne Rienner Publishers (Boulder, CO), reprinted with a critical essay and comprehensive notes by Edward Baugh and Colbert Nepaulsingh, 2004.

The Poet in the Theatre, Poetry Book Society (London, England), 1990.

The Antilles: Fragments of Epic Memory: The Nobel Lecture, Farrar, Straus (New York, NY), 1993.

Conversations with Derek Walcott, edited by William Baer, University of Mississippi (Jackson, MS), 1996.

(With Joseph Brodsky and Seamus Heaney) *Homage to Robert Frost,* Farrar, Straus (New York, NY), 1996.

What the Twilight Says (essays), Farrar, Straus (New York, NY), 1998.

Tiepolo's Hound, Farrar, Strauss (New York, NY), 2000.

Walker and Ghost Dance, Farrar, Straus (New York, NY), 2002.

CONTRIBUTOR

John Figueroa, editor, *Caribbean Voices,* Evans (London, England), 1966.

Barbara Howes, editor, *From the Green Antilles,* Macmillan (New York, NY), 1966.

Howard Sergeant, editor, *Commonwealth Poems of Today,* Murray (London, England), 1967.

O. R. Dathorne, editor, *Caribbean Verse,* Heinemann (London, England), 1968.

Anne Walmsley, compiler, *The Sun's Eye: West Indian Writing for Young Readers,* Longmans, Green (London, England) 1968.

Orde Coombs, editor, *Is Massa Day Dead?,* Doubleday (New York, NY), 1974.

D. J. Enright, editor, *Oxford Book of Contemporary Verse, 1945-1980,* Oxford University Press (New York, NY), 1980.

Errol Hill, editor, *Plays for Today,* Longman (London, England), 1985.

(Author of introduction) George Plimpton, editor, *Latin American Writers at Work,* Modern Library (New York, NY), 2003.

Also contributor to *Caribbean Literature,* edited by George Robert Coulthard; *New Voices of the Commonwealth,* edited by Howard Sergeant; and *Young Commonwealth Poetry,* edited by Peter Ludwig Brent.

Some of Walcott's personal papers are housed at the University of the West Indies in Saint Augustine, Trinidad.

SIDELIGHTS: Upon awarding Derek Walcott the Nobel Prize for Literature in 1992, the Swedish Academy, as quoted in the *Detroit Free Press,* wrote: "In him, West Indian culture has found its great poet." Walcott was the first native Caribbean writer to win the prize. Although born of mixed racial and ethnic heritage on St. Lucia, a West Indian island where a French/English patois is spoken, poet and playwright Derek Walcott was educated as a British subject. Taught to speak English as a second language, he grew skilled in his adopted tongue. His use of the language drew praise from critics, including British poet and novelist Robert Graves who, according to *Times Literary Supplement* contributor Vicki Feaver, "has gone as far to state that [Walcott] handles English with a closer understanding of its inner magic than most (if not all) of his English-born contemporaries." "Walcott has had to contend with the charge that he is so deeply influenced by Western tradition that he has yet to achieve his own voice. Yet this scion of African and European heritage embodies the cultural matrix of the New World. Thus, inevitable questions of origins, identity, and the creation of meaningful order in a chaotic world lead Walcott to themes that transcend race, place, and time," remarked Robert D. Hamner in the *Dictionary of Liter-*

ary Biography. "In his literary works," noted the Swedish Academy in its citation, "Walcott has laid a course for his own cultural environment, but through them he speaks to each and every one of us." Among Walcott's "central concerns," delineated Bruce King in *Contemporary Poets,* "are the existence of evil, especially in the form of political tyranny and racial hatred . . . his relationship to time, death, and God. . . . and his [feelings of] estrangement."

The major theme of Walcott's writing is the dichotomy between black and white, subject and ruler, and the elements of both Caribbean and Western civilization present in his culture and ancestry. In "What the Twilight Says," the introduction to *Dream on Monkey Mountain and Other Plays,* Walcott refers to his "schizophrenic boyhood," in which he led "two lives: the interior life of poetry [and] the outward life of action and dialect." In his study *Derek Walcott,* Robert D. Hamner noted that this "schizophrenia" is common among West Indians and comments further that "since [Walcott] is descended from a white grandfather and a black grandmother on both paternal and maternal sides, he is living example of the divided loyalties and hatreds that keep his society suspended between two worlds."

"As a West Indian . . . writing in English, with Africa and England in his blood," Alan Shapiro wrote in the *Chicago Tribune Book World,* "Walcott is inescapably the victim and beneficiary of the colonial society in which he was reared. He is a kind of Caribbean Orestes . . . unable to satisfy his allegiance to one side of his nature without at the same time betraying the other." Caryl Phillips described Walcott's work in much the same way in a *Los Angeles Times Book Review* essay. The critic noted that Walcott's poetry was "steeped in an ambivalence toward the outside world and its relationship to his own native land of St. Lucia."

One often-quoted poem, "A Far Cry from Africa," from *In a Green Night: Poems, 1948-1960,* deals directly with Walcott's sense of cultural confusion. "Where shall I turn, divided to the vein? / I who have cursed / The drunken officer of British rule, how choose / Between this Africa and the English tongue I love? / Betray them both, or give back what they give?" In another poem, "The Schooner Flight," from his collection *The Star-Apple Kingdom,* the poet used a Trinidadian sailor named Shabine to appraise his own place as a person of mixed blood in a world divided into whites and blacks. According to the mariner: "The first chain my hands and apologize, *History* the next said I wasn't black enough for their pride." Not white enough for whites, not black enough for blacks, Shabine sums up the complexity of his situation near the beginning of the poem, saying: "I had a sound colonial education, / I have Dutch, nigger and English in me,! / and either I'm nobody or I'm a nation."

It was Walcott, of course, who spoke, and *New York Review of Books* contributor Thomas R. Edwards noted how the poet suffered the same fate as his poetic alter-ego, Shabine. Edwards wrote, "Walcott is a cultivated cosmopolitan poet who is black, and as such he risks irrelevant praise as well as blame, whites finding it clever of him to be able to sound so much like other sophisticated poets, blacks feeling that he's sold his soul by practicing white arts."

Although pained by the contrasts in his background, Walcott chose to embrace both his island and his colonial heritage. His love of both sides of his psyche was apparent in his work. As Hamner noted in his study *Derek Walcott:* "Nurtured on oral tales of gods, devils, and cunning tricksters passed down by generations of slaves, Walcott should retell folk stories; and he does. On the other hand, since he has an affinity for and is educated in Western classics, he should retell the traditional themes of European experience; and he does. As inheritor of two vitally rich cultures, he utilizes one, then the other, and finally creates out of the two his own personalized style."

"Many of [Walcott's] early poems attempt to see both sides of his racial heritage," noted King, informing: "Walcott's volumes after *The Castaway* note his increasing alienation from the actual society of Saint Lucia while presenting him as part of Caribbean history, whether representative of a group of artists, a generation discovering West Indianness, or the alienated, nonconforming 'red' (colored) among blacks and whites. He often later returns to the same story, adding disillusionments, divorces, exile, nostalgia, and a larger body of acquaintances and places, commenting on the continuing injustices of a world in which the powerful enslave and suppress the weak; he is aware too that he is aging and threatened by the approach of death."

Walcott seems closest to his island roots in his plays. For the most part, he reserves his native language—patois or creole—to them. They also feature Caribbean settings and themes. According to *Literary Review* contributor David Mason, through his plays Walcott hopes to create a "catalytic theater responsible for social change or at least social identity."

Although a volume of poems was his first published work, Walcott originally concentrated his efforts on the theater. In 1950, two years after Walcott used two-hundred borrowed dollars to print and self-distribute (via street corners) his poetry debut, *25 Poems,* he and his twin brother founded St. Lucia Arts Guild. The importance of this, according to Hamner in *the Dictionary of Literary Biography,* was that it was "the first time Derek could cast, direct, and produce plays as he wrote them." Hamner explained, "The event is fortuitous because Walcott's creativity is evolutionary. His normal practice is to improvise and revise material even while it is in the middle of a production run."

During the fifties, Walcott wrote a series of plays in verse, including *Henri Christophe: A Chronicle in Seven Scenes, The Sea at Dauphin: A Play in One Act,* and *Ione: A Play with Music.* The first play deals with an episode in Caribbean history: ex-slave Henri Christophe's rise to kingship of Haiti in the early 1800s. The second marks Walcott's first use of the mixed French/English language of his native island in a play. Dennis Jones noted in the *Dictionary of Literary Biography Yearbook: 1981* that while Walcott uses the folk idiom of the islands in the play, the speech of the characters is not strictly imitative. It is instead "made eloquent, as the common folk represented in the work are made noble, by the magic of the artist."

In "What the Twilight Says" Walcott describes his use of language in his plays. In particular, he expresses a desire to mold "a language that went beyond mimicry, . . . one which finally settled on its own mode of inflection, and which begins to create an oral culture, of chants, jokes, folk-songs, and fables." The presence of "chants, jokes, and fables" in Walcott's plays caused critics such as Jones and the *Los Angeles Times* critic Juana Duty Kennedy to use the term "folk dramas" to describe the playwright's best pieces for theater. In *Books and Bookmen* Romilly Cavan observed the numerous folk elements in Walcott's plays: "The laments of superstitious fishermen, charcoal-burners and prisoners are quickly counter-pointed by talking crickets, frogs, and birds. Demons are raised, dreams take actual shape, [and] supernatural voices mingle with the natural lilting elliptical speech rhythms of downtrodden

natives." Animals who speak and a folk-representation of the devil, for example, were characters in the play *Ti-Jean and His Brothers.*

Walcott's most highly praised play, *Dream on Monkey Mountain,* is also a folk drama. It was awarded a 1971 Obie Award and called "a poem in dramatic form" by Edith Oliver in the *New Yorker.* The play's title is itself enough to immediately transport the viewer into the superstitious, legend-filled world of the Caribbean back country. In the play, Walcott draws a parallel between the hallucinations of an old charcoal vendor and the colonial reality of the Caribbean. Islanders subjected to the imposition of a colonial culture on their own eventually question the validity of both cultures. Ultimately, they may determine that their island culture—because it has no official status other than as an enticement for tourists—is nothing but a sterile hallucination. Conversely, as Jones noted, they may reach the conclusion at which Walcott wished his audience to reach: the charcoal vendor's "dreams connect to the past, and that it is in that past kept alive in the dreams of the folk that an element of freedom is maintained in the colonized world."

Reviews by some American critics have reflected their apparent unfamiliarity with the Caribbean reality which Walcott described in his plays. For example, while Walter Goodman wrote in the *New York Times* that Walcott's *Pantomime* "stays with you as a fresh and funny work filled with thoughtful insights and illuminated by bright performances," Frank Rich's comments on the play in the same newspaper were not as favorable. "Walcott's best writing has always been as a poet . . . ," Rich observed, "and that judgment remains unaltered by *Pantomime.* For some reason, [Walcott] refuses to bring the same esthetic rigor to his playwriting that he does to his powerfully dense verse."

In James Atlas's *New York Times Magazine* essay on Walcott, the critic confronted Rich's remarks head on, and explained that the poet would respond to Rich by commenting "that he doesn't conceive of his plays as finished works but as provisional effects to address his own people. 'The great challenge to me,' he says, 'was to write as powerfully as I could without writing down to the audience, so that the large emotions could be taken in by a fisherman or a guy on the street, even if he didn't understand every line.'"

If Walcott's plays reveal what is most Caribbean about him, his poetry reveals what is most English. If he hoped to reach the common person in his plays, the same cannot be said of his poetry. His poems are based on the traditional forms of English poetry, filled with classical allusions, elaborate metaphors, complex rhyme schemes, and other sophisticated poetic devices. In the *New York Times Book Review,* Selden Rodman called Walcott's poems "almost Elizabethan in their richness." The *New York Times* writer Michiko Kakutani also recognized British influences in Walcott's poetry, noting that "from England, [Walcott] appropriated an old-fashioned love of eloquence, an Elizabethan richness of words and a penchant for complicated, formal rhymes. In fact, in a day when more and more poets have adopted a grudging, minimalist style, [his] verse remains dense and elaborate, filled with dazzling complexities of style."

Some critics objected that Walcott's attention to style sometimes detracted from his poetry, either by being unsuitable for his Caribbean themes or by becoming more important than the poems' content. Denis Donoghue, for example, remarked in the *New York Times Book Review,* "It is my impression that his standard English style [is] dangerously high for nearly every purpose except that of Jacobean tragedy." In Steve Ratiner's *Christian Science Monitor* review of *Midsummer,* the critic observed that "after a time, we are so awash in sparkling language and intricate metaphor, the subject of the poem is all but obscured." *New York Review of Books* contributor Helen Vendleroks found an "unhappy disjunction between [Walcott's] explosive subject . . . and his harmonious pentameters, his lyrical allusions, his stately rhymes, [and] his Yeatsian meditations."

More criticism has come from those who thought that the influence of other poets on Walcott's work has drowned out his authentic voice. While Vendler, for instance, described Walcott as a "man of great sensibility and talent," she dismissed much of his poetry as "ventriloquism" and wrote that in Walcott's collection *The Fortunate Traveller* he seemed "at the mercy of influence, this time the influence of Robert Lowell." Poet J. D. McClatchy also noticed Lowell's influence in *The Fortunate Traveller* as well as two other Walcott poetry collections: *The Star-Apple Kingdom* and *Midsummer.* In his *New Republic* review, McClatchy not only found similarities in the two men's styles but also a similar pattern of development in their poetry. "Like Lowell," the critic noted, "Walcott's mode has . . . shifted from the mythological to the histori-

cal, from fictions to facts, and his voice has gotten more clipped and severe. There are times when the influence is almost too direct, as in 'Old New England,' [a poem from *The Fortunate Traveller*] where he paces off Lowell's own territory."

Both major criticisms of Walcott's poetry were answered in Sven Birkerts's *New Republic* essay. Birkerts observed: "Walcott writes a strongly accented, densely packed line that seldom slackens and yet never loses conversational intimacy. He works in form, but he is not formal. His agitated phonetic surfaces can at times recall Lowell's, but the two are quite different. In Lowell, one feels the torque of mind; in Walcott, the senses predominate. And Walcott's lines ring with a spontaneity that Lowell's often lack."

Other critics defended the integrity of Walcott's poems. Poet James Dickey noted in the *New York Times Book Review,* "Fortunately, for him and for us . . . Walcott has the energy and the exuberant strength to break through his literary influences into a highly colored, pulsating realm of his own." In his *Poetry* review of *Midsummer,* Paul Breslin wrote: "For the most part, . . . Walcott's voice remains as distinctive as ever, and the occasional echoes of Lowell register as homage rather than unwitting imitation."

Hamner wrote that when dealing with Walcott's poetry, the term *assimilation* rather than *imitation* should be used. The critic observed, "Walcott passed through his youthful apprenticeship phase wherein he consciously traced the models of established masters. He was humble enough to learn from example and honest enough to disclose his intention to appropriate whatever stores he found useful in the canon of world literature. . . . But Walcott does not stop with imitation. Assimilation means to ingest into the mind and thoroughly comprehend; it also means to merge into or become one with a cultural tradition."

In *Omeros,* whose title is the contemporary Greek word for Homer, Walcott paid homage to the ancient poet in an epic poem that replaced the Homeric Cyclades with the Antilles. Two of the main characters, the West Indian fishermen Achille and Philocte, set out on a journey to the land of their ancestors on the West African coast. The characters are concerned not with the events of the Trojan War, but rather with the array of civilization, from African antiquity to frontier

America and present-day Boston and London. Halfway through the book, the poet himself enters the narrative. *Los Angeles Times Book Review* critic Nick Owchar noted that "the message of *Omeros* grows with the poet's entrance." He wrote, "Walcott's philosophical intentions never come closer to being realized than when he turns . . . criticism on himself. Divestiture, as an artist, is Walcott's forte. He considers his own dangerous use of metaphors: 'When would I not hear the Trojan War / in two fishermen cursing?' he asked near the end. The poet's danger, like every person's, is to distance himself from human suffering by reinterpreting it."

Washington Post Book World reviewer Michael Heyward observed, "*Omeros* is not a translation or even a recreation of either of Homer's great epics. . . . The ancient work it resembles most . . . is Ovid's *Metamorphoses,* with its panoply of characters, its seamless episodic structure, and its panoramic treatment of a mythic world both actual and legendary." He concluded, "We are used to encountering the dynamic exploration of politics and history and folk legend in the contemporary novel, the domain—thanks to Rushdie, Marquez, Gaddis, and others—of modern epic. . . . *Omeros* is not a novel and it does not approximate the form of a novel, but it does rival the novel's mastery of a mythic, multidimensional narrative. Strenuous and thrilling, it swims against the tide."

The uniqueness of Walcott's work stems from his ability to interweave British and island influences, to express what McClatchy called "his mixed state" and do so "without indulging in either ethnic chic or imperial drag." His plays offer pictures of the common Caribbean folk and comment on the ills bred by colonialism. His poetry combines native patois and English rhetorical devices in a constant struggle to force an allegiance between the two halves of his split heritage. According to *Los Angeles Times Book Review* contributor Arthur Vogelsang, "These continuing polarities shoot an electricity to each other which is questioning and beautiful and which helps form a vision all together Caribbean and international, personal (him to you, you to him), independent, and essential for readers of contemporary literature on all the continents."

"Only a few poets at any given time are capable of distinctive style, much less a distinctive mature style; and Walcott's mature style, as evolved in *Midsummer*

and further perfected [in *The Bounty*], is his best," wrote Adam Kirch in a *New Republic* review of *The Bounty,* a collection of poems which, once again, showed that Walcott "is urgently concerned with the past and his place in it." Kirch thought that "the subject of History never comes up in Walcott's poetry without a strong note of ambivalence and longing." "Walcott," explained Kirch, "has never tried to escape the fact that the islands are, in the most neutral sense of the term, lacking in History with a glamorous (and ominous) capital 'H'; they lie outside the grand progression of classical and renaissance Europe, their culture and language imported, not to say imposed. What has troubled him, for most of his career, is whether this deprivation is to be mourned or celebrated. For many years he seemed committed to celebration; but he was always too honest to conceal his desire to mourn."

Some of Walcott's perspectives and thoughts are compiled in *What the Twilight Says,* "an insightful book for those with serious poetic interests," wrote *Library Journal* reviewer Scott Hightower. A range of writers, "almost exclusively male and lofty" were addressed in the 1998 collection of essays that Walcott first published between the years of 1970 and 1997. This "first prose collection" was praised by a *Publishers Weekly* critic who commented: "[What the Twilight Says] engages with literature, politics and their intersection. . . . [with writing] so intense that it threatens to disintegrate into lyric." A critic for *Publishers Weekly* praised "the beaut[iful] . . . sound" of Walcott's writing. "Reading Derek Walcott can be like listening to some grand cathedral music that's all tangled up in its own echoes: it's lovely, most definitely, but," stated Christian Wiman in a *Poetry* review of *The Bounty,* "it can sometimes be tough to tell one note from the next."

Music is not a foreign element to Walcott. Even though the playwright claimed in a 1997 interview with *Interview* contributor Brendan Lemon that he "hardly listen[s] to [and] . . . never play[s] music," he interwove his dramatic writing with music in a number of theatrical productions. For example, in his musical, *The Capeman,* Walcott collaborated with Paul Simon. *The Capeman,* described Lemon, was "a musical about 1950s Puerto Rican-gang member Salvador Agron." According to Margaret Spillane in *Progressive,* both creators "wanted *Capeman* to do what no other Broadway show had done before: consider the fears and terrors and raptures of New York's urban poor at a human scale—not some giant icon of the downtrodden in the manner of *Les Miz,* and not the outsized exotics of *West Side Story.* They insisted that their depiction of New York Puerto Rican life would be recognizable to people who actually inhabit New York Puerto Rican lives."

Reviews of the eleven million dollar *Capeman,* "the most expensive Broadway musical of all times," reported Spillane, were harsh and the show closed quickly. "The criticisms went beyond murmurs about unorthodox rehearsal expenditures," stated Spillane. In Celia Wren's *Commonweal* review the production was said to contain a "tide of blunders" and its "[musical] score seem[ed] to have been written first, and the drama patched in afterwards [which resulted in calamity]." When summarizing other criticisms, Spillane mentioned "the show didn't offer any monumental characters" and noted that some groups feared that the story "would glorify crime." "Journalists stiffened at the prospect of reckoning with the difficult material of the story," thought Spillane, believing the criticisms to be unfounded and adamantly defending *Capeman.* Spillane felt that political-like motives were at work when "the New York show biz press corps crushed *The Capeman.*" "I saw *The Capeman* twice," wrote Spillane, "and both times I kept swiveling my head in search of what journalists had reported: fidgeting, dissatisfied audience members. . . . But all I could see was people riveted or rocking, sometimes weeping, usually transfixed. At the curtain calls, people yelled and whooped and stomped out their pleasure."

In *Tiepolo's Hound* Walcott focuses on the painter Camille Pissarro. Pissarro experienced cultural confusion, similiar to Walcott's, in that Pissarro was a French Sephardic Jew living in the West Indies. Pissarro eventually left the West Indies for Europe to search for himself. It was while abroad that he established himself as one of the fathers of French Impressionism. When Walcott was a young man he learned to paint from "an old master," but he left his painting in order to focus his energies on poetry. Walcott's poem was a "spiritual journey" for him too, according a *Yomiuri Shimbun* reviewer, who noted Walcott's description of "his constant amazement at the potential and realization of art in poetry, music, and painting. His poem is . . . a tribute to Pissarro." Walcott combined his love for the islands, poetry, and painting to create the work, and yet his "catalyst" for the entire work was Pissarro and Walcott's interest in French Impressionism. *World Literature Today* writer Jim Hannan praised Walcott for reaching "most deeply into his and the reader's heart when he reflects on the calm and devastating clarity on his residual doubts, failures, and longings for an art greater than poetry."

The Haitian Trilogy was an ambitious three-part play that Walcott wrote early in his career, and was published in 2002 long after he established himself as a great poet. *Library Journal* contributor Thomas E. Luddy commented that it came from "a powerful imagination" and that it was "stuffed with historical characters." The plays begin with Columbus's third voyage to the New World and ends in the nineteenth century. *Booklist* critic Jack Helbig noted that Walcott's "Haitian Earth is more Brechtian in scope" and praised Walcott for his use and understanding of dialect as "remarkable."

BIOGRAPHICAL AND CRITICAL SOURCES:

BOOKS

Baugh, Edward, *Derek Walcott: Memory As Vision: Another Life,* Longman (London, England), 1978.

Bloom, Harold, *Derek Walcott,* Chelsea House (New York, NY), 1988.

Brown, Stewart, editor, *The Art of Derek Walcott,* Dufour (Chester Springs, PA), 1991.

Contemporary Literary Criticism, Gale (Detroit, MI), Volume 2, 1974, Volume 4, 1975, Volume 9, 1978, Volume 14, 1980, Volume 25, 1983, Volume 42, 1987, Volume 67, 1992, Volume 76, 1993.

Contemporary Poets, 6th edition, St. James Press (Detroit, MI), 1996.

Dictionary of Literary Biography, Volume 117: *Twentieth-Century Caribbean and Black African Writers,* Gale (Detroit, MI), 1992.

Dictionary of Literary Biography Yearbook, Gale (Detroit, MI), *1981,* 1982, and *1992,* 1993.

Dictionary of Twentieth-Century Culture, Volume 5: *African-American Culture,* Gale (Detroit, MI), 1996.

Goldstraw, Irma, *Derek Walcott: An Annotated Bibliography of His Works,* Garland Publishing (New York, NY), 1984.

Hamner, Robert D., compiler and editor, *Critical Perspectives on Derek Walcott,* Three Continents Press (Washington, DC), 1993.

Hamner, Robert D., *Derek Walcott*, Twayne (Boston, MA), 1981.

Hamner, Robert D., *Epic of the Dispossessed: Derek Walcott's "Omeros,"* University of Missouri Press (Columbia, MO), 1997.

Harper, Michael S., and Robert B. Stepto, editors, *Chant of Saints*, University of Illinois Press (Urbana, IL), 1979.

Herdeck, Donald E., editor, *Three Dynamite Authors: Derek Walcott (Nobel 1992), Naguib Mahfouz (Nobel 1988), Wole Soyinka (Nobel 1986): Ten Biocritical Essays from Their Works As Published by Three Continents Press*, Three Continents Press (Colorado Springs, CO), 1995.

King, Bruce Alvin, *Derek Walcott and West Indian Drama: Not Only a Playwright but a Company, the Trinidad Theatre Workshop, 1959-1993*, Oxford University (New York, NY), 1995.

Olaniyan, Tejumola, *Scars of Conquest/Masks of Resistance: The Invention of Cultural Identities in African, African-American, and Caribbean Drama*, Oxford University Press (New York, NY), 1995.

Parker, Michael, and Roger Starkey, editors, *Postcolonial Literatures: Achebe, Ngugi, Desai, Walcott*, St. Martin's Press (New York, NY), 1995.

Rodman, Selden, *Tongues of Fallen Angels*, New Directions (New York, NY), 1974.

Schomburg Center Guide to Black Literature, Gale (Detroit, MI), 1996.

Terada, Rei, *Derek Walcott's Poetry: American Mimicry*, Northeastern University Press (Boston, MA), 1992.

Thomas, Ned, *Derek Walcott, Poet of the Islands*, Welsh Arts Council (Cardiff, Wales), 1980.

Walcott, Derek, *In a Green Night: Poems, 1948-1960*, J. Cape (London, England), 1962.

Walcott, Derek, *Dream on Monkey Mountain and Other Plays*, Farrar, Straus (New York, NY), 1970.

Walcott, Derek, *The Star-Apple Kingdom*, Farrar, Straus (New York, NY), 1979.

Walcott, Derek, *Collected Poems, 1948-1984*, Farrar, Straus (New York, NY), 1986.

Wheatcroft, John, editor, *Our Other Voices: Nine Poets Speaking*, Bucknell University Press (Lewisberg, VA), 1991.

Wieland, James, *The Ensphering Mind: History, Myth, and Fictions in the Poetry of Allen Curnow, Nissim Ezekiel, A. D. Hope, A. M. Klein, Christopher Okigbo, and Derek Walcott*, Three Continents Press (Washington, DC), 1988.

PERIODICALS

African American Review, winter, 1999, "Conversations with Derek Walcott," p. 708.

American Poetry Review, May-June, 1978.

American Theatre, May-June, 1993, Patti Hartigan, "The Passions of Derek Walcott," p. 14.

Architectural Digest, January, 1997.

Art Journal, spring, 2001, review of *Tiepolo's Hound*, p. 107.

Atlanta Journal and Constitution, April 23, 1995.

Black Issues Book Review, May, 2001, Gregory A. Pardlo, review of *Tiepolo's Hound*, p. 34.

Booklist, April 15, 1997; December 1, 2001, Jack Helbig, review of *The Haitian Trilogy*, p. 625; August, 2002, Jack Helbig, review of *Walker and Ghost Dance*, p. 1912.

Books and Bookmen, April, 1972.

Book World, December 13, 1970; January 3, 1999, review of *What the Twilight Says*, p. 13.

Boston Globe, January 20, 1996; October 16, 1996; October 12, 1997; November 16, 1997.

Callaloo, spring, 1999, review of *Omeros*, p. 509; winter, 2001, review of *Omeros*, p. 276.

Caribbean Writer, Volume 13, 1999, review of *What the Twilight Says*, p. 234.

Chicago Tribune Book World, May 2, 1982; September 9, 1984; March 9, 1986.

Choice, March, 1995.

Christian Science Monitor, March 19, 1982; April 6, 1984.

Chronicle of Higher Education, April 19, 1996, p. A23.

Classical World, September, 1999, reviews of *Omeros*, p. 7, and *The Odyssey: A Stage Version*, p. 71.

Commonweal, April 10, 1998, review of *Capeman*.

Contemporary Literature, summer, 1979; winter, 1994, Graham Huggan, "A Tale of Two Parrots: Walcott, Rhys, and the Uses of Colonial Mimicry," p. 643.

Detroit Free Press, October 9, 1992.

Economist, September 6, 1997, review of *The Bounty*.

English Journal, March, 1994, p. 94.

Entertainment Weekly, February 13, 1998.

Georgia Review, summer, 1984.

Hudson Review, summer, 1984.

Interview, December, 1997, author interview.

Journal of Commonwealth Literature, December, 1976; August, 1981; August, 1986.

Library Journal, November 1, 1994, p. 127; June 1, 1996; April 15, 1997, review of *The Bounty*; October 15, 1998; May 15, 2000, Graham Christian, review of *Tiepolo's Hound*, p. 98; November 1,

2001, review of *The Haitian Trilogy*, p. 117; January, 2002, Thomas E. Luddy, review of *The Haitian Trilogy*, p. 105; July, 2002, Thomas E. Luddy, review of *Walker and the Ghost Dance*, p. 81.

Literary Review, spring, 1986.

London Magazine, December, 1973-January, 1974; February-March, 1977.

Los Angeles Times, November 12, 1986.

Los Angeles Times Book Review, April 4, 1982; May 21, 1985; April 6, 1986; October 26, 1986; September 6, 1987; January 20, 1991; October 20, 1996.

Nation, February 12, 1977; May 19, 1979; February 27, 1982.

National Review, November 3, 1970; June 20, 1986, James W. Tuttleton, review of *Collected Poems: 1948-1984,* p. 51.

New Criterion, March, 1998, Mark Steyn, review of *Capeman,* p. 38.

New Leader, March 11, 1991, Phoebde Pettingell, review of *Omeros,* p. 15; January 13, 1997, review of *Homage to Robert Frost;* September 8, 1997, review of *The Bounty.*

New Republic, November 20, 1976; March 17, 1982; January 23, 1984; March 24, 1986, J. D. McClatchy, review of *Collected Poems,* p. 36; October 29, 1990, Christopher Benfey, review of *Omeros,* p. 36; December 28, 1992; December 15, 1997, review of *The Bounty;* March 30, 1998, review of *Capeman.*

New Statesman, March 19, 1982; August 15, 1997, review of *The Bounty.*

New Statesman & Society, October, 16, 1992; July 21, 1995.

Newsweek, October 19, 1992.

New York, August 14, 1972; February 16, 1998.

New Yorker, March 27, 1971; June 26, 1971; December 12, 1992; February 9, 1998.

New York Review of Books, December 31, 1964; May 6, 1971; June 13, 1974; October 14, 1976; May 31, 1979; March 4, 1982; November 10, 1983; March 27, 1997.

New York Times, March 21, 1979; August 21, 1979; May 30, 1981; May 2, 1982; January 15, 1986; December 17, 1986; October 9, 1992; June 1, 1995; November 13, 1997.

New York Times Book Review, September 13, 1964; October 11, 1970; May 6, 1973; October 31, 1976; May 13, 1979; January 3, 1982; April 8, 1984; February 2, 1986; December 20, 1987; October 7, 1990; October 6, 1996; June 29, 1997.

New York Times Magazine, May 23, 1982; November 9, 1997.

Observer (London, England), October 11, 1992; February 14, 1999.

Paris Review, winter, 1986.

Poetry, February, 1972; December, 1973; July, 1977; December, 1984; June, 1986; August, 1998; August, 1999, review of *What the Twilight Says,* p. 286; April, 2001, Paul Breslin, review of *Tiepolo's Hound,* p. 38.

Progressive, June, 1998, review of *Capeman.*

Publishers Weekly, July 15, 1996, review of *Homage to Robert Frost;* May 26, 1997, review of *The Bounty;* August 31, 1998; February 7, 2000, review of *Tiepolo's Hound,* p. 69.

Research in African Literature, summer, 1994, Patrick Hogan, review of *Dream on Monkey Mountain,* p. 103; spring, 2003, Edward Baugh, "Derek Walcott and the Centering of the Caribbean Subject," p. 151.

Review, winter, 1974.

Sewanee Review, January, 1999, review of *What the Twilight Says,* p. R25.

South Carolina Review, fall, 1999, review of *Omeros,* p. 142.

Spectator (London, England), May 10, 1980.

Third World Quarterly, October, 1988.

Time, March 15, 1982; October 11, 1992; October 31, 1994, p. 78; July 14, 1997, Pico Iyer, review of *The Bounty,* p. 85; January 19, 1998; April 3, 2000, Paul Gray, "Islands in the Stream: Poet Derek Walcott Spins a Luminous Meditation on Visual Art," p. 81.

Times Literary Supplement, December 25, 1969; August 3, 1973; July 23, 1976; August 8, 1980; September 8, 1980; September 24, 1982; November 9, 1984; October 24, 1986; October 1, 1999, review of *What the Twilight Says,* p. 25.

Tribune Books (Chicago, IL), November 8, 1987.

TriQuarterly, winter, 1986.

Twentieth-Century Literature, summer, 2001, Charles W. Pollard, "Traveling with Joyce: Derek Walcott's Discrepant Cosmopolitan Modernism," p. 197; fall, 2001, Robert D. Hamner, review of *The Odyssey: A Stage Version,* p. 374.

Village Voice, April 11, 1974.

Virginia Quarterly Review, winter, 1974; summer, 1984; summer, 1999, review of *What the Twilight Says,* p. 84.

Vogue, January, 1998.

Wall Street Journal, October 9, 1992.

Washington Post Book World, February 21, 1982; April 13, 1986; November 11, 1990; April 26, 1995.

Western Humanities Review, spring, 1977.

World Literature Today, spring, 1977; summer, 1979; summer, 1981; winter, 1985; summer, 1986; winter, 1987; winter, 1989; winter, 1997; winter, 1998, review of *The Bounty,* p. 191; spring, 1999, review of *What the Twilight Says,* p. 339; autumn, 2000, Jim Hannan, review of *Tiepolo's Hound,* p. 797.

World Literature Written in English, April, 1973; April, 1977; November, 1977; spring, 1986; spring, 1987.

Yale Review, October, 1973.

Yomiuri Shimbun/Daily Yomiuri, August 22, 2000, "Walcott Turns an Artistic Eye to Colonialism in Epic Poem," p. YOSH12474972.

ONLINE

Academy of American Poets Web site, http://www.poets.org/ (June 3, 2003), author biography.

Boston University Web site, http://www.bu.edu/ (June 3, 2003), Derek Walcott faculty profile.

Nobel e-Museum Web site, http://www.nobel.se/ (June 3, 2003), author biographical material and interview.

Richmond Review Online, http://www.richmondreview.co.uk/ (June 3, 2003), Amanda Jeremin Harris, review of *Tiepolo's Hound.**

Ellen Stoll Walsh

*   *   *

WALSH, Ellen Stoll 1942-

PERSONAL: Born September 2, 1942, in Baltimore, MD; daughter of Joseph Adolphus (a businessman) and Nell (Orum) Stoll; married David Albert Walsh (a professor), August 25, 1964; children: Benjamin Martin. *Education:* Maryland Institute of Art, B.F.A., 1964; attended University of Minnesota, 1966-69.

ADDRESSES: Home—29 West St., Fairport, NY 14450.

CAREER: Writer and illustrator. Houghton Mifflin, Boston, MA, freelance illustrator, 1984—.

MEMBER: Authors Guild, Society of Children's Writers and Illustrators.

AWARDS, HONORS: Merit Award, Art Director's Club Fifty-ninth Annual Exhibition, and Award of Excellence, American Institute of Graphic Arts, both 1980, both for *Brunus and the New Bear;* Children's Choice selection, International Reading Association, 1982, for *Theodore All Grown Up;* Ezra Jack Keats Fellow at the Kerlan Collection, University of Minnesota, 1986; Reading Magic Award, *Parenting* magazine, 1989, for *Mouse Paint;* National Outdoor Children's Book Award for *Dot & Jabber and the Big Bug Mystery,* 2004.

WRITINGS:

SELF-ILLUSTRATED

Brunus and the New Bear, Doubleday (New York, NY), 1979.

Theodore All Grown Up, Doubleday (New York, NY), 1981.

Mouse Paint, Harcourt Brace (San Diego, CA), 1989.

Mouse Count, Harcourt Brace (San Diego, CA), 1991.

You Silly Goose, Harcourt Brace (San Diego, CA), 1992.

Hop Jump, Harcourt Brace (San Diego, CA), 1993.

Pip's Magic, Harcourt Brace (San Diego, CA), 1994.

Samantha, Harcourt Brace (San Diego, CA), 1996.

Jack's Tale, Harcourt Brace (San Diego, CA), 1997.

For Pete's Sake, Harcourt Brace (San Diego, CA), 1998.

Mouse Magic, Harcourt (San Diego, CA), 2000.

Dot & Jabber and the Great Acorn Mystery, Harcourt (San Diego, CA), 2001.

Dot & Jabber and the Mystery of the Missing Stream, Harcourt (San Diego, CA), 2002.

Dot & Jabber and the Big Bug Mystery, Harcourt (San Diego, CA), 2003.

ADAPTATIONS: Brunus and the New Bear was made into a filmstrip by Imperial Educational Resources, 1980; *Theodore All Grown Up* was made into a filmstrip by Spoken Arts, narrated by Frances Sternhagen, with music by Michael Barber, 1982.

WORK IN PROGRESS: Henry and Pell at the Beach.

SIDELIGHTS: Children's author and illustrator Ellen Stoll Walsh is the creator of over a dozen picture books focused on helping young readers learn important skills, such as counting, mixing colors, and overcoming fears. "I was born in Baltimore and grew up in the midst of a very large family," Walsh once told *CA.* "There were ten children in all, and those of us who were older shared the responsibility of looking after the younger ones. Life was often chaotic with so many people around, but there were many wonderful moments. We were all very close then, and though we are now scattered around the country, we feel closer than ever.

"As a child I loved to read and draw and was very fond of sports. I enjoyed being by myself and would spend hours alone in the woods, often practicing to be an Indian. One of my first great disappointments was learning that no matter how hard I practiced being an Indian, I could never grow up to be one. I loved summer camp, and when I was too old to be a camper, I worked as a counselor until I graduated from college.

"It never occurred to me to write children's books until my son, Ben, was three years old. Ben was curled up in my arms, and we were reading *Alexander and the Wind-Up Mouse* by Leo Leonni. And all of a sudden, I realized that I wanted to write and illustrate children's books more than anything else. I started immediately and from scratch. Since *Alexander* was a cut paper book, my first attempt was with cut paper. I experimented with a number of media and finally decided on colored inks. I was amazed to find out how difficult it is to write a good children's story. I quickly learned that no matter how nice the pictures are, if a story is not well thought out, an editor will not give it a second thought!"

Walsh's self-illustrated *Mouse Paint* and *Mouse Count,* published in 1989 and 1991 respectively, display the author's use of torn paper illustrations and her ability to write good children's stories. Both books provide creative ways to teach colors and counting to preschoolers. In *Mouse Paint,* three white mice camouflage themselves on a piece of white paper, remaining inconspicuous to a preying cat. When they decide to venture away from their safe haven, the mice stumble upon pots of red, blue, and yellow paint. Curiously, the mice dip their bodies into the paint, discovering that the original colors form new ones (green, orange, and purple) when blended. After bathing, the mice retreat to their white space to avoid contact with the cat. *School Library Journal* contributor Karen K. Radtke described *Mouse Paint* as a "real charmer that's great fun as well as informative." Isabel Schon, a reviewer for *Horn Book,* also noted that the book is "strikingly illustrated with torn paper collage in bright primary colors."

The mice reappear with seven new friends in *Mouse Count,* this time trying to escape a multicolored snake. The rodents find themselves trapped when the snake catches them during naptime and puts them in a jar, counting each mouse from one to ten. One of the mice deceives the snake by sending him away to find another mouse. While the snake is gone, the mice escape from the jar. Walsh's illustrations "display a naive charm and exuberance," wrote a *Publishers Weekly* reviewer. *Horn Book* reviewer Elizabeth Watson contended that the book provides "counting fun for two-year-olds."

"The first step in making a picture book is finding a good idea for a story," Walsh once explained to *CA.* "This is probably the most difficult time for me. During this 'waiting period,' I read a lot of other people's stories, talk and listen to children to find out what is important to them, and probe my childhood and my son's for interesting material. I always try out lots of ideas before settling down to one that I think is not only important to write about, but will be visually exciting as well.

"Once I have a good idea for a story, it grows so fast and in so many directions that I often have to remind myself to stop and remember what the original idea was all about. I find it almost impossible to confine myself to an outline, but write pages and pages trying to find the best way to tell my story."

Relaying a message of tolerance and diversity proves evident in Walsh's well-received children's book *Hop Jump.* Betsy's boredom with hopping and jumping like other frogs stimulates her need to experiment with different movements. The motion of leaves captivates Betsy, so she decides to pattern her own bodily rhythms after them. Betsy calls her new style "dance," but the other frogs proclaim that there is "no room for dancing." Betsy ignores them and continues to enjoy her newfound leaps and twirls. The frogs, however, gradually begin to join in on the fun. One frog still protests dancing and is quickly shunned by the converts who now oppose hopping. Betsy tries to unify the lone frog and the rest of the group by promoting dancing and hopping, thus eradicating the underlying discrimination. *School Library Journal* contributor Nancy Seiner praised *Hop Jump*'s "large, clearly seen figures and flowing language." Seiner continued by saying Walsh's book is "a popular and useful story time choice." According to a *Kirkus Reviews* contributor, *Hop Jump* is a "beautifully designed book that . . . yields new subtleties and visual delights with each reading."

Pip's Magic, published in 1994, touches on another subject that affects many children—the fear of the dark. Pip, an eager salamander, wants to combat his fear of darkness. A trio of frogs suggest he visit Old Abra, an omniscient wizard turtle, to help with his anxiety of the dark. Pip follows an obscure and lightless path to reach Old Abra, urged on by the frogs, a bird, a snake, and a mouse. Once the salamander reaches Old Abra, the turtle praises Pip and tells him that he has already conquered his fear by following the dark trail, in addition to gaining a little extra courage. Elated over his new sense of confidence, Pip retreats to a safe resting place. The book's "imaginative, boldly colored treatment of a common anxiety is

[Walsh's] best work yet," declared a contributor in *Kirkus Reviews.* Elizabeth Bush, writing in the *Bulletin of the Center for Children's Books,* praised Walsh's picture book, claiming the tale is "brief, simple, and direct, enlivened by neatly turned similes in Pip's soliloquies."

Walsh explores another common childhood occurrence in *Samantha,* published in 1996. Samantha, a young mouse, wishes her siblings would not play roughly with her. Samantha's thoughts are acknowledged when a fairy godmother appears and acts as her guardian. The fairy godmother takes her task very seriously and becomes overly protective of Samantha, thus eliminating the little one's fun. The unhappy mouse drives her protector away so that she can regain her normal lifestyle. Although Samantha begins to enjoy her siblings, she is once again susceptible to harm. The young mouse ends up falling in a snowdrift, but is rescued by her fairy godmother, who never ventured far away from her tiny friend. Samantha and her guardian reconcile their relationship by making a new rule: the fairy godmother promises to assist the mouse only in emergencies. Eunice Weech, a reviewer in *School Library Journal,* regarded *Samantha* as a "pleasing combination of a short, well-told story and simple but expressive illustrations." Deborah Stevenson asserted in the *Bulletin of the Center for Children's Books* that the story will make a "cozy but not suffocating readaloud."

In *For Pete's Sake,* Pete is an alligator who thinks he is a flamingo, whose green color just means that he is not "ripe" yet. When Pete meets two creatures who look like him, "Walsh reveals her originality by not settling for the easy resolution," wrote Nancy Vasilakis in *Horn Book.* Vasilakis concluded her review by calling the book "very cleverly done." Stephanie Zvirin of *Booklist* remarked that Walsh's illustrations "are pleasingly simple," while a *Kirkus Reviews* contributor found *For Pete's Sake* "a comforting, gladdening tale."

In 2001, Walsh began a series about a pair of detective mice, Dot and Jabber. In *Dot & Jabber and the Great Acorn Mystery,* the mice try to find why a tiny oak tree is growing so far away from a big oak tree on the other side of the meadow. They know that it was started by an acorn but wonder how the acorn ended up so far away from the tree. A *Publishers Weekly* reviewer noted that "these inquisitive mice [have] an appealing, comical quality." Other reviewers observed that *Dot & Jabber and the Great Acorn Mystery* gently introduces young readers to simple science concepts, with *Booklist* contributor Kathy Broderick remarking, Walsh's "graceful creatures transform the science lesson into something fun, thoughtful, and very special."

Water and insects are featured in two other "Dot & Jabber" books. In *Dot & Jabber and the Missing Stream,* the mice investigate the reasons a stream has suddenly dried up. They follow clues that include twigs and leaves that lead them to a dam. *School Library Journal* reviewer Be Astengo remarked favorably upon the collages in the book and commented that "Walsh successfully combines science and good storytelling" in the adventure. When all of the insects seem to disappear in *Dot & Jabber and the Big Bug Mystery,* the rodent sleuths attempt to find the creatures, finally discovering that the bugs never left but were just camouflaged from predators in the meadow's foliage.

"While I'm writing my stories," Walsh once remarked, "I begin to imagine what the characters who move through them look like, and I want to see them on paper. Drawing my characters helps establish their personalities and makes them and my stories come alive for me. It is unwise but often difficult to resist beginning to illustrate a story before it is finished, especially since the story is still undergoing change and a favorite illustration may no longer be appropriate when the story is finished. If you have ever tried to work around a well-turned sentence or paragraph in order to save it, even though it no longer fits in with what you are writing, then you can imagine how difficult it is to edit out a favorite illustration.

"It takes weeks of writing before a story will feel right to me, and after so much writing, the story is invariably too long. I must always keep in mind what the real point of my story is as I cut and chop my favorite paragraphs and sentences. After weeks of work, I hope to end up with a story that is no more than eight hundred words long and appears to have been written effortlessly.

"After my story is finished it will take me about nine months to complete the illustrations. I will often use black-and-white photographs to establish the way a person stands or sits in my illustrations. Once the basic proportions of a figure are set down, I put the photographs aside and work from nature and my imagination."

BIOGRAPHICAL AND CRITICAL SOURCES:

BOOKS

Walsh, Ellen Stoll, *Hop Jump,* Harcourt Brace (San Diego, CA), 1993.
Walsh, Ellen Stoll, *For Pete's Sake,* Harcourt Brace (San Diego, CA), 1998.

PERIODICALS

Booklist, November 15, 1981, p. 444; November 1, 1993, p. 532; February 15, 1996, p. 1027; October 15, 1998, Stephanie Zvirin, review of *For Pete's Sake,* p. 430; October 1, 2001, Kathy Broderick, review of *Dot & Jabber and the Great Acorn Mystery,* p. 330.
Bulletin of the Center for Children's Books, September, 1994, Elizabeth Bush, review of *Pip's Magic,* pp. 27-28; June, 1996, Deborah Stevenson, review of *Samantha,* p. 355.
Childhood Education, spring, 2003, review of *Dot & Jabber and the Mystery of the Missing Stream,* p. 180.
Horn Book, July-August, 1989, p. 479; May-June, 1991, Elizabeth Watson, review of *Mouse Count,* p. 325; January, 1993, p. 104; November-December, 1993, Isabel Schon, review of *Mouse Paint,* p. 769; June, 1995, p. 56; November, 1998, Nancy Vasilakis, review of *For Pete's Sake,* p. 722.
Junior Bookshelf, December, 1983, p. 238; December, 1985, p. 271; February, 1990, p. 19.
Kirkus Reviews, August 1, 1992, p. 995; October 15, 1993, review of *Hop Jump,* p. 1339; September 15, 1994, review of *Pip's Magic,* p. 1285; September 15, 1998, review of *For Pete's Sake,* p. 1391; August 15, 2002, review of *Dot & Jabber and the Mystery of the Missing Stream,* p. 1238.
New York Times Book Review, January 26, 1992, p. 21.
Publishers Weekly, December 24, 1979, p. 59; January 25, 1991, review of *Mouse Count,* p. 56; August 3, 1992, p. 70; September 20, 1993, p. 70; August 22, 1994, p. 54; October 26, 1998, review of *For Pete's Sake,* p. 65; January 31, 2000, review of *Mouse Magic,* p. 105; September 3, 2001, review of *Dot & Jabber and the Great Acorn Mystery,* p. 87; September 9, 2002, review of *Dot & Jabber and the Mystery of the Missing Stream,* p. 70; September 1, 2003, review of *Dot & Jabber and the Big Bug Mystery,* p. 117.

School Library Journal, October, 1979, p. 146; February, 1982, p. 71; June, 1989, Karen K. Radtke, review of *Mouse Paint,* p. 96; October, 1993, Nancy Seiner, review of *Hop Jump,* p. 113; November, 1994, pp. 92-93; May, 1996, Eunice Weech, review of *Samantha,* p. 101; October 26, 1998, Miriam Lang Budin, review of *For Pete's Sake,* p. 100; April, 2000, Carolyn Stacey, review of *Mouse Magic,* p. 116; September, 2001, Jody McCoy, review of *Dot & Jabber and the Great Acorn Mystery,* p. 208; November, 2002, Be Astengo, review of *Dot & Jabber and the Mystery of the Missing Stream,* p. 140; November, 2003, Shelley B. Sutherland, review of *Dot & Jabber and the Big Bug Mystery,* p. 117.

*   *   *

WEINTRAUB, William 1926-

PERSONAL: Born February 19, 1926, in Montreal, Quebec, Canada; son of Louis and Mina (Blumer) Weintraub; married Magda Landau, November, 26, 1967. *Education:* McGill University, B.A., 1947.

ADDRESSES: Home—3280 Ridgewood Avenue, Westmount, Quebec H3Y 3J4, Canada.

CAREER: Film producer, scriptwriter, novelist. *Montreal Gazette,* Montreal, Quebec, Canada, reporter, 1947-50; *Weekend Magazine,* Montreal, Quebec, copy editor, 1951-55; freelance writer, beginning 1955. National Film Board, producer, 1965-86; director, National Film Board studio, Nairobi, Kenya, 1975-76; director of English programming, 1976-78; has written and produced over 100 documentary films. Member of international jury, Cracow Film Festival, Poland, 1973; member of Canadian delegation visiting film industry in China, 1977; member of board of directors, Quebec council for the diffusion of cinema, 1971.

AWARDS, HONORS: Delegate to UNESCO Conference on Films and Television, Morocco, 1955; Canadian Council Senior Arts Fellowship, 1962.

WRITINGS:

Why Rock the Boat: A Novel, Little, Brown (Boston, MA), 1961.

The Underdogs, McClelland & Stewart (Toronto, Ontario, Canada), 1979.

City Unique: Montreal Days and Nights in the 1940s and '50s, McClelland & Stewart (Toronto, Ontario, Canada), 1996.

The Underdogs: A Play, Just For Laughs Press/Robert Davies Multimedia Publishers (Westmount, Quebec, Canada), 1998.

Getting Started: A Memoir of the 1950s; With Letters from Mordecai Richler, Mavis Gallant, and Brian Moore, McClelland & Stewart (Toronto, Ontario, Canada), 2001.

Author of scripts and commentaries for more than seventy-five productions by the National Film Board of Canada. Director and writer of *The Rise and Fall of English Montreal,* a documentary, 1993.

SIDELIGHTS: William Weintraub has written and produced, and/or directed over 100 documentary films. He is also the author of several books.

Why Rock the Boat is a comic novel satirizing the *Montreal Gazette,* where he worked as a young reporter. *National Post* reviewer Robert Fulford wrote, "Satire describing such a specific world usually dies young, but *Why Rock the Boat* reads well today. Seldom, before or since, has boredom been made so funny."

After working in journalism, Weintraub became interested in the new medium of television, took a two-week course in television scriptwriting and began working for the Canadian Broadcasting Corporation only three months after it was formed. He then worked as a freelance writer, and wrote short stories before becoming interested in film. In 1965, Weintraub began working for Canada's National Film Board; his relationship with them would last for several decades.

In *City Unique: Montreal Days and Nights in the 1940s and '50s,* Weintraub tells his own coming-of-age story. The book remained on Canadian best-seller lists for a year. In *Maclean's,* Anthony Wilson-Smith wrote that the book offered "a loving but clear-eyed look at the city" and noted that Weintraub's Montreal is "a wide-open, exuberant metropolis that dared to be many things, including great, and quite often succeeded." In *Canadian Geographic,* Joel Yanofsky commented that Weintraub "has a way with anecdotes and *City Unique* is packed with them, all lovingly told." Mike Kennedy wrote in the *Financial Post* that the book was "well-researched, entertaining," and that it "candidly portrays the good, the bad and the ugly aspects of two magical, almost unforgettable decades."

In *Getting Started: A Memoir of the 1950s; With Letters from Mordecai Richler, Mavis Gallant, and Brian Moore,* Weintraub describes how he and his friends, who later became noted Canadian writers, all dreamed of pursuing a life of writing and adventure while supporting themselves by working for various magazines and newspapers. In the *McGill News,* Jason Fowler praised Weintraub's use of amusing anecdotes, as well as his honest portrayal of his youthful insecurities about writing and his future. In addition, Fowler noted, the book "contains some fascinating bits of social history." In the *Montreal Review of Books,* Denis Sampson wrote, "The most extraordinary thing revealed in this book is the intimacy and solidity of the writers' friendships through tumultuous years of growing international recognition and success . . . displacement . . . and upheavals in personal lives."

BIOGRAPHICAL AND CRITICAL SOURCES:

PERIODICALS

Books in Canada, February, 1979, review of *The Underdogs,* p. 17; April, 1997, review of *City Unique: Montreal Days and Nights in the 1940s and '50s,* p. 16.
Canadian Book Review Annual, Volume 28, 1997, review of *City Unique,* p. 366.
Canadian Geographic, January-February, 1997, Joel Yanofsky, review of *City Unique,* p. 78.
Financial Post, April 19, 1997, Mike Kennedy, review of *City Unique,* p. 24.
Globe and Mail (Toronto, Ontario, Canada), September 22, 2001, review of *Getting Started: A Memoir of the 1950s; With Letters from Mordecai Richler, Mavis Gallant, and Brian Moore,* p. D4; November 24, 2001, review of *Getting Started,* p. D21.
Maclean's, February 26, 1979, review of *The Underdogs,* p. 57; March 25, 1996, p. 14; February 17, 1997, Anthony Wilson-Smith, review of *City Unique,* p. 75.
McGill News, winter, 2001-2002, Jason Fowler, review of *Getting Started.*
Montreal Review of Books, fall-winter, 2001-2002, Denis Sampson, review of *Getting Started.*

National Post, October 2, 2001.
Quill & Quire, December, 1996, review of *City Unique,* p. 30; February, 1997, review of *City Unique,* p. 50; September, 2001, review of *Getting Started,* p. 50.

*   *   *

WEISS, Jaqueline Shachter 1926-

PERSONAL: Born May 28, 1926, in San Antonio, TX; daughter of Albert O. (a businessman) and Yetta (a registered nurse and businesswoman; maiden name, Zalinsky) Nelson; married George Henry Weiss (a physician); children: Sherry Shachter Kandell, Ross David Shachter, Scott Jay Shachter, Steven Bertram Weiss. *Education:* University of Texas at Austin, B.A., 1946; University of Pennsylvania, M.S., 1963, Ed.D., 1969; attended National University of Mexico, summers, 1943, 1966. *Religion:* Jewish.

ADDRESSES: Home—3023 Dekalb Blvd., Norristown, PA 19401 (summer).

CAREER: Food, Tobacco, and Agricultural Workers Union, Houston, TX, business agent, 1946-47; Food, Tobacco, and Agricultural Workers Union, Philadelphia, PA, international representative, 1948-50; peace activist, 1951-62; elementary school teacher in Blue Bell, PA, 1963-68; Temple University, Philadelphia, assistant professor, 1968-72, associate professor of education, 1973-83; Philadelphia School District, Philadelphia, reading teacher, 1984—. High school Spanish teacher in Haverford, PA, fall, 1983.

MEMBER: Philadelphia Children's Reading Round Table (member of executive board), Phi Beta Kappa.

AWARDS, HONORS: Young Brer Rabbit was named a Notable Children's Trade Book in the Field of Social Studies by the National Council for the Social Studies and Children's Book Council, 1985.

WRITINGS:

Mexico: Spanish Selections Freely Translated and Augmented, University of Pennsylvania Press (Philadelphia, PA), 1967.

Jaqueline Shachter Weiss

(With Max Rosenfeld) *Old Testament Tales As Literature in Grades Three through Eight,* Sholom Aleichem (Philadelphia, PA), 1976.

Prizewinning Books for Children: Themes and Stereotypes in U.S. Prizewinning Prose Fiction for Children, Lexington Books (Lexington, MA), 1983.

(Collector and adapter) *Young Brer Rabbit, and Other Trickster Tales from the Americas,* illustrated by Clinton Arrowood, Stemmer House (Owings Mills, MD), 1985.

(With Carolyn W. Field) *Values in Selected Children's Books of Fiction and Fantasy,* Library Professional Publications (Hamden, CT), 1987.

Profiles in Children's Literature: Discussions with Authors, Artists, and Editors, foreword by Carolyn W. Field, Scarecrow Press (Lanham, MD), 2001.

Contributor of more than twenty articles to education and library journals.

SIDELIGHTS: Jaqueline Shachter Weiss is an educator specializing in children's literature. She has consequently published several reference works on the subject, as well as collected and adapted stories about the trickster rabbit who has become part of the folklore heritage of both North and South America. The author once commented, "I collected the *Young Brer Rabbit* stories over a five-year period, helped by my knowledge of Spanish and the children's literature study tours that I led to Central and South America while I was at Temple University. I hunted my elusive hero wherever I went. In Venezuela, I realized that Brer Rabbit is a current hero when I saw his costumes for puppet theater presentations of 'Brer Rabbit, Astronaut.' I studied Portuguese for a year so I could translate the marvelous stories that I received in Brazil. I also collected in the Caribbean area, making special trips to Puerto Rico and Cuba for that purpose."

Young Brer Rabbit, and Other Trickster Tales from the Americas includes fifteen stories derived from folk tales native to places such as Colombia and the West Indies, as well as adaptations of the Uncle Remus stories by Joel Chandler Harris. *School Library Journal* reviewer Kay McPherson objected to how Weiss rewrote these folk stories to make them similar to Harris's "Brer Rabbit" tales, thus ignoring "their rich and unique background," though the critic admitted that Weiss "has done a service" for librarians and other readers by collecting the tales in one source.

In the 1980s Weiss completed two major reference sources on children's literature: *Prizewinning Books for Children: Themes and Stereotypes in U.S. Prizewinning Prose Fiction for Children* and *Values in Selected Children's Books of Fiction and Fantasy,* the latter written with Carolyn W. Field. *Prizewinning Books for Children* includes over 700 titles arranged by theme and intended age of the audience. Margaret Mary Kimmel, writing in *School Library Journal,* unfortunately found a number of problems with this reference source, including an ill-defined explanation of just what "theme" means in the books discussed; also, Kimmel found fault with the organization of the appendix. "The most serious flaw, however," said the critic, "is the book's stated purpose." While Weiss states in the book that she is trying to provide a reference guide that will "give readers a sense of the 'completeness' of a work" by studying each story's themes, Kimmel asserted that the author fails to accomplish this task. *Journal of Academic Librarianship* contributor Anne Riley noted that Weiss's book will be "of limited interest to librarians outside the U.S." because of its focus on American literature.

According to Christine A. Behrmann in another *School Library Journal* assessment, Weiss's *Values in Selected*

Children's Books of Fiction and Fantasy suffers from a similar "lack of focus." Weiss and Field attempted to arrange the children's books in this reference source by the moral values they portray, such as friendship, cooperation, and bravery. However, Behrmann said that while the book "contains a seed of an interesting idea," its inability to organize the concept effectively results in a work that "simply serves as a list of high-quality children's books."

More recently, Weiss completed *Profiles in Children's Literature: Discussions with Authors, Artists, and Editors.* Though published in 2001, this work has its roots in a project the teacher began decades ago. While at Temple University, she conducted videotaped interviews of numerous children's authors for her class, which she has now transcribed. Of this experience, Weiss once told *CA,* "In the United States and on my recent trips to Israel, the Soviet Union, and Spain, I have been interviewing children's authors in order to publicize their books. In my own country and abroad I distribute 'Profiles in Literature,' videotaped interviews with more than fifty leading creators of books for children. Carolyn W. Field and I are interviewers, and I produce the programs. They have been enjoyed by more than one-hundred thousand viewers in the United States, Canada, and Australia." While *Bulletin of the Center for Children's Books* critic Janice M. Del Negro noted that the interviews in the subsequent book are all "safe" and "adulatory" without any sense of controversy, she concluded that the interviews with such authors as Margaret McElderry and Arna Bontemps "contain many, many gems."

BIOGRAPHICAL AND CRITICAL SOURCES:

BOOKS

Weiss, Jaqueline Shachter, *Prizewinning Books for Children: Themes and Stereotypes in U.S. Prizewinning Prose Fiction for Children,* Lexington Books (Lexington, MA), 1983.

PERIODICALS

Bulletin of the Center for Children's Books, May, 2002, Janice M. Del Negro, review of *Profiles in Children's Literature: Discussions with Authors, Artists, and Editors,* p. 347.

Journal of Academic Librarianship, May, 1985, Anne Riley, review of *Prizewinning Books for Children: Themes and Stereotypes in U.S. Prizewinning Prose Fiction for Children,* p. 107.
School Library Journal, December, 1983, Margaret Mary Kimmel, review of *Prizewinning Books for Children,* p. 34; January, 1986, Kay McPherson, review of *Young Brer Rabbit, and Other Trickster Tales from the Americas,* p. 71; June-July, 1988, Christine A. Behrmann, review of *Values in Selected Children's Books of Fiction and Fantasy,* p. 52.
Washington Post Book World, November 29, 1987, Vic Sussman, "Swinging with Mother Goose," p. 6.*

*　　　*　　　*

WICK, Walter 1953-

PERSONAL: Born February 23, 1953, in Hartford, CT; married. *Education:* Graduated from Paier College of Art (Hamden, CT), 1973.

ADDRESSES: Office—Winsted, CT. *Agent*—c/o Author Mail, Scholastic Press, 557 Broadway, New York, NY 10012.

CAREER: Photographer and writer of children's books, 1992—. Worked as a lab technician and photographer's assistant, Hartford, CT; photographer for magazines including *Discover, Psychology Today,* and *Games.*

AWARDS, HONORS: Boston Globe-Horn Book Award for Nonfiction, 1997, and Utah Beehive Award for Informational Book, Grades 3-6, 2000, both for *A Drop of Water: A Book of Science and Wonder.* Wick's books have been placed on recommended children's book lists by several organizations, including *Parenting* and the *New York Times.*

WRITINGS:

SELF-ILLUSTRATED

A Drop of Water: A Book of Science and Wonder, Scholastic (New York, NY), 1997.
Walter Wick's Optical Tricks, Scholastic (New York, NY), 1998.

Can You See What I See? Picture Puzzles to Search and Solve, Scholastic (New York, NY), 2002.

Can You See What I See? Dream Machine, Scholastic (New York, NY), 2003.

Can You See What I See? Cool Collections, Scholastic (New York, NY), 2004.

Can You See What I See? Seymour and the Juice Box Boat, Scholastic (New York, NY), 2004.

ILLUSTRATOR; "I SPY" SERIES; WRITTEN BY JEAN MARZOLLO

I Spy: A Book of Picture Riddles, Scholastic (New York, NY), 1992.

I Spy Christmas: A Book of Picture Riddles, Scholastic (New York, NY), 1992.

I Spy Mystery: A Book of Picture Riddles, Scholastic (New York, NY), 1993.

I Spy Fun House: A Book of Picture Riddles, Scholastic (New York, NY), 1993.

I Spy Fantasy: A Book of Picture Riddles, Scholastic (New York, NY), 1994.

I Spy School Days: A Book of Picture Riddles, Scholastic (New York, NY), 1995.

I Spy Spooky Night: A Book of Picture Riddles, Scholastic (New York, NY), 1996.

I Spy Super Challenger!: A Book of Picture Riddles, Scholastic (New York, NY), 1997.

I Spy Little Book, Scholastic (New York, NY), 1997.

I Spy Little Wheels, Scholastic (New York, NY), 1998.

I Spy Gold Challenger!, Scholastic (New York, NY), 1998.

I Spy Little Animals, Scholastic (New York, NY), 1998.

I Spy Treasure Hunt: A Book of Picture Riddles, Scholastic (New York, NY), 1999.

I Spy Little Christmas, Scholastic (New York, NY), 1999.

I Spy Little Numbers, Scholastic (New York, NY), 1999.

I Spy Extreme Challenger!: A Book of Picture Riddles, Scholastic (New York, NY), 2000.

I Spy Year-Round Challenger, Scholastic (New York, NY), 2001.

I Spy Little Bunnies, Scholastic (New York, NY), 2001.

I Spy Funny Teeth, Scholastic (New York, NY), 2003.

I Spy a Dinosaur's Eye, Scholastic (New York, NY), 2003.

I Spy Ultimate Challenger!: A Book of Picture Riddles, Scholastic (New York, NY), 2003.

I Spy a School Bus, Scholastic (New York, NY), 2003.

I Spy a Candy Cane, Scholastic (New York, NY), 2004.

Wick's works have been translated into Spanish and French.

ADAPTATIONS: The "I Spy" series has been adapted as a video game for the Nintendo Game Boy gaming system and to CD-ROM by Scholastic (New York, NY), including the titles *I Spy Fantasy, I Spy Spooky Mansion, I Spy Treasure Hunt, I Spy School Days, I Spy Junior: Puppet Playhouse,* and *I Spy Junior.*

SIDELIGHTS: Walter Wick's books for children are known for their inventive, original photography. He trained as a photographer and worked for magazines such as *Games* and *Psychology Today* before he got his start in children's books. Wick uses tricks of perspective and collage-like techniques to create intriguing puzzles and visual riddles in his work. Several critics have deemed Wick a photographic genius for his intriguing optical illusion puzzles.

Wick is well regarded for his work on the "I Spy" series, on which he collaborated with Jean Marzollo. In the "I Spy" books, Marzollo created riddles that the reader solves with visual clues in Wick's photographs. The first in the series, *I Spy: A Book of Picture Riddles,* was praised by a *Publishers Weekly* reviewer for its "excellent, sharp photographic work combined with ingenuity and imagination" that made the book's challenge "surprisingly great." Many reviewers have praised the series for its educational uses as well as its entertainment value; the books help children learn colors, numbers, shapes, patterns, and more. One of the most critically acclaimed in the series is 1993's *I Spy Fun House: A Book of Picture Riddles,* in which Janice Del Negro, writing for *Booklist,* praised Wick's use of "riotous color and cheerfully surreal designs." A reviewer for *Publishers Weekly* called this "I Spy" book the "best yet." For *I Spy Treasure Hunt: A Book of Picture Riddles,* Wick created a "stunningly detailed miniature village," as Lisa Gangemi Krapp wrote in *School Library Journal,* and readers of this book are challenged not only to find the hidden objects but also to solve a mystery involving pirate treasure.

As Carolyn Phelan wrote in a *Booklist* review of *I Spy Extreme Challenger!: A Book of Picture Riddles,* "once bitten by the 'I Spy' series bug, kids can find relief only in another volume." Expanding their collaborative efforts, Marzollo and Wick produced several "I Spy Challenger" books that combined favorite photo spreads from other volumes in the series with new, more challenging riddles. Some reviewers felt that these books were less interesting because of the reused pictures, but others appreciated the opportunity to look at familiar images in a new way. Wick and Marzollo also used sections of pictures from the "I Spy" books in "I Spy" board books, which generally have titles starting with *I Spy Little . . . .* Along with the "I Spy Junior" CD-ROMs, they introduce younger children to the "I Spy" concept with smaller, easier puzzles.

The first book that Wick both wrote and illustrated was *A Drop of Water: A Book of Science and Wonder.* In this book, Wick combines his interesting photographic techniques with an informative text about water in all its forms. A reviewer for *Resource Links* praised the "exceptional photographs . . . and well-written text" that draw in young readers and make the book "a truly aesthetic reading experience." In a review for *Booklist,* Carolyn Phelan noted Wick's use of simple techniques and unifying photographs to introduce complicated properties of water, such as capillary attraction and surface tension, calling *A Drop of Water* "a fine, eye-catching introduction to a well-focused topic."

Wick's next solo venture was *Walter Wick's Optical Tricks,* in which he uses a variety of photographic techniques to create illusions and visual surprises. At the end of the book, he reveals the tricks he used to make the puzzles. Some critics worried that the puzzles might be too difficult for younger readers, but others praised the book as fun for all ages. Daniel J. Brabander, writing for *Horn Book,* concluded that "Wick's elegant yet bold style of photography is ideally suited for the task of visual deception," and a *Publishers Weekly* reviewer called the book "visual catnip."

Wick followed this book with 2002's *Can You See What I See? Picture Puzzles to Search and Solve,* another book of photographic puzzles. Each themed picture puzzle in this book includes both a rhyme with objects to find, as in the "I Spy" books, and another kind of puzzle, such as a maze or optical illusion. In a *School Library Journal* review, Marianne Saccardi wrote that *Can You See What I See? Picture Puzzles to Search and Solve* would give children "hours of puzzle-solving fun," calling the book "'I Spy' and

much more." A *Kirkus Reviews* critic concluded that readers who enjoy the "I Spy" books "will be thrilled with a new challenge while newcomers will become immediate devotees."

Whether they are focused on science, optical illusions, or just plain fun, Wick's books are alike in their use of unique artwork and photography to enhance the reader's experience. Wick has found that children's books provide an outlet for his creative methods of photography, and that children are interested in subjects such as visual illusions and science just as he is. On his Web site, Wick wrote: "In all the years I've worked as a photographer, I've never had a more appreciative audience than children. I suspect I'll be doing children's books for a long time to come."

BIOGRAPHICAL AND CRITICAL SOURCES:

PERIODICALS

Booklist, May 15, 1993, Janice Del Negro, review of *I Spy Fun House: A Book of Picture Riddles,* p. 1694; February 1, 1997, Carolyn Phelan, review of *A Drop of Water: A Book of Science and Wonder,* p. 940; October 1, 2000, Carolyn Phelan, review of *I Spy Extreme Challenger!: A Book of Picture Riddles,* p. 342; April 15, 2002, Gillian Engberg, review of *Can You See What I See? Picture Puzzles to Search and Solve,* p. 1404; November 15, 2003, Ilene Cooper, review of *Can You See What I See? Dream Machine,* p. 598.

Horn Book, September-October 1998, Daniel J. Brabander, review of *Walter Wick's Optical Tricks,* p. 626.

Publishers Weekly, January 6, 1992, review of *I Spy: A Book of Picture Riddles,* p. 65; April 19, 1993, review of *I Spy Fun House: A Book of Picture Riddles,* p. 58; June 29, 1998, review of *Walter Wick's Optical Tricks,* p. 59; January 7, 2002, review of *Can You See What I See? Picture Puzzles to Search and Solve,* p. 63.

Resource Links, June, 1997, review of *A Drop of Water,* p. 214.

School Library Journal, January, 2000, Lisa Gangemi Krapp, review of *I Spy Treasure Hunt: A Book of Picture Riddles,* p. 124; March, 2002, Marianne Saccardi, review of *Can You See What I See? Picture Puzzles to Search and Solve,* p. 223; November, 2003, Genevieve Gallagher, review of *Can You See What I See? Dream Machine,* p. 132.

ONLINE

Walter Wick Home Page, http://www.walterwick.com/ (January 20, 2004).*

*   *   *

WILLIS, Charles
    See CLARKE, Arthur C(harles)

*   *   *

WINCHESTER, Simon 1944-

PERSONAL: Born September 28, 1944, in London, England; married Judy Winchester, 1966 (divorced); married second wife, 1989 (divorced, 1997); children: (first marriage) three sons; one daughter. *Education:* St. Catherine's College, Oxford, M.A., 1966. *Religion:* Church of England.

ADDRESSES: Home—Berkshire County, MA, and Luing, Western Isles of Scotland. *Agent*—Anthony Sheil Associates Ltd., 2-3 Morwell St., London WC1B 3AR, England.

CAREER: Writer and journalist. *Journal,* Newcastle upon Tyne, England, reporter, 1967-70; *Guardian,* London, England, correspondent in Northern Ireland, 1970-72, in Washington, DC, 1972-76, and in New Delhi, India, 1977-79; *Daily Mail,* London, chief U.S. correspondent in Washington, DC, 1979-80; *Sunday Times,* London, England, senior feature writer, 1981—. San Jose State University, CA, Lurie Professor, 2004.

AWARDS, HONORS: Journalist of the Year, England; AAPG Journalism Award.

WRITINGS:

NONFICTION

In Holy Terror: Reporting the Ulster Troubles Faber (London, England), 1974, published as *Northern Ireland in Crisis: Reporting the Ulster Troubles,* Holmes & Meier (New York, NY), 1975.

Simon Winchester

American Heartbeat: Notes from a Midwestern Journey, Faber (London, England), 1976.

Their Noble Lordships: The Hereditary Peerage Today, Faber (London, England), 1981, published as *Their Noble Lordships: Class and Power in Modern Britain,* Random House (New York, NY), 1982.

(With Jan Morris) *Stones of Empire: The Buildings of the Raj,* Oxford University Press (New York, NY), 1983.

Prison Diary, Argentina, Chatto & Windus (London, England), 1983.

The Sun Never Sets: Travels to the Remaining Outposts of the British Empire, Prentice-Hall (Englewood Cliffs, NJ), 1985, published as *Outposts,* Hodder & Stoughton (London, England), 1985.

Korea: A Walk through the Land of Miracles, Prentice-Hall (Englewood Cliffs, NJ), 1988.

Pacific Rising: The Emergence of a New World Culture, Prentice-Hall (Englewood Cliffs, NJ), 1991.

Hong Kong: Here Be Dragons, Stewart, Tabori & Chang (New York, NY), 1992.

Pacific Nightmare: How Japan Starts World War III: A Future History, Carol (New York, NY), 1992.

(With Martin Parr) *Small World,* Dewi Lewis (Stockport, England), 1995.

The River at the Center of the World: A Journey up the Yangtze and Back in Chinese Time, Holt (New York, NY), 1996.

The Professor and the Madman: A Tale of Murder, Insanity, and the Making of the Oxford English Dictionary, HarperCollins (New York, NY), 1998, published in England as *The Surgeon of Crowthorne,* Viking (New York, NY), 1998.

The Fracture Zone: A Return to the Balkans, Harper-Collins (New York, NY), 1999.

The Map That Changed the World: William Smith and the Birth of Modern Geology, HarperCollins (New York, NY), 2001.

Krakatoa: The Day the World Exploded, August 27, 1883, HarperCollins (New York, NY), 2003.

The Meaning of Everything: The Story of the Oxford English Dictionary, Oxford University Press (New York, NY), 2003.

Contributing editor of *Harper's.* Author of introduction to the 2002 edition of *A Dictionary of Modern Usage,* by Henry Fowler, Oxford University Press (New York, NY). Contributor of articles to magazines, including *Smithsonian, Conde Nast Traveler, National Geographic,* and *Salon.*

WORK IN PROGRESS: The Treasures of India, for Time-Life; *A History of Rioting in Britain,* a film for British Broadcasting Corp. (BBC), with a book expected to follow; a history of the San Francisco earthquake, to be published in 2006.

SIDELIGHTS: Simon Winchester is a journalist and writer as well as a trained geologist. Born in London and educated at Oxford, Winchester worked on oil rigs in the North Sea before turning his hand to journalism, writing as a correspondent for British newspapers around the world, covering stories from the Watergate affair to the Falklands War. In 1987 he became a full-time freelance writer, exploring topics from the urbane to the catastrophic. His surprise best-seller *The Professor and the Madman: A Tale of Murder, Insanity, and the Making of the Oxford English Dictionary* tells an intriguing behind-the-scenes story of the writing of the *Oxford English Dictionary,* while his 2003 work *Krakatoa: The Day the World Exploded, August 27, 1883* looks at a volcanic eruption that affected the entire world in the late nineteenth century. Other books from Winchester have examined topics from England's imperial past to the history of China. A thorough re-

searcher, Winchester confessed to "research rapture" in an interview with Adair Lara in the *San Francisco Chronicle Online.* "I'm in total rapture when I'm doing research," Winchester noted. "The temptation to get diverted into fascinating byways is enormous. You've got to keep these things measured and keep your eye on the real purpose of writing the book."

"I doubt that anybody has researched the British hereditary peerage as thoroughly or as entertainingly as Winchester," wrote Gerry Graber in a *Los Angeles Times* review of Winchester's 1981 book *Their Noble Lordships: Class and Power in Modern Britain.* In this book, the author explores the power and prestige of British peerage by way of fact and anecdote. Winchester's basic contention is that Britain, by clinging to the legislative rights of heredity, limits its chances to adapt to the dynamic, modern world. Unlike Japan, which abandoned its system of peerage after World War II, Britain maintained its institution in which lawmakers are selected by birth right. Now, if Britain is to "retain respect of the thrusting, grasping assertive countries of the globe that now surround her," the country must, noted Winchester in *Their Noble Lordships,* "develop a machinery of government that is in tune with the demands of the century."

Nine books and sixteen years later, Winchester told a strange but true story in *The Professor and the Madman: A Tale of Murder, Insanity, and the Making of the Oxford English Dictionary.* The professor behind the title is J. A. H. Murray, the determined editor who was behind the publication of the massive reference work of the title. Volunteers helped to create the dictionary by submitting definitions and illustrative quotations. One of the most prolific contributors was a Dr. W. C. Minor, who supplied more than 10,000 entries. After seventeen years of corresponding with Minor, Murray decided to visit his star worker. He was shocked to discover that Minor was confined to Broadmoor Asylum, a British prison for the criminally insane.

Minor had been born in Ceylon to American missionary parents. He acted as a surgeon in the Civil War. Perhaps as a result of the horrors he saw during that conflict, Minor became paranoid and schizophrenic. He left America for Europe, looking for a rest cure. Probably under the influence of his delusions, he shot and killed an innocent man, believing him to be an assassin. Once confined to Broadmoor, Minor was treated well; he had two cells and was allowed to keep his precious library in one of them. He was lucid most of the time, yet at night he was still plagued by hallucinations and terrible self-loathing, which eventually drove him to mutilate himself. A *Library Journal* reviewer rated *The Professor and the Madman* as a "delightful, simply written book" that "tells how a murderer made a huge contribution to what became a major reference source in the Western world." A *Publishers Weekly* writer noted, "Winchester celebrates a gloomy life brightened by devotion to a quietly noble, nearly anonymous task."

Reviewing the British edition of the book, which was published as *The Surgeon of Crowthorne*, an *Economist* reviewer called it "an extraordinary tale, and Simon Winchester could not have told it better. His fast pace means that the lexicographical details are never dull. He has an engaging sympathy with his main characters, and even the minor ones are painted with swift, vivid strokes. . . . Mr. Winchester has written a splendid book."

Winchester celebrates another solitary and underreported achievement in *The Map That Changed the World: William Smith and the Birth of Modern Geology*. In this book, Winchester presents the story of Smith, a mere surveyor and engineer, who created in 1815 the "world's first proper geological map," according to Kathryn Hughes, writing in the *New Statesman*. Smith labored for years on his own to create a more graphic representation of the world that showed geological strata, a finding that called into question the Genesis theory of creation. Robert Macfarlane, writing in the *Spectator*, found the book a "charming biography," while Hughes commented that Winchester "has written a wonderful book." Hughes also felt that Winchester was "particularly impressive" in the manner in which he "recreates the world picture of society tottering on the edge of an epistemological abyss." Writing in the *New York Times Book Review*, Malcolm C. McKenna had similar praise: "Winchester brings Smith's struggle to light in clear and beautiful language."

Geology on a grander scale comes into focus in Winchester's *Krakatoa*, a recounting of one of the most violent volcanic eruptions in the nineteenth century. The entire island was vaporized when its volcano exploded in 1883, sending shock waves around the world, killing scores of thousands of people, and providing brilliant sunsets around the world. So large was the explosion that it was heard 3,000 miles away; the tsunamis it generated killed people 2,000 miles from the blast. Winchester provides the background to the explosion in this "lavish rijstafel of a book," as a reviewer for the *Economist* described *Krakatoa*. The same critic further noted that Winchester has written an "engagingly discursive . . . account of the events leading up to the cataclysm." Lev Grossman, reviewing the same title in *Time*, observed that Winchester "takes an event that happened in a white-hot second and expands it in both directions, filling in the backstory and aftershocks to create a mesmerizing page turner." Grossman also called Winchester an "extraordinarily graceful writer." The *Spectator*'s Justin Marozzi also had praise for the book, remarking that "we learn a great deal in the course of this book and Winchester, storyteller to the core, wears his erudition lightly." And writing in the *New York Times Book Review*, Richard Ellis was full of superlatives: "[*Krakatoa*] is thrilling, comprehensive, literate, meticulously researched and scientifically accurate; it is one of the best books ever written about the history and significance of a natural disaster."

Winchester returns to the world of his breakout bestseller, *The The Professor and the Madman*, with his 2003 title *The Meaning of Everything: The Story of the Oxford English Dictionary*. While the former book focuses on two main players in the etymological endeavor, the latter book tells "the eventful, personality-filled history of the definitive English dictionary," as a critic for *Publishers Weekly* observed. Commissioned in 1857, the dictionary took seven decades and huge cost overruns to complete. Among the cast of characters in its completion are Murray and Minor from the earlier work, but also readers and researchers such as J. R. R. Tolkien. In the end, the dictionary was completed at over 15,000 single-spaced pages with over 400,000 words and almost 200,000 illustrative quotations. Winchester's book will be, according to the *Publishers Weekly*, reviewer, "required reading for word mavens." A contributor for *Kirkus Reviews* likewise found the book a "magnificent account, swift and compelling, of obsessions, scholarship, and, ultimately, philanthropy of the first magnitude." A reviewer for the *Christian Century* called the book a "fascinating account," while Robert McCrum, writing in the *Los Angeles Times Book Review*, found it "an affectionate and frankly partisan study of the making of a great dictionary." And for William F. Buckley, Jr., writing in the *New York Times Book Review*, the book "is teeming with knowledge and alive with insights."

BIOGRAPHICAL AND CRITICAL SOURCES:

BOOKS

Winchester, Simon, *Their Noble Lordships: Class and Power in Modern Britain,* Random House (New York, NY), 1982.

PERIODICALS

Asian Wall Street Journal Weekly, November 30, 1992, David Oyama, review of *Pacific Nightmare: How Japan Starts World War III: A Future History,* p. 13.
Booklist, November 1, 1996, Alice Joyce, review of *The River at the Center of the World: A Journey up the Yangtze and Back in Chinese Time,* p. 477; August, 1998, Brad Hooper, review of *The Professor and the Madman: A Tale of Murder, Insanity, and the Making of the Oxford English Dictionary,* p. 1941; August, 1999, Ted Hipple, review of *The Professor and the Madman* (audiobook), p. 2075; September 1, 2003, Mary Ellen Quinn, review of *The Meaning of Everything: The Story of the Oxford English Dictionary,* pp. 4-5.
Business Week, September 27, 1982, p. 12; September 3, 2001, review of *The Map That Changed the World,* p. 18.
Christian Century, October 4, 2003, review of *The Meaning of Everything,* p. 6.
Economist, May 16, 1992, review of *Pacific Nightmare,* p. 119; March 29, 2003, review of *Krakatoa: The Day the World Exploded.*
Far Eastern Economic Review, October 8, 1992, review of *Pacific Nightmare,* p. 50.
Kirkus Reviews, August 1, 2003, review of *The Meaning of Everything,* p. 1010.
Library Journal, May 1, 1986, Harold M. Otness, review of *The Sun Never Sets: Travels to the Remaining Outposts of the British Empire,* p. 121; April 15, 1991, review of *Pacific Rising: The Emergence of a New World Culture,* p. 110; September 1, 1992, Elsa Pendleton, review of *Pacific Nightmare,* p. 218; October 15, 1996, Caroline A. Mitchell, review of *The River at the Center of the World,* p. 81; March 15, 1999, Danna Bell-Russell, review of *The Professor and the Madman,* p. 126; September 1, 2003, I. Pour-El, review of *Krakatoa,* pp. 229-230.

Los Angeles Times, July 2, 1982, Gary Graber, review of *Their Noble Lordships.*
Los Angeles Times Book Review, May 11, 2003, Kenneth Reich, review of *Krakatoa,* p. 10; October 19, 2003, Robert McCrum, review of *The Meaning of Everything,* p. 6.
M2 Best Books, October 22, 2003, Darren Ingram, review of *The Meaning of Everything.*
National Review, December 21, 1998, Linda Bridges, review of *The Professor and the Madman,* p. 64.
New Statesman, July 2, 2001, Kathryn Hughes, review of *The Map That Changed the World,* p. 54.
New York Review of Books, September 24, 1998, John Gross, review of *The Professor and the Madman,* p. 13.
New York Times Book Review, June 1, 1986, Andrew Harvey, review of *The Sun Never Sets,* p. 14; April 28, 1991, review of *Pacific Rising,* p. 10; October 18, 1992, Malcolm Bosse, review of *Pacific Nightmare,* p. 11; December 8, 1996, David Willis McCullough, review of *The River at the Center of the World,* p. 31; August 30, 1998, David Walton, review of *The Professor and the Madman,* p. 12; August 5, 2001, Malcolm C. McKenna, review of *The Map That Changed the World,* p. 14; April 20, 2003, Richard Ellis, review of *Krakatoa,* p. 9; October 12, 2003, William F. Buckley, Jr., review of *The Meaning of Everything,* p. 13.
Publishers Weekly, March 14, 1986, review of *The Sun Never Sets,* p. 93; February 22, 1991, review of *Pacific Rising,* p. 206; July 27, 1992, review of *Pacific Nightmare,* p. 47; September 16, 1996, review of *The River at the Center of the World,* p. 59; November 2, 1998, review of *The Professor and the Madman,* p. 35; September 27, 1999, review of *The Fracture Zone: A Return to the Balkans,* p. 80; August 27, 2001, Yvonne Nolan, "Tracking the Mapmaker," pp. 44-45; March 10, 2003, Matt Nelson, "An Explosion of Attention," p. 64; July 14, 2003, review of *The Meaning of Everything,* p. 66
School Library Journal, March, 1999, Susan H. Woodcock, review of *The Professor and the Madman,* p. 233.
Science, August 24, 2001, David Oldroyd, review of *The Map That Changed the World,* p. 1439.
Smithsonian, April, 1987, David Lancashire, review of *The Sun Never Sets,* p. 156.
Spectator, July 7, 2001, Robert Macfarlane, review of *The Map That Changed the World,* p. 32; June 7, 2003, Justin Marozzi, review of *Krakatoa,* pp. 44-45.

Time, September 14, 1998, Jesse Birnbaum, review of *The Professor and the Madman,* p. 76; May 12, 2003, Lev Grossman, review of *Krakatoa,* p. 79.

Washington Post, May 22, 2003, George F. Will, review of *Krakatoa,* p. A35.

Wilson Library Bulletin, June, 1986, Sam Staggs, review of *The Sun Never Sets,* p. 87.

ONLINE

AAPG Web site, http://www.aapg.org/ (November 14, 2003).

Official Simon Winchester Web site, http://www.simonwinchester.com (November 14, 2003).

San Francisco Chronicle Online, http://www.sfgate.com/ (April 6, 2003), Adair Lara, "Q & A: Simon Winchester: Enraptured by Research, Intrigued by All."

San Jose State University Web site, http://www2.sjsu.edu/ (November 14, 2003), "Simon Winchester."*

*   *   *

WOLFER, Dianne 1961-

PERSONAL: Born October 28, 1961, in Melbourne, Australia; daughter of Donald (a manager) and Audrey (a teacher) Davidson; married Reinhard Wolfer (a systems manager), December 23, 1984 (died, 1995); children: Sophie. *Ethnicity:* "Australian." *Education:* Melbourne State College, Diploma of Teaching; Western Australian Institute of Technology (now Curtin University), Certificate of Fluency in Japanese and graduate study. *Hobbies and other interests:* Travel, reading, swimming, scuba diving, bush-walking, photography.

ADDRESSES: Home—P.O. Box 421, Denmark 6333, Western Australia, Australia. *E-mail*—dianne@denmarkwa.net.au.

CAREER: Western Australian Education Department, teacher, 1984-87; teacher at Japan International School and American School in Japan, Tokyo, 1987-90; Western Australian Education Department, teacher, 1991-92. Teacher of missionary children in remote western Nepal; TAFE International, lecturer to adults in Western Australia; workshop presenter and public speaker.

Member of Australian Conservation Foundation, Denmark Environment Centre, DenmarkArts, Peter Cowan Writers Centre, and Western Australia State Literature Office.

MEMBER: Australian Society of Authors, Society of Women Writers (Western Australia branch), Fellowship of Australian Writers, Children's Book Council, Amnesty International.

AWARDS, HONORS: Bronze Quill Award, Society of Women Writers, 1992, for short story "Gokiburi"; South-West Literary Award, South-West Development Authority, 1995, for *Christmas Lunch;* Furphy Award for best published novel, Fellowship of Australian Writers, 1995, for *Dolphin Song;* Mary Grant Bruce Short Story Award, Fellowship of Australian Writers, 1997, for "Donkey Ears."

WRITINGS:

BOOKS FOR YOUNGER READERS

Butterfly Notes, Thomson Learning Australia (Southbank, Victoria, Australia), 2002.

Ironkid, Thomson Learning Australia (Southbank, Victoria, Australia), 2003.

Being Billy, Thomson Learning Australia (Southbank, Victoria, Australia), 2003.

Scuba Kid, Thomson Learning Australia (Southbank, Victoria, Australia), 2004.

Village Rules!, Thomson Learning Australia (Southbank, Victoria, Australia), 2004.

OTHER

Dolphin Song (young adult), International Specialized Book Services (Portland, OR), 1995.

Border Line (young adult), International Specialized Book Services (Portland, OR), 1998.

Choices (young adult), International Specialized Book Services (Portland, OR), 2001.

Photographs in the Mud (picture book), Fremantle Arts Centre Press (Fremantle, Australia), in press.

Author of the one-act play *Christmas Lunch,* 1995. Work represented in anthologies, including *Going Down South,* 1992, and *Going Down South Two,* 1993.

Contributor of short stories, poetry, and articles to magazines, including *Decades, Lucky, Western Word, Nature and Health, Western Review, Let's Travel,* and *In Perspective.*

WORK IN PROGRESS: *Kokoda* (tentative title), a young adult novel; texts for picture books; stories for younger readers.

SIDELIGHTS: Dianne Wolfer once told *CA:* "I feel very lucky to be able to live in a beautiful area on the southwest coast of Western Australia. My home is surrounded by bushland, and it's a short drive to the dramatic beaches of the Southern Ocean. Parrots, wrens, and lorikeets feed outside my window, and if I'm up early I often see kangaroos nibbling on my lawn.

"The environment and unique beauty of the corner of Australia in which I live play an important part in my writing. I am interested in the conflicts that occur when humans meet nature, so my books have environmental undercurrents and themes. Friendship and the complex bonds between characters are also of great importance to me as a writer. I also enjoy writing books with parallel storylines, like *Choices,* my novel focusing on teenage pregnancy.

"I love traveling and have lived in several countries (Thailand, Nepal, and Japan). My family and friends are scattered around the world, and I hope that, through my writing, I can foster an interest in other countries and cultures."

Recently Wolfer added: "I am currently working on a novel set on the Kokoda Track in Papua New Guinea. Kokoda was the site of ferocious World War II battles between Japanese, Australian, and American soldiers. The novel is set in modern times with diary flashbacks to 1942.

"The aspect of writing I enjoy most is hearing from readers that my work has really touched them. I find that very special. I also love working my own hours and traveling to other communities to give workshops and speak about my work."

BIOGRAPHICAL AND CRITICAL SOURCES:

PERIODICALS

Australian Book Review, June, 1995, p. 62.
RRR Network News, summer, 2002, pp. 12-13.
School Library Journal, March, 2003, Sharon Rawlins, review of *Dolphin Song,* p. 243.

ONLINE

Dianne Wolfer Home Page, http://www.wn.com.au/dianne/ (April 12, 2004).

*   *   *

YORK, Lorraine (M.) 1958-

PERSONAL: Born November 21, 1958, in London, Ontario, Canada; daughter of Reginald Francis (an oil company employee) and Margaret (a teacher; maiden name, Waddell) York; married Michael Lawrence Ross (a professor of English), May 23, 1987. *Ethnicity:* "Anglo-Canadian." *Education:* Attended University of Waterloo, 1977-78; McMaster University, B.A., 1981, M.A., 1982, Ph.D., 1985; attended University of Toronto, 1982-83. *Politics:* New Democrat.

ADDRESSES: *Home*—Dundas, Ontario, Canada. *Office*—Department of English, McMaster University, Hamilton, Ontario L8S 4L9, Canada. *E-mail*—yorkl@cogeco.ca.

CAREER: McGill University, Montreal, Quebec, Canada, assistant professor of English, 1985-88; McMaster University, Hamilton, Ontario, Canada, assistant professor, 1988-91, associate professor, 1991-97, professor of English, 1997—.

MEMBER: Association of Canadian University Teachers of English, Association for Canadian Studies in the United States, Modern Language Association of America.

WRITINGS:

The Other Side of Dailiness: Photography in the Works of Alice Munro, Timothy Findley, Michael Ondaatje, and Margaret Laurence, ECW Press (Toronto, Ontario, Canada), 1988.
Front Lines: The Fiction of Timothy Findley, ECW Press (Toronto, Ontario, Canada), 1991.
(Editor) *Various Atwoods: Essays on the Later Poems, Short Fiction, and Novels,* House of Anansi Press (Toronto, Ontario, Canada), 1995.
Rethinking Women's Collaborative Writing, University of Toronto Press (Toronto, Ontario, Canada), 2002.

Contributor of more than a dozen articles and reviews to scholarly journals, including *Canadian Literature, University of Toronto Quarterly,* and *Essays on Canadian Writing.*

WORK IN PROGRESS: Literary Celebrity in Canada, a study of the star system in Canadian literary institutions.

SIDELIGHTS: Lorraine York once told *CA:* "I am interested in bringing the findings of other disciplines (the fine arts and political science) to bear on my own. The two main areas of literary thought which have been most important to me are feminist and Marxist theory. The interaction of literature and political ideology fascinates me.

"Feminist and Marxist theory have been important to my writing because I have become aware of the way in which conditions of production relate to the forms and types of literature written in a society. This concept is particularly relevant to a student of Canadian literature, I think, because that literature in itself was born out of rather harsh physical conditions in the nineteenth century and it survived in spite of some equally adverse political conditions of the twentieth century. The Canadian position—that of being a smaller power in direct proximity to a nation that has emerged in this century as a superpower—gives Canadians a special appreciation for marginal discourses. Acquaintances often ask me why there are so many prominent female writers in Canada, and students sometimes ask why so many writers we study together have been attracted to radical critiques of social structures. (Many twentieth-century Canadian poets, for instance, were at one time or another members of Communist or Marxist parties or groups.) My own response is that we as Canadians inevitably speak from the margins. And the teachings of feminist and Marxist theory remind us of how powerful this voice can be."

More recently York added: "As a scholar working in the Canadian literary academy, I've always been interested in the ways in which other systems of knowledge, material practices, or media intersect with the literary, be they photography, warfare, or collaborative forms of authorship. More recently, I have become influenced, like so many of my colleagues, by the influential study of culture now taking place in our universities: popular culture, material cultural practices, globalization. I've become excited by the possibilities of taking that concern into my own field of Canadian literature, and so I've been working on the way in which literary celebrity in Canada and, by extension, in the literary field in general. Influential thinkers include the late sociologist Pierre Bourdieu, film theorist Richard Dyer, and especially the work of P. David Marshall on celebrity and power.

"In the past, discussions of marketing and of consumer power have been seen to be outside the purview of traditional literary studies; now they are of increasing importance to many of us. In my work on Canadian literary celebrity, I focus on three contemporary case studies: writers Margaret Atwood, Michael Ondaatje, and Carol Shields, whose careers offer three narratives of the workings of literary celebrity in Canada. I also historicize this study, however, by focusing more briefly on several earlier Canadian literary 'stars': Pauline Johnson, the very popular turn-of-the-century poet and stage performer, comic writer Stephen Leacock, 'Jalna saga' author Mazo de la Roche, and *Anne of Green Gables* creator Lucy Maud Montgomery. I argue that, although many discussions of literary celebrity tend to emphasize its workings in more recent years, somehow assuming that earlier literary periods were less commercialized, many of the workings and tensions of literary celebrity are evident in these earlier figures in our literature.

"My next step is to move beyond the literary institutions—funnily enough, for a scholar trained in the literary—and to examine the workings of Canadian cultural celebrity in general. Focusing again on case studies—but now drawn from film, television, popular music, dance, and sport—I ask how the workings of celebrity in various fields of culture tend to construct notions of citizenship and entitlement. I feel as though I have grown as a scholar along with the evolution of what we still call 'English' literary studies. Now encompassing the field of culture, in all of its manifestations, we are poised to read the world around us: institutions, material practices, the often accepted and bypassed details of our quotidian lives. What could be more important, more exciting?"

BIOGRAPHICAL AND CRITICAL SOURCES:

PERIODICALS

Globe and Mail (Toronto, Ontario, Canada), September 3, 1987.